W9-BCF-012

Great Events from History

The 17th Century

1601-1700

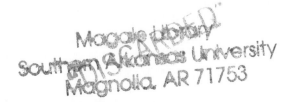

The 17th Century

1601 - 1700

Volume 1
1601-1652

Editor
Larissa Juliet Taylor
Colby College

SALEM PRESS
Pasadena, California   Hackensack, New Jersey

Editor in Chief: Dawn P. Dawson

Managing Editor: Christina J. Moose   *Production Editor:* Kathy Hix
Acquisitions Editor: Mark Rehn   *Graphics and Design:* James Hutson
Research Supervisor: Jeffry Jensen   *Editorial Assistant:* Dana Garey
Manuscript Editors: Desiree Dreeuws, Andy Perry   *Layout:* Eddie Murillo
Assistant Editor: Andrea E. Miller   *Photograph Editor:* Cynthia Beres

Cover photos: PhotoDisc, Corbis

(Pictured clockwise, from top left: Taj Mahal; 1650 map of the northern portion of the New World; Istanbul; Chateau de Versailles; Il Duomo; statue of Buddha; Jamestown settlement with ships)

Some of the essays in this work originally appeared in the following Salem Press sets: *Chronology of European History: 15,000 B.C. to 1997* (1997, edited by John Powell; associate editors, E. G. Weltin, José M. Sánchez, Thomas P. Neill, and Edward P. Keleher) and *Great Events from History: North American Series, Revised Edition* (1997, edited by Frank N. Magill). New material has been added.

Library of Congress Cataloging-in-Publication Data

Great events from history. The 17th century, 1601-1700 / editor, Larissa Juliet Taylor.

    p. cm.

Some of the essays in this work were originally published in Chronology of European history, 15,000 B.C. to 1997 and Great events from history : North American series. Rev. ed. 1997.

    Includes bibliographical references and index.

    ISBN-10: 1-58765-225-0 (set : alk. paper)

    ISBN-10: 1-58765-226-9 (v. 1 : alk. paper)

    ISBN-10: 1-58765-227-7 (v. 2 : alk. paper)

    ISBN-13: 978-1-58765-225-7 (set : alk. paper)

    ISBN-13: 978-1-58765-226-4 (v. 1 : alk. paper)

    ISBN-13: 978-1-58765-227-1 (v. 2 : alk. paper)

    1. Seventeenth century. I. Title: 17th century, 1601-1700. II. Title: Seventeenth century, 1601-1700. III. Taylor, Larissa. IV. Chronology of European history, 15,000 B.C. to 1997. V. Great events from history, North American series. 1997.

D246.G68 2005
909′.6—dc22

2005017362

First Printing

PRINTED IN THE UNITED STATES OF AMERICA

CONTENTS

1600's

1610's

1620's

1630's

1640's

CONTENTS

PUBLISHER'S NOTE

Great Events from History: The Seventeenth Century, 1601-1700, is the fourth installment in the ongoing *Great Events from History* series, which was initiated in 2004 with the two-volume *Great Events from History: The Ancient World, Prehistory-476*, followed in Spring 2005 with *The Middle Ages, 477-1453*, and in Fall 2005 with *The Renaissance & Early Modern Era, 1454-1600*. When completed, the series will extend through the twentieth century; subsequent volumes will address *The Eighteenth Century*, *The Nineteenth Century*, and *The Twentieth Century*.

EXPANDED COVERAGE

Like the rest of the series, the current volumes represent both a revision and a significant expansion of the twelve-volume *Great Events from History* (1972-1980), incorporating essays from the *Chronology of European History: 15,000 B.C. to 1997* (3 vols., 1997), *Great Events from History: North American Series, Revised Edition* (4 vols., 1997), and *Great Events from History: Modern European Series* (3 vols., 1973).

Each installment in the new series is being enlarged with a significant amount of new material—often more than half the original contents. *The Seventeenth Century* joins more than 236 new essays—commissioned especially for the new series and appearing for the first time—to 78 previously published core entries for a total of 314 essays on the century's major events. In addition, the new series features expanded and updated bibliographies, internal and external cross-references, a section containing maps of the world during the century, new appendices and indexes, plus numerous sidebars, quotations from primary source documents, maps, and illustrations throughout.

SCOPE OF COVERAGE

The century receives worldwide coverage with a priority for meeting the needs of history students at the high school and undergraduate levels. Events covered include the mandatory milestones in the geopolitics of the era—from the Thirty Years' War to the Wars of the League of Augsburg, from Europeans' arrival in Australia to the establishment of the Louisiana Colony. Also, however, the essays address key social developments in daily life: the

practice of birth control; the popularization of New World imports such as tobacco, coffee, and chocolate; the establishment of Tokyo's "Floating World" district; the ineradicable devastation of the Middle Passage and African American slavery. Students of this age of scientific revolution will learn the stories behind the development of the microscope, the earliest smallpox inoculations, the discovery of Saturn's rings, and the birth of modern chemistry. Those interested in the arts will learn what gave rise to Baroque music, the first modern libraries, British drama in an era of religious conservativism, and the Spanish Golden Age.

The emphasis of this collection, therefore, is on those turning points that redirected contemporary affairs and shaped the modern world, across a broad sweep of the following categories: agriculture (11 essays), architecture (15), art (9), astronomy (9), biology (11), colonization (49), communications (2), cultural and intellectual history (49), diplomacy and international relations (26), economics (45), education (3), engineering (3), environment (4), expansion and land acquisition (69), exploration and discovery (15), geology (2), government and politics (130), health and medicine (13), historiography (2), inventions (11), laws, acts, and legal history (27), literature (22), mathematics (9), music (5), natural disasters (6), organizations and institutions (26), philosophy (7), physics (13), religion and theology (58), science and technology (34), social issues and reform (41), theater (10), trade and commerce (50), transportation (4), and wars, uprisings, or civil unrest (107).

The scope of this set is equally broad geographically, with essays on events associated with the following countries or regions: Africa (23 essays), American Colonies (42), American Southwest (2), Angola (3), Australia (3), Austria (2), Balkans (2), Belgium (3), Benin (2), Bohemia (5), Brazil (6), Canada (12), Caribbean (4), China (13), Congo (2), Crete (1), Denmark (2), Egypt (1), England (73), Estonia (1), Ethiopia (1), Europe (22), Fiji (1), Finland (1), Flanders (1), France (26), Germany (10), Ghana (3), Hungary (2), India (9), Indonesia (8), Iran (5), Ireland (3), Italy (15), Jamaica (1), Japan (17), Lithuania (1), Livonia (1), Madagascar (1), Malaysia (1), Mali (2), Manchuria (1), Mauritania (1), Mauritius (1), Mexico (5), Middle East (20), Morocco (1), The Netherlands (19), New Guinea (1), New Zealand (1), Nigeria (3), Oman (1), Ottoman Empire (18), Outer Mongolia (1), Palestine (1), Paraguay (1), Peru (2), Poland (5), Portugal (6), Russia (12), Rwanda (1), Scotland (4), Senegal (2), Siberia (1), Slovakia (1), South Africa (1), South America (10), Southeast Asia (10), Spain (11), Sudan (2), Sweden (6), Tonga (1), Uganda (1), Ukraine (3), Uzbekistan (1), Vietnam (1), and Yemen (1). In addition, two essays cover developments with worldwide impact.

ESSAY LENGTH AND FORMAT

The essays have an average length of 1,600 words (2-3 pages) and adhere to a uniform format. The ready-reference top matter of every essay prominently displays the following information:
- the most precise *date* (or date range)
- the *name of the event*
- a *summary paragraph* that encapsulates the event's significance
- the *Locale*, or where the event occurred, including both contemporary and (where different) modern place-names
- the *Categories*, or the type of event covered, from Art to Wars and Civil Unrest
- *Key Figures*, a list of the major individuals involved in the event, with birth and death dates, a brief descriptor, and reign dates for rulers

The text of each essay is divided into the following sections:
- *Summary of Event*, devoted to a chronological description of the facts of the event
- *Significance*, assessing the event's historical impact
- *Further Reading*, an annotated list of sources for further study
- *See also*, cross-references to other essays within the *Great Events* set, and
- *Related articles*, which lists essays of interest in Salem's companion publication, *Great Lives from History: The Seventeenth Century, 1601-1700* (2 vols., simultaneously published in 2006).

SPECIAL FEATURES

A section of historical maps appears in the front matter of both volumes, displaying world regions in the seventeenth century for easy reference. Accompanying the essays are sidebars—including quotations from primary source documents—as well as maps and approximately 175 illustrations: images of artworks, battles, buildings, people, and other icons of the period.

A *Keyword List of Contents* appears in the front matter to both volumes and alphabetically lists all essays, permuted by all keywords in the essay's title, to assist students in locating events by name.

In addition, several research aids appear as appendices at the end of Volume 2:
- The *Time Line* lists major events in the seventeenth century; unlike the Chronological List of Entries (see below), the Time Line is a chronological listing of events by subject area and lists not only those events covered in the set but also a substantial number of other events and developments during the period.
- The *Glossary* defines terms and concepts associated with the period.
- The *Bibliography* cites major sources on the period.
- *Electronic Resources* provides URLs and descriptions of Internet sites and other online resources devoted to period studies.
- The *Chronological List of Entries* organizes the contents chronologically in one place for ease of reference.

Finally, four indexes round out the set:
- *Geographical Index* lists essays by region or country.
- *Category Index* lists essays by type of event (Agriculture, Architecture, Art, and so on).
- *Personages Index* includes major personages discussed throughout.
- *Subject Index* includes persons, concepts, terms, battles, works of literature, organizations, artworks, and many other topics of discussion.

USAGE NOTES

The worldwide scope of *Great Events from History* results in the inclusion of many names and words that must be transliterated from languages that do not use the Roman alphabet, and in some cases, more than one system of transliteration exists. In many cases, transliterated words in this set follow the American Library Association and Library of Congress (ALA-LC) transliteration format for that language. However, if another form of a name or word is judged to be more familiar to the general audience, it is used instead. The Pinyin transliteration is used for Chinese topics, with Wade-Giles variants provided for major names and dynasties; in a few cases, a common name that is not Pinyin has been used. Sanskrit and other South Asian names generally follow the ALA-LC transliteration rules, although again, the more familiar form of a word is used when deemed appropriate for the general reader.

Titles of books and other literature appear, upon first mention in the essay, with their full publication and translation data as known: an indication of the first date of publication or appearance, followed by the English title in translation and its first date of appearance in English; if no translation has been published in English, and if the context of the discussion does not make the meaning of the title obvious, a "literal translation" appears in roman type.

In the listing of Key Figures and in parenthetical material within the text, the editors have used these abbreviations: "r." for "reigned," "b." for "born," "d." for "died," and "fl." for flourished. Where a date range appears appended to a name without one of these designators, the reader may assume it signifies birth and death dates.

THE CONTRIBUTORS

Salem Press would like to extend its appreciation to all who have been involved in the development and production of this work. Special thanks go to Larissa Juliet Taylor, Professor of History at Colby College, who pored over the contents list, maintaining its balance and relevance to the student audience throughout the process of acquisitions in order to ensure that the curriculum was addressed fully.

The essays were written and signed by historians, political scientists, and scholars of regional studies as well as independent scholars. Without their expert contributions, a project of this nature would not be possible. A full list of their names and affiliations appears in the front matter of this volume.

CONTRIBUTORS

Amy Ackerberg-Hastings
*University of Maryland University
    College*

Richard Adler
University of Michigan—Dearborn

Peggy E. Alford
*Eastern Oregon University
Mesa Community College*

Thomas L. Altherr
Metropolitan State College of Denver

David L. Ammerman
Independent Scholar

Sharon L. Arnoult
Midwestern State University

James A. Baer
Northern Virginia Community College

Renzo Baldasso
Columbia University

Carl L. Bankston, III
Tulane University

John W. Barker
University of Wisconsin—Madison

Xavier Baron
University of Wisconsin—Milwaukee

Douglas Clark Baxter
Ohio University

Alvin K. Benson
Utah Valley State College

Donna Berliner
Southern Methodist University

Milton Berman
University of Rochester

Warren M. Billings
Independent Scholar

Nicholas Birns
New School University

Charlene Villaseñor Black
University of California, Los Angeles

Carol Blessing
Point Loma Nazarene University

William S. Brockington, Jr.
University of South Carolina—Aiken

Daniel A. Brown
California State University, Fullerton

Kendall W. Brown
Brigham Young University

James Burns
Clemson University

Joseph P. Byrne
Belmont University

Clare Callaghan
Independent Scholar

Jack Carter
University of New Orleans

Weston F. Cook, Jr.
*University of North Carolina at
    Pembroke*

David A. Crain
South Dakota State University

Steven Crawford
Independent Scholar

Laura A. Croghan
College of William and Mary

Bruce J. DeHart
*University of North Carolina at
    Pembroke*

Rene M. Descartes
*State University of New York at
    Cobleskill*

M. Casey Diana
*University of Illinois at Urbana-
    Champaign*

Desiree Dreeuws
Claremont Graduate University

Thomas Drucker
University of Wisconsin—Whitewater

John P. Dunn
Valdosta State University

John R. Elliott
Pepperdine University

Linda Eikmeier Endersby
Thomas A. Edison Papers

Robert F. Erickson
Independent Scholar

Randall Fegley
Pennsylvania State University

S. Annette Finley-Croswhite
Old Dominion University

Richard D. Fitzgerald
Onondaga Community College

Dale L. Flesher
University of Mississippi

Luminita Florea
University of California, Berkeley

George J. Flynn
*State University of New York—
    Plattsburgh*

C. George Fry
Winebrenner Theological Seminary

John G. Gallaher
*Southern Illinois University at
    Edwardsville*

Christopher E. Garrett
Texas A&M University

Mitchel Gerber
Southeast Missouri State University

Nancy M. Gordon
Independent Scholar

Kelley Graham
Butler University

Ronald Gray
Beijing Language and Culture University

Gretchen L. Green
Rockhurst College

M. Wayne Guillory
Georgia State University

Christopher E. Guthrie
Tarleton State University

David B. Haley
University of Minnesota

Irwin Halfond
McKendree College

Gavin R. G. Hambly
University of Texas at Dallas

Stephen Harmon
Pittsburgh State University

Peter B. Heller
Manhattan College

Mark C. Herman
Edison College

James F. Hitchcock
Independent Scholar

Hal Holladay
Simon's Rock College of Bard

John R. Holmes
Franciscan University of Steubenville

Lisa Hopkins
Sheffield Hallam University

Ronald W. Howard
Mississippi College

Raymond Pierre Hylton
Virginia Union University

Bruce E. Johansen
University of Nebraska at Omaha

Edward P. Keleher
Purdue University—Calumet

Grove Koger
Boise Public Library, Idaho

Paul E. Kuhl
Winston-Salem State University

Rebecca Kuzins
Independent Scholar

Ralph L. Langenheim, Jr.
University of Illinois—Urbana

Lawrence N. Langer
University of Connecticut

Eugene Larson
Los Angeles Pierce College

Abraham D. Lavender
Florida International University

Anne Leader
City College of New York, City University of New York

Christina H. Lee
San Jose State University

Thomas Tandy Lewis
Anoka-Ramsey Community College

Victor Lindsey
East Central University

Anne C. Loveland
Louisiana State University

Eric v.d. Luft
State University of New York, Upstate Medical University

R. C. Lutz
CII

Michael McCaskey
Georgetown University

James Edward McGoldrick
Greenville Presbyterian Theological Seminary

Kimberly Manning
Chaffey Community College

Joan E. Meznar
Eastern Connecticut State University

Diane P. Michelfelder
Utah State University

Timothy C. Miller
Millersville University of Pennsylvania

Bert M. Mutersbaugh
Eastern Kentucky University

Alice Myers
Simon's Rock College of Bard

John Myers
Simon's Rock College of Bard

Florentina Nicolae
Ovidius University, Constanta, Romania

Gary A. Olson
San Bernardino Valley College

Ayodeji Olukoju
University of Lagos, Nigeria

Joseph M. Ortiz
Princeton University

Meshak Owino
Bloomsburg University

Robert J. Paradowski
Rochester Institute of Technology

Jan Pendergrass
University of Georgia

Matthew Penney
Independent Scholar

Andy Perry
Independent Scholar

Marilyn Elizabeth Perry
Independent Scholar

George R. Plitnik
Frostburg State University

Marguerite R. Plummer
Louisiana State University, Shreveport

Clifton W. Potter, Jr.
Lynchburg College

Dorothy Potter
Lynchburg College

Shannon A. Powell
University of North Texas

George F. Putnam
Independent Scholar

Kevin B. Reid
Henderson Community College

Rosemary M. Canfield Reisman
Charleston Southern University

Betty Richardson
Southern Illinois University,
Edwardsville

William L. Richter
Independent Scholar

Edward A. Riedinger
Ohio State University Libraries

Edward J. Rielly
Saint Joseph's College of Maine

Charles W. Rogers
Southwestern Oklahoma State
University

Carl Rollyson
Baruch College, City University of
New York

John Alan Ross
Eastern Washington University

Wendy Sacket
Independent Scholar

José M. Sánchez
Independent Scholar

Kwasi Sarfo
York College of Pennsylvania

Randy P. Schiff
University of California, Santa
Barbara

Zoë A. Schneider
Georgetown University

William C. Schrader
Tennessee Technological University

Larry Schweikart
University of Dayton

R. Baird Shuman
University of Illinois at Urbana-
Champaign

Narasingha P. Sil
Western Oregon University

Shumet Sishagne
Christopher Newport University

Anna Sloan
Smith College

Richard L. Smith
Ferrum College

Sonia Sorrell
Pepperdine University

Joseph L. Spradley
Wheaton College, Illinois

Barbara C. Stanley
East Tennessee State University

Harold L. Stansell
Independent Scholar

August W. Staub
University of Georgia

Gerald H. Strauss
Bloomsburg University

Geralyn Strecker
Ball State University

Leslie Stricker
Park University

Fred Strickert
Wartburg College

Taylor Stults
Muskingum College

Charles R. Sullivan
University of Dallas

Glenn L. Swygart
Tennessee Temple University

Susan M. Taylor
Indiana University, South Bend

Moshe Terdiman
University of Haifa

Nicholas C. Thomas
Auburn University at Montgomery

Gale M. Thompson
Delta College

Leslie V. Tischauser
Prairie State College

Brian G. Tobin
Lassen College

Anatolii Trekhsviatskyi
Independent Scholar

Lisa Urkevich
American University of Kuwait

William T. Walker
Chestnut Hill College

Marcia J. Weiss
Point Park University

Richard Whitworth
Ball State University

Thomas Willard
University of Arizona

Michael Witkoski
University of South Carolina

Fatima Wu
Loyola Marymount University

Kristen L. Zacharias
Albright College

Yunqiu Zhang
North Carolina A&T State University

Lilian H. Zirpolo
Aurora: The Journal of the History
of Art

KEYWORD LIST OF CONTENTS

LIST OF MAPS, TABLES, AND SIDEBARS

AFRICA IN THE 17TH CENTURY

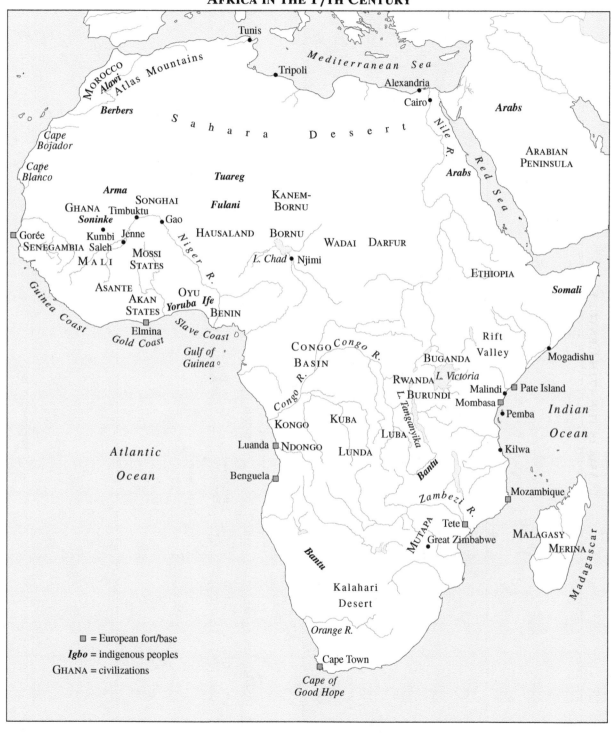

Tunis

Mediterranean Sea

Tripoli

Alexandria

Cairo

Arabs

MOROCCO
Alawi
Atlas Mountains

Berbers

*Cape
Bojador*

*Cape
Blanco*

S a h a r a   D e s e r t

Nile R.

Red Sea

ARABIAN
PENINSULA

Arabs

Tuareg

Arma
GHANA   SONGHAI   *Fulani*   KANEM-
BORNU
Soninke   Timbuktu
Gao
Gorée   Kumbi   Jenne   HAUSALAND   BORNU   WADAI   DARFUR
SENEGAMBIA   Saleh
M A L I   *Niger R.*
MOSSI
STATES   *L. Chad*   Njimi
ASANTE   ETHIOPIA
OYU   *Somali*
AKAN   *Yoruba*   *Ife*
STATES   BENIN
Elmina   *Slave Coast*
Gold Coast

Guinea Coast

*Gulf of
Guinea*

Mogadishu

Rift
Valley
CONGO   *Congo R.*   BUGANDA
BASIN   *L. Victoria*   Malindi   Pate Island
RWANDA   Mombasa
Congo R.   BURUNDI   Pemba
Atlantic   KUBA   *L. Tanganyika*   *Indian*
KONGO   LUBA
Ocean   Luanda   NDONGO   LUNDA   Kilwa   *Ocean*
Bantu
Benguela   *Zambezi R.*   Mozambique
MUTAPA   Tete   MALAGASY
Great Zimbabwe   MERINA
Bantu   *Madagascar*

*Kalahari
Desert*

Orange R.

☐ = European fort/base

Igbo = indigenous peoples

GHANA = civilizations

Cape Town

*Cape of
Good Hope*

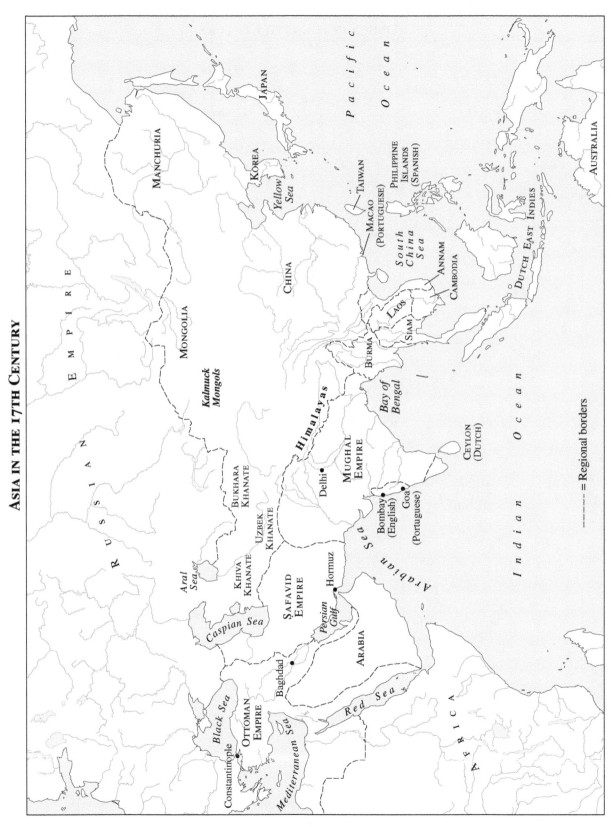

ASIA IN THE 17TH CENTURY

RUSSIAN EMPIRE

MANCHURIA

JAPAN

KOREA

Yellow Sea

MONGOLIA

Kalmuck Mongols

CHINA

TAIWAN

MACAO (PORTUGUESE)

PHILIPPINE ISLANDS (SPANISH)

South China Sea

ANNAM

CAMBODIA

LAOS

BURMA

SIAM

DUTCH EAST INDIES

AUSTRALIA

Pacific Ocean

Himalayas

Bay of Bengal

MUGHAL EMPIRE

Delhi

CEYLON (DUTCH)

Indian Ocean

BUKHARA KHANATE

UZBEK KHANATE

KHIVA KHANATE

Aral Sea

SAFAVID EMPIRE

Hormuz

Persian Gulf

Bombay (English)

Goa (Portuguese)

Arabian Sea

Caspian Sea

ARABIA

AFRICA

Baghdad

OTTOMAN EMPIRE

Black Sea

Constantinople

Mediterranean Sea

Red Sea

------ = Regional borders

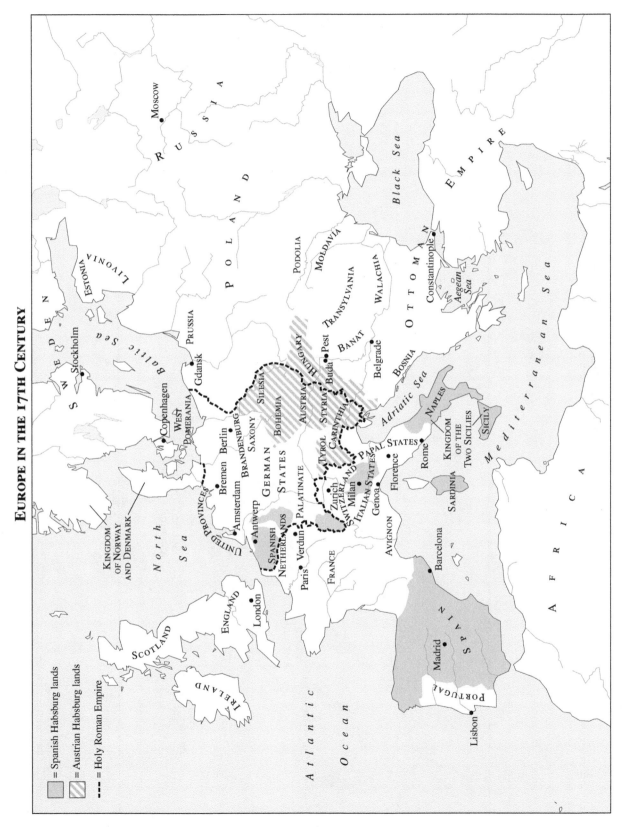

EUROPE IN THE 17TH CENTURY

= Spanish Habsburg lands

= Austrian Habsburg lands

= Holy Roman Empire

RUSSIA

Moscow

SWEDEN

Stockholm

ESTONIA

LIVONIA

Baltic Sea

POLAND

PRUSSIA

Gdansk

PODOLIA

MOLDAVIA

WALACHIA

Black Sea

OTTOMAN EMPIRE

Constantinople

Aegean Sea

TRANSYLVANIA

BANAT

HUNGARY

Pest

Buda

Belgrade

BOSNIA

Mediterranean Sea

Copenhagen

KINGDOM OF NORWAY AND DENMARK

WEST POMERANIA

Berlin

BRANDENBURG

SAXONY

Bremen

SILESIA

BOHEMIA

GERMAN STATES

AUSTRIA

STYRIA

CARINTHIA

TYROL

Adriatic Sea

NAPLES

KINGDOM OF THE TWO SICILIES

SICILY

North Sea

Amsterdam

UNITED PROVINCES

Antwerp

SPANISH NETHERLANDS

PALATINATE

Zurich

SWITZERLAND

Milan

ITALIAN STATES

Genoa

PAPAL STATES

Rome

Florence

SARDINIA

Verdun

Paris

FRANCE

AVIGNON

Barcelona

Atlantic Ocean

SCOTLAND

ENGLAND

London

IRELAND

SPAIN

Madrid

PORTUGAL

Lisbon

AFRICA

xxxix

European Colonization in the 17th Century

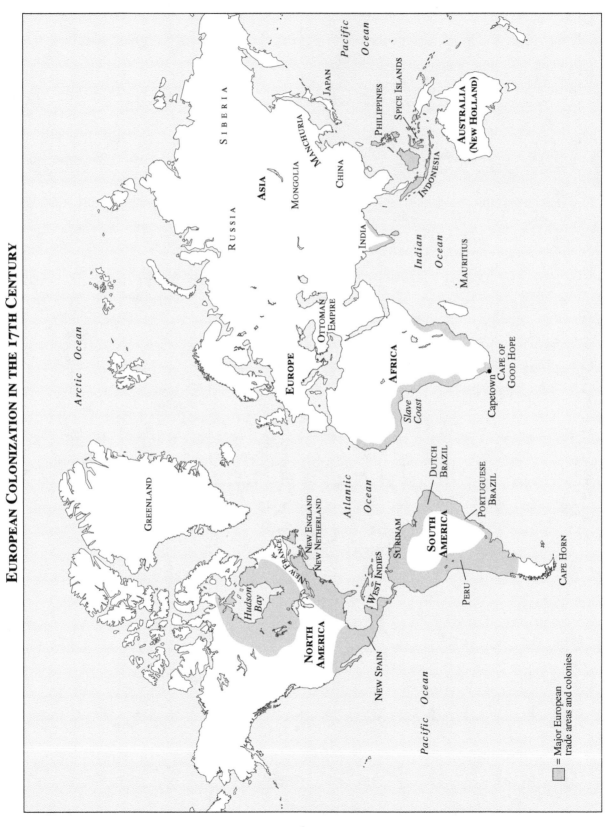

North America

Greenland

Hudson Bay

New France

New England

New Netherland

New Spain

West Indies

Atlantic Ocean

Pacific Ocean

Surinam

South America

Dutch Brazil

Portuguese Brazil

Peru

Cape Horn

Arctic Ocean

Europe

Ottoman Empire

Africa

Slave Coast

Capetown

Cape of Good Hope

Indian Ocean

Mauritius

India

Asia

Russia

Siberia

Mongolia

Manchuria

China

Japan

Philippines

Spice Islands

Indonesia

Australia (New Holland)

Pacific Ocean

☐ = Major European trade areas and colonies

NORTH AMERICA IN THE 17TH CENTURY

Athapascan = Native American language groups and related peoples

SOUTH AMERICA IN THE 17TH CENTURY

VENEZUELA

NEW
GRANADA

GUIANAS

San
Mateo
Bay

Amazon R.

NEW
HOLLAND

Palmares

Lima

Cuzco

PERU
Incas

PARAGUAY

Guaraní

São Francisco R.

BRAZIL

Salvador

Mato
Grosso

Rio de Janeiro

São Paolo

Pacific Ocean

Andes

Buenos Aires

Atlantic

Ocean

PATAGONIA

Cape Horn

The 17th Century

1601-1700

Early 17th century
REVENGE TRAGEDIES BECOME POPULAR IN ENGLAND

Beginning with Thomas Kyd's The Spanish Tragedy, *portrayals of the tragic consequences of seeking revenge became one of the dominant dramatic forms on the London stage for almost a century. Though William Shakespeare's* Hamlet, Prince of Denmark *is the major example of the genre, other revenge tragedies by such contemporaries as Thomas Middleton and John Webster were equally popular with theater audiences and continue to be performed.*

LOCALE: London, England
CATEGORIES: Theater; literature

KEY FIGURES

Thomas Kyd (1558-1594), English playwright and author of *The Spanish Tragedy*
William Shakespeare (1564-1616), English playwright, actor, and poet
John Webster (c. 1577/1580-before 1634), English playwright
Thomas Middleton (1580-1627), English playwright
James Shirley (1596-1666), prolific Caroline dramatist whose plays were revived and influential in the Restoration period

SUMMARY OF EVENT

When the Renaissance reached England in the sixteenth century, the study of Roman dramatists became part of school curricula. Prominent among these ancient playwrights was Seneca the Younger, whose plays probably were recited or read aloud by a single speaker. By the mid-1550's Seneca's plays were being translated from the Latin and performed at schools in England. In 1561, as part of a natural progression from translation to imitation, the first English tragedy—*Gorboduc* (pr. 1561, pb. 1565, authorized edition pb. 1570; also known as *The Tragedy of Ferrex and Porrex*)—was written by Thomas Sackville and Thomas Norton and presented to their fellow lawyers at London's Inns of Court. In 1576, the first of a number of public theaters opened, and about a decade later, Thomas Kyd's *The Spanish Tragedy* (pr. c. 1585-1589, pb. 1594?) introduced revenge tragedy to London audiences. A masterful blend of popular and academic traditions, *The Spanish Tragedy* may have been the most successful play of its age. It was often revived, and it begat a new genre that dominated the English stage for almost a century.

Generally set in royal courts, revenge tragedies portray intrigue and corruption thriving behind a facade of normality, conflicts spurred by sibling or political rivalry, and characters maneuvering for social or political advancement. Most of the plays are set in Italy or Spain, exotic and sinister locales about which most seventeenth century Englishmen knew little. These alien settings provided a useful distance from the action, enabling London audiences to observe parasitical flatterers with political aspirations and other evils of preferment at court with a comfortable detachment. At the same time, a London audience would have noticed parallels with the contemporary English court and the intrigues and political struggles of the day.

In the plays, people engage in private acts of revenge instead of relying upon the law, acts Elizabethans accepted when a son exacted revenge for the murder of his father, as in William Shakespeare's *Hamlet, Prince of Denmark* (pr. c. 1600-1601), or when a father avenged the killing of his son, as in *The Spanish Tragedy*. The latter play opens with a ghost revealing the details of a murder, as Hieronimo, a Spanish gentleman beset by melancholy and madness because of his son's murder, learns the identity of the villains and plots his revenge. He presents a play in which he and the unwitting culprits take part and in which he kills them and himself. Shakespeare in *Hamlet* used this play-within-a-play device, which Kyd introduced, as did John Marston in *Antonio's Revenge* (pr. 1599, pb. 1602). The concluding carnage in these plays also is present in most other revenge tragedies, such as Shakespeare's *Titus Andronicus* (pr., pb. 1594), Henry Chettle's *The Tragedy of Hoffman: Or, A Revenge for a Father* (pr. 1602, pb. 1631), and *The Revenger's Tragedy* (pr. 1606-1607, pb. 1607), which was once attributed to Cyril Tourneur but is now believed to be by Thomas Middleton.

A revenger was typically meant to command the sympathy of the audience, at least at the start, but his mental state or actions over the course of the play could cause this sympathy to fade or be tempered with other judgments. To increase dramatic tension, the playwright introduced obstacles that slowed the protagonist's pursuit of his goal, which may be why, in most of these plays (following Seneca's pattern), a ghost or the spirit of revenge was present to prod and encourage his vengeance. Many also had dumb shows or pantomimes between the acts to exemplify the action, but

1

these may have had their origin in medieval English drama.

There were other variations among the major Jacobean revenge tragedies: Some featured several revengers and conflicting intrigues. These include Marston's *The Malcontent* (pr., pb. 1604), in which only one of the attempted revengers succeeds, and *The Revenge of Bussy D'Ambois* (pr. c. 1610, pb. 1613) by George Chapman, a didactic play whose moral lessons almost overshadow the revenge framework of the plot. The medieval morality play tradition of personifying abstract qualities is apparent in *The Revenger's Tragedy*, whose characters' names are Italianate versions of such qualities. John Webster in *The White Devil* (pr. c. 1609-1612, pb. 1612) further expanded the parameters of the Kyd tradition by using events from the recent past for his plot, although he employed an Italianate setting to disguise his criticism of evils at the English court. In *The Duchess of Malfi* (pr. 1614, pb. 1623), largely a Kydian play, Webster made the revengers' victim the play's protagonist. The play's Bosola, nominally a villain and the revengers' instrument, is one of the most psychologically complex and indefinable characters in the genre.

Another departure from the Kyd tradition is exemplified by *The Changeling* (pr. 1622, pb. 1653), by Thomas Middleton and William Rowley, in which Beatrice cannot cope psychologically with the consequences of her crimes, confesses to adultery and murder, and is killed by her accomplice Deflores, who then commits suicide. The murder and suicide of the play's conspirators thwarts the proper revenger, denying him the satisfaction of taking his own revenge. By the 1620's, playwrights usually created revengers who were utter villains from the first act, making no attempt to encourage initial sympathy. Because audiences enjoyed seeing evil machinations perpetrated on the stage, playwrights catered to this predilection. Three plays of John Ford may serve as prime examples of this trend: *The Broken Heart* (pr. c. 1627-1631, pb. 1633), *'Tis Pity She's a Whore* (pr. 1629?-1633, pb. 1633), and *Love's Sacrifice* (pr. 1632?, pb. 1633).

As the decades passed, revenge tragedies, though increasingly imitative of earlier works, remained popular. Among the later plays in the genre is James Shirley's *The Cardinal* (pr. 1641, pb. 1652), which appeared just before the closing of the theaters in 1642 during the English Civil Wars and was often revived in the decades after the Stuart monarchy was restored in 1660. *The Spanish Tragedy*; *Hamlet, Prince of Denmark*; *The Duchess of Malfi*; *The Broken Heart*; and Cyril Tourneur's *The*

Atheist's Tragedy: Or, The Honest Man's Revenge (pr. c. 1607, pb. 1611) are obvious antecedents of *The Cardinal*, with such parallels as the murder of a rival by a jealous lover, support for the murderer by a Machiavellian villain eager for advancement or wealth, madness (real or feigned) as a result of grief, a play within a play, and revenge as an obsessive motive.

Shirley, however, departed from past practice with a lighthearted prologue that teased the audience about whether the play was a comedy or tragedy, even suggesting by his style and tone that it was the former. The prologue also engaged in self-mockery and made satiric comments about classical dramatic theory. These decisions may indicate that, in 1641, Shirley was sensitive to the risks of offering what was by then an old-fashioned revenge tragedy to sophisticated Londoners at a private theater. The ironic presentation of the genre by Shirley and other Restoration playwrights may account for their popularity on the Restoration stage.

SIGNIFICANCE

Revenge tragedy, which became the dominant Elizabethan dramatic form soon after public theaters began to open in the late English Renaissance, maintained its preeminent position as the decades passed, attracting almost all of the leading playwrights. The genre continued to develop in the hands of these playwrights, whose plays not only made structural changes to the basic generic template but also contained subtle allusions to current issues, such as the conflicts with Spain that had climaxed with the defeat of the Spanish Armada; to the controversies over Catholicism and the royal succession that dominated the seventeenth century; and to intrigues at court, which could not safely be addressed in a more direct and open manner.

The playwrights, after all, wrote for London's theatergoers, and they modified both the form and the content of revenge tragedies to cater to the interests of their audience. As the audience changed over the first half of the seventeenth century—becoming largely private and upper class by the late 1620's—the flexibility of the genre enabled revenge tragedy not only to survive but also to flourish, modifying its tone and concerns as necessary to accommodate new spectators. When the theaters reopened in 1660 after an eighteen-year hiatus, revenge tragedies by Shirley and others were revived, often with revisions, and they continued to influence new generations of dramatists into the eighteenth century.

—Gerald H. Strauss

FURTHER READING

Bowers, Fredson Thayer. *Elizabethan Revenge Tragedy, 1587-1642*. Princeton, N.J.: Princeton University Press, 1940. A seminal work that traces the origin of the form and sets the parameters for subsequent studies of revenge tragedy.

Braunmuller, A. R., and Michael Hattaway, eds. *The Cambridge Companion to English Renaissance Drama*. 2d ed. New York: Cambridge University Press, 2003. A valuable collection of essays by different specialists that reflects the latest scholarly reviews; also has useful biographies, bibliographies, and chronological tables.

Leggatt, Alexander. *English Drama: Shakespeare to the Restoration, 1590-1660*. London: Longman, 1988. Surveys English drama during its golden age, focusing upon individual playwrights and genres; useful appendices include biographical and bibliographical information as well as historical and cultural chronologies.

Ribner, Irving. *Jacobean Tragedy: The Quest for Moral Order*. London: Methuen, 1962. Chapters on six playwrights—George Chapman, Thomas Heywood, Cyril Tourneur, John Webster, Thomas Middleton, and John Ford—include close examinations of their plays with extensive focus upon textual analysis.

Sanders, Julie. *Caroline Drama: The Plays of Massinger, Ford, Shirley, and Brome*. Plymouth, Mass.: Northcote House, 1999. A brief study of how the plays of four major dramatists reflected the social and political milieu of Caroline London.

SEE ALSO: c. 1601-1613: Shakespeare Produces His Later Plays; Mar. 24, 1603: James I Becomes King of England; June 29, 1613: Burning of the Globe Theatre; Feb. 24, 1631: Women First Appear on the English Stage; 1642-1651: English Civil Wars; Sept. 2, 1642: Closing of the Theaters; May, 1659-May, 1660: Restoration of Charles II.

RELATED ARTICLES in *Great Lives from History: The Seventeenth Century, 1601-1700:* Charles I; Charles II (of England); James I; Thomas Middleton; James Shirley; Cyril Tourneur; John Webster.

Early 17th century
RISE OF RWANDA

The centralized kingdom of Rwanda gained prominence in east-central Africa and flourished for nearly a century under mythologized rulers Ruganza II Ndoori and Nyirarumaga. Despite the kingdom's rise, it also was plagued by conflicts that continued through the century—and beyond—among the region's Tutsi, Hutu, and Twa peoples.

LOCALE: Rwanda

CATEGORIES: Government and politics; expansion and land acquisition

KEY FIGURES

Ruganza II Ndoori (d. 1624), *mwami* of Rwanda, r. 1600-1624

Nyirarumaga (fl. seventeenth century), *nyiraruganza*, or Queen Mother, of Rwanda

SUMMARY OF EVENT

East-central Africa's Great Lakes region witnessed the rise of several powerful kingdoms in early modern times. Among these was the mountainous realm of Rwanda, populated by three groups whose origins are clouded in much mystery and controversy. Its earliest inhabitants were Twa Pygmies, who were hunter-gatherers and potters. Eventually forming a marginalized 1 percent minority of Rwanda's population, they were supplanted by Bantu-speaking migrants from the west, who make up more than 80 percent of all Rwandans.

Traditionally, the pastoral Tutsi, who dominated the area, were portrayed as a third people coming from the Horn of Africa in the fourteenth century. The Tutsi were dominant because they possessed cattle and had superior military and organizational skills, while the Bantu, whose original name remains unknown, became their servants, or *hutu*.

Fifteenth century Tutsi leader Ruganza Bwimba founded a kingdom near Rwanda's current capital, Kigali. To the north, the Nilotic-ruled kingdom of Bunyoro (a region in what is now Uganda), Rwanda's former overlord, remained dominant in the region, despite a series of droughts, devastating famines, political upheavals, and mass migrations that characterized the period from 1588 to 1621. In Rwanda, a political hierarchy emerged, dominated by Tutsi chiefs who were led by a Tutsi *mwami* (king), whose symbol was the *kalinga* (sacred drum). A *biru* (council of guardians) advised the *mwami* on his religious duties and court rituals. A council of great chiefs, the *batware b'intebe*, oversaw cattle chiefs and land chiefs, who collected the tribute all Rwandans paid the *mwami*.

Subservient to these chiefs were the subchiefs, each of whom governed an *umozozi* (hill). Military chiefs controlled frontier areas and raided neighboring tribes. In contractual arrangements known as *ubuhake*, Hutu farmers pledged their own and their descendants' homage, services, and crops to Tutsi lords in return for protection and the use of cattle and land. Though always unequal and comparable to medieval European manorialism, *ubuhake* was traditionally based on reciprocity, and it protected the Hutu from the arbitrary demands of other Tutsi.

Rwanda's royal court recorded its deeds in the *Icitekerezo* (bequest to posterity), a collection of oral histories and symbolic poetry. Said to have ancient origins, it relates humanity's divine origin and the superhuman status of savior-kings, who are able to mediate with God and engage in sacred warfare for their people's defense. However, such official histories are more often reflections of power than historical fact. According to the *Icitekerezo*, scattered Hutu and Twa groups inhabited Rwanda when the conquering Tutsi arrived from the north in the tenth century. Introducing centralized monarchy, cattle, iron, and other "advancements," the Tutsi (specifically, the royal Nyiginya clan) developed a powerful, cohesive state from chaos. In one of the *Icitekerezo*'s allegorical myths, the god Kigwa entrusts each of his three sons—Gatutsi, Gahutu, and Gatwa—with the safekeeping of milk overnight. By morning, Gatwa had drunk his milk, Gahutu had spilled his, and only Gatutsi returned his safely. Thus, only Gatutsi was qualified to rule.

The *Icitekerezo* provides evidence of one Hutu contribution to Rwanda's creation. When Tutsi prince Cyilima I Rugwe succeeded his father in the 1500's, he went to Hutu diviner Umurera, who refused the prince's gifts until Cyilima swore a blood pact with him. The prince relented and obtained wise advice, which led him to create an independent Rwanda by linking Tutsi military power with Hutu supernatural power. However, nowhere else are Hutu roles recognized, despite evidence that royal practices, such as the renewal of sacred fires and the reforging of ritual implements, were Hutu in origin.

In the early 1600's, Rwanda faced succession disputes and invasions from Bunyoro. According to the *Icitekerezo*, Ruganza II Ndoori, a herder of Nyiginya royal blood, had been journeying home from neighbor-

ing Karagwe (now a district in northwestern Tanzania) when he encountered a band of men who were sent by his greedy, usurping uncle Byinshi to assassinate him. Byinshi was trying to prevent Ruganza's return as rightful heir. Famed as a runner, Ruganza dashed away. A humble young woman named Nyirarumaga allowed him to hide in her home, which Byinshi's henchmen searched in vain. Ruganza, however, had escaped through a hole under the floor. Different versions of this tradition claim that the hole was a snake's den, a rabbit warren, a monkey's cave, or the underground lair of a mythical animal named Inyaga. The being that lived there, whether Inyaga or not, aided Ruganza by tunneling through the mountain into Rwanda.

Ruganza was able to claim the throne, but before his royal consecration, he needed a *nyiraruganza* (Queen Mother, or Lady Commander). Because his own mother was deceased, he needed an adoptive mother. The *mwami* sent for Nyirarumaga, the woman who earlier had saved Ruganza's life, considering her a second mother to Ruganza. Hence, a commoner was raised to be elective mother and consort of Rwanda's greatest early king, just as Ruganza had risen from the *umwoobo w'Inyaga* (hole of Inyaga) to the throne.

Ruling in peace and stability, Ruganza and Nyirarumaga revived Rwandan culture by collecting royal myths, rituals, poetry, and genealogies. Named *mwungura wunguye Ingoma Ubwenge* (augmenters of the kingdom's wisdom), they established the Intebe y'Abasizi (seat of poets), an institution for recording and teaching epics and training poets. The *Icitekerezo* was further developed by Nyirarumaga and Ruganza, both of whom composed some of its poems.

Building on Ruganza Bwimba's earlier state in central Rwanda, Ruganza Ndoori fended off Bunyoro and subdued outlying Hutu communities. Around 1700, Rwanda's growth was halted roughly at its current borders by increasingly powerful Burundi. Beset by succession disputes and rebellions, its early rival Bunyoro was eclipsed by Buganda by 1800.

During the nineteenth century reign of Mwami Kigeri IV Rwabugiri, *hutu* and *tutsi* became politically charged terms with ethnic meanings. The royal court established a complex network of centrally appointed chiefs. Backed by a military force, this centralization strained relations between Tutsi chiefs and their Hutu subjects. Later, Europeans became important allies of *mwami*, who submitted to German protection without resistance in 1899. Ruling through the *mwami*, Germans and later Belgians bolstered royal policies. The precolonial ideology of

Tutsi superiority was solidified under the Europeans, who transformed once-fluid categories into rigid, ethnic divisions. The gap grew between the rulers and ruled. *Ubuhake* became more coercive and inescapable.

SIGNIFICANCE

During the colonial era, Rwanda's first written histories entrenched Tutsi supremacy with the racially charged Hamitic hypothesis, which claimed that the Tutsi were of Hamitic origin, tied to the Caucasian Middle East, whereas the Bantu Hutu arose from an inferior "Black Africa." The Rwandan royal court adopted revised histories, which exaggerated tribal roles even further and gave spurious longevity and continuity to the Nyiginya Dynasty. Officially, the Hutu were only passive recipients of good, strong Tutsi government, presided over by *mwami*, whose divine attributes had been established by earlier myths, especially those associated with Ruganza II Ndoori. Physical characteristics distinguishing many Tutsi, such as tall, thin builds, thin noses, and light skin, provided evidence to confirm this view. However, these attributes, just as likely to have Nilotic origins, were common only among the 10 percent of Tutsi who were nobles.

Recent scholarship has demythologized Nyiginya and colonial versions of Rwanda's history. Identities were far more flexible and varied than previously thought. Successful or locally powerful Hutu were adopted into Tutsi lineages, and their origins were forgotten. All Rwandans speak the same Kinyarwanda language, and their clans contain Hutu, Tutsi, and even Twa, which suggests common descent or at least the inclusion of migrants into existing clans. Identities also appear to relate to one's proximity to the *mwami*. Those with loose ties to the court may not have distinguished Hutu and Tutsi at all. Hence, ethnic identities may be recent, political constructions.

After World War II, the Belgians reversed their policies and backed the increasingly politically active Hutu, undoing the system they helped build. *Ubuhake* was abolished in 1954, though Hutu dependence on Tutsi overlords continued. The Catholic Church supported the Hutu, many of whom had been schooled by Flemish priests who had been treated as second-class citizens in their own country.

Hutu activism, voiced in the 1957 Bahutu Manifesto, resurrected and reversed the Hamitic hypothesis, claiming that the Hutu's oppressors were the Tutsi, not the Europeans. Seeing the Tutsi as foreign threats, militant Hutu nationalists overthrew the system in 1959 and laid the groundwork for the genocide that would take place thirty-five years later, in 1994.

—*Randall Fegley*

FURTHER READING

Chrétien, Jean-Pierre. *The Great Lakes of Africa: Two Thousand Years of History*. Translated by Scott Straus. New York: Zone Books, 2003. An excellent history drawing on colonial archives, oral traditions, and archaeological, anthropological, and linguistic evidence.

Des Forges, Alison. *Leave None to Tell the Story*. New York: Human Rights Watch, 1999. This report links Rwanda's early history with the 1994 genocide.

Maquet, Jacques. *The Premise of Inequality in Ruanda*. London: Oxford University Press, 1961. Published immediately after Rwandan independence, Maquet's study details the Tutsi hierarchy's hold on Rwanda.

Newbury, Catharine. *The Cohesion of Oppression: Clientship and Ethnicity in Rwanda*. New York: Columbia University Press, 1988. This excellent work examines historical relationships among Rwanda's groups.

Prunier, Gérard. *The Rwanda Crisis: History of a Genocide*. New York: Columbia University Press, 1995. Chapter 1 is a survey of the myths and dynamics of early Rwanda.

Vansina, Jan. *Antecedents to Modern Rwanda: The Nyiginya Kingdom*. Madison: University of Wisconsin Press, 2005. Vansina guides readers through Rwanda's often-complicated history, analyzing and even correcting the records of early missionaries and court historians. He describes the formation of Hutu and Tutsi identities, explores their differences and their bitter feuds, and examines how Rwanda's past informs its twenty-first century identity as a nation.

SEE ALSO: 17th cent.: Emergence of Luba Governance; c. 1625: Formation of the Kuba Kingdom; Late 17th cent.: Rise of Buganda.

RELATED ARTICLE in *Great Lives from History: The Seventeenth Century, 1601-1700*: Njinga.

17th century
ADVANCES IN MEDICINE

The seventeenth century was a watershed in the evolution of medical knowledge and the practice of medicine. The development and perfection of the microscope opened new fields for the study of human anatomy and physiology, leading to greater understandings of reproduction, growth, disease, and decay.

LOCALE: England and continental Europe
CATEGORIES: Health and medicine; science and technology; biology; inventions; cultural and intellectual history

KEY FIGURES

Jan Swammerdam (1637-1680), Dutch anatomist and physiologist
William Harvey (1578-1657), English physician who discovered the circulation of blood
Antoni van Leeuwenhoek (1632-1723), Dutch lensmaker who perfected the microscope
Francesco Stelluti (1577-1646/1652), student of Galileo who coined the term "microscope"
Francesco Redi (1626-1697), Italian physician and poet who helped disprove spontaneous generation
Marcello Malpighi (1628-1694), Italian physician who developed the concept of glands
Nicolaus Steno (1638-1686), Danish physician and anatomist
Thomas Sydenham (1624-1689), English physician credited with reviving the Hippocratic view of medicine

SUMMARY OF EVENT

The development of the lens arguably represents the key element in scientific discovery during the seventeenth century. While Antoni van Leeuwenhoek is generally accredited with the microscope's perfection, it was Galileo who first developed a mechanism to observe the "small." Galileo is correctly associated with the telescope and its use in observations of the solar system, but he also used the same technology to observe microscopic objects. Early discoveries were made by students of Galileo, including Francesco Stelluti, who was the first to publish drawings of insects based upon his microscopic observations (1630), and the one who coined the term "microscope."

While the microscope did not originate with Leeuwenhoek, he developed it to the point that it became widely applicable in the field. Leeuwenhoek was born in Delft, Holland, in 1632, the son of a basket maker. Initially in the drapery business, by the 1650's he became increasingly interested in the production of lenses and their application in microscopy. In 1680, he would be elected as a fellow to the Royal Society of London; many of his letters and illustrations to the society were published in 1684. Even in Leeuwenhoek's old age, contemporaries noted the steadiness of his hands for his work.

Leeuwenhoek's work was primarily observational. The early sources for his specimens included water, plaque scraped from his teeth, and even fecal matter. His drawings appear to depict primarily protozoa and bacteria, though Leeuwenhoek never associated his "animalcules" with disease. Indeed, the germ theory of disease would not develop for another two centuries.

Contemporary with Leeuwenhoek was Jan Swammerdam, born in 1637 and among the first to apply Leeuwenhoek's microscope to the study of anatomy and physiology. Swammerdam is credited with the discovery of red blood corpuscles, though his ideas on their functions were primarily speculative. He studied insect anatomy mostly but also was one of the early anatomists to study the human reproductive system.

While the existence of a circulatory system was known as early as Galen in the second century, knowledge of its function remained nebulous for another fifteen hundred years. Galen understood the concept of blood vessels as well as a difference between arterial and venous blood based upon their color. In his view, however, circulation was an inherent function of arterial pumping; blood was created in the liver and was consumed by the organs.

It remained for William Harvey to provide a more modern explanation for blood circulation. First trained at Caius College in Cambridge, England, Harvey continued his medical training as a student of Italian anatomist Hieronymus Fabricius ab Aquapendente at Padua in Venice. Fabricius ab Aquapendente was a student of Italian anatomist Gabriele Falloppio, who discovered the function of what came to called the Fallopian tubes in a woman's body. Fabricius ab Aquapendente's discovery of valves within the venous system would later play an important role in Harvey's work on the process of circulation. Harvey received his diploma from Padua in 1602. Returning to England, in 1607, Harvey was elected fellow of the College of Physicians, maintaining a practice that had King James I and King Charles I as clients. He also did research in both anatomy and physiology.

Harvey utilized a variety of animals in his early studies on circulation, settling on snakes because the slow beating of their hearts allowed for a more precise observation. Harvey established that the contraction of the heart drives blood through the circulatory system. He also observed that the heart rested between beats, allowing it to be "refilled." Among other observations, Harvey noted that venous circulation occurs in a single direction: Using the heart as a pump, blood flows from arteries to veins, returning to the heart. Furthermore, by measuring the quantity of blood in an animal, Harvey demonstrated that blood is not produced continuously in the liver.

The primitive state of microscopy early in the century limited Harvey's ability to study the connections between arteries and veins. It remained for Marcello

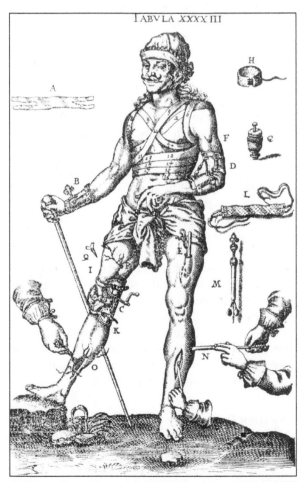

An illustration of the use of medical instruments, from a 1656 medical treatise on surgery. (Hulton\Archive by Getty Images)

Malpighi to discover the role of capillaries in the process. Born in Rome in 1628, ironically the same year Harvey published his work describing circulation, Malpighi earned his medical degree in 1653 from the University of Bologna. He spent much of his professional career there as a member of the medical faculty.

Malpighi is considered the father of comparative physiology, as he was among the first to utilize the microscope in the study of various systems in animals. Prior to Malpighi, physicians considered organ tissues to originate as coagulated fluids (coagulum), and hence referred to such tissue as parenchymal. Malpighi determined that such tissue is actually glandular, pockets of globular forms of cells. His observations encompassed numerous types of tissue. He discovered capillaries after observing that the lungs, for example, were composed of thin membranes with a variety of tiny vessels.

Malpighi observed similar "pockets" of cells in other tissues, including the spleen, liver, and kidneys (renal glomerulus), and was also the first to observe the layering of tissue that makes up the epidermis. Though he was a contemporary of Leeuwenhoek, Malpighi's attention to application—to practice—distinguished him from other scientific "observers."

Though Malpighi had discovered glands, it was the Danish anatomist Nicolaus Steno who determined how they function. Born in Copenhagen in 1638, Steno carried out his early anatomical studies at the university in that city. In 1661, while dissecting the head of a sheep, he observed the presence of excretory ducts originating from the salivary glands. The duct from the parotid (salivary) gland would be named the *ductus stenonianua* in his honor. Steno would continue his work in the field of anatomy, eventually discovering numerous glands and ducts in the mouth and nose.

Therapy for disease as it existed in the early seventeenth century was often a "hit or miss" phenomenon. The Aristotelian concept of "humors" as the basis for disease continued to dominate medical thought, and it often formed the basis for treatment that was as likely to kill as to cure; bleeding was a common practice. Thomas Sydenham, an English physician, is often credited with reviving the Hippocratic school of medicine, in which careful observation and "bedside manner" played an important role in diagnosis and recovery.

Sydenham received an excellent medical education at Oxford, though he came to believe clinical observation was more important than pharmacological treatments. His study of epidemics in the 1650's formed the basis of his theories on the role played by the environment in the

ADVANCES IN MEDICINE	
Date	*Event*
1628	William Harvey publishes *Exercitatio anatomica de mortu cordis et sanguinis in animalibus*, the description of blood circulation in animals
1630	Francesco Stelluti publishes the first microscopic drawings of insects
1632	Marco Severino authors the first illustrated text on surgical pathology
1652	Thomas Bartholin describes the presence of the thoracic duct in humans, demonstrating the presence of a lymphatic system
c. 1658	Jan Swammerdam observes red blood cells through a microscope
1661	Nicolaus Steno discovers excretory ducts in salivary glands
1661	Marcello Malpighi publishes his work on the physiology of the lung, including the existence of capillaries
1665-1666	Malpighi publishes his work on glandular structures
1666	Malpighi publishes the first description of Hodgkin's disease
1668	Francesco Redi demonstrates fallacies in the belief of spontaneous generation

outbreak of disease. For example, he was the first to associate fleas with typhus. He later concluded that certain illnesses resulted from iron deficiencies. Like the Hippocratic school, Sydenham believed fever itself was dangerous for the body, and he practiced methods of cooling the body to counteract its effects. Though skeptical about the drugs of the time, Sydenham did believe quinine would be useful in treating malaria. Because he insisted on careful observations in the diagnosis of medical problems, Sydenham became known as the English Hippocrates.

The idea that living matter could arise spontaneously from nonliving material, a concept called spontaneous generation, had been accepted since the time of Aristotle. Even the Church accepted some aspects of spontaneous generation. Recipes existed for the spontaneous production of mice (wheat plus dirty underwear), and frogs and eels could be generated from mud. Worms were thought to arise spontaneously in decomposing meat, a common sight during these times before refrigeration. In 1668, Francesco Redi demonstrated that such "worms," or maggots, arose not spontaneously but rather as a result of eggs laid by flies or other insects on the exposed food.

Redi carried out one of the earliest experiments using what are now referred to as "controls." He set up a series of flasks, into which were placed pieces of meat. The sur-

faces of several of the flasks were sealed completely or overlaid with gauze, which kept insects from the meat. Flasks were also left uncovered. Redi observed that the meat placed in the uncovered flasks became contaminated with maggots, and the covered flasks were free of maggots. Later, when he placed insect eggs obtained from the fine gauze on the previously covered meat, maggots formed.

Ironically, the development of microscopy would also lend support to the belief that the generation of microscopic animalcules could still occur spontaneously. The primitive state of microscopic observation meant that while relatively large objects could be observed in liquids, smaller objects could easily be overlooked. Consequently, even Redi could be "fooled" into mistaking contaminated liquids for those that were sterile. French scientist Louis Pasteur (1822-1895) ended the controversy of spontaneous generation through his own work in microbiology.

SIGNIFICANCE

Until the seventeenth century, medical knowledge and practice were guided by theories that originated with Hippocrates and Aristotle, and the study of anatomy was directed by the ideas of Galen. The single most important event for the century was arguably Leeuwenhoek's perfection of the modern microscope, which made clear some of the basic structures of plants as well as animals and opened the way for the sciences of anatomy and physiology. Researchers were able to see that microscopic elements—the "small"—were the necessary links to understanding organic processes such as reproduction, growth, disease, decay, and decomposition. Human anatomy and physiology, no longer speculative, were carried into the realm of modern science.

—Richard Adler

FURTHER READING

Conrad, Lawrence, et al., eds. *The Western Medical Tradition, 800 B.C. to A.D. 1800*. New York: Cambridge University Press, 1995. Andrew Wear's chapter, "Medicine in Early Modern Europe, 1500-1700," is an excellent introduction to early modern medicine.

Davies, Gill. *The Timetables of Medicine: An Illustrated Chronology of the History of Medicine from Prehistory to Present Times*. New York: Workman/Black Dog & Leventhal, 2000. Davies provides an illustrated time line for advances in medicine, covering a period of thousands of years. The detailed content makes for fascinating reading.

Fournier, Marian. *The Fabric of Life: Microscopy in the Seventeenth Century*. Baltimore: Johns Hopkins University Press, 1996. Examines work in microscopy and the reasons for the microscope's appearance in the seventeenth century.

Gest, Howard. *Microbes: An Invisible Universe*. Washington, D.C.: ASM Press, 2003. A history of microbiology from the time of its invention to the beginning of the twenty-first century.

McNeill, William. *Plagues and Peoples*. Wilmington, N.C.: Anchor, 1998. This work is primarily a sociological and geographic approach to the movement of disease through human history. McNeill follows the progression of disease as a function of human migration.

Nuland, Sherwin. *Doctors: The Biography of Medicine*. New York: Vintage Books, 1989. A history of medicine covering its beginnings with Hippocrates to modern times. Includes an excellent chapter on William Harvey and the context of his work.

Piccolino, Marco. "Marcello Malpighi and the Difficult Birth of Modern Life Sciences." *Endeavour* 23, no. 4 (1999). Examines Malpighi's contributions to science, including his pioneering work in microscopic medical anatomy, the composition of the human body, and the pathology of diseases.

Porter, Roy, ed. *Cambridge Illustrated History of Medicine*. New York: Cambridge University Press, 2001. As the title implies, this work is primarily an illustrated history, but it is a useful general history source.

Ruestow, Edward. *The Microscope in the Dutch Republic*. New York: Cambridge University Press, 1996. Ruestow explores the role of the microscope in the scientific discoveries of the seventeenth century. Emphasis is placed on the role of Leeuwenhoek.

SEE ALSO: 17th cent.: Birth Control in Western Europe; 1601-1672: Rise of Scientific Societies; 1612: Sanctorius Invents the Clinical Thermometer; 1617-1628: Harvey Discovers the Circulation of the Blood; 1660's-1700: First Microscopic Observations; 1664: Willis Identifies the Basal Ganglia; c. 1670: First Widespread Smallpox Inoculations; 1672-1684: Leeuwenhoek Discovers Microscopic Life; 1676: Sydenham Advocates Clinical Observation.

RELATED ARTICLES in *Great Lives from History: The Seventeenth Century, 1601-1700:* Galileo; William Harvey; Jan Baptista van Helmont; Robert Hooke; Christiaan Huygens; Antoni van Leeuwenhoek; Hans Lippershey; Marcello Malpighi; Santorio Santorio; Nicolaus Steno; Jan Swammerdam; Thomas Sydenham.

17th century
AGE OF MERCANTILISM IN SOUTHEAST ASIA

The theory and practice of mercantilism led to European—especially Dutch—expansion into Southeast Asia, where European powers and local states competed for control of the strong and profitable spice market. The age of mercantilism was a key period in the development of the European economy and in the establishment of European colonialism.

LOCALE: Southeast Asia, especially modern Indonesia
CATEGORIES: Economics; expansion and land acquisition; government and politics; colonization

KEY FIGURES
Abul Mafākhir (d. 1651), fourth sultan of Banten, r. 1596-1651
'Ala al-Dīn (d. 1639), sultan of Gowa, r. 1593-1639
Jan Pieterszoon Coen (1587-1629), officer of the Dutch East India Company and governor-general of the Dutch East Indies, 1619-1623 and 1627-1629
Arung Palakka (1634-1696), a prince of the Bugis and subject of Gowa who rebelled against Gowa and allied himself with the Dutch

SUMMARY OF EVENT
By the seventeenth century, Western Europe had developed into a region of competing nation-states, each with a central government, and each practicing mercantilism. According to the principles of mercantilism, the goal of trade is to increase the wealth of a nation. To increase and store wealth, according to mercantilist theory, states were encouraged to export more goods than they import.

Within a given country, mercantilism calls for individuals to be thrifty so that the amount of national wealth spent on consumer goods is minimized and the amount flowing to the country's treasury maximized. Internationally, export was key to a nation's wealth, as it led to the creation of a monopoly on vital goods and a monopoly on income. The strong armies made possible by increasing national wealth enabled states to establish colonies, to protect their markets, and to compete with one another directly in wars. In addition, rising states in other parts of the world followed economic practices similar to those of the competing European nations. Several of those non-European states were in the islands of Southeast Asia.

The Southeast Asian cluster of islands now known as Indonesia had long been the primary source of spices for Europe. The islands of the Moluccas were called the Spice Islands, and much of the European Age of Discovery during the sixteenth century involved European efforts to find sea routes to the Moluccas to obtain advantages in the spice trade. In 1511, the Portuguese established the first secure European foothold in the Spice Islands when Malacca fell to Portugal.

The Netherlands, along with Belgium and Luxembourg, had been ruled by the distant king of Spain until the end of the sixteenth century. While still throwing off Spanish control, Holland especially, as the dominant Dutch province, enjoyed rapid economic growth because of its access to the fishing territory of the North Sea and its central location along the trade routes of Europe. The strong Dutch economy helped the nation expand its shipping and trade economy to the area of the East Indies (Indonesia). In 1602, the Dutch established the Vereenigde Oost-Indische Compagnie (United East India Company), better known as the Dutch East India Company, to trade in the East Indies and to help secure wealth for the continuing struggle against Spain for Dutch independence. Although the Portuguese, Spanish, and other Europeans were active in the islands of Southeast Asia, the Dutch and the English became the primary competitors for control of the region.

Within Indonesia, local empires were expanding and, like the Europeans, trying to control trade and establish monopolies. The small kingdom of Banten (Bantam), founded in the mid-sixteenth century at the northwestern end of the island of Java, engaged in a series of wars and established control over some of the pepper-producing regions. As a result, Banten became a major pepper port. Bordering Banten, a Muslim ruling class took over central Java in 1600 and founded the kingdom of Mataram. Mataram sent out raiders, also attempting to take control of the profitable sea trade of the islands. In eastern Indonesia, the kingdom of Gowa had made itself the center of a loosely tied empire and a great trading power.

SOUTHEAST ASIAN TRADING REGION

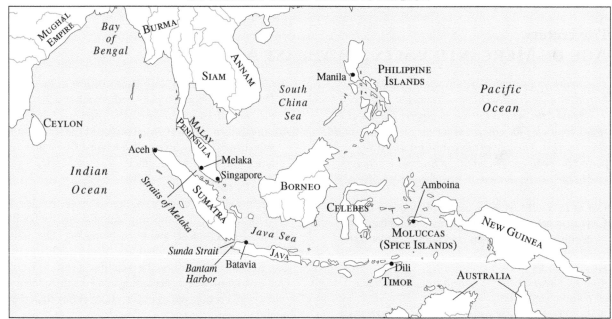

Mercantile policies brought the Dutch into Southeast Asia, putting the Dutch in contact with Southeast Asian powers who had similar monopolistic goals. This meant that the Europeans would not simply trade with the people of the Asian states, but would compete with the Asian rulers for the domination of commerce. At the beginning of the seventeenth century, the Dutch established a headquarters at Jacatra (Jakarta), on the northern coast of Java between Banten and Mataram. The ruler of Jacatra was a vassal of Sultan Abul Mafākhir of Banten. In 1617, Abul Mafākhir tried to expel the Dutch by laying siege to the European camp.

England also entered the competition for control of the spice trade in much the same way as the Dutch. Queen Elizabeth I granted a charter to the English East India Company in 1600. This brought England and Holland into fierce competition for spices. The Dutch tried to force local rulers to grant monopolies to their own company, and the Dutch called the English "smugglers" for attempting to set up trading posts.

Abul Mafākhir attempted to make use of the English-Dutch competition by encouraging the English admiral Sir Thomas Dale to take part in the attack on the Dutch camp outside Jacatra. Dale drove away a Dutch fleet under the command of Jan Pieterszoon Coen. Dale's forces were about to take the Dutch camp when soldiers of Banten arrived, took over Jacatra, and forced the English to leave. Although Abul Mafākhir wanted to get rid of the Dutch, he did not want to replace them with other European competitors. In May, 1619, Coen returned with a larger fleet, drove the Banten troops away, and destroyed Jacatra. The city was renamed Batavia, and it became the center from which Holland established its rule over the islands of the region. Coen became one of the most important Dutch figures in the region, serving as governor-general twice, from 1619 to 1623 and from 1627 to 1629.

After securing Batavia, Coen led an armed expedition against the Banda Islands, the world's primary producers of nutmeg and mace, in 1621. The people of the Banda Islands had a contract to sell exclusively to the Dutch, but they also had been trading with the English. Coen took the Banda island of Lonthor, killing or exiling most of its inhabitants. He returned to the Netherlands in 1623 to serve as head of the Dutch East India Company. After returning to Batavia four years later for his second term as governor-general, he defended the Dutch headquarters against two sieges by the ruler of neighboring Mataram, in 1628 and 1629.

In eastern Indonesia, the Gowa kingdom was an obstacle to Dutch attempts to create a monopoly and end smuggling. Sultan ʿAla al-Dīn, the ruler of Gowa until 1639, worked with traders from Asia and other European nations to undermine Dutch efforts to impose a trade monopoly. From 1615 until 1637, the Dutch East India Company and Gowa were in a state of sporadic warfare. In 1637, and again in 1655 and 1660, the Dutch and Gowa signed treaties. After 1660, though, the Dutch joined together with the Bugis prince Arung Palakka, a rebellious subject of the Gowa Empire. With the defeat of Gowa, the Dutch had eliminated most of the major hindrances to establishing a spice monopoly, although the subjugation of what would become known first as Dutch East India and then Indonesia would be a long process.

SIGNIFICANCE

The quest for monopolies of profitable goods and the surplus of wealth created by government efforts to increase national treasuries created capital for investment. Surplus wealth, which paid for large military forces in Western European nations, made possible European domination of other parts—and peoples—of the globe, leading to the establishment of European colonialism.

The Dutch gained control of the Spice Islands and the surrounding region, and out of this region came the nation of Indonesia. Other nations in Southeast Asia that were initially seeking spices seized other territories, creating other nations. To the north, much of the long southern peninsula of Southeast Asia fell under the English and became Malaya (now called Malaysia). To the west, the Spanish held on to islands they had taken in their quest for the spice market in the late sixteenth century, and these islands became the Philippines.

—*Carl L. Bankston III*

FURTHER READING

Magnusson, Lars. *Mercantilism: The Shaping of an Economic Language*. New York: Routledge, 1994. Magnusson looks at the development of mercantile theory and practice. Chapter 4 is devoted specifically to seventeenth century developments.

Ricklefs, M. C. *A History of Modern Indonesia Since c. 1200*. 4th ed. Stanford, Calif.: Stanford University Press, 2001. Part 2, "Struggles for Hegemony," explores the establishment of colonial power by the Dutch East India Company in the seventeenth century. Includes excellent maps.

Taylor, Jean Gelman. *Indonesia: Peoples and Histories*. New Haven, Conn.: Yale University Press, 2003. A general history of Indonesia. Chapters 5 and 6, on the entry of Europeans and on the Indonesian sultanates, deal directly with economics. Scattered throughout the book are capsules summarizing key topics.

SEE ALSO: 17th cent.: The Pepper Trade; Dec., 1601: Dutch Defeat the Portuguese in Bantam Harbor; 1602-1613: Japan Admits Western Traders; Mar. 20, 1602: Dutch East India Company Is Founded; Beginning Spring, 1605: Dutch Dominate Southeast Asian Trade; 1606-1674: Europeans Settle in India; Apr. 29, 1606: First European Contact with Australia; 1609:

Bank of Amsterdam Invents Checks; 1609: China Begins Shipping Tea to Europe; Jan. 14, 1641: Capture of Malacca; Apr., 1652: Dutch Begin to Colonize Southern Africa.

RELATED ARTICLES in *Great Lives from History: The Seventeenth Century, 1601-1700:* Piet Hein; John IV; Maurice of Nassau; Michiel Adriaanszoon de Ruyter; Abel Janszoon Tasman; Maarten Tromp; Zheng Chenggong.

17th century
BIRTH CONTROL IN WESTERN EUROPE

Historians and demographers believe that seventeenth century individuals in Europe understood the ramifications of large families during demographic crises and the risks to women of multiple pregnancies. Thus, couples used coitus interruptus, abstention, abortion, potions, condoms, prolonged lactation after the birth of a child, late marriage, and other methods of birth control.

LOCALE: Western Europe
CATEGORIES: Health and medicine; biology; historiography; cultural and intellectual history

SUMMARY OF EVENT
Modern historians have debated the idea that premodern peoples employed primitive forms of birth control. Many historians working in the 1960's and 1970's viewed any practice of contraception prior to the nineteenth century as unimaginable. Discussions related to premodern contraceptive behavior became tied to larger examinations of religious attitudes, sexual conduct, gender relations, family structures, and demographic fluctuations.

Using these avenues of research, historians gradually came to agree that rudimentary forms of birth control, including coitus interruptus, abstention, abortion, herbal potions and lotions meant to inhibit sexual ability, primitive condoms, prolonged lactation after the birth of a child, and late marriage to reduce fecundity were all forms of contraceptive technologies employed consciously in the seventeenth century to limit family size. E. A. Wrigley, a demographic and economic historian, has argued that the English in the sixteenth and seventeenth centuries limited family size by coitus interruptus, abortion, and infanticide, whereas Lawrence Stone, an early modern historian, determined that the English no-

bility was using some methods of birth control by the mid-seventeenth century.

Much contemporary evidence exists that premodern people practiced birth control. Catholic priests in the early Middle Ages, for example, issued prohibitions against coitus interruptus, popularly known as the "sin of Onan" from a story in the book of Genesis in which Onan "spilled his seed" instead of potentially impregnating his wife, Tamar. Cultural and medical historian Angus McLaren has argued that the sheer number of premodern penitentials referring to the sin of Onan undermines the argument of contraceptive ignorance. He further postulated that the growth of printing during the Reformation period and the publication of Bibles in the vernacular probably augmented general knowledge about coitus interruptus. In addition, there is some indication that couples may have practiced anal intercourse as a preventive measure against unwanted pregnancy. While anal intercourse was certainly viewed as a serious sin in the seventeenth century, it was not associated exclusively with homosexuality. Priests, pastors, and judges in the period discussed sodomy as an offense that both men and women might commit.

Knowledge of birth control methods in the seventeenth century was drawn not just from biblical sources but from ancient, medieval, and Islamic texts as well. Physicians in the Greek, Roman, and Islamic worlds wrote about contraception, and this knowledge was well known in the early modern period. Herbals and medical manuals in the sixteenth and seventeenth centuries reprinted age-old recipes that included oral potions meant to induce abortion, penis ointments used to promote abstinence, and recommendations for postcoital exercise. Oral contraceptives made from different combinations of ingredients, such as pepper, woodbine, rue, hemp, cumin, calamine, radish root, and castor oil, were meant to dampen the appetite for sexual intercourse.

Another form of abstinence involved refraining from sexual relations during certain months of the year. Demographers have argued that this was a conscious effort by agrarian peoples to limit births during the summer and early fall, when labor needs on the farm were most critical. Condoms made from animal bladders were also available to wealthy men in the seventeenth century. Historians, additionally, have identified a largely female subculture that disseminated knowledge about contraception. Midwives and wise women were familiar with techniques to prevent unwanted pregnancies and bring about abortions even though the seventeenth century midwife's oath included a statement against giving abortifacients.

Angus McLaren noted that early modern women secured abortions by magical, physical, pessary, and herbal means. Magical means might include a spell that could reverse a conception or involve an amulet to bring on a miscarriage. Physical means referred to bleedings, beatings, and vigorous exercise. Many of these recommendations actually were written in medical texts to reverse amenorrhea and prevent sterility, but remedies devised to restore menstruation might also be used to induce abortion. Pessaries, often made of iris root, almonds, or roots of lilies and sometimes mixed with vinegar, also were placed inside the vagina to induce abortion. Finally, women also used toxic and nontoxic substances in herbal potions to end unwanted pregnancies. The three most common abortifacients were pennyroyal, ergot of rye, and, the strongest, savin. In the seventeenth century, many women believed that an abortion was neither a sin nor immoral if it occurred before the "quickening," around the fifth month of pregnancy, when mothers become aware of fetal movement.

Dorothy McLaren, a historian of women's history, underscored that women in the seventeenth century knew of the contraceptive effects of frequent breast-feeding. She examined female marital fertility patterns in women of the upper class as well as the lower class in the seventeenth century and found that wealthy women who used wet nurses were more fertile than less wealthy women who breast-fed their own children. Prolonged breast-feeding produced amenorrhea of lactation in early modern women, making it harder for them to conceive and thus allowing them some mark of forethought in attempts to plan family size. Breast-feeding women tended to reproduce every twenty-four to thirty

months. This allowed women to space births over the course of their reproductive years. Wealthy women who used wet nurses, however, tended to have larger families because they became pregnant every twelve to fifteen months.

Recent statistical studies on northern European society in the seventeenth century also reveal one final observation of past contraceptive behavior. Wrigley and other members of the Cambridge Group for the History of Population and Social Structure developed an innovative technique called "family reconstitution" to study early modern European population shifts. Family reconstitution involves linking data drawn from parish records to reconstitute fertility and death rates for any given period. Rates of illegitimacy, premarital pregnancy, and family limitation practices can also be determined. These findings reveal a northern European marriage pattern predicated on late marriage, usually age twenty-five to twenty-seven for women and twenty-seven to twenty-nine for men. Late marriage was an especially effective form of premodern birth control that allowed for the adjustment of fertility to changing economic conditions. The later a woman married, the less time she spent in the childbed or birthing chair, thus reducing the number of pregnancies she experienced in her lifetime. Late age at marriage was not popular, however, in southern Europe, where women tended to marry between the ages of seventeen and nineteen.

SIGNIFICANCE

Twentieth century historical and demographic research reveals that people in seventeenth century Europe had a number of contraceptive options that they could pursue. The idea that they were ignorant of various aspects of reproduction and their abilities to prevent conception, affect the outcome of conception, or both is no longer tenable. While some of their methods of birth control were both crude and ineffective, others offered viable and successful means of limiting family size. This research shows that seventeenth century Europeans had real agency when it came to reproductive decision making and underscores that they did not always abide by religious strictures that linked intercourse with procreation only. Their behaviors indicate a willingness to use "family spacing" technologies that decreased fertility and allowed women more control over their bodies.

Some scholars have indicated, moreover, that even the more crude abortion potions, bloodletting regimes, and exercises might have been quite effective in the seventeenth century when pregnancies overall were more precarious because of diet and poor standards of living and miscarriages were much more commonplace than today. The most significant decline in fertility before the advent of the contraceptive pill occurred in the modern period between 1870 and 1920 in northern European urban centers. Nonetheless, Angus McLaren points out that this decline was based not on the development of new contraceptive knowledge or techniques but on increased use of methods that were already well known and employed in the seventeenth century.

—*S. Annette Finley-Croswhite*

FURTHER READING

McLaren, Angus. *A History of Contraception from Antiquity to the Present Day*. London: Basil Blackwell, 1990. Offers a key chapter on early modern contraceptive behavior.

_____. *Reproductive Rituals: The Perception of Fertility in England from the Sixteenth Century to the Nineteenth Century*. New York: Methuen, 1984. The author argues persuasively that premodern people employed rudimentary contraceptive practices.

McLaren, Dorothy. "Marital Fertility and Lactation, 1570-1720." In *Women in English Society, 1500-1800*, edited by Mary Prior. London: Methuen, 1985. This article argues that lactation amenorrhoea was a seventeenth century contraceptive "technology."

Stone, Lawrence. *The Family, Sex, and Marriage in England, 1500-1800*. London: Weidenfeld and Nicholson, 1977. Stone argues that marriages were loveless before the eighteenth century. He also discounts knowledge of contraception by the majority of the population before 1700. Current historians reject this thesis.

Wrigley, E. A., et al. *English Population History from Family Reconstitution, 1580-1837*. New York: Cambridge University Press, 1997. A major work exploring the logic between fertility and mortality.

SEE ALSO: 17th cent.: Advances in Medicine; 1689-1694: Famine and Inflation in France.

RELATED ARTICLES in *Great Lives from History: The Seventeenth Century, 1601-1700:* Louyse Bourgeois; Justine Siegemundin.

17th century
EMERGENCE OF LUBA GOVERNANCE

Institutions of royalty among the Luba of central Africa were among the earliest and most influential political traditions in medieval and early modern Africa, marking the first centralized state in the Congo region.

LOCALE: Upper Kasai River area, Democratic Republic of Congo

CATEGORIES: Government and politics; expansion and land acquisition

KEY FIGURES

Nkongolo (fl. seventeenth century), a legendary magical hunter, possible founder and then king of Luba

Mbidi Kiluwe (fl. mid-seventeenth century), a legendary magical hunter, whose son Kalal Ilunga was threatened with murder by King Nkongolo

Kalal Ilunga (fl. late seventeenth century), son of Mbidi who overthrew Nkongolo after he was threatened with death by the king

Mwine Kadilo (fl. early eighteenth century), Luba king

Ilunga Sungu (fl. late eighteenth century), grandson of Mwine, and Luba king, r. 1780-1810

SUMMARY OF EVENT

The Luba political system emerged after the fifteenth century among peoples of the grasslands of central Africa, on the shores of Lake Kisale, near the upper Kasai, a tributary of the Congo River. The founders of the Luba kingdom were probably immigrants from the north who spoke a language of the Bantu family. Settlers were initially drawn to the region by the opportunities for fishing in the marshes and streams.

By 1000, the economy of the region was expanding, with fishing communities being joined by farmers who raised sorghum, beans, and millets, and domesticated chickens and goats. The area had significant deposits of iron and salt, which were traded with neighbors who lived downstream. In addition to food production, hunting remained an important dietary supplement as well as a source of prestige for experts.

Economic diversification encouraged significant population growth, which in turn allowed for the social stratification that resulted in the emergence of the Luba kingdom. This is reflected in burials in the region, which by 1000 include copper grave goods, signifying the emergence of individuals with elite status. Since copper is not found in the immediate vicinity, its appearance likely means that trade existed with the mineral rich regions to the south. This suggests that by 1000 a political hierarchy had developed to deal with the challenges of allocating land and water resources, and to protect and foster commerce. Flood-plain agriculture and fishing both necessitated a degree of economic specialization and political centralization that encouraged the emergence of "big men," or authorities, who could organize and protect access to natural resources. Commerce also flourished best in areas where local leaders could assure the protection of traders and trade routes. Political authority fell naturally to religious leaders, those members of society who maintained connections to the ancestors and to the spirit world. Thus, the early Luba rulers successfully joined religious prestige with political power.

Luba oral traditions attribute the emergence of their political system to the conflict between their first ruler and a magical hunter. The first Luba king was Nkongolo, a mythical figure whose name means rainbow. Remembered as a tyrannical and barbarous ruler, Nkongolo and his people became civilized only with the arrival of a magical hunter named Mbidi Kiluwe, a foreigner who attempted to tutor the king. The two men quarreled, leading Mbidi to leave, but not before he had married and impregnated two of the king's sisters, each of whom bore sons: Kalal Ilunga and Kisulu Mabele. Suspicious of the stranger's children, Nkongolo tried to kill Kalal Ilunga, who escaped and returned to his father's village. Kalal returned with an army and overthrew the tyrannical Nkongolo.

This origin myth hints at the important political transformations that took place among the Luba after 1000. Socially stratified chiefdoms appear to have merged into a unitary state sometime during the fourteenth century. During this era, early Luba kings combined existing social institutions with novel political concepts to create a dynamic royal institution. Rulers over a relatively large population, and wealthy in salt and iron resources, the Luba kings established a confederation of tributaries over a wide swath of the eastern savanna, tributaries that recognized the authority and legitimacy of the Luba kingdom.

The Luba royal clan drew legitimacy from their founding myth, and the throne was available only to those who could claim to be descended in a line of male relatives from Kalal Ilunga. Because the great ancestor was believed to have been invested with magical powers, Luba kings also claimed to rule by divine right, which

was associated with an inherited magical property called *mulopwe*. However, all male members of the royal family were expected to rule as chiefs on behalf of their monarch, and the claims of Luba kings did not prevent weak or unpopular rulers from being challenged by rivals. To administer the kingdom, Luba rulers relied on members of the royal family as well as secret societies, social organizations that probably predated the rise of the monarchy and used to monitor the chiefs and their domains.

From its homeland, Luba influence expanded to the north and south along the trade routes linking the rain forest to the north with the copper belt of the southern savanna. The court grew wealthy from the tribute it exacted from neighboring peoples who accepted the authority of the Luba monarchs. Luba power came less from its military force (which was never very formidable) than from the immense prestige of its ruling dynasty. However, the actual influence of the Luba state was limited by the constraints on population and travel that were a fact of life in the region. The prestige of the monarch and his ability to exact tribute from his subjects diminished the farther one got from the Luba center. To assert their authority, Luba kings used a system of spies, administrators, and military men to keep its tributaries in line. Parties of warriors were sent by the king as a last resort to coerce tribute out of recalcitrant village leaders. Such parties also played an important role in disseminating Luba traditions into new regions.

Little is known about the early expansion of the Luba kingdoms. In approximately 1700, the first major expansion of one of the kingdoms began, led by King Mwine Kadilo. Upon his death, after a protracted succession dispute, this ruler's grandson Ilunga Sungu emerged as the ruler of the greatest Luba state. His raids expanded the wealth and authority of the Luba throughout the region. Some historians see the rapid Luba expansion of the seventeenth and eighteenth centuries as part of a "new" Luba kingdom brought about in part by a shift from matrilineal to patrilineal descent among some Luba communities. Luba political expansion reached its apex in the nineteenth century, and then the Luba rulers fell victim to the encroachment of Arab-Swahili raiders from the East African coast.

Significance

The emergence of Luba political institutions transformed the loosely affiliated farmers and fishing peoples who lived in the upper tributaries of the Congo River basin into the first centralized state in the region. Utilizing novel principles of divine kingship, Luba rulers were able to take advantage of a rising population and of economic diversification to claim tribute from and authority over the previously scattered peoples of the central African savanna. Luba governance proved easily adaptable by neighboring peoples. Thus, the most important result of the rise of the Luba dynasties was not in Lubaland itself, but in the adoption of Luba political traditions among the Lunda, their southern neighbors.

Under quite different environmental and geographic circumstances, the adaptation and reformulation of Luba kingship by the Lunda helped to create one of the most powerful empires of modern African history. The close connection between Luba and subsequent Lunda political traditions has encouraged scholars to speak of a Luba/Lunda political tradition. Lunda expansion in turn gave rise to other "copycat" states, such as Kazembe, which lies several hundred kilometers southeast of the Lunda heartland, or the more distant Bemba of Malawi, whose oral traditions also speak of Luba/Lunda origins. Thus, the emergence of Luba governance played a role in the rise of dynastic states throughout the central African savannas.

—James Burns

FURTHER READING

De Heusch, Luc. *The Drunken King: Or, The Origin of the State*. Bloomington: Indiana University Press, 1982. A structuralist comparison of central African oral traditions that treats Luba creation myths extensively.

Edgerton, Robert B. *The Troubled Heart of Africa: A History of the Congo*. New York: St. Martin's Press, 2002. Edgerton provides a thorough and complete history of the Congo region, from the arrival of the Portuguese in the 1500's through the twentieth century.

Ehret, Chris. *The Civilizations of Africa: A History to 1800*. Charlottesville: University of Virginia Press, 2002. A textbook that relies heavily on linguistics and archaeology in its reconstruction of Luba history and regional influence.

Gondola, Ch. Didier. *The History of Congo*. Westport, Conn.: Greenwood Press, 2002. A survey of Congo's history, covering the Kuba and other kingdoms and peoples. Provides, also, biographical sketches of key figures in the region's history.

Reefe, Thomas. *The Rainbow and the Kings: A History of the Luba Empire to 1891*. Berkeley: University of California Press, 1981. The only monograph devoted entirely to Luba history.

_____. "The Societies on the Eastern Savanna." In *History of Central Africa*, edited by David Birmingham and Phyllis M. Martin. Vol. 1. New York: Longman, 1983. Reefe continues his examination of the Luba kingdom and other societies of the region.

Vansina, Jan. *Kingdoms of the Savanna*. Madison: University of Wisconsin Press, 1968. The definitive work on state formation in central Africa, by an author of dozens of books on central African precolonial history, art, and politics.

SEE ALSO: Early 17th cent.: Rise of Rwanda; c. 1625: Formation of the Kuba Kingdom; 1644-1671: Ndongo Wars; Late 17th cent.: Rise of Buganda.

RELATED ARTICLE in *Great Lives from History: The Seventeenth Century, 1601-1700:* Njinga.

17th century
ENGLAND'S AGRICULTURAL REVOLUTION

Seventeenth century agricultural innovations included new cropping patterns, intensive and diversified fertilization techniques, extensive land reclamation, and new crops for human consumption and forages for livestock. In conjunction with increasingly complex marketing strategies and evolving industrial activity, these techniques elevated the overall nutritional levels of enlarging Western European populations. In England in particular, a favorable parliamentary environment encouraged this revolution.

LOCALE: England; the Low Countries, particularly the Netherlands

CATEGORIES: Agriculture; economics; science and technology; trade and commerce; inventions

KEY FIGURES

Francis Bacon (1561-1626), English scientist who was the first to apply science to agricultural concerns, particularly seeds and soil

Nehemiah Grew (1641-1712), English physician and botanist

John Evelyn (1620-1706), English writer and cofounder of the Royal Society

Robert Boyle (1627-1691), Irish chemist and cofounder of the Royal Society

SUMMARY OF EVENT

Nineteenth and early twentieth century historical accounts of the European Agricultural Revolution suggested 1760 as a starting date for the emergence of new agricultural practices. In fact, however, a number of processes— political, scientific, demographic, and economic—had coalesced more than a century earlier, ushering in a gradual institutionalization of new, primarily English, agrarian procedures. All areas of English agriculture were impacted, and agrarian evolution proceeded simultaneously with and provided both support and impetus for incipient industrial activity.

British scientists were among the first Europeans to use scientific observation and experimentation to investigate the potential for increased agricultural productivity. Francis Bacon initiated the study of soils and seed germination. Robert Boyle also worked on soil chemistry and authored *The Sceptical Chymist* (1661, rev. 1679). In 1662, Boyle contributed to the founding of the Royal Society. Another early member, John Evelyn, wrote the first British monograph on soil, *A Philosophical Dis-*

course of Earth (1676), while the London physician Nehemiah Grew published *The Anatomy of Vegetables Begun* (1672), by virtue of which he is considered one of the founders of the field of plant anatomy. These men and others, such as John Woodward (1665-1728), whose quantitative studies of plant physiology provided a basis for an understanding of plant nutrition, provided literate landowners with a comprehensive history of agricultural accomplishments, and their analyses made clear what other advances would be necessary before higher crop yields could be realized.

The English Civil Wars (1642-1651) allowed certain Royalist landowners to travel to the Low Countries, where varied farming and land reclamation practices were observed and ultimately imported to Britain. New crops in rotation and nitrogen-fixing plants were described in publications such as Walter Blith's *The English Improver Improved: Or, The Survey of Husbandry Surveyed* (1653). Multiple techniques were utilized by English farmers, including increased tillage, drainage, irrigation, and higher levels of manuring.

England's agricultural community profited from government support in the seventeenth century. After the Restoration of Charles II in 1660, Parliament included several influential members of the landed gentry who favored legislation that promised to enhance agricultural profit and productivity. The Corn Law of 1670 provided for duties on imported wheat to be determined by local pricing of English wheat. The Corn Bounty Act (1688), on the other hand, subsidized corn exports.

A series of Parliamentary acts beginning in 1604 allowed for the creation of enclosures, that is, the physical enclosing of agricultural land with fences or hedges, thereby amalgamating previously community-controlled holdings into larger, privatized, profit-oriented enterprises. Gradually, new crops and cropping patterns appeared, as did greater numbers of animals, which enhanced soil fertility. Animal numbers in pre-enclosure times were limited by the availability of common use pastures. Enclosures created more acreage for experimentation and gradually divorced farmers from ancient, community-oriented practices. Thus, the Agricultural Revolution altered England's rural social structure and land-use patterning, while increasing the supplies of food.

Incremental improvements and introductions defined the seventeenth century Agricultural Revolution, rather than mechanical breakthroughs. The enduring achieve-

Francis Bacon was the first Englishman to apply scientific methods to the study of agriculture. (Library of Congress)

ment of the century was the realization that livestock and cereal agriculture could be united by introducing new crops such as turnips, clovers, and grasses. The new crops coupled with new tillage practices raised outputs, elevated soil fertility, and complemented labor and cultivation inputs.

The seventeenth century witnessed more land under the plow, a positive remedy for both weedy fields and certain livestock diseases. Gradually, a tillage revolution came about whereby formally permanent grassland and inconsistent cultivation were replaced by up-and-down husbandry, that is, the plowing and sowing of new grassland. After several years of grazing or harvesting, the process was repeated. Hence, a rotational system replaced the medieval multifield pattern. Upon the grass, sheep and beef cattle were fattened, while milk and butter were produced in dairy areas. Greater supplies of animal forage meant that larger numbers of animals could be kept through the winter, thereby increasing supplies of manure as well as raising farm profits through new marketing strategies.

Industrial crops were grown experimentally, and then, if they proved successful, their culture was intensi-

fied. Woad, a dye crop, was extensively grown between 1590 and 1660. A by-product of the woad plant could be fed to sheep, so woad provided numerous benefits, including forage, ready cash through industrial sales, and a rationale for increased tillage. Additional crops destined for industrial usage included hemp, flax, and hops. Fertilized grassland provided up to four times the nutrients available in old common-use pastures. Forage productivity during the seventeenth century allowed livestock numbers to quadruple. Increased livestock numbers ultimately channeled more products into the industrial community, which in turn could provide those products, such as tallow, horn, and hides, more efficiently to existing markets, as well as developing new markets. Wool, long an important British product, was selectively altered during the seventeenth century to create a coarser type, destined for worsted cloth.

Soil fertility was a major concern of the agrarian program—manure, both animal and green manure, was liberally applied to the fields. Lime and marl, and any degradable material—bone, rags, ashes, chalk, and industrial wastes—were hauled to crop fields and tilled in.

Some farmers fattened sheep; mutton production rose. Others fed cattle or hogs on grasses, grains, and forage by-products. Marketable field crops included mustard, peas, beans, barley, lentils, carrots, peas, tobacco, and potatoes. Acreage devoted to English tobacco increased throughout the seventeenth century. Potatoes, previously grown in the sixteenth century for household usage, became an important crop for the cattle feeder by 1650. Turnips, initially a household root-crop, became a desirable crop for the cattle feeder and dairy farmer after 1660. By 1720, turnip cultivation accounted for about 8 percent of all tilled acreage. In the following century, the politician and agriculturalist Charles Townshend, second Viscount Townshend of Raynham (1674-1738), popularized the use of turnips as winter fodder and championed the four-course rotation system.

SIGNIFICANCE

The seventeenth century witnessed the dawn of specialization in English agriculture. Dairy farming, cattle feeding, industrial cropping, and sheep farming all appeared as specialties or as components in diversified farm operations. Market gardening of fruits and vegetables enhanced the profits for farmers living in proximity to growing urban areas. Population growth in England was yet another force that affected agricultural innovation: The 1540 national population of 2.8 million had enlarged to 5.2 million by 1650. In London as well, population growth mirrored the rise of nonfood producers; a population of 60,000 in 1534 rose to about 530,000 by 1696.

The challenge to achieve higher levels of agricultural efficiency was singularly addressed by England and Holland. The benefits of their innovations were legion. Foremost among these was a more balanced and nutritious diet, available not only to urbanites but to rural folk as well. Vitamin and caloric intake rose appreciably as the year-round availability of eggs, fruit, cereals, vegetables, and red meats, in addition to preserved foods, became commonplace.

Arable land benefited from increased fertilization practices and drainage. Land reclamation, ongoing since the Middle Ages, accelerated during the seventeenth century. Wetlands and fens were drained, and inland canal systems were improved, which in turn facilitated proto-industrial activity. Dutch engineers aided English landowners in technique; however, the revolution was largely an internal process, employing English resources and ingenuity and reinterpreting traditional and emerging problems.

The product of these labors was a more scientific, more productive form of agriculture. In the next century, mechanization would become widespread in planting and harvesting equipment.

—*Rene M. Descartes*

FURTHER READING

Beckett, J. V. *The Agricultural Revolution*. Oxford, England: Basil Blackwell, 1990. A thought-provoking survey examining English crop patterns, livestock systems, enclosures, productivity, and labor.

Kerridge, Eric. *The Agricultural Revolution*. London: Allen & Unwin, 1967. A classic study of English agrarian systems that concludes that the Agricultural Revolution was an English phenomenon transpiring between 1560 and 1690. Includes extensive bibliography and appendixes.

Mingay, G. E. *The Agricultural Revolution: Changes in Agriculture, 1650-1880*. London: A. & C. Black, 1977. A general history including forty-six separate documents attesting to Britain's primacy in agricultural change.

Riches, Naomi. *The Agricultural Revolution in Norfolk*. 2d ed. London: Frank Cass, 1967. An analysis of evolving Norfolk agrarian systems from the twelfth through the nineteenth centuries. Includes maps.

Russell, Sir E. John. *A History of Agricultural Science in Great Britain, 1620-1954*. London: Allen & Unwin, 1966. A comprehensive treatment that focuses upon scientific research in English agriculture.

Spencer, Colin. *British Food: An Extraordinary Thousand Years of History*. New York: Columbia University Press, 2002. A scholarly investigation into social dynamics, technology, the forces of proto-industrialization, and changing cuisines. Includes appendices.

Zuckerman, Larry. *The Potato*. New York: North Point Press, 1998. Historical review of the diffusion and importance of the tuber in Western culture.

SEE ALSO: 17th cent.: Rise of Proto-Industrial Economies; 1601-1672: Rise of Scientific Societies; 1612: Introduction of Tobacco Farming in North America; 1642-1651: English Civil Wars; May, 1659-May, 1660: Restoration of Charles II.

RELATED ARTICLES in *Great Lives from History: The Seventeenth Century, 1601-1700:* Robert Boyle; John Evelyn.

17th century
EUROPE ENDORSES SLAVERY

By the seventeenth century, slavery on European soil had been absent for four hundred years, but the reemergence of slavery in the New World forced Europeans to decide between condemning and condoning a practice that was as economically desirable as it was morally inexcusable.

LOCALE: Europe, the Mediterranean basin, and Africa
CATEGORIES: Economics; trade and commerce; social issues and reform

KEY FIGURES
Charles II (1630-1685), king of England, r. 1660-1685
Louis XIII (1601-1643), king of France, r. 1610-1643
Urban VIII (Maffeo Vincenzo Barberini; 1568-1644), Roman Catholic pope, 1623-1644
Jean-Baptiste Colbert (1619-1683), French controller general of finance, 1665-1683, minister of marine, 1669-1683, and secretary of state, 1669-1683

SUMMARY OF EVENT
Economic realities had essentially forced slavery out of Europe by the 1200's. Over the next four hundred years, however, as maritime advances opened up fresh sources and new markets for products, the preoccupation of European leaders with their intercontinental disputes and wars allowed for the reestablishment of the trade in human beings, this time in the Americas. The unique situations of colonial America and Africa made slavery not only feasible but also economically desirable, while the authorities in Europe were both slow to react against the creation of a global slave trade and impotent to regulate affairs on the other side of the world once they attempted to restrain the trade.

The institution of slavery goes back to the beginning of recorded history, but slavery faded in Europe between 800 and 1200, transitioning into feudalism. The latter system used serfs, who had some limited rights, instead of slaves, who were treated only as property. The absence of slavery in Europe had lasted a couple of centuries, when, once again, the potential profits of trading in forced servitude attracted Europeans. Portuguese mariners of the 1400's transformed the limited intra-African slave trade into an intercontinental market. Other Europeans followed suit, including the Spanish (1479), the English (1562), the Dutch (1625), and the French (1634).

The European hunger for sugar and to a lesser degree that for coffee, chocolate, and tobacco fueled the rise of slavery in the New World. The capture and deportation of generations of Africans was from the outset founded on the economics of gold. By the seventeenth century, it was a simple white substance that caused the stir. Sugar held two strong attractions: Economically, it was valuable enough to gain the label "white gold," and physically, it was almost addictive. The Arabs had taught the crusaders how to cultivate sugar on plantations around the Mediterranean. When it was brought back to the West, European consumers came to associate sugary products with wealth, increasing demand by imparting it with symbolic value in addition to its more obvious use-value. As a result, what had been profitable to cultivate at the edges of the Mediterranean became hugely valuable when installed in the tropical areas of the New World. From the middle of the seventeenth century to the middle of the eighteenth, sugar outdistanced grain as the world's most valuable commodity.

The Dutch demonstrated the profits that could be made from a wide range of associated commercial operations. In the port of Amsterdam, they built sugar refining and warehousing companies to complement the shipping industry. The three-stage journey required to provide "sugar in every cup of tea" began in seaports from Spain to Denmark. Ships left these ports bound for the west coast of Africa, where, with the help of African middlemen, the Europeans traded manufactured goods (especially guns) for slaves. Captive Africans were then taken to the Americas and exchanged for raw sugar cane. The cane was shipped to Europe for refining, thereby completing the commercial triangle. Entire cities, especially the ports of Seville, Lisbon, La Rochelle, Amsterdam, and London, profited enormously from this system.

The cultivation of these tropical crops relied upon two essential components, large expanses of land and large numbers of workers. In order to take advantage of innovations in seafaring and international trade, European nations organized legitimate commercial companies. These enterprises, often labeled with exotic names, ended up providing slaves to American plantations. In 1621, the Dutch formed the West India Company, which by virtue of its government-granted monopoly became one of the largest single slave-trading businesses in history. In 1660, King Charles II of England supported the launch of the Royal Adventurers into Africa. Twelve years later, the British created the Royal African Company, which set up and administered trading posts in western Africa. One task of this organization was to seize the occasional rogue British trader who, for private gain, tried to bypass the royal monopoly. Privateers and pirates also did their share of slave trading during this century.

Seventeenth century monarchs played an important role in deciding whether to move toward or away from slavery. The favorable economics of the enterprise usually outweighed moral considerations among European leaders. King Louis XIII of France was at first aghast that the refined French should follow Portugal and Spain in accessing the slave trade. Eventually, however, led by the promise of national profit and convinced that the Africans would benefit by converting to Christianity, the French became willing participants in human commerce. Jean-Baptiste Colbert, Louis XIV's finance minister, doubled national revenues over a ten-year period. One of his profit points was the establishment of France's own West Indian Company in 1664, complete with contracts for the delivery of slaves to the New World.

Most seventeenth century European heads of state were too worried about their own domestic or intercontinental disputes to involve themselves with the issue of slavery. The French, for example, fought among themselves in the Siege of La Rochelle (1627-1628) and battled the Spanish off and on between 1635 and 1659. Louis XIV went to war (1667-1668) against the country of his wife, Marie-Thérèse, daughter of Philip IV of Spain, in order to gain territory. The English, the Irish, and the Scots fought between the years 1641 and 1648. The Thirty Years' War (1618-1648) included a Danish phase (1625-1629), a Swedish phase (1630-1635), and a Franco-Swedish phase (1635-1648) before the Peace of Westphalia (1648). Thus, if the distracted European governments addressed the question of human servitude, they generally pronounced against it but then supported it indirectly by enacting trade motivations.

The positions of religious institutions vacillated on the question of slavery. The idea of bringing indigenous people a new and "right" religion was used to justify the subjugation of Africans. However, religious currents were usually a force *against* slavery, or at least for the mollification of its fierceness. In 1627, Father José de Anchieta, a Jesuit priest working peaceably among the Indians of Brazil, faced off with his compatriot colonizers who wanted to import slaves. The Jesuits in that same year announced to Europeans their belief that slavery combined humankind's worst qualities. In 1639, Pope Urban VIII forbade slavery in any New World colonies. Exemplifying the ambiguity of the time, the Quakers in

1676 admonished others to "treat kindly" their slaves and yet banned "negroes" from their own meetings. Further, the Roman Catholic Church, despite its official antislavery message, had a history of being associated with properties worked by slaves.

The Europeans received their first impressions of Africans by way of explorers' journals and various tales of travel. Along with missionaries, adventurers and often slavers wrote about their encounters with Africans. Thomas Phillips, a British slave trader of the late 1600's, admired "Negroes" who willfully drowned themselves rather than submit to slavery. Of all the original European perceptions of African peoples, the one that continued to prop up the system of brutality was the idea that the black man had a special resistance for working the hot and humid fields of sugar cane. Despite the obstacles of disease and oppression, and despite dying in shocking numbers, slaves did produce tropical crops in profitable quantities. The Europeans did not lose sight of this fact.

SIGNIFICANCE

Even apart from the mass genocide that results from the transport and abuse of slaves, slavery represents humankind at its worst. Many modern culture clashes have their roots in the transatlantic slave trade. Seventeenth century Europe, itself free from slavery for many years, became its instigator on the world stage, essentially for profit motives. Leading up to the seventeenth century, maritime and other technological advances made international slaving economically feasible on a large scale. Sea explorers were more intrepid and precise in their undertakings because of better ships, maps, and clocks.

Even if slavery had its historical origins already in place among African tribes, it never would have developed into the mass removal of peoples across the Atlantic without European technologies of agriculture and transportation and European political and social structures underpinning those technologies. If one considers that the institution of slavery was on the brink of extinction in the Western world, Europe's culpability in the foundation of the transatlantic slave trade becomes even clearer. It seems possible that some little impetus from a leader here or there might have been sufficient to prevent the trade from taking route and to allow it to progress toward obsolescence.

—Steven Crawford

FURTHER READING

Blackburn, Robin. "The Old World Background to European Colonial Slavery." *William and Mary Quarterly*, 3d ser. 54, no. 1 (January, 1997): 65-102. Treats the economic origins of sugar and slaves preceding transatlantic slave trade.

Bonnassie, Pierre. *From Slavery to Feudalism in South-Western Europe*. New York: Cambridge University Press, 1991. A close look at religious, military, and economic influences on the shift from slavery to serfdom in Europe, especially from 800 through 1100. Sets the stage for the events of the seventeenth century.

Deveau, Jean-Michel. *La France au temps des négriers*. Paris: Éditions France-Empire, 1994. Slavery from maritime point of view, as the author is from the French port of La Rochelle.

Gunther, Lenworth, ed. *Black Image: European Eyewitness Accounts of Afro-American Life*. Port Washington, N.Y.: Kennikat, 1978. Ranging from the 1400's to the 1960's, the editor provides first-person reports as to how opinions and stereotypes develop.

Klooster, Wim, and Alfred Padula. *The Atlantic World: Essays on Slavery, Migration, and Imagination*. Upper Saddle River, N.J.: Pearson Education, 2005. The introduction and chapter 2 deal extensively with the European take on seventeenth century slavery.

17th century
THE PEPPER TRADE

The rise and fall of the global economic system in the seventeenth century is directly connected to the production and distribution of pepper, which linked Southeast Asia to important markets in Western Europe, East Asia, and the Mediterranean. Pepper was a much-needed spice, used for food preservation as well as for masking the taste of spoiling food.

LOCALE: Southeast Asia
CATEGORIES: Economics; trade and commerce; organizations and institutions; transportation

KEY FIGURES
Elizabeth I (1533-1603), queen of England, r. 1558-1603, who chartered the British East India Company
Jan Pieterszoon Coen (1587-1629), a director of the Dutch East India Company
Tokugawa Ieyasu (1543-1616), shogun, r. 1603-1605, who organized and regulated Japan's Southeast Asian trade

SUMMARY OF EVENT
No other agricultural product had the vast market appeal of pepper. It became the first international cash crop purposely cultivated for world consumption. The sale of this important resource accelerated the expansion of the Southeast Asian economy, providing thousands of jobs and increasing the standard of living across the region. It was the foundation of the Southeast Asian sector of the new world economic order.

In an age without the ability to preserve food, spice, especially pepper, dominated the culinary world of early modern Eurasia. Combinations of spices could be used to preserve vegetables and meats and could also mask the unappetizing taste of food that was beginning to spoil. Pepper was the basic ingredient in most of these mixtures, thus allowing it to occupy the position at the top of the spice hierarchy.

China became involved in the pepper trade in the early years of the Ming Dynasty, when the country was able to establish a dominant position in the Indian Ocean complex. This newfound power helped energize the expansion of the Chinese economy and coincided with the introduction of large amounts of silver from mines in the Americas and Japan. This unprecedented economic growth led to a significant increase in the Chinese population. This in turn created a greater demand for the production of pepper, which was a major ingredient in Chinese cooking. Pepper would eventually become the first product of mass consumption in Chinese history.

Growth in the Chinese market also expanded the cultivation of pepper in the nations of Southeast Asia. This increased production and the wealth it generated affected every aspect of Southeast Asian society. Most of the region witnessed an increase in employment opportunities; this allowed people to marry earlier and have larger families, which triggered the growth of other sectors of the region's economy. The pepper trade also led to the migration of Chinese merchants to Southeast Asia, especially to Indonesia. Eventually, these entrepreneurs would become a dominant force in the region. This expanded Chinese presence was accompanied by neo-Confucian thought, which would play an important role in the creation of the bureaucratic sector of the new, powerful, highly centralized governments that came into existence in response to the need for the regulation and protection of the trade in pepper.

This global economic upturn also fostered urbanization in both China and Southeast Asia. Cities usually grew up around important ports and quickly became vibrant economic and cultural centers. Most of the cities supported not only educational institutions but also artists who were drawn to these locations because of their energy, freedom, patronage, and multicultural populations.

China also faced competition from the Islamic world. Fleets from Dar es Salaam maintained a powerful presence in the Indian Ocean and were part of a trading complex that extended to the Red Sea and the Persian Gulf. Originally the Mamlūk Empire, and eventually the Ottoman Empire, controlled both the sea lanes and the caravan routes that dominated the pepper trade in the Mediterranean region.

Like the Chinese experience, the Islamic participation in the pepper trade stimulated the migration of merchants to Southeast Asia. From the very beginning, Islam made great headway in the region, converting thousands of Southeast Asians to the Islamic faith. This was especially true among the merchant class, which favored a belief system that was open to international commerce. Muslim missionaries emphasized the fact that the Prophet Muḥammad came from a family of merchants in Saudi Arabia. The ethical teachings of Islam concerning commercial transactions also played a major role in the economy of Southeast Asia.

In addition, Europeans were attracted to the potential economic power of the pepper trade. The Portuguese broke the Chinese-Islamic monopoly when they gained control of the Indian Ocean. The Portuguese used their new, sophisticated marine and military technology to control the sea lanes by initiating oceanwide search and destroy missions, engaging and defeating the navies of both China and the Islamic world.

Other Atlantic states eventually would begin to compete for a share of the lucrative trade in pepper; the two most successful states were Great Britain (British East India Company) and the Netherlands (Dutch East India Company). Both nations were part of the European commercial revolution, which rested upon a triad of great trading companies, a strong and reliable banking system, and centralized, government economic planning. The move by the English and the Dutch into this global competition was accomplished by the formation of two powerful joint stock companies that focused on gaining control of the East Indian trading network. Both institutions were given unlimited government support and were allowed to initiate and conduct diplomatic and military operations. Both nations were willing to give these companies almost unlimited military support while allowing investors to make substantial profits from their trade.

In 1600, Queen Elizabeth I of England granted a charter to the British East India Company, giving it exclusive rights to trade in Asia. The company's initial success came from the substantial profits it made in the trade of pepper. Directors used this capital to increase the size of their fleet, which allowed them to expand the scope of their power. The Dutch followed suit in 1602 with the creation of the Dutch East India Company, and under the leadership of Jan Pieterszoon Coen the company made significant inroads in the region. Coen adopted an aggressive policy of colonization along with enforcing strict monopolistic control over the sale of pepper. By the early seventeenth century, England and the Netherlands controlled a substantial portion of the pepper trade.

Japan, too, played a major role in this new world system. Many historians mark this period as the start of the ascendancy of early modern Japan. The need for the regulation and protection of the pepper trade helped solidify the legitimacy of the newly established Tokugawa shogunate. Under the early leadership of Tokugawa Ieyasu, the new dynasty not only regulated the number of merchants that could take part in the trade but also created a powerful navy to protect its merchant fleet.

In turn, this stimulated the growth of Japan's urban sector. New cities became centers of Japanese commerce, and the merchant families located there grew in power and influence in the first half of the seventeenth century. This massive expansion of Japanese trade also

1600's

was driven by the substantial increase in the nation's production of silver, which was used to purchase pepper from Southeast Asian plantations.

The steady increase in the price of pepper that helped create the prosperity of the late 1500's peaked and began to decline in the third decade of the seventeenth century. One of the major factors that contributed to this economic decline was the reduction in the quantity of silver that entered the world system from the mines of Latin America and Japan. This lack of purchasing power led to a decrease in the demand for pepper, which in turn affected other areas of economic activity in the global economy.

Urban areas and the merchant class that dominated the trading system were especially hard hit, and port cities throughout the Indian Ocean complex experienced dangerous levels of civil unrest. This political and social chaos manifested itself in the revolutionary activity that traversed the entire Eurasian landmass, from the Ming Dynasty in the east to the British Isles in the west. This was particularly true in Southeast Asia, where this systemic shock reduced the standard of living, which accelerated a decline in both urban and rural areas. The new centralized governments that drew their strength from the regulation of the pepper trade lost much of their power and control. No other area of the world economic system suffered to the extent of Southeast Asia, and it would be centuries before the region would recover from this terrible calamity.

SIGNIFICANCE

The decline and virtual collapse of the Southeast Asian pepper trade was both a characteristic and a catalyst of the economic crisis of the seventeenth century. The hemispheric economic unsteadiness increased competition for control of a rapidly shrinking market. Most of the major nations would, in the end, use military force. The advanced technology possessed by the European states would allow them to dominate the armed forces of their competitors, and this moved the European nations into a position of prominence in the region.

In Asia the economic chaos hastened the collapse of the Ming Dynasty. It also sapped the once powerful states of Southeast Asia of their energy and pushed them into three centuries of impoverishment and colonial control.

—*Richard D. Fitzgerald*

FURTHER READING

Chaudhury, Sushil, and Michel Morineau. *Merchants, Companies, and Trade: Europe and Asia in the Early Modern Era*. New York: Cambridge University Press, 1999. The authors analyze Portuguese and Dutch trade competition within the European context of commercial and imperial strategies in Asia.

Emmer, P. C., and F. S. Gaastra. *The Organization of Interoceanic Trade in European Expansion, 1450-1800*. Aldershot, England: Variorum, 1996. This work examines the comparative mercantile, naval, and political strategies of various European powers for world trade, particularly in the Far East.

Fischer, Steven Roger. *A History of the Pacific Islands*. New York: Palgrave, 2002. Fischer emphasizes the degree to which the Dutch East India Company guarded its monopoly of commercial ventures and exploration.

Lieberman, Victor. *Strange Parallels: Southeast Asia in Global Context, c. 800-1830*. New York: Cambridge University Press, 2003. An excellent comparison of the economic and political development of Europe and Southeast Asia. Includes an index.

Reed, Anthony. *Expansion and Crisis*. Vol. 2 in *Southeast Asia in the Age of Commerce: 1450-1680*. New Haven, Conn.: Yale University Press, 1993. The most respected history of the impact of the age of commerce on Southeast Asia. Provides maps, charts, and an index.

Risso, Patricia. *Merchants of Faith: Muslim Commerce and Culture in the Indian Ocean*. Boulder, Colo.: Westview Press, 1995. An excellent overview of Muslim trade in the Indian Ocean complex, including Southeast Asia. Maps and an index provided.

SEE ALSO: 17th cent.: Age of Mercantilism in Southeast Asia; Dec., 1601: Dutch Defeat the Portuguese in Bantam Harbor; Mar. 20, 1602: Dutch East India Company Is Founded; Beginning Spring, 1605: Dutch Dominate Southeast Asian Trade; 1606-1674: Europeans Settle in India; Apr. 29, 1606: First European Contact with Australia; 1609: Bank of Amsterdam Invents Checks; Jan. 14, 1641: Capture of Malacca; 1642 and 1644: Tasman Proves Australia Is a Separate Continent; June 23, 1661: Portugal Cedes Bombay to the English.

RELATED ARTICLES in *Great Lives from History: The Seventeenth Century, 1601-1700:* Abel Janszoon Tasman; Tokugawa Ieyasu.

17th century
RISE OF PROTO-INDUSTRIAL ECONOMIES

Prior to the Industrial Revolution in the eighteenth century, Europe's population became largely accustomed to the conditions of manufacturing labor through work in peasant homes and small villages where the workers derived their support from wage labor.

LOCALE: Primarily Western Europe
CATEGORIES: Economics; trade and commerce; organizations and institutions

SUMMARY OF EVENT

The idea of proto-industrialism was advanced by scholars after World War II. The general outline of the concept was presented in an article by Franklin Mendels, a professor at the University of California at Berkeley, in an article published in the *Journal of Economic History* in 1972. In his article, based on his study of cottage manufacture in Belgium from the sixteenth to the eighteenth century, Mendels argued that the foundation of the Industrial Revolution of the eighteenth and nineteenth centuries lay in the creation of a laboring population accustomed to deriving its support not from agriculture but from manufacturing work in small shops and peasant homes. These sites existed in areas where the land was insufficient to support all those who lived in the area, either because the quality of the soil was not well suited to raising traditional crops or because the supply of good land was simply too restricted to support a large population.

Mendels supported his argument with some statistics derived from information about population in the area of Belgium south of the city of Ghent. This study suggested to Mendels that there were certain characteristic features of areas in which proto-industrialism took place. These included a fairly rapid increase in the population and the sale of manufactured goods on the international market. In the case of the area cited by Mendels, the manufacture of linen textiles was the defining feature, though he noted that although populations rose significantly in these areas, there was no discernible improvement in wages. At the same time, agriculture became increasingly commercialized, requiring large labor inputs only for short periods, so that a laborer could not rely solely upon such work to support a family.

Mendels's argument was picked up by historians in Europe, some of whom saw the concept as supporting the arguments of Karl Marx that the growth of an impoverished class of wage earners was an inevitable accompaniment of industrialization. Marx, indeed, had advanced a distinct but closely related argument to that of Mendels when he wrote that the "violent expropriation" of workers from the land was a necessary precondition of the Industrial Revolution, because it had created a large pool of potential unskilled laborers in urban centers, which alone made assembly-line manufacturing economically feasible. Whereas Marx looks at the issue from the point of view of the growing migration of former peasants from farmlands to urban areas, Mendels emphasizes that even the relatively rural pockets of proto-industrialization that developed in the seventeenth century provided a pool of workers already accustomed to working for wages barely above the subsistence level and therefore made the growth of factories in the eighteenth and nineteenth centuries easier.

Proto-industrialization is similar in important respects to what was once referred to as "cottage industry." Under this system, individual peasants who lacked sufficient land to support themselves through agriculture alone supplemented their income with small-scale manufacture, usually of textiles and often in their own homes. The early textile devices were very simple and inexpensive, so a peasant could easily afford, for example, a spinning wheel or even the simple looms common in the seventeenth century. Much cottage industry production consisted of turning common European fiber, either wool or flax, into textiles. With the growth of sheep raising in England, it became worthwhile for rural laborers to convert the wool first into yarn and then into woolen fabrics.

One common feature of the cottage industry was that it almost invariably occurred in the countryside. A major reason for this location was that, in many European towns in the seventeenth century, the guilds that had grown up in the Middle Ages still largely controlled manufacture; their authority, however, did not in most cases extend to the countryside outside the towns. Production outside towns was therefore not subject to the urban limitations imposed by the guilds to protect their economic position.

Historians differ over whether seventeenth century proto-industrialization can be seen as a consistent transitional step along a steady, systematic path of industrial evolution from the household manufacture of the late Middle Ages to the Industrial Revolution of the eigh-

25

teenth and nineteenth centuries. Research has demonstrated, for example, that population growth was encouraged as much by such things as the international trade in basic grains that emerged in the sixteenth century and the cost of living fluctuations related to that trade as by the opportunity to earn a living from wage labor. The specialization of agriculture, moreover, had as much to do with the variable productivity of the soil as with the existence of alternative means of support for a burgeoning population, and it was found that in some areas, where early cottage industry existed, changing commercial relations could also lead to de-industrialization.

The two industries in which examples of proto-industrialization were most prevalent were textiles and mineral production. As agriculture became less generalized and the raising of sheep became common in England in the fourteenth century, the crop the sheep produced, wool, was at first largely exported to the Low Countries and Italy. English production at first focused on the cities, where it was controlled by the guilds, but in the sixteenth century, production shifted away from the cities to the countryside. Woolen yarn and then textiles came to be produced in Yorkshire, East Anglia, the West Country, and even the southwest. In central England, hosiery knitting became extremely popular, because, although it was labor-intensive, it did not require much skill and therefore lent itself to the type of household industry that was characteristic of the earliest kinds of proto-industrialization.

In addition to the development of English proto-industrial textile manufacturing, small mining operations were also scattered over the English countryside. These operations produced iron, lead, and tin—the latter notably in Cornwall. The Kentish Weald was dotted with small iron furnaces in the seventeenth century, and in Derbyshire lead mining was common. In the West Midlands, many small metal objects were produced in modest shops, notably in Sheffield and Birmingham, areas that remained major producers of metal products in subsequent centuries.

The history of textile production in parts of the Low Countries was what led Mendels to develop his theory of proto-industrialization. While the area of modern Belgium had been known since the early Middle Ages for its woolen textiles, by the seventeenth century, it was more widely known for its linen goods. The flax that produced the fiber that was the basis of linen was grown throughout the Low Countries, and when agriculture became concentrated in the better lands, the peasantry living where the soil was less suited to commercial agriculture began to specialize in flax and linen production. Mendels found, in the area around Ghent, excellent examples of small-scale production of textiles, often in the homes of the workers; his concept, then, was a generalization of his study of this specific area.

Linen production was also found in many areas of what is now Germany. In parts of the Rhineland, particularly Silesia, there were numerous villages where the flax fiber was treated (a labor-intensive process) and then spun into linen yarn. The yarn was then passed on to the linen weavers, who enjoyed an international reputation. In the Swiss canton of Appenzell Outer Rhodes, the production of linen goods was widespread, since the mountainous countryside did not lend itself to raising crops. In the vicinity of Basel, there were households busily producing silk ribbon in the seventeenth century. In some areas, ownership of small agricultural plots was combined with textile production, as in the Oberlausitz region.

In Italy, where woolen textiles had been a major industry in the Middle Ages, production had shifted to silk by the seventeenth century. Silk was produced in the parts of Europe with a Mediterranean climate, especially in southern France and northern Italy. The combination of silkworms and mulberry trees, native to that region, was essential. Raising the silkworms to a level where the silk filaments could be captured and converted to thread was a labor-intensive business that was widespread in northern Italy and southern France. Woolen goods, which had been produced in the major Italian cities in the Middle Ages, became a cottage industry in the seventeenth century, particularly in the valleys of the lower Alps.

There were, also, many small producers of iron in the northern Italian valleys in the seventeenth century. Because the mountain streams provided sufficient water power to operate the bellows used in smelting the iron, the necessary ingredients were locally available. In the seventeenth century, metallurgical technology still allowed for small-scale production without heavy capital investments. Even as the technology came to call for greater investment, it still needed abundant producers of charcoal.

In Russia, where there were few towns, the production of manufactured goods necessarily took place in the countryside. As serfdom spread throughout the country, however, much cottage industry developed under the sponsorship of large landowners, although in some areas the produce of such enterprises was shared by owners and workers. The latter arrangement represented a logical extension of the not uncommon sharecropping used in agriculture to the rudimentary manufacturing industry that was just beginning to emerge.

SIGNIFICANCE

The notion of proto-industrialization was an attempt to develop a comprehensive model that would explain how a world that had been overwhelmingly agricultural for so many centuries came within a single century or so to be predominantly industrial. By suggesting that industrialization as it developed in the eighteenth and nineteenth centuries had deep roots particularly in the seventeenth century, the proponents of proto-industrialization theory offered historians a seamless picture of the gradual conversion of working lives from ones spent in the field to ones spent first in the rural workshop and then in the factory.

Further research has shown the simple, steady evolutionary version of the concept to be too neat, however. Many places that had thriving cottage industries did not become industrial centers when the technology changed. In some cases these regions became depopulated when other requirements of the industry compelled its location in urban areas. Thus, although the theory of proto-industrialization is appealing as a way of understanding the developing economies of seventeenth century Europe, reality often refuses to be stuffed into a single paradigm. Nevertheless, while the changes predating the eighteenth century may in fact have been uneven and inconsistent, theories such as those of Mendels and Marx are important, because they help to illustrate the extent to which the advent of the Industrial Revolution was simply not possible until significant prior demographic and lifestyle changes had already occurred within the European population.

—Nancy M. Gordon

FURTHER READING

Berg, Maxine, Pat Hudson, and Michael Sonnenscher, eds. *Manufacture in Town and Country Before the Factory.* New York: Cambridge University Press, 1983. Contains essays that call into question the restricted scope of the idea of proto-industrialization.

Coleman, D. C. "Proto-Industrialization: A Concept Too Many." *Economic History Review*, 2d ser. 36 (1983): 435-448. One of the numerous criticisms of the oversimplification implied by the concept of proto-industrialization.

The Economic Organization of Early Modern Europe. Vol. 5 in *The Cambridge Economic History of Europe.* New York: Cambridge University Press, 1977. General background to the proto-industrialization of Europe.

Knotter, Ad. "Problems of the 'Family Economy': Peasant Economy, Domestic Production, and Labour Markets in Pre-Industrial Europe." In *Early Modern Capitalism*, edited by Martin Prak. New York: Routledge, 2001. Knotter examines economics based on familial production in the century before work moved outside the home.

Kriedte, Peter, Hans Medick, and Jüürgen Schlumbohm. "Proto-Industrialization Revisited: Demography, Social Structure, and Modern Domestic Industry." *Continuity and Change* 8, no. 2 (1993): 217-252. The principal neo-Marxist supporters of the proto-industrialization concept modify their views to accommodate their many critics.

Mendels, Franklin F. "Proto-Industrialization: The First Phase of the Industrial Process." *Journal of Economic History* 32 (1972): 241-261. Mendels's original proposal of the concept.

Ogilvie, Scheilagh C. *State Corporatism and Proto Industry: The Württemberg Black Forest.* New York: Cambridge University Press, 1997. A detailed study of one area in Europe where pre-industrial cottage production was extensive.

Ogilvie, Scheilagh C., and Markus Cerman, eds. *European Proto-Industrialization.* New York: Cambridge University Press, 1996. A collection of fifteen articles covering Europe by most of the scholars involved in the issue.

SEE ALSO: 17th cent.: England's Agricultural Revolution; 1661-1672: Colbert Develops Mercantilism; Beginning 1689: Reforms of Peter the Great; July 25, 1698: Savery Patents the First Successful Steam Engine.

RELATED ARTICLE in *Great Lives from History: The Seventeenth Century, 1601-1700:* Thomas Savery.

17th century
RISE OF THE GUNPOWDER EMPIRES

One of the most notable worldwide developments of the seventeenth century was the emergence of several large-scale empires. Using newly developed firearms, especially cannon, a small number of states extended their control over the Americas, large parts of Asia, and central Eurasia. In addition to firearms, these empires were helped by expanding transportation and trade networks.

LOCALE: Worldwide
CATEGORIES: Expansion and land acquisition; science and technology; government and politics

KEY FIGURES
Akbar (1542-1605), Mughal emperor of India, r. 1556-1605
Mehmed II (1432-1481), Ottoman sultan, r. 1444-1446, 1451-1481
Mehmed IV Avci (1642-1693), Ottoman sultan, r. 1648-1687
Alexis (1629-1676), czar of Russia, r. 1645-1676
Ismāʿīl I (1487-1524), shah of Persia and founder of the Ṣafavid Dynasty, r. 1501-1524
ʿAbbās the Great (1571-1629), shah of Persia, r. 1587-1629
Shah Jahan (1592-1666), Mughal emperor of India, r. 1628-1658
Ivan the Great (1440-1505), grand prince of Moscow, r. 1462-1505
Philip II (1527-1598), king of Spain, r. 1556-1598, king of Naples and Sicily, r. 1554-1598, and king of Portugal, r. 1580-1598
Charles II (1661-1700), king of Spain, r. 1665-1700

SUMMARY OF EVENT
The term "gunpowder empire" is usually traced to the work of historian Marshall G. Hodgson, who sought to explain the rise of empires in the Islamic world. He used the term to describe new forms of states that appeared in Turkey, Persia, and Mughal India. According to Hodgson, artillery and other firearms had wide social and political consequences for these states. Because acquiring and maintaining guns demanded a highly developed government administration and extensive financial resources, the use of gunpowder tended to produce highly centralized governments that could buy large quantities of tin and copper, manufacture weapons, and train soldiers in the use of firearms. Other historians have

adopted this term to refer to states outside the Islamic region that used gunpowder technology to extend their control over territories that were less advanced technologically.

The Chinese appear to have been the earliest people to make use of gunpowder for warfare. In the thirteenth century, the Chinese developed gunpowder that was high in nitrates and made use of it in cylindrical metal barrels. By the end of the thirteenth or beginning of the fourteenth century, the Chinese were making use of small handguns. The technology quickly made its way to Europe, and the Europeans improved on it to create large cannon. The effectiveness of cannon in warfare led others to take them up eagerly.

The Turkish Ottoman Empire was one of the earliest and longest lasting of the gunpowder empires promoted by the spread of cannon and other firearms. The Turks had been pushed into the Near East from the eighth century onward by Mughal expansion in their original territory, around what is now Turkestan. At the beginning of the fourteenth century, the Turkish leader Osman I (c. 1258-1326) declared himself sultan, founding the Ottoman Empire. The Ottomans spread their control over the area formerly held by the Eastern Roman Empire, also known as the Byzantine Empire. In 1453, Sultan Mehmed II (r. 1444-1446 and 1451-1481) conquered Constantinople, bringing the Byzantine Empire to an end.

In their early years, Ottoman power was based on its cavalry. The Turks would make extensive use of firepower, using large cannon in their siege of Constantinople. They coordinated artillery with the use of cavalry and created an elite infantry corps known as the Janissaries. The Janissaries were child slaves taken from Christian parents, mostly in the Balkans, and raised as Muslims. They were trained to be expert in the use of firearms.

With its capital in Istanbul, as Constantinople became known, the Ottoman Empire developed into a centralized administration, funding the military use of firearms to spread its power through most of the Middle East and north and west into the Balkan Peninsula of Europe. For a time, it looked as if the guns of the Ottomans would carry them even farther. In 1529, the Turks laid siege to Vienna. Sultan Mehmed IV Avci attempted a second assault on Central Europe beginning in 1663, and he put Vienna under siege again in 1683. Although the

Turks continued to hold much of the territory they had taken by the end of the seventeenth century and fought other wars against the Europeans, their empire was in a state of decline until its end in the early twentieth century.

The Ṣafavid Empire of Persia also relied on the use of gunpowder for its power, and gunpowder seems to have shaped its structure. During the first half of the sixteenth century, Shah Ismāʿīl I led his Ṣafavid warriors to found a new Persian empire in Iran. The Ṣafavid Empire lasted until 1722, and the Shīʿite branch of the Islamic faith established by Ismāʿīl continues to be the dominant and contemporary religion of Iran today. Under Shah ʿAbbās the Great, at the end of the sixteenth and the beginning of the seventeenth centuries, Ṣafavid Persia took on the characteristics identified by Hodgson as those of a gunpowder empire. The Ṣafavids' hold on their territory had weakened considerably after the death of Shah Ismāʿīl. Shah ʿAbbās drove out foreigners, including Ottomans, who had made incursions into his territory. In doing this, he used a military force based on the use of gunpowder. He brought in an English adviser to help him reorganize and train his army. He divided this army into three bodies of troops—the slaves, the musketeers, and the artillerymen—all of whom were paid from a central treasury. He also created a strong, professionalized, central administration for organizing, training, and supplying this military force. To obtain the funds to maintain the political and military structures of the nation, the sixteenth century Ṣafavids fostered trade with Europe, industry, and an elaborate system of communication.

To the east of the Ottomans and the Ṣafavids, the Mughals shaped an Indian empire. The founder of this empire was Bābur (1483-1530), a Turkic prince of Central Asia said to be descended from the conquerors Tamerlane (Timur) and Genghis Khan. Bābur was driven out of Central Asia and descended into northern India, where he established Mughal rule. Bābur's grandson, Akbar, is considered the greatest of the Mughals. Akbar extended his empire to include all of northern and part of central India. His ability to do this resulted from the centralized organization of his political and military structures. The emperor ruled through high officials known as *mansabs*, who were top administrative or military officials who governed provinces, occupied key bureaucratic positions, or recruited and trained soldiers. Akbar's army relied heavily on the infantry, which was supplied with muskets, and on heavy artillery, using cannon. Much of his success came from the inability of competing powers in India to afford artillery or to train and maintain an armed infantry.

Akbar was succeeded by his son Jahāngīr and his grandson Shah Jahan, builder of the famous Taj Mahal. These two rulers maintained the army and administration created by Akbar. Under Jahan, the Mughal Empire is said to have reached its highest point culturally.

The concept of the gunpowder empire also has been extended to include non-Islamic nations that achieved wide territorial power through firepower and centralized administration. Russia, in the center of the Eurasian landmass, followed a pattern of expansion similar in ways to that of the Ottomans, the Ṣafavids, and the Mughals. Ivan the Great (1440-1505), grand prince of Moscow from 1462 to 1505, combined a centralized state with the new technology of artillery to begin Russia's rise from a marginal territory dominated by the Mughals in the south to a major empire.

Ivan's son, Ivan the Terrible, became the first czar of Russia. In the seventeenth century, the Romanov Dynasty came to power and accelerated the development of the state and the army. In particular, during the reign of Czar Alexis, the Russian army became a permanent, professional force, trained in the use of artillery and muskets. This made Russia successful in its wars against its western neighbors, Sweden and Poland, and prepared it for its spread across the east and southeast. Alexis's son, Peter the Great, on the throne from 1682 to 1725, pushed the centralization of authority, the organization of bureaucracy, and the professionalization of the military even further. Under Peter, Russia created an effective navy armed with artillery.

The maritime empires of the Iberian states, Portugal and Spain, also are frequently described as gunpowder empires. Both of these nations at the southwestern tip of Europe made use of ships designed to carry large cannon to dominate other parts of the world. During the reign of King Philip II, Spain's heavily armed ships made Spain one of the major European powers, as it took over much of the Americas. By 1600, the vast territories from New Mexico and Florida in the north to the tip of South America were under Spanish control. Only Brazil, taken by the Portuguese, was outside the Spanish Empire. Portugal had employed its own ships to establish itself in Goa, on India's Malabar Coast; in the Moluccas in the East Indies (now called Indonesia); and in Macao, off the coast of China. However, Portugal was forced into a union with Spain from 1580 to 1740. By the end of the seventeenth century, the period of the Iberian empires had passed. Following the death of Spanish king Charles II, in 1700,

29

other European powers became involved in fighting over who would succeed Charles, and Spain's period of greatness ended.

SIGNIFICANCE

By the seventeenth century, the advancement of firearms technology by well-organized military forces enabled a small number of states to spread their power over vast portions of the globe. The Ottoman Empire came to dominate much of the Islamic world. Even after centuries of decline, at the beginning of World War I, in 1914, the Ottoman Empire still controlled or influenced much of the Middle East. Although the Ṣafavid Dynasty did not conquer as wide a territory as did the Ottomans, or survive as long, the Ṣafavids had a lasting influence on the civilization of Iran and helped to establish Shīʿite Islam in several countries in the Middle East.

Similarly, weapons and centralized administration enabled Russia to begin its transformation from a weak marginal state under the grand prince of Moscow into one of the world's largest empires. The rise to power of Spain and Portugal, just before and during the seventeenth century, placed much of the Western Hemisphere under Iberian control and resulted in Spanish becoming one of the world's most widely spoken languages.

—Carl L. Bankston III

FURTHER READING

Diamond, Jared. *Guns, Germs, and Steel: The Fates of Human Societies*. New York: W. W. Norton, 1996. Offers an alternative to the gunpowder-empire explanation of political dominance, placing an emphasis on the role of the physical environment in shaping the development of nations.

Hodgson, Marshall G. S. *The Venture of Islam: Conscience and History in a World Civilization*. Vol. 3 in *The Gunpowder Empires and Modern Times*. Chicago: University of Chicago Press, 1974. The key work on gunpowder empires in the Islamic world and on the concept of the "gunpowder empire" in the development of civilizations around the world.

McNeill, William H. *The Age of Gunpowder Empires, 1450-1800*. Washington, D.C.: American Historical Association. Describes how different nations adapted the cultural, political, and military systems to the use of gunpowder and how gunpowder changed the global balance of power.

_____. *The Pursuit of Power: Technology, Armed Force, and Society Since A.D. 1000*. Chicago: University of Chicago Press, 1984. Considers how military conflict and technology have been connected in bringing about change in human societies.

_____. *A World History*. 4th ed. New York: Oxford University Press, 1998. A grand narrative of world civilizations. Part 3 explores gunpowder empires and world history.

SEE ALSO: 1602-1639: Ottoman-Ṣafavid Wars; 1623-1640: Murad IV Rules the Ottoman Empire; 1629: Ṣafavid Dynasty Flourishes Under ʿAbbās the Great; 1632-c. 1650: Shah Jahan Builds the Taj Mahal; Jan. 14, 1641: Capture of Malacca; 1642-1666: Reign of Shah ʿAbbās II; Aug. 22, 1645-Sept., 1669: Turks Conquer Crete; Feb. 13, 1668: Spain Recognizes Portugal's Independence; Beginning 1687: Decline of the Ottoman Empire.

RELATED ARTICLES in *Great Lives from History: The Seventeenth Century, 1601-1700:* ʿAbbās the Great; Alexis; Charles II (of Spain); Jahāngīr; Shah Jahan.

17th century
SONGHAI EMPIRE DISSOLVES

Invading Moroccans proved strong enough to destroy the Songhai Empire, but they did not assume control over the entire area of the former empire. Large chunks broke away and became independent, leaving the Arma, the descendants of the Moroccans, to rule a more modest state along the Middle Niger Valley.

LOCALE: Western Sudan, middle reaches of the Niger River Valley (now the Republic of Mali)

CATEGORIES: Wars, uprisings, and civil unrest; government and politics; expansion and land acquisition

KEY FIGURES

Abdullah al-Tilimsānī (d. 1618), first locally installed pasha, or leader, 1612-1618

Abdallah al-Hindī (d. 1623), *kaid*, or commander, of Bamba, r. 1623

ʿAbd al-Qādir (d. 1632), pasha, 1628-1632, who was defeated at Gao

SUMMARY OF EVENT

In 1591, a Moroccan army equipped with firearms crossed the Sahara Desert and attacked the Songhai Empire. In a series of battles, the Moroccans smashed the sword-and-bow army of the Songhai, killing two *askias* (Songhai emperors). The Songhai capital was then moved from Gao to Timbuktu, where the Moroccans set up their own administration, led by a pasha, who served as a military governor responsible to the Moroccan sultan in Marrakech. A remnant Songhai group retreated southward into the brush and forest country of Dendi, where they fought a successful guerrilla war that stopped the Moroccan advance.

The Moroccans proved strong enough to destroy, but not reconstruct, the Songhai Empire, which, before the invasion, had encompassed a huge area. Because the number of available Moroccan troops was never very large, some of the subject peoples of the empire, whom the Morrocan troops were to subdue, were able to revolt while groups who lived on the fringe of the empire began raids. Once the Moroccan advance ground to a halt in Dendi and the Moroccan aura of invincibility disappeared, whole populations of the empire began breaking away. However, the Moroccans retained control over the most commercially valuable parts of the empire, that is, the Niger River Valley between the cities of Jenne in the west and Gao in the east and the trans-Saharan trade corridor running north to the salt mine at Taoudenni.

After the death of the last of the great Saʿdian sultans in 1603 plunged Morocco into a series of dynastic wars, the government in Timbuktu began to change. In 1612, officers in Timbuktu overthrew the Marrakech-appointed pasha and appointed their own: Abdullah al-Tilimsānī. Abdullah al-Tilimsānī was then overthrown by his own men in 1618, but by this time even the rulers in Marrakech had come to realize that the government in Timbuktu represented an independent state. This state became known as a *pashalik*, and its ruler was elected by army soldiers. The Moroccans took wives and produced children who intermarried, creating a caste of soldier-rulers called the Arma. The Arma were divided into garrisons, or Casbahs (forts), scattered across the Middle Niger Valley.

The *pashalik*'s war against Dendi gradually ended. The Songhai made one final attempt to dislodge the Moroccans of the *pashalik* in an offensive launched between 1608 and 1612, which was stopped only after the Moroccans bribed the Songhai commander. In 1630, a treaty was signed between the *pashalik* and Dendi, in which the *pashalik* officially abandoned its goal of conquering the whole Songhai Empire. Within a few years, however, the two sides were raiding each other, and the *pashalik* was interfering in Songhai dynastic disputes. In 1639, an Arma army sacked the Dendi capital of Loulami and killed the *askia* but then withdrew. This proved to be the last major encounter between the two states. Arma interests turned elsewhere while Dendi plunged further into civil war, eventually disintegrating into petty states.

Dendi was downriver of Gao in the old empire's southeastern corner. To the southwest was the city of Jenne, which had traditionally been ruled by its own king, the *jenne-were*. The Moroccans and their Arma successors, who maintained a Casbah in Jenne, treated the *jenne-were* more like a glorified town chief than a king, which generated resentment and led to revolt on occasion. In the area between Jenne and Timbuktu lived the Fulbe (Fulani, Peul), a pastoral people who had migrated from the west. Had the *jenne-were* sought an alliance with the Fulbe, the *pashalik*'s power would have crumbled almost to the doorstep of Timbuktu. This was an option, however, that neither side seemed willing to consider. In 1599, for example, the *jenne-were* had remained loyal to the Moroccans, causing his city to come under siege by an anti-Moroccan coalition that included the Fulbe. In 1608, during the Songhai offensive, the two switched sides, with the Fulbe supporting the Moroccans and the *jenne-were* opposing them.

During the 1630's and 1640's, a series of incidents led to sporadic revolts in Jenne and attacks by the Fulbe. In 1645, the *pashalik* concluded a peace with one group of Fulbe, the Dialloube, who formed their own state in the inland delta region of Macina between Jenne and Timbuktu. Warfare, generally confined to raiding, continued on and off against the more pastoral Sanqare Fulbe, with the Arma launching an offensive against them as late as 1689.

Jenne was one of four great Casbahs, the others being located at Gao, Bamba, and the capital of Timbuktu. Smaller Casbahs also existed in smaller towns along the river. Control over the land between garrisons was inconsistent and unpredictable, and some people beyond the immediate vicinity of the Casbahs accepted the *pashalik*'s overlordship at least in theory. Areas such as Gurma on the south side of the river were kept in line by periodic expeditions to show the pasha's flag. Gurma was the home of a number of different non-Muslim peoples, including some fiercely independent groups such as the Dogon and Mossi. They were frequently raided for slaves, but the Arma made no attempt to incorporate them into the *pashalik*. North of the river lived nomads, the most important of which were tribes of Tuaregs. The Arma attempted to control them through treaties under which a chief agreed to recognize the pasha as his overlord, sometimes paying tribute, sometimes doing little more than professing allegiance.

During the seventeenth century, Gao, Bamba, and Jenne gradually asserted their independence from Timbuktu, a process that was more complete for Gao and Bamba than for Jenne, whose garrison needed strong support from Timbuktu in its sporadic struggles with the *jenne-were*. The Arma usually pulled together if threatened, but this did not keep the men from Bamba and Gao from engaging in acts of disobedience against Timbuktu. This occurred as early as 1623, when the *kaid* (commander) of Bamba, Abdallah al-Hindī, led his garrison in an unsuccessful attempt to overthrow the pasha. Al-Hindī's goal was not to split Bamba from the *pashalik* but to take control of the entire country for himself, but instead, he was killed.

In 1632, ʿAbd al-Qādir, one of the most powerful pashas, attempted to punish the garrison at Gao for insubordination. He led a force from Timbuktu but was defeated. In a second attempt that same year, his army

deserted him, and he was deposed and subsequently executed. In 1651, the soldiers at Gao began electing their own *kaid* in the same way Timbuktu elected the pasha; a year later Jenne followed suit. The garrisons gradually exerted more autonomy, and the pashas' interference in their affairs became increasingly rare. However, it cannot be assumed that the *pashalik* crumbled into city-states ruled by rival bands of Arma. No other garrison declared their *kaids* to be pashas, and in the scheme of things, *kaids* were subordinate to pashas, indicating that the garrisons were subordinate to Timbuktu, at least officially.

SIGNIFICANCE

Following the fall of the Songhai Empire, a large portion of the interior of West Africa underwent a slow process of political atrophy. With its frequent elections and the removal of pashas from control, the *pashalik* did not prove to be a very stable government. The Arma remained a closed caste and never constituted a significant portion of the population.

As a consequence, the peripheral regions of the old Songhai Empire broke away to become independent under new states. In the north, large areas came under the control of nomadic tribes that sometimes retained a fictional allegiance to the *pashalik*. As the imperial system folded, more ethnic-based polities emerged, such as the Fulbe state of Macina. Not until the late eighteenth and early nineteenth centuries, however, were such entities powerful enough to assume imperial structures, first under the Bambara, who had not been a part of the Songhai Empire, and, subsequently and more forcefully, by radicalized groups of Muslim Fulbe.

—*Richard L. Smith*

FURTHER READING

Abitbol, Michel. "The End of the Songhay Empire." In *General History of Africa*, edited by B. A. Ogot. Vol. 5. Berkeley: University of California Press, 1992. An excellent short summary of the *pashalik* and its neighbors.

Bourqia, Rahma, and Susan Gilson Miller, eds. *In the Shadow of the Sultan: Culture, Power, and Politics in Morocco*. Cambridge, Mass.: Harvard University Press, 1999. A collection that examines the relationship between power, legitimacy, and religion in the Moroccan monarchy.

El Fasi, M. "Morocco." In *General History of Africa*, edited by B. A. Ogot. Vol. 5. Berkeley: University of California Press, 1992. An excellent synopsis of the Moroccans in Africa.

Hunwick, John O. *Timbuktu and the Songhay Empire*. Boston: Brill, 1999. Hunwick notes the earliest examples of fringe groups that attacked and broke from the empire. The work also examines the situation in Jenne and the relationship between the *pashalik* and the Fulbe.

Kaba, Lansine. "Archers, Musketeers, and Mosquitoes: The Moroccan Invasion of the Sudan and the Songhay Resistance, 1591-1612." *Journal of African History* 22 (1981): 457-475. Kaba traces the origin of Dendi and the failure of the Moroccans in the early years to reunify the Songhai Empire.

Newman, James L. *The Peopling of Africa: A Geographic Interpretation*. New Haven, Conn.: Yale University Press, 1995. Newman offers a helpful analysis of the process of imperial fragmentation and the emergence of ethnic entities in Africa.

Thornton, John. *Warfare in Atlantic Africa, 1500-1800*. London: UCL Press, 1999. Includes a good discussion on the professional soldier (particularly the Arma) as opposed to the mass levies (conscriptions) common to other armies of the time.

SEE ALSO: Beginning c. 1601: Expansion of the Oyo Kingdom; 1612: Rise of the Arma in Timbuktu; 1640: Foundation of the Darfur Sultanate; Mid-17th cent.: Emergence of the Guinea Coast States; 1659: Expansion of the Alawis; Late 17th cent.: Decline of Benin.

RELATED ARTICLE in *Great Lives from History: The Seventeenth Century, 1601-1700:* Njinga.

1600's

1601
ELIZABETHAN POOR LAW

Passage of the Poor Law ended seventy years of legislative debate concerning ways to help the poor and infirm and to control the idle, wandering population of vagabonds who menaced individuals and social stability.

LOCALE: England and Wales

CATEGORIES: Laws, acts, and legal history; economics; government and politics; social issues and reform

KEY FIGURES
Elizabeth I (1533-1603), queen of England, r. 1558-1603
Mary I (1516-1558), queen of England, r. 1553-1558

SUMMARY OF EVENT
The Poor Law of 1601 represented the culmination of decades of wrangling, debating, and fine-tuning by the lawmakers of England. Parliament had spent the better part of the sixteenth century intermittently attempting to respond to the fallout generated by Henry VIII's dissolution of the monasteries (1536) combined with the changing demographics of the nation. The system of laws both punishing poverty and caring for the poor that evolved over the course of the century was consolidated at the beginning of the seventeenth century into one of the first modern, comprehensive welfare systems of the modern age.

Tudor monarchs from Henry VIII to Elizabeth I confronted two problems related to poverty. One was the problem of unemployed wandering vagabonds, generally young men, who, in an age before police and modern communication, posed a threat to isolated houses and villages and, in the city, threatened to swell the mobs that sometimes endangered the throne. The second was the problem of a growing number of impoverished people, especially after Henry VIII in 1536 began dissolution of the monasteries, which had been a traditional source of charity. In the same period that sources of charity decreased, poverty was increased as a result of economic depression and bad harvests. Attempts to improve agricultural production, moreover, caused land to be enclosed. Enclosure led to more unemployment, as farm laborers were forced from the land. Discontent with economic conditions, as well as resentment over changes in religious policy, led to occasional revolts, such as the Pilgrimage of Grace (1536-1537), a series of Catholic uprisings in the north.

With the death of Henry, England was ruled by a child king, Edward VI; juvenile monarchs had always been especially vulnerable to plots and rebellions. After Edward's brief reign, his half sister Mary I attempted to force England back to Roman Catholicism; her burning of Protestant martyrs created a wave of anti-Catholicism that was to last for centuries and generated new fears of civic disorder. Finally, Elizabeth I inherited a throne surrounded by plots and counterplots, especially after Pope Pius V excommunicated her in 1570, freeing Catholics from any allegiance to her rule. The maintenance of social order was thus, throughout this period, very much at issue. Two economic goals needed to be met if this order was to be maintained. First, the needy had to be given some means of subsistence. Second, vagabonds had to be suppressed.

Through the first half of the century, the second goal received the higher priority, possibly because the sheer number of vagabonds in the country was reaching menacing levels. According to historian Raphael Holinshed, seventy-two thousand thieves and vagabonds were hanged during the reign of Henry VIII. Laws passed in 1531 and 1536 attempted to force work on the unemployed, including children over five years of age. The most severe such law was passed in 1547, under Edward VI. Under this law, vagabonds could be made slaves for two years. Anyone loitering in the streets was compelled to ask for work, for money if anyone would pay him, or for food and drink if no one offered pay. If he still did not find work, anyone could request he be made a slave. If he fled, he was to be a slave for life. Children over five were to be taken from vagabond parents and made servants. Runaways were to be made slaves. This act was so punitive that it was repealed after three years, but its existence reflected a fear of mob and individual violence.

During the same period that these laws were enacted, however, steps were also taken toward forming England's first coherent public welfare policy. The act of 1536 created a parish-based relief system. Contributions to the poor were voluntary. The act of 1547, instituting the enslavement of vagabonds, also made local officials responsible for housing those poor people who were not vagabonds. When it was repealed in 1550, the basic concept of a workhouse was introduced, although that term was not yet used. One such house was to be established in each parish. There, the aged and "impotent" poor—that is, the disabled—were to engage in whatever labor they could manage.

From mid-century on, focus increasingly turned to aid for the poor. An act of 1552 marked the first step toward organized, as opposed to voluntary, poor relief. Parish registers were introduced, so an official count of the poor could be maintained. Alms collectors were to be named in each parish, and all inhabitants were to contribute. Enforcement of contributions was mandated by legislation in 1563. Anyone refusing to contribute would be summoned before a justice of the peace, who would assess a contribution. Those who still refused could be imprisoned. In an act of 1572, justices of the peace were to register names of the aged and impotent poor, decide how much they needed, and assess all inhabitants to meet those needs. Collectors of assessments and overseers of

the poor were to be appointed. (Scotland adopted this law in 1574; it remained in force until 1845.)

Another step was taken in legislation of 1576, which essentially provided two forms of poor relief. Outdoor relief meant that the poor were provided for in their homes. Indoor relief meant that the poor could be maintained in poorhouses, hospitals, and workhouses. To see that this relief was provided, overseers of the poor were to be elected; they were to act under the supervision of justices of the peace. Houses of correction were to be established in parishes and towns. Those admitted were to be whipped and set to work at hard labor. In Norwich, for example, prisoners began work in summer at 5:00 A.M. and ended at 8:00 P.M., with thirty minutes to eat and fifteen minutes to pray. Prisoners who balked could be whipped, and their food ration could be cut.

The 1576 act had serious consequences for unmarried women who gave birth. To prevent the child from becoming a burden on the parish, the mother was to be forced to name the father. According to historians Peter C. Hoffer and N. E. H. Hull, the number of murdered infants rose by more than 200 percent after passage of this law. The punishment for vagrancy remained harsh. Whereas slavery had been repealed in 1550, whipping and branding, legislated in 1531, were repeated in a statute of 1572. Two final acts in 1598 preceded the 1601 legislation. One abolished the death penalty for vagabonds, which was never restored in England. It was retained only for discharged soldiers convicted of crimes. They could be banished, and, if they returned without permission, they could be executed.

The 1601 act did not offer original legislation. Rather, it consolidated earlier laws, while fine-tuning certain aspects: for example, grandparents could take custody of poor relatives, the number of taxable persons was increased, and beggars were no longer necessarily to be viewed as criminals. While this law marked considerable progress toward organized relief, it included no administrative standards and no mechanism for enforcement.

SIGNIFICANCE

The 1601 Poor Law ended almost a century of Parliamentary debate over the responsibilities of the individual for his or her own maintenance and the responsibilities of the community for those who could not maintain themselves. It confirmed a mandatory system of poor relief unique to England. Frequently amended but never substantially changed, the legislation remained in force until 1834 and was the single most influential element in the establishment of a welfare system in the United States.

The Elizabethan debate concerning who among the poor should be forced to work and who should simply be assisted continued to be a serious point of argument well into modern times.

—*Betty Richardson*

FURTHER READING

Dean, David. *Law-Making and Society in Late Elizabethan England: The Parliament of England, 1584-1601.* New York: Cambridge University Press, 1996. A scholarly examination of legislative issues and processes.

Dodd, A. H. *Life in Elizabethan England.* Ruthin, North Wales: John Jones, 1998. First published in 1962, this work details care for the poor and examines institutional life.

Hibbert, Christopher. *The English: A Social History, 1066-1945.* New York: W. W. Norton, 1987. Chapter 14, "Villagers, Vagrants, and Vagabonds," examines the lives of the poor, using materials from contemporary accounts.

Jütte, Robert. *Poverty and Deviance in Early Modern Europe.* New York: Cambridge University Press, 1994. Compares English poverty and welfare with that in other European nations; contains a summary of legislation leading to the 1601 laws.

Morris, T. A. *Tudor Government.* New York: Routledge, 1999. Discussion of poor laws is part of a general discussion of Tudor policy in this pamphlet, part of the "Questions and Answers in History" series; contains extracts from the laws of 1563, 1572, 1575, and 1601.

Picard, Liza. *Elizabeth's London: Everyday Life in Elizabethan London.* New York: St. Martin's Press, 2004. A general history that includes a simple, clear summary of the welfare system.

Ridley, Jasper. *The Tudor Age.* New York: Carroll & Graf, 2002. Includes an examination of the social background underlying the 1601 legislation.

Slack, Paul. *The English Poor Law, 1531-1782.* New York: Cambridge University Press, 1995. Chapter 1 summarizes poor laws up to 1601; the appendix summarizes the most important laws from 1531 to 1782.

Thomas, Paul. *Authority and Disorder in Tudor Times, 1485-1603.* New York: Cambridge University Press, 1999. A brief study that relates poverty and political turmoil to reform legislation.

SEE ALSO: 17th cent.: Rise of Proto-Industrial Economies; 1646-1649: Levellers Launch an Egalitarian Movement.

RELATED ARTICLES in *Great Lives from History: The Seventeenth Century, 1601-1700:* Charles I; James I.

---

c. 1601
EMERGENCE OF BAROQUE MUSIC

A new musical style called Baroque, which induces strong moods or affections in its listeners, emerged at the end of the Renaissance period. Expressive solo lines began to dominate over group polyphony singing. The start of the Baroque era also saw a concern with contrasting timbres (sound colors) and an increase in dissonant tones. The new musical characteristics were meant to enhance a composition's affect.

LOCALE: Florence, Venice, Mantua (now in Italy)
CATEGORIES: Music; cultural and intellectual history

KEY FIGURES

Giulio Caccini (c. 1545-1618), Italian composer, singer, teacher, and member of the *camerata Bardi*
Claudio Monteverdi (1567-1643), Italian composer and instrumentalist
Jacopo Peri (1561-1633), Italian composer, singer, and instrumentalist

SUMMARY OF EVENT

Humanist philosophy of the Renaissance helped create rationalism, a way of thinking that was fast emerging in the early seventeenth century. Reason began to supersede Church authority and the authority of antiquity and other classical sources. Philosophers abandoned presuppositions and relied on empirical knowledge and logic. As intellectuals proposed new explanations about the world, musicians proposed a language that would meet the ideals of a new expressiveness.

"Baroque" is a term that describes the art, architecture, dance, literature, and music in the era from 1600 to 1750. The term was derogatory, originally used by observers of the later eighteenth century, who found the art and music of the seventeenth century to be gaudy, extreme, and excessive. Baroque artists and musicians did indeed turn to exaggeration, ornamentation, and contrast, but they did so to increase emotional expression in

their work. Their contributions were not fully acknowledged until the twentieth century, when a newfound appreciation for seventeenth century music emerged and
"baroque" was no longer a derogatory word in Western
culture.

In the seventeenth century, moods were known as "affections," and the theory about affections was tied to the
ancient Greek doctrine of "ethos." Affections were not
like emotions, which fluctuate, but were considered
fixed for a period of time. There were six core affections:
love, hate, joy, sorrow, wonder, and desire (and their
combinations). In the 1570's, a group of intellectuals and
musicians in Florence, Italy, who were known as the
camerata Bardi, discussed Italian art and philosophy and
the artistic practices of the ancients. *Camerata* members
examined how it would be possible to apply the artistic
processes of antiquity to contemporary culture. Consequently, they were concerned with how music could
clearly interpret or represent the affections.

Italian theorist and composer Vincenzo Galilei
(c. 1520-1591), father of scientist Galileo, was a leading
figure in the *camerata*. Galilei wanted to revive the ancient Greek ideal of music and poetry. He had learned
from his correspondence with a Roman scholar, Girolamo Mei (1519-1594), that ancient music was not polyphonic like that of the Renaissance, but instead focused

*Italian composer and organist Girolamo Frescobaldi was an
early innovator of the Baroque style of music.* (Hulton|Archive
by Getty Images)

on one line of sound. Galilei had reservations about Renaissance polyphony, especially in regard to the affections. Much Renaissance music called for several
singers, performing together, but each had independent
melodies and even different words. He felt that this old
"counterpoint" technique, that is, point against point, or
musical line against musical line, created confusion in
regard to the affections. Thus, he embraced the concept
of the "lone melody" to convey text. He proposed that the
new music of his time should consist of a single vocal
line with accompaniment on the lute or keyboard instrument. The *camerata* agreed, and asserted that such a new
musical idiom would be clearer and could vividly and
vigorously express moods or affections. The new musical style was called "monody": a solo song with an accompaniment featuring chords.

The composer most responsible for putting the ideas
of Galilei and the *camerata* into practice was Italian composer and singer Giulio Caccini, father of composer and
singer Francesca Caccini (1587-1641). In 1602, Giulio
Caccini published a collection of monodic songs called
Le nuove musiche (the new music), in which he sought to
"move the affect of the soul." An important aspect of
these new songs is their accompaniment. In the book,
Caccini explains the new notation that he uses for the
keyboard part (or, possibly, the lute part). Only the bass
line is written, but with numbers above, indicating additional notes that are to be filled in or flushed out. This
shorthand notation and the resulting practice of "impro-
vising" chords is known as basso continuo. Basso continuo, with a melody above it, results in monody. Basso
continuo pervades the entire Baroque period to the extent
that some modern scholars have referred to the Baroque
era as the basso continuo era.

The early seventeenth century also saw the development of the new sound ideal known as the *concertato*
style, that is, a style with contrasting timbres (sound
color). This concept developed in Venice in the late sixteenth century at St. Mark's Basilica. The church had several galleries in which separate choirs were placed, who
would sing at turn or, for climactic moments, sing simultaneously, thus producing a "surround sound" or stereo-
phonic effect. During the Baroque period, the physical
space was not necessary for the voices and instruments to
be mingled yet still play independent parts. So, for example, one passage of a piece might feature string instruments, another a group of voices, and another a soloist.
The *concertato* style was to make the music more expressive, invoking or reflecting the affections. Later in the
seventeenth century, a type of instrumental work would

MUSICAL WORDS AND THE BAROQUE

Baroque music is marked by its expressive, dramatic, and ornamented style. Composer Jacopo Peri, in the foreword to his opera Euridice *(1600), explains how speech in Baroque opera is embellished by song. Many words, he argues, are inherently musical and harmonious, and therefore lend themselves to the new style of music.*

Seeing that dramatic poetry was concerned and that it was therefore necessary to imitate speech in song (and surely no one ever spoke in song), I judged that the ancient Greeks and Romans (who, in the opinion of many, sang their tragedies throughout in representing them upon the stage) had used a harmony surpassing that of ordinary speech but falling so far below the melody of song as to take an intermediate form. . . .

I knew likewise that in our speech some words are so intoned that harmony can be based upon them and that in the course of speaking it passes through many others that are not so intoned until it returns to another that will bear a progression to a fresh consonance. And having in mind those inflections and accents that serve us in our grief, in our joy, and in similar states, I caused the bass to move in time to these, either more or less, following the passions, and I held it firm throughout that false and true proportions until, running through various notes, the voice of the speaker came to a word that, being intoned in familiar speech, opened the way to a fresh harmony.

Source: Jacopo Peri, foreword to *Euridice* (1600), excerpted in *A History of Western Musical Aesthetics*, by Edward Lippman (Lincoln: University of Nebraska Press, 1992), pp. 36-37.

---

by historians to be the first opera. However, *Dafne* does not survive intact. *Euridice* (pr. 1600, pb. 1601), also by Peri but with added music by Caccini, is the earliest surviving complete opera. It was considered quite innovative, containing a wide range of expressive techniques, including a mix of choral writing with passages for soloists (*concertato* style), simple rhyme schemes contrasting with freer rhymes, and lengthy recitative (a new invention of speech-song) that carried longer text. Because of its unique character, *Euridice* saw many performances.

The first masterpiece of opera, a pivotal work in music history, is Claudio Monteverdi's *La favola d'Orfeo* (pr. 1607, libretto pb. 1607, score pb. 1609, 1615). Monteverdi, who was the greatest composer of his time, debuted the opera in Mantua. It is replete with musical-dramatic insights, contains lavish orchestration for more than three dozen instruments, and includes closed musical forms like arias and dance songs, instrumental interludes, large choruses, and five-part harmonies.

emerge called the concerto, and it exploited the contrast between instruments and their sound colors. Some of the most famous Baroque concertos are the Brandenburg concertos of Johann Sebastian Bach (1685-1750).

Seventeenth century music showed more expressiveness also through the increased use of dissonance. In the Renaissance, music was viewed horizontally, as independent lines were heard simultaneously (counterpoint). However, since monody was introduced in the early Baroque period, music became viewed in a vertical fashion, and the melody and accompanying chords had to suit one another. Dissonance, created by a note that does not fit within a chord, sounds harsh and clashing. Placed with the right word, it can be quite expressive.

Monody, *concertato* style, and dissonance were employed in the expressive art form of opera, which was invented at the turn of the seventeenth century. The *camerata* had determined that Greek drama was sung throughout, and they felt that opera would work well to serve their new ideal of dramatic expression. Jacopo Peri, an Italian composer, singer, and instrumentalist who likely participated in the *camerata*, composed the music for *Dafne* (pr. 1597, partial pb. 1600), considered

It should be mentioned that although monody had taken hold in the early seventeenth century, Renaissance counterpoint was not abandoned, and composers frequently continued to write unaccompanied vocal music. Counterpoint was refashioned, however. The lines of musical sound as heard in Renaissance polyphony now had to fit the pattern of the chords that were either actually performed on a keyboard or were implied. This resulted in a new type of counterpoint, one that was harmonically driven, and it led eventually to the perfect balance for which Bach is so frequently lauded. His compositions achieve the most difficult task of being both horizontally rich (contrapuntal) and vertically strong (harmonic).

SIGNIFICANCE

Many significant changes took place during the early Baroque era, some that would develop throughout the period and later. Monody was an innovation with far-reaching consequences. Its prevalence caused a shift from a frequently polyphonic approach to one that was harmonic. This perspective, and the complementary character, or melodies, with harmonies, remains popular still in the West. Keyboard and lute performers became adroit improvisers within a fixed system. Monody compelled composers of the Baroque era to rethink their approach to polyphonic counterpoint and view the composition as a whole in connection with a harmonic scheme. The perfect balance between harmony and polyphony would be manifest later through the genius of Bach.

Opera proved to be an ideal outlet for dramatic and poetic expression through several epochs. Recitative (speech-song) has been employed in operas since opera's inception. The *concertato* principle contributed to the significant genres of concerto grosso in the later Baroque and solo concerto in the Classical era.

—Lisa Urkevich

FURTHER READING

Arnold, Denis, et al. *The New Grove Italian Baroque Masters*. New York: W. W. Norton, 1984. The definitive dictionary of Western music. Includes writings on Claudio Monteverdi, Girolamo Frescobaldi, Francesco Cavalli, Arcangelo Corelli, Alessandro Scarlatti, Domenico Scarlatti, and Antonio Vivaldi.

Blume, Friedrich. *Renaissance and Baroque Music: A Comprehensive Survey*. Translated by M. D. Herter Norton. New York: W. W. Norton, 1967. Includes a well-known encyclopedia essay on Baroque music by Blume, a noted musicologist, and places music in a cultural context. Includes discussion of national musical traits.

Grout, Donald Jay. *A History of Western Music*. 6th ed. New York: W. W. Norton, 2001. A standard college and music conservatory textbook on music history. Contains three chapters on Baroque music and comes with a recording.

Palisca, Claude V. *Baroque Music*. Englewood Cliffs, N.J.: Prentice Hall, 1991. A comprehensive text, good for some specific discussions and reviewing some pieces.

Schulenberg, David. *Music of the Baroque*. New York: Oxford University Press, 2001. A review of Baroque music with examples, and a discussion of instruments and important forms and genres. Includes some information on women composers.

SEE ALSO: Early 17th cent.: Revenge Tragedies Become Popular in England; c. 1601-1613: Shakespeare Produces His Later Plays; c. 1601-1620: Emergence of Baroque Art; c. 1601-1682: Spanish Golden Age; 1603-1629: Okuni Stages the First Kabuki Dance Dramas; Feb. 24, 1607: First Performance of Monteverdi's *La favola d'Orfeo*; Sept. 2, 1642: Closing of the Theaters; 1664: Molière Writes *Tartuffe*; c. 1666: Stradivari Makes His First Violin; c. 1673: Buxtehude Begins His Abendmusiken Concerts.

RELATED ARTICLES in *Great Lives from History: The Seventeenth Century, 1601-1700:* Francesca Caccini; Arcangelo Corelli; Girolamo Frescobaldi; Jean-Baptiste Lully; Marie de Médicis; Cosimo II de' Medici; Claudio Monteverdi; Henry Purcell; Heinrich Schütz; Barbara Strozzi.

c. 1601
EMERGENCE OF THE MERINA KINGDOM

During the 1600's, the Merina kingdom emerged as the dominant power in the central highlands of Madagascar. The early kings laid the foundation for the eventual unification and control of most of the island in the nineteenth century.

LOCALE: Madagascar
CATEGORIES: Government and politics; expansion and land acquisition

KEY FIGURES

Ralambo (d. 1610), founder of the Merina kingdom, r. 1575-1610
Andrianjaka (d. 1630), Merina king, r. 1610-1630
Andriantsitakatrandriana (d. 1650), Merina king, r. 1630-1650
Andriantsimitoviaminandriandehibe (d. 1670), Merina king, r. 1650-1670
Razakatsitakatrandriana (d. 1675), Merina king, r. 1670-1675
Andriamasinavalona (d. 1710), Merina king, r. 1675-1710

SUMMARY OF EVENT

By the thirteenth century, Vazimba tribes, most likely of African or Afro-Indonesian origin, were living in the central highlands of the Indian Ocean island of Madagascar. Each village had its own king or chief. By the mid-sixteenth century, the Hova, most likely Indonesian immigrants, began invading Vazimba territory. With the help of sages known as Marinh, some of the Vazimba and Hova resolved their disputes and consolidated power to form the early Merina society. Andriamanelo, son of a Vazimba queen, was the first king of the Andriana, or Merina, dynasty. He reigned from 1540 to 1575 and introduced the use of iron spears to the culture.

Andriamanelo's son, Ralambo, ruled from 1575 to 1610. Ralambo is considered the true founder of the Merina kingdom, which he consolidated through centralized rule, successful wars, territorial expansion, and new political and social institutions. He established a new capital at Ambohidrabiby, inherited from his mother, the daughter of a Vazimba chief. Thus, he inherited the chieftainships of both his father's and his maternal grandfather's tribes and united these to form the Merina state. Ralambo named his country Imerina, which means the "land where one can see far." The peo-

ple were called Merina ("highlanders"), referring to their residence in the central highlands.

Ralambo created a powerful, feudal, and secular foundation for his kingdom. He developed a caste system of four classes of *Andriana* (nobility). The *Zafindralambo* class were relatives or descendants of Ralambo and were the higher-ranking nobility. The other three noble castes collectively formed the *Andrianteloray* (nobility of three distinct fathers), who had no unique privileges but were rewarded for their service to the king. Ralambo also established two smith classes, silversmiths and ironsmiths. Eventually, ironsmiths became part of the army. He imposed a new capitation tax, or tax on each head or person. This *vadin-aina* ("price of secure life") made possible a standing army, which battled successfully against neighboring Vazimba tribes. Ralambo also introduced the use of firearms, which gave the Merina soldiers a significant advantage in battle.

Merina royalty was protected by twelve royal talismans, or amulet guardians, called *sampy*. The favorite of these twelve royal talismans were named *Mahavaly*, *Fantaka*, *Manjakatsiroa*, and *Kelimalaza*. Talismans were considered holy and had diverse functions, such as protecting the monarchy, striking the enemy in war, controlling the weather, and protecting against disease. Ralambo also affirmed royal status and power by performing royal circumcision rituals and establishing the divinity of ancestral kings. One of his most significant innovations was the annual royal bath celebration, the *fandroana* ("bath"), also called *taona tsara indrindra* ("the best moment of the year"). Performed at the end of each year, this ritual celebrated the beginning of the new year and reaffirmed the king's authority and puissance. It involved the sprinkling of water as a symbol of purification and blessing of the king and his people.

Ralambo radically changed the Merina diet when he introduced beef as a food. Previously, there was a taboo on eating beef, and cattle were used only as sacrificial or farm animals. Ralambo broke the taboo and changed the name of cattle from *jamoka* (oxen) to *omby* to emphasize their new status within his culture. He taught his people to roast the meat and commanded that the hump (or highest peak) and the rump (end piece) be reserved for royalty. Ralambo also made beef part of the royal feast that coincided with the year-end royal bath ritual.

A famous legend grew from Ralambo's choice of his younger son, Andrianjaka, as his successor. Fanorona was a traditional board game and has become the national game of Madagascar. It was probably derived from the game of Alquerque, popular in Arab countries and brought to Madagascar by traders. When Ralambo was ill and attempting to decide which of his two sons should inherit his kingdom, he decided to send for both sons. Whoever showed up first would claim the throne. Legend had it the older son was so immersed in a game of Fanorona that he ignored his father's envoy. The younger son, Andrianjaka, appeared first and thus became the next king of Merina.

In 1610, Andrianjaka ("the prince who rules") became the king of Merina and ruled until 1630. As a prince, he had already distinguished himself as a courageous soldier who had built up the kingdom's military arsenal and expanded his father's empire to the north and west. He also defeated another Vazimba tribe to seize a tall, natural rock fortress situated on a marshy plain. The fortress had been known as Analamanga (the "blue forest"), but Andrianjaka changed its name to Antananarivo ("the city of one thousand") to reflect the one thousand warriors stationed there. He made Antananarivo the new capital and constructed his wooden *rova*, or royal palace, strategically at the most elevated point on this hill.

During Andrianjaka's reign, divine status was given to the living monarch, whereas previously only ancestral or deceased monarchs had been considered divine. There were now three broad castes of Merinas, *andriana* (nobility), *hova* (plebeians or free citizens of established clans), and *andevo* (laborers or slaves with no ancestral tombs). Another significant achievement was the construction of canals and dikes to begin transforming the marshland into rice fields, providing both food and a trade commodity.

Andrianjaka's successor, King Andriantsitakatrandriana, continued building dams and rice plantations. From 1650 to 1670, Andrianjaka's grandson, Andriantsimitoviaminandriandehibe ("the prince not equaled by the great princes") ruled. His elder son, Razakatsitakatrandriana, ascended the throne in 1670 but proved incompetent and was overthrown in 1675. He was replaced by his younger brother, King Andriamasinavalona, who ruled from 1675 to 1710. Andriamasinavalona subdued various neighboring chiefs to expand the Merina kingdom outward to occupy all the lands within a 20- to 25-mile (32- to 40-kilometer) radius of the capital city. He also advanced rice cultivation further. These efforts established a firm foundation for Merina power and population growth. However, this sixth Merina king also decided to divide his kingdom among his four sons, which

led to rival, independent kingdoms forming after his death.

SIGNIFICANCE

The rivalries between Merina subkingdoms continued through most of the 1700's. However, the early Merina kings of the seventeenth century had laid the essential foundation for the later unification of the kingdom under King Andrianampoinimerina (r. 1787-1810), who controlled most of the central highlands of Madagascar. His son and successor, King Radama I, ruled from 1810 to 1828. Radama made a peace treaty with the British, who helped him conquer and unify nearly the entire island. He became recognized as the king of Madagascar and promoted a Europeanization policy on the island. Under Radama, a Merina nationalist elite began to develop.

By the second half of the nineteenth century, the Kingdom of Madagascar achieved formal recognition. The English-Malagasy Treaty of December 5, 1862, established recognition of the Malagasy state by foreign countries. However, in 1895 French troops captured the capital, exiled the Merina king and queen to Algeria, and took control of Madagascar. In August, 1896, France annexed the kingdom of Imerina, and on February 28, 1897, Madagascar officially became a French colony. In the twenty-first century, the Merina people remain the island's most populous ethnic group, and they account for the largest number of educated, middle-class citizens of Madagascar. The Merina dialect is also the principal Malagasy language. The modern capital of Madagascar is Antananarivo, the capital city established and named by Andrianjaka in the seventeenth century.

—Alice Myers

FURTHER READING

Bloch, Maurice. *From Blessing to Violence: History and Ideology in the Circumcision Ritual of the Merina of Madagascar*. New York: Cambridge University Press, 1986. Useful explanation of the myth of the origin of circumcision, beginning with the first Merina king. Illustrations, notes, and bibliography.

Brown, Mervyn. *A History of Madagascar*. Princeton, N.J.: Markus Wiener, 2002. This first complete history of Madagascar in English includes extensive coverage of the Merina kingdom. Illustrations, maps, and bibliography.

Cannadine, David. *Rituals of Royalty: Power and Ceremonial in Traditional Societies*. New York: Cambridge University Press, 1987. Includes a chapter on "The Ritual of the Royal Bath in Madagascar." Illustrations, index, and bibliography.

Green, Rebecca L. *Once Is Never Enough: Textiles, Ancestors, and Reburials in Highland Madagascar.* Bloomington: Indiana University Art Museum, 1998. Catalog of an exhibition that included pieces related to the rites and ceremonies of the Merina people. Illustrations, maps, bibliography, and notes.

Kent, Raymond. *Early Kingdoms in Madagascar, 1500-1700.* New York: Holt, Rinehart, and Winston, 1970. This well-researched study includes a detailed account of the early Merina kingdoms. Illustrations, maps, appendices, and bibliography.

Kottak, Conrad Phillip, et al., eds. *Madagascar: Society and History.* Durham, N.C.: Carolina Academic Press, 1986. Includes discussion of the evolution of the royal cult and bath. Illustrations and bibliography.

Stevens, Rita. *Madagascar.* Philadelphia: Chelsea House, 1999. A useful general source covering the history, geography, economy, people, and culture of Madagascar. Illustrations and glossary.

SEE ALSO: Early 17th cent.: Rise of Rwanda; 17th cent.: Emergence of Luba Governance; 17th cent.: Songhai Empire Dissolves; 1612: Rise of the Arma in Timbuktu; c. 1625: Formation of the Kuba Kingdom; Mid-17th cent.: Emergence of the Guinea Coast States; 1670-1699: Rise of the Asante Empire; Late 17th cent.: Decline of Benin; Late 17th cent.: Rise of Buganda; Beginning c. 1682: Decline of the Solomonid Dynasty.

RELATED ARTICLE in *Great Lives from History: The Seventeenth Century, 1601-1700:* Njinga.

Beginning c. 1601
EXPANSION OF THE OYO KINGDOM

The Yoruba state of Oyo, originally located in the savanna belt of northern Western Nigeria, expanded mostly south by deploying its cavalry and archers to subjugate Yoruba and non-Yoruba neighbors. Oyo grew into an empire of approximately 18,000 square miles by the end of the eighteenth century.

LOCALE: Yorubaland, Nigeria (West Africa)

CATEGORIES: Expansion and land acquisition; government and politics; wars, uprisings, and civil unrest

KEY FIGURES

Ajagbo (d. late 1690's), Oyo *alaafin*, or king, r. c. 1650-late 1690's, reputed for notable military innovations and victories

Abipa (late 1500's-mid-1600's), Oyo *alaafin*, r. early 1600's, who reoccupied the ancient capital of Oyo-Ile, c. 1600

Obalokun (late 1500's-mid-1600's), Oyo *alaafin*, r. first half of the 1600's, who consolidated the state

SUMMARY OF EVENT

The Oyo, a subgroup of the Yoruba, are located mainly in Western Nigeria and parts of the West African republics of Benin and Togo. Legend attributes the founding of Oyo to Oranmiyan, a son of Oduduwa, the acclaimed founder of the Yoruba nation. Oduduwa's sons were said to have dispersed from the ancient capital of Ile-Ife in the southern Yoruba forest to establish their own states. This tradition is consistent with attempts by Yoruba states to establish mythical relationships with Ile-Ife for political legitimacy.

Relations before the seventeenth century between the Oyo kingdom and its non-Yoruba neighbors, the Nupe and Borgu (Ibariba), were turbulent, climaxed by a rout by the Nupe in the early sixteenth century. Its capital at Oyo-Ile was abandoned, and its *alaafin* (king), Onigbogi, was driven into exile. The Igboho period, named after the town that served as the *alaafin*'s capital, witnessed a reconstruction of the state following the imposition of a new dynasty of *alaafins* of Borgu (Ibariba) origin, beginning with Alaafin Ofinran. The resurgent state, under Alaafin Ajiboyede, won a decisive military victory at Ilayi, which freed it from further pressure from its Nupe adversaries. This made it possible for Ajiboyede's successor, Abipa, to reoccupy the old capital of Oyo-Ile in about 1600, the prelude to the imperial phase of Oyo history.

A notable factor in the Oyo resurgence was the adoption of cavalry and the use of archers during the sixteenth century. The innovation, ascribed to an earlier *alaafin*, Orompoto, was owed to Oyo's northern neighbors, especially the Nupe. It is instructive that the legendary Alaafin Shango, who is also deified as the god of thunder, is represented as a rider on horseback. The military innovation did mark a turning point in the history of Oyo

A YORUBA PRAISE SONG

Sets of oriki, *poetic praise names, were given to every Yoruba, regardless of social stature, during the course of his or her life. The mother goddess Oshun, a healer, received the following* oriki, *which identifies her also with the Iyalode, the female chief of a Yoruba town.*

We call her and she replies with wisdom.
She can cure those whom the doctor has failed.
She cures the sick with cold water.
When she cures the child, she does not charge the father.
We can remain in the world without fear.
Iyalode who cures children—help me to have my own child.
Her medicines are free—she feeds honey to the children.
She is rich and her words are sweet.
Large forest with plenty of food.
Let a child embrace my body.
The touch of a child's hand is sweet.

Owner of brass.
Owner of parrots' feathers.
Owner of money.

My mother, you are beautiful, very beautiful.
Your eyes sparkle like brass.
Your skin is soft and smooth.
You are black like velvet.

Everybody greets you when you descend on the world.
Everybody sings your praises.

Source: The Horizon History of Africa, translated by Ulli Beier, edited by Alvin M. Josephy, Jr. (New York: American Heritage, 1971), p. 208.

Yoruba and non-Yoruba territories swelled the population of the state, in view of the refuge that its rising power offered, and contributed their skills and cultural capital to the development of the empire.

Territorial expansion proceeded through at least three stages, probably during the reign of Alaafin Obalokun. Expansion began with, first, the consolidation of the core of the state, which consisted of the metropolitan districts around the capital, inhabited by Oyo-speaking elements; second, the incorporation of non-Oyo Yoruba; and third, the incorporation of the non-Yoruba, such as the Nupe and the Fon (Dahomey). Beginning in the seventeenth century, Oyo subjugated the Igbomina-Yoruba communities of Ajase Ipo, Ila, Omu Aran, and Oyan; the northern Ekiti-Yoruba kingdom of Osi to the east; and the kingdoms of Ikirun, Ire, and Iragbiji on the boundary with the Ijesa-Yoruba to the southeast. To the west, Oyo expanded toward the territory of the Shabe, another Yoruba kingdom, with the Opara River forming their boundary. To the south, Oyo incorporated the Ibarapa (Yoruba) towns of Eruwa, Igangan, and Idere and marched with the Ketu (a western Yoruba kingdom) along the Oyan River and with the Egba to the east of the Ogun River. To the southwest, Oyo subdued the Egbado and incorporated the Awori kingdom of Ota to the southeast and the Anago settlements of Ihumbo, Ifonyin, Ipokia, and Takete across the Yewa River.

Although much of the territorial expansion of Oyo took place in the seventeenth and eighteenth centuries, the process had started in the sixteenth century. Oyo domination of the Igbomina and the expansion west of the Ogun River had begun or been accomplished by the latter date. After military subjugation, Oyo-Yoruba settled (colonized) those areas, especially during the seventeenth century. Thus, the Ibarapa kingdom of Eruwa is said to have been founded by an Oyo man from Igboho, an indication of the population movements and political consolidation that took place in the after-

and of its Yoruba and non-Yoruba neighbors by shifting the balance of power in the northern Yoruba savanna in favor of Oyo.

Another major innovation was the introduction of two important religious cults—Egungun (the cult of masqueraders representing the spirits of the ancestors) and Ifa (the god of divination)—from the Nupe country and Southern Yorubaland, respectively. These cultural institutions ensured social control and gave ideological and religious legitimacy to the state and to the *alaafin*.

Moreover, the population movements occasioned by the political and military reverses of the preimperial era contributed also to the reconstruction of the state in the subsequent period. First, important settlements emerged at Kusu and Igboho, successive temporary capitals of the *alaafin* in exile, and Ikoyi, which became the leading town outside the capital. Second, immigrants from

math of the return to the ancient capital of Oyo-Ile by 1600.

Oyo expanded into non-Yoruba territories to the far west in the second half of the seventeenth century, during the reign of Alaafin Ajagbo. He was reputed to have created the office of Are Ona Kakanfo (generalissimo), introduced the simultaneous despatch of four expeditions, and invaded the Egun state of Weme and the Aja kingdom of Allada in 1698. These military exercises suggest that by the late seventeenth century, Oyo had already secured firm control of the northern Egbado and Anago areas, from which it ventured into Dahomey. While Oyo control over Dahomey at this time was tenuous, the magnitude of Oyo colonization of the Egbado towns of Ilaro, Ibese, and Ijanna suggests that Egbado was Oyo's subject by the seventeenth century. Hence, the *alaafin* stationed colonial officials in those places to remit tribute to the metropolis.

In all, Oyo's expansion, starting in the early seventeenth century, was owed to the military, political, and cultural reorganization that followed the reoccupation of the ancient capital. The process of expansion involved conquest, absorption, and colonization, and extended the rule of the *alaafin* beyond the Oyo-Yoruba core to the non-Oyo-Yoruba and non-Yoruba periphery of the emergent empire.

SIGNIFICANCE

The rapid expansion of Oyo from its original location in the savanna in a general southward direction ensured its development. Oyo consolidated its hold on its Yoruba core and expanded in the eighteenth century into the Aja country to the southwest. This was achieved by the introduction of the cavalry corps, an innovation in Yoruba military technology and strategy, and of the ritual and spiritual institutions and practices that bolstered the power of the *alaafin* and the state. Military reforms, institutional innovations, and colonization helped Oyo rise to its apogee as the greatest Yoruba state by the eighteenth century.

Consequently, in the context of Yoruba history, the Oyo Empire was superseded in territorial extent only by the successor state of Ibadan in the nineteenth century. However, internal crises from the late eighteenth century and the rise of the Sokoto caliphate led to its collapse in the early 1800's. The events of the seventeenth century thus shed light on the dynamics of state formation and the evolution of political and social institutions among the Yoruba, a major nationality in Nigeria. These events also highlight the dynamics of imperial administration, intergroup relations, population movements, local and international trade, and the subsequent developments that culminated in the emergence of modern Nigeria in the twentieth century. Taken together, the expansion of Oyo in the 1600's, and its aftermath, provides insight into indigenous (pre-European) patterns of state formation, armaments, and statecraft.

—*Ayodeji Olukoju*

FURTHER READING

Ajayi, J. F. A., and Michael Crowder, eds. *History of West Africa.* 3d ed. Vol. 1. London: Longman, 1985. This work contains an authoritative account of Oyo expansion and the rise of Dahomey.

Akinjogbin, I. A. *Dahomey and Its Neighbours, 1708-1818.* Cambridge, England: Cambridge University Press, 1967. An authoritative, if slightly dated, text on the history of the Aja states, with sections on seventeenth century developments in Oyo.

Ikime, Obaro, ed. *Groundwork of Nigerian History.* Ibadan, Nigeria: Heinemann, 1980. This collection contains a succinct chapter on Yoruba history up to 1800.

Johnson, Samuel. *The History of the Yorubas: From the Earliest Times to the Beginning of the British Protectorate.* 1921. Reprint. Lagos, Nigeria: CSS, 2001. This is a standard text on Yoruba, and especially Oyo, history that contains a rich corpus of oral traditions.

Law, Robin. *The Oyo Empire, c. 1600-c. 1836: A West African Imperialism in the Era of the Atlantic Slave Trade.* Oxford, England: Clarendon, 1977. An authoritative study of the imperial phase of Oyo history, with a wider focus on developments in the Nigerian hinterland and the Atlantic basin.

Ogunremi, Deji, and Biodun Adediran, eds. *Culture and Society in Yorubaland.* Ibadan, Nigeria: Rex Charles, 1998. Contains two chapters with insights into the culture and society of Yorubaland before 1700.

SEE ALSO: 17th cent.: Songhai Empire Dissolves; 1612: Rise of the Arma in Timbuktu; 1619-c. 1700: The Middle Passage to American Slavery; Oct., 1625-1637: Dutch and Portuguese Struggle for the Guinea Coast; Mid-17th cent.: Emergence of the Guinea Coast States; 1670-1699: Rise of the Asante Empire; Late 17th cent.: Decline of Benin.

RELATED ARTICLE in *Great Lives from History: The Seventeenth Century, 1601-1700:* Njinga.

c. 1601-1606
APPEARANCE OF THE FALSE DMITRY

Russia's pretender to the throne, the False Dmitry, reigned briefly during an age of pretense, turmoil, and chaos, ultimately bringing about political change and the realization of Russia's need for a "good czar."

LOCALE: Moscow, Russia

CATEGORIES: Government and politics; wars, uprisings, and civil unrest

KEY FIGURES

Prince Dmitry Ivanovich (d. 1591), youngest son of Ivan IV (the Terrible), czarevitch of Russia, 1582-1591

Fyodor I (1557-1598), eldest surviving son of Ivan IV and his successor as czar of Russia, r. 1584-1598

Boris Godunov (c. 1551-1605), czar of Russia, r. 1598-1605

Ivan the Terrible (1530-1584), czar of Russia, r. 1547-1584

Grigory Otrepyev (d. 1606), called the False Dmitry, or "the Pretender," czar of Russia, r. 1605-1606

Vasily Shuysky (1552-1612), Russian boyar, later czar of Russia as Vasily IV, r. 1606-1610

SUMMARY OF EVENT

On July 18, 1605, the False Dmitry was crowned czar of Russia. The episode was part of an extended crisis that almost destroyed Russia between 1584 and 1613. Known in Russian history as the Time of Troubles, this period saw pretenders, civil wars, social revolt, famine so severe as to induce cannibalism, and, in its darkest hours, occupation of the Russian throne by Poland and the conquest of large sections of the country by Sweden.

The immediate cause of the catastrophic series of events was the extinction of the Rurik line of princes who had governed Russia for more than seven hundred years. More fundamental were the incredible strains imposed upon all segments of the Russian population by the Muscovites in their drive to solidify their hold on Russia and to expand its borders in the east and the west.

The culmination of the transformation of Russia into an absolute monarchy occurred during the reign of Ivan the Terrible. He waged merciless war against the powerful landed nobles, known as the boyars. By use of murder, pillage, rapine, torture, and exile, he ended their pretensions of independent political power in Russia. Unstable, violent, and probably mentally unbalanced, Ivan had killed his eldest son in a fit of rage and left as his heirs Fyodor, a physically frail and politically impotent twenty-six-year-old, and the toddler Dmitry. Given the greed and ferocity of the boyars; the discontent of the peasant, Cossack, and merchant populations; and the covetous aims of Sweden and Poland, Russia was deprived of a strong, legitimate ruler when one was desperately needed.

After Ivan's death in 1584, Fyodor was crowned czar, but because of his physical and mental weakness, he was dominated by various boyars and other men of military and administrative experience who struggled for power behind the scenes. The eventual winner in that struggle was Boris Godunov, who had been one of the most reliable henchmen of Ivan IV, "the Terrible," and was married to Fyodor's sister. In 1598, Boris became czar in his own right, despite the active opposition of the boyars and the leaders of the Russian Orthodox Church. Despite his success at making peace with Lithuania, the creation of a Russian patriarchate, deterring invasions from the Tatars, beginning diplomatic relations with Europe, and promoting trade, Godunov failed to establish himself on the throne as the initiator of a new line. This failure made it possible for the False Dmitry to play his part in Russian history.

In the period during which he had been the dominating force behind Fyodor, Boris had been faced with the ever-present possibility that the friends and relatives of Dmitry's mother would attempt to place the boy on the throne upon the expected death of Fyodor. Boris tried to forestall this by sending Dmitry and his mother, along with other members of the family, to the convent at Uglich on the northern reaches of the Volga River. There, under circumstances never completely explained, the nine-year-old boy died from a knife wound to his throat in 1591. He was epileptic and, according to his nurse, he suffered a fit and cut himself with a knife with which he had been playing. Within four days, Boris sent to Uglich a commission that conducted a thorough investigation and submitted a report verifying the nurse's story that the wounds were self-inflicted. The report was not widely circulated, however, and it soon came to be widely believed that Boris had arranged to have the boy killed.

Following Godunov's ascension to power, natural disasters of flooding and frost ruined harvests throughout Russia in 1601. These events signaled disaster for a country barely able to subsist. One-third of the population reportedly died. Although Godunov attempted to alleviate the problems of his country, he turned against the boyars. Unrest followed.

The first rumors of the False Dmitry occurred in 1598, and he was reported in Moscow as early as 1601 and 1602. He escaped, however, when it appeared he might be arrested when he claimed to be Dmitry. He then was seen in Poland in 1602 as a valet to a Polish landowner. Identified by Russian authorities as Grigory Otrepyev, the False Dmitry was a runaway monk who had formerly served the Romanovs and was a skilled transcriber and composer. He was a dignified, self-possessed man with much grace both on horse and afoot and was said to be courageous and intelligent. He knew a great deal about the circumstances under which Czarevitch Dmitry had lived. It is almost certain that he had come to believe that he was Dmitry, and during his brief period of glory, he acted with complete self-assurance and inner conviction. He convinced his noble master that he was genuine and gained, if not the support, at least the benevolent neutrality of King Sigismund III Vasa of Poland, who welcomed any excuse to make things difficult for the Russian czar. The False Dmitry acquired further support in Poland by marrying Marina Mniszech, the daughter of his Polish lord, and by becoming a convert to Roman Catholicism in the spring of 1604. Yet the Polish king neither instigated nor actively supported Dmitry's attack on and his eventual capture of the throne of Moscow.

At the head of a small army of less than four thousand freebooting Polish nobles and runaway peasants, the False Dmitry crossed the Dnieper River into Russia in October, 1604. In southern Russia, he quickly gained mass support from Cossacks, disaffected small landholders, and peasants. He was opposed by government troops and suffered some military defeats, but he advanced steadily toward Moscow at the head of an ever-growing swarm of disaffected Russians. In April, 1605, Godunov suddenly died, and the last barrier was removed. The mobs of Moscow murdered Godunov's supporters, and the great boyars of the capital, led by Vasily Shuysky, refused to swear allegiance to Godunov's son and successor, Theodore. Godunov's wife and son were murdered, and on June 20, 1605, the False Dmitry made a triumphal entry into Moscow. Shuysky, who had led the commission investigating Czarevitch Dmitry's death in 1591, now declared that the new arrival was Dmitry, as did the mother of the czarevitch, who was brought from the convent for that purpose. Shuysky also administered the oath to the False Dmitry. Russia, desperate for a Rurik, accepted the impostor as czar; another step had been taken toward civil war and anarchy.

SIGNIFICANCE

Once he was installed as czar, the False Dmitry's support ebbed rapidly. His manner was too frivolous and too "Western" for the Muscovites, who preferred their czars to be solemn and devoted to court and religious ritual. He and his Polish supporters lived too gaily, holding numerous balls and parties that upset the puritanical Muscovites. Moreover, he was a practicing Roman Catholic and brought with him Jesuit priests, who frightened and irritated the Russian Orthodox clergy and the population of Moscow.

Finally, Vasily Shuysky and the surviving boyars, who had hoped to use Dmitry as a tool, found that he served his own interests and feared that he might serve those of King Sigismund III Vasa of Poland. Their nationalistic emotions coincided with their desire for power, and they incited the nationalistic fervor of the inhabitants of Moscow. On May 17, 1606, the False Dmitry was murdered; on May 29, his body was burned, his ashes being fired from a cannon in the direction of Poland.

—*George F. Putnam and Marilyn Elizabeth Perry*

FURTHER READING

Barbour, Philip L. *Dimitry, Called the Pretender, Tsar, and Great Prince of All Russia, 1605-1606*. London: Macmillan, 1967. This excellent book is sound in scholarship and recounts an engrossing story.

Dunning, Chester S. L. *Russia's First Civil War: The Time of Troubles and the Founding of the Romanov Dynasty*. University Park: Pennsylvania State University Press, 2001. In this post-Marxist reassessment, Dunning maintains the Time of Troubles was not a Russian peasant rebellion but a long and violent civil war. Also recounts the story of the False Dmitry.

Emerson, Caryl. *Boris Godunov: Transpositions of a Russian Theme*. Bloomington: Indiana University Press, 1986. Emerson explores the Russian story in terms of historical, literary, and musical interpretations.

Florinsky, Michael T. *Russia: A History and an Interpretation*. 2 vols. New York: Macmillan, 1947, 1953. Florinsky's work is accepted by many as the best general history of Russia in English. Includes a glossary, a bibliography of principal sources, and, in each volume, an index.

Massa, Isaac. *A Short History of the Beginnings and Origins of These Present Wars in Moscow Under the Reign of Various Sovereigns Down to the Year 1610*. Translated by G. Edward Orchard. Toronto: University of Toronto Press, 1982. A Dutch eyewitness account of the historical events.

Perrie, Maureen. *Pretenders and Popular Monarchism in Early Modern Russia: The False Tsars of the Time of Troubles*. New York: Cambridge University Press, 1995. An in-depth study of a series of Russian pretenders to the throne and a comparison to other impostors in Europe.

Riasanovsky, Nicholas V., and Mark D. Steinberg. *A History of Russia*. 7th ed. New York: Oxford University Press, 2004. A comprehensive survey of Russian history that includes a chapter on the Time of Troubles and discussion of the False Dmitry.

Szvák, Gyula. *False Tsars*. Translated by Peter Daniel. Boulder, Colo.: Eastern European Monographs, 2000. This work examines pretenders to the Russian throne from the Time of Troubles to the end of the nineteenth century. Szvák, a Hungarian historian, describes how three men claimed to be Dmitry, the son of Ivan the Terrible.

SEE ALSO: Feb. 7, 1613: Election of Michael Romanov as Czar.

RELATED ARTICLES in *Great Lives from History: The Seventeenth Century, 1601-1700:* Michael Romanov; Sigismund III Vasa; Vasily Shuysky.

---

c. 1601-1613
SHAKESPEARE PRODUCES HIS LATER PLAYS

After establishing himself as one of the half-dozen great London playwrights at the end of the sixteenth century, William Shakespeare moved into a mature phase of darker tragedies. The few comedies of the period are equally dark problem plays or tragicomedies, a genre new to the English stage.

LOCALE: London, England
CATEGORIES: Theater; literature

KEY FIGURES

William Shakespeare (1564-1616), English playwright and actor
John Fletcher (1579-1625), English playwright who collaborated with Shakespeare
Francis Beaumont (c. 1584-1616), English playwright and Fletcher's writing partner
Robert Armin (c. 1568-1615), English comedic actor, writer, and playwright
William Kemp (d. c. 1603), English comedic actor and morris dancer

SUMMARY OF EVENT

With the start of a new century, and even more so with the death in 1603 of England's late sixteenth century figurehead, Queen Elizabeth I, the London stage turned ever more away from an Elizabethan optimism and toward a Jacobean grotesque. Taste in tragedy turned toward the Italianate, Senecan revenge tragedy, which Thomas Kyd (1558-1594) had Anglicized more than a decade earlier. Shakespeare met this vogue with *Hamlet, Prince of Denmark* (pr. c. 1600-1601), his own version

of a now lost play by Kyd. Hamlet's brooding melancholy seemed to personify the uncertainty of the era, and even the so-called comic relief of Hamlet's manic scenes, his toying with Polonius, and the joking gravediggers had a grim, gallows-humor edge.

Two other new vogues in theatrical taste in Stuart England, to which Shakespeare did not cater, were the domestic tragedy and the city comedy, both popular genres that tended to use a London setting. *Othello, the Moor of Venice* (pr. 1604, revised 1623), Shakespeare's first tragedy after the accession of James I, almost struck the opposite extreme, setting scenes on a world stage, in Christian Venice and "Turkish" Cyprus, with a Moorish tragic hero. Similarly, *Antony and Cleopatra* (pr. c. 1606-1607) straddles the Mediterranean, poised between masculine Rome and feminine Egypt. In contrast, *King Lear* (pr. c. 1605-1606) was indeed set in England but certainly not in London; instead it took place in a distant, mythic past.

Shakespeare's darker and darker explorations of the nature of evil do not descend to decadence as do the plays of his contemporaries, but evil seems increasingly universal, as the motives of the villains are increasingly ambiguous. Indeed, Iago in *Othello* refuses outright to explain his motives for tricking Othello into murdering his bride. In *King Lear*, the bastard Edmund blames his god, Nature, for his evil—implying, to viewers' horror, that evil is the human lot, a philosophy with which the despairing Gloucester concurs.

The seventeenth century political implications of Shakespeare's late plays were not all found on stage. On

The title page of the First Folio, Shakespeare's posthumously published collected works. (Folger Shakespeare Library)

May 19, 1603, the newly crowned King James issued an instruction declaring Shakespeare's acting company, the Lord Chamberlain's Men, the king's servants, with honorary titles of grooms of the royal chamber. Shakespeare acknowledged the favor of his monarch with a play set in the king's native Scotland, *Macbeth* (pr. 1606), in which one of James's ancestors, Banquo, is one of the noblest characters, and James's own writings on witchcraft are clearly a source.

The seventeenth century note of pessimism struck even the relatively few comedies that Shakespeare wrote after 1600, which, instead of the light, airy, fairy-tale mood of the 1590's, sounded a chord so gloomy that twentieth century critics did not even call them comedies but rather "problem plays." Not all of this change is attributable to national mood: Personnel changes in Shakespeare's company necessarily affected the type of

comedy he wrote. The company's leading comedian, William Kemp, had played the silly, zany, over-the-top clowns of the earlier, lighter comedies, but in 1600 he left the company. His place in the group was taken by Robert Armin, whose humor was more introspective, a brooding or bantering wit rather than Kemp's buffoonery. Armin appeared as Feste in *Twelfth Night: Or, What You Will* (pr. c. 1600-1602), Lavach in *All's Well That Ends Well* (pr. c. 1602-1603), Pompey in *Measure for Measure* (pr. 1604), and even the fool in *King Lear*.

The last of the vogues in Jacobean drama that occurred in Shakespeare's lifetime was that of the tragicomedy, associated with his younger contemporaries Francis Beaumont and John Fletcher. This dramatic form had implications for Jacobean politics, for Beaumont and Fletcher delighted in posing a conflict between the notion of the divine right of kings, requiring absolute obedience, and an evil king. Shakespeare had explored this problem even before he turned to the tragicomic form: In both *Hamlet* and *Macbeth*, he portrayed murdering, evil monarchs, as he had earlier in *Richard III* (pr. c. 1592-1593, revised 1623); in *King Lear*, his king is a fool, more criminally negligent than evil.

In Shakespeare's tragicomedy *The Winter's Tale* (pr. c. 1610-1611), Leontes is a misguided king whose baseless jealousy, like Othello's, causes the death of his wife, Hermione. Unlike Othello, however, Leontes has no Iago kindling his false jealousy, and unlike in any of the tragedies, Shakespeare resolves the tragic death with an unexpected, unexplained, miraculous resurrection. In this and his other three tragicomedies (modern critics call them "romances")—*Pericles, Prince of Tyre* (pr. c. 1607-1608), *Cymbeline* (pr. c. 1609-1610), and *The Tempest* (pr. 1611)—Shakespeare snatches a happy ending from the jaws of tragedy. More important, all four romances, as well as most of the tragedies of the period, explore changing Jacobean attitudes toward what Derek Hirst called "authority and conflict" in political relations.

Though 1601-1613 was largely a period of tragedies for Shakespeare, with the four romances tempering their tragedy with comic endings, even the two straight-out comedies of the period—*All's Well That Ends Well* (pr. c. 1602-1603) and *Measure for Measure* (pr. 1604)—have a tragic somberness that led critics to call them "dark comedies," "tragicomedies," or simply "problem plays." The moral assessment of both plays is obscured by the same device, "the bed trick," in which a husband goes to bed with his wife while mistakenly thinking she is another woman. Thus he is physically faithful to her though adulterous in intention.

MEASURE FOR MEASURE AND JACOBEAN COMEDY

Shakespeare's Measure for Measure *is exemplary of his later work: Nominally a comedy, it is nonetheless one of his darker plays, full of corruption, vice, and injustice. The following speech, a vivid expression of the horror of death spoken by a character condemned to be executed for having sex out of wedlock, demonstrates why this comedy is often labeled a "problem play."*

> Ay, but to die, and go we know not where;
> To lie in cold obstruction, and to rot;
> This sensible warm motion to become
> A kneaded clod; and the delighted spirit
> To bathe in fiery floods, or to reside
> In thrilling region of thick-ribbed ice;
> To be imprison'd in the viewless winds
> And blown with restless violence round about
> The pendant world; or to be worse than worst
> Of those that lawless and incertain thought
> Imagine howling—'tis too horrible!
> The weariest and most loathed worldly life
> That age, ache, penury, and imprisonment
> Can lay on nature is a paradise
> To what we fear of death.

Source: From Measure for Measure, *by William Shakespeare. In* The Riverside Shakespeare, *edited by G. Blakemore Evans (Boston: Houghton Mifflin, 1974), act 3, scene 1, ll. 117-131.*

The problem plays raise moral questions that they do not answer, another reflection of the uneasiness of an England in transition. In *Measure for Measure*, moreover, moral questions are pushed even further, particularly that of the balance of justice and mercy in absolute rulers. Vincentio is a duke of Vienna who feels he has been too lenient in punishing vice; Angelo, his deputy, is a puritanical moralist who goes to the other extreme. Angelo is brought to a balance only after the (to him) horrifying discovery of lust within himself brings him to wrong Isabella, the object of his desire. Isabella, in turn, is asked to do a wrong (give herself to Angelo) in order to prevent another wrong (the execution of her brother). She refuses, and it is only by the contrivance of the bed trick that her brother is saved.

SIGNIFICANCE

The late plays of Shakespeare, now thought of as the finest dramas in English, nearly universal in their appeal, are nevertheless reflective of the place and time in which they were written, England of the first decade-and-a-half of the seventeenth century. It was an age of changing images of the monarchy. Before James, Eliza-

beth I ruled by force of her individual personality. After James, Charles I's monarchy came into increasing conflict with Parliament, leading ultimately to civil war and the king's execution in 1642.

Between these two rulers, James and the plays of Shakespeare written in the first half of his reign represented an evolving corporate model of government. Coincidentally, the last plays to come from Shakespeare's pen mirrored that corporate model. Many Jacobean playwrights wrote in collaboration for their companies, but until the end of his career Shakespeare never wrote this way. In the last year of his active life in the theater, however, he collaborated with John Fletcher, who would in the ensuing decade replace him as chief writer for the King's Men, in a sort of dark comedy or romance called *The Two Noble Kinsmen* (pr. c. 1612-1613) and a history play, *Henry VIII* (pr. 1613). The moral clarity of the Elizabethan mind was replaced in Shakespeare's Jacobean drama with ambiguities that often had no solutions in the plays themselves.

—*John R. Holmes*

FURTHER READING

Bentley, G. E. *Shakespeare: A Biographical Handbook.* New Haven, Conn.: Yale University Press, 1961. A thorough compilation of original sources, with helpful interpretations, that has not been superseded.

Dollimore, Jonathan, and Alan Sinfield. *Political Shakespeare.* Ithaca, N.Y.: Cornell University Press, 1985. Demonstrates the political implications of Shakespeare's plays.

Gillies, John. *Shakespeare and the Geography of Difference.* New York: Cambridge University Press, 1994. An exploration of the expanded view of the world, especially in terms of "otherness," in Jacobean England, and how it affected Shakespeare's settings.

Hirst, Derek. *Authority and Conflict, 1603-1658.* Cambridge, Mass.: Harvard University Press, 1985. A study of the changing attitudes toward monarchy in seventeenth century England, observable in Shakespeare's plays.

Kenyon, J. P. *Stuart England.* New York: Penguin, 1978. A standard guide to the England in which Shakespeare wrote and produced his later plays.

McDonald, Russ. *The Bedford Companion to Shakespeare: An Introduction with Documents.* Boston: Bedford/St. Martin's Press, 1996. A wealth of background, documents, maps, and pictures to help understand the milieu in which Shakespeare wrote.

SEE ALSO: Early 17th cent.: Revenge Tragedies Become Popular in England; Mar. 24, 1603: James I Becomes King of England; June 29, 1613: Burning of the Globe Theatre; Mar., 1629-1640: "Personal Rule" of Charles I; 1642-1651: English Civil Wars.
RELATED ARTICLES in *Great Lives from History: The Seventeenth Century, 1601-1700:* John Fletcher; James I.

1600's

c. 1601-1620
EMERGENCE OF BAROQUE ART

The ultimate goal of Baroque art and architecture was to dazzle, draw in, and persuade, and its style was permeated with the desire to overwhelm the viewer's senses through naturalism and drama. The Baroque style emerged in different regions at different times but was well established throughout Europe by about 1620.

LOCALE: Western Europe, predominantly Italy, France, Spain, Flanders, and Holland
CATEGORIES: Art; cultural and intellectual history; architecture; religion and theology

KEY FIGURES

Caravaggio (1571-1610), Italian painter
Annibale Carracci (1560-1609), Italian painter
Gian Lorenzo Bernini (1598-1680), Italian sculptor, architect, and painter
Nicolas Poussin (1594-1665), French painter, active in Italy
Charles Le Brun (1619-1690), French painter and chancellor of the Royal Academy of Painting and Sculpture
Diego Velázquez (1599-1660), Spanish painter
Peter Paul Rubens (1577-1640), Flemish painter and diplomat
Rembrandt (1606-1669), Dutch painter
Jan Vermeer (1632-1675), Dutch painter
Jacob van Ruisdael (1628/1629-1682), Dutch painter

SUMMARY OF EVENT

Naturalism and high drama are the primary characteristics of the Baroque style. Used by painters and sculptors to great effect, these qualities imbued sacred and secular images alike with powerful messages conveyed through convincingly naturalistic characters acting out their dramas in believable settings.

Architects created grand spaces in which to stage the religious and political events of Baroque Europe, devising ever-more-majestic schemes to frame the pomp and ceremony of the Counter-Reformation Papacy as well as the French, Spanish, and English monarchies. The Baroque style also appealed to Protestant audiences, though typically on an intimate scale more appropriate to the well-appointed private homes typical of Holland and elsewhere in northern Europe.

Baroque art first flowered in Counter-Reformation Rome, where painters sought to satisfy the recommendations of the Council of Trent's twenty-fifth session (December, 1563), which decreed that religious images be clear and truthful. The two major trends in Baroque painting developed in the competing styles of Caravaggio and of Annibale Carracci, as shown by their works for the Cerasi Chapel (Santa Maria del Popolo, Rome). In 1601, Carracci painted the chapel's classicizing altarpiece, the *Assumption of the Virgin*, with the clear colors, bold volumes, idealism, and restrained drama of High Renaissance masters such as Raphael (1483-1520). Caravaggio painted two canvases in 1601 for the chapel's side walls depicting the *Crucifixion of Saint Peter* and the *Conversion of Saint Paul* with his signature rugged naturalism and dramatic contrasts of light and shadow, known as tenebrism. These images contain the brutally honest characters and stunning tenebrism that was disseminated by many artists throughout Europe, including the French painter Georges de La Tour (1593-1652) and the Spanish painters Francisco de Zurbarán (1598-1664) and Jusepe de Ribera (1588-1652, active in Italy). Although radically different in temperament, the Cerasi chapel paintings by Carracci and Caravaggio share a clarity of composition and content typical of Baroque sacred art.

While Baroque architects did design small, intimate churches, the enormous basilica of Saint Peter's exem-

The interior of St. Peter's Basilica in Rome, a classic of Baroque architecture. (R. S. Peale and J. A. Hill)

plifies the quintessential Roman Baroque church. Begun in the Renaissance after designs by Donato Bramante (1506) and Michelangelo (1546), St. Peter's was completed between 1606 and 1666 by Carlo Maderno (1556-1629) and Gian Lorenzo Bernini, whose magnificent piazza reaches out to visitors, drawing them to Maderno's classicizing facade and the spectacular church interior. In terms of scale, richness of material, and symbolic references to Rome reborn under the power and authority of the pope, St. Peter's rivals the propagandistic palaces and decorative programs of Baroque Europe's great monarchs.

Not only was he a great architect, Bernini was also one of the period's most talented sculptors. Whether pagan or Christian in subject, his marble statues epitomize the naturalism, drama, intensity, and immediacy of the Baroque style. Viewers see mythological and historical events unfold before their eyes, as in the miraculous transformation of human flesh to bark and leaves in his *Apollo and Daphne* of 1622-1624 or in his intense *Ecstasy of Saint Theresa*, created for the Cornaro family

chapel between 1645 and 1652. Bernini's decoration unites painting, sculpture, architecture, and stained glass to overwhelm and envelop chapel visitors in a profoundly mystical experience, drawing them toward Theresa to witness and share her miraculous vision of God.

Mythological dramas were quite popular in Baroque Italy, as seen in the frescoes painted for the Farnese and Barberini family palaces by Carracci and Pietro da Cortona (1596-1669), respectively. Grand allegories of love and power fill the ceilings of these elite Roman families' magnificent reception rooms, which find corollaries in the Baroque palaces of contemporary French and Spanish monarchs. Landscape painting by masters such as Domenichino (1581-1641) and the French-born Nicolas Poussin and Claude Lorrain (1600-1682) are typically filled with mythological or biblical scenes and offered another opportunity to employ the twin Baroque tastes for naturalism and classicism. While highly naturalistic in their light effects, colors, and forms, these compositions are in fact carefully orchestrated to create balanced, harmonious, and idealized views of nature.

Catholics and Protestants had decidedly different attitudes about the production and use of religious imagery. Unwilling to abandon centuries of visual tradition, the Catholic Church embraced sacred art as a means to communicate with and better understand God. Devotional images had to be both theologically correct and inspirational, and Baroque naturalism and drama served these demands well. Baroque altarpieces defended Catholic dogma, especially contested beliefs such as transubstantiation. The altar's symbolic function as sacrificial table that holds the body and blood of Christ miraculously transformed from bread and wine was reinforced by images that focused on Christ's crucified body, such as Caravaggio's *Entombment* of 1603 or Peter Paul Rubens's *Raising of the Cross* and the *Descent from the Cross* altarpieces of 1610-1612.

Protestants believed that religious images could lead to idolatry, and, in contrast, their churches were relatively bare. Religious beliefs and morals are not absent in northern works of art, however, as evidenced by the popular views of church interiors executed by Dutch painters such as Emanuel de Witte (1617-1692) and Pieter Saenredam (1597-1665), as well as the many stunningly naturalistic Dutch still life compositions, loved not only for their celebration of wealth and abundance, but also for their cautionary moral of *vanitas*, which reminds viewers that the pleasures derived from material success are fleeting and unimportant before God.

Loyal to the pope in Rome, Spanish artists also incorporated naturalism, truthfulness, and drama in their devotional works, as seen in engaging examples such as Zurbarán's *St. Serapion* (1628) or Ribera's *Martyrdom of St. Bartholomew*. Subject to the king of Spain, Flanders also saw the production of grand religious imagery, best exemplified by Rubens's riveting portrayal of Christ's crucifixion in his two grand altarpieces painted for Antwerp Cathedral. Of a decidedly different nature are the quiet devotional works by Spanish painter Bartolomé Esteban Murillo

(1618-1682) or French painter La Tour. La Tour's images adapt the tenebrism of Caravaggio with a serenity and silence not seen in his model's often brutal dramas. Murillo's pictures share this peaceful calm, but with a colorful palette, even lighting, and idealism not found in La Tour. These examples offer a glimpse of the range found in Baroque religious painting, underscoring the difficulty in identifying a single or singular Baroque style.

Baroque drama and naturalism also appealed to Europe's monarchs, who were keen to express and confirm their absolute power and control through numerous secular works. Rubens not only worked in his native Flanders but also found himself in high demand throughout Europe. His combination of naturalism, drama, and sensuality of color and form allowed him to create grand spectacles suitable for his royal patrons' aspirations, as exemplified by the series of twenty-one canvases painted for the Parisian palace of the queen regent Marie de Médicis of France (r. 1610-1617). These ostensibly biographical paintings portray her life as one of continuous triumph, magnificence, and splendor overseen and blessed by the classical pagan gods.

Spanish painter Esteban Murillo's A Girl and Her Duenna *(1665-1675) evokes the whimsical.* (Harry N. Abrams)

Beginning in 1669, her grandson, King Louis XIV (r. 1643-1715), would create the ultimate expression of Baroque grandeur with his palace and gardens at Versailles, intended to overwhelm visitors with their size and magnificence. Numerous references to Apollo remind viewers of Louis's claim to be the Sun King, while the extensive grounds designed by André Le Nôtre (1613-1700) and the opulent interiors overseen by Charles Le Brun suggest that in late seventeenth century France, the world truly did revolve around the monarch. Ironically, while Spain's political power declined in the seventeenth century, Spanish artistry achieved its Golden Age. As painter to king Philip IV (r. 1621-1665), Diego Velázquez created many royal portraits and battle scenes, such as *The Surrender of Breda* (1634-1635) and *Las Meninas* (1656), which impress viewers through their vibrant and immediate naturalism, while creating effective propagandistic images of royalty and power.

In the Baroque period, the Dutch Republic saw the accumulation of incredible wealth through thriving international trade and commerce. As a result, Holland's large merchant population, with the highest per-capita income in all of Europe, fueled a vibrant artistic economy. Because Calvinism forbade religious imagery in churches, Dutch artists specialized in secular picture types, including portraits, landscapes, still lifes, and genre scenes, all of which were well served by the Baroque interest in naturalism and clarity of composition. Portraiture reached new heights of immediacy and impact in the hands of artists such as Rembrandt and Frans Hals (c. 1583-1666), who relied on established conventions to reveal the sitter's social status yet captured their subjects' personalities with a new sense of intimacy and emotional power.

Proud and protective of their small territory, the Dutch loved landscape and coastal views of their native Holland. Artists such as Jacob van Ruisdael, Albert Cuyp (1620-1691), and Meindert Hobbema (1638-1709) exemplify the many painters who earned their reputations painting the flat terrain and vast, cloud-filled skies of their patrons' homeland. Genre painting and still life are two other picture types that were commonly displayed in middle-class Dutch homes. These scenes of daily life, painted with painstaking skill and unparalleled naturalism, frequently incorporated symbolism to remind viewers to be wary of vices such as avarice, gluttony, greed, envy, or lust. As their Netherlandish forebears, Baroque still life and genre were meant to be appreciated on many levels, aiming to be edifying as well as beautiful. Whether in the interiors of Jan Vermeer or in the collections of luxury items painted by still life masters such as Pieter Claesz (1597/1598-1661), Willem Heda (c. 1594-between 1680 and 1682), and Willem Kalff (1619-1693), Dutch genre and still life painting allowed patrons to take pride in their worldly accomplishments while remaining mindful of the ephemeral value of wealth and material goods.

SIGNIFICANCE

The word "baroque" was first used in the late eighteenth century as a derogatory term to distinguish the Neoclassical style from the art of the seventeenth century. While considerable debate remains as to the origin of the term, all etymological suggestions imply that Baroque art is somehow irregular, bizarre, or depraved.

Even though nineteenth century writers attempted to establish the

---

"OBSERVATIONS ON PAINTING"

As a genre with the goal of dazzling the senses while staying "true" to nature, the Baroque employed grandiose themes and striking forms and materials to produce spectacular effects. Baroque painter Nicolaus Poussin here describes the "grand manner" that is Baroque art.

On Some Characteristics of the Grand Manner; On Subject, Concept, Structure and Style: The grand manner consists of four elements: subject or theme, concept, structure, and style. The first requirement, fundamental to all the others, is that the subject and the narrative be grandiose, such as battles, heroic actions, and religious themes. But, if the subject which the painter endeavors to treat be grandiose, his first care should be to avoid minute details as much as he possibly can, in order not to violate the fitness of the theme, passing over the large and magnificent objects with a rapid brush by virtue of having neglected himself over vulgar and frivolous ones. . . . As for concept, it is a pure product of the mind which applies its efforts to the task. . . . The structure or composition of the parts should not be laboriously studied, nor *recherché*, nor labored, but true to nature. Style is a particular manner and skill of painting and drawing, born from the particular genius of each painter in the application and use of his ideas. This style, manner, or taste is a gift of nature and genius.

Source: Nicolaus Poussin, "Observations on Painting" (1672), excerpted in *Michelangelo and the Mannerists: The Baroque and the Eighteenth Century.* Vol. 2 in *A Documentary History of Art*, edited by Elizabeth G. Holt (New York: Anchor Books, 1958), p. 144.

value of the Baroque style, they also saw it as distinct from the classical tradition. More recently, the Baroque has been studied as an extension of and elaboration upon many themes and concerns prevalent in the Renaissance. Although Baroque art developed as a direct refutation of the graceful yet stilted forms of the Italian Mannerist style, Baroque artists and architects drew widely from ancient and High Renaissance sources, pursuing similar goals of naturalism, dramatic narrative presentation, and effective means of engaging the spectator.

—*Anne Leader*

FURTHER READING

Blunt, Anthony. *Art and Architecture in France, 1500-1700.* 5th ed. New Haven, Conn.: Yale University Press, 1999. An illustrated survey of French Renaissance and Baroque art.

Brown, Jonathan. *Painting in Spain: 1500-1700.* New Haven, Conn.: Yale University Press, 1998. An illustrated survey of Spanish painting with particular attention to Spain's Golden Age.

Held, Julius, and Donald Posner. *Seventeenth- and Eighteenth-Century Art.* New York: H. N. Abrams, 1972. A classic text on the development of Baroque art and architecture in Europe, organized by region and medium.

Martin, John Rupert. *Baroque.* London: A. Lane, 1977. A classic study that focuses on the major themes of Baroque art.

Minor, Vernon Hyde. *Baroque and Rococo: Art and Culture.* Upper Saddle River, N.J.: Prentice Hall, 1999. A well-illustrated exploration of Baroque art in its social, political, and cultural contexts.

Slive, Seymour. *Dutch Painting: 1600-1800.* New Haven, Conn.: Yale University Press, 1995. An illustrated survey of Dutch Baroque art.

Wittkower, Rudolph, Joseph Connors, and Jennifer Montagu. *Art and Architecture in Italy, 1600-1750.* 6th ed. New Haven, Conn.: Yale University Press, 1999. The standard, illustrated survey of Italian Baroque art.

SEE ALSO: c. 1601: Emergence of Baroque Music; c. 1601-1682: Spanish Golden Age; Mid-17th cent.: Dutch School of Painting Flourishes; 1656-1667: Construction of the Piazza San Pietro.

RELATED ARTICLES in *Great Lives from History: The Seventeenth Century, 1601-1700:* Gian Lorenzo Bernini; Claude Lorrain; Frans Hals; Georges de La Tour; Charles Le Brun; Marie de Médicis; Bartolomé Esteban Murillo; Philip IV; Nicolas Poussin; Rembrandt; Peter Paul Rubens; Diego Velázquez; Jan Vermeer; Francisco de Zurbarán.

1601-1672
RISE OF SCIENTIFIC SOCIETIES

The earliest scientific societies appeared in Italy but diminished there after the condemnation of Galileo in 1633. Informal scientific societies in England came under a single charter in 1662, when Charles II of England authorized the Royal Society of London to advance the cause of science. Louis XIV of France followed with the formation of the Paris Academy of Sciences in 1666 and the Royal Observatory in 1667.

LOCALE: Italy; Germany; London, England; Paris, France

CATEGORIES: Science and technology; organizations and institutions; cultural and intellectual history

KEY FIGURES

Charles II (1630-1685), king of England, r. 1660-1685, who founded the Royal Society

Louis XIV (1638-1715), king of France, r. 1643-1715, who founded the Academy of Sciences

Robert Boyle (1627-1691), Irish scientist and leader in early scientific societies

Robert Hooke (1635-1703), first curator of experiments at the Royal Society

Marin Mersenne (1588-1648), French priest and physicist who led early scientific societies in Paris

Galileo (1564-1642), Italian physicist and astronomer

SUMMARY OF EVENT

Increasing scientific activity in the seventeenth century led to the formation of scientific societies, first in Italy and Germany, and later in England and France. These often began as informal groups of scientists meeting privately, but some later developed into more formal societies when they came under the patronage of royalty. The most important of these were the Royal Society of London for the Promotion of Natural Knowledge (commonly known as the Royal Society) and the Royal Academy of Sciences (Académie Royale des Sciences) in Paris.

The earliest scientific societies began in Italy. In 1601, the Academy of the Lynxes (Accademia dei Lincei), named after the lynx because of its reputed keen eyesight, began meeting in Rome under the patronage of Duke Federigo Cesi. In 1609, it published the proceedings of its meetings, the earliest such publication by any scientific society. It had thirty-two members, including Galileo, who published two of his books under its sponsorship. However, the condemnation of the Copernican system by the Inquisition in 1615 began its demise, which was hastened by the death of its patron in 1630. The last of the seventeenth century Italian scientific societies was the Academy of Experiments (Accademia del Cimento), meeting in Florence from 1657 to 1667 under the patronage of the Medici brothers, Grand Duke Ferdinand II and Leopold de' Medici. It had about ten members, including disciples of Galileo, such as Giovanni Alfonso Borelli and Evangelista Torricelli.

Due to the condemnation of Galileo in 1633, scientists in Italy became more cautious, and leadership in science began to shift to northern and western Europe. Even the Accademia del Cimento worked mainly on experimentation to avoid controversial ideas. When Leopold de' Medici became a cardinal in 1667, the academy came to an end. German scientific societies carried on some activity at the time but did not match those in Italy. These included the Investigation Society (Societas Ereunetica), founded at the University of Rostock in 1622, and the College of Experimental Inquiry (Collegium Curiosum sive Experimentale), established in 1672 at Altdorf with Leopold I as patron. Neither of these, however, outlived its founders, and the more stable Berlin Academy did not begin until 1700, under the influence of Gottfried Wilhelm Leibniz. However, the most important scientific societies emerged in England and France.

In the early seventeenth century, the English philosopher Francis Bacon championed the ideals of experimental and institutional science. His ideas began to bear fruit in the 1640's in close conjunction with Puritanism and the English Revolution (1642-1660). The Irish scientist Robert Boyle was a leading figure in this movement, having close relations with Puritans, though he was himself a moderate Royalist. His group of associates in London became known as the Invisible College, because they had no fixed meeting place. They were influenced by the Puritan ideal of edification through mutual cooperation in groups and believed that science could further the glory of God and the welfare of humans.

As scientific activity spread in England in the first half of the seventeenth century, the Puritan clergyman John Wilkins began to popularize the Copernican system and harmonize it with Calvinist theology. He also promoted the application of science to crafts and industries along Baconian lines. Wilkins and Boyle were among the leaders in forming the Philosophical College in London and Oxford near the end of 1644, meeting weekly to discuss scientific theories and perform experiments. Of the ten known members of this group, six were Puritans siding with the Parliamentarians, and only one was definitely Anglican and Royalist.

With the Restoration of Charles II in 1660, many scientists appointed by the Commonwealth left Oxford and returned to London, which became the main center of science in England. A meeting at Gresham College in 1660 proposed the founding of a "College for the promoting of Physico-Mathematical Experimental Learning" and elected John Wilkins as chairman. In 1662, Charles II granted a Royal Charter incorporating the group as "The Royal Society for the Improvement of Natural Knowledge," with Wilkins as first secretary and Henry Oldenburg as second secretary. Oldenburg was a German businessman with extensive European connections who handled the society's correspondence and conceived the idea of publishing a scientific journal. In March of 1665, the first issue of *The Philosophical Transactions* appeared.

Membership in the Royal Society increased from about one hundred at its founding in 1660 to more than two hundred in the 1670's. The first Curator of Experiments was Robert Hooke, who proposed statutes in 1663 that were pervaded by Baconian influence and recommended against meddling in religion and politics. In the more open atmosphere of the Restoration, the Puritan affiliations of many of the members of the Royal Society became problematic. Out of the sixty-eight Fellows in 1663 for whom information is available, some forty-two (62 percent) had strong Puritan leanings, while twenty-six were Royalist.

In France in the 1640's, a Franciscan priest and disciple of Galileo, Marin Mersenne, initiated informal meetings in Paris with scientific enthusiasts such as Blaise Pascal and fellow priest Pierre Gassendi, and corresponded with Galileo and René Descartes. The wealthy Parisian Habert de Montmor organized later meetings at his house in Paris and formalized the Montmor Academy by a constitution in 1657 that declared its purpose to be the clearer knowledge of the works of God and the improvement of the conveniences of life. When the Montmor Academy requested aid from Louis XIV's minister, Jean-Baptiste Colbert, he decided to establish a

LEARNED SOCIETIES IN 17TH CENTURY EUROPE

• = Cities with universities, academies of science, or botanical gardens (or combinations thereof) founded in the seventeenth century

North Sea

Baltic Sea

Atlantic Ocean

Adriatic Sea

Mediterranean Sea

Edinburgh

Uppsala

Lund 1668

Harderwijk 1648
Rostock 1622
Amsterdam 1631
Groningen 1614
Cambridge
Osnabrück 1630
Oxford
Utrecht 1636
Paderborn 1614
London 1662
Halle 1694
Glessen 1607
Jena
Bamberg 1648
Paris 1663
Tyrnau 1635
Salzburg 1623
Linz 1669
Altdorf 1672
Florence 1657
Oviedo 1604
Rome 1601
Naples
Palermo 1637
Cagliari 1626

cruited from other countries, who were paid a salary by the king to work as a group on problems set by the royal ministers. The Dutch scientist Christiaan Huygens was a member of the academy who provided an early Baconian empirical influence, but this eventually gave way to a more philosophical influence inspired by the writings of Descartes.

SIGNIFICANCE

Much of modern scientific methodology began with the scientific societies of the seventeenth century. With increasing progress in science, these societies provided a rapid means of communicating ideas and discoveries between scientists through their meetings and scientific journals. The older universities, with their long traditions of formal learning, were often unable to adapt quickly to the new approaches of experimental science. The newer scientific societies were able to promote science effectively and bring scientists together from a variety of academic, commercial, and craft traditions. New scientific instruments began to be developed and tested, and new applications were commissioned.

Since the scientific societies were not restricted by hierarchical organizations or scholarly traditions, they were able to exchange ideas and test new discoveries more effectively. This activity was facilitated by their offering of awards and prizes for new discoveries and by the publication of new scientific journals. Discoveries that once were announced with anagrams to protect priority until they could be further tested could now be published openly. When scientific societies were recognized by government charters, they began to receive a degree of protection for the safe exchange of ideas, and some scientists in France even began to receive salaries for their work. Eventually, the scientific societies gave birth to new scientific specialties and new sources of funding.

—Joseph L. Spradley

new scientific society, complementing the Royal Academy of Inscriptions and Humanities (Académie Royale des Inscriptions et Belles-Lettres), which he had established in 1663.

Colbert founded the Académie Royale des Sciences in Paris on December 22, 1666, under the patronage of the Crown, followed in 1672 by the associated Paris Observatory (Observatoire de Paris). Like its English counterpart, the Académie Royale began publishing an important scientific journal, called *Mémoires*. The Académie began with twenty-one members, increasing to about fifty by the end of the century. In contrast with the self-supporting amateurs of the Royal Society, the academicians were professional scientists, several re-

FURTHER READING

Dear, Peter. *Revolutionizing the Sciences*. Princeton, N.J.: Princeton University Press, 2001. This book on European science from 1500 to 1700 includes in chapter 6 a discussion of scientific institutions and patrons.

Jacob, James. *The Scientific Revolution: Aspirations and Achievements*. New York: Humanity Books, 1999. Chapters 4 and 5 discuss seventeenth century science in France and England, including scientific societies in these countries and Italy.

Ornstein, Martha. *Role of Scientific Societies in the Seventeenth Century*. Chicago: University of Chicago, 1928. Reprint. London: Archon Books, 1963. The most complete study of scientific societies in the seventeenth century, including a chapter on scientific journals.

Rossi, Paoli. *The Birth of Modern Science*. Translated by Cynthia De Nardi Ipsen. Oxford, England: Blackwell, 2001. This translation from Italian includes a good discussion of scientific societies in chapter 16 on "Academies."

SEE ALSO: 17th cent.: Advances in Medicine; Sept., 1608: Invention of the Telescope; 1609-1619: Kepler's Laws of Planetary Motion; 1610: Galileo Confirms the Heliocentric Model of the Solar System; 1612: Sanctorius Invents the Clinical Thermometer; 1615-1696: Invention and Development of the Calculus; 1617-1628: Harvey Discovers the Circulation of the Blood; 1632: Galileo Publishes *Dialogue Concerning the Two Chief World Systems, Ptolemaic and Copernican*; 1643: Torricelli Measures Atmospheric Pressure; Dec. 6, 1648-May 19, 1649: Establishment of the English Commonwealth; 1654: Pascal and Fermat Devise the Theory of Probability; 1655-1663: Grimaldi Discovers Diffraction; Feb., 1656: Huygens Identifies Saturn's Rings; May, 1659-May, 1660: Restoration of Charles II; 1660-1692: Boyle's Law and the Birth of Modern Chemistry; 1664: Willis Identifies the Basal Ganglia; 1665: Cassini Discovers Jupiter's Great Red Spot; Late Dec., 1671: Newton Builds His Reflecting Telescope; 1673: Huygens Explains the Pendulum; Summer, 1687: Newton Formulates the Theory of Universal Gravitation.

RELATED ARTICLES in *Great Lives from History: The Seventeenth Century, 1601-1700:* Giovanni Alfonso Borelli; Robert Boyle; Charles II (of England); Jean-Baptiste Colbert; René Descartes; Ferdinand II; Galileo; Pierre Gassendi; Robert Hooke; Christiaan Huygens; Johannes Kepler; Gottfried Wilhelm Leibniz; Leopold I; Louis XIV; Marin Mersenne; Sir Isaac Newton; Blaise Pascal; Evangelista Torricelli.

c. 1601-1682
SPANISH GOLDEN AGE

Despite deeply troublesome social, economic, and political conditions, seventeenth century Spanish culture reached rare heights. The Golden Century (Siglo d'Oro), a cultural florescence that expressed itself most fully in drama and painting, began in the 1500's and reached its apex during the reign of the otherwise undistinguished King Philip IV.

LOCALE: Castile, Spain
CATEGORIES: Theater; literature; art; cultural and intellectual history

KEY FIGURES

Philip III (1578-1621), king of Spain, r. 1598-1621
Philip IV (1605-1665), king of Spain, r. 1621-1665
Count-Duke of Olivares (Gaspar de Guzmán y Pimental; 1587-1645), principal minister of Philip IV, 1621-1643
Charles II (1661-1700), king of Spain, r. 1665-1700
Lope de Vega Carpio (1562-1635), playwright and poet
Tirso de Molina (Gabriel Téllez; 1580?-1648), playwright
Francisco Gómez de Quevedo y Villegas (1580-1645), social critic and author
Luis de Góngora y Argote (1561-1627), poet
Pedro Calderón de la Barca (1600-1681), playwright
Diego Velázquez (1599-1660), painter
Francisco de Zurbarán (1598-1664), painter
Bartolomé Esteban Murillo (1618-1682), painter

SUMMARY OF EVENT

Spain's Golden Age, or Siglo d'Oro (golden century), was played out against a dreary backdrop of disruptive social change, economic stagnation and decline, and shrinking prestige and power on the stage of European affairs. Spain still ruled a far-flung empire, which included the Philippines and colonies in the New World as well as Portugal, Sicily, Naples and Milan in Italy, and the Spanish Netherlands, with pretensions to the Dutch provinces as well. Less creditable were the three Habsburg kings who ruled Spain from the death of Philip II in 1598 until 1700.

Philip III was a pleasure-loving ruler who quite consciously rejected his father's serious demeanor and attention to administration. His choice of ministers was unfortunate and included Francisco Gómez de Sandoval y Rojas, the duke de Lerma, who essentially ran the Spanish government for two decades, greatly enriching himself in the process. During Philip's twenty-three years as king, Spain entered a period of economic degeneration that was exacerbated by the expulsion of the Moriscos (converted Moors) in 1609 and the corruption and self-aggrandizing that was common at the highest levels of society.

Philip III's son, Philip IV, came to power at the age of sixteen. The first two decades of his reign benefited from the guiding hand of his principal minister, the count-duke of Olivares. Olivares was a cultured and serious student of governmental affairs who sought to revivify Spain's position in a Europe embroiled in the Thirty Years' War and to reform a society and ruling class that were gripped by corruption and lassitude. Philip resembled his father in his disinterest in administration, but Olivares shaped the young monarch into a passable ruler and a truly great patron of the arts, especially painting and theater.

The 1640's saw the Portuguese and Catalan rebellions, the fall of Olivares, and the defeat of the Habsburgs in the Thirty Years' War. By mid-century, it was clear that Spain had fallen as a major European power, despite its retention of Europe's greatest overseas empire. Habsburg inbreeding resulted in the tragic figure of King Charles II, who was both mentally and physically disabled. Only four years old when Philip died, Charles never quite outgrew his childhood and depended utterly on his mother, Mariana de Austria, and his ministers to direct Spain. Young and ambitious King Louis XIV of France took advantage of Spain's problems and pressed his advantage in the Netherlands (the War of Devolution and the French-Dutch War) and along the Spanish border, especially in the Wars of the Spanish Succession (1701-1714), which began following the death of the childless Charles.

Despite the steady income from its colonies, Spain's economy stagnated and people felt sharply the pangs of inflation and high taxation. Much Spanish wealth drained out of Iberia to pay for its wars and the constant flow of foreign goods. The large influx of silver from Potosí in the New World caused severe inflation, and subsequent government debasement of coins worsened the situation, causing a further drain of specie to pay foreign debts. Having but a small entrepreneurial middle class, Spain fell rapidly behind countries that were more advanced economically and technologically, such as England and the United Provinces. Better-designed foreign ships carried away Spanish goods, and Spanish industry slowly retarded as the wealthy diverted potential investment capital to foreign luxury goods.

As Madrid grew in prestige as the court's permanent home (after 1605), it drew nobles from their provincial seats, stripping the countryside of leadership and capital, and often leaving it in the hands of unscrupulous underlings. On the other hand, the congregation of competitive and often sophisticated aristocrats with deep pockets meant that Madrid, and to a lesser extent Seville and Toledo, would become even greater centers of artistic patronage and production.

Seventeenth century Spain was more than merely a Catholic country; it was the great force for militant, Counter-Reformation Catholicism. The Spanish took very seriously their Tridentine mission to thwart the heretic and convert the pagan, and authorities both secular and ecclesiastical tolerated little that smacked of dissent. Like Protestantism in England, Catholicism formed a core around which early Spanish nationalism was fostered, a very important step in creating a true Spain from Castile, Aragon, and their constituent parts. The Church served the state and the state the Church. The arts—theater no less than painting—served the interests of both, not least of all through popular entertainment that was both nationalistic and religious. This relationship was reinforced by the growing cultural legacy of Catholic Renaissance Italy and early Baroque Papal Rome that found its way to Iberia, often through Spanish Naples and Milan. All that was needed for the cultural flowering of the sixteenth century to continue were a few people of genius.

Although Miguel de Cervantes' novel *Don Quixote de la Mancha* (1605, 1615) casts a long shadow over early seventeenth century Spanish literature, the Siglo d'Oro produced numerous authors of the first caliber in lyric poetry and drama. The Salamanca-educated cleric and Royal Chaplain Luis de Góngora y Argote wrote complex poetry for a sophisticated, aristocratic audience. Góngora adopted strong, stylized, classical literary influences and utilized a very high and often pretentious tone, convoluted constructions, obscure or exotic vocabulary, and hidden, metaphoric meanings that constituted a novel poetic approach known as *culturanismo*. Together with *conceptismo*, a poetic approach that featured concision and brevity of expression studded with brilliant turns of phrase, *culturanismo* characterized what came to be called Gongorism and was manifested in Góngora's *Soledades* (1627; *The Solitudes of Don Luis de Góngora*, 1931; *The Solitudes*, 1964) and consciously classical *Fábula de Polifemo y Galatea* (1627; *Fable of Polyphemus and Galatea*, 1961).

Many poets and virtually all playwrights rejected the obscurity and artificial style of Gongorism. The Humanist Francisco Gómez de Quevedo y Villegas was an outspoken critic of Gongorism. As a propagandist for the Olivares government under Philip IV, Quevedo utilized a wide range of literary forms, including theological and philosophical tracts, history and fantasy, drama and political treatises, and satire and poetry, to point out Spanish society's ills. Even his staunch support of the regime,

Spanish writer Pedro Calderón de la Barca, following in the footsteps of dramatist Lope de Vega Carpio, wrote some of the greatest dramatic literature of the seventeenth century. (Library of Congress)

however, could not insulate him from censorship by a paranoid state, and he spent more than three years in prison for being an "enemy of the government."

Spanish drama, like that of other European traditions, had its roots in Catholic liturgical performances and classical theater. Madrid built its first permanent theaters in the 1580's, and by the seventeenth century, there had developed an insatiable hunger for daily performances in theaters in all of Spain's major cities and at the court in Madrid. With the work of the enormously prolific Lope de Vega Carpio, a native of Madrid and a superb poet, the Spanish *comedia*—a term used for any type of play in this period—received its classical shape and many of its best examples.

In his academic poem of 1609, *El arte nuevo de hacer comedias en este tiempo* (*The New Art of Writing Plays*, 1914), Lope de Vega supported the classical ideal that drama should entertain and teach, though he rejected classicism's many rules of composition, including the firm line between tragedy and comedy. In his more than one thousand plays, he blended a naturalistic treatment of society and language with a firm moralistic purpose that was often satirical or even mocking in tone. In works like *Fuenteovejuna* (1619; *The Sheep-Well*, 1936), he explored the developing notion that nobility was a matter of character and not birth. Like most playwrights, he supported the rigid and often brutal code of honor that demanded bloody revenge for serious slights. Generally conservative in his view of society and the regime, his plays tended to blend love, patriotism, religion, and the social code in a way that was primarily entertaining. In cape-and-sword (*capa y spada*) comedies he featured the loves, intrigues, and duels of the aristocrats, whom he often satirized to the delight of all classes. His vast output included plays based on Spanish and Italian stories, folk ballads, historical events, chivalric literature, the Bible, and saints' lives.

Lope de Vega's most prolific follower was Tirso de Molina, a well-educated cleric and masterful playwright who wrote some four hundred *comedias*. More intellectual than Lope de Vega, he carefully crafted his plots around well-formed characters and highlighted moral and theological issues where Lope de Vega emphasized action and social critiques. Tirso's *El burlador de Sevilla* (pb. 1630; *The Love Rogue*, 1924) featured his greatest creation, the unscrupulous lover Don Juan, a dramatic character who would have a long and fitful life on the European stage. Pedro Calderón de la Barca, a poet and playwright praised by Lope de Vega, carried on the tradition of the new comedy, reaching new rhetori-

Spanish painter Diego Velázquez's late work, The Maids of Honor *(1656), has been compared with the genre paintings of the contemporary Dutch school.* (Harry N. Abrams)

cal heights in his rich, dramatic poetry. Though he wrote for the popular stage, he revolutionized Spanish stagecraft in spectacular works produced in the Coloseo (1640), the fully equipped, Italian-style theater at Buen Retiro, Philip IV's new palace near Madrid. In later life, Calderón concentrated on public religious plays known as *autos sacramentales*, a genre that Lope de Vega had first developed from liturgical and morality plays into richly textured and sophisticated Christian dramas.

The Golden Age also produced some of Spain's greatest painters. In Toledo, El Greco dominated religious art until his death in 1614. Philip IV developed a strong taste for the work of Flemish and Italian artists, bringing to Madrid hundreds of paintings that stimulated the work of court painter Diego Velázquez and forms most of the Prado Museum collection. Working hard to raise the status of the Spanish painter, Velázquez blended what he learned from Roman, Venetian, and Flemish art into his native Spanish style, creating rich, complex, and expres-

sive courtly compositions such as *Las Meninas* (1656; the family of Philip IV). Though Seville was hit hard by Spain's economic downturn, its church and its cosmopolitan nobility sponsored scores of religious paintings. Most popular were the serene and idealized devotional images by Bartolomé Esteban Murillo. Francisco de Zurbarán served the tastes of the Sevillan aristocracy with paintings marked by forceful realism and accepted Philip IV's invitation to help decorate the king's Hall of Realms in the Buen Retiro palace.

SIGNIFICANCE

Like the Italian Renaissance or the Elizabethan era in England, the Golden Age of Spain saw the production of many of the early modern era's greatest artistic and dramatic masterpieces. Inspired by Late Renaissance Italian and Flemish masters, painters in Madrid and Seville found patrons among a generous royalty, a wealthy and powerful Church, and art-conscious nobility. Velázquez

59

and Zurbarán scaled new heights in lush naturalism, while Murillo created works perfectly suited to the bourgeois Tridentine piety of the later seventeenth century.

While the arcane sophistication of Gongorism died out with the Baroque Age, the naturalism and fundamental humanity of the *comedias* of Lope de Vega and Calderón found both willing imitators and satisfied audiences well into the eighteenth century. Like all cultural eras, the Siglo d'Oro came to a close, a point perhaps best marked by the deaths of Calderón and Murillo in 1681 and 1682.

—Joseph P. Byrne

FURTHER READING

Brown, Jonathan. *Painting in Spain, 1500-1700*. New Haven, Conn.: Yale University Press, 1998. A detailed overview of the major figures, trends, and monuments in seventeenth century Spanish painting.

_____. *Zurbarán*. New York: Abrams, 1991. A lavishly illustrated study of Zurbarán and his major works.

Casey, James. *Early Modern Spain: A Social History*. New York: Routledge, 1999. Casey explores the various classes that constituted Spanish society from about 1500 to 1800, the forces that shaped them, and the effects they had on Spanish history.

Defourneaux, Marcelin. *Daily Life in Golden Age Spain*. Stanford, Calif.: Stanford University Press, 1979. This work details urban and rural life and the customs, beliefs, and social structures of the period.

Elliott, J. H. *Spain and Its World, 1500-1700: Selected Essays*. New Haven, Conn.: Yale University Press, 1989. A collection of essays, some of which place Spanish decline in a broad context.

Jones, R. O. *The Golden Age: Prose and Poetry, the Sixteenth and Seventeenth Centuries*. New York: Barnes and Noble Books, 1971. A broad examination of the major authors, works, and trends in Spanish literature in the seventeenth century.

Kamen, Henry. *The Golden Age of Spain*. 2d ed. New York: Palgrave Macmillan, 2005. An updated version of a broad introduction to Spanish history in the seventeenth century.

Parker, Mary, ed. *Spanish Dramatists of the Golden Age*. Westport, Conn.: Greenwood Press, 1998. This work contains extended biographical essays on nineteen of Spain's most important dramatists from around 1500 to around 1700.

Wolf, Norbert. *Diego Velazquez, 1599-1660: The Face of Spain*. New York: Taschen, 2000. A well-illustrated overview of the artist's major works.

SEE ALSO: c. 1601: Emergence of Baroque Music; c. 1601-1620: Emergence of Baroque Art; 1605 and 1615: Cervantes Publishes *Don Quixote de la Mancha*; May, 1640-Jan. 23, 1641: Revolt of the Catalans; Mid-17th cent.: Dutch School of Painting Flourishes.

RELATED ARTICLES in *Great Lives from History: The Seventeenth Century, 1601-1700:* Pedro Calderón de la Barca; Charles II (of Spain); Luis de Góngora y Argote; Bartolomé Esteban Murillo; Count-Duke of Olivares; Philip III; Philip IV; Francisco Gómez de Quevedo y Villegas; Tirso de Molina; Lope de Vega Carpio; Francisco de Zurbarán.

February 7-19, 1601
ESSEX REBELLION

The Essex Rebellion, led by Robert Devereux, the earl of Essex, was the only armed uprising against Elizabeth I. However, the popular support expected by Essex did not materialize, and the rebellion was easily suppressed, leading to the execution of the earl and his chief followers. The failure of the rebellion demonstrated the solidity of the Tudor regime and the outdatedness of the earl's militaristic, chivalric credo.

LOCALE: London, England
CATEGORIES: Government and politics; wars, uprisings, and civil unrest

KEY FIGURES

Earl of Essex (Robert Devereux; 1566-1601), earl marshal of England, 1597-1600, and lord lieutenant and governor-general of Ireland, 1599-1600

Elizabeth I (1533-1603), queen of England, r. 1558-1603

Sir Robert Cecil (1563-1612), English secretary of state, 1590-1612, and first earl of Salisbury, 1605-1612

Third Earl of Southampton (Henry Wriothesley; 1573-1624), English noble, soldier, and rebel

Lady Penelope Rich (Penelope Devereux; 1562?-1607), Essex's sister

SUMMARY OF EVENT

Robert Devereux, the earl of Essex, was one of the most important figures of the late Elizabethan court. His father, Walter Devereux, first earl of Essex (sixth creation), had died while on active service in Ireland. His mother, Lettice Knollys, a cousin of Queen Elizabeth I, had then secretly married the queen's favorite, Robert Dudley, earl of Leicester. When the marriage eventually became public knowledge, Elizabeth was furious with Knollys, but she eventually forgave Leicester, and his handsome stepson thereafter shared in her favor, especially after Leicester himself died in 1588. Essex saw himself as the political and military heir of Leicester, of his own father, and of his friend Sir Philip Sidney, Leicester's nephew, whose widow he married after Sidney's heroic death at the Battle of Zutphen (1586).

Elizabeth, however, was unimpressed by military endeavors in general and by the cost of them in particular. Essex made several early attempts to attain military glory in France and by leading attacks on Spanish shipping, all of which were thwarted by the queen's parsimony and

her reluctance for him to be away from court. Finally, he was allowed to take up his father's command in Ireland as part of the ongoing English attempt to bring this rebel "colony" to heel. However, bad roads, difficult terrain, lack of local knowledge, and the difficulty of communicating with London meant that the earl, like others before him, struggled.

After Elizabeth objected to Essex's having met with the rebel leader, the earl of Tyrone, Essex returned to London, essentially deserting his post without permission, in order to explain himself in person. Legend has it that, arriving early in the morning, he surprised the queen without her wig and makeup; certainly, she was furious at his return and deprived him of his monopoly on the sale of sweet wines, his major source of income. Desperate to vindicate both his own reputation and the warrior culture that he saw himself as embodying, Essex, encouraged by his sister Lady Penelope Rich and his close friend the earl of Southampton, decided to lead an armed uprising against the queen.

The spark was lit on Saturday, February 7, 1601, when the earl received a summons to attend the Council. He feared that this was a pretext to arrest him, and it may indeed have been a provocative measure masterminded by Essex's principal enemy, Sir Robert Cecil, later the first earl of Salisbury, in an attempt to force him to show his hand. As he often had done in the past, Essex excused himself from the meeting on grounds of illness. To prime Londoners for the forthcoming coup, he also sent one of his followers, Sir Gelly Meyrick, to persuade the Lord Chamberlain's Men (the leading troupe of actors in London, whose principal dramatist was William Shakespeare) to perform a play about Richard II, who had been king of England from 1377 until his deposition in 1399.

It is not clear whether the company performed Shakespeare's *Richard II* (pr. c. 1595-1596) or another play on the same subject. In any event, reminding an English audience of the deposition of one monarch seemed like a good way of encouraging them to think of doing the same to another, and it further helped the earl's cause that Henry IV, who deposed Richard II, was his own ancestor. It was in response to this performance that Elizabeth uttered her famous remark, "Know ye not that I am Richard?"

Despite the performance, however, the rebellion that the earl launched the next day, Sunday, February 8, was an abject failure. The government had taken precautions

Robert Devereux, the earl of Essex. (Hulton|Archive by Getty Images)

make speeches. Essex walked on through the city, shouting out as he went that he was the victim of a plot, that there were plans to murder him, and that Sir Robert Cecil was determined to betray England by ensuring that the queen's successor would be the Spanish Infanta, daughter of England's hated enemy Philip II of Spain, who had sent the Armada against England in 1588. Even this had no effect.

Eventually, the earl turned back and made for Essex House again. He had to fight his way through Lud Gate, where the bishop of London had posted soldiers, but he eventually won through. Safely back at Essex House, he burned as many of his papers as he could and toyed with the idea of a desperate last stand, but when the lord admiral, Charles Howard, earl of Nottingham, appeared outside with guns, it was clear that the situation was hopeless, and Essex, reluctant to risk the safety of his sister and of the other women in the house, gave himself up without a fight. The Essex Rebellion was over.

Essex knew he was doomed. Elizabethan treason trials had only one possible outcome, a verdict of guilty, and the trial of Essex and his friend Southampton, held on February 19, 1601, was no exception. A particular betrayal was that the earl's cousin Sir Francis Bacon, to whom he had always been a friend, was one of the prosecutors. A little under a week later, on February 25, the earl was executed. Southampton, however, was spared the death penalty and ultimately pardoned, as was Penelope Rich.

SIGNIFICANCE

In one sense, the Essex Rebellion had no real significance, because the total failure of anyone but the earl's immediate circle to rally to his banner shows the extent to which his was an isolated and anachronistic viewpoint. Certainly, it confirmed that military leadership and personal valor counted for less in late Elizabethan society than did diplomacy and political skills, but that was already obvious to everyone except Essex and his most devoted followers. Culturally, however, the event had great impact.

Essex's friend Southampton was Shakespeare's patron, and *Hamlet, Prince of Denmark* (pr. c. 1600-1601) in particular has been seen as reflecting on the earl's fall. More generally, the rebellion and its failure made both topical and dangerous the Tacitean style of historiography (named after the Roman historian Cornelius Tacitus), which the earl was known to have favored and which interpreted events as being under the control of a capricious fortune rather than a benevolent Providence.

(which may well be evidence that Cecil had been in control of the situation from the outset): It doubled the guards at the palace at Whitehall, making it impossible for Essex and his followers to attempt to seize control of the court as they had originally planned; it sent messengers through the streets of London to tell the citizens to lock their doors and remain inside; and it sent four lords of the Council, including Essex's uncle, Sir William Knollys, and the lord chief justice, Sir John Popham, to Essex House to ensure the earl of a fair hearing if he would come with them peacefully.

Instead, a panicking Essex locked the four lords in a room, with his sister Penelope loudly calling for Popham's head, and decided to appeal directly to the citizens. He and his followers marched through Lud Gate and along the Strand to Saint Paul's Cathedral, a popular gathering place where books were sold in the churchyard and where the earl had planned to make a speech. However, the citizens, obeying the Council's orders, stayed resolutely indoors, and there was no one to whom to

The melancholy attitude to which this perspective gave rise remained fashionable, and indeed, when Elizabeth I died in 1603 (a death popularly attributed to grief at Essex's execution) and James VI of Scotland ascended the throne as James I, to be associated with the memory of the dead Essex became something of a passport to favor. More than forty years after his death, Essex did have an ironic revenge when his son Robert, the third earl, became a Parliamentary general fighting against and ultimately helping to depose King Charles I.

—*Lisa Hopkins*

FURTHER READING

Freedman, Sylvia. *Poor Penelope: Lady Penelope Rich.* London: Kensal Press, 1983. Although focusing on the earl's sister Penelope Devereux rather than on Essex himself, offers a detailed account of the rebellion.

Hammer, Paul E. J. *The Polarisation of Elizabethan Politics: The Political Career of Robert Devereux, Second Earl of Essex, 1585-1597.* New York: Cambridge University Press, 1999. Masterly and wide-ranging account of Essex's political career in its wider context.

Lacey, Robert. *Robert, Earl of Essex: An Elizabethan Icarus.* Rev. ed. London: Weidenfeld & Nicolson, 2001. A scholarly account of the earl's life and career.

Strachey, Lytton. *Elizabeth and Essex.* Reprint. New York: Oxford University Press, 1981. Dated but stylish psychological reading of the relationship between the queen and her favorite.

"The Trial of the Earls of Essex and Southampton, 1601." http://renaissance.dm.net/trial/index.html. Gives a full transcript of the trial of Essex and his friend and co-conspirator, the earl of Southampton.

SEE ALSO: Mar. 24, 1603: James I Becomes King of England; Nov. 5, 1605: Gunpowder Plot; 1620: Bacon Publishes *Novum Organum*; Mar.-June, 1639: First Bishops' War; Oct. 23, 1641-1642: Ulster Insurrection; 1642-1651: English Civil Wars; Mar. 12-14, 1655: Penruddock's Uprising; Aug. 13, 1678-July 1, 1681: The Popish Plot; Aug., 1682-Nov., 1683: Rye House Plot; Nov., 1688-Feb., 1689: The Glorious Revolution.

RELATED ARTICLES in *Great Lives from History: The Seventeenth Century, 1601-1700:* Charles I; James I.

July 5, 1601-April, 1604
SIEGE OF OOSTENDE

Following a siege of more than three years, the Spanish capture of Oostende, the last Dutch stronghold in the southern Netherlands, signaled the end of the Dutch Wars of Independence.

LOCALE: Oostende, Spanish Netherlands (now in Belgium)

CATEGORY: Wars, uprisings, and civil unrest

KEY FIGURES

Albert VII (1559-1621), archduke of Austria and governor of the Spanish Netherlands

Maurice of Nassau (1567-1625), prince of Orange, r. 1618-1625, and stadtholder of the Netherlands, r. 1585-1625

Johan van Oldenbarnevelt (1547-1619), landsadvocaat, or civil administrator, of the Estates-General of the Netherlands

Ambrogio Spinola (1569-1630), Genoese general who fought for Spain

Sir Francis Vere (1560-1609), English commander of Oostende's garrison

SUMMARY OF EVENT

Known in Europe as the Eighty Years' War, the Dutch Wars of Independence ravaged the Low Countries, northern Europe's most prosperous region. The oppressive policies of Spanish king Philip II sparked widespread rebellion in 1566. Led by Alessandro Farnese, Spanish forces reconquered what is now Belgium by 1588, but conflicts with England and France delayed Spanish campaigns against the mostly Protestant United Provinces of the northern Netherlands, allowing the Dutch, led by Stadtholder Maurice of Nassau, to reorganize.

Influenced by Maurice's interests in engineering and the advice of mathematician Simon Stevin, the army of the chief province of Holland was reduced in size, but its organization was improved. To avert mutiny—the perpetual curse of that era's armies—troops were promptly paid, properly equipped, and regularly trained. Systematically emphasizing siege warfare, Maurice captured several Spanish strongholds, beginning with Breda in 1590.

After Philip II appointed his son-in-law, Albert VII of Austria, governor of the Spanish Netherlands in 1595, Maurice was persuaded by his mentor, Landsadvocaat Johan van Oldenbarnevelt, to move south to reunite the Netherlands and aid Flanders in repelling its Spanish occupiers. A Spanish force of twelve thousand led by Albert clashed with eleven thousand Dutch troops deployed among sand dunes on the North Sea near Nieuwpoort on July 2, 1600. More numerous but weary from a twelve-hour march and outmaneuvered by greater Dutch mobility, Albert's army retired with losses exceeding four thousand troops, double those of his enemy. Despite this victory, Maurice also was compelled to withdraw because few Flemings rallied to his side. Attention was focused 10 miles northeast on Oostende, the last Dutch stronghold in the south. Originally Oostende-ter-Streepe, the town was founded about 814 as a fishing village. Fortified by Farnese in 1583, Oostende was defended by forts, bastions, and walls, and by ditches surrounding the town with seawater. By land, a web of streams and canals fed wide channels known as the Old Haven and Geule, on the west and east respectively.

Failing to convince Madrid to negotiate with the Dutch, Albert laid siege to Oostende with twenty thousand troops and fifty cannon on July 5, 1601. The Dutch garrison consisted of only two thousand men under Governor Vander Nood. However, the Estates-General (Dutch parliament) considered Oostende to be of utmost importance, and so it dispatched English general Sir Francis Vere to the besieged port with sixteen hundred troops. Facing them across the Old Haven, sixteen thousand of Albert's troops with thirty cannon encamped west of the town, while Count Bucquoy, with four thousand men and ten guns, took up positions across the broader and deeper Geule. Fordable for four hours every tide, the Old Haven was Oostende's weak side, and it included the Sand Hill, Porc Espic, and Helmond forts and several bastions.

Vere strengthened Oostende's defenses and dug ditches to the sea to maintain water levels. Drawing the Spanish away, he stationed two hundred men on rising ground to the south to fire on enemy boats coming from Bruges. Finding their supply lines threatened, the Spanish shelled the defenders mercilessly. Though his preparations proved successful, Vere was severely wounded by a cannon shot on August 4. Taken to Middelburg to recuperate, he returned to Oostende before his wounds properly healed. By August 8, some twelve hundred English troops arrived to bolster the defenders, who had been forced underground by cannon fire. Undistracted

by sorties led by Vere's brother, Sir Horace Vere, the besiegers erected a battery near the Old Haven and then opened fire on Sand Hill fort. Reinforcements continued to arrive, however, raising the garrison to forty-five hundred troops by late September.

Stunned by Oostende's stiff resistance, Albert engaged an English traitor named Coningsby to spy on the defenders. Captured when he attempted to bribe a sergeant to blow up a powder magazine, Coningsby confessed and was whipped out of town, an extraordinarily light punishment.

Through the autumn, the Spaniards built floating batteries in the Geule and sank sand-filled baskets in the Old Haven to allow passage of their troops. Late on December 4, they attacked suddenly. Igniting straw to see in the dark, the defenders fired on the besiegers as they crossed the mud, driving the Spaniards back with losses exceeding five hundred troops. Hard frosts thwarted further attacks but also prevented help from reaching the defenders. Ammunition fell short. The garrison dwindled. Only twenty-five hundred able-bodied men remained, though four thousand were required to guard the fortifications.

Correctly believing that a major Spanish assault was imminent once tides were low, Vere stalled for time. He sent Sir John Ogle to parley with Mateo Serrano, who agreed that he and another Spanish officer should go into Oostende, while Ogle and Sir Charles Fairfax would be held as hostages by the Spanish. Expecting a surrender, the Spanish were astonished when Vere proposed that Albert end the siege. Meanwhile, the three-day cease-fire, accompanying this parley (discussion of terms), enabled the defenders to repair the weakest of their fortifications. By night, five Dutch men-of-war ships anchored off Oostende. Sleeping in Vere's quarters, the Spanish envoys awoke to fire from their own side, vainly attempting to stop the disembarkation of four hundred men and great quantities of supplies. Breaking off negotiations, the envoys and hostages were returned to their respective sides.

On January 7, 1602, Spanish cannon fired more than 163,000 shots into Oostende. However, its complex fortifications were difficult to destroy, and the defenders, lying down in their earthworks, suffered little. That evening, 5,000 Italian and Spanish troops with ladders attacked the Porc Espic, Helmond, and Sand Hill forts. Closing sluices, Vere retained water in the channels. When the besiegers ceased firing to allow their guns to cool, 2,000 Spanish troops waded across the Old Haven, and a gun signaled Bucquoy to converge from the east. Stones, bricks, burning pitch, flaming hoops, grenades, and barrels of nails and ashes were hurled down on Albert's troops, who faltered at the foot of the walls. Meanwhile, Vere withdrew from and then recaptured a fort on the Geule to occupy Bucquoy's forces and prevent them from supporting Albert. Repulsed on all sides, the attackers retreated across the Old Haven as the tide rose. Vere reopened the sluices, carrying some Spaniards out to sea. Losing only 30 men, with 100 wounded, the garrison inflicted 2,000 deaths on the Spanish. Victorious, but worn by fatigue and numerous wounds, Vere resigned his command, retired to England, and was succeeded by his brother.

The siege continued. Open to the sea, Oostende's harbors allowed its stubborn defenders, some six thousand at their peak, to be resupplied and reinforced. A flotilla of Spanish galleys under Genoese Admiral Federico Spinola tried to blockade Oostende by sea and was attacked by Dutch warships, resulting in the admiral's death. A second land assault on April 13, 1603, also failed. Despite pressure from the Estates-General, Maurice, cautious after Nieuwpoort, refused to send a relief force. Both sides were distracted elsewhere.

Continuing the siege at his own expense, Ambrogio Spinola, Federico's older brother, took command in October of 1603. By April, 1604, he began to capture Oostende's outer defenses by attrition. Five Dutch governors died in battle that year. Following the loss of Sand Hill fort on September 14, 1604, the last Dutch governor, Daniel de Hertaing, surrendered the nearly destroyed town on September 20.

SIGNIFICANCE

Compared by its contemporaries to the Siege of Troy, the struggle for Oostende was the focal point of the final phase of the Dutch Wars of Independence. Despite the Dutch capture of Sluys, Spanish control of the southern Netherlands (Belgium) was reasserted. A lack of Flemish support had clearly caught Maurice of Nassau by surprise, revealing that intelligence had been overlooked by his military reforms.

Meanwhile, King James I of England anxiously pressed for peace. Negotiated by Albert, the Treaty of London (1604) ended sixteen years of Anglo-Spanish war. Albert and Spinola also urged Madrid to negotiate with the Dutch. Spain recognized the Netherlands' borders, but the Dutch refused to tolerate Catholicism or withdraw from conquests in the Americas and the East Indies. Having spent unprecedented sums in Flanders between 1604 and 1607, Spanish king Philip III was in no position to raise 300,000 ducats a month to continue the war. The Netherlands had secured its frontiers amid the expensive distraction of Oostende. The two sides concluded an armistice in 1607 and a twelve-year truce in 1609.

Maurice's increasingly tense relations with the impatient, overly optimistic Oldenbarnevelt led to Oldenbarnevelt's execution for treason in 1619. Hostilities resumed in 1621, and Spinola captured Breda in 1625. Embittered, Maurice died shortly thereafter. An important general in the Thirty Years' War and later governor of Milan, Spinola was killed in the War of the Mantuan Succession (1628-1631). Fearful of France's growing power, Spain finally recognized Dutch independence in 1648, and the Dutch-Belgian border, which has remained into the twenty-first century, was drawn.

Prospering under Austrian rule in the 1700's, Oostende became Belgium's most important fishing port and a fashionable seaside resort by the nineteenth century.

—*Randall Fegley*

FURTHER READING

Melegari, V. *The Great Military Sieges*. New York: Thomas Crowell, 1972. This work contains a good description of the Siege of Oostende.

Parker, Geoffrey. *The Dutch Revolt*. London: Penguin, 1990. A thorough history of the Dutch Wars of Independence.

Rady, Martyn. *From Revolt to Independence*. London: Hodder & Stoughton, 1990. A good general work on the Dutch Wars of Independence.

Vere, Sir Francis. *The Commentaries of Sir Francis Vere*. London: 1657. Published posthumously, this manuscript at Yale University includes Vere's account of Oostende, an account frequently quoted in books and electronic sources.

SEE ALSO: July, 1643-Oct. 24, 1648: Peace of Westphalia; Nov. 7, 1659: Treaty of the Pyrenees; Mar. 4, 1665-July 31, 1667: Second Anglo-Dutch War; May 24, 1667-May 2, 1668: War of Devolution; Apr. 6, 1672-Aug. 10, 1678: French-Dutch War; Aug. 10, 1678-Sept. 26, 1679: Treaties of Nijmegen; 1689-1697: Wars of the League of Augsburg.

RELATED ARTICLES in *Great Lives from History: The Seventeenth Century, 1601-1700:* James I; Maurice of Nassau; Philip III.

December, 1601
DUTCH DEFEAT THE PORTUGUESE IN BANTAM HARBOR

Portugal was the first European power to discover a maritime route around Africa to the riches of the East Indies. However, rising Dutch maritime power challenged and subdued Portuguese trade dominance in the region, transforming not only the East Indies but also Holland itself, which became a commercial and territorial power.

LOCALE: Northwestern Java (now in Indonesia)
CATEGORIES: Wars, uprisings, and civil unrest; trade and commerce; expansion and land acquisition; colonization

KEY FIGURES

Cornelis de Houtman (c. 1540-1599), Dutch sailor who pioneered the spice trade in Southeast Asia
Maulana Muhammad (1550?-1596), first ruler in Southeast Asia to make a treaty with the Dutch, defying Portuguese dominance in the region, r. 1580-1596
Steven van der Haghen (1563-1624), Dutch admiral who established, through a treaty with Maulana Muhammad, official Dutch trade in the Spice Islands
Wolfert Harmensz (fl. 1601), Dutch commander at Bantam Harbor battle
André Furtado de Mendonça (fl. 1601), Portuguese admiral at Bantam Harbor battle

SUMMARY OF EVENT

Forging a pioneer sea route around Africa to the riches of the East Indies, the Portuguese settled into the region beginning in the sixteenth century. They permanently circumvented Islamic control of a vast trade belt that extended from Morocco to Borneo. Negotiating trade agreements with local potentates but applying military force when necessary, the Portuguese set up fortified trading posts around the rim of the Indian Ocean and through Southeast Asia. They considered the region to be a "closed sea," exclusively under their control.

The Portuguese centered their regional operations in the city of Goa on the Malabar (western) coast of India, with many of their richest possessions lying farther east, in Southeast Asia. These constituted a crescent of fortified trading posts through the Straits of Malacca, which flowed between the Malay Peninsula and the island of Sumatra, past the island of Java, and on to the Celebes (now Sulawesi), Timor, and the Spice Islands (Moluc-

cas). This area beyond the Indian Ocean comprised the Java, Banda, and Timor Seas.

The Portuguese exploited an extraordinarily rich trade in nutmeg, mace, cloves, pepper, and other commodities. They maintained this trade in competition with Islamic mercantile influence, which, during the previous centuries, had invaded and come to dominate the mostly Hindu region. In 1580, however, an event occurred that would seriously jeopardize Portuguese dominance. In that year the Aviz Dynasty, which ruled Portugal, had died out, leaving the Portuguese throne vacant. It was immediately claimed and occupied by the then-most-powerful monarch in Europe, Philip II of Spain. With his ascension to the throne, Portugal acquired a rivalry with one of Spain's most bitter enemies in Europe, the Netherlands. The northern Protestant provinces of this region had begun a revolt against Catholic Spanish rule in 1572. This uprising would continue until 1648 and come to be known as the Eighty Years' War.

The most economically and technologically advanced of the Dutch provinces was the sea- and trade-based region of Holland, and it spearheaded the Netherlands into becoming a maritime power. Commercial power would strengthen the military endeavors of the Dutch, and the richest commercial advantages lay in Southeast Asia, especially the Spice Islands. To wrest a share of this trade from the Portuguese and assert the right of "open seas" became primary Dutch objectives.

For the Dutch to take over the Portuguese spice trade, they needed a special geopolitical strategy. All maritime trade over the Indian Ocean and the western edge of Southeast Asia depended on the monsoon trade winds. From Goa, Portuguese forces dominated this sphere, holding the east (Swahili) coast of Africa, the Persian Gulf, the Malabar Coast, and the Straits of Malacca. To circumvent this dominance, the Dutch resolved to approach the Spice Islands through the Straits of Sunda. This body of water connected the Indian Ocean and the Java Sea and lay between the southeastern tip of Sumatra and the northwestern point of Java. The principal harbor in the straits was Bantam, a major Muslim spice trading port, with the sultanate of Bantam extending the straits.

In 1595, Cornelis de Houtman, a Dutch sea trader who had sailed with the Portuguese and knew their trade routes, led a pioneer Dutch expedition to access the Spice Islands through the Straits of Sunda. Bantam's sultan, Maulana Muhammad, signed a trade treaty with the

Dutch. The offensive behavior of the Dutch alienated him, however, and they were routed away.

Because of the sultan's treaty, the Portuguese sent a fleet to Bantam in 1597, which the sultan defeated. Dutchman Houtman died in 1599 during a second voyage to the region by the Dutch. He was killed by the sultan of Aceh, a region on the northern edge of Sumatra, who had sent envoys to Europe to canvas intentions and strategies. Immediately after Houtman's death, however, the Dutch admiral, Steven van der Haghen, entered the Moluccas, signing treaties with local powers disaffected with the Portuguese.

Thoroughly alarmed by the mounting challenges to their dominance, the Portuguese sent a large fleet in 1601, led by André Furtado de Mendonça, to guard the Straits of Sunda against further Dutch incursions. On Christmas Day, the Portuguese encountered a small fleet of Dutch ships, commanded by Wolfert Harmensz. Combat between the two forces was sustained for several days. At first, the larger Portuguese fleet dominated. However, as the battles continued across the winds and currents of the bay around the harbor of Bantam, the lighter, more agile Dutch ships proved much more effective. The Dutch prevailed and the Portuguese retreated to Goa.

The following year, the Dutch East India Company was founded, an armed trading enterprise that was constituted to take control of the spice trade for the Netherlands. In 1603, it established a trading post at Bantam. Eventually, however, Jan Pieterszoon Coen established company headquarters east of this region, at Jacatra, which was renamed Batavia in 1619 (now called Jakarta).

It was not only because of Dutch success against the Portuguese that the company was founded. At the end of 1600, Queen Elizabeth I of England chartered the British East India Company, and the following year an English fortified trading post was established in the spice-rich Banda Islands, east of Timor. The Dutch would vanquish this initial English presence in the region.

Defeating and routing the Portuguese while suppressing English incursions into the East Indies, the Dutch

Dutch and Portuguese forces battled over the thriving trade port of Bantam Harbor, Java, in Southeast Asia in 1601. (Hulton|Archive by Getty Images)

changed the course of maritime and commercial history in Southeast Asia. They prompted the end of Portuguese dominance and delayed the rise of English influence. They succeeded in opening the seas against a Portuguese monopoly but ultimately would fail in attempting to apply their own such control.

SIGNIFICANCE

Portugal's loss of most of its commercial holdings in Asia to the Dutch during the first half of the seventeenth century brought an end to Portuguese dominance in the region. That decline accelerated even further as English and French competition penetrated the region later. Asia had been the wealthiest segment of the Portuguese maritime empire. With the loss of Asia, Brazil would become the economic center of Portuguese trade. Brazil was a vast, rich, sugar-producing Portuguese colony in South America.

Dutch commercial power in Asia endured from the seventeenth to the twentieth century. Out of the array of islands, kingdoms, and sultanates that it subdued in Southeast Asia, it formed what is now called Indonesia. The Dutch East India Company became one of the most successful enterprises of the seventeenth century. At its height after the middle of the century, it commanded nearly two hundred ships, a quarter of them warships. Of its tens of thousands of employees, a considerable number were soldiers. The company paid dividends to early investors that were many hundreds of times their initial investments.

Progressively, the Netherlands was transformed from a commercial enterprise to a territorial power. Nonetheless, by the following century, complacency, corruption, and accelerated regional competition bankrupted the Dutch East India Company, and it was dissolved in 1798.

As India became the jewel of the British Empire in Asia, so Indonesia was set as the rich center of the Dutch Empire. The modern independent country of Indonesia has its capital in Jakarta, the former Dutch imperial center of Batavia.

—*Edward A. Riedinger*

FURTHER READING

Chaudhury, Sushil, and Michel Morineau. *Merchants, Companies, and Trade: Europe and Asia in the Early Modern Era*. New York: Cambridge University Press, 1999. The authors analyze Portuguese and Dutch trade competition within the European context of commercial and imperial strategies in Asia. The Europeans confronted an Asian trading web of strategies and objectives.

Emmer, P. C., and F. S. Gaastra. *The Organization of Interoceanic Trade in European Expansion, 1450-1800*. Aldershot, England: Variorum, 1996. This work examines the comparative mercantile, naval, and political strategies of various European powers for world trade, particularly in the Far East.

Gaastra, F. S. *The Dutch East India Company: Expansion and Decline*. Zutphen, the Netherlands: Walburg, 2003. Reviews the development of the company, analyzing its initial policies, strategies, and resources for confronting and defeating the Portuguese in Asia in the early seventeenth century.

Kumar, Anne. *Java and Modern Europe: Ambiguous Encounters*. Richmond, England: Curzon, 1997. Kumar examines the historic complexity of economic interests and sociopolitical structures on Java and the island's relation with the Dutch East India Company and other competing European trading entities and interests.

Marques, António Henrique de Oliveira. *History of Portugal*. 2 vols. New York: Columbia University Press, 1972. Volume 1 focuses on the historic development of Portugal, detailing its origins as a nation-state and then as a global maritime empire.

SEE ALSO: 17th cent.: Age of Mercantilism in Southeast Asia; 17th cent.: The Pepper Trade; Mar. 20, 1602: Dutch East India Company Is Founded; Beginning Spring, 1605: Dutch Dominate Southeast Asian Trade; 1606-1674: Europeans Settle in India; Apr. 29, 1606: First European Contact with Australia; 1609: Bank of Amsterdam Invents Checks; Oct., 1625-1637: Dutch and Portuguese Struggle for the Guinea Coast; 1630-1660's: Dutch Wars in Brazil; Jan. 14, 1641: Capture of Malacca; 1642 and 1644: Tasman Proves Australia Is a Separate Continent; 1654: Portugal Retakes Control of Brazil; 1661-1672: Colbert Develops Mercantilism; c. 1690: Extinction of the Dodo Bird.

RELATED ARTICLES in *Great Lives from History: The Seventeenth Century, 1601-1700:* Jean-Baptiste Colbert; Piet Hein; Abel Janszoon Tasman.

1602-1613
JAPAN ADMITS WESTERN TRADERS

As part of his consolidation of the central authority of the shogunate, the first Tokugawa shogun, Ieyasu, set out to monopolize Japanese trade with European nations. He pursued trade links with the Spanish, Portuguese, English, and Dutch, causing a brief boom in Japanese-European contact as well as important linkages that would last the entire period of Tokugawa rule.

LOCALE: Japan
CATEGORIES: Trade and commerce; economics; diplomacy and international relations

KEY FIGURES
Tokugawa Ieyasu (1543-1616), Japanese shogun, r. 1603-1605
Tokugawa Hidetada (1579-1632), Japanese shogun, r. 1605-1623

SUMMARY OF EVENT

In 1549, Jesuit Francis Xavier visited Japan, which at the time was in a period of civil war and lacking a strong central ruler. Xavier established the nation's first Christian mission. Other missionaries followed Xavier, and in the following decades many Japanese, including the lords of several powerful fiefs in the south of the country, were converted to Christianity. Trade and other contact with Europeans accelerated from 1571, when Portuguese ships began to visit Nagasaki with greater frequency. Spanish ships also began frequent trading voyages.

In 1587, Toyotomi Hideyoshi, a military strongman who was continuing the consolidation of central power begun by his deceased lord, Oda Nobunaga, issued an edict ordering the expulsion of foreign missionaries. At the time, Hideyoshi was attempting to gain control of Kyūshū, the southernmost of the major Japanese islands and a center of Christian belief. There is evidence to suggest that he saw Christianity as a threat to his authority. There is also evidence that Hideyoshi was worried by reports that a missionary presence in other parts of Asia such as the Philippines had been a precursor to the expansion of European political control. At first, Hideyoshi's edict went unenforced, but the situation changed dramatically and came to have a negative impact on trade as well in 1596, when Hideyoshi ordered the confiscation of the Spanish ship *San Felipe* and the imprisonment of its crew.

The situation worsened in 1597, when twenty-six Japanese and foreign Christians were crucified on Hide-

yoshi's orders. Hideyoshi, however, died in the following year, prompting a struggle for authority, during which the powerful eastern lord Tokugawa Ieyasu gained authority over Japan's disparate domains after defeating his rivals at the Battle of Sekigahara in 1600. In 1603, Ieyasu assumed the political title of shogun and began to consolidate his position as Japan's absolute ruler. Ieyasu formally retired from the office of shogun in 1605 in favor of his son Tokugawa Hidetada, in order to guarantee the succession and ensure the establishment of a Tokugawa dynasty. He continued to wield authority from behind the scenes, however, remaining the effective ruler until his death in 1616.

One of Ieyasu's major projects was a redefinition of Japan's trading relations with the countries of Europe. He had taken bold steps to improve Japan's trading relationship with Spain even before he had become shogun. In 1602, Ieyasu welcomed the crew of a Spanish galleon that had blown ashore in Japan. This reception, contrasting markedly with the treatment of the *San Felipe* by Hideyoshi, was designed to facilitate a closer trading relationship with Spain and its New World colonies such as Mexico. In 1611, Ieyasu met with Sebastian Viscaino, the viceroy of New Spain, and it appeared as if Spanish-Japanese relations were entering an important period of development. This situation began to change rapidly, however, in 1612, when the Tokugawa shogunate began to return to Hideyoshi's policies by putting forward the first in a series of anti-Christian decrees. The shogunate's resistance to Christianity was to prove unacceptable to the Spanish, who eventually began to limit their trading relationship with Japan.

In the context of Spanish-Japanese relations, the decision to restrict Christianity may seem like a rash one. However, this decision was made in a larger international context. In 1600, a Dutch ship, the *Liefde*, landed in southern Japan. Despite the fact that the Dutch were denounced by the Spanish and Portuguese and said to be little more than pirates, Ieyasu eventually accepted overtures for the beginning of a trade relationship with them. In 1609, the Dutch were permitted to establish a factory at Hirado, in the south of the country. In 1613, the year after the ban on Christian missionary activities was enacted, English traders began to visit Japan, and they too were allowed to set up a factory on the southern Japanese island of Kyūshū.

The warm reception offered to the English and Dutch, who continued to enjoy special privileges after the enact-

A Dutch trader attempts to gain favor with Shogun Tokugawa Ieyasu by warning him against dealing with Spain and Portugal. The Dutch were the only Europeans who would maintain trade relations with Japan during the period of national seclusion. (Francis R. Niglutsch)

ment of the anti-Christian ordinances, was based in religious issues. England and Holland were Protestant nations, uninterested in missionary activities in Asia, which were then predominantly the provenance of the Jesuits and other Catholic orders. As a result, trade with these two countries was seen as more desirable than trade with the Catholic nations that were actively interested in transforming the religion and culture of Japan. Such a transformation would not merely disrupt Japan's traditional values and way of life: It was also likely to destabilize the power of the Tokugawa shogunate itself, as the shoguns well knew.

While Ieyasu had initially been indifferent and sometimes even receptive to Christianity and the Catholic missionary presence, the idea that foreign missionaries represented a threat to the central government's policies, a concept that had existed since Hideyoshi's day, was still an influential one in Japanese politics. In addition, recent research has suggested that, aside from limiting the ability of the outer lords to gain any advantage against the central government, it was the intention of Tokugawa Ieyasu to create the impression that the Euro-

peans were also subject to his authority. The missionary presence made this difficult with respect to the Spanish and Portuguese, but the Dutch in particular proved willing to accept the ceremonial conditions of a tributary relationship in exchange for trading privileges.

SIGNIFICANCE

The successor of Tokugawa Hidetada, Tokugawa Iemitsu, was far more aggressive in persecuting Christians—both Japanese and foreign missionaries—than Ieyasu and Hidetada had been. In 1624, the Spanish, whom Iemitsu suspected of both smuggling missionaries into Japan and supporting those who were living in the country in hiding, were banned from entering Japanese ports. In the 1630's, efforts were also made to ensure that Japanese citizens could not leave the country, and expatriates were prohibited from returning. In 1639, the Portuguese were barred from Japan. In short, the anti-Christian policies begun during Ieyasu's time in power eventually resulted in what is known as the *sakoku*, or "closed country," policy. Japanese were banned from going overseas, and contact with foreign traders was strictly controlled. The English, not finding the Japan trade to be profitable enough, left of their own accord in 1624. The Dutch, meanwhile, maintained the trading relationship with Japan that they had begun between 1600 and 1609. However, in 1641, all Dutch trade with Japan was confined to the island of Dejima in Nagasaki harbor.

Despite its limited scope, the continued Dutch presence was enormously influential. Through the Dutch factory at Dejima, Japan—a "closed country" according to official rhetoric—was afforded a window into international affairs and kept apprised of important European developments in areas such as medicine. In a similar vein, Europe was given a window into Japan. Important scholars—such as Engelbert Kaempfer, who visited Japan with the Dutch traders in the late seventeenth century, and Philipp Franz Von Siebold, who visited in the early nineteenth century—wrote voluminously about the Asian nation. This relationship between Japan and Holland continued to be very important until the 1850's, when American initiatives forced Japan to abandon its one-sided relationship with the Dutch and enter the larger world of international politics.

—*Matthew Penney*

FURTHER READING
Chaiklin, Martha. *Cultural Commerce and Dutch Commercial Culture: The Influence of European Material*

Culture on Japan, 1700-1850. Leiden, the Netherlands: Leiden University Press, 2003. Discusses the impact of the Dutch in Japan on a cultural level. Contains significant background on the Dutch contact in the early seventeenth century.

Hasselink, Reinier. *Prisoners from Nambu: Reality and Make-Believe in Seventeenth Century Japanese Diplomacy.* Honolulu: University of Hawaii Press, 2001. An extended discussion of the place of the Dutch traders in the worldview of the Japanese shogunate in the seventeenth century.

Totman, Conrad. *Early Modern Japan.* Berkeley: University of California Press, 1993. The most comprehensive single-volume treatment of the Edo period of Japanese history in English. Includes an extensive discussion of the trade between Japan and European countries in the sixteenth and seventeenth centuries.

SEE ALSO: 1603: Tokugawa Shogunate Begins; Jan. 27, 1614: Japanese Ban Christian Missionaries; 1615: Promulgation of the *Buke shohatto* and *Kinchū narabini kuge shohatto*; 1624-1640's: Japan's Seclusion Policy; 1651-1680: Ietsuna Shogunate; 1680-1709: Reign of Tsunayoshi as Shogun.

RELATED ARTICLES in *Great Lives from History: The Seventeenth Century, 1601-1700:* Tokugawa Ieyasu; Tokugawa Tsunayoshi.

1602-1639
OTTOMAN-ṢAFAVID WARS

For nearly four decades, the two most powerful states in the Islamic world, the Ottomans and the Ṣafavids, battled for control of Iraq and the Caucasus region. The wars ended with a division of the Caucasus, the Ottoman annexation of Iraq, and a permanent boundary treaty. Although Islamic doctrines continued to divide the Sunni Ottomans and Shia Ṣafavids, the two empires remained relatively at peace after 1639.

LOCALE: Iran, Iraq, Turkey, the Caucasus
CATEGORIES: Wars, uprisings, and civil unrest; expansion and land acquisition

KEY FIGURES
'Abbās the Great (1571-1629), shah of Persia, r. 1587-1629
Murad IV (1612-1640), sultan of the Ottoman Empire, r. 1623-1640

Osman II (1603-1622), sultan of the Ottoman Empire, r. 1618-1622
Mustafa I (1591-1639), sultan of the Ottoman Empire, r. 1617-1618, 1622-1623
Ṣafī (d. 1642), shah of Persia, r. 1629-1642

SUMMARY OF EVENT
From the establishment of Ṣafavid domination over Iran in 1514, antagonism marked relations between the new shahs of Persia and their western rival, the Ottoman Empire. The Ottoman sultans presented themselves as the champions of Sunni Islam, warriors against the infidels of Europe and Russia. The Ṣafavid shahs proclaimed themselves the regents for the Hidden Imam of the Shia (Shī'ite) Muslims.

These two states had already fought several vicious wars during the sixteenth century. In the early seventeenth century, however, the Ottoman-Ṣafavid wars were long, more destructive, and intermixed with domestic mutinies, peasant revolts, and urban rioting. The 1639 Treaty of Kasr-i Shirin brought an end to these wars and a balance of power between the two states that endured through the rest of the century.

In 1588, Shah ʿAbbās the Great came to power in Iran, confronting aggressive enemies at every point of the compass. These threats compelled ʿAbbās to accept a humiliating peace with the Ottomans that cost dearly in territory and tribute. Ottoman troops took over most of northern Iran, including the historical capital of Tabriz. However, ʿAbbās's strategic instincts and his steely patience eventually paid off. By 1602, the shah had pacified his northern and eastern borders. Spain and other European states furnished him modern firearms. Patiently enacted political and military reforms augmented Persia's traditional feudal armies (called *qizilbash*) and tribal horse levies with professional salaried soldiers.

Meanwhile, the Ottomans, embroiled in a war with Austria, lacked the strength and unity they enjoyed only a decade before. Simultaneously, civil unrest erupted throughout Ottoman Anatolia. Thousands of peasants, demobilized soldiers, and rural tribesmen joined freebooting private armies called Jelālī, seeking loot and protesting government financial burdens. The balance of power in the Middle East was shifting.

Starting in 1602, three years of tentative raids into Ottoman-occupied Iran began the Ottoman-Ṣafavid wars. The shah waited until September, 1605, to unleash his full army on his antagonists. Persian victory in a battle at Lake Urmiya shattered Ottoman forces in Iran. The liberation of Tabriz and the other cities of northern Iran followed rapidly. These successes put the shah in a solid position to launch an offensive into Ottoman Anatolia. Many of the Turkish and Kurdish tribes in the areas of Van, Kars, Diyarbakr, and Erzirum raised the Ṣafavid standard against the beleaguered Ottoman sultan. ʿAbbās was cautious, however, as he confined himself to raiding expeditions and sending his political agents, Shia Islamic missionaries, and other provocateurs to keep the "pot boiling." He knew the same rebels who welcomed him as a liberator in the morning might turn against him before nightfall. Moreover, in 1606, the Ottomans had made peace with Austria and Poland, which meant that Ottoman reinforcements would march Anatolian tribes east against the *Jelālī* and, then, perhaps, against Iran.

Success rewarded the shah's patience. Repressing the *Jelālī* rebels weakened the Ottomans. When the Ottoman invasion of Iran finally came in 1610, the expedition proved cumbersome and poorly organized. After win-

ning some minor skirmishes, the Ottomans invited the Ṣafavids to negotiate. Not eager to face a real invasion, the shah accepted the offer. The 1612 treaty basically restated an older agreement, the 1555 Treaty of Amasya. Under its terms, the Ottomans restored northern Persia, Azerbaijan, and parts of the Caucasus to ʿAbbās in exchange for peace on the borders of eastern Anatolia. As a bow toward Islamic solidarity, the two empires promised to coordinate operations against the growing threat from Russia to the north. In reality, the treaty was only a truce.

There was little peace in the peace of 1612. Border incidents escalated regularly until the Ottomans decided to launch a punitive expedition in late 1617. Before much could be accomplished against the Ṣafavids, a succession crisis exploded in Istanbul, the Ottoman capital. The listless Ottoman march against Tabriz failed against ʿAbbās's defenders. The 1612 treaty, therefore, was renewed virtually unchanged in September of 1618.

In the next several years, instability in the Ottoman Empire became volcanic. The murder of the reformist sultan Osman II in 1622 brought a lunatic, Mustafa I, to the throne. The next year, another violent faction installed Sultan Murad IV, though insurgencies continued to rock Ottoman lands, until even the Shia Muslims of southern and central Iraq rose up. For Shah ʿAbbās, self-proclaimed protector and first missionary of Shia Islam, the time seemed a godsend.

In late 1623, the Persians swept into Iraq. Baghdad fell in January, 1624, and only Basra and Mosul withstood the invasion. To dramatize that this war was a sectarian jihad, ʿAbbās massacred thousands of Sunni Muslims in Baghdad. He also launched a flotilla, seizing the Strait of Hormuz between the Persian Gulf and the Gulf of Oman. Rebels in eastern Anatolia made movement of troops, supplies, and weaponry too insecure for the Ottomans to march into Iraq. Nonetheless, the loss of Baghdad convinced the Ottoman ruling elites that the empire faced mortal danger. Setting quarrels and ambitions aside, they rallied to the new young sultan.

Swordsman, wrestler, and weightlifter, the charismatic young Murad IV inspired devotion and terror in his subordinates. His first military efforts successfully restored Ottoman order throughout much of the eastern region of Anatolia, ending the Ṣafavid threat to his flank. However, Murad's march on Baghdad in the fall of 1630 lacked the power to take the city. Russian intrigues in the Crimea, revolts in the Arab provinces of the empire, a lack of funds, and threats of mutiny by garrisons around Istanbul hampered the war effort. Still, pacifying Anatolia laid the critical groundwork for any future conquest of Iraq.

In 1629, ʿAbbās the Great died, passing the throne to his grandson, Ṣafī. A hedonistic adolescent, swayed by factions and indulgences, Shah Ṣafī tended to favor the bureaucrats in the state who raised money for him over the soldiers who seemed only to spend it. At the same time, the Persian position in Iraq remained tenuous. Ṣafavid occupation forces were small, Sunni resistance remained vigorous, and the northern routes into Iran remained vulnerable should the Ottomans again attempt Tabriz. Meanwhile, Murad strengthened his power in Istanbul, purging, impoverishing, or executing those who crossed him. The balance of forces began to tip away from the Persian side.

In the summer of 1634, Murad IV invaded northern Iran, ending his march with the capture of Tabriz that September. However, lacking enough forces to keep the long, tortuous supply lines open between the empire and Tabriz, the sultan had to abandon his prize. Ṣafī learned nothing from the experience. The Persians seemed reassured because the Ottomans did not return over the next years, but their complacency was misplaced. Murad first had affairs to settle in the Crimea and then on the Danube frontiers, but his resolve to reclaim Baghdad was undimmed.

Late in 1638, Murad IV, wearing the uniform of a common Janissary, led his troops to the plains of Baghdad. The Persians put up a stiff resistance. The battle lasted forty days, with Murad taking part in combat, gunnery, and even the dirty work of sapping the walls. At the same time, other Ottoman forces rode through northern Iraq, capturing other towns and often massacring Shia Muslims. Baghdad fell in late December, 1638, and the sultan began preparations for another campaign in the east.

With the arrival of spring, though, Ṣafavid and Ottoman diplomats began work on a comprehensive peace treaty that would secure the common frontiers of the two hostile empires. The 1639 Treaty of Kasr-i Shirin fixed the boundaries along commonly accepted lines and demilitarized some areas. Shah Ṣafī agreed to cease subversive activities along the border, punish raiders, and recognize Ottoman power in Iraq and the upper gulf area. In turn, the dispirited Murad recognized Azerbaijan as Persian territory. Religious concerns also were met. Shia Muslims in the empire, so long as they remained peaceful Ottoman subjects, were free to practice Shia Islam. The peace signed at Kasr-i Shirin lasted until the Ṣafavid Dynasty collapsed in the early 1700's.

SIGNIFICANCE

Ottoman-Ṣafavid wars set the final contest between the two empires, violent rivals since the 1510's. Under ʿAbbās the Great, Persia occupied Iraq, winning its greatest territorial extent in the modern era. Eventually, the Ottomans recovered Iraq, and the final treaty fixed the boundaries between Iran and the Arab-Turkish states. The 1639 treaty set a military and also religious balance of power in the Middle East ensuring that Shia Islam would endure in Iran and that Shia Muslims in Iraq would be tolerated under Sunni Ottoman rule. The Shia of modern Iraq owe their survival to this peace.

—*Weston F. Cook, Jr.*

FURTHER READING

Eskandar Beg Monshi. *The History of Shah ʿAbbās the Great.* 2 vols. Translated by Roger M. Savory. Boulder, Colo.: Westview Press, 1980. A concise, comprehensive history by the chief secretary of ʿAbbās's court and the most important source of Ṣafavid history in general. Ends with a discussion of ʿAbbās's death and funeral.

McCarthy, Justin. *The Ottoman Turks: An Introductory History to 1923.* New York: Longman, 1997. A sweeping historical overview of Ottoman history from the late thirteenth century to the early twentieth century.

Melville, Charles, ed. *Ṣafavid Persia: The History and Politics of an Islamic Society.* New York: St. Martin's Press, 1996. Contains fifteen essays that examine historiography, religious policies, and the silk industry under the Ṣafavids.

Murphey, Rhoads. *The Functioning of the Ottoman Army Under Murad IV.* 2 vols. Ph.D. dissertation. University of Chicago, 1979. This work focuses on a pivotal military era.

_____. *Ottoman Warfare, 1500-1700.* New Brunswick, N.J.: Rutgers University Press, 1999. Murphey provides excellent coverage of Ottoman warfare and an invaluable bibliography for detailed research.

SEE ALSO: 17th cent.: Rise of the Gunpowder Empires; 1603-1617: Reign of Sultan Ahmed I; Nov. 11, 1606: Treaty of Zsitvatorok; 1623-1640: Murad IV Rules the Ottoman Empire; 1629: Ṣafavid Dynasty Flourishes Under ʿAbbās the Great; Sept. 2, 1633: Great Fire of Constantinople and Murad's Reforms; 1638: Waning of the *Devshirme* System; 1642-1666: Reign of Shah ʿAbbās II; 1656-1662: Persecution of Iranian Jews.

RELATED ARTICLES in *Great Lives from History: The Seventeenth Century, 1601-1700:* ʿAbbās the Great; Jahāngīr; Kösem Sultan; Murad IV; Mustafa I; Shah Jahan.

March 20, 1602
DUTCH EAST INDIA COMPANY IS FOUNDED

The founding of the Dutch East India Company led to the founding of a large European empire in Asia and established the pattern of modern imperialism and colonialism.

LOCALE: United Provinces (now in the Netherlands)
CATEGORIES: Trade and commerce; organizations and institutions; economics; expansion and land acquisition; exploration and discovery; colonization

KEY FIGURES

Balthasar de Moucheron (1552-c. 1610), a merchant of the province of Zeeland
Johan van Oldenbarnevelt (1547-1619), landsadvocaat, or civil administrator, of the Estates-General of the Netherlands

SUMMARY OF EVENT

Although the Dutch East India Company was founded in 1602, its origins lay in the Netherlands' successful struggle to free itself from Spanish rule during the preceding century. This feat was accomplished in 1581, when the seven northern provinces of the Netherlands won independence. These seven combined to form an economically dynamic, although politically decentralized, seafaring power—one ready to challenge the control its rivals exercised over oceanic trade routes.

Spices from the East Indies had been vital to European cooking for centuries and were used to season food, to preserve it, and to disguise its flavor when preservation failed. The most common spices included pepper, cloves, nutmeg, and mace, the latter two derived from the seed of the same tree. Initially, European access to these spices was controlled by Muslim and Venetian merchants, most of whom had been supplanted by Portuguese traders in the fifteenth century. By the end of the following century, however, Portuguese power was waning.

Nine prosperous merchants from the province of Holland had formed the Company of Far Lands (in Dutch, the Compagnie van Verre) in 1594. Relying on information gathered by fellow countrymen who had sailed with the Portuguese, the company launched a small fleet of three ships under the command of Cornelis de Houtman the following year. The route Houtman had to follow was a long one—around Europe and the southern tip of Africa and across the Indian Ocean. Despite the loss of one ship and almost two-thirds of the ships'

crews, however, the company made a small profit on the cargo of pepper the expedition brought back from the island of Java.

This initial success encouraged other merchants throughout the Netherlands, and twenty-two ships were launched by five companies in 1598. These included a second expedition from the Company of Far Lands, which made the company an enormous profit, and one launched by a new company from the province that was Holland's greatest competitor. Zeeland merchant Balthasar de Moucheron had been active in seeking a northeast passage to the East Indies and had pioneered trade with West Africa and the Caribbean. So successful did his East Indies expeditions prove that he was in a position to threaten his competitors' subsequent efforts to bring the trade under control.

Dutch companies launched sixty-five ships in 1601, allowing them to surpass their old rivals, the Portuguese, after only a few years' effort. Yet, inevitably, such intense competition caused prices to rise at the sources of production in the East Indies and to fall in the Netherlands. So crowded was the field becoming that the Estates-General, the governing body of the Netherlands, encouraged the traders to join forces.

Representatives from the various provinces and companies gathered at the Inn of Brille in The Hague in December of 1601, with each party presenting a plan for coordinating trading efforts. Although the delegates came to agreement on a general structure, they were unable to set equitable terms for representation (and hence voting). Claiming that they were unable to negotiate further, the delegates from Zeeland withdrew. The Estates-General responded by calling a second meeting in The Hague on January 15, 1602. This session was led by Johan van Oldenbarnevelt, the landsadvocaat of the Estates-General, who forcefully warned the delegates that their traditional enemies, the Spanish, and new competitors, the members of the British East India Company, were prepared to take advantage of Dutch disunity. "It is therefore to the interest of the commonwealth," Oldenbarnevelt warned, "that all parties get together and place themselves under one organization."

The powerful Zeeland merchants, particularly Balthasar de Moucheron, remained reluctant and suspicious. Moucheron campaigned for a position as director of the proposed company and demanded sole rights to trade on the east coast of Africa. When the delegates voted to meet these conditions, and Oldenbarnevelt in turn hinted that further delay might well be interpreted as treason, opposition collapsed; Zeeland agreed to the compromise on March 16.

The Estates-General quickly moved to establish the United Netherlands Chartered East India Company (the Vereenigde Oost-Indische Compagnie, or VOC) four days later, on March 20, 1602. The company was to be run by a board of "Seventeen Gentlemen" (the Heeren XVII) apportioned to represent the various provinces, with eight of them coming from Holland. The latter number was a reflection of Holland's relative strength but was deliberately set one short of a majority. The Seventeen Gentlemen were to meet at each provincial capital in turn, further assuring that no province would assert undue control. This carefully balanced structure was primarily the work of Oldenbarnevelt, who, although a na-

tive of Holland, had deliberately chosen to limit his province's influence.

The Dutch East India Company was ostensibly a commercial enterprise, and any Dutch citizen had the right to buy shares in its operation. It was also given wide, almost absolute power over any territory it could annex east of the southern tip of Africa (the Cape of Good Hope) and west of the southern tip of South America (Cape Horn). It had the authority to wage war, establish diplomatic relations, sign treaties, coin money, and collect taxes, and it was granted a monopoly on Dutch trade in the same enormous area. In addition, it paid no import duties on the cargoes it brought back to the Netherlands.

SIGNIFICANCE

The company's formation led to the establishment of an enormous Dutch Empire in Southeast Asia, one that was

DUTCH TRADING ROUTES IN THE 17TH CENTURY

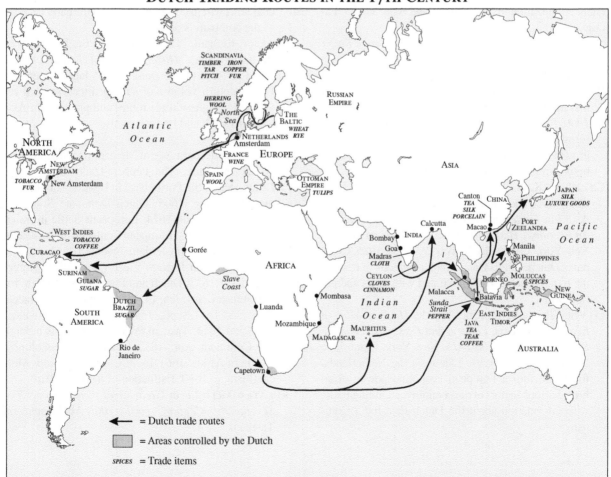

more than fifty times the size of the Netherlands. This empire would eventually include the large islands of Java, Sumatra, and Celebes; most of Borneo; the western half of New Guinea; and a host of smaller islands. The empire consolidated Dutch political strength and the economic status of its prosperous, middle-class population. It also laid the groundwork for the establishment of Indonesia, which exists largely within the cultural and geographic framework forced upon it by the Dutch. This framework came at great price, however, for the Dutch proved insensitive at best and ruthless at worst in exploiting their new subjects.

Historians have identified the Dutch East India Company and its competitor, the British East India Company, as setting the pattern for modern European imperialism. The Spanish and Portuguese had established colonial empires a century before, but these were largely expressions of their monarchist political systems. The Dutch East India Company embodied a representative, middle-class ethic that was to distinguish subsequent colonization in Africa, mainland Asia, and the Pacific.

—Grove Koger

FURTHER READING

Boxer, C. R. "The Eighty Years War and the Evolution of a Nation." In *The Dutch Seaborne Empire: 1600-1800*. New York: Alfred A. Knopf, 1965. Treats the formation of the Dutch East India Company as an outgrowth of the creation of the Netherlands. Boxer's book is regarded as a classic of popular history.

Chaudhuri, K. N. "The Dutch and English East India Companies and the Bureaucratic Form of Trade in Asia." In *Trade and Civilisation in the Indian Ocean: An Economic History from the Rise of Islam to 1750*. New York: Cambridge University Press, 1985. Compares Dutch, English, and French methods of trade in the Indian Ocean. Well illustrated with maps and period prints.

De Vries, Jan, and Ad van der Woude. *The First Modern Economy: Success, Failure, and Perseverance of the Dutch Economy, 1500-1815*. New York: Cambridge University Press, 1997. Examines the Netherlands' formation into a European economic power. Analyzes various sectors of the economy, including trade, with information about the Dutch East India Company.

Irwin, Douglas A. "Mercantilism as Strategic Trade Policy: The Anglo-Dutch Rivalry for the East India Trade." *Journal of Political Economy* 99 (December, 1991): 1296-1314. Argues that the Dutch prevailed in Southeast Asia because of managerial incentives inherent in the company's charter.

Israel, Jonathan Irvine. "The Breakthrough to World Primacy, 1590-1609." In *Dutch Primacy in World Trade, 1585-1740*. Oxford, England: Clarendon Press, 1989. Surveys the factors that made the Netherlands a preeminent mercantile power.

_____. *The Dutch Republic: Its Rise, Greatness, and Fall, 1477-1806*. Oxford, England: Clarendon Press, 1995. A comprehensive history. Includes information on the Dutch East India Company, Oldenbarnevelt, and the Dutch economy.

Masselman, George. "The Formation of the United East India Company." In *The Cradle of Colonialism*. New Haven, Conn.: Yale University Press, 1963. One of the most readable accounts available. Subsequent chapters chart in considerable detail the early decades of the company's development.

Pflederer, Richard. "Dutch Maps and English Ships in the Eastern Seas." *History Today* 44 (January, 1994): 35-41. Discusses the *Itinerario* of Jan Huygen van Linschoten, a volume of sailing directions that revealed Portuguese trade routes and practices in Asia to their Dutch and English rivals.

SEE ALSO: 17th cent.: Age of Mercantilism in Southeast Asia; 17th cent.: The Pepper Trade; Dec., 1601: Dutch Defeat the Portuguese in Bantam Harbor; Beginning Spring, 1605: Dutch Dominate Southeast Asian Trade; 1606-1674: Europeans Settle in India; Apr. 29, 1606: First European Contact with Australia; 1609: Bank of Amsterdam Invents Checks; 1617-1693: European Powers Vie for Control of Gorée; Oct., 1625-1637: Dutch and Portuguese Struggle for the Guinea Coast; Jan. 14, 1641: Capture of Malacca; Aug. 26, 1641-Sept., 1648: Conquest of Luanda; 1642 and 1644: Tasman Proves Australia Is a Separate Continent; Apr., 1652: Dutch Begin to Colonize Southern Africa; 1661-1672: Colbert Develops Mercantilism; c. 1690: Extinction of the Dodo Bird.

RELATED ARTICLE in *Great Lives from History: The Seventeenth Century, 1601-1700:* Abel Janszoon Tasman.

November, 1602
FIRST MODERN LIBRARIES IN EUROPE

The development of new ways to record, acquire, and house fast-accumulating knowledge and the shift from feudal to Humanistic values during the Renaissance combined to create a demand for more and better libraries throughout Europe. This movement began with the founding of the Bavarian State Library in 1558, gathered momentum with the founding of the Bodleian Library at Oxford University in 1602, and provided critical resources for the Enlightenment of the eighteenth century.

LOCALE: Western and Central Europe
CATEGORIES: Cultural and intellectual history; education; organizations and institutions

KEY FIGURES

Albert V (1528-1579), duke of Bavaria, r. 1550-1579
Thomas Bodley (1545-1613), English diplomat, founder of the Bodleian Library at Oxford
Federico Borromeo (1564-1631), Italian cardinal, founder of the Biblioteca Ambrosiana
Christina (1626-1689), queen of Sweden, r. 1644-1654
Ferdinand II (1578-1637), Holy Roman Emperor, r. 1619-1637
Frederick III (1609-1670), king of Denmark and Norway, r. 1648-1670
Gottfried Wilhelm Leibniz (1646-1716), German mathematician, philosopher, and librarian
Angelo Rocca (1545-1620), Italian Augustinian monk, bishop, and founder of the Biblioteca Angelica

SUMMARY OF EVENT

The modern public libraries that emerged from the urbanization of the Industrial Revolution in the nineteenth century were rooted in the royal, national, and academic libraries of the seventeenth century. Before the time of the Renaissance, libraries in Europe were made up of the private collections of kings, nobles, cardinals, and the wealthy, as well as a few collections that were affiliated with universities. These collections burgeoned after Johann Gutenberg invented printing with movable type about 1450.

In the next 150 years, better methods of recording and transmitting knowledge in turn led to an increase in how knowledge in natural science, social science, philosophy, art, literature, and politics was gained, analyzed, and used. Transcending the gulf between Roman Catholic and various Protestant worldviews that arose through the Reformation, the Humanistic, inquiring spirit of the times demanded new and larger repositories for its books and other written and artistic products. These new libraries helped to solidify cultural gains and promote further intellectual and artistic progress.

Duke Albert V of Bavaria, a prominent patron of intellectuals, artists, and musicians, founded the Wittelsbach Court Library in 1558 as an ornate home for his prolific book collection. Other rich nobles, who felt they needed to compete with him, quickly followed suit. This trend of aristocrats establishing libraries was well under way when University of Oxford alumnus Thomas Bodley, recalling the lack of a comprehensive library at Oxford during his student days in the 1570's, began in 1598 to collect books, donate money, and plan library facilities for his alma mater. The previous library at Oxford, that of Duke Humphrey of Gloucester, the youngest son of King Henry IV, dated from the 1440's but was mostly lost by the 1550's through a combination of carelessness and religious censorship. Bodley intended its replacement as a public library for everyone associated in any way with the university. Opened officially as the Oxford Public Library in November, 1602, it soon became known as the Bodleian, the Bodley, or just The Bod.

In 1610, Bodley arranged for the library to receive free copies of every title registered at Stationers' Hall, thus laying the foundation for legal deposit and, eventually, the concept of copyright. Legal deposit got a boost in 1624 when Holy Roman Emperor Ferdinand II decreed that a copy of every book published in the Holy Roman Empire or exhibited at the annual Frankfurt book fair be sent to the Habsburg Court Library in Vienna. The court library in Vienna had existed since the fourteenth century, but this change to a mandatory legal deposit library marked the beginning of its road toward becoming the Austrian National Library.

Several other national libraries in Europe originated around this time. The Swedish Royal Library under Queen Christina became one of the greatest collections in Europe, but when she abdicated and moved abroad in 1654, she took much of the collection with her. Some of this collection was dispersed, but most became part of the Vatican Library in 1690. What she left behind in Sweden was reestablished in 1661 and designated as the national legal depository library, but in 1697, a fire destroyed most of it. The collection was not redeveloped until the nineteenth century.

The Academy of Turku in Finland established its library in 1640. After a catastrophic fire in 1827, the school moved to the new Finnish capital, Helsinki, and since then the Helsinki University Library has been recognized as the national library. In 1653, King Frederick III established the Danish Royal Library, which evolved through a series of mergers into the national library. In Paris in 1692, the royal library, which dated from the fourteenth century, was first opened to the public, thus laying the groundwork for what would become the Bibliothèque Nationale de France.

As an integral component of the Roman Catholic Counter-Reformation in the late sixteenth and early seventeenth centuries, several popes supported initiatives for intellectual and cultural progress. The founding of the library of the Royal Monastery of El Escorial in 1575 in Madrid and the refounding of the Vatican Library in 1588 were part of this movement.

The Biblioteca Angelica, founded in Rome by Angelo Rocca and named for him, is generally acknowledged as the first truly public library in the modern world. Its predecessor, the library of the Convent of St. Augustine, had been collecting books and manuscripts since 1328. In the 1590's, the convent library's new director, Rocca, who had been in charge of the papal press, charted a completely different course for the library. He accumulated and donated about twenty thousand volumes to enrich its holdings, then opened it to the public, probably in 1604, although some sources say 1614.

Other Roman Catholic leaders followed Rocca's example. Archbishop of Milan Federico Borromeo, influenced by both Rocca and Bodley, bought the huge library of the estate of Gian Vincenzo Pinelli at auction in 1608, built a magnificent new home for it, and thus founded the Biblioteca Ambrosiana as a public library in 1609. It remains one of the greatest libraries in Italy.

Some of the most important Roman Catholic repositories began as libraries of religious orders. Most active were the Jesuits. In 1622, they transferred the collections of Charles University in Prague to their own Klemen-

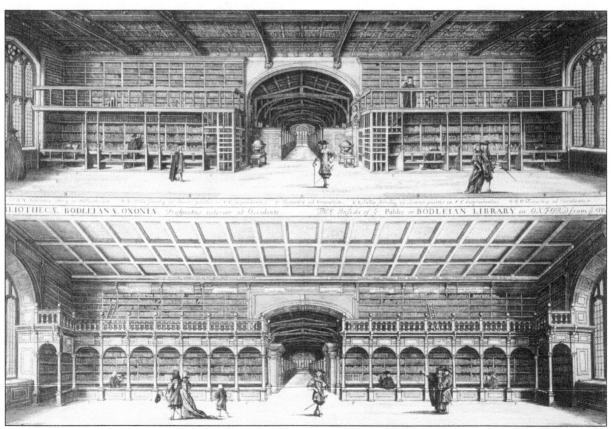

A 1675 depiction of the first modern, academic library in England, the Bodleian, which was founded by scholar Thomas Bodley at Oxford University. (The Granger Collection)

tinum, whose library evolved, with others, into the National Library of the Czech Republic. A Jesuit library accompanied the founding of the University of Malta in 1592, but many of its collections were lost through the expulsion of the Jesuits from Malta in 1768, Napoleon's closing of the university in 1798, and several wars, including World War II. The National Library of Malta began in 1649, when housing was built in Valleta for the books of the Order of St. John of Jerusalem, which had been collected since 1555.

The most celebrated Protestant thinker involved in the seventeenth century growth of libraries was Gottfried Wilhelm Leibniz. From 1676 until his death, he held a variety of positions in the service of the House of Hanover, including librarian to the dukes of Brunswick-Lüneburg and, from 1691, director of the Bibliotheca Augusta at Wolfenbüttel, Germany. His skill and vision in collecting, arrangement, cataloging, and general librarianship became so well regarded throughout Europe that major Roman Catholic libraries in the Vatican, Paris, and probably Vienna offered him directorships, all of which he refused because he would not convert. Unfortunately, most of his suggestions, though based on sound bibliographic and preservationist instincts, were ignored early in the eighteenth century when the dukes moved and reorganized the Bibliotheca Augusta.

SIGNIFICANCE

Many of the European libraries founded before 1700 remain among the world's most important repositories. The Wittelsbach Court Library evolved into the Bavarian State Library, which owns the world's largest collection of incunabula, or books printed before 1501. With 19,900 copies of 9,660 editions, this collection holds about one-third of all known surviving incunabula. The Bodleian Library has almost 7 million volumes, including 7,000 incunabula and 170,000 manuscripts. The other surviving libraries have smaller but highly specialized collections with exceptional research value, particularly manuscripts and incunabula. Together, these libraries provided the resources from which the Enlightenment emerged in the eighteenth century.

—*Eric v.d. Luft*

FURTHER READING

Battles, Matthew. *Library: An Unquiet History.* New York: W. W. Norton, 2004. An excellent exposition of the role of libraries as positive cultural forces and guardians of civilization.

Harris, Michael H. *History of Libraries in the Western World.* Metuchen, N.J.: Scarecrow Press, 1995. Fourth edition of a standard, popular work that first appeared in 1965, written by Elmer D. Johnson.

Stam, David H., ed. *International Dictionary of Library Histories.* Chicago: Fitzroy Dearborn, 2001. This dictionary features articles on library types and particular libraries around the world.

Tolzmann, Don Heinrich, Alfred Hessel, and Reuben Peiss. *The Memory of Mankind: The Story of Libraries Since the Dawn of History.* New Castle, Del.: Oak Knoll, 2001. A classic in its field, this edition is a revision and expansion of Peiss's 1950 translation of Hessel's 1925 scholarly German work.

Wiegand, Wayne A., and Donald G. Davis. *Encyclopedia of Library History.* New York: Garland, 1994. An excellent overview, but superseded by David Stam, especially for information about the world's largest libraries.

SEE ALSO: 1601-1672: Rise of Scientific Societies; 1638: First Printing Press in North America.

RELATED ARTICLES in *Great Lives from History: The Seventeenth Century, 1601-1700:* Christina; Ferdinand II; Gottfried Wilhelm Leibniz.

1603
TOKUGAWA SHOGUNATE BEGINS

After his victory at the Battle of Sekigahara, Tokugawa Ieyasu consolidated his power and was declared shogun of Japan by the emperor in 1603. By instituting political reforms designed to strengthen and preserve the centralized power of his shogunate and by passing nominal power to his son Hidetada while he himself was still alive and in control, Ieyasu forged a shogunal dynasty that lasted for 264 years.

LOCALE: Japan
CATEGORY: Government and politics

KEY FIGURES
Tokugawa Ieyasu (1543-1616), Japanese shogun,
     r. 1603-1605
Tokugawa Hidetada (1579-1632), Japanese shogun,
     r. 1605-1623

SUMMARY OF EVENT

The early history of the Tokugawa government is directly tied to the actions of its first two shoguns, Tokugawa Ieyasu and his son Tokugawa Hidetada. Ieyasu was born into a period of Japanese history that was just beginning to recover from many years of bloody civil conflict from roughly 1340. The era from 1477 to 1600 in particular is designated by scholars as the Japanese Warring States period. During this time, feudal barons fought savage wars of conquest as each attempted to establish his family as the premier power in the nation.

As a young warrior, Ieyasu distinguished himself in a number of important battles that had a significant impact on the fortunes of two powerful daimyos, Oda Nobunaga and his successor, Toyotomi Hideyoshi. Together with Ieyasu himself, these daimyos are known as the Three Unifiers, because they finally succeeded in conquering the other feudal lords and unifying the nation of Japan. Under the first two Unifiers, Ieyasu began to build an important base of power. They granted him extensive lands in eastern Japan that in turn became a great source of wealth to the Tokugawa clan. Ieyasu also took advantage of several governmental appointments, especially his place on the Council of Elders under Hideyoshi, to sharpen his political skills and to solidify important alliances with other powerful daimyos. The struggle for power after the death of Hideyoshi in 1598 eventually led to Ieyasu's victory at the Battle of Sekigahara (1600), after which Ieyasu effectively controlled the Japanese nation.

Tokugawa Ieyasu was officially appointed shogun of Japan by the emperor in 1603; he maintained that position until 1605, when he passed the title to his eldest son, Hidetada. He did this for essentially two reasons. Ieyasu was attempting to bring the entire nation for the first time into the modern era by centralizing national political power in the shogunate. To be successful, Ieyasu knew he had to concentrate on the political problems facing such a complete national transformation. He realized that Hidetada was competent enough to handle day-to-day military matters as shogun, so he felt confident enough to pass the title on to his eldest son. The second reason Ieyasu passed the shogunate to Hidetada was to establish the right of Tokugawan succession to this most powerful office. Until his death in 1616, Ieyasu was the real political force in Japan. He set into operation a system that transformed Japanese government and society.

Ieyasu's major political goal was to create a centralized government centered on the shogun who would be strong enough to withstand any political or military challenges from Japan's most powerful daimyos. Ieyasu placed these feudal barons into two distinct groups. The Fudai were the lords who were completely loyal to the Tokugawa clan, and the Tozama were the daimyos who had not proven their allegiance.

Ieyasu's first two actions as shogun were designed to isolate the Tozama in order to stifle the formation of any dangerous military or political alliances. He first created a system of land distribution that located any suspect baron between two loyal daimyos. Ieyasu also instituted a system of unequal taxation that placed a permanent strain on the finances of the suspect barons. Each had to contribute to the construction and repair of fortifications that were deemed necessary to maintain the national defense. They also had to furnish labor and materials for the building of roads and defenses in areas considered of great strategic importance.

However, the most extensive measures taken by Ieyasu and Hidetada were the implementation of two loyalty oaths, one in 1611 and the other in 1615, the year before Ieyasu's death, as well as the adoption of Neo-Confucian philosophy. These steps were the two most important pillars in the foundation of the autocratic Tokugawan society, and together they regulated just about every aspect of social and political behavior. In particular, they were both concerned with four different aspects of the Japanese state: national security, law, social morals, and the actions of the samurai warriors.

From a national security standpoint, the Tokugawa government was most concerned with domestic tranquillity and the creation of a well-functioning bureaucracy. The oaths directed authority figures to take harsh action against anyone who was suspected of treasonous actions or who had committed violent crimes such as murder. Failure to take appropriate action would itself be considered treason, and the offending parties would be severely punished, ensuring that national security would be a top priority for everyone in the Tokugawa government.

The impact of Neo-Confucian thought is evident in the other major area dealing with national security, the importance of a highly efficient national bureaucracy. Ieyasu and Hidetada both believed in the Confucian principle of staffing government agencies with men of great ability and honor. Neo-Confucianism also had a significant impact on the Tokugawa legal system. The Confucian social model of superior and subordinate was reflected in the expectation that all decrees issuing from the capital at Edo were to be obeyed without question. As in China, the Tokugawa government also followed Confucian economic principles. Iesayu and Hidetada both emphasized agricultural production as the basis of Japan's

economy. In turn, like their Chinese counterparts, they devalued the merchant class and took strict measures to control their economic and political power.

Tokugawan culture also reflected the conservative autocratic philosophy based upon a strict moral code and traditional values. The Loyalty Oath of 1615, in particular, emphasized the importance of traditional marriage in the operation of a well-functioning society. The oath also stressed that marriage brought a basic harmony to society and that anyone entering into this important institution should do so in a mature manner. The Tokugawa shogunate placed such great importance on this institution that the government had to approve all marriage contracts among the aristocratic class. The shogunate's regulation of marriage was also used to ensure that marriage between powerful families was not used to form political alliances against the Tokugawa government.

In addition, the Tokugawa government created strict guidelines for its warrior class, the samurai. It designed a tightly controlled Neo-Confucian system for the training and use of this warrior elite. First and foremost, the central government wanted a warrior who had both a powerful mind and a strong body. To this end, the shogunate ordered each samurai to read Japanese literature extensively. This mandate would ensure a deep respect for Japanese history and culture, as well as promoting the development of skills at reasoning that would pay enormous dividends on the battlefield. The samurai were also given extensive training in the martial arts, which made them potentially the most dangerous class in Japan; the Tokugawa government expected these elite warriors always to conduct themselves with honor, style, and grace. Any violation of their code of conduct, *Bushidō*, would be dealt with in a very harsh manner.

Early Tokugawa foreign policy began with an attempt to recover from the strained relations with China that had resulted from the Japanese invasion of Korea in 1592. Japan's navy had suffered an embarrassing defeat, and China had subsequently cut off trade relations with the island nation. This not only placed Japan in a precarious position with regard to

Tokugawa Ieyasu, by stepping down from the shogunal throne and handing over formal power to his heir while still alive, ensured the beginning of a dynasty that was to last until 1867. (Library of Congress)

81

East Asia's most powerful nation, but it also prevented the importation of silk and other trade goods that were extremely important to the Japanese aristocracy.

By the time the Tokugawa clan was securely in power, the Portuguese had expanded into East Asia and had developed an extensive trading relationship with China, which enabled them to supply Japan with much-needed goods in spite of China's embargo. Portugal was also the first European nation to introduce Japan to the power of Western technology. However, Ieyasu and his son became frustrated with the Portuguese, because the merchants refused to share their marine technology with the Tokugawa government. The shoguns also believed that Portugal was gaining too much political and economic influence in the region.

The shogunate reached out to Portugal's Iberian competitor, Spain, which had recently established a colonial presence in the Philippines. Unfortunately, the Tokugawas were unsuccessful in gaining access to Spain's technology and also faced the added burden of a great influx of Christian missionaries into Japan. In time, Roman Catholicism would pose such a challenge to Japan's neo-Confucian culture that Ieyasu would ban its practice. This suppression of Christianity in turn would strain relations with the West and would ultimately lead to the implementation of an isolationist policy.

SIGNIFICANCE

Ieyasu and his son Hidetada created a unified Japanese state after almost two centuries of bloody conflict, and they instituted a shogunal dynasty that lasted until 1867, when the emperor rather than the shogun again became the supreme ruler of Japan. The first Tokugawa shoguns initiated an operational paradigm that enabled the shogunate to govern 250 semi-independent feudal manors. They accomplished this by severely reducing the power of the feudal daimyos, thereby keeping Japan at peace for more than two centuries. This allowed Japan to grow and prosper politically, economically, and culturally. In addition, it set the stage for Japan's dominance of East Asia during the late nineteenth and twentieth centuries.

—*Richard D. Fitzgerald*

FURTHER READING

Jansen, Marius B. *The Making of Modern Japan*. Cambridge, Mass.: Harvard University Press, 2000. An excellent one-volume history of Japan from the Tokugawa shogunate to Japan's economic dominance in the 1970's. Maps, index.

Sansom, George. *A History of Japan, 1333-1615*. Stanford, Calif.: Stanford University Press, 1961. An excellent overview of feudal Japan by one of its most respected scholars. Maps, index.

Totman, Conrad. *Early Modern Japan*. Berkeley: University of California Press, 1993. The best single-volume account of early modern Japan. Charts, index.

1603-1617
REIGN OF SULTAN AHMED I

Changing trends in Ottoman governance and governmental structuring, which had been developing since the mid-sixteenth century, came to fruition during the sultanate of Ahmed I. Many scholars believe that these changes contributed significantly to internal decay and to the decline of the Ottoman polity in global affairs.

LOCALE: Ottoman Empire
CATEGORIES: Government and politics; wars, uprisings, and civil unrest

KEY FIGURES

Ahmed I (1590-1617), sultan of the Ottoman Empire, r. 1603-1617

Kösem Sultan (c. 1585-1651), favorite concubine of Ahmed, mother of sultans Murad IV and İbrahim

Mustafa I (1591-1639), brother and heir to Ahmed, sultan of the Ottoman Empire, r. 1617-1618, 1622-1623

Osman II (1603-1622), son of Ahmed and sultan of the Ottoman Empire, r. 1618-1622

Mehmed III (1566-1603), father of Ahmed, sultan of the Ottoman Empire, r. 1595-1603

'Abbās the Great (1571-1629), Ṣafavid shah, r. 1587-1629

SUMMARY OF EVENT

Long before the birth of the future sultan Ahmed I in 1590, the Ottoman Empire was undergoing certain radical changes, as long-standing traditions were being challenged. From the time of its foundation, the empire was a state not guided by the same "rules" as other states in the Middle East, Europe, and Africa. In theory, the sultan, as the head of the reigning Ottoman Dynasty, was the only free person in the realm. Legally, his subjects were his slaves, and, therefore, his power was theoretically absolute. Reality proved otherwise, particularly under weak sultans and in situations in which certain institutions and individuals had been able to take advantage of loopholes within the traditional system and amass a substantial amount of influence and power.

The Ottomans did not practice the system of automatic succession by primogeniture, that is, by the eldest son's inheritance of royal power. Instead, succession to the throne would devolve to the "dominant male" of the royal family, who would more often than not have to prove his mettle against siblings through victory in battle

or political intrigue. This tradition had fostered not only the rise of such competent rulers as Selim I (r. 1512-1520) and Süleyman the Magnificent (r. 1520-1566) but also destructive civil wars, such as those between brothers Bayezid II, sultan from 1481 to 1512, and his rival to the throne, Cem (1459-1495), during the 1480's. Another civil war raged among the three brothers Ahmed, Korkut, and Selim I from 1511 to 1512. As early as 1362, with the accession of Murad I, it came to be accepted that a sultan had to secure his title by fratricide, a decree by Sultan Mehmed II.

Eliminating all immediate family members—brothers in particular—became synonymous with assuring stability and perpetuating an undivided realm. The execution of family members became a more routine practice through the years. Even the secure and powerful ruler Süleyman the Magnificent felt compelled in his old age to execute his eldest son, Mustafa, for conspiring to seize the sultanate. In 1574, Murad III had done away with five younger brothers. The most horrific bloodletting was committed by Mehmed III in 1595 when his nineteen brothers—most of them infants and toddlers, none of them older than eleven years of age—were brutally murdered. For good measure—and certainly with a view to prevent the birth of rival male heirs—he eliminated each of his more than twenty sisters. The outcry was so great that fratricide would be changed in favor of confinement.

When Mehmed III died in 1603, he left two surviving sons: thirteen-year-old Ahmed and twelve-year-old Mustafa. Since both were minors (which was in and of itself an unprecedented situation for the Ottoman Empire), it was not a foregone conclusion that the elder sibling would inherit the crown. It appears that various court administrators, upon learning of Mehmed III's death, simply called a meeting of the Imperial Council, released young Ahmed I from the chamber where he was kept, and had him physically ascend the throne in their presence. Because it was possible that Ahmed could die before producing an heir, it therefore made no sense to eliminate Mustafa, the potential heir and only other surviving member of the dynasty. It also made sense to keep Mustafa alive at least as long as Ahmed's sons were below the age of adulthood. Others have speculated that Ahmed's sense of humanity was more acute than that of his predecessors, and so was reluctant to do away with Mustafa.

Whatever the true motivation, fratricide fell out of favor, so Mustafa, as only second in line to the sultanate, became the first victim of the *kafes* (the cage). *Kafes*, according to one persistent legend, did not involve being suspended above ground in a cage but instead being incarcerated within special quarters of the sultan's harem in Topkapi Palace, virtually isolated from human company. Mustafa would be granted the services of "sterile" concubines and would under no circumstances be allowed to father children until such time as he might succeed to the throne. Otherwise, he would be attended by certain servants who were both deaf and unable to speak. The walls of the *kafes* were devoid of windows, except for a few on the second floor that looked toward the sea. The new system of succession had the advantage of assuring that there would be an adult heir to the throne, but it also increased the chances that the new sultan would have faced mental and emotional challenges prior to becoming sultan. The years of sequestering, fear of execution, and lack of meaningful human companionship had driven Mustafa to insanity.

When Ahmed I abruptly died of typhus at the age of twenty-seven in 1617, his successor was to be either Mustafa or fourteen-year-old Osman II, who was Ahmed's eldest son by Greek concubine Mahfiruz. As an adult, Mustafa was retrieved from the cage and placed on the throne. Mustafa's rule was supported by another of Ahmed's Greek concubines, the powerful Kösem Sultan, who had borne Ahmed I three sons. She had outmaneuvered Osman by getting Mustafa on the throne. However, Mustafa proved so incompetent that he was deposed after three months in favor of Osman. Upon Osman's assassination in 1622, Mustafa was again withdrawn from the *kafes* to reign for fifteen months. He was once more deposed and confined—this time for good— and was replaced by Murad IV, the first of Kösem Sultan's three sons to become sultan.

Diminished leadership quality was further assured because Mehmed III had, with the advent of the *kafes*, terminated the practice of dispatching royal princes to serve apprenticeships as provincial governors (or *sanjak* beys), during which they would receive hands-on experience and instruction from established officials on the rudiments of political administration. Although ending these apprenticeships had the effect of denying potential competitors a political base and therefore diminishing the chances of civil conflict, it meant that future successors lacked practical administrative experience. Ahmed I, Mustafa I, and succeeding sultans who therefore lacked this experience had the tendency both to be more lacka-

daisical and out of touch with their people, and to rely on others to fulfill the day-to-day tasks.

Another sign that the sultanate was withdrawing from effective power was that, after Süleyman the Magnificent, rulers seldom, and then never, accompanied their armies on campaign. Mehmed III had done so half-heartedly in 1596, during the Austro-Turkish War of 1593-1606, with nearly disastrous results. Ahmed I resisted all attempts to persuade him to go on campaign. Signs of military decline manifested themselves in the Treaty of Zsitvatorok of 1606, when the sultan was first compelled to acknowledge the Austrian Habsburg emperor as an equal; the persistent Jelālī Revolts in Anatolia, led by Kalenderoglu Mehmed; and the gains made in the east by the armies of the Persian Ṣafavid shah ʿAbbās the Great.

Ahmed I, after a brief initial burst of interest in imperial affairs, became increasingly venal and self-indulgent, especially in regard to the pleasures of harem life; he was said to have wanted a different woman in his bed each night. In keeping with a continuing tradition, however, some of these concubines were favored over others and thus amassed tremendous political power. The Ottoman period of the late sixteenth and early seventeenth century has been popularly termed the "age of women." Among these powerful and influential women was the *buyuk valide*, or Grand Queen Mother, who had seniority and was usually the dominant force. However, *haseki sultanas*, or concubines who had given birth to sons, exercised varying degrees of influence. The famous Kösem Sultan, whose intelligence, personality, and skills in harem intrigue made her a dominant force for more than forty years, was the prime example of this phenomenon.

The harem's eunuchs also carved out their niches of power, foremost among them being the chief black eunuch (the *harem agasi*), whose responsibilities included the oversight of harem administration.

SIGNIFICANCE

In addition to the harem's rise in power and influence, the grand vizier and the divan (ruling council), as a matter of course, acquired greater autonomy as well, as the sultan's power receded. Even more disquieting was the increasing independence displayed by the army's elite Janissary corps, which became a self-compensating law unto itself and also maintained the capacity for overturning and even eliminating individual sultans who were deemed detrimental to their interests.

While many of the changes that are identified with the reign of Ahmed I had been in stages of development prior to 1603, the overlapping of forces that undermined the sultan's authority made his reign a watershed, in which the grand viziers, chief black eunuchs, *valide* and *haseki sultanas*, and Janissaries each carved out their power base and contributed to the general sense of uncertainty, confusion, and divided loyalties prevalent during the Ottoman Empire's declining years.

—*Raymond Pierre Hylton*

FURTHER READING
Cicek, Kemal, et al., eds. *The Great Ottoman-Turkish Civilisation*. 4 vols. Ankara, Turkey: Yeni Türkiye, 2000. The text includes an examination of the growing importance of Queen Mothers and their internal rivalries.
Davison, Roderic H. *Turkey: A Short History*. Huntingdon, England: Eothen Press, 1998. A detailed general history that ascribes Ottoman imperial decline to a slacking in religious fervor in the upper echelons of government after 1566, the year of Süleyman the Magnificent's death.
Eversley, Lord, and Valentine Chirol. *The Turkish Empire from 1288 to 1914, and from 1914 to 1922*. New York: Howard Fertig, 1969. Written in a lively and opinionated style. Ahmed I is depicted as an incompetent ruler who was excessively influenced by women at the palace.
Imber, Colin. *The Ottoman Empire, 1300-1650: The Structure of Power*. New York: Palgrave Macmillan, 2002. A detailed work on the Ottoman Empire of the late medieval-early modern era. Includes an excellent glossary of often-technical period terminology.
Inalcik, Halil, V. J. Parry, A. N. Kurak, and J. S. Bromley. *A History of the Ottoman Empire to 1730*. Edited by M. A. Cook. New York: Cambridge University Press, 1976. Contains good descriptions of the dilemmas of the succession.
Shaw, Stanford. *History of the Ottoman Empire and Modern Turkey*. Vol. 1. New York: Cambridge University Press, 1976. A painstakingly detailed account that stresses the importance and dynamics of palace intrigue.
Vucinich, Wayne S. *The Ottoman Empire: Its Record and Legacy*. Princeton, N.J.: D. Van Nostrand, 1965. Explains the basic history in a concise manner, even if it does not go into great detail over personalities.

SEE ALSO: 1602-1639: Ottoman-Ṣafavid Wars; Sept., 1605: Egyptians Rebel Against the Ottomans; Nov. 11, 1606: Treaty of Zsitvatorok; May 19, 1622: Janissary Revolt and Osman II's Assassination; 1623-1640: Murad IV Rules the Ottoman Empire; 1638: Waning of the *Devshirme* System; Aug. 22, 1645-Sept., 1669: Turks Conquer Crete; 1656-1676: Ottoman Empire's Brief Recovery; Beginning 1687: Decline of the Ottoman Empire.
RELATED ARTICLES in *Great Lives from History: The Seventeenth Century, 1601-1700:* ʿAbbās the Great; Merzifonlu Kara Mustafa Paşa; Kâtib Çelebî; Kösem Sultan; Murad IV; Mustafa I.

1603-1629
OKUNI STAGES THE FIRST KABUKI DANCE DRAMAS

Okuni created a new theatrical genre called Kabuki, combining music, dance, and drama in a unique fashion. These first performances reflected the tastes of Japan's emerging middle class and were highly influential in the development of several major performance genres during the Edo period.

LOCALE: Edo (now Tokyo), Japan
CATEGORIES: Theater; music

KEY FIGURES
Izumo no Okuni (1571-1658), performer regarded as the founder of Kabuki
Tokugawa Ieyasu (1543-1616), shogun of Japan, r. 1603-1605, who was the first to reign during the Edo period
Tokugawa Iemitsu (1604-1651), shogun of Japan, r. 1623-1651, under whose reign public performances by women were banned

SUMMARY OF EVENT
Kabuki began with the dances and songs of wandering female performers in Japan. It is likely that some of these performers had been displaced by the devastating civil wars in the years immediately preceding the victory of Tokugawa Ieyasu in the Battle of Sekigahara (1600), which enabled him to consolidate his power and become the first shogun of the Edo period. To earn a living, these displaced women alternated between prostitution and performing vernacular songs and dances of the day. Some of them were former Shinto shrine maidens or

Buddhist nuns who had been separated from their communities. Religious sentiment generally prohibited women from performing on stage on a regular basis, but after the war ended, an air of celebration and relief led to the relaxation of some of these restrictions. Also, the travel restrictions and military obligations imposed by the new shogun created an environment in which bored samurai and unmarried merchants, forced by decree or economic necessity to stay in the capital, were in need of recreation.

Izumo no Okuni, the most well known of the wandering female performers, was a prostitute and dancer. Her name indicated that she was from the well-known Izumo shrine, although this may have been her own assumed title. At the beginning of the seventeenth century, tradition holds that she danced on the dry riverbed of the Kamogawa River in Kyōto while her audience sat on the grass. Later, the government referred to Kabuki actors as "riverbank beggars." She sometimes danced on *kagura* stages (rectangular platforms used for sacred dances at Shinto shrines), and also on stages designed for Nō performances.

Okuni's repertoire included *yayako odori* (children's dance) and other popular genres. In 1603, she danced in Kyōto and toured throughout Japan. She became extremely popular, and in 1607 she danced in Edo. She wore very colorful costumes. Although a group of missionaries had been crucified in the preceding decade, and the current shogun was in the process of ridding Japan of foreign influence, Okuni often wore a cross and large golden rosary as a kind of ornament as she danced, and sometimes dressed completely in imitation of foreign clerics. In other dances included in her act, she dressed as a Shinto or Buddhist priest, ringing a bell with a small hammer as she danced. She created her own suggestive version of Nenbutsu, a popular dance genre that had evolved from Buddhist devotional practices.

Her dances were interspersed with skits that celebrated the hedonistic pursuits of the townspeople. In some of the skits, Okuni would dress up in

an animal skin jacket and brocade trousers, playing the part of a man flirting with women in the teahouses, procuring a partner for the evening, and other variations on the theme of courtship. Her troupe included men playing the parts of the women, presaging a trend that would eventually, through legislation and enforcement by the government, lead to Kabuki becoming an exclusively male tradition.

In her skits, Okuni employed stylized gestures that exaggerated, glamorized, and even idealized the conventions of sexual etiquette among cultured pleasure seekers in the capital. Her choreography became influential in the emergence of the geisha tradition. Okuni's performances formalized the elements and details of these conventions through costume and gesture, and (because she portrayed both men and women) they separated the performance of sexual gender roles from actual, physical gender. Okuni thereby personified and stimulated the fantasies of the many idle samurai who were kept in the

A rare image of a Kabuki performance before women were outlawed from the stage. (The Granger Collection)

area and of the community of merchants and prostitutes who served them. Because the cultural environment did not discourage homosexuality, sophisticated femininity could be viewed as a matter of cultivation and training rather than biological sex. It was something that could be learned and perfected as a skill by Kabuki female impersonators (*onnagata*) as easily as by actual female geisha.

The idea of creating and living in a fantasy world was a key element of Okuni's aesthetic and influenced the culture of Japan's pleasure districts in subsequent decades, especially the "floating world," that is, the Yoshiwara district of Edo. Okuni's song texts invited audiences to lose themselves in a dreamlike present. Her introduction of drama in conjunction with popular dance and music was eventually continued by her male counterparts, as subsequent generations of Kabuki actors and playwrights greatly expanded its plots and subject matter, while retaining the colorful essence of the tradition.

The term "kabuki" was first applied to Okuni's performances. At the time, the word was used as an adjective to describe something outlandish and scandalous. Part of Okuni's innovation was the juxtaposition of elements taken from elite culture with those taken from popular culture. By blending the stage and musical instruments (flute and drums) of Nō drama with the humor and brevity of her bawdy plays and dances, she appealed to a strengthening merchant class.

It is likely that the male roles in Okuni's shows were first performed by actors trained in the *kyōgen* genre, which favored concise, sometimes humorous plays that contrasted with the reserved formality of Nō drama. As Kabuki matured, this tension of coexisting elements continued, extending into musical style, creating a multilayered approach that deeply influenced musical structure in later genres such as *nagauta*. Whereas Okuni's earliest dances had used a more limited set of instruments, Kabuki productions quickly adopted the *shamisen*, a three-stringed, fretless plucked lute that became popular in all the major musical genres associated with the floating world district in the early 1600's.

The first Kabuki performances were a source of serious cultural conflict. The early Tokugawa shoguns promoted the restoration of Confucianism, a philosophy that emphasized social stability and family loyalty, yet the same rulers created the Yoshiwara district to satisfy the needs of the many samurai who were forced to live in the capital. Kabuki actresses and actors continued to serve as prostitutes, and as they grew in popularity, jealousies developed among their customers, and riots occasionally broke out during performances.

Seeking to curtail these disturbances, in 1629, the government under Tokugawa Iemitsu banned women from performing on the stage (although there were occasional reports of subsequent violations of this law). The official banishment of women from the stage led to a demand from audiences that young male actors personify their female predecessors with great accuracy. It soon became evident, however, that young men could arouse the same sorts of jealousies as female performers: The same kind of violent disturbances continued to be reported until 1652, when the government decreed that only mature male actors could appear on stage.

SIGNIFICANCE

Kabuki emerged as a genre of drama, dance, and music that combined elements of elite and vernacular culture that were previously separate. This allowed its audiences and performers at least temporarily (and sometimes permanently) to step out of conventional social and gender roles. Although it was created by people who lived at the margins of respectability and was initially suppressed by the Tokugawa government, Kabuki continued to be very popular, and it developed quickly into one of Japan's major performance genres. From the time of Okuni, Kabuki's focus has been on the actor, first as an object of desire but eventually as an artist able to evoke and personify familiar characters with great skill and presence.

Okuni's influence extended to other Edo performance traditions besides Kabuki. Closely related genres that draw upon the same colorful, dreamlike aesthetic include *bunraku* (puppet theater with music), *kouta* (self-accompanied song played by accomplished geisha), and *nagauta* (the larger musical ensembles). It is also likely that her gestures, colorful style of dress, and other performance elements influenced the practices of the geisha, the highly cultured courtesans of the floating world.

—*John Myers*

FURTHER READING

Downer, Lesley. *Women of the Pleasure Quarters: The Secret History of the Geisha.* New York: Broadway Books, 2001. Explains the shared roots of the Kabuki and geisha traditions. Glossary, index, illustrations.

Ernst, Earle. *The Kabuki Theatre.* Reprint. Honolulu: University Press of Hawaii, 1974. New preface. Includes discussions of Okuni, history of Kabuki, theater designs, performance, and actors. List of plays, glossary, fifty-eight illustrations, index.

Leiter, Samuel L., ed. *A Kabuki Reader: History and Performance.* Armonk, N.Y.: M. E. Sharpe, 2002. Essays by specialists in various aspects of Kabuki. Connects

Kabuki to earlier dramatic genres. Includes Okuni's performances. Detailed notes at ends of essays. Illustrated, selected bibliography.

Seigle, Cecilia Segawa. *Yoshiwara: The Glittering World of the Japanese Courtesan.* Honolulu: Hawaii University Press, 1993. Background, history of the Yosiwara district as a social environment. Includes Okuni. Glossary with kanji, extensive notes, illustrations, tables.

Swinton, Elizabeth de Sabato. *The Women of the Pleasure Quarter: Japanese Paintings and Prints of the Floating World.* New York: Hudson Hills Press, 1995. Includes history of Kabuki, with Okuni. Illustrated, mostly color plates. Glossary, checklist of prints, index.

Toita, Yasuji. *Kabuki: The Popular Theater.* Translated by Don Kenny. New York: Weatherhill/Tankosha, 1970. Kabuki from its origins through 1966. Illustrated, including photos. Chronology and detailed commentary on illustrations.

SEE ALSO: 1603: Tokugawa Shogunate Begins; Beginning 1607: Neo-Confucianism Becomes Japan's Official Philosophy; Jan. 27, 1614: Japanese Ban Christian Missionaries; 1617: Edo's Floating World District; 1624-1640's: Japan's Seclusion Policy.
RELATED ARTICLES in *Great Lives from History: The Seventeenth Century, 1601-1700:* Hishikawa Moronobu; Izumo no Okuni; Tokugawa Ieyasu.

March 15, 1603-December 25, 1635
CHAMPLAIN'S VOYAGES

Champlain explored Canada and New England, claiming land for New France and founding Quebec. He secured investors in the new colony and encouraged French settlers to immigrate to the Americas. By forging alliances with some Native American tribes against others, he fundamentally shaped the history of French, British, and American Indian relations for the next century.

LOCALE: New England and Canada
CATEGORIES: Exploration and discovery; colonization; expansion and land acquisition; diplomacy and international relations

KEY FIGURES
Samuel de Champlain (c. 1567/1570-1635), French explorer, cartographer, and founder of Quebec
Pierre du Gaust, Sieur de Monts (1560?-1628), French-born settler who helped establish the first French colony in America
Henry IV (1553-1610), king of France, r. 1589-1610, and Champlain's personal and financial supporter
François Gravé du Pont (1554-1629), commander of and investor in several French colonial voyages, and commander of Quebec

SUMMARY OF EVENT
At the end of the sixteenth century, distracted by civil war, France had not made any significant attempt to develop its claims in the New World for more than six de-

cades. In March, 1603, with the help of funds from King Henry IV of France, Samuel de Champlain traveled as an observer to eastern Canada with François Gravé du Pont. Champlain previously had traveled to the West Indies and Mexico as passenger on his uncle's ship. In May, 1603, Champlain and Gravé du Pont landed in Tadoussac, Canada, and sailed up the Saint Lawrence River to explore the surrounding areas.

In June, Champlain passed the future site of the city of Quebec. He was immediately impressed with the location, because it was well suited for shipping and military defense; its close proximity to friendly Canadian Indians was another advantage. He later suggested the area as a site for the first permanent settlement in Canada. Champlain and Gravé du Pont also explored the Richelieu River area, where they were met by Anadabajin, leader of the Montagnais Indians. The French became friends and trading partners with the Montagnais, trading with them for furs and cured fish before starting home in August, 1603.

Champlain returned to France with fish, furs, and descriptions of the lands and wildlife he had seen. He wrote about the voyage in *Des Sauvages: Ou, Voyage de Samuel Champlain, de Brouage* (1603). In it, he described the Native Americans, lands, and rivers he had seen in Canada. His talents for drawing and cartography were demonstrated in intricate maps of the regions he had explored and pictures of the indigenous people and culture he had witnessed. Champlain's descriptions of the Montagnais were the first detailed information Europeans had received of Montagnais dress, tools, religious ceremonies, hunting practices, and dance.

Champlain returned to the New World as a geographer in April, 1604. This voyage was under the command of Pierre du Guast, sieur de Monts, who also financed the expedition. In May, the party landed in Nova Scotia. Champlain traveled up and down the Atlantic coastline, drawing maps and searching for possible sites for a permanent settlement. Champlain explored the Bay of Fundy to Saint Croix Island and southward along the coast of New England to the Penobscot River, Cape Cod, and Boston Harbor.

In 1608, Champlain returned to Canada from France to establish a permanent settlement. On July 3, he planted the French flag in the soil of the site of Quebec, Canada, which became Canada's first successful permanent settlement. Champlain and his men set about felling trees, clearing ground, and building storehouses and cellars. He made friends and allies with the Huron and Algonquian Indians in the area. The Huron, Algonquian, and Montagnais tribes all had a common enemy in the Five Tribes of the Iroquois Confederacy. The three tribes asked Champlain and his men to demonstrate their loyalty by accompanying them in a campaign against the Iroquois. Champlain agreed, and so it was with a war party of sixty Indians that he reached the lake named after him, Lake Champlain, in July of 1609. Champlain shot two Mohawk chiefs on this victorious campaign, thus making enemies of the large and powerful Iroquois Confederacy, who would later side with the British against the French. The Hurons, Algonquians, and Montagnais continued to assist the French in trade and friendship.

Champlain returned to the New World in the spring of 1611, under the leadership of Captain Gravé du Pont. Finding the Quebec settlement progressing well, he traveled up the Saint Lambert River, past the La Chine rapids, and explored the surrounding area. Champlain made plans to establish another permanent settlement at Montreal; however, his plans were not carried out until 1642, seven years after his death. It was after this voyage that Champlain wrote *Les Voyages du Sieur de Champlain Xaintongeois* (1613), in which he shared his discoveries with the world in an attempt to encourage future investment, settlement, and exploration.

Champlain returned to Canada in March, 1613. He checked on the settlers at Quebec and traveled up the Ottawa River, through numerous rapids, to explore the Muskrat and Lower Allumette Lakes. Back in France in September of that year, Champlain wrote *La Quatrième Voyage du Sieur de Champlain* (1613), in which he de-

scribed his trip up the Ottawa River. He used his writings to encourage new investors in the New World. Investors were given exclusive rights to the fur trade in the Saint Lawrence River area for eleven years. In return, Champlain received a salary. Each investor would arrange for six families to move to Canada to begin a permanent population there. Champlain also agreed to take four Franciscan priests with him to the New World in an attempt to convert the Native Americans to Catholicism.

In 1615, Champlain again moved up the Ottawa River to Lower Allumette Lake and the mouth of the Mattawa River to Lake Nipissing. He traveled up the French River into Lake Huron. He later landed near Penetanguishene, where he discovered numerous Huron Indian settlements. He went from village to village, meeting and gathering tribesmen for a war party against the Iroquois. With several hundred Hurons in his party, Champlain traveled west to Lake Ontario. They then moved southward to Lake Oneida, where the party came upon the Onondaga tribe at an Iroquois fortress.

Champlain and the Huron chiefs immediately attacked the fortification and laid siege to the stronghold. However, they were unable to take it, and Champlain was wounded in the leg and knee in the battle. On their journey homeward to Quebec, the Huron Indians stopped for a month to hunt deer. Champlain later described the intricacies of their deer hunt and other experiences in *Voyages et descouvertures faites en la Nouvelle France* (1619). During the winter of 1615-1616, Champlain spent four months with the Huron tribe. By the time he returned to Quebec, Champlain had explored large undiscovered regions of interior lands surrounding the Great Lakes.

French friars were finding it impossible to convert the Native American populations to Catholicism. Champlain contended that a permanent French population of at least three hundred families was needed to demonstrate the benefits of French civilization to the Canadian Indians. He encouraged the building of more trading posts in Canada, the development of fisheries, and the exploitation of Canada's mineral wealth of iron, lead, and silver. Champlain warned that failure to develop these areas might mean losing French holdings in the New World to the English or Dutch.

On successive trips to the New World, Champlain monitored the progress of the habitation at Quebec and encouraged improvements. He brought cattle, oxen, seeds, building materials, and necessary annual provisions. He encouraged settlers to till their own fields instead of depending on unreliable annual shipments for

CHAMPLAIN'S NORTH AMERICAN EXPEDITIONS, 1603-1616

their survival. Champlain also was called upon to settle disputes among the tribal allies, the French, and the Iroquois. In 1632, Champlain published *Les Voyages en la Nouvelle France Occidentale*, detailing his most recent travels and experiences.

SIGNIFICANCE

Champlain returned to Canada for the last time in 1633. His significance to the history of New France can be seen encapsulated in the many achievements of that final visit: He brought permanent colonists and saw to the rebuilding of Quebec, which had been burned down during an English attack. He reestablished trade with the Montagnais and Algonquians, who had been trading with the English, and built trading posts on Richelieu Island and Saint Croix Island. He helped, then, to rejuvenate an entire nascent culture and to reestablish ties with other vital cultures of Canada. Champlain did not merely find and found Quebec; in a very real sense, he was the spirit of the colonial community.

Champlain died in Canada on Christmas Day in 1635. His contributions remained in the settlement of the territories he explored and the many descriptions of Canadian lands and Native American culture that he left.

—Leslie Stricker

FURTHER READING

Biggar, Henry P., ed. *The Works of Samuel de Champlain*. Toronto: The Champlain Society, 1922-1936. An eight-volume English translation of Champlain's works.

Grant, W. L., ed. *Voyages of Samuel de Champlain, 1604-1618*. New York: Barnes & Noble Books, 1959. An English translation of Champlain's *Voyages*.

Heidenreich, Conrad E. "The Beginning of French Exploration out of the Saint Lawrence Valley: Motives, Methods, and Changing Attitudes Towards Native People." In *Decentring the Renassiance: Canada and Europe in Multidisciplinary Perspective, 1500-1700*, edited by Germaine Warkentin and Carolyn Podruchy. Toronto: University of Toronto Press, 2001. Compares Champlain's exploration of Canada to exploration by Jacques Cartier and Jean-François de la Rocque, sieur de Roberval.

Lanctot, Gustave. *A History of Canada*. Cambridge, Mass.: Harvard University Press, 1963. Canadian history from a French historian. Focuses on the last ten years of Champlain's work.

Morison, Samuel Eliot. *Samuel de Champlain: Father of New France*. Boston: Little, Brown, 1972. Focuses on Champlain's voyages and personal life.

Parkman, Francis. *Pioneers of France in the New World*. Vol. 1 in *France and England in North America*. New York: Literary Classics of the United States, 1983. Canadian history by an English historian noted for his narrative style.

SEE ALSO: Spring, 1604: First European Settlement in North America; Beginning June, 1610: Hudson Explores Hudson Bay; 1611-1630's: Jesuits Begin Missionary Activities in New France; Apr. 27, 1627: Company of New France Is Chartered; 1642-1684: Beaver Wars; May, 1642: Founding of Montreal; Aug., 1658-Aug. 24, 1660: Explorations of Radisson and Chouart des Groseilliers; May 2, 1670: Hudson's Bay Company Is Chartered; Beginning 1673: French Explore the Mississippi Valley; Dec., 1678-Mar. 19, 1687: La Salle's Expeditions; May 1, 1699: French Found the Louisiana Colony.

RELATED ARTICLES in *Great Lives from History: The Seventeenth Century, 1601-1700:* Samuel de Champlain; Saint Isaac Jogues; Sieur de La Salle; Jacques Marquette.

March 24, 1603
JAMES I BECOMES KING OF ENGLAND

James VI of Scotland ascended the English throne, founding the Stuart Dynasty and beginning a century-long battle between the monarchy and Parliament over the proper powers of each. James's uneasy relationship with Catholicism and his antagonism of Puritans would also prove to foreshadow much of seventeenth century English history.

LOCALE: England and Scotland
CATEGORY: Government and politics

KEY FIGURES
James I (1566-1625), king of Scotland as James VI, r. 1567-1625, king of England, r. 1603-1625, and cousin of Elizabeth I

Elizabeth I (1533-1603), queen of England, r. 1558-1603

Lord Beauchamp (Edward Seymour; 1561-1612), cousin of James and Elizabeth and possible claimant of the British throne

Arabella Stuart (1575-1615), cousin of James and Elizabeth and possible claimant of the British throne

Earl of Essex (Robert Devereux; 1566-1601), Elizabeth I's favorite until 1601

George Villiers (1592-1628), a favorite of James and later first duke of Buckingham, 1623-1628

Robert Carr (c. 1587-1645), a favorite of James

First Earl of Salisbury (Robert Cecil; 1563-1612), Elizabeth I's chief minister

Sir Edward Coke (1552-1634), attorney general of England, 1594-1606, and later lord chief justice

Robert Parsons (1546-1610), English Jesuit missionary and conspirator

Guy Fawkes (1570-1606), Catholic conspirator in the Gunpowder Plot of 1605

SUMMARY OF EVENT
Henry VIII of England was survived by three children, each of whom succeeded him in turn. Edward VI died at the age of sixteen; he never married and left no children. Mary I was married to Philip II of Spain, but she was already past childbearing age at the time of her marriage. Upon her death, Mary was succeeded by her half sister Elizabeth, who likewise left no children. With Elizabeth's death in 1603, the Tudor Dynasty, which had occupied the English throne since 1485, came to an end. Henry's VIII's sister Margaret had been the wife of James IV of Scotland and the mother of James V, who was in turn the father of Mary, Queen of Scots, the mother of James VI. Thus in 1603, it was James VI of the House of Stuart who possessed the best claim to the English throne.

James had been born on June 19, 1566, and he had been only fifteen months old when he succeeded his mother to the Scottish throne. His Catholic mother had been driven out of Scotland by the Calvinist nobility for marrying James Hepburn, earl of Bothwell, shortly after the unsolved murder of her estranged husband, Lord Darnley. Mary, Queen of Scots had fled to her cousin Elizabeth I in England, but Elizabeth had made Mary a prisoner for nineteen years. In 1587, Mary, Queen of Scots was executed for her alleged involvement in several plots to regain her throne and possibly to gain the throne of England as well.

James VI became king of Scotland from the time of his mother's exile (he never saw her after 1567) and was reared under the strict supervision of the leading nobles. Eager to succeed the childless Elizabeth I to the English throne, he merely lodged a formal protest when his mother was executed for treason against Elizabeth in 1587. James had taken no measures to prevent his mother's execution, and he maintained generally good relations with Elizabeth. He spent twenty years successfully attesting his position as head of church and state in Scotland, outwitting nobles who conspired against him. This experience was to serve him well as monarch of England.

The question of the succession to the English throne was widely discussed almost from the beginning of Elizabeth's reign, when it was assumed that she would marry. She apparently had no intention of marrying, however, and in time forbade discussion of the question by her subjects. She also refused to discuss the succession, perhaps to allow herself as much flexibility as possible in diplomatic dealings concerning proposals of marriage.

James, the only child of Mary, Queen of Scots, was the first king to rule both England and Scotland and appears to have had his mind set on attaining the English throne from an early date. More than once, he complained about Elizabeth's long life, and following the execution of his mother he demanded that Elizabeth recognize his claim formally in order to wipe out the dishonor done to his family. There were two other possible claimants to the English throne. James's cousin Arabella Stuart was also a descendant of Margaret Tudor. Arabella had been born and reared in England, and this circumstance appeared to give her an advantage, but a female succession was favored by few people, and Arabella was not considered suitable to rule. Henry VIII had actually excluded the descendants of his sister Margaret from the throne in favor of those of his younger sister Mary. Mary's last surviving heir, Lord Beauchamp, was also considered unfit to rule because the validity of his parents' marriage was in question.

James's expectations were therefore realistic. At the time of Mary, Queen of Scots's execution, Elizabeth had told James that she would not oppose his claim if his behavior toward her continued to be correct. In 1589, James went to Scandinavia to marry Anne of Denmark, who bore him several children, three of whom survived. He expended considerable energy in diplomatic negotiations with the rulers of Europe, seeking their support for his candidacy. In general, they gave him their approval but did nothing active to further his cause.

In 1594, the English Jesuit Robert Parsons published *A Conference on the Next Succession to the Crown of England*, in which he argued against all prevailing claims, especially those of James. His intention was to further the cause of the Infanta of Spain, Carla Eugenia, who was a descendant of Edward III of England. The claim put forth by Parsons was absurdly farfetched and could have been realized only by a successful Spanish invasion, but James was sufficiently disturbed about it to publish a reply.

In their dealings with the Catholic rulers of Europe, James's emissaries were instructed to promise secretly that James would grant toleration to English Catholics if he should come to the throne. He was greatly concerned, however, that news of these promises should not reach the English, who might thereby be prejudiced against him. In his dealings with Pope Clement VIII, James even held out the possibility of his own conversion (his wife, Anne of Denmark, was already a Catholic), a matter that would in all probability have ended his hope of being crowned if it had become known in England.

As it was, James almost lost his chance through his involvement with Robert Devereux, earl of Essex, Elizabeth's favorite, who fell from favor after a quarrel with her in 1601 and who fomented a foolish and unsuccessful rebellion for which he was subsequently executed. James had solicited friendship with Essex while that nobleman was still powerful. When Essex fell, Elizabeth threatened to deny James the succession. His claim was revived unexpectedly by Robert Cecil, the first earl of Salisbury, Elizabeth's chief minister. Salisbury had been hostile to James, but he secretly promised to aid him after the fallout from the Essex Rebellion. Both sides maintained complete secrecy, lest Elizabeth discover the alliance and turn against them. Salisbury was able to soothe Elizabeth's feelings toward James, who also wrote her a series of unctuous letters.

Elizabeth I died early on the morning of March 24, 1603. There were rumors that on her deathbed she had

King James I of England. (Library of Congress)

who criticized episcopacy. He declaimed, "No bishop, no king," and ordered the Puritans to conform to the regulations of the Church of England within ten months. Eventually, ninety of them were dismissed from their posts. The only positive outcome of the conference was that it led to the creation of the King James Version of the Bible.

The king's major quarrels, however, were with the House of Commons, which contained a substantial Puritan element. In his first Parliament, held in 1604, he was unable to secure the proclamation of total union between England and Scotland that he desired, and he had to suffer complaints about his methods of raising money and his attitudes toward the Puritans. He lectured Parliament sternly on its duties of obedience.

James's firm stand against the Puritans did not necessarily indicate good relations with Catholics, however, toward whom he was unable to fulfill the promises he had made before his accession. In the Gunpowder Plot of 1605, a small group of Catholic nobles and a Catholic mercenary named Guy Fawkes plotted to blow up the Houses of Parliament on the opening day of the session; the plan was to kill the king and the leading men of the kingdom. The conspirators believed that this would cause spontaneous Catholic uprisings throughout the country, resulting in the seizure of the government and the institution of Catholic rule. The plot was discovered ahead of time, and the leading conspirators were executed.

James also had trouble with the lord chief justice of the Court of Common Pleas, Edward Coke, who believed strongly that the courts and the law should be independent of royal control. They clashed several times over James's interference in Coke's jurisdiction. The king attempted to overcome Coke's resistance by promoting him to lord chief justice of the King's Bench, which resulted in Coke losing jurisdiction over the kinds of cases that were the source of greatest contention between them. Ultimately, Coke was dismissed from the King's Bench in 1616. He would be instrumental in framing the Petition of Right in 1628, asserting limitations upon the powers of James's successor, Charles I.

The king's major problem was financial, for his need for funds made him dependent on Parliament, which alone had the legal right to levy new taxes. In 1610, the House of Commons proposed the Great Contract, by which James would surrender his extra-Parliamentary means of taxation in return for a guaranteed annual in-

named James as her successor, but they were never confirmed. Within eight hours of her death, the Privy Council, the body of chief advisers to the Crown, proclaimed James I king of England, and within two days the news reached him in Edinburgh. His trip to London was a triumphal procession lasting a month, during which he was entertained lavishly by many of the great people of England, and he knighted more than three hundred individuals. James was crowned on July 25, 1603.

In the beginning, James made a good impression on most of the people he met in England. Friction arose, however, when the large number of Scots he brought with him were given English titles and offices that aroused jealousy among the English nobility. In January, 1604, the first serious conflict of James's English reign occurred at the Hampton Court Conference, a discussion between the king and the leading clergy of the Puritan wing of the Anglican Church. The Puritans had presented James with a petition during his journey from Scotland in which they called for an end to all ritual and vestments in church services and for a better-educated clergy. James, an avid theologian, showed his autocratic nature at the conference by violently abusing delegates

come. King and Commons again quarreled, and James dismissed Parliament.

The earl of Salisbury died in 1612. He had been a moderating influence on James's policies, and henceforth the greatest political influence at court was wielded by two of the king's personal favorites, Robert Carr, who was created Viscount Rochester in 1611 and earl of Somerset in 1613, and George Villiers, who was successively created earl (1617), marquis (1618), and duke (1623) of Buckingham. The favorites were intensely disliked, both by their rivals and by the populace at large, and the moral tone of the court was a scandal to the Puritans. In the Parliament of 1614, the so-called Addled Parliament, the king's advisers were severely criticized. In a rage, James again dissolved that body.

The Parliaments of the early 1620's concerned themselves with foreign affairs, with the strong Puritan element in the Commons urging the king to aid the Protestants in the Thirty Years' War. In return for grants of revenues, James was forced to grant concessions to the Commons, although he did not become involved in the war to any great extent.

One of the king's major quarrels with Parliament involved the use of monopolies, a royal prerogative. Before Parliament abolished monopolies in 1624, James exercised his rights to start colonies in North America; Virginia was established in 1607, and Plymouth was founded in 1620. In Ireland, the early submission of the earl of Tyrone was followed by enforcement of the English legal and administrative systems. When Tyrone and the earl of Tyrconnel fled their country under suspicious circumstances a few years later, six of the northern counties were declared forfeit to the crown, and English and Scottish settlers were sent to set up plantations on the best Irish land. There were to be long-lasting repercussions both in North America and in Ireland resulting from the king's acts.

Toward the end of his reign, James tried to conclude a marriage contract between his son and heir, Charles, and a Spanish princess. Negotiations were protracted but ultimately fruitless, and the duke of Buckingham and Charles returned from a visit to Spain determined to declare war on that country. Parliament was in favor of doing so, but James was not. In any case, the suggestion of a marriage alliance with Spain was abhorrent to Englishmen, so James and Charles started to negotiate with France for a marriage between Charles and Henrietta Maria, sister of Louis XIII, even though it involved a secret agreement to promise toleration for English Catholics. Negotiation of this marriage treaty, which was later

to involve Charles in war with France, was one of James's last acts before he died on March 27, 1625. At his death, he rightly warned his son and heir, Charles I, of future dangers to the monarchy from Parliament. Charles lost a civil war against Parliament and was beheaded in 1649.

SIGNIFICANCE

In his lifetime, James wrote poetry and books about kingship, theology, witchcraft, and tobacco. Many of his strongest historical associations are literary or cultural rather than political. James commissioned the English translation of the Bible that is named for him. William Shakespeare spent much of his writing career as playwright to James I, and there is a distinct difference between the plays of his Elizabethan period and those of his Jacobean period of production. The term "Jacobean" has, indeed, become strongly associated with the dark, bloody, and vengeful tragedies the were written during James's reign.

James was also the founder of the English Stuart Dynasty, the most controversial and contentious of English ruling families. Of the first four Stuart kings, one was overthrown in the bloody Civil Wars, and a second was deposed in the bloodless Glorious Revolution. The issues raised by James's reign—the proper constitutional relationship between the Crown and Parliament and the proper attitude of the state toward Puritanism, Catholicism, and other non-Anglican religions—would be the two issues that defined seventeenth century English politics. The century would end with both issues settled, a constitutionally limited monarchy firmly established and an Act of Toleration allowing freedom of Christian worship.

—*James F. Hitchcock and M. Casey Diana*

FURTHER READING

Bergeron, David M. *Royal Family, Royal Lovers: King James of England and Scotland*. Columbia: University of Missouri Press, 1991. Psychological profile that presents James in the familial roles of son, husband, and father. Although it is sometimes complicated by literary theory, the book nevertheless provides an in-depth account of James, the man. Illustrated.

Bingham, Caroline. *James I of England*. London: Weidenfeld & Nicolson, 1981. Approachable historical account of James I's reign. Although this volume is a sequel to *James VI of Scotland*, which traces James's life to his thirty-seventh year, it can stand alone and provides an adequate prologue. Highly illustrated with bibliography and family tree.

Croft, Pauline. *King James*. New York: Palgrave Macmillan, 2003. Balanced and perceptive account of James's life and reign, focusing on his attempts to rule Scotland and Ireland as well as England.

Davies, Godfrey. *The Early Stuarts, 1603-1660*. Vol. 9 in *The Oxford History of England*. Oxford, England: Clarendon Press, 1959. Provides an exhaustive account of James's economic, political, and religious policies. Emphasizes Parliament's increasing power.

Lee, Maurice. *Great Britain's Solomon: James VI and I in His Three Kingdoms*. Urbana: University of Illinois Press, 1990. In-depth and scholarly biographical account of James that questions James's reputation. Includes bibliographical references.

Newton, Diana. *The Making of the Jacobean Regime: James VI and I and the Government of England, 1603-1605*. Rochester, N.Y.: Boydell, 2005. Surveys the early years of James I's reign and describes how these years were crucial in shaping his approach to English rule. Newton argues that after some initial misunderstandings, James proved his political acumen and ability to rule both England and Scotland.

Stewart, Alan. *The Cradle King: The Life of James VI and I, the First Monarch of a Unified Great Britain*. New York: St. Martin's Press, 2003. Focuses on how James VI of Scotland became James I of England.

Stewart maintains James was an able ruler of Scotland, but the tactics that served him well in that country were not applicable for governing England and a unified Great Britain.

SEE ALSO: Early 17th cent.: Revenge Tragedies Become Popular in England; c. 1601-1613: Shakespeare Produces His Later Plays; Feb. 7-19, 1601: Essex Rebellion; Nov. 5, 1605: Gunpowder Plot; May 14, 1607: Jamestown Is Founded; 1611: Publication of the King James Bible; 1618-1648: Thirty Years' War; 1619-1622: Jones Introduces Classicism to English Architecture; Dec. 26, 1620: Pilgrims Arrive in North America; Dec. 18, 1621: The Great Protestation; May 6-June 7, 1628: Petition of Right; Mar., 1629-1640: "Personal Rule" of Charles I; 1642-1651: English Civil Wars; Aug. 17-Sept. 25, 1643: Solemn League and Covenant; May, 1659-May, 1660: Restoration of Charles II; 1688-1702: Reign of William and Mary; Nov., 1688-Feb., 1689: The Glorious Revolution; May 24, 1689: Toleration Act.

RELATED ARTICLES in *Great Lives from History: The Seventeenth Century, 1601-1700:* First Duke of Buckingham; Charles I; Sir Edward Coke; James I; Mary II; William III.

1604-1680
RISE OF CRIOLLO IDENTITY IN MEXICO

After defeating the Aztecs, the Spanish divided the population of New Spain into two separate legal entities, one for Spaniards and the other for indigenous peoples. By the end of the sixteenth century, however, the Spanish, African, and indigenous cultures had become intermingled. This mixing of cuisines, art, and customs produced a distinctive variant of Spanish civilization, called criollo, that would blossom into full-fledged Mexican consciousness by 1810.

LOCALE: Continental heartland of the viceroyalty of New Spain (now in Mexico)

CATEGORIES: Cultural and intellectual history; colonization

KEY FIGURES

Bernardo de Balbuena (c. 1562-1620), poet, author, and bishop of Puerto Rico

Philip of Jesus (Felipe de Jesús de las Casas; 1572-1597), patron saint of Mexico City

Carlos de Sigüenza y Góngora (1645-1700), scientist, antiquarian, and author

SUMMARY OF EVENT

In the Kingdom of New Spain, the Spaniards and their descendants of unmixed Spanish lineage constituted the ruling class and technically enjoyed legal equality. Those born in New Spain called themselves criollos, and some Spanish immigrants caught the "criollo spirit," identifying more with their American habitation than with their homeland. The word derived from the verb *criar*, which can mean to breed, raise, rear, or nourish, and it signified the vitality of the new and distinctive culture that developed among the immigrants and indigenous inhabitants of New Spain.

One of the Spaniards who caught the criollo spirit was

Bernardo de Balbuena, who was born in Valdepeñas in the early 1560's and was educated in Mexico City. While in Jamaica, Balbuena wrote *Grandeza mexicana* (1604; the grandeur of Mexico), which described Mexico as a floral paradise populated with beautiful women of superior intellect. This 1604 text helped to found a sense of a distinctive Mexican or criollo identity. The paradise described in the book had been the perfect setting for the appearance of the Virgin Mary to an indigenous youth at Tepeyac, a hill outside Mexico City, in 1531. By the middle of the seventeenth century, criollos had named the apparition the Virgin of Guadalupe, because the image resembled the pictures of the Virgin of Gualdalupe in Extremadura, Spain. The Virgin of Guadalupe became regarded as the spiritual mother of all of the ethnic groups in Mexico.

When Balbuena died in 1620, he was the bishop of Puerto Rico. He received his education in one of the many schools established in New Spain by the Catholic Church to prepare criollos for the priesthood. The most famous of the schools was the Royal Pontifical University (later renamed the University of Mexico), run by the Augustinian order. Modeled after the University of Salamanca in Spain, the Royal Pontifical University began enrolling students in 1553. By 1650, there were about six thousand priests, both diocesan and secular, from the Franciscan, Dominican, Augustinian, and Jesuit orders. Most of the priests were criollos, but most of the bishops were Spaniards.

One of the criollos who became a Franciscan priest was Philip of Jesus, who was born in Mexico City in 1572. He entered the Reformed Franciscan Convent of Santa Barbara in Puebla, Mexico, but left after one year, moving to Manila in the Philippines, where he returned to his vocation. While on a return voyage to New Spain, Philip's ship wrecked on the coast of Japan. When the survivors refused to renounce Christianity, they were crucified on February 5, 1597, at Nagasaki. Philip of Jesus was beatified on September 14, 1627, and canonized on June 8, 1862, as the Patron Saint of Mexico City. He was the first North American to become a saint in the Catholic Church.

The criollo priest Carlos de Sigüenza y Góngora earned secular renown as a scholar and a writer. Born in Mexico City on August 20, 1645, Sigüenza y Góngora was home-schooled by his father, who had been tutor to King Philip IV. Sigüenza y Góngora took vows as a Jesuit in 1662 in Tepotzotlán and, after being expelled from the College of the Holy Spirit in Puebla, he enrolled in the Royal Pontifical University. He was later appointed to the university's chair of mathematics and astronomy. An avid student of the indigenous past, he learned indigenous dialects and amassed an impressive collection of documents and artifacts. He reconstructed the Aztec dynasties and studied Mesoamerican mathematics, astronomy, and cosmography.

Sigüenza y Góngora also produced significant literary works. *Primavera Indiana* (1668; Indian spring) and *Teatro de virtudes políticas* (1680; theater of political virtues) both glorify the American past and Aztec emperors. In other writings, he speculated about a link between the apostle Saint Thomas and the Aztec deity Quetzalcóatl. He regarded the conversion of the Mexican Indians as the greatest accomplishment of the Spaniards. His literary and scientific works, including a map of Pensacola Bay, circulated widely in Spain and combined with Balbuena's works to establish Mexico as a center of Spanish culture.

Although individual criollos distinguished themselves as leaders in the literary realm, full-blooded Spaniards—both on the Iberian Peninsula and in New Spain—continued to regard the mass of criollos as second-class Spaniards, because they were born in a distant realm populated by *gente vil* (despicable people). The Spaniards had conceived of New Spain as one land inhabited by two nations, meaning two homogeneous ethnic groups with common languages, customs, and physical features.

From 1600 to 1700, the white population of New Spain grew from about 60,000—including *peninsulares* and criollos—to about 400,000. The indigenous population dropped to a low point of 1 million in 1625 and began to recover thereafter. By 1646, there were 35,089 blacks in Mexico and more than 100,000 Afromestizos, people of mixed African and indigenous or Spanish ancestry. Persons with mixed ancestry were presumed to be illegitimate. The Spaniards placed them in an indeterminate category between the Spanish and Indian nations and referred to them as belonging to the *sociedad de castas*, or caste society. Spaniards regarded themselves as racially superior to the Indians and the castes and superior to the criollos because of their birth in the caste-ridden Americas.

Criollo resentment toward Spanish attitudes was fueled by economic conditions in the seventeenth century. The Spanish crown declared bankruptcy in 1575, 1596, and 1607, and Spain entered a period of prolonged economic depression. Spaniards continued to dominate the bureaucracies of the Catholic Church, the government, and the military, but Spain could no longer support their imperial enterprises in the Americas. Criollos began to take the lead in developing the economy of New Spain. They expanded the viceroyalty's activities in mining, ranching, textiles, sugar, and finances. While Spain stagnated, New Spain flourished; yet, the Spaniards treated the criollos and Mexican society with contempt. In turn, the criollos despised the Spaniards and referred to them as *gachupines*, an insulting word of uncertain meaning but thought by some to refer to the spur on fighting cocks. Criollo resentment of Spanish contempt would fuel the Mexican independence movement.

SIGNIFICANCE

Criollo accomplishments in all realms of society continued to go unrecognized and unrewarded by the Spaniards from the seventeenth century to the end of the colonial period. During Spain's first constitutional crisis in 1808, the criollos, despite their resentments, largely remained loyal to the vacated throne until the return of King Ferdinand VII. Emblematic of Spain's attitude toward the criollos was King Ferdinand's refusal to reward Agustín Iturbide for suppressing a rebellion. Iturbide received neither a knighthood nor a commission in the Spanish army, partly because he was a criollo.

During the second Spanish constitutional crisis in 1821, Iturbide joined forces with the *castas*, who had also been born and reared in New Spain. Iturbide agreed with the Afromestizo leader Vicente Guerrero to break from Spain, end the caste system by establishing a single legal code for all Mexicans, and retain the protected status of the Catholic Church. The criollo affections for their true homeland and their sense of autonomy as a society that had been developing since the turn of the seventeenth century made possible this independence movement. After taking a critical leadership role in the movement, criollos made themselves the elite class of the new nation of Mexico, which became a country with a heterogeneous population governed by autonomous institutions.

—Paul E. Kuhl

FURTHER READING

Bennett, Herman L. *Africans in Colonial Mexico: Absolutism, Christianity, and Afro-Creole Consciousness, 1570-1640*. Bloomington: Indiana University Press, 2003. Study focusing on African slave society, particularly in the cities, and the creolization of free persons of African descent.

Boyer, Richard. "Mexico in the Seventeenth Century: Transition of a Colonial Society." *The Hispanic American Historical Review* 57, no. 3 (August, 1977): 455-478. Important article that first drew scholarly attention to the emergence of the mestizo character of the society that became Mexico.

Brown, Jonathon C. *Latin America: A Social History of the Colonial Period*. 2d ed. Belmont, Calif.: Wadsworth, 2005. The four chapters in Part 2 of this very fine text use scholarship since the Boyer article to treat seventeenth century Latin America, including New Spain. Extremely helpful reading lists at the ends of the chapters.

Lafaye, Jacques, et al. *La Pintura de Castas [Painting Castes]*. No. 8, 2d rev. ed. With translations by Lorna Scott Fox et al. Mexico City: Artes de Mexico y del Mundo, 1998. Insightful discussions of the evolution of colonial society with more than forty photographs of paintings illustrating fifty-three of the castes that emerged from the mixing of Europeans, Africans, Indigenes, and their offspring in Mexico.

SEE ALSO: c. 1601-1682: Spanish Golden Age; Nov. 28, 1607: Martin Begins Draining Lake Texcoco; Jan. 27, 1614: Japanese Ban Christian Missionaries; 1615: Guamán Poma Pleas for Inca Reforms; 1619-c. 1700: The Middle Passage to American Slavery; 1630's-1694: Slaves Resist Europeans at Palmares; 1648: Cult of the Virgin of Guadalupe; Beginning 1680's: Guerra dos Bárbaros.

RELATED ARTICLES in *Great Lives from History: The Seventeenth Century, 1601-1700:* Sor Juana Inés de la Cruz; Philip IV.

Spring, 1604
FIRST EUROPEAN SETTLEMENT IN NORTH AMERICA

Saint Croix Island was the site of the first European community established in North America, on the boundary of what is now Maine and New Brunswick.

LOCALE: Saint Croix Island, New France (now in Maine)

CATEGORIES: Colonization; expansion and land acquisition; trade and commerce

KEY FIGURES

Pierre du Guast, Sieur de Monts (1560?-1628), French founder of the first European community in North America

Samuel de Champlain (c. 1567/1570-1635), French explorer and cofounder of the Saint Croix settlement

Henry IV (1553-1610), king of France, r. 1589-1610

SUMMARY OF EVENT

In 1603, Pierre du Guast, sieur de Monts, a Protestant merchant and representative of the French king Henry IV, proposed creating a colony to the south of the Saint Lawrence River in North America. The following year, on March 7, 1604, Monts, with a royally granted monopoly on the fur trade firmly in hand, set sail with geographer and cartographer Samuel de Champlain. The expedition departed from Havre-de-Grâce, France, aboard the *Bonne Renommée* with a crew of approximately one hundred male artisans, including blacksmiths, stonemasons, brick makers, and carpenters, as well as a Roman Catholic priest, a Protestant minister, and prisoners recruited from French prisons. Another captain, François Gravé du Pont, and shipowner Jean de Biencourt de Poutrincourt, also made up part of the expedition.

A second ship left on March 10, 1604. Four years earlier, in 1600, Monts had explored Canadian New France with Pierre de Chauvin to ascertain the prospects for colonization. The ostensible goal of this colonization effort was to convert the native population to Christianity, but they also intended to search for silver and gold such as the Spanish had found in Mexico and South America and to initiate a viable fur trade.

In May, 1604, the colonists reached Nova Scotia, and although they first entertained a site they called Port Royal in the Annapolis Basin, they were not altogether satisfied and shortly set off again to look for a site in the Bay of Fundy, which they named la Baie Française. Ultimately, they set sail south once more to Passamaquoddy Bay, where they chose a seven-acre (three-hectare) island in the Saint Croix River that they named Saint Croix Island. The island today forms the Canada-United States border between New Brunswick and Maine. The area had an abundance of hunting and fishing, its soil was fertile and supported brick making, and its secluded location protected the colony from invasion by the British. Before long, the new settlers became friendly with the region's indigenous people, the Etchemin. Significantly, this colonial enterprise occurred three years before the 1607 Jamestown Settlement in Virginia and sixteen years before the Pilgrims arrived from England at Plymouth, Massachusetts, in 1620.

Although the majority of the settlers stayed on at Saint Croix, Champlain continued to explore the coast of Maine and the Penobscot River, mapping the New England coast as far south as Cape Cod. This was Champlain's third expedition to the New World: He had first voyaged to the West Indies in 1599 and had explored the Saint Lawrence River in 1603. The detailed maps he produced as geographer and cartographer as part of the Saint Croix expedition were used by North American navigators throughout the seventeenth century.

Some buildings within the Saint Croix settlement were joined by protective palisades that placed a screen between the settlers and local wildlife (or, for that matter, British invaders). The settlement's two streets crossed a square providing access to the storehouse, carpenter's, and blacksmith's shops, as well as the bakery, cookhouse, chapel, and captain's quarters. The entire colony featured twenty wooden buildings with stone and clay foundations, in addition to the gardens. In the fall of 1604, seventy-nine settlers remained at the Saint Croix Island colony.

The burgeoning colony in New France almost failed to make it through the exceptionally bitter winter of 1604-1605, for which it was utterly unprepared. Because New France was located on the same latitude as France itself, the French settlers simply assumed that the region's weather would be similar to the mild climate of their homeland. They were shocked to see snow fall in October as a result of the glacial air stream. It was so cold that the drinking water froze. The colonists had barely enough food and ran short of firewood and fresh water. Almost half the colony died, primarily of scurvy, a disease caused by lack of vitamin C. Thanks to the Etchemin, though, some colonists did manage to stay alive by trading bread for meat.

After barely surviving the horrendous winter, Monts sailed down the coast of Maine in search of a more hospitable site for a permanent colony. As they traveled south, the crew noticed larger native dwellings and more advanced agricultural sites. After rounding Cape Cod, they stopped at Nauset Harbor, which they called Mallebarre, or "Bad Bar," and which was populated by the Armouchiquois. However, they did not remain long and returned to Saint Croix after only five weeks. In reality, the settlement had already effectively failed, since more than half the settlers had died during the winter of 1604-1605. However, their determination laid the basis for later settlements in Nova Scotia (1605) and Quebec (1608).

In time, Monts decided to relocate the settlement to Port Royal, on the north side of the Annapolis Basin,

where indeed the colony prospered. King Henry IV had earlier called the area—the lands between the 40th and 46th parallels—"La Cadie," named for the mythical Arcadia, and soon it came to be called Acadia. The king named Monts lieutenant-general and presented him with a ten-year exclusive right to found additional settlements, along with a monopoly in the fur trade. In return, Monts promised to bring sixty new colonists each year to settle in Acadia.

Today, this territory includes the Canadian Maritime Provinces and sections of New England and the mid-Atlantic coast as far south as Philadelphia. In time, it was taken by the British and later divided into American states and Canadian provinces. Saint Croix Island became known as Bone Island in the eighteenth century after ero-

SAINT CROIX ISLAND

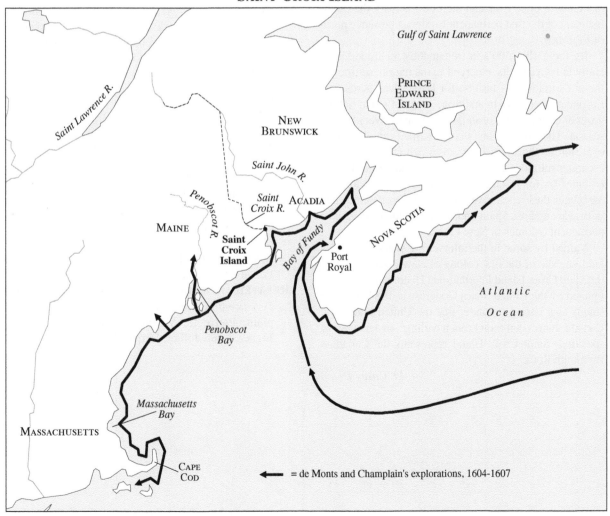

= de Monts and Champlain's explorations, 1604-1607

sion exposed the settlers' graves. In 1797, after a boundary dispute between England and the United States, Saint Croix Island was deemed to be a part of the United States when the results of a scientific survey demonstrated that the island was on the western side of the Saint Croix River Channel. In 1812, the island was named the Neutral Island, since it remained a place where United States citizens could trade with the British in peace.

SIGNIFICANCE

Often, it is the British who are thought of as founding the first European colony in North America. However, the French colony on Saint Croix Island predates the 1620 landing of the English Pilgrims at Plymouth Rock by seventeen years. Indeed, before the Pilgrims founded the first New England colony and even before the Virginia Company established an English colony in Jamestown, the French had mapped the northeast coast from the Bay of Fundy to Cape Cod, and their efforts mark the establishment of the first permanent European presence north of Florida.

By the early 1600's, a tremendous fur trade, especially in beaver pelts, emerged in the region, setting off the era's ubiquitous fashion for beaver hats across the European continent. In addition, America's rich fishing grounds enticed fleets of ships from Europe every fishing season. The French king's coffers filled rapidly. However, unlike the English colonists, who were intent on escaping religious persecution by founding permanent colonies in, for instance, Pennsylvania, Delaware, and Maryland, the French government found itself entrenched with wars against Spain and hardly heeded the idea of permanent colonies in New France.

Named by some in the intervening years Dochet Island, the site of the first colony of New France is today the Saint Croix Island International Historic Site, so designated by the United States Congress in 1984. The site stands as a lasting reminder that the United States and Canada share a common French heritage. In a manner of speaking, Saint Croix Island represents the Canadian Plymouth Rock.

—M. Casey Diana

FURTHER READING

Bumsted, J. M. *A History of the Canadian Peoples*. New York: Oxford University Press, 2004. Provides a comprehensive overview of Canadian history, beginning with the first settlement at Saint Croix Island.

Ganong, William Francis. *Champlain's Island: Ste-Croix Dochet Island*. Fredericton, N.B., Canada: Goose Lane Editions, 2004. Good overview of the Saint-Croix Island's history and development.

Mancall, Peter. *American Encounters: Natives and Newcomers from European Contact to Indian Removal, 1500-1850*. New York: Routledge, 1999. Although it does not supply abundant coverage of Canada, the book provides chapters regarding encounters with natives, intermarriage, religion, trading, disease, and experiences the Saint Croix settlement might have encountered.

Nester, William R. *The Great Frontier War: Britain, France, and the Imperial Struggle for North America, 1607-1755*. New York: Praeger, 2000. Historical account of what happened between Britain and France after the Saint Croix Island settlement as both struggled to dominate the region.

SEE ALSO: Mar. 15, 1603-Dec. 25, 1635: Champlain's Voyages; May 14, 1607: Jamestown Is Founded; Beginning June, 1610: Hudson Explores Hudson Bay; 1611-1630's: Jesuits Begin Missionary Activities in New France; Dec. 26, 1620: Pilgrims Arrive in North America; Apr. 27, 1627: Company of New France Is Chartered; 1642-1684: Beaver Wars; May, 1642: Founding of Montreal; May 2, 1670: Hudson's Bay Company Is Chartered; Beginning 1673: French Explore the Mississippi Valley; Dec., 1678-Mar. 19, 1687: La Salle's Expeditions; May 1, 1699: French Found the Louisiana Colony.

RELATED ARTICLES in *Great Lives from History: The Seventeenth Century, 1601-1700:* Samuel de Champlain; Pierre Le Moyne d'Iberville; Saint Isaac Jogues; Louis Jolliet; Jacques Marquette.

1605 and 1615
CERVANTES PUBLISHES *DON QUIXOTE DE LA MANCHA*

Spanish Golden Age writer Miguel de Cervantes' major work, Don Quixote de la Mancha, *is considered the first modern novel.*

LOCALE: Madrid, Spain
CATEGORIES: Literature; cultural and intellectual history

KEY FIGURES
Miguel de Cervantes (1547-1616), Spanish writer
Philip II (1527-1598), king of Spain, r. 1556-1598, king of Naples and Sicily, r. 1554-1598, and king of Portugal, r. 1580-1598
Philip III (1578-1621), king of Spain, r. 1598-1621

SUMMARY OF EVENT
Spanish writer Miguel de Cervantes' *El ingenioso hidalgo don Quixote de la Mancha* (pb. 1605, 1615; *The History of the Valorous and Wittie Knight-Errant, Don Quixote of the Mancha,* 1612-1620; better known as *Don Quixote de la Mancha*) is one the most influential works of world literature and one of the most widely translated books. Most literary historians consider it to be the very first modern novel, a claim that remains prevalent despite some disagreements. Critic Lionel Trilling, in *The Moral Obligation to Be Intelligent* (2000), asserts that "all prose fiction is a variation on the theme of Don Quixote."

Cervantes wrote *Don Quixote de la Mancha* in two parts. The first part became an instant best-seller after its publication in 1605, so naturally there was a demand for a second part. However, it was not until another writer, using the pseudonym Alonso Fernández de Avellaneda, published a spurious second part in 1614 that Cervantes decided, one year later, to publish the anticipated sequel.

Set at the beginning of the 1600's, *Don Quixote de la Mancha* is a novel about an aging country gentleman, Alonso Quijano, who is an obsessive reader of books of chivalry. The heroes of these books were valiant warriors with supernatural powers who could defeat any adversary in defense of truth and justice. Quijano identifies with these heroes so closely that he deludes himself into believing that he is also a chivalric knight. He abandons his home, dons rusty old armor, and sets out to save the world from evil. He finds a more impressive alias for himself, Don Quixote de la Mancha. Don Quixote then convinces a simpleminded peasant, Sancho Panza, to join him in his adventures. In broad terms, the novel is built upon two characters' sharply differing attitudes toward life: Don Quixote's romantic idealism and Sancho's down-to-earth pragmatism.

Don Quixote de la Mancha is considered a valuable work not only to literature buffs but also to those interested in understanding what life was like in Spain during the reigns of Kings Philip II and Philip III. The novel is a compendium of fictional accounts of social, political, and economic issues of the time. Among these, two topics are developed at length: the Spaniards' growing obsession with purity of religion and ethnic blood, and the emergence of a social order ruled by money.

The society to which *Don Quixote de la Mancha* belongs was obsessed with ethnic and religious purity. Before 1492, Spain did not have an official language and religion. The Iberian Peninsula was composed mainly of a number of Muslim and Christian territories. When the Catholic monarchs unified the peninsula and established the Spanish Empire at the end of the fifteenth century, they imposed Roman Catholicism as the official religion.

Miguel de Cervantes. (Library of Congress)

All Jews and Muslims had the choice either to convert or to leave Spain. The *conversos* (descendants of Jews) and Moriscos (descendants of Moors, or Muslims) who converted became known as the New Christians, and those who came from Christian lineage were called Old Christians. The Old Christian majority controlled all the centers of political power and took official measures to ensure that the New Christians remained members of the underclass. Spain's obsession with purity of blood culminated with the expulsion of all of the Moriscos in 1609.

Although Cervantes was a devout Catholic and a strong supporter of the Spanish Empire, in his novel he exposed the tragic consequences of an absolutist and intolerant regime. Many of his New Christian characters are shown as true followers of the Christian faith, and they cannot be distinguished from Old Christians other than by their physical appearance. For instance, in part 2 of the novel, Cervantes tells the moving story of what happens to a Morisco named Ricote and his daughter Ana Félix after they are expelled from Spain. Ironically, these two characters are presented as Christian exemplars who, even after their expulsion, question neither their belief in the Catholic faith nor their loyalty to the Spanish king. Some literary historians believe that Cervantes was particularly interested in the topic of purity of blood because he, too, was a *converso*, a claim that has not been definitely confirmed.

Cervantes also exposes in *Don Quixote de la Mancha* the impact of the changing economic landscape on the common person. Traditionally, Spain had been a rural society whose economy had depended on agriculture, but this started to change toward the end of the seventeenth century. With the imminent development of a capitalistic system, more and more peasants who owned lands moved out of their farms and became employees of rich lords. They became seasonal laborers or artisan manufacturers, went to the New World, or, like *Don Quixote de la Mancha*'s character Sancho, joined the service sector.

Sancho is a poor and illiterate peasant who decides to leave his village and become a squire because he can no longer survive only on the work of his land. Sancho is representative of the lowest social rank (about 80 percent of the population) that comprised mainly poor peasants. At first, Sancho agrees to be Don Quixote's squire because of the salary he is promised. Sancho does not think that Don Quixote is crazy when he

---

DON QUIXOTE DE LA MANCHA

Don Quixote, influenced by a world of books and imagination, transformed himself into a knight errant. His "squire," Sancho Panza, a peasant with the common sense that Don Quixote lacks, attempts to convince his master that what Don Quixote sees as giants are actually windmills. Don Quixote suffers when his imagination collides with reality and he is badly injured after attacking the "giants." Ever true to his image of himself, he responds, "And if I do not complain of the pain, it is because a knight errant is not allowed to complain of any wounds, even though his entrails may be dropping out through them."

In a certain village in La Mancha, which I do not wish to name, there lived not long ago a gentleman, . . . in the times when he had nothing to do—as was the case for most of the year—gave himself up to the reading of books of knight errantry. . . . He filled his mind with all that he read in them, with enchantments, quarrels, battles, challenges, wounds, wooings, loves, torments and other impossible nonsense. . . . [N]ow that he had utterly wrecked his reason, he fell into the strangest fancy that ever a madman had in his whole world. He thought it fit and proper, both in order and to increase his renown and to serve the state, to turn knight errant and travel through the world with horse and armour in search of adventures. . . .

[Don Quixote and Sancho Panza] caught sight of some thirty or forty windmills, which stand on that plain, and as soon as Don Quixote saw them he said to his squire: "Fortune is guiding our affairs better than we could have wished. Look over there, friend Sancho Panza, where more than thirty monstrous giants appear. I intend to do battle with them and take all their lives. With their spoils we will begin to get rich, for this is a fair war, and it is a great service to God to wipe such a wicked brood from the face of the earth."

"What giants?" asked Sancho Panza.

"Those you see there," replied his master, "with their long arms. Some giants have them about six miles long."

"Take care, your worship," said Sancho; "those things over there are not giants but windmills. . . .

"It is quite clear," replied Don Quixote, "that you are not experienced in this matter of adventures. They are giants, and if you are afraid, go away and say your prayers, whilst I advance and engage them in fierce and unequal battle."

Source: Miguel de Cervantes, *The Adventures of Don Quixote*, translated by J. M. Cohen (Baltimore: Penguin Books, 1968), pp. 31, 68.

makes promises of great riches, which supposedly would come from his master's victorious battles against evil. For the naïve Sancho, his master's discourse sounds just like the propaganda about New World riches used for recruiting people to go to the Americas.

Currency's importance is a topic that arises throughout the book. Don Quixote's idealism prevents him from understanding the need for money. He does not understand why he needs money to survive because money is never mentioned by the knights he reads about in books. It is ironic that when Don Quixote manages to escape difficult situations for which he needs money, it is often because Sancho has some coins in his pocket to rescue him. In fact, the greatest disappointment for Don Quixote occurs when, in what looks like a dream, he finally faces his muse, Dulcinea. Dulcinea is interested only in borrowing six *reales* (Spanish currency). Don Quixote has only four *reales*, which were earned earlier by Sancho, and gives those to her. This episode serves to show that Don Quixote's ideals cannot have victory over a world in which money is lord. Thus, we could say that the real enemy of Don Quixote is a growing social order ruled by money.

Don Quixote de la Mancha *is considered the first European novel and is a classic of world literature. In this wood engraving, Don Quixote and Sancho Panza look for adventure.* (The Granger Collection)

After his encounter with a debased Dulcinea, Don Quixote's behavior is marked by a pessimistic attitude, which culminates in a defeat in a duel with the Knight of the Mirrors (a disguised neighbor). Don Quixote, disillusioned and humiliated, returns home, quickly recovers his sanity, but then dies. Critics generally agree that within the logic of the novel, the death of the main character was inevitable because Don Quixote's existence was possible only in an ideal world. Some also believe that Cervantes killed his protagonist to ensure that no one could write another unauthorized sequel to the novel.

SIGNIFICANCE

Don Quixote de la Mancha, a model for subsequent modern novels, addresses important, sometimes controversial, issues in their historical context from more than one perspective. In *Don Quixote de la Mancha*, Cervantes almost always allows his reader to interpret the episodes from different points of view. In this way, he differs radically from writers of his time, who favored moralistic and authoritarian stances. Through irony and ambiguity, Cervantes never makes clear to his audience the nature of his own position on any particular issue. Cervantes' relativistic approach to writing is one of his greatest achievements, leading many to believe that relativism is the most important element defining the modern novel. It is quite possible, however, that Cervantes approached his work through a relativistic lens as the way to avoid censure by the Spanish Inquisition. Because of its relativistic focus, *Don Quixote de la Mancha* could be considered a novel that either supports or subverts dominant ideology, or the status quo, but it is Cervantes' modern readers who are entrusted with the last word.

—Christina H. Lee

FURTHER READING

Anderson, James M. *Daily Life During the Spanish Inquisition*. Westport, Conn.: Greenwood Press, 2002. Anderson surveys the effects of the Inquisition on every aspect of mundane existence, from the royal court to rural farming communities, from military life to the daily experience of students. Includes illustrations, bibliographic references, and index.

Bloom, Harold, ed. *Cervantes' Don Quixote*. Philadelphia: Chelsea House, 2000. A collection of essays by renowned writers, including Thomas Mann, Franz Kafka, Vladimir Nabokov, and Jorge Luis Borges.

Cascardi, Anthony, ed. *The Cambridge Companion to Cervantes*. New York: Cambridge University Press, 2002. This work provides good historical, political, and cultural context for understanding Cervantes' life and most important works. Written by leading scholars in the field.

Cervantes, Miguel de. *Don Quixote*. Translated by Edith Grossman. New York: HarperCollins, 2003. An updated translation of the novel that is more accessible to the general reader than are earlier translations.

Fuentes, Carlos. Introduction to *The Adventures of Don Quixote de la Mancha*. New York: Farrar, Straus & Giroux, 1986. This introduction by Mexico's leading novelist discusses the influence of Desiderius Erasmus on Cervantes and the duality of realism and imagination in *Don Quixote de la Mancha*. Argues

that the novel can be considered the beginning of a modern way of looking at the world.

Hart, Thomas R. *Cervantes' Exemplary Fictions: A Study of the "Novelas Ejemplares."* Lexington: University Press of Kentucky, 1994. A reading of Cervantes' stories in the context of the knowledge of everyday life and literary conventions shared by Cervantes' contemporaries.

McCrory, Donald P. *No Ordinary Man: The Life and Times of Miguel de Cervantes*. Chester Springs, Pa.: Peter Owen, 2002. A thorough biography of Cervantes. Includes bibliographical references and an index.

Quint, David. *Cervantes' Novel of Modern Times: A New Reading of Don Quijote*. Princeton, N.J.: Princeton University Press, 2003. Quint focuses on how *Don Quixote de la Mancha* reflects the political, social, and economic changes that Spain was experiencing in the sixteenth century.

Williamson, Edwin, ed. *Cervantes and the Modernists: The Question of Influence*. London: Tamesis, 1994. Williamson explores the novelist's impact on such twentieth century writers as Marcel Proust, Thomas Mann, Primo Levi, Carlos Fuentes, and Gabriel García Márquez. No index or bibliography.

SEE ALSO: c. 1601-1620: Emergence of Baroque Art; c. 1601-1682: Spanish Golden Age; June 30, 1680: Spanish Inquisition Holds a Grandiose *Auto-da-fé*.

RELATED ARTICLES in *Great Lives from History: The Seventeenth Century, 1601-1700:* Pedro Calderón de la Barca; Luis de Góngora y Argote; Bartolomé Esteban Murillo; Philip III; Philip IV; Francisco Gómez de Quevedo y Villegas; Tirso de Molina; Lope de Vega Carpio; Francisco de Zurbarán.

1605-1627
MUGHAL COURT CULTURE FLOURISHES

Upon his accession to the throne in 1605, Emperor Jahāngīr set out to refine Mughal court culture through his patronage of the luxury arts and architecture. He also developed a royal painting workshop, called the Jahāngīr school.

LOCALE: Āgra, India

CATEGORIES: Cultural and intellectual history; art; architecture; government and politics

KEY FIGURES

Jahāngīr (1569-1627), Mughal emperor of India, r. 1605-1627

Nūr Jahān (Mihr-un-Nisāʾ; d. 1645), Mughal empress of India, r. 1611-1645, and consort of Jahāngīr

Akbar (1542-1605), Mughal emperor of India, r. 1556-1605

Abū al-Ḥasan (fl. seventeenth century), a painter who served Jahāngīr

SUMMARY OF EVENT

Upon the death of Mughal emperor Akbar in 1605, his son Jahāngīr assumed the imperial throne. During his twenty-two-year reign, Emperor Jahāngīr waged few military campaigns. Residing in the largely consolidated empire established by his father, Jahāngīr and his influential wife, Nūr Jahān, refined the visual culture of the Mughal court.

Although Jahāngīr patronized the construction of many buildings, he is best known for being a connoisseur of painting and for his consolidation of artists at the Mughal painting workshop, devoted to the production of books and the paintings that illustrated them. With his support, artists from both Persian and Indian backgrounds continued to flourish at the Mughal court, becoming increasingly recognized for their distinct individual styles. A detailed record of Jahāngīr's reign remains in his own memoirs, the *Jahāngīrnāmah* (*The Jahangirnama*, 1999), which documents contemporary political events and personal observations, along with accounts of the ruler's active involvement in courtly painting.

As Akbar lay dying in 1605, his heir was brought to his side and invested with a turban, robes, and the emperor's own dagger. A week after Akbar's death, during his accession ceremony at the Āgra fort, the prince mounted the emperor's throne, placed the turban on his own head, and accepted the royal title Jahāngīr (world conqueror). These two events were recorded in contemporary court chronicles, including Jahāngīr's memoirs, where they served to underscore the transfer of official imperial power. Most significantly for modern times, the episodes reveal the critical role played by luxury objects and court ceremonial in bestowing the right to rule.

Like Mughal emperors before him, Jahāngīr used artistic patronage to proclaim legitimacy by reference to his family's impressive dynastic lineage—a practice that linked Mughal court culture to the power and artistic patronage of the central Asian ruler Tamerlane (or Timur; r. 1370-1405) and his descendants. Unlike his predecessors, however, Jahāngīr turned away from grand-scale public building projects, urban foundations, and extravagantly illustrated dynastic histories. His patronage was concentrated instead on more personal architectural sites, such as gardens, tombs, and hunting pavilions, and on the enrichment of Mughal court culture, witnessed most particularly in his refinement of the imperial painting workshop.

After his accession, Jahāngīr established his imperial center at his father's former capital city of Āgra, although the royal encampment often shifted for extended periods of time to temporary headquarters such as Kabul, Lahore, Ajmer, and Mandu. During the hot season, Jahāngīr made frequent trips to northern sites such as Kashmir, where he patronized formal gardens and other structures. His most imposing architectural project was the tomb built for Akbar at Sikandra (1605-1614), near Āgra. In keeping with Mughal precedent, Akbar's tomb is set at the center of a vast, formally planned garden. The cross-axial watercourses that divide the site's walled garden follow a well-established type known as a *char bagh* (four-fold garden), an Iranian plan long associated with paradisal imagery. Though the tomb's setting and its highly decorated gateway are modeled on Mughal prototypes, its pyramidal arrangement of five stories represents a sharp deviation from earlier dynastic tombs.

Jahāngīr's patronage of painting, like his patronage of architecture, benefited from the achievements of his forebears while forging new artistic directions. At the onset of his rule, Jahāngīr inherited from his father a vibrant painting workshop. Under Jahāngīr's grandfather, Emperor Humāyūn (r. 1530-1540 and 1555-1556), the practice of painting was consolidated within a courtly workshop, or *kitabkhana* (book house), an institution established under the Mughal and Timurid dynasties to provide a space for the collection and production of books. During the reigns of both Humāyūn and Akbar, Persian painters and calligraphers were brought into the workshop, where Iranian styles and techniques quickly commingled with indigenous Indian painting.

Whereas the illustration of grand state-sponsored histories had dominated production during Akbar's reign, Jahāngīr tended to commission smaller books with very fine illustrations, often by a single artist. He also embraced portraits and other single-folio paintings, which were often gathered in albums alongside specimens of calligraphy, reviving a practice of collecting that had been popular in Timurid central Asia. In keeping with what appears to have been a trend toward specialization during Jahāngīr's reign, several artists in his workshop specialized in portraiture. The seventeenth century artists Manohar and Bishandās, among others, were renowned for producing studies of courtiers, rulers, and holy men that emphasized individual physiognomic details. The fashion for naturalism was also expressed in meticulous animal studies and botanical illustrations, both of which thrived at Jahāngīr's court.

Jahāngīr is often remembered for his passions—as a connoisseur of jewels, a hunter, and a great consumer of wine and opium. Yet, his memoirs suggest that he was also a keen observer of the world around him, and, certainly, the cultivation of individual masters such as Manṣūr (seventeenth century), who specialized in illustrations of the natural world, was due to the emperor's personal interests. By his own account, Jahāngīr was heavily involved in the activities of his painting workshop, and he claimed the ability to identify the artist responsible for a detail as small as an eye or eyebrow in any painting brought before him.

While many of the paintings produced for Jahāngīr seem to have suited his personal whims, others were clearly constructed as political statements, intended to present the ruler as a commanding and venerable figure. Abū al-Ḥasan, the son of the Persian painter Āqā Rezā (sixteenth-seventeenth century), produced a series of allegorical paintings of the emperor that owe more to fantasy than to reality. A renowned example presents Jahāngīr embracing a frail version of the Ṣafavid shah ʿAbbās the Great (r. 1587-1629), with whom he fought repeatedly over Qandahār in Afghanistan. Contrary to the historical record, Jahāngīr's rival is shown in a gesture of submission, while the two stand upon a globe bearing the images of a lamb and lion lying together, a symbol of peaceful resolution. In almost diametric opposition to the realism that typifies nature studies commissioned by the emperor, allegorical paintings produced in his reign present figures in a purely symbolic

The court of the Mughal Empire was centered at the magnificent fort in Āgra. (George L. Shuman)

context, an innovation that was inspired by English paintings brought to India by ambassadors and other visitors.

Jahāngīr's reign is marked not only by his own character but also by the power of his wife, Mihr-un-Nisā', whom he married in 1611. Mihr-un-Nisā' was the daughter of a high-ranking Persian nobleman at his court, and she quickly became Jahāngīr's favored wife. She was given the title Nūr Jahān (light of the world). A talented clothing and textile designer, inventor of perfume, poet, and patron of architecture, Nūr Jahān had a notable impact on Mughal culture. She was also given unprecedented influence over state policies. She followed in her father's footsteps and was appointed the state's finance minister, and she even had coins minted in her name—a symbol of royal prerogative in Islamic kingdoms. By 1622, poor health and an addiction to wine and opium had rendered Jahāngīr incapable of governing, and Nūr Jahān stepped in to maintain control of the empire until her husband's death in 1627, when Jahāngīr's heir, Shah Jahan, ascended the throne.

SIGNIFICANCE

While Jahāngīr made few territorial gains during his reign, the prosperity he inherited at his father's death allowed the emperor to focus on refining his court's cultural achievements. As a connoisseur and patron, Jahāngīr brought his innate interest in the natural world to bear on artistic production, continuing his father's enthusiastic support of painters within the royal workshop. Artists' signatures and the emperor's own written accounts reveal the identities of court-sponsored painters. Alongside the influx of images imported from European lands, this mix of Persian and Indian artists provided the workshop with sources of new innovation. In keeping with the experimentations of Akbar's reign, Jahāngīr's workshop continued to formulate a distinctive synthetic idiom, and in the process created many of the artistic masterpieces of the Mughal era.

—*Anna Sloan*

FURTHER READING

Asher, Catherine B. *Architecture of Mughal India*. New Cambridge History of India 1. New York: Cambridge University Press, 1992. This thorough study organized by regnal eras contains a chapter on Jahāngīr's architectural patronage. Includes a glossary, maps, plates, site plans, and a series of interpretive bibliographical essays.

Beach, Milo Cleveland. "Jahāngīr's *Jahāngīr-Nama*." In *The Powers of Art: Patronage in Indian Culture*, edited by Barbara Stoler Miller. New York: Oxford University Press, 1992. Beach discusses the role of painted illustrations in Jahāngīr's memoirs.

Crowe, Sylvia, et al. *The Gardens of Mughal India*. London: Thames & Hudson, 1972. This work contains documentation and analysis of Jahāngīr's garden projects. Includes illustrations, maps, and plans.

Richards, John F. *The Mughal Empire*. Cambridge History of India 1. Reprint. New Delhi, India: Foundation Books, 1995. An analysis of Mughal institutions, military organization, ideologies, and cultural policies from the reign of Bābur through the accession of Muhammad Shah. Includes a glossary, maps, and a bibliographic essay.

Stronge, Susan. *Painting for the Mughal Emperor: The Art of the Book, 1560-1660*. London: V & A Publications, 2002. Stronge discusses painting under emperors Akbar, Jahāngīr, and Shah Jahan. Includes color plates.

Thackston, Wheeler M., trans. and ed. *The Jahangirnama: Memoirs of Jahangir, Emperor of India*. New York: Oxford University Press, 1999. The best translation, including annotations, of Jahāngīr's personal memoirs. Illustrated with plates showing contemporary paintings and objects.

SEE ALSO: 1632-c. 1650: Shah Jahan Builds the Taj Mahal; 1658-1707: Reign of Aurangzeb.
RELATED ARTICLES in *Great Lives from History: The Seventeenth Century, 1601-1700:* 'Abbās the Great; Aurangzeb; Jahāngīr; Shah Jahan.

Beginning Spring, 1605
DUTCH DOMINATE SOUTHEAST ASIAN TRADE

The seventeenth century saw the Dutch establish control over the Spice Islands—later known as Indonesia—and thereby dominate the lucrative world of Southeast Asian trade.

LOCALE: Indonesia

CATEGORIES: Economics; trade and commerce; expansion and land acquisition; colonization

KEY FIGURES

Cornelis de Houtman (c. 1540-1599), leader of the first major Dutch expedition to Southeast Asia

Abul Mafākhir (d. 1651), fourth sultan of Banten, r. 1596-1651

Jan Pieterszoon Coen (1587-1629), officer of the Dutch East India Company and governor-general of the Dutch East Indies, 1619-1623 and 1627-1629

Sir Thomas Dale (d. 1619), English admiral who led the attack on the Dutch camp at Jacatra

'Ala al-Dīn (d. 1639), sultan of Gowa kingdom, r. 1593-1639

SUMMARY OF EVENT

The islands of Southeast Asia (East Indies) in the region now known as Indonesia were of great significance to European trade in late medieval and early modern times. In 1511, Portugal took the island of Malacca, beginning the long European presence in Southeast Asia. The Indonesian archipelago would produce many spices for European markets, earning for the islands the moniker Spice Islands.

A Dutch expedition of four ships left for the East Indies under the command of Cornelis de Houtman in 1595. The Houtman expedition dropped anchor in Banten (Bantam), the largest port for pepper in the islands, the following year, and also managed to sign a trade treaty with Banten's sultan, Maulana Muhammad (r. 1580-1596). Visiting Sumatra and Bali, as well as Banten, this early expedition experienced great difficulties, but the survivors of the voyage did manage to return to Holland with spices in 1597. The next year, five expeditions under the command of Admiral Jacob van Neck left Holland for the Indies.

The ruler of Banten, Sultan Abul Mafākhir, saw the newly arrived Dutch as potential valuable allies against the Portuguese, and the sultan even helped the Dutch fill ships with pepper. The spice yielded a great profit in Europe, prompting a second Dutch expedition to the region.

The Portuguese became concerned over the Dutch incursions, so the governor of Goa, a Portuguese colony on the west coast of the Indian peninsula, sent a fleet to stop Dutch trade in the area in 1601. Close to the Straits of Sunda, five Dutch ships defeated the Portuguese fleet in December.

Within the following year, the Dutch attempted to centralize their commercial presence in Southeast Asia by combining several different companies into the Vereenigde Oost-Indische Compagnie (the United East India Company), better known as the Dutch East India Company. Under the company, the Dutch began to strike back against and displace the Portuguese. In 1603, company forces began to attack Portuguese interests in the region. In February of 1605, the company took the Portuguese post at Amboina and then attacked the Portuguese at Tidore. By the spring of 1605, the defeated Portuguese left for Spanish-held Manila. Although the Portuguese managed to hang on in some locations, their era of dominating trade in Southeast Asia had essentially ended.

The English became the primary competitors with the Dutch for control of the region. Spaniard Pedro Acuña invaded and conquered Ternate in the spring of 1606, leading the Spanish to control Ternate for another sixty years. However, Queen Elizabeth I's granting of a charter to the English East India Company in 1600 created the main rival to the Dutch East India Company.

In addition to competing with the English, the company also had to contend with the local rulers. The kingdom of Banten, one of the first places in the region to receive Dutch ships, had established control over some of the pepper-producing regions. Bordering Banten, a Muslim ruling class took over central Java in 1600 and founded the kingdom of Mataram. Mataram sent out raiders, also attempting to take control of the profitable sea trade of the islands. In eastern Indonesia, the kingdom of Gowa had made itself the center of a loosely tied empire and a great trading power.

Sultan Abul Mafākhir tried to play the English and Dutch against each other by encouraging the English admiral Sir Thomas Dale to take part in an attack on the Dutch camp outside Jacatra (Jakarta). In 1619, Admiral Dale drove away a Dutch fleet under the command of their leader, Jan Pieterszoon Coen, who later became governor-general of the Dutch East India Company. Dale's forces were about to take the Dutch camp when soldiers of Banten showed up, took over Jacatra from its ruler, and forced the English to leave. Although Abul Mafākhir wanted to get rid of the Dutch, he did not want to replace them with other European competitors. In May, 1619, Coen returned with a larger fleet, drove the Banten troops away, and destroyed Jacatra. The city was soon renamed Batavia and became the center from which Holland established its control over the islands of the region.

From Batavia, Coen led an armed expedition in 1621 against the Banda Islands, the world's primary producers of nutmeg and mace. The people of the Banda Islands had a contract to sell exclusively to the Dutch, but they had been trading with the English. Coen and his men attacked the Banda island of Lonthor, killing or exiling most of its inhabitants. Coen went back to the Netherlands in 1623 to serve as head of the Dutch East India Company. After returning to Batavia for his second term as governor-general, he defended the Dutch headquarters against two sieges by the ruler of neighboring Mataram (1628 and 1629).

Gowa remained the main obstacle to a Dutch monopoly on trade in Southeast Asia. Sultan ʿAla al-Dīn, the ruler of Gowa until 1639, worked with traders from other European nations as well as Asian traders to undermine Dutch efforts to impose a trade monopoly. From 1615 until 1637, the Dutch East India Company and Gowa were in a state of sporadic warfare. In 1637, and again in 1655 and 1660, Gowa signed treaties with the Dutch. In 1666, the company sent a fleet under Admiral Cornelis Speelman against Maluku and Gowa. Two years later, Gowa territories were placed under company control. During the last part of the seventeenth century, the Dutch played the local rulers against each other, signing protection treaties to achieve control of trade. In 1686, Banten gave the Dutch control of all its pepper trade. At the very end of the century, the company brought coffee cultivation to the islands, establishing what would become one of the major cash crops of the region.

SIGNIFICANCE

The Dutch trade domination in Indonesia helped to make Holland, then still a province of the United Provinces of the Netherlands, a wealthy colonial, economic, and territorial power in the seventeenth century. They controlled the region until the twentieth century, shaping the development of the islands of Southeast Asia. The nation of Indonesia emerged from the territories over which

DUTCH EXPEDITIONS TO SOUTHEAST ASIA	
Date	*Event*
Apr. 2, 1595	Dutch expedition led by Cornelis de Houtman leaves for the East Indies. Within the next two years, Dutch ships reach Sumatra, Banten (Bantam), and other locations.
1598	Five expeditions—twenty-two Dutch ships—set out for the East Indies.
Dec. 25-27, 1601	Dutch ships defeat a Portuguese fleet at Banten.
Mar. 20 1602	Dutch East India Company is founded.
1616	Company forces attack Banda.
1618	Jan Pieterzoon Coen is appointed governor-general of the company.
Jan., 1619	After an initial defeat by English forces at Jayakerta, Dutch forces from Banten retake Jayakerta.
Spring, 1619	Jayakerta renamed Batavia by the Dutch.
Aug., 1619	Dutch begin building the city of Batavia.
1620	Jan Pieterzoon Coen attacks Banda and has much of its population killed to enforce the company's monopoly on trade.
Sept. 20, 1629	Coen dies.
1633	War between Banten and the company.
1641	The company, in alliance with the sultan of Johore, attacks the Portuguese at Malacca.
1666	The company sends a fleet under Admiral Cornelis Speelman against Maluku and Gowa.
1668	Gowa signs a treaty, placing its territories under company control.
Feb. 15, 1686	A treaty between the company and Banten gives the Dutch a monopoly on Banten's pepper trade.
1699	The Dutch introduce coffee cultivation in Java.

the Dutch East India Company established its control. Batavia, the city built by the Dutch, became Jakarta, the capital and still the most important city of Indonesia.

—Carl L. Bankston III

FURTHER READING

Ames, Glenn Joseph. *Renascent Empire? The House of Braganza and the Quest for Stability in Portuguese Monsoon Asia, c. 1640-1683*. Amsterdam: Amsterdam University Press, 2000. Based on extensive archival research, Ames describes Portugal's imperial losses in Asia and the attempts to recover its lucrative possessions in South Asia and Southeast Asia.

Chaudhury, Sushil, and Michel Morineau. *Merchants, Companies, and Trade: Europe and Asia in the Early Modern Era*. New York: Cambridge University Press, 1999. The authors analyze Portuguese and Dutch trade competition within the European context of commercial and imperial strategies in Asia. The Europeans confronted an Asian trading web of strategies and objectives.

Gaastra, F. S. *The Dutch East India Company: Expansion and Decline*. Zutphen, the Netherlands: Walburg, 2003. Gaastra examines the development of the company, analyzing its initial policies, strategies, and resources for confronting and defeating the Portuguese in Asia in the early seventeenth century.

Hall, D. G. E. *A History of Southeast Asia*. 4th ed. New York: St. Martin's Press, 1981. Chapter 16 explores the Anglo-Dutch struggle for the spice trade, and chapters 17 and 18 examine the expansion, zenith, and decline of the company.

Kumar, Anne. *Java and Modern Europe: Ambiguous Encounters*. Richmond, England: Curzon, 1997. Kumar examines the historic complexity of economic interests and sociopolitical structures on Java and the island's relation with the Dutch East India Company and other competing European trading entities and interests.

Ricklefs, M. C. *A History of Modern Indonesia Since c. 1200*. 4th ed. Stanford, Calif.: Stanford University Press, 2001. Part 2, "Struggles for Hegemony," addresses the establishment of colonial power by the Dutch East India Company in the seventeenth century. Includes good maps at the end of the book.

Taylor, Jean Gelman. *Indonesia: Peoples and Histories*. New Haven, Conn.: Yale University Press, 2003. A general history of Indonesia. Chapter 5, on European colonization, examines the expansion of Dutch power. Scattered throughout the book are capsules summarizing key topics.

SEE ALSO: 17th cent.: Age of Mercantilism in Southeast Asia; 17th cent.: The Pepper Trade; Dec., 1601: Dutch Defeat the Portuguese in Bantam Harbor; 1602-1613: Japan Admits Western Traders; Mar. 20, 1602: Dutch East India Company Is Founded; 1606-1674: Europeans Settle in India; Apr. 29, 1606: First European Contact with Australia; 1609: Bank of Amsterdam Invents Checks; 1609: China Begins Shipping Tea to Europe; Beginning c. 1615: Coffee Culture Flourishes; July, 1625-Aug., 1664: Founding of New Amsterdam; Oct., 1625-1637: Dutch and Portuguese Struggle for the Guinea Coast; Jan. 14, 1641: Capture of Malacca; Apr., 1652: Dutch Begin to Colonize Southern Africa; Mar. 22, 1664-July 21, 1667: British Conquest of New Netherland.

RELATED ARTICLES in *Great Lives from History: The Seventeenth Century, 1601-1700:* Piet Hein; John IV; Maurice of Nassau; Michiel Adriaanszoon de Ruyter; Abel Janszoon Tasman; Maarten Tromp; Zheng Chenggong.

September, 1605
EGYPTIANS REBEL AGAINST THE OTTOMANS

The Ottoman Empire's governor of Egypt was killed by rebels in a series of revolts that reflected growing tensions between foreign governors and local revenue (or tax) farmers under pressure to provide tribute to Constantinople. The empire's Janissary military corps, having integrated into Egyptian society, would take control of the region because of a weakened sense of allegiance to the Ottoman capital, but the empire eventually prevailed and retook Egypt.

LOCALE: Shubra, near Cairo, Egypt
CATEGORIES: Government and politics; wars, uprisings, and civil unrest

KEY FIGURES
Ahmed I (1590-1617), sultan of the Ottoman Empire, r. 1603-1617
İbrahim Paşa (d. 1605), Ottoman viceroy of Egypt, 1604-1605
Muḥammad Paşa (d. 1611), Ottoman viceroy of Egypt, 1607-1611
Koja Mustafa (fl. 1609), commander of loyalist forces responsible for quelling the revolt

SUMMARY OF EVENT
In 1517, Sultan Selim I (r. 1512-1520) extended the territory of the Ottoman Empire by conquering Egypt. A brief period of expansion was followed by seven decades of quiet and general acceptance of Ottoman rule; then unrest erupted. The common pattern for the Ottomans had been to replace local government institutions, including the military. However, in Egypt, Selim offered pardon to many of the defeated Mamlūks, that is, to the rulers with slave origins. Those who were willing to profess loyalty to the new regime were incorporated into the new administration. During the sixteenth century, the Ottomans continued to purchase military slaves from the Caucasus, known also as Circassians.

The military system was somewhat complex. Janissaries were elite infantry troops who guarded Cairo and the military governor, known as a viceroy. However, there were also many other units of former Mamlūks in the rural areas. Among these units were the *sipahi*, cavalry who fought with bows and arrows. They were often supported by an additional local tax known as the *tulba*. As the size of the military increased, tax revenues were thus divided and diminished. The Ottoman procedure was to give beys, military commanders, responsibility over a portion of land from which they raised troops and exacted taxes. Originally twelve in number, by the beginning of the seventeenth century the number of beys had increased to forty. This increase in number led to a decentralized local government and helped raise questions about restoring self-rule.

In September, 1605, these autonomous Egyptian forces assassinated the Ottoman viceroy İbrahim Paşa, threatening to overthrow imperial rule. This uprising was caused by a number of factors. First, the entire Ottoman Empire was faced with massive inflation because of an influx of silver from the Spanish Americas. With their own silver currency debased, the Ottomans were unable to meet payroll obligations for their growing bureaucracy and extensive military. The Ottomans compounded this crisis through a series of costly wars against the Habsburg Dynasty in Europe (1593-1606). Revolts among soldiers were common.

In Egypt, revolts had begun as early as 1586, when a viceroy initiated an investigation concerning the delivery of revenues to the sultan, a significant act because Egypt paid much more than its fair share in finances to run the empire. In turn, the imperial soldiers removed the viceroy from the citadel, put him under house arrest, and suspended his rule. His successor attempted to deal with the soldiers but instead aggravated them to the point of their revolt in 1589, in which the soldiers obtained a number of concessions. More revolts followed. The confidence of the rural troops grew as discontented soldiers from elsewhere in the empire sought refuge in Egypt.

When İbrahim Paşa arrived to take up the office of viceroy in 1604, he was determined to restore the authority of his office. It had been the custom of arriving viceroys to present a financial gift to the military upon taking office, but İbrahim chose to ignore this tradition. The soldiers responded first by collapsing his tent on top of him and then by taking the gift by force. İbrahim situated himself in the citadel and slowly began a campaign of revenge against the offending soldiers. The following year, in September of 1605, he was no longer secure, as the annual Nile River floods forced him to leave the citadel. Fifteen *sipahi* (armed cavalry) surrounded his house at Shubra on the outskirts of Cairo and broke in with drawn swords to kill him. They proceeded to parade through the streets of Cairo bearing the head of the slain İbrahim and the heads of three of his elite Janissary soldiers, finally displaying them on the Zuwayla Gate, a place reserved for the heads of the worst criminals.

The assassination of the sultan's representative was a major threat to the Ottoman Empire. Sultan Ahmed I responded by sending a tough new viceroy, a formidable foe named Muḥammad Paşa. He would be known as Kul Kiran (the breaker of the Mamlūks). Upon assuming office, he assembled the beys (military commanders) and regimental leaders in order to inquire into the death of Viceroy İbrahim. The beys were accused of involvement in the murder, and thirteen of them, about half, were removed from their leadership positions and exiled. Perhaps the most severe reaction to İbrahim's murder was the discontinuation of the *tulba*, the traditional tax that was raised in the rural areas of Egypt to support the *sipahi*. Since this tax was local, and not a practice in other parts of the empire, the decision of the viceroy seemed to make sense from an administrative standpoint. However, the decision incited even more soldiers to oppose the viceroy.

Matters continued to worsen until 1609, when the *sipahi* named their own sultan and government ministers. In essence, the *sipahi* were announcing their secession from the Ottoman Empire. Swearing an oath of allegiance to this separatist movement on the grave of a revered Sufi leader, they marched on Cairo in order to take on the viceroy's Janissaries. The *sipahi* singled out Koja Mustafa, who was marked for assassination. Along the way they gathered support in every village.

Viceroy Muḥammad was not deterred. Rounding up sympathizers to the separatist movement, he put some to death immediately. He called upon the beys to make an oath of loyalty, and he appointed Koja to command the loyal forces against the rebels. Confronting the rebel forces at Al-Khanqa near Cairo, a well-organized and highly disciplined Ottoman army, equipped with cannon and guns, proved a formidable threat. Many of the rebels surrendered without hesitation, and others were systematically rounded up. Fifty were beheaded on the spot to instill terror. Captured leaders, humiliated and in chains, were paraded before the crowds. The names of the rest of the captured rebels were recorded, and their weapons were confiscated. With the rebellion thwarted, the loyalist troops returned to Cairo in triumph. Because of the intervention of the chief judge, the lives of rebel leaders were spared on the condition that they be exiled to Yemen.

SIGNIFICANCE

The success of Muḥammad Paşa was such that the Arab chronicler Muḥammed ibn Abī al-Surūr referred to the thwarting of the rebellion as the second Ottoman conquest of Egypt. Although Muḥammad served as viceroy for only four years, he was able to crush the revolt convincingly, thereby putting a stop to future unrest. There would be no further revolts in Egypt for more than a century. As a final gesture, he ordered the people of Cairo to dig out a cubit's depth (about 18 inches) in front of their houses to forever remove the footprints of the rebels.

The beys—reduced in number to their original twelve—not only continued to play a role in government but also were soon designated with new leadership functions. Prior to 1604, judges had been responsible for transitions between one viceroy and another. However, beys would now have this important task. Their influence was evident in 1623, when troops loyal to the bey were successful in refusing a replacement for a viceroy recalled by Constantinople.

Likewise, beys would be appointed *amīr-al-Hajj*, the overseer of the safe passage of pilgrimage caravans to Mecca. Also, beys would be appointed *amīr-al-Khazna*, the overseer of the safe delivery of the annual tribute to Constantinople. So, rather than providing a check to this source of local power, the rebellions of the early seventeenth century helped to bring the bey to a dominant position in eighteenth century Egyptian politics.

—*Fred Strickert*

FURTHER READING

Daly, M. W., ed. *Modern Egypt from 1517 to the End of the Twentieth Century*. Vol. 2 in *The Cambridge History of Egypt*. New York: Cambridge University Press, 1998. In chapter 1, Michael Winter describes the organization of the administration and the army. In chapter 2, Jane Hathaway describes the seventeenth century as an age of transformation.

Goodwin, Godfrey. *The Janissaries*. London: Saqi Books, 1994. A highly recommended history of the elite Janissary corps.

Goodwin, Jason. *Lord of the Horizons: A History of the Ottoman Empire*. New York: Henry Holt, 1998. A popular survey of the Ottoman Empire.

Holt, P. M. *Egypt and the Fertile Crescent, 1516-1922: A Political History*. Ithaca, N.Y.: Cornell University Press, 1966. Includes a thorough description of the revolt along with causes, results, and significance of this event.

_____. "The Pattern of Egyptian Political History from 1517 to 1798." In *Political and Social Change in Modern Egypt*, edited by P. M. Holt. London: Oxford University Press, 1968. Provides a context for the rebellion of 1605 by dividing the period into four distinct phases: acquisition, 1517-1525; quiescence, 1525-1586; internal conflict, 1586-1711; and the ascendancy of the grandees, 1711-1798.

Imber, Colin. *The Ottoman Empire, 1300-1650: The Structure of Power.* New York: Palgrave Macmillan, 2002. A detailed work on the Ottoman Empire of the late medieval-early modern era. Includes an excellent glossary of often-technical period terminology.

SEE ALSO: 1603-1617: Reign of Sultan Ahmed I; 1638: Waning of the *Devshirme* System; 1640: Foundation of the Darfur Sultanate; 1659: Expansion of the Alawis; 1660-1677: A Jihad Is Called in Senegambia; Beginning 1687: Decline of the Ottoman Empire.

RELATED ARTICLES in *Great Lives from History: The Seventeenth Century, 1601-1700:* 'Abbās the Great; Merzifonlu Kara Mustafa Paşa; Kâtib Çelebî; Kösem Sultan; Murad IV; Mustafa I.

November 5, 1605
GUNPOWDER PLOT

A group of English Catholics conspired to blow up the houses of Parliament with King James and all the members inside. The Gunpowder Plot not only failed but also intensified Protestant suspicions of Catholics and reduced religious tolerance of Catholicism in England.

LOCALE: England

CATEGORIES: Government and politics; religion and theology

KEY FIGURES

Robert Catesby (1573-1605), leader of the Gunpowder Plot

Guy Fawkes (1570-1606), conspirator in the Gunpowder Plot

James I (1566-1625), king of England, r. 1603-1625, and king of Scotland as James VI, r. 1567-1625

Francis Tresham (c. 1567-1605), conspirator who revealed the existence of the Gunpowder Plot

SUMMARY OF EVENT

The Gunpowder Plot was a conspiracy by a small group of English Roman Catholics who were discontented with the policies of King James I. Their plan was to blow up the king, his ministers and family, and the entire legislature during the opening of Parliament on November 5, 1605. After the destruction of the monarchy and the government, the conspirators had hoped that an uprising by English Catholics would follow and enable them to take over the country.

Under Queen Elizabeth I, persecution of Catholics had been widespread. Executions and imprisonments were not uncommon in extreme cases. The introduction of recusancy laws, which fined people for failure to attend Anglican church services, was also extremely un-

popular among English Catholics. Some individuals were forced to pay thousands of pounds in recusancy fines over the years. The accession of James I to the throne in 1603 brought hopes of greater tolerance for Catholics and that the persecutions would soon end. Conflict between the king and Parliament, however, resulted in little relaxation of the recusancy laws. James's nationality—the idea of a Scottish monarch ruling England—as well as his failure to obtain religious freedom for Catholics led Robert Catesby to initiate the Gunpowder Plot conspiracy.

Catesby had seen his family persecuted for years under Queen Elizabeth, and he was quite willing to seek violent revenge on the Protestant government. In March of 1604, Catesby told fellow Catholics Thomas Percy and Thomas Winter of his plans to blow up Parliament. They were shocked by the plan at first and suggested trying to secure relief for the English Catholics through peaceful means by seeking assistance from foreign governments. When King Philip III of Spain failed to convince James to relax the recusancy laws, however, violence seemed to be the only alternative left for the conspirators to consider.

Returning to England in May, Winter brought with him Guy Fawkes, a man he believed would be an asset to their plans because of his military experience. Later that month, the conspirators rented rooms near the Houses of Parliament. The conspiracy had grown to include John Wright, Christopher Wright, Robert Winter, and John Grant. The following year, Ambrose Rokewood, Francis Tresham, and Sir Everard Digby were added to help finance the operation. The conspirators' plan, to dig a tunnel to the House of Lords and place a large quantity of gunpowder there, was fraught with problems from the start. With the exception of Fawkes, who had some experience in mining operations, the conspirators were members of the gentry with no experience of digging. Consequently, they found their task to be quite challenging physically.

Finances, too, were a problem, but the problem was lessened somewhat by the addition of Rokewood, Digby, and Tresham, to whom the full details of the plot were not revealed. Although the opening of Parliament was delayed many times, the workers began to despair of the tunnel. In February of 1605, however, they learned of a cellar for rent under the House of Lords. They abandoned the tunnel and rented the cellar, supposedly for the storage of coal and wood. By April, they had succeeded in storing some twenty barrels of gunpowder in the cellar. The conspirators disbanded and arranged to meet later in the year to discuss the final steps in their plot.

While the conspirators waited for Parliament to commence, several of them began to have second thoughts. Catesby, however, managed to convince most of the conspirators to continue with the plot as planned. He also acquired a small number of horses and weapons, which he stationed in small groups throughout the West Midlands. These forces were to be used in the uprising he believed would naturally follow once their plan had been executed.

When Tresham learned the full details of the plot and that his brother-in-law, William Parker, fourth baron Monteagle and eleventh baron Morley, would be a victim of the explosion, he was shocked. Unable to convince Catesby to seek a less violent means to achieve their political goals, Tresham decided to reveal the plot by warning his brother-in-law not to attend the opening of Parliament. On October 26, Monteagle held a dinner party at his home. During the evening, a messenger delivered an anonymous letter to him, which he instructed to be read aloud. The letter warned of a plot to blow up Parliament, although no names of the conspirators were mentioned.

It has been suggested that both Tresham and Monteagle conceived the idea of the "anonymous" letter and believed that by having it read in public, the government could be alerted to the plot without implicating Tresham as a conspirator. It was Tresham's hope that, once alerted to the plot, the government would intercede and prevent a horrible tragedy from occurring. In addition, Tresham believed, news that the plot had been discovered would reach his fellow conspirators in time for them to abandon their plans and flee to safety abroad.

Between October 26 and November 4, little action was taken by the authorities. As a result, it was only during the few days prior to November 5 that most of the conspirators decided to abandon the plot and flee. When the authorities eventually searched the cellar containing the concealed gunpowder, they met a man named Johnson who claimed to be Thomas Percy's servant. According to Johnson, his master was using the area for coal storage. Moments before midnight on November 4, the cellar was visited again by authorities. This time, the concealed gunpowder casks were discovered and Johnson was arrested. Johnson was interrogated over several days and was even subjected to some allegedly mild tortures. He eventually revealed his true name to be Guy Fawkes.

Shortly after Fawkes was discovered, the king appointed a commission to investigate the Gunpowder Plot. The commission comprised the attorney general, Sir Edward Coke, and seven privy councillors. Over a period of about two weeks, Fawkes

---

THE LETTER TO MONTEAGLE

On October 26, William Parker, fourth baron Monteagle and eleventh baron Morley, received the following letter, warning him of the plot to blow up the Houses of Parliament. The letter was unsigned, but it is generally believed that it was written by Francis Tresham, one of the conspirators and Monteagle's brother-in-law.

My lord,

Out of the love I bear to some of your friends, I have a care of your preservation. Therefore, I would advise you as you tender your life to devise some excuse to shift of your attendance at this Parliament, for God and man hath concurred to punish the wickedness of this time; and think not slightly of this advertisement but retire yourself into your country, where you may expect the event in safety, for, though there be no appearance of any stir yet, I say they shall receive a terrible blow this Parliament, and yet they shall not see who hurts them. This counsel is not to be contemned, because it may do you good and can do you no harm, for the danger is passed as soon as you have burnt the letter, and I hope God will give you the grace to make good use of it—to whose holy protection I commend you.

Source: From the Archives of the Gunpowder Plot Society. http://www.gunpowder-plot.org/. Accessed April 26, 2005. Orthography and punctuation modernized by the editors.

Guy Fawkes and his co-conspirators plotted to blow up the Houses of Parliament when the king and all the members of Parliament were present. (R. S. Peale and J. A. Hill)

eventually provided most of the details of the plot, including the names of the conspirators. Even without Fawkes's early cooperation, the identities of many of the conspirators were suspected. Many of them, including Catesby, Percy, Grant, Thomas Winter, and Christopher Wright, were well-known Catholic sympathizers, and warrants were issued for their arrest.

Around the time of Fawkes's arrest, the remaining conspirators had participated in what they hoped would be the outbreak of rebellion in other parts of the country. The fighting was short-lived, however, and many of the conspirators were killed, including Catesby, Percy, and both of the Wright brothers. Thomas Winter was wounded and arrested together with the others shortly after. Those who survived were tried and executed at the end of January, 1606.

SIGNIFICANCE

Over the centuries since the Gunpowder Plot, studies of the early Stuart administration and of the plot itself have been hindered by a fire in 1619 that destroyed many of the Privy Council's records. Although unlikely, there

have long been rumors that the plot was actually instigated by members of the government who were attempting to discredit the Catholics. In retrospect, it is easy to understand the source of those rumors: The conspiracy was in fact disastrous for the Catholic cause in England. Public exposure of the conspiracy led England's Protestants to grow more suspicious of Catholics than ever. They harbored greater resentment toward them, and the unpopular recusancy law was enforced even more rigorously. Since 1606, November 5 has been a day of public thanksgiving in Great Britain and is often celebrated with displays of fireworks.

—Nicholas C. Thomas

FURTHER READING

Edwards, Frances. *Guy Fawkes: The Real Story of the Gunpowder Plot?* London: Rupert Hart-Davis, 1969. An introductory account of the plot, emphasizing the role of Guy Fawkes.

Fraser, Antonia. *Faith and Treason: The Story of the Gunpowder Plot.* New York: Doubleday, 1996. Fraser, an author of popular English histories, examines the causes and events that led to November 5, 1605, comparing the Gunpowder Plot to modern acts of religion-inspired terrorism.

Gardiner, Samuel R. *What the Gunpowder Plot Was.* Reprint. New York: AMS Press, 1969. Based on a century-old first printing by a great scholar, this work examines historical evidence for the plot and discounts high-level government involvement.

Haynes, Alan. *The Gunpowder Plot: Faith in Rebellion.* Stroud, Gloucestershire, England: Sutton, 1994. Provides information about Guy Fawkes and the other plotters and explains why these Catholics attempted to kill the Protestant members of Parliament and King James I.

Nicholls, Mark. *Investigating the Gunpowder Plot.* New York: St. Martin's Press, 1991. Examines how King

James and his Privy Council approached the investigation of the plot. Contains a useful bibliography.

Wormald, Jenny. "Gunpowder, Treason, and Scots." *The Journal of British Studies* 24 (1985): 141-168. Attempts to explain why the conspirators resorted to violence to address their grievances.

SEE ALSO: Feb. 7-19, 1601: Essex Rebellion; Mar. 24, 1603: James I Becomes King of England; 1611: Publication of the King James Bible; Aug. 13, 1678-July 1, 1681: The Popish Plot; Aug., 1682-Nov., 1683: Rye House Plot; May 24, 1689: Toleration Act.

RELATED ARTICLES in *Great Lives from History: The Seventeenth Century, 1601-1700:* Sir Edward Coke; James I; Philip III.

1606-1674
EUROPEANS SETTLE IN INDIA

Spurred by the lucrative spice trade and the success of Portuguese traders in Asia, merchants from the Netherlands, Britain, France, and Denmark established trading footholds on the subcontinent of India.

LOCALE: India

CATEGORIES: Trade and commerce; economics; expansion and land acquisition; exploration and discovery; government and politics

KEY FIGURES

Sir Thomas Roe (c. 1581-1644), English diplomat

William Hawkins (d. 1612 or 1613), English sea captain

François Martin (1634-1706), director of the French East India Company

Elizabeth I (1533-1603), queen of England, r. 1558-1603

Jean-Baptiste Colbert (1619-1683), controller general of finance under King Louis XIV of France

Jahāngīr (1569-1627), Mughal emperor of India, r. 1605-1627

SUMMARY OF EVENT

Lured by the prospect of easier access to spices, whose cost had risen when the Ottoman Empire had assumed control of overland trade routes, Portuguese explorers reached India by sea in the late fifteenth century. Sailing

around the southern tip of Africa, Vasco da Gama arrived at the port of Calicut on the southwest or Malabar Coast of India in 1498. In the decades that followed, the Portuguese seized the port of Goa and set up trading stations, or "factories," at several other ports.

Anxious to reap the rewards of the lucrative Asian trade, four other European nations—the Netherlands, Britain, France, and Denmark—moved to establish their own factories in southern Asia. They did so through the formation of joint stock companies in which wealthy merchants bought shares and distributed proportionate profits. The companies were in competition (and sometimes at war) with each other, and they brought an end to more than one century of Portuguese dominance in the region. Not only did they assume control of trade between Asia and Europe but also took over much of the Indian Ocean trade market. Despite the companies' initial interest in spices, they had discovered that the many textiles and other manufactures of India offered significant commercial opportunities as well.

The Dutch East India Company (Verenigde Oost-Indische Compagnie, or VOC) was formed in 1602 from remnants of previous Dutch trading companies. One of the VOC's ships reached India three years later, and its agents established factories at the southeast or Coromandel Coast ports of Petapuli and Masulipatnam in 1606, Tirupapaliyur in 1608, and Pulicat in 1610. The Dutch also established a factory at Surat, the major port of the

A drawing of the British trading post Surat, India, which served as the center of operations for the British East India Company until the latter part of the seventeenth century, when the company moved its main post to Bombay. (Hulton|Archive by Getty Images)

Gujarat region in northwest India, in 1617, and at Calcutta in northeast India. Like the Portuguese before them, the Dutch concentrated their efforts on trade in Ceylon (now Sri Lanka) and the islands of the Malay Archipelago (now Indonesia and Malaysia). Yet, the Dutch eventually supplanted their Portuguese competitors on both the islands and the mainland, driving the Portuguese out of Ceylon by 1658 and out of most of their settlements on the Malabar Coast by 1663.

Queen Elizabeth I chartered the British East India Company on the final day of 1600, granting it exclusive trading rights between Britain and southern Asia. Captain William Hawkins reached Surat in 1608, but it was not until 1612 that another agent, Thomas Best, obtained formal trading rights. The company went on to set up a factory in Surat in 1613. Two years later, Sir Thomas Roe negotiated a far-reaching treaty with Mughal emperor Jahāngīr, who ruled nearly three-fourths of India. Under the treaty's assurance of commercial rights and le-

gal protection, the company established several other factories.

One of the most important bases of the British East India Company turned out to be the former Portuguese stronghold of Bombay. Situated farther down the west coast of India, Bombay passed into the hands of English king Charles II in 1661 as part of the dowry of Princess Catharine of Braganza of Portugal. In turn, Charles leased it to the company in 1668 for a nominal fee. Blessed with a fine natural harbor, Bombay supplanted Surat as the company's headquarters in 1687.

The English were active on the Coromandel Coast as well. They established a base in 1611 at Masulipatnam, where the Dutch had been active for five years, and built Fort Saint George. Fort Saint George would become the city of Madras on a site ceded by the raja (prince) of Chandragiri, Damarla Venkatadri, to company agent Francis Day in 1639. The first piece of Indian territory actually owned by the English, Madras soon surpassed

117

AN ACCOUNT OF DUTCH HOSTILITY TOWARD THE ENGLISH IN INDIA

Competition among European traders in Southeast Asia and India was fierce and often deadly. A decidedly partial account by a French witness gives readers an idea of the hostilities between the Dutch and the English in Bantam, India.

A relation of the Frenchmen which lately arrived into France in a ship of Dieppe out of the East Indies concerning the wrongs and abuses which the Hollanders [the Dutch] had lately done to the English there (1617):

At Bantam the English and the Hollanders had great disputes, insomuch as it was verily thought they would have fought together in the road, for the general of the Hollanders had brought thither fourteen great ships, ready to fight, where the English had nine, which they fitted for defense; but they fought not, for the governor of Bantam forbade them to fight in his road, and threatened them that if they did fight contrary to his command he would cut the throats of all their men that he should find upon the land.

The 27th of November the Hollanders proclaimed war against all the English at the Mulluccoes, Banda, and Amboyna, threatening to make one and all prize and to put them to the edge of the sword. . . .

Source: Excerpted in *Readings in European History*, edited by James Harvey Robinson (Boston: Atheneum Press, 1906), pp. 400-401.

Masulipatnam as the major English factory in Coromandel and along with Bombay became one of the most important English bases in India.

Danish merchants organized their own trading company, the Danish East India Company, in 1616, modeling it closely on the Dutch company. After a failed attempt to set up a post in Ceylon, the Danes built a fort at Tranquebar on the Coromandel Coast in 1620, and in 1625, as did so many other European traders, established a factory at Masulipatnam. After a brief period of prosperity, however, the company went into decline and was dissolved by Danish king Frederick III in 1650. A second Danish trading company was established in 1670, but it proved equally unsuccessful.

Spurred on by their Dutch and English competitors, French merchants had attempted several largely unsuccessful trading voyages to India by the time the French East India Company was established in 1642 under the sponsorship of controller general Jean-Baptiste Colbert. The company's first expedition sailed to the island of Madagascar, off the southeastern coast of Africa, but in 1668, its director François Martin established a factory at Surat, where representatives of the British East India Company had been active for years. The French also set up a trading post at Masulipatnam in 1669, but their most important settlement would prove to be south of Madras

at Pondicherry, where Martin established a base in 1674 and went on to become its first governor.

SIGNIFICANCE

By the end of the seventeenth century, European trading companies had ringed the Indian subcontinent with factories. Although the Europeans who reached India were initially interested in trade, their ambitions slowly turned to the acquisition of land. The Mughal Dynasty, which had ruled India since 1526, slid into a slow decline in the last decade of the seventeenth century, and as a result, its constituent states, which were spread across the great subcontinent of India, became virtually independent.

Although the Dutch East India Company eventually drove the Portuguese and the English from the Malay Archipelago, the Dutch lost Ceylon and India to the English and French. The Danish East India Company was eventually dissolved in 1729, with Denmark taking over direct control of Tranquebar, but the country lacked the resources to maintain its factory effectively. These developments meant that the French and English companies (and their parent states) were poised to expand throughout the subcontinent. Although the French East India Company increased its holdings in southern India in the early years of the eighteenth century, England asserted its supremacy in the three Carnatic Wars (1746-1783), and so it went on to assume control of virtually the entire country.

—Grove Koger

FURTHER READING

Bowen, H. V., Margarette Lincoln, and Nigel Rigby, eds. *The Worlds of the East India Company*. Rochester, N.Y.: D. S. Brewer, 2002. A multidisciplinary collection of essays concentrating on the British East India Company but touching on its Dutch counterpart as well. Includes black-and-white and color illustrations.

Chaudhury, Sushil, and Michel Morineau, eds. *Merchants, Companies and Trade: Europe and Asia in the Early Modern Era*. New York: Cambridge University Press, 1999. This collection includes several essays assessing the European impact on trade in the Indian Ocean during the seventeenth century, supplemented with bibliographies and tables.

Judd, Denis. *The Lion and the Tiger: The Rise and Fall of the British Raj, 1600-1947*. New York: Oxford University Press, 2004. An illustrated history of the British East India Company from its earliest days, incorporating many extracts from contemporary accounts.

Keay, John. *India: A History*. New York: Atlantic Monthly Press, 2000. Keay places the period of European intrusion in the broader context of Indian history. Includes black-and-white and color illustrations, maps, tables, and a bibliography.

Prakash, Om. *European Commercial Enterprise in Pre-Colonial India*. New York: Cambridge University Press, 1998. The most authoritative modern work on the subject, which surveys the operations of European traders from the late fifteenth through the eighteenth centuries. Supplemented with maps, tables, and a bibliographic essay.

SEE ALSO: 17th cent.: The Pepper Trade; Dec., 1601: Dutch Defeat the Portuguese in Bantam Harbor; Mar. 20, 1602: Dutch East India Company Is Founded; Beginning Spring, 1605: Dutch Dominate Southeast Asian Trade; 1609: Bank of Amsterdam Invents Checks; 1639-1640: British East India Company Establishes Fort Saint George; Jan. 14, 1641: Capture of Malacca; 1661-1672: Colbert Develops Mercantilism; June 23, 1661: Portugal Cedes Bombay to the English; c. 1666-1676: Founding of the Marāthā Kingdom.

RELATED ARTICLES in *Great Lives from History: The Seventeenth Century, 1601-1700:* Catherine of Braganza; Jean-Baptiste Colbert; Piet Hein; Jahāngīr; William Kidd; Śivājī.

April 29, 1606
FIRST EUROPEAN CONTACT WITH AUSTRALIA

In the first decade of the seventeenth century, Dutch and Portuguese navigators explored the Pacific islands near Australia, with the Dutch making landfall on the Australian coast in 1605. Europeans thus moved toward a geographical knowledge of the actual outlines of the elusive sixth continent.

LOCALE: New Hebrides; New Guinea; New Holland (now Australia); Batavia, Java (now Jakarta, Indonesia)

CATEGORIES: Exploration and discovery; expansion and land acquisition; economics; trade and commerce; organizations and institutions; environment

KEY FIGURES
Willem Jansz (c. 1570-1630), Dutch commander of the *Duyfken*, credited with first landfall on Australia
Pedro Fernández de Quirós (c. 1565-1615), Portuguese navigator in the service of Spain
Luis Vaez de Torres (fl. 1605-1607), European discoverer of what is now called the Torres Strait
Dirk Hartog (fl. 1616), Dutch sea captain who made landfall on western Australia

SUMMARY OF EVENT
The first contact with Australia by Europeans was not a single event but a series of discoveries, often made quite by chance. The landings on the shores of Australia made it possible to map the outline of the huge landmass and to identify it, eventually, as the sixth continent.

In the sixth century B.C.E., Greek philosophers had hypothesized that if Earth were indeed round, as they believed, there must then be a large landmass in the Southern Hemisphere of the round Earth to balance the landmass in the Northern Hemisphere. It was not until the early sixteenth century that Terra Australis Incognita, the "unknown" land to the south, first appeared on a map, though it was represented as a vast area that stretched along the entire southern part of the globe.

In December, 1605, Pedro Fernández de Quirós left Callao, Peru, as the leader of a Spanish expedition comprising three ships, whose mission was to locate and colonize Terra Australis Incognita. On April 29, 1606, he sighted the islands now called the New Hebrides, which appeared to him to be a single landmass. Believing that he had reached his goal, Quirós christened the land La Australia del Espíritu Santo, thus crediting his success to the guidance of the Holy Spirit. Despite skirmishes between the indigenous peoples of the islands and his men, Quirós sent a contingent ashore to establish a colony. However, just three weeks later, without explanation, he ordered his ships back to sea. When his flagship became separated from the other two ships in the expedition,

Quirós sailed his ship back to the Americas, leaving two at Espíritu Santo.

Taking command of the two vessels that remained in harbor at Espíritu Santo, Luis Vaez de Torres, the chief pilot, first sailed along the coast far enough to ascertain that Espíritu Santo was an island and not the continent they had been seeking. Then he headed northwest, becoming the first explorer to make the difficult passage through the strait between New Guinea and Australia. Although it is most likely that he did not see Australia, Torres had discovered that New Guinea was not attached to land to the south. After his arrival in Manila in May, 1607, Torres submitted a report on his findings, but the Spanish concealed it, fearing that it might enable the Dutch or the British to find new trade routes. Nothing more is known of Torres, but in 1762, when the British took Manila from the Spanish, they found his report and renamed his discovery the Torres Strait.

With Torres's death came the end of the era of Spanish and Portuguese exploration of the Pacific and the beginning of Dutch domination of the area. Unlike the Spanish, the Dutch did not aim to establish colonies nor to convert the indigenous to Christianity; their interests were purely commercial. In 1602, the Dutch East India Company was founded, and it began to operate as *the* Dutch presence in Southeast Asia.

In 1605, the Dutch East India Company sent Willem Jansz and his small ship *Duyfken* (little dove) to look for sources of gold on the southern side of New Guinea, but only the northern coast of New Guinea had been mapped. Along the way, Jansz failed to see the western entrance to the strait that Torres would discover five months later. Instead, the *Duyfken* sailed south into the Gulf of Carpenteria. Crewmen were sent ashore to explore what is now called the Cape York Peninsula, which they described as a desolate area populated by cannibals, who had attacked them and killed several crew members. Neither Jansz nor his men could have guessed that they would be remembered as the first Europeans to make landfall on the Australian continent.

In 1611, the Dutch sea captains discovered that they could travel from Africa to the East Indies in half the usual time if they took a more southerly route. Inevitably, those who made a slight miscalculation as to when to turn back north found themselves facing an unfamiliar land. However, they did not realize that they had found the continent so many had sought. Thus, on October 25, 1616, when Captain Dirk Hartog of the *Eendracht* landed on a sandy island, looked around, and nailed an engraved pewter plate to a post before sailing on, he had no idea that he had discovered the west coast of Australia.

Dutch ships on their way to Java (Indonesia) soon began to delay turning north until they had reached this landmass, which the company named New Holland to distinguish it from Terra Australis, which everyone still thought lay farther south. Thus, more and more of the western coast was revealed. In 1619, after high waves prevented his ship's landing near what is now Perth, Frederick de Houtman continued northward and later reported seeing 150 miles of unbroken coastline on the western side of New Holland. In 1629, after the ship *Batavia* went aground in the same area that Houtman attempted to land, its captain, François Pelsaert, sailed 500 miles along the coast on his way to Batavia to find help for those he had to leave behind. His notes were the most detailed reports yet on a sizeable area of northwestern Australia.

Two years earlier, another captain had explored the southwestern shoreline. When he realized that his ship, the *Gulden Zeepaert*, was hopelessly off course, its captain, François Thijssen, decided to do a little investigating. He sailed eastward along the coast for 1,000 miles, stopped long enough to name two island groups—St. Francis and St. Peter—then turned back and found his way to Batavia.

Meanwhile, the Dutch East India Company had not forgotten about southern New Guinea. In 1623, Jan Carstenz was placed in command of two ships, the *Arnhem* and the *Pera*, to explore the coast. However, like Jansz, he missed the strait and landed at Cape York Peninsula. Venturing westward, the crew of the *Arnhem* found a new coastal area, which they named Arnhem Land. However, the company was not impressed. All Carstenz could report about southern New Guinea was that it had no commercial possibilities.

In 1636, the company sent another expedition to see whether there was a strait between New Guinea and New Holland. After the expedition's commander was killed by tribesmen, though, the enterprise ended. There would be no more such ventures until 1642-1644, when Abel Janszoon Tasman was able to prove, unwittingly, however, that Australia indeed was a separate continent after his circumnavigation of the landmass.

SIGNIFICANCE

In the early decades of the seventeenth century, Europeans believed they could locate a sixth continent. Those who actually happened upon Australia did not realize the significance of their discoveries; but find the sixth continent they did, whether by exploratory expeditions or by accidental landfall. One of the most valuable and significant discoveries of the period, the existence of a strait that separated New Guinea from the area to the south, would not be made public for 150 years.

Most of the reports sent to the Dutch East India Company by the leaders of expeditions or by ship captains involved in trade described New Holland as an uninviting land, populated by hostile and savage peoples if populated at all. Later explorers, venturing inland, would discover the commercial possibilities of this huge and varied land.

—*Rosemary M. Canfield Reisman*

FURTHER READING

Allen, Oliver E. *The Pacific Navigators*. Alexandria, Va.: Time-Life Books, 1980. A lavishly illustrated book that is an ideal starting point for a study of Pacific explorations.

Beaglehole, J. C. *The Exploration of the Pacific*. 3d ed. Stanford, Calif.: Stanford University Press, 1966. One of the most detailed sources available. Map inserts.

Day, Alan Edwin. *Historical Dictionary of the Discovery and Exploration of Australia*. Lanham, Md.: Scarecrow Press, 2003. A good source with a range of details, cross references, and an extensive bibliography.

Estensen, Miriam. *Discovery: The Quest for the Great South Land*. New York: St. Martin's Press, 1999. Describes the search for the sixth continent from the time of the ancient Greeks to the eighteenth century. Maps and illustrations.

Fischer, Steven Roger. *A History of the Pacific Islands*. New York: Palgrave, 2002. Emphasizes the degree to which the Dutch East India Company guarded its monopoly of commercial ventures and exploration in the Pacific.

Flannery, Tim F., ed. *The Explorers: Stories of Discovery and Adventure from the Australian Frontier*. New York: Grove, 2000. Among the sixty-seven firsthand accounts in this volume are those of explorers Janz, Carstenz, and Pelsaert. Includes an introduction by the editor and a comprehensive bibliography.

Gaastra, F. S. *The Dutch East India Company: Expansion and Decline*. Zutphen, the Netherlands: Walburg, 2003. Reviews the development of the company, analyzing its initial policies, strategies, and resources for confronting and defeating the Portuguese for trade dominance in the early seventeenth century.

Robert, Willem C. H. *The Dutch Explorations, 1605-1756, of the North and Northwest Coast of Australia*. Amsterdam: Philo Press, 1973. Extracts from journals, logbooks, and other documents relating to the voyages of Dutch explorers of Australia. Includes original Dutch texts, edited and with English translations, a critical introduction, and notes. Also includes appendices, a bibliography, and indexes.

SEE ALSO: 17th cent.: The Pepper Trade; Dec., 1601: Dutch Defeat the Portuguese in Bantam Harbor; Mar. 20, 1602: Dutch East India Company Is Founded; Beginning Spring, 1605: Dutch Dominate Southeast Asian Trade; Oct., 1625-1637: Dutch and Portuguese Struggle for the Guinea Coast; Jan. 14, 1641: Capture of Malacca; 1642 and 1644: Tasman Proves Australia Is a Separate Continent; Apr., 1652: Dutch Begin to Colonize Southern Africa.

RELATED ARTICLES in *Great Lives from History: The Seventeenth Century, 1601-1700:* William Dampier; Engelbert Kämpfer; Abel Janszoon Tasman; Zheng Chenggong.

September, 1606-June, 1609
GREAT JELĀLĪ REVOLTS

Landholders who were branded deserters by the Ottoman government for failing to serve the empire as soldiers revolted after imperial officials confiscated their lands and the sultan condemned them to death. The Jelālī forces, first organized in 1596 with the help of a rebel Ottoman soldier, were joined by other disaffected persons in the empire's Anatolian provinces in 1602. In 1606, the revolt gained momentum, but within three years, the Ottoman army eradicated Jelālī leaders, ending the revolts.

LOCALE: Anatolian provinces in the Ottoman Empire (now in Turkey)
CATEGORY: Wars, uprisings, and civil unrest

KEY FIGURES
Kuyucu Murad Paşa (1535-1611), military leader and Ottoman grand vizier, 1606-1611
Kalenderoglu Mehmed (fl. 1605-1609), supreme leader of the Great Jelālī Revolts
Janbuladoglu (d. 1610), Jelālī leader in Aleppo

SUMMARY OF EVENT
Seeds of the Great Jelālī Revolts were planted in late October, 1596, just after the resounding Ottoman victory against the Habsburg Dynasty at the Battle of Mezö Kerésztés in central Europe. The battle was part of the Fifteen Years' War against the Habsburgs that began in 1591 along the Hungarian border and continued through 1606, ending with the Treaty of Zsitvatorok. Military leader and future grand vizier Kuyucu Murad Paşa ordered that all the *sipahi* (landholders) who had not been present at the roll call before the 1596 battle be hunted down and killed as deserters. Their land was confiscated and then reverted to central government control, and then it was doled out to court favorites.

In response to these brutal disciplinary measures, the *sipahi* fled to Anatolia and formed the Jelālī forces, rebel groups that also had unemployed and dissident Ottoman soldiers, including *sekhans*, musketeers who were unpaid in peace time, and brought together by soldier Kara Yaziji. Also part of the Jelālī forces were nomadic Kurds and Turkmens, and *suhtes*, unemployed madrasa (religious school) graduates. Often, peasants joined the Jelālī rather than flee or face the wrath of Ottoman officials. Even provincial army forces sent to suppress the Jelālīs sometimes joined the rebel forces. By December of that

year, the first rebellions had begun, and Anatolia was thrown into anarchy.

The first major Jelālī uprisings in 1598 were not attempts to overthrow the Ottoman government, but rather reactions to the social and economic crises in Anatolia. This changed in 1606, as new groups of Jelālīs formed under the leadership of Janbuladoglu in Aleppo and Kalenderoglu Mehmed in western Anatolia.

Initially, Janbuladoglu was considered the more serious threat by the Ottoman government. His family had controlled land along the Syrian border for generations. As he gathered forces in September of 1606, he seemed poised to initiate the first secession from the Ottoman Empire. Instead, he requested the military governorship of Aleppo and continued to consolidate power in the area, installing his own men in local government positions. Kuyucu, realizing what Janbuladoglu was up to, was determined to stop him.

In January of 1607, Kalenderoglu's Jelālī forces moved into western Anatolia. They spread the Jelālī Revolts throughout Anatolia, initiating the Great Flight. Peasants abandoned their villages in confusion and terror. Fleeing from the Jelālīs, they sought refuge in fortified cities. The rich, who could afford it, fled to Constantinople, Rumeli, and even the Crimea to escape the Jelālīs and the Ottoman troops.

In June, Grand Vizier Kuyucu Murad Paşa moved his troops into Anatolia and began his campaign to eliminate the Jelālīs. He refused to incorporate them into the Ottoman army as had been earlier policy. Kuyucu offered Kalenderoglu a governorship if he would stop fighting, but Kalenderoglu refused. In March, Kuyucu offered a second governorship, but Kalenderoglu's troops continued their fighting, and the offer was soon retracted.

Kuyucu turned his attention to Janbuladoglu. As he poised his troops to attack Janbuladoglu, he wrote to all the other minor Jelālī leaders, offering them government positions and eliminating them as allies for Janbuladoglu. He wrote to Kalenderoglu once again and offered him the governorship of Ankara, but Kalenderoglu had found nothing but trouble there. While Kuyucu was busy in Aleppo, Kalenderoglu had problems subduing Ankara. He faced great opposition from the residents, who requested Ottoman troops to drive off the Jelālīs. Other Jelālī bands came to aid Kalenderoglu and help him defeat the government troops in Ankara. When all else failed, the residents of Ankara bought off the Jelālīs with 200,000 ducats. Kalenderoglu then took his troops and headed toward Bursa and Constantinople, the empire's capital, which made the Ottoman government feel the Jelālī threat as real and far too near. Kuyucu was still in the eastern part of Anatolia fighting Janbuladoglu, so the government called out forty thousand citizens and a small number of regular troops to protect Constantinople and Bursa.

Kalenderoglu's forces reigned havoc on the mixed army, so that only six thousand men returned to Constantinople. Kalenderoglu then turned south and set up a winter camp instead of finishing off Constantinople. As he was leaving the area, Kalenderoglu sent a message to the sultan, asking for a good government position as a reward for turning away from Constantinople.

In October of 1607, Kuyucu pounced on Janbuladoglu's Jelālīs. The two forces met north of Aleppo, and the Ottoman forces slaughtered the mercenaries. Kuyucu had tens of thousands of men beheaded, and wells were sunk to contain the heads. This action earned him the title Kuyucu (the well-sinker). He sent the heads of forty-eight Jelālī leaders back to Constantinople.

By November, Aleppo was firmly under Ottoman control once more. Kuyucu had managed to buy off all the other minor Jelālī leaders with governorships or other government positions, while continuing his battle with Janbuladoglu. The buy offs also eliminated any other potential allies for Kalenderoglu. After defeating Janbuladoglu, Kuyucu aimed his sights at his other audacious Jelālī nemesis, Kalenderoglu.

In January of 1608, Kalenderoglu's Jelālīs defeated an Ottoman force and ambushed troops carrying Kuyucu's treasury. Kuyucu suddenly faced huge problems trying to muster his campaign against the remaining Jelālī leader. The harsh winter and spring of 1608 delayed supplies, the farmlands devastated by battles were not supplying food, and his treasury and additional troops failed to arrive. Kuyucu's advance was stalled and remained so until summer. When supplies and reinforcements finally arrived, the Ottoman army hunted the Jelālīs.

In August of 1608, Kuyucu's Ottoman forces defeated Kalenderoglu's Jelālīs at Alacajayir, and in September, Kuyucu's troops finished off the Jelālīs at Şebinkarahisar. Kalenderoglu fled east after his final defeat and joined the Persian troops of the Ṣafavid shah. Once the Ottoman troops had crushed the forces of the supreme Jelālī commander, Kalenderoglu, the Ottoman army moved quickly through the rest of Anatolia, suppressing further revolts and eliminating Jelālī forces.

By December, Kuyucu had returned to Constantinople. With the two major Jelālī leaders defeated and out of the way, Kuyucu could put the rest of his master plan to work. One by one, he recalled all those minor Jelālī leaders from the government posts he had offered them while fighting Janbuladoglu. One by one, he had them murdered, as they reported to his camp like the loyal underlings they were. By June of the following year, Kuyucu's elimination of the remnants of the Jelālī leaders was complete and the Great Jelālī Revolt was put to rest.

SIGNIFICANCE

The Great Jelālī Revolts affected the Ottoman Empire profoundly. They weakened the Ottoman response to an invading Persia, devastated Anatolian agriculture, and eliminated separate provincial authority. By using violence, political subterfuge, and his army, Grand Vizier Kuyucu Murad Paşa successfully consolidated power in the central Ottoman government, eliminating any provincial independence by purging the Jelālīs.

Unfortunately, the battles left Anatolia and its farmland in ruins. The Anatolian peasants had abandoned their small holdings, and they did not return. The land remained uncultivated and famines swept the Anatolian plateau. Military leaders who settled in the Anatolian provinces after the revolts created large private ranches. They ran livestock rather than plant crops, which further disrupted the agrarian tradition.

The long-lasting effects on rural life left the Ottoman provinces defenseless against an encroaching Persian army. The Ottoman government had to spend its resources quelling the Jelālī Revolts that it had little left to create an imperial army to send against Persia. In 1603, Persia had launched an offensive against the Ottoman Empire. By 1608, Persia had regained many of the provinces it had previously lost to the Turks, including the Caucasus, thereby taking away from the Turks an agricultural region. By 1612, Persia imposed a peace settlement that forced the Turks to relinquish most of the territory they had gained in 1590. Eradicating the revolts caused the Ottoman Empire to lose many inhabitants as well. The empire was just beginning its long and painful decline.

—*Peggy E. Alford*

FURTHER READING

Barkey, Karen. *Bandits and Bureaucrats: The Ottoman Route to State Centralization*. Ithaca, N.Y.: Cornell University Press, 1994. An in-depth look at the dynamics of Ottoman state centralization and the roles played by the Jelālīs.

Faroqhi, Suraiya. *Coping with the State: Political Conflict and Crime in the Ottoman Empire, 1550-1720.* Istanbul, Turkey: Isis Press, 1995. A collection of previously published articles by Faroqhi that outline the impact of the Jelālī Revolts on the Ottoman government and the people of Anatolia.

Kinross, Lord. *The Ottoman Centuries: The Rise and Fall of the Turkish Empire.* New York: Morrow Quill, 1977. Kinross explains the circumstances that brought the Jelālīs together and their devastating effects on Anatolian agriculture and society.

McCarthy, James. *The Ottoman Turks: An Introductory History to 1923.* New York: Addison Wesley Longman, 1997. McCarthy supplies extensive background information on the Jelālī Revolts and their effects on the Ottoman Empire.

SEE ALSO: 1602-1639: Ottoman-Ṣafavid Wars; 1603-1617: Reign of Sultan Ahmed I; Nov. 11, 1606: Treaty of Zsitvatorok; May 19, 1622: Janissary Revolt and Osman II's Assassination; 1623-1640: Murad IV Rules the Ottoman Empire; 1638: Waning of the *Devshirme* System; 1656-1676: Ottoman Empire's Brief Recovery; July 14-Sept. 12, 1683: Defeat of the Ottomans at Vienna.

RELATED ARTICLES in *Great Lives from History: The Seventeenth Century, 1601-1700:* ʿAbbās the Great; Merzifonlu Kara Mustafa Paşa; Murad IV.

November 11, 1606
TREATY OF ZSITVATOROK

The treaty between the Ottoman Empire and the Holy Roman Empire, which ended the Fifteen Years' War fought in Hungary and Transylvania, laid the groundwork for the constitutional rights and self-administration of the restored Hungarian Estates, and revived the long-vacant office of Palatine. In addition, virtual freedom of religion was guaranteed throughout the kingdom and principality.

LOCALE: Zsitvatorok, near Komáron, Hungary (now Slovakia)

CATEGORIES: Wars, uprisings, and civil unrest; government and politics

KEY FIGURES

Murad III (1546-1595), Ottoman sultan, r. 1574-1595

Mehmed III (1566-1603), Ottoman sultan, r. 1595-1603

Ahmed I (1590-1617), Ottoman sultan, r. 1603-1617

Rudolf II (1552-1612), Holy Roman Emperor, r. 1576-1612

Matthias (1557-1619), Rudolf's younger brother, archduke of Austria, king of Hungary, and Holy Roman Emperor, r. 1612-1619

Sigismund Báthory (1572-1613), prince of Transylvania, r. 1581-1599

István Bocskay (1557-1606), prince of Transylvania, r. 1605-1606

Gabriel Bethlen (1580-1629), prince of Transylvania, r. 1613-1629

SUMMARY OF EVENT

Upon the death of Süleyman the Magnificent (r. 1520-1566), the sprawling medieval kingdom of Hungary consisted of three parts: southern and southwestern Hungary, ruled from Buda, was part of the Ottoman Empire; the principality of Transylvania, ruled from Gyulafehérvár (now Alba Iuria, Romania), was an Ottoman vassal; and the north, with its capital at Pozsony (now Bratislava), was under Habsburg, rule as Royal Hungary, for which the emperor paid an annual tribute to the sultan. Frontiers remained porous, and there was periodic raiding from both sides. All these lands suffered severely from the ravages of war, depopulation, enslavement, famine, plague, and starvation.

Such was the background to the Fifteen Years' War, which began in 1591 and lasted until the Treaty of Zsitvatorok in 1606. From 1591, frontier incidents intensified, but expanded to all-out war when the aged Ottoman grand vizier Koca Sinan Paşa, conscious of a loss of momentum under the feeble rule of Murad III and sensing danger on the northern frontier, took the field in person in 1593. This danger came not from the somnolent and increasingly erratic emperor Rudolf II but from the sadistic prince of Transylvania, Sigismund Báthory, who regarded as his religious mission the end of his subordination to Constantinople. Báthory's stance implied an alliance with the Habsburgs, something previous princes of Transylvania had avoided. With Gyulafehérvár equal distance from Constantinople and Vienna, it made sense to the rulers of

Transylvania to balance each powerful neighbor against the other.

By 1594, Sinan Paşa had captured Györ, the gateway to Vienna. Sensing a renewed threat to the heart of Christendom, Pope Clement VIII launched a Holy League and provided funds for Rudolf to lead a grand alliance against the Turks. Meanwhile, in his initial advance into Hungary, Sinan Paşa summoned Báthory as the sultan's vassal to support him, but Báthory failed to appear, despite the urging of the pro-Ottoman faction among the Transylvanian nobility. Sinan Paşa unleashed the Crimean Tatars on Transylvania, and Báthory abdicated in 1593, only to reappear in 1594 and stage against the pro-Ottoman faction a bloodbath horrible enough to silence opposition.

For the moment, Báthory had a loyal lieutenant in a distant kinsman, István Bocskay, whom he sent to Prague to conclude an agreement with Rudolf (January 28, 1595). Báthory would recognize Rudolf as king of Hungary, while Rudolf would recognize Báthory and his descendants as hereditary princes of Transylvania, an agreement to be sealed by marriage with a Habsburg princess. The marriage was a disaster, as Báthory proved to be impotent, further imperiling his fragile sanity. He therefore threw himself into frenetic military action. Transylvanian forces, under the command of Bocskay, expelled the Ottomans from Transylvania, pursued them as far as Bucharest in Walachia, and won a victory over Sinan Paşa at Giurgiu on the lower Danube. To the west, imperial forces retook Visegrád, Vác, and Esztergom.

These victories were momentary successes. A new sultan, Mehmed III, took the field, the first sultan to do so since Süleyman the Magnificent, and advanced to Eger, where the Ottomans had been repulsed in 1552. On October 13, 1595, the great fortress surrendered to the sultan's forces. A powerful imperial army was approaching and Mehmed's forces engaged it at Mezö Kerésztés. The Ottoman army, perhaps 100,000 strong, although wearied by its long march and the Siege of Eger, threw itself upon the entrenched imperial position, and there followed a punishing three days of one of the bloodiest battles of the century. The fabled reputation of the Janissary corps was upheld, and Mezö Kerésztés came to be regarded as one of the greatest Ottoman victories. However, the Turks were too exhausted to press home the advantage, although for the remaining decade, the military edge lay mainly with them.

Meanwhile, Báthory, utterly unpredictable, traveled with Bocskay to Prague in January of 1597 to negotiate with Rudolf a divorce, his abdication in return for an an-

nuity and two duchies in Silesia, and the promise of a cardinal's hat. In April, 1598, imperial commissioners took over Transylvania on behalf of the emperor. These arrangements were most unpopular in the principality, where the pro-Ottoman faction reasserted itself. Rudolf, however, faced with resistance, subjected Transylvania to the tender mercies of a brutal Transylvanian mercenary, Giörgio Basta (1550-1607), and the unhappy country was exposed to a savage pacification.

This was Bocskay's moment. He was one of the most remarkable men of the age, and without him the Treaty of Zsitvatorok might never have happened. Born in 1557 in Kolozsvár (Cluj-Napoca, Romania) and a Protestant, he had served Báthory loyally until that prince's erratic behavior became impossible to condone. Despite, however, Bocskay's former friendly relations with the Habsburgs, Rudolf's commissioners dismissed him from command of the army in 1598, and in October, 1604, they sought to seize him and confiscate his estates on the grounds that he had been in communication with the leader of the pro-Ottoman faction, Gabriel Bethlen, who was later prince of Transylvania.

The attempt to seize Bocskay was part of a vicious policy pursued by Rudolf's agents to harass and dispossess the greater Hungarian nobility in the interests of fiscal gain, thereby alienating the class the Habsburgs should have been conciliating. Bocskay, however, had previously recruited a private army of ruthless freebooters known as *hajdus*, in some ways resembling the Ukrainian Cossacks, whom he had recruited for just such a day. The *hajdus* dispersed the imperial forces and marched on Kassa (Košice, Slovakia), where Bocskay, as their leader, made a ceremonial entry on November 11, 1604. He was greeted by Bethlen, who presented him with a sword of office and a *farman* (sultanic degree) from Ahmed I, appointing him prince of Transylvania.

Much of the Hungarian nobility joined Bocskay, imperial garrisons were expelled, and by autumn he was said to have commanded forty thousand men. On February 21, 1605, the Transylvanian diet elected Bocskay their prince, and on April 20, the Hungarian diet, meeting at Szerém (Syrmia, Croatia), named him prince of Hungary. In Constantinople, Ahmed I appointed him king, and on November 11, 1605, the grand vizier, Lala Mehmed, brought Bocskay a jewel-encrusted crown. However, Bocskay was a cautious man, and while he accepted the crown as a personal gift, he hesitated to alienate the Habsburgs by accepting the office.

By this time, the war had dragged on for more than a decade, with both sides exhausted. Archduke Matthias of

Austria, devious and ambitious, was bent on supplanting his brother, the near-insane Rudolf, and sought to woo the Hungarian nobility. Representatives of the latter came to Vienna in 1606 to negotiate the settlement, which made possible the Treaty of Zsitvatorok and finally brought to an end the Fifteen Years' War. With Bocskay as mediator, Ahmed I agreed that a single payment of 200,000 thalers from the emperor should replace the annual tribute. Significant for the future, Rudolf's title as emperor received official Ottoman recognition, the first time a sultan had ever recognized an infidel ruler as a near equal. Territorially, the frontiers remained much as they had been in 1591, except that the Ottomans retained Eger and Nagykanizsa. Shortly afterward, Bocskay died mysteriously in Kassa (December 29, 1606), said to have been poisoned on Matthias's orders, and on November 16, 1608, Matthias himself was crowned king of Hungary in Pozsony.

SIGNIFICANCE

The Fifteen Years' War, with its immense loss of life and devastation, marked a historical turning point. In the course of the war, the Ottomans modified their practice of annual expeditions from Constantinople in favor of leaving garrisons permanently in the country, with disastrous consequences for its inhabitants. Vast areas were depopulated, many villages were permanently abandoned, and agricultural land reverted to pastoralism. The central Hungarian lands and Transylvania suffered most from the incessant campaigning, whereas those border regions inhabited by Slovaks, Romanians, and Serbs were much less affected. This had important consequences for future patterns of settlement and demographic growth.

As for the treaty itself, in the words of Denis Sinor in his *History of Hungary* (1959), the Ottomans, whose resources were less threadbare than those of their opponents, and "though [they were] still redoubtable, had to recognize, . . . that their enemies must be treated with a modicum of consideration."

—*Gavin R. G. Hambly*

FURTHER READING

Finkel, C. *The Administration of Warfare: The Ottoman Military Campaigns in Hungary, 1693-1606*. Vienna, Austria: VWGO, 1988. A detailed account from the Ottoman perspective.

Greene, Molly. *A Shared World: Christians and Muslims in the Early Modern Mediterranean*. Princeton, N.J.: Princeton University Press, 2000. Greene explores the Crete of the time of the Ottoman conquest and after.

Makkai, Laszlo, and Zoltan Szasz. *History of Transylvania*. Vol. 2. Toronto: Hungarian Research Institute of Canada, 2002. A detailed account of the Ottoman presence in Transylvania.

Murphey, Rhoads. *Ottoman Warfare, 1500-1700*. New Brunswick, N.J.: Rutgers University Press, 1999. A penetrating study of tactics, logistics, and military psychology.

Shaw, Stanford J. *History of the Ottoman Empire and Modern Turkey*. 2 vols. New York: Cambridge University Press, 1976. A detailed survey of Ottoman history.

Sinor, Denis. *History of Hungary*. London: George Allen & Unwin, 1959. An excellent summary of the war.

Sugar, Peter F. *Southeastern Europe Under Ottoman Rule, 1354-1804*. Seattle: University of Washington Press, 1977. An authoritative account of Ottoman involvement in the Balkans.

_____, ed. *A History of Hungary*. Bloomington: Indiana University Press, 1990. A thoughtful presentation of the war in a broader setting.

Wheatcroft, Andrew. *Infidels: A History of the Conflict Between Christendom and Islam*. New York: Random House, 2004. Examines the continuing religious conflicts between the Christian West and the Islamic Middle East.

SEE ALSO: 1602-1639: Ottoman-Ṣafavid Wars; 1603-1617: Reign of Sultan Ahmed I; Sept., 1606-June, 1609: Great Jelālī Revolts; 1638: Waning of the *Devshirme* System; Aug. 22, 1645-Sept., 1669: Turks Conquer Crete; Summer, 1672-Fall, 1676: Ottoman-Polish Wars; July 14-Sept. 12, 1683: Defeat of the Ottomans at Vienna; Jan. 26, 1699: Treaty of Karlowitz.

RELATED ARTICLES in *Great Lives from History: The Seventeenth Century, 1601-1700:* Merzifonlu Kara Mustafa Paşa; Bohdan Khmelnytsky; Kösem Sultan; Leopold I; Murad IV; Mustafa I.

Beginning 1607
NEO-CONFUCIANISM BECOMES JAPAN'S OFFICIAL PHILOSOPHY

The scholar Hayashi Razan designed a philosophical system based upon Chinese Neo-Confucianism that helped create a stable hierarchical structure for the Tokugawa shogunate, its national bureacracy, its samurai warriors, and Japanese society as a whole. Neo-Confucianism remained the state philosophical system of Tokugawa Japan until that dynasty came to an end in 1867.

LOCALE: Japan
CATEGORIES: Cultural and intellectual history; government and politics

KEY FIGURES
Tokugawa Ieyasu (1543-1616), Japanese shogun, r. 1603-1605
Hayashi Razan (1583-1657), Japanese Neo-Confucian scholar
Kumazawa Banzan (1619-1691), Japanese political philosopher and chief minister of Okayama prefecture, 1647-1656
Tokugawa Hidetada (1579-1632), Japanese shogun, r. 1605-1623
Tokugawa Iemitsu (1604-1651), Japanese shogun, r. 1623-1651
Yamaga Sokō (1622-1685), Japanese military scholar, teacher, and philosopher who developed the samurai code of *Bushidō*

SUMMARY OF EVENT
Neo-Confucianism was the intellectual progeny of a sophisticated system of thought originally put forward by China's great philosophical sage, Confucius, in the sixth century B.C.E. Using his ideas as their foundation, Neo-Confucian scholars of the Song Dynasty (Sung; 960-1279) created an intellectual paradigm based upon three philosophical concepts. The primary premise of this new system was that the universe and human society were based upon natural laws and that these laws could be discovered and understood through the use of reason. Furthermore, Neo-Confucian philosophers believed that the laws governing the world and society represented objective truths that were both universal and unchanging.

Most Chinese Song intellectuals were not concerned with the great metaphysical questions, however, but focused instead on how the rational Confucian model could help solve the problems of the human condition. Most important, they wanted to develop a model that would ensure good government, peace, and prosperity, which in turn would maintain a secure social and political order. These scholars also believed in the importance of history. They wanted to use the records of past dynasties, both their accomplishments and their failures, as a source of knowledge and as a learning tool for future generations. Study of these records would enable historians to discover the natural laws of history, which then could be used to create a well-ordered and prosperous nation. The Neo-Confucians also used historical biography. They wanted to present the actions of historical figures as examples of the importance of high moral and ethical standards to the well-being of society.

As it spread, however, Neo-Confucianism also fostered a negative xenophobic and ethnocentric response in the cultures that embraced it. This response was based upon the belief that Neo-Confucianism was the only true philosophical system and any culture that followed a different paradigm was necessarily inferior to Neo-Confucian cultures. In the case of Japan, this belief would first manifest itself in the nation's isolationist tendencies during the early modern period and later in its aggressive, militaristic attitude toward the rest of East Asia.

In 1603, when the emperor appointed Tokugawa Ieyasu as shogun, Japan was still suffering from two centuries of civil conflict and the bloody wars of unification fought by Ieyasu's two predecessors, Oda Nobunaga and Toyotomi Hideyoshi. Ieyasu knew he needed to adopt a philosophical model that would bring stability to his ravaged nation. China had long been the cultural center of East Asia, and its philosophical systems and historical analyses had an impact on scholars of every nation in the region. It is no surprise, then, that Ieyasu looked to Chinese philosophy for his model.

Ieyasu had plans not only to stabilize the nation, but also to create a stable and lasting shogunal dynasty for his family. In 1605, he officially retired from the shogunate, passing the title to his son, Tokugawa Hidetada, but he continued to wield power from behind the scenes until his death in 1616. Ieyasu decided that he would attempt to apply Neo-Confucian principles to the operation of the Tokugawa government. He hoped this Chinese philosophical system would provide the government with the necessary skills to bring peace and prosperity to Japan.

In 1607, Ieyasu turned to an orthodox Neo-Confucian scholar, Hayashi Razan, who in time would serve four Tokugawa shoguns, becoming the Tokugawas' top adviser.

127

Hayashi created a Japanese form of Neo-Confucianism based upon his belief in natural law and in an orderly universe. He created a cosmic model centered on the Confucian "Great Chain of Being" paradigm, which asserted that the universe originated with a heavenly power known as the Supreme Ultimate. This creative energy set into motion a process that brought into existence the basic cosmic harmony, Yang (motion) and Yin (lack of motion). It was from these two forces of nature that the five basic elements of the universe—wood, fire, earth, metal, and water were created. In turn, all life on earth evolved from these same elements.

Hayashi was convinced that he had created a philosophical model that proved the connection between heaven, the Supreme Ultimate, and all life on earth. He also stated that this order extended to the five basic Confucian social relationships that created a social hierarchy governing the interactions of the shogun and his subjects, patriarchal family relations, and the intercourse among friends. Hayashi, like Confucius, believed that a nation's success could be guaranteed if it remained faithful to this social orthodoxy.

Most important, Hayashi believed that the natural laws governing the social order, which could assure the well-being of Japan, could be discovered and comprehended by the use of reason. He thus emphasized the importance of the empirical scientific study of all aspects of the natural world and human relationships. He also stated that if in fact these natural laws could be discovered, understood, and applied, it followed logically that this knowledge could be used to create a group of elite scholar-bureaucrats that would form the foundation of a well-ordered government, ensuring peace and prosperity for the Japanese people. To this end, in 1630 Hayashi convinced Tokugawa Iemitsu, the third Tokugawa shogun, to create a national university where the best and the brightest from Japanese society could obtain the education needed to become members of this Neo-Confucian elite. The creation of a Neo-Confucian educational system was Hayashi's greatest achievement, and members of his family controlled the National University well into the modern era.

Later in the century, Kumazawa Banzan, a follower of the Confucian sect known as the School of the Mind, challenged Hayashi's philosophical model. Kumazawa also believed in natural law and in the power of the Supreme Ultimate, but he differed from Hayashi in his assertion that the mind intuitively knew the good and that, through the practice of disciplined introspection, one could know the will of heaven. This belief in using intuition and introspection to guide conduct directly challenged Hayashi's

premise that one must engage in rational, empirical investigation of the world beyond the self in order to gain an understanding of the natural laws one should follow.

Kumazawa also developed a political philosophy that advocated developing a benevolent government guided by a class of talented but very humble bureaucrats. Many of his writings foreshadow the concept of the welfare state, in which government agencies control prices, execute social programs, and equitably manage the nation's resources. Ultimately, however, Kumazawa lost the intellectual battle for the direction of Neo-Confucianism to Hayashi and his followers; he spent the last years of his life under house arrest.

In spite of philosophical challenges by men like Kumazawa, the success of the Neo-Confucian system designed by Hayashi and perpetuated by the Tokugawa shoguns did create a period of peace and prosperity in Japan. Ironically, this very prosperity posed a unique problem for the Tokugawas: Japan's warrior class, the samurai, and their warlords, the daimyos, had been occupied fighting each other for centuries, but with relative peace inside the nation, the idle warriors represented a potential danger to their military ruler, since there was no one else for them to fight. This threat was finally defused by reinforcing the principles of a hierarchical class structure found in the writings of Neo-Confucian scholars.

The most important philosopher dealing with this question of the potential danger of the samurai was Yamaga Sokō, who was a masterless samurai, or *rōnin*. Yamaga used the Confucian social model to create a distinct warrior class that would follow a strict martial code, *Bushidō*, which itself was based upon the Neo-Confucian social structure. Tokugawa Ieyasu had already helped to form the underpinnings of this warrior code when he issued the *Buke shohatto* (1615), an imperial edict that governed the actions of the samurai class. The edict had also established the samurai as the only group in Japanese society that was allowed to bear arms. This in turn prevented any rival daimyo from arming thousands of peasants and creating a potentially destabilizing army.

Over time, the *Bushidō* code would have a far-reaching impact on Japanese society. Yamaga envisioned the samurai becoming an example of the highest standards of Neo-Confucianism, which would reinforce the social structure of the Tokugawa shogunate as a whole. First and foremost, *Bushidō* emphasized duty and self-sacrifice on the part of the warrior. His first concern was loyalty to his daimyo, and he was always ready to give up his life in the service of his lord. Like Neo-Confucianism, *Bushidō* also regulated a samurai's actions among his family and friends. He was always regarded as an individual that both family and friends could count on to be steadfast and loyal.

SIGNIFICANCE

Neo-Confucianism created a political system that enabled the Tokugawa clan effectively to govern a nation that in essence was made up of 250 independent feudal regions. It also helped create a national social structure whose hierarchal characteristics supported the Tokugawa autocracy. Neo-Confucianism formed the basis of the code of *Bushidō*, which created a paradigm of loyalty and self-sacrifice that controlled the potential danger posed by Japan's warrior elite. Finally, the Neo-Confucian emphasis on empirical scientific study ensured the success of Japan's eventual transition to industrialization during the Meiji Period (1868-1912).

—*Richard D. Fitzgerald*

FURTHER READING

De Bary, William Theodore. *Sources of Japanese Tradition.* Vol. 2. New York: Columbia University Press,

1963. An excellent collection of primary source documents.

Jansen, Marius B. *The Making of Modern Japan.* Cambridge, Mass.: Harvard University Press, 2000. An excellent one-volume history of Japan from the Tokugawa shogunate to Japan's economic dominance in the 1970's. Maps. Index.

Totman, Conrad. *Early Modern Japan.* Berkeley: University of California Press, 1993. The best single-volume account of early modern Japan. Charts. Index.

SEE ALSO: 1603: Tokugawa Shogunate Begins; 1615: Promulgation of the *Buke shohatto* and *Kinchū narabini kuge shohatto*; 1624-1640's: Japan's Seclusion Policy; Oct., 1637-Apr. 15, 1638: Shimabara Revolt; 1651-1652: Edo Rebellions; 1651-1680: Ietsuna Shogunate; 1680-1709: Reign of Tsunayoshi as Shogun.

RELATED ARTICLES in *Great Lives from History: The Seventeenth Century, 1601-1700:* Seki Kōwa; Tokugawa Ieyasu; Tokugawa Tsunayoshi; Wang Fuzhi; Yui Shōsetsu.

February 24, 1607
FIRST PERFORMANCE OF MONTEVERDI'S *LA FAVOLA D'ORFEO*

Between 1597 and 1600, the first operas were performed. However, these tentative forays into the emerging genre failed to employ music as a dramatic, rather than a merely ornamental, element. The first work to realize the potential of operatic performance fully was Monteverdi's La favola d'Orfeo, *considered the first masterpiece of the genre.*

LOCALE: Florence and Mantua (now in Italy)
CATEGORIES: Theater; music

KEY FIGURES

Claudio Monteverdi (1567-1643), composer of *La favola d'Orfeo*
Alessandro Striggio the Younger (1573?-1630), librettist of *La favola d'Orfeo*
Jacopo Peri (1561-1633), composer of *Dafne* and *Euridice*, the first operas
Ottavio Rinuccini (1562-1621), poet and librettist of *Dafne* and *Euridice*
Girolamo Mei (1519-1594), Florentine scholar who wrote a treatise on ancient music

Giovanni Bardi (1534-1612), Florentine aristocrat who hosted the meetings of the *camerata Bardi*, a group of scholars, artists, and musicians

SUMMARY OF EVENT

In the last two decades of the sixteenth century, several groups of literati, comprising poets, musicians, philosophers, and members of the Florentine aristocracy, assembled at each others' houses on a regular—albeit informal—basis to discuss the current state of Italian culture. A favorite meeting place was the palace of Count Giovanni Bardi, himself a musician, writer, and scientist. The group that met at the count's palace became known as the *camerata Bardi*, and it included Vincenzo Galilei (c. 1520-1591), lutenist, composer, music theorist, and father of Galileo; Giulio Caccini (1545-1618), composer, singer, and a protege of Cosimo I de' Medici; the poet Ottavio Rinuccini; the composer Jacopo Corsi (1561-1602), himself a noted patron of the arts; and the composer and singer Jacopo Peri. The discussions among these learned people, their correspondence, and their published writings became the theoretical basis on which the first entirely sung dramatic spectacles were composed and performed during the last decade of the sixteenth century and the first years of the seventeenth century.

A strong influence on the ideas of the *camerata Bardi* was Girolamo Mei, a Florentine by birth but a resident of Rome since about 1560. Mei and Vincenzo Galilei corresponded extensively on topics ranging from descriptions of musical composition and performance in the works of classical authors to the present state of sixteenth century music. Mei believed that monody was a more suitable way of setting words to music than the excessive polyphony that was the fashion of the day—and which, by virtue of its contrapuntal intricacies, obscured not only the individual words being sung but also the general meaning of the text being set.

Galilei, in his *Dialogo della musica antica, et della moderna* (1581; *Dialogue of Ancient and Modern Music*, 2003), concluded that, based on reports by ancient authors, the emotional response of the ancients to monody must have been much more intense than the response of sixteenth century listeners to contrapuntal music. To recapture the intense emotional effects of ancient music, Galilei recommended that singers study the techniques of declamation practiced by actors. He believed that such a course of study would help singers discover what inflections of the voice best matched particular emotions expressed in a text, as well as enabling them to understand how such inflections could appropriately reflect the social, economic, and marital status of the characters they portrayed through song.

The first staged operatic performances took place in conjunction with major social events, such as carnivals and aristocratic marriages: for the Carnivals of 1591 Emilio de' Cavalieri (c. 1550-1602) set to music and staged two works, now lost; of these, one was *La disperazione di Fileno* (pr. 1591), including a superb performance by the renowned singer Vittoria Archilei (1550-c. 1620). Cavalieri's works are called opera by some scholars, but they are usually categorized as intermezzi or pastorals, which anticipate but do not yet achieve the status of opera. For the Carnival of 1597, Rinuccini and Peri collaborated, at the urgings of Jacopo Corsi, in the making of the text and music for *Dafne* (pr. 1597, partial pb. 1600), the first work to count as opera in the estimation of most historians.

On October 6, 1600, at the Palazzo Pitti, the wedding of Henry IV of France and Marie de Médicis was celebrated with a splendidly staged performance of Rinuccini and Peri's *Euridice* (pr. 1600, pb. 1601), the story of Orpheus told in verse with the text sung in its entirety.

Claudio Monteverdi, composer of the first great opera, La favola d'Orfeo. *(Library of Congress)*

The dramatic structure of the libretto was modeled on ancient Greek tragedy—a genre intentionally and artfully emulated by Italian humanists. The Prologue was sung by Lady Tragedy, who introduced the story and the characters. The subject matter was most appropriate for a musical play, as the legend centered around a legendary musician of the ancient world, the tragic story surrounding the death of his wife, Euridice, on their wedding day, and Orpheus's journey to the Underworld to rescue her.

Contemporary writers described the lavish sets, which included serene pastoral landscapes filled with light for the nuptial scenes and the burning flames of hell for Orpheus's descent to Inferno in search of his beloved Euridice. The costumes were kept simple, elegant, and of classic cut. The dramatic structure, the music—both vocal and instrumental—and the stage setting were in perfect harmony with the nature of the subject and designed to address an audience whose members were not only of the upper classes, but also well acquainted with ancient and modern literature and music. In other words, refined *cognoscenti* were the opera's target audience. *Euridice* is the earliest opera still extant in its entirety, including both music and libretto.

The new genre took root, and interest in it spread from Florence to other Italian cities and courts. One of these was Mantua, which on February 27, 1607, played host to the work that is regarded by many as the first fully realized opera, *La favola d'Orfeo* (pr. 1607, libretto pb. 1607, score pb. 1609, 1615). The work featured libretto by the poet and Humanist Alessandro Striggio the Younger and music composed by Claudio Monteverdi. It was designed in conjunction with the long-planned marriage between Francesco Gonzaga, the heir to the ducal throne of Mantua, and Margaret of Savoy. This marriage was postponed several times for political reasons, however, and ultimately took place in 1608, a year after the opera was first performed. Monteverdi would compose a second opera, *Arianna* (pr. 1608, partial pub. 1608, 1623), for the actual wedding.

La favola d'Orfeo, like its predecessor *Euridice*, included a prologue (sung by Lady Music) and comprised five acts incorporating arias, recitatives, orchestral interludes, dances, and choral numbers, all preceded by an opening instrumental overture, which Monteverdi called a *toccata*. The singers for its initial performance were some of the best that the country had to offer. The tenor Francesco Rasi sang the part of Orfeo; the castrato Girolamo Bacchini sang Euridice's part; and the famous Florentine castrato Giovan Gualberto Magli, a pupil of Caccini, sang the character that personified Music. The backdrops, representing the plains of Thrace and the Inferno, were painted and hung on the walls of a large room in the ducal palace. Due to the immense success of this first performance, Francesco Gonzaga ordered a second one to be given on March 1.

SIGNIFICANCE

La favola d'Orfeo is the earliest work that historians of opera routinely evaluate as a masterpiece or a work of genius. The qualities that justify such evaluations are notoriously difficult to define, but in the case of this opera they have several sources. *La favola d'Orfeo* skillfully combines themes and tropes of ancient myth and classical tragedy with musical conventions of the sixteenth and seventeenth centuries, creating a truly new form that is nevertheless in substantial dialogue with its source material. Music does not merely comment on or heighten the drama but becomes an integral part of the dramatic technique of the work. This integration occurs both within specific moments—as when two characters' vocal parts emphasize different chords to indicate lack of understanding between them—and on a larger scale, as repeated musical patterns are used to unify specific sections or entire acts of the opera.

Opera continued to evolve throughout the seven-

teenth century. For example, while *La favola d'Orfeo* and its Florentine predecessors addressed a limited, aristocratic audience and were performed as a rule in the homes of the noble and wealthy, Venetian opera took a different direction. In 1637, the Teatro San Cassiano opened its doors to anyone who could afford the price of a ticket. This in turn had a tremendous impact on the development of the genre. For the Florentine literati, the libretto had reigned supreme, and music was simply meant to enhance the meaning of the text; the more numerous and somewhat more plebeian Venetian public, however, demanded sumptuous spectacles and elaborate musical numbers. In 1678, following in the footsteps of Venice, Hamburg was the second European city to open a public opera house.

Opera at Venice grew into a grandiose affair that included large orchestras, choruses, and elaborate machinery allowing gods to descend from the sky (*deus ex machina*) and sieges and naval battles to be represented onstage. Two of Monteverdi's later operas, *Il ritorno d'Ulisse* (pr. 1641; Ulysses' homecoming) and *L'Incoronazione di Poppea* (pr. 1642; the coronation of Poppea) were composed for and set in Venice. The extent to which the demand for opera in Venice grew is best illustrated by the extraordinary output of one of Monteverdi's pupils, Pier Francesco Cavalli (1602-1676), who composed no less than forty-one works in the genre.

The tradition of lavish performances involving extremely complex stage effects was exported to other European cities and courts: A famous example is the performance of *Il pomo d'oro* (pr. 1668; the golden apple) by Antonio Cesti (1623-1669) and Francesco Sbarra (1611-1668), written for the 1666 wedding between Emperor Leopold I and Margaret of Spain but not performed until Margaret's birthday in 1668.

England developed its own brand of opera, a private, aristocratic entertainment called a masque, comprising closed numbers such as dances, songs, recitatives, and choruses. Of the surviving masques, the most elaborate was *Cupid and Death* (pr. 1653, rev. 1659), a collaboration between playwright James Shirley (1596-1666) and composers Christopher Gibbons (1615-1676) and Matthew Locke (c. 1621/1622-1677).

—Luminita Florea

FURTHER READING

Arnold, Denis. *Monteverdi*. 3d ed., rev. by Tim Carter. London: Dent, 1990. Examines Monteverdi's life and works and devotes several chapters to Monteverdi's dramatic music.

Carter, Tim. *Monteverdi's Musical Theatre*. New Haven, Conn.: Yale University Press, 2002. An exhaustive survey of Monteverdi's compositions involving drama, music, and dance, including discussions of his true operas.

Ossi, Massimo M. *Divining the Oracle: Monteverdi's Seconda Prattica*. Chicago: University of Chicago Press, 2003. A detailed discussion of the old versus the new style of vocal writing in the works of Monteverdi, focusing especially on his madrigals, but touching upon his other vocal works such as the operas.

Pirotta, Nino, and Elena Povoledo. *Music and Theatre from Poliziano to Monteverdi*. 1969. Translated by Karen Eales. New York: Cambridge University Press, 1982. Traces the early history of opera, from Angelo Poliziano's *Orfeo* to the *Orfeo* of Monteverdi; the book won the Otto Kinkeldey Award of the American Musicological Society.

SEE ALSO: Early 17th cent.: Revenge Tragedies Become Popular in England; c. 1601: Emergence of Baroque Music; c. 1601-1613: Shakespeare Produces His Later Plays; c. 1601-1620: Emergence of Baroque Art; 1603-1629: Okuni Stages the First Kabuki Dance Dramas; Sept. 2, 1642: Closing of the Theaters; 1664: Molière Writes *Tartuffe*; c. 1673: Buxtehude Begins His Abendmusiken Concerts.

RELATED ARTICLES in *Great Lives from History: The Seventeenth Century, 1601-1700:* Gian Lorenzo Bernini; Thomas Betterton; Francesca Caccini; Girolamo Frescobaldi; Jean-Baptiste Lully; Claudio Monteverdi; Henry Purcell; Heinrich Schütz.

May 14, 1607
JAMESTOWN IS FOUNDED

Jamestown was the first permanent English settlement in the New World. While not considered a success, the English experience of founding the colony informed all subsequent endeavors, and the colony thus established the patterns and practices through which the British Empire would come to dominate North America.

LOCALE: Jamestown, Virginia
CATEGORIES: Colonization; expansion and land acquisition

KEY FIGURES

John Smith (1580-1631), second president of the council of Jamestown

Powhatan (Wahunsenacawh; c. 1550-1618), head of the Powhatan Confederacy, r. late sixteenth century-1618

Pocahontas (Matoaka; c. 1596-1617), daughter of Powhatan and wife of John Rolfe

Thomas Smythe (1558?-1623), merchant and treasurer of the London Company, 1609-1618

John Rolfe (1585-1622), English-born Virginia colonist and official

Opechancanough (c. 1545-1644/1646), Pamunkey chief, r. before 1607-1644/1646, and head of the Powhatan Confederacy, r. 1618-1644/1646

Sir Edwin Sandys (1561-1629), member of Parliament and treasurer of the London Company, 1619-1620

Christopher Newport (1561-1617), English captain of the first expedition to Jamestown

James I (1566-1625), king of England, r. 1603-1625, and king of Scotland as James VI, r. 1567-1625

SUMMARY OF EVENT

On December 20, 1606, the London Company (also known as the Virginia Company of London), a stock company acting under a charter granted by King James I, sent out three ships, the *Godspeed*, the *Discovery*, and the *Susan Constant*, under the command of Christopher Newport. The ships carried 144 settlers who were to establish a trading post in Virginia. Investors in the company, which was modeled after the highly successful East India Company, hoped to profit from trade with Native Americans, the discovery of precious metals, and the production of goods in short supply in England. The settlers hoped to make their fortune in the New World. The English government saw a chance to establish a foothold in North America. During the eighteen years of the London Company's existence, however, one disaster followed another; the investors lost their money and four out of five of the settlers died of disease or Indian attacks. Nevertheless, by the time the company's charter was annulled in 1624, Virginia had evolved the pattern of settlement through which the British Empire would spread over much of North America.

On May 13, 1607, Captain Newport selected a low-lying peninsula some sixty miles inland from the coast as

John Smith believed that Powhatan was about to have him killed when the sachem's daughter, Pocahontas, intervened to save him. Modern scholars believe she may merely have been playing her assigned role in a tribal ritual Smith did not understand. (Gay Brothers)

the site of the new settlement and disembarked the one hundred men and four boys who had survived the voyage. With water on three sides and a narrow neck, the site chosen was militarily defensible, though the stagnant swamps nearby would pose significant health hazards. It soon became clear that the settlers were poorly adapted for their task. Too many of the colonists were gentlemen and their personal servants who were unwilling to work with their hands; too few were farmers or ordinary laborers willing to work in the fields. Unable or unwilling to raise their own food, the English depended on Virginia Indians for supplies. When they could not buy food, the settlers seized it by force, setting off a series of small-scale guerrilla wars between the two groups. Soon after Newport left the settlement, men began to sicken and die. When he returned in January, 1608, with more supplies and settlers, only thirty-eight colonists were still alive.

Under the forceful leadership of John Smith, a veteran of European wars against the Ottoman Empire, the colony was able to secure itself during the following year. When Smith assumed control in the winter of 1608-1609, he made it the rule "that he that will not worke shall not eate (except by sicknesse he be disabled)." Smith had

previously established friendly relations with local Indian tribes. While exploring north of Jamestown in December, 1607, he had been captured by a band of Powhatan Indians. Smith believed that he had been condemned to death by Powhatan and saved only by the personal intervention of the chief's favorite daughter, Pocahontas. Modern scholars have suggested that Smith misunderstood an adoption ceremony in which Powhatan, impressed by Smith's bravery, had him ritually killed and reborn as a member of the tribe. In either case, Smith's relations with Powhatan enabled him to get vital supplies of corn for the settlers. Under his command, only seven or eight men died that winter.

As it became clear that Virginia had no easily extractable mineral wealth, usable native labor force, or significant trade opportunities with the Indians, the London Company began to rethink its strategy. Led by its treasurer, Sir Thomas Smythe, the company decided to try to increase the population of the colony and have the colonists produce goods such as sugar, dye woods, and naval stores (masts, tar, pitch, and resin), which might be profitably sold in England. More shares of stock were issued and prospective settlers were promised one hundred acres of land if they would work for the company in Virginia for seven years. In June, 1609, the company sent a new fleet with five hundred men and one hundred women, as well as large quantities of equipment and supplies. The four hundred settlers who survived the voyage arrived weakened and debilitated. Again they failed to plant crops; Smith, who had been wounded in a gunpowder explosion, had returned to England. At the end of the winter of 1609-1610, the sixty colonists who were still alive decided to abandon the settlement. By chance, when they set sail for England, they were met by a new fleet bringing more men and supplies and turned back to Jamestown.

Sir Thomas Smythe continued to raise money and send out settlers. The imposition of a harsh disciplinary code prevented further starvation in Jamestown, but the company still did not show any profit. Finally, the stockholders revolted and replaced Smythe as treasurer in 1619 with Sir Edwin Sandys. Unwilling to abandon the colony, Sandys organized a last great effort. To induce settlers to migrate, the company offered "headrights" of fifty acres to any person who settled or brought settlers to Virginia. Settlers could pool their land holdings into jointly owned tracts or "private plantations." The military discipline previously imposed under Smythe was replaced with a more normal system of civil courts and a representative assembly, the first in America. In the next six years the company sent some forty-five hundred new settlers and tried, still with little success, to get them to provide desirable products for the British market.

Although the company never realized a profit, individual settlers did. After John Rolfe demonstrated in 1614 that West Indian species of tobacco could be grown in Virginia and profitably exported to England, the colony experienced a boom. The company tried and failed to discourage production of what they considered an obnoxious weed. Settlement spread out beyond Jamestown along the banks of the James and other rivers as planters sought to increase their production. By making land freely available, the company had opened the way to wealth for those who could find labor to exploit. Virginians who could afford to buy indentured servants worked them as hard as they dared. A shipload of Africans arrived in 1619. Africans were apparently more expensive than English servants and few were then imported; as late as 1640, there were only 150 blacks in Virginia, some of whom were freemen and landowners.

The spread of population beyond Jamestown was also encouraged by a season of relatively peaceful relations with the Indians after Rolfe married Pocahontas in 1614. The Indians' resentment of the growing expansion of the English simmered under the surface, however. After Powhatan's death, his successor, Opechancanough, organized a massive attempt to drive out the Europe-

---

CAPTAIN JOHN SMITH'S INSTRUCTIONS FOR SETTLING VIRGINIA

In the early 1600's, Captain Smith wrote a detailed treatise instructing the future founders of Jamestown how to go about establishing a colony in Virginia. The following excerpt discusses the selection of a site for the colony.

When it shall please God to send you on the coast of Virginia, you shall do your best endeavour to find out a safe port in the entrance of some navigable river, making choice of such a one as runneth farthest into the land, and if you happen to discover divers portable rivers, and amongst them any one that hath two main branches, if the difference be not great, make choice of that which bendeth most toward the North-west for that way you shall soonest find the other sea.

When you have made choice of the river on which you mean to settle, be not hasty in landing your victuals and munitions; but first let Captain *Newport* discover how far that river may be found navigable, that you [may] make election of the strongest, most wholesome and fertile place; for if you make many removes, besides the loss of time, you shall greatly spoil your victuals and your casks, and with great pain transport it in small boats.

But if you choose your place so far up as a bark of fifty tuns will float, then you may lay all your provisions ashore with ease, and the better receive the trade of all the countries about you in the land; and such a place you may perchance find a hundred miles from the river's mouth, and the further up the better. For if you sit down near the entrance, except it be in some island that is strong by nature, an enemy that may approach you on even ground, may easily pull you out: and if he be driven to seek you a hundred miles [in] the land with boats, you shall from both sides of the river where it is narrowest, so beat them with your muskets as they shall never be able to prevail against you.

Source: From "Instructions by Way of Advice, for the Intended Voyage to Virginia," by John Smith. Quoted in *History of the London Virginia Company*, by E. D. Neill (Albany, N.Y.: 1869), p. 8. The Virtual Jamestown Project. http://etext.lib.virginia .edu/etcbin/jamestown-browse?id=J1039. Accessed April 26, 2005.

VIRGINIA IN 1607

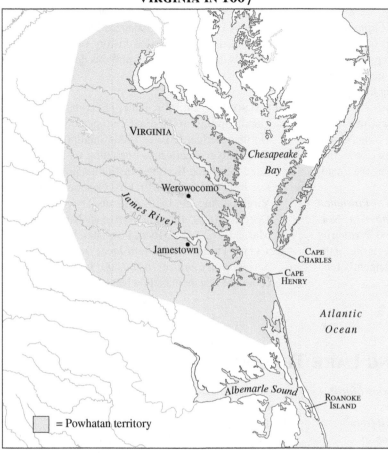

VIRGINIA

Chesapeake Bay

Werowocomo

James River

Jamestown

CAPE CHARLES

CAPE HENRY

Atlantic Ocean

Albemarle Sound

ROANOKE ISLAND

☐ = Powhatan territory

ders and disasters of its first two decades, and the basic pattern for the future had emerged. The British empire in North America would consist of settlement colonies, following the rule of law and practicing self-government, with easily available land acting as a magnet for immigrants.

—*Milton Berman*

FURTHER READING

Abrams, Ann Uhry. *The Pilgrims and Pocahontas: Rival Myths of American Origin*. Boulder, Colo.: Westview Press, 1999. Examines two myths about American origins, one about Jamestown and Pocahontas, the other about the Pilgrims and Plymouth Rock. Compares and contrasts these myths and the messages they convey.

Billings, Warren M., John E. Selby, and Thad W. Tate. *Colonial Virginia: A History*. White Plains, N.Y.: KTO Press, 1986. The section on Jamestown captures the drama of the early decades there.

Bridenbaugh, Carl. *Jamestown, 1544-1699*. New York: Oxford University Press, 1980. This brief (200-page) history emphasizes what Bridenbaugh describes as the "people—red, white, and black—who lived on or near Jamestown Island."

Hawke, David Freeman, ed. *Captain John Smith's History of Virginia: A Selection*. Indianapolis, Ind.: Bobbs-Merrill, 1970. Reprints sections on Virginia from Smith's *Generall Historie of Virginia, New-England, and the Summer Isles*. A major primary source, if suspect given its discrepancies with Smith's more contemporaneous account in his *True Relation*.

Hume, Ivor Noël. *The Virginia Adventure: Roanoke to James Towne*. New York: Alfred A. Knopf, 1994. Historical archaeologist Hume provides an extremely detailed account of the settling of Virginia, comparing primary documents as well as physical evidence and deftly teasing out fact from legend.

Josephy, Alvin M., Jr. *Five Hundred Nations: An Illustrated History of the North American Indians*. New York: Alfred A. Knopf, 1994. Powhatan and Smith are covered in chapter 4 of this lavishly illustrated his-

ans. In March, 1622, the Indians attacked along the rivers, killing at least 347 English. In retaliation, the settlers took up arms and proceeded to destroy the towns and food supplies of the Powhatan Confederacy. Food was short for both Indians and English that winter, and both groups suffered in the near famine conditions. Shocking accounts of the savage treatment of the Indians and of the cruel and brutal treatment of the indentured servants reached England and led to an investigation that recommended revocation of the company's charter.

SIGNIFICANCE

When King James moved to annul the charter in 1624 and assume direct control of the first royal colony in North America, Jamestown appeared to be a failure. The London Company was bankrupt, the shareholders had lost their investment, and only some 1,275 of the approximately 8,500 people who had settled in Virginia remained. The colony, however, had survived all the blun-

tory of North America written from the viewpoint of its original occupants.

LeMay, J. A. Lee. *The American Dream of Captain John Smith*. Charlottesville: University Press of Virginia, 1991. The author provides a step-by-step account of Smith's activities in Virginia, arguing that his writings were essentially truthful, including the episode with Pocahontas.

Price, David A. *Love and Hate in Jamestown: John Smith, Pocahontas, and the Heart of a New Nation*. New York: Random House, 2003. Draws on period letters, chronicles, and documents to relate the founding of the Jamestown colony.

Rountree, Helen C. *Pocahontas's People: The Powhatan Indians of Virginia Through Four Centuries*. Norman: University of Oklahoma Press, 1990. Written by an ethnohistorian and anthropologist, this is one of the best studies of Jamestown and the settlement's relationship to the Powhatan Confederacy.

Vaughan, Alden T. *American Genesis: Captain John Smith and the Founding of Virginia*. Boston: Little, Brown, 1975. A short, balanced biography of Smith combined with a detailed history of Virginia from Smith's departure in 1609 until his death in 1631.

SEE ALSO: Mar. 24, 1603: James I Becomes King of England; Spring, 1604: First European Settlement in North America; 1617-c. 1700: Smallpox Epidemics Kill Native Americans; Beginning c. 1619: Indentured Servitude Becomes Institutionalized in America; July 30-Aug. 4, 1619: First General Assembly of Virginia; Aug. 20, 1619: Africans Arrive in Virginia; Dec. 26, 1620: Pilgrims Arrive in North America; Mar. 22, 1622-Oct., 1646: Powhatan Wars.
RELATED ARTICLES in *Great Lives from History: The Seventeenth Century, 1601-1700:* James I; Opechancanough; Pocahontas; Powhatan; John Smith.

November 28, 1607
MARTIN BEGINS DRAINING LAKE TEXCOCO

Luis de Velasco the Younger entrusted Enrico Martin with the daunting task of draining the lakes surrounding the City of Mexico to protect it from floods and to provide much-needed land for an expanding population. The project was underfunded, and although Martin worked on it for more than twenty years, it was ultimately insufficient to prevent the destruction of the city by flood in 1629.

LOCALE: Mexico City, New Spain (now in Mexico)
CATEGORIES: Science and technology; engineering

KEY FIGURES

Enrico Martin (Henrico Martinez; d. 1632), European hydraulic engineer and cosmographer
Luis de Velasco (Velasco the Elder; 1511-1564), viceroy of New Spain, 1550-1564, who helped found the University of Mexico in 1553
Luis de Velasco (Velasco the Younger; 1534-1617), viceroy of New Spain, 1590-1595, 1607-1611, and viceroy of Peru, 1595-1604

SUMMARY OF EVENT

Although the water projects of seventeenth century Spaniards helped make Mexico City into a great metropolis, modern urban planners and environmentalists have pointed out that the city's less-than-ideal location made it a poor choice for a megalopolis. The Spanish colonists built their capital on unstable drained lake beds, and the surrounding mountain ranges hampered access to resources and markets. In pre-Columbian Mexico, the Aztecs had settled this high plateau peppered with lakes out of historical necessity, and during rainy seasons their settlements were often flooded.

The Aztecs built their capital of Tenochtitlán on an island in Lake Texcoco, one of the five principal lakes in a valley of 3,000 square miles (7,770 square kilometers). Because Texcoco was the lowest of the lakes, heavy rains and mountain runoff would often lead to overflows from the higher lakes into Texcoco, with a consequent inundation of Tenochtitlán. The Aztecs actually instituted projects to control these floods, but their technologies were inadequate for the task. After the Spanish conquest, the settlers, who began building their capital on the wreckage of Tenochtitlán, realized that they, too, would have to bring the unruly waters of the valley under control if their City of Mexico was to prosper.

Because the first viceroys of New Spain were involved with extending and consolidating the military conquests of Hernán Cortés, they had neither the resources nor the will to tackle such long-range infrastructure problems as the periodic flooding of the Valley of Mexico. Luis de Velasco the Elder, New Spain's second viceroy, devoted his energies to the pacification of Native Americans, an aim that also characterized the rule of his son, Luis Velasco the Younger, who, as eighth viceroy, believed that advanced European technologies would foster the city's economic success. After serving as viceroy of New Spain and Peru, Velasco the Younger retired to his Mexican estate in 1604, but in 1607, he agreed to serve again as New Spain's eleventh viceroy. During his final four-year rule, Velasco initiated a water-control project for the Valley of Mexico as part of his plan to protect the capital and improve its economy.

Velasco entrusted the engineer Enrico Martin with solving the valley's water problems. Martin, who is also known as Henrico Martinez, was in fact most likely a Frenchman named Henri Martin who had Hispanicized his name. He had received his technical training in Europe and understood the valley's basic problem: excess water from the higher lakes had nowhere to go but into Lake Texcoco, resulting in the destructive flooding of the city.

Martin had a plan to construct a canal that would provide an outlet for the water overflowing from Lake Zumpango. This canal would result in a reduction of water flowing into Lake Texcoco and a consequent drop in its water level. On November 28, 1607, a large number of workers began digging a tunnel that would channel Lake Zumpango's surplus water into the Tula River. Martin's project was plagued with problems during its first year. The soft, spongy soil and the constant pressure of flowing water caused corrosion of the tunnel's walls and roof, precipitating cave-ins that obstructed water flow. Consequently, the desired reduction of the water volume in Lake Texcoco did not take place.

Colonial government officials as well as Philip III, the king of Spain, became concerned about the rising costs of the project and the impracticality of Martin's plan. Luis de Velasco retired permanently as viceroy in 1611 and was replaced by Garcia Gurerra, who served only a year. Martin wrote to the king, defending his work, but his project was terminated in May of 1609. The king also sent an official, Diego Fernandez de Cordoba, marqués de Guadalcazar, who, in 1612, became the thirteenth viceroy, with special instructions regarding the work of draining the valley. Meanwhile, Philip III tried to find a competent engineer for the project, eventually selecting a Dutchman, Adrian Boot, who arrived in Mexico in 1614. Following the new viceroy's suggestion, both Boot and Martin submitted reports on the status of the canal, which Martin found salvageable and Boot inade-

quate. Boot also presented the viceroy with a plan whose execution would cost $185,900. Martin offered to complete his plan with three hundred men at a cost of only $100,000. Boot's plan was rejected and Martin's proposal was approved by King Philip on April 3, 1616.

For the next seven years, Martin tried to finish his project, but when, in 1623, a new viceroy ordered a test of his canal, the results were unsatisfactory. Indeed, floods continued to occur, and in the late 1620's, overflows from the lakes imperiled the city. Martin was blamed for exacerbating the problem when he sealed the opening of the drainage canal. He did this because he feared that the canal would be unable to handle the increased water flow, leading to the destruction of all that he had built. The action resulted in Martin's imprisonment, but the court later accepted his argument that inadequate funding for the project had caused delays in necessary repairs, and he was freed.

Since Martin was the only person who had extensive knowledge of the project, he was put to work repairing the tunnel, but it was too little, too late. A catastrophic flood struck the valley in 1629. Scholars estimate that more than thirty thousand people died in the flood, and the resulting massive property damage crippled the city's economy for several years. Martin became the scapegoat for this disaster, and the aged engineer, who had labored on his project for twenty-five years, died a disappointed man, having never fulfilled his plans for the valley.

SIGNIFICANCE

After Enrico Martin's death, Spanish authorities in the seventeenth and eighteenth centuries continued to be concerned with the drainage of the Valley of Mexico, and engineers, building on Martin's work, managed to reduce the water level of Lake Texcoco, creating land for the rapidly increasing population of Mexico City, which, by 1800, was the largest city of the Western Hemisphere. By this time, Martin's tunnel had been converted into an open canal.

When Mexico became an independent nation in 1821, its capital city still suffered from periodic flooding. Throughout the nineteenth century, engineers proposed various projects involving tunnels, canals, and culverts, but politics prevented anything from being done. By 1900, some claimed that, with a new canal and tunnel, Mexico City's battle with the lakes was won, but in the twentieth century, major floods still occurred, despite the widening of existing canals and the extension of the canal system. During the 1970's, an elaborate structure of deep drainage tunnels contributed significantly to alleviating the capital's centuries-old flooding problems.

Modern environmentalists have pointed out that solving the valley's flooding problems by draining its lakes created other problems. The rich plant and animal life dependent on the lakes was largely destroyed. Because much of downtown Mexico City was constructed on the clay bottom of the drained Lake Texcoco, many of its buildings suffered damage as they sank at the rate of several inches a year. Some structures collapsed completely during earthquakes. The ancient Mexicans had adapted their way of life to nature, whereas modern Mexicans have tried to force nature to conform to contemporary lifestyles, often with disastrous results. Martin's tunnel, which still exists as a canal, began the destruction of the valley's lakes, but at the beginning of the twenty-first century, Lake Texcoco was being rejuvenated as part of a plan to solve Mexico City's immense pollution problems.

—*Robert J. Paradowski*

FURTHER READING

Foster, Lynn V. *A Brief History of Mexico*. Rev. ed. New York: Facts On File, 2004. Contains material relevant to sixteenth and seventeenth century Mexico City in chapters 4 and 5. Illustrated, with tables and maps.

Appendices, including a bibliography and a "suggested reading" list. Index.

Priestley, Herbert Ingram. *The Mexican Nation: A History*. New York: Cooper Square, 1969. Chapter 7 on the viceroyalty and chapter 8 on seventeenth century New Spain provide the political background needed to understand Enrico Martin's achievements. A bibliography of "sources, authorities, and additional readings" and an index.

Simonian, Lane. *Defending the Land of the Jaguar: Natural History of Mexico*. Austin: University of Texas Press, 1996. This "Book of the Year" traces the history of environmentalism in Mexico from the pre-Columbian period to the end of the twentieth century. Enrico Martin is depicted as a person who understood the environmental problems of the Valley of Mexico.

SEE ALSO: 1604-1680: Rise of Criollo Identity in Mexico; 1615: Guamán Poma Pleas for Inca Reforms; June-Aug., 1640: *Bandeirantes* Expel the Jesuits; 1648: Cult of the Virgin of Guadalupe; Mar. 31, 1650: Earthquake Destroys Cuzco; June 8, 1692: Corn Riots in Mexico City.

RELATED ARTICLE in *Great Lives from History: The Seventeenth Century, 1601-1700:* Philip III.

1608
JESUITS FOUND PARAGUAY

Members of the Society of Jesus established the first missions to the Guaraní Indians in the interior of what is now Paraguay, converting the Guaraní to Christianity and encouraging their self-sufficiency.

LOCALE: Paraguay, South America, including parts of modern Argentina, Bolivia, Peru, and Brazil
CATEGORIES: Religion and theology; colonization; social issues and reform

KEY FIGURES

Alonzo de Barcena (1528-1598), Jesuit missionary to Peru and Paraguay
Hernando Arias de Saavedra (Hernandarias; 1561-1634), provincial governor, 1597-1599, 1602-1608, and national governor, 1608-1609, 1614-1618, of Paraguay
Francisco de Victoria (d. 1592), bishop of Tucuman, 1583

Francisco de Angulo (d. 1620), Jesuit missionary to Peru and Paraguay
Francisco de Alfaro (1551-1644), judge who issued ordinances protecting the Guaraní
Diego de Torres (1551-1638), Jesuit who advised Francisco de Alfaro

SUMMARY OF EVENT

Spanish and Portuguese exploration and exploitation in South America during the sixteenth and seventeenth centuries affected the interior region known as Paraguay less than any of its neighboring regions. This landlocked area at the beginning of the seventeenth century occupied about half of South America stretching from Peru south to Patagonia. It was bordered on the east and south by Brazil, on the west and south by Argentina, and on the north by Bolivia. In 1600, its northern border was Peru. Sixteenth century explorers were interested in the riches of Peru and Mexico. They found little to tempt them in

Paraguay. In comparison to Peru and Mexico, Paraguay was a sprawling wasteland with virtually no enticing mineral deposits to attract colonizers seeking gold and silver. Thus, it escaped some of the colonial strife that befell its neighbors to the east and west.

The territory that became Paraguay belonged to the Guaraní Indians. The predominant method for traveling within this territory was by means of its rivers, notably the Parana, which forms the border between Paraguay and Brazil, and the Paraguay, South America's fifth largest river. A major problem for the Guaraní was that slave raiders from Brazil, *mamalucos*, invaded their villages, captured the residents, and sold them as slaves. The Indians' villages had only meager fortifications, and the Indians themselves lacked weapons that could compete with the fire power of the *mamalucos*.

Under Spanish law, Paraguayan Indians were outside the jurisdiction of the colonial government. They were forbidden to have guns, so they could not acquire the means to defend themselves effectively. The few missionaries that reached the Guaraní in the late sixteenth century, mostly Dominicans and Franciscans, essentially sprinkled them with holy water and considered them Christian converts, although these Indians did not embrace Christianity in any deep or active way. They viewed these early missionaries with suspicion and disdain.

The Society of Jesus, more familiarly called the Jesuit order, which had been in existence for less than a century, was just beginning to make inroads into South America at the beginning of the seventeenth century. Its novices, essentially vigorous young men, were subjected to fifteen years of intensive training before they were admitted to full membership in the order. They were considered the most intellectually elite group within the Roman Church.

A contingent of twenty Jesuits was sent to Peru in the late sixteenth century to work with the Indians. They learned native languages, and besides converting the indigenous people to Christianity, they helped them to bring about reforms within their society and to become self-sufficient. They also protected the natives from the *mamelucos*, who sought to enslave them. When Francisco de Victoria, bishop of Tucuman in Paraguay, discovered what the Jesuits had accomplished in Peru, he begged the provincial to send him missionaries for Paraguay. In 1588, three Jesuits arrived from Peru in the Paraguayan town of Santiago del Estero. Father Francisco de Angulo remained in town, but Father Alonzo de Barcena, accompanied by his secretary, Brother Villegas, struck

out into the wilderness seeking Indians to convert to Christianity.

Barcena and Villegas quickly won over the Indians because of their willingness to fit into the Guaraní communities, sharing with the Indians—essentially a peaceful and simple people—the hunger, illnesses, and dangers that were part of everyday Guaraní life. Having worked among the Peruvian Indians for twenty years before they came to Paraguay, these missionaries were fluent in the languages the Guaraní spoke.

By 1600, the Jesuits had begun to organize some 150,000 Indians into productive farming communities called *reducciones*. The purpose of the missionaries was not merely to bring the Guaranís to an acceptance of the Christian faith but also to provide education for them and to help them improve their lots by becoming self-sufficient. Property in the *reducciones* was held in common, but the missionaries reserved the right to make important decisions. The average work day in the *reducciones* was six hours. The Guaraní spent their nonworking hours praying or perfecting skills such as art, music, wood carving, and clock making. The Guaraní, guided by the Jesuits, built within their *reducciones* cathedrals, churches, schools, hospitals, libraries, and dwellings for widows. Guaraní villages were carefully planned communities with central squares, public buildings and churches, and meticulously plotted residential areas. The Jesuits strove to reinforce the family structures of the natives. Chiefs within each mission were appointed to head blocks of several families. Some *reducciones* had as many as twenty thousand inhabitants.

In 1597, Hernando Arias de Saavedra became the first native-born governor of Paraguay. He served three nonconsecutive terms as governor between 1597 and 1618. Under his leadership, the Jesuit Province of Paraguay was established in 1604. Paraguay became a nation in 1608. In 1609, at Arias de Saavedra's instigation, the first Jesuit mission in Paraguay, the Loreto Reduccion, was established, followed in 1611 by the Reduccion Santa Ignacio Miri. By 1630, eleven more *reducciones* had been established in Paraguay, and by the end of the century, there were some thirty such settlements in Paraguay, Peru, Argentina, and Brazil.

Diego de Torres, a Jesuit, became an adviser to Francisco de Alfaro, a judge who, with Torres's guidance, issued ordinances to benefit the Guaraní. On January 30, 1607, he issued the *Cedula Real*, which guaranteed any Guaraní who converted to Christianity a ten-year exemption from paying taxes. On March 6, 1609, in the *Cedula Magna*, he affirmed that the Guaraní enjoyed the same freedoms that were accorded to Spaniards, thereby reaffirming their freedom from slavery, although in actuality many of the Guaraní lived in virtual slavery, because, when they could not meet externally imposed financial obligations, they became indentured servants. (It is important to remember that nearly all the existing information about the Jesuit missions and the Guaraní was produced by Jesuits, so the viewpoint informing these reports was most likely slanted in favor of the Europeans.)

In essence, the *reducciones* were a society within a society. These settlements were viewed by many as Utopias, privileged communities that existed for the protection of their inhabitants. Although Paraguay did not have the number of Spanish settlers that other South American countries had attracted, there were in the larger society numerous Creole farmers, called *peninsulares*, native-born citizens of Spanish lineage. As the *reducciones* spread throughout the region, these Creole farmers became resentful of them because they were in competition with the *reducciones*, especially in the profitable *yerba mate* trade. As a result, in 1767 the Spanish king expelled the Jesuits from all of South America's Spanish colonies.

SIGNIFICANCE

The Jesuit missions in Paraguay were remarkable entities that brought to the indigenous people an order, a prosperity, and a self-respect that they had been lacking before the missionaries arrived. Although the Jesuits taught the Guaraní a great deal about Western culture and traditions, they did not do so at the expense of weakening the Indians' own traditions.

From the beginning, the Jesuits became one with the Guaraní, first learning their languages and then living on an equal basis with them within the communities they inhabited. The Guaraní had not had favorable contact with prior Christian missionaries, but they sensed quite

quickly that the Jesuits were a different breed from the Dominicans, Franciscans, and Benedictines who had come into their villages earlier.

The Guaraní needed the kind of guidance and structure that the Jesuits provided. It is significant that when the Jesuits were finally expelled from Paraguay by the king of Spain in 1767, the *reducciones* quickly deteriorated, and the Guaranís entered a period of decline.

—*R. Baird Shuman*

FURTHER READING

Haverstock, Nathan A. *Paraguay in Pictures*. Minneapolis, Minn.: Lerner, 1995. Directed toward adolescents, this book provides helpful background and mentions the Jesuit missions briefly but cogently.

Morrison, Marion. *Paraguay*. Chicago: Children's Press, 1994. Written for a juvenile audience, this book presents a solid overview of the country and devotes several pages to the Jesuit missions.

Reiter, Frederick J. *They Built Utopia: The Jesuit Missions in Paraguay, 1610-1768*. Potomac, Md.: Scripta Humanistica, 1995. This remarkably detailed account of the Jesuit missions in Paraguay is comprehensive. By far the best source in the field, it is well written and easily accessible.

SEE ALSO: 1604-1680: Rise of Criollo Identity in Mexico; 1611-1630's: Jesuits Begin Missionary Activities in New France; 1615: Guamán Poma Pleas for Inca Reforms; 1630-1660's: Dutch Wars in Brazil; June-Aug., 1640: *Bandeirantes* Expel the Jesuits; 1654: Portugal Retakes Control of Brazil; Early 1690's: Brazilian Gold Rush.
RELATED ARTICLES in *Great Lives from History: The Seventeenth Century, 1601-1700:* Saint Isaac Jogues; Saint Rose of Lima; Kateri Tekakwitha.

September, 1608
INVENTION OF THE TELESCOPE

The telescope's invention has been attributed to several individuals, but, whatever its precise provenance, the scope quickly diffused throughout Europe and became the chief device by which astronomers such as Galileo, especially early on, explored the previously unseen wonders of the universe.

LOCALE: Middleburg, Zeeland, United Provinces (now in the Netherlands)

CATEGORIES: Science and technology; inventions; astronomy

KEY FIGURES

Hans Lippershey (c. 1570-c. 1619), Dutch inventor and maker of spectacles who is traditionally credited with the invention of the telescope

Zacharias Janssen (1580-c. 1638), Dutch optician, coiner, and counterfeiter, whose invention of the microscope is more solidly established than his purported invention of the telescope

Galileo (1564-1642), Italian mathematician, astronomer, and physicist who became the first scientist to make extensive telescopic observations of extraterrestrial objects

SUMMARY OF EVENT

Ancient and medieval astronomers used instruments to map the positions of stars and to follow the paths of planets through the heavens, but these instruments were limited because all of them relied on the human eye unaided by any optical device. The magnifying power of lenses had been observed in the Middle Ages, and by the thirteenth century convex lenses were being used as reading glasses. Several medieval natural philosophers speculated about the possibility of using such lenses to enlarge distant objects, but these speculations did not result in practical instruments.

By the sixteenth century, Tycho Brahe, the greatest observer of the heavens to work without an optical device, continued to make use of such apparatus as astrolabes, quadrants, and armillary spheres, although his instruments were larger and much more sophisticated than their medieval predecessors. The German astronomer Johannes Kepler used Brahe's precise data on Mars to discover that it, like the other planets, orbited the sun in elliptical, not circular orbits, thus helping him, without the aid of a telescope, to revolutionize astronomy.

Much controversy exists over the questions of where, when, and by whom the telescope was first invented. Claims have been made for Leonard Digges in England, Giambattista della Porta in Italy, and James Metius (also known as Jacob Adriaanzoon) in Holland, but scholars have found these affirmations, often put forward by relatives or friends of the claimants, are often unsubstantiated. Most historians of science and technology make Holland the country of the telescope's origin and 1608 as the year of its development.

Persuasive documentary evidence exists for a Dutch genesis of this invention, though some uncertainty exists about the actual inventor. These uncertainties are further complicated by the debate over what constitutes the "discovery" of this instrument. Is it finding that two lenses that are held an appropriate distance apart magnify distant objects? Or is it the actual construction of what would later be called a "refracting telescope" by fitting two lenses into a tube in which one lens (the objective) collects light and brings it to a focus while a second lens (the eyepiece) becomes the conduit of the magnified image to the observer?

Dutch lens grinder Hans Lippershey is credited with the invention of the first telescope. (Library of Congress)

Although most scholars credit Hans Lippershey with the telescope's discovery, the evidence for this attribution is not as unequivocal as scholars would like. Characterized by some as an illiterate artisan, Lippershey was a master of the techniques of lens grinding, for he was a successful maker of spectacles. In the traditional story, which has several versions, either an apprentice or two children, while playing with long and short focus convex lenses, noticed that the lenses, when held a certain distance apart, made the weather vane on a church across the street they were on appear larger and closer. Upon his return to his shop, Lippershey, when informed of this exciting observation, verified it, and then arranged the lenses in a metal tube, in effect creating the first refracting telescope.

Unlike other claimants for the glory of the telescope's discovery, Lippershey, realizing its potential military value, quickly applied for a patent. On September 25, 1608, a committee of councilors in Zeeland wrote a letter to the States-General in The Hague, informing this governing body of The Netherlands that Lippershey had invented a device by means of which things at a great distance could be seen as if they were nearby. On October 2,

1608, Lippershey formally petitioned the States-General for a thirty-year patent for what he called a *kijker* (looker). Because of its potential utility for Dutch naval security, Lippershey requested that his invention be kept secret. He wanted an annual pension to enable him to manufacture these devices, which he promised to sell only in Holland. Prince Maurice of Nassau, head of the Belgian army, tested Lippershey's monocular instrument from a tower on his palace and declared that it would be of value to the Dutch state, especially if a binocular version could be built.

The telescope proved to be too valuable an invention (and too easy to duplicate) to remain a secret for long. In Alkmaar, about 20 miles north of Amsterdam, James Metius sent a petition to the States-General in which he claimed that he had made a magnifying device equal in power to Lippershey's, but his request for a patent was denied, and his case for having invented the telescope independently of Lippershey was weakened by his refusal to show his device even to his closest friends.

Another possible Dutch inventor of the telescope, at least according to his son, was Zacharias Janssen who, like Lippershey, was an optician in Middleburg. Long af-

Venetian senators and nobles around 1608, high above Venice, sharing a telescope to see the city from a new perspective. (Hulton Archive by Getty Images)

ter Zacharias Janssen's death, his son claimed that his father had invented the telescope in 1590, but according to some scholars' estimate of the father's birth date, this would mean he invented the telescope when he was just ten years old, and just two years old if, as some believe, he was born in 1588. According to his daughter, Zacharias Janssen invented the telescope in 1611 or 1619, several years after Lippershey's documented discovery. Some scholars think that the children may have confused their father's invention of the microscope with the invention of the telescope. Zacharias Janssen led an unconventional life. He was convicted twice for counterfeiting and was forced to flee when his conviction resulted in a sentence of death by immersion in boiling oil. Research indicates that he never sought credit for the telescope's discovery and this false claim was mainly his son's doing.

> ## GALILEO ON THE FIRST TELESCOPE
>
> *Spectacle maker Hans Lippershey is credited with inventing the first telescope in 1608. Galileo was so inspired by the instrument's possibilities that he ventured to build his own. He wrote that the scope he constructed enabled him to see objects "magnified nearly a thousand times, and more than thirty times nearer than if viewed by the natural powers of sight alone." Here, Galileo writes of the telescope's powers in his* The Sidereal Messenger *(1610).*
>
> About ten months ago a report reached my ears that a Dutchman [Lippershey] had constructed a telescope, by the aid of which visible objects, although at a great distance from the eye of the observer, were seen distinctly as if near. . . .
>
> It would be altogether a waste of time to enumerate the number and importance of the benefits which this instrument [the telescope Galileo constructed after Lippershey] may be expected to confer, when used by land or sea. But without paying attention to its use for terrestrial objects, I betook myself to observations of the heavenly bodies; and first of all, I viewed the Moon as near as if it was scarcely two semidiameters of the Earth distant. After the Moon, I frequently observed other heavenly bodies both fixed stars and planets, with incredible delight.
>
> *Source:* Excerpted in *An Editor's Treasury: A Continuing Anthology of Prose, Verse, and Literary Curiosa*, vol. 2, edited by Herbert R. Mayes (New York: Atheneum, 1969), pp. 1181-1182.

Because the States-General declined to grant a patent to Lippershey, he saw his invention spread to France, Germany, and Italy without any remuneration coming to him. These instruments were called optic tubes, Dutch cylinders, optic glasses, or Dutch perspectives (the term "telescope" was a later, Italian coinage). Early in 1609, the telescopes were on sale in Paris and, later that year, they were being sold in Germany at a Frankfurt fair.

In Italy, Galileo first heard of Lippershey's invention in May of 1609. Not only did this forty-five-year-old professor of mathematics re-create the Dutch invention, he was also able to make advanced models with greater magnifying powers than Lippershey's device. His gift of a telescope to the Paduan senate resulted in a substantial salary increase for him at his university. So famous were the Galilean telescopes that he was often referred to as its inventor, an appellation he himself always denied, reserving that title for "the Dutchman." However, he did claim for himself the serious, extensive, and intelligent use of the device to make many important astronomical discoveries.

Early in 1610, he found that his telescope revealed that the Moon, like the Earth, had mountains and plains (which he named "seas") and, unlike the Earth, numerous craters. He found that the Milky Way was not a cloud but myriad unknown stars. He was the first to behold Jupiter's spherical shape and its four satellites (now called "Galilean Moons" in his honor). He was also the first to bring to light the phases of Venus, which he used to support his longstanding belief in the Copernican heliocentric system. His publication of the *Sidereus nuncius* (*The Sidereal Messenger*, also known as *The Starry Messenger*) in March of 1610 made his telescope discoveries famous not only in Italy but in other countries as well.

In Germany, Johannes Kepler, who read and wrote about Galileo's book, invented a new type of telescope that he described in his *Dioptrice* (partial translation of the preface, 1880) in 1611. The Keplerian telescope came to dominate astronomy for more than a century.

SIGNIFICANCE

The history of astronomy has been heavily populated with instruments, but none of these has had the dramatic and dominating influence of the telescope. Many scientists date modern astronomy from 1610, the year Galileo turned his telescope toward the heavens and expanded manyfold the frontiers of the observable universe.

Early telescopes were hampered by chromatic and spherical aberrations, in which white objects appeared colored and out of focus, but Isaac Newton's invention of the reflecting telescope corrected these aberrations, and astronomers of the eighteenth and nineteenth centuries developed larger and larger reflectors. In 1781, the German-English astronomer William Herschel used his large reflecting telescope to discover the planet Uranus. In the nineteenth century, the Irish astronomer William Parsons built a seventy-two-inch reflecting telescope with which he was able to discern the spiral shapes of nebular objects. Seventy-five years later, the American astronomer Edwin Hubble, using the hundred-inch Mount Wilson telescope in the mountains of Southern California, showed that these nebular objects actually were systems of stars far beyond our Milky Way galaxy. Named in his honor, the Hubble Space Telescope has continued the long and glorious history of this instrument in revealing the great mysteries of the universe.

—*Robert J. Paradowski*

FURTHER READING

Asimov, Isaac. *Eyes on the Universe: A History of the Telescope*. Boston: Houghton Mifflin, 1975. A chronicle of astronomy by a skillful and knowledgeable popularizer that centers on the evolution of increasingly sophisticated telescopes.

King, Henry C. *The History of the Telescope*. New York: Dover, 1979. This reprint of a classic work originally published in 1955 has been called by Owen Gingerich, a distinguished historian of astronomy, "the last word" on this topic. This extensively illustrated book

contains much information unavailable elsewhere, along with many references to primary sources and a detailed index.

Moore, Patrick. *Eyes on the University: The Story of the Telescope*. New York: Springer-Verlag, 1997. Written to commemorate the fortieth anniversary of the British television series "The Sky at Night," this illustrated account of the telescope's history is intended for general readers and amateur astronomers.

North, John. *The Norton History of Astronomy and Cosmology*. New York: Norton, 1995. North, a professor in the history of the exact sciences, discusses the telescope as part of the evolution of astronomy. Includes an index and a thirty-four page bibliographical essay.

SEE ALSO: 1609-1619: Kepler's Laws of Planetary Motion; 1610: Galileo Confirms the Heliocentric Model of the Solar System; 1632: Galileo Publishes *Dialogue Concerning the Two Chief World Systems, Ptolemaic and Copernican*; Feb., 1656: Huygens Identifies Saturn's Rings; 1660's-1700: First Microscopic Observations; 1665: Cassini Discovers Jupiter's Great Red Spot.

RELATED ARTICLES in *Great Lives from History: The Seventeenth Century, 1601-1700:* Gian Domenico Cassini; Galileo; Robert Hooke; Christiaan Huygens; Johannes Kepler; Hans Lippershey; Maurice of Nassau; Sir Isaac Newton.

1609
BANK OF AMSTERDAM INVENTS CHECKS

The Netherlands' Bank of Amsterdam helped make possible the modern trading economy by streamlining the deposit and transfer of monetary assets by creating transactions by bank note, or check. Also, as a public rather than private bank, it gained integrity and depositor trust.

LOCALE: The Netherlands
CATEGORIES: Economics; trade and commerce; organizations and institutions

SUMMARY OF EVENT

By the seventeenth century, the Dutch were the leading traders in the world. Their ascent to this position of dominance had its roots in the Middle Ages, when the revival of international trade first led to the creation of currencies

and then to bills of exchange, bills that allowed for payments from one kind of currency to another. Finally, international trade led to the creation of banking institutions in the Low Countries, particularly the northern provinces.

Dutch trade dominance came about as a result of several factors. The first of these was their preeminence in Europe's grain trade in the late sixteenth and early seventeenth century. The Dutch, who had developed the *fluyt*, a far more capacious cargo ship that made possible the shipment of raw materials in bulk, came to dominate the trade in grain from the Baltic region. As Europe's population rose, local agricultural crops were often insufficient to feed entire populations. So, Dutch warehouses in the port of Amsterdam became the back-up source of food for all of western Europe.

As European trade expanded from the Continent to the world, trade that was made possible by voyages to the Americas and to South and East Asia in the sixteenth century, there came a need for institutions to facilitate the transfer of trading profits from one trader, or one trading business, to another. The leaders of the city of Amsterdam recognized this need, and in 1609, they created the Bank of Amsterdam. Many of the leading commercial figures of Antwerp, including those who would help found the bank, had fled northward after 1585, especially to Amsterdam, after Spain had attempted to reconquer provinces in the southern Low Countries. (The Low Countries had been trying to shake off Spanish control.) Those who fled and resettled in Amsterdam contributed their expertise and their financial resources to the city's commercial leadership.

Prior to the establishment of the Bank of Amsterdam, the usual method of making "international" payments had been through the bill of exchange. The bill of exchange was a financial instrument that signified the amount of debt owed by one individual merchant to another, as a result of the transfer of some goods. Although rudimentary bills of exchange had been developed in antiquity, the modern bill of exchange was essentially created in Italy in the fourteenth century; it specified the debt owed by one individual to another, generally in a "foreign" currency. Indeed, technically, bills of exchange could only operate in the case of such a currency transfer. Over time, however, bills of exchange could be assigned to a third party, each bill guaranteeing the payment to the party who eventually claimed the cash.

This system of "assigning" bills of exchange had developed into the preferred instrument of foreign commerce, especially in the Antwerp of the sixteenth century. When the commercial center of Europe shifted to Amsterdam after 1585, of concern was institutionalizing this somewhat informal method of transferring obligations from one party to another. The city fathers of Amsterdam created the Bank of Amsterdam—an official institution of the city—to formalize the transfer of funds.

The bank's primary purpose was to establish accounts for the principal traders active in Dutch international trade. Traders could—indeed, they were required to—deposit their various currency holdings into the accounts they held at the bank, a feature that eliminated the risk of cash transactions. Once a trader had an account at the bank, he could settle his obligations to others not through cash payments but by ordering the transfer—by check—

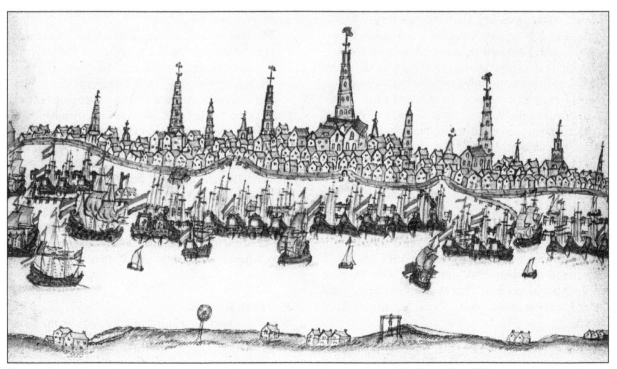

The creation of checks for use among traders and merchants helped Amsterdam, and the Dutch Republic, become the major import center in Western Europe. This depiction shows a thriving Amsterdam harbor around 1670. (Hulton\Archive by Getty Images)

THE BANK OF AMSTERDAM AND DEPOSITOR TRUST

The Bank of Amsterdam gained depositor trust by emphasizing its public status and its function as an institution that transfers funds between accounts through checks. Contemporary English commentator Onslow Burrish noted the importance of this trust in 1728.

Without doubt, the only reason why persons are contented to deposit their money upon such terms is a firm belief that it remains sacred, untouched and unapplied to any use [as in lending] whatsoever. The magistrates of Amsterdam, all those concerned in the government of the Bank and in general the whole body of the Seven Provinces, take pains to propagate this opinion and appear, at least, to be of the same mind themselves.

Source: Quoted in *The Embarrassment of Riches: An Interpretation of Dutch Culture in the Golden Age*, by Simon Schama (Berkeley: University of California Press, 1988), p. 345.

did, however, make loans to the municipal authorities of the City of Amsterdam and to the Dutch East India Company, which was founded in 1602. In 1612, the City of Amsterdam added a municipally sponsored insurance system, called the Chamber of Assurance, to the financial facilities available to traders, thus helping to mitigate the risks of international trade.

About 1700, the Bank of Amsterdam developed a system to provide payments throughout the world. This capability of settling financial obligations anywhere made Amsterdam the financial capital of the world in the seventeenth century.

of some of his credit at the bank to the accounts of other traders, who also held accounts at the bank. Moreover, unlike the bill of exchange, financial commitments avoided transfers between different currencies. Initially, all transactions of more than 600 guilders (the Dutch currency) had to be processed by the bank; the limit on cash transactions was later reduced to 300 guilders.

Each transaction entailed a fee that was determined by the size of the transaction. The bank grew very profitable from these fees; it also benefited when new accounts were opened. Those individuals with multiple accounts (for example, separate accounts relating to trading ventures with different individuals) had to open separate accounts from which the bank also received a fee.

In addition, the bank accepted deposits of coins of various denominations and origin, thus helping to reduce the losses traders experienced from the constant devaluation of coins by clipping and other measures. The bank also accepted gold and silver bullion, which circulated in large quantities in sixteenth and seventeenth century Europe, thanks to the amounts of gold and silver won by the Spanish and other adventurers in the New World. Coins and bullion brought to the bank were credited to the depositor at 5 percent below their nominal amount, which also contributed to the bank's profits. In 1683, the bank created special receipts for the deposits of currency and bullion, receipts called *recipis*. The *recipis*, in turn, could be traded.

Initially, the Bank of Amsterdam did not make loans; this function was provided by another bank, established in 1614, although it did advance funds to the lending bank (also a municipal institution) up until 1640. The bank

SIGNIFICANCE

By creating an institution that could handle all of Europe's international trading transactions, the Bank of Amsterdam gave a significant boost to the expansion of international trade in the seventeenth century. By making it possible to transfer financial assets from one individual to another through the use of paper notification—an early form of the bank check—the bank in effect created a new international currency.

The ease with which such transactions could be carried out eliminated a good deal of the risk that had previously plagued international trade, and by so doing facilitated the economic expansion of Europe.

The success of the Bank of Amsterdam inspired other cities in the Netherlands to create their own banks, but those banks never achieved the international success of Amsterdam's. The Bank of Amsterdam, however, continued to play an important part in the economy of the Netherlands and the world, until the Napoleonic conquests made it impossible for the bank to carry out its international role. The Bank of Amsterdam was liquidated in 1820. Nevertheless, the system of settling debts by direct payment from one account to another prevails in Europe, where it is called the giro system.

—*Nancy M. Gordon*

FURTHER READING

Barbour, Violet. *Capitalism in Amsterdam in the Seventeenth Century*. Ann Arbor: University of Michigan Press, 1963. This small volume gives an overview of the growth of the Dutch economy during the seventeenth century.

De Vries, Jan, and Ad van der Woude. *The First Modern Economy: Success, Failure, and Perseverance of the Dutch Economy, 1500-1815*. New York: Cambridge University Press, 1997. This broad survey by two Dutch scholars provides detailed information about the Bank of Amsterdam's origins and practices.

Einzig, Paul. *The History of Foreign Exchange*. London: Macmillan, 1962. This work examines the historical origins of bills of exchange.

Glamann, Kristof. "European Trade, 1500-1750." In *The Sixteenth and Seventeenth Centuries*, vol. 2 in *The Fontana Economic History of Europe*, edited by Carlo M. Cipolla. New York: Barnes and Noble Books, 1977. An overview of the economic development of the period.

't Hart, Marjolein, Joost Jonker, and Jan Luiten van Zanden, eds. *A Financial History of the Netherlands*. New York: Cambridge University Press, 1997. A detailed description by three Dutch scholars of the development of the Dutch financial market.

SEE ALSO: 17th cent.: Age of Mercantilism in Southeast Asia; 17th cent.: The Pepper Trade; Mar. 20, 1602: Dutch East India Company Is Founded; Beginning Spring, 1605: Dutch Dominate Southeast Asian Trade; 1606-1674: Europeans Settle in India; 1623-1674: Earliest Calculators Appear; 1661-1672: Colbert Develops Mercantilism; Early 1690's: Brazilian Gold Rush; July 27, 1694: Bank of England Is Chartered.

RELATED ARTICLES in *Great Lives from History: The Seventeenth Century, 1601-1700:* Maurice of Nassau; William Paterson; Maarten and Cornelis Tromp; Gerrard Winstanley.

1609
CHINA BEGINS SHIPPING TEA TO EUROPE

The introduction of tea as a commodity from China into seventeenth century Europe had far-reaching social, physical, and economic consequences. It led to the development of a "tea culture" that shaped social interactions throughout polite society in Britain and elsewhere, and it became a major source of revenue for nations that imposed a special tax upon the new commodity.

LOCALE: China, India, Europe, American colonies
CATEGORIES: Trade and commerce; economics; agriculture

KEY FIGURES
Catherine of Braganza (1638-1705), queen consort of England, r. 1662-1685, and regent of Portugal, r. 1704-1705
Giovanni Battista Ramusio (1485-1557), Venetian diplomat and author
Oliver Cromwell (1599-1658), lord protector of England, 1653-1658
Peter Stuyvesant (c. 1610-1672), director-general of New Netherland, 1647-1664

SUMMARY OF EVENT
Although by the third century C.E., the benefits of tea drinking were well documented in China, tea did not become popular in Europe until the seventeenth century.

The first European reference to tea (also called chai) appears in Venetian diplomat Giovanni Battista Ramusio's *Delle navigationi et viaggi* (1559; of the voyages and travels), while the first ship known to have brought tea to Europe arrived from Macao around 1609. The ship's port of origin is uncertain, but it may have been Dutch. By 1615, the English were aware of tea, as it is mentioned in a letter from June 27 of that year written by Mr. Wickham, an agent of the East India Company, and sent from Japan to Macao.

First referred to in England as "cha" (from a Cantonese slang term for the beverage), the drink's name changed later to "tay" or "tee" when the British changed trading locales from Guangzhou (Canton) to Xiamen (Amoy), where the word for tea is *te* (Wade-Giles, *t'e*). In 1662, tea was still so uncommon in England that when Portugal's Catherine of Braganza arrived at Portsmouth to marry King Charles II, a cup of tea could not be found. The new queen's predilection for tea, however, soon transformed it into a sensation at the English court, and the English affinity for tea increased substantially over time. Between 1650 and 1700, tea imports to Britain totaled only 181,545 pounds, but during the next fifty years, Britain would import 40 million pounds. The Netherlands would also import large amounts of tea in the eighteenth century, consuming by 1770 almost two-thirds as much as Britain. Moreover, from the day that

Peter Stuyvesant first brought tea to the Dutch settlement of New Amsterdam, tea consumption also developed rapidly in the British colonies in America.

Drinking tea became a social activity, and as a tea culture developed in Europe, that culture provided a context for social interaction, especially between the sexes. British men cultivated business and literary connections in coffeehouses, sites believed to be less morally objectionable than alehouses or other public gathering places. Women, conversely, acted as hostesses to create gathering places in their private homes, and the tea table became a center of this domestic space. The originally Chinese drink was to become the British drink par excellence, and the tea table and the ritualized ceremony surrounding it were to define British civility, refinement, and family togetherness.

Far from a mere pastime, tea drinking acquired a set of formal, socially coded interactions that provided participants with opportunities both to display and to confirm their social status. By 1732, families and friends would spend social evenings out dancing, listening to music, or watching fireworks at new entertainment venues known as tea gardens, the most popular being Vauxhall or Ranelagh in London. In these popular tea gardens, men and women could meet and take tea together or take in the amusements accompanying the "tea craze."

Beyond its social functions, tea improved the health of Europeans, as it had helped the Chinese for many centuries. Originally introduced into Europe as an exotic medicinal agent said to relieve headache and indigestion, tea provided an alternative to alcoholic drinks. Because water was often unsafe, beer and wine were served with most meals, even to children. Tea became a safe, nonalcoholic beverage, since, whether they knew it or not, Europeans sterilized their tea water by boiling it.

During the seventeenth century, tea also became a powerful economic factor by providing large sources of government revenue. From the first arrival of tea in Europe, taxes on tea provided a means of enriching the royal coffers. Oliver Cromwell was the first to tax tea, and in 1660, the Restoration court imposed a tea tax as well. From an exotic luxury, tea quickly became a mass-produced staple commodity, and it came in time to account for one-tenth of British tax revenue. By the middle of the eighteenth century, the tax on tea had grown to 119 percent. However, by 1684, the extreme expense of legitimate, taxed tea created a black market for the drink, and smuggling became widespread.

SIGNIFICANCE

The introduction of tea as a commodity from China into seventeenth century Europe had far-reaching social, physical, and economic effects. In addition to creating new cultural practices and giving Europeans new ways to interact, tea provided a major new source of revenue for the British government and trade in tea helped to forge important diplomatic relationships between the East and the West.

The complexity of importing tea from China to Europe, however, ultimately created a need to grow tea in other areas of the world. When the nineteenth century saw an imbalance of trade between Britain and China, the East India Company began to pay for its tea with opium grown in its India colonies and smuggled to China in the company's ships. This situation led to the Opium Wars of 1839-1842. When these wars depleted the tea supply from China, Britain escalated its tea imports from Assam, India, where tea originally grew wild. Tea was also grown in Ceylon (Sri Lanka) from 1867 and in Africa from the late nineteenth century. By 1900, there were four thousand estates growing tea in India and two thousand in Sri Lanka. Tea consumption also increased the demand for the sugar grown on American plantations, which in turn increased the demand for slave labor on those plantations.

Caffeinated tea would also contribute to the rise of capitalism by becoming an invaluable drink for urban factory workforces during the Industrial Revolution. Inexpensive and nonalcoholic, when mixed with sugar, it provided nutritional sustenance for those working long hours in factories. In addition, tea later played an important role in the nineteenth century temperance or "teetotal" movement's fight against alcohol abuse, with tea meetings emerging as a means to convert drinkers to sobriety.

Among the most well known of tea's unpredictable effects on Western history is the role it played in the advent of the American Revolution. The Townshend Revenue Act, passed by Parliament in 1767 on Britain's American colonies, led to a protest meeting in Boston that culminated in the adoption of a nonimport agreement. In 1773, colonial merchants loyal to the British crown were granted the right to sell tea without paying the tax. However, this agreement merely eliminated the colonial middlemen and passed the cost on to American consumers.

The New England colonists rebelled against the tea tax imposed upon them without their consent, and angry patriots who called themselves the Sons of Liberty disguised themselves as Native Americans and boarded East India Company ships at Griffen's Wharf on December 16, 1773, where they threw 342 chests of tea from the London firm of Davison and Newman into Boston Harbor. The event, which in time came to be known as the Boston Tea Party, was organized by Samuel Adams with support from John Hancock and led by the wealthy Boston merchant Lendall Pitts. Silversmith Paul Revere also participated. As a result of the Boston Tea Party, King George III closed the Boston harbor, and royal troops occupied the city. The colonial leaders came together to resist the occupation, and the American Revolution was underway.

—*M. Casey Diana*

FURTHER READING

Forrest, Denys. *Tea for the British: The Social and Economic History of a Famous Trade*. London: Chatto & Windus, 1973. Contains historical facts regarding tea and statistical figures to put its role in sharp historical perspective.

MacFarlane, Alan. *The Empire of Tea: The Remarkable History of the Plant That Took Over the World*. New York: Overlook Press, 2004. A personal account of life on a tea estate in India and the hardships suffered by the laborers, followed by a history of tea and the economic events contributing to the growth of the empire.

Moxham, Roy. *Tea: Addiction, Exploitation, and Empire*. London: Carroll & Graf, 2003. A scathing account of how the addictive properties of tea contributed to imperialism. Deals with the role tea played in England's loss of its American colonies.

Pettigrew, Jane. *A Social History of Tea*. London: National Trust, 2002. Explores tea's enormous influence on society and history. Includes lively accounts of the Boston Tea Party, smuggling, and clipper ships.

SEE ALSO: 17th cent.: England's Agricultural Revolution; 17th cent.: The Pepper Trade; 17th cent.: Rise of Proto-Industrial Economies; Beginning Spring, 1605: Dutch Dominate Southeast Asian Trade; 1642-1651: English Civil Wars; Dec. 16, 1653-Sept. 3, 1658: Cromwell Rules England as Lord Protector; 1656: Popularization of Chocolate; May, 1659-May, 1660: Restoration of Charles II.

RELATED ARTICLES in *Great Lives from History: The Seventeenth Century, 1601-1700:* Catherine of Braganza; Charles II (of England); Oliver Cromwell; Peter Stuyvesant.

1609-1617
CONSTRUCTION OF THE BLUE MOSQUE

Constantinople's Blue Mosque is a landmark in Ottoman architecture because of its monumental size, noted interior decoration and design, interior illumination, and six minarets. It was inspired partly by the Byzantine Empire's sixth century church complex Hagia Sophia, also in Constantinople, and symbolizes the deep Islamic faith of the Ottomans.

LOCALE: Constantinople, Ottoman Empire (now Istanbul, Turkey)

CATEGORIES: Architecture; cultural and intellectual history; religion and theology; organizations and institutions

KEY FIGURES

Ahmed I (1590-1617), Ottoman sultan, r. 1603-1617, who ordered construction of the Blue Mosque

Mehmed Ağa (fl. early seventeenth century), chief Ottoman architect, who designed the Blue Mosque

Sinan (1489-1588), chief royal architect to Sultan Süleyman the Magnificent, whose earlier mosques inspired the design of the Blue Mosque

SUMMARY OF EVENT

The Blue Mosque, built on the prominent site of the Great Palace of Byzantium near the former Hippodrome on the European side of the Bosporus, is the masterwork of Ottoman architect Mehmed Ağa. The architect was inspired both by Byzantine emperor Justinian's sixth century Christian church complex, the Hagia Sophia (Ayasofya)—before the empire's conquest by the Ottomans—and also by aspects of Sinan's famous Süleymaniye Mosque of the sixteenth century.

Fired by a deep religious feeling and compensating for the humiliating treaties that the young Sultan Ahmed I was compelled to sign with Persia and Austria, Ahmed decided to erect a complex worthy of his ancestors. The Blue Mosque, also known as the Mosque of

The Ottoman-built Blue Mosque in Constantinople (now Istanbul), Turkey. (Digital Stock)

Sultan Ahmed (Ahmediye), is the largest of all the imperial mosques and surpasses all of its predecessors in the lavishness of its decoration. Like previous imperial complexes, the Blue Mosque physically dominates the diverse social institutions attached to it.

However, the mosque's proposed construction was protested by ulema (teachers of Islamic law), who claimed that a mosque should be built only from the spoils of conquest and not under the tight circumstances of political defeat and increasingly heavy taxation. The ulema also objected to the Blue Mosque's six minarets because the usual four minarets were meant to symbolize the four corners of the world. They asserted that six minarets was not canonical. The mosque and its minarets would be built starting in 1609, however, in the distinctive Ottoman style of tall, tapering towers with conical tops indicating the sultan's patronage of the mosque.

The Blue Mosque takes its name from the predominant color of its interior, namely its blue Iznik (Anatolia) tile work and blue stencils. The imperial complex—more

than just a house of worship—includes three schools for religious instruction at various levels, a service kiosk, and rows of single- and double-storied shops. There is also a public bath; a soup kitchen, bakery, and larder for the poor; a hospital; fountains; and Sultan Ahmed's imperial tomb. These civic institutions, scattered seemingly haphazardly around the southern and eastern borders of the square, show that Ottoman mosque complexes were centers not only of religious life but also of educational, charitable, social, and even commercial activity.

The mosque is surrounded on three sides by a broad, nearly square, courtyard of some 175 yards on each side. Access is provided by eight portals. The inner court is reached through three gates and surrounded in turn by domed or vaulted colonnades enclosing the courtyard. A fountain for ablutions takes up the center of the courtyard, and is surrounded by six marble columns. Of the six minarets, four have three balconies and two have two balconies each, totaling sixteen, to allow the muezzins (Muslim crier of daily prayers) to call the faithful to prayer.

Exceeding Hagia Sophia in size, the Blue Mosque proper covers an area of some 70 by 78 yards, even though its central dome is slightly smaller than Sinan's Süleymaniye or Selimiye Mosques. This central dome is supported by four corner arches with corner pendentives, which are in turn set on four large round and fluted piers about 1.75 yards in diameter. Four semidomes, one on each side of the central dome, and small cupolas in the corners complete the roof system of the mosque. It is this construction of semidomes and turrets that reaches a climax with the major dome from all four sides. Another original feature of the mosque is the 260 windows allowing light to enter the interior. Some of the Venetian glass through which the light filtered in was later replaced to generate even more illumination.

The walls and piers are covered with glazed earthenware for one-third of their height to the level of the upper consoles. A total of 21,043 tiles were used, producing the bluish hue. The glazed earthenware bears floral motifs of various colors on white background, suggesting architect Mehmed Ağa's skill as an inlayer as well. The calligraphy of Qurʾānic verses and professions of faith was created by Ahmeti Kasim Gubari, considered the greatest calligrapher of the time. Additionally, there are bronze and wooden decorations. Eight volumes of records meticulously kept track of the cost of construction materials and other expenses.

SIGNIFICANCE

Grand royal complexes like the Blue Mosque completed (in 1617) in the postclassical period after 1600 would become rare. Political instability, military reverses, and economic setbacks—already evident under Ahmed I— all served to limit the number and size of new imperial mosques through most of the seventeenth and eighteenth centuries. In the meantime, however, the Blue Mosque came to be considered the first mosque of the Ottoman Empire, the people's favorite with its oversized courtyard, the largest in the land. During its construction, the entire output of the tile factories in Iznik was used in the mosque's decoration, even though much of what looks like tiles is in fact stencil work. The construction of the mosque involved so much material that it used up the empire's entire production of stone and marble, in addition to available tiles. Still, various construction materials were plundered from other buildings.

Critics are divided in their evaluation of the complex. Some see it as comparable to the magnificence of the Byzantine Hagia Sophia, while others highlight its lack of originality (even monotony), the mosque's heavy handed interior, and the garishness of the altered lighting arrangement. Still others view its external profile as the most successful pyramidal composition of all the great Ottoman mosques, with the large dome cascading into smaller ones. To many visitors, the Blue Mosque is one of the most noteworthy of Constantinople's landmarks.

It is paradoxical that Sultan Ahmed I, during whose tenure the Ottoman Empire had already seen its peak, was to order the construction of one of Constantinople's most distinctive monuments. Furthermore, the great Sinan's "pupil," Mehmed Ağa, should have come to equal his former master in building skills even though Mehmed Ağa paid his former mentor the highest of compliments when he replicated his vaulting scheme for the Sehzade Mosque. A final seeming contradiction is that Atatürk (1881-1938), the founder and hero of modern republican Turkey in the 1920's, who espoused secularism, should have been unable to diminish the symbolic significance of this or any other mosque, having to resign himself into converting Hagia Sophia from a mosque into a museum in 1934. The Blue Mosque, however, remains a "working" mosque but is open to visitors.

—*Peter B. Heller*

FURTHER READING

Aksit, Ilhan. *Treasures of Istanbul*. Istanbul: Haset Kitabevi Tunel, 1982. This handsomely illustrated survey by a Turkish archaeologist includes a chapter entitled "The Mosque and Tomb of Sultanahmet," stressing the beauty of the Blue Mosque.

Bierman, Irene A., et al., eds. *The Ottoman City and Its Parts: Urban Structure and Social Order*. New Rochelle, N.Y.: Aristide D. Caratzas, 1991. A collaborative work by Islamic, Ottoman, and art historians, pointing to the role of Ottoman Islam in architecture, urban development, and civic life. Illustrations, including the plan of the Blue Mosque complex, glossary, index.

Frishman, Martin, and Hasan-Uddin Khan, eds. *The Mosque: History, Architectural Development, and Regional Diversity*. New York: Thames & Hudson, 1994. Chapter 8 by Gulru Necipoglu, "Anatolia and the Ottoman Legacy," compares the Blue Mosque with others in the classical and postclassical period (pre- and post-1600). Bibliography, glossary, chronology, illustrations, index.

Goodwin, Godfrey. *A History of Ottoman Architecture*. New York: Thames & Hudson, 1987. An authoritative work that includes one of the best illustrated descriptions of the Blue Mosque. Glossary, bibliography, illustrations, index.

_____. *Sinan: Ottoman Architecture and Its Values Today.* London: Saqi, 1993. Goodwin suggests the architectural training that Sinan gave to Mehmed Ağa is evident in a number of the Blue Mosque's features. Illustrations, glossary, notes, maps, index.

Macauley, David. *Mosque.* Boston: Houghton Mifflin, 2003. A simple but graphic description of how, why, and by whom Ottoman mosque complexes were built up to the seventeenth century. Well illustrated in color

(including the blue Iznik tiles that decorate the Blue Mosque) and includes a glossary.

SEE ALSO: 1619-1636: Construction of Samarqand's Shirdar Madrasa; 1632-c. 1650: Shah Jahan Builds the Taj Mahal; 1656-1667: Construction of the Piazza San Pietro; July 13, 1664: Trappist Order Is Founded; 1675-1708: Wren Supervises the Rebuilding of St. Paul's Cathedral.

RELATED ARTICLES in *Great Lives from History: The Seventeenth Century, 1601-1700:* Kösem Sultan; Murad IV; Mustafa I.

1609-1619
KEPLER'S LAWS OF PLANETARY MOTION

Johannes Kepler, using the extremely accurate astronomical data inherited from Tycho Brahe, and over years of diligent persistence, single-handedly derived the three laws of planetary motion. Without these laws, Sir Isaac Newton might not have realized his law of universal gravitation.

LOCALE: Prague, Bohemia (now in the Czech Republic), and Linz, Austria
CATEGORIES: Science and technology; astronomy; mathematics; physics; cultural and intellectual history

KEY FIGURES
Johannes Kepler (1571-1630), astronomer who derived the three laws of planetary motion
Tycho Brahe (1546-1601), astronomer who brought mathematical precision to observational astronomy
Sir Isaac Newton (1642-1727), used Kepler's third law to deduce in mathematical form the universal law of gravitation
Nicolaus Copernicus (1473-1543), postulated a Sun-centered universe, a model Kepler championed

SUMMARY OF EVENT
The first serious challenge to the earth-centered universe of the ancient Greeks was Nicolaus Copernicus's sun-centered (heliocentric) model, published in 1543 as *De revolutionibus orbium coelestium* (*On the Revolutions of the Heavenly Spheres*, 1939; better known as *De revolutionibus*). Unfortunately, because Copernicus, like the Greeks, assumed the planets moved in circular orbits, his theory was inaccurate and offered no practical

improvement on the ancient model. Johannes Kepler, by shear dogged persistence over many years, derived the correct mathematical form of planetary orbits—his first law—as well as two additional laws of planetary motion.

Tycho Brahe, the first person since the Greeks to improve astronomy, devoted his life to the patient observation of planetary motion, measuring this motion with incredible accuracy years before the invention of the telescope. Kepler assisted Tycho during Tycho's last two years of life, acquiring his voluminous collection of data upon Tycho's death in 1601. Kepler had long been convinced of the correctness of the Copernican theory, but he knew that it was seriously flawed. He therefore turned his considerable mathematical skills to solving the problem of planetary orbits. To Kepler this was a religious quest; the key to God's mind was harmony and simplicity manifested in geometric order. To solve the mysteries of the solar system was to understand the grand secret of the universe.

Kepler assumed Tycho's post of imperial mathematician to Emperor Rudolf II of Bohemia in 1601, a position he occupied until Rudolf's death in 1612. Although there were royal astrological duties to attend to, the position gave him status, a salary, and, most important, time to pursue his scientific interests. During this most fruitful period of his professional life, he single-handedly founded scientific astronomy and invented instrumental optics.

He began the astronomical analysis of planetary orbits almost immediately by attempting to meld Tycho's data on the orbit of Mars into a Copernican system of simple uniform circular motion about the Sun. Over the next four years Kepler failed repeatedly; Tycho's data placed the orbit eight minutes of arc outside the predicted Copernican orbit, an error exceeding the accuracy of the measurements by at least a factor of four. Not willing to overlook this difference, Kepler had to assume that the Copernican scheme was seriously flawed. To rectify it he had to abandon the one assumption Copernicus had lifted directly from the ancient Greeks: that the planets moved in circular paths (or combinations of circles) at uniform speeds. By trial and error he discovered that the planetary orbits corresponded to a simple geometrical figure known to mathematicians since the third century B.C.E. as the ellipse. Kepler's first law of planetary orbits, building on this ancient knowledge, states that all planets move in elliptical paths, with the Sun at one of the foci of each ellipse. (Mathematically, an ellipse is a curve for which the sums of the distances of any point on the curve from two

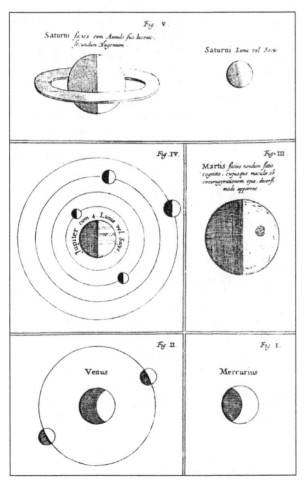

A 1611 drawing by Johannes Kepler, outlining his revolutionary model of planetary motion. (The Granger Collection)

internal fixed points, the foci, are equal to the sums of distances from the foci to any other point on the curve.)

Kepler realized that his first law by itself was incomplete because it provided absolutely no information about how the speed of a planet in its orbit was related to its orbital position. If such a relationship could be found the features of any planet's motion could be elegantly and succinctly summarized. Although Kepler had no guarantee that such a relationship even existed or could be found, such was his faith in the order of the universe that he proceeded on the basis that it lay hidden in Tycho's voluminous data. By sheer persistence and ingenuity Kepler revealed another simple law, to be called the second law of planetary motion: During any given time interval, the imaginary line connecting a planet and the Sun sweeps out the same area anywhere along the elliptical path. As a result of this law, it follows that the distance from the Sun to a planetary position multiplied by the speed at that point is equal to a constant, thus giving Kepler his simple relationship. His second law establishes the possibility of accurate astronomical prediction, without resort to the multiplicity of geometric artifices employed by previous systems utilizing circular orbits.

Kepler labored for several years on a book detailing these laws, readying it for publication in 1606. Three more years were required to find a publisher and to raise the money to pay the printing costs, an expenditure he had to assume since no wealthy patron offered support. Printing began 1608, and the book was released the following summer as *Astronomia nova* (1609; *New Astronomy*, 1992).

During the time he was theorizing planetary orbits, Kepler also researched optics, particularly lenses, publishing *Ad Vitellionem paralipomena, quibus astronomiae pars optica traditur* (1604, also known as *Astronomiae pars optica*; *Optics*, 2000). This work showed that light intensity decreases as the inverse square of the distance from a source, explained the principle of the camera obscura (precursor to the photographic camera), elucidated how spectacles for near and far sightedness worked, explained light refraction by lenses, and showed that the eye's lens projects an inverted image on the retina. This was followed by another great work on optics, *Dioptrice* (1611; partial English translation of preface, 1880), which applied the principles discussed in the earlier work to the newly invented telescope.

Kepler's first and second laws of planetary motion were discovered by a bizarre combination of blundering intuition and an astute alertness for hidden clues. The laws were phenomenally successful at predicting planetary positions, but Kepler remained dissatisfied because no overall pattern connecting the orbits of different planets existed. Although there was no good reason why the motions of unrelated planets should be connected, Kepler, who was obsessed with the conviction that nature was simple and harmonious, believed a relationship did exist. Consequently, he spent a decade relentlessly pursuing this quest despite the many personal misfortunes that plagued the latter part of his life. (After Rudolf II died, Kepler lost his position at court and was forced to accept a lesser position in Austria.)

After years of unceasing toil, he found that there was indeed a pattern connecting the orbits of different planets: the third law of planetary motion. This law states that the square of the period of revolution of a planet about the Sun is proportional to the cube of the mean radius of the planetary orbit. Produced against the backdrop of European turmoil and personal tragedy, Kepler published *Harmonices mundi* (1619; *The Harmony of the World*, 1997), with no intended irony.

SIGNIFICANCE

Not only are Kepler's three laws the foundation upon which modern astrophysics was constructed, but the intervening centuries has verified their accuracy for all types of orbits, including those followed by charged particles moving under the action of electrical forces.

Kepler never realized the true significance of his laws, because without differential calculus (invented by Isaac Newton), the three laws show no apparent connection to each other. The connection was revealed eighty years later when Newton proved that an elliptical orbit is one of the logical consequences of his laws of motion and gravitation. The objective importance of Kepler's third law to Newton is inestimable, as it provided the final clue for Newton to deduce and verify his law of universal gravitation.

Although Kepler is honored for his work in astronomy, a subtle and perhaps even more important contribution was his innovative attitude toward astronomy, an attitude destined to have profound effects on the future of the physical sciences. This was a shift from attempting to fit the universe to preconceived geometrical models to a new emphasis on the mathematical relationships underlying the observations. His successful attempt to formulate physical laws in mathematical form, based on precise quantitative data, established the equation as the prototypical essence of physical law.

—*George R. Plitnik*

FURTHER READING

Applebaum, William. "Keplerian Astronomy after Kepler: Researches and Problems." *History of Science* 34, no. 4 (December, 1996): 451. Applebaum argues that Kepler was more influential on astronomy in his own time than is commonly thought.

Casper, Max. *Kepler*. New York: Abelard-Schuman, 1959. A translation of the 1947 edition of the definitive biography of Kepler and his time, including discussions of his laws and how he arrived at them. Includes an index and excellent bibliography.

Ferris, T. *Coming of Age in the Milky Way*. New York: Doubleday, 1989. Chapter 4 of this well-written summary of science history presents a comprehensive overview of how Copernicus, Tycho, and Kepler advanced human understanding of the solar system.

Hathaway, N. *The Friendly Guide to the Universe*. New York: Penguin Books, 1994. This entertaining, idiosyncratic synopsis of astronomy, among other areas, explains Kepler's laws with easy-to-read prose and simple diagrams.

Koestler, Arthur. *The Sleepwalkers*. New York: Penguin Books, 1989. An easy to read compendium tracing the evolution of human understanding of astronomy from the ancient Greeks through Isaac Newton. Eleven chapters are devoted to Kepler.

SEE ALSO: Sept., 1608: Invention of the Telescope; 1610: Galileo Confirms the Heliocentric Model of the Solar System; 1615-1696: Invention and Development of the Calculus; 1632: Galileo Publishes *Dialogue Concerning the Two Chief World Systems, Ptolemaic and Copernican*; 1665: Cassini Discovers Jupiter's Great Red Spot.

RELATED ARTICLES in *Great Lives from History: The Seventeenth Century, 1601-1700:* Galileo; Johannes Kepler; Gottfried Wilhelm Leibniz; Sir Isaac Newton.

1610

GALILEO CONFIRMS THE HELIOCENTRIC MODEL OF THE SOLAR SYSTEM

Galileo, through his observations and analyses, confirmed Copernicus's heliocentric model of the solar system, which led to an inevitable clash between scientific inquiry and the traditional geocentric beliefs of Aristotelian philosophy.

LOCALE: Italy

CATEGORIES: Astronomy; physics; science and technology; cultural and intellectual history

KEY FIGURES

Nicolaus Copernicus (1473-1543), Polish astronomer who developed the heliocentric model of the solar system

Galileo (1564-1642), Italian astronomer, mathematician, and physicist

Cosimo II de' Medici (1590-1621), grand duke of Tuscany, 1609-1621, and patron and protector of Galileo

Paul V (Camillo Borghese; 1552-1621), Roman Catholic pope, 1605-1621, who suppressed Copernican heliocentric theory

Urban VIII (Maffeo Vincenzo Barberini; 1568-1644), Roman Catholic pope, 1623-1644, who forced Galileo to renounce the heliocentric theory

SUMMARY OF EVENT

Galileo's *Sidereus nuncius* (1610; *The Sidereal Messenger*, 1880; also known as *The Starry Messenger*) created a sensation throughout Europe, with poets comparing his scientific discoveries to the feats of explorer Christopher Columbus during the Renaissance. In the book, Galileo reported observing the heavens through a spyglass, later called a refracting telescope. After improving the magnification of the original Dutch spyglass, Galileo made additional observations during 1609-1610 and, for the first time, diagramed the distant stars of the Milky Way, the constellation Cancer, and the nebula Praesepe. He also proclaimed that Earth's moon was not as smooth as previously believed by Aristotle and his supporters. Instead, the Moon was pitted with mountains, valleys, and craters. Within a two-month period, Galileo watched and sketched the horned moon change its shape.

Turning his telescope on distant Jupiter, he observed strange lights nearby that changed positions over several weeks and deduced that they orbited Jupiter as the Moon orbits Earth. These objects were, in fact, the moons of Ju-

piter. Galileo named them the "Medicean stars" to honor his patrons, the Medici rulers of Florence. Galileo also observed lights around Saturn, later identified as the rings of Saturn.

Galileo's book also advanced his own career, for he was appointed mathematician-philosopher to Cosimo II de' Medici, the grand duke of Tuscany, who became a strong patron and protector of Galileo during the next ten years. More important, *The Sidereal Messenger* became a milestone in Galileo's march toward total acceptance of the heliocentric theory of the solar system as espoused by Nicolaus Copernicus. At first, Galileo had not questioned the traditional beliefs of Aristotelian philosophy that state that Earth stood stationary at the center of the universe, with the stars and Sun revolving around it. By 1597, however, he found Copernicus's ideas of planetary motion around the Sun more plausible. Galileo's telescopic observations of the changing moon, of Jupiter and Saturn, and of other stars during 1609-1610 provided ample evidence that Aristotle's claims were false.

Galileo's conviction that the heliocentric model was correct deepened in late 1610, when he observed through his telescope the sunlight on Venus, which glided across that planet in similar fashion to that of Earth's moon. He noted the phases of sunlight on Venus, changing from a sliver to a full circle. To Galileo, Aristotle's beliefs could not account for these changes, but Copernicus's heliocentric theory could.

Galileo became so enamored with heliocentricity and his telescopic discoveries that he cast caution aside in promoting the unorthodox heliocentric theory. In doing so, he inadvertently challenged the Roman Catholic Church, which held firmly to Aristotle's beliefs because Aristotelian concepts supported biblical accounts of the universe. In 1611, for example, Galileo displayed his telescope to Pope Paul V, who made strong objections to Galileo's scientific observation of the heavens. In a series of letters made public by Galileo's enemies in 1613-1614, Galileo offended Church leaders by arguing that the heliocentric theory was compatible with Catholic doctrine and proper interpretation of the Bible. When Galileo's letters on sunspots (1613) appeared, he contradicted the Church's views that the heavens were perfect and unchanging, since his telescope revealed black blemishes randomly scudding across the Sun's sur-

A statue of Galileo. (George L. Shuman)

esy and teachings contrary to Church doctrine. The Church feared unauthorized ideas, so it banned speeches, burned books, and even resorted to burning blasphemers at the stake.

In 1616, Pope Paul V officially denounced the heliocentric theory and placed the works of Nicolaus Copernicus on the Index of Forbidden Books, reasoning that Copernican ideas endangered Church tenets. The pope also summoned Galileo to Rome to determine the orthodoxy of Galileo's views. In spite of Galileo's protests, Pope Paul forbade Galileo to hold or defend the heliocentric theory, either orally or in writing. When the Holy Office threatened to bring formal charges if he disobeyed, Galileo—a devout Catholic, reluctantly promised to do so.

Galileo continued to study the heavens privately through his telescope. He also turned his energies to perfecting the microscope and to studying magnets, flood control, condensation of water, navigational problems, and even the chance factors in a roll of dice. He wrote *The Assayer* (1623; also known as *Saggiatore*) and *Dialogo sopra i due massimi sistemi del mondo, tolemaico e copernicano* (1632; *Dialogue Concerning the Two Chief World Systems, Ptolemaic and Copernican*, 1661). The latter publication, a best-selling book that had been approved by Church censors, presented the witty dialogue of three acquaintances. Each represented a specific posture for and against the scientific and religious worldviews and the debate over the center of the universe, Sun or Earth. On the surface, Galileo treated the three characters impartially. Nevertheless, he cleverly disguised the Aristotelian-Copernican controversy within the dialogue, making sure that the character holding the heliocentric view came off best in the end.

In 1632, when enemies of Galileo pointed out to Pope Urban VIII (successor to Paul V) that Galileo had violated the 1616 papal order forbidding the discussion of heliocentric theory, Urban immediately stopped the sale of the book and ordered that Galileo be prosecuted for disobedience of a Church order. To make matters worse, Galileo's enemies claimed that the book ridiculed Church teachings, hinting that one dim-witted character in the book appeared to be the pope himself. To avoid the threat of torture on the rack, Galileo publicly confessed his heresy and the falseness of the heliocentric theory before the pope and the entire Congregation of the Holy Office. Condemned to life imprisonment, never to utter a word about cosmology, the disgraced Galileo saw *Dialogue Concerning the Two Chief World Systems* prohibited from distribution and burned as trash.

face. Galileo arrogantly dismissed the swelling ranks of angry priests and professors who resented and envied him, belittling them as ignorant and inadequate. In turn, these individuals accused Galileo of spreading evil doctrine, crossing over into theology, contradicting Scripture, and even challenging the authority of the Catholic Church.

Between 1613 and 1631, the Catholic Church warned Galileo to abandon the heliocentric model of the heavens. The Church felt threatened by Reform movements sweeping Protestant Germany, the Netherlands, England, and Scandinavia, along with the unrest seething in France. The Catholic Church checked further threats to its power and influence by means of the Inquisition, a tribunal established to discover, suppress, and punish her-

Broken in spirit, arthritic, and confined in isolation to his house outside Florence for the remainder of his life, Galileo spent his later years engaged in pure science, thus avoiding theological speculation. In spite of blindness, Galileo wrote his masterwork, *Discorsi e dimostrazioni mathematiche intorno a due nuove scienze atteneti alla meccanica* (1638; *Discourses Concerning Two New Sciences*, 1914), a book on physics that provided mathematical proofs on his theory of projectile motion, laws of free-falling bodies, and studies on uniform acceleration and the tensile strength of materials. Somehow, he managed to smuggle the book to the Netherlands for publication. Nearly three decades later, this work by Galileo aided Sir Isaac Newton, an English mathematician, in discovering the laws of gravity and motion.

When Galileo died in 1642, an unforgiving Pope Urban refused to allow the erection of a statue in Galileo's memory, thus embarrassing the Catholic Church over the next three hundred years for its antiscience and antiintellectual stance.

SIGNIFICANCE

In 1835, the Catholic Church finally removed its ban on Galileo's *Dialogue Concerning the Two Chief World Systems*, long after the heliocentric theory became accepted science. In 1984, a papal commission released secret documents in the Galileo case and admitted that Galileo should not have been condemned.

Galileo's continuing fame rests on his mathematical theories, his work in physics, his inventions, and his unsuccessful battles with the Catholic Church. More important, his stature increased over the years because of his stubborn questioning of false ancient beliefs and his demand for verification of "truths" through observation and experimentation. These basic principles, as espoused by Galileo, became the foundation of modern science.

—*Richard Whitworth*

FURTHER READING

Blackwell, Richard J. *Galileo, Bellarmine, and the Bible*. London: University of Notre Dame Press, 1991. Blackwell's work examines the complexities of the Galileo affair from the perspective of his contemporary Catholic opponents.

Drake, Stillman. *Galileo: Pioneer Scientist*. Toronto: University of Toronto Press, 1990. A scholarly account that traces Galileo's journey from Ptolemaic astronomy to full belief in the heliocentric theory.

Finocchiaro, Maurice A., ed. *The Galileo Affair: A Documentary History*. Berkeley: University of California Press, 1989. Provides the actual correspondence of Galileo, his friends, and his enemies from 1613 to 1633. Includes a chronology of events and a biographical glossary.

Machamer, Peter, ed. *The Cambridge Companion to Galileo*. New York: Cambridge University Press, 1998. Collection of essays exploring the many facets of Galileo's work and his relationship with the Church. Chapter 7 examines "Galileo's Discoveries with the Telescope and Their Evidence for the Copernican Theory."

Reston, James. *Galileo: A Life*. New York: HarperCollins, 1994. A lively, dynamic portrayal of Galileo's life, temperament, and accomplishments.

Ronan, Colin A. *Galileo*. New York: G. P. Putnam's Sons, 1974. A synthesis of modern scholarship on Galileo's life in Renaissance Italy. Lavishly illustrated.

Rowland, Wade. *Galileo's Mistake: A New Look at the Epic Confrontation Between Galileo and the Church*. New York: Arcade, 2003. Rowland argues that Galileo and Church officials disagreed about something more significant than whether Earth revolved around the Sun: He argues that in reality they were in dispute about the nature of truth and how people acquire the truth.

Sharratt, Michael. *Galileo: Decisive Innovator*. Oxford, England: Blackwell, 1994. A concise biography that closely examines Galileo's masterworks.

SEE ALSO: Sept., 1608: Invention of the Telescope; 1609-1619: Kepler's Laws of Planetary Motion; 1615-1696: Invention and Development of the Calculus; 1632: Galileo Publishes *Dialogue Concerning the Two Chief World Systems, Ptolemaic and Copernican*; Feb., 1656: Huygens Identifies Saturn's Rings; 1665: Cassini Discovers Jupiter's Great Red Spot; Dec. 7, 1676: Rømer Calculates the Speed of Light.

RELATED ARTICLES in *Great Lives from History: The Seventeenth Century, 1601-1700:* Gian Domenico Cassini; Galileo; Robert Hooke; Christiaan Huygens; Johannes Kepler; Hans Lippershey; Maria Celeste; Cosimo II de' Medici; Sir Isaac Newton; Paul V; Urban VIII.

1610's

1610-1643
REIGN OF LOUIS XIII

*King Louis XIII's government, under the leadership of
Cardinal de Richelieu, laid the foundations of royal
absolutism, economic development, and French
military hegemony in Europe. The government also
patronized artists and writers and established the
French Academy to standardize the French language.*

LOCALE: France

CATEGORIES: Government and politics; economics;
cultural and intellectual history; wars, uprisings, and
civil unrest

KEY FIGURES

Louis XIII (1601-1643), king of France, r. 1610-1643

Marie de Médicis (1573-1642), Louis's mother, queen
regent, r. 1610-1617

Cardinal de Richelieu (Armand-Jean du Plessis; 1585-
1642), chief minister, 1624-1642

Concino Concini (d. 1617), chief minister during
Marie's regency

Duke de Luynes (Charles d'Albert; 1578-1621),
government director, 1617-1621

Gaston d'Orléans (1608-1660), brother of Louis XIII

Anne of Austria (1601-1666), queen of France,
r. 1615-1643, and queen regent, r. 1643-1651

Jules Mazarin (1602-1661), Richelieu's assistant and
successor as chief minister

Louis XIV (1638-1715), king of France, r. 1643-1715

Jean Martin de Laubardemont (1590-1653), ruthless
agent of Richelieu

SUMMARY OF EVENT

In 1610, the assassination of King Henry IV plunged
France into a period of political instability, religious
quarrels, and aristocratic rebellion. The new monarch,
Louis XIII, was only nine years old. His mother, Marie
de Médicis, despite her sympathies with the Spanish
Habsburg Dynasty (she sought alliances with them),
controlled the government as regent. Her pro-Spanish
sentiments presented problems and alienated the king
and the French people because France had been at war
with the Habsburgs for more than a century.

The Queen Mother rebuilt the Luxemburg Palace and
hired Flemish artist Peter Paul Rubens to paint twenty-
one portraits of the royal family. She showed little af-
fection for her son, however, who spent much of his
time on hunting excursions with his falconer, Charles
d'Albert, duke de Luynes. At the age of fourteen, Louis

was obliged to enter into a political marriage with Anne
of Austria, daughter of the king of Spain.

The great nobles and the judges of the courts took advantage of the weakness of the Crown to assert their independent powers. Attempting to rally support for the
Crown, Anne in 1614 called a meeting of the Estates-
General, the national representative assembly. Some of
the delegates to the assembly hoped it might acquire
powers like those of England's Parliament, but the conflicts among its three social orders—clergy, nobility, and
middle-class commoners—prevented it from getting institutional vetoes over taxes or spending.

During her regency, Marie de Médicis turned over
many governmental functions to her Italian favorite,
Concino Concini, marquis d'Ancre. She also relied on
the assistance of Cardinal de Richelieu (Armand-Jean du
Plessis), the young bishop of Luçon and an efficient administrator who had trained for a military career before
entering the priesthood. In November, 1616, Richelieu
was named secretary of state for foreign affairs. By then,
however, Louis was becoming dissatisfied with the situation. In April of 1617, encouraged and assisted by the
duke de Luynes, he arranged the assassination of the unpopular Concini. The police and courts quickly accepted
claims of Concini's treason, despite a lack of evidence.
Louis sent his mother into exile under house arrest in
Bloise, and he also dismissed Richelieu, who temporarily returned to his bishopric tasks.

For the next four years, Louis's chief adviser was the
duke de Luynes, who was promoted to constable of the
country. After Luynes reduced the pensions of the nobles,
they revolted and rescued the Queen Mother. Luynes defeated the nobles in battle and then ended the rebellion by
negotiations. Like most rulers of the century, Louis and
Luynes assumed that religious unity was necessary for
public order. When Luynes tried to restore Catholicism
to Navarre and other regions of France, the Protestant
Huguenots revolted. Luynes led successful campaigns
against them in 1620 and 1621. Following Luynes's
death, the principal government adviser was Charles de
La Vieuville, the superintendent of finance.

After reconciling with his mother in 1621, Louis read-
mitted Richelieu into his government. Richelieu became
a cardinal and joined the royal council in 1624. After La
Vieuville's disgrace, the ambitious cardinal emerged as
the dominant minister in the government—a position he
would hold until his death eighteen years later. Although

Louis allowed Richelieu a great deal of discretion, he usually oversaw the overall direction of governmental policies, rarely allowing his minister to forget who was king.

Richelieu's memoirs and political testament (both probably compiled by assistants) indicate that his policies included three major objectives: to deprive the French Protestants (Huguenots) of their fortresses, to reduce the independence of the great nobles, and to check the power of the Habsburgs in Germany, Spain, and Italy. Although he sometimes spoke of France's natural borders (the Rhine River, Alps, and Pyrenees), he was primarily concerned with securing strategic bridgeheads for protection against external enemies.

At home, Richelieu soon faced the challenge of overcoming a series of insurrections. In 1626, a revolt of nobles involved the king's younger bother and heir, Gaston d'Orléans. Richelieu reacted ruthlessly, executing one conspirator, Henri de Talleyrand. The Huguenot insurrections were even more dangerous. In October of 1628, royal troops captured the fortress port at La Rochelle.

Louis XIII. (Library of Congress)

Once Richelieu captured their southern strongholds, the resulting Peace of Alais (1629) deprived the Huguenots of military power, while allowing them limited freedom to exercise their religion. Ignoring religion in his foreign policy, he intervened militarily in the duchy of Mantua in an effort to oppose Habsburg power in northern Italy.

Richelieu's policies of allowing religious freedom for Protestants and opposing the Habsburgs infuriated the French ultra-Catholics, called *devots*. The Queen Mother, who had close ties with them, turned against the cardinal. In 1630, during a life-threatening illness, Louis XIII yielded to his mother's pressures and promised to dismiss Richelieu. After the famous Day of Dupes (November 10), however, Louis recovered and decided to retain Richelieu. The Queen Mother fled into the arms of France's enemies in the Spanish Netherlands. Gaston also fled into exile, and two years later he invaded France with foreign troops. The governor of Languedoc, Duke Henri de Montmorency, joined the invasion, but Richelieu's forces prevailed. Montmorency was executed and others on his side were brutally punished.

With his belief in royal absolutism and the divine rights of kings, Richelieu would not tolerate illegal acts or opposition to the regime. He insisted that the death penalty for dueling be enforced. When the abbot of Saint-Cyran, a leader of the Jansenist movement, criticized French foreign policy for not supporting international Catholicism, the cardinal had him imprisoned for nearly a decade. Often he commissioned the sinister baron Jean Martin de Laubardemont as a special prosecutor against opponents of the regime, as in the Loudun witch trial of Urbain Grandier, who was an opponent of royal policies.

As the Thirty Years' War progressed, Richelieu expanded his efforts to check the power of the Habsburgs. He did not hesitate to subsidize Protestant leaders, such as Swedish king Gustavus II Adolphus. In 1635, France formally declared war against Spain. After some initial reverses, French troops won a series of significant victories. By 1640, they were in possession of Alsace, Artois, and other regions that they would acquire in treaties of 1648 (Peace of Westphalia) and 1659 (Treaty of the Pyrenees). Richelieu's military operations were extremely expensive, however. In order to raise money, he resorted to a variety of means, including skyrocketing taxation, loans, and the sale of offices.

In industrial policy, Richelieu supported mercantilist schemes to make France self-sufficient. He constructed a network of canals and established commercial companies to trade overseas, especially in Canada. An enthusiastic builder, he renovated the palace at Fontainbleau and constructed a number of famous buildings, including the large residential complex, the Palace Cardinal, now called the Palace Royale. His educational projects included the beginning of the College du Plessis and enlargement of the Sorbonne.

In this age of outstanding cultural accomplishments, Richelieu used both his own great wealth and funds of the state to patronize an exceptionally large number of artists, architects, playwrights, and philosophers. For instance, he sponsored the so-called Society of Five Authors, of whom the most famous was dramatist Pierre Corneille, author of *Le Cid* (1636-1637; *The Cid*, 1637). The artists he patronized included Louis Le Nain, who painted the realistic life of peasants; Jacques Callot, who realistically depicted the miseries of warfare; Georges de La Tour, who emphasized religious themes; and painter Philippe de Champaigne, who produced many portraits of the period. Among philosophers, Richelieu supported René Descartes, perhaps the most influential philosopher of the period; Marin Mersenne, defender of orthodox Christianity; Pierre Gassendi, who did much to popularize Epicurean ethics; and Tommaso Campanella, who had spent many years in Italian prisons for his unorthodox views.

Throughout his tenure, Richelieu never lost sight of his long-term objective of concentrating as much authority as possible into institutions controlled by the Crown. In 1635, he established the French Academy in an effort to bring about national standards for a common language throughout the kingdom. Also, he began to strengthen the royal agents in the provinces by making them permanent residents, called intendants, with authority to supervise the police force under French marshals. He also spent considerable funds for an informal system of spies to provide information about possible threats to the Crown. He easily prevented a calling of the Estates-General, but to limit the powers of the powerful courts, called *parlements*, was more difficult. He particularly opposed their traditional practice of making remonstrances, or formal protests, of royal edicts, and by 1641, he had temporarily checked this power.

Louis XIII never had a very close relationship with Queen Anne. Early in the reign he was greatly disappointed by her three miscarriages. With age, the king had a series of platonic as well as sexual relationships with both women and men. After he learned of Anne's indiscretions with the duke of Buckingham in 1625, he avoided her company. During the war with the Habsburgs in the 1630's, her continuing association with the enemy was an additional source of hostility. Richelieu had her interrogated and closely supervised. In December of 1637, however, a storm reportedly obliged the king to stay with Anne in the Louvre, apparently resulting in the birth of the future king Louis XIV.

After 1639, the king's favorite was a young courtier, Henri Coeffier-Ruzé d'Effiat, marquis de Cinq-Mars. Richelieu's spies discovered that Coeffier-Ruzé d'Effiat had entered into a conspiracy with Gaston and Habsburg agents. On September 12, 1642, at Richelieu's insistence, the marquis was executed, and his death produced coolness between the king and his minister. Three months later, Richelieu died from overwork and chronic illness, and the king died of tuberculosis on May 14, 1643. Four-year-old Louis XIV inherited the throne. Anne of Austria assumed the powers of the regency. As chief administrator, she relied on another strong cardinal, Jules Mazarin, who had been trained by Richelieu.

SIGNIFICANCE

Encouraged by Louis XIII, Cardinal de Richelieu initiated a process of centralization that later developed into a system of near-absolute monarchy during the reign of Louis XIV. The cardinal's accomplishments included the limitations on the *parlements* and the establishment of residential intendants in the provinces. In the realm of religious unity, Richelieu's subduing of the Protestants made it possible for Louis XIV in 1685 to abolish religious freedom for Protestants.

The Battle of Rocroi, which occurred shortly after the deaths of Louis XIII, usually is considered to have inaugurated French military domination of Europe. Although Louis XIII's reign was less spectacular than that of his son, it was a part of France's Great Century, with impressive accomplishments in economic development and cultural achievements.

—Thomas Tandy Lewis

FURTHER READING

Bercé, Yves-Marie. *The Birth of Absolutism: A History of France, 1598-1661*. Translated by Richard Rex. New York: St. Martin's Press, 1996. Bercé argues that absolutism was a modern creation growing out of the disorders and political conflict of the period.

Bergin, Joseph. *The Rise of Richelieu*. New Haven, Conn.: Yale University Press, 1991. A detailed account of the cardinal's early career until his joining the royal council in 1624.

Church, William. *Richelieu and Reasons of State*. Princeton, N.J.: Princeton University Press, 1972. A scholarly work dealing with how the cardinal tried to harmonize his ideals of a Christian statesman with the exigencies of a monarchical system.

Hayden, J. Michael. *France and the Estates General of 1614.* New York: Cambridge University Press, 1974. A scholarly monograph that provides an excellent analysis about why the Estates-General failed to meet again until 1789.

Knecht, Robert. *Richelieu.* London: Longman, 1991. An outstanding synthesis of the cardinal's life and career, especially good on the topics of absolutism and the patronage of the arts. Highly recommended.

Marvick, Elizabeth. *Louis XIII: The Making of a King.* New Haven, Conn.: Yale University Press, 1987. A detailed account of the king's complex personality and his life before the coup of 1617.

Moote, A. Lloyd. *Louis XIII, the Just.* Berkeley: University of California Press, 1989. A controversial work because of its thesis that Louis was an efficient monarch and more intelligent than usually thought. Moote includes interesting information about the king's personal life.

Ranum, Orest. *Richelieu and the Councilors of Louis XIII.* London: Oxford University Press, 1963. A standard and useful work that describes the internal workings of Louis's government.

Rapley, Robert. *Case of Witchcraft: The Trial of Urbain Grandier.* Montreal, Canada: McGill-Queens University Press, 1998. The story of a famous witch trial that reveals much about the judicial system of the time and Richelieu's ruthlessness in dealing with his enemies.

SEE ALSO: 1618-1648: Thirty Years' War; Nov. 10, 1630: The Day of Dupes; 1637: Descartes Publishes His *Discourse on Method*; July, 1643-Oct. 24, 1648: Peace of Westphalia; June, 1648: Wars of the Fronde Begin; Nov. 7, 1659: Treaty of the Pyrenees; 1661: Absolute Monarchy Emerges in France; 1661-1672: Colbert Develops Mercantilism; May 24, 1667-May 2, 1668: War of Devolution.

RELATED ARTICLES in *Great Lives from History: The Seventeenth Century, 1601-1700:* Anne of Austria; Jacques Callot; Tommaso Campanella; Charles I; Jean-Baptiste Colbert; The Great Condé; Pierre Corneille; René Descartes; Pierre Gassendi; Gustavus II Adolphus; Cornelius Otto Jansen; Georges de La Tour; Louis XIII; Louis XIV; Marie de Médicis; Marin Mersenne; Jules Mazarin; Axel Oxenstierna; Philip IV; Cardinal de Richelieu; Urban VIII.

Beginning June, 1610
HUDSON EXPLORES HUDSON BAY

Hudson's explorations established the main water route to northwestern Canada, a route that would be exploited throughout the next two centuries for trade and settlement. His expeditions would lead indirectly to the creation of the Hudson's Bay Company, arguably the most successful and most powerful of all privately chartered European colonial corporations.

LOCALE: Hudson's Bay (now Hudson Bay, Canada)
CATEGORY: Exploration and discovery

KEY FIGURES
Henry Hudson (1560's?-1611), English explorer and navigator
Robert Juet (d. 1611), mate aboard the *Discovery* and leader of the mutiny against Hudson
Médard Chouart des Groseilliers (1625-1698), French explorer and cofounder of the Hudson's Bay Company
Pierre Esprit Radisson (c. 1636-1710), French fur trader, explorer, and cofounder of the Hudson's Bay Company

Martin Frobisher (c. 1535-1594), English explorer thought to be the first European to sail into Hudson Strait
Prince Rupert (1619-1682), prince of Bavaria, cousin of Charles II of England, and an early supporter of the Hudson's Bay Company

SUMMARY OF EVENT
On April 27, 1610, Henry Hudson and a crew of twenty-three men, including his son, embarked from London in the ship *Discovery* to search for the fabled Northwest Passage to Asia. Bold and determined, Hudson had made several earlier attempts to locate the Northwest Passage. Among these was a voyage in 1608 for the Dutch that resulted in the exploration of the Hudson River when his crew lost confidence in his plans to sail through Hudson Strait. On the 1610-1611 expedition, his final voyage to the New World, Hudson established the existence of Hudson Bay; the Hudson Strait, which is the main conduit to Hudson Bay; and James Bay, the southern appendix to Hudson Bay. Others, including Martin

161

Frobisher, had made earlier, less conclusive attempts to explore the territory, but Hudson was the most successful.

Over the next three months, Hudson and his crew sailed north from London past Iceland and Greenland, arriving in Ungava Bay in June, 1610. They entered the strait and were in the bay proper at the end of June. By September, they had pushed south and begun to explore James Bay, still desperately persisting in the belief that they could find the Northwest Passage. Following the eastern coast of James Bay, the decision was made to winter on the southern shores, near the mouth of the Rupert River. Hudson and crew passed an uncomfortable and fractious winter, troubled by too few provisions and unexpected cold. The arrival of spring found the crew uncertain of Hudson's leadership and unwilling to trust his promises of an immediate return to England. They mutinied in June, 1611, led by Robert Juet, and Hudson, his son, and seven sailors, including several sick crew members, were placed in an open boat and set adrift. Hudson and the others were never seen again, and they are believed to have died soon afterward. Only eight of Hudson's crew returned to England six months later, carrying with them Hudson's records, including a fragment of his logbook. Four of these men were tried and acquitted by the Admiralty for their part in the mutiny.

Several times between 1612 and 1616, the *Discovery* returned to Hudson Bay, with crews that included some of Hudson's men, to retrace Hudson's route, confirm his findings, and look for survivors. Other explorers—Robert Bylot and Luke Foxe (1631) and Thomas James (1631)—would follow Hudson's route, trying yet again to find the elusive passage to Asia. However, permanent European settlement of the area would not begin for more than fifty years. The bare and heavily forested regions of the Canadian Shield would prove somewhat inhospitable to Europeans, and their main settlements continued to be in the area of the Saint Lawrence River Valley and the coastal regions to the east.

Native settlement in the area of Hudson Bay, however, was fairly extensive. Ringing Hudson Bay to the north and on the east and west sides were the Inuit. To the south, the Cree, an Algonquian people, made their home, and to the west lived the Chipewyan. The company undoubtedly encountered native peoples on this voyage, especially the Cree, in whose territory the company camped for the winter. Hudson's hope to rely on native peoples for food through the winter failed, however,

An artist's rendering of Hudson making contact with Native Americans during his expedition. The explorer is shown introducing Canadian Indians to alcohol. (Gay Brothers)

HUDSON'S VOYAGE OF 1610-1611

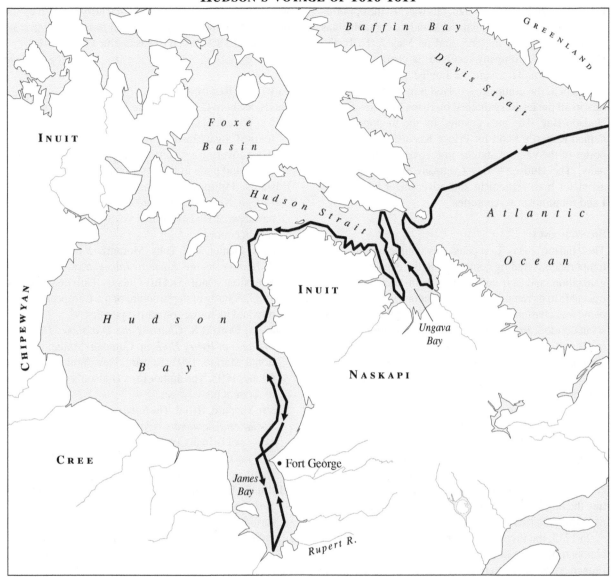

which is why food was so scarce in the 1610-1611 winter. In addition, it seems that the crew was fatally attacked while retreating through the strait after the mutiny, and several crew members were lost.

Ultimately, the English would settle Hudson Bay, drawn to brave the harsh winters by the lucrative fur trade. While the fur trade had begun in the early part of the sixteenth century as a subsidiary to European coastal fishing, by century's end the seemingly insatiable European demand for furs guaranteed the independence of the trapping industry. Competition between the Dutch and

the French in the Saint Lawrence region proved the profitability of the industry but also left some areas nearly depleted of animals. The English, eager to stake their share in the fur trade, sought their own opportunity in the northwest.

In 1688, an English trading post was established at the opening of the Rupert River by Médard Chouart des Groseilliers, who, with Pierre Esprit Radisson, sought further funding to develop the venture. The two Frenchmen had first offered their venture to their own government, but France had declined, as their settlement farther south along the Saint Lawrence River was firmly established. For the English, though, this was just the opportunity they had sought. A joint stock trading company was formed in England in 1665, and on May 2, 1670, the Hudson's Bay Company received its charter from the English crown. To assure the English presence against the French, the company received a monopoly to trade furs in all the territory drained by rivers that flowed into Hudson Bay. The area covered by the monopoly was named Rupert's Land for Prince Rupert, an early supporter of the venture and the first governor of the company. The Hudson's Bay Company was the primary agent for both settlement and government in Rupert's Land for almost two centuries.

SIGNIFICANCE

The Hudson's Bay Company was unique among contemporaneous trading companies in the degree of its organization and self-sufficiency, both of which were traceable to its remoteness from London, where the company was chartered. Basic policy and procedures were set in London; an elected governor acted for the company in Rupert's Land. A series of posts was built at the mouths of important rivers. Each post—part military fortress, part trade town—was led by a chief factor aided by a council of officers. The presence of the company and its success in securing pelts for the European market seem to have raised the ire of the French fur traders along the Saint Lawrence River. For fifty years, the French traders moved westward and upward in their search for beaver and other animals, encroaching on lands claimed by the company. Several times, the French campaigned to capture the English posts as part of their attempts to claim all of North America.

In 1713, the French were forced to recognize English claims to the area as part of the Treaty of Utrecht. The French government completely withdrew from the competition in 1763, when it ceded its holdings in North America at the close of the French and Indian War. Taking its place in competition for furs was an English trading company based in Montreal, the North West Company. Established in the 1760's by Scottish immigrants to Canada, the North West Company in 1790 challenged the Hudson's Bay Company, attempting to end the latter's monopoly. By establishing inland posts and exploring the unexploited western regions of Rupert's Land, the North West Company gained the upper hand. The Hudson's Bay Company was forced to respond, and a rivalry for land, loyalty, and furs ensued. The competition culminated in a merger of the two companies in

1821, engineered and approved by the British Parliament, which furthermore extended the territory covered by the original monopoly. Rupert's Land remained in private hands until 1869, when it was claimed by Canada.

—*Kelley Graham*

FURTHER READING

Davis, Richard C., ed. *Rupert's Land: A Cultural Tapestry*. Waterloo, Ont.: Wilfrid Laurier University Press for the Calgary Institute for the Humanities, 1988. Articles covering a variety of subjects relating to exploration and trade in Rupert's Land.

Edwards, Philip. *Last Voyages: Cavendish, Hudson, Ralegh*. New York: Oxford University Press, 1988. A narrative of Hudson's final voyage, using contemporary accounts.

Francis, Daniel, and Toby Morantz. *Partners in Fur: A History of the Eastern James Bay, 1600-1870*. Kingston, Ont.: McGill-Queens University Press, 1983. A study of the structure of the European fur empire and its impact on native peoples.

Johnson, Donald S. *Charting the Darkness: The Four Voyages of Henry Hudson*. Camden, Maine: International Marine, 1993. Reprint. New York: Kodansha Globe, 1995. The author uses Hudson's original logs to recount his voyages.

Krech, Shepard, III, ed. *The Subarctic Fur Trade: Native Social and Economic Adaptations*. Vancouver: University of British Columbia Press, 1984. Detailed articles on the effects of the fur trade from the seventeenth century onward.

Millman, Lawrence. "Looking for Henry Hudson." *Smithsonian* 30, no. 7 (October, 1999): 100. Describes Hudson's search for a northwest passage, providing information on the *Half Moon*'s voyage, the mutiny on Hudson's final trip, and Hudson's impact on the fur trade.

Shuster, Carl. "Into the Great Bay." *Beaver* 79, no. 4 (August/September, 1999): 8. The article, published in the journal of the Canadian National Historical Society, recounts Hudson's exploration in Canada.

Stewart, Gordon. *History of Canada Before 1867*. Washington, D.C.: Association for Canadian Studies in the United States, 1989. Presents a concise and detailed picture of conflicts and issues in early Canadian history.

Woodcock, George. *A Social History of Canada*. Markham, Ont.: Viking, 1988. An introductory work on the history of the people of Canada, including the indigenous peoples.

SEE ALSO: Mar. 15, 1603-Dec. 25, 1635: Champlain's Voyages; Spring, 1604: First European Settlement in North America; 1611-1630's: Jesuits Begin Missionary Activities in New France; Apr. 27, 1627: Company of New France Is Chartered; 1642-1684: Beaver Wars; May, 1642: Founding of Montreal; Aug., 1658-Aug. 24, 1660: Explorations of Radisson and Chouart des Groseilliers; May 2, 1670: Hudson's Bay Company Is Chartered.

RELATED ARTICLES in *Great Lives from History: The Seventeenth Century, 1601-1700:* Henry Hudson; Pierre Esprit Radisson; Prince Rupert.

1611
PUBLICATION OF THE KING JAMES BIBLE

King James I authorized an official translation of the Bible into English, an undertaking that involved six committees of scholars in three cities. Once the King James Bible was published, it quickly transformed the Anglican Church and more gradually influenced the history of the English language itself.

LOCALE: London, Oxford, and Cambridge, England
CATEGORIES: Religion and theology; literature; cultural and intellectual history

KEY FIGURES
James I (1566-1625), king of England, r. 1603-1625, and king of Scotland as James VI, r. 1567-1625
Lancelot Andrewes (1555-1626), dean of Westminster and later bishop of Winchester
Richard Bancroft (1544-1610), bishop of London and later archbishop of Canterbury
John Rainolds (John Reynolds; 1549-1607), a leading Puritan scholar and president of Corpus Christi College, Oxford

SUMMARY OF EVENT
Portions of the Bible were translated into English or at least paraphrased in the current vernacular beginning perhaps as early as the seventh century. Such efforts, however, were far from producing any complete English translation of the Bible. It was not until the late fourteenth century and the stirring in England of a pre-Lutheran Protestantism that a movement toward a complete translation of the Bible would begin. The founder of the movement was a priest named John Wyclif, who emphasized the Bible alone as the rule of faith for Christians. His followers, called Lollards by their enemies, were condemned by the Catholic Church, and the movement was gradually all but destroyed by persecution. Only a few remnants survived until the Reformation.

The Lollards successfully completed two translations of the Bible. Like previous partial English translations, however, they were based not on the original Hebrew, Aramaic, and Greek texts but on the Latin Vulgate, the Bible the Catholic Church had derived from the translation by Jerome in the late fourth and early fifth centuries. For nearly 150 years, the Wyclif translations were the only English versions of the Bible. Having been produced without Church approval and before the invention of the printing press, they circulated only in handwritten copies.

For the great majority of the English, the Bible remained inaccessible and illegal in their native tongue, and relatively few could read Latin. The Church feared the vernacular Bible, because it believed the laity might misinterpret it and fall into heresy. In England, possession of even a fragment of a vernacular Bible was taken as evidence of heresy, although in other countries, such as Germany, there were a number of translations of the Bible made before Luther.

Early in the sixteenth century, William Tyndale, a young English priest, made a vow to a more powerful cleric, "If God spare my life, ere many years I will cause a boy that driveth the plough should know more of the scriptures than thou dost." Intending to keep his vow, Tyndale applied unsuccessfully to Cuthbert Tunstall, the bishop of London, for permission to translate the Bible in 1523. The following year, Tyndale went to Hamburg, Germany, where he completed his translation of the New Testament from Greek and attempted to print it in Cologne in 1525. Catholic authorities intervened, and Tyndale fled to Worms, where he published his New Testament in 1525 or 1526. In 1530, translating from Hebrew and starting with the Pentateuch (Genesis through Deuteronomy), he began issuing his Old Testament, which was printed at Antwerp in the Netherlands.

Copies of Tyndale's Bible were smuggled into England and were eagerly bought, although many copies were seized and burnt by the authorities. A royal proclamation was issued reinforcing the prohibitions on reading the Scriptures in the vernacular. Tyndale himself was arrested by Catholic officials at Antwerp in May of 1535, was jailed for more than a year, and was strangled and then burned at the stake in 1536 at Vilvorde, near Brussels. Henry VIII's break with the papacy in 1534, however, produced a huge change in English Christianity. Although Henry remained staunchly orthodox in much of his theology, he was willing to allow certain innovations, including an English Bible.

In 1535, there appeared on the Continent a vernacular Bible by the former English monk Miles Coverdale, who had once served as Tyndale's assistant and who relied on Tyndale's translations, as well as on other derivative texts. The English crown permitted the use of this Bible in churches, and it was the first complete edition to be printed (rather than handwritten) in English. At Antwerp in 1537, an edition appeared that was also authorized and came to be called the Matthew Bible. It was ostensibly edited by a man named Thomas Matthew but was actually compiled by John Rogers, a friend of Tyndale, from Tyndale's and Coverdale's versions. In 1539, the English Church produced the so-called Great Bible, a large volume edited by Coverdale and intended for reading aloud at public worship services.

The Great Bible remained essentially unrevised throughout the reigns of the Protestant King Edward VI (1547-1553) and the Catholic Queen Mary I (1553-1558), the latter of whom forbade public Bible readings but did not revert to the policies of some of her predecessors in prohibiting all vernacular Bibles.

During Mary's reign, a number of Protestants had fled to the Continent, and a group at Geneva, headed by William Whittingham and advised by Coverdale, published a Calvinist translation in 1560 generally called the Geneva Bible. When the Protestant Elizabeth I ascended the English throne in 1558, these exiles returned home, where their Bible became enormously popular, going through some 150 editions between 1560 and 1640.

In 1568, another translation, called the Bishops' Bible, was published, largely as a result of the energy of Matthew Parker, archbishop of Canterbury. The city of publication was London, which before the middle of the sixteenth century had not had a printing industry developed enough to undertake a major project such as the Bible. The Bishops' Bible, authorized for oral readings in church, was heard all over the realm but never achieved the popularity of the Geneva Bible.

A translation for Catholics of the Latin Vulgate was made by English refugees in France in two parts: They published the New Testament at Reims in 1582 and the Old Testament at Douay in 1609-1610. This Douay-

Reims version, revised in the eighteenth century by Richard Challoner, became an important Catholic Bible.

At the Hampton Court Conference, a meeting between James I and the leaders of the English clergy in January of 1604, the Puritan John Rainolds, president of Corpus Christi College, Oxford, suggested to the king that a new translation of the Bible be prepared. James readily agreed, stating that all existing English versions were unsatisfactory and the highly popular Geneva was the worst.

Richard Bancroft, the bishop of London and initially an opponent of Rainolds's proposal, was appointed to help find suitable translators, and by June 30, James had approved a list of fifty-four scholars, of whom forty-seven are actually known to have participated in the work. They were divided into six committees, two of which met at Westminster, two at Oxford, and two at Cambridge. Each committee was assigned to translate a specific part of the Bible (with the Apocrypha included). One of the most notable scholars involved with the project was Lancelot Andrewes, then dean of Westminster, who headed one of the Westminster committees. Rainolds himself worked on an Oxford committee, but he died before the completion of the project.

Through Bancroft, James issued a set of rules that the translators were to follow. He pointedly forbade tendentious marginal notes in the finished Bible on the grounds that the Calvinistic notes in the Geneva Bible were "erroneous and treasonable." In general, the Bishops' Bible was to be taken as the guide, but most of the translators were apparently casual about that rule, and the influence of Tyndale and Coverdale, whether direct or indirect, is evident in the final product. Familiar proper names and familiar ecclesiastical titles such as "Church" were not to be changed even for the sake of greater accuracy.

The translators generally followed a procedure by which each of the scholars in a given committee would prepare a translation of the same passage, and the translations would then be compared. When an entire book of the Bible was considered satisfactory to one committee, it was sent to other committees. Disagreements among different committees were settled by meetings of the principal scholars from the various committees. In the final editing, two translators from each of the three translation centers met in London, where they followed a systematic procedure. Miles Smith and Thomas Bilson were the scholars who supervised the printing.

The work was completed by 1611, and the King James Bible was published in that year by Robert Barker, the king's printer. The title page bore the phrase "appointed to be read in the churches," and thus this translation came to be commonly known as the Authorized Version. In the United States, this edition has generally been known as the King James Version.

Acceptance of the Authorized Version took some time, since editions of the Geneva Bible continued to appear after 1611, and even Lancelot Andrewes continued to use it. With the defeat of Puritanism and the Restoration of Charles II in 1660, however, the Authorized Version replaced the Geneva Bible as the most popular English Bible. Until well into the twentieth century, the Authorized Version was almost the only Protestant Bible used in English-speaking lands. It went through small revisions from 1611 to 1616, including some that corrected printer's mistakes, and other revisions in 1629, 1638, 1762, and 1769.

In 1982, a New King James Version was published as the work of devout scholars, who wished to replace archaic wording with modern but who still wished not only to preserve the grandeur and reverence characterizing the old King James Version but also to translate faithfully what they considered the most reliable texts in the original languages.

SIGNIFICANCE

As the appearance of the New King James Version suggests, the influence of the old version has been immeasurable, not only in religion but also in literature and in the development of the English language, since its fine literary qualities, as well as its familiarity, have accounted for much of its popularity. The simple availability of a standard, authorized version of the Bible in English has had profound consequences for the history of Christianity, as it has made an achievable reality for the Anglophone world of the Protestant ideal of a "priesthood of all believers." Moreover, the diction, rhythm, and imagery of the King James Bible, even divorced from its content, have significantly influenced Western civilization. It is among the most quoted texts in the English language, and as such, it has shaped every native speaker's idea of the poetic, regardless of his or her religion.

— *James F. Hitchcock and Victor Lindsey*

FURTHER READING

Bobrick, Benson. *Wide as the Waters: The Story of the English Bible and the Revolution It Inspired.* New York: Penguin, 2002. Comprehensive history of the English Bible, focusing on translators John Wyclif and William Tyndale and on other contributors to what eventually became the King James Bible. Bobrick argues that the Bible's concepts of liberty and free will guided the English revolutionaries who overthrew Charles I.

"The History of the King James Bible." In *Holy Bible: The New King James Version Containing the Old and New Testaments.* Nashville, Tenn.: Thomas Nelson, 1982. A detailed account that includes all revisions to date of the King James Version of the Bible.

Lawton, David. *Faith, Text, and History: The Bible in English.* Charlottesville: University Press of Virginia, 1990. Chapter 3 contains a historical account, ending with the King James Version, and a discussion of "style and transparency in English Bible translation."

McGrath, Alister E. *In the Beginning: The Story of the King James Bible and How It Changed a Nation, a Language, and a Culture.* New York: Doubleday, 2001. Recounts the history of the King James Bible from Gutenberg's invention of the printing press to its publication. McGrath focuses on the politics of translation and the various biblical texts and describes how the King James Bible has influenced the English language, literature, art, and music.

Partridge, A. C. *English Biblical Translation.* London: Andre Deutsch, 1973. A scholarly account of most biblical translations into English from the early Middle Ages to 1970, with numerous comparisons of translated passages.

Robertson, Edwin. *Makers of the English Bible.* Cambridge, England: Lutterworth, 1990. An account of persons who played important roles in various translations of the Bible into English.

SEE ALSO: Mar. 24, 1603: James I Becomes King of England; May, 1659-May, 1660: Restoration of Charles II.

RELATED ARTICLES in *Great Lives from History: The Seventeenth Century, 1601-1700:* Lancelot Andrewes; James I.

1610's

1611-1630's
JESUITS BEGIN MISSIONARY ACTIVITIES IN NEW FRANCE

Beginning in 1611, Jesuits endured countless hardships and dangers in their attempts to convert and educate the indigenous peoples of Quebec and Acadia (present-day Nova Scotia).

LOCALE: Quebec, Acadia, and other locations in New France (now in Canada)
CATEGORIES: Religion and theology; colonization

KEY FIGURES

Samuel de Champlain (c. 1567/1570-1635), French explorer and founder of Quebec
Pierre Biard (c. 1567-1622), Jesuit missionary to Acadia
Enemond Massé (1574-1646), Jesuit missionary to Acadia and Quebec
Joseph Le Caron (c. 1586-1632), Recollect priest and first missionary to the Huron Indians
Gabriel Sagard (c. 1590-1637), Recollect missionary and historian
Denis Jamet (Denis Jamay; d. 1625), Recollect missionary and first superior of the mission to New France
Jean Dolbeau (1586-1652), Recollect missionary
Saint Jean de Brébeuf (1593-1649), famous Jesuit who was brutally killed in 1649
Charles Lalemant (1587-1674), Jesuit missionary to Quebec
Paul Le Jeune (1592-1664), Jesuit leader and writer

SUMMARY OF EVENT

For more than a century before French Jesuits arrived in Canada, their colleagues from Spain and Portugal had been in the vanguard of missionary activities in Mexico, South America, Asia, and Africa. In the 1570's, a few Spanish Jesuits were even active in Virginia. Inspired by the example set by their colleagues, many Jesuits in France were anxious to contribute to the expansion of Catholicism into non-European cultures.

Shortly after French merchants in 1604 opened a trading station at Port Royal, Acadia, the Jesuit leadership made arrangements to send missionaries to the station. Moreover, as soon as explorer Samuel de Champlain founded Quebec in 1608, he asked French Jesuits to send missionaries to the small settlement. The Jesuits declined, however, because of their prior commitment to Port Royal. They had good reasons to question the viability of Quebec in any case: Only nine of the twenty-eight

original colonists survived the winter of 1608-1609, and Quebec's first permanent resident, Louis Hébert, would not arrive for another seven years.

In 1611, two Jesuits, Pierre Biard and Enemond Massé, landed at Port Royal. They were the first two priests in New France proper. Soon, they were joined by other priests of the black gown, Jacques Quentin, Joseph Le Caron, and Jean Dolbeau. Because the merchants in Port Royal thought proselytizing efforts were bad for business, the Jesuits moved their mission to Mount Desert Island in nearby Maine. In 1614, before the Jesuits were able to accomplish very much, sixty English soldiers from Virginia, led by Captain Samuel Argall, destroyed the settlements of Port Royal and Mount Desert Island. Some of the priests and merchants were set adrift in a boat, while others were taken prisoner and shipped to France. After returning home, Father Biard published an account of the goals and history of the mission, encouraging his fellow Jesuits to return to North America.

During a visit to France in 1614, Champlain asked the Recollect Fathers, the most austere branch of the Franciscans, to send missionaries to the region around Quebec. When the Recollects agreed, the sieur de Monts's Company of Merchants, which possessed a monopoly of the fur trade, contracted to support them. The Estates-General of France also agreed to provide economic assistance.

In 1615, four Recollects—Jean Dolbeau, Joseph Le Caron, Denis Jamet, and Pacifique Duplessis—arrived in Quebec. Father Dolbeau's assignment was to the nomadic Montagnais Indians of the lower Saint Lawrence River, Le Caron chose to labor among the semisedentary Hurons in the region of Georgian Bay (in present-day Ontario), and the other two "gray friars" stayed in Quebec, ministering to the colonists and Native Americans who entered the village. Soon, additional Recollects arrived, including Gabriel Sagard, the first true historian of New France. In 1619, a group of Recollects attempted missionary activities in Acadia, but after a series of disasters, they were forced to abandon this project in 1624.

Missionaries in New France faced immense problems, including the disruptions of intertribal warfare, the necessity of learning unwritten languages, and considerable hostility from French traders. Even more, most Indians were firmly committed to their traditional religions, and they were not prepared to accept Christian principles of sexual morality. After a decade in Canada, the Recollects had little to show for their work. Clearly, they had not been prepared for the gargantuan undertaking. In addition to a lack of resources, they had almost no experience in dealing with alien cultures. The powerful Jesuit order, in contrast, could benefit from its long record of building foreign missions. Acknowledging the need for help, the Recollects in 1624 invited the Jesuits to send missionaries as soon as possible.

In April, 1625, three Jesuit priests—Enemond Massé, Charles Lalemant, and the future Saint Jean de Brébeuf—arrived in Quebec. More than the Recollects, they recognized the importance of adopting the Indian lifestyle and learning native languages. Brébeuf's residence among the Hurons became a model for later missions. Rather than emphasizing differences between Christianity and Indian religions, the Jesuits concentrated on their spiritual similarities. Most of the Jesuits' efforts were directed at the Montagnais, Algonquians, and Hurons. Their relationship to these tribes brought them into conflict with the Five Nations of the Iroquois Confederation. Believing that the presence of French Protestants (Huguenots) hindered their work, the Jesuits delegated Father Lalemant to go to France and convince the government of the need for religious uniformity among the settlers. Before he could return, however, the English conquered Quebec in 1629, which ended Jesuit missions for the next three years.

In the Treaty of Saint-Germain-en-Laye (1632), however, France regained sovereignty over Quebec and Acadia. Under Cardinal de Richelieu, the French government gave the Jesuits a monopoly over the religious affairs of both settlers and Indians. That summer, the new Jesuit superior for Quebec, Paul Le Jeune, arrived with several of his associates. A steady stream of Jesuit missionaries soon followed.

Le Jeune initiated the writing of annual reports, called the *Relations*, which for forty years stimulated great interest in the mother country and helped bring forth a steady stream of donations and new missionaries. Under his leadership, the Jesuits continued to live among the Indians, learning their languages and cultures. The Jesuits, however, had already learned the futility of trying to make long-term converts of nomadic individuals, so they wished to promote a sedentary way of life among Native Americans. To accomplish this goal, the Jesuits decided that it was necessary to instruct Indians in agricultural skills. They also recognized the importance of educating young people during their impressionable years. In 1635,

the Jesuits founded a college in Quebec. Two years later, they established a village reserved for Christian Indians in nearby Sillery. Within a few years, they were operating similar missions in Three Rivers and elsewhere.

SIGNIFICANCE

During the seventeenth century, the Jesuits were the most energetic and successful group of missionaries in North America. Although they converted a relatively small percentage of the indigenous peoples, many of these converts and their children, especially among the Hurons, remained committed to Catholicism. An unknown number married French settlers and became assimilated into the colonial society. Even in the twenty-first century, descendants of Native Americans continue to live in communities that can be traced back to the Jesuit missions.

The Jesuits' missionary activities and devotion to social services profoundly influenced the subsequent political and cultural life of Quebec. For several centuries, the population of the province was recognized for its piety and firm commitment to the Catholic Church. To some extent, this development can be traced back to the devotion and sacrifices of the 115 Jesuit missionaries of the seventeenth century.

The works of the Jesuits are significant for secular as well as religious reasons. Their knowledge and transcription of Indian languages played an important role in the development of the French empire in North America. Modern historians recognize, moreover, that Jesuit ethnographic writings are among the best sources of knowledge about seventeenth century Native American culture.

—*Thomas Tandy Lewis*

FURTHER READING

Axtell, James. *Invasion Within: The Context of Cultures in Colonial North America*. New York: Oxford University Press, 1985. Argues that in contrast to English settlers, the Jesuits' commitment to conversion caused them to learn to appreciate indigenous ways of life.

Donnelly, Joseph. *Jean de Brébeuf, 1594-1649*. Chicago: Loyola University Press, 1976. Detailed study of the celebrated Jesuit martyr who was canonized as a saint.

Francis, R. Douglas, Richard Jones, and Donald Smith. *Origins: Canadian History to Confederation*. Toronto: Harcourt Canada, 2001. Includes a helpful summary of the Jesuits' influences within the context of Canadian history.

Grant, John W. *Moon of Wintertime: Missionaries and the Indians of Canada.* Toronto: University of Toronto Press, 1984. An interesting account emphasizing the cultural differences between the Europeans and American Indians.

Jennings, Francis. *The Invasion of America: Indians, Colonialism, and the Cant of Conquest.* Chapel Hill: University of North Carolina Press, 1975. Highly critical of all colonial missionaries as espousing "conquest religions," but Jennings acknowledges the Jesuits' curiosity and knowledge of indigenous cultures.

Moore, James T. *Indians and Jesuits: A Seventeenth Century Encounter.* Chicago: Loyola University Press, 1982. An interesting summary, taking a favorable view of the Jesuits and emphasizing their empathetic approach to American Indian cultures.

Morision, Samuel Eliot. *Samuel de Champlain: Father of New France.* Boston: Little, Brown, 1972. A standard work that includes information about Champlain's support of missionary activities.

Roustang, François, ed. *An Autobiography of Martyrdom: Spiritual Writings of the Jesuits in New France.*

Bruges, Belgium: B. Herder, 1964. Select writings by Brébeuf, Le Jeune, and others with perceptive historical analysis.

Thwaites, Reuben, ed. *The Jesuit Relations and Allied Documents: Travels and Jesuit Missionaries in New France, 1610-1791.* 73 vols. New York: Pageant, 1959. A massive and extremely valuable collection of original documents. The first three volumes have good introductions that summarize the early missionary efforts of the Recollects and Jesuits.

Wright, Jonathan. *God's Soldiers: A History of the Jesuits.* New York: Doubleday, 2004. Chronicles the story of the religious order, with an emphasis on its work in education and foreign missions.

SEE ALSO: Mar. 15, 1603-Dec. 25, 1635: Champlain's Voyages; Spring, 1604: First European Settlement in North America; 1617-c. 1700: Smallpox Epidemics Kill Native Americans; Apr. 27, 1627: Company of New France Is Chartered; 1642-1684: Beaver Wars; May, 1642: Founding of Montreal.

RELATED ARTICLES in *Great Lives from History: The Seventeenth Century, 1601-1700:* Samuel de Champlain; Saint Isaac Jogues; Cardinal de Richelieu.

1612
INTRODUCTION OF TOBACCO FARMING IN NORTH AMERICA

Tobacco, already gaining popularity in Europe, was introduced as a commercial crop in Jamestown, Virginia. The New World plant's cultivation corresponded with the rise of tobacco culture in Europe, provided America with a fundamental economic underpinning by which plantation owners gained immense fortunes, and aided in the destruction and displacement of Native Americans.

LOCALE: Jamestown Colony (now in Virginia)
CATEGORIES: Agriculture; trade and commerce; economics; health and medicine

KEY FIGURES

John Rolfe (1585-1622), English-born colonial official and first North American tobacco farmer
Sir Walter Ralegh (c. 1552-1618), English explorer who popularized tobacco in England
James I (1566-1625), king of England, r. 1603-1625, and king of Scotland as James VI, r. 1567-1625

SUMMARY OF EVENT

Tobacco was first introduced into Europe from North America before its establishment as a crop in Virginia. Native Americans consumed wild tobacco, which was plentiful in the Americas, rather than cultivating tobacco fields. The growing European desire for the New World plant, or "weede," as it was initially referred to, literally saved the lives of the struggling British colonists and provided a means for their colonies to grow and prosper. While tobacco was widespread during the sixteenth and early seventeenth centuries, it was not until the second half of the seventeenth century that the price of tobacco fell drastically and tobacco became truly popular. The addictive desire for tobacco in Europe and eventually the rest of the world brought about enormous social, physical, and economic change.

It is difficult to imagine Europeans' initial response when they first viewed pipe smoking or snuff inhalation. They simply had no referential context whatsoever by which to understand the practice, so it is hardly any

By the early 1660's, tobacco was the driving force behind Virginia's economy. In this depiction, a small fleet of ships is loaded with barrels bound for England; a single ship would be insufficient to meet the demand back home. (Hulton\Archive by Getty Images)

wonder such phrases as "drinking smoke" or "drinking fog," were invented for lack of better terms. Native Americans viewed tobacco as a medicine and used it also within social frameworks to bring people together in peace and camaraderie. With electrifying speed, Europeans, and soon after the rest of the world, borrowed American cultural and social practices surrounding the use of tobacco.

Tobacco, which gained an early reputation as a medicinal panacea, was introduced to France in 1556, Portugal in 1558, Spain in 1559, and finally to England in 1565. The explorer Christopher Columbus is actually credited with bringing tobacco to Europe at the end of the 1400's, but it did not become popular until the middle of the sixteenth century, when diplomats like France's Jean Nicot, for whom nicotine is named, began to use it as a curative. In France, where tobacco could only be purchased with a prescription, Queen Catherine de Médicis was so favorably impressed when it reportedly cured her headaches that she decreed that it be called Herba Regina, the "queen's herb."

After tobacco use moved beyond the medical arena, a culture of smoking, initially based on Native American social practices, sprung up in Europe. Pipes were ritually passed around from person to person in communal camaraderie by Native Americans to pledge an oath or ratify a treaty. This practice inspired the phrase "peace pipe." When Hernán Cortés landed in Mexico (1519), the natives offered him tobacco as "a pledge of peace and good will." Similarly, in early seventeenth century Europe, tobacco was "drunk" from a communal pipe that was handed from man to man around the table. In time, tobacco etiquette demanded that people of both genders cultivate the proper manner of smoking, which included a delicate hand.

Both genders and all ages smoked, including children, and, while smoking was the English nicotine delivery method of choice during the Stuart and Cromwellian eras, like many other imported French court manners, inhaling snuff gained in popularity after the Restoration of Charles II. Among aristocrats, it was common to have a different, enormously expensive snuff box for every day of the week.

In addition to the tobacco culture—smoking, snuff taking, and their accompanying mannerisms and accoutrements—tobacco also had a physical influence on seventeenth century bodies. Its ability to diminish the appetite led it to be used often in place of food. As a result, a reduction in the intake of meat, milk, and cheese accompanied Europeans' consumption of tobacco and allowed workers to work longer hours. Tobacco also played a role in major military conflicts, permitting soldiers to fight longer by increasing energy while keeping their bodies relaxed. In fact, seventeenth century European soldiers carried pipes in their caps, and tobacco constituted part of their daily rations.

The famous pipe smoker Sir Walter Ralegh is credited with popularizing tobacco in England during the reign of Queen Elizabeth I (r. 1558-1603). In 1587, Ralegh established a settlement on Roanoke Island in Virginia. After its failure, he attempted to colonize Guiana, rumored to be the mythical El Dorado, but instead of gold, he returned to England with tobacco.

The first successful commercial tobacco crop was cultivated in Virginia in 1612 by Englishman John Rolfe, secretary and recorder of the fledgling Jamestown Colony. Rolfe, who is also well known for marrying the Powhatan princess Pocahontas in 1614, obtained tobacco seeds in the Caribbean and planted them in Virginia in lieu of the more bitter native tobacco. This act literally saved the starving colonists. Two years later, he sent to England 4 hogsheads (252 dry gallons) of tobacco, weighing about 2,600 pounds (1,180 kilograms). The colony exploded with the growing and selling of tobacco. In the Chesapeake region of Virginia, tobacco was used as a medium of exchange by some Native Americans: It became a form of currency for the colonists as well, with everything bought and sold with tobacco.

Concern about his subjects' health had led the English king James I to issue *A Counterblaste to Tobacco* (1604), condemning tobacco as a "heathenish" poison. However, the tobacco market continued to expand, and, by 1617, Virginia had shipped around 10 tons (9,100 kilograms) of tobacco to England. The European demand for tobacco grew at a bewildering rate. In 1603, England had imported a total of only 25,000 pounds (11,300 kilograms) of the plant, but by 1640, tobacco had risen to first place among London's imports. In 1700, the nation imported almost at

38 million pounds (17 million kilograms) and in 1771, over 100 million pounds (45 million kilograms).

SIGNIFICANCE

The introduction of tobacco crops as a commercial crop in seventeenth century North America had far-reaching social, physical, and economic significance. Its cultivation spurred the developing tobacco culture in Europe and throughout the world. Tobacco joined sugar and other plantation crops to form the heart of the colonial American economy, binding the colonies to developing world markets and providing an ever-greater impetus to import slaves to work the plantations. Historians agree that tobacco made more fortunes than all the silver in North and South America.

Although mild when compared with today's hard narcotics, nicotine's advance into Britain during the seventeenth and eighteenth centuries marked a major step in the development of global, imperialist capitalism. Tobacco, as an ever-increasing commodity, ensured the ongoing development of Virginia and provided an economic incentive for further expansion and settlement of the New World.

Furthermore, tobacco greatly influenced the displacement of Native Americans. Since it is a crop that is exhausting to the soil, virgin land must be cultivated continuously to keep up production. Thus, more and more land was needed to fulfil the rapidly expanding worldwide desire for tobacco. In order to meet the need for new territory, settlers took advantage of the Native Americans: By trading for mere pots and pans, the Indians lost control of their lands. The European and colonial craving for tobacco therefore played a major role in imperial acquisition and colonial expansion.

—M. Casey Diana

FURTHER READING

Gately, Iain. *Tobacco: A Cultural History of How an Exotic Plant Seduced Civilization*. New York: Grove Press, 2003. Traces the history of tobacco from pre-Columbian America through the litigation of the 1990's. Fascinating account of tobacco in literature, film, and society.

Goodman, Jordan. *Tobacco in History: The Cultures of Dependence*. New York: Routledge, 1994. A far-reaching analysis of the culture and business of tobacco. Explores the chemical addictive nature of tobacco, details the introduction of tobacco to Europe, and examines the role of government and the enormous economic impact worldwide. Provides a forty-page bibliography.

Middleton, Arthur Pierce. *Tobacco Coast: A Maritime History of the Chesapeake Bay in the Colonial Era.* Baltimore: Johns Hopkins University Press, 1984. Scholarly history of tobacco's role in the Chesapeake Bay economy. Discusses how the early colonists thrived on the cultivation of tobacco and the plant's increasing importance as the area's primary economic mainstay.

Schivelbusch, Wolfgang. *Tastes of Paradise: A Social History of Spices, Stimulants, and Intoxicants.* Translated by David Jacobson. New York: Pantheon Books, 1992. Although this book deals primarily with coffee, tea, and alcohol, it contains a highly informative section on the history of tobacco and its cultural and economic impact.

SEE ALSO: 17th cent.: England's Agricultural Revolution; May 14, 1607: Jamestown Is Founded; Beginning c. 1619: Indentured Servitude Becomes Institutionalized in America; 1619-c. 1700: The Middle Passage to American Slavery; July 30-Aug. 4, 1619: First General Assembly of Virginia; Aug. 20, 1619: Africans Arrive in Virginia; Mar. 22, 1622-Oct., 1646: Powhatan Wars; May 6, 1626: Algonquians "Sell" Manhattan Island; 1642-1684: Beaver Wars; 1642-1700: Westward Migration of Native Americans; Mar., 1661-1705: Virginia Slave Codes.

RELATED ARTICLES in *Great Lives from History: The Seventeenth Century, 1601-1700:* Charles I; Charles II (of England); Oliver Cromwell; James I; Pocahontas; Powhatan; John Smith.

1612
RISE OF THE ARMA IN TIMBUKTU

The Arma, a military caste that descended from Moroccan soldiers who conquered the Songhai Empire, built the pashalik, *a state that endured for almost two centuries.*

LOCALE: Niger River Valley (now in the Republic of Mali)

CATEGORIES: Government and politics; expansion and land acquisition; wars, uprisings, and civil unrest

KEY FIGURES

Abdullah al-Tilimsānī (d. 1618), first pasha, 1612-1618, locally appointed but later overthrown by his own men

'Abd al-Qādir (d. 1632), pasha, 1628-1632, who made the most serious, albeit unsuccessful, attempt to centralize the *pashalik*

Judar Paşa (d. 1606), commander of Moroccan troops who overthrew the Songhai Empire

SUMMARY OF EVENT

In 1591, the sultan of Morocco, Ahmad al-Manṣūr, sent an army commanded by Judar Paşa across the Sahara to attack and conquer the Songhai Empire. Although Judar's army of between three thousand and four thousand fighting men, plus auxiliaries, was vastly outnumbered, it defeated the Songhai in a number of engagements because the Moroccans were equipped with muskets and cannon; the Songhai had swords and bows

only. Within a decade, the Moroccans came to control most of the Niger River Valley between the cities of Jenne and Gao, making Timbuktu their capital.

Morocco, however, drifted into rebellion and civil war following the death of al-Manṣūr in 1603. In 1612, soldiers in Timbuktu overthrew the sultan-appointed pasha (commander) and placed Abdullah al-Tilimsānī in control. Abdullah al-Tilimsānī was then overthrown in 1618 by fellow officers, after which the Moroccan government decided unofficially to abandon its enterprise in the West African interior. In theory, the conquered territory remained part of the Moroccan Empire, at least as long as the Saʿdi Dynasty ruled in Morocco. In fact, however, the pashas became independent sovereigns elected by their soldiers.

Judar's original force was comprised mostly of professional soldiers and had a distinct ethnic division. One thousand of the musketeers were Andalusians, refugees from Muslim Spain who had been forced into exile during the Christian Reconquista. Another thousand musketeers were *uluj*, or renegades, European Christians who converted to Islam. The musketeers were augmented by Turkish mercenaries and some Christian prisoners of war and freely hired European Christians who had particular skills in operating artillery, among other skills. A contingent of 1,500 lancers was recruited from certain loyal tribes in Morocco, and support personnel, including camel drivers, sappers, and physicians, were also Moroccans. In the following years, most of the reinforcements were drawn from the southern part of Morocco, largely tribesmen the sultan distrusted and wanted to get out of his own country. By one account the total number of troops sent from Morocco to conquer and rule the Songhai amounted to 23,000.

The Moroccan army brought along no women, and local women were among the victims of war. For several years Moroccan soldiers accumulated large numbers of concubines. Once it became apparent that they were stranded in the interior of West Africa and not likely to return to Morocco, the soldiers began establishing families. Their children married each other, founding their own group that became known as the Arma, or Ruma (from the Arabic *al-rumat*).

From the beginning, half of the Arma gene pool was Sudanese, mostly Songhai, but it also included Soninke, Fulbe, and others. The Moroccans brought with them some preferences retained by the Arma. In architecture, for example, the Arma preferred the Maghribian style—introducing such innovations as grilled windows—and

in music they transplanted their love of the violin. In other matters, however, the Arma soon became more West African than north African. This clearly shows in the language of the Arma. Judar's army was comprised largely of Arabic and Spanish speakers, but subsequent generations of Arma learned their language from their mothers, and soon the descendants of the original conquerors spoke only Songhai. They did not, however, see themselves as Songhai. They remained a people apart, a ruling military caste that believed they were superior to the sea of peoples over which they ruled.

The state the Arma created is known in history as the *pashalik*. Soldiers were divided into units supposedly based on their origins, the most important being the divisions of Fés and Marrakech, comprising the right and left wings of the army. This military distinction gradually evolved into a political one, the divisions becoming parties and eventually clans, reflecting their exclusiveness and cohesiveness. The office of pasha alternated between divisions. In turn, the high officers of each division selected a candidate, who was then endorsed by the rank-and-file. This system discouraged pashas who were too ambitious or too capable. When the pasha succeeded in alienating enough of his fellow officers, they came together and deposed him.

Twenty-one pashas ruled between 1612 and 1660. Following their reigns, many were killed, imprisoned, or exiled. The *pashalik* was not a stable system, and it would get worse. The most notable attempt to introduce a stronger and more centralized government occurred during the reign of ʿAbd al-Qādir. When he set out to put down a rebellion by the garrison at Gao, however, his army deserted him, and he was subsequently overthrown and beheaded in 1632.

In 1659, the last of the Saʿdian sultans was killed. Henceforth, the people of the *pashalik* no longer officially recognized the sultan of Morocco as their overlord. The pasha became, in theory, the final arbiter of power along the Middle Niger. This did not, however, lead to a stronger, more stable system. On the contrary, during the second half of the seventeenth century, the average reign of a pasha dropped from over two years to eleven months. Some pashas ruled for several weeks or days only. In 1697, one was elected and deposed on the same day. The situation for pashas did not improve during the following century. Be-

TIMBUKTU, AFRICA, AND ENVIRONS

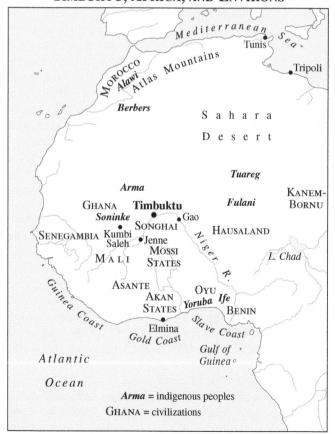

Arma = indigenous peoples
GHANA = civilizations

tween 1671 and 1750, the *pashalik* experienced 114 regime changes. After 1750, there were long periods of interregnum until the system faded into oblivion at the end of the century.

SIGNIFICANCE

The descendants of a Moroccan army cut off deep in the West African interior assumed the role of ruling caste over a state created by default. Sometimes described as a military republic, the *pashalik* is a good study in the disadvantages associated with a government controlled by its own army. Although the pasha was, in theory, elected, the government was a military oligarchy with power in the hands of certain families that provided the high officers. The officers vied for power among themselves, but collectively they opposed the centralizing tendencies of ambitious pashas.

For a people bred in the military tradition, the Arma proved to be quite factious. As a result, the *pashalik* was never as large, powerful, or well-ruled as the Songhai Empire it replaced. Nevertheless, the *pashalik* endured for almost two centuries, providing at least some measure of security for the maintenance of an orderly society across much of the middle portion of the Niger Valley. Most of the time it also protected the trans-Saharan and trans-Sudanese trading systems. In the end, the *pashalik* succumbed to its own internal inconsistencies, but the descendants of the Arma remain a proud people who still inhabit many of the former garrison towns along the river.

—Richard L. Smith

FURTHER READING

Abitbol, Michel. "The End of the Songhay Empire." In *Africa from the Sixteenth to the Eighteenth Century*, edited by B. A. Ogot. Vol. 5 in General History of Africa. Berkeley: University of California Press, 1992. Abitbol's studies are the most complete of the Arma period, but most are available only in French. However, his main findings are adequately covered in the chapter of this work, which is part of a multivolume set on African history.

Hunwick, John O. *Timbuktu and the Songhay Empire.* Boston: Brill, 1999. Hunwick, the foremost Songhai scholar in North America, provides useful primary source documents together with a lengthy interpretative essay and extensive comments and notes.

Saad, Elias. *Social History of Timbuktu.* New York: Cambridge University Press, 1983. Saad explores the Arma regime and its relation with the civilians who lived in the main *pashalik* town.

Thornton, John. *Warfare in Atlantic Africa, 1500-1800.* London: UCL Press, 1999. Thornton explores the professional soldier (particularly the Arma) and his role and effectiveness in contrast to the mass levies (conscriptions) common to other armies of the time.

SEE ALSO: 17th cent.: Songhai Empire Dissolves; Beginning c. 1601: Expansion of the Oyo Kingdom; Mid-17th cent.: Emergence of the Guinea Coast States; 1659: Expansion of the Alawis; 1670-1699: Rise of the Asante Empire; Late 17th cent.: Decline of Benin.

RELATED ARTICLE in *Great Lives from History: The Seventeenth Century, 1601-1700:* Njinga.

1612
SANCTORIUS INVENTS THE CLINICAL THERMOMETER

The clinical thermometer was invented by Sanctorius, an Italian physician and physiologist, who described in his 1612 book his use of the heat-measuring device. Sanctorius's thermometer, although not the first to observe heat, was the first to measure it.

LOCALE: Padua and Venice (now in Italy)
CATEGORIES: Health and medicine; biology; inventions; science and technology

KEY FIGURES

Santorio Santorio (Sanctorius; 1561-1636), Italian physician, physiologist, and inventor of medical instruments

Giovanni Alfonso Borelli (1608-1679), Italian physicist and physiologist

Robert Boyle (1627-1691), Irish mathematician, physicist, and chemist

Cornelis Drebbel (1572-1633), Dutch glassblower, chemist, and inventor

Gabriel Daniel Fahrenheit (1686-1736), German physicist

Ferdinand II de' Medici (1610-1670), grand duke of Tuscany, r. 1621-1670, scientist, and inventor

Robert Fludd (1574-1637), English physician, chemist, and mystic

Galileo (1564-1642), Italian physicist and astronomer

Otto von Guericke (1602-1686), German architect, engineer, physicist, and inventor

Robert Hooke (1635-1703), English mathematician and general scientist

Athanasius Kircher (1601-1680), German Jesuit priest, general scientist, and inventor

Jean Leuréchon (1591-1624), French Jesuit priest and mathematician

Jean Rey (1583?-1645?), French physician and chemist

Evangelista Torricelli (1608-1647), Italian mathematician and physicist

SUMMARY OF EVENT

Before the last decade of the sixteenth century, there was no known way to quantify heat. All means of measuring it were subjective. About 1593, Galileo began experimenting with possible solutions to this problem, and by 1596, he had invented a device that showed differences in temperature. His device showed a rising or falling column of water in an unsealed glass tube, rather like a thin Florence flask inverted in a bowl of water. As air in the bulb at the top of the tube heated and expanded, it pushed the water down; as it cooled and contracted, it allowed the water to rise.

This instrument, commonly called the air thermometer, was sensitive but inaccurate. Its inaccuracy mainly came from the unrecognized effects of barometric pressure on the unsealed system. Barometric pressure was unknown until Evangelista Torricelli described it in the 1640's and Otto von Guericke, Robert Hooke, and Robert Boyle investigated it in the 1650's.

Galileo did not invent the familiar, decorative Galileo thermometer, which indicates temperature with liquid-filled glass balls rising and falling in a liquid sealed inside a glass column. This was developed later, probably by Athanasius Kircher, from a principle Galileo discovered. The principle stated that the density, and therefore the buoyancy, of a liquid varies according to its temperature.

In the second and third decades of the seventeenth century, Sanctorius (Santorio Santorio) invented several variations of the air thermometer, at least three of which had clinical applications. The first mention of a clinical thermometer, and one of the earliest published mentions of any thermometer, is in Sanctorius's 1612 book *Commentaria in artem medicinalem Galeni* (commentary on the art of medicine of Galen). He did most of his work on thermometry when he was professor of theoretical medicine at the University of Padua from 1611 to 1624, and he published his results shortly thereafter. His 1625 book *Commentaria in primam fen primi libri canonis Avicennae* (commentaries on the first part of the first book of the Canon of Avicenna) describes and illustrates one uncalibrated and three calibrated clinical air thermometers.

The first of these four woodcut illustrations shows a Florence flask with an unusually long and thin neck inverted in an open vessel of water. The patient's hand would enclose the bulb of the flask and within a few minutes the thermometer would react. Even though it had no scale, two threads tied around the neck could be slid up or down to record temperatures. The second woodcut is the most remarkable, as it illustrates the world's first oral thermometer. It had a tiny bulb at the top that was placed in the patient's mouth. The scaled neck was even longer and had four switchback curves. The length improved accuracy and the curves saved space. The third woodcut depicts a similar instrument, but with a larger bulb at the top to take the temperature of the patient's hand. The fourth woodcut shows the least successful of the three calibrated models, with the bulb at the top replaced by a funnel into which the patient would exhale.

Sanctorius believed that quantifying the heat of healthy as well as diseased bodies could help medical diagnoses. Keener instruments were required because correlating temperatures and other symptoms with specific ailments was the key to clinical progress in this area and because differences in body heat could be quite small. Sanctorius was one of the originators of the idea that, to be effective, medicine and its instruments must be precise. He was an iatromechanist in medicine. Iatromechanism is a theory that states the phenomena of human physiology, health, and disease can be quantified and are best understood numerically. Iatromechanism reduced physiology to physics, mechanics, and mathematics, while its main ideological rival, iatrochemism, reduced physiology to chemistry and alchemy.

Sanctorius's greatest achievement in thermometry was being the first to attempt to quantify heat by adding a

Physician, scientist, and scholar Santorio Santorio, best known as Sanctorius, invented medical instruments of precision, including the clinical thermometer. (Library of Congress)

scale. A Latin manuscript called *Mathematica maravigliosa*, written in Rome and dated 1611, contains the earliest known illustration of a calibrated air thermometer. This instrument, attributed to Sanctorius, consists of two volumetric flasks, the thinner-necked flask inverted as far as possible into the thicker-necked flask, with the column of liquid at about the midway point of the two necks. The outer neck is scaled in eight divisions of six degrees each.

Sanctorius's experiments with calibration led to the first genuine thermometer. Strictly speaking, what Galileo invented was the thermoscope, not the thermometer, because it allowed its user to see heat but not to measure it. In 1624, Jean Leuréchon coined the word *thermomètre* from two Greek words, *thermos* (hot) and *metron* (measure), to name the calibrated device and distinguish it from the noncalibrated variety.

Robert Fludd independently invented a calibrated air thermometer in London around 1615. By the late 1630's, this "weather glass" was a popular commercial item in Britain. Cornelis Drebbel developed a calibrated J-shaped air thermometer in the Netherlands before 1625. Other early experimenters with air thermometers include Kircher in the 1640's and Guericke about 1660.

Thermometry entered an important new phase when Jean Rey invented the first practical liquid thermometer between 1630 and 1632, a Florence flask with a long calibrated neck and a small bulb at the bottom. Heating or cooling the liquid in the bulb would expand or contract it in the neck, but since the top was open the instrument was still subject to air pressure. The next step was to seal the thermometer and close the system. Duke Ferdinand II de' Medici of Tuscany built the first sealed liquid thermometer in 1641 and by 1654 had much improved its design. Hooke's *Micrographia* (1665) describes his sealed, four-foot, wine-filled thermometer, for which he attempted to standardize a scale with one fixed point, the freezing point of water.

SIGNIFICANCE

By 1709, Gabriel Daniel Fahrenheit had invented the sealed alcohol thermometer, followed in 1714 by the sealed mercury thermometer. He published his familiar temperature scale in 1724, setting five key points: zero as the temperature of a mixture of equal weights of snow and dehydrated sea salt, 32 as the temperature of the equilibrium of ice and water, 96 as the axillary temperature of the human body, 212 as the boiling point of water, and 600 as the boiling point of mercury. Normal healthy human body temperature is between 98.2 and 98.6 degrees (now called degrees Fahrenheit) and the boiling point of mercury is really 675.1, but the Fahrenheit scale remains acceptable for many applications, especially in the United States, even though the Celsius and Kelvin scales have been the standards in science since the nineteenth century.

Developing the means to measure changes in body temperature paved the way for rapid progress in physiology and in the clinical methods that depend upon accurate functional knowledge of physiology. Sanctorius's contribution led directly to better understanding of the respiratory and cardiovascular systems. Iatromechanism made further progress when Giovanni Alfonso Borelli's clinical and animal experiments in the 1660's challenged and overturned the ancient Galenic idea that the heart heats the body and the lungs cool it, thus maintaining ideal body temperature within a healthy balance of the four humors.

—Eric v.d. Luft

FURTHER READING

Castiglioni, Arturo. "Life and Work of Sanctorius." *Medical Life* 38 (1931): 730-785. The standard biography and the most detailed treatment of Sanctorius in English.

Chang, Hasok Chang. *Inventing Temperature: Measurement and Scientific Progress*. New York: Oxford University Press, 2004. A philosophical and historical analysis of the several theories of measuring temperature.

Major, Ralph H. "Santorio Santorio." *Annals of Medical History*, n.s. 10 (1938): 369-381. A eulogistic biography that highlights the development of the thermometer and other instruments. Major's photograph collection at the Clendening History of Medicine Library, University of Kansas Medical Center, Kansas City, contains images and descriptions of several seventeenth century thermometers, including three from Santorio.

Middleton, William Edgar Knowles. *A History of the Thermometer and Its Use in Meteorology*. Baltimore: Johns Hopkins University Press, 2003. A reprint of the well-reviewed 1966 edition, which, despite its title, also contains much information on the history of clinical thermometers and three chapters on the seventeenth century.

Mitchell, S. Weir. *The Early History of Instrumental Precision in Medicine*. New York: Burt Franklin, 1971. A reprint of a groundbreaking medical historiography that considers the contributions of Sanctorius to the development of accurate diagnosis.

SEE ALSO: 17th cent.: Advances in Medicine; 1601-1672: Rise of Scientific Societies; 1617-1628: Harvey Discovers the Circulation of the Blood; 1620: Bacon Publishes *Novum Organum*; 1623-1674: Earliest Calculators Appear; 1660's-1700: First Microscopic Observations; c. 1670: First Widespread Smallpox Inoculations; 1672-1684: Leeuwenhoek Discovers Microscopic Life; 1676: Sydenham Advocates Clinical Observation.

RELATED ARTICLES in *Great Lives from History: The Seventeenth Century, 1601-1700:* Giovanni Alfonso Borelli; Robert Boyle; Robert Fludd; Galileo; Otto von Guericke; William Harvey; Jan Baptista van Helmont; Robert Hooke; Marcello Malpighi; Santorio Santorio; Thomas Sydenham; Evangelista Torricelli.

February 7, 1613
ELECTION OF MICHAEL ROMANOV AS CZAR

Michael Romanov's election as czar ushered in a new Russian dynasty that followed several decades of internal confusion, civil war, and foreign occupation.

LOCALE: Moscow, Russia
CATEGORY: Government and politics

KEY FIGURES

Michael Romanov (1596-1645), czar of Russia,
    r. 1613-1645
Filaret (d. 1633), patriarch of the Russian Orthodox
    Church and coruler of Russia with his son Michael
    Romanov, r. 1619-1633
Sigismund III Vasa (1566-1632), king of Poland,
    r. 1587-1632, father of Władysław, and also a
    claimant to the Russian throne
Władysław (1595-1648), Polish claimant to the
    Russian throne, 1610-1612, and subsequently king
    of Poland as Władysław IV Vasa, r. 1632-1648

SUMMARY OF EVENT

Michael Romanov's ascension to the throne of Russia marked the end of the Time of Troubles (1584-1613), a period of tremendous upheaval both domestically and in Russia's relations with its western neighbors. Internal problems following the death of Ivan the Terrible in 1584 and controversy surrounding the rule of Boris Godunov (r. 1598-1605) led to widespread peasant discontent, Cossack unrest, power struggles of political factions within Russia seeking to take power in Moscow, plus the added pressures resulting from foreign invasion by Sweden and Poland and their occupation of Russian territory.

These years had witnessed the rapid rise and fall of numerous pretenders to the Russian throne, including two Polish claimants, Polish king Sigismund III Vasa and his son Władysław. Sigismund had taken advantage of the internal chaos in Russia to send troops to help elements of the Russian nobility who supported his efforts to secure the Russian throne for Władysław. By 1610, the Poles had occupied Moscow, where a hastily gathered assembly gave its approval to the accession of Władysław as czar. When Sigismund immediately sought to remove his young son and take the crown for himself, the Muscovite nobles, confident of their ability to control Władysław, feared that the powerful Polish king would ignore the interests of Russia and the Russian Orthodox Church in favor of those of Poland and Roman Catholicism. Consequently, a national reaction to the Polish in-

fluence developed in Russia, which had been spearheaded by leaders of the Russian Church and loyal Cossacks, whose army encircled Moscow and drove the Polish garrison within the walls of the Kremlin fortress. By October, 1612, the Polish troops had capitulated, and the capital once again passed into Russian hands.

An attempt by Sigismund to recapture Moscow in December, 1612, failed. Two months later, in February, 1613, an assembly of notables, the *zemskii sobor*, or council, met in Moscow to formally elect a new czar. Potential candidates included several Russians as well as at least one Swedish prince. The winning candidate was sixteen-year-old Michael Romanov, who came from a well-established aristocratic family. Michael's great aunt Anastasia had married Ivan the Terrible (r. 1547-1584) and was the mother of Fyodor I (r. 1584-1598). This Romanov connection provided a link with Russia's former ruling dynasty, and several scholars maintain that this influenced the choice of the new ruler who was installed as czar in July, 1613.

The reluctant Michael's two other outstanding qualities, which recommended his election by the *zemskii sobor*, were his Russian nationality and his inability to rule. The second of these qualities meant that Michael spent much of his long reign watching others use the power that was rightfully his. During the first several years of his reign, the czar relied on the *zemskii sobor* for its guidance during the period of national reconstruction and unification. Eventually the most important influence over Michael was his father Filaret, who from 1619 to 1633 ruled with, or more accurately for, him and was patriarch of the Russian Orthodox Church.

Released in 1619 from several years of Polish captivity, Filaret returned to a nation that had barely begun to recover domestically from the Time of Troubles and had recently been forced to surrender extensive western territories to Poland and Sweden. Michael was more than content to stand aside, allowing Filaret to administer the affairs of state and institute vitally needed reforms, among which were a new tax system to ensure increased revenues, the training of a new army along western lines, and the establishment of munitions plants to supply Russia with modern implements of war. In addition, Filaret, in his capacity as patriarch, sought to improve the education of the clergy of the Russian Orthodox Church.

The death of Filaret in 1633 found Michael little more competent to rule than he had been in 1613, and so the czar

Russian czar Michael Romanov was the first ruler of the Romanov Dynasty (1613-1917). (Francis R. Niglutsch)

soon fell under the influence of court favorites. One significant event in the closing decade of his reign was that in 1634, Władysław, now king of Poland, agreed at the end of an inconclusive two-year war with Russia to renounce all claims to the Russian throne. Otherwise, Poland emerged from the conflict apparently as strong as before.

SIGNIFICANCE

While Russia under Michael Romanov was barely able to hold its own against Poland, under subsequent Romanov rulers in the seventeenth and eighteenth centuries, Russia participated in the weakening and eventual destruction of the Polish state.

The Romanov Dynasty also moved gradually toward the creation of an absolute monarchy. By Michael's death, the *zemskii sobor* rarely met or had any authority over the monarch. When Michael's young grandson Peter the Great came to power in 1682, he developed an autocratic political system that remained as the dominant practice in Russia until the early twentieth century.

—*Edward P. Keleher and Taylor Stults*

FURTHER READING

Bain, R. Nisbet. *The First Romanovs, 1613-1725: A History of Muscovite Civilization and the Rise of Modern Russia Under Peter the Great and His Forerunners.* New York: Russell & Russell, 1967. A reprint of an early twentieth century assessment of the first years of the Romanov Dynasty.

Cowles, Virginia. *The Romanovs.* New York: Harper & Row, 1971. Good character studies of the famous Russian dynasty through its long history (1613-1917), supplemented by excellent illustrations.

Dunning, Chester S. L. *Russia's First Civil War: The Time of Troubles and the Founding of the Romanov Dynasty.* University Park: Pennsylvania State University Press, 2001. In this post-Marxist reassessment, Dunning maintains that the Time of Troubles was not a Russian peasant rebellion but a long and violent civil war. Includes information about Michael Romanov's election to the throne.

Florinsky, Michael T. *Russia: A History and Interpretation.* 2 vols. New York: Macmillan, 1947, 1953. This detailed work is considered by many to be the best account of the complex history of early seventeenth century Russia. Includes a glossary, bibliography, and an index in each volume.

Lincoln, W. Bruce. *The Romanovs: Autocrats of All the Russias*. New York: Dial Press, 1981. Lincoln's solid research traces the dynasty from its beginnings.

Platonov, S. F. *The Time of Troubles: A Historical Study of the Internal Crisis and Social Struggle in Sixteenth and Seventeenth Century Muscovy*. Translated by John T. Alexander. Lawrence: University Press of Kansas, 1970. A leading Russian scholar describes the devastating effects of the Time of Troubles on Russia's government and society.

Riasanovsky, Nicholas V., and Mark D. Steinberg. *A History of Russia*. 7th ed. New York: Oxford University Press, 2004. A comprehensive overview of Russian history that includes information about Michael Romanov's ascension to the throne and his reign as czar.

Skrynnikov, R. G. *The Time of Troubles: Russia in Crisis, 1604-1618*. Edited and translated by Hugh F. Graham. Gulf Breeze, Fla.: Academic International Press, 1988. A detailed account of Russia's problems in the time period, including Michael's early years as the Russian czar.

Soloviev, Sergei M. *The First Romanov: Tsar Michael, 1613-1645*. Edited and translated by G. Edward Orchard. 2 vols. Gulf Breeze, Fla.: Academic International Press, 1991-1995. An English translation of an important biography by a noted Russian historian of the czarist period.

SEE ALSO: c. 1601-1606: Appearance of the False Dmitry; 1632-1667: Polish-Russian Wars for the Ukraine; Apr., 1667-June, 1671: Razin Leads Peasant Uprising in Russia.

RELATED ARTICLES in *Great Lives from History: The Seventeenth Century, 1601-1700:* Alexis; Michael Romanov; Sigismund III Vasa; Sophia; Vasily Shuysky.

1610's

June 29, 1613
BURNING OF THE GLOBE THEATRE

The first Elizabethan theater fire occurred when the Globe Theatre, south of London, rapidly burned to the ground during a performance of William Shakespeare and John Fletcher's history play, Henry VIII. *The firing of a special effects cannon into the thatched roof caused the fire. Within a year, the Globe was rebuilt on the same spot.*

LOCALE: near London, England
CATEGORY: Theater

KEY FIGURES
William Shakespeare (1564-1616), English playwright and actor
John Fletcher (1579-1625), English playwright
James Burbage (c. 1530-1597), English theater owner
Richard Burbage (c. 1567-1619), English actor and theater shareholder
Matthew Brend (1600-c. 1637), English landlord of the Globe property

SUMMARY OF EVENT
Built in 1599, the Globe Theatre was located in Southwark, south of the Thames River from London proper. The theater was important as the venue for many of William Shakespeare's plays, as well as those of other Elizabethan and Jacobean playwrights. Its design was similar to but larger than that of the Rose Theatre of the same era: Called "the Wooden O," the Globe was round or polygonal in shape and open in the middle. Wealthier audience members sat in covered seats around the theater's perimeter, while those who could not afford seats (the so-called groundlings) stood by the stage itself. The roofed portion of the stage was covered in thatch, a material made of dried straw.

It was in this straw that the fire started. Burning wadding, the packing material used in loading munitions, was fired from a sound effects cannon, caught by the wind, and blown into the ceiling, igniting the very flammable thatch. The cannon was employed during a production of Shakespeare and John Fletcher's collaborative play *Henry VIII* (pr. 1613), probably to signal the appearance of the King in act 1 at Cardinal Wolsey's house. The catastrophe took place on the third day of the play's performance by the King's Men theatrical company under its original title, *All Is True*. Within an hour or so, the entire theater had burned to the ground. This was the first London theater fire in the time of Shakespeare; it would not be the last.

Fortunately, there were no fatalities from the incident and perhaps only a few injuries. Several eyewitness accounts tell the tale. One, a letter from diplomat Sir Henry Wooten to his nephew Sir Edmund Bacon, reported that a male audience member's breeches caught fire, only to be put out by some ale. Another witnessed some burns on a man who returned to pull a child out of the blaze. An anonymous broadside ballad, written within a day of the fire, tells of Richard Burbage, actor and co-owner of the theater, running out of the burning building and of the grief of actor John Heminges.

Reports differ concerning how much property was lost in the fire. Besides damage to the wood and thatch structure itself, Wooten's letter mentions only coats burning. Some historians have speculated that the King's Men's costumes and promptbooks were presumably saved, but other historians claim playbooks and other properties were lost. Shakespeare's manuscripts, however, were certainly safely stored elsewhere.

The destruction of the first Globe Theatre, which had been so closely associated with Shakespeare's drama, coincided with his departure from the world of playwriting. Shakespeare had, in fact, been one of the shareholders who financed the construction of the original Globe Theatre, together with the heirs of James Burbage, his sons Cuthbert and Richard, and four other actors. The elder Burbage had owned The Theatre, the first building in England erected specifically to house dramatic productions, and the original Globe had been built from the timbers of The Theatre after Burbage's death. The Globe was home to Shakespeare's acting company, known first as the Lord Chamberlain's Men while Elizabeth I was ruler and then as the King's Men under James I.

The Globe Theatre was not to disappear from the London scene. The land lease for the first Globe stipulated that a new theater would have to be constructed within a year. The shareholders were concerned that rebuilding might not be financially rewarding, however, as there were only fifteen years left on the original land lease. They worked with the landholder, Sir Matthew Brend, to ex-

tend the lease for another fifteen years, on the condition that they spend at least £1,000 to rebuild the Globe; the original Globe had cost only £700. The leasees claimed to invest £1,400 to £1,500 of their own money in the new theater, although Brend alleged later in a lawsuit, initiated because he wanted to revoke the lease to earn more money from the property, that they had spent only £500.

The second Globe was built on the foundations of the first in the spring of 1614; the construction must have been rapid, as it was open that same summer. Philip Henslowe, a rival theater investor, tried to build his nearby Hope Theatre at the same time to capture the Globe's lost market. There is some speculation that the second Globe was somewhat larger and more elaborate than the first, but just how similar it was to the original Globe is unknown. A 1634 Southwark survey reported the theater to be built of timber, as the first one had been, upon an old foundation. Some of the wood may have been reclaimed from the original Globe; the rest was probably imported fir.

One important change in the Globe's construction was in the roofing material: Costlier but more fire-resistant

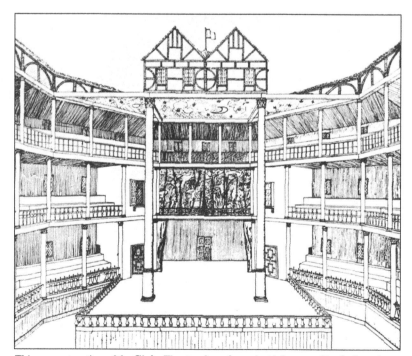

This reconstruction of the Globe Theatre, based on what is known of its design, shows several features of the theater that influenced the plays written to be performed within it. The upper stage was the setting for the balcony scene in Shakespeare's Romeo and Juliet, *and the recessed "discovery space" at the back was used in such plays as his* The Winter's Tale *and* The Tempest. *(Folger Shakespeare Library)*

tiles replaced the thatch of the original roof. This change was advisable, but it was no guarantee of safety. Another London public playhouse, the Fortune Theatre, located near the Globe, burned down on December 9, 1621. Unfortunately, its tiled roof did not save it.

The burning of the Globe was not the first time that the theater had to be closed down, nor would it be the last. From time to time, whenever a plague spread through the city of London causing at least thirty deaths, all the theaters were closed until the danger was past; plague had closed the theater for an entire year starting in late summer of 1608. After the second Globe was finished in June of 1614, it was used for twenty-eight years, until the English Civil Wars and the beginning of the Puritan Commonwealth. The Puritans viewed stage plays as sinful, and the Puritan Parliament officially closed all the theaters in London in 1642. The Globe was demolished in 1644.

SIGNIFICANCE

The burning of the first Globe Theatre may have led to Shakespeare's retirement, as he wrote no more plays following its destruction. Whether it was coincidental with his decision to leave the theater or not, biographers of Shakespeare comment on the irony of the blaze that brought his career to an end.

With the Globe's brief closure, the private Blackfriars Theatre, built by James Burbage, which was a more intimate, enclosed venue, increased in popularity and was used by such early seventeenth century playwrights as John Webster. At Blackfriars, plays could be performed at night in an interior lit by torches and candles, allowing a darker setting for the Jacobean dark tragedies of the era than was possible in the daylight open-air setting of the Globe. Despite the precariousness of open flames used to illuminate the Blackfriars, surprisingly, it never burned. However, there is evidence that the second Globe continued to be a popular venue as well following its reconstruction. It was used for the summer theater season and the Blackfriars for the rest of the year.

—Carol Blessing

FURTHER READING

Adams, John Cranford. *The Globe Playhouse: Its Design and Equipment*. 2d ed. New York: Barnes & Noble, 1961. Brief discussion of the fire includes eyewitness accounts.

Bate, Jonathan, and Russell Jackson, eds. *Shakespeare: An Illustrated Stage History*. New York: Oxford University Press, 1996. A good guide to original staging;

contains a concise but thorough overview of the 1613 fire.

Berry, Herbert. "Playhouses." In *A Companion to Renaissance Drama*, edited by Arthur F. Kinney. Malden, Mass.: Blackwell, 2002. This comprehensive volume includes essays by numerous scholars on staging, context, playwrights, and genres. Berry's chapter provides good information on the rebuilding and use of the Second Globe.

_____. *Shakespeare's Playhouses*. New York: AMS Press, 1987. Using early seventeenth century primary documents, Berry uncovers a lawsuit about the rebuilding of the burned Globe. His chapter on the lawsuit provides information on the land lease, rebuilding expenses, landowner, and investors.

Gurr, Andrew. *The Shakespeare Company, 1594-1642*. New York: Cambridge University Press, 2004. An excellent, thoroughly researched resource for background to Shakespeare's productions, this contains information on the Globe fire and all the playhouses, including the Second Globe. Includes reprints of primary documents about the fire and the theater rebuilding.

Gurr, Andrew, and John Orrell. *Rebuilding Shakespeare's Globe*. London: Weidenfeld and Nicolson, 1989. Discusses the construction of the present-day Globe Theatre in London but includes extensive backgrounds on the first and second Globe Theatres, including information on the fire, as well as early and contemporary illustrations of the theaters.

Knutson, Roslyn Lander. *The Repertory of Shakespeare's Company, 1594-1613*. Fayetteville: University of Arkansas Press, 1991. Coverage of the Globe fire conjectures that the event caused a significant loss of King's Men properties.

Wells, Stanley. *Shakespeare: For All Time*. London: Macmillan, 2002. Briefly discusses the fire and its impact on Shakespeare, and contains three stanzas of the 1613 ballad written to commemorate the event.

SEE ALSO: c. 1601-1613: Shakespeare Produces His Later Plays; Mar. 24, 1603: James I Becomes King of England; 1642-1651: English Civil Wars; Sept. 2, 1642: Closing of the Theaters; Dec. 6, 1648-May 19, 1649: Establishment of the English Commonwealth; Sept. 2-5, 1666: Great Fire of London.

RELATED ARTICLES in *Great Lives from History: The Seventeenth Century, 1601-1700:* Richard Burbage; Oliver Cromwell; John Fletcher; James I; John Webster.

1610's

1614-1615
SIEGE OF ŌSAKA CASTLE

After the Battle of Sekigahara in 1600, Hidegori, the son and heir of Toyotomi Hideyoshi, was one of the last individuals in Japan capable of mounting a challenge to the Tokugawa shogunate. Tokugawa Ieyasu used a trivial excuse to mount a campaign against Hideyori's Ōsaka castle in 1614 and captured the fortress, driving his rival to suicide in the following year and eliminating the last obstacle to the establishment of a Tokugawa dynasty.

LOCALE: Ōsaka, Japan
CATEGORIES: Wars, uprisings, and civil unrest; expansion and land acquisition; government and politics

KEY FIGURES
Tokugawa Ieyasu (1543-1616), Japanese shogun, r. 1603-1605
Tokugawa Hidetada (1579-1632), Japanese shogun, r. 1605-1623
Toyotomi Hideyori (1593-1615), Japanese warlord
Yodogimi (1577-1615), Japanese noblewoman and mother of Hideyori

SUMMARY OF EVENT
After nearly 150 years of civil war, central power in Japan was once again restored by a trio of military strongmen, known as the Three Unifiers, in the late sixteenth century. The process was begun by Oda Nobunaga, the lord of a small domain in central Japan who expanded his power and gained control of half the country, including Kyōto, the imperial capital. Nobunaga died as a result of the rebellion of one of his own generals, Akechi Mitsuhide, in 1582. Another of his followers, Toyotomi Hideyoshi, a man who had risen from humble beginnings to become one of Nobunaga's most capable commanders, defeated and killed Akechi in battle and set himself up as Nobunaga's successor. Hideyoshi further consolidated Nobunaga's gains but died in 1598, leaving his son, Hideyori, as heir in the care of a council of five regents. The most powerful of the regents, Tokugawa Ieyasu, decided, however, to seize power for himself and, after defeating his rivals at the Battle of Sekigahara in 1600, established the Tokugawa shogunate that was to rule Japan until the nineteenth century. Hideyori was given substantial landholdings and allowed to take up residence at Hideyoshi's castle in Ōsaka.

In the 1610's, however, Tokugawa Ieyasu considered Toyotomi Hideyori to be the most serious threat to the Tokugawa shogunate, and the 1614 and 1615 Ōsaka campaigns are thought to have begun because of Ieyasu's desire to eliminate him. Ōsaka Castle was a massive construction. It was similar in size and defensive strength to the Tokugawa bastion in Edo. Legislation enacted by Ieyasu in the 1610's shows that he was concerned with limiting the ability of the daimyos, or feudal lords, of various fiefdoms to build and repair castles. It is clear that Ōsaka Castle, arguably the most substantial fortress in Japan at the time, was one of the few remaining threats to the Tokugawa polity. Ieyasu also feared that Hideyori, while lacking the military prowess and leadership abilities of his father, could nonetheless serve as a rallying point for those opposed to or disenfranchised by the new system of Tokugawa rule.

Scholars are almost unanimous in their agreement that the Shomei Incident of 1614 was simply a pretext that Ieyasu used to launch a preemptive strike against Hideyori. Hideyori had bankrolled the restoration of the temple Hokoji in Kyōto. The inscription on the temple bell that Hideyori commissioned was interpreted as a possible insult to Ieyasu and a call for rebellion against the Tokugawa. Ieyasu immediately called for the young man's complete surrender. When Hideyori refused, Ieyasu launched the first of the Ōsaka campaigns.

Hideyori and his mother, Yodogimi, called upon the various daimyos to fight against the Tokugawa, but the system of domains and alliances that Ieyasu had cemented after 1600 proved stable, and none of the daimyos came to the aid of Hideyoshi's heir. Instead, it was individuals who had lost their social place or political power in the post-1600 reorganization of Japan's feudal system who stood to gain from a rebellion, and thousands of *rōnin*, or masterless samurai, as well as former vassals of Hideyoshi such as Ono Harunaga, rallied to Hideyoshi's banner. In the ranks of the *rōnin* were men like Sanada Yukimura, who proved to be an able commander during the fighting.

While the figures may have been exaggerated by contemporary chroniclers, it is estimated that Hideyori's forces eventually came to number more than 100,000. Ieyasu, on the other hand, was able to call on the various daimyos from all over Japan for military support because of the alliance system that he had developed. Ieyasu's

JAPAN C. 1615

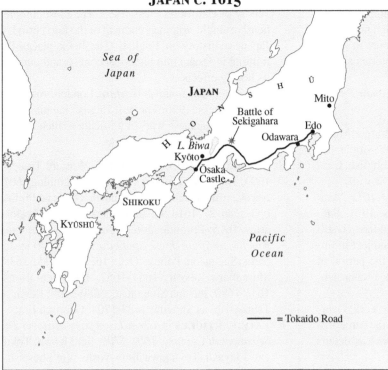

Sea of
Japan

JAPAN

Mito

Battle of
Sekigahara

Edo

Odawara

L. Biwa
Kyōto
Ōsaka
Castle

SHIKOKU

KYŪSHŪ

Pacific
Ocean

—— = Tokaido Road

the *natsu no jin*, or "summer campaign," began. The Ōsaka Castle's defenses were now far less effective than they had been in the previous year, and Hideyori's forces decided to engage Ieyasu's men in sporadic fighting around Ōsaka rather than rely on the castle alone to protect them. Poorly equipped and suffering from morale problems because of the reversal of their fortunes, Hideyori's troops were easily crushed by the Tokugawa army. Ōsaka Castle fell to Ieyasu's siege parties in early June of 1615. Hideyori and his mother, Yodogimi, were protected by holdouts but took their own lives before the last part of the fortress fell.

SIGNIFICANCE

The fall of Ōsaka Castle is typically regarded as the end of large-scale resistance against the new Tokugawa government and a final end to the century and a half of civil strife that had prevented the formation of a strong central authority in Japan. The elimination of Hideyori allowed Ieyasu and his son Hidetada to rule virtually unchallenged. While Ieyasu died shortly after the end of the Ōsaka campaigns, his victory over Hideyori gave his successors an ability, unparalleled in previous Japanese history, to promulgate laws to support the Tokugawa power system. Ever suspicious of the other feudal lords, the Tokugawa went on to introduce a series of laws governing their conduct. The laws barred alliances between daimyos and eventually introduced a system of alternate attendance at the shogun's capital of Edo whereby the families of important daimyos were kept hostage to ensure their loyalty.

In 1624, a policy of national seclusion was introduced. Japanese trade with foreign countries was strictly regulated, and travel abroad was made impossible. These measures were designed to limit Christian influence and also to ensure that the powerful domains on the fringes of Japan could not gain an advantage against the shogunate by engaging in trade with Europeans. In short, rebellion was made next to impossible, and these measures allowed the Tokugawa to remain in power until the arrival of America and other Western powers in the 1850's

forces are said to have numbered more than 200,000. He led these forces along with his son Tokugawa Hidetada, who held the official title of shogun at the time.

The first siege, called the *fuyu no jin*, or "winter campaign," ended in mid-January of 1615. Despite his superior numbers, Ieyasu was able to make little headway as a result of Ōsaka Castle's nearly impregnable defenses and the tenacious resistance of Hideyori's supporters. Ieyasu negotiated a withdrawal. Under the terms of the withdrawal, Hideyori granted Ieyasu permission to fill in the castle's outer moats and dismantle the fortress's perimeter defenses.

Ieyasu went too far, however. In violation of the terms of the agreement, Ieyasu had his men begin work dismantling and burying some of Ōsaka Castle's inner defenses as well as the outer ones. As a result of these measures, Hideyori's security was severely compromised. When he protested, Ieyasu requested that he remove himself from Ōsaka Castle and take up residence in another part of Japan. This demand was totally unacceptable to Hideyori and his supporters, and the young man chose once again openly to challenge Ieyasu.

The Tokugawa for their part were able once again to assemble a fighting force of more than 200,000 men and

sparked internal dissent and caused the system to collapse. The Tokugawa shogunate finally came to an end in 1867. Despite this end, however, the Tokugawa ruled for more than 250 years, and this long tenure in power was made possible in part by Ieyasu's victories against Hideyori at Ōsaka.

—*Matthew Penney*

FURTHER READING

Berry, Mary Elizabeth. *Hideyoshi.* Cambridge, Mass.: Harvard University Press, 1982. The best single volume treatment of Hideyoshi's career in English. Contains information about Hideyori's life as well.

Sansom, George. *A History of Japan, 1334-1615.* Stanford, Calif.: Stanford University Press, 1961. Sansom's three volume history of premodern Japan is still the most authoritative coverage of the subject in English. Provides extensive coverage of the period of civil war and the events leading up to the Ōsaka campaigns.

Sato, Hiroaki. *Legends of the Samurai.* New York: Overlook Press, 1995. Contains accounts of the careers of Nobunaga, Hideyoshi, and Ieyasu as well as details about their battles.

Totman, Conrad. *Early Modern Japan.* Berkeley: University of California Press, 1993. The most comprehensive single-volume treatment of the Edo period of Japanese history in English. The book places the fighting in Ōsaka into historical context and outlines its lasting effects.

Turnbull, Stephen. *Samurai Warfare.* London: Arms and Armour Press, 1996. The best English language history of the Japanese wars of unification. Includes details about the Ōsaka campaigns.

SEE ALSO: 1602-1613: Japan Admits Western Traders; 1603: Tokugawa Shogunate Begins; Beginning 1607: Neo-Confucianism Becomes Japan's Official Philosophy; Jan. 27, 1614: Japanese Ban Christian Missionaries; 1615: Promulgation of the *Buke shohatto* and *Kinchū narabini kuge shohatto*; 1624-1640's: Japan's Seclusion Policy; Oct., 1637-Apr. 15, 1638: Shimabara Revolt; 1651-1652: Edo Rebellions; 1651-1680: Ietsuna Shogunate; 1680-1709: Reign of Tsunayoshi as Shogun; 1688-1704: Genroku Era.

RELATED ARTICLES in *Great Lives from History: The Seventeenth Century, 1601-1700:* Seki Kōwa; Tokugawa Ieyasu; Tokugawa Tsunayoshi; Yui Shōsetsu.

January 27, 1614
JAPANESE BAN CHRISTIAN MISSIONARIES

Christian missionaries arrived in Japan in the mid-sixteenth century and began to win converts, but in 1614, the Japanese government banned Christianity— executing some Christians and exiling others. Japan remained a closed society until the 1850's.

LOCALE: Japan
CATEGORIES: Religion and theology; cultural and intellectual history; government and politics

KEY FIGURES

Oda Nobunaga (1534-1582), Japanese daimyo and national unifier
Toyotomi Hideyoshi (1537-1598), Japanese daimyo and national unifier
Tokugawa Ieyasu (1543-1616), Japanese shogun, r. 1603-1605
Tokugawa Hidetada (1579-1632), Japanese shogun, r. 1605-1623
Tokugawa Iemitsu (1604-1651), Japanese shogun, r. 1623-1651

SUMMARY OF EVENT

Prior to the sixteenth century, the islands of Japan were relatively isolated from world events. The exception to this trend was Japan's long relationship with China and its sometime vassal state of Korea. Japanese writing was based on that of China, and seventh century Chinese Buddhist missionaries shaped Japanese religious history. Even with these influences, however, Japan's relative geographical isolation resulted in a unique and largely self-contained Japanese culture. The culture's native religion was Shintoism, or the "way of the gods," and Japan's emperor was claimed to be descended from the sun goddess, Amaterasu. Most Japanese in the sixteenth century practiced a combination of Shintoism and Buddhism.

In 1542, Portuguese sailors landed in Japan, and Christian missionaries soon followed, notably Saint Francis Xavier in 1549. Western Christianity was a great contrast to the religion and culture of Japan, not only theologically but also culturally. Nevertheless, the Japanese were initially accepting of westerners, probably more because of their technology (especially gunpowder) than because of their religious beliefs and practices. Sixteenth century Japan was a society in violent upheaval. The emperor, though believed to be divine, did not rule. The actual ruler was the shogun, or chief military general, but by the 1500's, the Ashikaga shogunate, established in 1333, was in decline. Into the resulting power vacuum emerged three seminal figures, known to history as the Three Unifiers, all of whom had an impact upon Christianity in Japan.

The first of the Three Unifiers, Oda Nobunaga abolished the Ashikaga shogunate in 1573. Because he was in a bitter feud with bands of Buddhist warrior monks, Nobunaga allowed the missionaries, most of them initially Catholic Jesuits, to propagate Christianity among the population. At the time of his death in 1582, it is estimated that there were approximately 150,000 Japanese Christians, mostly in southern Japan. These included common people but also members of the samurai, or warrior, caste and some daimyo, or feudal lords. Some Japanese were undoubtedly sincere converts to the theology and morality of Christianity. Others associated the Western religion with superior Western technology and an exotic culture. Still others were attracted to the religion for economic and political reasons.

Nobunaga's successor as Japan's unofficial ruler, Toyotomi Hideyoshi, placed severe restrictions upon Christians, or *kirishitan*. In 1587, he demanded that all foreign missionaries leave Japan within twenty days. His decree was not rigorously enforced for a number of years, but in 1597, just before his death, he ordered the execution by crucifixion of twenty-six missionaries and Japanese converts. One reason for these executions was an influx of additional Christian missionaries, in spite of the 1587 expulsion edict.

The Jesuits were consummate diplomats, and in China they confined their activities mainly to the imperial court. However, in the 1580's, other Catholic religious orders, including the Franciscans and Augustinians, arrived in Japan, many from the Spanish-ruled Philippines. These new arrivals were allowed to enter Japan but only on the condition that they not preach Christianity. Once in the country, they ignored the prohibition and began preaching in the major cities of Kyōto, Nagasaki, and Ōsaka, as well as in the countryside. Not only did monotheistic Christianity contradict the beliefs of Shintoism and imperial divinity, but it also potentially threatened the political and social order of feudal Japan, and the insistence of the missionaries upon proselytizing

in direct violation of the law served only to heighten this threat.

The third unifier was Tokugawa Ieyasu. A supporter of Hideyoshi but also a rival, Ieyasu became the de facto ruler of Japan after the Battle of Sekigahara in 1600. Although he had promised to remain loyal to Hideyoshi's son and heir, Toyotomi Hideyori, Ieyasu had the powerless emperor appoint Ieyasu himself as shogun in 1603. Ieyasu's son, Tokugawa Hidetada, was proclaimed shogun in 1605, but Ieyasu retained actual power until his death in 1616. In the 1614-1615 Siege of Ōsaka Castle, Ieyasu defeated Hideyori, who committed suicide, removing the last major obstacle to Tokugawa rule.

In the early years of his reign, Ieyasu encouraged foreign trade, especially with the Portuguese and the Dutch, and was tolerant of Christian worshipers in Japan, whether native or foreign. However, in 1611, the shogunate reversed its policies and prohibited the preaching and practice of Christianity. In 1612, orders were given to punish certain individuals, followed in June, 1613 by an edict warning all religious monasteries and shrines to avoid Evil Sects, including Christians and heterodox Buddhist groups. Finally, on January 27, 1614, a decree was promulgated completely abolishing Christianity in Japan. Christian churches in the capital of Kyōto were destroyed, missionaries were imprisoned, and some Christian daimyo were driven into exile. Ultimately, all Japanese were required to register as worshipers in Buddhist temples.

Ieyasu's anti-Christian motives were mainly political. He was less concerned with what the peasants and other commoners believed than with the issue of whether Christian samurai and daimyo could be trusted to remain loyal to their feudal lords and overlords. Ieyasu, who was in the process of founding a dynasty, brooked no challenges to his authority, and he and other members of the ruling shogunate came to believe that Christianity was a threat to Japan's feudal hierarchy and its warrior code of *Bushidō*. The decision to abolish Christianity, moreover, was linked to the close relationship between the Catholic religious orders and Spain and Portugal. By 1614, Ieyasu no longer had to rely upon Spain and Portugal for trade; he had found viable alternatives in the Protestant Dutch and English merchants who were far less concerned with converting others to their faith than were the Catholics. While Ieyasu ruled, however, no foreign missionaries were put to death.

After Ieyasu's death, the government of his successors pursued a more relentless policy toward Christians, Japanese and foreign alike. Hidetada, who was shogun

187

until his death in 1623, and his successor, Tokugawa Iemitsu, were lesser figures than Ieyasu and consequently more fearful of possible Christian resistance to Tokugawa rule. In October, 1616, the daimyos were ordered not to allow any of their people to practice Christianity, not even the lowliest peasant farmer. In 1622, the year of the so-called Great Martyrdom, thirty Christians were beheaded and twenty-five others were burned at the stake. An English merchant described the burning of fifty-five Japanese Christians, including children five and six years old, at Miyako. However, in spite of the prohibitions, Catholic missionaries continued to be secretly smuggled into Japan from the Philippines, and in reaction Japanese officials discussed the possibility of launching a military assault to destroy the Catholic base of missionary activity in Luzon, a threat that was not carried out.

By 1625, Christianity in Japan had been either destroyed or driven underground. Those Christians living in urban areas, under greater direct pressure, recanted first, while peasant farmers in rural regions were able publicly to practice their adopted religion longer. In 1637-1638, the Shimabara Revolt occurred near Nagasaki on the southern island of Kyūshū, mainly caused by economic grievances, but inasmuch as a number of the participants were Christians and some of the rebels waved banners with the names of Christian saints upon them, the government viewed the revolt as inspired by the Christian religion rather than economics. The *fumie* was introduced, by which anybody suspected of being a Christian was required to stamp on the Christian cross to prove they were not Christians. The following year, in 1639, a decree was issued that stated that any foreign vessel with Christian priests on board that landed in Japan would be destroyed and its passengers and crew executed. In 1640, a Portuguese ship arrived on a diplomatic mission. Fifty-seven members of the crew were subsequently beheaded.

SIGNIFICANCE

Tied to Japan's anti-Christian campaign was the policy of excluding all foreign shipping from Japan. The only exceptions to this policy were ships from China and the Netherlands. The Spanish were expelled in 1624, the En-

glish focused upon India, and the Portuguese were driven out in the aftermath of the Shimabara uprising. Only the Dutch among Europeans were still allowed to trade with Japan, and the Dutch were restricted in the number of ships they could send per year and were confined to the island of Dejima, in Nagasaki Harbor. After 1637, Japanese were prohibited from leaving Japan, and Japanese living abroad were forbidden to return. Through this seclusion policy, Japan intentionally cut itself off from much of the Western world and culture until an American, Commodore Matthew C. Perry, forcibly opened it in 1853.

—*Eugene Larson*

FURTHER READING

Boxer, C. R. *The Christian Century in Japan, 1549-1650.* Berkeley: University of California Press, 1951. A well-written survey of Japan from the arrival of Christianity to its near-demise.

Elison, George. *Deus Destroyed: The Image of Christianity in Early Modern Japan.* Cambridge, Mass.: Harvard University Press, 1973. A classical study of Christianity in Japan during the sixteenth and seventeenth centuries.

Jansen, Marius B. *The Making of Modern Japan.* Cambridge, Mass.: Harvard University Press, 2000. This work, by one of the most eminent American historians of Japan, includes a discussion of the expulsion of western Christians from Japan.

McClain, James L. *Japan: A Modern History.* New York: W. W. Norton, 2002. Another recent history of Japan, beginning with the Tokugawa shogunate and which includes a discussion of the exclusion of Christian missionaries.

SEE ALSO: 1602-1613: Japan Admits Western Traders; 1603: Tokugawa Shogunate Begins; 1614-1615: Siege of Ōsaka Castle; 1615: Promulgation of the *Buke shohatto* and *Kinchū narabini kuge shohatto*; 1624-1640's: Japan's Seclusion Policy; Oct., 1637-Apr. 15, 1638: Shimabara Revolt.

RELATED ARTICLE in *Great Lives from History: The Seventeenth Century, 1601-1700:* Tokugawa Ieyasu.

Beginning c. 1615
COFFEE CULTURE FLOURISHES

Coffee, which became popular first among the Sufis in the early fifteenth century, reached the Middle East in the early 1600's and was soon exported to Europe and cultivated in Southeast Asia and Latin America. Within a few decades, coffee became a popular drink, as coffeehouses—and the culture they spawned—spread from Arabic and North African countries to the European continent, England, and the New World.

LOCALE: Middle East and Europe

CATEGORIES: Cultural and intellectual history; economics; health and medicine; trade and commerce

KEY FIGURES

'Abd al-Qāder Jazīrī (1505/1506-c. 1569), Arab chronicler, who wrote of the possible origins of coffee drinking

'Alī ibn 'Umar al-Shādhilī (fl. fifteenth century), Sufi leader in Yemen, reportedly the first to make coffee consumption popular among the Sufis

Murad IV (1612-1640), Ottoman sultan, r. 1623-1640, who attempted to prohibit coffee drinking

SUMMARY OF EVENT

Coffee's stimulating effects, according to one popular legend, were first realized by a ninth century Ethiopian shepherd who observed the excited behavior of the animals he was tending after they had eaten parts of a coffee plant. It is not surprising that this legend exists, given that the coffee plant is believed to be indigenous to Ethiopia in northeast Africa and possibly to Yemen on the southern Arabian peninsula. Coffee beans come from the flowering shrub *Coffea arabica* and its related species.

The tale of the Ethiopian shepherd, however, has been much disputed, and it remains legend. Historians agree, though, that coffee as some sort of consumable, most likely ground and eaten, originated in Ethiopia, and there is general agreement that coffee's origins as a drink lie in fifteenth century Yemen. Why coffee became so popular in the Middle East and then in Europe remains a mystery.

Coffee, called the new drug by French cultural historian Fernand Braudel, first appeared in Europe by way of Venice around 1615. Along with tea, cocoa, and sugar, it was considered something exotic, something only the rich could afford and enjoy. It took another thirty years or so for coffee beans, and for specialty coffee cups and pots from the Muslim world, to reach Marseilles and Paris in

France. It did not take long for coffee to become popular, and to change social life as it did in the Middle East possibly a century before. Usually, coffee was publicly consumed, making it a social drink, but it also was popular because it was supposed to be healthy. Ibn Kāshif al-Dīn Yazdī, a seventeenth century Persian pharmacologist and physician, recommended easing a hangover by taking an opium pill with coffee. Some, however, called coffee an "antiaphrodisiac" and a "eunuch's drink." Still others, doctors namely, believed coffee "dried up the cerebrospinal fluid and the convolutions . . . the upshot being general exhaustion, paralysis, and impotence."

Because history writing has traditionally meant recording monumental events, the story of seemingly trivial and mundane topics such as coffee and coffee drinking remains mostly undocumented. Cultural historians often must use as a starting point the time when something such as coffee consumption was first talked or written about. Historian Ralph Hattox, however, believes that in the case of coffee and coffeehouses, there is ample discussion in recorded history, though coffee history is not always detailed, and it is often made up of just "historical table scraps."

In the sixteenth century, 'Abd al-Qāder Jazīrī chronicled two legends about how coffee drinking started. In his posthumously published work *'Umdat al-Ṣafwah fī ḥall al-qahwah* (c. 1588), Jazīrī writes that *qahwa* or *qahva* (coffee) was brought to the region from Ethiopia by Jamāl al-Dīn Abū 'Abdallāh Moḥammad ibn Sa'īd Dabḥānī, a jurist in the early fifteenth century, who apparently witnessed the "use" of *qahwa* (which, if true, would mean coffee drinking could have originated in Africa). *Qahwa*, an Arabic term, and *qahva*, a Persian term, predate coffee use, and have been used to describe any drink made of plants that causes stimulation or intoxication, such as wine. Indeed, Europeans first called coffee from the Middle East the "wine of Islam," especially its dark, rich, and thick Turkish blend.

Jazīrī also writes of a second origin story, one that is accepted by most historians. Jazīrī reports that Sufi leader 'Alī ibn 'Umar al-Shādhilī was the first to make coffee consumption popular among the Sufis in Yemen, giving coffee its earliest reputation as a stimulating drink. The Sufis embraced coffee because it allowed them to stay awake through the evening and night to devote their unbridled time and energy in prayers to God. Al-Shādhilī became, according to modern historian 'Alī

Āl-e Dāwūd, "a kind of patron saint of coffee growers and coffeehouse owners."

It is most likely that the spread of coffee culture into the rest of the Islamic world—and then into Europe and the New World—originated with the Sufi orders of Yemen, and inherent in that coffee culture was not just the drinking of coffee but the drinking of coffee with others: In its earliest stages, coffee drinking was a social event. Coffee drinking soon moved out of the strictly religious, pious realm and into the realm of pleasure, becoming a part of public gatherings. These public gatherings became fledgling "coffeehouses," and were modeled on existing wine taverns.

From Yemen, coffee consumption spread rapidly to other areas of the Middle East, including Mecca and Cairo, and later to Baghdad, Damascus, Constantinople, and other major cities. The Ottomans, whose territory stretched to southern Yemen in the early sixteenth century, exported coffee beans throughout their vast empire. The Ottoman capital, Constantinople, opened the world's first-known coffeehouse around 1554-1555. According to historian Heinrich Éduard Jacob, the early Turkish coffeehouses were called *mekteb-i-'irfan* (schools of the cultured) and coffee was called "the milk of chess-players and of thinkers." So popular was coffee drinking that the Ottoman court established a coffee "department" called a *qahva-kāna*, the same name for "coffeehouse." The court's *qahva-kāna* was supervised by a *qahvačī-bāšī*.

Muslim pilgrims, starting in the early 1600's, would smuggle the beans of the highly regulated—and much desired—crop to other parts of the Middle East, and it

THE MIGRATION OF COFFEE CONSUMPTION

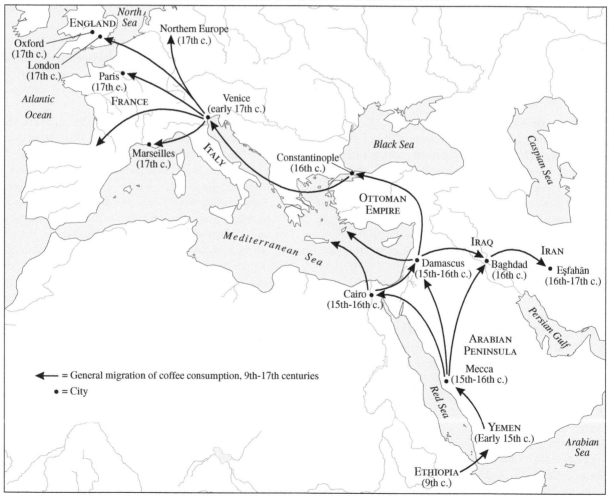

← = General migration of coffee consumption, 9th-17th centuries

● = City

made its way to ports busy with European traders and merchants. The trade in coffee began, as the British East India Company and the Dutch East India Company exported the coffee bean from Middle Eastern and North African ports and traded it within the region; it did not take long to reach Europe. The Dutch were the first to bring the beans to areas such as Ceylon (Sri Lanka), Indonesia, and, in the early 1700's, South America, for cultivation.

Opposition to *qahwa*'s intoxicating effect came swiftly in the form of civil unrest, and official condemnation came in the form of fatwas (legal-moral opinion). The coffeehouses persisted, though, despite their reputation as nothing more than taverns. According to Hattox, the coffeehouses were different from taverns in one fundamental way: "the coffeehouse was a tavern without wine, and as such . . . it was not a cause of shame to be caught in one." Fearing no public condemnation or shame, people could patronize the coffeehouses, and soon they became more and more popular. Ottoman sultan Murad IV tried to prohibit coffeehouses, along with tobacco and wine shops and the use of opium, but the prohibitions did not last.

Europeans began writing extensively about coffee and Middle East coffee culture in the seventeenth century. English poet George Sandys (1577-1644) in 1610 thought coffee "black as soote, and tasting not much unlike it," adding, "it helpeth, as they say digestion, and procureth alacrity." Pope Clement VIII was asked to outlaw coffee, but after trying it himself, he reportedly said, "Why, this Satan's drink is so delicious that it would be a pity to let the infidels have exclusive use of it. We shall fool Satan by baptizing it and making it a truly Christian beverage." Pietro della Valle wrote in 1615 that coffee "prevents those who consume it from feeling drowsy. For that reason, students who wish to read into the late hours are fond of it." Thomas Herbert visited Persia in the 1620's and wrote, "There is nothing of which the Persians are fonder than 'coho' or 'copha,' which the Turks call 'caphe.' This beverage is so black that one might suppose it to have come from the River Styx. . . . Drunk very hot, it is said to be wholesome, dispelling melancholy, drying tears, allaying anger, and producing cheerfulness."

COFFEE AND HEALTH

In The Manner of Making of Coffee, Tea, and Chocolate *(1671), physician Philippe Sylvestre Dufour outlines what he believes are the health benefits of coffee. Readers most likely will be overjoyed to hear that coffee "drives away wind" and cures other ills—even (contrary to modern medical science) stomachaches.*

It dries up all cold and damp humours, drives away wind, strengthens the liver, relieves dropsies by its purifying quality; sovereign equally for scabies and impurity of the blood, it revives the heart and its vital beat, relieves those who have stomach ache and have lost their appetite; it is equally good for those who have a cold in the head, streaming or heavy. . . . The vapour which rises from it [helps] watering eyes and noises in the ears, sovereign remedy also for short breath, colds which attack the lungs, pains in the spleen, worms; extraordinary relief after over-eating or over-drinking. Nothing better for those who eat a lot of fruit.

Source: Quoted in *Civilization and Capitalism: Fifteenth to Eighteenth Century.* Vol. 1 in *The Structures of Everyday Life: The Limits of the Possible*, by Fernand Braudel (New York: Harper & Row, 1981): p. 257.

Other seventeenth century works that mention coffee include Francis Bacon's *Historia vitae et mortis* (1637; *The Historie of Life and Death*, 1638) and *Sylva sylvarum* (1627; *Sylva Sylvarum: Or, A Natural History*, 1664), Richard Burton's *Anatomy of Melancholy* (1632), the botanical description in John Parkinson's *Theatricum Botanicum: The Theater of Plants* (1640), and physician Philippe Sylvestre Dufour's *De l'usage du café, du thé et du chocolat: Dialogue entre un médecin, un Indien, et un bourgeois* (1671; *The Manner of Making of Coffee, Tea, and Chocolate: As It is Used in Most Parts of Europe, Asia, Africa, and America, With Their Vertues*, 1685). Persian physician Yazdī dedicated to Shah ʿAbbās II (r. 1642-1666) a treatise on coffee and tea called *Resāla-ye čūb-e čīnī wa qahva wa čāy* in 1664.

Coffeehouses and coffee drinking profoundly affected society, first in the Middle East and then in Europe. In Persia, the coffeehouses were called *qahva-kāna*, or coffee rooms, according to contemporary chronicler Adam Olearius, a German scholar and embassy secretary, in his work *The Voyages and Travels of the Ambassadors* (1662), regarding his travels through Persia in the seventeenth century. The larger, more elaborate establishments took shape also as smaller shops and as market stalls and street carts. They often were "grand" or "luxurious" places, located in gardenlike or park settings, with both indoor and outdoor seating. Most significant in the development of a specifically coffee culture was that it afforded a place to see and be seen, to hear music, poetry, and narration (storytelling, speeches, drama), to play games, and to discuss politics and other controversial subjects. Talking politics, and not coffee drinking itself, turned coffeehouses into salons of a sort. Coffeehouses also were places for conducting business, for drug use, for sitting and staring, for arranging sex between males, and for idle talk, rumor, and innuendo, especially regarding women. Women were not permitted in coffeehouses of the time, except, on some occasions, as performers. To some the establishments were reputable, innocent places, but to others, especially local governments, religious leaders, and the deeply pious, they were disreputable, seditious, and subversive. The coffeehouses would hold the attention of authorities.

Coffee changed the makeup of everyday, public life. Coffee culture came to be accepted more and more, and the gatherings soon included men from all walks of life. Also, coffee roasting and brewing introduced new smells to a city, town, or village, and, "where formerly the lights at night burned mostly from the mosque, and there usually only at times of festival, the lights burned far into the night in the coffeehouses," mainly because they were "packed with people." Coffee as it was brewed and served in the Middle East, especially in Turkey, was too strong and bitter for many in the West. European consumers of the drink wanted something more "tasty" and palatable, so they often added milk and sugar.

Ṣafavid shah ʿAbbās the Great (r. 1587-1629) responded to the popularity of coffeehouses in Persia, and to their reputation for the irreligious and immoral, by placing a mullah in a well-known coffeehouse in Eṣfahān. The mullah would give talks about religion, law, literature, and history but would see to it that patrons went about their daily lives, too, discouraging people from "hanging out." The Persian government, in effect, ensured that patrons remained "civil." Mystics and other religious figures soon followed the mullahs, and the places often became sanctuaries of a sort for those in need of guidance, spiritual or otherwise.

The idea of the coffeehouse in Europe was modeled on the inns and monasteries that catered, since the twelfth century, to Christian travelers and pilgrims in need of a place to eat and rest. European coffeehouses also were modeled on cook shops, an early form of the restaurant, which thrived in Europe beginning in the fifteenth century as urban populations expanded. Not until the second half of the seventeenth century did coffee drinking become popularized, as it moved into ordinary cafes. In these cafes, one could find men of all classes and income levels, and women were welcomed in female-only establishments.

Exactly when the first coffeehouse in Europe opened is not clear. Some say 1645 in Venice (when it was called a *caffé*), others say around 1650 in Oxford, England. Still others place the first Venice coffeehouse as late as 1685. Another opened at St. Michael's Alley, Cornhill, London, in 1652. An extant handbill, or flyer, from this London shop reads, "The Vertue of the COFFEE Drink." In Canada, the Hudson's Bay Company held its first public sale of fur at Garraway's Coffee House in 1672. Coffee was sold from carts in Venice by the 1650's as well. Another early coffeehouse on the European continent most likely opened in 1671 in Marseilles, with another opening in Paris the next year. By about 1670, there were possibly as many as five hundred coffeehouses in England, albeit in all forms, from carts to stalls to shops. Also by the end of the century, coffee made its way to Germany and to the Netherlands.

As in the Middle East, with coffee drinking in Europe came great controversy. Citing concerns over its health consequences as well as its general affect on society and culture, pamphlets and broadsides such as *A Coffee Scuffle* (1662) and *The Character of a Coffee House . . . by an Eye and Ear Witness* (1665) raged against the "seminaries of sedition." *The Women's Petition Against Coffee* (1674) argued, "We find it of late a very sensible *Decay* of that true *Old English Vigour. . . .*" This "decay" came from "the Excessive use of that Newfangled, Abominable, Heathenish Liquor called *Coffee*, which . . . has so *Eunucht* our Husbands, and *Crippled* our more kind *gallants. . . .* They come from it with nothing *moist* but their snotty Noses, nothing *stiffe* but their Joints, nor *standing* but their Ears." England's king Charles II even intervened, or tried to, when he issued an order to suppress the coffeehouses in 1675. The order was rescinded, and the places kept serving coffee.

SIGNIFICANCE

Coffee culture flourished and gained widespread popularity at a time that saw the expansion and dissemination of knowledge as well as an influx of consumables from around the globe. Coffee became a major commodity of exchange in world trade and commerce.

Not knowing the story of *qahwa*'s origins would make it easy to discount its significance to cultural and, indeed, world history. After all, it is just a drink. However, coffee's introduction into the Middle East and Europe forever transformed the global marketplace, affecting economics, politics, literature, the arts, urban life, and the way information was distributed; the coffee-house became a library of sorts for "newsbooks," newspapers, and political papers. Coffee culture brought to everyday life new tastes and smells and a new culinary experience, and people gathered for reasons other than religious, a novelty at the time.

By the end of the seventeenth century, coffee drinking was more common than ever, and it reached well beyond the coffeehouse into cafes, restaurants, and homes. It also jumped across the Atlantic Ocean to the Americas, where it was first sold in the colonies of North America around 1670, possibly in Boston. It became not only a favorite pastime but also a majòr crop, especially in Latin America.

In the first years of the twenty-first century, coffee was second only to petroleum in world trade, and coffee remains one of the most-consumed drinks. The business of coffee, from growing, trading, manufacturing, and selling, employs millions of people worldwide.

—Desiree Dreeuws

FURTHER READING

Albrecht, Peter. "Coffee-Drinking as a Symbol of Social Change in Continental Europe in the Seventeenth and Eighteenth Centuries." *Studies in Eighteenth Century Culture* 18 (1988): 91-103. A social and cultural history of coffee consumption and coffee culture's transformative effects.

Dāwūd, ʿAlī Āl-e. "Coffee" and "Coffeehouse." *Encyclopaedia Iranica*. http://www.iranica.com. Accessed April, 2005. Two brief but fact-filled articles detailing the origins and later histories of coffee and coffeehouses in the Middle East, especially Persia (Iran). Each article includes a bibliography of primary and secondary sources.

Hattox, Ralph S. *Coffee and Coffeehouses: The Origins of a Social Beverage in the Medieval Near East*. Seattle: University of Washington Press, 1985. An already-classic study on the beginnings of coffee drinking and coffeehouses in the Middle East. Includes some discussion of coffee in Europe and of coffee culture in the seventeenth century. Includes a glossary, bibliography, and an index.

Jacob, Heinrich Eduard. *The Saga of Coffee: The Biography of an Economic Product*. Translated by Eden Paul and Cedar Paul. London: Allen & Unwin, 1935. Another classic study of coffee culture, especially its economic history. Includes illustrations, a bibliography (mostly of non-English sources), and an index.

Lillywhite, Bryant. *London Coffee Houses: A Reference Book of Coffee Houses of the Seventeenth, Eighteenth, and Nineteenth Centuries*. London: Allen & Unwin, 1963. A comprehensive work on the social, political, and economic history of coffee and coffeehouses.

Liss, David. *The Coffee Trader*. New York: Random House, 2003. A fictionalized historical account of a seventeenth century Portuguese-Jewish trader who, after losing a fortune in the sugar trade, attempts to introduce coffee—illegally—to Amsterdam in partnership with a local woman, but not without conflict.

Pendergrast, Mark. *Uncommon Grounds: The History of Coffee and How It Transformed Our World*. New York: Basic Books, 1999. Pendergrast explores the world of coffee in a style ideal for general readers. Includes an extensive bibliography and an index.

Schivelbusch, Wolfgang. *Tastes of Paradise: A Social History of Spices, Stimulants, and Intoxicants*. Translated by David Jacobson. New York: Pantheon Books, 1992. Schivelbusch examines primarily coffee, tea, and alcohol consumption, as well as the history and cultural and economic impacts of these popular intoxicants.

Smith, Woodruff D. "From Coffeehouse to Parlour: The Consumption of Coffee, Tea, and Sugar in Northwestern Europe in the Seventeenth and Eighteenth Centuries." In *Consuming Habits: Drugs in History and Anthropology*, edited by Jordan Goodman, Paul E. Lovejoy, and Andrew Sherratt. New York: Routledge, 1995. A collection of articles examining the cultural history of coffee in Europe. Includes a bibliography and an index.

Sommerville, C. John. "Surfing the Coffeehouse." *History Today* 47, no. 6 (June, 1997): 8-10. A brief article on the dissemination of media—news, political, and so forth—in seventeenth century coffeehouses.

Ukers, William H. *All About Coffee*. New York: Tea and Coffee Trade Journal Company, 1935. This classic work on the economic and cultural history of coffee includes a "coffee thesaurus" called "Encomiums and Descriptive Phrases Applied to the Plant, the Berry, and the Beverage."

SEE ALSO: Beginning Spring, 1605: Dutch Dominate Southeast Asian Trade; 1609: China Begins Shipping Tea to Europe; 1623-1640: Murad IV Rules the Ottoman Empire; 1629: Ṣafavid Dynasty Flourishes Under ʿAbbās the Great; Sept. 2, 1633: Great Fire of Constantinople and Murad's Reforms.

RELATED ARTICLES in *Great Lives from History: The Seventeenth Century, 1601-1700:* ʿAbbās the Great; Robert Burton; Charles II (of England); Murad IV.

1610's

1615

GUAMÁN POMA PLEAS FOR INCA REFORMS

In the early seventeenth century, a native Andean named Felipe Guamán Poma de Ayala sent a twelve-hundred-page, richly illustrated book to Philip III, recounting the history of his people before the Spanish conquest, the trauma and abuse inflicted upon them by the conquistadors, and the resulting disintegration of their society. Although he hoped to spur the king to implement reforms, it is unlikely the monarch ever received the letter.

LOCALE: Viceroyalty of Peru
CATEGORIES: Social issues and reform; colonization; literature

KEY FIGURES

Felipe Guamán Poma de Ayala (c. 1635-c. 1615), Andean interpreter, collaborator, writer, and activist
Philip III (1578-1621), king of Spain, Naples, Sicily, and Portugal, r. 1598-1621
Francisco de Toledo (1515-1584), Spanish viceroy of Peru, 1569-1581
José de Acosta (1540-1600), Spanish Jesuit missionary to Peru

SUMMARY OF EVENT

Almost everything known about the first years following the arrival of Spanish conquistadors in South America comes from European sources. In 1908, however, a startling tome was found in the Royal Library of Copenhagen. It was an extensive account, with almost four hundred illustrations, written by a native Andean in a mix of Spanish and Quechua. The book recounted the history of Peru before the arrival of the Spaniards and provided a detailed account of the problems that had beset the region when the Europeans established political control. This volume, written by a former Andean collaborator in the conquest named Felipe Guamán Poma de Ayala, took the form of a letter to King Philip III of Spain. It was meant to elicit sympathy from the monarch, as well as his support for governmental reforms to improve the lives of the people of Peru.

Titled *Primer nueva corónica y buen gobierno de las Indias* (1615; *Letter to a King*, 1978, better known as *The First New Chronicle and Good Government*), Guamán Poma's twelve-hundred-page work at first elicited mixed reactions from scholars. While the history it recounted was deemed flawed, the drawings provided valuable visual images that provided unusual insight into

local Peruvian culture immediately following the conquest. At the end of the twentieth century, historians, anthropologists, and students of literature continued to assess the extraordinary contributions of Guamán Poma's work. By then, a consensus had been reached that the text and drawings allow for a far better understanding of the tensions and contradictions that emerged among individuals like Guamán Poma as the Spanish colonization of Peru proceeded. These Andean Indians at first had cooperated with the Spaniards, but when they later realized the cost of the conquest to their people, they sought redress.

In the immediate aftermath of the conquest, groups that had been subjugated by the Incas found opportunities to rise socially by allying themselves with the Spaniards. Inca noblemen also struggled to maintain their status as the world they knew drastically changed. Infighting among the conquistadors themselves further complicated the political situation. Political unrest, native revolts, and civil wars among the Spanish raged in the Andes from the 1530's to the 1560's. Only with the arrival of Viceroy Francisco de Toledo and the execution of the last Inca emperor in 1571 did the turmoil subside. At last, a more effective, centralized colonial government emerged. Even so, navigating the new political landscape remained challenging for many native Andeans. Guamán Poma, a member of an important Inca family, became an interpreter for and supporter of both the Spanish religion and the Spanish crown in Peru. His career as a Spanish interpreter, his subsequent change of heart, and above all his chronicle of the period provide crucial insight into the uncertainties Andeans faced in the years following the conquest.

Ironically, before the Spanish conquest of Peru, Guamán Poma's family had served the Inca government as ambassadors to newly conquered regions of the Inca Empire. Their job was to move to a new region and persuade local inhabitants to submit to the new government. While this was a prestigious appointment, indicating that they were trusted subjects, it also separated them from their clan attachment to land and ancestors. When the Spaniards arrived, then, the Pomas were fairly recent migrants to the region in which they lived. These loyal servants of the Inca eventually transferred their allegiance to the Spaniards. Guamán Poma embraced Christianity: Taking on a Christian first name and surname, he became Felipe Guamán Poma de Ayala. He was acculturated as well to Spanish ways, learning the language and collaborating with colonial authorities.

When Viceroy Toledo organized a campaign to subdue a revolt that had spread through old religious networks, Guamán Poma accompanied priests on their tours of inspection and eradication of idolatry, acting as an interpreter for the Spaniards. In his travels with Spanish authorities, he witnessed both the good and the ill the newcomers brought to his homeland. He was appalled by the depopulation that resulted from the relocation of Andeans in order to make them more readily available for service in the new silver and mercury mines. This forced labor required of native communities, although based on Inca precedent, proved far more onerous under the Spaniards, and many were injured or even killed in the dangerous mines. Guamán Poma was also troubled

by the violence and venality of some churchmen, yet he admired the Jesuits, particularly the well-known missionary José de Acosta.

Although he was tightly connected to Spanish authorities, Guamán Poma also experienced the vulnerability of native Andeans under this new colonial order. In the late 1580's, a group of Peruvian Indians who had in the 1540's helped the Spanish crown establish control over rebellious conquistadors petitioned and won claim to a parcel of land. The Poma family had also been granted that same land, however. For almost fifteen years, the two groups struggled to assert their competing claims, until Guamán Poma's ties to the colonial church and state bureaucracies seemed to provide his family with the upper hand. By 1600, he believed the dispute had been settled in his family's favor, but the other claimants to the land exploited the Pomas' crucial weakness: As relative newcomers to the region, they had no local clan ties. Therefore, no one would vouch for them or support their claims to noble status. The Pomas' opponents asserted that Guamán Poma was in reality a low caste Indian who had falsely passed himself off as a nobleman. When this most likely fraudulent allegation was upheld, Guamán Poma was publicly punished with a whipping of two hundred lashes and then exiled from the region for four years.

This setback, which Guamán Poma must have seen as a betrayal on the part of those he had served so faithfully, changed his view of colonial government. It was probably when he began his period of exile that he also started to pen his letter to the king of Spain. In *The First New Chronicle and Good Government*, he sought first to establish his noble lineage by providing a history of Peru's pre-Spanish past and his own family's place in it. Guamán Poma, who was only Inca on his mother's side, claimed that his father descended from a royal dynasty that predated the Incas themselves. He then enumerated a series of abuses carried out by Spanish authorities and advised

---

GUAMÁN POMA'S LETTER TO PHILIP III

Guamán Poma's twelve-hundred-page chronicle of the Peruvian people and their mistreatment by the Spanish, The First New Chronicle and Good Government, *took the form of a "letter" to Philip III, king of Spain. In the following excerpt, dated February 14, 1615, Guamán Poma sets forth his reason for writing.*

It has occurred to me to prepare a chronicle or general history of everything that I have come to know and understand in the age of my time, for I am eighty years old. . . . For which inquiry and satisfaction of informing myself about the truth of all that with my very own eyes, it has been necessary for me to have spent thirty years in the task, having traveled on foot personally throughout the provinces of these kingdoms, taking down in writing, in spite of my poor understanding, the truth that all the afore-mentioned lords and authorities, older than myself and even more than one hundred years of age, have been able to affirm to me. And all this, so that Your Majesty might be served in the mentioned amount of time and occupation, during which I, my wife and children have suffered great necessity, poverty, and nakedness on account of not being able to have access to my herds and fields, in doing everything with great patience, with the goal of doing a great service to God our Lord and to Your Majesty by giving a long account of the manner in which the natives of these kingdoms have been treated ever since they were conquered and their lands peopled by the Spaniards, in order that Your Majesty be informed of the truth of everything, and so that Your Majesty order that remedy be sent to the call of the great damage done, because only to Your Majesty pertains looking after them as their king and natural lord, which Your Majesty in fact is, and who is distressed by their misery, calamities, bad treatment, and worse payment that they continually receive in general from every class of people, who treat them worse than slaves who have come from Africa (because even these are treated better, costing their masters the price that they actually pay for them).

Source: From *The Guamán Poma Website: A Digital Research Center for the Royal Library, Copenhagen, Denmark.* http://www.kb.dk/elib/mss/poma/. Accessed February 22, 2005.

---

the king on changes that were required to assure good government (and Indian support) in the viceroyalty of Peru. This twelve-hundred-page letter, most likely composed over a twenty-year period, was written mostly in Spanish, interspersed with a few passages in Quechua, the imperial language of the Inca. Having learned to draw under the instruction of Spanish priests, Guamán Poma included almost four hundred illustrations, possibly believing that the images would convey to the king even more strongly than his prose the urgency of the situation in Peru.

SIGNIFICANCE

Guamán Poma's letter in all probability never reached Philip III. In fact, it disappeared, resurfacing only in 1908 in an archive in Copenhagen. Given its fate, the letter may somehow have fallen into the hands of the Dutch ambassador to Spain. The discovery of Guamán Poma's letter revitalized Andean studies by providing scholars with an unusual, extensive view from a native's perspective of the harsh realities of the century following the conquest.

The First New Chronicle and Good Government provides invaluable insight into the struggles of an early generation of acculturated Indians to adjust to the system brought by the Spanish conquest. It illustrates the extent to which competing interests on all sides made for a complex and unpredictable world. The best public servants could see themselves punished rather than rewarded for their service to the crown. More than anything, Guamán Poma's chronicle allows us entry into the mind of a descendant of the Incas at a time when it still seemed possible that Indians and Spaniards might share authority in the New World.

—*Joan E. Meznar*

FURTHER READING

Adorno, Rolena. "Felipe Guamán Poma de Ayala: Native Writer and Litigant in Early Colonial Peru." In *The Human Tradition in Colonial Latin America*, edited by Kenneth J. Andrien. Wilmington, Del.: Scholarly Resources, 2002. Focusing on the land litigation as the probable reason Guamán Poma wrote to Philip III, this essay provides excellent background on Guamán Poma and his world.

_____. *Guamán Poma: Writing and Resistance in Colonial Peru*. 2d ed. Austin: University of Texas Press, 2000. Considers Guamán Poma's letter as an early, uniquely Latin American critique of Spanish colonialism. Provides excellent insight into ways in which Guamán Poma used what he had learned from the Spaniards to attack the Spanish system.

Guamán Poma de Ayala, Felipe. *Letter to a King: A Peruvian Chief's Account of Life Under the Incas and Under Spanish Rule*. Edited by Christopher Dilke. New York: E. P. Dutton, 1978. English translation of excerpts from the *Primer nueva corónica y buen gobierno*.

Stern, Steve J. *Peru's Indian Peoples and the Challenge of Spanish Conquest: Huamanga to 1640*. Madison: University of Wisconsin Press, 1982. Excellent account of the transformation of the region of the viceroyalty of Peru that was home to Guamán Poma, giving good background to both the opportunities and the problems Guamán Poma faced.

SEE ALSO: Nov. 28, 1607: Martin Begins Draining Lake Texcoco; 1608: Jesuits Found Paraguay; June-Aug., 1640: *Bandeirantes* Expel the Jesuits; Mar. 31, 1650: Earthquake Destroys Cuzco.

RELATED ARTICLES in *Great Lives from History: The Seventeenth Century, 1601-1700:* Philip III; Saint Rose of Lima.

1615

PROMULGATION OF THE *BUKE SHOHATTO* AND *KINCHŪ NARABINI KUGE SHOHATTO*

In order to consolidate centralized power in Japan, Tokugawa Ieyasu, the founder of the Tokugawa shogunate, ordered Zen and Confucian scholars to compile the Buke shohatto *and* Kinchū narabini kuge shohatto, *a pair of codes of conduct designed to control the actions of the great warrior houses and the court nobles in Kyōto.*

LOCALE: Japan

CATEGORIES: Government and politics; laws, acts, and legal history; literature

KEY FIGURES

Tokugawa Ieyasu (1543-1616), Japanese shogun, r. 1603-1605

Hayashi Razan (1583-1657), Japanese Neo-Confucian scholar

Tokugawa Hidetada (1579-1632), Japanese shogun, r. 1605-1623

SUMMARY OF EVENT

In the late sixteenth century, after nearly 150 years of civil war and disorder, a series of three military strongmen, known as the Three Unifiers, consolidated central power in Japan. The first of the unifiers, Oda Nobunaga, began from a small fiefdom in central Japan and eventually increased his sphere of influence to include most of the central island of Honshū. Nobunaga was assassinated in 1582 and succeeded by Toyotomi Hideyoshi, his most able general. Hideyoshi completed the process of national unification by force of arms, and the entire country was loyal to him at the time of his death in 1598. Hideyoshi's heir, Toyotomi Hideyori, was supplanted by another powerful warlord, Tokugawa Ieyasu, who had served under both Nobunaga and Hideyoshi and, after defeating his rivals at the Battle of Sekigahara in 1600, he was declared shogun of Japan by the emperor in 1603. In 1605, seeking to establish a lasting Tokugawa dynasty, Ieyasu turned over the title of shogun to his son, Tokugawa Hidetada, just two years into his reign. Ieyasu continued to wield the real power from behind the scenes, however, until his death in 1616.

Ieyasu was an able and ambitious administrator. He knew that Nobunaga and Hideyoshi, who had achieved national unification thought force of arms, had been unable to pass on power to their heirs. He wanted to ensure that the Tokugawa family would enjoy a perpetual reign,

so, in addition to securing his son's succession while he was still alive, he took legal measures to consolidate Tokugawa power and to ensure that it would remain consolidated. After the Battle of Sekigahara, he reorganized the nation's feudal domains to his advantage. In 1615, Ieyasu defeated Toyotomi Hideyori, who he believed could serve as a rallying point against him, and he enacted a series of codes of conduct called the *Buke shohatto* and *Kinchū narabini kuge shohatto*, governing the warrior houses and the court nobility, respectively, in order to further entrench Tokugawa power.

Ieyasu had long been aware of the potential for Neo-Confucian thought, with its emphasis on rigid social structures and hierarchy, to support his vision of a new regime. Accordingly, in 1615, he recruited Neo-Confucian scholar Hayashi Razan along with Zen monks from the major Kyōto temples to go over existing Japanese and Chinese codes of law and behavior in order to formulate a new series of directives to support Tokugawa power. The *Buke shohatto* and the *Kinchū narabini kuge shohatto* were the result.

Promulgated in 1615, the *Buke shohatto* was a simple series of precepts designed to ensure the continued loyalty of regional lords to the Tokugawa family. It began by stating that members of the warrior class should cultivate both culture and literature (*bun*) and the military arts (*bu*). The *bun/bu* dichotomy was an important one during the Edo period (1603-1867), during which members of the samurai class evolved from hereditary fighters into a sort of new bureaucratic class. The inclusion of this provision at the start of the code, however, while recognizing the new role of the samurai in a time of peace, also continued to play up their role as warriors, an essential element of class identity for the whole of the period.

The stipulations requiring that the samurai remain warrior-scholars were followed by a ban on lewd conduct for members of the warrior aristocracy and a number of directives designed to defeat the possibility of rebellion. Domains were instructed not to shelter criminals, a measure that gave primacy to Tokugawa interpretations of law over all of Japan and ensured that conspirators against the shogunate could not be sheltered in sympathetic regions without fear of reprisal. The measure also provided a means by which the central government could mobilize local forces to take care of these

197

Under the Buke shohatto, *only members of the warrior class were permitted to carry weapons in Japan.* (Hulton|Archive by Getty Images)

types of problems without becoming directly involved.

In order to emphasize the importance of the new directives, a further regulation stated that daimyos, the feudal lords of the various fiefs, had to turn over willingly anyone accused of murder or treason. Other regulations were issued to eliminate the possibility of rebellion. Plots against the shogunate were to be reported, and men from one domain were forbidden to interact with individuals from another region. In a similar vein, in order to prevent the formation of alliances between different feudal lords, the Tokugawa reserved the right to approve all marriages. During the period of civil war (the Sengoku Jidai, or Warring States period, 1477-1600) that led up to the consolidation of power under the Tokugawa, strategic alliances cemented by marriage were the norm among the daimyo families. Specific regulations in the *Buke shohatto* were designed to prevent this type of political maneuvering from continuing.

Just as strategic marriage was an important element of the landscape of power during the Warring States period, castle building was an important symbol of regional strength. The Tokugawa were weary of castles not under their direct control, and after the reduction of Hideyori's Ōsaka castle in 1615, a direct statement forbidding new castle construction and requiring lords to report all re-

pairs to existing fortifications was included in the *Buke shohatto*. The document concluded with a number of more general stipulations, including a directive that the samurai should be frugal in both lifestyle and dress and that lords must follow proper rules of etiquette when calling on the shogun.

Ieyasu and the other Tokugawa shoguns theoretically received their mandate to rule from the emperors at Kyōto. The rulers of the ancient imperial court were largely powerless figureheads by the beginning of the seventeenth century, but Ieyasu was well aware of their ability to serve as a rallying point for those opposed to the shogun's rule. For this reason the *Kinchū narabini kuge shohatto* was issued at the same time as the *Buke shohatto*, in the interests of placing similar restrictions on the court itself. The emperor was effectively told to occupy himself with scholarship and the arts and to ignore politics. In addition, the political role of the emperor and his court were limited to tasks explicitly outlined by the shogun.

SIGNIFICANCE

The Tokugawa controlled Japan from 1603 until the Meiji Restoration (1868), which followed the renewal of contact between Japan and the Western powers after the end of the seclusion policy enacted by Ieyasu's successors. While other elements of the Tokugawa polity, such as their policy of national seclusion, which effectively placed all foreign trade in the hands of the shogunate, had a lot to do with the longevity of the Tokugawa Dynasty, the provisions laid down in the *Buke shohatto* and *Kinchū narabini kuge shohatto* undoubtedly played a leading role as well.

The *Buke shohatto* was expanded in 1631 and again in 1635 under the auspices of the third Tokugawa shogun, Tokugawa Iemitsu, but its overall content remained largely unchanged from Ieyasu's day. The provisions of the code limited the ability of individual daimyos to form alliances and made organized action against the shogunate next to impossible. Any violation of the provisions spelled out in the *Buke shohatto* could result in the confiscation of a lord's domains or forced suicide. This was enough to keep the various domains in check until the entire system was shaken by the reappearance of the West in the 1850's. The nearly 250-year rule of the Tokugawa, long by Japanese and indeed world standards, was made possible, then, by the restrictions put forth in the *Buke shohatto* and *Kinchū narabini kuge shohatto* in 1615.

—*Matthew Penney*

FURTHER READING

Sansom, George. *A History of Japan, 1334-1615.* Stanford, Calif.: Stanford University Press, 1961. Sansom's three volume history of premodern Japan is still the most authoritative coverage of the subject in English. Details the early Tokugawa system and the enactment of the codes of conduct.

Sato, Hiroaki. *Legends of the Samurai.* New York: Overlook Press, 1995. A detailed work on the samurai tradition that contains early codes of conduct and coverage of the formation of a new social order under the Tokugawa.

Totman, Conrad. *Early Modern Japan.* Berkeley: University of California Press, 1993. The most compre-

hensive single volume treatment of the Edo period of Japanese history in English. Includes a discussion of the intellectual climate that resulted in the formation of the Tokugawa codes of conduct.

Turnbull, Stephen. *Samurai Warfare.* London: Arms and Armour Press, 1996. Extensive coverage, not only of samurai warfare but also of the philosophy and codes of behavior of the samurai class from the Sengoku period until Edo.

SEE ALSO: 1602-1613: Japan Admits Western Traders; 1603: Tokugawa Shogunate Begins; Beginning 1607: Neo-Confucianism Becomes Japan's Official Philosophy; 1614-1615: Siege of Ōsaka Castle; Jan. 27, 1614: Japanese Ban Christian Missionaries; 1624-1640's: Japan's Seclusion Policy; Oct., 1637-Apr. 15, 1638: Shimabara Revolt; 1651-1652: Edo Rebellions; 1651-1680: Ietsuna Shogunate; 1680-1709: Reign of Tsunayoshi as Shogun; 1688-1704: Genroku Era.

RELATED ARTICLES in *Great Lives from History: The Seventeenth Century, 1601-1700:* Seki Kōwa; Tokugawa Ieyasu; Tokugawa Tsunayoshi; Yui Shōsetsu.

1615-1696
INVENTION AND DEVELOPMENT OF THE CALCULUS

Sir Isaac Newton and Gottfried Wilhelm Leibniz, working independently and building on the work of predecessors, created the calculus, a new branch of mathematics.

LOCALE: England and continental Europe
CATEGORIES: Mathematics; physics; inventions; science and technology; cultural and intellectual history

KEY FIGURES

Sir Isaac Newton (1642-1727), English natural philosopher and mathematician
Gottfried Wilhelm Leibniz (1646-1716), German philosopher and mathematician
John Wallis (1616-1703), English mathematician
Blaise Pascal (1623-1662), French mathematician and physicist
Pierre de Fermat (1601-1665), French mathematician
Bonaventura Cavalieri (1598-1647), Italian Jesuit priest and mathematician
Johannes Kepler (1571-1630), German astronomer and mathematician

Isaac Barrow (1630-1677), English mathematician and theologian

SUMMARY OF EVENT

No person, even a genius, creates in a vacuum. Sir Isaac Newton recognized this when he stated, "If I have seen further than other men, it is because I stood on the shoulders of giants." Even though the creation of the calculus has been associated more closely with Newton than with any other mathematician, his work depended on the contributions of others. That seventeenth century mathematicians had been primed for the calculus is evidenced by its independent discovery by Gottfried Wilhelm Leibniz, who also used the contributions of his mathematical precursors.

It is no accident that the calculus originated during the Scientific Revolution, since the calculus provided scientists with efficacious ways of solving such problems as centers of gravity, instantaneous velocities, and projectile trajectories. The calculus was also different from such previous disciplines as geometry and algebra, since it involved a new operation by which, for example, a circle's area could be calculated by means of the limit of the areas of inscribed polygons, as their number of sides increased indefinitely.

During the first half of the seventeenth century, several mathematicians devised new methods for determining areas and volumes. For example, Johannes Kepler, stimulated by the problem of discovering the optimum proportions for a wine cask, published in 1615 a treatise in which he used immeasurably minute quantities, or "infinitesimals," in his volumetric calculations. Some scholars have seen Kepler's achievement as the inspiration for all later work in the calculus.

In 1635, Bonaventura Cavalieri published a book that challenged Kepler's in popularity, and some mathematicians attribute the development of the calculus to its appearance. Cavalieri used extremely small segments called "indivisibles" to devise theorems about areas and volumes. Although he compared these indivisibles to pages in a book, he made use of an infinite number of them in solving various problems. Blaise Pascal also used indivisibles in calculating the areas under various curves, but in his method he neglected "differences" of higher order, which some scholars see as the basic principle of the differential calculus.

Building on the work of Pascal, his friend Pierre de Fermat formulated an ingenious method for determining the maximum and minimum values of curves.

In England, John Wallis, who had studied the mathematical methods of Fermat and others, attempted to arithmetize the geometric treatment of areas of volumes in his *Arithmetica infinitorum* (1655; arithmetic of infinitesimals), but Isaac Barrow was critical of Wallis's work. Barrow favored a geometric approach in determining tangents to curves, and his advocacy of geometry influenced Newton. In studying problems of tangents and quadratures (constructing squares equal in area to a surface), Barrow recognized the basic inverse relationship between differentiations and integrations, but he never generalized his method. This became the principal mathematical achievement of his pupil, Isaac Newton.

According to Newton's personal testimony, he began the steps that led to his invention of the calculus while he attended Barrow's lectures at Cambridge University. He was also studying Wallis's work and the analytic geometry of René Descartes. Because of an outbreak of the bubonic plague, Newton returned to his home in Lin-

Sir Isaac Newton circulated his version of the calculus in the 1669 manuscript De analysi per aquationes numero terminorum infinitas. *(Library of Congress)*

colnshire where he derived a method of using infinite series to express the area of a circle. He also devised a differentiation method based not on ultimately vanishing quantities but on the "fluxion" of a variable. For example, Newton was able to determine instantaneous speeds through fluxions of distance with respect to time. Fluxions, Newton's name for the calculus, were descriptive of the rates of flow of variable quantities.

During the next four years, Newton made his methods more general through the use of infinite series, and he circulated his discoveries among his friends in a work titled *De analysi per aquationes numero terminorum infinitas* (1669; on analysis by means of equations with an infinite series of terms), which was not formally published until 1711 (in *Analysis per quantitatum series, fluxiones, ad differentias: Cum enumeratione linearum tertii ordinis*). Not only did Newton describe his general method for finding the instantaneous rate of change of one variable with respect to another but he also showed that an area under a curve representing a changing variable could be obtained by reversing the procedure of finding a rate of change. This notion of summations being obtained by reversing differentiation came to be called the fundamental theorem of the calculus. Though Newton's predecessors had been groping toward it, he was able to understand and use it as a general mathematical truth, which he described fully in *Methodus fluxionum et serierum infinitarum* (*The Method of Fluxions and Infinite Series*, 1736), written in 1671 but not published until after Newton's death. In this work, he called a variable quantity a "fluent" and its rate of change the "fluxion," and he symbolized the fluxion by a dot over the letter representing the variable.

Newton's third work on the calculus, *Tractatus de quadratura curvarum* (treatise on the quadrature of curves), was completed in 1676 but published in 1711 (also part of *Analysis per quantitatum series*). He began this treatise by stating that, instead of using infinitesimals, he generated lines by the motion of points, angles by the rotation of sides, areas by the motion of lines, and solids by the motion of surfaces. This work exhibits Newton's mastery of the increasingly sophisticated and powerful methods he had developed. Though he made sparse use of fluxions in his greatest work, *Philosophiae naturalis principia mathematica* (1687; *The Mathematical Principles of Natural Philosophy*, 1729, best known as the *Principia*), he did offer three ways to interpret his new analysis: using infinitesimals (as he did in *De analysi*), limits (as he did in *De quadratura*), and fluxions (as he did in *Methodus fluxionum*). The *Principia* was Newton's last great work as a mathematician.

The chief work on the calculus that rivaled Newton's work was that of Leibniz. Leibniz's early mathematical interests were arithmetic and geometry, but in studying the problem of constructing tangents to curves he used a "differential triangle" (used earlier by Pascal, Fermat, and Barrow) to arrive at solutions. He recognized that the ratio of the differences in the horizontal and vertical coordinates of a curve was needed to determine tangents, and by making these differences infinitely small, he could solve these and other problems. He also realized that the operations of summation and determining differences were mutually inverse. In a 1675 manuscript on his "inverse method of tangents," Leibniz used an integral sign for the sum and "dx" for the difference. With his new notation he was able to show that integration is the inverse of differentiation. Like Newton, Leibniz did not circulate his ideas immediately, but, in 1682, he published his discoveries in a new journal, *Acta eruditorum* (proceedings of the learned). In this and later articles he presented his methods of determining integrals of algebraic functions and solving differential equations.

SIGNIFICANCE

Both Newton and Leibniz saw the calculus as a general method of solving important mathematical problems. Though their methods were essentially equivalent, Newton, the geometer, and Leibniz, the algebraist, developed and justified their discoveries with different arguments. They both reduced such problems as tangents, rates, maxima and minima, and areas to operations of differentiation and integration, but Newton used infinitely small increments in determining fluxions whereas Leibniz dealt with differentials. Scholars have attributed this contrast to Newton's concern with the physics of motion and Leibniz's concern with the ultimate constituents of matter.

Initially, no priority debate existed between Newton and Leibniz, both of whom recognized the basic equivalence of their methods. Controversy began when some of Newton's disciples questioned Leibniz's originality, with a few going so far as to accuse Leibniz of plagiarism (since Leibniz had seen Newton's *De analysi* on a visit to London in 1676). Nationalism played a part in the controversey as well. The English and the Germans desired the glory of the calculus's discovery for their respective countries. Though the controversy generated

Gottfried Wilhelm Leibniz demonstrated that integration was the inverse of differentiation in an unpublished manuscript of 1675. (Library of Congress)

many hurt feelings and some unethical behavior on both sides in the seventeenth century, scholars now agree that Newton and Leibniz discovered the calculus independently.

The significance of this priority controversy was not a question of victor and vanquished but the divisions it created between British and Continental mathematicians. The English continued to use Newton's cumbersome fluxional notation, whereas Continental mathematicians, using Leibniz's superior formalism, were able to systematize, extend, and make a powerful mathematical discipline of the calculus. Consequently, for the next century, British mathematicians fell behind the mathematicians of Germany, France, and Italy, who were able to develop the calculus into a powerful tool capable of helping mathematicians, physicists, and chemists solve a wide variety of important problems.

—*Robert J. Paradowski*

FURTHER READING

Berlinski, David. *A Tour of the Calculus*. New York: Vintage Books, 1997. This book was written for general readers "who wish to understand the calculus as an achievement in human thought." Though the author's emphasis is on the concepts and formalism of the calculus, he also makes use of historical analysis, with many references to Newton and Leibniz. Includes an index.

Boyer, Carl B. *The History of the Calculus and Its Conceptual Development*. New York: Dover, 1959. This reprint of a classic work makes available for a wide variety of readers an authoritative and comprehensive treatment of the entire history of the calculus. Includes an extensive bibliography and an index.

Cohen, I. Bernard, and George E. Smith, eds. *The Cambridge Companion to Newton*. New York: Cambridge University Press, 2002. Several prominent scholars examine Newton's principal achievements. A. Rupert Hall's "Newton Versus Leibniz" is particularly relevant. Includes a thematic bibliography and an index.

SEE ALSO: 1601-1672: Rise of Scientific Societies; 1609-1619: Kepler's Laws of Planetary Motion; 1610: Galileo Confirms the Heliocentric Model of the Solar System; 1632: Galileo Publishes *Dialogue Concerning the Two Chief World Systems, Ptolemaic and Copernican*; 1637: Descartes Publishes His *Discourse on Method*; 1654: Pascal and Fermat Devise the Theory of Probability; 1673: Huygens Explains the Pendulum.

RELATED ARTICLES in *Great Lives from History: The Seventeenth Century, 1601-1700:* René Descartes; Pierre de Fermat; Johannes Kepler; Gottfried Wilhelm Leibniz; Sir Isaac Newton; Blaise Pascal; John Wallis.

1616-1643
RISE OF THE MANCHUS

Juchen warlord Nurhaci conquered and united all the Manchu tribes under his banner. His son, Abahai, invaded China just as the Ming Dynasty was crumbling. Abahai founded the Qing Dynasty and began the process of installing that dynasty as China's new rulers. However, his sudden death left it to his brother and son to complete the conquest.

LOCALE: Liaodong (now in Liaoning and Jilin Provinces), China

CATEGORIES: Expansion and land acquisition; government and politics; wars, uprisings, and civil unrest

KEY FIGURES

Nurhaci (Qing Taizu; 1559-1626), Manchu uniter and leader, r. 1586-1626

Abahai (Qing Taizong; 1592-1643), Manchu leader, r. 1626-1643, and emperor of China, r. 1636-1643

Dorgon (1612-1650), Manchu prince and imperial regent

Chongzhen (Ch'ung-chen; 1611-1644), emperor of China, r. 1628-1644

Shunzhi (Shun-chih; 1638-1661), first Qing emperor of China, r. 1644-1661

SUMMARY OF EVENT

After the Juchens of the Jin Dynasty (Chin, 1115-1234) were defeated by the Mongols in 1234, they retreated back to the northeastern part of China outside the Great Wall. With the Chinese, they served as subordinates to the khans during the Mongolian Yuan Dynasty (1260-1368). Not until the appearance of Nurhaci and his son

Abahai would the Juchens, later called the Manchus, succeed in again controlling China, launching a longer period of alien rule by the Qing Dynasty (Ch'ing, 1644-1911).

During the Ming Dynasty (1368-1644), trade markets were set up in Liaodong for the Mongols and Juchens, who came with silver, pearls, sable, horses, and ginseng in exchange for Chinese grains, textiles, pigs, farming tools, and iron implements. To ensure peace, guard points were established at major locations. The Jianzhou Guard of 1403 incorporated five Juchen tribes who lived to the east of Liaodong and north of the Yalu River. Nurhaci, the self-proclaimed first emperor of Hou Jin or the Later Jin Dynasty, came from the Jianzhou confederates.

Nurhaci belonged to the Aisin Gioro clan. His mother died when he was young, and he made a living by collecting ginseng and selling it at the trade markets. Nurchaci once lived in the Ming general Li Chengliang's household and had accompanied him on tribute missions in Beijing. As a young adolescent, Nurhaci learned Chinese and was interested in Chinese history and military strategy. In 1583, Nurhaci's father Tashi (Taksi) and grandfather, Giocanagga, a secondary chieftain, were massacred by Nikan Wilan (d. 1586), another strong leader in the Juchen confederation and a Ming ally. Nurhaci swore revenge and demanded compensation from the Ming, who allowed him to succeed his grandfather's title. In 1583, Nurhaci defeated Wilan, who fled to the Ming for protection. In his rage, Nurhaci turned to subdue the cities in the vicinity of Jianzhou, as well as the smaller Juchen tribes. To appease him, the Ming administration named Nurhaci assistant commissioner in chief and, in 1595, "Dragon General."

Nurhaci's relationship with China aroused jealousy and conspiracy from the neighboring Juchen groups such as the Hoifa, Hada, Ula, and Yehe, together called the Four Hulun States. In 1593, the Hulan States allied with five other Mongol tribes to attack Nurhaci, but Nurhaci defeated them. Between 1599 and 1619, Nurhaci conquered the Hulun tribes one by one. In the meantime, the Manchu leader tried to ally with the Mongol tribes in his campaigns against the Ming. The Mongol chiefs from the Korchins, Chahars, and Five Khalakas exchanged women with Nurhaci in marriage, but their relationship was one more of mutual opportunism than of political solidarity.

The Mongols needed to trade their horses with the Ming government to survive. Finally, though, Nurchaci decided to break with the Ming, risking the loss of trade and tribute gifts that were important to his people. In

1616, he announced his independence from the Ming, proclaimed himself khan, and called his dynasty Hou Jin. He assumed the title of Brilliant Emperor, Nurturer of All Nations. In the next ten years, Nurhaci launched his campaigns against the Ming towns in the Liaodong area. Fushun, a major Ming trading post, fell in 1618. When the cities of Liaoyang and Shenyang (Mukden) submitted to Nurhaci in 1621, the Liaodong area was effectively under Manchu rule. Nurhaci first made Liaoyang the capital of Hou Jin, then transferred the capital to Shenyang in 1625.

In building his Manchu empire, Nurhaci reorganized his people into military units called banners, differentiated by the colors yellow, white, red, and blue. Each banner was headed by a beile, or wise prince, usually a son, brother, uncle, or grandson of Nurhaci, followed by a banner commander and two vice-commanders. At first there were four banners, a number later expanded to eight. As a result, the Manchus were sometimes referred to as the Baqi or Eight Banner Men. Nurhaci and the beiles had personal guards who could be deployed for war. Members of the banners were made up not just of Manchus, but also of Mongols and Chinese. Nurhaci himself controlled three banners and all the beiles reported to him in meetings held every five days.

Between 1623 and 1626, Nurhaci was faced with imminent problems. His neighbors, the Koreans, allied with the Ming forces against him. Moreover, famine led to rebellions in the Liaodong area, and widespread banditry emerged. In 1626, Nurhaci led his army into Liaoxi hoping to take the town of Ningyuan, but the Ming army's Portuguese cannons caused the Manchus great losses and they wounded Nurhaci himself, who died later in September.

Nurhaci's eighth son, Abahai, was elected his successor by three senior beiles, with the understanding that his imperial position paralleled that of the three princes. Like his father, Abahai possessed significant military and political talents. He knew he had to pacify the Mongols and gain the support of the Koreans in order to realize his father's vision of conquering China. In 1627, Abahai signed a treaty with the Koreans, who agreed to become trade partners. The most important point in this treaty was that Korea would remain neutral in future Chinese-Manchu conflicts.

To avoid the cannons in the Chinese army, Abahai thought of entering China through Inner Mongolia in the southwest. Instead of fighting battles on open fields, the Manchu leader called for besieging strategic strongholds. To achieve this end, the Manchus drove the Chahar troops westward. In 1629, Abahai reached the outskirts of Beijing and occupied four major cities inside the Great Wall. But the greatest prize he obtained in this campaign, however, was the group of Chinese cannon experts he managed to kidnap. The new weapons his hostages designed proved their worth in 1631, during the Siege of Dalinghe, an important town that linked the Northeast to China proper. After the defeat of the last khan of the Chahar Mongols in 1634, Abahai changed the name of the dynasty from Hou Jin to Da Qing or Great Purity in 1636 and proclaimed himself to be emperor of China. A year earlier, he began to use the name Manchu, an old nomenclature from Juchen history, in reference to his people.

With Korea and Inner Mongolia under his control, Abahai now concentrated in his campaigns against the Ming, who had already been severely weakened by internal rebellion and piracy. There were now two Chinese emperors, the Ming emperor Chongzhen and the Qing emperor Abahai. Between 1636 and 1643, the Manchus launched three major attacks to eliminate Chongzhen once and for all. One attack garnered huge amounts of silver, gold, and 400,000 captives, which provided a significant boost to the worsening economy in Liaodong. Abahai succeeded in taking over the Ming city of Jinzhou in 1643, leaving only one more Ming defense garrison between the Manchus and the throne, but he died on September 6 before reaching this goal. In June, 1644, after overcoming the Ming rebel Li Zicheng (Li Tsu-ch'eng), Prince Dorgon, another son of Nurhaci, accompanied the six-year-old Fulin (r. 1644-1661), Abahai's son, who ascended the throne in Beijing as the Shunzhi emperor and began the uncontested rule of the Qing Dynasty.

SIGNIFICANCE

Both Nurhaci and Abahai were the pioneers in establishing the long-lasting Qing Dynasty. From an insignificant ethnic group in the northeast, they led their people, the Manchus, in the conquest of imperial China. Nurhaci, not contented with only wealth and local power, had the ambition and vision to build an empire. Abahai's victorious campaigns against the Mongols and the Chinese prompted him to consider a multinational empire seriously.

Abahai advocated equality between the Manchu and the Chinese people. Some Manchu laws were modified according to Chinese standards. For example, civil exams were used to recruit capable people, forming the basis of a meritocracy. The Manchu law requiring a man to

marry the wife of a deceased uncle or brother was eliminated, as it went against the Confucian value of *li*, or decorum. Abahai even criticized Nurhaci's reckless killing of the Chinese after their 1625 rebellion. Loyal Chinese officials were promoted and respected by Abahai. Even before the Manchus had control over China, they had a strong military and administrative system based closely on the Chinese model, and perhaps for that very reason, this small ethnic group of approximately one million was able to rule about 300 million Chinese for the next 267 years.

—*Fatima Wu*

FURTHER READING

Crossley, Pamela Kyle. *The Manchus*. Cambridge, Mass.: Blackwell, 1997. The chapters on Nurhaci and the history of the Manchus are especially useful.

Elliott, Mark C. *The Manchu Way: The Eight Banners and Ethnic Identity in Late Imperial China*. Stanford, Calif.: Stanford University Press, 2001. Has detailed information on the origin and structure of the eight banners system. The book covers banner life, Manchu cities in China and the crisis of Qing in the eighteenth century.

Michael, Franz. *The Origin of Manchu Rule in China*. New York: Octagon Books, 1972. A book devoted to the history, politics, and social structure of the Manchus before their conquest of Ming China.

Peterson, Willard. *The Ch'ing Empire to 1800*. Vol. 9 in *The Cambridge History of China*. New York: Cambridge University Press, 2002. The first chapter by Gertraude Roth Li gives a comprehensive history of the Juchens since the twelfth century Jin Dynasty.

Sinor, Denis, ed. *The Cambridge History of Early Inner Asia*. New York: Cambridge University Press, 1990. Chapter 15 gives the origin and history of the Khitans and Juchens in the Liao state from the tenth to the seventeenth century. It also covers areas of religion, customs, and language.

SEE ALSO: 1631-1645: Li Zicheng's Revolt; Apr. 25, 1644: End of the Ming Dynasty; June 6, 1644: Manchus Take Beijing; 1645-1683: Zheng Pirates Raid the Chinese Coast; Feb. 17, 1661-Dec. 20, 1722: Height of Qing Dynasty; 1670: Promulgation of the Sacred Edict; Dec., 1673-1681: Rebellion of the Three Feudatories.
RELATED ARTICLES in *Great Lives from History: The Seventeenth Century, 1601-1700:* Abahai; Chongzhen; Dorgon; Shunzhi; Zheng Chenggong.

1617
EDO'S FLOATING WORLD DISTRICT

The newly established Tokugawa shoguns, who were consolidating power in Japan, also legalized and regulated a blended urban environment of prostitution and the arts, including drama, dance, and music. Idle samurai and merchants of the capital were thus relieved from boredom and tension, which also kept them out of trouble. Through several centuries, the unique atmosphere of the Floating World district stimulated the development of major genres of fine and performing arts in Japan that blended traditions of elite Japanese culture with more-colorful popular styles.

LOCALE: Edo (now Tokyo), Japan

CATEGORIES: Cultural and intellectual history; organizations and institutions; laws, acts, and legal history; government and politics

KEY FIGURES

Jinemon Shoji (1576-1644), a Japanese brothel owner and first administrator of the Yoshiwara district

Tokugawa Ieyasu (1543-1616), Japanese warrior, founder of the Tokugawa shogunate, and shogun, r. 1603-1605

Hishikawa Moronobu (1618-1694), a Japanese painter and print designer, founder of the *ukiyo-e* genre

Izumo no Okuni (1571-1658), a Japanese performer, regarded as the founder of Kabuki theater

Tokugawa Hidetada (1579-1632), son of Ieyasu and second shogun of the Tokugawa shogunate, r. 1605-1623

SUMMARY OF EVENT

With peace and prosperity in the first decade of the seventeenth century, the capital of the new Tokugawa shogunate in Japan, Edo, expanded rapidly and was soon bustling with merchants as well as samurai, the feudal knights that were now united in the shogun's service. To maintain power, the shogun required that the samurai stay in the capital for extended periods, which attracted prostitutes, some of whom also were skilled in dance or other forms of art. With peace, though, came boredom and a demand for entertainment. One of the earliest of the popular entertainers in Edo was Izumo no Okuni, a former shrine maiden and courtesan. Okuni created provocative dances that celebrated the sexually charged atmosphere of the time. Out of her creation came Kabuki theater.

It did not take long for government authorities to become concerned about the criminal behavior and public disturbances associated with the brothels, dance performances, and skits. They preferred an orderly and controllable society, and so decided to license and restrict prostitution and popular entertainment to special zones near major cities. These walled areas were based on Chinese models developed during China's Ming Dynasty (1368-1644). Edo's entertainment center, established in a wetland area by Shogun Tokugawa Hidetada in 1617, was called the Yoshiwara (field of reeds). To manage the Yoshiwara, Hidetada chose Jinemon Shoji, a prominent brothel owner who had led a group of associates in petitioning Shogun Tokugawa Ieyasu for the regulation of prostitution. Similar entities existed in other Japanese cities: the Shimabara in Kyōto and the Shinmachi in Ōsaka.

The first Yoshiwara was relatively small. The entire structure, with high walls and a single gate for entry and exit, was designed to make it easy for government agents to keep track of potentially troublesome characters and for brothel owners to prevent their prostitutes (many of whom were kept against their will) from escaping. From the beginning, the rules were very strict. Courtesans could not travel except to visit gravely ill relatives, and they could go beyond the walls of the district only once per year to attend the cherry blossom festival. No guest could stay beyond a single evening, and brothel keepers were required to report any suspicious person immediately.

In spite of these restrictions, culture flourished in this new environment. While the government encouraged an inflexible division of classes and social functions, the Yoshiwara offered a chance for people to step outside these roles. With the right combination of beauty, artistic skill, and psychological manipulation, a clever prostitute could rise to the status of *tayu*, who would be showered with gifts but could decline propositions. There was a considerable overlap between the roles of the most prestigious courtesans and female hostess-entertainers known as geisha, who were talented in the arts and well versed in poetry, chess, and other subjects. At the other extreme were those forced to serve multiple clients in a single evening. In general, an air of mystery and glamour prevailed, in which patrons could hide their identities under straw hats sold for that purpose. A complex system of etiquette emerged, which prolonged and delayed the consummation of relationships, often causing wealthy merchants to lose their entire fortunes in the pursuit of pleasure.

Encouraged by Jinemon Shoji, performers of music and dance flourished in the district as well. A special genre of song, the *kouta*, was developed by the geisha. *Kouta* performers would accompany their own singing with the samisen. Rather than use the heavy plectrum to play the instrument, the geisha would pluck the strings with her fingers, producing a more delicate sound. Both male and female actors built upon the popular dances and plays developed by Izumo no Okuni, who had blended upper-class and vernacular elements in a style that was described as *kabuki*. At first, *kabuki* was an adjective suggesting something outside the norm, but the word was eventually applied to the exciting new genre that combined music, dance, and theater. Kabuki became the main performance genre in the district. In 1629, after samurai began fighting over the Kabuki actresses (who were also prostitutes), the government, under the third Tokugawa shogun Iemitsu (r. 1623-1651) banned women from performing on the stage, and public performances were taken over by all-male troupes of actors, including handsome young boys playing female roles.

This society and lifestyle of sensual pleasure soon came to be known as the *ukiyo* (floating world), a term used by the writer Asai Ryōi (1612-1691) in his tales of the Floating World district. Originally a Buddhist term denoting the transience of everything, *ukiyo*'s meaning changed (or evolved) to "transient pleasure seeking." It also came to represent a new genre of art called *ukiyo-e* (pictures of the floating world). Depicting everyday life in Edo (scenes with courtesans, Kabuki actors, and dancers), these pictures, mostly woodblock prints, were popular with the townsman class of merchants and artisans. Hishikawa Moronobu, the "father" of *ukiyo-e*, refined the technique of woodblock printing for mass production, thus generating affordable artwork. The *ukiyo-e* tradition continued into the next century with artists such as Hiroshige, Hokusai, and Utamaro.

In 1657, a terrible fire destroyed the entire Yoshiwara complex. The district was then rebuilt in a much larger area of almost 20 acres, with its walls enclosed in a moat. Its streets were lined with willow trees—associated in literature with prostitution—and cherry trees, whose blossoms suggested the transient beauty of life. The people of Yoshiwara set trends in fashion, arts, and language that spread through urban Japan. While most people could not afford courtesans, Kabuki theater was very accessible. *Ukiyo-e* glamorized the Yoshiwara celebrities, stimulated the fantasies of the general population, and fascinated observers with gossip and stories about the actors, courtesans, and patrons.

SIGNIFICANCE

By the early nineteenth century, the Yoshiwara was declining because of competition from illegal prostitution. However, its art forms flourished in new contexts. On March 31, 1854, Japan and the United States signed the Treaty of Kanagawa, which opened Japan to foreign trade, thus ending more than two centuries of Japanese isolation. Soon, Japanese objects and woodblock prints flowed into Europe, where a craze developed for all things Japanese. In 1872, the French art critic Philippe Burty coined the term "Japonisme" to describe the Japanese influence on French art and design. Many Impressionist and Post-Impressionist artists admired Japanese woodblock prints and assimilated *ukiyo-e* subject matter, modeling, and design elements into their own works. The Japanese influence is apparent in works by Monet, Toulouse-Lautrec, Degas, Gauguin, and Van Gogh.

The Yoshiwara burned to the ground during the bombing of Tokyo by the United States in March, 1945, and hundreds of the women who were locked inside perished. Yoshiwara later opened for business, but it was shut down after prostitution became illegal in Japan in 1958. However, some illicit sex trade continued in the neighborhood, now officially renamed Senzoku. The more positive cultural achievements of the old Yoshiwara live on worldwide through the continued cultivation and oral transmission of Yoshiwara's artistic and performance genres, including Kabuki and *kouta*.

—*Alice Myers*

FURTHER READING

American Haiku Archives. *The Floating World: An Evocation of Old Japan*. New York: Universe Books, 1989. A collection of Edo period poetry. Illustrated with *ukiyo-e* prints.

De Becker, J. E. *The Nightless City of the Geisha*. New York: Kegan Paul, 2002. A fascinating in-depth account of the Yoshiwara geishas and courtesans. Illustrated. Bibliography.

Downer, Lesley. *The Secret History of the Geisha: Women of the Pleasure Quarters*. New York: Broadway Books, 2002. A very readable intimate portrait, including stories of the Yoshiwara geisha. Illustrated. Glossary and bibliography.

Kita, Sandy et al. *The Floating World of Ukiyo-e: Shadows, Dreams, and Substance*. New York: Harry N.

Abrams, 2001. This text showcases *ukiyo-e* works in the Library of Congress. Illustrated. Bibliography.

Lane, Richard. *Images from the Floating World: The Japanese Print.* New York: Dorset Press, 1978. An illuminating account of *ukiyo-e*. Illustrated dictionary. Bibliography.

Neuer, Roni, and Herbert Libertson. *Ukiyo-e: Two Hundred Fifty Years of Japanese Art.* New York: Mayflower Books, 1979. A comprehensive book with beautiful color illustrations, a chronology, and a bibliography.

Seigle, Cecilia Segawa. *Yoshiwara: The Glittering World of the Japanese Courtesan.* Honolulu: University of Hawaii Press, 1993. An impartial, comprehensive study based on both historical and literary sources. Illustrated. Bibliography.

Swinton, Elizabeth de Sabato. *The Women of the Pleasure Quarter: Japanese Paintings and Prints of the Floating World.* New York: Hudson Hills Press, 1995. This book features more than two hundred pieces of artwork depicting the Edo pleasure quarters. Includes a bibliography.

SEE ALSO: 1603: Tokugawa Shogunate Begins; 1603-1629: Okuni Stages the First Kabuki Dance Dramas; 1688-1704: Genroku Era.

RELATED ARTICLES in *Great Lives from History: The Seventeenth Century, 1601-1700:* Hishikawa Moronobu; Tokugawa Ieyasu.

1617-1628
HARVEY DISCOVERS THE CIRCULATION OF THE BLOOD

William Harvey's discovery of the circulation of the blood was one of most important discoveries of the Scientific Revolution and of the history of medicine. Quickly accepted by the medical community, it led doctors and scientists to rethink the blood and heart's physiology, as well as general therapeutic strategies.

LOCALE: London, England

CATEGORIES: Health and medicine; biology; cultural and intellectual history

KEY FIGURES

William Harvey (1578-1657), English physician

Hieronumus Fabricius ab Aquapendente (1537-1619), Paduan professor whose lectures Harvey attended

René Descartes (1596-1650), French philosopher

Jean Riolan (1580-1657), French physician

SUMMARY OF EVENT

William Harvey's discovery of the circulation of the blood was not a punctual event. Rather, it was the product of a decade of observations, reflections, speculations, and writings, beginning in 1617 and ending in 1628, when Harvey published *Exercitatio anatomica de motu cordis et sanguinis in animalibus* (1628; *Anatomical Exercise on the Motion of the Heart and Blood in Animals*, 1653; commonly known as *De motu cordis*). This slim book, published in Frankfurt, formally announced the discovery, which turned accepted notions about the heart and blood upside down. These accepted notions sprung from the ideas of Galen (129-c. 199), a second century Greek physician whose work was influential throughout the Middle Ages and Renaissance.

The dissections Harvey performed while lecturing on surgery at the Royal College of Physicians gave him the opportunity to study the heart, although he originally intended to focus his research on the heartbeat, and convinced him that the Galenic understanding of the function and motion of the heart and blood needed to be revised. In fact, while Renaissance dissections had considerably expanded the knowledge of human anatomy—epitomized by Andreas Vesalius's *De humani corporis fabrica* (1543; *On the Fabric of the Human Body*, books I-IV, 1998; better known as *De fabrica*)—they had not revealed how or why the heart moves, nor elucidated the circulation of the blood. Indeed, the cardiovascular system and cardiac movements are very complex phenomena that cannot be easily observed.

Although the Renaissance physician Realdo Colombo (1516?-1559) had already raised doubts about Galen's description of the heart's function, when Harvey first considered the anatomical evidence, he was a convinced Galenist, like most of his colleagues. In Galenic medicine, blood was considered to be one of the four humors whose balance determined the health of an individual. It was thought of, not as circulating in a closed system, but rather as being continuously produced and destroyed. Galen believed that the liver produced blood to provide nourishment to the body; therefore, blood was consumed and had to be regenerated. This nourishing plasma was identified with the darker, venous blood.

Red, arterial blood, according to Galen, had instead the function of carrying *pneuma*, the vital spirit that was infused when the blood mixed with air in the lungs. A minimal exchange between the two blood types was believed to occur only in the heart's septum. The lack of a circulatory process in this model demanded that blood flow very slowly, allowing time for its generation and destruction. Similarly, the heart was not considered responsible for the motion of blood, which was instead thought to be attracted by the various organs and passageways, each at its own rate.

One reason Galen's model had endured so long was that oxygen-rich arterial blood in fact transforms into depleted venous blood in the capillaries, which are so small that they are visible only under a microscope. Since this process was beyond contemporary observational abilities, it neither required explanation nor stood as a recognizable contradiction to Galen's system. The capillaries would not be observed until Marcello Malpighi discovered them in 1660.

The chain of ideas and observations that led Harvey to challenge and undo the Galenic system remains a matter of speculation, because his notes and papers were lost during the Great Fire of London (1666). Any reconstruction of the exact history of Harvey's discovery must therefore rely primarily on circumstantial evidence. Harvey wrote the crucial chapters of *De motu cordis* between 1617 and 1619, and in the 1628 work's introduction, he claims to have discovered the circulation of the blood nine years earlier.

Harvey's introduction also indicates that it was thinking about the properties of venous valves that originally compelled him to doubt Galenic notions, study the heart's function and movement, and hypothesize that blood circulates through the body. Discovered by Hieronumus Fabricius ab Aquapendente and illustrated, albeit without understanding their true function, in his *De venarum ostiolis* (1603; on the veins' little doors), venous valves prevent the blood from flowing away from the heart, forcing it toward the heart. Recognizing this action of the valves in the veins and realizing that arteries lack such valves, Harvey concluded that the blood must somehow pass from the arteries to the veins and therefore circulate in the body.

Harvey's book uses metaphoric language and relies repeatedly on analogies of microcosm to microcosm and of the meteorological cycle of water. Beyond such abstract reasoning, however, Harvey devised a series of clever experiments to support his daring claim that blood circulates and is somehow transferred from the arteries to the veins. For example, by ligating an arm and regulating the blood flux in veins and arteries with a finger, he presented a visual demonstrations that valves prevent the blood from flowing away from the heart. These experiments are the only ones illustrated in *De motu cordis*, a book that includes only two plates.

Harvey also calculated the amount of blood that is expelled by the heart per hour: Even with conservative estimates for the average heartbeat and for the ventricles' size and volume, he concluded that about 1,000 fluid ounces, or almost 8 gallons (29.5 liters), of blood emerge from the heart each hour. Since it seemed impossible for the body to produce and consume fluid at that rate, this figure seemed to prove that the same blood must pass through the heart repeatedly. Harvey's combined rhetorical arguments, experimental evidence, and quantitative observations ultimately proved convincing.

Harvey demonstrating his theory of blood circulation to King Charles I. (Hulton| Archive by Getty Images)

The fact of the blood's circulation correlates with the notion that the heart must function as a pump. Harvey therefore studied the heart's motion and function, although he never actually used that often repeated comparison between the organ and the machine. Human cardiac movements remain unclear when observed in a heart beating at a normal rate, so Harvey performed vivisections of cold-blooded animals, whose hearts beat more slowly. He also examined dying mammals' hearts as they slowly stopped beating. These experiments allowed him to understand systolic and diastolic movements and thus to revise Galenic notions about cardiac anatomy and the function of the heart's four valves.

Harvey's claims and ideas were bold and challenged the status quo of medicine. Not surprisingly, they gave rise to heated debates in which he himself took part, as did prominent intellectuals of the seventeenth century, including Robert Fludd, Kenelm Digby, Thomas Hobbes, and René Descartes. The two most interesting opposing views were presented by Jean Riolan, a famous French physician and anatomist, and by Descartes. Riolan ingeniously attempted to reconcile Harvey's circulation of the blood with the Galenic model, allowing for the blood to circulate in a smaller circuit of the heart and lungs, though at a much slower rate of one complete cycle per day.

Conversely, Descartes fully supported circulation, but he disputed Harvey's account of the relationship of the blood to the heart. Following his belief that the body is a machine, Descartes tried to theorize the cardiovascular system and cardiac motions in mechanical terms, with the heart powered by the passage of the blood. Although significant, Riolan's hybrid system and Descartes's mechanical reinterpretation did not have a lasting impact; they were quickly disproved by experimental evidence.

SIGNIFICANCE

Harvey's discovery of the circulation of the blood is often compared in tenor and importance to Galileo's discoveries and to Sir Isaac Newton's theories. Although it was certainly revolutionary, however, it is important to underscore that Harvey's discovery did not reflect or incorporate the basic tenets of the Scientific Revolution. In fact, Harvey remained a convinced Aristotelian; his explanations are generally qualitative rather than quantitative, and they all embody the causal scheme proper in Aristotelian natural philosophy. In fact, he conceived his research to be part of a program, which he shared with many of his colleagues, aimed at reviving Aristotelian medical theories. It is within this framework that his attitude toward dissection and experimentation should be viewed.

Despite many authoritative attempts to disprove it, Harvey's discovery became mainstream medical knowledge within four decades of its publication. His discovery had both theoretical and practical implications. Accepting that the blood circulates not only demanded that physicians rethink their notions of blood and cardiac physiology, but it also proved a death blow to Galenic medicine. Therapeutic strategies were also affected. For instance, the practice of bloodletting, previously meant to rid the body of a presumed excess of blood and to reestablish the balance among the four humors, lost meaning.

—*Renzo Baldasso*

FURTHER READING

Bylebyl, Jerome. "Harvey." In *Dictionary of Scientific Biography*, edited by C. C. Gillispie. Vol. 4. New York: Charles Scribner's Sons, 1972-1990. Seven pages of this informative article focus on Harvey's discovery.

_____, ed. *William Harvey and His Age: The Professional and Social Context of the Discovery of the Circulation*. Baltimore: Johns Hopkins University Press, 1979. Important collection of essays.

Conrad, Lawrence, et al., eds. *The Western Medical Tradition, 800 B.C. to A.D. 1800*. New York: Cambridge University Press, 1995. Andrew Wear's chapter, "Medicine in Early Modern Europe, 1500-1700," is the best introduction to early modern medicine; it dedicates fifteen pages to Harvey's achievements.

French, Roger. *William Harvey's Natural Philosophy*. New York: Cambridge University Press, 1994. The best analysis of Harvey's work and ideas. Dedicates several chapters to Harvey's discovery and its reception in the medical and philosophical communities. Includes an extensive bibliography.

Fuchs, Thomas. *The Mechanization of the Heart: Harvey and Descartes*. Rochester, N.Y.: University of Rochester Press, 2001. Detailed study of the controversies of the circulation of the blood.

Gregory, Andrew. *Harvey's Heart: The Discovery of Blood Circulation*. London: Totem Books, 2001. Short, clear, and precise: The best monograph on this subject. It also offers a useful glossary.

Harvey, William. *The Circulation of the Blood and Other Writings*. Translated by Kenneth J. Franklin. London: J. M. Dent, 1990. The best translation of Harvey's works, with an insightful introduction by Andrew Wear.

SEE ALSO: 17th cent.: Advances in Medicine; 1610: Galileo Confirms the Heliocentric Model of the Solar System; 1612: Sanctorius Invents the Clinical Thermometer; 1632: Galileo Publishes *Dialogue Concerning the Two Chief World Systems, Ptolemaic and Copernican*; 1637: Descartes Publishes His *Discourse on Method*; 1660's-1700: First Microscopic Observations; 1664: Willis Identifies the Basal Ganglia; Sept. 2-5, 1666: Great Fire of London; c. 1670: First Widespread Smallpox Inoculations; 1672-1684: Leeuwenhoek Discovers Microscopic Life; 1676: Sydenham Advocates Clinical Observation; Summer, 1687: Newton Formulates the Theory of Universal Gravitation; 1693: Ray Argues for Animal Consciousness.

RELATED ARTICLES in *Great Lives from History: The Seventeenth Century, 1601-1700:* René Descartes; Robert Fludd; Galileo; Thomas Hobbes; Sir Isaac Newton.

1617-1693
EUROPEAN POWERS VIE FOR CONTROL OF GORÉE

For more than three centuries, strategically important Gorée Island was a contested base for Portuguese, Dutch, British, and French slave traders. As the transatlantic slave trade became more and more significant over the course of the seventeenth century, the value of the island and the struggles to control it similarly increased.

LOCALE: Senegal, West Africa

CATEGORIES: Trade and commerce; wars, uprisings, and civil unrest; social issues and reform

KEY FIGURES

André Brüe (1654-1738), French merchant and administrator

Jean d'Estrées (1624-1707), French admiral

SUMMARY OF EVENT

A basalt massif sheltered by the Cape Verde Peninsula, Gorée Island lies two miles off Senegal, opposite its present-day capital, Dakar. Called Bir or Beseguiche locally, Gorée was intermittently inhabited by fishermen from the nearby coast. In 1444, a company of soldiers dispatched by Portuguese navigator Denis Dias claimed the island for Lisbon and named it Palma. That same year, the first African slaves exported by Europeans arrived in Portugal from Mauritania. Astride major trade routes, the 45-acre (18-hectare) island was the deepest and safest anchorage on West Africa's coast, so it became a natural launching point for ships laden with slaves and other cargo.

By 1500, demand for slave labor increased with the establishment of sugarcane plantations on the Canaries, Madeira, São Tomé, and the Azores. Slaves were also sent from Palma to Portugal as domestic servants and agricultural laborers. In 1510, the first slaves were shipped across the Atlantic to South America via Spain. By 1532, slave ships began sailing direct routes to the Americas from Africa. The coasts near Palma are thought to have supplied one-third of all African slaves exported before 1600. However, Portugal's decline brought the strategically placed island many years of turmoil, as successive European powers sought to control the lucrative transatlantic trade.

In 1588, Palma was seized by the Dutch in the course of a long series of raids on Portuguese trading stations that accompanied Protestant Holland's assertion of independence. The Dutch renamed the island Goede Reede, meaning "good anchorage," which a later French corruption rendered as "Gorée." (An alternative explanation of the name claims that the island was named after the Goree peninsula in Zeeland.)

Around 1594, Gorée became a way station for ships plying routes between Holland and the West Indies, the Gold Coast, and the Indian Ocean. Holland's involvement intensified with the establishment of the Dutch East India Company in 1602. The Dutch bought Gorée from a local chief in 1617. As with Manhattan nine years later, they purchased the island for a pittance, a few iron nails. By 1621, the construction of docks and forts had transformed it into the world's most important slaving center. The island's tiny size and deep surrounding waters enabled a small garrison to control hundreds of captives. The Dutch built Fort Orange on Gorée's southern high ground and Fort Nassau to guard the docks on the island's northern tip. Falling briefly to Portugal and England, the island increased in value with the advent of Dutch colonization at the Cape of Good Hope in 1652.

Emerging from the Wars of the Reformation as a major power, the Netherlands became embroiled in several of Europe's dynastic conflicts. In 1677, during a war between France and Holland, French admiral Jean d'Estrées captured Dutch possessions in Senegal. On November 1, his fleet seized Gorée after a ten-month battle. Estrées reconstructed the existing fortifications under new names: Fort Orange became Fort Saint-Michel, and Fort Nassau became Fort Saint-François (later renamed Fort d'Estrées). French power in the region increased. The Compagnie Normande had established a post at the mouth of the Senegal in 1638 and founded Saint-Louis on a nearby island in 1659. Over the next half century, France's Senegalese possessions were governed by numerous companies, including the Compagnie du Cap Vert et du Sénégal (1658), Compagnie des Indes Occidentales (1664), Compagnie de Sénégal (1672), Compagnie d'Afrique (1682), Compagnie de Guinée (1684), Compagnie de Rouen (1710), and the Compagnie des Indes Orientales (1718).

Successively local director of the Compagnie de Sénégal, Compagnie de Rouen, and Compagnie des Indes Orientales, André Brüe extended French influence into Senegal's interior and increased slave, ivory, and gum arabic exports. Not only were French colonies in Haiti, Guiana, Guadeloupe, and Martinique supplied with labor, but Gorée also became the transit point for slaves bound to other parts of the New World from Nigeria, Gabon, and Angola. As soldiers, sailors, traders, and bureaucrats were forbidden from bringing wives to Senegal, numerous marriages and other liaisons occurred between European men and African women. As a result, a mulatto class, known as *signares*, emerged to play an important role in trade and local society.

The British governor of Gambia, James Booker, held Gorée for six months in 1693, before French forces reoccupied it, and the island would continue to change hands in the next century. Gorée would prosper, moreover, as transatlantic slaving reached its peak in the 1780's. Seven stone houses, built in 1763, replaced earlier thatched huts. By 1784, Gorée would boast eighty-one stone buildings, which would numbered over a hundred in the early 1800's. The entire island would become covered with trading compounds, offices, and dwellings.

SIGNIFICANCE

The European struggle for Gorée Island in the seventeenth century was a struggle to seize and hold the single most strategically important base of operations for the exploitation, plunder, and rape of the West African coast. The island's historical significance has come to be symbolized by the massive eighteenth century edifice, the

Maison des Esclaves (slave house). Up to two hundred chained captives were packed in this building's dark, unpainted, ground floor cells, while slave merchants and *signares* lived and worked on its spacious upper floors. Sorted like produce, men, women, and children were separated from one another. Held sometimes for weeks, slaves were herded onto ships through the Door of No Return, a portal in the building's outer, seaward wall. Voyages of indescribable horror and brutal captivity in strange lands followed.

In the nineteenth century, Gorée Island's function and significance underwent a dramatic reversal. Abolitionist pressure and successful slave uprisings were profoundly affecting public opinion in Europe and America. One European power after another outlawed the slave trade, beginning with Denmark in 1804. In 1831, Gorée became a base for antislaving naval patrols. By then, as many as 2 million slaves had passed through the island's horrific cells. Britain made slave ownership illegal in 1834. Taken from a captured slave ship and landed on Gorée in 1846, 250 ex-slaves were resettled in Gabon, where they founded Libreville. Slavery ended in Sweden, Denmark, and France in 1848, then in Dutch colonies (1863), the United States (1865), Portugal (1869), Cuba (1886), and finally Brazil (1888).

With the abolition of slavery and the founding of Dakar as Senegal's capital in 1857, Gorée's population decreased dramatically. The island once again began a new life, this time as a center for education and remembrance. The Lafitte House was transformed into the William Ponty School, French West Africa's first teacher training college. Later, the elite Mariama Ba School was founded to educate Senegal's highest achieving girls. Joined to Dakar in 1927, Gorée was regarded as a historic monument as early as 1944. Part of French West Africa, Senegal gained independence in 1960.

In 1978, Gorée was placed on the World Heritage List of the United Nations Educational, Scientific, and Cultural Organization (UNESCO), which launched an appeal to restore the island in 1980. These efforts and increasing visits by day-tripping tourists arriving on hourly ferries have assured Gorée's preservation. Often compared to San Francisco's Alcatraz, the entire island is a museum complex, hosting the Historical Museum of Senegal, a maritime museum, a women's museum, and, above all, the Slave House, a place of pilgrimage for Africa's diaspora. Visitors to its somber slave quarters and elegant houses have included Pope John Paul II, Nelson Mandela, and three American presidents. Though a physical reminder of past human exploitation, Gorée is

1610's

also tranquil and beautiful. Its cafés, art galleries, and beach have made it a refuge from Dakar's urban bustle and the host of numerous conferences, ranging from HIV/AIDS workshops to meetings of the heads of United Nations peacekeeping missions.

—Randall Fegley

FURTHER READING

Clark, Andrew Francis, and Lucie Colvin Phillips. *Historical Dictionary of Senegal*. Lanham, Md.: Scarecrow Press, 1995. A good reference to Senegal's history.

Gorée, Richard Harrison. *Gorée Island: Island of No Return*. Detroit, Mich.: Gold Leaf Press, 1997. These reflections on Gorée by an African American particularly emphasize the *signares*.

Northrup, David. *Africa's Discovery of Europe*. New York: Oxford University Press, 2002. Much material on the slave trade and Gorée is presented in this groundbreaking book on African-European interactions between 1450 and 1850.

Renaudeau, Michel, J. C. Blachere, and Maquette S. Coreth. *Goree*. Paris: Hachette, 1978. A short book of reflections on Gorée.

SEE ALSO: 17th cent.: Europe Endorses Slavery; 1619-c. 1700: The Middle Passage to American Slavery; Aug. 20, 1619: Africans Arrive in Virginia; May 6, 1626: Algonquians "Sell" Manhattan Island; Nov., 1641: Massachusetts Recognizes Slavery; Apr., 1652: Dutch Begin to Colonize Southern Africa; Mar., 1661-1705: Virginia Slave Codes; Beginning 1671: American Indian Slave Trade; Apr. 6, 1672-Aug. 10, 1678: French-Dutch War.

RELATED ARTICLES in *Great Lives from History: The Seventeenth Century, 1601-1700:* The Great Condé; Frederick Henry; Louis XIV; Marquis de Louvois; Maurice of Nassau; Njinga; Michiel Adriaanszoon de Ruyter; Maarten and Cornelis Tromp; Viscount de Turenne.

1617-c. 1700
SMALLPOX EPIDEMICS KILL NATIVE AMERICANS

Introduced to the east coast of North America with the arrival of European explorers and colonists, a series of smallpox epidemics decimated the Native Americans of the region during the first half of the seventeenth century. The disease killed as much as 90 percent of the indigenous population as it spread from New England into the Great Lakes region.

LOCALE: Northeastern North America
CATEGORIES: Health and medicine; biology; colonization

KEY FIGURES

Pocahontas (Matoaka; c. 1596-1617), Powhatan princess and diplomat
Increase Mather (1639-1723), Puritan clergyman and president of Harvard College
John Winthrop (1588-1649), cofounder of Massachusetts Bay Colony
Miles Standish (c. 1584-1656), soldier who arrived on the *Mayflower*

SUMMARY OF EVENT

Smallpox was first introduced to the Americas, probably by accident, during the conquest of the Aztec Empire by Hernán Cortés beginning in 1519. The Native American populations of Mexico and the Southwest were devas-

tated by the disease, dying in such great numbers that a small force of Spanish conquistadors was able to conquer an empire of as many as 5 million people in less than two years. The smallpox virus, however, is maintained only in humans and cannot be carried or transmitted by animals. Consequently, the relatively isolated populations of southwestern North America did not provide a focus of infection for the Native American tribes of the Northeast, who remained unaffected by the disease during the sixteenth century.

The introduction of smallpox to the eastern coast of North America followed explorations by French, Dutch, or English explorers. The first recorded epidemic appeared between 1617 and 1619 along the Massachusetts coast. The death rate among the Narragansett tribe alone probably exceeded 90 percent. Seven years prior to the epidemic, the Narragansetts were reportedly able to muster at least three thousand warriors from a population estimated at some seventy-five hundred persons. The absence of any form of natural immunity, however, resulted in disease taking a deadly toll: By the time Captain Miles Standish arrived in 1620, the only survivors present were a "few straggling inhabitants." What had been villages in the region between Narragansett Bay and the Kennebec River had become devastated sites containing only burial grounds and graves. The Wampanoag village of Pawtuxet, for example, had been completely abandoned. While there is some question as to whether this devastation was the result of an outbreak of smallpox, the description by Captain Thomas Dermeer of sores and spots on the faces of survivors supports that theory. Standish believed the outbreak to be a "blessing in disguise," as it provided an opportunity for the Pilgrims to establish a colony in the absence of native competition.

A second major epidemic occurred in 1633 in the vicinity of Plymouth Colony. The epidemic appears to have originated with Dutch traders moving between the colonies and the native tribes along the Connecticut River. Within a year, it infected the surviving Narragansetts and Connecticuts, spreading through New York into both the Great Lakes and Saint Lawrence regions of North America. Whole communities of Native Americans were devastated. By 1641, out of an estimated 160,000 members of the Five Nation Iroquois Confederacy in New York, approximately 20,000 had survived. The Iroquois fell victim to the epidemic itself, as well as to its indirect consequences, including famine. Nearly 80 percent of eighty-one hundred Mohawks died within two years of the outbreak. The epidemic was not confined to the native tribes; twenty *Mayflower* Pilgrims also died. The Puritan clergyman Increase Mather described the disease as an act of God, a divine punishment for disputes between the settlers and natives. "God ended the controversy," he said.

By 1634, smallpox had spread into the Great Lakes region, the epidemic lasting until 1640. The Hurons, with an estimated population of between twenty thousand and thirty-five thousand persons living in twenty-eight villages in 1620, had lost 50 percent of their members by 1650. Further incursions into Huron territory by hostile Iroquois from New York resulted in their absorption into other tribes and the effective elimination of the Huron tribe as a distinct entity. Nor were the Iroquois themselves spared: Between 1649 and 1679, at least three major epidemics of smallpox were reported within the Confederation. At least one Iroquois war party in 1649 was forced to turn back from an assault on the French in Montreal as a result of the disease.

Jesuit missionaries reported a significant number of baptisms among the dying natives. Ironically, however, it is likely that spread of the disease was exacerbated by the practice of kissing the crucifix as priests moved from village to village. Also, while not widespread, there is some evidence of the intentional infection of natives by the French and English. There exists at least one report of a trader intentionally presenting a keg of rum wrapped in a smallpox contaminated flag to a tribe as revenge for a recent raid.

The absence of densely populated villages in the Middle Colonies limited the outbreak of diseases such as smallpox. The Powhatan Confederacy, which surrounded the 1607 settlement at Jamestown, numbered some eighty-five hundred persons spread among an estimated thirty tribes occupying one-fifth of present day Virginia and representing approximately one-half of the native population in the region. Only a single isolated smallpox epidemic was recorded in the region during the century, in 1667. Nevertheless, by the end of the century, fewer than two thousand Powhatans were believed to have survived. In this case, however, the devastation was a consequence of military conflicts.

The tragedy of Pocahontas represents a small example of the effects of European diseases on a population lacking any form of immunity. Pocahontas, daughter of Powhatan, chief of the tribe, is most noted for having twice saved the Jamestown colony from attack. In 1614, she married Jamestown colonist John Rolfe, converted to Christianity, and returned with him to England, where three years later she was exposed to smallpox and died at the age of twenty-one.

By the end of the seventeenth century, smallpox and other diseases had played a significant role in reducing the populations of native villages to a fraction of what they had been at the beginning of European settlement. Europeans were not universally immune to these diseases. In 1630, for example, John Winthrop sailed from England on the flagship *Arbella* with nine hundred persons, eventually founding a number of towns, including Boston, along Massachusetts Bay. Smallpox broke out on board ship, but death was limited to a single child. Winthrop would later record (1636) that smallpox had wiped out the native population, opening the way for European settlement. The endemic nature of the presence of diseases such as smallpox throughout Europe ensured that these settlers would have a distinct advantage when outbreaks did occur.

SIGNIFICANCE

The size of the Native American populations in North America at the time of initial European settlement is subject to dispute, though it probably numbered in total in the tens of thousands. The absence of any previous exposure to European diseases resulted in minimal immunity to even the more benign forms of illness imported by the colonists. Even among Europeans who presumably had some level of immunity, however, smallpox epidemics often produced mortality rates of 70 percent or higher. Decimated by disease, native populations were unable to resist encroachment by the ever-growing numbers of Europeans arriving in the New World. As their populations declined, peaceful tribes were sometimes overrun by more hostile neighbors. The Hurons of the Great Lakes region, for example, became vulnerable to attacks by the more warlike Iroquois from New York and eventually ceased to exist as a unique tribe.

Repeated epidemics resulted in the loss of villages long present in the eastern regions of the continent. In many cases, the few survivors simply abandoned the dead, being unable even to bury them. Native American villages were either absorbed by their neighbors or were dispersed, or the villagers simply ceased to exist as distinct tribes. Many of the natives continued to resist European settlement for another century or more, but declining numbers resulting from a combination of disease, starvation, and warfare made the result inevitable.

—*Richard Adler*

FURTHER READING

Fenn, Elizabeth. *Pox Americana: The Great Smallpox Epidemic of 1775-1782*. New York: Hill and Wang, 2001. Discusses the eighteenth century smallpox epidemics that began with the Revolutionary War. The dynamics of smallpox epidemics were similar in the preceding century.

Grob, Gerald. *The Deadly Truth: A History of Disease in America*. Cambridge, Mass.: Harvard University Press, 2002. The author provides a historical review of disease in America, spanning the period from the first arrival of Europeans to the twenty-first century.

Emphasis is on social factors relating to development and spread of illness.

Hopkins, Donald. *Princes and Peasants: Smallpox in History*. Chicago: University of Chicago Press, 1983. A historical account of the presence and movement of smallpox from its likely origins in Africa to its presence throughout the world. Effects of the disease on human history are also recounted.

Robertson, R. G. *Rotting Face: Smallpox and the American Indian*. Caldwell, Idaho: Caxton, 2001. Graphic account of a smallpox outbreak among the tribes along the Missouri River during the 1830's.

Stearn, E. W., and A. E. Stearn. *The Effect of Smallpox on the Destiny of the Amerindian*. Boston: Bruce Humphries, 1945. Using contemporary accounts, the authors describe the spread of disease through the Great Lakes region.

Williams, H. U. "The Epidemic of the Indians of New England, 1616-1620." *Johns Hopkins Hospital Bulletin* 20 (1909): 340-349. Review of contemporary accounts of the outbreak of disease among Native Americans.

SEE ALSO: May 14, 1607: Jamestown Is Founded; 1611-1630's: Jesuits Begin Missionary Activities in New France; Dec. 26, 1620: Pilgrims Arrive in North America; Mar. 22, 1622-Oct., 1646: Powhatan Wars; 1642-1700: Westward Migration of Native Americans; c. 1670: First Widespread Smallpox Inoculations; Beginning 1671: American Indian Slave Trade.

RELATED ARTICLES in *Great Lives from History: The Seventeenth Century, 1601-1700:* Canonicus; Saint Isaac Jogues; Pocahontas; Powhatan; John Smith; Squanto; Miles Standish; Kateri Tekakwitha; John Winthrop.

1618-1648
THIRTY YEARS' WAR

The Thirty Years' War, the major European military conflict of the seventeenth century, was a struggle that began as a religious conflict but ended as a confrontation waged for secular political reasons. By its close, the political power of the Holy Roman Empire was weakened severely and France emerged as the predominant power in Europe.

LOCALE: Western and Central Europe
CATEGORIES: Wars, uprisings, and civil unrest; diplomacy and international relations; religion and theology

KEY FIGURES

Matthias (1557-1619), Holy Roman Emperor, r. 1612-1619
Frederick V (1596-1632), elector of the Palatinate, 1610-1623
Ferdinand II (1578-1637), Holy Roman Emperor, r. 1619-1637
Count Johan Tserclaes Tilly (1559-1632), commander of the imperial army
Christian IV (1577-1648), king of Denmark and Norway, r. 1588-1648
Albrecht Wenzel von Wallenstein (1583-1634), commander of the imperial army, 1625-1630 and 1632-1634
Gustavus II Adolphus (1594-1632), king of Sweden, r. 1611-1632
Axel Oxenstierna (1583-1654), Swedish chancellor and regent, 1612-1654
Cardinal de Richelieu (Armand-Jean du Plessis; 1585-1642), chief minister of France, 1624-1642

SUMMARY OF EVENT

In the sixteenth century, the rise of Lutheranism and Calvinism led to numerous wars and conflicts among the advocates of the new reformed churches and those who defended Catholicism. In 1555, the Peace of Augsburg recognized Lutheranism and established the principle of *cuius regio, eius religio*, literally, "whose rule, his the religion." In other words, the religion of a prince or political leader determined the religion that was to be practiced within a given realm. The Peace of Augsburg, however, failed to legitimize Calvinism; that factor, and the emergence of a dedicated Counter-Reformation (also known as the Catholic Reformation), led to the Thirty Years' War.

Another reason for continued conflict has to do with the way the Peace of Augsburg was applied within the religiously and ethnically diverse Holy Roman Empire. During the reign of Emperor Rudolf II, the Catholic Habsburgs sought to impose their religious views on those under their control, but regional and local Protestant leaders resisted these efforts. Decades of mutual mistrust and antagonism crystallized with the formation of the Evangelical (Protestant) Union in 1608 and the Catholic League the following year. The immediate cause of the outbreak of the war in 1618 was the closing of Protestant churches in Bohemia by representatives of Holy Roman Emperor Matthias. Subsequently, the emperor's representatives in Prague were thrown out of a palace window, in an action known as the Defenestration of Prague.

THE BOHEMIAN PHASE (1618-1625). The initial phase of the war, the Bohemian Phase (1618-1625), was marked by the repudiation of Emperor Matthias's authority. The Evangelical Union sprang into action to denounce the emperor's closing of Protestant churches. In the initial skirmishes and battles, the Protestants scored one victory after another. In early 1619, the Evangelical Union approached Vienna and threatened to lay siege to the Habsburg capital, but they had an inadequate force. In that same year, Protestant leaders named Elector Frederick V of the Palatinate, son-in-law of King James I of England, as the king of Bohemia; the Catholic claimant was the new Holy Roman Emperor, Ferdinand II, who had replaced Matthias upon his death. Ferdinand II capitalized upon growing dissent with the Protestant camp and took the offensive that resulted in the Habsburg victory at the Battle of White Mountain (Weisserberg) on November 8, 1620. The Protestants were devastated by this defeat, but they regrouped in the spring of 1622 to win the Battle of Wiesloch, their only major victory in this phase of the war. After Wiesloch in April, 1622, the imperial Habsburg forces prevailed; the Evangelical Union was dissolved and the Palatinate and Bohemia were returned to the control of the emperor.

THE DANISH PHASE (1625-1629). Christian IV, king of Denmark and Norway, emerged as the leader of the Protestant cause in 1625, marking the start of the Danish phase of the war. Christian knew that he would benefit from eliminating Habsburg control in northern Germany. From the very outset of this phase of the war, however, it was evident that Christian had made a strategic mistake that would be compounded by a series of tactical errors. Habsburg imperial armies under Albrecht Wenzel von Wallenstein and Count Johan Tserclaes Tilly defeated the Protestant forces in the Battles of Dessau Bridge (April 25, 1626) and Lutter (August, 1626). Habsburg victories were followed by the Edict of Restitution on March 6, 1629, an imperial decree that specified that all land seized from Catholics since the Peace of Augsburg was to be returned to the Catholic family from which it had been seized, and that only the Catholic and Lutheran religions were acceptable—all others were subject to persecution.

During 1629-1630, Wallenstein conducted a violent persecution of Calvinist and other dissenters. The Danish phase of the war came to an end with the Peace of Lübeck (May 22, 1629). In that agreement between Ferdinand II and Christian IV, the Danish king received almost all of his lands back in return for a pledge to remove himself from German political and religious affairs.

THE SWEDISH PHASE (1630-1635). In the summer of 1630, the war was resumed when King Gustavus II Adolphus of Sweden arrived with an army to champion the Protestant cause. Gustavus refused to accept the Treaty of Lübeck and wanted to acquire territory in Pomerania and other north German coastal areas to secure his previously won acquisitions in Finland and the Baltic Sea. In 1631, Tilly defeated German forces and seized Magdeburg (May 20, 1631), but the imperial army was defeated by Gustavus's Swedes, supported by a Saxon force, at the Battle of Breitenfeld on September 17, 1631. In 1632, Tilly died in the failed defense of Munich; the Swedes and their allies were in Bavaria. Gustavus was killed during the Battle of Lützen (November 16, 1632).

Axel Oxenstierna, the Swedish chancellor, assumed command of the Swedish army and continued the offensive, receiving the military assistance of Bernard, duke of Saxe-Weimar. While the offensive continued, Oxenstierna, a diplomat, recognized the vulnerability of the Swedish position near the Danube River, so he initiated contact with the French chief minister Cardinal de Richelieu, which resulted eventually in transforming this original religious war to a modern political struggle. Wallenstein, who had alienated many of his officers and troops through his Catholic radicalism, was assassinated on February 25, 1634. Later that year, the imperial armies under Prince Ferdinand (later Ferdinand III) scored a major victory over the Swedish-German army at the Battle of Nördlingen (September 6, 1634). By that

THE THIRTY YEARS' WAR: MAJOR EVENTS	
Date	*Event*
1618-1625	**Bohemian Phase**
May 23, 1618	Defenestration of Prague, War Begins
1618	Frederick V named head of Protestant Union
July 3, 1620	Treaty of Ulm
Nov. 8, 1620	Battle of White Mountain
Apr., 1622	Battle of Wiesloch
1625-1629	**Danish Phase**
Apr. 25, 1626	Battle of Dessau Bridge
Aug. 26, 1626	Battle of Lutter
May-July, 1628	Siege of Strasund
Mar. 6, 1629	Edict of Restitution
May 22, 1629	Peace of Lübeck
July-Nov., 1630	Electoral Assembly at Regensburg
1630-1635	**Swedish Phase**
July 6, 1630	Swedish army arrives in Pomerania
May 20, 1631	Fall of Magdeburg
Sept. 17, 1631	Battle of Breitenfeld
Nov. 16, 1632	Battle of Lützen, death of Gustavus II Adolphus
Feb. 25, 1634	Assassination of Wallenstein
Sept. 6, 1634	Battle of Nördlingen
May 30, 1635	Peace of Prague
1635-1648	**French-Swedish Phase**
Oct. 4, 1636	Battle of Wittstock
Mar. 2, 1638	Battle of Rheinfelden
Dec. 1, 1640	Frederick William becomes elector of Brandenburg
Nov. 2, 1642	Second Battle of Breitenfeld
Nov. 24-25, 1643	Battle of Tuttlingen
1643-1645	**Swedish-Danish War**
Mar. 14, 1647	Truce of Ulm
May 17, 1648	Battle of Zusmarshausen
Aug. 20, 1648	Battle of Lens
Oct. 24, 1648	Peace of Westphalia (war ends)

THE PEACE OF WESTPHALIA ENDS THE WAR

The Peace of Westphalia, which is actually two treaties—one signed at Münster, the other at Osnabrück—is made up of dozens of pages addressing, among other things, the future of church lands under dispute between Catholics and Protestants. Most critically, the peace put an end to the Thirty Years' War (1618-1648). The following excerpt is from the opening remarks of the treaty signed at Osnabrück.

In the name of the Holy and Indivisible Trinity. To all whom these presents may concern, be it known: When the divisions and disorders which began several years ago in the Roman Empire had grown to a point where not only all Germany but some of the neighboring kingdoms as well, especially Sweden and France, found themselves so involved that a long and bitter war resulted . . . [there also began] a great effusion of Christian blood and the desolation of divers provinces, until at last, through the movings of the Divine Goodness, it came about that both parties began to turn their thoughts toward the means of reestablishing peace. . . .

Source: From the Peace of Westphalia (1648), excerpted in *Readings in European History*, edited by James Harvey Robinson (Boston: Atheneum Press, 1906), pp. 346-347.

time, both sides were exhausted and the populace (both Catholic and Protestant) clamored for peace. The subsequent Peace of Prague (May 30, 1635) curtailed the implementation of the Edict of Restitution (1629) and returned some lands to Protestant leaders.

THE FRENCH-SWEDISH PHASE (1635-1648). Even before the Peace of Prague was signed, the fourth and final phase of the Thirty Years' War began. Unlike the initial three phases, the French-Swedish phase—sometimes called simply the French phase—commenced outside the German realm. Cardinal de Richelieu, chief minister to King Louis XIII of France, attacked Spain in May, 1635. Spain had been held by the Habsburgs, and Richelieu believed that French security required the defeat and containment of the Habsburgs. Catholic France went to war with the Catholic Habsburgs—in Spain and in Central Europe. The tenor of the final phase of the war was set in 1636, when Spanish military efforts were repelled by French forces, and at Rheinfelden (March 2, 1638), when the Habsburgs were defeated by a Swedish-German coalition.

During the French-Swedish phase, there was some realignment of allies. Christian IV of Denmark became an ally of the Habsburgs and was defeated during a two-year Swedish-Danish War (1643-1645). Despite occasional setbacks, such as the defeat at Tuttlingen on November 24-25, 1643, French forces were ultimately successful. The Swedes won a decisive victory at the Second Battle of Breitenfeld (November 2, 1642). The Habsburgs lost their Bavarian ally when it entered a separate peace (Truce of Ulm) with France and Sweden on March 14, 1647, but within six months Bavaria had reentered the war. Ferdinand III continued the war until the Habsburgs were defeated at Zusmarshausen on May 17, 1648, and at Lens on August 20, 1648. During September and October, Emperor Ferdinand III moved toward accepting the terms of the peace treaty that had been developed.

THE PEACE OF WESTPHALIA (1648). Negotiations to bring the Thirty Years' War to a close were protracted and difficult. While numerous states and principalities were involved, the principal negotiators were France and Sweden on one hand and the Holy Roman Empire and its ally Spain on the other. Initial discussions began in 1644 in Münster and Osnabrück, both in Westphalia, and were continued intermittently until October 24, 1648, when the Peace of Westphalia was signed. The specific terms of the peace included the following:

- France received almost all of Alsace and much of Lorraine and several small towns on the Rhine.
- France and Sweden received the right to vote in the Diet (assembly) of the Holy Roman Empire.
- Sweden gained control of the Baltic Sea and a foothold in Germany by gaining Western Pomerania and Baltic islands; the Swedes also gained control over the Bremen and Verden.
- The United Provinces of the Netherlands and the Swiss Confederation were recognized as independent states.
- Brandenburg received compensation for the loss of Western Pomerania through the acquisition of several towns.
- The operational terms of the Peace of Augsburg were reaffirmed and extended—the religion of the prince determined the religion to be practiced by the people and Calvinism was made an acceptable form of Christianity.

While the Holy Roman Empire remained as an institution until its dissolution by Napoleon Bonaparte in 1806,

1610's

THE THIRTY YEARS' WAR: BATTLE SITES

it was no longer a meaningful factor in European affairs after the Peace of Westphalia was signed in 1648.

SIGNIFICANCE

The Thirty Years' War was a defining moment in the history of early modern Europe. In the sixteenth century, the Protestant Reformation of Martin Luther, John Calvin, and other reformers, as well as advancing nationalism, transformed the organization of Europe radically. The medieval unifying concept of Christendom was replaced by competing religious views that were frequently identified with dynastic or national interests.

The reformers opposed one another and all of them were targeted by the Catholic Counter-Reformation that took shape with the Council of Trent (1545-1564) and with the establishment of new religious orders, such as the Jesuits. At the outbreak of the Thirty Years' War with the Bohemian phase in 1618, the conflict was based on religion, and the contenders' motivation and actions were delineated on religious lines. Those same factors clearly were primary in the second, Danish, phase. However, during the Swedish phase in the 1630's, the alignment of forces began to be predicated on dynastic or national priorities rather than religion. Catholic France joined Protestant Sweden against the Catholic Holy Roman Empire. After 1648, no major European war would be fought primarily over religious differences.

The impact of the Thirty Years' War was substantial, for it altered the geopolitical orientation of European affairs. France would be the predominant power for more than two centuries and Central Europe witnessed a struggle between the Habsburgs of Austria and the Hohenzollerns of Prussia, a struggle that resulted in the establishment of the Prussian dominated German Empire in 1871. Also, the independence of the Netherlands and Switzerland were recognized at the Peace of Westphalia.

In human terms, the war was devastating. Estimates of the direct and indirect casualties of the war run as high as eight million. The Thirty Years' War is also significant because of a growth of secularism in Europe; while religion and churches continued to have meaning for Europeans after 1648, the influences of Christian values and institutions declined.

The war paralleled another significant movement—the scientific and intellectual revolution of the seventeenth century—where the thought of Francis Bacon, René Descartes, Johannes Kepler, Isaac Newton, Thomas Hobbes, and John Locke presented a new worldview that was founded upon an extension of human values and a hope for a new society that would be based upon reason and not religion or spirituality alone.

—William T. Walker

FURTHER READING

Asch, Ronald G. *The Thirty Years' War: The Holy Roman Empire and Europe, 1618-48.* New York: St. Martin's Press, 1997. Asch argues that the essential points of contention in the Thirty Years' War were religion and the constitutional crisis in the German world—the battle over sovereignty between the Habsburgs and the northern German princes. A solid introduction to the war.

Benecke, Gerhard, ed. *Germany in the Thirty Years' War.* New York: St. Martin's Press, 1979. A relatively brief but valuable study of Germany's role in the Thirty Years' War from the Peace of Augsburg in 1555 through the late 1640's. Includes both narrative and excerpts of primary sources on politics and the constitution, economics and the military system, religion and propaganda, and sections on the war's social impact.

Bireley, Robert. *The Jesuits and the Thirty Years' War: Kings, Court, and Confessors.* New York: Cambridge University Press, 2003. A valuable study by a Jesuit on the focus among the Catholic and increasingly nationalist dynasties in Madrid, Paris, Vienna, and Munich. The text is based on a wealth of primary sources and is geared toward the reader with some historical familiarity with the war.

Guthrie, William P. *Battles of the Thirty Years' War: From White Mountain to Nordlingen, 1618-1635.* Westport, Conn.: Greenwood Press, 2002. The best and most comprehensive account of the military actions during the Bohemian, Danish, and Swedish phases of the Thirty Years' War. Guthrie's excellent appendices provide valuable information on many aspects of the battles.

_____. *The Later Thirty Years' War: From the Battle of Wittstock to the Treaty of Westphalia.* Westport, Conn.: Greenwood Press, 2003. Guthrie's account of the French phase of the Thirty Years' War is the best and the most detailed account in English. Provides excellent, detailed appendices.

Lockhart, Paul D. *Denmark in the Thirty Years' War, 1618-1648: King Christian IV and the Decline of the Oldenburg State.* Selinsgrove, Pa.: Susquehanna University Press, 1996. A well-written and well-researched account of Christian IV's lamentable misunderstanding of Denmark's strategic position and military capabilities and his miscalculated intervention in the name of national and dynastic defense. Lockhart is at his best when examining the impact of the conflict on the Danish political system and the subsequent success of absolute monarchy over the shared governance of the king with the aristocracy.

Maland, David. *Europe at War, 1600-1650.* Totowa, N.J.: Rowman and Littlefield, 1980. An excellent survey of the causes, outbreak, development, and consequences of the Thirty Years' War. An ideal introductory study for the general reader and student, which combines an understanding of the historical forces that were at play with the most significant facts associated with the struggle.

Osborne, Toby. *Dynasty and Diplomacy in the Court of Savoy: Political Culture and the Thirty Years' War.* New York: Cambridge University Press, 2002. This is the only study in English of the role of Savoy in the Thirty Years' War. The work is centered on the role of diplomacy, the aims of the House of Savoy, and the interests of the elite during the war.

Parker, Geoffrey. *The Thirty Years' War.* New York: Routledge and Kegan Paul, 1987. An excellent introduction to the war, well-written, fully documented, and supported by valuable maps. Parker's study is one of the best general histories of the conflict.

Polisenský, Josef V., and Frederick Snider. *War and Society in Europe, 1618-1648*. New York: Cambridge University Press, 1978. This excellent study examines the contemporary and later historical sources on the Thirty Years' War, the problems associated with studying the conflict, and the effects of the war.

Ringmar, Erik. *Identity, Interest, and Action: A Cultural Explanation of Sweden's Intervention in the Thirty Years' War*. New York: Cambridge University Press, 1996. A seminal study that argues that Sweden's entrance into the war in 1630 was based on reasons of identity rather than a rational choice based on dynastic and national interests. Ringmar's interpretation suggests new approaches for the study of the war.

SEE ALSO: May 23, 1618: Defenestration of Prague; July, 1620-Sept., 1639: Struggle for the Valtelline Pass; Nov. 8, 1620: Battle of White Mountain; Mar. 6, 1629: Edict of Restitution; 1630-1648: Destruction of Bavaria; May 30, 1635: Peace of Prague; July, 1643-Oct. 24, 1648: Peace of Westphalia; Oct., 1651-May, 1652: Navigation Act Leads to Anglo-Dutch Wars; 1667: Pufendorf Advocates a Unified Germany.

RELATED ARTICLES in *Great Lives from History: The Seventeenth Century, 1601-1700:* The Great Condé; Ferdinand II; Frederick V; Gustavus II Adolphus; James I; Jules Mazarin; Samuel von Pufendorf; Cardinal de Richelieu; Lennart Torstenson; Viscount de Turenne; Albrecht Wenzel von Wallenstein.

May 23, 1618
DEFENESTRATION OF PRAGUE

The Defenestration of Prague precipitated the Thirty Years' War after Catholic representatives of the Holy Roman Emperor were thrown out of a window by Bohemian Protestant nobles after a heated confrontation between Catholics and Protestants. The defenestration was the last straw in a series of ongoing conflicts concerning religion, politics, and dynastic struggle in Europe.

LOCALE: Hradcany Castle in Prague, Bohemia (now in the Czech Republic)

CATEGORIES: Government and politics; wars, uprisings, and civil unrest; religion and theology; social issues and reform

KEY FIGURES

Baron Colona von Fels (fl. 1618), Protestant instigator of the defenestration plot

Ferdinand II (1578-1637), archduke of Inner Austria, king of Bohemia, r. 1617-1637, and Holy Roman Emperor, r. 1619-1637

Frederick V (1596-1632), elector of the Rhenish Palatinate, king of Bohemia, r. 1619-1620, and head of the Protestant Union

Jaroslav Borsita von Martinitz (1582-1649), Catholic deputy governor of Bohemia and representative of the Holy Roman Emperor

Matthias (1557-1619), Holy Roman Emperor, r. 1612-1619

Rudolf II (1552-1612), Holy Roman Emperor, r. 1576-1612, ruler of Habsburg Austrian possessions, including Bohemia

Wenceslaus Ruppa (fl. early seventeenth century), Protestant leader of the Bohemian nobility

Wilhelm Slavata (1572-1652), Catholic deputy governor of Bohemia and representative of the Holy Roman Emperor

Heinrich Matthias Thurn (1580-1640), Protestant leader of the Bohemian nobility

SUMMARY OF EVENT

The Protestant Reformation, which began with Martin Luther nailing his ninety-five theses to the Wittenberg church door in 1517, began a century and a half of religious and political strife in the Holy Roman Empire. While the issues were initially theological, various princes saw the controversy as an opportunity to weaken the power not only of the Roman Catholic Church but also of the Holy Roman Emperor. Increasingly, the struggle became a constitutional one with religious differences marking the boundaries between the opponents. Further complicating the situation was the emergence of a militant Calvinism that challenged both the Lutheran princes and the Catholic Habsburg monarchs of the sixteenth century.

By 1618, religious lines had been drawn throughout the Holy Roman Empire. Catholic princes had formed a Catholic League that ostensibly looked to the emperor

Bohemian Protestant rebels threw Catholic imperial councillors out a window in Prague, an act—called a defenestration—that encouraged Protestant rebellion and marked the start of the Thirty Years' War. (Francis R. Niglutsch)

for leadership, but only for as long as the emperor did not assert too much royal power. Protestant princes were far less united, distrusting each other almost as much as they distrusted the emperor. The Habsburgs regarded themselves as the apostles of the Catholic-led Counter-Reformation; by 1600, they had largely eliminated Protestantism from Austria. Bohemia was the next target for their reforming zeal. However, Bohemia had, since the age of Church reformer Jan Hus (1372-1415), been markedly reformist. Most of the influential nobility were anti-Catholic. As was typical of the age, most nobles viewed Habsburg actions as an advance of royal power at their expense.

Some temporary relief had been afforded in 1607, when the incompetent Emperor Rudolf II quarreled with his brother, Archduke Matthias, over control of the Habsburg lands. Rudolf needed the support of the Bohemians against his brother, and in order to buy this support, he granted the Bohemian Estates a Letter of Majesty in 1609. Under this decree, religious toleration was granted to Bohemians, along with the right to construct churches and schools on royal domains. Rudolf even

agreed to allow a standing committee, the Defensors, to be selected from the Bohemian Estates, which was to be responsible for making sure that the agreement was enforced. Yet these concessions did little to strengthen Rudolf's position; in 1611, Matthias deprived him of Bohemia, and upon Rudolf's death succeeded him as Holy Roman Emperor.

The reign of Emperor Matthias once again brought the religious issue in Bohemia to the forefront, but it was now coupled with a political issue, the search for a successor to the childless emperor. Although Matthias lost little time in reconfirming the Letter of Majesty, the Bohemian Estates soon had cause to wonder if the reconfirmation meant anything inasmuch as the emperor quickly removed Protestant officials from key offices in Bohemia and replaced them with Catholics.

A more serious threat to Bohemian religious liberty rested in the decision of Matthias to name his cousin, Archduke Ferdinand of Inner Austria, the most fanatical Habsburg exponent of the Catholic Reformation, as his successor. The divided Bohemian Estates, lacking a candidate of their own, reluctantly agreed on June 17, 1617,

221

to "accept" Ferdinand as their king, a title he shared with Matthias until the latter's death two years later. The use of the term "accept" by the Bohemian nobility avoided the question of whether the Habsburgs held the crown of Bohemia on the basis of hereditary right or by the electoral consent of the Estates. To soothe the religious sensitivities of the Bohemian Estates, Ferdinand on the following day confirmed the Letter of Majesty.

Within a few months, a dispute developed over the interpretation of the Letter of Majesty, a quarrel that resulted in a Bohemian revolt against the Habsburgs and that ultimately led to the Thirty Years' War. Two Protestant churches, one in Hrob (Klostergrab) and the other in Broumov (Braunau), had been built on Catholic Church land, which in Bohemia was customarily regarded as royal domain. The Protestants felt that they were within their rights as set forth in the Letter of Majesty. The Habsburg authorities, however, rejected this argument. By order of the regent, Ferdinand, in 1617, the churches were ordered closed; the one at Hrob was even torn down. The Defensors summoned the Bohemian Estates to assemble in Prague on March 5, 1618, to discuss the anti-Protestant actions by the Habsburgs.

Although a decree had been promulgated forbidding Protestant assemblies, most Bohemian nobles considered the meeting legal under the agreement of 1609. The Prague Assembly petitioned the emperor for a change of policy, but Matthias refused and ordered the nobles to disperse.

Two months later, on May 21, 1618, the Protestant nobles met again in defiance of this ban. On May 22, they demanded a redress of grievances arising out of the religious dispute, but the Habsburg government rejected their demands. The deputy governors of Bohemia, Jaroslav Borsita von Martinitz and Wilhelm Slavata, who were also leaders of the Catholic, pro-Habsburg faction in the Bohemian Estates, then ordered the assembly to disperse. The demand caused such an uproar that a radical wing of the Bohemian Estates, led by

Heinrich Matthias Thurn, Baron Colona von Fels, and Wenceslaus Ruppa, raised the standard of revolt against the Habsburgs.

The incensed Protestant leaders were determined to deal with the threat, by force if necessary. On May 23, an armed band of more than one hundred men marched to Hradcany Castle for a formal confrontation with Martinitz and Slavata. Both officials denied any personal involvement in rejection of the Protestant demands. Heated words were exchanged. Suddenly, Thurn and others stepped forward, seized the two deputy governors, and hurled them through a castle window into the refuse-filled moat forty feet below. Incredibly, the victims survived the fall and managed to escape. Protestants quickly noted that the two had been lucky that their fall had been softened by the "mist" into which they had fallen; Catholics immediately retorted that their lives had been saved by angels and that it was nothing short of a miracle.

RUSHWORTH ON THE DEFENESTRATON OF PRAGUE

English historian John Rushworth (1618?-1690) gives an account of the Defenestration of Prague on May 23, 1618, a day that marked the beginning of the Thirty Years' War.

The clouds gather thick in the German sky; jealousies and discontents arise between the Catholics and the Evangelics, or Lutherans, of the Confession of Augsburg. Both parties draw into confederacies and hold assemblies; the one seeking by the advantage of power to encroach and get ground, the other to stand their ground and hold their own. The potency of the house of Austria [the Habsburgs], a house devoted to the persecution of the reformed religion, became formidable. . . .

The Bohemian troubles took their first rise from the breach of the edict of peace concerning religion and the accord made by the emperor Rudolf [Letter of Majesty, 1609] whereby the Protestants retained the free exercise of their religion, enjoyed their temples, colleges, tithes, patronages, places of burial, and the like, and had liberty to build new temples and power to choose defenders to secure these rights and to regulate what should be the service in their churches. . . .

On the 23d of May the chief of the Evangelics went armed into the castle of Prague, entered the council chamber, and opened their grievances; but, enraged by opposition, they threw Slabata, the chief justice, and Smesansius, one of the council, and Fabricius, the secretary, from a high window into the castle ditch; others of the council, temporizing in this tumult and seeming to accord with their demands, were peacefully conducted to their own houses. Hereupon the assembly took advice to settle the towns and castle of Prague with new guards. . . . They chose directors, governors, councilors provincial to govern affairs of state. . . .

Source: Quoted in *Readings in European History*, edited by James Harvey Robinson (Boston: Atheneum Press, 1906), pp. 340-342.

SIGNIFICANCE

This confrontation is known in history as the Defenestration of Prague, and it precipitated widespread revolt against the Habsburg regime beyond the religious issue, beyond Bohemia, and beyond the year 1618. Thurn and Ruppa became leaders of a revolutionary government in Bohemia and mobilized fighting forces that fought with imperial troops between 1618 and 1620. In August of 1619, Bohemia led a confederation with Moravia, Silesia, and Lusatia, crownlands with which it had been affiliated in the past. This confederation proceeded to arrange a pact of mutual assistance with the Protestant states of Upper and Lower Austria. What completed the revolt was the deposition of Ferdinand on August 22, 1619, by this extended confederation. The election on August 26 of Frederick V, Calvinist prince elector of the Rhenish Palatinate, filled the vacancy.

Because of its brevity, Frederick's rule is known as "the reign of the Winter King." In March of 1619, Emperor Matthias died, and in August, Ferdinand was elected to succeed him. As Habsburg emperor, Ferdinand was determined to quell religious nonconformity in Bohemia and to regain the Bohemian crown. His army, augmented by a large Spanish force, decisively defeated the Bohemian army at the Battle of White Mountain on November 8, 1620. This victory ended Bohemia's bid for autonomy. For the losers, defeat meant death, and to the leaders, defeat meant the confiscation of property of sympathizers and the recatholicization of Bohemia.

Although fighting ceased in Bohemia, the manner of the Habsburg reconquest evoked fear throughout the Holy Roman Empire and beyond. It was the start of the Thirty Years' War in Europe.

—*Edward P. Keleher and William S. Brockington, Jr.*

FURTHER READING

Asch, Ronald G. *The Thirty Years' War: The Holy Roman Empire and Europe, 1618-1648.* New York: St. Martin's Press, 1997. Asch focuses on the Holy Roman Empire's role in the war, including the empire's disagreements with Bohemia that precipitated the conflict.

Bireley, Robert. *The Refashioning of Catholicism, 1450-1700: A Reassessment of the Counter Reformation.* Washington, D.C.: Catholic University of America Press, 1999. Bireley demonstrates how the Counter-Reformation was an active response to profound changes taking place in the sixteenth century.

Carsten, F. L. *Princes and Parliaments in Germany from the Fifteenth to the Eighteenth Century.* London: Oxford University Press, 1959. Carsten provides information and significant generalizations regarding the various assemblies and their composition.

Evans, R. J. W. *The Making of the Habsburg Monarchy, 1550-1700: An Interpretation.* 3d ed. New York: Oxford University Press, 1991. Evans examines, primarily, Austria and the Holy Roman Empire and offers significant information on changes in Austrian lands during the period.

Grell, Ole Peter, and Bob Scribner, eds. *Tolerance and Intolerance in the European Reformation.* New York: Cambridge University Press, 1996. Chapter 7, an essay by historian Euan Cameron, examines Protestant identities in Germany during the later Reformation.

Lee, Stephen J. *The Thirty Years' War.* London: Routledge & Kegan Paul, 1991. Lee provides an excellent introduction to the causes and major issues of the war. He examines the motives of the participants, their gains and losses, and the religious, military, social, and economic aspects of the war.

Parker, Geoffrey, ed. *The Thirty Years' War.* 2d ed. New York: Routledge, 1997. Parker incorporates new research to update the 1984 edition of this narrative and analytical account of the conflict. Includes maps, a six-nation chronology, genealogies, and an index with the birth date and other pertinent facts about each person listed.

Pursell, Brennan C. *The Winter King: Frederick V of the Palatinate and the Coming of the Thirty Years' War.* Burlington, Vt.: Ashgate, 2003. A biography of Frederick V, providing his perspective of the causes and initial battles of the war.

Wedgwood, C. V. *The Thirty Years' War.* London: Jonathan Cape, 1938. While some of the interpretations are dated, this highly readable account of the period still merits a read.

SEE ALSO: 1618-1648: Thirty Years' War; July, 1620-Sept., 1639: Struggle for the Valtelline Pass; Nov. 8, 1620: Battle of White Mountain; Mar. 6, 1629: Edict of Restitution; 1630-1648: Destruction of Bavaria; May 30, 1635: Peace of Prague; July, 1643-Oct. 24, 1648: Peace of Westphalia.

RELATED ARTICLES in *Great Lives from History: The Seventeenth Century, 1601-1700:* Ferdinand II; Frederick V; Frederick William, the Great Elector; Gustavus II Adolphus; Cardinal de Richelieu; Albrecht Wenzel von Wallenstein.

Beginning c. 1619
INDENTURED SERVITUDE BECOMES INSTITUTIONALIZED IN AMERICA

To meet the need for unskilled labor in the American colonies, European colonists imported poor people who were willing to agree to a limited period of servitude in return for passage to the New World and a parcel of land once their servitude ended. This practice began the reliance upon unfree labor that would shape the history of American agriculture well into the nineteenth century.

LOCALE: English North American colonies, including the West Indies

CATEGORIES: Colonization; social issues and reform; agriculture; trade and commerce

KEY FIGURES

Sir George Peckham (d. 1608), early English advocate of exporting the unemployed to the New World

Sir Edwin Sandys (1561-1629), treasurer of the London Company

SUMMARY OF EVENT

The American colonies were started by early capitalistic enterprises, such as the London Company (also known as the Virginia Company of London), which had been assigned the southern portion of the American coastline as a trading post by King James I. Between 1607 and 1618, several attempts were made to establish a settlement on the James River, but their original concept failed, and by 1618 the company had been converted into a system for encouraging the settlement of Englishmen in America.

The concept of "indentured servitude" was based on the common practice in England of "service in husbandry," in which individuals bound themselves or their children to work on the farms of the larger landowners for a period of a year or more. Adapting this concept to the peopling of the New World was first suggested by Sir George Peckham and picked up by Sir Edwin Sandys, treasurer of the London Company, which established the first colony in Virginia in 1607. In the case of indentured servants in America, the idea was for impoverished Englishmen to take passage on a ship to the colonies and to repay those who financed the sea voyage with their labor for a fixed period of time. After they had worked off their debt, indentured servants became freemen with the ability to own land of their own, an ability that would have been beyond them back in their home country.

The opening up of land in America occurred at a time in Europe when the population had been expanding more rapidly than wages, and there was in consequence a significant surplus of agricultural workers. In Elizabethan England, these workers were classified as "rogues and vagabonds," and were regarded as a superfluous population. Many wandered into the rapidly growing cities, such as London and Bristol, and the authorities in those cities were anxious to get rid of them. As accomplish this goal, laws were passed and strictly enforced mandating heavy punishments for relatively minor crimes, and the large number of convictions that resulted provided an instant, exportable pool of labor for the colonies. Furthermore, the religious conflicts of the period resulted in many military prisoners, and "transportation" was the easiest way to dispose of them. Likewise, the many orphans roaming city streets could be rounded up and sent to America.

In the earliest years, the need for labor was greatest in the southern colonies on the American continent and in the West Indies. The enormous profitability of sugar led to many indentured servants being sent to the sugar plantations in such colonies as Barbados, but the tropical climate killed many, and by the middle of the century, indentured servants were used in the sugar colonies chiefly as supervisors of the African slaves who began arriving in large numbers at that time. On the mainland, the need for indentured servants was greatest in the tobacco colonies, Virginia and Maryland, for next to sugar, tobacco was the most profitable product of America.

Though some indentured servants went to the Carolinas, the combination of a semi-tropical climate and the character of the chief agricultural product, rice, soon led to their displacement by African slaves. Although slaves came during the seventeenth century to provide much of the field labor in the tobacco fields, however, there continued to be a demand for white indentured servants to fill other roles in the Carolina colonies. In the middle colonies, where the chief crop was wheat, the need was not so great, and the indentured servants who worked there continued to be used for agricultural labor. In New England, the earliest immigrants had large families and used them for a workforce, so few indentured servants were needed.

Over the course of the seventeenth century, the legal requirements of indentured servitude came to be codified, chiefly by the colonial legislatures. As early as 1619, the Virginia General Assembly tried to encourage indentured servants to immigrate by promising that, following their period of service (four years unless the servant was very young), servants would qualify for a land grant, normally 50 acres (20 hectares). Many who qualified never actually acquired the land, however, finding it easier to sell their "headright" (as the land grant was called) to those who already had sufficient capital to exploit the land. In the West Indies, because there was no surplus of land to grant, cash incentives were sometimes offered.

One of the biggest problems with which colonial legislatures had to deal was the relatively high risk that an indentured servant, having reached America, would run away, thus depriving the person who had paid his transatlantic passage of the return on his investment. Heavy penalties, including increased time of servitude, were levied on runaways, who could be legally pursued until they were caught and returned to their "owner." Because convicts were particularly prone to running away, the colonial legislatures attempted to stop the transporting of convicts, but the English government overturned such laws: The English were more interested in getting rid of their downtrodden masses than they were in aiding their colonial subjects.

In the late seventeenth century and early eighteenth centuries, to aid in keeping track of bonded servants, bureaucratic offices were created where documentation of indenture was to be formally registered. This bureaucratic system was not uniform throughout England, but Bristol, for example, had such a registration service for a number of years. In the eighteenth century, registration became virtually automatic, especially in the case of those who came as families, known as "redemptioners."

In the seventeenth century, especially in the early years, the majority of the indentured servants were male unskilled laborers who were put to work performing agricultural labor. Some women came as well, and they were normally used as household servants. Not a few became the wives of landowners, and their children sometimes rose in social standing. By the late seventeenth century, however, the greatest demand was for men with recognizable skills, including blacksmiths, masons, carpenters, and wheelwrights, as well as literate individuals who could manage the accounts of plantations. Unskilled labor had begun to be provided predominantly by slaves.

SIGNIFICANCE

Although the system of indentured servitude undoubtedly made it possible for many individuals without capital to emigrate to the new colonies in the New World, it ultimately served to perpetuate the social system that prevailed at the time, with a small elite at the top and large numbers at the bottom of the social scale. Some indentured servants, even some black indentured servants did indeed between landowners, who ironically employed indentured and enslaved laborers themselves on their new lands. The vast majority, however, merely changed the venue in which they lived hand-to-mouth and ended their lives with substantially the same means they had had when they emigrated from England.

More important than the maintenance of traditional European social hierarchies, indentured servitude gave legitimacy to a system in which individuals, brought to the New World at the expense of others, constituted a capital asset that could be bought and sold. It laid the foundations for the practice of African slavery in America.

—Nancy M. Gordon

FURTHER READING

Galenson, David. *White Servitude in Colonial America: An Economic Analysis.* New York: Cambridge University Press, 1981. Provides a detailed look at the economic underpinnings of the system of indentured servitude.

Games, Alison. *Migration and the Origins of the English Atlantic World.* Cambridge, Mass.: Harvard University Press, 1999. Documentation on indentured servitude is sorely lacking, but Games has made effective use of London port registers of 1635 to track some five thousand indentured servants who came to America.

Menard, Russell R. "From Servant to Freeholder: Status Mobility and Property Accumulation in Seventeenth Century Maryland." *William and Mary Quarterly,* 3d ser. 30 (1973): 37-64. Using local documents, Menard traces the post-servitude careers of some of the seventeenth century immigrants to Maryland, a major destination of indentured servants.

Pagan, John Ruston. *Anne Orthwood's Bastard: Sex and Law in Early Virginia.* New York: Oxford University Press, 2003. The fascinating story of one female indentured servant whose fate is known because she became entangled with the law.

Smith, Abbot Emerson. *Colonists in Bondage: White Servitude and Convict Labor in America, 1607-1776.* Chapel Hill: University of North Carolina Press, 1947. The classic account of indentured servitude in America, though a few conclusions have been questioned by later scholars.

1610's

Van der Zee, John. *Bound Over: Indentured Servitude and American Conscience.* New York: Simon and Schuster, 1985. Vignettes of the lives of indentured servants.

SEE ALSO: 17th cent.: Europe Endorses Slavery; 1612: Introduction of Tobacco Farming in North America; 1617-1693: European Powers Vie for Control of Gorée; 1619-c. 1700: The Middle Passage to American Slavery; July 30-Aug. 4, 1619: First General Assembly of Virginia; Aug. 20, 1619: Africans Arrive in Virginia; Dec. 26, 1620: Pilgrims Arrive in North America; May 14, 1625-1640: English Discover and Colonize Barbados; Nov., 1641: Massachusetts Recognizes Slavery; May 10, 1655: English Capture of Jamaica; Mar., 1661-1705: Virginia Slave Codes; Mar. 24, 1663-July 25, 1729: Settlement of the Carolinas; May 10-Oct. 18, 1676: Bacon's Rebellion.

RELATED ARTICLES in *Great Lives from History: The Seventeenth Century, 1601-1700:* Nathaniel Bacon; John Smith.

1619-1622
JONES INTRODUCES CLASSICISM TO ENGLISH ARCHITECTURE

Well into the seventeenth century, English architecture was dominated by the native Tudor and the Gothic Flemish styles. London first encountered a new style between 1619 and 1621, when craftspeople under the direction of the royal architect Inigo Jones built the Banqueting House for Whitehall Palace in Westminster. The first classically influenced Renaissance building in England, it effectively introduced classicism, or Palladianism, to English architecture.

LOCALE: Westminster, London, England
CATEGORY: Architecture

KEY FIGURES
Inigo Jones (1573-1652), architect and surveyor of the King's Works, 1615-1649
James I (1566-1625), king of England, r. 1603-1625, and king of Scotland as James VI, r. 1567-1625
Peter Paul Rubens (1577-1640), Flemish painter who decorated the ceiling of the Banqueting House
Andrea Palladio (1508-1580), Italian architect

SUMMARY OF EVENT
During the later fifteenth and sixteenth centuries, many aspects of Italian Renaissance culture were introduced into England and became incorporated into British life. Despite this general cultural trend, however, English architecture and architectural tastes remained largely untouched during the Renaissance. Both noble and royal palaces followed the eccentricities of what is often called the Tudor-Gothic style, characterized by rambling construction in brick or half-timbering that sported medieval turrets, towers, spires, gables, crockets, and finials.

Stonework on these buildings was rare, and when present it was quite Gothic in style and technique.

Some new public buildings, such as Thomas Gresham's Royal Exchange in the City of London (1567), and private palaces like Somerset House (1550) were inspired by late Gothic and Northern Renaissance Flemish models. Indeed, craftspeople had to be imported from Antwerp to build the Exchange, so strange was this new style to English workers. John Shute's *The First and Chief Grounds of Architecture* (1563) introduced readers to some of the classicizing decorative elements and details that characterized the Italian Renaissance style, but it contained no formal analysis of either classical or Italian architecture and espoused no coherent theory of architectural form. Some English Renaissance buildings contained classical bits, but these isolated elements were sporadic and often seemed out of place in the context of the building as a whole. The very notion that a building might be designed by someone other than a carpenter or a master mason was completely alien to the English: Indeed, the word "architect" appeared in English for the first time only in the mid-sixteenth century.

Inigo Jones is widely regarded as the first classical English architect and the one who initiated English Palladianism. He was the son of a cloth worker and is said to have been apprenticed to a London joiner or carpenter as a young man, although little is known of his early life. By the age of twenty-six, though, he had left his home country, and he traveled through northern Italy between 1599 and 1603. In Venice and nearby Vicenza and Padua, he would have been able to visit the villas and churches designed by the great Vicentine Renaissance architect Andrea Palladio. In many ways, Palladio's work, both in stone and on paper, was the culmination of the revival of classical architecture that began in the mid-fifteenth century with the efforts of the Florentine Leon Battista Alberti (1404-1472).

Both Alberti and Palladio studied and imitated the classical Roman architect Marcus Vitruvius Pollio (fl. first century B.C.E.), whose *De architectura* (after 27 B.C.E.; *On Architecture*, 1914) proved an important model to generations of Renaissance and Neoclassical architects and patrons. They also studied classical structures, or their ruins, and portrayed them—and their own ideas—in their treatises, Alberti's *De re aedificatoria* (1485; *Ten Books on Architecture*, 1955) and Palladio's *I quattro libri dell'architettura* (1570; *The Four Books of Architecture*, 1738), a copy of which Jones purchased in Venice for two ducats.

A visit to France in 1609 allowed Jones to study Roman architectural remains at places like Nîmes, and in 1613 and 1614 he accompanied Thomas Howard, earl of Arundel, on a tour of Italian cities, an early version of the continental Grand Tour. On this trip, he befriended the Italian architect Vincenzo Scamozzi, a student of Palladio. Given its role in embedding the classical ideal in Jones and providing him with experience and models

Inigo Jones. (Library of Congress)

from which to build, the historian of the Grand Tour, Edward Chaney, wrote that Jones's was arguably the most important one ever taken.

Once he returned from the Continent full of ideas, Jones needed a patron and a project, and he found both in London. England's King James I and his court resided in Whitehall Palace in Westminster, outside London proper. Early in his reign, it had become customary to sponsor one or more extravagant court entertainments known as masques each year. These included music, dancing, and panegyric speeches written by the likes of Ben Jonson and George Chapman, as well as elaborate sets and costumes. Jones began designing the sets and costumes of the Jacobean court masques in 1604.

The masques were performed in the palace's banqueting hall, a large ceremonial chamber first built during Queen Elizabeth I's reign. This decrepit timber structure was demolished, and a new, grander one in brick and timber was completed in 1609, perhaps according to a plan by Jones. The hall's interior was open in the center with galleries on three sides. Following classical principles, Doric columns held up the galleries, while the higher Ionic order was employed in the interior. The banqueting hall burned to the ground on January 12, 1619.

As a result of the fire, Jones got his chance to design and construct a fully Palladian building. The king required a new banqueting house, and Jones had been appointed surveyor of the King's Works in late 1615, a position that placed him in charge of all royal construction. James I had no particular taste in architecture, though he may have been impressed by Jones's Palladian designs for the Queen's Palace at Greenwich and the new Star Chamber, neither of which was completed. The sale of two English port towns in Flanders provided the roughly £2,000 needed for construction, so Jones had virtually a free hand. The first function held in the new Banqueting House was a reception for the Knights of the Garter on April 21, 1621.

Palladio's mature version of classical architecture was based upon clear order, mathematical proportion, functionality, and clean lines, and Jones incorporated all of these elements into his new hall. He designed it as a Roman basilica with the proportions of a double cube, 55 by 110 feet (17 by 34 meters). Like its predecessor, it had a cantilevered gallery around three sides, leaving one end open for the king's throne. The Ionic order was used on the ground floor, while the higher Corinthian appeared above. He left the ceiling flat with compartments into which Peter Paul Rubens's famous ceiling would be inserted between 1634 and 1638.

Due to later remodeling, little else is known about the building's original interior, although it was probably thoroughly whitewashed, both to aid in nighttime illumination and to provide a neutral backdrop for the Raphael-inspired tapestries that adorned the walls. The exterior featured clean lines of simple stonework and pilasters whose capitals echoed the orders used inside. Simple garlands topped each second-story window, and an equally simple balustrade crowned the street-front façade. All of these features signaled the arrival of a new architectural style at the very heart of the kingdom. Surrounded by the Tudor-Gothic buildings of Whitehall, the Palladian Banqueting House seemed thoroughly out of place: It was a sign that the king and his architect planned further changes to London's principle royal residence.

SIGNIFICANCE

The royal plans to continue rebuilding Whitehall were never realized. Despite being the only Palladian building in the palace, however, the Banqueting House served as an impetus for the application of classicism to English structures from garden pavilions to Saint Paul's Cathedral. Initially, the Banqueting House struck many as odd, since the English retained a largely medieval aesthetic that could not appreciate the beauty inherent in its classical form and elements. Moreover, the hall soon became a symbol of royal decadence in a very Puritan city: It was no accident that Parliament chose it as the site of the execution of Charles I in 1649.

Nonetheless, the Banqueting House and several buildings inspired by it survived the Puritan Commonwealth to become models for Restoration, Baroque, Georgian, and Neoclassical designs well into the eighteenth century. The effects of Jones's embrace of the classical Roman and Palladian Renaissance styles rippled through the plans and buildings of such outstanding architects as Sir Christopher Wren, Nicholas Hawksmoor, James Gibbs, Thomas Jefferson, and John Soane.

—*Joseph P. Byrne*

FURTHER READING

Jones, Inigo. *The Theatre of the Stuart Court: Including the Complete Designs for Productions at Court.* 2 vols. Berkeley: University of California Press, 1973. Contains sketches and drawings by Jones of costumes and sets for many of the court masques held in the Banqueting House during the rule of James I and Charles I.

Leapman, Michael. *Inigo: The Troubled Life of Inigo Jones, Architect of the English Renaissance.* London: Review, 2003. Detailed biography of Jones that concentrates on his masques.

Palme, Per. *Triumph of Peace: A Study of the Whitehall Banqueting House.* London: Thames & Hudson, 1957. Classic study of the building and its famous ceiling.

Strong, Roy. *Britannia Triumphans: Inigo Jones, Rubens, and Whitehall Palace.* New York: W. W. Norton, 1981. Expanded version of lectures, primarily on the Banqueting House ceiling and Jones's role in its Solomonic imagery and design.

Summerson, John. *Inigo Jones.* New Haven, Conn.: Yale University Press, 2000. Nicely illustrated short study of Jones's architecture.

Worsley, Giles. *Classical Architecture in Britain: The Heroic Age.* New Haven, Conn.: Yale University Press, 1995. Places Inigo Jones's introduction of classicism in the context of later developments in English architectural classicism.

SEE ALSO: c. 1601-1620: Emergence of Baroque Art; Mar. 24, 1603: James I Becomes King of England; 1605-1627: Mughal Court Culture Flourishes; 1609-1617: Construction of the Blue Mosque; 1619-1636: Construction of Samarqand's Shirdar Madrasa; 1632-c. 1650: Shah Jahan Builds the Taj Mahal; 1642-1651: English Civil Wars; 1656-1667: Construction of the Piazza San Pietro; Sept. 2-5, 1666: Great Fire of London; 1670: Popularization of the Grand Tour; 1673: Renovation of the Louvre; 1675-1708: Wren Supervises the Rebuilding of St. Paul's Cathedral.

RELATED ARTICLES in *Great Lives from History: The Seventeenth Century, 1601-1700:* James I; Inigo Jones; Ben Jonson; Peter Paul Rubens; Sir Christopher Wren.

1619-1636
CONSTRUCTION OF SAMARQAND'S SHIRDAR MADRASA

The construction of the Shirdar Madrasa marked a renaissance of grand-scale architectural patronage in Samarqand. With the earlier Ulūgh Beg Madrasa and later Tila Kari Madrasa, the Shirdar Madrasa formed the city's renowned Registan Square ensemble.

LOCALE: Samarqand, Central Asia (now in Uzbekistan)

CATEGORIES: Architecture; cultural and intellectual history; religion and theology

KEY FIGURES

Yalangtush Bahador (fl. early seventeenth century), Tuqay-Timurid general and governor of Samarqand, r. early seventeenth century

Imām Qulī Khan (d. 1642), great khan of the region in northern Afghanistan and western-central Asia that included the oasis cities of Samarqand and Bukhara, r. 1612-1642

Abdul Jabbar (fl. 1619), architect of the Shirdar Madrasa

SUMMARY OF EVENT

Between 1619 and 1636, the Shirdar Madrasa was constructed in Samarqand as a residential college for the study of Islamic sciences. The second of three theological colleges that form the city's renowned Registan (place of sand) ensemble, the structure mirrors the appearance of the Ulūgh Beg Madrasa (1417-1421), which sits directly opposite it. The construction of the Shirdar Madrasa under the auspices of the Tuqay-Timurid general Yalangtush Bahador marks a continuation of the grand scale architectural projects initiated two centuries earlier under the central Asian conqueror Tamerlane (also known as Timur). Its form reiterates the Timurid Dynasty's emphasis on colossal scale, symmetry, and prolific decoration.

The three structures built on the Registan Square embody the political and cultural ideals of Tamerlane and his descendants, who forged a dynastic identity that combined Turko-Mongol and Islamic values. For the Timurids, the patronage of Islamic institutions served not only to buttress the appearance of Islamic religious piety but also to maintain dynastic affiliation. Tamerlane's extensive conquests in Iran, Anatolia, and Mesopotamia were modeled on the campaigns of the Mongol leader Genghis Khan, and Timurid claims to Genghizid ancestry were expressed in titles, inscriptions, political

rhetoric, and artistic production. The Timurid concern with genealogy infused central Asian arts and architecture with motifs intended to appropriate political legitimacy through their associations with traditional Mongol formula, and it established a model of artistic patronage that would inspire central Asian rulers through the seventeenth century.

After the fall of the Timurid Dynasty in the early sixteenth century, western-central Asia was organized into a political system led by descendants of Genghis Khan's eldest son Jochi Tuqay-Timur. The first period of Jochid rule, also known as Shibanid rule, lasted through the sixteenth century under descendants of Genghis Khan's grandson, and Jochi's son, Shiban. It was followed in the seventeenth century with the rule of another grandson, named Tuqay-Timur as well, who gained sovereignty and initiated a period of prosperity centered in the oasis cities of Samarqand and Bukhara.

Under the Tuqay-Timurid branch, new investments in public architecture benefited from the wealth generated by trade routes through western-central Asia. These sources of income allowed for the construction of civic structures such as bazaars, hostels, bridges, and reservoirs, as well as religious structures such as madrasas and hospices that supported a learned class of Muslim scholars and Sufi brotherhoods. The patronage of religious institutions was an integral component of a symbiotic relationship between the state and the learned class, which offered legitimacy to the khans and tribal leaders who governed local populations.

The madrasa gained popularity in Islamic lands beginning in the eleventh century. As an institution for higher learning, it supported scholarship and instruction in Islamic law and sciences, and often provided residence for scholars. The Shirdar Madrasa was ordered in the second decade of the seventeenth century by Yalangtush Bahador, a Tuqay-Timurid general who served as the governor of Samarqand under the region's great khan, Imām Qulī Khan. The location and orientation of the madrasa were carefully chosen to appropriate the symbolic value of earlier buildings on the site constructed under Timurid rulers. Initially, in the fourteenth century, the site had housed a large trading market built by Tamerlane's consort Tuman Aqa. Between 1417 and 1421, however, Tamerlane's grandson Ulūgh Beg had replaced the market with a Sufi hospice and a madrasa, the latter of which remains on the site into the twenty-first century. By the end of the sixteenth century, the site had accrued a funerary madrasa as well as a congregational mosque and madrasa complex.

The construction of the Shirdar Madrasa utterly changed the appearance of the site, replacing its fifteenth century hospice with a massive structure mirroring Ulūgh Beg's madrasa in its positioning, scale, and form. The madrasa, known as the Shirdar, or lion bearing, because of the lionlike tigers that decorate its entry portal, was built atop a hill of rubble and sand. A barely decipherable inscription attributes the structure to the architect Abdul Jabbar and its decoration to Muḥammad ʿAbbās. Its general form is based upon the four-*iwan* plan, a standard Iranian formula in which each of a structure's four walls is marked by a monumental portal, or *iwan*. The spatial composition of the college consisted of students' cells stacked in two stories around a central courtyard. Three of the structure's monumental arched portals would have been used as open-air classrooms.

The college's main entrance facade was oriented directly onto the Registan Square, and its rectangular entrance facade and twin minarets were composed to echo Ulūgh Beg's madrasa directly opposite it. On either side of the structure's entrance *iwan*, a ribbed dome sits high upon a cylindrical drum—a configuration that became popular in Timurid architecture of the fifteenth century and served to enhance a structure's visibility from afar. The building, like that of Timurid prototypes, is cloaked in a tapestry of polychrome ceramic tiles. Its highly decorated facade mimics the zigzagging compartments and geometric Arabic inscriptions that cover the Ulūgh Beg Madrasa across the square. The zoomorphic forms over the Shirdar's portal, on the other hand, represent a major deviation from the earlier structure's program. In the spandrels over the madrasa's arched portal, an unusual program presents symmetrical images of deer chased by lions with human-faced suns rising from their backs.

Together with the Tila Kari Madrasa, built between 1646 and 1660, the two symmetrically opposed madrasas form a three-sided facade overlooking Samarqand's renowned Registan Square. Despite the additive nature of building activities on the site, which spanned more than two centuries, the three surviving structures retain a unified appearance. Possibly inspired by the U-shaped complex (1620) in Bukhara known as the Lab-i Haws (edge of the reservoir), the square's unity is owed to the harmonious proportions, symmetry, and coherent decorative programs of the three madrasas. The transformation of the site that was initiated with the construction of the Shirdar Madrasa left a legacy that would last long after the Tuqay-Timurid state declined in the late seventeenth century.

SIGNIFICANCE

The construction of the madrasas at Registan Square reflects the complex political dynamics in central Asia between the fall of the Timurid Dynasty in the early sixteenth century and the ascendancy of the Russians in the nineteenth century. Religious institutions such as colleges and hospices were constructed under the auspices of the ruling khans (descendants of Genghis Khan), but were patronized at the local level by members of tribal groups who held military and administrative ranks. Institutions such as the Shirdar Madrasa were built to support a third powerful group, composed of Islamic scholars and religious leaders who, in turn, legitimized ruling khans and governors with their support.

In its colossal silhouettes, virtuoso domes and minarets, and profuse ornamentation, the Shirdar Madrasa typifies the aesthetic of high visibility and extravagance that was defined by Timurid architects and designers in the fourteenth and early fifteenth centuries. It represents the culmination of an architectural tradition that lasted for four centuries in central Asia, and would have significant resonance in the architectural achievements of the Mughal emperors in India (1526-1857) and the Ṣafavid Dynasty (1501-1736) in Iran.

—*Anna Sloan*

FURTHER READING

Blair, Sheila S., and Jonathan M. Bloom. *The Art and Architecture of Islam: 1250-1800.* New Haven, Conn.: Yale University Press, 1994. Blair and Bloom provide a concise introduction to the Registan ensemble in a chapter on central Asian art and architecture between the sixteenth and nineteenth centuries. Includes photographs, maps, and site plans.

Bosworth, Clifford Edmund. *The New Islamic Dynasties.* New York: Columbia University Press, 1996. This revised edition of a classic genealogical manual offers complete bibliographies and tables of dates, titles, and names.

Bulatova, V., and G. Shishkina. *Samarkand: A Museum in the Open.* Tashkent, Uzbekistan: Izdatel'stvo literatury i iskusstva imeni Gafura Guliama, 1986. A monograph on Samarqand's urban history and architectural sites. Contains nineteenth century photographs of city life and contemporary photographs showing multiple views of monuments.

Kalter, Johannes, and Margareta Pavaloi, eds. *Uzbekistan: Heirs to the Silk Road.* New York: Thames &

Hudson, 1997. A catalog for a large exhibition of objects from central Asia. An essay by Thomas Leisten provides a general introduction to Islamic monuments of central Asia in the territory that is now called Uzbekistan. Includes photographs, maps, and site plans.

Knobloch, Edgar. *Monuments of Central Asia: A Guide to the Archaeology, Art, and Architecture of Turkestan*. London: I. B. Tauris, 2001. An introduction to architectural sites in central Asia, with illustrations, photographs, maps, and plans.

McChesney, Robert D. "Central Asia, VI: In the Tenth-Twelfth/Sixteenth-Eighteenth Centuries." *Encyclo-paedia Iranica* 5 (1985): 176-193. An introduction to the central Asian political system, which also provides an economic and historical context for Tuqay-Timurid architectural patronage. Contains tables of the Shibanid and Tuqay-Timurid Dynasties.

SEE ALSO: 1609-1617: Construction of the Blue Mosque; 1632-c. 1650: Shah Jahan Builds the Taj Mahal.

RELATED ARTICLES in *Great Lives from History: The Seventeenth Century, 1601-1700:* Aurangzeb; Shah Jahan.

1619-c. 1700
THE MIDDLE PASSAGE TO AMERICAN SLAVERY

In the British North American colonies, slavery arrived late, and then only after a significant transitional period, during which chattel slavery gradually supplanted the system of indentured servitude that had supplied the main source for manual plantation labor. By 1700, chattel slavery had become legally institutionalized throughout British North America, but it flourished primarily in the Chesapeake region and the Carolina Low Country.

LOCALE: West Africa, Atlantic Ocean, and colonial North America

CATEGORIES: Social issues and reform; trade and commerce; economics; agriculture; colonization

KEY FIGURES

John Punch (d. after 1640), first documented African in Virginia to be enslaved for life

Sir John Yeamans (1611-1674), British planter and colonial governor of Carolina, 1672-1674, who imported the first African slaves into the Carolina Low Country

Anthony Johnson (Antonio, a Negro; d. after 1660), African-born indentured servant who became a prominent Virginia landowner

Sir George Yeardley (1587?-1627), Virginia's acting governor, 1616-1617, and governor, 1619-1621, 1626-1627

SUMMARY OF EVENT

The Middle Passage long predated the year 1619, which is traditionally denoted as the occasion of the arrival of the first African slaves in the British North American colonies. In point of fact, the two phenomena—the Middle Passage and chattel slavery—would never truly coincide until much later, though by the end of the seventeenth century, chattel slavery would indeed be established as the pattern for British North America.

The Middle Passage may be defined as the second "leg" of the Atlantic world's Triangular Trade which, briefly stated, consisted of European articles being shipped to and exchanged for African trade items, including slaves; African items (mainly slaves) being transported across the Atlantic to the New World; and American-produced or refined items, such as rum, tobacco, and molasses, then being carried back to Europe and sold. This is, of course, a more simplified overview of an extremely complex process, but slavery became such an integral part of the transatlantic socioeconomic system and so affected the movement of so many millions of people that it has become synonymous with the term Middle Passage.

As it developed from the time of initial contact between West Africans and Portuguese mariners around the late fifteenth century, the Middle Passage began with the actual capture of individuals within Africa itself and their immediate transformation into marketable chattel labor. Though some Africans (mainly those who dwelled closest to the coast) were kidnapped by Europeans, many were taken by other Africans, either as the traditional spoils of warfare between tribal and national units or as captives to be transported to the trading posts and fortresses on the coast and sold to Europeans. It was in the course of the actual abduction, and the often long, always arduous trek to the coast, that the first fatalities (some

231

African captives were often held in coastal stockades for days or weeks, forced to wait for the next slave ship to take them to the New World. (Library of Congress)

cannons of these fortresses were invariably pointed seaward so as to provide defense from other Europeans rather than to counter any threat from the Africans—which was considered negligible.

To avoid disputes over ownership at busy ports where several slave ships might be harbored at the same time, all simultaneously loading their human cargo, slaves were branded with hot irons, receiving the mark of their ship's captain or of the company that owned the sailing vessel. The slaves were then placed below deck, in holds where they were chained lying on their backs to the planks. In order to increase their profits, some ship captains advocated "tight" packing, that is, cramming as many individuals in as small a space as possible so as to assure that, by sheer weight of numbers, more Africans would complete the journey alive. Those who favored "loose" packing, for their part, argued that a higher survival rate would exist when the captives were placed into less cramped and, theoretically, less unhealthy conditions.

With at most five feet from floor to ceiling, minimal lighting, stagnant air, and very basic, haphazard facilities for the disposal of human waste, the slave ships were prime for the spread of diseases on these voyages. Many captives died from dysentery, smallpox, scurvy, measles, malaria, yellow fever, suicide, and in slave mutinies, which were occasionally successful. The diet was usually minimal and most often consisted of water served with yams or rice. With lack of sanitation, whippings, and malnutrition, and despite the captives being occasionally taken on deck for air and forced to do "exercises," the death rates on the Middle Passage were high. Anywhere from 10 percent to 50 percent of the captives perished en route. Bodies were tossed overboard, and it became the norm for a slave ship to be so identified on the high seas by the sighting of scavenging sharks following in its wake.

sources assert as many as half the numbers involved) occurred. Some died resisting or were killed attempting to escape; others might be chained together and forced to march—some were even strapped to poles and carried along—and these latter captives might succumb to the beatings they received to keep them moving or to the exhaustion of the forced march itself.

Once on the coast, some captives were sold right then and there to be immediately loaded into waiting slave ships, although it was more often the case that European-controlled redoubts would open their gates and the slaves would be hustled into semi-underground prisons to await loading and transport aboard the next available ship. The

The actual numbers involved have always been a source of controversy from the moment that W. E. B. Du Bois put forward a figure of fifteen million individuals who were transported to the Americas (this did not account for fatalities along the way). Though initially the tendency was to reduce this figure, the estimate began to increase over the course of the late twentieth century. By the beginning of the twenty-first century, commonly accepted estimates ranged between twenty million and thirty million people transported from Africa to the Americas. Basil Davidson has speculated that the Middle Passage cost Africa fifty million people, including fatalities en route. With smooth sailing, the Atlantic crossing might take less than a month, though it might also last sixty to ninety days. Those who survived would be disembarked and auctioned to the highest bidder in the New World.

In 1619, when the first "twenty and odd" Africans were recorded to have been sold in Virginia, and for years thereafter, chattel slavery as practiced in the Iberian-settled colonies was not established in the British colonies. Initially, the Africans brought to these colonies were indentured servants, on a par with white indentured servants and with at least the nominal, legal right to freedom when their terms of indenture (the "contract periods" during which they were required to labor under the direction of their masters) expired. The "contract period" generally lasted seven years. Most of these indentured Africans had been purchased under these terms from a Dutch ship by then-governor of Virginia Sir George Yeardley and some of his associates. The best known of these African servants, Anthony Johnson, who was originally documented in 1625 as "Antonio, a Negro," had arrived in Virginia in 1621, and, having served his indenture, had by 1651 acquired a 250-acre (100-hectare) farmstead on the Eastern Shore of Virginia at the Pungoteague River.

Even during Johnson's lifetime, however, attitudes were shifting toward discontinuing the indentured labor system and supplanting it with chattel slavery based on race. In 1640, John Punch, the only black man among three indentured servants who had attempted to escape from their master, was sentenced to servitude for life by the court at Jamestown, while his two white accomplices received lesser sentences. Indentured servitude could provide only a temporary, increasingly restive and unreliable, source of labor, while chattel slavery placed at the plantation

1610's

A SLAVER DESCRIBES THE BEGINNING OF THE MIDDLE PASSAGE

Slaves in Benin bound for the New World were taken to ports such as Fida to await their ships. They were usually unaware of where they were going or even of whether they were to be executed or eaten by the alien, white-skinned men they encountered there. In the passage below, a slave merchant named John Barbot describes processing enslaved Africans who were about to embark on the Middle Passage.

As the slaves come down to Fida from the inland country, they are put into a booth, or prison, built for that purpose, near the beach, all of them together; and when the Europeans are to receive them, every part of every one of them, to the smallest member, men and women being all stark naked. Such as are allowed good and sound, are set on one side, and the others by themselves; which slaves so rejected are there called Mackrons, being above thirty five years of age, or defective in their limbs, eyes or teeth; or grown grey, or that have the venereal disease, or any other imperfection. These being set aside, each of the others, which have passed as good, is marked on the breast, with a red-hot iron, imprinting the mark of the French, English, or Dutch companies, that so each nation may distinguish their own, and to prevent their being chang'd by the natives for worse, as they are apt enough to do. In this particular, care is taken that the women, as tenderest, be not burnt too hard.

The branded slaves, after this, are returned to their former booth, where the factor is to subsist them at his own charge, which amounts to about two-pence a day for each of them, with bread and water, which is all their allowance. There they continue sometimes ten or fifteen days, till the sea is still enough to send them aboard; for very often it continues too boisterous for so long a time, unless in January, February and March, which is commonly the calmest season: and when it is so, the slaves are carried off by parcels, in bar-canoes, and put aboard the ships in the road. Before they enter the canoes, or come out of the booth, their former Black masters strip them of every rag they have, without distinction of men or women; to supply which, in orderly ships, each of them as they come aboard is allowed a piece of canvas, to wrap around their waist, which is very acceptable to those poor wretches.

Source: From *A Description of the Coasts of North and South Guinea.* In *Collection of Voyages and Travels,* edited by Awnsham Churchill. Vol. 5. London: Churchill, 1746. UNESCO Slave Route Project. http://www.vgskole.net/prosjekt/slavrute/ slavnarrative.htm. Accessed February 18, 2005.

owner's beck and call a racially and legally distinct population that could be more readily controlled.

During the course of the seventeenth century, nine colonies endorsed and codified slavery into law, Massachusetts (1641), Connecticut (1650), Virginia (1661), Maryland (1663), New York (1664), New Jersey (1664), South Carolina (1682), Pennsylvania (1700), and Rhode Island (1700). Antimiscegenation laws were also enacted by most colonies, and a Virginia statute of 1669 dictated that henceforth a master might under certain circumstances hold the power of life or death over his slaves. During the last quarter of the century, large numbers of Africans were imported via the Middle Passage into the colonies, particularly into the South Carolina Low Country, where in 1671 the future Carolina governor Sir John Yeamans established a plantation into which he introduced African slaves.

Except for certain rare instances, newly arrived slaves were displayed for auction, inspected, and sold after bidding. They were then taken to wherever they were to dwell and work. Conditions and circumstances varied from master to master and from region to region. In the two main areas of southern colonization, the Chesapeake and the South Carolina Low Country, slaves were engaged almost exclusively in the plantation economy, mainly in tobacco or rice and indigo, respectively. For the "field slaves," who were certainly in the majority, housing was provided but in simple wooden structures with beaten-earth floors, and work went on from morning to dark (if the moon were shining, it was not unheard of to labor well into the night). Clothing was rough, practical, and basic; shoes might be distributed once a year, if at all.

The "house slaves," who had the fortune of living near the plantation house and usually working indoors, sheltered from the elements, were nevertheless subject to constant supervision by the master and his family. Life as a slave, then and later, was a life punctuated by constant

TRANSATLANTIC SLAVE TRADE ROUTES

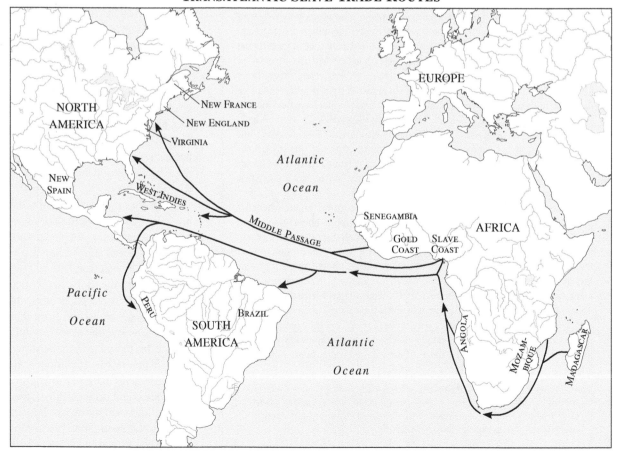

labor, tight restriction, and the ever-present possibility of physical and emotional abuse. Attempts to achieve literacy were certainly discouraged and in many instances subject to severe, exemplary punishment. While its application varied from master to master, use of the whip, either to punish offenses or to discourage slacking on the job, was standard procedure.

Though pains were usually taken to see that not too many Africans from the same nation were placed together on the same plantation (the rationale was that a common language would make it easier for them to plot revolts and escapes), the influx of slaves was so massive and sudden in Carolina that this proved an impossible goal, and it was there that African cultural remnants (language such as Gullah, steep-roofed structures for slave quarters, foodways, music) endured most tenaciously. The fact that the African population of the Carolina Low Country was so culturally integrated within itself and far outnumbered the white population led of necessity to a much stricter and more oppressive system there than in the Chesapeake region. Everywhere, however, the threat of slave uprisings and the presence of African or African-Native American (so-called maroon) communities, formed by escaped slaves and existing in remote areas, were facts of life in the South that lasted into the years of the American Civil War (1861-1865).

SIGNIFICANCE

The Middle Passage was a crucial part of the greatest mass movement of humanity in history, the molding of the Atlantic world. The displacement of millions of African people depleted that continent of much of its human resources and made possible its later vulnerability to colonial domination and "underdevelopment." On the other side of the Atlantic, the institutionalized slave trade arguably determined the course of history in the Americas. Certainly, without the labor supplied by enslaved Africans, the southern North American, Caribbean, and Latin American plantation system could not have existed as it did, and the economic development and subsequent history of the Americas would have been much altered. However, the legacy and issues of racism and exploitation that the trade in human bondage brought in its wake have not been resolved to this day.

—*Raymond Pierre Hylton*

FURTHER READING

Craven, Wesley Frank. *White, Red, and Black: The Seventeenth Century Virginian*. New York: W. W. Norton, 1977. Describes the advantages and limits of the extant sources and tries to formulate statistical data on what is available regarding race relations in seventeenth century Virginia.

Davidson, Basil. *The African Slave Trade: Precolonial History, 1450-1850*. Boston: Little, Brown, 1961. Focuses on the effects of the slave trade on Africa itself and concludes that the population losses made African states all the more vulnerable to nineteenth century imperial conquest.

Davis, David Brion. *Slavery in the Colonial Chesapeake*. Williamsburg, Va.: Colonial Williamsburg Foundation, 1986. Basic account of the actual, ground-level operation of chattel slavery in the Tidewater Virginia region.

Eltis, David, Stephen Behrendt, David Richardson, and Herbert S. Klein. *The Trans-Atlantic Slave Trade: A Database on CD-ROM*. New York: Cambridge University Press, 1998. Provides documentation for more than twenty-seven thousand slaving voyages between 1519 and 1867, including names of ships, captains, tonnages, fatalities, destinations, and outcomes.

Morgan, Edmund S. *American Slavery, American Freedom: The Ordeal of Colonial Virginia*. New York: W. W. Norton, 1975. Seminal study that examines the paradox of the establishment of slavery and the simultaneous emergence of constitutional ideas.

Northrup, Daniel, ed. *The Atlantic Slave Trade*. Boston: Houghton Mifflin, 2002. Collection of documents touching on the various issues relating mainly to the actual trade and the economic factors underpinning it.

Thomas, Hugh. *The Slave Trade: The Story of the Atlantic Slave Trade, 1440-1870*. New York: Touchstone Press, 1997. One of the most detailed descriptions of the mechanics of the Middle Passage and its interfunctioning with the New World plantation systems.

SEE ALSO: 17th cent.: Europe Endorses Slavery; 1612: Introduction of Tobacco Farming in North America; 1617-1693: European Powers Vie for Control of Gorée; Beginning c. 1619: Indentured Servitude Becomes Institutionalized in America; Aug. 20, 1619: Africans Arrive in Virginia; Nov., 1641: Massachusetts Recognizes Slavery; Mar., 1661-1705: Virginia Slave Codes; Mar. 24, 1663-July 25, 1729: Settlement of the Carolinas; Beginning 1671: American Indian Slave Trade.

RELATED ARTICLES in *Great Lives from History: The Seventeenth Century, 1601-1700:* Nathaniel Bacon; Aphra Behn; Jacob Leisler; Njinga; John Smith; António Vieira.

1610's

July 30-August 4, 1619
FIRST GENERAL ASSEMBLY OF VIRGINIA

Under instructions from the London Company, Virginia governor George Yeardley called a General Assembly at Jamestown, thereby creating the first representative political body in the British colonies and beginning the long evolution of democracy in America.

LOCALE: Jamestown, Virginia
CATEGORIES: Government and politics; colonization

KEY FIGURES

Samuel Argall (c. 1572-c. 1626), deputy governor of
Virginia, 1617-1619
Sir George Yeardley (1587?-1627), Virginia's acting
governor, 1616-1617, and governor, 1619-1621,
1626-1627
Sir Edwin Sandys (1561-1629), treasurer of the
London Company who instructed Yeardley to call
the first General Assembly
John Pory (1572-1636), secretary of the Virginia
colony and speaker of the first General Assembly

SUMMARY OF EVENT

The first permanent English colony in America was established at Jamestown, Virginia, in 1607. By 1618, the colony had neither prospered greatly nor realized the full expectations of the London Company (also known as the Virginia Company of London), which had been responsible for its founding. Twice, the London Company had been reorganized in unsuccessful efforts to make the Virginia venture turn a profit, but by 1618, it was again on the verge of bankruptcy. In 1617, as an inducement to settlement, the company had sanctioned the introduction of private land tenure and the creation of particular plantations, which had resulted in widely scattered settlements and confused land titles.

The emergence of private landowners in Virginia soon made feasible the establishment of a representative assembly, but the colony's economic base was still insecure. The colonists grew more restive, especially after 1617, when Sir Samuel Argall became deputy governor and returned the colony to stricter discipline by rigorously enforcing the *Lawes, Divine, Morall, and Martiall*, which had been adopted by the Virginia Company in 1612 and provided for partial government by martial law.

Against this background, the London Company resolved anew in 1618 to revitalize its Virginia venture. Led by Sir Edwin Sandys, the company embarked on an ambitious course of action that aimed at a comprehensive reorganization of the entire colonial operation. The company embodied its plans in a series of instructions and commissions, the so-called Great Charter, which was designed to reform land tenure, improve local administration, and replace the *Lawes, Divine, Morall, and Martiall* with English common law and a more representative and resident government.

In 1619, Deputy Governor Argall was accused of self-interested dealings, including being responsible for the importation of the first African slaves into Virginia, which had put the Virginia Company heavily in debt. Argall was relieved of his duties by the London Company; he escaped arrest only by fleeing Virginia with most of his wealth before the arrival of his replacement, Sir George Yeardley. Yeardley had lived in Virginia from 1610 to 1617 and had been acting governor for his last two years in the colony, after which he had returned to England. In 1618, he was knighted and sent back to Virginia officially to assume the governorship, which he did the following year.

Yeardley was instructed to call an assembly consisting of himself, a council of state appointed by the London Company, and burgesses elected by the freemen of the colony. The assembly would meet not more than once a year, except on "very extraordinary and important occasions." It would serve as a court of justice, and it was to have the power to enact such general laws and ordinances for the colony's welfare as should be deemed necessary. These laws were to be subject to a gubernatorial veto and to review by the London Company. The legal name for the new assembly was The Treasurer and Company of Adventurers and Planters of the City of London, for the First Colony in Virginia.

Following his return to Jamestown, Yeardley issued a call for the assembly, and on July 30, 1619, the first meeting of a representative legislative body in the New World convened in the church in Jamestown. This church, measuring only 50 feet by 20 feet (15 meters by 6 meters), had been built in 1617 by Argall to replace one that had collapsed. It was apparently situated along the James River, outside the protective walls of James Fort. The assembly was composed of the governor, six councilors, and twenty-two burgesses—two from each of eleven settlements (plantations, "hundreds," and towns). The burgesses had been elected by the votes of all freemen who were seventeen years of age or older. After selecting

John Pory (secretary of the colony and one of the councilors) as speaker and taking the necessary oaths of allegiance and supremacy, the General Assembly proceeded to its business.

After deliberating the qualifications of its members, a tradition followed by the later Congress of the United States, two members were rejected pending clarification of the patents from the London Company. Beginning its legislative work, the assembly adopted several revisions of the Great Charter that the company suggested. It then enacted a series of laws dealing with relations with the Indians, the dress and conduct of the settlers, church attendance, and measures to promote certain industries, including flax, hemp, silk, and wine. With the completion of the legislative work, the assembly switched to a court of justice and resolved several criminal cases.

This first session of the General Assembly was remarkably short, lasting only six days. Yeardley, "by reason of extream heat, both paste and likely to ensue," which had apparently caused the illness of several burgesses and the governor himself, ordered a review of all that had been accomplished and then adjourned on August 4, 1619. The next session was scheduled for March 1, 1620.

SIGNIFICANCE

Despite the brevity of the meeting, the first General Assembly of Virginia made an important beginning. It ushered in a new era in colonial government and transformed Virginia from a plantation colony, supported and governed by a trading company largely for profit, into a self-supporting and partially self-governing political community. Although the assembly would undergo modifications in its functions and its right to exist would be challenged after the London Company lost its charter in 1625, that first meeting in July, 1619, established the precedent for the development of representative political institutions in British North America. However, this House of Burgesses, as the General Assembly is sometimes called, did not represent a radical departure from European political institutions. It was essentially the transplanting to America of the traditional European form of representative government.

Although its legality was questioned when the Virginia Company was dissolved in 1624 and Virginia became a royal colony controlled directly by the king, the General Assembly survived and nurtured the elusive goal of self-government until it bore fruit in 1776.

—Warren M. Billings and Glenn L. Swygart

FURTHER READING

Andrews, Matthew Page. *Virginia: The Old Dominion.* Richmond, Va.: Dietz Press, 1949. Chapters 7 and 8 detail the beginning and the early history of the General Assembly.

Billings, Warren M. *A Little Parliament: The Virginia General Assembly in the Seventeenth Century.* Richmond: Library of Virginia, 2004. Describes the founding and evolution of the Virginia General Assembly, demonstrating how the legislative body established in seventeenth century Jamestown formed the basis of America's representative government.

Bridenbaugh, Carl. *Jamestown, 1544-1699.* New York: Oxford University Press, 1980. Chapter 7 explains the problem of self-interest in relation to the establishment of the General Assembly.

Hume, Ivor Noël. *The Virginia Adventure: Roanoke to James Towne.* New York: Alfred A. Knopf, 1994. Chapter 13 covers the problems and conditions that spurred the creation of the first assembly.

Morton, Richard L. *The Tidewater Period, 1607-1710.* Vol. 1 in *Colonial Virginia.* Chapel Hill: University of North Carolina Press, 1960. Chapter 4 describes the land distribution in 1617 that made possible a representative assembly.

Randolph, Edmund. *History of Virginia.* Charlottesville: University of Virginia Press, 1970. Chapter 3 covers events relating to the assembly from 1619 until the end of the Virginia Company in 1624.

Tyler, Lyon Gardiner, ed. *Narratives of Early Virginia, 1606-1625.* New York: Charles Scribner's Sons, 1907. Includes the proceedings of the assembly in 1619, taken from primary accounts, plus editorial comments. Lists the original burgesses.

Willison, George F. *Behold Virginia: The Fifth Crown.* New York: Harcourt, Brace, 1952. Chapter 15 details problems in Virginia preceding the first meeting of the General Assembly.

SEE ALSO: May 14, 1607: Jamestown Is Founded; Aug. 20, 1619: Africans Arrive in Virginia; Mar., 1661-1705: Virginia Slave Codes; May 10-Oct. 18, 1676: Bacon's Rebellion.

RELATED ARTICLES in *Great Lives from History: The Seventeenth Century, 1601-1700:* Nathaniel Bacon; George Calvert; Opechancanough; Pocahontas; Powhatan; John Smith.

1610's

August 20, 1619
AFRICANS ARRIVE IN VIRGINIA

The arrival of between twenty and thirty African indentured servants in Virginia marked the beginnings of what would ultimately become a firmly entrenched institution of slavery in the British North American colonies and a plantation economy dependent upon slave labor for its existence.

LOCALE: Point Comfort, Virginia
CATEGORIES: Social issues and reform; colonization

KEY FIGURES

Anthony Johnson (Antonio, a Negro; d. after 1660), African-born indentured servant who became a prominent Virginia landowner

John Punch (d. after 1640), first documented African in Virginia to be enslaved for life

SUMMARY OF EVENT

In August of 1619, a Dutch warship carrying "20 and odd" Africans landed at Point Comfort, Virginia. These Africans, the first to arrive in the British colonies, most likely were put to work not as slaves but as indentured servants. Neither the laws of the mother country nor the charter of the colony established the institution of slavery, although the system was developing in the British West Indies at the same time and was almost one hundred years old in the Spanish and Portuguese colonies.

To be sure, African indentured servants were discriminated against early on—their terms of service were usually longer than those of white servants, and they were the object of certain prohibitions that were not imposed on white servants—but in the early seventeenth century, at least some black indentured servants, like their white counterparts, gained their freedom and even acquired some property. Anthony Johnson, who labored on Richard Bennett's Virginia plantation for almost twenty years after he arrived in Virginia in 1621, imported five servants of his own in his first decade of freedom, receiving 250 acres (100 hectares) on their headrights. Another former servant, Richard Johnson, obtained one hundred acres for importing two white servants in 1654. These two men were part of the small class of free blacks that existed in Virginia throughout the colonial period.

Such cases as the two Johnsons were rare by mid-century. As early as the 1640's, some African Americans were in servitude for life, and their numbers increased throughout the decade. In 1640, in a court decision involving three runaway servants, the two who were white

were sentenced to an additional four years of service, while the other, an African named John Punch, was ordered to serve his master "for the time of his natural Life." Punch is the earliest African enslaved in Virginia for whom documents still exist. In the 1650's, some African servants were being sold for life, and the bills of sale indicated that their offspring would inherit slave status. Thus, slavery developed according to custom before it was legally established in Virginia.

Not until 1661 was chattel slavery recognized by statute in Virginia and then only indirectly. The House of Burgesses (or General Assembly) passed a law declaring that children followed the status of their mothers, thereby rendering the system of slavery self-perpetuating. In 1667, the assembly strengthened the system by declaring that, in the case of children that enslaved at birth, "the conferring of baptisme doth not alter the condition of a person as to his bondage or freedome; that divers masters, freed from this doubt, may more carefully endeavor the propagation of christianity." Until this time, Americans had justified enslavement of Africans on the grounds that they were "heathen" and had recognized conversion as a way to freedom. This act closed the last avenue to freedom, apart from formal emancipation, available to African American slaves.

In 1705, Virginia would establish a comprehensive slave code, completing the gradual process by which most African Americans were reduced to the status of chattel. Slaves could not bear arms or own property, nor could they leave their plantation without written permission from their master. Capital punishment was provided for murder and rape; lesser crimes were to be punished by maiming, whipping, or branding. Special courts were established for the trials of slaves, who were barred from serving as witnesses, except in the cases in which slaves were being tried for capital offenses.

In the other British colonies, the pattern was similar to that of Virginia. African racial slavery existed early in both Maryland and the Carolinas. Georgia attempted to exclude slavery at the time of settlement, but yielding to the protests of the colonists and the pressure of South Carolinians, the trustees eventually repealed the prohibition in 1750. The Dutch brought slavery to the Middle Colonies early in the seventeenth century. The advent of British rule in 1664 proved to be a stimulus to the system in New York and New Jersey, but in Pennsylvania and Delaware, the religious objections of the Quakers delayed its growth somewhat and postponed legal recognition of slavery until the early eighteenth century.

In seventeenth century New England, the status of Africans was ambiguous, as it was in Virginia. There were slaves in Massachusetts as early as 1638, possibly before, although slavery was not recognized by statute until 1641, the first enactment legalizing slavery anywhere in the British colonies. New England became heavily involved in the African slave trade, particularly after the monopoly of the Royal African Company was revoked in 1698. Like Virginia, all the colonies enacted slave codes in the late seventeenth or early eighteenth century, although the New England codes were less harsh than those of the Middle or Southern colonies. In all the colonies, a small class of free blacks developed alongside the institution of slavery, despite the fact that formal emancipation was restricted.

The first Africans to arrive in Virginia were most likely set to work as indentured servants rather than slaves. Some eventually earned freedom and even became landowners. Later, these involuntary immigrants from Africa were sold into permanent slavery. (The Granger Collection)

1610's

SIGNIFICANCE

Slavery in Virginia grew slowly in the first half of the seventeenth century. In 1625, there were twenty-three Africans in Virginia, most of whom were probably servants, not slaves. By mid-century, a decade before the statutory recognition of slavery, the black population was only three hundred, or 2 percent of the overall population of fifteen thousand. In 1708, there were twelve thousand African Americans and sixty-eight thousand whites. In a little more than fifty years, the black population had jumped from 2 percent to 15 percent of the total Virginia population. In the Carolinas, blacks initially made up 30 percent of the population but within one generation outnumbered whites, making South Carolina the only mainland colony characterized by a black majority. In New England, blacks numbered only about one thousand out of a total population of ninety thousand.

Although slavery developed haphazardly, as it developed, it became more and more entrenched. Plantation owners and others who used slaves developed ideologies justifying the institution of slavery at the same time that economic structures developed that depended upon slavery for their success. Moreover, as the Virginia colony developed its own distinctive culture, separate from the British culture that had been left behind, slavery came to be an integral part of that culture. Thus, by the time of the American Civil War (1861-1865), the end of slavery would become synonymous in the minds of many Southerners with the demise of a way of life.

—*Anne C. Loveland and Laura A. Croghan*

FURTHER READING

Davis, David Brion. *The Problem of Slavery in Western Culture*. Ithaca, N.Y.: Cornell University Press, 1966. The first in a trilogy examining slavery. Analyzes the sources of the ideas in Western culture that justified slavery.

Faggins, Barbara A. *Africans and Indians: An Afrocentric Analysis of Contacts Between Africans and Indians in Colonial Virginia*. New York: Routledge, 2001. Examines social relations between Africans and Native Americans. Describes Africans' life in Point Comfort and Jamestown.

Jordan, Winthrop D. *White over Black: American Attitudes Toward the Negro, 1550-1812*. New York: W. W. Norton, 1968. Examines the British colonists' attitudes toward Africans, particularly their views on African religions and skin color. Characterizes the establishment of slavery as an unthinking decision.

Morgan, Edmund S. *American Slavery, American Freedom: The Ordeal of Colonial Virginia*. Reprint. New York: W. W. Norton, 2003. Argues that the switch to black slavery was intended to curb the growth of a discontented lower class by decreasing the number of freemen coming out of indentures and looking for land.

Morgan, Philip D. "British Encounters with Africans and African-Americans, Circa 1600-1780." In *Strangers Within the Realm: Cultural Margins of the First British Empire*, edited by Bernard Bailyn and Philip D. Morgan. Chapel Hill: University of North Carolina Press, 1991. Posits a useful model to distinguish between a slave-owning society and a slave society. Maintains Virginia made the transition from slave-owning to slave society in 1710, when slaves represented 20 percent of the population.

Parent, Anthony S., Jr. *Foul Means: The Formation of a Slave Society in Virginia, 1660-1740*. Chapel Hill: University of North Carolina Press, 2003. Refutes previous historians' views that racial slavery created a Golden Age in Virginia. Instead, Parent maintains the institution of racial slavery was a calculated move by the emerging planter class to consolidate its power, with invidious consequences for Virginia and American society.

Vaughan, Alden T. "The Origins Debate: Slavery and Racism in Seventeenth Century Virginia." *Virginia Magazine of History and Biography* 97 (July, 1989): 311-354. Comprehensive examination of the scholarly literature on the origins of slavery and racism.

SEE ALSO: 17th cent.: Europe Endorses Slavery; 1617-1693: European Powers Vie for Control of Gorée; 1618-1648: Thirty Years' War; Beginning c. 1619: Indentured Servitude Becomes Institutionalized in America; 1619-c. 1700: The Middle Passage to American Slavery; Nov., 1641: Massachusetts Recognizes Slavery; Mar., 1661-1705: Virginia Slave Codes; Beginning 1671: American Indian Slave Trade.

RELATED ARTICLES in *Great Lives from History: The Seventeenth Century, 1601-1700:* Nathaniel Bacon; John Smith.

1620
BACON PUBLISHES *NOVUM ORGANUM*

Bacon's Novum Organum *established an impressive agenda for modern science and inspired the work of later groups, such as the Royal Society of London.*

LOCALE: London, England
CATEGORIES: Science and technology; cultural and intellectual history; literature

KEY FIGURES

Francis Bacon (1561-1626), lord chancellor of England, 1618-1621
James I (1566-1625), king of England, r. 1603-1625, and king of Scotland as James VI, r. 1567-1625
First Duke of Buckingham (George Villiers; 1592-1628), lord high admiral of England, favorite of James I, and first duke of Buckingham

SUMMARY OF EVENT

Even by the standards of its age, Francis Bacon's *Novum Organum* (1620; English translation, 1802) was an outrageously ambitious book. England was still full of "Renaissance men" with the financial means to avoid narrow specializations and, in Bacon's famous phrase, to take all knowledge for their province. A number of learned women thrived as well—including Bacon's mother, who translated a religious work from Latin—and the next generation saw the emergence of "female virtuosos" such as the poet and chemist Margaret Cavendish, duchess of Newcastle. Bacon, however, undertook to organize the new learning and to mobilize the students for the monumental task of perfecting God's creation.

The first part of Bacon's great plan was a survey of the arts and sciences. He made his preliminary survey in *The Twoo Bookes of Francis Bacon of the Proficience and Advancement of Learning, Divine and Humane* (1605; enlarged as *De Augmentis Scientiarum*, 1623; best known as *Advancement of Learning*), which he dedicated to the new king of England, James I. In the treatise, he judged certain sciences to have reached a degree of "proficiency," detailed the "deficiency" of others, and made recommendations for their improvement. It was like attempting to write an entire university catalog from scratch.

In 1620, the second part of his plan was ready, a description of his method for the brave new world of learning. He called his method the *Novum Organum*, or new system of rules, and in doing so, he announced that his method would replace the old rules. Ever since the rise of the universities in the Middle Ages, the six books of Aristotle's logic had dominated the curriculum. Collectively known as the *Organum* or *Organon*, they were enshrined as the final authority in all debate under the Elizabethan Statutes at Cambridge University, where Bacon had studied. Aristotle's logic was based on syllogism and on deduction from universal precepts to specific conclusions. Bacon's method, by contrast, worked by induction from observations to axioms.

Bacon wrote in Latin so he could reach an international office. He planned a Latin translation of the *Advancement of Learning* and presented the *Novum Organum* as the second part of a vast work that he called the *Instauratio Magna* (great restoration). He explained that he wanted to help restore human knowledge to the condition that Adam was said to have had in Paradise, before the Fall, and to restore human communication to the universal language that humankind was said to have had at Babel, before the confusion of tongues described in the Old Testament book of Genesis. The large folio volume, printed in London, had an engraved title page that showed a ship sailing beyond the Pillars of Hercules, as the Straits of Gibraltar were once called, and thus going beyond the lands known to the ancient world. The motto on the title page was taken from a prophecy in the Book of Daniel, translated in the King James Bible to read "Many shall run to and fro, and knowledge shall be increased." The implication was that the discoveries in the new age of science along with the geographical discoveries in the Age of Exploration would lead humankind into a golden age.

The *Novum Organum* began with a personal statement, "Francis of Verulam reasoned thus with himself and judged it to be for the interest of the present and future generations that they should be made acquainted with his thoughts." Bacon voiced his fear that the thoughts would die with him if they were not written down and made public. In the preface that followed, he explained that his great work would have six parts. The first was his survey of learning to date, which had not yet been translated from English. The second part was "The New Organum; or directions concerning the interpretation of nature," and provided the method for what was to follow.

The third part would record the "histories" of all the natural and experimental sciences. The fourth would be a set of "instances" discovered about the sciences and pointing to further experiments. The fifth would be a list of axioms that could be inferred provisionally from these instances. The sixth, which would have to be written by Bacon's heirs in a later age, would be the true science toward which he looked. This was a sign of modesty on Bacon's part. His fragmentary notes for part three included 130 subjects for "histories." Here were proposed histories of the elements he knew: fire, air, water, and earth. It would take a later age to talk about hydrogen, oxygen, and carbon.

The *Novum Organum* itself was divided into two books, each of which was written in a series of numbered paragraphs, called "aphorisms" in the translation. The first book discussed the nature of knowledge and the obstacles to knowledge, and among these obstacles in-

1620's

BACON ON MODERN AND ANCIENT WISDOM

Bacon's Novum Organum *laid out a fundamentally modern approach to the sciences, contesting the status that had been accorded to the ancients throughout the Middle Ages and the Renaissance. In the passage reproduced below, Bacon argues that the moderns are in fact older than the ancients, since they lived later in history, and their wisdom is therefore superior to the "youthful" wisdom of the ancients.*

As for antiquity, the opinion touching it which men entertain is quite a negligent one, and scarcely consonant with the world itself. For the old age of the world is to be accounted the true antiquity; and this is the attribute of our own times, not of that earlier age of the world in which the ancients lived; and which, though in respect of us it was the elder, yet in respect of the world it was the younger. And truly as we look for greater knowledge of human things and a riper judgment in the old man than in the young, because of his experience and of the number and variety of the things which he has seen and heard and thought of; so in like manner from our age, if it but knew its own strength and chose to essay and exert it, much more might fairly be expected than from the ancient times, inasmuch as it is a more advanced age of the world, and stored and stocked with infinite experiments and observations.

Source: From Novum Organum, *by Francis Bacon, quoted in* The Age of Reason: The Culture of the Seventeenth Century, *edited by Leo Weinstein (New York: George Braziller, 1965), p. 326.*

cluded the "idols" that people fashion—distortions that can be tracked to human nature or to individual quirks, to the use of language or the abuse of a philosophical system. The second book was a demonstration of the inductive method he proposed. Here, Bacon investigated the property of heat and created separate "tables" for studying the presence of heat, the absence of heat, and the increase or decrease of heat. He dedicated his work, once again, to King James. The king wrote a letter of thanks, promising to read the book, but probably never did.

Two centuries later, Thomas Macauley remarked, famously, that Bacon wrote philosophy like a lord chancellor. Bacon was actually appointed lord chancellor of England in 1618, reaching the peak of the legal profession and marking the end of a long ascent that had taken him from solicitor general to attorney general and lord keeper of the seal. Bacon thought he was in a unique position to dispense justice. At times in his writings, he seems quite highhanded as he presides over the arts and sciences. At times, he is dead wrong. For example, he is sometimes said to underestimate the importance of mathematics.

Bacon was made Lord Verulam in 1618, when he became lord chancellor, and he received the further title of Viscount Saint Albans in 1621. Later that year, he was accused of accepting bribes in court cases. He admitted his guilt and apologized profusely, but his public career was over. Banished from court by an act of Parliament, he was imprisoned briefly in the Tower of London. His family's house in London was given to his old ally, the marquis of Buckingham (who would become duke of Buckingham in 1623). Bacon retired to the country house his father had built and married an heiress. He spent his last years making experiments and notes for experiments. He is said to have died of a chill he caught while conducting an experiment with ice.

An expanded Latin version of *Advancement of Learning* appeared in 1623, and the projected volume on natural history appeared posthumously as *Sylva sylvarum* (1627). Bacon never wrote the rest of his masterwork except in fragments, but he left a science-fiction story that suggests what his dream looked like toward the end. In *New Atlantis* (1627), he imagined a kingdom of science, presided over by a second Solomon. King James was no Solomon; his grandson, Charles II, dabbled in chemistry, however, and became the first patron of the Royal Society. When the society's official history was published in 1667, the frontispiece showed the lord chancellor seated in a room full of books and scientific instruments; at his

feet was the motto *artium instaurator*, which may be translated "the restorer of science."

SIGNIFICANCE

Francis Bacon's *Novum Organum* reversed the accepted, Aristotelian methodology of science. Aristotle advocated applying universal rules, known in advance, to specific instances in order to determine their scientific meaning. Bacon, on the other hand, advocated a new empiricism, observing nature in all its manifestations in order to deduce new hitherto unknown rules or principles. The *Novum Organum*, then, is an important part of the Scientific Revolution, in which Sir Isaac Newton would deduce the laws of gravitation and the heirs of Nicolaus Copernicus, Johannes Kepler, and Galileo would establish empirically that the earth was not the center of the universe. Although Bacon's work was not a necessary precursor of any of these other thinkers' triumphs, it was nevertheless a singular and influential expression of a crucial seventeenth century cultural trend, one that informed both the history of science and the broader philosophical Enlightenment of the next century.

—*Thomas Willard*

FURTHER READING

Bacon, Francis. *The New Organon and Related Writings*. Edited by Fulton H. Anderson and translated by James Spedding. New York: Liberal Arts Press, 1960. The standard translation with an excellent introduction by the editor.

Eiseley, Loren. *The Man Who Saw Through Time*. Reprint. Boston: Houghton Mifflin, 1973. Beautifully written by an American naturalist, this short book celebrates Bacon's achievement. First published as *Francis Bacon and the Modern Dilemma* (1962).

Lynch, William T. *Solomon's Child: Method in the Early Royal Society of London*. Stanford, Calif.: Stanford University Press, 2000. Describes how Royal Society members relied upon Bacon's scientific method to perform and articulate their work.

Peltonen, Markku, ed. *The Cambridge Companion to Bacon*. New York: Cambridge University Press, 1996. Collection of essays exploring Bacon's philosophy of science, the classification of knowledge, religion, rhetoric, history, morality, and politics.

Snider, Alvin. *Origin and Authority in Seventeenth-Century England: Bacon, Milton, Butler*. Toronto: University of Toronto Press, 1994. This wide-ranging and often challenging book includes a detailed analysis of the *Novum Organum*.

Webster, Charles. *The Great Instauration*. London:

Duckworth, 1975. Offers a detailed account of Bacon's legacy to a century of revolution and apocalyptic thought, culminating in the formation of the Royal Society.

Whitney, Charles. *Francis Bacon and Modernity*. New Haven, Conn.: Yale University Press, 1986. Drawing on literary theory and scholarship, the author shows how Bacon helped to shape the sense of what is modern.

Williams, Charles. *Bacon*. New York: Harper & Bros., 1933. Written by a novelist and poet, this classic biography re-creates Bacon's intellectual life.

Wormald, B. H. G. *Francis Bacon: History, Politics, and Science, 1561-1626*. New York: Cambridge University Press, 1993. Detailed study places Bacon's thought in its historical context.

SEE ALSO: 1601-1672: Rise of Scientific Societies; Sept., 1608: Invention of the Telescope; 1609-1619: Kepler's Laws of Planetary Motion; 1610: Galileo Confirms the Heliocentric Model of the Solar System; 1612: Sanctorius Invents the Clinical Thermometer; 1637: Descartes Publishes His *Discourse on Method*; 1643: Torricelli Measures Atmospheric Pressure; 1660's-1700: First Microscopic Observations; 1660-1692: Boyle's Law and the Birth of Modern Chemistry; Late Dec., 1671: Newton Builds His Reflecting Telescope; Summer, 1687: Newton Formulates the Theory of Universal Gravitation.

RELATED ARTICLES in *Great Lives from History: The Seventeenth Century, 1601-1700:* Charles II (of England); Galileo; James I; Johannes Kepler; Duchess of Newcastle; Sir Isaac Newton.

July, 1620-September, 1639
STRUGGLE FOR THE VALTELLINE PASS

For twenty years during the early stages of the Thirty Years' War, the Habsburgs in Spain and Austria struggled with the French-supported Grisons for control of the Alpine pass through which Spanish troops from Milan could travel into Germany and points north. The Capitulation of Milan in 1639 left the pass open to the passage of Spanish troops.

LOCALE: Italian Alpine Valtelline and neighboring counties of Bormio and Chiavenna

CATEGORIES: Wars, uprisings, and civil unrest; diplomacy and international relations

KEY FIGURES

Cardinal de Richelieu (Armand-Jean du Plessis; 1585-1642), principal minister of France under King Louis XIII, 1624-1642

George Jenatsch (1596-1639), Grison preacher, patriot, and military leader

Henri de Rohan (1579-1638), French nobleman and military commander in the Valtelline, 1635-1637

Rudolf Planta (fl. c. 1615-1640), Catholic Valtelline nobleman and political leader

Count-Duke of Olivares (Gaspar de Guzmán y Pimental; 1587-1645), foreign minister to King Philip IV of Spain

SUMMARY OF EVENT

Historically, the Valtelline region—from Lake Como to the Inn River—functioned as a major passageway through the Alps that linked Lombardy with northern Europe. Because of its strategic importance, it has often been the site of conflict for its control. In 1335, the region was annexed by the duke of Milan, and it remained in Milanese hands until 1500, when King Louis XII of France drove out the Milanese and established France as protector over the region, a situation that held for a dozen years.

In 1512, the pope, with the Holy League and the League of the local Alpine Grisons (Graubünden, Grigioni, or Grays, a federation of three regional leagues who were unaffiliated with the Swiss cantons), ousted the French garrisons and established an "eternal union" of the Valtelline with the Grison confederacy in 1513.

During the sixteenth century, many of the Grisons and Valtellinese converted to Calvinism and, by the end of the century, leaned politically toward the France of King Henry IV, a stance necessitated by the seizure and control of Milan by the Spanish Habsburgs. Spain sought a right to unimpeded passage through the region, which would link Spanish Milan with Habsburg Austria and the Spanish Netherlands in the lower Rhine region.

Around 1600, the Spanish built El Fuente at Monticchio, a powerful fortress at the southern entrance to the valley, and sought to isolate the Grisons by prohibiting trade with the region. Despite a 1603 alliance with the French and with Venice, the Grisons agreed to allow the Spanish to use the pass and to recruit troops in the area.

Tensions among the region's politico-religious factions intensified in the later 1610's. The majority desired political alignment with France against Spain, while smaller groups of Protestants sought Venetian help and the pro-Spanish group remained satisfied. Meanwhile, arguments between the Austrian (Habsburg) and Spanish thrones ended when the Habsburgs and Spain concluded an agreement of cooperation in March, 1617, setting the scene for intense coordination between the two Catholic dynasties. The duchy of Savoy controlled the western passes, and neutral Swiss cantons, generally unfriendly to the Catholic Spaniards, held the central passes, which left a single corridor between Milan and the north.

In July, 1618, Protestant communities that were led by preachers such as the fiery George Jenatsch banded together and formed an assembly, at which many pro-Spanish Catholic leaders were condemned in absentia and a few were executed. The Catholic leaders, including Rudolf Planta, fled to Milan and Innsbruck, at which they plotted their return. Two years later, in July, 1620, one hundred armed men, led by a Valtelline aristocrat, entered the Valtelline and moved through the countryside for two weeks, massacring Protestant leaders and others at random—perhaps as many as 600—in the so-called Sacred Slaughter.

An army of Protestant Swiss and Grisons, led by the charismatic pastor Jenatsch, marched into the region to restore order, at which the Spanish declared the Valtelline under its own protection and dispatched into the valley an army of twenty thousand men under the command of the duke of Feria. The Austrians blocked the northern entrance to the valley, so Bern and Zurich sent more than three thousand men to support the Grisons. On September 17, 1620, two armies met at Tirano in a bloody if indecisive battle that left the Spanish in control of the pass. With the death of Spain's Phillip III, Spanish resolve weakened and Pope Gregory XV brokered the Treaty of Madrid (April, 1621), which returned all to conditions that existed before the hostilities. Spain's new king, Philip IV, did not press his claims further lest he draw in the French. Nonetheless, the Catholics sent diplomats to Rome and Madrid to plead the case for Protestant oppression in the Valtelline and their fear of Protestant reprisals.

Since Europe was rapidly sliding into the Thirty Years' War, Spanish access to Germany had never been more vital. Through a 1622 treaty, the Grisons retained control of the Valtelline but Spain obtained full rights of passage. Five weeks later, France, Venice, and the duchy of Savoy formed a league against Spain to enforce the Treaty of Madrid, which had limited Spain's options in the Valtelline. In October, the count-duke of Olivares named a new chief minister under Philip IV, but the minister would not risk war with France because of an Alpine pass, regardless of that pass's importance. In early 1623, the pope stepped in again, and both sides agreed to allow a force of papal troops to control the pass and guarantee the liberties of the people. Though some considered making the valley a feudatory of the Papacy, France blocked the idea.

As the war to the north continued, the French minister Cardinal de Richelieu saw to it that the French-Venitian-Savoy league was renewed (1624) and the effort made to return the pass to the Protestant Grisons. Citing violations of the most recent agreement, Swiss troops working for Richelieu invaded Grison territory, including the Valtelline, which secured the area for the French, who then used it as leverage to aid the Savoyards in their struggle to control Genoa (spring, 1625). One year later, Richelieu found his position among the warring states of Europe to be untenable, and he decided to quit the conflict and his Savoyard and Venetian allies. The Treaty of Monzon (1626) granted the Valtelline self-rule guaranteed by the Papacy, Spain, and France, with Spain and France having de facto right of passage. The Grisons and Valtelline Protestants received nothing. Through the next decade, tens of thousands of imperial and pro-imperial troops marched through the Valtelline, fueling the Habsburg cause in the great European struggle and ravaging the area.

To halt this aggression, Richelieu appointed the gallant Huguenot general Henri de Rohan. Imperial troops had abandoned the Valtelline according to the terms of the Treaty of Cherasco (1630) and Rohan was to support the Grisons in reestablishing Grison/French dominance. With Jenatsch as an important local agent, Rohan marched into the region in March and April, 1635. The Austrians and Spaniards rapidly responded and invaded the Valtelline in June, but Rohan defeated both forces during the next few months and secured the Valtelline for France. The Grisons soon realized that the French were not about to relinquish to them control of the area. On September 24, 1636, many of the Grison leaders, including Jenatsch, met at Silvaplana and decided to abandon the French and seek an Austrian alliance. The emperor promised religious freedom and Grison rule in Valtelline in return for free passage, and the deal was struck. The Grison leaders treated Rohan with dignity as they escorted him out of the valley following the anti-French uprising of March, 1637. After Spain was included in further negotiations, the agreement was sealed in September, 1639, in the Capitulation of Milan.

SIGNIFICANCE

Control of the Valtelline, Bormio, and Chiavenna was a matter of local interest until the Thirty Years' War and the Spanish-Austrian alliance gave this important passageway its international importance. The fortunes of all the major powers—and several minor ones—in the war depended upon which side held the passes. For the Grisons, however, the only matter of importance was local autonomy, regardless of who guaranteed it. Jenatsch, a Calvinist, took the step to become Roman Catholic as part of his deal with the Austrians, abandoning his confessional loyalty to further his patriotic cause. The struggle over the Valtelline was thus both a matter of grand military strategy and of local aspirations for self-rule. In the end, the French failed to thwart the Spanish-imperial interests and the Grisons proved tolerant and tolerable lords of the region until the 1815 Congress of Vienna.

—*Joseph P. Byrne*

FURTHER READING

Elliott, J. H. *Richelieu and Olivares*. New York: Cambridge University Press, 1991. Elliott's work includes a discussion of the role of the Valtelline struggle in French-Spanish relations in the early years of the Thirty Years' War.

Levi, Anthony. *Cardinal Richelieu and the Making of France*. New York: Carroll & Graff, 2000. Levi discusses the Valtelline and Spain in the context of the foreign policy of Richelieu's France.

Osborn, Toby. *Dynasty and Diplomacy in the Court of Savoy: Political Culture and the Thirty Years' War*. New York: Cambridge University Press, 2002. A bold study of the roles of Savoy in the war, including the League of Lyon.

Parker, Geoffrey. *The Thirty Years' War*. New York: Routledge, 1997. A standard account of the war in English, with discussion of the Valtelline wars.

SEE ALSO: 1618-1648: Thirty Years' War; Mar. 31, 1621-Sept. 17, 1665: Reign of Philip IV.

RELATED ARTICLES in *Great Lives from History: The Seventeenth Century, 1601-1700:* Louis XIII; Count-Duke of Olivares; Philip IV; Cardinal de Richelieu.

1620's

November 8, 1620
BATTLE OF WHITE MOUNTAIN

In the first truly decisive battle of the Thirty Years' War, the Protestant revolt in Bohemia came to an ignominious end when the combined forces of the Holy Roman Empire and the Catholic League overwhelmed the Bohemian rebels.

LOCALE: White Mountain (Bílá Hora), just outside Prague, Bohemia (now in the Czech Republic)

CATEGORIES: Wars, uprisings, and civil unrest; religion and theology

KEY FIGURES

Ferdinand II (1578-1637), Holy Roman Emperor, r. 1619-1637, and king of Bohemia, r. 1619-1637

Frederick V (1596-1632), king of Bohemia, r. 1619-1620, and elector palatine of the Rhine, 1610-1623

Christian of Anhalt (1568-1630), Calvinist prince of Anhalt, 1603-1630

Ambrogio Spinola (1569-1630), Spanish general who fought in the Palatinate

Count Johan Tserclaes Tilly (1559-1632), commander of the Catholic League

Karel Bonaventura Buquoy (1571-1621), aristocrat and leading general of the Holy Roman Empire

Maximilian I (1573-1651), duke of Bavaria, elector, and founder and head of the Catholic League

Gabriel Bethlen (1580-1629), Calvinist prince of Transylvania, 1613-1629

SUMMARY OF EVENT

The Thirty Years' War began in 1618 with a Bohemian revolt against the authoritarian rule of the Holy Roman Empire. The kingdom of Bohemia was one of more than three hundred principalities and cities within the predominantly Germanic empire, which was divided along religious lines—Roman Catholic, Lutheran, and Calvinist. The Treaty of Augsburg (1555) had allowed Catholic and Lutheran princes to determine an established church, but the Calvinists had no legal recognition. In 1608, a group of Protestant rulers formed the Evangelical Union to defend their interests, and this encouraged the creation of the opposition, the Catholic League, the following year.

Before 1618, the kingdom of Bohemia had enjoyed more religious toleration than most other areas in the empire. About two-thirds of the population was Protestant, and it included Lutherans, Calvinists, and followers of Jan Hus (1372-1415), a Bohemian reformer. The Catholic minority included many prominent nobles. King Matthias, who was also Holy Roman Emperor, disliked the idea of religious diversity, but he felt too weak to enforce uniformity. When the aging and childless king was in bad health, the Bohemian diet proclaimed in 1617 that the next king would be Ferdinand of Styria, who had a record of keeping non-Catholics from living in his duchies.

Almost immediately, Ferdinand, with Matthias's blessings, began efforts to re-Catholicize Bohemia and to consolidate powers of the Crown. On May 23, 1618, Protestant nobles in the kingdom expressed their displeasure by hurling two imperial commissioners (Catholics) from a window of the Prague Castle, an act known as the Defenestration of Prague. Protestant estates of Bohemia would further defy the Crown by appointing their own local administrators, setting up a national militia, and seeking assistance from neighboring states of the empire. Matthias was slow to react.

After Matthias died in March of 1619, Ferdinand succeeded him as both king of Bohemia and the Holy Roman Emperor. In July, pro-Protestant representatives of Bohemia, Moravia, Lusatia, and Silesia agreed to an Act of Confederation. Among the terms, the signatories pledged to continue Bohemia's policy of religious toleration and its tradition of an elective monarchy. They planned to finance the confederation with confiscated properties of the Crown and the Catholic Church. In August, 1619, a new Diet of the Bohemian kingdom met and formally repudiated the Habsburg succession. On August 26, the Diet offered the throne to a fervent German Protestant, Frederick V, elector of the Palatinate.

Frederick accepted the crown and arrived in Prague in October after being encouraged by his adviser, Christian of Anhalt, a firm Calvinist and skilled diplomat. Meanwhile, rebel and imperial armies fought inconclusive battles at the Vyšši Brod pass in southern Bohemia. Frederick was hoping for significant financial and military assistance from the Protestant Union and from his father-in-law, James I, the king of England. However, the Protestant Union and the English king, given the military balance, were unprepared to promise any significant as-

sistance. The Dutch and the duke of Savoy agreed to provide some military support, amounting to about seven thousand soldiers. Frederick also made an alliance with Prince Gabriel Bethlen of Transylvania, who invaded Hungary.

Emperor Ferdinand was much more successful in his search for allies. Many rulers feared that the spirit of revolt would spread if the Bohemians prevailed, and conservative Catholics were further motivated by the religious issue. Philip III gave assistance to Ferdinand from the inception of the Bohemian revolt, and in early 1620, he committed twelve thousand elite Spanish troops to the cause. Likewise, Maximilian of Bavaria, the head of the Catholic League, agreed to send money and troops in exchange for territorial compensation and the title of elector. The Lutheran elector of Saxony, John George I, also supported Ferdinand because of his disdain for Calvinism and his desire for additional territory.

On April 30, 1620, the emperor ordered Frederick to leave Bohemia. Spanish general Ambrogio Spinola led his troops into Frederick's most prized territory, the Lower Palatinate on the left bank of the Rhine River. Imperial forces then moved into Hungary to oppose Gabriel Bethlen. Frederick's hopes that the Protestant Union might enter the fighting were dashed on July 2, when it agreed to an armistice with the Catholic League in the Treaty of Ulm. By early September, Catholic League troops under Count Johan Tserclaes Tilly had suppressed most supporters of the rebels in Austria. The Saxons also captured rebel strongholds in Lusatia.

On September 20, the imperial coalition, which was organized into two professional armies, crossed the Bohemian border. The army of the Holy Roman Empire, commanded by General Karel Bonaventura Buquoy, had about fifteen thousand soldiers. The Catholic League's army, led by Tilly, numbered about ten thousand, and their strategy was to concentrate on capturing Prague and then pacifying the rest of the country. The outnumbered Bohemians were unable to stop the march toward Prague, where Christian of Anhalt commanded about fifteen thousand soldiers, including many Bohemian volunteers with little training. When Christian learned that the enemy was approaching, he led his forces outside the city to intercept the invaders.

On November 8, 1620, the two opposing armies faced each other on White Mountain, which is really a large hill on the western outskirts of Prague. Anhalt's army occupied a favorable defensive position on high ground. His right flank was protected by a hunting castle, and his left flank was covered by a large brook. Tilly ordered his well-trained and well-equipped soldiers to attack the center of the enemy line directly. Within two hours, the imperial forces had won a decisive victory, and the rebels were fleeing in all directions. Frederick, learning of the defeat, went into exile in the Netherlands, where he would live for the remainder of his life.

Imperial soldiers looted Bohemia and summarily executed an unknown number of suspected rebels without trials. In a public ceremony, twenty-seven leaders of the rebellion were beheaded in Prague's Old Town Square. The rector of Prague University, Jan Jesensky, and others were cruelly tortured before being killed. The heads of twelve of those executed were displayed on the tower of the Charles Bridge for ten years. The property belonging to supporters of the rebellion, whatever their social status, was confiscated and sold cheaply to Catholic loyalists. About three-quarters of the privately owned land changed hands.

SIGNIFICANCE

The Battle of White Mountain marked the end of the Bohemian rebellion. Ferdinand unleashed the forces of the Counter-Reformation. He issued a royal decree giving Protestants the choice of conversion to Catholicism or banishment from Bohemia. About one-fifth of the nobles and burghers of the kingdom chose to move elsewhere. Many outstanding intellectuals, such as historian Pavel Stransky and Humanist Jan Komenský settled in Holland. Prague University was transformed into a Jesuit seminary. For a time, all Bohemian books published between 1414 and 1620 were prohibited.

With military control over Bohemia, Ferdinand greatly limited the kingdom's autonomy and integrated its institutions into those of the Holy Roman Empire. The Czech chancellery was moved to Vienna and then given additional powers in a new Land Constitution. The powers of the Bohemian diet were severely curtailed. Although retaining the right to veto taxes, the diet only was allowed to deliberate on matters proposed by the king. It also lost its longstanding right to assent to each new king. Decisions of Bohemian courts could henceforth be appealed to the high courts in Vienna.

Ferdinand's conquest of Bohemia did not end the Thirty Years' War. The fighting moved to Denmark and then into northern Germany. Imperial forces began to suffer major defeats after 1631, and the destructive war would continue until 1648, ending with the Peace of Westphalia.

—Thomas Tandy Lewis

FURTHER READING

Bonney, Richard. *Thirty Years' War, 1618-1648*. Oxford, England: Osprey, 2002. A helpful summary of the war in less than one hundred pages.

Guthrie, William P. *Battles of the Thirty Years' War: From White Mountain to Nordlingen, 1618-1635*. Contributions in Military Studies 213. Westport, Conn.: Greenwood Press, 2003. This volume describes the battles fought in the early years of the war, with detailed accounts of their armies, strategies, weapons, leadership, and unforeseen developments.

Langer, Herbert. *The Thirty Years' War*. Poole, England: Blandford Press, 1978. This book is actually an account of European cultural and political history during the war years, an includes abundant illustrations.

Mortimer, Geoff. *Eyewitness Accounts of the Thirty Years' War, 1618-48*. New York: Macmillan, 2004. An interesting account based on diaries, memoirs, and chronicles of citizens and soldiers who witnessed the war.

Parker, Geoffrey. *The Thirty Years' War*. 2d ed. New York: Routledge, 1997. A clearly written survey that describes major personalities and emphasizes the horrors of the war.

Sayer, Derek. *The Coasts of Bohemia: A Czech History*. Translated by Alena Sayer. Princeton, N.J.: Princeton University Press, 2000. Taking its title from a Shakespeare play, this lively account emphasizes Bohemia's central place in European conflicts. The Czech author is highly critical of Ferdinand's religious policies after 1620.

Teich, Mikulas, ed. *Bohemia in History*. New York: Cambridge University Press, 1998. A collection of excellent essays, including one devoted to the theme of the White Mountain battle "as a symbol of modern Czech history."

Wedgwood, C. V. *The Thirty Years' War*. 2d ed. London: Jonathan Cape, 1963. A standard narrative account that gives considerable detail about leaders and campaigns.

1620's

December 26, 1620
PILGRIMS ARRIVE IN NORTH AMERICA

The arrival of the Pilgrims in North America established a second sphere of influence of English American colonists and offered another haven for English citizens fleeing religious or political oppression at home.

LOCALE: Plymouth, Massachusetts
CATEGORIES: Colonization; expansion and land acquisition; religion and theology

KEY FIGURES

William Bradford (1590-1657), governor of the Plymouth Colony, 1621-1632, 1635, 1637, 1639-1643, 1645-1656

William Brewster (1567-1644), Puritan layman and religious leader

Massasoit (Ousamequin; c. 1580-1661), Wampanoag grand sachem, r. before 1620-1661

John Carver (c. 1576-1621), first elected governor of the Plymouth Colony, 1620-1621

Christopher Jones (1570?-1622), captain of the *Mayflower*

Samoset (c. 1590-c. 1653), Pemaquid Indian who aided the Pilgrims

Squanto (Tisquantum; c. 1590-1622), Pawtuxet interpreter

Miles Standish (c. 1584-1656), a non-Puritan leader of the Plymouth Colony

Edward Winslow (1595-1655), a Puritan layman who won the friendship of Massasoit for the Pilgrims

SUMMARY OF EVENT

In 1534, as the Protestant Reformation swept across Europe, King Henry VIII separated the Christian Church in England from the Roman Catholic Church. Under his daughter, Elizabeth I, the national Church of England was created by combining some Roman Catholic traditions and doctrines with the beliefs and practices of the new Protestant churches on the continent. Elizabeth's goal was an independent church where all Englishmen would feel at home. However, some opposed the retention of Roman Catholic ritualism within the new Anglican Church and advocated "purifying" the church of that ritualism. The Puritans, as they were soon called, included both nonseparatists, who wanted to remain in a purified Church of England, and separatists who saw no alternative but to create a new, pure church of their own.

By the early seventeenth century, the Separatist Puritans were being persecuted by the Church of England and by the English government. In 1607, many of them, including the Scrooby Congregation, sought refuge in the Netherlands. Within a few years, however, conditions in the Netherlands became unsatisfactory, and the Scrooby Congregation decided to seek a better home in the new land of America, where the Jamestown Colony had been established in Virginia in 1607. The Scrooby Congregation returned to England in 1620 and received permission to settle in the northern part of Virginia, where the boundary had only vaguely been surveyed. After arranging financial backing from London merchants, the group secured two vessels, the *Speedwell* and the *Mayflower*, to transport some of

The Mayflower. (R. S. Peale and J. A. Hill)

them to their new home. The leaders of the initial group were William Bradford and William Brewster.

The original departure date for the Pilgrims' voyage to America was August 5, 1620. This journey was aborted six days later, however, when the *Speedwell* proved unfit for an Atlantic crossing. On September 6, the *Mayflower* sailed alone from Plymouth, in southwestern England. Aboard were 102 passengers. Since one person died and one person was born en route, they arrived in America with the same number. The passengers were divided into two categories. The thirty-five Puritans, led by Bradford and Brewster, were called Saints. The remaining sixty-seven, mostly young men sent by the London merchants to guarantee the economic success of the colony, were called Strangers. The leader of the Strangers was Miles Standish.

THE MAYFLOWER COMPACT

Upon their arrival in Plymouth, the Pilgrims signed the following contract, known as the Mayflower Compact. The compact both formed and declared the signatories' allegiance to the Plymouth Colony.

IN THE NAME OF GOD, AMEN. We, whose names are underwritten, the Loyal Subjects of our dread Sovereign Lord King *James*, by the Grace of God, of *Great Britain, France*, and *Ireland*, King, *Defender of the Faith*, &c. Having undertaken for the Glory of God, and Advancement of the Christian Faith, and the Honour of our King and Country, a Voyage to plant the first Colony in the northern Parts of *Virginia*; Do by these Presents, solemnly and mutually, in the Presence of God and one another, covenant and combine ourselves together into a civil Body Politick, for our better Ordering and Preservation, and Furtherance of the Ends aforesaid: And by Virtue hereof do enact, constitute, and frame, such just and equal Laws, Ordinances, Acts, Constitutions, and Officers, from time to time, as shall be thought most meet and convenient for the general Good of the Colony; unto which we promise all due Submission and Obedience. IN WITNESS whereof we have hereunto subscribed our names at *Cape-Cod* the eleventh of November, in the Reign of our Sovereign Lord King *James*, of *England, France*, and *Ireland*, the eighteenth, and of *Scotland* the fifty-fourth, *Anno Domini*; 1620.

Source: From the Yale Law School Avalon Project. http://www.yale.edu/lawweb/avalon/amerdoc/mayflower.htm. Accessed April 27, 2005.

After a rough voyage of sixty-four days in a leaky ship, the weary occupants of the *Mayflower* rejoiced to sight land on November 9. They had intended to land near the mouth of the Hudson River, then within the boundary of the London Company's territory, in what later became New York City, but the violent storms of the Atlantic Ocean had blown the vessel much farther north. The land they saw on that day was Cape Cod, in what later became Massachusetts. After a brief attempt to sail south failed because of the dangerous coastline, the leaders decided to seek a landing site near Cape Cod. After five weeks of scouting and several landing parties, they choose an area near the western end of Cape Cod, which a 1614 map by Captain John Smith of the Jamestown Colony had already called Plymouth. It was here that the *Mayflower* landed on December 16, 1620. (This was the date by the Julian calendar then in use; by the present-day Gregorian calendar, the date would be December 26.) A large rock near the landing site was later named Plymouth Rock.

Before disembarking from the *Mayflower*, realizing the need for unity and order, the leaders of the expedition drew up the Mayflower Compact. This historic document was then signed by all of the adult men, who thereby agreed to obey all laws passed by their elected leaders. Some historians classify this compact as the beginning of democracy in America. John Carver was elected as the first governor of the colony.

Soon after landing, the Pilgrims were ravaged by disease and starvation. Their hardships were similar to those of the Jamestown colonists in 1607 but complicated by more severe weather. Although they built crude shelters, they had to spend most of the winter aboard the *Mayflower*. Christopher Jones, the captain of the *Mayflower*, refused to abandon the colonists during the harsh winter, even though he and his crew suffered the same afflictions as the Pilgrims. Jones died of chills and a fever a few months after returning to England. By early spring, only about fifty of the colonists were still alive. Warm weather brought new hope, however, and when the *Mayflower* sailed for England in April, not one of the survivors was on board.

In March of 1621, the colonists were shocked when a young Native American walked into their village and addressed them in English. He identified himself as Samoset, a sachem, or chief, of the Pemaquid tribe in what later became the state of Maine. Samoset had apparently learned some English from fishermen along the coast. Two weeks later, Samoset returned with Tisquantum, better known as Squanto. Squanto was a

The Pilgrims holding their first Sabbath service after landing in the New World. (Gay Brothers)

member of the Pawtuxet tribe, which occupied much of present-day Massachusetts and Rhode Island.

In 1605, Squanto and two other Pawtuxet Indians had been kidnaped and taken to England by English adventurers. He was returned to his tribe in 1614 by Captain John Smith, during Smith's mapmaking explorations. Nine years of residence in England enabled Squanto to become fluent in the English language, making him a valuable interpreter between the English colonists and the native tribes. Before Smith could make use of his services, however, Squanto was again captured, this time by Thomas Hunt, a ship's captain left behind by John Smith. He was sold as a slave in Spain but escaped to England and returned thence to America in 1619, only to find that his tribe had been wiped out by disease, probably smallpox brought by Europeans. The site of Squanto's village became the location of the Plymouth Colony.

Samoset, Squanto, and Edward Winslow of Plymouth soon arranged a meeting between Governor John Carver and Massasoit, grand sachem of the Wampanoags who controlled southeastern Massachusetts. At this historic meeting, Carver and Massasoit signed a treaty of friend-

ship that lasted until Massasoit's death in 1661. Carver's contribution to Plymouth was strong but short. His wisdom helped guide the colonists through their first winter, but he died soon after his meeting with Massasoit, only four months after landing at Plymouth Rock. William Bradford was then elected governor, serving in that position all but five of the years between 1621 and his death in 1657.

During the summer of 1621, with the aid of their native friends and Miles Standish, the Pilgrims planted, hunted, and fished. By fall, their harvest was so bountiful that Governor Bradford proclaimed a thanksgiving celebration. The Pilgrims invited their friends among the local Indian tribes to join them, and about ninety, led by Massasoit, arrived, bringing five deer for the feast.

SIGNIFICANCE

From 1621 to 1630, the colony experienced slow but steady growth. Periodically, ships from England brought more settlers and more supplies. The debts to the London merchants, with their exorbitant interest rates, were paid off. By 1643, the colony included ten towns and about twenty-five hundred people. The Plymouth Colony continued growing until 1691, when it became part of the larger Massachusetts Bay Colony. In the course of that merger, the Separatist Puritans of Plymouth were absorbed by the more numerous nonseparatists, who had established the Puritan Congregational church while still officially recognizing the Anglican Church.

Along with other English North American colonies, the Plymouth Colony proved to be of great economic value to England. By providing such products as cotton, timber, and furs and creating a market for English manufactured goods, these colonists helped pave the way for England's growth as a world leader. The subsequent British acquisition of Dutch New Netherland and of French Canada secured that position. At the same time, the establishment of a Puritan theocracy in Massachusetts meant that the religious freedom of the Pilgrims was earned at the expense of English colonists of other faiths. As Puritanism became the state religion of Massachusetts, English immigrants fled from the Puritans own brand of religious persecution to found colonies in Connecticut, Rhode Island, and elsewhere.

—*Glenn L. Swygart*

FURTHER READING

Ames, Azel. *The Mayflower and Her Log, July 15, 1620-May 6, 1621*. With new additions by Jeffrey A. Linscott. Bowie, Md.: Heritage Books, 1998. Originally published in 1901, the book contains the *Mayflower*'s log and information about the ship, its crew, and itspassengers. Linscott has added a preface and index.

Bradford, William. *Of Plymouth Plantation, 1620-1647*. Edited by Samuel Eliot Morison. New York: Alfred A. Knopf, 1970. A primary source by one of the major participants of the Plymouth Colony. Includes notes and an introduction by Morison, a noted historian, and valuable appendices.

Caffrey, Kate. *The Mayflower*. Briarcliff Manor, N.Y.: Stein & Day, 1974. Provides background for the *Mayflower* and its historic voyage. Many appendices, including passenger lists and the Mayflower Compact.

Deetz, James, and Patricia Scott Deetz. *The Times of Their Lives: Life, Love, and Death in Plymouth Colony*. New York: W. H. Freeman, 2000. Describes how the Plymouth colonists lived, including how they maintained order, their relations with Native Americans, gender relations, and hearth and home.

Dillon, Francis. *The Pilgrims*. New York: Doubleday, 1975. Presents the economic, political, and religious background of the Puritan exodus from England. Explains the difficulties of a frontier settlement.

Fiore, Jordan D., ed. *Mourt's Relation: A Journal of the Pilgrims of Plymouth*. Plymouth, Mass.: Plymouth Rock Foundation, 1985. A primary account of the early years at Plymouth, from accounts by Bradford and others. Illustrations and maps, including the 1614 map by John Smith.

Goodwin, John A. *The Pilgrim Republic*. New York: Houghton Mifflin, 1879. Reprint. New York: Kraus Reprint, 1970. A historical review of the Plymouth Colony that compares it to other New England colonies. Goodwin provides an explanation of Puritan beliefs.

Stratton, Eugene Aubrey. *Plymouth Colony: Its History and People, 1620-1691*. Salt Lake City, Utah: Ancestry, 1986. A concise chronological and topical history, describing life in the colony. Contains more than three hundred biographical sketches of colonists.

SEE ALSO: May 14, 1607: Jamestown Is Founded; 1617-c. 1700: Smallpox Epidemics Kill Native Americans; July, 1625-Aug., 1664: Founding of New Amsterdam; May, 1630-1643: Great Puritan Migration; Fall, 1632-Jan. 5, 1665: Settlement of Connecticut; June, 1636: Rhode Island Is Founded; Nov., 1641: Massachusetts Recognizes Slavery; 1642-1700: Westward Migration of Native Americans; Sept. 8, 1643: Confederation of the United Colonies of New England; Mar. 22, 1664-July 21, 1667: British Conquest of New Netherland; June 20, 1675: Metacom's War Begins; June, 1686-Apr., 1689: Dominion of New England Forms; June 2, 1692-May, 1693: Salem Witchcraft Trials.

RELATED ARTICLES in *Great Lives from History: The Seventeenth Century, 1601-1700:* William Bradford; Massasoit; Metacom; Squanto; Miles Standish.

1620's

March 31, 1621-September 17, 1665
REIGN OF PHILIP IV

Determined to revive a declining monarchy's fortunes, Philip IV and his chief minister guided Spain into almost fifty years of uninterrupted war. This ill-advised bellicosity exhausted Spain's resources and accelerated its decline as a European Great Power. Philip's patronage nonetheless nurtured the Spanish Golden Age in poetry, drama, and painting.

LOCALE: Iberian peninsula

CATEGORIES: Government and politics; wars, uprisings, and civil unrest; art; cultural and intellectual history

KEY FIGURES

Philip IV (1605-1665), king of Spain, r. 1621-1665

Count-Duke of Olivares (Gaspar de Guzmán y Pimental; 1587-1645), royal favorite and unofficial chief minister, 1623-1643

Mariana de Austria (1634-1696), queen of Spain, r. 1649-1665, and queen regent for son Charles II, r. 1665-1696

Luis de Haro (1598-1661), unofficial chief minister, 1643-1661

María de Ágreda (1602-1665), royal correspondent and confidant

Diego Velázquez (1599-1660), painter

Pedro Calderón de la Barca (1600-1681), poet and playwright

SUMMARY OF EVENT

On March 31, 1621, sixteen-year-old Philip IV became ruler of a "mixed" monarchy, which included the Iberian crowns of Aragon, Castile, and Portugal, each jealous of its constitutional liberties (*fueros*): the duchy of Milan and kingdoms of Naples and Sicily in Italy, the Low Countries, or Flanders (an area approximating modern Belgium), and an American empire stretching from California to Cape Horn at the southern tip of South America. Few contemporaries doubted that Philip had ascended the throne of the world's greatest economic and military power.

A conflux of negative socioeconomic and demographic trends nonetheless led royal ministers, self-styled *arbitristas* (reformers), and foreign observers to describe Spain as a monarchy in decline. Spain's seventeenth century crisis had numerous causes, but prominent among them were its inequitable tax structure and the Crown's chronic, insatiable need for cash. Huge sums were required to administer and defend a far-flung empire, to maintain the court in suitable splendor, and to satisfy the constant demands of a nobility that viewed royal *mercedes* (mercies) as its just reward for a largely passive loyalty. Castilian resources (supplemented by booming imports of American silver) had sustained Spanish arms and expansion during the sixteenth century.

By the 1620's, harvest failures and famines, epidemics of bubonic plague, and, above all, onerous taxation of an already overstressed peasantry had combined to crush Castile's underdeveloped, primarily agricultural economy and depopulate its countryside. Silver from Mexican and, especially, Peruvian mines still provided vital infusions of ready cash, but these windfalls became progressively smaller and more erratic as the century progressed. Bullion from the treasure fleets returning from New Spain (Mexico) and Tierra Firme (South America) never provided more than 10 percent—and usually far less—of Philip's needs in any given year. Despite the vastness of its territories, the Crown had few alternative sources of income. There was wealth, but too much of it was sheltered in and beyond Castile by noble and ecclesiastic immunities. The corporate *fueros* of Philip's dissimilar subject territories all but ensured that non-Castilian receipts remained in the hands of the landed nobilities and urban oligarchies of the provinces.

Neither Philip nor his chief minister and mentor, Gaspar de Guzmán y Pimental, the count-duke of Olivares, understood Spain's crisis in such straightforward, secular terms. An intensely Roman Catholic court that was also incongruously sensual regarded Spain's earlier greatness as a divine reward for the monarchy's militant, missionary advancement of the true faith. The withdrawal of providential favor was attributed to Spain's loss of crusading zeal, especially during the ostentatiously corrupt and politically passive reign of Philip's indolent father, Philip III (r. 1598-1621). Philip and Olivares accordingly planned to restore the monarchy's power and prestige (*reputación*) by resuming the struggle against the traditional—albeit not exclusively Protestant—European enemies of the Habsburgs and by resurrecting the military virtues of Spain's luxuriating and self-interested nobility. The Calvinist, rebellious United Provinces (now the Netherlands) would be subjugated by military, naval, and economic pressure, while the predominance of the Austrian Habsburgs and Catholicism in Germany would be assured by decisive intervention in what became known as the Thirty Years' War (1618-1648).

Unstinting artistic patronage and a new palace (the spacious Buen Retiro, constructed during the 1630's) propagandized Habsburg greatness and enabled Philip to live (for a time) in unparalleled splendor. Philip's reign became associated with a golden age in Spanish poetry, drama, and painting. The king contributed significantly to this artistic efflorescence through lavish but discriminating patronage. The aging poet Lope de Vega Carpio (1562-1635) was succeeded as Spain's premier writer by

A statue in Madrid of Spanish king Philip IV. (George L. Shuman)

Pedro Calderón de la Barca, a popular court playwright who penned more than one hundred "cloak-and-dagger" dramas and *autos sacramentales* (one-act religious plays). Arriving at court in 1623, the portrait painter Diego Velázquez became the foremost representative of an impressive array of commission-seeking luminaries.

Olivares and his enthusiastic pupil benefited politically from a widespread aristocratic and popular clamor for restoration of the monarchy's fortunes, as well as from reforms initiated near the end of Philip III's reign by Olivares's uncle and sponsor, Baltasar de Zúñiga (d. 1622). The first years of the new reign witnessed a dizzying succession of military and naval triumphs, crowned by three widely trumpeted victories in 1625: the recapture of the Portuguese sugar colony of Bahia from the Dutch; the defeat of an English expedition against Cádiz; and a successful but staggeringly expensive siege of the Dutch fortress of Breda.

Philip and Olivares were obsessed with foreign affairs, but they failed to carry through the leveling fiscal reforms needed to sustain Spain's military efforts. Equitable redistribution of the tax burden would have necessitated the curtailment of noble, clerical, and regional immunities, a policy understandably anathema to non-productive elites already mortgaged beyond their means. The Crown instead invoked politically and economically damaging expedients with increased frequency. There were issues of debased copper coinage (*vellón*), sequestrations of private (merchants') shares of registered American bullion, alienation of royal jurisdictions, and the creation and (sometimes forced) sale of public offices. There also were extortions of compulsory "gifts" (*donativos*) and sales of prorated "pardons" (*indultos*) to merchants who engaged in (and submitted financial estimates of) smuggling. The military strain on the monarchy's resources was insupportable, leading the Crown to declare a first bankruptcy in 1627. Fiscal crisis was compounded by the catastrophic capture of the entire American treasure fleet by the Dutch in the Cuban bay of Matanzas (1628) and an ill-conceived conflict with France over the succession to the Italian duchy of Mantua (1627-1631). By the early 1630's, Spain's military prestige was again in tatters, its finances rapidly descending into permanent chaos.

Olivares obtained only limited cooperation from the separate *cortes*, or estates, of Aragon and Valencia (and none from the *cortes* of Catalonia) in imposing his project for a Union of Arms, wherein Philip's various provinces would separately enlist, outfit, and pay troops in proportion to their estimated populations and wealth.

1620's

253

During the 1630's—especially following the outbreak of full-scale war with France in 1635—Olivares therefore began to order select (often disliked) grandees to raise regiments at their own expense. This attempt to mobilize the resources of Spain's greatest nobles reaped a few positive results, but it also engendered a veritable flight of alienated *títulos* (titled nobles from Madrid), which was a development deeply troubling to a monarch as conscious of the need for courtly "luster" as Philip IV.

Revolts in Catalonia and Portugal sealed Olivares's political fate. Longstanding tensions between Crown and Catalans exploded in a peasant jacquerie during the winter of 1640, initially directed against ill-disciplined Spanish troops billeted upon the Catalans since 1635; the municipal council of Barcelona quickly appealed to France for protection (from the mob and from expected Spanish reprisals). Late that year the small but cohesive Portuguese aristocracy, disenchanted by declining prospects for advancement, took advantage of mass discontent to launch its own coup, enthroning the compliant duke of Bragança as King John IV (r. 1640-1656). When it was discovered that there was a conspiracy by Andalusian grandees to secede and establish an independent kingdom, Philip could no longer deny the gathering threat to his own position. Olivares was dismissed to his estates with honor, where the spurned favorite (*valido*) soon went mad and died.

By now mature, thoughtful, and self-willed, Philip was doomed to spend the remainder of his life fighting to recover his patrimony. Philip invariably justified his wars as defensive (he only lamented the War of Mantua), but what was undoubtedly an aggressive attempt to restore Spanish preponderance in Europe became instead a grinding struggle for the monarchy's survival following the disasters of the early 1640's. Buttressed by regular missives from the renowned mystic and Carmelite abbess Sor María de Ágreda, the king vowed to exercise personal sovereignty and never again place unlimited trust in a *valido*. Philip showed noticeable dedication, at least initially, but the reams of paperwork generated by Europe's largest bureaucracy soon compelled him to entrust Olivares's self-effacing nephew, Luis de Haro, with almost all the count-duke's former duties.

Philip managed to reconcile his Castilian grandees, and he briefly benefited from public sympathy following the deaths of Queen Isabella (Elizabeth) of France (1603-1644) and the *infante* (heir) Baltasar Carlos (1629-1646). His hold on power remained precarious, though, thanks to Spain's uncertain military fortunes and a spate of desperate popular rebellions from Naples to Andalusia.

The already depressed Indies trade all but collapsed in the 1640's; royal bankruptcies followed in 1647, 1653, and 1662. Determined in principle to fight on until he secured favorable terms, Philip nonetheless recognized that Spain's parlous finances no longer permitted him to confront several hostile powers at once. He grudgingly conceded Dutch independence by the Treaty of Münster (1648) so that he could focus Spain's dwindling resources on the struggle with France. Concentration of effort bore fruit; Catalonia was recovered after a plague-assisted siege of Barcelona in 1652. Hoping to press his seeming advantage, Philip rejected peace overtures from the temporarily weakened French. The reward for Philip's obstinacy was disaster. In 1655, a war weary Spain was attacked by Puritan England. Defeated on land and at sea, with his communications to the Americas severed and his treasure fleets shattered by roving English squadrons, Philip was forced to accept the humbling Treaty of the Pyrenees (1659) to escape from a now unwinnable conflict with France.

The incorrigibly bellicose Philip thereupon shifted his gaze to Portugal, determined not to treat with "rebels" or their English ally (from 1661). Yet Philip was able to muster only small armies of Italian and German mercenaries, while all classes (especially in Castile) groaned under the king's unceasing demands for revenue. As his armies and health failed, Philip fell into a devastating depression. The king died in Madrid on September 17, 1665, bequeathing an empty treasury and enfeebled realm to Mariana de Austria, his second queen and the regent for their son, the sickly King Charles II (r. 1665-1700). Mariana de Austria finally ended a half century of uninterrupted warfare by negotiating peace with England and recognizing Portuguese independence (1668).

SIGNIFICANCE

Spain did not enjoy a single day of peace during the long reign of Philip IV. Committed to restoring the monarchy's *reputación*, Philip and his officials sapped the dwindling resources of their vast but underdeveloped realms in a doomed effort to secure Spain's strategic position against the growing threats posed by powerful and aggressive enemies (England, France, and the Netherlands). Unwilling to recognize that his reach exceeded Spain's grasp, Philip exacerbated and prolonged economic, social, and demographic crises through the rapacious confiscations, conscriptions, and fiscal extortions needed to sustain his unending campaigns. He thereby ensured that a frail child, his son Charles II, would inherit a diminished and utterly exhausted kingdom, shorn of its former status as Europe's greatest power.

Philip demonstrated artistic and intellectual sensitivity, but the material benefits of the Spanish Golden Age were enjoyed primarily by a parasitical nobility; the masses lived in a state of abject, malnourished want that astounded foreign contemporaries. Philip viewed Spain as the patrimony and instrument of his Habsburg Dynasty, dimly understanding and never addressing his downtrodden subjects' needs. Although recent historiography has portrayed Olivares as a frustrated apostle of centralizing absolutism (and thus a modernizer), the count-duke fully shared (in fact, he shaped) his king's dynastic views and sought means to wage war with an imperious single-mindedness that nearly destroyed the monarchy. Draining the domestic foundations of their power to pursue unrealistic dreams of imperial glory, Philip and his ministers profoundly misunderstood the roots of, and thereby hastened, Spain's seventeenth century decline. Queen Mariana would be the one who ended decades of warfare.

—M. Wayne Guillory

FURTHER READING

Brown, Jonathan, and J. H. Elliott. *A Palace for a King: The Buen Retiro and the Court of Philip IV*. Rev. and expanded ed. New Haven, Conn.: Yale University Press, 2003. A comprehensive history of the artistic and cultural showcase of the Spanish Golden Age.

Darby, Graham. *Spain in the Seventeenth Century*. London: Longman, 1994. Reviews the economic, political, and military conditions of the reign of Philip IV in relation to his Habsburg predecessors and successor.

Elliott, John Huxtable. *The Count-Duke of Olivares: The Statesman in an Age of Decline*. New Haven, Conn.: Yale University Press, 1986. A masterful account of the political strategies and personal flaws of the failed administration of the most important minister of Philip IV's reign.

Kamen, Henry. *The Golden Age of Spain*. 2d ed. New York: Palgrave Macmillan, 2005. An updated version of a broad introduction to Spanish history, namely its golden age, in the seventeenth century.

Lobell, Steven E. *The Challenge of Hegemony: Grand Strategy, Trade, and Domestic Politics*. Ann Arbor: University of Michigan Press, 2003. Lobell analyzes Philip's reign and other topics to demonstrate how changing strategic environments influence the policies of declining world powers.

Stradling, R. A. *Philip IV and the Government of Spain, 1621-1665*. New York: Cambridge University Press, 1988. A positive treatise on Philip's reign, which emphasizes the king's independence after Olivares's dismissal.

SEE ALSO: c. 1601-1682: Spanish Golden Age; July, 1620-Sept., 1639: Struggle for the Valtelline Pass; May, 1640-Jan. 23, 1641: Revolt of the Catalans; Nov. 7, 1659: Treaty of the Pyrenees; Feb. 13, 1668: Spain Recognizes Portugal's Independence.

RELATED ARTICLES in *Great Lives from History: The Seventeenth Century, 1601-1700:* Anne of Austria; Pedro Calderón de la Barca; Charles II (of Spain); Frederick Henry; John IV; John of Austria; Louis XIV; Marie-Thérèse; Count-Duke of Olivares; Philip III; Philip IV; Lope de Vega Carpio; Diego Velázquez.

1620's

December 18, 1621
THE GREAT PROTESTATION

In opposition to the monarchy, the English parliament asserted its authority over judicial and legislative affairs, intensifying the conflict between the king and Parliament that would eventually culminate in the English Civil Wars.

LOCALE: London, England
CATEGORIES: Government and politics; laws, acts, and legal history

KEY FIGURES
James I (1566-1625), king of England, r. 1603-1625, and king of Scotland as James VI, r. 1567-1625
Sir Edward Coke (1552-1634), member of Parliament and former lord chief justice of the King's Bench
Sir Giles Mompesson (1584-1651?), royal commissioner who owned several monopolies
John Pym (1584-1643), member of Parliament and later leader of the Long Parliament
John Selden (1584-1654), member of Parliament and political theorist
Third Earl of Southampton (Henry Wriothesley; 1573-1624), patron of Shakespeare

SUMMARY OF EVENT
Following the death of Queen Elizabeth I in 1603, James VI of Scotland ascended the throne as James I of England. Almost immediately upon his ascension, the king sought to increase his influence over the country's legislative, judicial, and ecclesiastical affairs. While Puritan radicalism had been a thorny political issue throughout Elizabeth's reign, James's perceived sympathies toward Catholicism raised the pitch of religious debate considerably. As a result, political and religious opposition to the crown became more regular and overt, and the period from 1621 to 1642 was marked by a series of attempts by Parliament to curtail royal power.

In defense of his claims to authority, James frequently cited the doctrine of the divine right of kings, according to which rulers of nations were anointed by God and therefore above religious or parliamentary scrutiny. James was successful in increasing the scope of his authority, perceived or actual, in part because he was able to use fines and imprisonment to enforce his proclamations and in part because most of his judges regularly sided with him on questions of jurisdiction. James also relied on his power both to call and to dissolve sessions of Parliament.

At the same time, however, although Parliament could only meet at the behest of the king, James was increasingly dependent upon Parliament to raise money for his foreign campaigns, since under British law, only Parliament could levy new taxes. The king was thus often compelled to call a Parliament despite himself, and once called, Parliament was able to pass laws in its own interests contradicting the will of the king. James had routinely been in need of money throughout his reign, and when Spanish troops invaded the Palatinate in 1620, the possibility of war preparations made the issues of royal funds even more pressing. It was in this context that James called the two parliamentary sessions of 1621.

The Parliament of 1621, instead of dedicating most of its time to the money-raising campaigns that James had hoped to instigate, ultimately devoted its energy to a series of actions designed to reform those aspects of James's leadership that had become especially contentious. During this time, Sir Edward Coke became one of the leading members of Parliament who sought to advance these reforms. One of the more successful efforts by Parliament in this process was a series of impeachments of James's royal officers. Following a legal precedent that had been in existence since the Middle Ages, the House of Commons began to exercise its power to impeach a government officer before the House of Lords.

In February, the Commons impeached one of the king's commissioners, Sir Giles Mompesson, on the grounds that he had illegally used his administrative authority over certain monopolies to extort funds from the government. Mompesson was successfully impeached and sentenced to life imprisonment. The success of this trial made impeachment a popular method for dealing with James's most controversial ministers, including the first duke of Buckingham a few years later, and the practice continued well into the eighteenth century.

The controversial role of monopolies in England's economy had long been a sticking point for many members of Parliament, so the actions taken against Mompesson were hardly surprising. James, following his usual habit of trying to negotiate with contending factions in the government (at least for a while), had in fact made known his willingness to hear arguments in favor of reforming monopolies. In the spirit of this attitude of cooperation, James made several conciliatory gestures, including canceling several monopolies and loosening trade regulations. During a second session of Parliament in the same year, however, James angered the House of Commons by restricting them from any discussion of foreign policy. He made the additional mistake of putting forth an official statement reminding Parliament (correctly, but unwisely) that its authority had only been instituted in recent history by a royal grant and was therefore, presumably, contingent upon the Crown's power.

Parliament responded quickly and vehemently to the king's bravado and, during this same session, made one further significant attempt to mitigate the king's authority over judicial and legislative affairs. On December 18, a bill was passed declaring that "the liberties, franchises, privileges, and jurisdictions of parliament are the ancient and undoubted birthright and inheritance of the subjects of England, and that the arduous and urgent affairs concerning the king, state, and defense of the realm . . . are proper subjects and matter of council and debate in parliament." By this official act of "protestation," Parliament hoped to secure their influence on judicial appointments, as well as interject themselves into the daily legislative activities of the government, both of which James had aggressively sought solely to control since his accession.

This act of open defiance immediately incurred James's anger. Upon reading the official journal of the parliamentary session, it is reputed that he tore out the page containing the act of protestation in a rage. The king quickly denied the legality of Parliament's claims to authority (in part, he claimed, because correct parliamentary procedure had not been followed), and he dissolved the session shortly afterward. In addition, James had several of the leading members of Parliament imprisoned, including Sir Edward Coke, John Selden, and Henry Wriothesley, third earl of Southampton (whose son, the fourth earl of Southampton, would become a staunch supporter of Charles I). Also arrested for a short time was John Pym, who by that time had already established himself as a fierce opponent of Roman Catholicism and who would go on to become one of the most influential opponents of the king during the English Civil Wars, leading the Long Parliament of 1640. Although most of these members were soon released, the conflict was viewed as a breakdown of the English constitution, paving the way for further tensions between Parliament and Charles I upon his accession in 1625.

SIGNIFICANCE

Although the king's power to dissolve Parliament meant that the 1621 session was not able to realize its stated claims to authority immediately, the Great Protestation set down in unambiguous language many of the political arguments that Parliament was to draw upon over the next few decades in their attempt to wrest power from the monarch. More important, the 1621 Parliament had the effect of galvanizing anti-Royalist sentiment, which had already been developing in the Puritan faction in England since the sixteenth century. For this reason, the Great Protestation is often identified as the beginning of the Puritan Awakening, a period of intense opposition to the royal court that would culminate in the English Civil Wars and the execution of Charles I in 1649.

—*Joseph M. Ortiz*

FURTHER READING

Cogswell, Thomas. *The Blessed Revolution: English Politics and the Coming of War, 1621-1624*. New York: Cambridge University Press, 1989. Analyzes the immediate effects of the Great Protestation, particularly as an antecedent to the English Civil Wars. Index, bibliography.

Coward, Barry. *The Stuart Age: England, 1603-1714*. New York: Longman, 1994. An excellent analysis of the period that contextualizes the Great Protestation within the larger political and social movements in seventeenth century England. Bibliography, timeline.

Croft, Paula. "Capital Life: Members of Parliament Outside the House." In *Politics, Religion, and Popularity in Early Stuart Britain*, edited by Thomas Cogswell, Richard Cust, and Peter Lake. New York: Cambridge University Press, 2002. Interesting discussion of the meeting habits and customs of Parliament members during the Jacobean period.

Tanner, Joseph R. *Constitutional Documents of the Reign of James I, A.D. 1603-1625*. Cambridge, England: Cambridge University Press, 1930. Includes the full text of the 1621 protestation, along with a general commentary.

Thrush, Andrew. "The Personal Rule of James I, 1611-1620." In *Politics, Religion, and Popularity in Early Stuart Britain*, edited by Thomas Cogswell, Richard Cust, and Peter Lake. New York: Cambridge University Press, 2002. Analyzes the king's treatment of Parliament in the years immediately preceding the Great Protestation.

Tite, Colin. *Impeachment and Parliamentary Judicature in Early Stuart England*. London: Athlone Press, 1974. Analyzes the political maneuverings of the 1621 Parliament in its opposition to the Crown. Index, bibliography.

1620's

SEE ALSO: Mar. 24, 1603: James I Becomes King of England; May 6-June 7, 1628: Petition of Right; Mar., 1629-1640: "Personal Rule" of Charles I; Nov. 3, 1640-May 15, 1641: Beginning of England's Long Parliament; 1642-1651: English Civil Wars; Dec. 6, 1648-May 19, 1649: Establishment of the English Commonwealth; Dec. 16, 1653-Sept. 3, 1658: Cromwell Rules England as Lord Protector; May, 1659-May, 1660: Restoration of Charles II; Dec. 19, 1667: Impeachment of Clarendon; 1679: Habeas Corpus Act; Apr. 4, 1687, and Apr. 27, 1688: Declaration of Liberty of Conscience; Nov., 1688-Feb., 1689: The Glorious Revolution; Feb. 13, 1689: Declaration of Rights.

RELATED ARTICLES in *Great Lives from History: The Seventeenth Century, 1601-1700:* First Duke of Buckingham; Charles I; Sir Edward Coke; James I; John Pym.

March 22, 1622-October, 1646
POWHATAN WARS

After the death of Powhatan, who had worked to maintain peace between his people and the English colonists in Virginia, the tensions between the Virginian Indians and European settlers erupted into all-out war. The tribes of the Powhatan Confederacy were greatly reduced by the wars, after which they ceased to represent a serious obstacle to European expansion in Virginia.

LOCALE: Virginia
CATEGORIES: Wars, uprisings, and civil unrest; colonization; diplomacy and international relations

KEY FIGURES

Powhatan (Wahunsenacawh; c. 1550-1618), head of the Powhatan Confederacy, r. late sixteenth century-1618
Opechancanough (c. 1545-1644/1646), Pamunkey chief, r. before 1607-1644/1646, and head of the Powhatan Confederacy, r. 1618-1644/1646
Necotowance (fl. 1646), head of the Powhatan Confederacy, r. 1644/1646-before 1676
John Smith (1580-1631), Jamestown founder who established trade relations with the Powhatans
John Rolfe (1585-1622), English-born American colonist and tobacco farmer
Pocahontas (Matoaka; c. 1596-1617), daughter of Powhatan and wife of John Rolfe
Sir Francis Wyatt (1575?-1644), governor of Virginia, 1621-1626, 1639-1641
Sir William Berkeley (1606-1677), governor of Virginia, 1641-1649, 1660-1677

SUMMARY OF EVENT

In 1607, the twenty-eight horticulturally based, egalitarian Powhatan tribes residing between the Potomac River and the James River of the Chesapeake Bay region of Virginia were the first American Indians to interact with the settlers at Jamestown. Jamestown was the first permanent English settlement in the New World. The Powhatan Confederacy was composed of approximately nine thousand individuals who resided in perhaps two hundred palisaded, sedentary villages along the Chesapeake Bay. The leader of the confederation was Powhatan, a high priest and paramount chief, described by Captain John Smith as a tall, well-proportioned man. Powhatan had inherited the office of chief upon his father's death, probably in the mid-1570's, and he began to expand his own power and authority through intimidation and force over nonaligned contiguous tribal groups. Some Europeans considered Powhatan to be a king, while others referred to him as an emperor. The English addressed his daughter Pocahontas as "empress."

Although the success of the Jamestown colony was dependent upon the accommodation and often-needed assistance of the Powhatans, conflict commenced almost immediately and continued in varying degrees, ultimately resulting in a sustained sense of tension and even hostility between the two very different cultures. There is no indication of why the powerful Powhatan chief did not simply annihilate the small group of early colonists, but he chose rather to save the English from famine on several occasions with generous contributions of food. In fact, Powhatan had his people teach the early settlers how to farm, hunt, and fish successfully in the unfamiliar terrain of Virginia.

Despite continual encroachment by the settlers and a swelling of their numbers as more and more British subjects immigrated to Virginia, the Powhatans continued to refrain from exercising any concerted military power against the English. Even Powhatan's half brother, Opechancanough, who had captured Captain John Smith, chose not to kill the Englishman, indicating Powhatan's respect for the settlement leader. There has been speculation that Powhatan may have believed the British would later assist him in absorbing other tribes of the area into the Confederacy. It soon became apparent to Powhatan and certainly to others of his tribe that the primary intent of the English was to possess and control their lands.

The uncertain relationship between the Powhatan tribes and the English settlers was exacerbated by several factors, including intermittent armed conflict, the dire effects of newly introduced diseases and alcohol upon the natives, a general sense of deprivation resulting from white encroachment, and the increased immigration of Europeans to Virginia. Because of intermarriage, it also was apparent that many English were attempting to assimilate the Powhatans into the Anglo culture.

In 1614, Pocahontas, who had converted to the Anglican religion and been baptized as Lady Rebecca, married the very literate entrepreneur John Rolfe, who first introduced West Indian tobacco to the colonies in 1612. This celebrated marriage probably helped to ameliorate overt hostility, as did the realization that the number of Powhatan warriors had been reduced through armed conflict. Consequently, for eight years prior to the Powhatan Wars, relative peace existed between the English and the Powhatan people, undoubtedly a reflection of Powhatan's policy of accommodation. As early as 1609, he realized the potential threat posed to his people by the English, with their firearms and edged steel weapons. Nevertheless, from 1609 to 1614 relations with the settlers generally deteriorated, and warfare intensified. However, Powhatan claimed he wanted to live in peace, and he managed to maintain peaceful relations between his people and the colonists from 1614 until April, 1618, when he died and his half brother, Opechancanough, succeeded him.

As paramount chief of the Powhatan Confederacy, Opechancanough attempted to continue the policy of accommodation, despite the colonists' increasing refusal to respect the Powhatans' unqualified sovereignty. However, with the realization that the English settlers were expanding their claim to and use of lands, as well as their constant attempts to proselytize and assimilate his people, Opechancanough began to resent these incursions and planned to drive the English from Powhatan territory with a major uprising. His plan required that he convince the thirty tribes of the Powhatan Confederacy to join with him in expelling the English. The plan was implemented on March 22, 1622, when the highly regarded prophet and warrior Nemattanow was murdered by the British, who suspected he had killed a white trader. Opechanca-

nough took advantage of his people's anger and organized an attack on the colonists.

The surprise Indian attack annihilated 347 settlers, nearly a third of the English settlement in Virginia. It is believed that more would have died had they been completely unprepared for the attack. However, a Pamunkey servant forewarned his master, who was able to alert some of the other settlers of Jamestown and the surrounding communities in time. Thus, many settlers were able to coordinate a defense. Even more devastating, however, was the counterattack by the English, who conducted military expeditions against many Powhatan villages, which they burned, destroying crops and great quantities of stored foodstuffs.

The London Company, holders of the Virginia colony's charter, took advantage of the massacre, using it as an excuse to dispossess of their land most Powhatans who lived in and near the various settlements. The company even encouraged the enslavement of young girls and boys. In fact, the assembly and the governor, Sir Francis Wyatt, initiated a policy of extermination, writing, "Wee have anticipated your desire by settinge uponn the Indiyans in all places." After a decade of almost continual fighting, a treaty was negotiated in 1632, ending the Powhatan Wars, but even during the peace ceremony, poison was placed in the Indians' wine.

The truce was effective for approximately twelve years, until Opechancanough, now nearly one hundred years old and quite debilitated and feeble, was able to persuade the Powhatan Confederacy tribes again to wage war against the English. On April 18, 1644, the combined tribes staged a coordinated attack against the English, killing nearly five hundred. The Indians' efforts to expel the English were futile, however, for the settlers in Virginia now numbered approximately eight thousand. The renewed fighting continued for another two years. Warfare ceased in October, 1646, when the colonial assembly joined in a peace agreement negotiated by Governor Sir William Berkeley and Necotowance, Opechancanough's successor.

SIGNIFICANCE

The treaty between Berkeley and Necotowance recognized the York River as the line of demarcation separating the Powhatans and the English, and only with the colonial governor's permission could a member of one group enter the other group's territory. Despite this recognition of Powhatan sovereignty within their own lands, however, the Powhatan Wars conclusion spelled the end of the Powhatan Confederacy's ability to stand in

1620's

259

the way of English colonial expansion in Virginia. Two decades of conflict, along with introduced diseases, had greatly reduced the Powhatan population at the same time that immigration caused the English population to increase every year. The English would ultimately take control of Powhatan lands and resources, and the indigenous people of Virginia began a difficult period of deculturation as a result.

—John Alan Ross

FURTHER READING

Craven, Wesley Frank. *White, Red, and Black: The Seventeenth Century Virginian.* Charlottesville: University Press of Virginia, 1971. A comprehensive study of different groups resident in Virginia.

Gleach, Frederic W. *Powhatan's World and Colonial Virginia: A Conflict of Cultures.* Lincoln: University of Nebraska Press, 1997. Outlines the cultural differences between the Powhatans and the British colonists.

Josephy, Alvin M., Jr. *Five Hundred Nations: An Illustrated History of the North American Indians.* New York: Alfred A. Knopf, 1994. Chapter 4 covers the conflict, placed in the context of European colonization. Lavishly illustrated.

Lowe, William C. "Powhatan Confederacy" and "Powhatan Wars." In *Ready Reference: American Indians.* Vol. 2. Pasadena, Calif.: Salem Press, 1995. Brief but informative accounts of the development of intertribal internal functions and tribal conflict with white settlers.

Paredes, J. Anthony, ed. *Indians of the Southeastern United States in the Late Twentieth Century.* Tuscaloosa: University of Alabama Press, 1992. An excellent ethnographic compendium of the effects of Euro-American socioeconomic and political policies upon Native Americans of this area.

Rountree, Helen C. *Pocahontas's People: The Powhatan Indians of Virginia Through Four Centuries.* Norman: University of Oklahoma Press, 1990. A thorough, well-presented ethnographic history of the Powhatan Indians.

Rountree, Helen C., and E. Randolph Turner III. *Before and After Jamestown: Virginia's Powhatans and Their Predecessors.* Gainesville: University Press of Florida, 2002. A comprehensive history of the Powhatans from their earliest contact with Europeans to the present. Includes a chapter discussing the Jamestown colony from a Powhatan perspective.

Townsend, Camilla. *Pocahontas and the Powhatan Dilemma.* New York: Hill and Wang, 2004. Depicts Pocahontas and Powhatan not as naive or innocent but as people who were able to confront British colonists with sophistication, and diplomacy, but also violence.

SEE ALSO: May 14, 1607: Jamestown Is Founded; 1612: Introduction of Tobacco Farming in North America; 1617-c. 1700: Smallpox Epidemics Kill Native Americans; July 30-Aug. 4, 1619: First General Assembly of Virginia; July 20, 1636-July 28, 1637: Pequot War; 1642-1700: Westward Migration of Native Americans; June 20, 1675: Metacom's War Begins; Aug. 10, 1680: Pueblo Revolt.

RELATED ARTICLES in *Great Lives from History: The Seventeenth Century, 1601-1700:* Opechancanough; Pocahontas; Powhatan; John Smith.

May 19, 1622
JANISSARY REVOLT AND OSMAN II'S ASSASSINATION

Members of the elite Ottoman Janissary corps assassinated Sultan Osman II after they mutinied and overthrew his government. The Janissaries were deeply opposed to planned corps reform.

LOCALE: Constantinople, Ottoman Empire (now Istanbul, Turkey)

CATEGORIES: Government and politics; organizations and institutions; wars, uprisings, and civil unrest

KEY FIGURES
Osman II (1603-1622), Ottoman sultan, r. 1618-1622
Kösem Sultan (c. 1585-1651), Queen Mother and Osman's stepmother
Dilawar Paşa (d. 1622), Ottoman grand vizier, 1621-1622
Davud Paşa (d. 1623), Ottoman grand vizier, 1622

SUMMARY OF EVENT
In 1617, Sultan Ahmed I died after a reign of fourteen years. Best remembered for his monumental Blue Mosque (Ahmediye Mosque), his reign epitomized the dynastic flaccidity that had set in since the death of Süleyman the Magnificent in 1566. Until this time, sons of reigning sultans had been sent to the provinces to learn administrative skills as *sanjak beys* (provincial governors). Ahmed I was the first sultan to not have had this experience, and his successors, like him, were brought up in the harem, learning only what the women and eunuchs cared to teach them.

Ottoman succession practices in earlier times had been based upon the law of fratricide, the practice whereby a new ruler ordered the execution of his brothers and their male children, and also the execution of pregnant imperial concubines (*haseki*). With Ahmed's accession to the throne, this practice ceased because the sultan was only fourteen. The execution of his half brother, Mustafa, would have endangered the Ottoman succession. Eventually, Ahmed had three sons who survived: Osman II, by a concubine, Mahfiruz; and Murad IV and İbrahim, by another concubine, Kösem Sultan. Under usual circumstances, Osman should have succeeded, but a palace clique preferred the late sultan's half brother Mustafa, whose reign of a few months (1617-1618) proved so incompetent that the *sheyhülislam* (chief judge), Esat Efendi, working with Osman's mother, Mahfiruz, managed Mustafa's deposition and his substitution by Osman II. Osman possessed considerable energy and de-

termination, which was unusual for seventeenth century sultans.

A simmering problem for the new administration was the frontier with Poland. In 1615, landowners in southeastern Poland invaded Moldavia (an Ottoman vassal) to intervene in the succession. In 1617, Iskender Paşa, *beylerbey* (governor-general) of Özü (Ochakov), retaliated, taking ten thousand men into Moldavia to a stand off with the Poles at Busza, where an agreement was signed. Poland agreed to not interfere in Moldavia, Walachia, and Transylvania and to curb Cossack depredations, while the Ottomans were to do the same regarding the Crimean Tatars. This treaty, however, was disregarded by the Polish king, Sigismund III Vasa, who, staunchly pro-Habsburg, attacked the prince of Transylvania, Gabriel Bethlen, an Ottoman protege. On September 18, 1620, Iskender Paşa attacked a Polish force under its commander, Stanislas Zolkiewski, at Cecora, overwhelming it and sending Zolkiewski's head to Constantinople. However, the Poles rallied and established a strong bridgehead at Khotin (now in the Ukraine).

Sultan Osman II then led his own troops (an increasingly rare phenomenon during the seventeenth century). For weeks, the Ottomans tried to assail the Polish defenses, with a final, unsuccessful assault on September 28, 1621. Irritated by the conduct of the Janissaries, whom he berated publicly, Osman renegotiated the 1617 Treaty of Busza.

Osman's brief experience in the field came at a time when Ottoman reformers were advocating fundamental internal changes. The moment seemed ripe for the sultan to take the initiative, but reform programs inevitably threaten vested interests, and the inexperienced sultan soon faced major opposition. Traditionally, the *sheyhülislam* made all clerical appointments, but Osman transferred this function to himself. Esat Efendi was left with his juridical authority intact, but he soon became a bitter opponent, along with dismissed officials from Mustafa's brief reign and the entourage of his stepmother, Kösem.

More serious, however, was his conflict with the army—the Janissaries and the *sipahi* of the palace (cavalry units stationed in the capital)—recruited from non-Turks, mainly through the *devshirme* system, the so-called tribute of Christian slave-boys from the Balkan provinces. Osman had been angered by the performance of these units on campaign (and they were disappointed with his leadership), but the issue transcended mere irri-

1620's

tation. Since the glorious days of Süleyman the Magnificent, great changes had come over military life. The days of highly mobile border warfare had come to an end with the virtual closing of the Hungarian and Caucasian frontiers. In war zones far distant from Constantinople, where siege warfare was replacing mobile raiding, the actual fighting was becoming arduous and dangerous, with little expectation of booty. The disgruntled soldiers still were recruited through the *devshirme*, which could no longer provide the numbers of troops needed. Osman thought that he knew the solution.

It is by no means certain that the ideas for reform originated with the sultan himself, who, in 1621, was still a teenager, although he had learned much in the past three years. More probably, the ideas came from his grand vizier, Dilawar Paşa, appointed in September, 1621. A *devshirme* boy of Croat origin, he had risen through the ranks of the palace service to enjoy successively the offices of *beylerbey* of Cyprus, Baghdad, Erivan, and Di-

Two Ottoman Janissary corps members wearing elaborate headdress. (The Granger Collection)

yarbakir. He had accompanied the sultan to the Siege of Khotin (1621), where the sultan elevated him to the grand viziership. It was Dilawar who proposed a practical solution to the problem of military recruitment: Abolish the *devshirme*, which could not provide sufficient recruits but instead created a corporate truculence toward authority, and expand the Janissaries' numbers with free-born Turkish recruits from Anatolia and Syria. Dilawar urged the sultan to leave Constantinople for Anatolia for his own safety, since the reform would be highly controversial. The sultan's pretext for leaving would be the pilgrimage to Mecca. This was logical but dangerous advice, only to be implemented if the sultan could secretly escape from his capital, a hotbed of Janissary discontent, including growing resentment of the sultan.

Hearing a rumor that Osman planned to leave for Mecca, the Janissaries, along with discontented *ulama* and bureaucrats, assembled in the Blue Mosque in May, 1622, to demand that he forgo his pilgrimage, but the meeting quickly got out of hand: The *sheyhülislam* produced a *fetva* (a religious decree) declaring the sultan's evil advisers worthy of death. The sultan agreed to abandon his pilgrimage, but the Janissaries demanded the grand vizier's death, and a mob broke into the palace and lynched him and other high officials (May 19). The sultan was then deposed and taken to Yedikule, the Castle of the Seven Towers, Constantinople's bastille.

The Janissaries and the city mob were being secretly manipulated by Davud Paşa, a Bosnian product of the *devshirme* system, and a one-time *beylerbey* of Rumelia, who had served briefly as Kapudan Paşa (grand admiral) and had accompanied Osman on the Khotin campaign. He had married a sister of deposed sultan Mustafa I and was now acting on behalf of the future valide sultan, Kösem. As Osman's stepmother, she was eager to be rid of him, fearing that, in the Ottoman tradition, he would order the execution of his half brothers. For the present, with her own sons mere children, she and Davud arranged to have the deposed Mustafa I brought from his gilded captivity and restored to the throne (May 20), at which time she appointed Davud grand vizier.

Osman clearly could not be left alive, and Davud promptly departed with his accomplices for Yedikule. Osman must have known why he had come, but he was young and put up a tremendous struggle. According to the Ottoman writer, Evliya Çelebi, it took several men to overcome him. One of the late sultan's ears was sent to the vengeful Kösem, and a finger was lopped off to obtain a valuable ring. As the English ambassador Sir Thomas Roe astutely observed, "this was . . . the first emperour that they ever laid violent hands on; a fatal signe, I think, of their declynation."

SIGNIFICANCE

Although fratricide within the palace was an Ottoman tradition, Osman's execution was, as Roe remarked, the first time that a sultan had been murdered by his subjects. It set a grim precedent, often repeated in the years that followed. Above all else, it illustrated the arrogance of the Janissary corps and its growing appetite for mutiny and mayhem. The *devshirme* system itself, which Osman and Dilawar had rightly identified as the problem, was abolished by Osman's half brother, Murad IV, but the corps survived, passing through various mutations until Mahmud II (1808-1839) ordered in 1826 its disbandment and the massacre of its rank-and-file.

Not long after the wretched Osman had been murdered, the Janissaries, with the waywardness typical of mobs, displayed overwhelming remorse for what they had done. The feeble-minded Mustafa I survived only a few months (1622-1623) and was soon returned to isolation. Davud was dismissed from the grand viziership (1622) and later executed (1623), along with his associates. In the ensuing chaos, widespread protests by the *ulama* led to the accession of the eleven-year-old Murad IV with his mother, Kösem Sultan, acing as regent on his behalf.

—*Gavin R. G. Hambly*

FURTHER READING

Goodwin, Godfrey. *The Janissaries*. London: Saqi Books, 1997. An excellent account of the rise and fall of the Janissary corps.

Imber, Colin. *The Ottoman Empire, 1300-1650: The Structure of Power*. New York: Palgrave, 2002. An updated overview of the period.

Kinross, Lord. *The Ottoman Centuries*. New York: Morrow Quill, 1977. A popular account of Ottoman history, including Osman II's misadventures.

Murphey, Rhoads. *Ottoman Warfare, 1500-1700*. New Brunswick, N.J.: Rutgers University Press, 1999. A sophisticated analysis of the Ottoman war machine, in which the Janissaries played a central role.

Pierce, Leslie P. *The Imperial Harem: Women and Sovereignty in the Ottoman Empire*. Oxford, England: Oxford University Press, 1963. A groundbreaking study of the central institution of the Ottoman Empire. Essential reading.

SEE ALSO: 1603-1617: Reign of Sultan Ahmed I; 1609-1617: Construction of the Blue Mosque; 1623-1640: Murad IV Rules the Ottoman Empire; 1638: Waning of the *Devshirme* System; 1677-1681: Ottoman-Muscovite Wars.

RELATED ARTICLES in *Great Lives from History: The Seventeenth Century, 1601-1700:* Kösem Sultan; Murad IV; Sigismund III Vasa.

1623-1640
MURAD IV RULES THE OTTOMAN EMPIRE

In seventeen years as sultan, Murad reversed the decline that threatened to destroy the Ottoman Empire; however, to revive and strengthen the empire, Murad imposed repressive measures and draconian penalties, including death, upon his subjects.

LOCALE: Ottoman Empire and Iran
CATEGORIES: Wars, uprisings, and civil unrest; government and politics

KEY FIGURES

Murad IV (1612-1640), Ottoman sultan, r. 1623-1640
Mustafa I (1591-1639), Ottoman sultan, r. 1617-1618, 1622-1623
Kösem Sultan (c. 1585-1651), mother of Murad IV and İbrahim
İbrahim (1615-1648), Ottoman sultan, r. 1640-1648

ʿAbbās the Great (1571-1629), shah of Persia, r. 1587-1629

SUMMARY OF EVENT

Although the official reign of Murad IV as sultan began in 1623, when he was eleven years old, his role as an active and independent leader did not commence until 1632, when he definitively grasped the reins of power. The Ottoman Empire and much of the western world were in decline when Murad was thrust into the sultancy after the forced deposition of his predecessor, the mentally unfit Mustafa I, who became sultan on November 22, 1617. Murad was replaced by his half brother Osman II on February 26, 1618, after serving for only three months.

Osman served for four years but was deposed in 1622. When this happened, the Janissary corps (an elite military), which had gained considerable control over the Ottoman Empire, forced Mustafa to resume the sultancy, which he did on May 19, 1622. He was deposed a second time on September 10, 1623 when his mental problems rendered him unfit to rule.

Eleven-year-old Murad IV took control in this chaotic political climate. For the next nine years, he ruled with his mother, Kösem Sultan, who served as his regent. Kösem, chastened by the influence the harem had exerted over Selim II and Murad III, nudged Murad IV toward homosexuality so that the harem could not influence him and thus regain control and reestablish what had been derisively dubbed the Sultancy of Women during previous reigns.

Kösem sought suitable advisers, called *viziers*, to guide her son's sultancy, but often she found herself in a political maelstrom as the Janissaries, the guard of the empire that became shamelessly corrupt, worked strenuously to direct the way she was grooming the sultan for his role as leader of his people. The Ottoman Empire suffered several major defeats during the first years of Murad's reign.

Among these defeats was a revolt of the Janissaries, whose leader received support and encouragement from the Iranian shah ʿAbbās the Great. Another defeat was the loss of Baghdad and parts of Iraq to ʿAbbās in 1624. At this time, the Ottoman treasury was virtually empty. The government's inability to pay the Janissaries their stipends triggered a revolt. The adolescent sultan, even though the official ruler of the empire, seemed powerless to stem the tide that was leading his people and empire toward destruction.

Finally, in 1632, facing a distrustful and discontented central government, Murad had to act decisively. Members of the cavalry, the *sipahi*, stormed the sultan's palace and demanded that the grand vizier and sixteen of Murad's most important officials be executed; and they were. Murad took immediate control, marking the "true" start of his reign. Murad, at this time twenty years old, overcame his mother's dominating regency and was now sultan alone.

Among his early acts was the closing of Turkey's coffeehouses and taverns, places Murad believed to be seditious. He imposed curfews, prohibited homosexuality, and banned the use of alcohol, tobacco, and coffee. The enforcement of these mandates was draconian and immediate. Murad's executioner was not far from his side, carrying the hardware required to torture and execute "criminals" on the spot. Those who disobeyed the law—or were even suspected of disobeying it—were summarily executed without a trial.

Murad IV. (Hulton|Archive by Getty Images)

Murad became the most brutal and sadistic of rulers. He would himself kill those who came too close to his palace or who annoyed him in any way. He also was an excellent archer, and from the gardens of his palace he regularly shot arrows into crowds of people outside the palace walls merely to watch them suffer after being hit and then die. He demonstrated little regard for human life, as his actions in the provinces and in Iran would soon tell.

As his empire declined during the first nine years of his reign, Murad's government officials, most of whom had paid bribes to secure their appointments, became increasingly corrupt. His provincial governors, who were expected to send tax moneys to Constantinople (the empire's capital), often kept such revenues for themselves, which brought the empire to the point of insolvency.

Murad personally journeyed into rebellious Ottoman provinces in the Balkans and Anatolia, where he made examples of dissident officials by executing them in public. In one case, he had the legs of a province official amputated while the assembled throng watched this once-powerful person bleed to death. He also redistributed land, making sure that every new recipient swore loyalty to him and was firmly committed to serving in his army.

In 1635, Murad began a military assault on Iran that lasted until the fall of Baghdad in December of 1638. He was determined to retake Ottoman lands that had been claimed by Iran under the leadership of Shah ʿAbbās the Great. His enormous army left Constantinople in May, 1638, and marched to Baghdad. Murad's first assault upon the city occurred on November 16. The fighting continued fiercely until December 25.

The strong, resolute, and brave Murad set an example for his soldiers by fighting beside them in the battlefield, eating what they ate, and sleeping on the ground beside them. His brutality came to light again when, after his conquest of Baghdad, he ordered the execution of all Persian (Iranian) soldiers in the garrison, by some estimates as many as thirty thousand. This slaughter apparently was accomplished in the period of one or two days. Only three hundred of the garrison's soldiers survived. Shortly thereafter, when a powder magazine exploded accidentally and killed some of Murad's army, he ordered the execution of an estimated thirty thousand more Persians, mostly women and children.

Finally, in May of 1639, having regained Baghdad, the Ottoman lands of the Caucasus that had been lost to Iran, and the portion of Iraq held by the Ṣafavids, Murad and the Iranians agreed to the Treaty of Kasr-i Shirin, which established boundaries between the Ottoman Empire and Iran. The boundaries specified in this treaty continued intact for more than two centuries.

Having restored the strength of the Ottoman Empire, although at the expense of the populace that he shamelessly oppressed, Murad fell ill early in 1640. He died on February 9, 1640, felled ironically by cirrhosis of the liver, which resulted from his excessive drinking. Because, at age twenty-eight, he died without issue, his brother, İbrahim, was next in line of succession. From his deathbed, Murad ordered İbrahim's execution. Kösem, Murad and İbrahim's mother, overruled Murad's order. At Murad's deathbed, she assured him that his execution order had been carried out (though it was not), whereupon Murad smiled cruelly and died.

SIGNIFICANCE

Murad IV was a gifted and intelligent leader, physically strong, capable of assessing difficult situations and turning them to his and his empire's advantage. Despite this, he had gone through life never having his ideas challenged. One dared not disagree with the sultan because the penalty for disagreement was death. He was, after 1632, an absolute ruler who insisted that his every wish become everyone's command.

As a result of his rule, the Ottomans regained the lands they had lost to Iran during the ineffective reigns of several previous sultans. From the sultancies of Selim II to Mustafa I, a period of sixty-two years, the position of the empire in world politics declined precipitously, and its treasury teetered on the brink of collapse. By assessing the situation and acting decisively to eliminate its causes, Murad single-handedly turned the empire around. When he died, he left behind an empire of renewed vigor and financial integrity but with a demoralized populace that almost universally rejoiced at his death.

—*R. Baird Shuman*

FURTHER READING

Barber, Noel. *The Sultans.* New York: Simon and Schuster, 1973. Barber presents a detailed account of the life of Murad IV, with vivid descriptions of his atrocities.

Goodwin, Godfrey. *The Janissaries.* London: Saqi Books, 1997. A comprehensive overview of the Janissaries and the role they played in the early life of Murad IV.

_____. *Ottoman Turkey.* London: Scorpion, 1977. Goodwin offers a detailed presentation of the politics and intrigues in the empire under Murad IV.

Mansel, Philip. *Constantinople: City of the World's Desire, 1453-1924.* New York: St. Martin's Press, 1996. A brief but insightful account of Murad's rule.

Somel, Selcuk Aksin. *Historical Dictionary of the Ottoman Empire.* Lanham, Md.: Scarecrow Press, 2003. An important work on Ottoman history.

SEE ALSO: 17th cent.: Rise of the Gunpowder Empires; 1602-1639: Ottoman-Ṣafavid Wars; 1603-1617: Reign of Sultan Ahmed I; Sept., 1606-June, 1609: Great Jelālī Revolts; Nov. 11, 1606: Treaty of Zsitvatorok; Beginning c. 1615: Coffee Culture Flourishes; May 19, 1622: Janissary Revolt and Osman II's Assassination; 1629: Ṣafavid Dynasty Flourishes Under ʿAbbās the Great; Sept. 2, 1633: Great Fire of Constantinople and Murad's Reforms; 1638: Waning of the *Devshirme* System; 1642-1666: Reign of Shah ʿAbbās II; Aug. 22, 1645-Sept., 1669: Turks Conquer Crete; 1656-1662: Persecution of Iranian Jews; 1656-1676: Ottoman Empire's Brief Recovery.

RELATED ARTICLES in *Great Lives from History: The Seventeenth Century, 1601-1700:* ʿAbbās the Great; Merzifonlu Kara Mustafa Paşa; Kâtib Çelebî; Kösem Sultan; Murad IV; Mustafa I.

1623-1674
EARLIEST CALCULATORS APPEAR

Schickard, Pascal, and Leibniz built the first mechanical calculators. These machines marked the beginning of automatic computation, as mechanical levers, gears, and wheels replaced the human mind, performing more quickly and, in many cases, more accurately.

LOCALE: Tübingen, Württemberg (now in Germany); Rouen and Paris, France
CATEGORIES: Science and technology; inventions; mathematics

KEY FIGURES
John Napier (1550-1617), Scottish mathematician and eighth lord of Merchiston
Wilhelm Schickard (1592-1635), German minister and mathematician
Blaise Pascal (1623-1662), French scientist and religious philosopher
Gottfried Wilhelm Leibniz (1646-1716), German philosopher and mathematician

SUMMARY OF EVENT
In the seventeenth century, a great leap in methods of calculation occurred with the introduction of the first mechanical calculating machines and the beginning of automatic computation. Mechanical levers, gears, and wheels were built to perform the tedious, laborious calculations involved in mathematics, astronomy, surveying, financial transactions, and other areas.

The struggle to develop quicker and more accurate methods of calculations had been occurring for centuries. The earliest physical aids to calculation included the abacus, tally sticks, quadrants, sectors, compasses, and slide rules. In the early seventeenth century, John Napier developed logarithms, an ingenious method for multiplying and dividing used in the early calculators. Napier's *Rabdologiae, seu Numerationis per Virgulas Libri Duo* (1617; *Study of Divining Rods, or Two Books of Numbering by Means of Rods*, 1667) described a device referred to as "Napier's bones," a precursor of the slide rule. Developments in clock making and the building of automata in the seventeenth century also aided the development of mechanical calculators to perform the four standard arithmetic functions, addition, subtraction, multiplication, and division.

The Lutheran minister Wilhelm Schickard became a professor of biblical languages at the University of Tü-

bingen, Württemberg in 1619. His research also encompassed astronomy and mathematics. Schickard worked with the astronomer Johannes Kepler, and their discussions regarding Napier's logarithms inspired Schickard to design a calculator to automate the process of multiplication. His research in astronomy had driven him to develop skills as a mechanic as he struggled to build his own astronomical instruments. Those skills enabled him to build a mechanical calculator in 1623.

Schickard's machine used wheels with ten teeth, one for each of the digits 0-9. Each wheel represented a "place" in a numeral: There was a units wheel, a tens wheel, a hundreds wheel, and so forth. The machine's carry mechanism carried from each wheel to the next higher wheel when the lower wheel turned from 9 to 0. However, the carry mechanism only worked for up to six digits. The force required to produce a carry from six to seven digits (that is, from 999,999 to 1,000,000) would have damaged gears on the unit wheel. To compensate for this limitation, the machine incorporated brass rings: Every time a carry was propagated past 6 digits, a bell would ring, and the operator could slip a brass ring on his finger to remind him how many times the carry had propagated past six digits. Thus, each ring on the operator's finger stood for one million units.

Blaise Pascal, a mathematician, also struggled with the laborious methods of calculation. While Pascal was not aware of Schickard's machine, he was inspired to design a calculator to relieve the boring routine of calculations his father needed for tax assessing and collecting in Rouen, France. Like Schickard, Pascal was dissatisfied with the skills of local craftspeople and taught himself the mechanical skills necessary to create a calculating device. Pascal also delved into blacksmithing to experiment with different materials for the gears.

Pascal built about fifty calculators. Most of these calculators had eight wheels, but one had as many as ten. The top of the machine contained toothed wheels and two series of windows above them to show results. The upper windows showed results for addition and the lower for subtraction. Subtraction was accomplished using a method called "nines complement addition," because the wheels in the machine could not be turned backward.

Due to its use of the technical "nines complement" method, Pascal's device required more mathematical knowledge by the operator than did Schickard's machine. Pascal's versatile machines operated in French monetary units (livres, sols, and deniers) as well as decimals, however. His machines, like Schickard's, performed multiplication and division, but the process was awkward and unwieldy, using repeated additions or subtractions. Unlike Schickard, Pascal did not rely on a single-tooth gear for the carry mechanism. Pascal's solution used falling weights rather than gears. Thus, the strain on gears that limited Schickard's machine did not limit Pascal's. His machines, however, were susceptible to producing inaccurate results by generating extra carries.

Another mathematician and philosopher, Gottfried Wilhelm Leibniz, set out to improve upon Pascal's work. Leibniz served as adviser to the elector of Mainz, and he needed to plan a way to distract the French from their focus on attacking German lands. He intended to draw France's attention to Egypt by campaigning for a united European effort to conquer the non-Christian world. Leibniz traveled extensively during this campaign and became aware of Pascal's work while in Paris. Leibniz designed a device to be attached to the top of a machine like Pascal's and allow it to do multiplication more easily. However, Leibniz either did not have enough information on Pascal's machine or did not understand it properly, and the device would not have worked.

Leibniz developed his own mechanical multiplier around 1671. The key component of this machine was the stepped drum, or reckoner, which had cogs of varying lengths. The problem of a correct propagation of a carry plagued Leibniz, as it had Schickard and Pascal. The carry mechanism Leibniz designed did not properly handle the calculation if a carry from one digit to the next then produced another carry to the next higher digit. Leibniz handled this problem by designing the mechanism so that a point from a disk in the mechanism would protrude if a propagating carry occurred. The operator would then notice the point and push the disk to propagate the carry manually. Thus, Leibniz's machine was not fully automatic.

Leibniz demonstrated his machine in 1672 at the Royal Society in London. Because of comments on his machine, Leibniz began work on improvements and alterations. However, the same problems that Schickard and Pascal had encountered, inadequate workmen and materials, also hindered Leibniz. After tracking down a highly skilled clockmaker to assist in the construction, Leibniz built a new machine in 1674. This machine design incorporated a mechanical version of the shift-and-add procedure used on digital electronic computers in the twentieth century. Leibniz's stepped drum remained the

1620's

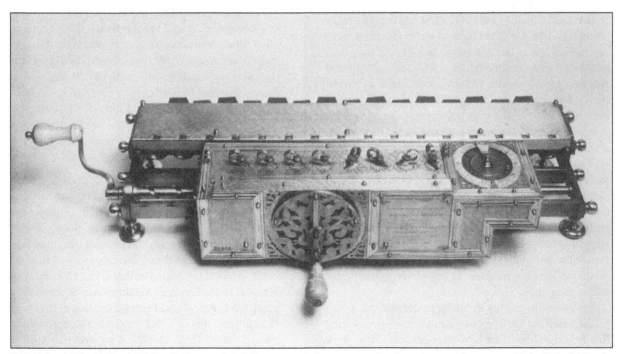

Leibniz's mechanical multiplying device was not fully automatic because carries that propagated across multiple digits had to be handled manually. (The Granger Collection)

only practical means to build a workable calculator until the development of variable-toothed gears in the late nineteenth century.

Leibniz never achieved his goal of building a larger machine to mechanize all human reasoning processes by assigning a number to all possible thoughts and thus end fruitless arguing. However, he did develop binary arithmetic. While he never connected this system with his mechanical calculator, binary arithmetic would provide a system particularly suited to the electronics used in twentieth century computers.

SIGNIFICANCE

While there had been attempts to mechanize calculations before 1623, they had required substantial human intervention. The machines invented in the seventeenth century differed significantly from their predecessors, because they attempted to automate the entire process, including the carry mechanism. The appearance of these earliest automatic calculators influenced intellectual and mathematical development, since the designers needed to develop calculation techniques to get levers, gears, and wheels to move in the ways required to do simple arithmetic.

The early calculators responded to a growing need for more, and more precise, calculations resulting from a significant increase in astronomical data, financial bureaucracies, colonial land acquisition, and other forms of numerical data generated by new technologies of measurement, such as the barometer. In addition, they both responded and contributed to a scientific culture that was developing precise scientific laws, such as Robert Boyle's law, Johannes Kepler's laws of planetary motion, and Sir Isaac Newton's laws of motion and gravitation, which understood the physical world in terms of mathematical formulas.

The computers of the twentieth century owe the most to the work of Leibniz, his stepped reckoner, his development of binary arithmetic, and the shift-and-add procedure for multiplication. However, one of the earliest programming languages used on the electronic computers was named after Pascal in recognition of his accomplishments. Pascal built his machine at the age of nineteen and produced the first mechanical calculator available for sale to the public.

Seventeenth century calculators constituted a significant step in the efforts to automate human reasoning that would follow in the next three centuries. The work of Schickard, Pascal, and Leibniz inspired and influenced the work of later inventors in the seventeenth,

eighteenth, and nineteenth centuries who would achieve the goal of fully automating (and accurately performing) the standard arithmetic functions of addition, subtraction, multiplication, and division. This work provided the foundation for the electronic computers of the twentieth century, which automated far more than these functions but continued using basic techniques developed in the seventeenth century.

—*Linda Eikmeier Endersby*

FURTHER READING

Adamson, Donald. *Blaise Pascal: Mathematician, Physicist, and Thinker About God*. New York: St. Martin's Press, 1995. Biography of Pascal that includes information on Pascal's calculator and minor information on Schickard and Leibniz.

Aspray, William, ed. *Computing Before Computers*. Ames: Iowa State University Press, 1990. A series of essays describing developments in computational technology before the modern computer. The first essay in particular provides coverage of pre-nineteenth century developments.

Spencer, Donald D. *Great Men and Women of Computing*. Ormond Beach, Fla.: Camelot, 1996. Accessible essays on individual contributors to the history of computing, including Pascal and Leibniz.

_____. *The Timetable of Computers: A Chronology of the Most Important People and Events in the History of Computers*. 2d ed. Ormond Beach, Fla.: Camelot, 1999. Illustrated chronology of events in the development of computing from the earliest days to the twentieth century. Includes comprehensive index.

Williams, Michael R. *A History of Computing Technology*. 2d ed. Los Alamitos, Calif.: IEEE Computer Society Press, 1997. A survey of the development of calculating and computing machines and technology from earliest times to the twentieth century.

SEE ALSO: 1601-1672: Rise of Scientific Societies; Sept., 1608: Invention of the Telescope; 1609-1619: Kepler's Laws of Planetary Motion; 1610: Galileo Confirms the Heliocentric Model of the Solar System; 1612: Sanctorius Invents the Clinical Thermometer; 1615-1696: Invention and Development of the Calculus; 1637: Descartes Publishes His *Discourse on Method*; 1643: Torricelli Measures Atmospheric Pressure; 1654: Pascal and Fermat Devise the Theory of Probability; 1660's-1700: First Microscopic Observations; 1660-1692: Boyle's Law and the Birth of Modern Chemistry; Late Dec., 1671: Newton Builds His Reflecting Telescope; 1676: Sydenham Advocates Clinical Observation; Dec. 7, 1676: Rømer Calculates the Speed of Light; Summer, 1687: Newton Formulates the Theory of Universal Gravitation; July 25, 1698: Savery Patents the First Successful Steam Engine.

RELATED ARTICLES in *Great Lives from History: The Seventeenth Century, 1601-1700:* Robert Boyle; Galileo; Johannes Kepler; Gottfried Wilhelm Leibniz; Sir Isaac Newton; Blaise Pascal; Wilhelm Schickard.

1624-1640's
JAPAN'S SECLUSION POLICY

Japan's Tokugawa shogunate introduced a series of laws, referred to collectively as the sakoku, *or seclusion policy, that placed limits on foreign trade and outlawed foreign travel. The policy sought to eliminate the influence of Christianity in Japan and to prevent daimyos from gaining an advantage against the central authorities by trading directly with the West.*

LOCALE: Japan

CATEGORIES: Diplomacy and international relations; government and politics; trade and commerce; economics; cultural and intellectual history

KEY FIGURES

Tokugawa Iemitsu (1604-1651), Japanese shogun, r. 1623-1651

Toyotomi Hideyoshi (1537-1598), Japanese daimyo and national unifier

Tokugawa Ieyasu (1543-1616), Japanese shogun, r. 1603-1605

SUMMARY OF EVENT

The Tokugawa shogunate was established by Tokugawa Ieyasu in 1603. After nearly 150 years of civil war, Ieyasu defeated all of his major rivals, consolidated central power, and began to take legal and administrative steps to ensure that power would remain in the hands of his family. To this end, disruptive influences like Toyotomi Hideyori, the son of Ieyasu's predecessor, Toyotomi Hideyoshi, were eliminated. Legal codes like the *Buke shohatto*, a series of laws governing the samurai warrior houses, were also enacted in order to ensure the continued loyalty of the various feudal lords, or daimyos, to the Tokugawa family. Other elements in Japanese society proved harder to control, however.

Christianity, since its arrival in Japan in the 1540's, had made major gains, particularly in the southern island of Kyūshū. Since the time of Hideyoshi, however, Christianity was believed by the Japanese elite to be a dangerous influence and an obstacle to the centralization of

power. Hideyoshi began to persecute Christians in 1587, and while Ieyasu was initially sympathetic to the faith because of his desire to trade with European nations, persecution of Christianity began again in earnest in the 1610's. Under Tokugawa Iemitsu, the third Tokugawa shogun, who inherited the office in 1623, the persecution of Christians in Kyūshū increased in severity. The Spanish, suspected by the government of transporting priests to Japan and supporting those hiding in the country, were expelled from Japan and banned from entering Japanese ports in 1624. This prohibition is considered the beginning of the legal measures that eventually became a comprehensive formal policy of national seclusion known as *sakoku*, or the "closed country" edicts.

After the expulsion of the Spanish, Iemitsu's persecution of Japanese Christians increased in intensity. Torture was used to force believers to abandon their faith or to inform on their fellows. Efforts to find and eliminate foreign priests hiding in Japan also increased. In 1633, another edict was promulgated requiring a license for anyone wishing to leave or enter Japan. Japanese who had lived abroad were banned from returning unless they met certain strict conditions or had been unavoidably detained for a short period. A stricter system of searches for foreign priests was commenced, and significant cash rewards were offered to those who would turn them in. Another, more strict edict was promulgated in the following year. Sailing abroad was forbidden. Japanese caught trying to enter the country were to be executed. These harsh measures enacted against Japanese trying either to leave or to enter the country were intended to block any further Christian influence.

In 1637, as a result of persecution and oppressive land taxes, peasants in the Shimabara region of northern Kyūshū revolted against the local lords and the shogunate. The revolt was brutally suppressed and all thirty-seven thousand participants were massacred in the following year. During the revolt, the Dutch, whose Protestant beliefs the shogun Iemitsu did not see as dan-

JAPAN C. 1640

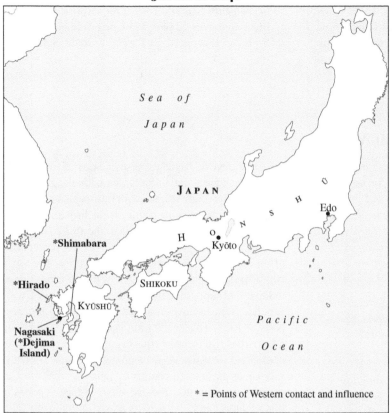

* = Points of Western contact and influence

While scholars often focus on the anti-Christian elements of Japan's policy of national seclusion, Tokugawa Iemitsu's *sakoku* edicts may also be seen as an attempt to reorient power relations in the region. The Dutch, Koreans, and Chinese were required to pay tribute to the shogun, and this requirement has been increasingly interpreted as an attempt by the Japanese leadership to create the illusion of a total primacy of Japanese rule in world affairs. In the context of Japanese domestic politics, this type of illusion proved useful, as it allowed the government to claim a greater level of authority and legitimacy. Also important in the context of domestic power relations was the shogunate's monopoly on trade. Trade was strictly controlled by the central authorities, ensuring that regional lords could not gain an advantage in technology by trading with the West or gain a financial advantage through the lucrative trade with Asian nations. In short, not only was the *sakoku* policy a means of controlling and eventually stamping out Christian influence, it was also a means by which the shogunate was able to increase its power over the rest of Japan's daimyos.

gerous, were recruited to assist the shogunate by bombarding the rebels from the sea.

After the rebellion was put down, the final elements of the policy of national seclusion were put into place. In 1639, the Portuguese, former strong trading partners, were barred from entering Japanese ports because of suspicion that they were continuing to transport foreign priests to Japan. In 1641, the Dutch were moved from their factory at Hirado to the island of Dejima in Nagasaki harbor. The Dutch, along with Chinese and Korean merchants, were allowed to continue trading with Japan, but their actions were strictly controlled. These groups continued to be very influential in Japan: The Dutch imported scientific and medical knowledge, as well as information about events in the outside world, while the Chinese influenced the nation's artistic and literary culture. Together, they made Nagasaki into something of a cosmopolitan center. However, with the exception of this carefully controlled center of cosmopolitanism, Japan had effectively closed its borders to contact with other nations.

SIGNIFICANCE

The policy of seclusion, while by no means total, had a great impact on the character of Japanese society during the Edo period (1603-1867). The strict control of information from the outside world combined with the prohibitions keeping most of the individual domains from engaging in international trade or travel helped to maintain the power structure established by Tokugawa Ieyasu in the early seventeenth century. The *sakoku* policy was a major factor in the shogunate's ability to maintain a rigid social order for over 250 years. The policy also effectively forced Japan's burgeoning Christian community underground. Japanese Christians still practiced their faith in hiding but were unable to worship publicly until the 1870's. This was seen as a necessary measure to maintain order by the Tokugawa.

Trade with the Dutch, as well as with Chinese and Korean merchants, was still carried out under strict conditions. Despite the official seclusion policy, foreign knowledge was studied by a small number of Japanese scholars. European languages and medicine proved influential. In addition, Chinese painting and verse continued to form the main cultural pursuits of a small intellectual elite. Despite this limited contact, however, the seclusion policies ultimately resulted in the deterioration of Japanese science and military technology, which had rivaled that of the Western powers in the seventeenth century. Developments in the West eventually led to the reopening of Japan to foreign contact through gunboat diplomacy, which neither the Tokugawa nor individual domains were able to resist.

—*Matthew Penney*

FURTHER READING

Chaiklin, Martha. *Cultural Commerce and Dutch Commercial Culture: The Influence of European Material Culture on Japan, 1700-1850.* Leiden, the Netherlands: Leiden University Press, 2003. Discusses the impact of the Dutch under the *sakoku* system.

Hesselink, Reinier. *Prisoners from Nambu: Reality and Make-Believe in Seventeenth-Century Japanese Diplomacy.* Honolulu: University of Hawaii Press, 2001. An extended discussion of the place of the

Dutch traders in the world view of the Japanese shogunate in the seventeenth century.

Toby, Ronald. *State and Diplomacy in Early Modern Japan: Asia in the Development of the Tokugawa Bakufu.* Princeton, N.J.: Princeton University Press, 1984. A discussion of the role of Asia in the formation of Japan's seclusion policies and the continued relationship between Japan and China and Korea in the early Edo period.

Totman, Conrad. *Early Modern Japan.* Berkeley: University of California Press, 1993. The most comprehensive single-volume treatment of the Edo period in English. Includes a comprehensive discussion of the development of the policy of seclusion and its lasting effects.

SEE ALSO: 1602-1613: Japan Admits Western Traders; 1603: Tokugawa Shogunate Begins; Jan. 27, 1614: Japanese Ban Christian Missionaries; 1615: Promulgation of the *Buke shohatto* and *Kinchū narabini kuge shohatto*; 1617: Edo's Floating World District; Oct., 1637-Apr. 15, 1638: Shimabara Revolt; 1651-1680: Ietsuna Shogunate; 1680-1709: Reign of Tsunayoshi as Shogun.

RELATED ARTICLES in *Great Lives from History: The Seventeenth Century, 1601-1700:* Tokugawa Ieyasu; Tokugawa Tsunayoshi.

c. 1625
FORMATION OF THE KUBA KINGDOM

The Kuba kingdom formed a centralized military and commercial power developed out of the diverse ethnic communities along the savanna and rain forest border of the upper Congo River. The kingdom emerged through a process of migration, population growth, political innovation, and the introduction and adaptation of several New World crops brought to Africa by the Portuguese. Also, Kuba art remains among the most influential cultural achievements of the early modern era, and is highly valued.

LOCALE: Central Africa, Democratic Republic of Congo

CATEGORIES: Government and politics; expansion and land acquisition; wars, uprisings, and civil unrest; economics; agriculture

KEY FIGURE

Shyaam the Great (fl. c. 1625), founder of the Kuba kingdom and its first ruler, r. c. 1625

SUMMARY OF EVENT

The Kuba kingdom was one of several new African states that emerged in central Africa during the sixteenth and seventeenth centuries. Their concurrent development suggests that shared economic influences and common political innovations contributed to their rise.

The Kuba state emerged on the fringe of the equatorial rain forest, in the modern Democratic Republic of Congo in the 1600's. The Kuba area lay between the Sankuru and Kasai Rivers, parallel tributaries of the Congo that rise south of the river. Linguistic and archaeological evidence suggest that the founders of the Kuba kingdom were Mongo-speaking immigrants who drifted from the rain forest to the north into the border of the savanna. On the savanna-forest fringe, these immigrants encountered ethnically diverse peoples, the dominant power among them being the Bushong, a Mongo-speaking community that lived along the Sankuru River.

Because there are no written records of Kuba history before the eighteenth century, little is known about this crucial period. However, Kuba myth and oral tradition provide insight into the origins of the state. The Kuba believe they are descended from a heroic ancestor named Woot. In one tradition, Woot stole a magic basket from the Kuba's creator god, only to have it returned to the Kuba king by a Pygmy. This tradition reflects the integration of the aboriginal Pygmy, or Twa, peoples of the region into the community that eventually became the Kuba kingdom. The story of Woot and his family form a central motif in Kuba rituals and art.

Kuba traditions attribute the kingdom's rise to the arrival of a great immigrant warrior and leader named Shyaam the Great, believed to have been the son of a local queen whose travels in the Kongo kingdom to the west brought him magical knowledge, which he employed to establish the kingdom. In a heroic tale similar to that told of the neighboring Luba Empire, Shyaam returned home from his travels, unseated a despotic ruler, and founded a new dynasty.

Under Shyaam and his successors, Kuba royalty tied together many diverse ethnic groups, though the chiefly clan was the Bushong. Bushong tradition tells of a process whereby the Bushong were chased from their homeland near the mouth of the Kwango River by the Yaka, a shadowy group of raiders involved in the wars with the neighboring state of Kongo and the Portuguese, some time after 1568, on the west African coast.

With Shyaam's arrival came the adoption of crops from the New World, such as maize and cassava, which Portuguese traders brought to Africa. Indeed, the introduction of New World crops appears to have played a critical role in the Kuba economy's expansion and diversification. Though the Kuba were not in direct contact with traders from the Atlantic coast, they were able to adapt many useful and lucrative new crops for trade shortly after they first appeared on the African continent. In addition to the staples maize and cassava, Kuba farmers grew peanuts, chili peppers, tobacco, and other crops for export. The expansion of agriculture encouraged population growth among the Kuba. It also fostered the growth of long-distance trade, strengthening Kuba rulers.

In the Kuba state, the Bushong clan successfully claimed a monopoly on royal power. However, the Bushong rulers had councils made up of representatives from the kingdom's major ethnic groups. At the state's height, the Kuba rulers relied on an administration of tax collectors and administrators to run their affairs. The Kuba economy supported not only the extensive Bushong royal family but also a class of wealthy aristocrats.

According to Jan Vansina, a Kuba historian, pre-Kuba politics in the region was focused on the collections of villages, which shared a common chief. These chiefs ruled with councils of elders and village leaders. Shyaam and his followers were able to play the rulers against one another, throwing their weight on one side in a power struggle between two leading chiefdoms. Between 1625 and 1680, this new Kuba state successfully integrated villages and chiefdoms from throughout the region.

KUBA POETRY THROUGH SONG AND DANCE

The Kuba ncok *is a lighthearted form of poetry accompanied by singing and dancing. Although the following three* ncok *were documented in 1953, the genre has existed for hundreds of years.*

The rooster sings during the night
The cuckoos provoked the rising of the moon
The rooster sang his cry
The rooster the Bushoong have taken.

The crocodile is dying in the water
The crocodile has become deaf
The huge crocodile has become blind.

The land of the goat, we are trampling it
The heaven of God, we touch it with the hand
I will go to the village of the dead, borne on the arms of men.
One day in the future, during the heat
The day of my death, don't bury me at the foot of the *ngum* tree
I fear its spines;
at the foot of the *buncweemy*
I fear the drops of water;
One day in the future, bury me on the main square near the tree *bushaang*
I want to hear the beat of the drumming and the rattles of the dancers!

Source: Jan Vansina (1953), excerpted in *The Horizon History of Africa*, edited by Alvin M. Josephy, Jr. (New York: American Heritage, 1971), p. 382.

The wealth of Kuba, which flowed from the trade and industry of the growing agricultural population of the region, sustained also one of the most fertile artistic traditions of central Africa. It supported commercial and aristocratic classes that identified themselves through the patronage and consumption of locally produced art. Kuba cloth weavers and designers were supported by aristocratic and royal patrons, who used the elaborate clothes, made from animal pelts, beads, woven fabric, and other exotic materials, as markers of royal and aristocratic status. Kuba masks were another important expression of the culture's artistic genius and were central to Kuba religious and social ceremonies.

Kuba wooden sculpture in particular was an art form that was brought to a remarkable degree of refinement by the craftspeople of this civilization. Most famous were the sculptures called *ndop*, which were commissioned as portraits of Kuba monarchs. This artistic tradition is associated with King Shyaam, who is said to have introduced the genre around 1700.

In addition to providing prestige to the ruling classes, Kuba art also played an important role in regional trade. Kuba textiles, woven from raffia cloth, were a highly valued trade good in regional commerce. Kuba traders conducted a brisk commerce in textiles with their neighbors, particularly with the Luba to the south.

The Kuba empire fell into decline in the nineteenth century and was incorporated into Belgian king Leopold II's Congo Empire by century's end (1884-1885). It was annexed to Belgium in 1908. Today the Kuba are considered an ethnic group in the Democratic Republic of Congo that traces its antecedents to the precolonial Kuba kingdom.

SIGNIFICANCE

The Kuba state was one of several similar centralized political entities to emerge in central Africa during the seventeenth century. Before this period, this region had been populated by scattered farming and fishing villages and by hunter-gatherer peoples. Under the leadership of monarchs of the Bushong clan, the Kuba kings forged a centralized state from a host of disparate ethnic groups, including the Kel, Pyaang, Ngeende, Bieeng, Ilebo, Kaam, Idiing, and Ngoombe.

Like the Lunda Empire to the south, Kuba state formation was encouraged by a process of migration, population growth, political innovation, and the introduction

and adaptation of several New World crops. These processes allowed Kuba monarchs to develop a powerful dynasty whose wealth was based on taxation from agriculture, manufacturing, and trade. However, the Kuba developed a highly specialized and distinctive artistic tradition that reflects its unique development. Kuba art showed the wealth, centralization, and social stratification that were hallmarks of this civilization. This artistic tradition played an important role in the formation of elite identity among the Kuba, and Kuba sculpture today is well-known and highly prized. It is often at the center of museum collections worldwide.

—*James Burns*

FURTHER READING

Edgerton, Robert B. *The Troubled Heart of Africa: A History of the Congo*. New York: St. Martin's Press, 2002. Edgerton provides a thorough and complete history of the Congo region, from the arrival of the Portuguese in the 1500's through the twentieth century.

Gondola, Ch. Didier. *The History of Congo*. Westport, Conn.: Greenwood Press, 2002. A survey of Congo's history, covering the Kuba and other kingdoms and peoples. Provides, also, biographical sketches of key figures in the region's history.

Vansina, Jan. *The Children of Woot*. Madison: University of Wisconsin Press, 1978. The standard text on Kuba history. Vansina is the author of dozens of books on the precolonial history, art, and politics of central Africa.

_____. *Kingdoms of the Savanna*. Madison: University of Wisconsin Press, 1968. An early and important work on state formation in central Africa.

_____. "The Peoples of the Forest." In *History of Central Africa*, edited by David Birmingham and Phyllis M. Martin. Vol. 1. New York: Longman, 1983. An excellent article about the Congo region.

SEE ALSO: Early 17th cent.: Rise of Rwanda; 17th cent.: Emergence of Luba Governance; Aug. 26, 1641-Sept., 1648: Conquest of Luanda; 1644-1671: Ndongo Wars; Apr., 1652: Dutch Begin to Colonize Southern Africa; Oct. 29, 1665: Battle of Mbwila; Late 17th cent.: Rise of Buganda; Beginning c. 1682: Decline of the Solomonid Dynasty.

RELATED ARTICLE in *Great Lives from History: The Seventeenth Century, 1601-1700:* Njinga.

1620's

1625

GROTIUS ESTABLISHES THE CONCEPT OF INTERNATIONAL LAW

Grotius's major work, On the Law of War and Peace, *is widely considered the first definitive text on international law. It provides a systematic description and prescription of the behavior of national communities, which, he argues, have legal rights as well as duties. The work anticipated the advent of the modern state system after 1648.*

LOCALE: Paris, France

CATEGORIES: Laws, acts, and legal history; cultural and intellectual history; literature

KEY FIGURES

Hugo Grotius (Huig de Groot; 1583-1645), Dutch jurist, theologian, statesman, diplomat, poet, and author of works on law and jurisprudence, theology, and cultural history

Maurice of Nassau (1567-1625), Dutch stadtholder, or chief executive, and commander-in-chief who employed Grotius as legal counsel in 1604 but had him arrested and brought to trial for sedition in 1618-1619

Louis XIII (1601-1643), king of France, r. 1610-1643, who granted Grotius safety and a modest stipend when Grotius fled to Paris in 1621

Christina (1626-1689), queen of Sweden, r. 1644-1654, who dismissed Grotius from the Swedish diplomatic service in 1644

Maria van Reigersbergh de Groot (1589-1653), wife of Hugo Grotius, who helped Grotius escape to France

SUMMARY OF EVENT

Known as the father of international law, Huig de Groot, who used the Latinized version of his name, Hugo Grotius, was born to an old and distinguished Dutch family in Delft, Holland, in 1583. Grotius was a child prodigy who wrote Greek and Latin poetry, matriculated at the University of Leiden at age eleven, received a doctor of laws degree from the University of Orléans (France) at fifteen, and was admitted to the Dutch bar at sixteen.

Grotius became his country's official historiographer at eighteen and legal counsel to the Dutch ruler, Prince Maurice of Nassau, at twenty-one. He continued advancing in public and diplomatic posts until 1618 when, becoming involved in a political-religious controversy, Grotius, along with other senior officials, was arrested

and sentenced to life imprisonment in Loevestein fortress for treason.

Yet in March of 1621, with the help of his wife, Maria van Reigersbergh, and his maid, Grotius managed to escape from the castle where he was held and to flee to France where, at first, he was well received and got the moral and financial support of King Louis XIII. Beginning in 1622, in a Paris suburb, he began drafting his magnum opus in Latin, *De jure belli ac pacis libri tres* (1625) translated into English as *On the Law of War and Peace* (1654). Other well-known works by Grotius in law and jurisprudence include *Apologeticus eorum qui Hollandiae Westfrisiaeque et vicinis quibusdam natioibus ex legibus praefuerunt* (defense of the lawful government of Holland and West Friesland, together with some neighboring provinces, as it was before the change occurring in 1618), *Inleidinge tot de Hollandsche Rechts-geleerdheyd* (pb. 1631; *Introduction to Dutch Jurisprudence*, 1845), *De jure praede commentarius*

Dutch scholar and politician Hugo Grotius wrote the first major work in international law, On the Law of War and Peace, *presenting his concept of the just war.* (Library of Congress)

(wr. c. 1604-1606; *Commentary on the Law of Prize and Booty*, 1950), and *Mare liberum* (1609; *The Freedom of the Seas*, 1916). Yet his great versatility is evidenced by his publications in other fields as well.

In 1631, Grotius returned to Holland in defiance of his outlaw status but was forced to flee the following year. He at first took refuge in Germany but then moved to Stockholm where, in 1634, he was offered the Swedish ambassadorship to Paris. He helped to negotiate the Franco-Swedish Treaty of 1635 and others but was relieved of his post by the newly ascended Queen Christina of Sweden in 1644. In 1645, Grotius returned to Stockholm but declined the alternative employment offered him in the Swedish service. On his way to Rostock, Germany, he was shipwrecked in the Baltic Sea and died of exhaustion two days later on August 28, 1645. Grotius was subsequently buried in his home town of Delft.

On the Law of War and Peace, a work in international law, is an expansion of Grotius's ideas outlined in his earlier work. The book is premised on his idea of civil society governed by the *ius gentium*, the law of nations. The latter in turn is based on common natural law, fundamental to human nature and discoverable by human reason. This law of nations should dictate relations between communities not yet organized as units of political society as well as between national states since no community can exist without law. The theme, heralded by a long line of thinkers from classical times on, is developed in Grotius's three-volume treatise, the original 1625 edition running to 786 pages. It falls into two major parts: first, the legal obligations of human societies, including those with sovereign power; and second, how to enforce such obligations and punish violations of law—vital features of Grotius's message. This message declares that communities have legal rights and duties, and that war is a law-enforcement procedure similar to judicial remedies.

Book 1 (five chapters) of *On the Law of War and Peace* inquires whether war is ever justified. Grotius's

---

GROTIUS ON WAR AND PEACE

Hugo Grotius laid the foundation of international law, believing mostly in peace over war. However, he also believed that war is just in some instances, notably when a nation's rights have been violated or when a country seeks to remedy those violations, if no legal recourse is available.

It is not, then, contrary to the nature of society to look out for oneself and advance one's own interests, provided the rights of others are not infringed; and consequently the use of force which does not violate the rights of others is not unjust. This thought Cicero also has presented: "Since there are two ways of settling a difference, the one by argument, the other by force, and since the former is characteristic of man, the latter of brutes, we should have recourse to the second only when it is not permitted to use the first. . . ." Now war is of the utmost importance, seeing that in consequences of war a great many sufferings usually fall upon even innocent persons. Therefore in the midst of divergent opinions we must lean towards peace.

[D]uring the entire administration of a war the should cannot be kept serene and trusting in God unless it is always looking forward to peace. Sallus[t] most truly said, "The wise wage war for the sake of peace." With this the opinion of Augustine agrees: "Peace is not sought that war may be followed, but war is waged that peace may be secured." Aristotle himself more than once condemns those nations which made warlike pursuits, as it were, their end and aim. Violence is characteristic of wild beasts, and violence is most manifest in war; therefore the more diligently effort should be put forth that it be tempered with humanity, lest by imitating wild beasts too much we forget to be human.

Source: Grotius, *On the Law of War and Peace*, books 1, 2, and 3, translated by Francis W. Kelsey, edited by James Brown Scott (New York: Bobbs-Merrill, 1925), pp. 54, 560, 861.

1620's

---

answer, contradicting pacifist opinion and many Christian theologians, is that it is justified when an injury of some sort is the cause. Book 2 (twenty-six chapters) holds that there can therefore be as many just causes of war as there are types of injuries. Grotius also admonishes against going to war too hastily, even for just cause, and recommends conferences and arbitrations, even contests among the leaders themselves, as preferred alternative methods of settling disputes. To reach his conclusions, Grotius reviewed the entire gamut of substantive rights under municipal law, for "there is a common law among nations, which is valid alike for war and in war." Book 3 (twenty-five chapters) deals with the actual conduct of war, that is, the humanitarian rules that belligerents must observe during hostilities. Grotius's counsels of moderation flow from his basic belief in rights common to all humans, which were often ignored in the barbarities of the Thirty Years' War.

The work abounds in references to the Bible, ancient orators and statesmen, classical historians, philosophers, even poets, but avoids contemporaneous controversial matters. Many of the references are to establish historical authenticity or clarity but some are for adornment. Whatever the purpose, the influence of Greek, Roman, and medieval thinking on Grotius's formulation of international law is unmistakable.

SIGNIFICANCE

The elaboration of "rules" in *On the Law of War and Peace* by Grotius could not have come at a better time. For the bloody Thirty Years' War leading to the Peace of Westphalia in 1648 transformed numerous petty principalities into separate sovereign states. Grotius's great work provided a body of laws to regulate their relations.

In addition to the timing of his writing, Grotius's persona and his scholarly reputation contributed to the success of his treatise. Another factor in this success was his Dutch heritage. Holland was one of the dominant countries of Europe that had spearheaded the idea of the nation-state. It is not surprising, then, that since its publication, the book crafted by the one dubbed "the wonder of Holland" and "the jurisconsult of humankind" has gone through about one hundred editions and numerous translations.

—*Peter B. Heller*

FURTHER READING

Bull, Hedley, Benedict Kingsbury, and Adam Roberts, eds. *Hugo Grotius and International Relations*. Oxford, England: Clarendon Press, 1992. A collection of essays based on a series of commemorative lectures at Oxford University in 1983. Several of the contributions touch on Grotius's seminal work.

Dumbauld, Edward. *The Life and Legal Writings of Hugo Grotius*. Norman: University of Oklahoma Press, 1969. This brief book by an American judge includes an excellent critical essay on Grotius's major text.

Edwards, Charles S. *Hugo Grotius, the Miracle of Holland: A Study in Political and Legal Thought*. Chicago: Nelson-Hall, 1981. This book examines Grotius's works on the basis of his most eminent concepts—the law of nature, the law of nations, and the law of war. Includes extensive notes and a bibliography.

Gellinek, Christian. *Hugo Grotius*. Boston: Twayne, 1983. The author, a corresponding member of the journal *Grotiana* published in the Netherlands, includes a critical evaluation of Grotius's major work in chapter 5, "Legal Treatises." Also contains an excellent and detailed tabulation of the body of Grotius's writings.

Grotius, Hugo. *On the Law of War and Peace*. Translated by Francis W. Kelsey, et al. New York: Bobbs-Merrill, 1925. Based on the 1646 edition of the Latin original, the last edition to be revised by Grotius, this 1925 translation is the translation used most frequently by international lawyers and scholars and is widely accessible.

Haakonssen, Knud, ed. *Grotius, Pufendorf, and Modern Natural Law*. Brookfield, Vt.: Ashgate, 1999. This work discusses various aspects of the philosophies of Grotius and his contemporary Samuel von Pufendorf, including their ideas on the modern state.

Knight, William S. M. *The Life and Work of Hugo Grotius*. 1925. Reprint. Dobbs Ferry, N.Y.: Oceana, 1962. An authoritative work by an Oxford scholar and lawyer. Despite the many intervening years, Knight's work is one of the few biographies on Grotius written in English.

Onuma, Yasuaki, ed. *A Normative Approach to War: Peace, War, and Justice in Hugo Grotius*. Oxford, England: Clarendon Press, 1993. The revised and translated version of a book by six Japanese professors of international law that examines various aspects of Grotius's output. The translated and indexed list of key Latin terms used by Grotius adds to the book's significance.

Tuck, Richard. *The Rights of War and Peace: Political Thought and the International Order from Grotius to Kant*. New York: Oxford University Press, 1999. Tuck examines the work of numerous philosophers who laid the foundation for modern theories of international law. He focuses on seventeenth and eighteenth century thinkers, including Grotius, Thomas Hobbes, and John Locke.

Vollenhoven, Cornelis van. *The Framework of Grotius' Book "De Iure Belli ac Pacis," 1625*. Amsterdam: Noord-Hollandsche, 1931. A perceptive and detailed analysis of *On the Law of War and Peace* by perhaps the foremost modern Dutch expert on Grotius.

SEE ALSO: 1618-1648: Thirty Years' War; July, 1643-Oct. 24, 1648: Peace of Westphalia; 1667: Pufendorf Advocates a Unified Germany.

RELATED ARTICLES in *Great Lives from History: The Seventeenth Century, 1601-1700:* Christina; Sir Edward Coke; Frederick Henry; Pierre Gassendi; Hugo Grotius; John Locke; Louis XIII; Maurice of Nassau; Axel Oxenstierna; Nicolas-Claude Fabri de Peiresc; Samuel von Pufendorf; Anna Maria van Schurman.

1625-October 28, 1628
REVOLT OF THE HUGUENOTS

Fearing the whittling away of their rights by the centralizing, pro-Catholic policies of King Louis XIII's regime, the Protestant Huguenots launched the last of the French Wars of Religion. However, in overcoming an English expeditionary force, the powerful French chief minister Cardinal de Richelieu besieged and captured the Huguenot stronghold of La Rochelle to end the conflict.

LOCALE: Béarn, southern France, and Aunis and
   Saintonge on the French Atlantic coast
CATEGORIES: Wars, uprisings, and civil unrest;
   government and politics; religion and theology

KEY FIGURES
Louis XIII (1601-1643), king of France, r. 1610-1643
Charles I (1600-1649), king of England, r. 1625-1649
Seigneur de Soubise (Benjamin de Rohan; 1583-1642),
   Huguenot commander at La Rochelle
Henri de Rohan (1579-1638), brother of Benjamin de
   Rohan and leader of the Huguenots in southern
   France
Cardinal de Richelieu (Armand-Jean du Plessis; 1585-
   1642), chief minister of France, 1624-1642
First Duke of Buckingham (George Villiers; 1592-
   1628), court favorite of King Charles I and
   commander of English forces aiding the Huguenots
Jean Guiton (1585-1654), militant Calvinist mayor of
   La Rochelle

SUMMARY OF EVENT
The 1598 Edict of Nantes, proclaimed by King Henry IV, provided a measure of religious freedom to the minority Huguenot population. It also guaranteed them *places du surete*, fortified towns the Huguenots were authorized to garrison and maintain in southern and western France. They were given the right to mount what was effectively an independent army and to operate as a state within the French state.

As long as Henry IV (r. 1589-1610) was on the throne, there existed a laissez-faire atmosphere with regard to religious practice, and the Huguenots even were represented on the Royal Privy Council, notably by Maximilien de Béthune, the duke de Sully. This changed after Henry's assassination, when the Huguenots were forced out from governmental decision-making. Sully quickly became alienated and resigned in 1611 out of disgust.

Queen Mother Marie de Médicis, regent for the nine-

year-old monarch Louis XIII, was a devout Catholic. When Louis came of age, his own Catholic sensibilities made him anything but sympathetic to his Protestant subjects. He reportedly expressed his desire privately to eradicate Huguenot worship from his realm. The Huguenots saw their rights under the Edict of Nantes challenged bit by bit until their power and influence in court circles were eroded completely. To worsen the situation, most of their principal leaders, such as Sébastien Chateillon of the sixteenth century, François de Bonne (duke de Lesdiguières), and the Condés defected to Catholicism (usually for political reasons). By the 1620's, the powerful de Rohan family was among the very few significant families of the upper nobility to cling to the ancestral Calvinist faith. It was an uncertain time of incompetent and corrupt royal favorites, assassinations, and attempted coups.

In 1617, the king's Edict of Restitution to restore Catholic worship in predominantly Protestant Béarn led to a Huguenot assembly at the formidable fortified city of La Rochelle. This assembly was dominated by a militant element and it openly defied the king. Royal military campaigns in 1620, 1621, and 1622 through southern France could not break Huguenot power. However, the Huguenots did lose some important ground: Benjamin de Rohan, seigneur de Soubise, was heavily defeated at Île de Ries in 1622 and lost Poitou Province, while his brother Henri de Rohan was compelled to sign the Peace of Montpellier, which stipulated that the Huguenot garrisons would be dismantled in 1625. Only the Atlantic port of La Rochelle remained defiant.

Early in 1625, Soubise seized the Île de Ré and the Île d'Oléron near La Rochelle and appealed for assistance from King Charles I of England. Charles's marriage to Louis XIII's sister Henrietta Maria seemed to calm the situation, but the French-English alliance broke apart and the French government made a pact of friendship with ultra-Catholic Spain. In July of 1627, Soubise and his brother Henri were promised help by Charles's royal favorite, George Villiers, the duke of Buckingham, and an English fleet was accordingly sent to the area. Many believed that Buckingham's influence had been instrumental in driving France and England into conflict in the first place.

Cardinal de Richelieu became first minister of France in 1624 and set out energetically to surround and then to invest La Rochelle in a siege, recognizing the city as key

French minister Cardinal de Richelieu, with his aides, planning an end to the Protestant Huguenots' siege of La Rochelle. (Francis R. Niglutsch)

to the struggle. Wearing his own unique armor and personally directing the actual operations—including the construction of a dike to block the port—the cardinal maintained constant pressure on the will and morale of the townspeople. However, a former admiral in the French navy named Jean Guiton was chosen as mayor and became the inspirational heart and soul of the city's resistance. The actual siege began on August 10, 1627, and, almost simultaneously, Buckingham's fleet appeared.

The English force made its first attempt to break the siege by trying to secure a base on the nearby Île de Ré, which was held by a smaller French contingent at Fort St.-Martin. After some initial success, Buckingham's momentum broke down, and on November 6, 1627, he launched a suicidal attack on the battlements, suffered appalling casualties, and was promptly driven out by a French counterattack. Buckingham returned to England and from May to June, 1628, a second English fleet under William Feilding, the first earl of Denbigh, hovered around the fortifications, only to turn back without attempting a breach. Buckingham, increasingly unpopular, sought to recoup his fortunes by organizing a third—

and larger—relief expedition. However, on August 23, 1628, he was stabbed in the chest by an assassin, John Felton, and died minutes later. His death marked the end of serious involvement by the English.

Meanwhile, in Béarn and Guyenne, Henri de Rohan held his own against superior forces but, without English assistance, he had no hope of breaking through to La Rochelle. Hemmed in at all sides and racked by starvation and disease, the population had reduced to 5,000 from an estimated 25,000 at the beginning of the siege, La Rochelle surrendered on October 28, 1628. Finally, on November 1, Louis and Richelieu triumphantly rode into town.

SIGNIFICANCE

After La Rochelle's capitulation, Henri de Rohan, in Béarn, was forced to come to terms two months later. The settlement, called the Peace of Alais (1629) completely stripped the Huguenots of their fortresses and independent military power. Richelieu, however, proved willing to affirm the basic rights they enjoyed as Protestant Frenchmen under the Edict of Nantes, and they would remain unharmed as long as the cardinal remained in control. The reduction of Huguenot autonomy went a long way toward realizing Richelieu's dream of a powerful, united French state under a centralized and absolute monarchy.

—*Raymond Pierre Hylton*

FURTHER READING

Burckhardt, Carl J. *Richelieu: His Rise to Power*. New York: Vintage Books, 1964. A still-useful study that, at times, reads like a novel. Oriented very much in favor of Richelieu.

Holt, Mack P. *The French Wars of Religion, 1562-1629*. New York: Cambridge University Press, 1995. A unique and comprehensive account of French sectarian conflict that ties in the seventeenth century war (1610-1629) with the better-known wars of the sixteenth century.

Levi, Anthony. *Cardinal Richelieu and the Making of France*. New York: Carroll & Graf, 2000. Richelieu is improbably described as a benevolent reformer. Still, the author's treatment is reasonably even-handed.

Lockyer, Roger. *Buckingham: The Life and Political Career of George Villiers, First Duke of Buckingham, 1592-1628*. New York: Longman, 1981. Lockyer attempts a more sympathetic and complex analysis of one of the most maligned political figures of the early seventeenth century.

Lublinskaya, A. D. *French Absolutism: The Crucial Phase, 1620-1629*. Cambridge, England: Cambridge University Press, 1968. A classic study that depicts the Huguenots as obstacles to the irresistible trend of the centralization of governmental power.

O'Connell, D. P. *Richelieu*. New York: World, 1968. In similar fashion to Burckhardt's book, O'Connell depicts Richelieu quite sympathetically, while emphasizing the weaknesses of Buckingham and his Huguenot allies.

Treasure, G. R. R. *Cardinal Richelieu and the Development of Absolutism*. New York: St. Martin's Press, 1972. Another work that largely sings the praises of Richelieu. Makes a case for the cardinal being more in sympathy with the moderate Huguenots and less of a Catholic extremist than some sources assert.

SEE ALSO: 1610-1643: Reign of Louis XIII; July, 1620-Sept., 1639: Struggle for the Valtelline Pass; May 6-June 7, 1628: Petition of Right; Mar. 6, 1629: Edict of Restitution; 1661: Absolute Monarchy Emerges in France; Apr., 1670: Charles Town Is Founded; 1685: Louis XIV Revokes the Edict of Nantes; Sept. 20, 1697: Treaty of Ryswick.

RELATED ARTICLES in *Great Lives from History: The Seventeenth Century, 1601-1700:* First Duke of Buckingham; Charles I; The Great Condé; Henrietta Maria; Louis XIII; Cardinal de Richelieu; Duke de Sully.

1620's

May 14, 1625-1640
ENGLISH DISCOVER AND COLONIZE BARBADOS

Captain John Powell claimed Barbados for England in 1625. In 1627, Sir William Courteen established England's second Caribbean colony on the island. Barbados's settlers founded a plantation economy based on tobacco and cotton, but in the 1630's, sugar supplanted tobacco as the primary cash crop.

LOCALE: Barbados, Caribbean Sea
CATEGORIES: Colonization; expansion and land acquisition; exploration and discovery

KEY FIGURES

John Powell (fl. 1624-1625), English captain and governor of Barbados, 1629
Henry Powell (fl. 1627-1628), English captain and governor of Barbados, 1627-1628
Sir William Courteen (1572-1636), English merchant and lord proprietor of Barbados, 1625-1627
Henry Hawley (fl. 1630's), governor of Barbados, 1630-1633, 1634-1638, 1639
Charles Wolferston (fl. 1628-1629), governor of Barbados, 1628-1629
Philip Herbert (d. 1669), earl of Pembroke and supporter of Courteen
James Hay (1612-1660), earl of Carlisle and lord proprietor of Barbados, 1627-1652

SUMMARY OF EVENT

On May 14, 1625, Captain John Powell stopped at Barbados on his voyage from Brazil to England. Finding the island uninhabited, Powell claimed it for England and King James I. He named the landing site Jamestown (now Holetown). On Powell's return trip to England, he stopped at Saint Christopher (Saint Kitt's), settled by the British in 1624, to report his claim to Sir William Courteen, a wealthy merchant who controlled an important English trading company. Courteen, his brother Peter Courteen, John Mounsay, and Captains John Powell and Henry Powell launched the first expedition to occupy Barbados.

On February 17, 1627, Captain Henry Powell arrived with eighty settlers and ten African slaves at Jamestown. The settlers immediately felled trees and built log houses along the seashore. They found tropical fruits in abundance and wild hogs for meat. While the settlers cleared land, Powell went to Essequibo, Guiana, to obtain seeds and foodstuffs from his old friend Adrian Groenewegen, the governor of the Dutch colony there. With Groenewegen's permission, thirty-two Arawak Indians returned with Powell to Barbados, to provide seeds and expertise in cultivation. The Arawaks were supposed to remain free men and receive land for themselves but eventually were reduced to slavery.

In May of 1627, Captain John Powell arrived with a cargo of supplies and ninety men and women—mostly indentured servants. By mid-1627, the Courteen colony had cleared land 7 miles (11 kilometers) inland, built one hundred houses, and started five plantations. The Arawaks helped plant food crops of fruits, cassava, corn, and potatoes, along with cash crops of tobacco, cotton, ginger, and indigo. Barbados's population increased rapidly, and soon there were a dozen thriving plantations, along with numerous small farms. European indentured servants, African slaves, and Caribbean Indians made up the labor force.

English politics interfered with Barbados's development, however. James Hay, earl of Carlisle, petitioned King Charles I for title to Barbados. His creditors, primarily a syndicate of London merchants headed by Marmaduke Royden, supported his petition in order to use Carlisle to gain a foothold in the lucrative island trade. In July, 1627, Charles I awarded Carlisle a patent to the "Caribee" Islands, including Barbados, and named him lord proprietor of the island. To clear his debts, Carlisle leased 10,000 acres (4,045 hectares) to Royden's syndicate.

When Sir William Courteen discovered this intrigue, he sought help from Philip Herbert, earl of Pembroke, who claimed Barbados under a patent from King James I. On February 25, 1628, Pembroke persuaded King Charles to grant him the islands of Trinidad, Tobago, Barbados, and Fonseca in trust for Courteen. In response, Carlisle obtained another grant from Charles confirming that Barbados was included in his Caribee Islands patent. The

lord keeper Coventry ruled that Carlisle's patent was valid, so a royal edict went to the governor of Barbados in May, 1629, declaring the earl of Carlisle's title to the island to be in full force. Thus, Carlisle obtained sovereign rights over Barbados. He received all subsidies, customs, and taxes for ten years and could select the estates he desired for his private domain. The planters, who paid the taxes and subsidies, were caught up in the war of intrigue and litigation between Carlisle and Courteen.

On March 19, 1628, Lord Proprietor Carlisle commissioned Captain Charles Wolferston as governor and commander-in-chief of Barbados for three years. Wolferston arrived in Barbados in June, 1628, with sixty-four men, took over as governor, and claimed jurisdiction over Courteen's planters. When Governor John Powell opposed this action, Wolferston put him in prison. In October, 1628, Carlisle sent two merchants named Havercamp and Mole with twenty men to start a new plantation. They persuaded some of the Courteen planters to accept Carlisle's sovereignty, established Carlisle's private plantation, and returned to England.

On February 26, 1629, Henry Powell arrived with a cargo of supplies and about one hundred men and women. Angered at his brother's imprisonment, Powell seized Wolferston and William Deane, a planter who had defected to Carlisle, then released John Powell from prison and reinstated him as governor. All of the Royden syndicate's possessions were confiscated, including servants and tobacco. Henry Powell secured a shipload of tobacco from the Courteen planters, along with their pledges of allegiance, and sailed for England, with Wolferston and Deane aboard as prisoners.

Carlisle retaliated in August of 1629 by sending Henry Hawley to Barbados as governor. Hawley tricked John Powell and loyal Courteen planters aboard his ship, chained them to the mainmast, and departed for the Leeward Islands, leaving Robert Wheatley in charge as deputy governor. Enraged, Courteen planters mounted an armed attack on Wheatley, but Wheatley won the battle and confiscated all plantations that fell within the Carlisle acreage. Hawley returned in triumph to resume his role as governor in 1630, but the conflict, compounded by severe drought in 1629 and Carlisle's failure to send supplies from Europe, wrought such devastation in Barbados that the years 1630-1631 became known as the Starving Time.

Barbados regained the lost ground of the Starving Time when it transitioned to sugar production in the 1630's. Dutchmen from Guiana brought sugarcane for planting and technology for producing sugar, and sugar soon supplanted tobacco as Barbados's chief export. Like tobacco and cotton plantations, sugar plantations were dependent upon slaves and indentured servants. Dutch merchants supplied slaves from West Africa, and poor English whites came to Barbados as indentured servants. Some servants were kidnap victims, and on occasion, convicted criminals were shipped to Barbados as laborers. Descendants of the white slaves and indentured laborers were known as Red Legs. Visitors to Barbados during the early 1630's reported the poor conditions in which slaves and servants lived, as well as widespread drunkenness and immorality among the planters. These evils were attributed to the lack of sufficient clergy and a failure to maintain a strong religious influence on standards of behavior.

In December, 1634, the lords commissioner for the plantations ordered that no more "subsidy men" (that is, men of substance who might pay taxes) be allowed to emigrate. In 1635, a total of 707 men and 36 women left London for Barbados. Among these were very few planters but numerous tradesmen, craftspeople, and servants. By 1639, the population in Barbados had reached ten thousand, and the planters had retrieved their political power. The island's first Parliament was held in 1639, making Barbados's Parliament the third oldest legislative body in the Commonwealth, after the British House of Commons and Bermuda House of Assembly. Barbados held so closely to English government, laws, and traditions that it became known as Little England.

SIGNIFICANCE

Barbados was important to the British for its strategic location, lying to windward (east) of the island chain of the Lesser Antilles and not so vulnerable to attack by the Spanish. The colony proved increasingly profitable as a sugar producer and trading post for the British in the Caribbean. In 1651, Barbados was besieged by Oliver Cromwell's military forces and forced to sign Articles of Capitulation in 1652. The Parliament, however, turned the articles into a Charter for Barbados and used the charter to win a measure of independence from the English monarchy when it was restored in 1660. From 1640 to 1700, despite periodic slave unrest and destructive hurri-

canes, Barbados maintained a successful sugar plantation society and economy, and moved ever further toward home rule.

—*Marguerite R. Plummer*

FURTHER READING

Barbados Tourism Encyclopedia. "The Abbreviated History of Barbados." *History Archives*. Available at http://axses.com/encyc/bta/archives. Accessed October 18, 2004. A chronology of Barbados history with links to *The Barbados Saga* on-line.

Gragg, Larry. "The Pious and the Profane: The Religious Life of Early Barbados Planters." *Historian* (Winter, 2000): 1-15. Available at http://www.findarticles.com. Accessed October 11, 2004. Examines the effects of neglect of religion on Barbados plantation society.

Handler, Jerome. *The Unappropriated People: Freedmen in the Slave Society of Barbados*. Baltimore: Johns Hopkins University Press, 1974. Documents occupations, customs, traditions, and relationships of freedmen and slaves.

Harlow, Vincent T. *A History of Barbados, 1625-1685*. New York: Negro Universities Press, 1926. Using primary sources, details the early history of Barbados.

Puckrein, Gary A. *Little England: Plantation Society and Anglo-Barbadian Politics, 1627-1700*. New York: New York University Press, 1984. Discusses the effects of political struggles on plantation economy.

Sheppard, Jill. *The "Redlegs" of Barbados*. Millwood, N.Y.: KTO Press, 1977. A social history of Barbados's white indentured servants and slaves and their descendants.

SEE ALSO: 1642-1651: English Civil Wars; Dec. 6, 1648-May 19, 1649: Establishment of the English Commonwealth; Dec. 16, 1653-Sept. 3, 1658: Cromwell Rules England as Lord Protector; May 10, 1655: English Capture of Jamaica; May, 1659-May, 1660: Restoration of Charles II; Mar. 24, 1663-July 25, 1729: Settlement of the Carolinas; Apr., 1670: Charles Town Is Founded.

RELATED ARTICLES in *Great Lives from History: The Seventeenth Century, 1601-1700:* Charles I; Oliver Cromwell; James I.

1620's

July, 1625-August, 1664
FOUNDING OF NEW AMSTERDAM

The Dutch West India Company built New Amsterdam, the capital of its American colony of New Netherland, and designed it to resemble Dutch cities back home. The population of the colony, however, was more ethnically and religiously diverse than was the Dutch homeland.

LOCALE: Manhattan Island, New Netherland (now in New York)

CATEGORIES: Colonization; expansion and land acquisition; exploration and discovery

KEY FIGURES

Peter Minuit (c. 1580-1638), director-general of New Netherland, 1626-1632

Willem Kieft (1597-1647), director-general of New Netherland, 1638-1647

Peter Stuyvesant (c. 1610-1672), director-general of New Netherland, 1647-1664

Adriaen van der Donck (1620-1655), Dutch-born colonial American lawyer

SUMMARY OF EVENT

In July, 1625, the Dutch West India Company decided to move its trading post on the lower Hudson River from Nut Island (now Governors Island) to the tip of Manhattan Island and to erect a fort there. The company had sent an expedition in 1624 to claim the entire area between the Connecticut and Delaware Rivers as the colony of New Netherland. When early leadership proved incompetent, the colonial council selected Peter Minuit as New Netherland's first director-general in May, 1626. He decided to concentrate the sparse population of the colony around the fort as New Amsterdam, leaving only small garrisons and fur traders at Fort Orange (now Albany) and on the Delaware and Connecticut Rivers. To legitimize the move, Minuit arranged to purchase Manhattan Island from the resident Indians for sixty guilders worth of trade goods.

The most persistent myth about the history of New York City is that Minuit cheated the Manhattan Indians by buying such valuable real estate for twenty-four dollars worth of beads and trinkets. The dollar figure is meaningless, since satisfactorily calculating the present value of seventeenth century guilders is close to impossible. Although specific records of what the Indians received have not survived, both sides had reason to be satisfied with the bargain. Comparable later land sales between

European settlers were close to what Minuit paid. The Indians, who thought in terms of temporary, not permanent, rights to occupy land, did not settle for beads. Trade goods accepted by Indians in other land purchases included desirable European textiles and metal products—blankets, kettles, axes, hoes, and drilling awls usable to carve shells into wampum (accepted as money by both Indians and colonists).

When the company dismissed Minuit in 1632, New Amsterdam was a tiny settlement of some three hundred people, most of them living in small wooden houses with reed roofs, clustered close to the protection of the fort. A windmill used to saw lumber reminded the residents of the Dutch homeland. From the beginning, Manhattan had a very diverse ethnic and linguistic population. The first settlers sent by the company were thirty Walloon families, French-speaking Protestant refugees from the Catholic-controlled southern Netherlands who stubbornly refused to learn Dutch. They would soon be joined by German, English, Spanish, Scandinavian, and Portuguese colonists, rendering the colony extremely polyglot. Slaves imported by the company added Africans to the mixture; by the 1660's, three hundred slaves and seventy-five free blacks lived in the city. When the future Saint Isaac Jogues visited New Amsterdam in 1643, he was told that eighteen different languages were spoken there. Probably only a bare majority of the population during the life of the colony was Dutch; the Netherlands was at the peak of its prosperity in the seventeenth century, and few of its citizens chose to leave it for the New World.

The settlement came close to extinction in the 1640's due to the mistaken, brutal Indian policy of director-general Willem Kieft. An attempt to collect taxes from nearby Indians led to stiff resistance and sporadic violence. Fighting intensified after Kieft, over the vigorous objections of the colonists, organized a nighttime massacre of Indians, including women and children, in February, 1643. In response nearly all local tribes joined the war; farmsteads and settlements in upper Manhattan and the Hudson Valley were destroyed and the population of New Amsterdam had shrunk below three hundred when the war ended in August, 1645. Complaints by settlers led the West India Company to replace Kieft with Peter Stuyvesant in May of 1647.

Stuyvesant began a vigorous policy of improvements that, during the 1650's, transformed the bedraggled settlement into a small, distinctly Dutch city containing three hundred buildings and fifteen hundred residents. What had been wandering paths were surveyed and organized into regular streets. A small creek running through the city was widened, its sides were straightened, and it was turned into a canal (later Broad Street) crossed by three stone bridges. The canal, two windmills, and newly built, gable-ended brick residences, roofed with imported Dutch tiles, reminded residents of Holland. A Sunday market held on the banks of the canal permitted farmers from Brooklyn to bring their produce into the center of the settlement. A city pier on the East River led to a busy two-block commercial district of warehouses, workshops, and taverns. In 1653, Stuyvesant established an almshouse for the aged poor, in 1654, an orphan asylum was constructed, and in 1658, a hospital followed. Fearing attack from New England during the first Anglo-Dutch War, Stuyvesant built a high stockade fence (later Wall Street) along the northern border of the city in 1653.

A 1660 map of New Amsterdam located nineteen licensed taverns and three breweries. Merchants met to socialize and conduct business at the stone City Tavern, which became City Hall after the municipal government

organized. The rectangular fort enclosed a stone barracks, a guard house, a church, and the governor's residence. A wide street, later named Broadway, ran north from the fort to the Land Gate in the wall. As the city grew, it clustered around the fort and the East River dockside; much of the land directly south of the wall was planted with vegetable gardens and orchards.

While doing his best to turn New Amsterdam into a neat, orderly Dutch town, Stuyvesant refused to accept the policy of religious toleration that made the Netherlands unique in Europe. Zealously protective of the privileges of the Dutch Reformed Church, the only denomination permitted to erect church buildings in the city, Stuyvesant angrily prohibited Lutheran attempts to worship openly. When twenty-three Jewish refugees reached the city in 1653, only a direct order from the company prevented Stuyvesant from driving them out of his colony. Quaker preachers suffered the worst from his bigotry, being physically harassed and punished before being forced into exile.

Stuyvesant's dictatorial governing style infuriated many colonists, who accused him of arbitrary rule and

Governor Peter Minuit purchasing the island of Manhattan from Algonquian Indians. (Francis R. Niglutsch)

political favoritism and complained that he placed the profits of the Dutch West India Company ahead of the colony's welfare. Led by Adriaen van der Donck, the only New Netherland resident who had studied law in Holland, the colonists appealed to the Dutch Estates-General to recall Stuyvesant, abolish the company, and grant New Amsterdam a municipal charter. The Estates-General refused the first two requests but in 1653 ordered Stuyvesant to establish a local government resembling those in Dutch cities and giving New Amsterdam burghers control of their own affairs. The structure of New Amsterdam's new city government provided for a slate of elected officials bearing familiar Dutch titles while recognizing an emerging class structure. Great burghers—a few dozen merchants with close ties to leading Amsterdam families—dominated overseas trade and exercised political privileges; small burghers—artisans and shopkeepers—actively participated in local affairs.

When an English fleet appeared in the harbor in August, 1664, Stuyvesant wanted to fight, but the leading burghers refused to support him, and he reluctantly capitulated. In negotiating the terms of surrender, the citizens induced the English to maintain the existing city structure and to guarantee the continuance of all the rights and freedoms they enjoyed.

SIGNIFICANCE

Stuyvesant successfully guided the transformation of a struggling settlement into a solidly established European society, imitating its Dutch model. By 1664, New Amsterdam had become a small but vibrant commercial city with the most diverse population in North America. Successful merchants, although still junior partners of the great Dutch magnates, were involved in all aspects of Atlantic commerce. Immigration had increased and the demographic makeup of the immigrants was markedly different: In the colony's first decades, the colonists were overwhelmingly rootless males. Now, young couples, many with children, chose to join the colony. Citizens became accustomed to managing the affairs of their city.

Dutch New Amsterdam became British New York, but the original city would transmit a heritage of freedom and self-sufficiency to its new incarnation. Parts of its political structure would endure into the nineteenth century. More important, the city would demonstrate that people of different ethnic, linguistic, and religious traditions could live together, for the most part peacefully. As a conspicuous example of successful diversity, New Amsterdam prefigured the future of New York City and the United States.

—*Milton Berman*

FURTHER READING

Burns, Ric, and James Saunders. *New York: An Illustrated History*. New York: Alfred A. Knopf, 1999. Lavishly illustrated chapter on New Amsterdam helps visualize life in the colony.

Burrows, Edwin G., and Mike Wallace. *Gotham: A History of New York City to 1898*. New York: Oxford University Press, 1999. Five chapters provide a succinct history of New Amsterdam.

Cantwell, Anne-Marie, and Diana diZerega Wall. *Unearthing Gotham: The Archaeology of New York City*. New Haven, Conn.: Yale University Press, 2001. Archaeological digs in lower Manhattan reveal details about daily life in New Amsterdam.

Rink, Oliver A. *Holland on the Hudson: An Economic and Social History of Dutch New York*. Ithaca, N.Y.: Cornell University Press, 1986. Rink carefully analyzes immigration patterns to New Netherland and stresses the importance of private merchants' activities.

Shorto, Russell. *The Island at the Center of the World: The Epic Story of Dutch Manhattan and the Forgotten Colony That Shaped America*. New York: Doubleday, 2004. Shorto argues that the social and political practices of New Amsterdam's inhabitants powerfully influenced the development of American democracy.

SEE ALSO: Spring, 1604: First European Settlement in North America; Beginning June, 1610: Hudson Explores Hudson Bay; 1611-1630's: Jesuits Begin Missionary Activities in New France; Dec. 26, 1620: Pilgrims Arrive in North America; May 6, 1626: Algonquians "Sell" Manhattan Island; June, 1636: Rhode Island Is Founded; Apr. 21, 1649: Maryland Act of Toleration; Oct., 1651-May, 1652: Navigation Act Leads to Anglo-Dutch Wars; Summer, 1654-1656: First Jewish Settlers in North America; Mar. 22, 1664-July 21, 1667: British Conquest of New Netherland.

RELATED ARTICLES in *Great Lives from History: The Seventeenth Century, 1601-1700:* Saint Isaac Jogues; Peter Minuit; Peter Stuyvesant.

Dutch and Portuguese Struggle for the Guinea Coast

October, 1625-1637
DUTCH AND PORTUGUESE STRUGGLE FOR THE GUINEA COAST

The Portuguese fort of São Jorge da Mina, once a major entry point for the gold trade, was already in decline when it was captured by the Dutch in 1637. This operation was part of a larger war that spanned three continents.

LOCALE: Costa da Mina (Gold Coast), Republic of Ghana

CATEGORIES: Trade and commerce; wars, uprisings, and civil unrest

KEY FIGURES
Salvador Correia de Sá e Benevides (1594-1688), Portuguese commander on the Angolan coast

Francisco Sotomaior (fl. 1625), governor of São Jorge da Mina in 1625

Nikolaas van Ypren (fl. 1637), Dutch commander at Fort Nassau in 1637 and director-general of the fort, now called Elmina, 1638-1639

SUMMARY OF EVENT
By the early seventeenth century, the empire of the Portuguese on the African coast stretched from Morocco to Kenya. In West Africa, Portuguese power was anchored by the great fort of São Jorge da Mina on the Costa da Mina, or Gold Coast. São Jorge, built in 1482, was essentially a medieval castle adapted to the use of cannon. Its function was to tap into the trade of the Akan gold fields, the richest in West Africa. Satellite forts were built at Shama and Axim. At Mina, African merchants traded gold for a variety of European manufactured goods, with textiles and copper-based products leading the list.

By the seventeenth century, however, the post at Mina was suffering chronic problems. The government's attempt at a complete trade monopoly had led to widespread corruption and smuggling. The Portuguese system proved too cumbersome and archaic to adapt to new economic conditions, often resulting in a failure to supply Mina with sufficient or acceptable trade goods. The climate on the Guinea coast was unhealthy for Europeans, and few in the Portuguese military volunteered for duty there. The ranks became filled with convicts and other social undesirables. Military discipline sagged, and morale hit bottom. On the positive side, the local Africans, particularly those in the nearby village of Dondou, developed an intense loyalty to Portugal, greatly augmenting Portuguese power in the area.

In 1580, Portugal came under the rule of the Spanish royal family, binding the two states together until 1640. Henceforth, Spain's enemies were Portugal's enemies, especially the Dutch, the most implacable. Dutch ships began arriving in Guinea waters in the 1590's. The Dutch could provide goods the Africans wanted because metal products and cloth were manufactured in the Netherlands and neighboring areas. Dutch financiers and merchants had the capital for such enterprises, and the Dutch had bigger, better, and more ships than the Portuguese.

In 1612, the Dutch built their own castle, Fort Nassau, 12 miles down the coast from São Jorge. From there a Dutch force set out in October of 1625 with fifteen ships and twelve hundred European soldiers, augmented by African allies, to drive the Portuguese from the Mina coast. The garrison in São Jorge consisted of fifty-six soldiers, but Governor Francisco Sotomaior knew the attack was coming, and so he secured the help of the men of Dondou. Sotomaior also bribed nearby African rulers into neutrality by emptying the castle's storerooms of trade goods. The Dutch opened the siege with a naval bombardment, which did no real harm to São Jorge. The sides of the castle, it seemed, were so unevenly matched that Dutch confidence became cockiness. On ordering a land assault, the Dutch commander did not bother to send scouts. When the Dutch reached a clearing known as Pilicada near the castle, Portuguese crossbowmen caught them in a cross fire, throwing confusion into their ranks. Before the Dutch could reorganize, the men of Dondou appeared, fighting hand-to-hand with axes and spears. The Dutch admitted to losing more than four hundred soldiers; Portuguese casualties, including the Dondou allies, reportedly were less than thirty. The Dutch fleet retaliated with a concentrated bombardment, which was ineffectual. In mid-November, it sailed away.

In Lisbon, the Battle of Pilicada was greeted as a great victory. However, this did not rekindle a new interest in the distant outpost, and Mina was soon forgotten. The trade goods used to buy the neutrality of local rulers were not replenished. Neglect became the norm, and the garrison went without pay, sometimes for years. In 1634, the soldiers decided they had suffered enough. They refused to recognize the newly appointed governor and elected one of their own. The townspeople of Dondou, however, refused to recognize the usurper. Portuguese power was unraveling, a good time for the Dutch to renew their aggression.

The new Dutch commander at Fort Nassau, Nikolaas van Ypren, had been busy taking care of matters ignored

CENTERS OF SLAVE TRADE ALONG THE GUINEA COAST

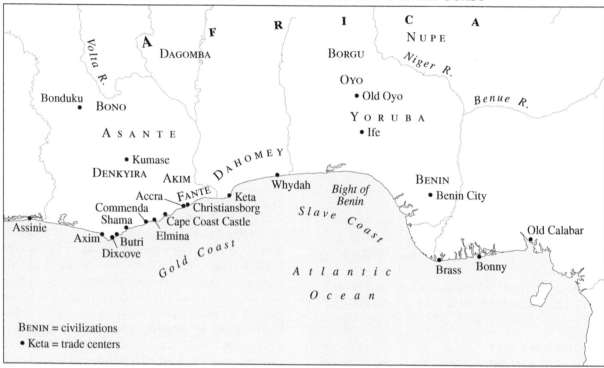

BENIN = civilizations
• Keta = trade centers

by his predecessor. He used a wealth of Dutch trade goods to bribe virtually all the African states in the area into alliances or neutrality. He also secured the support of a large Dutch fleet then operating in Brazil. In August of 1637, a Dutch force of eight hundred soldiers and more than one thousand African auxiliaries marched on São Jorge. This attack was much more determined and carefully planned. This time there was no ambush on the road. The initial clash was over control of a small hill near the castle, from which the Dutch hoped to position their artillery. At the base of the hill, the Portuguese had stationed the ever-loyal Dondou men. It is unclear which governor was actually in charge of the Portuguese effort.

The Dutch attacked the hill, were repulsed in fierce fighting, and suffered heavy casualties. The Dondou men returned to their town to celebrate, assuming the battle was over. As soon as they were gone, however, a second Dutch force moved in and occupied the hill, from which they bombarded the castle. Nevertheless, the walls of the old fort held firm. In the meantime, the African allies of the Dutch attacked and overran Dondou. If, however, the Portuguese situation seemed hopeless, the Dutch also were in fairly bad shape. Their recently arrived army was quickly becoming incapacitated from sickness and

would be good for a siege of only a few days. As a bluff, Dutch commander van Ypren demanded that the Portuguese surrender or be put to death once the castle fell. At first the Portuguese refused, but soon thereafter they reconsidered and surrendered.

The castle of São Jorge was still intact, suffering little damage. Inside was a large inventory of weapons, most of which qualified as antiques. Under the terms of surrender the Portuguese were not allowed to take anything from the castle. Even gold crosses from the church were to be left behind. When the Dutch searched the fortress, they found no gold, no trade goods, and no provisions.

SIGNIFICANCE

The loss of São Jorge da Mina was not a crippling blow to Portugal. One century earlier it had been the single richest source of gold in the world. The huge quantity of bullion that flowed from the Americas, though, made West African production pale in comparison, and by the early seventeenth century Mina, had slipped into irreversible decline. In some years, the expense of maintaining the post was greater than the income it provided.

The Dutch conquest of Mina and occupation of the surrounding coast were part of a much larger conflict spanning across decades of the seventeenth century that some historians consider the first real "world war." Alliances shifted, but generally the Dutch, English, and French were pitted against the empires of Spain and Portugal. For the most part, the Dutch were successful in Asia, but the reverse was true in South America, where the Portuguese retained control over Brazil.

In Africa, the results were mixed. As early as 1598-1599, the Dutch had raided São Tomé and Principe, the sugar-producing islands in the Gulf of Guinea that were also important as slave emporiums. Farther south along the Angolan coast, the Dutch attacked and occupied the slaving ports of Luanda and Benguela in 1641. However, seven years later, a Portuguese expedition from Brazil recaptured Luanda largely because of the leadership of Salvador Correia de Sá e Benevides, governor of Rio de Janeiro and subsequent captain-general of Angola. São Tomé and Principe, which had also come under Dutch control, were likewise retaken. When a peace treaty was finally signed in 1663, the Dutch kept Mina, but the Portuguese stayed in Angola and on the islands.

—*Richard L. Smith*

FURTHER READING

Boxer, C. R. *The Portuguese Seaborne Empire, 1415-1825.* 2d ed. Manchester, England: Carcanet Press, 1991. A detailed survey by the author of an equally useful book, *The Dutch Seaborne Empire.*

Hair, P. E. H. "Discovery and Discoveries: The Portuguese in Guinea, 1444-1650." *Bulletin of Hispanic Studies* 69 (1992): 11-28. A broad look at the Portu-

guese in West Africa, with helpful historiographical information.

Russell-Wood, A. J. R. *A World on the Move: The Portuguese in Africa, Asia, and America, 1415-1808.* New York: St. Martin's Press, 1992. A topical examination of the Portuguese Empire that assumes some basic knowledge of the period.

Volt, John. *Portuguese Rule on the Gold Coast, 1469-1682.* Athens: University of Georgia Press, 1979. Still the best place to start for a basic understanding of this topic.

Winius, George D., ed. *Portugal the Pathfinder: Journeys from the Medieval Toward the Modern World, 1300-ca. 1600.* Madison, Wis.: Hispanic Seminary of Medieval Studies, 1995. This work provides a context for understanding the Portuguese colonial enterprise.

SEE ALSO: Beginning c. 1601: Expansion of the Oyo Kingdom; Dec., 1601: Dutch Defeat the Portuguese in Bantam Harbor; Mar. 20, 1602: Dutch East India Company Is Founded; Apr. 29, 1606: First European Contact with Australia; 1630-1660's: Dutch Wars in Brazil; Aug. 26, 1641-Sept., 1648: Conquest of Luanda; Mid-17th cent.: Emergence of the Guinea Coast States; Mar. 4, 1665-July 31, 1667: Second Anglo-Dutch War; Oct. 29, 1665: Battle of Mbwila; 1670-1699: Rise of the Asante Empire; Late 17th cent.: Decline of Benin; Beginning 1680's: Guerra dos Bárbaros.

RELATED ARTICLES in *Great Lives from History: The Seventeenth Century, 1601-1700:* Piet Hein; Njinga; Michiel Adriaanszoon de Ruyter.

1626-1673
CIVIL WAR RAVAGES VIETNAM

The northern Trinh battled the southern Nguyen for control of Vietnam, ultimately resulting in a stalemate and the partitioning of the country. Europeans sold weapons to both sides in the civil war and sent missionaries and traders, yet the Vietnamese successfully resisted foreign control.

LOCALE: Vietnam
CATEGORIES: Wars, uprisings, and civil unrest; expansion and land acquisition

KEY FIGURES

Trinh Trang (1577-1657), lord of the Trinh, r. 1623-1657
Trinh Tac (1606-1682), lord of the Trinh, r. 1657-1682

Phuc Nguyen (1563-1635), lord of the Nguyen, r. 1613-1635
Phuc Lan (1601-1648), lord of the Nguyen, r. 1635-1648
Phuc Tan (1623-1687), lord of the Nguyen, r. 1648-1687
Dao Duy Tu (1572-1634), military strategist of the Nguyen
Le Than Tong (1607-1662), emperor of Vietnam, r. 1619-1643, 1649-1662
Alexandre de Rhodes (1591-1660), French bishop and missionary to Vietnam

SUMMARY OF EVENT

In the seventeenth century, a civil war effectively divided Vietnam into two parts. The war was rooted in the rivalry of two clans, the Trinh in the North and the Nguyen in the South. Both families rose to power in the aftermath of the decline of the Le Dynasty. Since 1533, the Le emperors had been figureheads, while the Trinh and the Nguyen had fought for real control of the Vietnamese empire. The two families were actually related, but this did little to cool their rivalry.

In the early 1600's, the Trinh lords controlled northern Vietnam. Their leader was Trinh Trang. In 1570, his father had made himself hereditary lord, or *chua*. At age twenty-three, in 1600, Trinh Trang married Nguyen Ngoc Tu, apparently cementing an alliance between the rival clans. However, when Ngoc Tu's brother, Phuc Nguyen, became Lord Sai and ruler of southern Vietnam in 1613, Trinh Trang secretly allied himself with two other brothers of his wife. In 1620, Phuc Nguyen caught his two disloyal brothers and put them in jail to die. Trinh Trang avoided seizure, and in 1623 became Lord Thanh Do Vuong.

In 1626, Trinh Trang moved five thousand soldiers to the south, just outside of Dong Hoi, where the lands of his Nguyen enemies began. Trinh Trang ordered the southern lord to pay tribute and to help fight anti-Le rebels in the north. To buy time, Phuc Nguyen pretended to agree, but he had his military counselor, Dao Duy Tu, build a defensive wall at Dong Hoi that eventually ran for 6 miles (10 kilometers) inland from the coast and reached a height of 20 feet (6 meters). The partition between the Trinh and the Nguyen domains was close to where North and South Vietnam would be divided from 1954 until 1976.

Angered by Phuc Nguyen's delays, Trinh Trang finally attacked in 1627. Contemporary sources speak of 200,000 soldiers, 500 war elephants, and 500 warships. Trinh Trang was defeated, as Phuc Nguyen's gunners employed their Portuguese cannons to kill and frighten the elephants, who trampled his soldiers to death. The Nguyen victory highlighted the importance of European arms. Portuguese missionaries and traders had been active in southern Vietnam since 1540, and they had used the gun trade to form alliances in the south of the country. This also frustrated the ambitions of the English, who could not gain a foothold of their own in the south once the Portuguese connection with the Nguyen was established.

In the north, the French sought an alliance with the Trinh. At first, they sent primarily missionaries, who doubled as traders and scientific advisers. One of the most famous of these was Alexandre de Rhodes, who ar-

rived in 1624. He was welcomed at the Trinh capital of Thang Long (modern Hanoi), and by the time of the first battle, he claimed to have baptized sixty-seven hundred Vietnamese people. Rhodes's missionary work angered the Trinh, and in 1630 he was officially expelled, only to sneak back many times.

During the dry season of 1631, Dao Duy Tu advised Phuc Nguyen to launch an attack against the north. Nguyen forces captured the border district of Nam Bo Chinh. The Nguyen also forbade Christian preaching, while continuing to buy arms from the Portuguese. To strengthen his position in the south, where Vietnamese settlers and soldiers were in conflict with the Chams and the Khmer (Cambodians), Phuc Nguyen married Princess Ngoc Khoa to the king of Champa in 1631. Princess Ngoc Van had already married the Cambodian king in 1620. In 1634, Trinh Trang sought revenge by allying himself with a traitorous son of Phuc Nguyen. However, the son, Nguyen Anh, was replaced as commander of the border district of Quang Binh, preventing him from being of use to Trinh Trang. When the disappointed Trinh Trang attacked anyway, he was defeated.

After Phuc Nguyen died in 1635, his second son, Phuc Lan, succeeded him. Nguyen Anh responded by rebelling against the family order. This time, he sought the help of Japanese traders. The Nguyen soldiers caught him, however, and an uncle decided to have him executed. In 1639, Phuc Lan fell in love with a prince's widow, Tong Thi. She moved in with him and he ended his family's tradition of not mistreating their subjects, extorting valuables from his rich followers to give as gifts to his paramour.

Trinh Trang attacked again in 1643 and was again defeated. The Trinh were allied with the Protestant Dutch, whom the Catholic Portuguese had successfully barred from Nguyen territory. Since 1637, the Dutch had held a trading post at Pho Hien, near modern Hanoi, and had sold arms to the Trinh. In 1641 and 1642, the Dutch and the Vietnamese under Nguyen lordship clashed. Late in 1643, the Dutch attacked near Da Nang with three battleships. The Vietnamese counterattacked with smaller boats. One Dutch warship ran aground and sank. When the Vietnamese boarded the flagship, Dutch captain Pierre Baeck blew it up, killing most of his crew. The last ship escaped to the north, signaling a Vietnamese victory over a European fleet.

This naval victory hardened Vietnamese attitudes toward Christianity. In 1644, missionaries were martyred in Da Nang. In 1645, Alexandre de Rhodes was expelled permanently. Even as the warring Vietnamese used European arms, they vigorously resisted any attempts at colonization and remained unrelentingly suspicious of Christianity.

In 1648, Trinh Trang launched a land and sea border attack. Even though Phuc Lan died of illness during the fighting, his son Phuc Tan led one hundred war elephants on a decisive nighttime attack. The Trinh forces were defeated and fled but not before losing three thousand men. Phuc Tan succeeded his father as Lord Hien, the Wise Lord. Emboldened, the Nguyen attacked the Trinh in 1655. Initially, they were successful. In 1657, Trinh Trang died at age 80 (counted as 81 in Asia). Perhaps to give his successor a chance for peace, Phuc Tan halted the Nguyen offensive. Trinh Tac succeeded his father, but he was disliked for his contemptuous attitude and had a brother tortured to death in 1657.

In the late 1650's, rivalry among Nguyen generals led to the loss of all territory the Nguyens had conquered since 1631. In 1661, moreover, Trinh Tac invaded. Emperor Le Than Tong was ordered to accompany the invasion. Exemplary of the Trinh's power over the imperial family, the emperor's father had been forced to commit suicide by Trinh Tac's grandfather, whose daughter was Le Than Tong's mother. Later, Trinh Tac's father forced his daughter and the emperor to marry, even though she was the ex-wife of the emperor's uncle and had borne the latter four children.

By 1662, Trinh Tac had to leave the south in defeat. He took Le Than Tong to Hanoi, where he died and was replaced by a son. In 1673, Trinh Tac launched his final attack. Defeated again in front of the wooden wall at Dong Hoi, he gave up. A tenuous peace was established between the Nguyen and the Trinh that would last for the next one hundred years.

SIGNIFICANCE

The seventeenth century civil war in Vietnam, which divided the country into a northern and southern part, darkly foreshadowed the Vietnam War in the twentieth century. Even though the Trinh had physical possession of the Le emperors, controlled about four-fifths of Vietnam's population, and had twice as many soldiers, they could not defeat the Nguyen. The inability of the Trinh to achieve victory was due in part to the Nguyen's use of Portuguese weapons, their relatively small and defensible front line, and the high morale of their soldiers.

In spite of the civil war, the Nguyen lords extended their territory in the mid-seventeenth century at the expense of the Chams and Khmer. In 1653, Phuc Tan annexed the province of Khan Hoa, extending his domain to-

ward modern Saigon and the fertile Mekong Delta. This expansion attracted both Vietnamese settlers and Chinese immigrants to Nguyen territories, increasing Nguyen economic power, as well as the sheer percentage of Vietnamese subjects under their authority. In 1679, a Chinese general with a fleet of fifty ships asked for asylum. Phuc Tan welcomed him and his three thousand soldiers and settled them in the Saigon area. In the twenty-first century, the Cho Lon district of Saigon still retains a Chinese character stemming from these seventeenth century migrations.

The civil war between the Trinh and the Nguyen provided imperialist Europe with several opportunities, particularly in the sale of weapons and dispensation of scientific advice. Despite these inroads, the Europeans failed to subdue the Vietnamese in the seventeenth century. National resistance to outside colonialism was too strong even in times of fratricide. The most influential European was Alexandre de Rhodes. Convinced that he needed Vietnamese priests, he transcribed the Vietnamese language using the Roman alphabet together with diacritical remarks to help pronunciation. His system, called *quoc ngu*, is still in use. It has made Vietnamese the only Asian language that uses the Roman alphabet.

—*R. C. Lutz*

FURTHER READING

Chapuis, Oscar. *A History of Vietnam*. Westport, Conn.: Greenwood Press, 1995. Chapters 5, "The Vietnamese Shoguns," and 7, "Western Involvement," offer detailed narratives of the period. Maps, bibliography, index.

Ha, Van Thu. *A Brief Chronology of Vietnam's History*. Hanoi, Vietnam: The Gioi, 2000. Brief biographies of all the major players. Gives full diacritical remarks for Vietnamese names.

Karnow, Stanley. *Vietnam: A History*. New York: Viking Press, 1983. Still the most widely available source in English. Chapter 3 discusses the seventeenth century. Photos, chronology, index.

Lamb, Helen. *Vietnam's Will to Live*. New York: Monthly Review Press, 1972. Perceptive account of Vietnamese resistance to European colonialism. Notes, bibliography.

SEE ALSO: 17th cent.: Age of Mercantilism in Southeast Asia; 17th cent.: The Pepper Trade; Dec., 1601: Dutch Defeat the Portuguese in Bantam Harbor; Beginning Spring, 1605: Dutch Dominate Southeast Asian Trade; Jan. 14, 1641: Capture of Malacca.

1620's

May 6, 1626
ALGONQUIANS "SELL" MANHATTAN ISLAND

The Dutch secured a legal claim to their primary stronghold in North America by giving trade goods to the Canarsee Indians in exchange for the island of Manhattan. Four decades later, the Dutch would be forced in turn to relinquish control of the island to the British, who would rename it New York.

LOCALE: Manhattan Island, New Netherland (now in New York)

CATEGORIES: Expansion and land acquisition; colonization; trade and commerce

KEY FIGURES

Henry Hudson (1560's?-1611), English n.avigator who explored the Hudson River for the Dutch East India Company

Cornelius Jacobsen May (fl. 1624-1625), first governor of New Netherland, who brought settlers to the area

Willem Verhulst (fl. 1625-1626), second governor of New Netherland

Peter Minuit (c. 1580-1638), director-general of New Netherland, 1626-1632

Willem Kieft (1597-1647), director-general of New Netherland, 1638-1647

Peter Stuyvesant (c. 1610-1672), director-general of New Netherland, 1647-1664

SUMMARY OF EVENT

In the early seventeenth century, the Netherlands, like other nations of northern Europe, sent out explorers to search for a sea route around North America to the riches of eastern Asia. The principal explorer for the Dutch was Henry Hudson, an Englishman who, in 1609, explored the river that bears his name. When Hudson and other navigators failed to find the Northwest Passage, the Dutch, like other Europeans, decided to claim the lands that they had found in the Americas and exploit their resources. While hoping to discover gold and silver, as the Spanish had done to the south, the Dutch soon found that furs were the most readily exploitable resource of the middle Atlantic coastal region that they claimed. The Dutch could obtain these furs by trading with the Native Americans, who would do most of the trapping in exchange for European goods. The demand for pelts was so great in Europe that one shipload could make its investors wealthy.

In the interests of further discovery and to stimulate trade, the Dutch legislative body, the States-General,

granted to its traders and explorers the exclusive right to make four voyages to any new lands that they might explore. Under this grant, in 1614, five ships visited the Hudson River, which the Dutch then called Mauritius. Later that same year, these traders combined as the United New Netherland Company and received a monopoly on the trade of the Hudson Valley from the States-General. Ignoring Manhattan Island, these early traders sailed up the Hudson River to the site of present-day Albany, where they erected Fort Nassau on Castle Island as a base of operations. There they exchanged their goods for furs with the Mohican tribal peoples. Following the expiration of the charter of the United New Netherland Company in 1618, a succession of different companies plied the Hudson River fur trade.

In 1621, a number of influential merchants obtained from the States-General a charter for the Dutch West India Company with the sole right to trade on the Atlantic coasts of Africa and North and South America for twenty-four years. Although the new company organized primarily to challenge Spanish control of Latin America, it was also interested in the Hudson River area. In 1624, the company dispatched Captain Cornelius Jacobsen May with a shipload of thirty families to settle in North America. Opposite Castle Island, the group founded a trading post they named Fort Orange; to the south, they formed a settlement on the Delaware River. They also may have established a trading house on Governor's Island, in what would become New York City's harbor. Coastal Algonquian tribes probably were in the process of forming a coalition when the Dutch arrived and disrupted that maneuver.

The first two governors of New Netherland, Cornelius Jacobsen May and Willem Verhulst, lived at the Delaware River site and administered the colony from there. Peter Minuit, the first director-general of New Netherland, shifted his center of operations to Manhattan Island. A native of Wesel, then in the Duchy of Cleves, Minuit was probably of French or Walloon descent. He impressed many as a shrewd and somewhat unscrupulous man.

One of Minuit's first acts after arriving on Manhattan Island early in 1626 was to buy the rights to the island from an Algonquian tribe, the Canarsee, for trinkets worth about sixty guilders, or about twenty-four dollars. There is some debate whether Minuit actually arranged the purchase himself or if his predecessor, Verhulst, did, but a May, 1626, letter revealed Minuit's intentions to buy the island. Controversy also surrounds the morality of the purchase. Tradition commonly calls the sale an unconscionable steal or a tremendous bargain. However, some historians suggest that the conversion to twenty-four dollars is too low and that, refiguring the payment in 1986 dollars, the Dutch paid $31 billion.

The Canarsee, moreover, certainly placed a different value on the beads, other trade goods, and land than did the Europeans. Value is a human creation, and if the Canarsee in fact believed that the island was equal in worth to the trinkets they received for it, it is difficult to find a basis from which to argue that they were incorrect. Certainly, to claim that European judgments of the relative value of land and trade goods was more accurate than Native American judgments is to tread dangerous ground. To be sure, however, the concept of land ownership did not exist among most indigenous people or, at the least, it had a meaning completely different from that of Europeans. As a result, the Canarsee may have though they were selling temporary rights, or some set of permanent rights to the land less exhaustive than the Dutch believed they were buying.

Because the Manhattan tribe, whose name the island inherited, had a better claim to it than did the Canarsee, Minuit later apparently also bought the island from them.

Through this, their first major land purchase from the Native Americans, the Dutch secured the semblance of a legal title to Manhattan. At the time of the purchase, it was a beautiful island, covered with a great forest and abounding with wildlife and wild fruits.

Minuit made New Amsterdam, at the southern tip of Manhattan, the nucleus of Dutch activity in the area. A large fort, pentagonal in shape, surrounded on three sides by a great moat and fronting on the bay, was one of the first structures to be built. When it was complete, Minuit brought several families from Fort Orange to settle in the town. He also ordered the evacuation of Fort Nassau on the South River, near present-day Gloucester, New Jersey, and transferred the fort's garrison to New Amsterdam. Despite his vigorous administration of the colony, the parent country recalled him for examination in 1632 and dismissed him from the Dutch West India Company's service.

In the meantime, in 1629, the directorate of the company, with the approval of the States-General, had issued a charter of Freedoms and Exemptions that provided for the grant of large estates, called patroonships, to those members of the company who would recruit at least fifty settlers more than fifteen years of age to settle their lands

1620's

The Algonquian inhabitants of Manhattan Island before contact with Europeans. (Gay Brothers)

New Amsterdam, c. 1651, about twenty-five years after the Dutch acquired the island. (Library of Congress)

within four years. These grants ostensibly were to promote farming in New Netherland, but their primary intention was to encourage settlers to go up the Hudson River to settle and make additional contacts with the Native Americans, thereby extending the fur trade. Traders presumably would ship the furs down the river to New Amsterdam, whence the Dutch West India Company had the sole right to export them. With one exception, Rensselaerwyck, these patroonships never measured up to Dutch expectations.

SIGNIFICANCE

After the purchase of Manhattan Island, relations between the Dutch and the Native Americans of the region remained mostly harmonious and the fur trade continued to prosper until 1641, when hostilities broke out. The fighting, called Kieft's War after Director-General Willem Kieft, resulted from his attempt to collect taxes from the Algonquian tribes for Dutch "protection." The conflict ended with a treaty on August 29, 1645, but it had already disrupted the fur trade and forced Kieft to relinquish some of his power to advisory bodies in order to obtain popular support for the prosecution of the war.

In 1647, Peter Stuyvesant succeeded Kieft and became the last Dutch director-general of New Netherland. It was he who surrendered the colony to the British in

1664. The brightness of the early promise of New Netherland, lustrous with the purchase of Manhattan in 1626, faded within the half century. With its fading, however, the promise of the island as a British outpost shone all the brighter. Although the Dutch would retain significant economic and cultural influence in the renamed New York, the English would benefit even more from their possession of one of the world's best harbors.

—William L. Richter and Thomas L. Altherr

FURTHER READING

Brasser, Ted J. "The Coastal New York Indians in the Early Contact Period." In *Neighbors and Intruders: An Ethnohistorical Exploration of the Indians of Hudson's River*, edited by Laurence M. Hauptman and Jack Campisi. Ottawa, Ont.: National Museums of Canada, 1978. Argues that the coastal Algonquians were probably in the process of forming a coalition when the Dutch obtained Manhattan.

Condon, Thomas J. *New York Beginnings: The Commercial Origins of New Netherland.* New York: New York University Press, 1968. Examines the Dutch purchase decision as part of a wider commercial policy.

Francis, Peter, Jr. "The Beads That Did Not Buy Manhattan Island." *New York History* 67, no. 1 (January, 1986): 4-22. Asserts that the trinkets the Dutch paid for the island were much more valuable than is commonly assumed.

Gehring, Charles. "Peter Minuit's Purchase of Manhattan Island: New Evidence." *De Halve Maen* 54 (Spring, 1980): 6ff. Discusses a letter from Minuit suggesting his intention to buy Manhattan Island.

Rink, Oliver A. *Holland on the Hudson: An Economic and Social History of Dutch New York*. Ithaca, N.Y.: Cornell University Press, 1986. Argues strongly for Minuit's mastery in establishing New Amsterdam.

Shorto, Russell. *The Island at the Center of the World: The Epic Story of Dutch Manhattan and the Forgotten Colony That Shaped America*. New York: Doubleday, 2004. Minuit's purchase of Manhattan is included in this history of New Netherland. Shorto argues that America owes a debt to the Dutch colony, because it was the first place in the New World where people of different races and creeds lived together in relative harmony.

Trelease, Allen W. *Indian Affairs in Colonial New York: The Seventeenth Century*. Ithaca, N.Y.: Cornell University Press, 1960. Places the Dutch purchase in the context of other relations with Native Americans around New Netherland. Argues that the money paid was worth more to the Canarsee tribal people than usually is presumed.

Weslager, C. A. "Did Minuit Buy Manhattan Island from the Indians?" *De Halve Maen* 43 (October, 1968): 5-6. Questions whether it was Minuit who actually purchased the island, suggesting that Verhulst did instead.

SEE ALSO: Beginning June, 1610: Hudson Explores Hudson Bay; July, 1625-Aug., 1664: Founding of New Amsterdam; 1630-1660's: Dutch Wars in Brazil; 1642-1684: Beaver Wars; Mar. 22, 1664-July 21, 1667: British Conquest of New Netherland; May 2, 1670: Hudson's Bay Company Is Chartered.

RELATED ARTICLES in *Great Lives from History: The Seventeenth Century, 1601-1700:* Henry Hudson; Peter Minuit; Peter Stuyvesant.

April 27, 1627
COMPANY OF NEW FRANCE IS CHARTERED

A powerful and influential group of investors sought to benefit from Cardinal de Richelieu's reorganization of French colonial charters in 1627. Founding the Company of New France, the group constituted the most important French colonizing power in North America until 1663.

LOCALE: New France (now in Canada)
CATEGORIES: Economics; organizations and institutions

KEY FIGURES
Samuel de Champlain (c. 1567/1570-1635), founder of Quebec in 1608
David Kirke (c. 1597-1654), Anglo-Scots privateer
Cardinal de Richelieu (Armand-Jean du Plessis; 1585-1642), French chief of the royal council, 1624-1628, and first minister of France, 1624-1642

SUMMARY OF EVENT
France's first permanent settlements in the Western Hemisphere were Acadia—which included parts of present-day Nova Scotia, New Brunswick, Prince Edward Island, and Maine and was founded in 1605—and New France,

founded in 1608 with its capital at Quebec. These colonization efforts were fledgling and precarious. Both were financed by merchant investors, who expected profits in fishing and the fur trade. Harsh winters, underfunding, and conflicts between colonial leaders and the private companies that had been granted fur monopolies resulted in weak development. New France, on the Saint Lawrence River, fared better than did Acadia, which suffered from its physical isolation, but even New France had a population of fewer than one hundred by 1627. Its residents were mostly clerks, interpreters, and missionaries, with only one actual settler family present.

In 1627, Cardinal de Richelieu, King Louis XIII's chief policymaker and the de facto ruler of France, carried out widespread reforms in colonial policy with the goal of increasing the prestige, wealth, and power of the Crown. He revoked all previous charters and concessions given for New France and initiated the chartering of a new and much more powerful group of investors, the Company of New France (la Compagnie de la Nouvelle-France) or, as it came to be known, the Company of One Hundred Associates (la Compagnie des Cent Associés). This company was so named, because initially one hundred men and women, the latter being wealthy widows, invested 3,000 livres each (one livre was roughly equal to four U.S. dollars in 1990), creating a capital pool of 300,000 livres for the initial investment. Many of the shareholders were government officeholders, merchants, and clergy. Some of the latter were motivated by religion as much as or more than by the drive for profit. The charter granted the new organization full title to all lands from the Arctic Circle to Florida and from Newfoundland in the Atlantic Ocean to the Great Lakes.

The charter was issued by Richelieu in April, 1627, and received official approval the following month. It required the new company to bring two hundred to three hundred settlers to New France in 1628 and at least four thousand more over the following fifteen years. The company's highest priorities were to be encouraging settlement and maintaining and expanding the fur trade, New France's only important export trade.

The charter discriminated against Huguenots (French Protestants), who had been instrumental in the establishment of Acadia. Only Roman Catholics were now allowed to colonize New France. Surprisingly, and probably uniquely in the history of European colonization of North America, Article XVII of the charter stated that native people in the colonized area who became Catholic "will be considered and reckoned natural born subjects of France, and as such will be allowed to settle in France whenever they please, acquire property therein, make wills, inherit, accept donations and legacies, in the same manner as those born in France." It is difficult to imagine a North American Indian pursuing these privileges, and none is known to have done so, but that it was allowed in the charter demonstrates an openness on the part of French colonizers at that time.

The Company of New France's tenure over the colony had a rocky start. War broke out between France and England in 1628, and the initial convoy sent to Quebec in the spring of that year was captured in the Gulf of Saint Lawrence by an English privateering force led by David Kirke. Those waiting for the ships to arrive at Quebec waited in vain and barely survived the following winter by subsisting on wild plants. Samuel de Champlain, who had been governing the colony for years, was forced by hunger and lack of supplies to surrender to Kirke's English forces in the summer of 1629. The Company of One Hundred Associates depleted its treasury in futile attempts to recapture the colony for France, and by 1630, the investment group Richelieu had initiated was nearly bankrupt.

In the Treaty of Saint-Germain-en-Laye, signed by the English and French in 1632, the colony of New

France was returned to the French, and the company was allowed to continue its efforts to develop the colony. Champlain was named governor once again. The royal government was pre-occupied with the Thirty Years' War in Europe for the next few decades and therefore neglected its fledgling colony in North America. In the absence of strong leadership on the part of the company and the French crown from the 1630's to 1663, the Roman Catholic Church, particularly religious orders such as the Jesuits, took a prominent role in governing New France. In the 1640's, Montreal was founded as a religious community of nuns and missionaries, and Jesuit missionary efforts influenced much of what transpired in northeastern North America throughout the mid-seventeenth century.

The company lacked the funds to satisfy its obligations as stated in the charter, so its directors farmed out land grants to wealthy French investors, who agreed, in turn, to settle these lands with colonists who would farm on the banks of the Saint Lawrence River. The number of colonists who came for this purpose would be credited to the company's quota of four thousand. Hence, what became known as the seigneurial system in New France was inaugurated. By 1642, there were still only three hundred people in the colony, although the number climbed to two thousand by 1653.

One of the reasons for such slow population increase was that, although the fur trade was a much more lucrative way to make a living than settling down to farm, fur trading meant traveling into the interior to live with Canadian Indians. Thus, while colonial furriers perhaps contributed to the growth of the indigenous population, they did not enlarge New France's population or increase the number of French families in the New World. Also, the French had allied with many native nations along or near the Saint Lawrence River, including Algonquians, Montagnais, Hurons, and had, through these alliances, gained a formidable set of enemies. The powerful Iroquois Confederacy of Five Nations—the Senecas, Cayugas, Onondagas, Oneidas, and Mohawks—were the enemies of the Saint Lawrence Valley tribes and by extension of the colonists of New France.

These Iroquois nations, particularly the Mohawks, were determined to undermine the French or even to expel them from the Saint Lawrence Valley altogether, and the mutual hostility that developed between Iroquois and colonists resulted in frequent surprise attacks mounted by each on the other's communities. The French attacked Iroquois civilian populations at times, and the Iroquois reciprocated in like fashion from the 1630's through the 1650's. This situation made further immigration by French colonists from the mother country a frightful proposition. It contributed to a lack of enthusiasm for crossing the Atlantic even by those in France who lived on the economic margins and might have benefited from farming on a seigneurial estate, which would have given them an improved standard of living and more autonomy than peasant farming back home.

Significance

The Iroquois' ability to undermine the colony made the Company of One Hundred Associates look bad in France, and the company struggled until 1663. By then, colonization under the auspices and guidance of a private company was considered a failure, and New France became a royal colony under the direct control of the Crown. Despite this eventual judgment, the company chartered in 1627 had been more successful than any previous attempt to promote French settlement in the Saint Lawrence Valley, and it had arguably made the royal colony possible. The Company of New France was responsible for bringing thousands of French people to the New World and for nurturing the fledgling American Francophone culture that would go on significantly to influence the history of Canada and Louisiana.

—Gretchen L. Green

Further Reading

Adair, E. R. "France and the Beginning of New France." *Canadian Historical Review* 13 (September, 1944): 3-37. A detailed and highly respected account of the early years of New France.

Bumsted, J. M. *The Peoples of Canada: A Pre-Confederation History.* 2d ed. Vol. 1. Don Mills, Ont.: Oxford University Press, 2003. The first of two volumes recounts Canadian history from the country's indigenous peoples to the confederation of 1867. Includes information about European exploration in the sixteenth and seventeenth centuries and colonial settlement in the Atlantic provinces, the Saint Lawrence Valley, and New France.

Delâge, Denys. *Bitter Feast: Amerindians and Europeans in Northeastern North America, 1600-1664.* Translated by Jane Brierley. Vancouver: University of British Columbia Press, 1993. A native perspective on the history of French and Dutch colonization in northeastern North America.

Eccles, William J. *France in America.* Rev. ed. East Lansing: Michigan State University Press, 1998. Account of French colonization in North America, including a brief mention of the 1627 company chartered for New France.

Lescarbot, Marc. *The History of New France.* Edited by W. L. Grant and H. P. Biggar. 3 vols. Toronto: Champlain Society, 1907-1914. An important primary source on the history of New France. Volume 1 deals with the Company of New France.

Moogk, Peter. *La Nouvelle France: The Making of French Canada, a Cultural History.* East Lansing: Michigan State University Press, 2000. Examines life in New France, demonstrating how the area's social institutions and the experiences and character of its settlers have set it apart from the rest of Canada.

Thwaites, R. G., ed. *The Jesuit Relations and Allied Documents.* 73 vols. Cleveland, Ohio: Burrows, 1896-1901. A collection of letters written by Jesuit missionaries in New France and Acadia, primarily dealing with seventeenth century events. An invaluable source of information on the native nations, both allied and enemy, with which the priests dealt.

Zoltvany, Yves F., ed. *The French Tradition in America.* New York: Harper & Row, 1969. A collection of documents related to the French presence in North America. Includes an English translation of the text of the charter of the Company of One Hundred Associates.

See also: Mar. 15, 1603-Dec. 25, 1635: Champlain's Voyages; Spring, 1604: First European Settlement in North America; 1610-1643: Reign of Louis XIII; Beginning June, 1610: Hudson Explores Hudson Bay; 1611-1630's: Jesuits Begin Missionary Activities in New France; 1618-1648: Thirty Years' War; 1642-1684: Beaver Wars; May, 1642: Founding of Montreal; May 2, 1670: Hudson's Bay Company Is Chartered; Beginning 1673: French Explore the Mississippi Valley; May 1, 1699: French Found the Louisiana Colony.

Related articles in *Great Lives from History: The Seventeenth Century, 1601-1700:* Samuel de Champlain; Pierre Le Moyne d'Iberville; Saint Isaac Jogues; Louis Jolliet; Sieur de La Salle; François Laval; Jacques Marquette; Cardinal de Richelieu; Kateri Tekakwitha.

1620's

May 6-June 7, 1628
PETITION OF RIGHT

The Petition of Right allowed the English parliament to voice its grievances against King Charles I, marking a significant step in the evolution of constitutional monarchy in England.

LOCALE: London, England
CATEGORIES: Government and politics; laws, acts, and legal history; social issues and reform

KEY FIGURES

John Eliot (1592-1632), leader of the House of Commons, 1626-1629
Sir Edward Coke (1552-1634), former lord chief justice of the King's Bench who helped draw up the Petition of Right
Charles I (1600-1649), king of England, r. 1625-1649
First Duke of Buckingham (George Villiers; 1592-1628), chief minister of Charles I, 1625-1628
Thomas Wentworth (1593-1641), member of Parliament and first earl of Strafford, 1640-1641

SUMMARY OF EVENT

At the beginning of the seventeenth century, Parliament's relations with the English monarch were guided by the principle that the king could do no wrong. Under common law, the Crown could not be sued, for the monarch, as supreme lord of the courts, was not subject to their jurisdiction. There was, however, a tradition of petitioning a monarch for restitution or redress that dated back to the Magna Carta (1215). Such petitions were an accepted legal remedy for disputes with the Crown.

Ultimately, Parliament found mounting petitions to be an effective technique in dealing with recalcitrant monarchs, especially when combined with their power of the purse: By tying petitions to money bills, Parliament could coerce monarchs into agreeing to limitations on the royal prerogative. The laws of England forbade the king from levying taxes: only Parliament could tax the people. The advantage of a petition, moreover, was that, as it merely confirmed existing rights, Parliament could secure significant concessions from the king while maintaining the appearance of a status quo. That is, when Parliament used this ploy, there would seem to be no extension of parliamentary rights at the expense of the Crown.

By the time of the accession of Charles I in 1625, the monarchy and Parliament had long been at odds over the royal prerogative. The issue was simple: Was there to be a balance between king and Parliament (constitutional monarchy), or was the king to be supreme in his realm (absolutist monarchy)? Although not unusually learned, Charles I inherited from his father an authoritarian streak, stubbornness, and a tendency toward duplicity in dealing with those whom he considered to be his inferiors. Charles demonstrated little or no patience for Parliament, whose desires to limit his prerogative he saw as utterly without legitimacy, and he drastically underestimated the practical power of Parliament to enforce its desires, whether philosophically legitimate or not.

The first Parliament of Charles's reign, which met in 1625, expressed its displeasure with the duke of Buckingham, who was head of the navy, for blundering and misusing resources in his conduct of the war against Spain. As an expression of its dissatisfaction, the House of Commons voted the tax known as "tunnage and poundage" for only one year. The tax, an import and export duty, had habitually been voted for each king's entire reign, and limitation of the grant to one year indicated that Parliament did not trust Charles.

The House of Commons of 1625 also severely criticized Arminianism in the Church of England. William Laud, then bishop of London and a privy councillor to Charles, was a strong supporter of episcopacy and church discipline. As the theory of divine right of kings rested upon the concept of one king, one church, the king either controlled his established church as its Supreme Head, or he saw the diminution of his religious authority coincide with a diminution of his royal power. Laud was also High Church, which meant he favored a more ceremonial liturgy in the Church. These ideas were anathema to the Puritan Anglicans, who wanted to "purify" the Church of England along Calvinist lines. To them, lack of austerity and excessive ritualism smacked of "popery." Puritans wanted less state interference in local matters and a simplified church service. Thus, for the Puritans no less than for the king, religious issues were also political issues.

Disgusted at what he regarded as the radicalism of the 1625 Parliament, Charles dissolved it. Before summoning a new one the following year, he eliminated certain radical members prominent in the previous Parliament by making them sheriffs and thus forcing them to remain in their own counties instead of coming to London. The leadership of the Commons passed by default, however, to an even more radical group led by John Eliot. The 1626 Parliament attempted to impeach Buckingham on charges of misconduct in the war. The impeachment was of questionable legality but showed the increasing boldness of the House of Commons. Once more failing to obtain grants of taxes to carry on the war, Charles soon dissolved Parliament again.

For two years Charles attempted to rule without Parliament. Unfortunately, Buckingham foolishly entangled England in a war with France while the nation was still at war with Spain. Claiming that England should aid French Huguenots, in 1627 the duke personally led an expedition to La Rochelle. It was an unmitigated disaster: The expedition was costly, troops were quartered in the homes of English citizens until they were ready to sail, and nothing was accomplished. To raise money, Charles attempted to secure a huge forced loan from the more substantial men of the kingdom, an expedient that had been used in England before but never on so large a scale. More than seventy rural landowners, including Eliot, were jailed for refusing to pay. They petitioned the courts, which ultimately upheld the king but only after the case had been thoroughly publicized and had aroused considerable opposition.

Without taxes, Charles's financial situation was becoming desperate, and in 1628, he again summoned Parliament. Prominent among the new members were Eliot, who had recently been released from prison, Sir Thomas Wentworth, who had also been imprisoned in connection with the loan but was more moderate and later became Charles's chief adviser, and the elderly Sir Edward Coke, the former lord chief justice who had been removed from office by James I. The king again requested taxes for the support of the war, but Eliot and others asserted that the war was going badly because of Buckingham and demanded that he be removed before Parliament would consider granting money. In the meantime, the House of Commons discussed the grievances which it had against the king's government.

For more than a month, the Commons debated the drawing up of a Bill of Rights guaranteeing fundamental liberties to English subjects against the encroachments of royal power. Private conferences were held with members of the House of Lords, who also had to approve bills. On April 28, the king summoned the Lords and the Commons together and assured them of his respect for traditional English liberties embodied in Magna Carta and other documents, but some members still distrusted him. By May 5, however, it was decided that the Bill of Rights had no future, because the king and the Lords would never accept it.

On May 6, Sir Edward Coke suggested that the Commons attempt to join with the Lords in presenting the king with a Petition of Right. This petition would not have the status of a bill but would take the form of a plea to the king, which Parliament had the right to present without limit. Wentworth supported the suggestion and so did Eliot. The Petition of Right was formally drawn up the same day. It was a protest against those actions of the king's officers that the Commons claimed violated the fundamental rights of Englishmen, the taking of forced loans, arbitrary arrest and imprisonment without charge and without trial, and the forced billeting of soldiers in private houses. On May 8, a fourth clause was added protesting the proclamation of martial law in peacetime.

1620's

THE PETITION OF RIGHT

In the Petition of Right, Parliament set out for King Charles I a list of grievances over his actions as king and required him to promise that he would refrain from continuing to perform such actions. The first paragraph of the petition, reproduced below, sets out the specific laws limiting the king's powers that Parliament believed Charles to have violated.

Humbly show unto our Sovereign Lord the King, the Lords Spiritual and Temporal, and Commons in Parliament assembles, that whereas it is declared and enacted by a statute made in the time of the reign of King Edward I, commonly called Stratutum de Tellagio non Concedendo, that no tallage or aid shall be laid or levied by the king or his heirs in this realm, without the good will and assent of the archbishops, bishops, earls, barons, knights, burgesses, and other the freemen of the commonalty of this realm; and by authority of parliament holden in the five-and-twentieth year of the reign of King Edward III, it is declared and enacted, that from thenceforth no person should be compelled to make any loans to the king against his will, because such loans were against reason and the franchise of the land; and by other laws of this realm it is provided, that none should be charged by any charge or imposition called a benevolence, nor by such like charge; by which statutes before mentioned, and other the good laws and statutes of this realm, your subjects have inherited this freedom, that they should not be compelled to contribute to any tax, tallage, aid, or other like charge not set by common consent, in parliament.

Source: From http://www.constitution.org/eng/petright.htm. Accessed April 26, 2005.

The king's chief minister, the duke of Buckingham, who had supported the policies that led Parliament to adopt the Petition of Right in protest, was assassinated less than three months after Charles I accepted the petition. (R. S. Peale and J. A. Hill)

In the Commons, Eliot gave a long speech detailing the maladministrations of Charles's servants, especially Buckingham. On June 5, Charles sent word that the Commons should not engage in any speeches that cast aspersions on the government or its ministers, a message which the delegates took to be an illegal interference with their right of free discussion. Protracted debate followed over whether to submit a formal protest to the king, but on June 7, he summoned the two Houses of Parliament unexpectedly, had the Petition read, and in a brief statement in French indicated his acceptance of it.

Continuing in session for the consideration of several tax bills, the Commons then drew up a less formal remonstrance to the king, in which Buckingham was again mentioned in connection with a number of grievances throughout the kingdom. Charles received it with sarcasm and did nothing about it. He had obtained the taxes that he had sought, so he adjourned Parliament, though he did not dissolve it. One of Parliament's major grievances was soon removed, when Buckingham was assassinated by John Felton, a disappointed office-seeker, on August 23.

When Parliament met again in 1629, however, feelings still ran high. When the king realized the mood of the Commons, he ordered Parliament dissolved, but the radical party, led by Eliot, held the speaker in his chair, thereby keeping the House officially in session, while protests were passed against Arminianism and against tunnage and poundage, which Charles had been collecting without authorization. Eliot was prosecuted for this act and died in prison in 1632. Wentworth, alarmed at what he regarded as the radicalism of his colleagues, went over to the king's side. Charles made it clear that he would not summon another Parliament unless he were in dire financial necessity, and for the following eleven years, he attempted to rule without the cooperation of Parliament.

The absence of Parliament provided only one inconvenience for Charles, namely the difficulty of raising money. He resorted to a number of extralegal or dubious methods, including revival of forgotten medieval feudal dues, and extending existing taxes beyond the limits intended for them. "Ship money," for instance, was ordinarily collected from coastal towns, but it was now extended to the entire kingdom. He also imposed

The Lords were ready to concur in the Petition until a letter arrived from the king promising never again to imprison men arbitrarily, especially in connection with forced loans. On May 17, the Upper House proposed adding a clause to the petition proclaiming that the king's power would in no way be diminished. The Commons refused to accept the amendment, and the Lords finally gave in and passed the unamended petition on May 26. Two days later, the Petition of Right was formally presented to the king. He was promised new taxes if he agreed to accept the restrictions of royal power set forth in the petition. On June 2, Charles met with the two Houses of Parliament, and although he promised that he would do nothing contrary to the laws of the kingdom, he made no mention of the Petition of Right.

various customs duties. Fierce resentment against these expedients grew throughout the country, especially when those who refused to pay were prosecuted and imprisoned. Resentment increased when Charles refused to intervene on the Protestant side in the Thirty Years' War in Germany.

A second major source of grievance in these years was renewed activity against the Puritans, instigated by Charles's most trusted adviser, Bishop Laud, who had become archbishop of Canterbury. Although Puritans were still members of the established church, Laud forced Puritan ministers from their pulpits and dealt brutally with the more outspoken Puritan pamphleteers, who were imprisoned and mutilated. King Charles and Archbishop Laud were suspected, unfairly, of being secret Catholics.

In 1637, Laud attempted to impose a revised Book of Common Prayer on Scotland. The Scots resisted and swore to the National Covenant, in open defiance of the king's authority over ecclesiastical affairs. Charles decided to fight, and in 1639 the First Bishops' War erupted. It was this conflict that, in 1640, forced the king to end his eleven years of absolutist rule. Desperate for money, he summoned Parliament, but the so-called Short Parliament was too aggressive and was quickly dissolved. A second Parliament proved to be no less aggressive, for the Long Parliament sat for thirteen years and brought about the most sweeping changes in English history. Civil war, the abolition of the monarchy, and the execution of Charles I clearly limited the royal prerogative. Unfortunately, Parliament without king proved to be as absolute as king without Parliament. Only in 1688, with the Glorious Revolution, were England's constitutional and religious issues finally resolved.

SIGNIFICANCE

The seventeenth century is arguably the most significant period in the evolution of a constitutional monarchy in England. It was the Petition of Right that began this period of constitutional development. In English government, no single document exists that establishes a separation of powers with checks and balances. The Petition of Right, coupled with the Bill of Rights of 1689, which was passed after the Glorious Revolution of 1688, are two of the most significant documents limiting the power of the monarchy. Both draw heavily upon the Magna Carta of 1215, which asserted that no one in England, not even the king, was above the law. This understanding of constitutional mon-

archy is one of the great legacies of Great Britain to the world.

—*James F. Hitchcock and William S. Brockington, Jr.*

FURTHER READING

Cust, Richard. *The Forced Loan and English Politics, 1626-1628*. New York: Longman, 1987. Provides a detailed analysis of the issues and personalities that led to the Petition of Right.

Guy, J. A. "The Origins of the Petition of Right Reconsidered." In *Law, Liberty, and Parliament: Selected Essays on the Writings of Sir Edward Coke*, edited by Allen D. Boyer. Indianapolis, Ind.: Liberty Fund, 2004. Reexamination of the Petition of Right and Coke's role in its creation.

Hirst, Derek. *Authority and Conflict: England, 1603-1658*. Cambridge, Mass.: Harvard University Press, 1986. Analysis of the forces, religious and political, that resulted in war between king and Parliament.

Hulme, Harold. *The Life of Sir John Eliot*. New York: New York University Press, 1957. Detailed account of Eliot's parliamentary motivations and maneuvers.

Kenyon, J. P., ed. *The Stuart Constitution, 1603-1688: Documents and Comments*. 2d ed. New York: Cambridge University Press, 1986. Includes the Petition of Right.

Mosse, George L. *The Struggle for Sovereignty in England*. East Lansing: Michigan State University Press, 1950. Argues that the rule of Parliament theoretically involved arbitrary and absolute power to the same degree as rule by the king.

Reeve, L. J. *Charles I and the Road to Personal Rule*. New York: Cambridge University Press, 1989. Studies the motivations of Charles I and analyzes the historical forces with which he dealt.

Sharpe, Kevin. *The Personal Rule of Charles I*. New Haven, Conn.: Yale University Press, 1992. Examines Charles's personality, principles, and political views to explain his decision to dissolve Parliament.

SEE ALSO: 1618-1648: Thirty Years' War; Dec. 18, 1621: The Great Protestation; Mar., 1629-1640: "Personal Rule" of Charles I; Mar.-June, 1639: First Bishops' War; Nov. 3, 1640-May 15, 1641: Beginning of England's Long Parliament; 1642-1651: English Civil Wars; Aug. 17-Sept. 25, 1643: Solemn League and Covenant; Dec. 6, 1648-May 19, 1649: Establishment of the English Commonwealth; May, 1659-May, 1660: Restoration of Charles II; Dec. 19, 1667: Impeachment of Clarendon; 1673-1678: Test Acts; 1679: Habeas Corpus Act; Apr. 4, 1687, and Apr. 27, 1688: Declaration of Liberty of Conscience; 1688-1702: Reign of William and Mary; Nov., 1688-Feb., 1689: The Glorious Revolution; Feb. 13, 1689: Declaration of Rights; May 24, 1689: Toleration Act.

RELATED ARTICLES in *Great Lives from History: The Seventeenth Century, 1601-1700:* First Duke of Buckingham; Charles I; Sir Edward Coke; John Eliot; James I; William Laud; John Pym; First Earl of Strafford.

1629
ṢAFAVID DYNASTY FLOURISHES UNDER ʿABBĀS THE GREAT

The latter part of the reign of ʿAbbās the Great saw the Ṣafavid Empire of Persia reach a high point of military organization and the centralization of government. The Persian empire's territory reached a peak around this time, and culture, the arts, and philosophy flourished as well.

LOCALE: Iran
CATEGORIES: Government and politics; cultural and intellectual history; trade and commerce; art; organizations and institutions; science and technology; philosophy; literature

KEY FIGURES
ʿAbbās the Great (1571-1629), shah of Persia, r. 1587-1629
Rezā ʿAbbāsī (1575?-1635?), major artist of the Eṣfahān school of Persian miniature painting
Mīr Dāmād (d. 1631 or 1632), Persian philosopher
Mullā Ṣadrā (c. 1571-1640), Persian philosopher and mystic, and a disciple of Mīr Dāmād
Iskandar Beg Munshī (c. 1560-c. 1632), Ṣafavid historian and biographer of ʿAbbās the Great

SUMMARY OF EVENT
The Ṣafavids were members of an Islamic military and religious order established in the late 1200's by Persian mystic Ṣafī al-Dīn (1252/1254-1334). By the middle of the 1400's, the Ṣafavid order was becoming increasingly successful in warfare. Shah Ismāʿīl I (1487-1524) led his Ṣafavid warriors to found the Ṣafavid Empire, which existed from 1501 until 1722. Ismāʿīl also established the Shīʿite branch of the Islamic faith as the state religion, which continues to be the dominant faith of Iran.

Ismāʿīl, though, experienced a serious defeat at the hands of the Ottoman Turks in 1514. After he died in 1524, Ṣafavid control of the empire weakened considerably, so foreign powers, including the Ottoman Turks,

were able to make incursions on Ṣafavid territory. Shah ʿAbbās the Great, who came to the throne in 1587, reorganized the Iranian military and strengthened Ṣafavid rule. By the end of ʿAbbās's rule—the first three decades of the seventeenth century—the Ṣafavids had reached a military, political, and cultural zenith.

The shah had taxed the country heavily to pay for a professional military, a reorganized standing army that made possible the rise of the Ṣafavid Empire militarily. He moved away from using traditional chieftains as commanders and staffed the army with troops that owed personal loyalty to the Crown. Foreign advisers, notably from England, helped to train the new forces. Robert Sherley and his brother Anthony arrived from Elizabethan England in 1598, and in the early seventeenth century they helped reorganize the Ṣafavid military into three bodies of troops: the slaves, the musketeers, and the artillerymen, all of whom were paid from a central treasury and managed by a central administration. This modernized military eagerly adopted firearms and advanced military technology.

With the new military, Ṣafavid Persia was able to strike back against its neighbors, the Ottoman Turks. Between 1603 and 1607, Ṣafavid forces fought several battles against the Ottomans and won back much of the land that earlier had been lost. In 1623, the Ṣafavid army under ʿAbbās the Great invaded Iraq and retook Baghdad. The English, in return for privileges to trade in Iran, helped the Ṣafavids push the Portuguese out of Hormuz in 1622.

The military and commercial ties to the English were part of Ṣafavid Iran's widening circle of diplomatic connections. Reflecting the religious tolerance of this period in Iranian history, a number of the contacts were with European Christianity. Pope Clement XIII sent a Carmelite mission from Rome in 1604. French chief minister Cardinal de Richelieu sent representatives to

Iran in 1627, and the French missionaries, in turn, received permission to establish Capuchin missions in Baghdad and Eṣfahān.

The city of Eṣfahān became a center of Ṣafavid civilization in the early 1600's. Eṣfahān was an ancient city with a long history, but it entered its golden age after 1598, when ʿAbbās the Great made it his capital and began a massive program of building and rebuilding. Eṣfahān became renowned for its public buildings and public baths, mosques, and religious schools. At the center of the city, ʿAbbās's architects and builders constructed the Maydan-i Shah, a huge courtyard and central square. The Ali Qapu, or the royal palace, was a building in the shape of an arch on the western side of the courtyard. Across from the Ali Qapu, on the eastern side of the courtyard, stood the mosque that ʿAbbās used for his own prayers and devotions. At the southern end was another mosque, the Masjed-i Shah, or royal mosque. To the north, a gateway led into the mile-long royal bazaar.

The royal bazaar of Eṣfahān was one of the grand public places of the early modern world. At its main entrance, there was a gallery for musicians, who played at sunrise and sunset on days ʿAbbās was in the city. The bazaar itself was divided into different sections, with each section having its own gate and each devoted to a specific trade. The sections contained receiving areas for storing goods, and had shopping arcades, where buyers

ṢAFAVID IRAN IN THE 17TH CENTURY

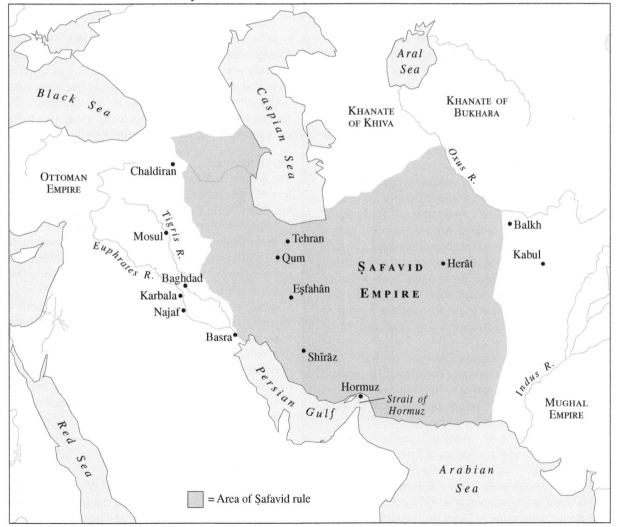

1620's

= Area of Ṣafavid rule

could view and select goods. In addition to commercial places, the royal bazaar contained public baths, mosques, and other buildings.

The main avenue into Eṣfahān, the Chahar Bagh, or four gardens, was a spacious route shaded by trees, and had water basins and fountains at intervals to refresh travelers. The avenue was named Chahar Bagh because gardens were located on both sides of the road; lattice walls on each side of the route enabled travelers to look into the gardens. On one side was the Garden of the Dervishes, the Mulberry Garden, and the Nightingale Garden. On the other side was the Octagonal Garden, the Throne Garden, and the Vineyard.

The visual arts, as well as architecture, reached a peak during ʿAbbās's reign. Miniature painting had been a Persian art form for centuries, but Eṣfahān became the home of its last great school under ʿAbbās's patronage. The most highly regarded miniature painter of the Eṣfahān school was Rezā ʿAbbāsī, who was supported and protected by ʿAbbās. Unlike many approaches to the visual arts in Islam, Rezā and his contemporary miniature painters emphasized the human form.

Carpetweaving, an Iranian art form that dates to antiquity, reached a new level of artistry in the Ṣafavid era, which crafted the finest of all Persian carpets. The weaving of carpets also became a national industry after ʿAbbās founded carpet-making factories in Eṣfahān and other cities. Factory production made it possible for wealthy individuals other than royalty to buy the carpets, which also were exported, reaching European courts.

The early seventeenth century also saw the flourishing of textiles. The Ṣafavid royal government established textile factories in a number of provinces, in which workers made silks, brocades, velvets, and embroidered work in great quantities. They also made cotton fabrics printed with blocks in a wide variety of designs. Painters such as Rezā ʿAbbāsī offered their designs for use in prints for fabrics, which connected the crafts and the visual arts.

There was also substantial Chinese influence on Iranian pottery design, especially porcelains. To produce ceramics that would appeal to the European market, ʿAbbās is said to have brought three hundred Chinese potters and their families to Iran.

Eṣfahān in the early seventeenth century also was known as a center of intellectual activity. The philosopher and teacher Mīr Dāmād made his home in the city and became known as the father of the school of Eṣfahān. Mīr Dāmād wrote many works of Islamic philosophy and poetry, attempting to blend the rationalist philosophy derived from Aristotle with religious ideas based on revelation. His writings are noted for their difficulty and obscurity. Most of his philosophical and religious writings were in Arabic, but the poems were in Persian. Mīr Dāmād's major disciple, Mullā Ṣadrā, was more mystical in his philosophy. The philosophical thought of the Ṣafavid period is generally considered to have reached its climax with Mullā Ṣadrā's works, about fifty of which are extant. Mullā Ṣadrā expressed himself with greater clarity than had Mīr Dāmād, and this may have been one of the reasons the younger thinker came under attack as a heretic.

ʿAbbās, who encouraged the work of poets, often visited coffeehouses to hear them read their poetry. He appointed poets to the office of poet laureate of his court and rewarded those whose verse he enjoyed. The shah is said to have appreciated one poet so much that he paid him the amount of the poet's weight in gold.

ʿAbbās's reign saw the work of one of the Islamic world's greatest historians. Iskandar Beg Munshī is known primarily for *The History of Shah ʿAbbās the Great*, a work long admired for the beauty of its prose style, and it continues to be regarded as one of the most important sources on the history of Iran under the Ṣafavid Dynasty. Iskandar worked as a secretary to the shah, giving him a special perspective on the shah's life.

SIGNIFICANCE

The Ṣafavid Empire marked a flourishing era in the history of Iran. The empire achieved great, lasting success not only in military technology and warfare but also in the arts, architecture, literature, poetry, philosophy, and studies of religion. Its greatest achievements were in organizing the structure and administration of government and in controlling its vast territories through centralized political control.

Many of the buildings of the time, such as those in Eṣfahān, continue to stand as lasting monuments. Diplomatic and trade connections brought Iran into closer contact with Europe. Persian carpets, often considered one of the characteristic artistic products of Iranian civilization, not only reached a high level of quality but also were produced in large quantities in carpet-making factories throughout Iran.

—*Carl L. Bankston III*

FURTHER READING

Daniel, Elton L. *The History of Iran*. Westport, Conn.: Greenwood Press, 2001. Part of the Greenwood Histories of Modern Nations series, this is an excellent general history of Iran for students and general readers. The work covers Iran from antiquity to the present, with chapter 4, "Early Modern Iran," examining the Ṣafavid era. One section in this chapter, "Zenith and Decline of Ṣafavid Iran," discusses ʿAbbās the Great and his reign.

Dimand, M. S. "Ṣafavid Textiles and Rugs." In *Highlights of Persian Art*, edited by Richard Ettinghausen and Ehsan Yarshater. New York: Wittenborn Art Books, 1981. Surveys sixteenth and seventeenth century production, with emphasis on achievements during the reigns of ʿAbbās and others.

Iskandar Beg Munshī. *The History of Shah ʿAbbās the Great*. 2 vols. Translated by Roger M. Savory. Boulder, Colo.: Westview Press, 1978. A translation of the most important primary source on Ṣafavid life and culture at its highest point. Most modern works on Iran in the early seventeenth century draw heavily on this book.

Floor, Willem. *Safavid Government Institutions*. Costa Mesa, Calif.: Mazda Publishers, 2001. Using materials from Iranian archives and accounts from sixteenth century European travelers, Floor thoroughly analyzes the military and political institutions of the Ṣafavid Empire. The work is scholarly in its treatment and might be too advanced for general readers.

Jackson, Peter, and Laurence Lockhart, eds. *The Timurid and Safavid Periods*. Vol. 6 in *The Cambridge History of Iran*. New York: Cambridge University Press, 1986. An authoritative work on Iranian history from late medieval to early modern times. Chapter 5, "The Safavid Period," provides a general history of the period. Other chapters cover religious and philosophical thought, carpets and textiles, architecture, the arts, and literature.

Morgan, David. *Medieval Persia, 1040-1797*. New York: Longman, 1988. A concise history, which places the Ṣafavid period in a larger historical context.

Savory, Roger. *Iran Under the Safavids*. New York: Cambridge University Press, 1980. One of the best sources on the Ṣafavid Dynasty, from its rise to its fall. Chapter 4 looks at the empire under ʿAbbās the Great. Other chapters consider relations with the West, the flowering of the arts, the construction and design of Eṣfahān, the social and intellectual structure of Ṣafavid Iran, and intellectual life during the period.

SEE ALSO: 17th cent.: Rise of the Gunpowder Empires; 1602-1639: Ottoman-Ṣafavid Wars; Beginning c. 1615: Coffee Culture Flourishes; 1623-1640: Murad IV Rules the Ottoman Empire; 1642-1666: Reign of Shah ʿAbbās II.

RELATED ARTICLES in *Great Lives from History: The Seventeenth Century, 1601-1700:* ʿAbbās the Great; Shah Jahan.

1620's

March, 1629-1640
"PERSONAL RULE" OF CHARLES I

Charles I's dissolution of Parliament in 1629 began an eleven-year period known as the Personal Rule, during which the king governed without calling Parliament and pursued political, fiscal, and religious policies that generated tremendous discontent.

LOCALE: England
CATEGORIES: Government and politics; religion and theology

KEY FIGURES
Charles I (1600-1649), king of England, r. 1625-1649
William Laud (1573-1645), privy councillor, 1626-1645, bishop of London, 1628-1633, and archbishop of Canterbury, 1633-1645
First Duke of Buckingham (George Villiers; 1592-1628), chief minister of Charles I, 1625-1628

Thomas Wentworth (1593-1641), lord president of the north, 1628-1641, privy councillor, 1629-1641, lord deputy of Ireland, 1632-1641, and first earl of Strafford, 1640-1641

SUMMARY OF EVENT
In the four years that followed Charles I's ascent to the English throne in 1625, relations between him and Parliament, in particular the House of Commons, steadily deteriorated. Charles's early reign was characterized by two situations that had carried over from the reign of his father, James I. He continued the English war with Spain, which the Commons endorsed, and he relied heavily upon George Villiers, first duke of Buckingham, whom the Commons detested. Parliament blamed Buckingham for mismanagement of the war,

Royalists donating valuables to support the army. Charles I required such gifts during the period of "personal rule," because without Parliament he was unable to levy taxes. (Francis R. Niglutsch)

which, after 1627, involved France as well. Charles supported Buckingham and, for his part, blamed the Commons for desiring war but refusing to fund it adequately.

Funding was perhaps the single greatest point of contention between Charles and the Commons. By English law, only Parliament could levy new taxes, so the king was dependent upon the Commons to pay for the war. The relationship between Parliament and the Crown grew worse when Charles attempted by bypass this obstacle: He resorted to forced loans to augment his revenue, and he imprisoned those who refused to loan him money. Parliament, believing that Charles was violating the rights of his subjects, in 1628 refused to grant him any monies until he agreed to the Petition of Right, which guaranteed freedom from unparliamentary taxation and from imprisonment without cause. Although Charles signed the Petition, the Commons continued to prepare resolutions protesting his financial and religious policies, and in March, 1629, Charles, rather than let these resolutions pass, dissolved Parliament, quietly resolving never to summon it again.

Charles's resolution meant that he would have to conduct his government without any new taxes. He ended the expensive wars with France and Spain in 1629, but that was not enough to bring Charles's income into balance with his expenditures. As he continued working to improve the royal finances, Charles also instituted a new administrative policy designed to demonstrate to his subjects the benefits of monarchical rule without Parliament. This administrative policy, called "Thorough,"

combined a scrupulous and strict enforcement of the law with effective supervision of local government. The policy was associated with Thomas Wentworth, eventually created earl of Strafford, who had entered Charles's service in 1628. When Wentworth was put in charge of northern England and, later, Ireland, he made them models for the exercise of real, effective, and severe royal authority.

The Thorough policy provided Charles with the revenues he needed, as he rigorously enforced long neglected laws to his financial benefit. For example, beginning in 1630, Charles began to enforce distraint of knighthood, an old medieval law that required any man owning land worth a certain amount to present himself to be knighted. This law had been long disregarded, but Charles began to apply it, fining men who owned qualified properties but had failed to present themselves for knighthood. Between 1630 and 1635, Charles raised £165,000 from distraint of knighthood. Similarly, in 1634 he collected fines for violations of the medieval "forest laws" and began to exploit "ship money," the right of the king to demand funds to maintain the navy. Only coastal areas were supposed to pay ship money, but Charles began to levy the funds from inland counties as well. Charles also ruthlessly exploited his feudal rights and dues and continued the unpopular practices of selling monopolies and levying impositions, or special customs taxes.

As a result of these measures, by 1640 Charles had significantly augmented his income. However, while every one of Charles's fund-raising tactics was technically legal, the king was widely perceived to be engaging in non-parliamentary taxation, a violation of both the oversight rights of Parliament and the property rights of British subjects. If not the letter of the law, Charles was certainly violating the spirit of the English constitution. Moreover, his attempt to tighten supervision over local government was resented by the lords and gentry who actually ran local government and who, not coincidentally, were the chief victims of Charles's financial policies.

Discontent over Charles's political and fiscal program was joined by concern over his religious policy, which was most closely associated with William Laud, whom Charles promoted to archbishop of Canterbury in 1633. As Supreme Head of the Church in England, Charles stressed the importance of the sacraments, especially communion. He increased ceremony and ritual in general in the services of the Church of England, discouraged and decreased preaching, and emphasized the importance of the clergy, especially bishops, arguing that bishops had a divine right to govern the Church similar

Charles I. (R. S. Peale and J. A. Hill)

to the king's divine right to govern the state. English Puritans were outraged by Charles's ecclesiastical reforms. As strict Calvinists, the Puritans believed that the Anglican Church was already too soft on doctrine, had too much ceremony and not enough preaching, and should not be governed by bishops. Those critics who spoke out against Charles or Laud were brutally suppressed by the Court of Star Chamber, headed by Laud himself.

The combination of Charles's religious policies with his political and fiscal ones raised anxiety and discontent in England to unprecedented levels. Not only the liberty of British subjects, but also their very souls seemed increasingly to be in danger. Charles's policies drove all sorts of people into opposition, creating unlikely allies. Many people who had had no sympathies with the Puritans before the 1630's became Puritan supporters as a result of Charles's ceremonial innovations, which seemed to shift Anglicanism in the direction of Catholicism. Propertied gentlemen, who would ordinarily cheer to see "subversives" punished for attacking those in authority, found themselves siding with the "subversives," as the gentlemen themselves felt threatened by a new, combined clerical and monarchical power that expanded divine right beyond the king to the Church hierarchy.

Even as these fears and anxieties arose, the legal means for their expression and redress, Parliament, was in abeyance. Englishmen believed that their liberty could only be protected by Parliament, and the longer time passed without Charles calling a Parliament, the more men realized that he never intended to call one again. This realization slowly became part of the general perception that the king was constructing a tyranny of church and state.

How long this might have gone on is unknown. That there was deep discontent in the 1630's is certain; that the English would ever have acted on that discontent, outside of the venue of Parliament, is not. In any case, the matter was decided for all concerned when Charles attempted to extend his religious policies to Scotland, which was adamantly opposed to episcopacy, or a bishop-governed church structure. The result was a revolt by the Scots. Charles's attempt to suppress this revolt, the First Bishops' War of 1639, failed, and without new taxes, there was no way to raise an army capable of defeating the Scots. As a result, in 1640, the king was forced to call a Parliament, and the era of Personal Rule came to an end.

1620's

SIGNIFICANCE

Charles's Personal Rule revealed important things about England in the 1630's. The discontent generated by Charles's policies showed how deeply attached the English had become to their political system, a constitutional or limited monarchy. Already, the English were beginning to think of themselves as having political rights, at least in embryonic form. These included the right not to be taxed without parliamentary consent and the right to be represented in Parliaments that met regularly. This sense of entitlement on the part of English subjects explains the feelings of betrayal that resulted when Charles continued to govern without calling a Parliament and raised funds through legal but questionable means. That sense of betrayal was all the more acute as Charles was perceived as bringing unwanted innovations into the Anglican Church as well.

The Personal Rule, then, destroyed any trust between Charles and most of his subjects. The reaction of those subjects demonstrates the extent to which, even before it was legally established as such, the English saw their proper system of government as a constitutional monarchy, rather than an absolutist one. They did not believe, in other words, that divine right gave the king unfettered powers, and they saw his divine right to rule as placing upon him a corollary obligation to protect the civil rights of the ruled. Englishmen did not overlook the fact that Charles had agreed to the Petition of Right, signed it, and then violated it. They were acutely aware that he was using the law to attack their rights and denying them the means to amend the law or codify those rights. Such a king was simply not to be trusted. This issue of trust, or rather, the lack of trust, was perhaps the single most important factor in bringing about the English Civil Wars in 1642 and Charles's eventual execution in 1649.

—Sharon L. Arnoult

FURTHER READING

Davies, Julian. *The Caroline Captivity of the Church: Charles I and the Remoulding of Anglicanism, 1625-1641*. Oxford, England: Clarendon Press, 1992. This work focuses on Charles's religious policies.

Hughes, Ann. *The Causes of the English Civil War*. 2d ed. New York: St. Martin's Press, 1998. The best short account of how Charles's policies helped bring on the English Civil Wars.

Merritt, J. F., ed. *The Political World of Thomas Wentworth, Earl of Strafford, 1621-1641*. New York: Cambridge University Press, 1996. This collection of essays examines many facets of the Personal Rule, from the political thought that motivated it to its execution in practice and its results.

Sharpe, Kevin. *The Personal Rule of Charles I*. New Haven, Conn.: Yale University Press, 1992. A massive and comprehensive study of the period.

Young, Michael B. *Charles I*. New York: St. Martin's Press, 1997. Scholarly biography of the king that takes issue with some of Sharpe's interpretations of the Personal Rule.

SEE ALSO: Dec. 18, 1621: The Great Protestation; May 6-June 7, 1628: Petition of Right; Mar.-June, 1639: First Bishops' War; Nov. 3, 1640-May 15, 1641: Beginning of England's Long Parliament; 1642-1651: English Civil Wars; Dec. 6, 1648-May 19, 1649: Establishment of the English Commonwealth; Dec. 16, 1653-Sept. 3, 1658: Cromwell Rules England as Lord Protector; May, 1659-May, 1660: Restoration of Charles II; Nov., 1688-Feb., 1689: The Glorious Revolution.

RELATED ARTICLES in *Great Lives from History: The Seventeenth Century, 1601-1700:* First Duke of Buckingham; Charles I; John Eliot; James I; William Laud; John Pym; First Earl of Strafford.

March 6, 1629
EDICT OF RESTITUTION

The Edict of Restitution marked the high point of the Counter-Reformation and of Habsburg imperial power during the Thirty Years' War.

LOCALE: Holy Roman Empire
CATEGORIES: Laws, acts, and legal history; religion and theology

KEY FIGURES
Ferdinand II (1578-1637), Holy Roman Emperor, r. 1619-1637
Gustavus II Adolphus (1594-1632), king of Sweden, r. 1611-1632
John George I (1585-1656), elector of Saxony, 1611-1656
William Lamormaini (1570-1648), Ferdinand's Jesuit confessor
Maximilian I (1573-1651), elector of Bavaria, 1623-1651
Cardinal de Richelieu (Armand-Jean du Plessis; 1585-1642), chief minister of France, 1624-1642
Count Johan Tserclaes Tilly (1559-1632), commander of the army of the Catholic League
Albrecht Wenzel von Wallenstein (1583-1634), commander of the imperial army

SUMMARY OF EVENT
During the first phases of the Thirty Years' War (1618-1648), it appeared that Emperor Ferdinand II would be at least partly successful in emulating the powers of Western Europe by establishing a stronger national state based on monarchical authority and religious conformity. The Edict of Restitution, issued in 1629, marked the turning point after which achievement of these ambitions became increasingly unlikely.

Hitherto, the war had been predominantly a religious contest between the Catholic Habsburg Empire on the one side, and several Protestant powers of Europe, including Bohemia, the Palatinate, and Denmark, on the other. During the course of the Bohemian phase of the war from 1618 to 1625, Ferdinand ruthlessly crushed religious and political rebellion in Bohemia while his brother-in-law, Maximilian I of Bavaria, and the army of the Catholic League overran the Palatinate. Similarly, the Danish phase of the war from 1625 to 1629 witnessed the Habsburg conquest of Denmark, which had entered the conflict to shore up the faltering Protestant cause and promote Danish dynastic interests in northern Germany.

The year 1629 found Catholicism and Habsburg Austria triumphant. For Ferdinand II, the moment had arrived to crown his success by taking steps to strengthen the Roman Catholic Church and the sovereign power of his dynasty within the Holy Roman Empire. Acting upon the advice of William Lamormaini, his Jesuit confessor, the emperor promulgated the Edict of Restitution on March 6, 1629.

Imperial law governing the recognition of religious confessions, the control of the numerous and often wealthy ecclesiastical principalities, and the ownership of Church property was settled by the Peace of Augsburg in 1555. Under that agreement, only the Catholic and Lutheran Churches were recognized as legal. The princes reigning in the ecclesiastical principalities were required under a provision known as the ecclesiastical reservation to be Catholic, and the ownership of Church properties was assigned to whichever of the legal confessions actually had possession at the time of the Truce of Passau on August 2, 1552.

The three-quarters of a century between the Peace of Augsburg and the Edict of Restitution had seen the arrival of the Reformed (Calvinist) church, the widespread avoidance of the ecclesiastical reservation in northern and eastern Germany, and the loss of considerable property by the Catholics.

Ferdinand decreed that all Church properties that had been acquired by the Protestants since the Truce of Passau were to be restored, and all ecclesiastical principalities were to receive Catholic rulers. This decree affected the two archbishoprics of Magdeburg and Bremen; twelve bishoprics, three of which were subsequently left in the hands of John George I of Saxony, a Lutheran supporter of the imperial cause; and numerous abbeys, churches, and estates. The edict further stated that only adherents of the Catholic faith or the faith of the Augsburg Confession, meaning Lutherans, were to enjoy free exercise of religion. The Reformed or Calvinist faith was thus placed outside imperial protection.

Yet even the religious tolerance extended to the Lutherans was qualified by the edict's strict adherence to the terms of the Peace of Augsburg, ignoring the secret promise of toleration extended to Lutherans in the ecclesiastical lands made by Emperor Ferdinand I. This clause represented the widest application to date of the principle *cuius regio, eius religio*—literally, "whose rule, his the religion." Ferdinand had previously made extensive use of this principle against the Protestants of Inner Austria (Styria, Carinthia, Carniola), Bohemia, and Upper and Lower Austria.

Ferdinand's decision to require restitution by means of an imperial edict rather than by calling for an imperial Diet, and his enforcement of the edict by imperial commissioners backed by the imperial army under Albrecht

An astrologer forecasts the assassination of imperial general Albrecht Wenzel von Wallenstein (right), who was killed by his own emperor's officers after Wallenstein had secretly met with Protestant leaders, the Catholic empire's enemies. (R. S. Peale and J. A. Hill)

Wenzel von Wallenstein and that of the Catholic League under Count Johan Tserclaes Tilly were all aspects of his attempt to strengthen the monarchical power in Germany. These measures raised a storm of controversy and numerous other problems as well. The Protestant princes of the empire, even those who were excluded from the provisions of the edict, such as John George of Saxony and George William of Brandenburg, now had cause to fear a new wave of religious persecution at the hands of the triumphant Catholic forces, which were then concluding military operations against defeated Denmark. Both Protestant princes and Catholic princes, such as Maximilian of Bavaria, feared that the emperor would use the edict to subject them to the absolute power of the Habsburg Dynasty.

A Holy Roman Empire unified behind a Habsburg ruler also presented a definite threat to France, now asserting its strength under the guidance of Cardinal de Richelieu and ready to resume its contest with the emperor's ally, Habsburg Spain. Furthermore, violent arguments broke out among Catholic princes and religious orders as to which of the restored territories they would receive. Finally, the emperor failed to take into consideration the insufficient number of Catholic clergy available in relation to the large territories they would be forced to take over.

Such problems, combined with the ruthless execution of the edict by Wallenstein and Tilly, served to undercut Ferdinand's support from Catholics as well as Lutherans. At the same time, it inspired many of the Protestant princes to look abroad for assistance from King Gustavus II Adolphus of Sweden and from Richelieu's France. Ferdinand, in an attempt to salvage the support of his former staunch ally Maximilian of Bavaria, who was in the process of negotiating an alliance with France, agreed on August 13, 1630, to dismiss Wallenstein but not to modify the Edict of Restitution. The dismissal of Wallenstein also represented an unsuccessful attempt to prevent the Protestant princes from rallying behind Gustavus II Adolphus, who two weeks earlier had landed with his forces at Peenemünde in Pomerania. Within a year, Gustavus II Adolphus had secured the somewhat reluctant support of John George of Saxony and George William of Brandenburg and had made an alliance with Cardinal de Richelieu of France.

SIGNIFICANCE

Consequently, the international nature of the war was significantly strengthened by Swedish and subsequent French participation, and the conclusion of peace was made more difficult. Not until 1648 was peace restored in Germany, while the conflict between France and Spain lasted until 1659.

—*Edward P. Keleher and William C. Schrader*

FURTHER READING

Bireley, Robert. *The Refashioning of Catholicism, 1450-1700: A Reassessment of the Counter Reformation.* Washington, D.C.: Catholic University of America Press, 1999. Bireley demonstrates how the Counter-Reformation was an active response to the profound changes taking place in the sixteenth century.

_____. *Religion and Politics in the Age of the Counterreformation: Emperor Ferdinand II, William Lamormaini, S. J., and the Formation of Imperial Policy.* Chapel Hill: University of North Carolina Press, 1981. A detailed account of the role of Ferdinand's confessor.

Gagliardo, John G. *Germany Under the Old Regime, 1600-1790.* London: Longman, 1991. Provides a coherent overview of the political, cultural, social, and economic trends in the Holy Roman Empire during its last two centuries.

Grell, Ole Peter, and Bob Scribner, eds. *Tolerance and Intolerance in the European Reformation.* New York: Cambridge University Press, 1996. Chapter 7, an essay by historian Euan Cameron, examines Protestant identities in Germany during the later Reformation.

Holborn, Hajo. *The Reformation.* Vol. 1 in *A History of Modern Germany.* New York: Alfred A. Knopf, 1959. Still the best overall history of Germany in English for this period, and a standard source.

Ingrao, Charles W. *The Habsburg Monarchy, 1618-1815.* New York: Cambridge University Press, 1994. A well-balanced and literate work, without being ponderous, covering the formation of the Habsburg dynastic empire.

Parker, Geoffrey. *The Thirty Years' War.* London: Methuen, 1985. Places the events in their military context.

Sturdy, David J. *Fractured Europe, 1600-1721.* Oxford, England: Blackwell, 2002. This thorough overview of European history includes a chapter on the Edict of Restitution.

Wedgwood, C. V. *The Thirty Years' War.* New Haven, Conn.: Yale University Press, 1949. An extremely readable account of the war, including its German as well as international ramifications.

SEE ALSO: 1618-1648: Thirty Years' War; 1625-Oct. 28, 1628: Revolt of the Huguenots; 1630-1648: Destruction of Bavaria; May 30, 1635: Peace of Prague; July, 1643-Oct. 24, 1648: Peace of Westphalia.

RELATED ARTICLES in *Great Lives from History: The Seventeenth Century, 1601-1700:* Ferdinand II; Frederick William, the Great Elector; Gustavus II Adolphus; Cardinal de Richelieu; Albrecht Wenzel von Wallenstein.

1620's

1630's-1694
SLAVES RESIST EUROPEANS AT PALMARES

For much of the seventeenth century, African slaves who fled from the sugar plantations along the coast of northeast Brazil journeyed to Palmares, a multiracial and multiethnic community built by former slaves. Although Dutch and Portuguese slaveholders mounted numerous well-armed attacks, the inhabitants of Palmares bravely resisted for nearly a century.

LOCALE: Territory on the border of Alagoas and Pernambuco in northeast Brazil

CATEGORIES: Government and politics; social issues and reform; wars, uprisings, and civil unrest

KEY FIGURES

Zumbi (1655-1695), black leader of Palmares
Ganga Zumba (d. 1680), black leader of Palmares
Domingos Jorge Velho (1614?-1703), Brazilian-Portuguese explorer, adventurer, and slave catcher

SUMMARY OF EVENT

In the second half of the sixteenth century, Portuguese settlers in Brazil began to plant and process sugarcane, and by the early seventeenth century, northeast Brazil supplied most of Europe's sugar. In order to staff the plantations, the Portuguese expanded the slave trade from Africa. As sugar production increased, so did the numbers of Africans brought in bondage to Brazil.

Life on the sugarcane plantations was brutal for slaves, who often worked sixteen-hour days, toiling in the fields. Working in the boiling rooms where the juice of the cane was transformed into sugar was not much better: The heat generated by the copper cauldrons in which the cane syrup was boiled was so intense the experience was compared to life in hell. Not surprisingly, slaves fled the plantations. Finding it impossible to make their way back to Africa, they established communities in the interior of Brazil, where they re-created, as much as possible, the life they had known before being brought to Brazil and enslaved. Slaves on Brazilian sugarcane plantations came from many different regions in West Africa. Thus, runaway communities saw a variety of blended African customs and traditions. Because African women were always in short "supply" (Brazilian planters preferred to purchase men for the hard labor on sugar plantations), runaway slaves often formed families with indigenous and mixed-race women. Thus, these communities became multiracial and multiethnic, combining a variety of African, indigenous, and European ways.

Africans clearly despised life on sugar plantations, but Europeans coveted the wealth generated by the Portuguese. In 1624, a Dutch naval expedition attacked the Brazilian capital city of Salvador, hoping to take over control of both the production and the supply of sugar. Repulsed by the Portuguese settlers in 1625, the Dutch struck again in 1630, this time farther north, successfully taking the cities of Recife and Olinda in the captaincy of Pernambuco. For twenty-four years, the Dutch remained in possession of this rich sugar area in northeast Brazil. The Portuguese did what they could to expel them.

African slaves took full advantage of the fighting between the Portuguese and the Dutch in Pernambuco. Between 1630 and 1654, the largest runaway slave community in Brazilian history expanded to become a thriving alternative to colonial society. By the 1650's, Palmares included eleven villages, the largest of which was home to eight thousand people living in fifteen hundred households. Palmares at that time had a total population of between twenty thousand and thirty thousand.

By all accounts, Palmares was much more than a hideout for runaway slaves. It was a thriving community organized in a fair and representative manner (the chief was elected by a council of warriors). Because those who lived in Palmares were not interested in supplying the European market, they used their rich soil to plant food such as manioc, maize, and many varieties of fruits and vegetables. This bountiful production nourished healthy inhabitants, while Palmares's leaders trained security forces to protect the community from outside attack. Their crops produced such an abundance that *palmarinos* engaged in trade with the plantations, supplying food for masters and slaves in return for firearms and other goods they could not produce. When unsuccessful at getting supplies through trade, *palmarinos* raided plantations and took what they needed. Over time, Palmares became a beacon for the oppressed plantation slaves, an alternative to their life in captivity. As such, the village threatened the control of slave masters and the authority of the Portuguese and Dutch colonial states.

The Dutch sent several expeditions to destroy Palmares, yet none succeeded, and the expulsion of the Dutch in 1654 encouraged the Portuguese to turn military attention against Palmares as well. In a 1655 raid, the Portuguese captured some of the children born in Palmares, including an infant who would later become the greatest leader of Palmares, the warrior Zumbi. This child was taken in and raised by a priest, who gave him the Christian name Francisco. He was taught to read and write both in Portuguese and in Latin. Apparently, Francisco was treated well by his foster father, for many years later, once back in Palmares, Zumbi sent the priest gifts on several occasions. Despite a more pleasant life than that of most slaves, once he became a teenager, he decided to cast his lot with the *palmarinos*. In 1670, he returned to Palmares and took the name Zumbi. He proved to be an exceptional warrior, rising quickly to become one of Palmares's most accomplished generals.

By the time of Zumbi's return, Palmares had become an armed encampment. Portuguese attempts to destroy the community had intensified; authorities were even encouraging *bandeirantes*, mixed-race individuals who hunted the indigenous for enslavement in the south of Brazil, to come north with their men and help eliminate the "black republic."

In 1678, following a costly Portuguese raid, the elected leader of Palmares, Ganga Zumba, negotiated a peace settlement with Portuguese authorities. In return for guarantees of land for himself and for his followers who had never been slaves, he agreed that slaves taken from plantations would be returned to their owners. Many in Palmares thought he was foolish to trust the white men, and some believed that turning over any black man to a slave master was betrayal. Zumbi, who helped to organize resistance to Ganga Zumba, eventually became the leader of the faction that chose to continue to defend Palmares.

Although Ganga Zumba was given land, he and his followers soon discovered they were not free from raids by settlers searching for new slaves. Blacks living in the community continued to be viewed as potential slaves. Not long after leaving Palmares, Ganga Zumba was poisoned (possibly on Zumbi's orders), and he died. It became clear to *palmarinos* that any negotiation with the whites would lead only to disaster. Peace was no longer an option. As the state mounted a number of attacks on Palmares, the former slaves dug in and resisted. They repulsed at least fourteen well-organized military attacks as they struggled to maintain their vision of an alternative way of life for black men and women in Brazil.

In the 1680's, a notorious *bandeirante*, Domingos Jorge Velho, was invited to bring his men and reinforce local government troops in a concerted attack on Palmares. When he and his men arrived in 1693, they mounted a serious challenge to Palmares. After a number of unsuccessful attempts, the five thousand troops took Macaco, the capital of Palmares. Zumbi escaped and began to regroup. One of the captured *palmarinos* under torture agreed, however, to take the troops to Zumbi. Thus, betrayed by a friend, he was captured and killed on November 20, 1695. Permanently destroyed was his free community where Africans, indigenous, and mulattoes (mixed race) worked for their own well-being.

SIGNIFICANCE

Palmares has become the ultimate symbol of black resistance in Brazil. Those who lived in Palmares created a viable alternative to a colonial system that abused Africans and Amerindians in order to supply agricultural commodities to the European market. At Palmares, African slaves organized their own government and forged a more equitable economic system than the one established by Europeans. In the face of numerous attacks, the inhabitants of Palmares organized armies and held back the raids of Europeans for almost a century. Their last leader, the great Zumbi, refused to believe the false promises of the Europeans and died rather than betray his people. In the twenty-first century, the slaves who escaped to Palmares continue to provide Brazilians with proud examples of the capacity of Africans and their descendants to engage in a noble struggle against racism and economic oppression.

—*Joan E. Meznar*

FURTHER READING

Anderson, Robert Nelson. "The Quilombo of Palmares: A New Overview of a Maroon State in Seventeenth-Century Brazil." *Journal of Latin American Studies* 28, no. 3 (October, 1996): 545-566. Focusing on rigorous translations of documents by contemporary observers describing Palmares, this article examines the mixture of African, indigenous, and Portuguese influences on that community. It raises the possibility that, had Zumbi not led an opposition movement to Ganga Zumba, the peace treaty might have established an enduring settlement of free blacks in northeast Brazil.

Diggs, Irene. "Zumbi and the Republic of Os Palmares." *Phylon* 14, no. 1 (1953): 62-70. An early overview in English of the history of Palmares.

Karasch, Mary. "Zumbi of Palmares: Challenging the Portuguese Colonial Order." In *The Human Tradition in Colonial Latin America*, edited by Kenneth J. Andrien. Wilmington, Del.: Scholarly Resources, 2002. An excellent account of the life of Zumbi and of the challenge Palmares posed to Portuguese colonial government.

1630's

Kent, R. K. "Palmares: An African State in Brazil." *Journal of African History* 6 (1965): 161-175. The classic account in English of the development and destruction of Palmares.

Nascimento, Abdias do. "Sortilege II: Zumbi Returns." In *Crosswinds: An Anthology of Black Dramatists in the Diaspora*, edited by William B. Branch. Bloomington: Indiana University Press, 1993. This play by one of Brazil's leading black dramatists illustrates the enduring appeal of Zumbi and Palmares.

SEE ALSO: 1617-1693: European Powers Vie for Control of Gorée; 1619-c. 1700: The Middle Passage to American Slavery; Oct., 1625-1637: Dutch and Portuguese Struggle for the Guinea Coast; 1630-1660's: Dutch Wars in Brazil; June-Aug., 1640: *Bandeirantes* Expel the Jesuits; 1654: Portugal Retakes Control of Brazil; Beginning 1680's: Guerra dos Bárbaros.
RELATED ARTICLE in *Great Lives from History: The Seventeenth Century, 1601-1700:* António Vieira.

1630-1648
DESTRUCTION OF BAVARIA

Military operations during the Thirty Years' War led to major destruction in many parts of Germany, notably in Bavaria, leading to a realignment of political and economic power in Germany and further divisions based on religion.

LOCALE: Central and Western Europe
CATEGORIES: Wars, uprisings, and civil unrest; diplomacy and international relations; religion and theology; government and politics; economics; organizations and institutions

KEY FIGURES
Ferdinand II (1578-1637), Holy Roman Emperor, r. 1619-1637
Gustavus II Adolphus (1594-1632), king of Sweden, r. 1611-1632
Bernhard (1604-1639), duke of Saxe-Weimar and leader of Protestant forces
Albrecht Wenzel von Wallenstein (1583-1634), duke of Friedland and commander of the imperial army

SUMMARY OF EVENT
Inhabitants of frontier areas have long been at higher risk from military action than those living in interior provinces. The inhabitants of the province of Bavaria thought they were among the latter group in the seventeenth century, but during the Thirty Years' War (1618-1648), Bavaria was among the former.

The Protestant Reformation was the great popular upheaval of the sixteenth century. Most supporters of Protestantism in Germany came from the central and northern parts of the region, but Protestantism, especially its more radical version, Calvinism, had attracted some followers in southern Germany as well. Calvinism was supported even though the Peace of Augsburg (1555) had given religious authority to the predominant Reformed faith, Lutheranism, in those areas where the ruler was Lutheran. The lack of a provision for Calvinism, together with the revival of the Catholic Church through the Counter-Reformation (1560-1648), led to the Thirty Years' War, in which the forces of Catholicism sought to reclaim all of Germany for Catholicism. The war had been spearheaded by Holy Roman Emperor Ferdinand II (the Habsburg ruler in Vienna) in alliance with the duke of Bavaria, Maximilian I.

All of the region's Protestant rulers—whether Calvinist or Lutheran—fought to defend the Peace of Augsburg. The Catholics had two armies, the imperial army and that of the Catholic League, led by Duke Maximilian, and the Protestants had armies commanded by various princes, including the king of Sweden, Gustavus II Adolphus.

The Catholics, for the most part, prevailed in the first ten years of the war (1618-1628). This trend prevented the Bohemians from choosing as their ruler the Calvinist Frederick William, elector of the Palatinate, at the Battle of White Mountain in November of 1620. The Catholic victories also kept the ruler of Denmark from intervening on behalf of the Protestants. However, the overreaching Catholics, led by Emperor Ferdinand II, reclaimed for the Catholic Church the former ecclesiastical principalities that had been secularized after the Peace of Augsburg through the Edict of Restitution (1629). This action enraged and energized the Protestant rulers and led to the intervention of King Gustavus.

Beginning in 1630, the Protestants were the ones who most often prevailed. Gustavus won major victories for them before being killed in battle at Lützen in 1632. Infighting among the Catholics, whose brilliant general Albrecht Wenzel von Wallenstein was assassinated in 1634 at the command of Ferdinand II, led to battlefield losses and the restoration of a balance of power among the German princes. Meanwhile, the Protestant forces had carried the fighting to southern Germany, notably Bavaria, which was invaded repeatedly by Protestant forces.

The nature of the fighting and its consequences led to substantial destruction. Because both sides in the conflict ran out of money, it was common practice to rely on the occupied lands' inhabitants to support the troops. The troops were generally quartered in the countryside, and the locals were forced to be supportive by providing the troops a place to rest and by giving them food. This system of "contributions" affected especially those who raised the food: the peasantry. Towns "contributed" to

the war effort to prevent military depredation (plunder), though Nuremberg, for example, which had a healthy municipal treasury before the war, wound up with heavy indebtedness after the war.

Military strategy often called for troops to deliberately ravage the areas through which they marched. This was particularly the case in Bavaria, which was invaded by Protestant forces under Gustavus in 1632. In April, 1632, at the Battle of the Lech (a river flowing from the Austrian Alps through central Bavaria), Gustavus defeated the imperial forces, which had withdrawn and moved toward Ingolstadt. The Protestant army marched through the countryside until it reached Munich, the German capital, and wreaked devastation as it advanced. By the fall of 1632, Gustavus and his troops were at the gates of Nuremberg, one of Bavaria's most prosperous cities. The Protestant army ravaged the area around the city, though they did not invest Nuremberg. In the winter and spring of 1633, despite the death of Gustavus the preceding fall, the Protestant forces reorganized under their new leader, Bernhard of Saxe-Weimar, and marched through northern Bavaria, devastating the areas around Würzburg and Bamberg and capturing Regensburg. Some peasants, desperate at their loss of lands and crops, staged a brief revolt.

This devastation was enhanced by outbreaks of the plague in the early 1630's, outbreaks that were brought on by the military's destruction of the countryside and the subsequent movement to the towns and cities of refugees seeking safety. It is not known how many deaths resulted from starvation, disease, or military action, but the number was substantial.

By the mid-1630's, both sides in the war were prepared to call a truce, but the negotiations proved difficult. The intervention of France gave new life to the Protestant cause, but Catholic Bavaria suffered again in 1645, when Protestant forces invaded the region once more. Protestant victories convinced combatants that it was time to stop fighting, and peace

Swedish king and Protestant commander Gustavus II Adolphus was killed by Catholic forces in the fall of 1632 near Nuremberg, Bavaria, during the Thirty Years' War. (R. S. Peale and J. A. Hill)

Protestantism, a popular religion in the German states, including Bavaria, was gaining even more adherents, which angered the already concerned Catholic Church. A contemporary depiction shows Protestant preaching in the streets around the time of the Thirty Years' War. (R. S. Peale and J. A. Hill)

was negotiated at Münster and Osnabrück between 1645 and 1648, treaties now known collectively as the Peace of Westphalia.

SIGNIFICANCE

Historians have debated the extent of the devastation and destruction described in writings of and about the period, especially those descriptions by authors such as Hans Jakob Christoffel von Grimmelshausen in his popular novel *Der abentheuerliche Simplicissimus* (1669; *The Adventurous Simplicissimus*, 1912; best known as *Simplicissimus*). Lacking any official population statistics, historians have generally concluded that the population of Germany declined during this period by about 30 percent, though some later estimates have reduced that figure. Some historians argue that the country was already in decline prior to 1618, when the growth of international trade caused the economic center of gravity in Europe to move to the western periphery of the Continent. There can be no doubt, however, that the war af-

fected the population severely, and Bavaria did not recover its population numbers until the next century.

The devastation of the Thirty Years' War might also have played a part in changing the role of armies in the century that followed. Armies were of limited size and were supported by taxes. They fought battles on limited fields, and the results tended to be confined to the exchange of territorial ownership among governments that were more or less absolutist in character.

—*Nancy M. Gordon*

FURTHER READING

Beller, E. A. "The Thirty Years' War." In *The New Cambridge Modern History*, edited by J. P. Cooper. Cambridge, England: Cambridge University Press, 1970. A good synthesis of accounts that noted Bavaria's devastation.

Guthrie, William P. *Battles of the Thirty Years' War: From White Mountain to Nordlingen, 1618-1635*. Contributions in Military Studies 213. Westport,

Conn.: Greenwood Press, 2003. This first volume of two books describes the battles fought in the early years of the war.

_____. *The Later Thirty Years' War: From the Battle of Wittstock to the Treaty of Westphalia.* Contributions in Military Studies 222. Westport, Conn.: Greenwood Press, 2003. Guthrie concludes his examination of the Thirty Years' War with a description of the battles fought between 1636 and 1648.

Holborn, Hajo. *A History of Modern Germany: The Reformation.* New York: Knopf, 1959. A general history of Germany by one of the foremost scholars in the field.

Hughes, Michael. *Early Modern Germany, 1477-1806.* Philadelphia: University of Pennsylvania Press, 1992. Hughes is more skeptical of the extent of the devasta-

tion, noting that most of the description of it was by German authors.

Parker, Geoffrey, ed. *The Thirty Years' War.* 2d rev. ed. New York: Routledge, 1997. A comprehensive and authoritative history of the war. Like Hughes, Parker is somewhat skeptical of the extent of the destruction.

SEE ALSO: 1618-1648: Thirty Years' War; May 23, 1618: Defenestration of Prague; Nov. 8, 1620: Battle of White Mountain; Mar. 6, 1629: Edict of Restitution; May 30, 1635: Peace of Prague; July, 1643-Oct. 24, 1648: Peace of Westphalia; 1667: Pufendorf Advocates a Unified Germany.

RELATED ARTICLES in *Great Lives from History: The Seventeenth Century, 1601-1700:* Christina; Ferdinand II; Gustavus II Adolphus; Leopold I; Lennart Torstenson; Albrecht Wenzel von Wallenstein.

1630-1660's
DUTCH WARS IN BRAZIL

The Dutch West India Company, determined to take Spanish and Portuguese colonial holdings in the Americas and Africa for its own trading monopoly, successfully occupied Portugal's rich sugar-producing colonies in the northeast of Brazil. The Dutch named the region New Holland. The company also took Portuguese slaving posts in West Africa, which provided labor for New Holland.

LOCALE: Northeastern Brazil

CATEGORIES: Wars, uprisings, and civil unrest; colonization; trade and commerce; economics; expansion and land acquisition; organizations and institutions

KEY FIGURES

John Maurice of Nassau (1604-1679), principal governor of New Holland

Felipe Camarão (1600-1648), Indian leader allied with the Portuguese against the Dutch

Salvador Correia de Sá e Benevides (1594-1688), Brazilian-born governor who led the reconquest of Portuguese colonies in Africa

Henrique Dias (d. 1662), black military leader allied with the Portuguese against the Dutch in Brazil

SUMMARY OF EVENT

The Dutch Wars in Brazil pitted the rising maritime power of the Netherlands against the declining sea power

of Portugal. The king of Spain was also king of Portugal, and Spain was the bitterest enemy of the Netherlands. Catholic Spanish kings resolutely suppressed the Protestant-inspired movement for Dutch independence. In capturing Brazil, the Dutch enhanced their own resources while weakening those of their enemy.

The Dutch West India Company was established in 1621 as a privately funded, government-sponsored monopoly trading enterprise. It was authorized to organize its own armed forces to acquire the treasure and lands of Spain and Portugal in the Caribbean, South America, and Africa for Dutch colonization and commerce. Its enemies considered it no more than organized piracy on the high seas. The prizes it first sought were the rich, sugar-producing colonies of Brazil. These curved along the coast of northeast South America, descending from the equator to the Tropic of Capricorn.

The capital of Brazil was Salvador, located on the coast in the province of Bahia. Northward lay the richest colony, Pernambuco, with its coastal cities of Olinda and Recife. Far south of Salvador lay Rio de Janeiro and São Paulo. The initial objective of the Dutch West India Company was to capture Salvador. With a force of two dozen ships and more than three thousand soldiers, the company took Salvador in May of 1624.

The capture of Salvador sent shock waves through both Portugal and Spain. The rich sugar plantations of Brazil were lost, and the silver mines of Upper Peru

(Bolivia) were now exposed to enemy routes. Philip IV, king of Spain, ordered a multinational force that massed nearly five dozen ships and more than twelve thousand soldiers to recapture Salvador, doing so the following year.

The Dutch West India Company, however, did not desist in its objectives for Brazilian sugar. It was determined to capture the richest sugar colony, Pernambuco. In early 1630, with a force of more than five dozen ships and nearly seven thousand troops, the Dutch launched a two-front attack, capturing the provincial capital of Olinda and the nearby port city to the south, Recife. The wealthy landowners of Pernambuco organized guerrilla resistance to the Dutch, restraining them from moving beyond the coast. Inadequate arms and supplies, together with betrayals and desertions, hindered this local resistance. The Dutch, from their base at Recife, advanced up and down the coast. By 1637, they held key settlements and forts from Rio Grande in the north, to several settlements near Recife in the south.

Named New Holland, the region experienced its peak period beginning in 1637, when the Dutch West India Company appointed Prince John Maurice of Nassau as civil governor and military commander. Enamored of Brazil, he governed New Holland until 1644, providing an administration of singular skill and effectiveness. He also expanded the Dutch hold on Brazil. Moving westward along Brazil's northern coast, the Dutch occupied Fortaleza, in the province of Ceará, by the end of 1637. Advancing farther toward the mouth of the Amazon River, they occupied São Luis, in Maranhão, four years later. In 1638, the Dutch attempted once more to conquer the Portuguese capital, Salvador, but the Portuguese soundly defeated them. New Holland, or Dutch Brazil, therefore, never extended farther south than above Bahia.

Essential to sugar production was African slave labor, so the Dutch captured and occupied Portugal's slave territories in Africa. In 1637 and 1641, they occupied Portuguese slave settlements in west-central Africa (Ghana) and southwest Africa (Angola).

Dominating now the former Portuguese strongholds around the rim of the South Atlantic, the Dutch West India Company reaped considerable rewards from New Holland. Developing new methods of sugar cultivation and marketing, the Dutch increased their wealth. John Maurice of Nassau invested in Recife's infrastructure, improving its streets, bridges, ports, and physical amenities. Although a Protestant, he followed the Dutch practice of tolerating all religions to secure peaceful conditions for commerce. Recife had a sizable Jewish community that built the first synagogue in Latin America.

However, the Dutch could not keep their hold on Brazil. In 1640, Portugal regained its independence from Spain, restoring its own monarchy and removing the Spanish king from Portugal's throne. Of paramount importance to the restored Portuguese monarchy was reasserting control over its wealthiest colony, Brazil. This restoration also was critical to Portuguese landowners in New Holland. The conflict between the Dutch and Portuguese had allowed many slaves to mutiny and flee into the interior to establish independent communities known as *quilombos*. To get new slaves, landowners had to "purchase" them through Dutch-controlled markets. While revenue became unstable and costs increased for some Portuguese landowners, the Dutch collected taxes regularly and thoroughly. These economic difficulties exacerbated the sociocultural differences between the Portuguese and their Protestant and Jewish, Dutch-speaking occupiers.

John Maurice returned to the Netherlands in 1644, and the vulnerability of New Holland increased. By 1647, the Portuguese mounted two fleets, one to retake Recife, the other to retake Luanda. The first attacked Recife, supporting the guerrilla movement besieging the city from the interior. This movement was made up of a historic alliance of landowners with blacks, Indians, and mixed-blood contingents, who were dependent on the landowners. Blacks were led by Henrique Dias, and the Indians were led by Felipe Camarão. In 1648 and 1649, in two battles in the heights of Guararapes outside Recife, this local alliance defeated the Dutch. The second fleet, led by the governor of Rio de Janeiro, Salvador Correia de Sá e Benevides, reoccupied Luanda, eventually driving the Dutch from nearly all occupied Portuguese African territories.

Besieged in Recife beginning in 1650, the Dutch surrendered Recife and all the territories of New Holland to Portugal at the beginning of 1654. Conclusive treaties, involving Portuguese indemnities to the Dutch, were signed a decade later.

SIGNIFICANCE

The Dutch Wars significantly changed both the Dutch and Portuguese empires. The Dutch had initial success holding Brazil, but once they lost Brazil, they were successful only in securing peripheral areas in the Americas. These areas were Suriname, the region west of the Amazon River, Curaçao, and some other small Caribbean islands. In Africa, the Dutch ultimately kept a hold on the southern tip of the continent only. The heart of the Dutch empire moved to Asia, where it fortified its position in the country that became Indonesia.

Portugal made the restored Brazil the heart of its empire, and progressively the colony became more critical economically. The colonies that Portugal regained in Africa were subordinate to Brazil as the source of its labor supply. The alliance of Portuguese landowners with black and Indian leaders to expel the Dutch led to forging Brazilian nationalism and the Brazilian interracial national character.

Both empires had been brief maritime powers. In the seventeenth century, they steadily became subordinate to the rising sea power of Britain. During the eighteenth century, Britain became the dominant maritime empire and, in its global conflicts with France, it fortified itself strategically by alliances with Portugal and the Netherlands.

—Edward A. Riedinger

FURTHER READING

Boxer, Charles R. *The Dutch Seaborne Empire, 1600-1800*. New York: Knopf, 1965. A classic account of the rise of the Dutch maritime empire in competition with that of Portugal. Follows their rivalries in South America, West Africa, and Southeast Asia.

Price, J. L. *The Dutch Republic in the Seventeenth Century*. New York: St. Martin's Press, 2002. A concise overview of internal economic, political, and sociocultural issues propelling international expansion of the Netherlands in the seventeenth century.

Von Donselaar, J. "On the Vocabulary of the Dutch in Their Seventeenth-Century South American Colonies." In *The Low Countries and the New Worlds: Travel, Discovery, Early Relations*, edited by Johanna C. Prins et al. Lanham, Md.: University Press of America, 2000. Examines the social and economic factors of Dutch settlement in Brazil, Suriname, and Berbice (now Guyana) that affected the development of the Dutch language, particularly in relation to terms for flora and fauna.

Whitehead, Peter James Palmer. *A Portrait of Dutch Seventeenth Century Brazil: Animals, Plants, and People by the Artists of Johan Maurits of Nassau*. Amsterdam: North Holland, 1989. A collection of detailed plant, animal, and anthropologic images, some in color, from Dutch scientific expeditions in Brazil.

SEE ALSO: Dec., 1601: Dutch Defeat the Portuguese in Bantam Harbor; 1608: Jesuits Found Paraguay; 1617-1693: European Powers Vie for Control of Gorée; 1619-c. 1700: The Middle Passage to American Slavery; July, 1625-Aug., 1664: Founding of New Amsterdam; Oct., 1625-1637: Dutch and Portuguese Struggle for the Guinea Coast; 1630's-1694: Slaves Resist Europeans at Palmares; June-Aug., 1640: *Bandeirantes* Expel the Jesuits; Jan. 14, 1641: Capture of Malacca; Aug. 26, 1641-Sept., 1648: Conquest of Luanda; 1644-1671: Ndongo Wars; Mid-17th cent.: Emergence of the Guinea Coast States; 1654: Portugal Retakes Control of Brazil; Feb. 13, 1668: Spain Recognizes Portugal's Independence; 1670-1699: Rise of the Asante Empire; Beginning 1680's: Guerra dos Bárbaros; Early 1690's: Brazilian Gold Rush.

RELATED ARTICLES in *Great Lives from History: The Seventeenth Century, 1601-1700:* Maurice of Nassau; Njinga; Philip IV; António Vieira.

1630's

May, 1630-1643
GREAT PURITAN MIGRATION

In the 1630's, English Puritans sought a home beyond the practical reach of King Charles I, the Supreme Head of the Church of England, who not only persecuted the Puritans but also changed Church doctrine and practice in ways that they despised. As a result, twenty thousand Puritans migrated to New England, founding the Massachusetts Bay Colony as a Puritan theocracy.

LOCALE: Massachusetts Bay
CATEGORIES: Colonization; religion and theology; expansion and land acquisition

KEY FIGURES
John Winthrop (1588-1649), governor of
    Massachusetts, 1629-1633, 1637-1640, 1642-1644,
    1646-1649
Charles I (1600-1649), king of England, r. 1625-1649
John Cotton (1584-1652), teacher at the First Church
    in Boston and an eminent clergyman
Thomas Hooker (1586-1647), theologian and framer of
    the constitution of Connecticut
Roger Williams (c. 1603-1683), one of the founders of
    Rhode Island
Anne Hutchinson (1591-1643), prominent religious
    dissenter and Antinomian preacher

SUMMARY OF EVENT
Credit for the successful establishment of a Puritan commonwealth in North America belongs as much to Charles I, king of England and Puritan antagonist, as to any other single individual. Resentful of any limitations or contradiction of either his political or his religious authority, Charles dissolved Parliament on March 2, 1629, thereby denying the Puritans, or any of his subjects, a public forum from which to continue their agitation for reforming the Church of England. A few days later, on March 14, he granted a royal charter to the Puritan-controlled Massachusetts Bay Company to establish a colony in the New World. By thus harassing the Puritans in old England even as he allowed them to procure a beachhead in New England, Charles virtually guaranteed the success of their colonizing venture.

The charter granted to the Massachusetts Bay Company contained, contrary to established custom, no clause stipulating that the company should hold its meetings in England. This omission enabled several leading Puritan stockholders to carry the charter with them to the New World and so transfer control of both company and colony to North America. Massachusetts thus became an autonomous commonwealth, the government of which evolved out of a transplanted joint-stock company. The stockholders who emigrated to Massachusetts became the voting citizens of the state; the board of directors, known as assistants, developed into a legislative assembly; and the company president served as governor of the colony. John Winthrop was the first such governor, elected to the position in 1629, even before the colonists left England.

The first contingent of settlers came to America in 1630, the earliest ships arriving in May and June. Over the course of the Great Migration, which lasted until 1643, some twenty thousand people came to Massachusetts, constituting the greatest colonizing exodus that England has ever known. They came mainly in family groupings, sometimes from the same parish, and largely from the east of England, especially East Anglia. Most were middle-class farmers or tradesmen. Religious reasons played a major role in their coming, although economic hard times and political problems influenced them as well.

Those who moved through Boston and settled the land, as most of the early migrants did, generally favored the open-field system of land tenure. Under that plan, quite common in England, each household had a village lot where it built its home and raised its garden, living in close proximity to its neighbors. Village life centered on the meeting house, where in town meetings the villagers discussed issues of common interest with the elected selectmen. The meeting house also was the church, and although the settlers of the Great Migration had different experiences that brought them to New England, they more or less shared the religious outlook that was called Puritanism. As the first governor of Massachusetts Bay, John Winthrop made it clear to those traveling with him in 1630 that they were on a mission for God. Their objective was not just to settle a new land: It was to establish a "City upon a Hill," a holy commonwealth that would serve as an example for their countrymen back home.

Winthrop realized soon after his arrival in the colony that too few members of the company had emigrated to provide a secure basis for government. In 1631, therefore, he arranged for the admission of more than a hundred settlers to the status of freemen, as stockholders were then called in England, and this number was gradually increased as the colony grew. Although the original stockholders had hoped to contain the rights of these newly created citizens within definite limits, such restrictions proved to be increasingly difficult to enforce. By 1644, the freemen had broadened their participation in the legislative process through the establishment of a lower house in the legislature. Consisting of two deputies from each town, the lower house shared with the governor and assistants in the enactment of laws for the affected territory.

Despite these changes in the structure of government and the remarkable growth of the colony, Massachusetts remained safely under the control of a Puritan oligarchy. A law in 1636 helped to maintain this alliance of the church and the state by providing that only members of an approved congregation could apply for the status of freemen. Moreover, Puritan political theory held that although the people had a right to elect their leaders, once magistrates were installed in office, they held a commission from God and were responsible to the deity rather than to the electorate. Therefore, as Boston's influential minister John Cotton repeatedly pointed out, the freemen had no right to deprive a man of elective office unless they found him guilty of some grave offense. The remarkable durability of Puritan magistrates attests to the effectiveness of this doctrine.

The difficulty of maintaining orthodoxy in a congregational system of church government presented the Puritan commonwealth with its greatest challenge during the early years of settlement. Despite John Winthrop's efforts to maintain unity within the colony, zealots such as Roger Williams, one of the founders of Rhode Island, and Anne Hutchinson, an enthusiastic disciple of John Cotton, threatened to divide the province into warring factions by convincing their respective congregations that the church stood in need of further purification. Since each congregation was presumably independent of outside authority, it was difficult to discipline any "heretic" who succeeded in winning support from his or her local church.

Williams arrived in Massachusetts in 1631 and almost immediately began to challenge the purity of the New England churches, as well as the basis on which the Puritans had erected their civil government. He contended that the Massachusetts congregations retained too many contacts with the Church of England, that the civil government had no right to enforce religious uniformity, and that the king had acted illegally in granting a charter to the colony. These arguments threatened established authority, and yet, because Williams enjoyed the confidence of his congregation at Salem, both the magistrates

and the ministers found it difficult to deal with him.

Hutchinson presented an even greater problem. She argued that personal revelation might supplant the teachings of the ministers and that each person must obey the voice of God rather than the commands of either church or state (a philosophy that came to be known as Antinomianism). Although she held no official church position, she enjoyed the support of a majority in the Boston congregation and, like Williams, proved a thorny problem for the ministers and magistrates.

The ultimate expulsion of both Williams and Hutchinson demonstrated that orthodoxy would continue to protect itself in Massachusetts. Williams pioneered the colony of Rhode Island; Hutchinson joined him before going on to Long Island, then under Dutch jurisdiction. Her son-in-law, John Wheelwright, would head north to what became New Hampshire, founding the town of Exeter. Others who had differences with the Puritan oligarchs left Massachusetts Bay of their own accord.

Thomas Hooker, a Puritan clergyman whose eminence almost equaled John Cotton's, may have led a portion of his Cambridge congregation to the Connecticut Valley in 1636 because of his rivalry with Cotton, whose influence on John Winthrop clearly made Hooker increasingly uncomfortable with the blending of church and state in Winthrop's colony. Others followed the remarkable Hooker, who penned the most elaborate of early America's constitutions, the Fundamental Orders of Connecticut (1639). Unlike Hooker, the Reverend John Davenport and his rich patron, merchant Theophilus Eaton, believed that the relationship between church and state in Massachusetts was not close enough. In 1638, Davenport and Hooker, inspired by a vision of a religious utopia based on the Mosaic, founded New Haven.

SIGNIFICANCE

The Puritans of Massachusetts Bay brought with them to the New World stark Calvinist values and a belief in religious governance. At the same time, however, they also brought a surprisingly diverse group of religious voices and viewpoints. As a result, the early colonial history of New England became almost immediately a history of struggle between advocates of specific dogmas and advocates of religious toleration. Massachusetts became the center of belief in dogmatic government and close cooperation of church and state. Other colonies, such as Rhode Island and Maryland, became traditional havens for dissenters.

The lawmakers and clergy of Massachusetts continued to insist upon the autonomy of each congregation,

1630's

but they managed to maintain uniformity through their control of the government. In theory, the ministers of the colony exercised no authority over a particular congregation except through persuasion. They could, however, declare a person a heretic, and it then became the duty of the civil government to see that that person was punished. Through this partnership of the church and the state, formalized by the Cambridge Platform of 1649, the Puritans maintained virtually unchallenged control of Massachusetts throughout the first half of the seventeenth century.

—*David L. Ammerman and Ronald W. Howard*

FURTHER READING

Anderson, Virginia DeJohn. *New England's Generation: The Great Migration and the Formation of Society and Culture in the Seventeenth Century.* New York: Cambridge University Press, 1991. A searching analysis of who came, why they came, and what they hoped to do in Massachusetts Bay.

Battis, Emery. *Saints and Sectaries: Anne Hutchinson and the Antinomian Controversy in the Massachusetts Bay Colony.* Chapel Hill: University of North Carolina Press, 1962. A detailed study of the Antinomian controversy, with suggestions about its psychological, sociological, and physiological undercurrents.

Bremer, Francis J. *John Winthrop: America's Forgotten Founding Father.* New York: Oxford University Press, 2003. Bremer, editor of the Winthrop papers for the Massachusetts Historical Society, draws upon those papers to produce this exhaustively detailed biography.

Cressy, David. *Coming Over: Migration and Communication Between England and New England in the Seventeenth Century.* New York: Cambridge University Press, 1987. Emphasizes the essential English nature of the Puritan enterprise in New England.

Fischer, David Hackett. *Albion's Seed: Four British Folkways in America.* New York: Oxford University Press, 1989. Argues that Puritan folkways were transferred largely from East Anglia and remained a potent force throughout U.S. history.

Games, Alison. *Migration and the Origins of the English Atlantic World.* Cambridge, Mass.: Harvard University Press, 1999. Tracks the movements of about five thousand migrants who traveled from London to the Americas in 1635, providing information about their backgrounds and lives in New England and the West Indies. Features vignettes about many of the settlers.

Miller, Perry. *Orthodoxy in Massachusetts, 1630-1650.* Cambridge, Mass.: Harvard University Press, 1933. Comprehensive account of Miller's theories of the establishment of congregationalism in Massachusetts Bay.

Morgan, E. S. *The Puritan Dilemma: The Story of John Winthrop.* 2d ed. New York: Longman, 1999. Relates with eloquence and precision the "middle way" that Winthrop chose as he and other Puritans sought to build a society upon biblical principles.

Winship, Michael P. *Making Heretics: Militant Protestantism and Free Grace in Massachusetts, 1636-1641.* Princeton, N.J.: Princeton University Press, 2002. Thorough and accessible study of the politics of the Antinomian controversy.

SEE ALSO: Dec. 26, 1620: Pilgrims Arrive in North America; Mar., 1629-1640: "Personal Rule" of Charles I; Fall, 1632-Jan. 5, 1665: Settlement of Connecticut; June, 1636: Rhode Island Is Founded; Mar.-June, 1639: First Bishops' War; Oct. 23, 1641-1642: Ulster Insurrection; 1642-1651: English Civil Wars; Sept. 8, 1643: Confederation of the United Colonies of New England; Dec. 6, 1648-May 19, 1649: Establishment of the English Commonwealth; Apr. 21, 1649: Maryland Act of Toleration; 1652-1689: Fox Organizes the Quakers; Mar. 4, 1681: "Holy Experiment" Establishes Pennsylvania; June, 1686-Apr., 1689: Dominion of New England Forms; Apr. 4, 1687, and Apr. 27, 1688: Declaration of Liberty of Conscience.

RELATED ARTICLES in *Great Lives from History: The Seventeenth Century, 1601-1700:* Charles I; John Cotton; John Davenport; Thomas Hooker; Anne Hutchinson; William Laud; Roger Williams; John Winthrop.

November 10, 1630
THE DAY OF DUPES

The Day of Dupes exposed the intrigue of the French chief minister Cardinal de Richelieu against his enemies, ended France's medieval trappings, and allowed France to emerge as an absolute monarchy at the forefront of European nations.

LOCALE: Paris and Versailles, France
CATEGORY: Government and politics

KEY FIGURES

Anne of Austria (1601-1666), queen of France, r. 1615-1643, queen regent, r. 1643-1651, and daughter of King Philip III of Spain

Duke de Sully (Maximilien de Béthune; 1559-1641), soldier, diplomat, and minister to King Henry IV

Concino Concini (marquis d'Ancre; d. 1617), appointed marshal of France in 1613 by Marie de Médicis

Third Prince of Condé (Henry II de Bourbon; 1588-1646), Protestant nobleman

Louis XIII (1601-1643), king of France, r. 1610-1643, son of Marie de Médicis and Henry IV

Louis de Marillac (1573-1632), French marshal and brother of Michel

Michel de Marillac (1563-1632), councillor of state who opposed Cardinal de Richelieu

Marie de Médicis (1575-1642), second wife of Henry IV, and, after his death, dowager queen of France and regent until 1617

Gaston d'Orléans (1608-1660), brother of Louis XIII

Cardinal de Richelieu (Armand-Jean du Plessis; 1585-1642), chief minister of Louis XIII, 1624-1642

SUMMARY OF EVENT

After King Henry IV's assassination in 1610, his nine-year-old son succeeded him as Louis XIII. Marie de Médicis, widow of Henry IV and mother of Louis, became regent. She was a distant relative of Catherine de Médicis, who had been regent a generation earlier, and both were descended from the great Medici family of Florence. French statesman Maximilien de Béthune, the duke de Sully and minister to the late Henry IV, was on poor terms with the regent and retired early in 1611. Left without a reliable minister, Marie depended for advice mainly upon the papal *nuncio* and the Spanish ambassador. Such reliance on foreign advice increased Marie's unpopularity because she was herself a foreigner.

During the reigns of Henry IV and Louis XIII, the government of France consisted of a national elective body called the Estates-General. The Estates-General included the first state, the clergy; the second state, the nobility; and the third state, the middle-class commoners.

In 1614, at the demand of Protestant nobleman Henry II de Bourbon, third prince of Condé, the Estates-General met to consider various grievances against the government and one another. The nobles and the clergy demanded suppression of the *paulette*, a practice begun by Sully, which allowed middle-class officeholders to treat their offices as private property if they paid an annual tax on them. The third state, composed almost exclusively of officeholders, then demanded the abolition of all government pensions to the nobility and drew up a declaration denying the pope's right to intervene in French affairs.

In January, 1615 (in a move foreshadowing the event that began the French Revolution of 1789), the queen locked the third state out of its meeting place and dissolved the Estates-General. That same year, however, Henry II announced his support of the popular grievances, including opposition to foreigners and to Marie's supposed pro-papal sentiments. Henry II took to the field with armed forces, so that a royal army was needed to protect the king when he journeyed to Bordeaux to marry Anne of Austria in 1615. Peace was made in 1616, but Marie had Henry II imprisoned in the Bastille shortly afterward.

Marie's most trusted adviser at the time was the Italian statesman Concino Concini, the marquis d'Ancre, whom she had made a marshal of France in 1613. Although Concini was the husband of Marie's best friend, Leonora Galigai, he behaved arrogantly toward everyone, including Louis XIII. Early in 1617, Louis plotted with several noblemen to overthrow Concini, and in April, Louis ordered the marshal's arrest; when Concini resisted, he was shot to death.

The assassination of Concini marked the turning point of Louis XIII's reign. The new royal favorite and chief adviser in this period was Louis's falconer, Charles d'Albert, duke de Luynes, who had played a key role in the plot against Concini. In 1617, Louis exiled Marie to Blois, effectively ending her regency. When she allied with some powerful noblemen, she threatened civil war. Yet, the duke de Richelieu, then bishop of Luçon and a member of Marie's own entourage who had played an important role in the meeting of the Estates-General in 1614, arranged a truce.

In 1621, the French Protestant leaders met to divide France into eight "circles" for purposes of fund-raising and military defense. Alarmed at what seemed an attempt to establish a state within the state, Louis seized all but two of the armed cities that had been guaranteed to the Protestants (the Huguenots) by the Edict of Nantes in 1598. Authorized by Henry IV, the Edict of Nantes allowed French Protestants to hold government office and provided special courts to adjudicate disputes between the faiths.

The duke de Luynes died in 1621, creating another gap in the circle of royal advisers. Richelieu had been made a cardinal in 1622 through Marie's influence, but despite his obvious political ability, Louis distrusted him. Louis declined to make Richelieu his minister until 1624, when a crisis in foreign affairs demanded his presence. Until his death in 1642, Richelieu dominated both the king and his government. A diplomat of rare skill in both foreign and domestic affairs, Cardinal de Richelieu maintained his position at court despite his enemies, who included some of the most powerful men in the kingdom. Factions and intrigues abounded. The king's

Marie de Médicis. (Hulton|Archive by Getty Images)

own brother, Gaston d'Orléans, plotted against Louis and Richelieu on a number of occasions.

Between 1627 and 1628, Richelieu engineered the fall of the last two Huguenot strongholds, the most important of which, La Rochelle, fell on October 28, 1628. Thereafter, the Huguenots ceased to be an independent force within France. Until 1630, France fought Germany and Spain over border territories, to France's detriment. Moreover, resentful at Richelieu's duplicity in leaving her service and entering that of the king, Marie de Médicis championed her younger son Gaston.

In September, 1630, Louis became violently ill, and for almost a month he was barely conscious; at one point, he seemed near death. Marie hoped for the childless Louis's death so that his younger brother, Gaston, might succeed him. Louis revived, however, and made a slow recovery. Undismayed, Marie reconciled herself to Louis. She argued incessantly against Richelieu, blaming him for all the evils that France suffered while at the same time preventing Richelieu from seeing the king. Louis's wife, Anne of Austria, who also resented the cardinal's influence over the king, joined Marie in her insidious campaign.

In mid-October came news from Germany that the French ambassadors, alarmed by Louis's expected death, had made peace with the Holy Roman Emperor on unfavorable terms. Richelieu repudiated the treaty and warned Louis that it was the equivalent of surrender. Because of strong popular desires for peace, however, Marie and Anne pressed Louis to accept it. The recovering King Louis spent most of his time in Paris with his mother and his wife, and he refused to grant Richelieu an audience. By early November, the cardinal's fall seemed certain. On November 10, 1630, Louis was in conference with Marie, having left strict orders that no one was to disturb them. Richelieu, however, entered their chamber through an unused door, the only one left unlocked. Falling on his knees before the king, he begged forgiveness for any offense he might have given. Marie screamed with rage until the king, angry with both of them, stalked out of the room.

Louis went to his hunting lodge at Versailles and, later in the day, summoned Richelieu. The cardinal offered to resign, but Louis insisted that he valued Richelieu's services highly and that Marie had interfered with affairs of state. That evening, Louis met with members of his council and stated that for a year the conspiracy against the cardinal had disrupted state business. He ordered Michel de Marillac, Richelieu's chief opponent, to resign, and had him conducted to a distant fortress, where he died

The court of the influential French minister Cardinal de Richelieu, who was a dominant figure during the reign of Louis XIII and whose politics led to years of factions and intrigue. (Francis R. Niglutsch)

several years later. Then Louis summoned Michel's brother, Louis de Marillac, a marshal commanding the French forces fighting in Germany, to be brought to Paris under armed guard. After charging Louis de Marillac, probably unjustly, with corruption, Louis beheaded him in May, 1632.

Outraged and dismayed at the unexpected turn of events, Marie remained away from the king and raged against the cardinal. One of her courtiers remarked, "This is the day of dupes." Subsequently, the phrase came to be accepted as an apt description of the king's sudden change of heart.

Upon hearing of the sudden revival of Richelieu's power, Gaston d'Orléans went to the king and renounced his allegiance to Marie, promising instead complete loyalty to Louis and to Richelieu. A short time later, however, he fled to Orléans and threatened rebellion unless Richelieu was dismissed. Louis still supported his minister and, fearful of his mother, took her with him when his court moved from Versailles to Comprègne. She was supposed to have said, "If I had not forgotten one lock that day in Paris, the cardinal would have been lost." Al-

though the king planned to imprison her at Moulins, Marie pled illness and remained at Comprègne for several months. On July 18, 1631, she fled secretly, hoping to capture a town from which she could negotiate with the king. Her allies deserted her, however, and she crossed over into the Spanish Netherlands instead. For eleven years, she wandered among the courts of Europe, friendless and unhonored, dying at Cologne in 1642. Louis, who was in the last year of his own life, showed no grief at her passing.

Meanwhile, Richelieu had marched against Gaston, who also fled the country. In 1632, Gaston invaded France and was defeated. His leading followers were put to death, but he was reconciled with his brother. Gaston continued to intrigue against the Crown even after Louis's death and late in life was pardoned by Louis's son, King Louis XIV.

SIGNIFICANCE

The Day of Dupes and its aftermath left Cardinal de Richelieu for the first time entirely free to pursue the foreign policy that was his greatest achievement and to engineer the emergence of France as the greatest nation of Europe.

—*James F. Hitchcock and Barbara C. Stanley*

FURTHER READING

Bergin, Joseph. *Cardinal Richelieu: Power and the Pursuit of Wealth.* New Haven, Conn.: Yale University Press, 1985. A good portrait of the political Richelieu.

_____. *The Rise of Richelieu.* New Haven, Conn.: Yale University Press, 1991. Bergin discusses Richelieu's success based on his being both an ecclesiastical figure and a figure in the royal court.

Boulenger, Jacques. *The Seventeenth Century in France.* New York: Capricorn Books, 1963. A good history of life and politics in seventeenth century France.

Burckhardt, Carl J. *Richelieu: His Rise to Power.* Translated and abridged by Edwin and Willa Muir. London: Allen & Unwin, 1940. An excellent overview of Richelieu's spheres of influence.

Church, William. *Richelieu and Reason of State.* Princeton, N.J.: Princeton University Press, 1972. A good overview of the government of France under Richelieu.

Knecht, Robert. *Richelieu.* New York: Longman, 1991. Knecht's work is not a complete biography, but instead is a reassessment of Richelieu that focuses on the major features, achievements, and failures of his career.

Levi, Anthony. *Cardinal Richelieu and the Making of France.* New York: Carroll & Graf, 2000. Levi argues that Richelieu sought to create a French national unity as much through cultural symbolism as through political means.

Lough, John. *An Introduction to Seventeenth Century France.* New York: David McKay, 1954. A useful general survey that places Richelieu's career in the context of seventeenth century French politics.

Tapié, Victor Lucien. *France in the Age of Louis XII and Richelieu.* Edited and translated by D. Lockie. New York: Cambridge University Press, 1984. Translation of a monumental study, recounting the two men's policies and how their actions affected the French people and the nation's culture.

SEE ALSO: 1610-1643: Reign of Louis XIII; 1625-Oct. 28, 1628: Revolt of the Huguenots; Mar. 6, 1629: Edict of Restitution; 1661: Absolute Monarchy Emerges in France; 1685: Louis XIV Revokes the Edict of Nantes.

RELATED ARTICLES in *Great Lives from History: The Seventeenth Century, 1601-1700:* Anne of Austria; Charles I; The Great Condé; Gustavus II Adolphus; Cornelius Otto Jansen; Louis XIII; Louis XIV; Marie de Médicis; Jules Mazarin; Axel Oxenstierna; Cardinal de Richelieu; Urban VIII.

1631-1645
LI ZICHENG'S REVOLT

Thriving in an environment marked by despair and famine, Li Zicheng became a powerful rebel leader who eventually captured Beijing, leading to the suicide of the Chongzhen emperor. This event hastened the collapse of the Ming Dynasty, which asked its enemies, the Manchus, to help it fight Li; soon, the Manchus both defeated Li and overthrew the Ming, establishing their own Qing Dynasty in China.

LOCALE: Northern China
CATEGORIES: Wars, uprisings, and civil unrest; government and politics

KEY FIGURES

Li Zicheng (Li Tzu-ch'eng; 1605?-1645), Chinese rebel leader who captured Beijing
Wu Sangui (Wu San-kuei; 1612-1678), Ming general who allied himself with the Manchus

Chongzhen (Ch'ung-chen; 1611-1644), last Ming emperor of China, r. 1628-1644
Zhang Xianzhong (Chang Hsien-chung; 1606-1647), Chinese bandit leader and Li's occasional ally
Dorgon (1612-1650), Manchu prince and regent who captured Beijing
Shunzhi (Shun-chih; 1638-1661), first Qing emperor of China, r. 1644-1661

SUMMARY OF EVENT

In the 1620's, China's Ming Dynasty faced a series of military and economic challenges that led to a deteriorating living situation for the population. The Manchus threatened in the northeast. China's silver supply via the Spanish Philippines was disrupted. Continuous tax increases, official corruption, and inertia did not help to overcome the crisis. The situation was particularly hard on the peasants of China's northwestern provinces. Two years of bad harvests in 1627 and 1628 created famine conditions. Many desperate peasants became bandits.

Li Zicheng was one of the young rural men who became outlaws. Born in northern Shaanxi (Shensi) province, just south of the Great Wall, probably in 1605, Li had worked in a wine shop and at an ironworker's and had gotten laid off as a post-station messenger before joining the military in 1630. He had a reputation as a skilled cavalry archer and as a violent man. In 1631, the government did not resupply Li's unit, and he deserted with his troops. Crossing into Shanxi (Shansi) province, Li joined his bandit uncle Gao Ying Xian (d. 1636) and quickly became an outlaw leader.

Li called his fellows Chuang Zei, "dashing bandits," and himself Chuang Chiang, "dashing general." The Ming government struck back in response to their raids, and by the end of 1633, Li had to retreat south. In 1634, he was captured, but through either bribery or a false promise to leave Shaanxi province, Li was freed. He soon resumed his raids.

In 1635, Li and twelve other bandit leaders met to coordinate their operations, but the meeting ended inconclusively. Defeated by Ming troops, Li moved into Henan (Honan) and joined forces with fellow outlaw Zhang Xianzhong. The government captured his uncle Gao in 1636 and had him beheaded. Li assumed his uncle's title of Chuang Wang, "Dashing King." Li and Zhang moved into Sichuan (Szechuan) province in 1637. Defeat in 1638 had them retreat into a remote borderland.

When drought and famine struck Henan in 1639, the peasants became desperate, and the scholar Li Yen joined Li Zicheng. Under Li Yen's intellectual influence, Li Zicheng styled his movement as a peasant revolt and called for tax relief and land reform. As bandits turned into rebels, Li Zicheng forbade them to harm ordinary people and restricted pillaging to the wealthy and government officials.

When a Manchu invasion weakened the Ming government, Li Zicheng struck. In March, 1641, he captured Luoyang (Lo-yang), a historically important city in Henan province. To impress the people, Li ordered a hated prince executed, slaughtered, and eaten. In 1642, Li continued his conquest of Henan. Cities that surrendered were spared; others were savagely pillaged. Li's old bandit comrade Zhang established himself in Chengdu (Ch'eng-tu) in Sichuan. Severe natural catastrophes such as droughts, floods, and epidemics continued to plague northwestern China, increasing Li's alternative appeal as a savior. Li captured Xi'an (Hsi-an), capital of his native province of Shaanxi, in November, 1643.

By early 1644, Li Zicheng had founded his kingdom, named Da Shun Gao (great Shun state), calling himself King Li Sheng, and tried to establish a Shun dynasty. He issued his own coins and royal proclamations. In Chengdu, Zhang Xianzhong followed this example, founding Da Xi Guo (great western state). Li continued his conquests, capturing Shanxi province by March, 1644. To conquer Beijing (Peking; then called Jingchen, "capital city"), Li divided his army. Most troops went north, capturing Datong (Ta-t'ung). A smaller army went south, capturing Baoding (Pao-ting) in April, 1644. Beijing was encircled on April 23, 1644.

Faced by Li's rebel army, the Chongzhen emperor despaired. He took leave of Princess Chang and walked into the imperial Jingshan Park, where he hanged himself on a tree in the first hour of April 25, 1644, ending the Ming Dynasty. Li Zicheng entered Beijing unopposed later that day. Initially, Li's army showed restraint. Discovering an empty imperial treasury, Li agreed on May 1 to confiscate the fortunes of high-ranking Ming officials. His soldiers tortured captive Ming officers, killing many. Horrified by the murders, on May 12 Li ordered the release of the prisoners. Now his soldiers turned against the merchants and engaged in widespread looting and pillaging, which aroused the hatred of the people.

Ming loyalists looked to General Wu Sangui. Wu held the strategic Ningyuan garrison, defending the easternmost part of the Great Wall against the Manchus. The isolated Wu could either ally himself with Li and support the new regime or ask the Manchus to help him defeat Li. In Beijing, Li held hostage the general's father, Wu Xiang. According to popular history, Li also captured Wu Sangui's favorite concubine, Chen Yuanyuan, and made her his own. Traditionally, it was this act that persuaded Wu to ally with Manchu prince Dorgon to defeat Li. Contemporary historians speculate that Wu may have hoped to use the Manchus to defeat Li, restore the Mings to power, and secure a high position for himself in a restored Ming government. The excesses of Li's army may also have persuaded Wu that alliance with the Manchus was the better of his two options.

On May 18, 1644, Li left Beijing to confront Wu, and their forces clashed at Shanhaiguan (Shan-hai-kuan). Contemporary historians assume that about eighty thousand men of infantry, cavalry, and artillery participated in the battle on Li's side, opposed by thirty thousand of Wu's soldiers and sixty thousand Manchus, Han Chinese, and Mongols under Prince Dorgon, including cavalry and artillery. While some historians argue that Wu defeated Li only to have to surrender to Dorgon when the latter took Wu's base at Shanhaiguan, most scholars believe that Li and Wu fought an inconclusive pitched battle until Dorgon led his forces around the combatants and, aided by a sandstorm, attacked Li's left flank. Caught by surprise, Li's forces were defeated and fled back to Beijing. Exactly when Wu Sangui shaved his forehead and submitted to the Manchus is debated, but this took place around the time of this battle.

Defeated, Li returned to Beijing. He executed Wu Xiang, and he crowned himself emperor on June 3, 1644. His troops left Beijing on June 4, and by June 6, Prince Dorgon had taken control of the city. Dorgon placed on the imperial throne the six-year old Fulin, who took the reign name of Shunzhi (obedient ruler), formally founding the Qing Dynasty.

Dorgon sent his brother Dodo to hunt down Li Zicheng, who fled to Xi'an. In January, 1645, under pressure from the Manchu armies, Li abandoned Xi'an and fled into the mountains of northwestern Jiangxi (Kiangsi) province. Li's end remains uncertain, however. Some sources state that villagers whom he tried to rob in June, 1645, beat him to death. Others tell that he committed suicide around the same time. A third, more romantic narrative states that Li escaped to a monastery, where he died peacefully. In January, 1647, Manchu forces killed Li's former ally Zhang Xianzhong in Chengdu, eliminating the last remnants of the former rebel army.

SIGNIFICANCE

Li Zicheng's rise from bandit to rebel leader to conqueror of Beijing had a vast impact on modern Chinese history. Li's revolt effectively ended the Ming Dynasty, which had ruled China since 1368. It allowed the northern Manchus, a people of two million, to conquer one hundred million Chinese and establish a dynasty that would last until 1912.

If Li's early years were marked by banditry, the influence of Li Yen transformed him into a popular hero whose avowed goal was to better the lot of the peasants. As such, Li can be seen in a long tradition of peasant rebel leaders, even foreshadowing the victory of the Chinese Communists in the twentieth century. As people were starving and the government did not help, desperate peasants and anguished scholars flocked to Li Zicheng.

Many contemporary historians hold that Li Zicheng's inability to control his looting and murdering soldiers in Beijing demonstrated a lack of leadership. Certainly, the excesses of his army cost him the sympathies of the Chinese people. His treatment of Wu Sangui and his family alienated the powerful Ming general and drove him into the arms of the Manchu leader Dorgon. In the end, Li Zicheng failed to rule successfully the nation he had conquered.

—R. C. Lutz

FURTHER READING

Graff, David A. "State Making and State Breaking." In *A Military History of China*, edited by David A. Graff et al. Boulder, Colo.: Westview Press, 2002. Discusses Li Zicheng's role in the downfall of the Ming Dynasty and Li's failure to establish a dynasty of his own. Maps, chronology, index.

Hsu, Immanuel C. Y. *The Rise of Modern China.* 6th ed. New York: Oxford University Press, 2000. Places Li's revolt in the context of the fall of the Manchu dynasty and focuses on Li's end. Notes, bibliography, index.

Parsons, James Bunyan. *Peasant Rebellions of the Late Ming Dynasty.* Tucson: University of Arizona Press, 1970. Thorough discussions of causes and history of Li Zicheng's revolt. Maps, notes, bibliography, and index.

Spence, Jonathan. *The Search for Modern China.* 2d ed. New York: Norton, 1999. Most widely available book in English on modern Chinese history. The chapter "Conquest and Consolidation" discusses Li Zicheng's revolt. Maps, illustrations, notes, bibliography, index.

Wakeman, Frederic, Jr. "The Shun Interregnum of 1644." In *From Ming to Ch'ing*, edited by Jonathan Spence and John Wills, Jr. New Haven, Conn.: Yale University Press, 1979. Vivid description of the brief reign of Li Zicheng as self-proclaimed emperor. Notes.

February 24, 1631
WOMEN FIRST APPEAR ON THE ENGLISH STAGE

Since the Middle Ages, women were banned from the stage in England. That tradition was broken when women appeared in Ben Jonson and Inigo Jones's court masque Chloridia. *Indeed, Henrietta Maria, queen consort of England, performed in the masque as Chloris. England thus joined in the reintroduction of actresses into the theater that had been taking place across Europe throughout the seventeenth century.*

LOCALE: London, England
CATEGORIES: Theater; cultural and intellectual history

KEY FIGURES

Henrietta Maria (1609-1669), queen consort of England, r. 1625-1649
Mary Betterton (née Saunderson; c. 1637-1712), English actress and company co-manager
Elizabeth Barry (1656/1658-1713), English actress
Mrs. Anne Bracegirdle (c. 1663-1748), English actress
Nell Gwyn (1650-1687), English actress and mistress of Charles II
Ben Jonson (1573-1637), English playwright and poet
Inigo Jones (1573-1652), English architect and set designer
Armande Béjart (1642-1700), French actress and company director
Marie Champmeslé (1642-1698), French actress
Isabella Andreini (1562-1604), Italian *commedia dell'arte* actress and company manager
Maria Calderon (La Calderona; fl. 1623-1672), Spanish actress and mistress of Philip IV
Jusepa Vaca (fl. 1602-1634), Spanish actress

SUMMARY OF EVENT

An English court masque was a special theatrical event usually produced at court for a holiday or some other festive occasion. Inigo Jones, who had studied in Italy, was a theatrical producer and visual designer who teamed with the playwright Ben Jonson to produce some thirty court masques between 1608 and 1631. It was in their final effort, *Chloridia* (pr., pb. 1631), that a woman first appeared on the English stage in the role of Chloris. That woman was none other than Henrietta Maria, queen consort of England and the sister of King Louis XIII of France. According to the first edition's title page, Chloris and her nymphs were "personated in a masque, at Court, by the Queenes Majesty and her ladies, at Shrove-Tide, 1630." (Because the Julian year began on March 25

rather than January 1, Shrovetide, or February 14-16, 1630, in the Julian calendar took place February 24-26, 1631, according to the modern Gregorian calendar.)

The first performance of *Chloridia* thus ended a centuries-long tradition of banning women from the stage under stricture from the Church. England thus joined other European countries, such as Italy, Spain, and France, that had allowed actresses in professional companies for many years. Indeed, throughout Europe in the seventeenth century, women were slowly becoming not only professional actresses but important leaders of major acting troupes as well. Despite the importance of Queen Henrietta Maria's theatrical performance as a first step in this direction, however, the tradition of men performing in women's roles would not change in England until after the Restoration in 1660.

It is difficult to say exactly when the first actresses appeared on the European continent, but women were prominent members of Italian *commedia dell'arte* companies as early as the latter half of the sixteenth century. One of the most important *commedia* actresses was Isabella Andreini, who debuted on stage in 1577. Andreini and her husband, Francesco Andreini, jointly managed the famous Gelosi Company, which toured throughout Italy and France. When Francesco died, Isabella took over as manager of the company until her death in 1604. She thus set the standard for actresses to measure up to in the seventeenth century.

In 1587, a license was issued by the Church in Spain making it legal for women to appear on stage. Many women took advantage of this new freedom, including Jusepa Vaca, the leading lady of the great Spanish playwright Lope de Vega Carpio, who is considered the "Spanish Shakespeare." Perhaps the most famous actress of seventeenth century Spain was Maria Calderon, known as La Calderona. Maria Calderon ultimately became mistress to the king and mother of the famous Don Juan of Austria.

It was French actresses, however, who would have the most important influence on English theater, and there is some evidence that as early as 1629 women appeared in a French acting company that was touring England. Among the earliest of the French seventeenth century actresses was Marie Venier (fl. 1590-1619), who was featured at the Hotel D'Argent Theater, but it was Armande Béjart, wife of the great actor-playwright Molière, who would become the most influential of the French actresses. Upon Molière's death in 1673, Béjart became the virtual head of his acting company and remained in that position until the creation of the Comédie Française in 1680. Thereafter and for most of the rest of the century, Marie Champmeslé became the greatest star on the French stage.

During the Puritan Commonwealth in England, Prince Charles had taken refuge in France. When the Stuart monarchy was restored in 1660, the newly crowned King Charles II imported several French conventions, including allowing female theatrical performers. The innovation made in 1631 by the former Queen Henrietta Maria, herself a member of the French nobility, was almost immediately renewed and expanded. When William Davenant formed the first professional acting company of Restoration England, he hired Mary Saunderson as his leading actress, so that it is possible that the distinction of being the first professional English actress may fall to her. Davenant's leading man was Thomas Betterton, now thought to be the greatest actor of his day. Saunderson and Betterton soon married, and Mary Betterton played all the major roles opposite her husband, in addition to assuming the co-management of his theatrical troupe, the United Company. She was most applauded for her Lady Macbeth to Betterton's Macbeth.

Soon, Mary Betterton acquired several important rivals, the most renowned of whom was Elizabeth Barry. Considered among the greatest actresses of her day, Barry performed both serious roles, in plays such as John Dryden's *All for Love: Or, The World Well Lost* (pr. 1677, pb. 1678), and roles in Restoration comedies by writers such as Aphra Behn, England's first professional woman playwright. Barry also performed in so-called breeches roles, that is, male roles played by women performers, so that the actresses could reveal their legs. (Men's breeches at the time typically ended at the knee and revealed the lower leg, while women's legs were always hidden under long skirts.)

Two other actresses were known for breeches roles, Nell Gwyn and Mrs. Anne Bracegirdle. Gwyn began her career selling oranges to theater audiences. When she finally obtained a breeches role in 1665 at the age of fifteen, she was immediately hailed for her beauty and comic timing. Before long, she became the mistress of King Charles II and bore him a son, who was created duke of St. Albans.

It was Bracegirdle, however, who was to become the most praised actress of her generation and who was to bring the seventeenth century to its close. She

Mrs. Anne Bracegirdle, one of the most successful actresses of the seventeenth century English stage, portraying an American Indian princess. (The Granger Collection)

flourished as an actress from 1688 to 1707. Like her contemporaries, Bracegirdle played some breeches roles, but she was mainly known for her "good woman" creations, such as William Shakespeare's Ophelia in *Hamlet, Prince of Denmark* (pr. c. 1600-1601) and Desdemona, in *Othello, the Moor of Venice* (pr. 1604, revised 1623). By the time Bracegirdle retired from the stage, at least one hundred women had acted professionally in England.

SIGNIFICANCE

When Henrietta Maria decided to appear in a court masque, she broke a long-standing taboo in English society. In doing so, the queen consort most likely saw herself merely as following the precedent of female performers already prevalent in her home country of France. Her boldness, however, planted the seeds for the English ban on female performers to be shattered in the second half of the seventeenth century, as female performers instead of boys began to play women's parts.

Indeed, in seventeenth century continental Europe, women not only performed on stage but also managed several of the major acting companies. When Charles II returned from exile in France, he followed Queen Henrietta Maria's lead and insisted that women be allowed on stage. There followed in England a great blossoming of female theatrical talent, led by Mary Betterton. Although no actresses were performing in England in 1660, the next forty years saw almost one hundred actresses at work on the London stage, and, indeed, this wealth of female talent helped to establish the career of Aphra Behn, the first professional female playwright in England, and to open the door for women in other related professional pursuits.

—*August W. Staub*

FURTHER READING

Brockett, Oscar G., and Franklin J. Hildy. *History of the Theatre.* 9th ed. Boston: Allyn and Bacon, 2002. The standard reference on all aspects, periods, and regional traditions of theater history.

Duerr, Edwin. *The Length and Depth of Acting.* New York: Holt, Rinehart, Winston, 1963. A thorough study of the history of European and American acting and actors until the mid-twentieth century.

Ficher-Lichte, Erika. *History of European Drama and Theatre.* New York: Routledge, 2002. A recent study of theater history emphasizing the art from ancient Greece to the present day on the European continent.

The attention given to women in theater history is especially useful.

Howe, Elizabeth. *First English Actresses: Women and Drama, 1660-1700.* Cambridge, England: Cambridge University Press, 1992. This work gives special attention to social attitudes toward women in the Restoration and how the actresses made gains for women's rights.

Wilson, John Harold. *All the King's Ladies: Actresses of the Restoration.* Chicago: University of Chicago Press, 1958. A thorough and well-documented study of English actresses from 1660 to 1700. Great attention is given to detail, and there is a separate discussion of the life and achievements of more than ninety actresses in a special appendix.

SEE ALSO: Early 17th cent.: Revenge Tragedies Become Popular in England; c. 1601-1613: Shakespeare Produces His Later Plays; June 29, 1613: Burning of the Globe Theatre; 1642-1651: English Civil Wars; Sept. 2, 1642: Closing of the Theaters; Dec. 6, 1648-May 19, 1649: Establishment of the English Commonwealth; May, 1659-May, 1660: Restoration of Charles II.

RELATED ARTICLES in *Great Lives from History: The Seventeenth Century, 1601-1700:* Aphra Behn; Thomas Betterton; Mrs. Anne Bracegirdle; Charles II (of England); John Dryden; Nell Gwyn; Inigo Jones; Ben Jonson; Louis XIII; Henrietta Maria; Philip IV.

1630's

1632
GALILEO PUBLISHES *DIALOGUE CONCERNING THE TWO CHIEF WORLD SYSTEMS, PTOLEMAIC AND COPERNICAN*

Galileo published his great work Dialogue Concerning the Two Chief World Systems, *leading to widespread acceptance of the heliocentric system of Copernicus while precipitating condemnation of Copernican theory by the Roman Catholic Church.*

LOCALE: Rome and Florence (now in Italy)
CATEGORIES: Science and technology; astronomy; physics; cultural and intellectual history; literature

KEY FIGURES

Galileo (1564-1642), Italian mathematician who began the swing toward accepting Copernicus's theories
Tycho Brahe (1546-1601), Danish astronomer who modified the geocentric system of planets

Nicolaus Copernicus (1473-1543), Polish astronomer who developed the heliocentric system
Johannes Kepler (1571-1630), German astronomer who formulated new laws of the planets
Sir Isaac Newton (1642-1727), English physicist who established a scientific basis for the heliocentric system

SUMMARY OF EVENT

Although Galileo's *Dialogo sopra i due massimi sistemi del mondo, tolemaico e copernicano* (1632; *Dialogue Concerning the Two Chief World Systems, Ptolemaic and Copernican,* 1661) was condemned by the Roman Catholic Church and placed on the Index of Forbidden Books, it fueled the Scientific Revolution and led to increasing acceptance of the heliocentric (sun-centered) system of Nicolaus Copernicus, culminating in the Newtonian synthesis and the eighteenth century Enlightenment. The classic Greek system of the planets was completed by Ptolemy in about the year 150. This Ptolemaic system was geocentric (Earth-centered) and could accurately account for the positions of the planets by a complicated combination of circles known as epicycles. It was further developed by Arabic scientists and was incorporated into Catholic theology by Thomas Aquinas in the thirteenth century.

The heliocentric system was developed by Copernicus and published in 1543 as *De revolutionibus orbium coelestium* (*On the Revolutions of the Heavenly Spheres*, 1939; better known as *De revolutionibus*), in an attempt to simplify astronomy; but it still required complicated combinations of circles to match the accuracy of Ptolemy, and it provided no explanation of how Earth could rotate on its axis and revolve around the sun. The annual revolution of Earth about the sun implied that the positions of the stars should shift as Earth moves, but no such shifting of the stars was observed. Since motion of Earth also seemed to contradict the philosophical and theological ideas of the time, only a few astron-

omers gave serious consideration to the Copernican system.

The last great astronomer before the introduction of the telescope was Tycho Brahe. By building very large instruments for measuring celestial positions, he increased the accuracy of astronomy about ten times that of the Greeks. However, he was still unable to measure the annual shifting of the stars required by the Copernican system. He recognized the mathematical advantages of heliocentric astronomy but could not accept the idea of a moving Earth. Thus, he proposed a compromise system in which the sun revolved around a stationary Earth, but all the other planets revolved in circular orbits around the sun. The Tychonic system gained a significant following among astronomers, so that by the end of the sixteenth century there were three competing systems of the world: the Ptolemaic (geocentric) system, the Copernican (heliocentric) system, and the Tychonic (combined geo-heliocentric) system.

The two great champions of the Copernican system at the beginning of the seventeenth century were Galileo and Johannes Kepler, even though neither was able to detect direct evidence of Earth's motion. Kepler became Tycho's assistant in 1600. A year later, Tycho died

Galileo faces a Catholic Church tribunal for his writings on heliocentrism, ideas condemned as heretical. He later wrote an apology to the Church for his views and renounced his own work. (R. S. Peale and J. A. Hill)

and Kepler began to develop the Copernican system using the accurate data Tycho had accumulated. In 1609, he published his analysis of the orbit of Mars in his *Astronomia nova* (*New Astronomy*, 1992), which established that the planets move in elliptical orbits. This simplified the Copernican system, since only a single ellipse was required to account for the motion of each planet rather than a complicated combination of circles.

Although Galileo corresponded with Kepler and shared many of his heliocentric views, he never endorsed elliptical orbits and retained a strong emphasis on the importance of circles in astronomy. Galileo was born at Pisa in northern Italy in the same year that Michelangelo died. His father, Vincenzo Galilei, was a musician whose book *Dialogo della musica antica, et della moderna* (1581; *Dialogue of Ancient and Modern Music*, 2003) was used by Kepler

---

GALILEO RECANTS HIS HELIOCENTRIC THEORY OF THE UNIVERSE

Galileo's "On Demand of the Inquisition, a Recantation" (June 22, 1633) denounces his own radical theory that the sun, and not the Earth, is the center of the universe. The scientist swears off any allegiance to his own work and submits "to all the pains and penalties" of the Church should he ("which God forbid!") fall from this promise.

[A]fter having been admonished by this Holy Office entirely to abandon the false opinion that the Sun was the centre of the universe and immovable, and that the Earth was not the centre of the same and that it moved, and that I was neither to hold, defend, nor teach in any manner whatever, either orally or in writing, the said false doctrine; and after having received a notification that the said doctrine is contrary to Holy Writ, I did write and cause to be printed a book in which I treat of the said already condemned doctrine, and bring forward arguments of such efficacy in its favour, without arriving at any solution: I have been judged guilty of heresy, that is, of having held and believed that the Sun is the centre of the universe and immoveable, and the Earth is not the centre of the same, and that it does move. . . . I abjure with a sincere heart and unfeigned faith, I curse and detest the said errors and heresies, and generally all and every error and sect contrary to the Holy Catholic Church.

Source: Galileo, excerpted in *An Editor's Treasury: A Continuing Anthology of Prose, Verse, and Literary Curiosa*, vol. 2, edited by Herbert R. Mayes (New York: Atheneum, 1969), pp. 1938-1939.

---

in his attempt to apply the principles of harmony to astronomy. In 1581, Galileo went to the University of Pisa in the Republic of Venice to study medicine, but after four years he had to drop out for lack of funds. After further private study of mathematics, he was appointed as a professor of mathematics at the University of Pisa in 1589. Conflict with Aristotelian colleagues led him to resign after three years and take an appointment at the University of Padua, where he concentrated on the study of motion.

Galileo interrupted his work on motion in July of 1609 when word reached Venice about a magnifying tube made with a combination of lenses by a Dutch lens grinder, Hans Lippershey. After hearing these reports, Galileo ground lenses and tried several arrangements before finding a combination that gave a magnifying power of about thirty. When he presented one of his telescopes to the Venetian senate, it renewed his professorship for life and doubled his salary. He loaned another telescope to Kepler, who worked out the geometry of image formation by two lenses. Galileo recognized that the primary value of the telescope was in astronomy, opening up new vistas of space. Few of his contemporaries realized how valuable this would be for astronomy, and some even op-

posed its use as deceitful. In 1610, Galileo published his initial discoveries, including the four largest moons of Jupiter, in a small booklet called *Sidereus nuncius* (*The Sidereal Messenger*, 1880; also known as *The Starry Messenger*). This success led to his appointment as chief mathematician of the University of Pisa and recognition in Rome by Pope Paul V.

Galileo's successes with the telescope led him into a bolder polemic for the Copernican system, bordering on propaganda. Although none of his observations provided conclusive evidence for a moving Earth, taken together they began to turn the tide toward its wider acceptance. Resistance to Galileo's ideas began to build. In 1616, he was warned by the Holy Office in Rome that the idea of the moving Earth was expressly condemned. After the election of Pope Urban VIII in 1623, Galileo went to Rome, where he had several audiences with the new pope and received permission to write about the motion of Earth as a scientific hypothesis. During the next six years, he worked on his masterpiece, the *Dialogue Concerning the Two Chief World Systems*. Supposedly an evenhanded comparison of the Copernican and Ptolemaic systems, it ended up as a highly persuasive book in favor of the heliocentric system while largely ignoring the Tychonic system. To make matters worse for him, Galileo wrote it in vernacular Italian, accessible to a wide audience, instead of the usual scholarly Latin.

Using the dialectical form of Plato, Galileo developed his arguments through the voices of three persons: the traditional Simplicio, the Copernican Salviati, and the open-minded Sagredo. On the first of four days (chapters), the dialogue compares Simplicio's Aristotelian (geocentric) arguments on celestial perfection with telescopic evidence of such apparent imperfections as sunspots, mountains on the moon, and bulges (rings) on Saturn. The phases of Venus are given as evidence against the Ptolemaic system and for the Copernican system without mention of the rival Tychonic system, which could also account for them. The second and third days include arguments on the rotation and revolution of Earth, indicating his failure to detect the annual shift in the positions of the stars as evidence for large stellar distances. The moons of Jupiter are offered as an example of a nongeocentric system. On the fourth day, Salviati presents Galileo's erroneous theory of the tides as conclusive evidence for the Copernican system.

Galileo submitted his manuscript to the chief censor at Rome in 1630. After several delays and minor revisions, permission was finally granted in both Rome and in Florence, where it was published in 1632. The closing paragraph of the dialogue included a statement suggested by Pope Urban that the Copernican theory was "neither true nor conclusive" and that no one should "limit the divine power and wisdom to one particular fancy of his own." Unfortunately, Galileo put these words in the mouth of Simplicio, leading to the accusation that all of his views represented those of the pope. Sale of the book was stopped, and Galileo was summoned to Rome.

SIGNIFICANCE

In the winter of 1633, the gravely ill Galileo was carried by litter to Rome. After trial by the Inquisition, in which he vigorously denied that he had intended to teach the truth of the heliocentric system, he was judged guilty and the *Dialogue Concerning the Two Chief World Systems* was totally forbidden. He was then sentenced to house arrest at his country estate near Florence, with no visitors allowed except by special permission. Although he lost his eyesight in the last decade of his life, he returned to the study of matter and motion, which was eventually developed by Isaac Newton to establish the physical basis for the Copernican system.

—Joseph L. Spradley

FURTHER READING

Alioto, Anthony. *A History of Western Science*. Englewood Cliffs, N.J.: Prentice Hall, 1993. Chapter 15 gives a succinct historical account of Galileo's work.

Boorstin, Daniel J. *The Discoverers*. New York: Random House, 1983. In chapters 40 and 41, Boorstin provides a brief but authoritative historical account of Galileo's scientific work.

Drake, Stillman. *Galileo at Work: His Scientific Biography*. Chicago: University of Chicago Press, 1978. An excellent biography of Galileo written by a noted scholar.

Galileo Galilei. *Dialogue Concerning the Two Chief World Systems*. Translated by Stillman Drake. Berkeley: University of California Press, 1967. The standard English translation of Galileo's chief work.

Koyré, Alexandre. *Galileo Studies*. Translated by John Mepham. Atlantic Highlands, N.J.: Humanities Press, 1978. Ably translated into English, these scholarly studies of Galileo provide intriguing insights into Galileo's work.

Machamer, Peter, ed. *The Cambridge Companion to Galileo*. New York: Cambridge University Press, 1998. A collection of essays exploring the many facets of Galileo's work. Chapter 7 discusses "Galileo's Discoveries with the Telescope and Their Evidence for the Copernican Theory."

Rowland, Wade. *Galileo's Mistake: A New Look at the Epic Confrontation Between Galileo and the Church*. New York: Arcade, 2003. Rowland argues that Galileo and Church officials disagreed about something more significant than whether Earth revolved around the sun: They were really in dispute about the nature of truth and how people acquire the truth.

Sharratt, Michael. *Galileo: Decisive Innovator*. Oxford, England: Blackwell, 1994. Concise biography that closely examines *Dialogue Concerning the Two Chief World Systems*.

SEE ALSO: Sept., 1608: Invention of the Telescope; 1609-1619: Kepler's Laws of Planetary Motion; 1615-1696: Invention and Development of the Calculus; Feb., 1656: Huygens Identifies Saturn's Rings; 1665: Cassini Discovers Jupiter's Great Red Spot; Dec. 7, 1676: Rømer Calculates the Speed of Light.

RELATED ARTICLES in *Great Lives from History: The Seventeenth Century, 1601-1700:* Gian Domenico Cassini; Galileo; Robert Hooke; Christiaan Huygens; Johannes Kepler; Hans Lippershey; Maria Celeste; Sir Isaac Newton; Paul V; Urban VIII.

1632-c. 1650
SHAH JAHAN BUILDS THE TAJ MAHAL

The grand Taj Mahal was built by Mughal emperor Shah Jahan, according to one popular legend, to remember the love he shared with his favorite wife, Mumtaz Mahal. The building has come to represent not only this love but also dynastic splendor and, as another legend tells it, the emperor's piety and his devotion to Islam.

LOCALE: Āgra, India

CATEGORIES: Architecture; government and politics; religion and theology

KEY FIGURES

Shah Jahan (1592-1666), Mughal emperor of India, r. 1628-1658

Mumtaz Mahal (1593-1631), Shah Jahan's favorite wife, for whom he built the Taj Mahal

Ustad Ahmad Lahori (fl. mid-seventeenth century), chief architect of the Taj Mahal

Amanat Khan (fl. early seventeenth century), calligrapher of the Taj Mahal

SUMMARY OF EVENT

On January 5, 1592, Shah Jahan was born to the Mughal emperor Jahāngīr (r. 1605-1627) and Princess Manmati in Lahore, India. In 1611, Jahāngīr married Nūr Jahān, whose brother, Asaf Khan, was a high-ranking military officer. Asaf Khan had a daughter named Arjumand Banu Begum (Mumtaz Mahal), born in Āgra in 1593. According to legend, Shah Jahan was sixteen when he first saw Arjumand. He wanted to marry her immediately, but for political reasons, he first married a Persian princess around 1608. Four years later, in 1612, Shah Jahan married Arjumand, whose name became Mumtaz Mahal, which means "chosen one of the palace." She was his favorite wife and bore his only children, and she would become the inspiration for the famous Taj Mahal.

Shah Jahan rebelled against his father Jahāngīr in 1623. Jahāngīr died in 1627 and was succeeded by Shah Jahan, who was proclaimed emperor on January 28, 1628, and resided in the early years of his reign in Āgra.

The inseparable Mumtaz and Shah Jahan traveled together on early military expeditions to recover lost ancestral territories. Little is known about Mumtaz except that she was of legendary beauty and the emperor loved her deeply. He entrusted her with the royal seal, and she influenced him on behalf of the needy. Although pregnant, she traveled with Shah Jahan in 1631 to fight the Lodi Empire in the Deccan. On June 17, 1631, Mumtaz died after giving birth to their fourteenth child, a daughter. Mumtaz was buried temporarily, while the grief-stricken Shah Jahan proceeded to build the most beautiful mausoleum possible: the Taj Mahal, constructed as a lasting symbol of the love between himself and Mumtaz.

Construction on the mausoleum began in 1632. According to official Mughal histories, the chief architect was Ustad Ahmad Lahori, an Indian of Persian descent, who also designed the Red Fort in Delhi. A renowned mathematician and astronomer, he became the royal architect. The master calligrapher was Amanat Khan, whose signature is inscribed on the gate. Amanat Khan came to India from Shiraz, Persia, in 1608, and was already the preeminent calligrapher during Jahāngīr's reign.

More than one thousand elephants transported building materials, including twenty-eight types of gemstones, such as lapis lazuli, turquoise, and jade, which were used for the *pietra dura*, or decorative floral and geometric designs, inlaid in the white marble. More than twenty thousand laborers from India, the Ottoman Empire, Persia, and Europe worked on the Taj Mahal.

There is controversy regarding the exact date of its completion. According to Abdul Hamid Lahori, Shah Jahan's official chronicler, the Taj Mahal was completed in twelve years (1644). However, an inscription on the main gate shows a date of 1648, seventeen years after Mumtaz's death. Yet another source, an account of travels in India by the French jewel merchant Jean-Baptiste Tavernier (1605-1689), states that after mourning for two years, Shah Jahan began construction: sixteen years of building for the main mausoleum and an additional five to six years to complete the other structures, which would indicate a completion date of 1654-1655.

The 42-acre Taj Mahal complex has five principal parts: the main gateway, mausoleum, mosque, garden, and *jawab* (a building mirroring the mosque). The redstone gateway has a main arch, flanked by two pairs of smaller arches, which contain black Qurʾānic calligraphy inlaid in white marble paneling. The white marble mausoleum rests on a square podium, with a minaret, or tower, at each corner, a large dome surrounded by four smaller domes in the center, and four identical facades, each with a central arch. Inside, an octagonal marble

1630's

333

The magnificent Taj Mahal, viewed from the garden side of the immense compound. (George L. Shuman)

chamber contains the "false" tombs of Shah Jahan and Mumtaz Mahal, whose real coffins lie underneath at the garden level. The redstone mosque and *jawab* flank the mausoleum, and the garden is divided into four equal parts by canals.

Generally, architecture and the arts flourished under Shah Jahan. In 1634, he commissioned the creation of a magnificent imperial throne to symbolize the glory of his court. No longer in existence, the Peacock Throne was reportedly made entirely of gold and jewels from the royal treasury and took seven years to complete. It was flanked by the gilded tails of two peacocks, inset with rubies, diamonds, and other gems. The throne was supported by twelve emerald-covered pillars and had an enameled canopy. The underside was covered with rubies, garnets, diamonds, and emeralds.

In 1638, Shah Jahan moved his capital from Āgra to Shahjahanabad (now Old Delhi) on the Yamuna River. At Delhi he built the famous Red Fort, named for its gateways and high walls of red sandstone. The Red Fort contained the grand imperial palace made of white marble, and the Peacock Throne stood in the palace's public audience hall.

Shah Jahan also built the Moti Masjid (the Pearl Mosque) within Āgra Fort, northwest of the Taj Mahal. Constructed between 1646 and 1653, this mosque has been compared to a perfect pearl because of its translucent white marble and perfect proportions. There are three domes, a large courtyard, and a rectangular prayer hall divided into three aisles, each with seven bays.

By 1656, construction was finished on the Jama Masjid (the Great Mosque), the largest mosque in India. Situated across from the Red Fort in Delhi, the Jama Masjid has three giant gateways and two minarets, each 130 feet high. The courtyard is large enough to accommodate more than twenty thousand worshipers. It is believed that the mosque holds some hair, considered sacred, from the prophet Muḥammad and a chapter of the Holy Qurʾān.

When Shah Jahan became gravely ill in 1657, four sons—Dara Shukoh, Shuja, Aurangzeb, and Murad—fought for succession to the throne. Shah Jahan designated Dara Shukoh as his successor, but Aurangzeb defeated his brothers. He then deposed Shah Jahan and confined him to Āgra Fort. According to legend, Shah Jahan spent the last eight years of his life staring at the

Taj Mahal through a window at the fort. On January 22, 1666, he died and joined his beloved queen, Mumtaz Mahal, at the Taj Mahal.

SIGNIFICANCE

Shah Jahan's reign is considered the golden age of Mughal architecture and art. The Pearl Mosque at Āgra and the palace and Great Mosque at Delhi stand as monumental achievements of this period. Shah Jahan introduced the broad use of white marble instead of red sandstone in building construction.

His solid gold Peacock Throne, however, no longer exists. In 1739, Persian king Nāder Shāh (r. 1736-1747) plundered Delhi and took the Peacock Throne to Persia, where it was eventually dismantled and lost. The throne and its later reproductions would become symbols of the Persian (Iranian) monarchy.

Shah Jahan's architectural masterpiece, the Taj Mahal, is considered one of the world's most beautiful buildings and is a popular tourist attraction. The delicate white marble, harmonious forms, intricate decorative details, and structural symmetry epitomize the Mughal aesthetic style, which combines Islamic, Indian, and Persian elements. The love story and mythology of the Taj Mahal have also endured through the years, so that this opulent building has become one of the most celebrated symbols of love.

In 1983, the United Nations Educational, Scientific, and Cultural Organization (UNESCO) designated the Taj Mahal a World Heritage Site, a recognition given to a place or building of major import to the common heritage of humankind and, thus, worthy of preservation. Although controversy surrounds the exact dates of the Taj Mahal's construction, India celebrated the 350th anniversary of this famous monument to love in September of 2004.

—*Alice Myers*

FURTHER READING

Asher, Catherine. *Architecture of Mughal India*. New York: Cambridge University Press, 1992. An excellent account of Shah Jahan as a builder and patron of architecture, with accompanying ground plans, diagrams, and photographs.

Begley, W. E., and Z. A. Desai, eds. *The Shah Jahan Nama of Inayat Khan*. New York: Oxford University Press, 1990. In this first complete English translation of the official court chronicles of Shah Jahan, thirty chapters record each year of his reign. Illustrations, bibliography, appendices, and index.

_____, comps. and trans. *Taj Mahal, the Illumined Tomb: An Anthology of Seventeenth-Century Mughal and European Documentary Sources*. Cambridge, Mass.: Aga Khan Program for Islamic Architecture, 1989. A great resource for contemporary documents about the Taj Mahal. Includes illustrations and bibliographical references.

Kumar, Raj. *India Under Shah Jahan*. New Delhi: Anmol, 2000. A biography of Shah Jahan, covering his life and achievements. Includes a bibliography.

Nou, Jean-Louis, Amina Okada, and M. C. Joshi. *Taj Mahal*. New York: Abbeville Press, 1993. A comprehensive study of the Taj Mahal, with color plates, a glossary, and a bibliography.

Pal, Pratapaditya. *Romance of the Taj Mahal*. London: Thames & Hudson, 1989. The story of Shah Jahan, the Taj Mahal, and the architecture, art, and painting of his reign. Includes an extensive bibliography and 262 illustrations.

Stierlin, Henri. *Islamic Art and Architecture from Isfahan to the Taj Mahal*. New York: Thames & Hudson, 2002. Chapter 7 examines the masterpieces created during Shah Jahan's reign. Includes illustrations, a glossary, and a bibliography.

Stronge, Susan. *Painting for the Mughal Emperor: The Art of the Book, 1560-1660*. New York: V & A Publications, 2002. Chapters examine "Painting for Jahangir" and "Painting for Shah Jahan." Includes color plates, notes, and a glossary.

SEE ALSO: 1605-1627: Mughal Court Culture Flourishes; 1609-1617: Construction of the Blue Mosque; 1619-1636: Construction of Samarqand's Shirdar Madrasa; 1642-1666: Reign of Shah 'Abbās II; 1658-1707: Reign of Aurangzeb; 1679-1709: Rājput Rebellion.

RELATED ARTICLES in *Great Lives from History: The Seventeenth Century, 1601-1700:* 'Abbās the Great; Aurangzeb; Jahāngīr; Kösem Sultan; Murad IV; Shah Jahan; Śivājī.

1630's

1632-1667
POLISH-RUSSIAN WARS FOR THE UKRAINE

The Smolensk War (1632-1634) and the Thirteen Years' War (1654-1667) between the Polish-Lithuanian Commonwealth and Muscovy contributed to the former's decline and the emergence of Muscovy as a Great Power.

LOCALE: Polish-Muscovite borderlands

CATEGORIES: Wars, uprisings, and civil unrest; expansion and land acquisition; religion and theology; government and politics; diplomacy and international relations

KEY FIGURES

Władysław IV Vasa (1595-1648), king of Poland, r. 1632-1648

John II Casimir Vasa (1609-1672), king of Poland, r. 1648-1668

Michael Romanov (1596-1645), czar of Muscovy, r. 1613-1645

Alexis (1628-1676), czar of Muscovy, r. 1645-1676

Sigismund III Vasa (1566-1632), king of Poland, r. 1587-1632

Bohdan Khmelnytsky (c. 1595-1657), hetman of Zaporozhian, or Dnieper, Cossacks, r. 1648-1657

Charles X Gustav (1622-1660), king of Sweden, r. 1654-1660

Frederick William, the Great Elector (1620-1688), elector of Brandenburg, r. 1640-1688

SUMMARY OF EVENT

In 1600, the Polish-Lithuanian Commonwealth was the largest state in eastern Europe, with frontiers stretching from the Baltic Sea almost to the Black Sea. The core of Muscovy, consisted of what is now northeastern Russia. Ukraine was dominated by the Tatar khanate of the Crimea and the Cossacks—frontiersmen, runaway serfs, and adventurers of all kinds—unwilling to bow to king, czar, khan, or sultan. The Zaporozhian Cossacks of the Dnieper, however, had long been within the Polish sphere of influence.

The Polish-Muscovite rivalry had two aspects. Territorially, the borderlands between the two states, including the cities of Smolensk and Kiev on the Dnieper, were in dispute. Ideologically, the Polish-Lithuanian Commonwealth had come to embody the spirit of the Counter-Reformation in eastern Europe, but the Muscovy czars claimed the spiritual heritage of Orthodox Constantinople, which had been lost to the Ottomans in 1453.

Poland's staunchly Catholic king Sigismund III Vasa intervened in the Muscovite Time of Troubles (1584-1613): In September, 1610, the Poles fought their way into Moscow, and, in June of 1611, they captured Smolensk after a protracted siege. The expulsion of the Poles from Moscow (August, 1612) led to the enthronement of Czar Michael Romanov, the first monarch of the Romanov Dynasty. That the new government remained weak was reflected in the Peace of Deulino with the Polish-Lithuanian Commonwealth (December, 1618), which left Smolensk in Polish hands.

For the Muscovites, however, the treaty was not the end of the matter. Czar Michael's father, Metropolitan Filaret, the patriarch of the Russian Orthodox Church and coruler of Muscovy with his son (1619-1633), was soon planning for a renewal of hostilities, hiring Protestant foreign mercenaries and raising new regiments. In 1632, a Muscovite army commanded by Michael Shein, after some initial successes, settled down to besiege Smolensk. However, disease and hunger took their toll on the besiegers, troops had to be diverted against Tatar raiders and local insurgents, and before long, the besieging army found itself encircled by the Poles. In 1633, Filaret died, and the Moscow government opened negotiations. Shein himself surrendered to the Poles in February of 1634. By the Peace of Polianovka (June, 1634), Poland retained Smolensk and other towns taken during the Time of Troubles (1584-1613), but Władysław IV Vasa renounced claims to the Muscovite throne, which had been first advanced in 1610. Shein was tried and executed for treason, paying the price of failure. Muscovy's new regiments were disbanded and their foreign officers expelled, thus ending the Smolensk War of 1632-1634.

Between 1648 and 1654, the Dnieper Cossacks, led by Bohdan Khmelnytsky, revolted against Polish overlordship. The quarrels between Poles and Cossacks ran deep, fueled by the determination of the Polish magnates of the southeast to reduce the Ukrainians to serfdom, to strip the Cossacks of their independence, and to enforce Catholicism upon the Orthodox. The uprising was of unparalleled ferocity, as was Polish retaliation. The conflict raged back and forth, amid carnage and devastation. Neither Władysław IV Vasa nor his successor John II Casimir Vasa could suppress the rebellion, but Khmelnytsky's forces could not retain the initiative, so he was forced to turn to Moscow. By the Treaty of

Pereyaslavl (January, 1654), the Zaporozhian Cossacks acknowledged the overlordship of Czar Alexis, although the treaty's terms were interpreted differently by the signatories.

Thus, the czar became embroiled with the Polish-Lithuanian Commonwealth in the Thirteen Years' War (1654-1667), involving campaigns of great ferocity fought over repeatedly devastated lands. Alexis's prime objectives were to recover Smolensk and Kiev; Casimir's objective was to lose as little territory as possible. Hostilities opened in the spring of 1654 with Muscovite forces in the north advancing into Lithuania, taking a number of towns. By July, they had captured Smolensk, and by the following year, they had taken Minsk, Vilna, Kaunas, and Grodno. In the south, in collaboration with the Cossacks, they had besieged Lviv and entered Lublin.

These Polish reverses, exposing Polish military weakness, soon tempted another predator. Charles X Gustav of Sweden launched a preemptive invasion of Poland, fearing that his own Baltic provinces would be exposed to Muscovite invasion and determined to force the abrogation of the Polish Vasa's long-standing claim to the Swedish throne. By September of 1655, Charles X had occupied Warsaw, and by October, he had occupied Kraków. Many Polish nobles had defected to the Swedes, and John II was a refugee in Silesia. The greatest magnates in Lithuania, the Radziwills, submitted to Charles in recognition of virtual independence; Brandenburg's Frederick William, the Great Elector, sought to occupy Ducal Prussia; and György II Rákóczi, prince of Transylvania, was preparing to invade from the south. It seemed that one century before the First Partition, Poland was to be wiped off the map.

However, in a startling reversal of fortune, the tide turned, symbolized by the heroic defense of the shrine of the "Black Madonna" at Czestochowa against the Swedes (December, 1655). Charles had been too successful, and a hostile coalition consisting of the Habsburg emperor, Denmark, and the Netherlands was forming. Alexis, too, was fearful of Swedish expansion and was willing to negotiate with the Poles for recognition of his territorial gains. Muscovy was experiencing severe financial hardship, and the upheavals associated with the reforms of Patriarch Nikon were beginning. One improbable bargaining chip was that Alexis should succeed the childless John II as king of Poland.

In any case, the course of events gave Poland breathing space: Rákóczi's incursion of 1657 ended in his forces being crushed by the Poles and their new allies, the Crimean Tatars. Frederick William abandoned his

Swedish ally, and the Poles ceded Ducal Prussia to him (Treaty of Wehlau, September, 1657). The opportune death of Charles X in February of 1660 hastened the end of the First Northern War (1655-1661) with the Treaty of Oliva (May, 1660) and the Treaty of Kardis (June 21, 1661). Poland was free to concentrate on the eastern front, where circumstances were also changing in its favor.

Khmelnytsky had died in 1657, and his successor as hetman (leader) of the Zaporozhian Cossacks, Ivan Vyhovsky, disillusioned with the harshness with which Moscow interpreted the terms of Pereyaslavl, turned back to Poland, initiating the Treaty of Hadiach (September 16, 1668), which anticipated a Ukrainian principality as the equal partner of the Polish kingdom and the grand duchy of Lithuania. However, the bitterness between the Poles and Cossacks could not be assuaged, so the agreement was not implemented.

Several months earlier, a Muscovite army of some 150,000, commanded by Prince Alexis Trubetskoi, was decisively defeated at Konotop (June 19, 1658). There was panic in Moscow, and many fled the city, fearing a Polish-Cossack or Tatar advance, which never happened. Significantly, however, the defeat led Czar Alexis to begin modernizing his forces. Vyhovsky's failure to follow up on his victory left the Muscovites firmly in control of the Left Bank. In October, the hetman resigned and retired to Poland.

Vyhovsky's success at Konotop was repeated by his Polish allies, who, as a result of the Peace of Oliva, could divert troops eastward. Near Polotsk, Hetman Paweł Jan (c. 1610-1665) defeated Prince Ivan Khovansky, who left 19,000 men dead or captive on the field (June 27, 1660). The Poles recaptured Vilna, Grodno, and Mogilev (1661). In the south, 40,000 troops in the Ukraine were defeated at Chudnovo by a combined Polish-Tatar force and had to capitulate (October 17, 1660). The failed army, which consisted of traditional gentry cavalry, further justified the case for radical military reform.

The Poles had regained the entire Right Bank except for Kiev, but they could make no headway east of the Dnieper. Plenipotentiaries eventually met at Andrusovo, near Smolensk. In the light of Moscow's losses, Czar Alexis anticipated little good from the negotiations, but he was elated by the favorable terms his principal diplomat, Afansasy Lavrentyevich Ordyn-Nashchokin, extracted from the Poles. John II, however, was facing unrest at home, planning his abdication (September 16, 1668), and planning his retirement to France.

1630's

SIGNIFICANCE

The Treaty of Andrusovo (January of 1667), which included a thirteen-year armistice, laid out the future map of eastern Europe until the First Partition of Poland in 1772. By its terms, Muscovy gained permanent control of the Left Bank (much of what is now Ukraine), while Poland retained its traditional rights to the Right Bank. Kiev was to remain in Muscovite hands for two years only, but the Poles never regained it. Moscow kept Smolensk. In 1686, Alexis's daughter Sophia, queen regent, signed a Perpetual Peace (the Treaty of Moscow) with the Polish king, John III Sobieski, which confirmed Moscow's possession of Kiev and its right to intervene on behalf of the Commonwealth's Orthodox subjects, marking the death knell of Poland as a Great Power.

—*Gavin R. G. Hambly*

FURTHER READING

Davies, Norman. *God's Playground: A History of Poland.* 2 vols. New York: Columbia University Press, 1982. An excellent source for studies of seventeenth century Poland.

Florinsky, Michael T. *Russia: A History and Interpretation.* 2 vols. New York: Macmillan, 1947, 1953. This detailed work is considered by many to be the best account of the complex history of early seventeenth century Russia. Includes a glossary, a bibliography, and an index in each volume.

Frost, Robert I. *After the Deluge: Poland-Lithuania and the Second Northern War, 1655-1660.* New York: Cambridge University Press, 1993. A detailed chronological narrative and analysis of the political and military aspects of the Polish phase of the war.

Korduba, M., and W. Tomkiewicz. "The Reign of John Casimir." In *The Cambridge History of Poland to 1696.* Cambridge, England: Cambridge University Press, 1950. The authors provide a detailed narrative of John II Casimir Vasa's reign.

Longworth, Philip. *Alexis, Tsar of All the Russias.* New York: Franklin Watts, 1984. The definitive biography of Alexis, an underestimated ruler.

Majewski, W. "The Polish Art of War in the Sixteenth and Seventeenth Centuries." In *A Republic of Nobles,* edited by J. K. Fedorowicz. New York: Cambridge University Press, 1982. Essential reading for studies of Polish military history.

Stevens, Carol Belkin. *Soldiers of the Steppe.* De Kalb: Northern Illinois University Press, 1995. Essential for studying the military history of seventeenth century Muscovy.

Subtelny, Orest. *Ukraine: A History.* 3d ed. Toronto: University of Toronto Press, 2000. An authoritative overview of Ukrainian history.

SEE ALSO: Feb. 7, 1613: Election of Michael Romanov as Czar; Jan. 29, 1649: Codification of Russian Serfdom; 1652-1667: Patriarch Nikon's Reforms; July 10, 1655-June 21, 1661: First Northern War; 1672-c. 1691: Self-Immolation of the Old Believers; Summer, 1672-Fall, 1676: Ottoman-Polish Wars; 1677-1681: Ottoman-Muscovite Wars.

RELATED ARTICLES in *Great Lives from History: The Seventeenth Century, 1601-1700:* Alexis; Charles X Gustav; Christina; Frederick William, the Great Elector; John III Sobieski; Bohdan Khmelnytsky; Ivan Stepanovich Mazepa; Nikon; Michael Romanov; Sigismund III Vasa; Sophia.

February 22-27, 1632
ZUÑI REBELLION

Upon completion of a missionary church in the Zuñi village of Hawikuh, site of the first Spanish massacre of the Zuñi almost a century earlier, the people of the village murdered a Christian priest and then fled from their homes. Although the colonial government retaliated quickly and brutally, the incident succeeded in eliminating missionaries from Zuñi territories for the next three decades.

LOCALE: Zuñi pueblos, New Mexico
CATEGORIES: Wars, uprisings, and civil unrest; colonization

KEY FIGURES
Francisco Letrado (d. 1632), first priest killed by the Zuñi
Martín de Arvide (d. 1632), second priest killed in the rebellion

SUMMARY OF EVENT
Zuñi Indian contact with Spanish explorers began in violence. The Zuñi lived in six pueblos widely scattered across what is now western New Mexico. They occupied communities of apartment houses built on the sides or tops of mesas. They had no central government, and each pueblo spoke a distinct language. Spaniards first entered this territory in 1539. They came north from Mexico, hunting for great cities of gold reported to be in the area.

The legend of the Seven Cities of Gold, called Cíbola, had spread through Spanish possessions in the New World three years earlier, when Álvar Núñez Cabeza de Vaca—a sailor who had spent eight years wandering through Texas and the Southwest after a shipwreck on the Gulf Coast—brought to Mexico City the story he had been told by native peoples. The governor of New Spain sent an expedition led by a Franciscan priest, Marcos de Niza, and a former slave named Estevanico (also known as Estevan) into the region to verify the story. Estevanico reached a Zuñi pueblo a few days before the priest. By the time Fray Marcos arrived, the Zuñi had killed Estevanico, reportedly for taking liberties with Zuñi women. The priest returned south and, contrary to all evidence, told the governor what the latter wanted to hear, that the Seven Cities of Cíbola did exist and were as magnificent as legend had held.

In the summer of 1540, the Spanish launched an expedition of more than a hundred men, including several priests, led by Francisco Vásquez de Coronado, the gov-

ernor of Nueva Galicia, a state in western Mexico. After six months of travel, the explorers reached the Zuñi villages previously visited by Fray Marcos and were greatly disappointed by the poverty they discovered. The Zuñi, fearing that the invaders were looking for slaves, met the Spaniards in front of their village and warned that trying to enter their homes meant death. Coronado explained through an interpreter that he had come on a sacred mission to save souls for Christ. A priest then read the *requerimiento*, a statement read by a priest before all battles, warning the Zuñi that if they did not accept Spain's king, Charles V, as their ruler, and if they did not embrace Christianity, they would be killed or enslaved.

The Zuñi responded with arrows, killing several Spaniards, but Spanish muskets and steel swords proved far superior to native weapons, and Coronado's forces quickly destroyed much of the village. The Zuñi fled, leaving behind large quantities of corn, beans, turkeys, and salt, but no gold. Coronado, who had traveled much of the way in full armor, received several wounds during the battle but survived. He concluded that Cíbola must be somewhere else. Before continuing his search, however, he destroyed the village, called Hawikuh by the Zuñi. Despite the victory, no Spaniard returned to Zuñi territory until 1629.

By 1629, Franciscan missionaries had more than fifty churches in the area of New Mexico. Their headquarters in Santa Fe had been built by Pueblo Indian laborers in 1610. Most of the mission churches had been constructed by native labor, with women building the walls and men doing the carpentry. The priests decided to reestablish contact with peoples living farther to the west. In 1629, eight priests traveled to Acoma, a village built on top of a 400-foot (122-meter) mesa, where they erected a church. The next year, Fray Estevan de Pereá, sixty-four years of age, was sent to Hawikuh, about 60 miles (100 kilometers) west of Acoma. He found a village of eight hundred people, who greeted him peacefully. An interpreter told the Zuñi that the expedition had come to free them from slavery and the "darkness of idolatry." This was the same message brought to them a hundred years before by Coronado, and it had led to bloodshed. This time, however, the Zuñi allowed the Spanish to remain and build a church. Three years later, the church was completed.

Zuñi religious leaders, called sorcerers by the Christian fathers, fought the new religion from the very beginning. In their religion, there were many gods, not just one, who lived on the earth in trees, mountains, plants, and various animals. The Zuñi worshiped water gods, according to Coronado, because water made the corn grow and sustained life in a very harsh climate. Water seemed almost as valuable to them as gold did to the Spaniards, something the Spaniards could not understand. Zuñi priests taught that people should live in harmony with the earth and learn to live with nature, not conquer it as Christians seemed to believe.

Zuñi sought harmony in every aspect of their lives, which to them meant compromise and getting along with everything. They did fight wars, especially with Apache raiders, but violence and aggression were to be avoided when possible. The Spaniards found little of value in these teachings and believed their God had chosen them to conquer the heathens, bring light to those living in darkness—which meant anyone who was not Christian—and then grow rich, as God meant them to do. Compromise meant weakness to the Spanish; conquest was the highest good. These conflicting values would finally lead the Zuñi to rebellion and violence.

Another source of conflict between Zuñi and Spaniards was the system of labor that developed under the Europeans. Zuñi and other native peoples did most of the manual labor on construction projects; they also worked in mines and in the fields. Spanish nobles, government officials, and settlers simply did not perform this type of work; hard labor was considered beneath their dignity. Native Americans were forcibly recruited for this back-breaking labor. Under the *encomienda* system, wealthy Spanish landlords were entitled to tribute from all Indians living on "their" land. This tribute, in theory, could take the form of money, goods, or labor—in practice, the *encomienda* system evolved into a system of slavery and forced labor. The landlords did, however, also receive tributary goods from all the families on their extensive properties, usually 1.6 bushels (56 liters) of maize (corn) and a cotton blanket or deer or buffalo hide each year. In times of drought, these payments were especially onerous and deeply resented.

Native peoples also hated the compulsory labor demanded of them by Spanish authorities. Thousands of Pueblo Indians, including the Zuñi, had built Santa Fe under this system. They were supposed to be paid for their work, but many were not. In other places, the native peoples were used largely as pack animals to carry logs and heavy mining equipment across the desert. Many mines used slaves captured on frequent slaving expeditions into tribal territory. Slavery and economic exploita-tion added to Native American resentment of the Europeans.

On February 22, 1632, according to Spanish government records, Zuñi warriors killed Fray Francisco Letrado, the missionary at Hawikuh, during a mass he was celebrating to honor the completion of his church. The Zuñi then abandoned the pueblo and did not return for several years. Upon hearing of the killing, Governor Francisco de la Mora Ceballas sent a party of soldiers after the Zuñi. The soldiers found the Zuñi's hiding place and took revenge on the population, killing some and enslaving others. Five days after the murder of Fray Letrado, the Zuñi killed another priest, Fray Martín de Arvide, at a pueblo fifty miles west of Hawikuh. Two soldiers in Fray Martín's party also were killed. The governor sent another military expedition to avenge these deaths. Several Zuñi were killed in battle, and at least one was later executed for participating in the murders.

SIGNIFICANCE

As with the first encounter between the Zuñi and the Spanish, the latter seemed to achieve the clear victory, but they then left the Zuñi alone for a number of years. Thus, while the Zuñi Rebellion spread no further than the murder of two priests and two soldiers, Christian missionaries did not return to the Zuñi pueblos until 1660. Those missionaries would remain among the Zuñi until the Pueblo Revolt of 1680, when violence between Spaniards and Zuñi again broke out and the Zuñi mission churches again were destroyed.

—*Leslie V. Tischauser*

FURTHER READING

Barrett, Carole A., ed. *American Indian History*. 2 vols. Pasadena, Calif.: Salem Press, 2002. An overview of the Zuñi Rebellion is included in volume 2 of this survey of Native American history from the fifteenth through the twentieth centuries.

Crampton, C. Gregory. *The Zuñis of Cíbola*. Provo: University of Utah Press, 1977. A general history of the Zuñi people. Black-and-white photographs illustrate how the pueblos have changed over time.

Ganner, Van Hastings. "Seventeenth Century New Mexico." *Journal of Mexican American History* 4 (1974): 41-70. Provides a pro-Indian view of tribal relations with the Spanish. Includes a brief description of the events leading up to 1632.

Hodge, Frederick Webb. *History of Hawikah, New Mexico: One of the So-Called Cities of Cíbola*. Los Angeles: Southwest Museum, 1937. Contains translations of Spanish mission records and early histories of

Spanish-Zuñi relations. The only detailed history of the revolt.

Scholes, France V. *Church and State in New Mexico, 1610-1650.* Historical Society of New Mexico Publications in History 7. Albuquerque: University of New Mexico Press, 1942. Takes a pro-Spanish point of view, treating Native Americans in a condescending manner. Based on translations of Spanish documents.

Weber, David J. *The Spanish Frontier in North America.* New Haven, Conn.: Yale University Press, 1992. A general overview and detailed history of the Spanish presence in North America, from the early 1500's to

the 1830's. A balanced view of relations between Native Americans and the Spanish, with much useful information on religion, social structure, and culture.

SEE ALSO: 1617-c. 1700: Smallpox Epidemics Kill Native Americans; 1648: Cult of the Virgin of Guadalupe; Aug. 10, 1680: Pueblo Revolt.

RELATED ARTICLES in *Great Lives from History: The Seventeenth Century, 1601-1700:* Canonicus; Sor Juana Inés de la Cruz; Massasoit; Metacom; Opechancanough; Pocahontas; Powhatan; Squanto; Kateri Tekakwitha.

Fall, 1632-January 5, 1665
SETTLEMENT OF CONNECTICUT

A second wave of Puritans, seeking the prime land that had already been occupied in Massachusetts by the first wave of settlers, found and colonized the Connecticut River Valley, expanding British holdings in the Americas and creating a new government markedly different from the one developing in the Massachusetts Bay.

LOCALE: Connecticut River Valley and the coast of Long Island Sound

CATEGORIES: Expansion and land acquisition; colonization

KEY FIGURES

John Davenport (1597-1670), founder and coleader of the New Haven colony

Theophilus Eaton (1590-1658), English merchant and cofounder of the New Haven colony

Thomas Hooker (1586-1647), pastor and leader of the Hartford settlement

Roger Ludlow (1590-1666), leader of the settlement at Windsor

Second Earl of Warwick (Robert Rich; 1587-1658), president of the Council for New England

Edward Winslow (1595-1655), Plymouth colonist who explored the Connecticut River Valley

John Winthrop, Jr. (1638-1707), founder of the settlements at Saybrook and New London and governor of Connecticut

SUMMARY OF EVENT

As more and more settlers poured into Massachusetts Bay as part of the Great Puritan Migration, towns that at

first had seemed only partly settled began to seem congested. The first settlers obtained the best agricultural land; those who came later were left with second-best. New groups often brought their favorite pastor with them, but these Puritan pastors often found their ideas of the Puritan way of life somewhat at odds with those espoused by the earlier groups. Both these forces worked to motivate the groups coming later to seek new ground to found settlements of their own.

In the fall of 1632, Edward Winslow of the Plymouth Colony explored westward and discovered the Connecticut River Valley, the site of some of New England's most productive farmland. Moreover, the most desirable land was cleared land, and the river valley contained extensive meadows that had few trees because of the frequent flooding. News of the rich meadows to the west rapidly reached the congested settlements in Massachusetts Bay, and a number of settlers attached to the minister Thomas Hooker resolved to move to the new area. Although the Dutch traders centered at Albany had earlier laid claim to the portion of the river valley near the present site of Windsor, the English settlers chose to ignore this claim. Instead, they bought the claim Winslow's explorations had created from Plymouth, and in 1635, they moved to the site of the present city of Hartford. Other groups soon followed, settling at Windsor and Wethersfield on the Connecticut River.

Robert Rich, second earl of Warwick and president of the Council for New England, had secured a patent for at least part of what is now Connecticut; the boundaries of the patent were ill-defined, however. In 1635, Warwick and his associates authorized John Winthrop, Jr., son of

1630's

the leader of the Massachusetts Bay Colony, to build a fort and create a settlement at the mouth of the Connecticut River, where it flows into Long Island Sound. He negotiated an agreement with the followers of Thomas Hooker, proposing to settle in the Connecticut River Valley, as a result of which Winthrop became governor of the colony.

Because Winthrop's authority did not include the right to establish a governing body, he secured the cooperation of the Massachusetts General Court, which authorized the establishment of basic government institutions similar to those existing in the Massachusetts Bay Colony. These institutions provided for the participation of all Christian freeholders in the election of individuals to office in the towns and in the General Court for Connecticut. This franchise—relatively broad compared to that in the older colony, which restricted participation to those who were recognized members of a church—has led many commentators to view Connecticut as fundamentally more democratic than the Massachusetts Bay Colony.

In 1637, the first General Court of Connecticut met at Hartford, comprising representatives of the towns of Hartford, Windsor, and Wethersfield. This general court prepared for war against the powerful Pequots, whose lands lay between these settlements and the coast. In a three-week campaign, the settlers vanquished the Pequots and eliminated them as a threat to the new colony. Shortly after the victory over the Pequots, a new group of settlers, under the leadership of John Davenport and Theophilus Eaton, founded a new colony at New Haven. The coastal settlement proved successful, and soon other groups settled in the vicinity.

The settlers in the Connecticut River Valley, flush with their victory over the Pequots, immediately turned their attention to creating a stable government for the colony. They drew up a constitution, called the Fundamental Orders, that provided for a General Court, or legislature, to meet twice a year and created the office of governor. Representatives of the towns sat in the General Court; every qualified householder could vote in the Town Meeting to choose the town's representatives, but only settlers who were freemen and held substantial property were eligible to serve in the General Court. The settlers around New Haven were not included, as they were a separate colony. Attempts were made to include representatives from the settlements on the eastern end of Long Island, but the difficulties of travel ensured that they would rarely participate in governmental decisions. The formal drafting of the Fundamental Orders relied heavily on the advice of Roger Ludlow, the only one of the earlier settlers with legal training.

All these settlements flourished under the neglect of the British government, for during most of the first thirty years of Connecticut settlement, the British were wholly preoccupied with their own Civil Wars and the Protectorate under Oliver Cromwell. With the restoration of the Stuart monarchy in 1660, the lack of a royal charter for any group in Connecticut (in contrast to Massachusetts Bay) became an urgent issue. In 1661, John Winthrop, Jr., was commissioned to go to England and secure a royal charter. Winthrop proved to be a highly successful maneuverer, and in 1662, he won for Connecticut the desired charter, issued on May 3. On January 5, 1665, although somewhat reluctantly, the independent colony at New Haven agreed to be incorporated into Connecticut. The conquest of New Amsterdam by the English that same year eliminated any foreign competition for control of Connecticut.

SIGNIFICANCE

Overall, the first thirty years of settlement in Connecticut brought many new émigrés from England, although new immigrants were few during the 1640's. The supply of good land during these years ensured that this overwhelmingly agricultural society would remain relatively homogeneous socially. Although some who came subsequently left, those who stayed were soon able to acquire enough land for a "competency," that is, a standard of living that enabled them and their families to live with modest comfort. Few would have been able to achieve this level had they remained in England. For them, living in Connecticut was the realization of a dream.

Connecticut is also particularly important to the history of colonial America as a result of the Fundamental Orders, framed by Hooker and Ludlow. This document, one of the most important and elaborate early American constitutions, was a model for later such documents and enshrined the principle of separation of church and state that was eschewed by the nearby theocracy of Massachusetts Bay.

—Nancy M. Gordon

FURTHER READING

Andrews, Charles M. *The Settlements*. Vol. 2 in *The Colonial Period of American History*. New Haven, Conn.: Yale University Press, 1964. Still a valuable account, with chapters 3 through 5 presenting a straightforward narrative of the settlement of Connecticut and its political organization. Argues that the availability of cleared land along the river was a major motivation for settlement.

Canny, Nicholas, and Alaine Low, eds. *The Origins of Empire: British Overseas Enterprise at the Close of the Seventeenth Century*. Vol. 1 in *The Oxford History of the British Empire*, edited by William Roger Lewis. New York: Oxford University Press, 1998. Collection of essays by noted historians exploring numerous aspects of Britain's worldwide colonial expansion. Explains the founding and governance of individual American colonies, and several essays focus on British colonies in New England, the Carolinas, the mid-Atlantic, and the Chesapeake Bay area.

Jones, Mary Jean Anderson. *Congregational Commonwealth: Connecticut, 1636-1662*. Middletown, Conn.: Wesleyan University Press, 1968. Argues that the search for religious freedom was the primary motive behind the settlement of Connecticut. In addition, the desire for new, uninhabited land drove some early settlers to move to the Connecticut River Valley. Asserts that the rudimentary government created for Connecticut was less democratic than is usually depicted.

Lucas, Paul R. *Valley of Discord: Church and Society Along the Connecticut River, 1636-1725*. Hanover, N.H.: University Press of New England, 1976. Describes the deep dissension within the churches of the first Connecticut settlements.

Main, Jackson Turner. *Society and Economy in Colonial Connecticut*. Princeton, N.J.: Princeton University Press, 1985. An innovative study presenting details of the economic and social conditions of the early settlers of Connecticut, based on an extensive collection of statistical materials. Concludes that the colonial society of Connecticut was substantially homogeneous.

Martin, John Frederick. *Profits in the Wilderness: Entrepreneurship and the Founding of New England Towns in the Seventeenth Century*. Chapel Hill: University of North Carolina Press, 1991. Argues that individuals of means played a larger role in the creation of new towns in New England than has previously been recognized, and that the founding of new towns was driven as much by profit as by religious motives.

SEE ALSO: Dec. 26, 1620: Pilgrims Arrive in North America; May, 1630-1643: Great Puritan Migration; June, 1636: Rhode Island Is Founded; July 20, 1636-July 28, 1637: Pequot War; 1642-1651: English Civil Wars; Sept. 8, 1643: Confederation of the United Colonies of New England; Dec. 16, 1653-Sept. 3, 1658: Cromwell Rules England as Lord Protector; May 10, 1655: English Capture of Jamaica; May, 1659-May, 1660: Restoration of Charles II.

RELATED ARTICLES in *Great Lives from History: The Seventeenth Century, 1601-1700:* Charles II (of England); Oliver Cromwell; John Davenport; Thomas Hooker; Roger Ludlow; John Winthrop.

September 2, 1633
GREAT FIRE OF CONSTANTINOPLE AND MURAD'S REFORMS

Constantinople's great fire of 1633, which destroyed one-fifth of the city and led to increased social upheaval, spurred Sultan Murad IV's reforms of the empire. His reign of terror, aided by his deeming the fire divine wrath, restored order by coercively imposing decrees and prohibitions, including the shutting down of coffeehouses and wine taverns, meant to consolidate his authority and uphold the Islamic ideals of morality.

LOCALE: Constantinople, Ottoman Empire (now Istanbul, Turkey)

CATEGORIES: Wars, uprisings, and civil unrest; social issues and reform; government and politics; architecture

KEY FIGURES
Murad IV (1612-1640), Ottoman sultan, r. 1623-1640
Kösem Sultan (c. 1585-1651), Murad's mother
Koçu Bey (d. c. 1650), councillor of the sultan
Abaza Mehmed Paşa (d. 1634), Turkish commander
Kadizade Mehmed Efendi (d. 1635), preacher of the Hagia Sophia
Nef'i (c. 1572-1635), poet

SUMMARY OF EVENT

Murad IV's seventeen-year reign, which began when he was eleven years old, can be divided into two stages. During the first nine years, in which Murad was under the authority of his mother, Kösem Sultan, the empire was beleaguered by much internal upheaval, such as the revolt led by Abaza Mehmed Paşa, who raised an army of forty thousand soldiers against the Ottoman capital, Constantinople. Other upheavals included the riot of the Crimean Tatars and the Anatolian uprisings.

One the most terrible epidemics to have swept across Constantinople—the plague—decimated as many as one thousand people per day. Further blows were dealt to the empire by Egypt's inability to pay annual tribute and the Persians' recapture of Baghdad in 1623-1624 after eighty-nine years of Ottoman reign. In addition, the Turkish fleet in the Black Sea would incur damages from the Kazakh raids.

In 1632, when Murad took control of the empire on his own, marking the second stage of his reign, socioeconomic difficulties and the Ottoman army's lamentable condition led to revolts by the *sipahi* of the palace (feudal cavalry stationed in the capital) and the Janissary corps, threats as much to the sultan's life as to Constantinople's economic and commercial life: Stores, the port, and state institutions came to a standstill; the rebels plundered and threatened the civilians even during Ramadan. Murad had to assume full state control, and a reign of terror commenced through his coercive methods, which juxtaposed executions and prohibitions of all sorts.

First, Murad had the grand vizier Regeb Paşa, the sultan's brother-in-law, executed for secretly supporting the rebels. Then, the capital and provinces were drastically purged of rebels, and the sultan had all the members of the *askeri* class (which included the government and the army) take their oath of allegiance to him. Furthermore, he reorganized the empire's administrative and financial systems with a view to eliminating corruption and bribery. In so doing, Murad drew heavily on the theoretical model provided by his councillor Koçu Bey's treatise on government (1631). In effect, this treatise laid the foundation for the reform movement supported by sultans who reigned after Murad IV. Koçu Bey argued that state decline was triggered by the sultan's weakening authority and by harem and palace administration intrigues; by the oppressed populace's urban migration, which resulted in decreased revenues; by financial corruption; and by inefficient organization of the military.

The sultan was aided in his campaign by an unforeseen event. A fire, which erupted in a café on September 2, 1633, grew to engulf and destroy one-fifth of Constantinople, including the state archive, the *sipahi* barracks, two thousand wooden buildings—among which were superb manor houses—and private collections of manuscripts and documents. Deeming the disaster a sign of the divine wrath, Murad used the effects of the fire in

The Ottoman capital of Constantinople suffered a devastating fire in 1633 that destroyed one-fifth of the city and led to repressive social reforms by Sultan Murad IV. (The Granger Collection)

his campaign for upholding the Islamic ideals of purity and austerity, such as wearing distinctive Muslim garb, and for reorganizing state institutions.

All cafés, coffeehouses, wine stores, and wine taverns were closed down by Murad, who believed they posed threats of rebellion. Taking his cue from the religious fanatism of a preacher named Kadizade Mehmed Efendi of the Hagia Sophia, and his followers, the Kadizadeler (sons of the cadi), the sultan banned coffee, opium, and tobacco by declaring them *haram*, that is, canonically prohibited. Brought into the empire from Yemen near the end of the sixteenth century, coffee had already been banned several times, and the priests had fulminated against tobacco ever since its introduction in 1601.

On August 5, 1635, the sultan banned alcohol and ordered the closure of all taverns and wine stores, personally supervising the enforcement of the decree. He would walk the streets incognito by day and by night and pierce his sword through anyone caught consuming the prohibited products. Murad caused so much terror that people would not dare to even utter his name, even in private. Yet, alcohol prohibition notwithstanding, Murad himself indulged in drinking wine—and forcing his entourage, the priests included, to join him—in the upper chambers of his palace. During the last seven years of his reign, he became an alcoholic, which, compounded with sciatica and hereditary gout, led to the sultan's untimely death at age twenty-eight. The decree prohibiting coffee, opium, and tobacco was enforced only during Murad's reign.

The destruction of the state archive in the 1633 fire called for the reorganization of the taxation registers; alongside the enforcement of regular tax collection, this contributed to the rebalancing of the state treasury. Another positive measure was the strict record of and improvement in the status of the *tīmār*-holding *sipahi* (*tīmārli sipahi*), that is, the fief-holding cavalrymen, by entering their names and *tīmārs* in registers (*defterler*), as well as by rewarding the brave ones and their male descendants. With his newly reorganized army, Murad IV was able to conquer Yerevan from the Iranians (1635) and then reconquer Baghdad (1638), which earned him the name Bagdat Fatihi (conqueror of Baghdad), a name by which he has been known in Ottoman history.

Yet the cultural life of the empire suffered greatly in the wake of the sultan's prohibitions. Free speech was censured, and many public figures were executed for minor offenses, among them the poet Nef'i, who was sentenced to death for writing satirical verse. Spiritual leaders, too, died upon the sultan's orders, including the Islamic religious leader Ahizade Huseyin Efendi, charged with treason and strangled in 1634, and the Greek Orthodox patriarch of Constantinople, Cyril Lukaris (1620-1638), one of the most important reformers of the patriarchal academy. Murad would not refrain from having his own brothers killed—all cold-blooded murders owing more to his choleric temperament than to administrative reform.

The internal reforms in the aftermath of the 1633 fire brought about economic improvement and expanding commercial exchanges with the European states; demographic increase followed, as Constantinople became the most populated European city with as many as 600,000 inhabitants. However, Murad IV's military and tax reforms—buttressing as they did an authority not seen since the reign of Süleyman the Magnificent—delayed the Ottoman Empire's fall only temporarily, and this was primarily because of the sultan's determination and cruelty.

SIGNIFICANCE

The consequences of the great fire of 1633 affected not only Constantinople but also the entire Ottoman state, as Murad IV's politics of building reconstruction affected institutional rebuilding as well. During his reign, religious fanaticism and cultural censorship reached high levels, while the economy and finances could be restored only by prohibitions and coercive means; transgression led to excessively cruel penalties. For example, as many as twenty thousand people were executed for various offenses.

Financial recovery enabled Murad to strengthen the military and buy its loyalty, which contributed significantly to diminishing the number of uprisings in the provinces. The sultan's legendary bravery and cruelty were important assets in slowing down the deterioration of both Turkish society and the Ottoman state. However, his reforms proved to be short-lived. His brother and successor, İbrahim (r. 1640-1648), ruined virtually everything Murad had accomplished in matters of state consolidation. Yet, it must be admitted that the Ottoman Empire's waning started in the second part of Murad's reign, the time made more tumultuous by the devastating 1633 fire.

—*Florentina Nicolae*

FURTHER READING

Coco, Carla. *Secrets of the Harem*. New York: Vendome Press, 1997. Using well-documented texts, photos, and paintings, the author examines the erotic world of the Turkish harem.

Inalcik, Halil, and Donald Quataert, eds. *An Economic and Social History of the Ottoman Empire, 1300-1914*. 2 vols. New York: Cambridge University Press, 1994. A highly specialized history, with many maps and tables.

McCarthy, Justin. *The Ottoman Turks: An Introductory History to 1923*. New York: Longman, 1997. A sweeping historical overview of Ottoman history from the late thirteenth century to the early twentieth century.

Mansel, Philip. *Constantinople: City of the World's Desire, 1453-1924*. New York: St. Martin's Press, 1996. A brief but insightful account of Murad's rule and the state of the Ottoman capital.

Mantran, Robert, ed. *Histoire de l'Empire Ottoman*. Paris: Fayard, 1989. Mantran investigates the economic, social, and political evolution of the Ottoman

1630's

state from its inception to the nineteenth century. Special attention is paid to the Balkan and Arab provinces and to cultural life. Includes maps.

Shaw, Standford J. *History of the Ottoman Empire and Modern Turkey.* 2 vols. New York: Cambridge University Press, 1994-1995. The first volume of this comprehensive history analyzes the rise and decline of the Ottoman Empire between 1280 and 1808.

Stiles, Andrina. *Russia, Poland, and the Ottoman Empire, 1450-1700.* London: Hodder and Stoughton, 1991. Stiles employs contemporary evidence in this brief work to investigate the Ottoman period and the

reciprocal impact of Islamic and European civilizations.

SEE ALSO: 1602-1639: Ottoman-Ṣafavid Wars; Beginning c. 1615: Coffee Culture Flourishes; 1623-1640: Murad IV Rules the Ottoman Empire; 1638: Waning of the *Devshirme* System; Jan. 18-20, 1657: Meireki Fire Ravages Edo; Sept. 2-5, 1666: Great Fire of London.

RELATED ARTICLES in *Great Lives from History: The Seventeenth Century, 1601-1700:* Kösem Sultan; Murad IV.

May 30, 1635
PEACE OF PRAGUE

The Peace of Prague marked a critical stage in the Thirty Years' War, revealing the desire of the Austrian Habsburgs to achieve success and inaugurating the last phase of the war.

LOCALE: Prague, Bohemia

CATEGORIES: Diplomacy and international relations; wars, uprisings, and civil unrest

KEY FIGURES

Ferdinand II (1578-1637), Holy Roman Emperor, r. 1619-1637

John George I (1585-1656), elector of Saxony, 1611-1656

Axel Oxenstierna (1583-1654), chancellor of Sweden, 1612-1654

Cardinal de Richelieu (Armand-Jean du Plessis; 1585-1642), chief minister of France, 1624-1642

SUMMARY OF EVENT

By 1635, the Thirty Years' War had reached a critical stage, for with the defeat of the Swedish army and its allies by the imperial forces under the king of Hungary at Nördlingen on September 6, 1634, the way seemed open for peace. Swedish power, which had been dominant in Germany since 1630, was now seriously diminished, and even though Cardinal de Richelieu, chief minister of France, and Count Axel Oxenstierna, chancellor of Sweden, arranged a new treaty of alliance at Compiègne in April, 1635, it did not appear that the arrangement enlisted much sympathy among the German princes. Instead, a peace movement grew in Germany itself, born of the general weariness and devastation of warfare and of

the genuine fear among the German princes of domination by Sweden or the rising power of France. From their point of view, it was far better to arrange a German peace and permit the German people to reconstruct their devastated society.

The lead in arranging such a peace was taken by the leading Protestant power allied with Sweden, the Elector John George I of Saxony, who had been negotiating for peace throughout much of 1634. The Battle of Nördlingen enhanced Habsburg power in the eyes of the German princes and served to further the momentum toward their agreement with the emperor. As early as November of 1634, Saxon and imperial agents reached agreement on the preliminaries of a treaty, and the king of Hungary signed a military truce with the Saxons at Laun in February, 1635. These measures resulted in the agreement called the Peace of Prague, which represented a compromise between John George and Emperor Ferdinand II.

By the terms of the treaty, the Edict of Restitution of March 6, 1629, was superseded by the provision that disputed church properties were to remain in the hands of those who possessed them on November 12, 1627, for a period of forty years, after which litigation in the imperial courts might challenge this ownership. The ecclesiastical principalities east of the Elbe River were to remain in Protestant hands, with the important archbishopric of Magdeburg reserved for a son of John George, but those in Lower Saxony and Westphalia were to remain as they had been restored to Catholic hands. Ferdinand II ceded the province of Lusatia to Saxony and made some concessions to the Lutherans in his remaining province of Silesia. In accordance with Saxon policy,

Axel Oxenstierna, chancellor of Sweden, negotiated with French minister Cardinal de Richelieu for peace after the previously dominant Swedes were defeated by imperial forces. The peace did not last, however, as the French and Swedes battled in the final phase of the Thirty Years' War. (Library of Congress)

the concessions made to Protestants were restricted to the Lutherans.

Despite these concessions, the emperor stood to gain significantly from this peace. All the German powers were invited to subscribe to its terms, and to join in a national effort to exclude the Swedes and French from the empire. The empire was to raise an army for this purpose that would be under imperial command, and no prince was to keep an army of his own or to engage in military alliances. This would have increased the powers of the emperor considerably. To encourage other leading German princes to accept these terms, Maximilian I of Bavaria was guaranteed his electoral dignity and possession of most of the Palatinate, while George William of Brandenburg was enticed by the prospect of the succession in Pomerania. Only the family of the deposed elector Palatine and the so-called Bohemian exiles were excluded from the general amnesty offered to the emperor's foes. Before long, apart from those excluded from its aegis, only Bernard of Saxe-Weimar, William of Hesse-Cassel,

and the city of Strassbourg refused to accede to the terms of the Peace of Prague, which had been formally promulgated at Vienna.

John George of Saxony, Maximilian of Bavaria, and many of the other German princes were motivated primarily, and Emperor Ferdinand at least somewhat, by a genuine desire for peace and the good of the German nation. However, in the eyes of Ferdinand this goal was parallel with that of cooperating with his Spanish cousin in another round of their interminable dynastic wars. On May 21, 1635, in accordance with the terms of its alliance with Sweden, France had declared war on Spain. For the German rulers and for the German people of the numerous towns that adhered to the Peace of Prague, it soon became obvious that the treaty had not brought peace but had drawn the whole of Germany into an enlarged struggle between the Habsburgs and the Bourbons. France, appearing on the left bank of the Rhine as the ally of Sweden, was now the major enemy of the empire. The German states, far from achieving a position in which their only task would have been to assist the Habsburg emperor in ridding Germany of the Swedish menace, now found that they were obliged to fight all the battles of both the Austrian and the Spanish Habsburgs.

SIGNIFICANCE

At the Diet of Regensburg in 1640-1641, a last effort was made to achieve a peace based on the Peace of Prague. The abandonment of the emperor by the new elector of Brandenburg, Frederick William, shattered any remaining hopes of success. The support of the Austrian Habsburgs for their Spanish relatives, along with the entrance of France into the struggle, had completely altered the nature of the war. The Peace of Prague, far from bringing peace, actually prolonged the war in Germany and elsewhere for another thirteen years.

—*Robert F. Erickson and William C. Schrader*

FURTHER READING

Asch, Ronald G. *The Thirty Years' War: The Holy Roman Empire and Europe, 1618-1648.* New York: St. Martin's Press, 1997. This work focuses on the Holy Roman Empire's role in the war, including the disagreements with Bohemia that precipitated the conflict and the Peace of Prague.

Bireley, Robert. *The Jesuits and the Thirty Years' War: Kings, Courts, and Confessors.* New York: Cambridge University Press, 2003. The author recounts the role the Jesuits played during the war at the Catholic courts of Vienna, Munich, Paris, and Madrid. He describes how Jesuit leaders in Rome confronted the challenges of running an international organization during the three-decade religious conflict.

Gagliardo, John G. *Germany Under the Old Regime, 1600-1790.* London: Longman, 1991. The author provides a coherent overview of the political, cultural, social, and economic trends in the empire during its last two centuries.

Holborn, Hajo. *The Reformation.* Vol. 1 in *A History of Modern Germany.* 3 vols. New York: Alfred A. Knopf, 1959. Reprint. Princeton, N.J.: Princeton University Press, 1982. Still the best overall history of Germany in English for this period and a standard source.

Ingrao, Charles W. *The Habsburg Monarchy, 1618-1815.* New York: Cambridge University Press, 1994. A well-balanced and literate work without being ponderous, covering the formation of the Habsburg Empire.

Parker, Geoffrey. *The Thirty Years' War.* London: Methuen, 1985. Parker places the events of the war in their military context.

Polienský, Josef V. *War and Society in Europe, 1618-1648.* Cambridge, England: Cambridge University Press, 1978. A leading scholar on the Thirty Years' War considers events from a central European perspective.

Wedgwood, C. V. *The Thirty Years' War.* London: J. Cape, 1938. Reprint. London: Folio Society, 1999. An extremely valuable account of the war, including its German and international ramifications.

SEE ALSO: 1618-1648: Thirty Years' War; Mar. 6, 1629: Edict of Restitution; 1630-1648: Destruction of Bavaria; 1640-1688: Reign of Frederick William, the Great Elector; July, 1643-Oct. 24, 1648: Peace of Westphalia; 1667: Pufendorf Advocates a Unified Germany.

RELATED ARTICLES in *Great Lives from History: The Seventeenth Century, 1601-1700:* Ferdinand II; Frederick William, the Great Elector; Axel Oxenstierna; Samuel von Pufendorf; Cardinal de Richelieu; Albrecht Wenzel von Wallenstein.

June, 1636
RHODE ISLAND IS FOUNDED

Dissatisfied members of the Massachusetts Bay Colony sought freedom from the Puritan oligarchy and religious intolerance.

LOCALE: Narragansett Bay (now in Rhode Island)
CATEGORIES: Colonization; expansion and land acquisition; religion and theology

KEY FIGURES

Roger Williams (c. 1603-1683), colonial American religious leader who founded Providence

Massasoit (Ousamequin; c. 1580-1661), Wampanoag grand sachem, r. before 1620-1661

Canonicus (c. 1565-1647), grand sachem of the Narragansett tribe, r. before 1600-1647

Anne Hutchinson (1591-1643), colonial American religious leader who cofounded Portsmouth

William Coddington (1601-1678), founder of the Aquidneck Island settlements of Portsmouth and Newport

Samuel Gorton (1592-1677), controversial supporter of Anne Hutchinson who established Warwick

John Clarke (1609-1676), physician and minister who was Rhode Island's agent in England

SUMMARY OF EVENT

The founding of Rhode Island was more complicated than the founding of most of the other American colonies because it involved five separate settlements and unusual leaders bent on expressing their individualistic beliefs. The earliest settlers in Rhode Island migrated to the area from the Massachusetts Bay Colony. Some had been forced out of that colony for their "dangerous" opinions, and others had left of their own accord, because they were dissatisfied with the Puritan oligarchy that controlled Massachusetts.

The first European settler of Rhode Island, with the exception of the recluse William Blakston, was Roger Williams, who was ordered to leave the Massachusetts Bay Colony on October 9, 1635. He managed to avoid deportation back to England for three months, but in January of 1636, he became aware that he would soon be arrested. Three days before his planned arrest, Williams left his home and set out on foot for what would become Rhode Island during a blinding blizzard. Walking 80-90 miles (130-145 kilometers) through the worst of a New England winter, Williams suffered immensely and would likely have died of exposure were it not for the aid of his friends among the Wampanoag Indians.

Williams managed to reach the lodge of Massasoit, grand sachem of the Wampanoags, at Mount Hope. Williams had first met the Wampanoag sachem when the latter was about thirty years of age, and he considered Massasoit to be a great friend. Near the end of his trek, Williams also lodged with the Narragansett grand sachem Canonicus and his family, whom Williams also counted as friends. Canonicus and Massasoit enabled Williams to survive his flight from Massachusetts. Nevertheless, his winter trek left Williams with permanent scars that hindered his health for the rest of his life.

Soon after purchasing land near the Seekonk River from Massasoit, Williams was joined by five other men. A warning from the governor of Plymouth that they were trespassing forced them to establish a new settlement on the Great Salt River in June, 1636, which they called Providence Plantations. It is not known whether Williams had an actual plantation in mind or simply envisioned a trading post or mission, but other outcasts soon arrived at Providence and were welcomed, and each new

settler was allotted a home lot and a farm from the land that Williams had purchased from the natives.

Providence was strictly an agricultural community. The colony was built without capital or outside assistance, and its population and economy grew slowly. The heads of families participated in a town-meeting type of government and signed a compact agreeing to obey the laws passed by the will of all. The compact was intended to be operative "only in civil things," signifying a commitment to the separation of church and state—one of the central issues that had driven many of the settlers from the theocratic colony of Massachusetts.

Williams's house at Providence Plantations quickly became a transcultural meeting place. He lodged as many as fifty Indians at a time, including travelers, traders, and sachems on their way to or from treaty conferences. If a Puritan needed to contact a native or vice versa, he more than likely did so with Williams's aid. Among the Indian nations at odds with each other, Williams became known as "a quencher of our fires." When the citizens of Portsmouth needed an American Indian agent, they approached Williams. The Dutch did the

Roger Williams says goodbye to his family before fleeing Massachusetts to avoid arrest. (Gay Brothers)

1630's

Roger Williams arrives in what will become Providence, Rhode Island, and is welcomed by the Narragansett Indians. (Francis R. Niglutsch)

same thing after 1636. Williams often traveled with Canonicus, Massasoit, and their warriors, lodging with them in the forest. The Narragansetts' council sometimes used Williams's house for its meetings.

In April, 1638, another band of exiles, led by William Coddington, left Boston in search of religious freedom. They had been preceded in March by Anne Hutchinson, whose Antinomian emphasis on "grace" over "works" elevated personal revelation and thus diminished the clergy's role in religious practice. Arriving at Providence, the exiles arranged to purchase the island of Aquidneck from the natives, and by the following spring they had established the new settlement of Pocasset (Portsmouth). By seventeenth century standards, the settlement had a democratic form of government, with Coddington serving as judge.

Two such dominant personalities as Coddington and Hutchinson could not exist in harmony for long, however. When their two factions split over Hutchinson's eccentric supporter Samuel Gorton, Coddington was ousted and, with his followers, began the new plantation

of Newport. In March, 1640, he succeeded in uniting the two settlements on Aquidneck so that they could manage their own affairs apart from Providence. The union, the most orderly civil organization in the Narragansett region, was to endure for seven years. By today's standards, the democracy that they proclaimed in 1641 was limited, because it excluded half the adult males from participating in government. Probably because Coddington was unsuccessful in obtaining a patent for Aquidneck, the people of Portsmouth became disillusioned and broke away from Newport in 1648.

Meanwhile, the controversial Gorton, driven from both Portsmouth and Providence for defying the authority of the government, purchased Indian lands to establish Warwick. After enduring harassment and imprisonment by Massachusetts officials, he obtained an order compelling Massachusetts to cease molesting him and lived in peace as an honored citizen of Warwick.

Of all the Rhode Island leaders, Williams emerged as the dominant figure. His efforts to maintain peace among the tribes were of inestimable service to the whole of

New England, yet the ambitions of other political leaders in the British settlements in and around Rhode Island were to remain his chief problem. Convinced that the settlements of Rhode Island had to cooperate in order to remain intact, he worked selflessly for a federation of the four main towns. When the formation of the United Colonies of New England in 1643 threatened Rhode Island's integrity, Williams sailed for England to obtain a charter from the Long Parliament. The patent that he brought back in September, 1644, authorized the union of Providence, Portsmouth, and Newport as "The Incorporation of Providence Plantations." Warwick was included later.

The political instability caused by the English Civil Wars back home caused a delay in putting the newly authorized government into effect, but in May, 1647, an assembly of freemen met at Portsmouth to organize the government and to draft laws. A federalist system, whereby the towns maintained their individual rights as parts of the larger community, was created. Their code of laws was one of the earliest in the American colonies and was the first to embody in all its parts the precedents set by the English legal system. By 1650, a representative assembly composed of six delegates from each town was operating. The assembly also served as a judicial body, until a separate court for trials was established in 1655. Town courts preserved the local peace.

Coddington continued to deal underhandedly in an attempt to separate Aquidneck from the union. In 1651, he succeeded in obtaining a lifetime appointment as governor of Aquidneck and Conanicut Islands from the Council of State. However, the residents of the islands supported Williams's successful mission to England, which resulted in the annulment of Coddington's patent in 1652. Distrust of central government and antagonism between the mainland and the islands persisted until 1654, when Williams, with the support of Oliver Cromwell, restored the atmosphere of cooperation between the towns.

The 1660 restoration of the Stuart monarchy in England imperiled the validity of Rhode Island's charter of 1644. As a result, John Clarke, the colony's agent in London, petitioned the Crown for confirmation. Meanwhile, Charles II confirmed Connecticut's grant, including half of Rhode Island's territory, so it became necessary to submit the matter to arbitration. The arbitration was decided in Rhode Island's favor, and the new colonial charter of July 18, 1663, also confirmed the colony's policy of complete liberty of conscience. It was the only colonial charter to do so.

SIGNIFICANCE

Rhode Island was one of several colonies founded in a search for religious toleration and freedom. Other such colonies included Maryland, primarily a haven for Catholics, and Pennsylvania, which was founded by Quakers. Rhode Island, however, included the right to freedom of conscience in its charter, becoming the first colony to codify in its core document what would ultimately become a core principle of the United States. Moreover, Rhode Island was founded not by colonists fleeing persecution in the Old World, but by those fleeing a new kind of persecution in the New World. By breaking off from the theocratic Puritan government of Massachusetts Bay, Roger Williams and others successfully prevented that government from controlling the fate of New England as a whole.

Although Williams advocated and fought primarily for religious freedom, his ideas were relevant to political freedom as well, and his legacy helped to shape the debates that would ultimately drive the colonies to rebel against the English crown in the eighteenth century. Williams espoused such values as "soul liberty," political freedom, and economic equality: He not only presaged the American Revolution but also created a community in which his prescient philosophy could but put into practice, win adherents, and flourish.

—Warren M. Billings and Bruce E. Johansen

FURTHER READING

Andrews, Charles M. *Our Earliest Colonial Settlements: Their Diversities of Origin and Later Characteristics.* New York: New York University Press, 1933. Chapter 4 details the political turmoil of the early years and the lives of the colony's principal leaders.

_____. *The Settlements.* Vol. 2 in *The Colonial Period of American History.* New Haven, Conn.: Yale University Press, 1964. Chapters 1 and 2 present a detailed overall account of Rhode Island's founding.

Greene, Theodore P., ed. *Roger Williams and the Massachusetts Magistrates.* Boston: D. C. Heath, 1964. This collection of readings presents disparate views from the seventeenth century to the present on the question of Williams's banishment.

Grinde, Donald A., Jr., and Bruce E. Johansen. *Exemplar of Liberty: Native America and the Evolution of Democracy.* Los Angeles: University of California, Los Angeles, Native American Studies Center, 1991. Includes a chapter on Williams's founding of Rhode Island and his use of Native American aid and ideas about political society.

1630's

James, Sydney V. *The Colonial Metamorphoses in Rhode Island: A Study of Institutions in Change*. Edited by Sheila L. Skemp and Bruce C. Daniels. Hanover, N.H.: University Press of New England, 2000. Examines how the founders of Rhode Island created the local institutions that shaped their lives. Based upon extensive archival research, the book details the development of town and colony governments, the courts, and land companies from Rhode Island's founding until the American Revolution.

LaPlante, Eve. *American Jezebel: The Uncommon Life of Anne Hutchinson, the Woman Who Defied the Puritans*. San Francisco, Calif.: HarperSanFrancisco, 2004. LaPlante, an eleventh-generation granddaughter of Hutchinson, examines Hutchinson's life, including her move to Rhode Island and her role in founding the colony.

Miller, Perry. *Roger Williams: His Contribution to the American Tradition*. New York: Atheneum, 1962. Liberally interspersed with selections from Williams's writings, Miller's study contends that Williams was concerned basically with theology, not democratic political reforms.

Morgan, Edmund S. *Roger Williams: The Church and the State*. New York: Harcourt Brace & World, 1967. Concentrating upon the thought of Roger Williams as presented in his writings, Morgan seeks "to expose the symmetry of the ideas that lay behind the polemics."

Williams, Roger. *The Complete Writings of Roger Williams*. 7 vols. New York: Russell & Russell, 1963. The most complete collection of Williams's writings on the founding of Rhode Island.

_____. *A Key into the Language of America*. 5th ed. Reprint. Providence, R.I.: Tercentenary Committee, 1936. Williams's views on religion, politics, and society are presented in the context of a guide to Native American languages.

SEE ALSO: Dec. 26, 1620: Pilgrims Arrive in North America; May, 1630-1643: Great Puritan Migration; Fall, 1632-Jan. 5, 1665: Settlement of Connecticut; 1642-1651: English Civil Wars; Sept. 8, 1643: Confederation of the United Colonies of New England; Apr. 21, 1649: Maryland Act of Toleration; Dec. 16, 1653-Sept. 3, 1658: Cromwell Rules England as Lord Protector; May, 1659-May, 1660: Restoration of Charles II; Mar. 4, 1681: "Holy Experiment" Establishes Pennsylvania; June, 1686-Apr., 1689: Dominion of New England Forms.

RELATED ARTICLES in *Great Lives from History: The Seventeenth Century, 1601-1700:* Canonicus; Charles II (of England); Oliver Cromwell; Anne Hutchinson; Massasoit; Roger Williams.

July 20, 1636-July 28, 1637
PEQUOT WAR

The Pequot War represented the first major conflict between Native Americans and New England settlers. The settlers allied with several other New England Indian tribes and utterly defeated the once-dominant New England indigenous nation, killing or enslaving many of its members. The war marked the beginning of a forty-year period of violence and conflict between Europeans and Native Americans in New England.

LOCALE: Connecticut
CATEGORIES: Wars, uprisings, and civil unrest; colonization

KEY FIGURES
Sassacus (c. 1560-1637), sachem of the Pequots
John Endecott (1588-1665), first governor of the Massachusetts Bay Colony
John Mason (1600-1672), soldier who led the combined Massachusetts-Connecticut force
John Underhill (1597?-1672), trained warrior and Massachusetts militia captain
Uncas (c. 1606-c. 1682), leader of the Mohegans and son-in-law of Sassacus
Miantonomo (c. 1600-1643), sachem of the Narragansetts
Roger Williams (c. 1603-1683), cofounder of Rhode Island

SUMMARY OF EVENT
As suggested by their name (from *pekawatawog*, "the destroyers"), the Pequots were once the most formidable tribe in New England. Part of the Eastern Algonquian language family, by the dawn of the seventeenth century they were well established in what is now Connecticut.

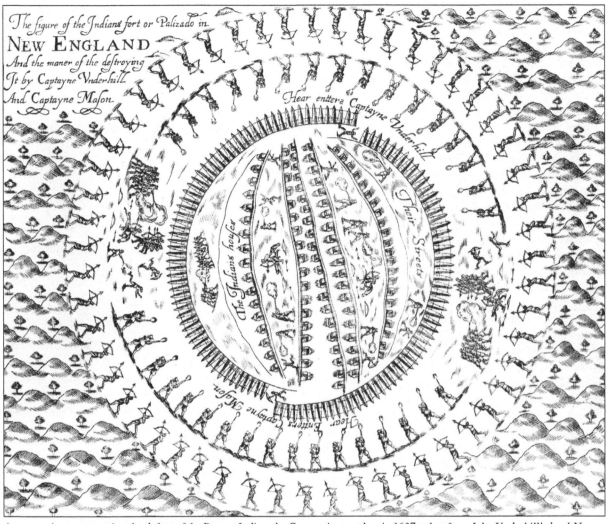

An engraving representing the defeat of the Pequot Indians by Connecticut settlers in 1637, taken from John Underhill's book Newes from America *(1638).* (Library of Congress)

Their powerful leader, or sachem, was the venerable Sassacus, who was born near what is now Groton. Despite his many years of experience, Sassacus faced, in his seventies, the biggest crisis in his people's history. Although the Pequots had a virtual hegemony over their adjacent nations—a leader among the Mohegans, Uncas, was married to the daughter of the Pequot sachem—the Pequots had trouble coping with the impact of European colonists in the Connecticut Valley. The Pequots found themselves caught between the Dutch, who were moving eastward from New Netherland, and the English, moving westward from the Massachusetts Bay Colony and Connecticut. European competition for control over trade on the Connecticut River proved to be a destabilizing factor in intertribal relationships, threatening the Pequot hegemony.

The political climate was therefore ripe for violence, which finally erupted after two English traders were killed in Connecticut. John Stone was killed in 1633, and John Oldham died on July 20, 1636. It has never been firmly established that the Pequots were in fact the ones responsible for the traders' deaths. John Gallup, an English merchant, found Native Americans in control of Oldham's ship, anchored off Block Island, in July of 1636. Gallup fought with the Indians for control of the vessel.

Upon hearing of the skirmish for Oldham's ship, Massachusetts governor John Endecott led ninety sol-

353

diers on a punitive raid on the Indians of Block Island. They killed every man on the island. Although most of the casualties were Narragansetts, not Pequots, Endecott pushed eastward along the Connecticut coast, indiscriminately demanding reparations from the Pequots as well. The tribe refused, resisted the Massachusetts troops, and suffered at least one death, as well as the destruction of several villages.

Sassacus, outraged, invited the Narragansetts to join him in war on the English, but the Narragansett sachem, Miantonomo, was favorably disposed toward the colonists and refused. He was probably influenced by Roger Williams, the founder of Rhode Island, who had cultivated a close relationship with the Narragansett people. Even without Narragansett support, Sassacus acted, laying siege to Fort Saybrook, on the Connecticut River, during the winter of 1636-1637 and concurrently attacking several outlying English settlements, including Wethersfield, where at least nine settlers were killed.

Puritan retaliation was not long in coming. Captains John Mason and John Underhill shared command. Born in England, Mason had served as an army officer in the Netherlands before his arrival in Massachusetts in 1632. From Hartford, he set forth with a band of eighty, supported by warriors of the Mohegan, Narragansett, and Niantic tribes. Uncas had allied with the English against his father-in-law, Sassacus. Like Mason, Underhill had been born in England, and he then was reared in the Netherlands, where his father had fought the Spanish. Since 1630, he had lived in Massachusetts. Mason and Underhill initially went eastward, by ship, along the Connecticut coast, making landfall at Narragansett Bay. Then, with their native allies, they moved westward by land. After crossing the Pawcatuck and Mystic Rivers, they were poised to attack the main Pequot village at sunrise on May 25, 1637.

The Puritan forces divided, with each half attacking one of the village's two main gates, located at opposite ends of the stockaded native settlement. The English did not profit as much as expected by their surprise attack; their opening forays were successfully repulsed. The Europeans then set fire to the wigwams, however, and as the village burned, the Pequots faced horrible alternatives. Some, mostly women and children, remained inside the fort, perishing in the flames. Those who fled, mostly the warriors, were cut down by the English and their Narragansett, Mohegan, and Niantic allies. Between six hundred and one thousand Pequots perished in this massacre. Only two colonists were lost, and a mere twenty were wounded. Underhill rejoiced in the "mighty vic-

tory," comparing his annihilation of the Pequots to David's destruction of his foes in biblical times.

A large group of Pequot refugees sought sanctuary in a swamp near New Haven, only to be discovered and destroyed on July 28, 1637. In the subsequent confusion, Sassacus and a handful of followers fled, seeking asylum in Mohawk territory. Desiring to prove their loyalty to the English, however, the Mohawks beheaded Sassacus.

SIGNIFICANCE

As a consequence of the Pequot War, Uncas, the son-in-law of Sassacus, seized control of the Mohegan tribe. With English support, Uncas began a career of conquest that made him the most powerful sachem in New England. Miantonomo, sachem of the Narragansetts, was killed by command of Uncas in 1643, perhaps at the request of his English allies. Although Uncas initially prospered as a prominent warrior and ruler, however, he ultimately discovered his English allies to be unpredictable. When he attacked Massasoit in 1661, the Puritans forced him to give up prisoners and plunder; later, during Metacom's War (King Philip's War; 1675-1676), Uncas surrendered his sons as hostages to the colonists, who, defeating Metacom of the Wampanoags, effectively ended the New England Indians' resistance to European settlement.

The Pequot War began a period of almost constant conflict between the Puritan settlers and the Indians of New England that lasted until the time of Metacom's War. The conflict was ultimately tragic for all the Native Americans. The Pequots, who (together with the Mohegans) had numbered perhaps four thousand men when the English arrived at Plymouth Rock in 1620, steadily declined. An estimate made in 1643 suggested that there were twenty-five hundred men in their group. Following their defeat, many of the Pequots were massacred or enslaved. Pequot slaves were shared between the Europeans and other tribes, and some were deported as far from home as Boston or the island of Bermuda. Others were assimilated into other tribes, by being resettled among their former enemies. In 1655, the Pequots were moved to two reservations on the Mystic River. By 1674, there were only three hundred men in this once-proud nation. Pequot place names disappeared: The Pequot River, for example, became the Thomas River. Their power had been forfeited and their identity nearly eradicated. In 1990, there were between nine hundred and sixteen hundred Pequots.

—C. George Fry

FURTHER READING

Cave, Alfred. *The Pequot War*. Amherst: University of Massachusetts Press, 1996. Cave explains how the English Puritans transformed petty squabbles between themselves, the Pequots, other Native American nations, and the Dutch traders into a cosmic struggle of good and evil in the wilderness.

De Forest, John W. *History of the Indians of Connecticut from the Earliest Known Period to 1850*. Hartford, Conn.: W. J. Hammersley, 1851. Reprint. Hamden, Conn.: Shoestring Press, 1988. A classic study of the native peoples of Connecticut.

Hauptman, Laurence M., and James D. Wherry. *The Pequots in Southern New England: The Fall and Rise of an American Indian Nation*. Norman: University of Oklahoma Press, 1990. Collection of essays, including essays on the Pequots in the seventeenth century, the Pequot War and its legacies, and Indians and colonists in southern New England after the Pequot War.

Josephy, Alvin M., Jr. *Five Hundred Nations: An Illustrated History of the North American Indians*. New York: Alfred A. Knopf, 1994. This generously illustrated volume is sympathetic to the point of view of the Native Americans. References to the situation in New England revise earlier accounts.

Orr, Charles, ed. *History of the Pequot War: The Contemporary Accounts of Mason, Underhill, Vincent, and Gardener*. Cleveland, Ohio: Helman-Taylor, 1897. A valuable anthology of eyewitness reporting on the Pequot War from the Puritan perspective, drawing on the recollections of major English participants.

Peale, Arthur L. *Memorials and Pilgrimages in the Mohegan Country*. Norwich, Conn.: Bulletin, 1930. Peale, author of a groundbreaking study of Uncas, was celebrated for his knowledge of the Mohegans and the Pequots. Eloquent.

Salisbury, Neal E. *Manitou and Providence: Indians, Europeans, and the Making of New England, 1500-1643*. New York: Oxford University Press, 1982. A thorough, objective study of the contrasting attitudes and values of the Native Americans and the Europeans during a century and a half of contact and conflict.

Vaughan, Alden T. *New England Frontier: Puritans and Indians, 1620-1675*. Boston: Little, Brown, 1965. This helpful study of a half century of relationships between Native Americans and European settlers is a fine starting point for research.

SEE ALSO: 1617-c. 1700: Smallpox Epidemics Kill Native Americans; Dec. 26, 1620: Pilgrims Arrive in North America; Mar. 22, 1622-Oct., 1646: Powhatan Wars; July, 1625-Aug., 1664: Founding of New Amsterdam; Fall, 1632-Jan. 5, 1665: Settlement of Connecticut; June, 1636: Rhode Island Is Founded; 1642-1700: Westward Migration of Native Americans; June 20, 1675: Metacom's War Begins; Aug. 10, 1680: Pueblo Revolt.

RELATED ARTICLES in *Great Lives from History: The Seventeenth Century, 1601-1700:* Canonicus; Massasoit; Metacom; Roger Williams.

1630's

1637

DESCARTES PUBLISHES HIS *DISCOURSE ON METHOD*

Descartes's Discourse on Method *articulated his rational-mathematical philosophical system, one that would influence philosophers and scientists—and thought in general—through the seventeenth century and beyond.*

LOCALE: Leiden and other cities in the Netherlands
CATEGORIES: Philosophy; cultural and intellectual history; science and technology; literature

KEY FIGURE
René Descartes (1596-1650), French philosopher and mathematician

SUMMARY OF EVENT

With the publication of the *Discours de la méthode* (1637; *Discourse on Method*, 1649), philosophy was reoriented toward the practical and the deductive. René Descartes's quasi-autobiographical essay both described one person's progress in teaching himself the sciences and attempted to establish a new universal philosophy based upon the most essential foundations. In this way, the *Discourse on Method* was a conscious separation from those aspects of the medieval traditional reliance on authority—especially Aristotelianism—that had survived into the Renaissance as well as an explication of a scientific method that was opposite to the inductive process of formulating hypotheses from the observation of evidence as espoused by the Renaissance thinker Francis Bacon.

Descartes was born into a family of the lower French nobility and raised by his maternal grandmother. He was educated in a Jesuit college between the ages of ten and fourteen and took a law degree from the University of Poitiers in November of 1616. His travels took him to the Netherlands, where he served as a volunteer soldier and experienced a famous vision on November 10, 1619, in which he dreamed of a universal science of nature to which the key was mathematics.

In the 1620's, Descartes continued to travel and to write scientific treatises. He settled in the Netherlands in 1628 for full-time and intense research, meditation, and writing. Three examples of the method of Descartes came out of this period of study: the *Optics, Meteorology,* and *Geometry.* The *Discourse on Method* was written to be the preface to those essays. A mechanical explanation of biology and the universe was also prepared during this time, but Descartes abandoned plans for publication when Galileo was condemned by the Inquisition. The metaphysical aspects of this work in natural philosophy reappeared in the *Discourse on Method,* which was published anonymously along with the three essays in mid-1637 in the hope of finding an open-minded lay audience.

Although the material making up the *Discourse on Method* was written at different times, the outlines of the philosophical system are relatively clear and readily grasped. To Descartes, the sovereign good was scientific knowledge, and the sovereign tool was reason. Unlike many of his predecessors, he explicitly distinguished between reason and faith. His means for increasing knowledge then utilized all the advantages of logical, algebraic, and geometrical procedures—Euclidean geometry was Descartes's favorite discipline, and mathematics the model for all other knowledge. First, Descartes set aside all learning in order to start at an absolute beginning. The most basic fact he could know, Descartes realized, was his own existence, the often-quoted "I think, therefore I am" (*Cogito, ergo sum*), and, since his mind could conceive infinity even though it was itself finite, he then deduced the existence of an infinite and perfect God who created Descartes's idea of infinity.

Another deduction was that there was a distinction or dualism between the mind and the body. Similarly, Descartes explained, the natural philosopher must always start with a firm central theory and proceed from there into the explication of more detailed phenomena, as a chain of truths was formed. The method depended upon preservation of the proper order or sequence and was tied together by observational evidence.

This approach can be concentrated into the following four rules, as Descartes himself did in the second part of the *Discourse on Method:*

1. The philosopher must never accept anything as true without evidence of its truth.
2. Each philosophical or scientific problem should be divided into as many parts as possible to make the attack on the problem easier and more effective.
3. The process is carried out in an orderly manner, beginning with the simplest steps and progressing to the most complicated.
4. The philosopher should be careful and thorough, so that nothing is left out of the chain of reasoning.

DESCARTES'S *DISCOURSE ON METHOD*

René Descartes's work laid the foundation for a new method of certainty that uses mathematics to get at the truth of things. For Descartes, what mattered was the first causes of nature, the greater plan and its mechanics, not the details of particular occurrences. In this excerpt, he sets out the four precepts of his new method of certainty.

Among the different branches of Philosophy, I had in my younger days to a certain extent studied Logic; and in those of Mathematics, Geometrical Analysis and Algebra—three arts of sciences which seemed as though they ought to contribute something to the design I had in view. But in examining them I observed in respect to Logic that the syllogisms and the greater part of the other teaching served better in explaining to others those things that one knows . . . than in learning what is new. And although in reality Logic contains many precepts which are very true and very good, there are at the same time mingled with them so many others which are hurtful or superfluous, that it is as almost as difficult to separate the two as to draw a Diana or a Minerva out of a block of marble which is not yet roughly hewn. . . . [S]o, instead of the great number of precepts of which Logic is composed, I believed that I should find the four which I shall state quite sufficient, provided I adhered to a firm and constant resolve never on any single occasion to fail in their observance. [These four precepts are:]

1. Accept nothing as true which I did not clearly recognise to be so.
2. Divide up each of the difficulties which I examined into as many parts as possible.
3. Carry on my reflections in due order, commencing with objects that were the most simple and easy to understand.
4. Make enumerations so complete and reviews so general that I should be certain of having omitted nothing.

Source: Descartes, *Discourse on Method* (1637), in *Descartes: Selections,* edited by Ralph M. Eaton (New York: Charles Scribner's Sons, 1927), pp. 15-17.

When the final draft of the *Discourse on Method* was written in the winter of 1635-1636, Descartes divided the essay into six parts. In the first section, Descartes gave some of his reflections upon the sciences. This and the beginning of the second part are the most explicitly autobiographical sections of the work. The second part also contains the rules for Descartes's method, while part three shifts to considerations of moral rules. There is another change of topics in part 4, where Descartes placed the foundations of his metaphysics, such as his proofs for the existence of God and the human soul. The fifth section includes summaries of Descartes's mechanical biology and mechanical physics. Finally, in part 6, Descartes introduced *Meteorology* and *Optics* in order to explain why the *Discourse on Method* was a necessary preface to those works. In other words, this section dealt with his ideas about theory construction.

The three essays published with the *Discourse on Method* were influential scientific treatises in their own right, as well as illustrations of the Cartesian method. The *Optics* was largely practical, containing instructions for the construction of optical instruments. Descartes also included his theory that light was an impulsive force transmitted instantaneously along a straight line, as well as the sine-law of refraction. *Meteorology* was the most like a textbook of the three works, with explanations of various weather phenomena in addition to some features of Descartes's physics, which was based upon a full, material universe. In *Geometry*, Descartes defined algebraic operations for geometry; that is, he combined algebra and geometry into analytic geometry.

There are some problems with Descartes's ideas. For example, his own practice of science often did not follow his method. His philosophy also loses rigor when it is based on assumptions outside mathematics, although Descartes corrected some of the difficulty with an independent argument in the section of *Discourse on Method* dealing with metaphysics. Descartes's contemporaries criticized the circularity of the method, and Descartes responded to the comments of critics such as Pierre Gassendi and Antoine Arnauld in later publications and occasionally in correspondence, even though he was not one who reacted particularly positively to criticism. Finally, the autobiographical nature of *Discourse on Method* is problematic and deceiving. Descartes is not a reliable source for the precise details concerning the development of his ideas.

SIGNIFICANCE

The scientific method of Descartes, along with aspects of his ideas about nature, including an optimistic belief in progress and an argument for a constant amount of motion in the universe, influenced both other natural philosophers and Descartes's own later works. His *Medita-*

1630's

René Descartes. (Library of Congress)

tiones de prima philosophia (1641; *Meditations on First Philosophy*, 1680) and *Principia philosophiae* (1644; *Principles of Philosophy*, 1983) extended his writings on metaphysics and science. When reactions to his ideas became increasingly virulent, Descartes traveled to France in 1644, but he returned to the Netherlands later that year. He accepted an invitation to the court of Queen Christina of Sweden in 1649, where he died of pneumonia the following February.

The rationalism, skepticism, and scientific method of Descartes can be found in many of his successors, as his name quickly became attached to anyone who attempted to follow his rules for a universal philosophy. For example, individuals such as Robert Hooke and Jan Swammerdam carried out Descartes's program of the mechanization of physiology, much of which was described in the *Discourse on Method*. Meanwhile, numerous philosophers tried to clarify Descartes's metaphysics in the second half of the seventeenth century, while John Locke, George Berkeley, and David Hume led a British revision of certain Cartesian theories. Later, the *philosophes* of the French Enlightenment sought to present themselves as heirs of Descartes and his rejection of tradition. In general, the problem of attaining a wholly objective under-

standing of any subject matter proved to have universal human appeal.

—*Amy Ackerberg-Hastings*

FURTHER READING

Bordo, Susan, ed. *Feminist Interpretations of René Descartes*. University Park: Pennsylvania State University Press, 1999. A four-part collection exploring Descartes's philosophy and its impact on feminist and gender theory, epistemology, ideas on women, passion, wonder, embodiment, and more. Includes a select bibliography on Descartes, Cartesianism, and gender, and an index.

Cottingham, John, ed. *The Cambridge Companion to Descartes*. New York: Cambridge University Press, 1992. One in a series of references for students and nonspecialists that contains essays on Descartes by leading experts in the field.

_____. *A Descartes Dictionary*. Cambridge, Mass.: Blackwell Reference, 1993. Primarily describes what Descartes meant by his use of certain terms. Should be used as an aid in elucidating Descartes's writings.

Cottingham, John, Robert Stoothoff, and Dugald Murdoch, trans. *The Philosophical Writings of Descartes*. 2 vols. New York: Cambridge University Press, 1984-1985. Comprehensive and readable, this is the standard, modern English translation of Descartes's writings.

Davies, Richard. *Descartes: Belief, Skepticism, and Virtue*. Studies in Seventeenth Century Philosophy 3. New York: Routledge, 2001. Analyzes Descartes's thoughts on credulity, skepticism, and the search for reason and eternal truth.

Garber, Daniel. *Descartes Embodied: Reading Cartesian Philosophy Through Cartesian Science*. New York: Cambridge University Press, 2001. Garber links Descartes's ideas about science to his overall philosophy. Chapter 2 is titled "Descartes and Method in 1637."

Gaukroger, Stephen. *Descartes: An Intellectual Biography*. Oxford, England: Clarendon Press, 1995. A noted scholar illuminates Descartes's intellectual pursuits and explains their rationale. Written in reasonably clear language.

Schouls, Peter A. *Descartes and the Enlightenment*. Kingston, Ontario, Canada: McGill-Queen's University Press, 1989. Schouls, a professor of philosophy, treats Descartes as a progenitor of the Enlightenment by highlighting the concepts of freedom, mastery, and progress in his works.

Srathern, Paul. *Descartes in Ninety Minutes*. Chicago: Ivan Dee, 1996. A quick but helpful introductory overview of Descartes's thought.

SEE ALSO: 1601-1672: Rise of Scientific Societies; 1615-1696: Invention and Development of the Calculus; 1617-1628: Harvey Discovers the Circulation of the Blood; 1620: Bacon Publishes *Novum Organum*; 1623-1674: Earliest Calculators Appear; 1651: Hobbes Publishes *Leviathan*; 1654: Pascal and Fermat Devise the Theory of Probability; 1660-1692: Boyle's Law

and the Birth of Modern Chemistry; 1664: Willis Identifies the Basal Ganglia; Late Dec., 1671: Newton Builds His Reflecting Telescope; Summer, 1687: Newton Formulates the Theory of Universal Gravitation; 1693: Ray Argues for Animal Consciousness.

RELATED ARTICLES in *Great Lives from History: The Seventeenth Century, 1601-1700:* Christina; Pierre de Fermat; Pierre Gassendi; William Harvey; Thomas Hobbes; Robert Hooke; Christiaan Huygens; Johannes Kepler; Gottfried Wilhelm Leibniz; Sir Isaac Newton; Blaise Pascal; John Ray; Jan Swammerdam.

October, 1637-April 15, 1638
SHIMABARA REVOLT

In response to economic exploitation and religious persecution, Christians rose in revolt against the Japanese feudal power structure. Gathering troops from all over Japan and calling on their Dutch allies for aid, the Tokugawa shogunate successfully quashed the rebellion. Virtually all of the more than thirty-seven thousand people who participated in the revolt were killed in the fighting or put to death in its aftermath.

LOCALE: Shimabara and Asakusa regions of northern Kyūshū (now in Nagasaki Prefecture), Japan

CATEGORIES: Wars, uprisings, and civil unrest; government and politics

KEY FIGURES

Amakusa Shiro (1622-1638), Japanese religious leader and rebel

Matsukura Shigeharu (d. 1638), daimyo of Shimabara

Tokugawa Iemitsu (1604-1651), Japanese shogun, r. 1623-1651

SUMMARY OF EVENT

From the mid-sixteenth century, the regions around Nagasaki, in the northern part of the Japanese island of Kyūshū, were bastions of Christian belief. The faith was brought to the region by Portuguese and Spanish missionaries beginning in the 1540's. When prominent local lords converted to Christianity, most of the population of the area followed suit. In the late sixteenth century, however, Toyotomi Hideyoshi, a military strongman who was attempting to restore a measure of central authority after nearly a century and a half of civil war, began to see Christianity as a threat to his efforts to consolidate power. He introduced edicts banning the faith, and while

enforcement was not consistent, there were periodic persecutions of Christian believers.

After Hideyoshi's death, another general, Tokugawa Ieyasu, completed the process of consolidating central power. The Tokugawa shogunate was formed in 1603, and while Ieyasu and his advisers were initially friendly to foreign traders and preachers, this attitude began to change in the 1610's. Tokugawa Iemitsu, the third of the Tokugawa shoguns, began to persecute Christians in earnest. Spanish traders were expelled from Japan in 1624, and from 1633, a system of searches for foreign priests living in hiding in Japan was instituted. The persecutions were particularly harsh in the area around Nagasaki. In October, 1637, a revolt broke out in the largely Christian Shimabara region.

The immediate cause of the Shimabara Revolt is considered by many to have been taxation. The daimyo, or feudal lord, of the region, Matsukura Shigeharu, was notorious for overtaxing the local peasants. During the seventeenth century, while central power lay in the hands of the Tokugawa family, the daimyos were allowed to maintain fiefs where they exercised a great deal of autonomous control. There was no system of national taxation, and individual lords decided the tax rates of their domains. As a result, some areas of Japan, such as the Shimabara and Asakusa regions of Kyūshū, were subject to far more oppressive taxes than other areas of the country. Thus, although Christian persecution was a major factor behind the beginning of the rebellion, some scholars believe that heavy taxes were the most important immediate catalyst triggering the outburst of violence and that many of the rebels began to consider their revolt in Christian terms only after it had already begun.

In all likelihood, however, the revolt was brought about by a number of disparate factors. Aside from oppressive tax rates and religious persecution, the Shimabara peasants had been caught up in a type of millennial movement centered around a local youth, Amakusa Shiro (also known as Masuda Shiro Tokisada). The locals entertained a mixture of Christian belief and superstition. They believed that the emergence of paradise on earth had been foretold, and this belief lent a millennial character to the Shimabara Rebellion. Scholars also see Amakusa Shiro as the equivalent of the leaders of peasant revolts in Europe—a charismatic youth who was believed by his followers to possess a divine power and the potential to deliver them from hardship. While reports differ, Amakusa was considered to be either an angel or a divine presence by his followers. This is a testament to the fact that the beliefs of the rebels were quite far from those preached by orthodox Christians.

Many historians describe the Tokugawa period (1603-1867) as a time of peace, and it is true that the Shimabara Revolt was a rare occurrence of violence. It represents the largest mobilization of armed force between the Ōsaka campaigns of the 1610's and the events of the Meiji Restoration in the 1860's. The Tokugawa raised an army of more than 200,000, mainly from the domains of northern Kyūshū but eventually encompassing troops from all over Japan. When even this force could not defeat the rebels, a ship of the shogunate's Dutch allies was also requested to join in the fighting. The scale of the mobilization is an indication of how serious the revolt was considered to be by Shogun Iemitsu and his advisers.

The fighting was difficult for the shogunate. While the majority of the rebels were peasants, their ranks also contained *rōnin*, masterless samurai who had lost their social rank as a result of the Tokugawa execution of their master, the daimyo Konishi Yukinaga, following the Battle of Sekigahara in 1600. The shogun's forces experienced setbacks on a number of occasions, including a bad defeat in February of 1638, when more than two thousand warriors from the domain of Hizen were killed by rebel fighters. As the fighting stretched on, however, the rebels began to run low on provisions and were besieged by the Tokugawa forces at Hara Castle. The Dutch ship bombarded the fortress with artillery fire, and the castle fell in mid-April of 1638. Amakusa Shiro is said to have been killed and his head taken to Nagasaki. All thirty-seven thousand participants in the revolt, including women and children, are said to have been massacred by the forces of the shogun.

SIGNIFICANCE

The Shimabara Revolt effectively put an end to the open practice of the Christian faith in northern Kyūshū, the area of Japan that had once been a bastion of Catholic belief. Christianity continued to endure in the region, but it was forced underground. Because of their isolation, these "Hidden Christians" began to practice a version of the faith far different from that originally carried to Japan by missionaries in the sixteenth century. When Japan once again began to engage in open relations with Western nations in the 1850's, many Japanese Christians came out of hiding only to experience another period of persecution. The advent of the new Meiji government in the late 1860's represented a new consolidation of power like the one that took place in the early period of Tokugawa rule. As in the seventeenth century, Christians were seen as a dangerous element and a threat to the consolidation of central power. It was only in the 1870's, partially as a result of the complaints of the Christian nations of the West, that Japanese believers were allowed to practice their faith freely.

Apart from the Christian situation, the Shimabara Revolt had an impact on Japanese foreign relations. Partially as a result of the rebellion, the shogun continued to enact regulations restricting foreign travel and trade, provisions that eventually came to constitute a policy of national seclusion. The Dutch participation on the side of the authorities, however, helped to cement a trading agreement between Japan and the Netherlands that lasted through the period of seclusion. Having shown their willingness to put aside matters of religion and even actively to attack Japanese Christians, Dutch traders were allowed to maintain special privileges, and until the 1850's, the Dutch were the only Westerners allowed to trade with Japan, albeit under strict regulation. In effect, the massacre of Japanese Christians at Shimabara helped to keep open the only window on Western affairs, language, and scientific advances enjoyed by the Japanese elite during the Edo period.

—*Matthew Penney*

FURTHER READING

Totman, Conrad. *Early Modern Japan*. Berkeley: University of California Press, 1993. The most comprehensive single-volume treatment of the Edo period of Japanese history in English. Discusses the factors that led up to the Shimabara Revolt and its impact.

Turnbull, Stephen. *The Samurai Sourcebook*. London: Arms and Armour Press, 1998. Offers encyclopedic coverage of the important figures in the history of the samurai, as well as aspects of their military culture, including coverage of the Shimabara Revolt.

_____. *Samurai Warfare*. London: Arms and Armour Press, 1996. The best English-language history of the fighting techniques of the samurai.

SEE ALSO: 1602-1613: Japan Admits Western Traders; 1603: Tokugawa Shogunate Begins; 1614-1615: Siege of Ōsaka Castle; Jan. 27, 1614: Japanese Ban Chris-

tian Missionaries; 1615: Promulgation of the *Buke shohatto* and *Kinchū narabini kuge shohatto*; 1624-1640's: Japan's Seclusion Policy; 1651-1652: Edo Rebellions; 1651-1680: Ietsuna Shogunate; 1680-1709: Reign of Tsunayoshi as Shogun.

RELATED ARTICLES in *Great Lives from History: The Seventeenth Century, 1601-1700:* Tokugawa Ieyasu; Tokugawa Tsunayoshi; Yui Shōsetsu.

1638
FIRST PRINTING PRESS IN NORTH AMERICA

Stephen Day, assisted by his son Matthew, established North America's first printing press in Cambridge, Massachusetts, and used it to publish various works, including the first book in the British colonies.

LOCALE: Cambridge, Massachusetts Bay Colony (now in Massachusetts)

CATEGORIES: Communications; literature; science and technology

KEY FIGURES

Jose Glover (d. 1638), English clergyman responsible for bringing the first printing press to North America

Stephen Day (c. 1594-1668), traditionally considered the first printer in North America

Matthew Day (c. 1620-1649), Stephen Day's son and possibly North America's first printer

Samuel Green (1615-1702), Harvard College printer, 1642-1692

John Eliot (1604-1690), colonial American clergyman known as the Apostle to the Indians

Henry Dunster (1609-1659), first president of Harvard College

SUMMARY OF EVENT

The New World's first printing presses were established in the Spanish colonies of Central and South America during the sixteenth century. The first printing press in North America belonged to British settlers in New England during the mid-seventeenth century. A Puritan clergyman, Jose Glover (also called Joss, Josse, or Joseph), purchased a printing press in England for £20, along with paper and type, and brought all this aboard the *John of London*, a ship bound for Boston, in the summer of 1638. Glover had been rector of a church in Sutton,

County Surrey, but he found government restrictions on his religion burdensome, and he saw the press as a way of spreading his religious views in the New World.

Before embarking, Glover signed a contract with Stephen Day, a locksmith, who agreed to work for Glover in America for two years. Both men traveled with their families: Glover brought his wife and five children, and Day brought his wife and two sons. Unfortunately, Reverend Glover died of a fever during the transatlantic voyage, and his wife became the owner of the printing equipment. The widow chose to settle in Cambridge, Massachusetts, and set up the printing press near the newly founded Harvard College. She left the work of running the business to Stephen Day, and Day relied on the skills of his eighteen-year-old son, Matthew Day, who had been apprenticed to a printer in England.

Their first publication, which was the first printed material created in the British colonies, was "The Oath of a Free-Man" (c. 1638-1639), a half-sheet containing the words of the oath required by the colony of those who wished to become legal citizens. (Only men twenty years of age and older who had owned their homes for six months or longer were eligible to take the oath.) Not one of these broadsheets has survived, and scholars learned of them only through later accounts. For the same reason, it is uncertain whether the freeman's oath was printed late in 1638 or early in 1639.

The second publication of the Cambridge press (sometimes called, despite its modest length, the first English book printed in America) was *An Almanack for 1639: Calculated for New England by Mr. William Pierce, Mariner* (1639). This and the other almanacs the Days published from 1640 to 1645 were very successful, because they provided New Englanders with helpful information on tides, weather, and important astronomical data.

1630's

361

Many scholars consider the third publication of the Days to be English America's first true book because of its substantial length (296 pages), the number of copies printed (seventeen hundred, of which eleven have survived), and its frequent reprints. *The Whole Booke of Psalmes Faithfully Translated into English Metre* (1640; better known as the *Bay Psalm Book*) was the work of some of the chief clergymen of the Massachusetts Bay Colony, including Richard Mather and Thomas Weld. Though the book was poorly printed—with many typographical errors, eccentric spellings, and irregular spacings—it filled a need, since many Puritan divines used psalms for communal singing in their churches. The clergy of the colony praised the translators' faithfulness to the Hebrew originals.

In 1641, the Days were responsible for printing the Body of Liberties, a code of laws that for many years served as the foundation of legislation in Massachusetts Bay Colony. The code has the dubious distinction of containing the first legal recognition of the institution of slavery in the colony. In this same year, Glover's widow married Henry Dunster, who was then president of Harvard College, and Dunster thereby gained control of the press. Harvard's first commencement was held in 1642, and the press published the names of the first class; it also published material for several succeeding commencements. After his wife's death in 1643, Dunster retained the Days to run the printing business.

Later publications included a spelling book, catechisms, and collections of sermons. The last publication under Stephen Day's directorship was a 1646 almanac compiled by Samuel Danforth. Friction between Day and Dunster caused the former to leave the Cambridge press, but his son Matthew continued to manage the press until his tragically early death in 1649. After Matthew Day's death, Dunster asked Samuel Green, a former militia captain, to run the business, despite his lack of printing experience. For the next forty-three years, Green oversaw the

publication of many books of religious, academic, and legal importance. For example, *The Platform of Church-Discipline* (1649), published under Green's direction, has been called the cornerstone of American Congregationalism.

Green's most productive period was from 1660 to 1674, and his most significant publication during this time was John Eliot's Bible for Native Americans. For nearly thirty years, Eliot had been working on the conversion of Native Americans, and he had mastered the Algonquian language. To aid in his missionary activities, he translated the Bible into Algonquian, and he applied to the London Society for the Propagation of the Gospel among the Indians of New England for financial help, since projected sales would not cover printing expenses. He also needed specialized type, such as a ligatured double "o." Samuel Green also

The first printing press in North America was purchased and transported by Jose Glover, who died during the Atlantic crossing. Once installed in Cambridge, Massachusetts, the press was operated by Glover's employee, Stephen Day. (The Granger Collection)

needed help in completing this monumental printing task, and he hired Marmaduke Johnson, a skilled journeyman printer. Native American converts, provided by Eliot, also assisted in the printing of fifteen hundred copies of this twelve-hundred-page book, commonly called the Indian Bible but also known as the Eliot Bible. Contemporaries saw the Eliot Bible as the press's most notable production, but some revisionist scholars have interpreted this Bible as "an instrument of domination" over Native Americans already demoralized by conquest and disease.

SIGNIFICANCE

North America's first printing press became the locus for training several colonial printers who would go on to spread printing technology through the colonies. Through books, pamphlets, and broadsides, the Cambridge printers contributed to the spread of information, both secular and religious, to an increasingly literate populace. After his work in Cambridge, Marmaduke Johnson received permission from colonial government officials to set up a printing business in Boston, which was purchased by John Foster, a Harvard graduate who became Boston's first printer.

Boston was also the site of America's first newspaper. Printing spread to the Middle Colonies when William Bradford, a London Quaker, set up the first press in Philadelphia in 1685. He later established a printing business in New York City. The seventeenth century growth of the printing industry in New England and the Middle Colonies prepared the way for the spectacular and influential expansion of publishing in the eighteenth century. A good example of publishing's success during this time was the work of Benjamin Franklin. His publication of *Poor Richard's Almanack* in editions of more than ten thousand copies from 1732 to 1757 made him financially independent enough to pursue his political interests. By 1775, fifty printers were active in the American colonies, and some scholars have compared the role that printing played in the American War of Independence to the role that it had earlier played in the Protestant Reformation in Europe.

—*Robert J. Paradowski*

FURTHER READING

Armory, Hugh, and David D. Hall, eds. *The Colonial Book in the Atlantic World.* Vol. 1 in *A History of the Book in America.* New York: Cambridge University Press, 2000. This work, whose theme is the connection between the book trade in the New and Old Worlds, traces the emergence of the book industry in early America.

Bigmore, E. C., and C. W. H. Wyman. *A Bibliography of Printing.* Reprint. New Castle, Del.: Oak Knoll Press, 2001. A modern reprint of a classic work originally published in three volumes from 1880 to 1886. This new edition, illustrated with woodcuts, contains a comprehensive index.

Clement, Richard W. *The Book in America with Images from the Library of Congress.* Golden, Colo.: Fulcrum, 1996. Traces the history of the book in both colonial America and the United States, making excellent use of rare images from the Library of Congress. Chapter 1 deals with colonial book production from 1638 to 1783. Section on further reading and an index.

Steinberg, S. H. *Five Hundred Years of Printing.* Reprint. New Castle, Del.: Oak Knoll Press, 1996. This standard work, long available as a Pelican Book (1956), has been revised and copiously illustrated. Select bibliography and index.

Winship, George Parker. *The Cambridge Press, 1638-1692: A Reexamination of the Evidence Concerning "The Bay Psalm Book" and the Eliot Indian Bible.* Philadelphia: University of Pennsylvania Press, 1945. This narrative history of how printing arrived, spread, and flourished in seventeenth century Massachusetts also includes an analysis of the development, variety, and quality of early American printing. Selective bibliography and index.

SEE ALSO: Dec. 26, 1620: Pilgrims Arrive in North America; May, 1630-1643: Great Puritan Migration; Nov., 1641: Massachusetts Recognizes Slavery; Sept. 8, 1643: Confederation of the United Colonies of New England; May 30-31, 1650: First College in North America.

RELATED ARTICLE in *Great Lives from History: The Seventeenth Century, 1601-1700:* John Eliot.

1630's

1638
WANING OF THE *DEVSHIRME* SYSTEM

The devshirme, *a periodic levy of Christian boys from the subject population of the Balkans, supplied most of the Ottoman Empire's soldiers. The system, unique to the Ottomans and in stark contrast to the hereditary aristocracies of contemporary Europe, provided the empire's ruling elite, military commanders, and high officers of state. Devshirme was abandoned gradually during the seventeenth century because of internal abuses.*

LOCALE: The Balkans and the Ottoman Empire
CATEGORIES: Organizations and institutions; wars, uprisings, and civil unrest; government and politics; social issues and reform

KEY FIGURES
Osman II (1603-1622), Ottoman sultan, r. 1618-1622
Murad IV (1612-1640), Ottoman sultan, r. 1623-1640
Evliya Çelebi (1611-c. 1684), Ottoman traveler
Sir Paul Rycaut (1628-1700), English historian

SUMMARY OF EVENT
Unique to medieval Islamic society was the slave-soldier (*mamlūk* in Arabic, *ghulam* in Persian), a non-Muslim boy acquired by capture in war or through the slave trade. Islamic law forbade the enslavement of Muslims, so others were acquired, especially Christian boys from the Balkans. A boy would be converted to Islam, undergo a *cursus honorum* in military training, assimilate into Islamic society, and adopt its cultural norms.

The eleventh century Seljuk grand vizier Niẓñām al-Mulk described in his manual of government (*Siyasatnama*) the way in which a slave-boy was trained to be both a soldier and a courtier of his master until seniority and experience qualified him for high command or a provincial governorship. Several Islamic dynasties consisted of men who had made their mark as military slaves: In Egypt, for example, between 1250 and 1517, the ruling sultans advanced through the slave army, as did the first sultans of Delhi (1206-1290).

These facts illustrate the background to the institution known as the *devshirme* (collection), which provided troops and bureaucrats for the Ottoman Empire through the fifteenth and seventeenth centuries. The *devshirme* levied Christian male children, mainly from the Ottoman Balkan provinces. Ottoman tradition, anachronistically, tells that the practice originated in the time of Ottoman ruler Orhan Gazi (r. 1326-c. 1360), but the oldest ref-

erence dates from 1395, with the reign of Bayezid I (r. 1389-1402), and the next dates from 1430, with the reign of Murad II (r. 1421-1451). It seems likely that, coinciding with his reorganization of the Janissaries (elite troops), Murad conceived the *devshirme* as the foundation for Janissary recruitment.

There were several theoretical justifications for the practice, one being that because nonbelievers had been conquered by force, the *devshirme* was permitted in Islamic law. A counterargument was that the practice went against Islamic law because it infringed upon the specific rights of *dhimmis* (nonbelievers of revealed religions). This counterposition, however, was in turn countered by the argument that *dhimmi* status did not apply to those Christians whose faith came after Qurʾānic revelation, which includes most of the rural population of the Balkans. Theory and practice with regard to the *devshirme*, however, were often at odds.

A *devshirme* was supported by many because it met a specific need for soldiers. A Janissary officer, accompanied by a secretary, went into the district where the levy was to be made, carrying official authorization, two registers, a supply of uniforms, and soldiers to enforce his orders. In the district where the *devshirme* was proclaimed, male children, along with their fathers and the village clergy, who brought with them the boys' baptismal records, were required to assemble at a designated location. European sources held that the children's ages ranged between eight and twenty, but Ottoman records imply that those selected were teenagers.

Not all children, however, were eligible. Those with poor health and disabilities were exempted because the Ottomans wanted strong and sturdy peasants (*reaya*) only. Also excluded were urban craftspeople's sons and those who already were married (leading some communities to practice early marriage), but the methods used for the *devshirme* varied from region to region and from time to time. Once the boys were selected, their names, ages, physical features, and parentage were entered in the two registers, one of which was retained by the recruiting officer and the other by the *suruju* (drover), who transported the boys to Constantinople.

Usually, *devshirme* boys were ethnic Greeks, Macedonians, Albanians, Bulgarians, Serbs, Bosnians, or Croats. Some areas were exempt from the *devshirme* because they had submitted voluntarily to Ottoman rule. Others had exempt status presumably because their populations consisted of city dwellers. Also, the *devshirme* was not levied in Walachia or Moldavia. A peculiar case involved the Muslims of Bosnia, who converted en masse in 1463 but requested that their sons should still qualify for the *devshirme*.

After the *devshirme* boys had been selected and registered, they were escorted to Constantinople and then inspected again for their physical and mental qualities. (Medieval Islamic tradition held that a person's moral qualities and even his destiny might be read in his physiognomy.) Those of superior intelligence were transferred to the palace service, where, after being converted to Islam, they learned Turkish and acquired the ʿadet-i othmaniyye (the cultural values of Ottoman society) as well as secretarial and other bureaucratic skills. The remainder were sent to landholders' estates in Anatolia, where they grew robust working the land, learned Turkish, and acquired some exposure to indigenous culture.

Thereafter, they would be recalled, as needed, to Constantinople and enrolled in the Janissary corps, the Kapikulu cavalry (made up of six regiments of the *sipahi* and forming the household cavalry), or the Bostancis (guards of the palace establishments), with expectations of unlimited future advancement. It was a unique aspect of Ottoman government (in contrast to the hereditary aristocracies of contemporary Europe) that its ruling elite, military commanders, and high officers of state, recruited by the *devshirme* and enrolled as Kapikulus of the Sublime Porte (Ottoman government), were not Turks at all but came from the subject population. The Köprülü family of grand viziers, for example, were Albanian by descent.

To Europeans, the *devshirme* was evidence of the inherent barbarity of the Turks. There is, of course, no disputing the anguish involved in the separation of parents and children, made worse by the certainty that baptized Christians automatically became Muslims, but there must have been times when large peasant families living between bare subsistence and starvation were relieved to have one less mouth to feed, and there was always the hope that a "lost" boy would end up a *serder* or *serasker* (military commander), an agha of the Janissaries, or a grand vizier. To what extent *devshirme* boys retained ties with their families is uncertain, but there is some anecdotal evidence.

İbrahim Paşa, the Greek-born grand vizier under Sultan Süleyman the Magnificent (r. 1520-1566), when disgraced, was accused of advancing family interests. Mehmed Sokollu, Serbian-born grand vizier (1564-1579), favored fellow Serbs and reestablished the metro-

politanate of Peć with his Christian brother as archbishop. These are high-level examples, but there must have been many more.

When the Ottoman Empire was a world power, the *devshirme* was the main instrument for recruiting its seemingly invincible armies, especially the dreaded Janissaries, who were the terror of Christendom. Change set in, though, during the late sixteenth century. In the beginning of Süleyman the Magnificent's reign (1520-1566), the Janissary corps had numbered about 7,900; by 1609, it had risen to more than 39,000. By this time, the corps included recruits from all walks of life and were not made up exclusively of troops trained through the *devshirme* system. A reformer of the 1630's, Mustafa Kochi Bey, denounced the new corps as consisting of "city boys of unknown religion, Turks, gypsies, Tats, Kurds, outsiders, Lazes, Turkomans, muleteers and camel-drivers, porters and confectioners, highwaymen and pickpockets." His solution was to return to the classical institutions of the earlier empire, including the *devshirme*.

However, a return to the past was hardly possible, not least because the *devshirme* no longer could provide the numbers needed. Meanwhile, the Janissaries had declined in fighting capacity and discipline and became a source of urban mayhem and rabble-rousing in the capital, threatening the foundations of the state. In 1621, Osman II and his grand vizier Dilawar Paşa planned the total abolition of the *devshirme* as the first step on the road to radical reform; the second step was to open the Janissary corps to free-born Turks recruited in Anatolia and Syria. The idea cost them their lives.

Thereafter, the *devshirme* was levied less and less often. It seems that no sultanic decree ordained its abolition, although Osman's half brother, Murad IV, was said to have ordered that abolition in 1638. It seems that the protests that met Osman's proposed abolition died as the Janissary corps became a corporation that was increasingly hereditary (the old prohibition on Janissaries marrying had long been ignored). The Ottoman writer Evliya Çelebi supposed that the *devshirme* still occurred every seven years, but Sir Paul Rycaut, the first historian of the Ottoman Empire to write in English, who was in Constantinople in 1660, thought that the practice had been abandoned for the most part. This cannot be the case because the Ottoman-Polish Treaty of Buczacz (1672) includes the stipulation that the inhabitants of Podolia, newly annexed to the Ottoman Empire, were to be exempt from the *devshirme*. A *devshirme* had certainly occurred before Buczacz treaty, in 1666, and another after, in 1674, although the latter was for palace-service only. When, in 1703, Ahmed III (r. 1703-1730) decided to transfer one thousand unruly Bostancis into the Janissary corps, he ordered a *devshirme* to recruit their replacements. Perhaps connected with Ahmed's order was a *devshirme* ordered for Greece in 1705, the last known instance.

SIGNIFICANCE

Turkish slave-soldiers and the Janissary corps itself predated the *devshirme* and survived long after its demise. Like other elite units (for example, the Roman praetorian guards or the Muscovite *streltsi*), the Janissaries deteriorated over time, and the *devshirme* became an anachronism, lingering on to the end of the seventeenth century. The Janissaries survived until 1826, when they finally were disbanded, many of them massacred by order of Mahmud II (1808-1839).

—Gavin R. G. Hambly

FURTHER READING

Goodwin, Godfrey. *The Janissaries.* London: Saqi Books, 1994. A highly recommended history of the elite Janissary corps.

Imber, Colin. *The Ottoman Empire, 1300-1650.* New York: Palgrave, 2002. An excellent history of Ottoman institutions from the beginning of the fourteenth to the mid-seventeenth century.

Miller, Barnette. *The Palace School of Muhammad the Conqueror.* Cambridge, Mass.: Harvard University Press, 1941. Reprint. New York, 1973. A useful account of the training of the Kapikulus, the palace guard.

Murphey, Rhoads. *Ottoman Warfare, 1500-1700.* New Brunswick, N.J.: Rutgers University Press, 1999. Perhaps the best account of the Ottoman war machine.

Suger, Peter F. *Southeastern Europe Under Ottoman Rule, 1354-1804.* Seattle: University of Washington Press, 1977. The author provides sensible observations about the significance of the *devshirme*.

SEE ALSO: 17th cent.: Rise of the Gunpowder Empires; 1602-1639: Ottoman-Ṣafavid Wars; 1603-1617: Reign of Sultan Ahmed I; Sept., 1605: Egyptians Rebel Against the Ottomans; Nov. 11, 1606: Treaty of Zsitvatorok; May 19, 1622: Janissary Revolt and Osman II's Assassination; 1623-1640: Murad IV Rules the Ottoman Empire; Sept. 2, 1633: Great Fire of Constantinople and Murad's Reforms; Aug. 22, 1645-Sept., 1669: Turks Conquer Crete; Summer, 1672-Fall, 1676: Ottoman-Polish Wars; Beginning 1687: Decline of the Ottoman Empire; 1697-1702: Köprülü Reforms of Hüseyin Paşa.

RELATED ARTICLES in *Great Lives from History: The Seventeenth Century, 1601-1700:* Merzifonlu Kara Mustafa Paşa; Murad IV; Mustafa I.

1638-1639
URGA BECOMES THE SEAT OF THE LIVING BUDDHA

Zanabazar, the son of a Mongol nobleman and reportedly a descendant of Genghis Khan, was proclaimed the leader of Mongolian Buddhism in 1639, residing in Urga, now known as Ulan Bator. Urga grew out of the encampment around Zanabazar's monastery.

LOCALE: Urga and Shireet Tsagaan Nuur in Outer Mongolia

CATEGORIES: Religion and theology; government and politics

KEY FIGURES

Sonam Gyatso (1543-1588), Tibetan lama, the first to be known as the Dalai Lama, 1578-1588

Gombodorj (1594-1655), a khan of the Khalka Mongols and father of Zanabazar

Zanabazar (1635-1723), the first *bogd gegen*, or supreme leader, of Buddhism in Mongolia, 1639-1723

SUMMARY OF EVENT

Under the leadership of Genghis Khan (1155/1162-1227), the Mongols became one of the most powerful peoples in the world. However, after the death of the last Mongol emperor in 1259, the Mongols split into a variety of different groups. During the fifteenth century, Mongolia was ravaged by civil war between the eastern clans of the Khalka and the western clans of the Oirad. During the sixteenth century, the Khalka leader Altan Khan managed to unite the Khalkas and defeat the Oirad.

Buddhism had entered Mongolia as early as the third century B.C.E., when silk traders from India brought with them the teachings of the Buddha. By the time of Altan

Khan, many Mongolians already had adopted Buddhism. During the 1570's, Altan Khan met with a Tibetan Buddhist lama, or teacher, named Sonam Gyatso. The Mongolian leader converted to Tibetan Buddhism in 1578 and made Buddhism the religion of the Mongolians. Altan Khan gave Sonam Gyatso the title Dalai Lama, frequently translated as "ocean of wisdom." The title also was bestowed on Sonam Gyatso's two predecessors, making Sonam Gyatso the Third Dalai Lama. The Dalai Lama, in turn, named Altan Khan the "king of the turning wheel and wisdom." With Buddhism, then, Mongolia began to recover some measure of political and religious unity.

In 1580, the Dalai Lama met with another important Mongolian leader, Avtai Khan of the Tusheet khanate, who also converted to Tibetan Buddhism. Avatai Khan was succeeded as ruler of the Tusheet khanate first by his son and then by his grandson, Gombodorj. The birth of Gombodorj's own son, in 1635, become the subject of legends and tales. This son was given the name of Zanabazar, which is frequently translated as "thunderbolt of wisdom."

Zanabazar is said to have begun speaking and reciting prayers at the age of three. His father enrolled him in a monastery as a lama in 1638. According to tradition, both the Buddhist hierarchy and the secular leaders of Mongolia heard about the extraordinary gifts of the child, and they became convinced that he was destined to play a historic part in Mongolian Buddhism. According to some modern historical interpretations, the nobility used the young lama as a rallying point for unifying the Mongolian nobility. Zanabazar's rise to religious supremacy is believed to be the result of the political and military power of his father, Gombodorj, and as a consequence of Gombodorj's desire to establish his own control over Mongolia.

A convocation was held in the territory of Gombodorj at Shireet Tsagaan Nuur, or White Throne Lake, in 1639 to enthrone Zanabazar as the head of Mongolian Buddhism. The gathering took place at the small lake, surrounded on three sides by hills covered with sand dunes, with a great rock massif on one side. There were probably several thousand people at the convocation, with khans from all the khanates of Mongolia. The four-year-old Zanabazar was first given the title of *gegen*, meaning "supreme holiness" or "enlightened one." *Bogd gegen*, the full title he later received, is usually translated as "holy enlightened one." It became the title held by Zanabazar and by all of his successors as head of Mongolian Buddhism.

Near the lake, there was a traditional Mongolian tent, known as a *ger*. The name of the spot, Urga, is a Russian pronunciation of *ger*. A Buddhist lama carried little Zanabazar up to the *ger* and placed him on a throne inside, symbolizing that the child was now the head of Buddhism in Mongolia. The *ger* was sanctified as a temple and became the new *bogd gegen*'s own monastery. Those assembled swore allegiance to the child leader and gave him offerings, including a dozen *ger* and property associated with them. They ended the ceremonies with celebratory games.

The year after Zanabazar was named *bogd gegen*, another, purely secular assembly gathered. The Mongolian ruler Baatar Khongtaiji called together Mongolian groups from all around Asia. He argued that they should form a union against their foreign enemies, including the Russians, Manchus, and Chinese.

The *bogd gegen*, then five years old, was probably not present at the gathering called by Baatar Khongtaiji. However, Mongol-Tibetan Buddhism was an important element of unity in the Mongolian coalition. Baatar Khongtaiji encouraged his fellow Mongol leader Gushri Khan. In 1642, Gushri Khan overthrew the king of Tibet and made the fifth Dalai Lama the ruler of that land in secular as well as religious matters.

If Buddhism offered a means of uniting the Mongols, it also divided them. While some Mongol factions saw themselves as the representatives of Buddhism under the Tibetan Dalai Lama, the Khalkas clung to their own supreme leader, the *bogd gegen*. The connections between the Dalai Lama and the *bogd gegen* continued, but Buddhism did not provide a way to revive the Mongol Empire. After Zanabazar studied the Buddhist teachings for years under the most learned teachers in Mongolia, he traveled to Tibet for further studies in 1649, at about the age of fourteen. There, he met the fifth Dalai Lama, whom Gushri Khan made leader. In 1650, Zanabazar received the Tibetan title of *javzandamba hutagt*, which became the title for all the living Buddhas of Urga in the years that followed until the death of the eighth *javzandamba* in 1924. Zanabazar made a second trip to Tibet in 1655, strengthening the religious connections between the Mongols and the Tibetans.

The proclamation of Zanabazar as religious and national leader of Mongolia did not prevent the Mongols from falling under foreign political domination. Mongolia had been under pressure from the Russians, the Chinese, and the Manchus. Inner Mongolia fell under Manchu administration a few years before the convocation at Shireet Tsagaan Nuur. By the late seventeenth and

1630's

early eighteenth century, the Manchus, who became rulers of China, established an uneasy domination of Outer Mongolia. Some modern Mongolian historians have criticized the first *bogd gegen* for reportedly collaborating with the Manchus and allowing Manchu political influence over his country.

As *bogd gegen*, Zanabazar was the most important Buddhist figure in Mongolia. He also became a sculptor of religious figures. He is credited with having developed the *soyombo*, a mystical image including a yin and yang symbol with horizontal bars and arrows above and below and vertical bars on each side. The *soyombo* is often regarded as the symbol of Mongolian nationhood, and using the *soyombo* as a foundation, Zanabazar is said to have created a writing system for the Mongolian language. The temple and palace that grew around his *ger* developed into the city that was later known as Ulan Bator, the modern capital of Mongolia.

SIGNIFICANCE
The convocation at Shireet Tsagaan Nuur in 1639 created one of the key figures in Mongolian history, the Living Buddha of Urga. As first Living Buddha of Urga, Zanabazar played an important part in spreading Tibetan Buddhism in Mongolia. As a sculptor and painter of religious images, the first *bogd gegen* became one of Mongolia's most influential artists. Contemporary museums in Ulan Bator still display his works.

Because the Mongolian capital of Ulan Bator grew around the monastery and palace of the Living Buddha,

the convocation of 1639 also marked a central event in the political geography of Mongolia. Although Mongolia did fall under foreign domination, Ulan Bator continued to be the nation's main center as well as its political heart. The successors of Zanabazar continued as the official religious and political heads of Mongolia until the early-twentieth century.

—*Carl L. Bankston III*

FURTHER READING
Heissig, Walther. *The Religions of Mongolia*. Translated by Geoffrey Samuel. Berkeley: University of California Press, 1980. A good overview of Mongolian religions. Includes a bibliography, an index, and a map of the region.

Kaplonski, Christopher. *Truth, History, and Politics in Mongolia: The Memory of Heroes*. New York: RoutledgeCurzon, 2004. Kaplonski explores modern interpretations of important figures in Mongolian history. Chapter 7 focuses on interpretations of the role of Zanabazar.

Spuler, Bertold. *History of the Mongols*. Translated by Helga Drummond and Stuart Drummond. New York: Dorset Press, 1988. One of the best general histories of the Mongol people.

SEE ALSO: 1616-1643: Rise of the Manchus.

RELATED ARTICLE in *Great Lives from History: The Seventeenth Century, 1601-1700:* Abahai.

1638-1669
SPREAD OF JANSENISM

Spurred by rigorous Catholic Reformation piety and set against the contemporary religious leniency and relativism of the Jesuits, the Jansenists, who were adherents of Augustinian theology and Saint-Cyran's demanding piety, gained many followers in France. Despite intense official opposition, Jansenism grew and prospered.

LOCALE: France
CATEGORIES: Religion and theology; wars, uprisings, and civil unrest

KEY FIGURES
Cornelius Otto Jansen (1585-1638), Dutch theologian, church reformer, and bishop of Ypres

Jean Duvergier de Hauranne (1581-1643), French abbot and religious leader, also known as Saint-Cyran

Antoine Arnauld (1612-1694), French Jansenist theologian

Angélique Arnauld (1591-1661), abbess of Port-Royal

Blaise Pascal (1623-1662), French philosopher and scientist

SUMMARY OF EVENT
The Catholic Reformation of the mid-sixteenth century spawned two religious movements that had a major impact on French religious life in the seventeenth century: the Society of Jesus (the Jesuits) and an intensification of personal spirituality. The broader Reform movements also had given new life to Saint Augustine,

the fourth-fifth century theologian and doctor of the Church.

Saint Augustine had championed religious predestination against contemporary Pelagians, who had emphasized a person's own role in salvation, while downplaying that of God's grace. Augustine's doctrine of predestination—that God has decided each person's ultimate fate, and one can do nothing about it—had traditionally been set aside by the Catholic church but was resurrected by Martin Luther and John Calvin and was at the heart of French Huguenot (Protestant) theology.

The Council of Trent, and consequently, the Jesuits, stressed the role of human free will in salvation and rejected Protestant predestination. Many Catholics, including clergy and theologians, championed Augustine's ideas, however, and argued against the Church's newly clarified position and its Jesuit defenders. Among them was Antoine Arnauld, an attorney who had a hand in the French *parlements*' expulsion of the Jesuits in the 1590's. However, the Jesuits' power was strong and growing stronger, as they gained influential positions as confessors and advisers of Europe's Catholic courts. At a university like that of Louvain in the Spanish Netherlands, the theology faculty and students tended to split into pro- and anti-Jesuit factions.

Cornelius Otto Jansen, who studied theology at Louvain, came to reject Jesuit scholasticism and was determined to present the "real" Augustine to the world. As a faculty member at Louvain and later bishop of Ypres, he spent his last seventeen years writing *Augustinus*, an immense and powerful study of the Church fathers' doctrines of grace and predestination as Jansen understood them. Published posthumously at Louvain in 1640 and Paris in 1641, the work was quickly condemned as heretical by Church authorities and Jesuit theologians. Nonetheless, it represented the beliefs of a considerable faction among French Catholics, including the pastor of Saint-Cyran, Jean Duvergier de Hauranne.

The Jesuit-trained, Basque/French Duvergier had been a colleague of Jansen at the Sorbonne, and the two studied Augustine together for nearly five years at Duvergier's family home near Bayonne. Adopting the title Saint-Cyran, the charismatic and sophisticated Duvergier joined the religious and political life of Paris, flirting with the fringes of a circle of Catholic reformers that included Vincent de Paul and Francis de Sales. Eventually, he became the spiritual adviser to a number of influential men and women as well as to the female convent of Port Royal near Paris, a Cistercian monastery and later the center of the short-lived Institute of the Holy Sacrament (1633-1638).

The founder of Jansenism, Cornelius Otto Jansen. (Library of Congress)

In 1621, he had been introduced to the convent's abbess, Mother Angélique Arnauld, by her brother, both members of the large and influential Arnauld family. Mother Angélique had joined the convent as a child and became abbess as a flighty teenager, but she converted to reform in 1608. Under the direction of Saint-Cyran she adopted an even stricter "Augustinian" moral and liturgical rigor that clearly and purposefully ran counter to the relative laxity of the secular and even monastic society at large. The convent was soon filled to bursting, and laypersons who wanted to live the same sort of life gathered on convent property outside Paris, living like hermits. The ascetic life of Port Royal was becoming quite popular.

In 1638, the year of Jansen's death, the institute was dissolved and Saint-Cyran was arrested on May 14 by order of Cardinal de Richelieu, a onetime friend. With the "martyrdom" of Saint-Cyran, the direction of the movement, which centered on Port Royal and Saint-Cyran's version of Augustinianism, fell to the brothers Antoine Arnauld the younger, a theology student at the Sorbonne, and Robert Arnauld d'Andilly, a courtier and staunch devotee. Shortly after Richelieu's death in November,

1642, the authorities released Saint-Cyran, who would die within the year.

Jansen's *Augustinus* would soon draw both enthusiastic support and withering criticism from individuals such as Richelieu. Authorities quickly linked the controversial work to the "Augustinian" movement of Saint-Cyran, and the official Church had clergy preach against both in the Advent series of sermons of 1642 and the Lenten series in 1643. Ironically, this served to generate great interest in both book and movement, which together constituted "Jansenism," a term of opprobrium coined by Jesuit opponents. Antoine Arnauld finished his doctorate in theology at the Sorbonne and then became Jansenism's champion.

The papal response to Jansen's book took the form of the bull *In eminenti*, which was released in June, 1643, and published in Paris in December, thanks to pro-Jansenists in the *parlement* of Paris. Pope Urban VIII pointed out in the bull the errors in Jansen's work that his predecessors had condemned in previous papal statements. Jansenist leaders were dismayed but not surprised. Though Jansenists continued to consider themselves Catholics, they blamed Jesuit influence for the pope's misguided stance.

In 1644, Arnauld published *De la frequente communion* (on frequent Communion), in which he argued from Church tradition that taking Communion often led to contempt for the sacrament. This had an immediate impact in Parisian churches, as Jansenism took hold. Sixteen French bishops approved of Arnauld's work, and one even joined Port Royal. When these and other bishops met at Cardinal Jules Mazarin's insistence, the group narrowly approved *De la frequente communion*, but the cardinal attacked the decision and directed Arnauld to Rome to defend his work. At this point, the *parlement* and University of Paris joined to protest any appeal to the foreign power of the Papacy in a matter concerning the French church. For more than a century the French government and clergy had insisted on its so-called Gallican liberties, the right to handle its own internal religious affairs. Arnauld remained in France, and the movement—by this time recognized as a sect—continued to prosper.

In 1651 and 1652, Pope Innocent X received requests from the Spanish and French courts to have five specific propositions derived from the *Augustinus* condemned as heretical. Innocent condemned the following in his bull *Cum occasione* (May 31, 1653):

1. Even the just lack the grace to obey all of God's commandments.

2. Fallen humanity cannot resist interior grace.
3. Freedom from constraint, not freedom from necessity, are necessities.
4. Prevenient grace can be neither resisted nor obeyed.
5. Christ did not die to save all people.

Anti-Jansenist forces moved against Port Royal and had Arnauld fired from the Sorbonne. Jansenists fought back by refusing to recognize the condemnation, and, in 1656, the philosopher and mathematician Blaise Pascal became an active controversialist, defending Jansenism and attacking the Jesuits in a series of anonymous letters now known as *Lettres provinciales* (1656-1657; *The Provincial Letters*, 1657). Official pressure, including new condemnations by Pope Alexander VII, continued until four recalcitrant bishops finally bowed to the softer touch of pro-French pope Clement IX in mid-1667. On October 8, 1668, Clement's Peace of the Church was declared in Paris, and on October 23, King Louis XIV forbade any further public discussion of the controversy. Port Royal and the Jansenists were left in peace.

SIGNIFICANCE

For nearly two centuries Jansenism entrenched itself in French social, religious, and even political life, making extrication by Church and political authorities more difficult with each passing generation. Unlike Protestant reformers, Jansenist leaders remained firmly attached to Roman Catholic tradition and the Church's hierarchy, while insisting upon adherence to strict interpretations of Saint Augustine and other theological heavyweights. In doing so, they challenged from the inside the tradition and the teaching power of the Church, which they saw as having been corrupted by modern movements.

Since members of the movement could be neither convinced nor coerced during their first thirty years, the relaxation of official pressure in 1668 ensured that new disciples would continue to appear. More and more bishops and lower clergy adopted Jansenism, and its tenets influenced alike the laity in the pew as well as the confessional. Yet, neither pope nor king could long endure the practically schismatic nature of Jansenism, and its successes would generate several official condemnations in the eighteenth century. Even so, French Jansenists championed the French church's Gallican liberties against internationalist interference by Jesuits and the Papacy. Perhaps the Jansenists' greatest triumph was aiding the destruction of the Jesuit order itself in the 1770's.

—*Joseph P. Byrne*

FURTHER READING

Delumeau, Jean. *Catholicism Between Luther and Voltaire: A New View of the Counter-Reformation.* Philadelphia: Westminster Press, 1977. A translation of a French work from 1971 that explores Jansenism as an outgrowth of the Catholic Reformation.

Doyle, William. *Jansenism: Catholic Resistance to Authority from the Reformation to the French Revolution.* New York: St. Martin's Press, 1999. A brief, balanced view of Jansenism, including a discussion of Jansen's *Augustinus* and how the book's publication deepened the feud between French Jesuits and more-established Catholic orders. Include a broad biography.

Kolakowski, Leszek. *"God Owes Us Nothing": A Brief Remark on Pascal's Religion and on the Spirit of Jansenism.* Chicago: University of Chicago Press, 1995. A well-written theological discussion of the heart of Jansenist thought.

Lubac, Henri de. *Augustinianism and Modern Theology.* Translated by Lancelot Sheppard. New York: Crossroad, 2000. Discusses Jansen's principal work, *Augustinus*, and his role in creating Jansenism. Originally published in 1969, this reprint includes a new introduction.

Pascal, Blaise. *Selected "Pensees" and Provincial Letters/ Pensees et Provinciales choisies: A Dual-Language Book.* Edited and translated by Stanley Applebaum. Mineola, N.Y.: Dover, 2004. Selected translations of Jansenist Blaise Pascal's famous letters in defense of his friends and his religion. Includes selected translations from Pascal's classic work *Pensées* (1670).

SEE ALSO: 1618-1648: Thirty Years' War; 1625-Oct. 28, 1628: Revolt of the Huguenots; 1664: Molière Writes *Tartuffe*; July 13, 1664: Trappist Order Is Founded; June 30, 1680: Spanish Inquisition Holds a Grandiose *Auto-da-fé*.

RELATED ARTICLES in *Great Lives from History: The Seventeenth Century, 1601-1700:* Angélique Arnauld; François de Salignac de La Mothe-Fénelon; Innocent XI; Cornelius Otto Jansen; Jan Komenský; Duchesse de Longueville; Louis XIV; Jules Mazarin; Blaise Pascal; Jean Racine; Cardinal de Richelieu; Urban VIII; Saint Vincent de Paul.

1639-1640
BRITISH EAST INDIA COMPANY ESTABLISHES FORT SAINT GEORGE

British East India Company employee Francis Day established a factory, or trading station, for the company at what would become Fort Saint George, Madras. The fort became a major center for trade, with thousands of inhabitants and wide-reaching commercial interests.

LOCALE: Madras, southeast India
CATEGORIES: Trade and commerce; expansion and land acquisition

KEY FIGURE
Francis Day (fl. 1625-1652), British East India Company employee who founded the fort at Madras

SUMMARY OF EVENT

In the early seventeenth century, British East India Company merchants were drawn to the Bay of Bengal, where traditions of maritime trade with Southeast Asia reached back for centuries. For European shipping, however, this coast presented problems. From Cape Comorin to Orissa, the coastline stretched north in an almost unbroken line of sandy beaches upon which giant waves beat incessantly. There were virtually no safe anchorages, and with the wind blowing incessantly landward, no ship could safely anchor close to shore during the fury of the monsoon. The only significant port on the entire east coast was Masulipatam, at the mouth of the Godavari River in the domain of the sultan of Golconda.

As early as 1611, the British East India Company had established a factory, or trading station, in Masulipatam. The mouth of the Godavari River was gradually filling up with silt, however, preventing large ships from reaching the port. In 1625, a company employee, Francis Day, established an alternative settlement at Armagaon down the coast, but it proved a wretched place, all too easily overmatched by the Dutch at nearby Pulicat. So Day sought an alternative site, which he found at Madras. It had a narrow strip of land, about 6 miles long and 1 mile deep, backed on the inland side by the small Cooum River, which flowed circuitously to the coast, creating an island approximately 400 yards long and 100 yards wide, on which was to be constructed Fort Saint George.

1630's

The hinterland was fertile, and the local population consisted of highly skillful weavers. The land on which Madras stood belonged to the local *naik* (a petty raja, or ruler) of Chingleput, with whom Day struck a deal in 1639 or 1640. The annual rent was to be 1,200 pagodas (a south Indian coin of silver or gold), or 600 pounds. This arrangement was confirmed by the *naik*'s superior, Damarla Venkatadri, the raja of Chandragiri, but above him was the more formidable figure of the sultan of Golconda. The Golconda sultans (1512-1687) ruled the entire southeastern Deccan region and were steadily encroaching on the Carnatic, the territory between the Eastern Ghats and the coast. The English in Madras would have to learn to deal with these greedy rulers.

The fort was begun in 1644, for security was an immediate concern. Fort Saint George's warehouses were soon bulging with valuable merchandise, mainly muslin and calico piece-goods, of which the finest came from the Carnatic. The fort was essential to defend the settlement from raiders from the interior and from pirates. The eastern seas swarmed with buccaneers of every nation, including English swashbucklers such as John Avery and William Kidd.

Once completed, Fort Saint George enclosed a number of official buildings, private residences, and warehouses, and in the center was the governor's mansion. Beyond the fort's northern ramparts lay what was called the Black Town, with a resident population of weavers, craftspeople, and local merchants. During the 1660's, a Catholic church was built in the fort. Such toleration offended the Anglican clergy but reflected the company's desire to lure Portuguese from the nearby town of San Thomé. Furthering this policy was a colorful French Capuchin missionary, Father Ephraim, a linguist and mathematician who, on visiting the court of Golconda, found in the sultan a kindred spirit. Settling for missionary work in Madras, he proved a magnet for drawing Portuguese merchants from San Thomé to such an extent that the Portuguese authorities contrived his kidnapping and incarceration by the Inquisition at Goa: It proved impossible to secure his release until the sultan of Golconda threatened to destroy San Thomé. Ephraim was subsequently returned to Madras in 1652, and he left his mark upon the community for the next several decades. The Anglican garrison church of St. Mary's was constructed by Governor Streynsham Master between 1678 and 1681, and, in 1687, Governor Elihu Yale provided the church plate.

Finally, in 1688, King James II granted a charter, making Madras the first municipal corporation in India.

The administration of the settlement consisted of the governor's executive council, which met twice weekly. The council's secretary maintained the minutes of the meetings, which were regularly submitted to the authorities in London, many months' sailing-time away. The members of council ranked as "merchants"; under them were the "factors," then the "writers," then the "apprentices." Salaries were pitifully low, although the company provided board and lodgings. All employees illicitly supplemented their salaries by private trading, often at the company's expense, and the London authorities were consequently profoundly suspicious of their servants in India.

Increasingly, over the century, officials were married. Few English women were available for marriage (one, Catherine Nicks, in Governor Yale's time, was an enterprising businesswoman in her own right), but wives and mistresses were recruited from among Portuguese, Eurasian, and Indian women. (Yale's mistress and the mother of his illegitimate son, Hieronima de Paivia, was a Portuguese Jew.) The inhabitants of Fort Saint George constituted a thoroughly cosmopolitan community.

In 1674, when Madras had four decades of growth behind it, the physician and traveler John Fryer visited Fort Saint George. His ship, as was customary, anchored a mile or so out in the roadsteads, and he was brought to land through the tremendous surf in a *mussoola* made of planks sewn with coir twine. As he reached the breakers, he was swung onto the shoulders of one of the boatmen, who then plunged into the sea, so that both reached the shore soaked through. (This was how Europeans would continue to arrive in Madras well into the nineteenth century.) Fryer's first sight of the fort impressed him. There were strong walls thick enough to withstand cannon. Beside the gate facing the sea, a half-moon bastion bristled with ordnance, and two more bastions on the south wall protected St. Thomas's Gate. Two gateways on the northern wall led into Black Town. Inside the fort, Fryer was impressed by the tree-lined streets, all very clean, with rows of fine mansions built of brick or stone and with fine classical porticos.

He estimated that the fort contained three hundred English and perhaps three thousand Portuguese inhabitants, including a mixed garrison of seven hundred soldiers, and he reckoned the population of Black Town at around thirty thousand individuals, almost all of them Hindus. The governor, Sir William Langhorn, "a gentleman of indefatigable industry and worth," maintained a considerable state and a ceremonial persona suitable for a representative of the company.

SIGNIFICANCE

In the last quarter of the seventeenth century, Madras evolved from a factory on the shore to a thriving settlement with far-flung commercial interests. A succession of shrewd and hardheaded governors had done much to advance the process: Langhorn (1670-1677); Streynsham Master (1677-1681); William Gyfford (1681-1687), whom the London authorities described as "our too easy agent"; the Boston-born Elihu Yale (1687-1692), who was to give his name to Yale University; the Connecticut-born Nathaniel Higginson (1692-1697); and the poacher-turned-gamekeeper, the notorious "interloper" Thomas Pitt (1697-1709), nicknamed Diamond Pitt for his acquisition of the famous stone, and who also was the grandfather and great-grandfather of two British prime ministers.

These men guided the settlement through perilous times. It was not enough for them to be good businessmen; they also had to be astute politicians and dexterous diplomats. The rivalries of the European companies in the eastern seas often led to open conflict, while in the last quarter of the century, the hinterland became acutely unstable. In 1687, after years of encroachment, the Mughals finally overthrew the sultanate of Golconda, and southeastern India was integrated into the Mughal Empire. It was in Yale's time that Madras had to come to terms with the new masters of the Carnatic. Worse still, Śivājī, the Marāthā king and the implacable enemy of the Mughals, invaded the Carnatic in the 1670's, seizing major forts such as Tanjore and Gingee. Between 1689 and 1698, Gingee was closely invested by Mughal forces. That Madras was able to keep its distance from these quarrels was a measure of a newfound maturity.

Beginning around 1709, when Thomas Pitt returned to England, Madras entered into a period of solid growth and prosperity, far exceeding in size Calcutta in Bengal or Bombay on the west coast. English visitors waxed enthusiastic in their impressions of Madras, its straight brick- and tree-lined streets, with public buildings such as the town hall, St. Mary's Church, the college, the hospital, and the governor's lodgings—and all within Fort of Saint George. Visitors admired the rustic outskirts of the town as well as the company's garden, designed for recreation, and they enjoyed the opulent country houses commissioned by the wealthier Europeans in the surrounding countryside.

—*Gavin R. G. Hambly*

FURTHER READING

Bingham, Hiram. *Elihu Yale.* Hamden, Conn.: Archon Books, 1968. A splendid account of this tough, colorful governor of Madras.

Foster, William. "The East India Company, 1600-1740." In *The Cambridge History of India,* edited by H. H. Dodwell. Vol. 5. Cambridge, England: Cambridge University Press, 1929. A detailed narrative of the company's early history.

Love, Henry D. *Vestiges of Old Madras, 1640-1800.* 4 vols. London: Indian Records Series, 1913. Early records of Fort Saint George. This and other titles on the early history of Madras were written by Anglo-Indian antiquarians before World War I. A few titles have been reprinted in India.

Spear, Percival. *The Nabobs.* Oxford, England: Oxford University Press, 1968. An excellent account of the early social history of the English in India.

Temple, Richard Carnac. *Diaries of Streynsham Master.* 2 vols. London: Indian Records Series, 1911. Discusses the administration of the important Madras governor.

Wheeler, James Talboys. *Madras in the Olden Times.* 3 vols. Madras, India, 1861-1862. A collection of records from early Madras history.

SEE ALSO: 1606-1674: Europeans Settle in India; Jan. 14, 1641: Capture of Malacca; 1658-1707: Reign of Aurangzeb; June 23, 1661: Portugal Cedes Bombay to the English; c. 1666-1676: Founding of the Marāthā Kingdom.

RELATED ARTICLES in *Great Lives from History: The Seventeenth Century, 1601-1700:* Aurangzeb; James II; William Kidd; Śivājī.

1630's

March-June, 1639
FIRST BISHOPS' WAR

Consisting of little more than skirmishing, the First Bishops' War was a failed attempt by King Charles I to subdue Scotland, which had exploded into rebellion in the face of religious changes imposed by the king. The cost of the war forced Charles to call a Parliament, ending eleven years of Personal Rule and precipitating the English Civil Wars.

LOCALE: England and Scotland
CATEGORIES: Wars, uprisings, and civil unrest; government and politics; religion and theology

KEY FIGURES
Charles I (1600-1649), king of England, r. 1625-1649
William Laud (1573-1645), archbishop of Canterbury, 1633-1645
Archibald Campbell (1607-1661), eighth earl, 1638-1641, and first marquis, 1641-1660, of Argyll
Alexander Leslie (c. 1580-1661), commander of the Covenanters' army and first earl of Leven, 1641-1661
James Hamilton (1606-1649), third marquis of Hamilton, 1625-1643, and first duke of Hamilton, 1643-1649

SUMMARY OF EVENT
There were two causes of the First Bishops' War. First, although Charles I had assumed the thrones of both England and Scotland when his father, James I, died in 1625, Charles in fact had little understanding of his northern kingdom, which he had left when he was only two years old. The other, more immediate cause of the war was Charles's determination, as Supreme Head of the Church of England, to institute uniformity of worship in both of his kingdoms. This determination caused him to impose a new liturgy in Scotland in 1637.

The Church of Scotland, known as the Kirk, was staunchly Calvinist, with a plain and unadorned Sunday service that consisted mainly of a sermon and a few prayers composed by the minister himself. In Anglican services, by contrast, the minister was required to follow the Book of Common Prayer, with its prayers, creeds, confession, Bible reading, hymns, and canticles. This left little time for a sermon, even if a minister was licensed to preach, which most were not, and it left little room even in the prayers for the minister's personal faith to shape the service.

The lack of preaching was a cause of complaint by England's strict Calvinists, the Puritans; they objected as well to the increasing use of ceremony and ritual in English church services under the religious policies pursued by Charles and his archbishop of Canterbury, William Laud. For English Puritans, the services of the Kirk of Scotland were far superior to those of England, and the Scots certainly believed their church services represented a "truer" and "purer" religion than did England's. Moreover, Charles was a strong proponent of episcopacy, a system of church governance in which the bishops held all authority: He saw an episcopal church as the religious equivalent of a strong or even absolute monarchy. On the other hand, Charles believed that Presbyterianism, a more democratic system of church governance favored in Scotland, smacked of the constitutionally limited monarchy that he fought so hard to prevent Parliament from instituting.

Despite the traditions and wishes of his Scottish subjects, Charles insisted that a version of the English liturgy be used throughout Scotland. This Scottish Prayer Book, as it was known, was even more ceremonial and ritualistic, and closer to the Roman Catholic mass, than its English counterpart. As he prepared to impose this new liturgy in Scotland, Charles made it clear that no other forms of service would be tolerated and that there would be no more extemporaneous prayers or preaching without a license. To the Scots, this seemed like nothing less than an attempt to bring Catholicism to Scotland, and when the new Scottish Prayer Book was first used, at Saint Giles' Cathedral in Edinburgh on July 23, 1637, the result was a riot.

Charles had done many of the same things in Scotland that were causing unrest in England: He placed bishops in government office, threatened property rights, and generally acted without consultation or consent of religious, aristocratic, or legislative authorities. The Scottish Prayer Book, though, was the last straw. The riots in Edinburgh continued, and by the fall of 1637, royal authority in the Scottish capital was at an end. The rebels began to set up an alternative government, which culminated in the signing of the National Covenant in February, 1638. While this document claimed that its signers were still loyal to Charles, it denounced his religious innovations and pledged the Covenanters' determination to maintain "true religion." The powerful leader of the Campbell clan, Archibald Campbell, eighth earl of Argyll, quickly emerged as a leader of the Covenanters. By the fall of 1638, not just Edinburgh but all of Scotland was essentially under the Covenanters' control.

Charles sent his chief Scottish adviser, James Hamilton, third marquis of Hamilton, to negotiate with the Covenanters but with little hope of success. If he could do nothing else, though, Hamilton was instructed to stall for time as, during the winter of 1638-1639, Charles began to arrange for a military force to subdue his rebellious northern kingdom. The Covenanters also made military preparations, raising an army commanded by Scotland's greatest soldier, Alexander Leslie, later the first earl of Leven. By the spring of 1639, the Covenanters' army numbered some twenty thousand men, most of whom were veterans of continental wars, and it had secured every important military site north of the border, including Edinburgh Castle.

Charles, on the other hand, was severely limited in what military might he could muster, because he was determined not to call Parliament, which had not met in England since he dissolved it in 1629. Only Parliament could grant the king the necessary taxes to raise and equip an army; without Parliament, Charles's resources were extremely limited. Although the king had, barely, been able to keep royal finances afloat, there was simply no money in the treasury for an army, so Charles exercised his feudal right to summon his nobles to meet him with armed troops, while also directing the lords lieutenant of the northern counties to mobilize the local militias. The king also appealed to Englishmen, in particular the city of London, for voluntary monetary aid. In March, 1639, Charles arrived in York to head up his royal army, which by June, 1639, numbered some eighteen thousand men.

Compared to the Covenanters, however, the English army was a motley, ill-equipped, undertrained affair. The truth was that most Englishmen had no desire to fight the Scots, who at this point were making no move to invade England itself. In fact, sympathy for the Covenanters ran high among the English, especially those who were alienated by Charles's fiscal, political, and religious policies at home. Indeed, the very fact that Charles would prepare for war without summoning a Parliament—something unprecedented since the thirteenth century—drove home to many Englishmen the nature of the king's royal absolutism. Thus, the English nobility either stayed away or showed up with unsavory and unprepared recruits. The militia—the so-called trained bands—were in fact very poorly trained, inadequately armed, and completely unprepared to fight. No voluntary donations to the enterprise were forthcoming from the city of London, either, or from anywhere else in England.

As the royal army moved north, desertion became rampant. It was clear even to the king that his army had neither the ability nor the will to fight the Scots. After some unsuccessful skirmishing, Charles consented to the Pacification of Berwick on June 19, 1639; both sides agreed to disarm, and Charles promised to summon the Scottish parliament and the General Assembly of the Kirk to settle the matters in dispute between himself and his Scottish subjects. Although the Pacification of Berwick ended the First Bishops' War, however, neither side saw it as ending the overall conflict.

SIGNIFICANCE

The First Bishops' War exposed the underlying weakness of Charles's seemingly secure reign, and it showed as well the depth of the discontent in England with his rule. The king's inability to command his northern kingdom, his failure to bring it to heel, was both humiliating and ominous. The military campaign, besides being embarrassing, had left Charles bankrupt. The king would have no option now but to call a Parliament.

Although the First Bishops' War had left Charles politically weakened, however, the king was determined neither to abandon his policies nor to concede any of his principles, either to the Scots or to his own people. In the aftermath of the First Bishops' War, Charles did change his advisers, but in that process he eliminated the more moderate voices and enhanced the roles of the extreme Royalists William Laud and Thomas Wentworth, first earl of Strafford. The latter was the author of the policy of "Thorough," whereby royal authority was severely exercised over all levels of English government by means of a scrupulous and strict enforcement of the law combined with effective supervision of local and regional governments.

Moreover, as Charles was forced to call Parliament, the ensuing elections provided a forum in which the discontent growing over the last eleven years could finally be discussed. Issues became clearer, and the extent to which grievances with Charles's regime were national, not merely local, became apparent. This situation, combined with Charles's intransigence, did not bode well for relations between the king and the Parliament that assembled in April of 1640. Civil war was nearly at hand.

—*Sharon L. Arnoult*

FURTHER READING

Donald, Peter. *An Uncounselled King: Charles I and the Scottish Troubles, 1637-1641.* New York: Cambridge

University Press, 1990. Focuses on the immediate causes of the First Bishops' War.

Fissel, Mark Charles. *The Bishops' Wars: Charles I's Campaigns Against Scotland, 1638-1640.* New York: Cambridge University Press, 1994. Chronicles the progress of the war itself.

Lee, Maurice. *The Road to Revolution: Scotland Under Charles I, 1625-37.* Urbana: University of Illinois Press, 1985. Focuses on the Scottish background of the events that led to the First Bishops' War.

Woolrych, Austin. *Britain in Revolution, 1625-1660.* New York: Oxford University Press, 2002. Authoritative study of the period of Charles I's reign; important for understanding the context and result of the First Bishops' War.

Wormald, Jenny. "One King, Two Kingdoms." In *Uniting the Kingdom: The Making of British History*, edited by Alexander Grant and Keith J. Stringer. New York: Routledge, 1995. Examines the problem of a "dual monarchy" that helped lead to conflict.

SEE ALSO: Mar. 24, 1603: James I Becomes King of England; Dec. 18, 1621: The Great Protestation; May 6-June 7, 1628: Petition of Right; Mar., 1629-1640: "Personal Rule" of Charles I; Nov. 3, 1640-May 15, 1641: Beginning of England's Long Parliament; 1642-1651: English Civil Wars; Aug. 17-Sept. 25, 1643: Solemn League and Covenant; July 2, 1644: Battle of Marston Moor; Dec. 6, 1648-May 19, 1649: Establishment of the English Commonwealth; Dec. 16, 1653-Sept. 3, 1658: Cromwell Rules England as Lord Protector; May, 1659-May, 1660: Restoration of Charles II; May 19, 1662: England's Act of Uniformity; 1673-1678: Test Acts; Apr. 4, 1687, and Apr. 27, 1688: Declaration of Liberty of Conscience; May 24, 1689: Toleration Act.

RELATED ARTICLES in *Great Lives from History: The Seventeenth Century, 1601-1700:* Richard Cameron; Charles I; James I; William Laud; First Earl of Strafford.

December, 1639
RUSSIANS REACH THE PACIFIC OCEAN

The seventeenth century was a century of rapid Russian expansion eastward: In just six decades, Cossacks and fur traders moved across the whole of Siberia, exploring the valleys of Siberian great rivers. In 1639, they reached the coast of the Pacific Ocean for the first time. Subsequent Russian explorations rounded the Arctic coast of Asia and passed through the straits separating Asia and North America.

LOCALE: Siberia, northern Asia, Russia
CATEGORIES: Expansion and land acquisition; exploration and discovery

KEY FIGURES
Yermak Timofeyevich (d. 1584/1585), Russian Cossack conqueror of the Siberian Khanate
Ivan Moskvitin (fl. seventeenth century), Russian explorer
Vasily Poyarkov (d. 1668), Russian explorer
Semyon Ivanov Dezhnyov (c. 1605-1673), Russian Cossack navigator
Vladimir Atlasov (c. 1652-1711), Russian Cossack, senior clerk of Anadyr, 1695, and conqueror of Kamchatka
Kuchum (d. after 1598), khan of Siberia, r. 1556-1598

Peter Beketov (fl. 1632), founder of the Siberian *ostrog* (town) Yakutsk
Fedot Alekseyev (fl. seventeenth century), a trader who accompanied Dezhnyov

SUMMARY OF EVENT
Russian penetration of Siberia began during the Middle Ages, when the Novgorodians sent expeditions to barter with the indigenous peoples for furs in the Northern Trans-Ural region. After the conquest of the Kazan Khanate in 1552, Russia began to expand eastward. In 1582-1585, Yermak Timofeyevich, at the head of 850 Cossacks, crossed the Urals and defeated Kuchum, the khan of the Siberian Khanate, one of the remnants of the Golden Horde. In 1587, the fort of Tobolsk was founded on the Tobol River. Tobolsk remained the capital of Russian Siberia for a long time.

Cossacks, runaway peasants, traders, trappers, and adventurers rushed to Siberia in search of furs and other riches. These prospectors were also explorers, venturing into uncharted territories. Usually, these territories were donated to the czar soon after their discovery. At the end of the seventeenth century, the whole of Siberia was covered with the thick network of *ostrogs* (stockaded towns), where offices of *voevodas* (governors) were located. The indigenous peoples of Siberia were forced to pay a *yasak* (tribute in furs).

The geography of Siberia contributed to a relatively easy Russian advance eastward: The major Siberian rivers flow from the south to the north, and their tributaries flow from the west to the east. By moving "toward the sun" via the Ob, Yenisey, and Lena Rivers, the Russians, over the course of only a few decades, were able to traverse thousands of miles through enormous spaces of the taiga and tundra.

Around 1620, from Turukhansk, founded in 1607 on the banks of the Turukhan River, one of the Yenisey River's branches, a freeman by the name of Pantelei Demidov Penda led forty Russian adventurers in search of the great Lena River. This legendary journey continued for several years; its participants traversed more than 6,000 miles (9,650 kilometers). The band ascended the Lower Tunguska River, overcoming cliffs and rapids. After portaging the boats, they reached the Lena River and descended to the place where the *ostrog* of Yakutsk was later founded. Then they turned back, reached the Lena River's source, and through the Buryat steppes emerged onto the Angara River. They were the first Russians to sail down that river. Having overcome its terrible rapids, Penda and his companions returned to Turukhansk by a familiar road along the Yenisey River.

At the end of the 1620's, the way was opened from the Angara River—via its tributary, the Ilim River, and the Lena River's portage—to the Kuga River, a tributary of the Lena River. This route from the Angara River to the Kuga River soon became the main eastward one through Siberia. In 1632, the Yenisey Cossack *sotnik* (cavalry-captain) Peter Beketov established Yakutsk on the bank of the Lena River. Yakutsk was to become the base of Russian expansion in eastern Siberia.

The 1630's and 1640's were the most significant years in the history of Russian explorations, culminating in Siberian explorers' arrival at the Pacific Ocean. In 1638, Russians heard from an Evenk shaman about a great river in the south with a silver mountain on its banks. Reports of this mountain caught their attention, since Cossacks had an official order to search for silver deposits in new lands. In the seventeenth century, Russia had no silver mines of its own and had to import silver from Europe to coin money. In the spring of 1639, Ivan Moskvitin, at the head of thirty Cossacks, left Yakutsk in search of the silver mountain.

Having ascended various rivers and crossed the Dzhugdzhur Range, the Cossacks reached the Ulia River, which flowed into the Sea of Okhotsk, an inlet of the Pacific Ocean, by the end of 1639. They built two 50-foot (15-meter) *koches* (Russian sailing vessels), and in the summer of 1640, sailing along the coasts of eastern Siberia, they reached the Amur delta. They gave up trying to enter the delta, since many native Siberian boats were gathered there, and turned back. Moskvitin and his Cossacks returned to Yakutsk in the spring of 1641. Moskvitin did not find silver, but through his expedition, Russia had gained an outlet to the Pacific: The port of Okhotsk, the main Russian port in the Pacific and a gateway to Kamchatka, Alaska, and Russian America, was founded in 1647.

The Russians succeeded in reaching the Amur River in 1644, when a military expedition, under Vasily Poyarkov, numbering 143 men, left Yakutsk and, ascending the Aldan River, reached the Zeia River, a tributary of the Amur River. However, Poyarkov's mistakes in organizing a winter camp combined with hostile indigenous peoples resulted in a tragedy: Between eighty and one hundred of his Cossacks starved to death. The next summer, the survivors descended the Amur River and emerged onto the Sea of Okhotsk. Retracing Moskvitin's route, they returned to Yakutsk in 1646, bringing back news of the "great river Amur" and its riches. Two *ostrogs* were built to capitalize on this discovery. In 1658, Nerchinsk was established on the Shilka River, the Amur River's tributary, and in 1665, Albazin was constructed on the Amur River itself. They became the headquarters of Russian annexation and economic development efforts in the Amur area.

The Russian explorers from Yakutsk also traveled north to the Arctic Ocean. Bands of Cossacks descended the Lena River and sailed along the Arctic coasts of Siberia, searching for furs and walrus tusks. The voyage of Semyon Ivanov Dezhnyov, a Russian Cossack navigator, and Fedot Alekseyev, a trader, around the Chukchi Peninsula to the Bering Sea in 1648 was the culmination of these expeditions and had significant historical impact: Dezhnyov and Alekseyev discovered and passed the straits separating Asia and America.

In June, 1648, ninety men on six *koches* descended from the Kolyma River into the Arctic Ocean and sailed east, rounding a cape, the northeasternmost point of the Asian continent, which Dezhnyov referred to in his report as a "large rock nose" (in 1898, it was named Cape Dezhnyov in honor of the navigator). Only thirteen men including Dezhnyov survived this voyage, however, af-

1630's

RUSSIAN EXPANSION IN THE 17TH CENTURY

ter storms, shipwrecks, and bloody clashes with the warlike local tribes of the Chukchi. Having wintered at the Anadyr estuary, the survivors ascended the river and founded the Anadyr *ostrog*, from which they collected tribute from the local people. The Anadyr *ostrog* became the center of Russian conquest of Chukotka and Kamchatka.

The Russian exploration and territorial expansion in the seventeenth century culminated with the conquest of Kamchatka. Vladimir Atlasov, a Cossack captain and senior clerk of the Anadyr *ostrog*, with sixty Cossacks and sixty Yukaghir natives, left Anadyr in December, 1696, went out to Penzhina Bay, and, having crossed the Koryak Range, reached the Bering Sea. He collected tribute from local tribes of the Koryaks throughout the journey. Part of Atlasov's band entered Kamchatka, moving along the Pacific coast of the peninsula. Meanwhile, Atlasov returned to the west coast and continued south. Atlasov ravaged the entire peninsula with fire and sword, conquering the native Itelmens and forcing them to pay tribute. In commemoration of Kamchatka's annexation, on July 13, 1697, he set a cross on the banks of the Kamchatka River, where he built two forts. He visited Moscow in 1701 and had an audience with Peter the Great. His detailed geographical and ethnographical de-

scription of Kamchatka was highly valued and was used for further explorations.

SIGNIFICANCE

There is no doubt that Russian explorations in Siberia and northeastern Asia in the seventeenth century were part of the great voyages of discovery, considerably broadening Europeans' knowledge of the unknown world of "Tataria" lying to the north of the Chinese Empire. Specifically, the discoveries of Russian pioneers made it possible for Europeans to draw much more accurate maps of Asia. They paved the way for the First (1725-1730) and Second (1733-1743) Kamchatka Expeditions led by Captain Vitus Bering on the initiative of Peter the Great. Advancing farther to the Kuril and Aleutian Islands and to Alaska in the eighteenth century, the Russian Empire gained strategic control of the North Pacific.

For a long time, Siberia remained a colony of the Russian Empire, which, in contrast to the colonies of other European states, was not situated overseas but instead directly adjoined the mother country. Siberia supplied furs, one of the most important sources of public revenue. As industrialization developed, moreover, the region's mineral resources came to play a significant role. In the twenty-first century, Siberia remains Russia's treasure house: Siberian metals, diamonds, and, above all, oil and gas, represent the economic foundation of that country. According to estimates, about 40 percent of world mineral resources are concentrated in Siberia.

—*Anatolii Trekhsviatskyi*

FURTHER READING

Bobrick, Benson. *East of the Sun: The Epic Conquest and Tragic History of Siberia.* New York: Poseidon Press, 1992. The emotional narrative of Russia's conquest of Siberia.

Forsyth, James. *A History of the Peoples of Siberia.* New York: Cambridge University Press, 1992. The first comprehensive ethnohistory of Siberia in English.

Examines the impact of Russian explorations on the natives of Siberia.

Lincoln, Bruce W. *The Conquest of a Continent: Siberia and the Russians.* New York: Random House, 1994. A detailed description of Siberia's history. Part 2 discusses the Russian explorations in Siberia.

SEE ALSO: July 10, 1655-June 21, 1661: First Northern War; Beginning 1689: Reforms of Peter the Great; Aug. 29, 1689: Treaty of Nerchinsk Draws Russian-Chinese Border.

RELATED ARTICLES in *Great Lives from History: The Seventeenth Century, 1601-1700:* Alexis; Michael Romanov; Sophia.

1640
FOUNDATION OF THE DARFUR SULTANATE

The founding of the Darfur sultanate made complete a succession of Islamic states across the Sudan, opening a pilgrimage route to the holy city of Mecca and extending trade not only with Africa and the Middle East but also with Europe.

LOCALE: Darfur, Sudan
CATEGORIES: Expansion and land acquisition; religion and theology; trade and commerce

KEY FIGURES

Ahmed el-Makur, the legendary ancestor of the Keira Dynasty
Dali, the legendary first ruler of the Keira Dynasty
Sulayman Solong (d. 1637), sultan of Darfur, r. 1596-1637
Ahmad Bakr (d. 1722), sultan of Darfur, r. 1682-1722

SUMMARY OF EVENT

Darfur is located between the Nile and Chad Rivers in western Sudan. In this huge area, which was inhabited mostly by nomads, only the Jebel Marra Mountains were suitable for the formation of a central government. The trade routes, passing since ancient times through this area, brought about the expansion of three successive dynasties far beyond its homeland in the mountains. These three dynasties, derived mainly from oral and written traditions that passed from father to son, were the Daju, the Tunjur, and the Keira.

By the sixteenth century, the Tunjur Dynasty established an empire that extended to Darfur and Wadai, and it even established political and commercial contacts

with Ottoman Egypt. However, the Tunjurs disappeared in the seventeenth century and were succeeded by the Keira Dynasty in Darfur and by the Maba Dynasty in Wadai.

According to local traditions, the disappearance of the Tunjur Dynasty and the rule of the Keira there is associated with the figure of Ahmed el-Makur, an Arab from North Africa, who, by the authority of one local tradition, came to the court of a Fur chief called Kurooma. Kurooma had married a daughter of the Keira chief. Later, Kurooma divorced her and gave her to Ahmed. From this marriage came Dali, the first ruler of the Keira Dynasty.

Dali, described by local traditions as having established some of the most fundamental of the Darfur sultanate institutions, divided the state into five provinces. These provinces would remain the territorial units of the Keira administration until the nineteenth century. Dali also codified the laws and customs of the Keira sultanate in the so-called book of Dali.

Local traditions credit Sulayman Solong, who lived eight generations after Dali, as the second founder of the Keira state. Sulayman ruled between 1596 and 1637, the year of his death. He and his grandson, Ahmad Bakr, expanded the sultanate, probably to maintain long-distance caravan trade with Egypt and the rest of Sudan, trade that was well established by the end of the seventeenth century.

Good political and commercial contacts between Darfur and the Nile Valley were made because of the "forty-days' road" (*darb al-arba'in*), which served as a route to supply slaves from the inner African continent to the Ottomans in Egypt. Slaves, a main export for Darfur, were seized from the pagan peoples south of the sultanate through raids acknowledged by the authorities. These raids, called *ghazwa* in Arabic, were organized and led by the noblemen, who sought permission from the sultan and then led a volunteer search group. The captured slaves not only faced export but also served as soldiers, agricultural laborers, bureaucrats, and even "gifts."

The *darb al-arba'in* was the main link connecting Darfur with the outside world. The Keira Dynasty made Kobbe, located at the southern end of the *darb al-arba'in*, the first commercial and political capital of the dynasty, attesting to the road's significance.

A second trading axis passing through the sultanate ran from west to east and formed part of the pilgrimage route from the western Sudanic belt to the holy cities Mecca and Medina. The Sudan Road, as it came to be known, was increasingly traveled in the seventeenth century because Darfur and Wadai provided security for pilgrims. Also, Darfur was located along an important trade route to Tripoli and Tunis in north Africa. It is no accident that Darfur was established in a location busy with traveling Muslim holy men from West Africa and the Nile Valley and along a major trade route.

Sulayman wanted to expand his territories to increase his catchment area for slaves, who could be bartered for arms, armor, horses, and fine cloth with Egyptian and Sudanese merchants. Kordofan in central Sudan fell to Sulayman, and local traditions even credit him with expanding the borders of the sultanate to the Atbara River in the east and to the deserts of the north.

Sulayman is said to have introduced Islam to the region. He built mosques for his subjects and encouraged Islamic practices. However, the Islamization of the Darfur sultanate was a very slow process, in which indigenous, animistic beliefs expressed in rituals coexisted with the practice of Islam.

However, the most significant expansion of the Darfur sultanate took place under the reign of Sulayman's grandson, Ahmad Bakr, expanding beyond the Jebel Marra area. Ahmad Bakr's reign began in 1682, and by the time of his death in 1722, the sultanate reached almost to the boundaries of what is now Darfur province. Ahmad Bakr also tried to spread Islam, which until his rule was limited to court circles, throughout the sultanate by introducing teachers of Islam and by building mosques and schools.

SIGNIFICANCE

The legacy of the founding of the Darfur sultanate is still popular in the region. Islamization continued during the eighteenth and nineteenth centuries, as holy men, pilgrims, and traders influenced the religious practices of the peoples of the region.

The slave trade with Egypt and with the rest of Sudan increased as well, but the trade, which brought prosperity to the elite, also brought an end to the sultanate by the Egyptians. Egypt, or more correctly, the Turco-Egyptian administration in Khartoum, conquered the sultanate of Darfur in 1874, but the Keira Dynasty, continuing its fight to remain independent, retreated to its base at Jebel Marra. The British conquered Darfur in 1916, and it became part of Sudan.

—Moshe Terdiman

FURTHER READING

Arkell, A. J. *The History of The Sudan from the Earliest Times to 1821*. London: University of London Press, 1966. A short survey of the circumstances of the foundation of the Darfur sultanate.

Ewald, Janet J. *Soldiers, Traders, and Slaves: State Formation and Economic Transformation in the Greater Nile Valley, 1700-1885*. Madison: University of Wisconsin Press, 1990. A description of the trade links of the sultanate of Darfur in the eighteenth and nineteenth centuries.

O'Fahey, R. S. "The Conquest of Darfur, 1873-1882." *Sudan Notes and Records* (1997): 47-67. A description of the decline of the Darfur sultanate.

_____. "A Hitherto 'Unknown' Darfur King List." *Sudanic Africa*, no. 6 (1996): 157-169. A detailed description of the legendary rulers of Darfur.

O'Fahey, R. S., and J. L. Spaulding. *Kingdoms of the Sudan*. London: Methuen, 1974. A detailed survey of the traditions surrounding the sultanate's founding, its history, institutions, and its trade links.

SEE ALSO: 17th cent.: Songhai Empire Dissolves; Sept., 1605: Egyptians Rebel Against the Ottomans; 1612: Rise of the Arma in Timbuktu; 1617-1693: European Powers Vie for Control of Gorée; 1619-c. 1700: The Middle Passage to American Slavery; 1660-1677: A Jihad Is Called in Senegambia.

1640-1688
REIGN OF FREDERICK WILLIAM, THE GREAT ELECTOR

The reign of Frederick William, the Great Elector, led to the rise of Brandenburg-Prussia as a major state in northern Germany, paving the way for the emergence of Prussia as a leading European power in the eighteenth century.

LOCALE: Brandenburg-Prussia (now Brandenburg, Germany) and northern Germany

CATEGORIES: Government and politics; expansion and land acquisition

KEY FIGURES

Frederick William, the Great Elector (1620-1688), elector of Brandenburg, r. 1640-1688

Louise Henrietta (1627-1667), first wife of Frederick William

Dorothea of Hanover (1636-1689), second wife of Frederick William

Frederick (1655-1713), elector as Frederick III, r. 1688-1700, king of Prussia as Frederick I, r. 1701-1713, and son of Frederick William

SUMMARY OF EVENT

When Frederick William succeeded his father, George William, as the elector of Brandenburg in 1640, he faced a host of challenges. Beginning in 1356, each ruler of Brandenburg had been one of seven electors who chose the emperors of the Holy Roman Empire, dominated by the Austrian Habsburg Dynasty. Since 1415, the Hohenzollerns had been the ruling family of Brandenburg, a small state in northern Germany, that was relatively poor in resources. The Hohenzollerns had other lands that were geographically separated from Brandenburg. To the east was Prussia, of which the kings of Poland were the nominal overlords, and to the west the small states of Cleves and Mark. Frederick William, later known as the great elector, assumed power in the midst of the catastrophic Thirty Years' War (1618-1648).

The Hohenzollerns, who were Protestant Calvinists, were unpopular among the majority Protestant Lutheran population. Initially, Sweden was the immediate threat to the territorial integrity of the elector's lands, and the elector's small army of five thousand was no match for the Swedes. One of the continuing challenges facing the great elector throughout his reign was to increase the size and professional competence of his army, and given the poverty of his lands, he often relied upon subsidies from foreign governments that came at the cost of forcing the elector into numerous temporary alliances.

Frederick William also faced opposition from the estates, or parliaments, of the various Hohenzollern lands. Representing local elites of landowners and merchants, the several estates opposed increasing taxes to fund the military and diplomatic ambitions of the elector, particularly if those taxes were to be spent elsewhere than where they were raised. On occasion, he simply authorized the seizure of taxes without the consent of the estates. In the seventeenth century, there was little "German" nationalism, and localism reigned supreme. Even the elector was largely motivated by dynastic rather than nationalistic considerations.

The Peace of Westphalia ended the Thirty Years' War in 1648, and although the Calvinists in the empire were guaranteed religious toleration, Frederick William's territorial gains were minimal. His lands were still divided, and Swedish power still loomed large. Building up his army and his alliances, by the end of the 1650's it appeared that Sweden would be forced to abandon lands claimed by the elector, but France backed the Swedes as a counterweight to the imperial Habsburgs, and Frederick William had to settle with being recognized as the duke of Prussia.

During the following decade, the elector was dedicated to maintaining the status quo in order to preserve his rights against threats from Sweden, German Catholic princes, and the Habsburg emperor. However, the ultimate danger came from France's King Louis XIV, who seized the Spanish Netherlands in the name of his Spanish wife. Louis's ambitions threatened the Dutch Republic as well as Frederick William's principalities of Cleves and Mark. He had married Louise Henrietta, princess of Orange and daughter of the Dutch stadtholder William of Orange (later King William III), partially for religious reasons—the Dutch were Calvinist—but also to get Dutch support for his territorial claims to the small principalities of Julich-Berg.

The elector initially allied with the Dutch during the French-Dutch War (1672-1678), but Louis's victories led Frederick William to abandon the Dutch and join France. However, he switched sides again when promised French subsidies did not arrive. In 1675, he defeated the invading Swedes at the Battle of Fehrbellin, winning for himself the title of the "great elector," later the title of a biography by Samuel von Pufendorf, one of his advis-

Refugee Huguenots, who fled France after King Louis XIV revoked official toleration of Protestantism, were welcomed into Protestant Brandenburg by Great Elector Frederick William. Many of the refugees were professionals and skilled artisans. (Francis R. Niglutsch)

ers. Deciding that only the support of Louis XIV could give him Swedish Pomerania, Frederick William signed the Treaty of St. Germain with France in 1679 in exchange for an annual subsidy, but his anticipated territories were restored to Sweden. In 1685, fearing French ambitions and concerned about the security of Protestantism after Louis revoked religious toleration for the Protestant Huguenots, he again changed sides, joining the Dutch and the Swedes in a pact against France. Before conflict broke out, the elector died in 1688.

Frederick William's wars and diplomacy were allied with his desire to create a powerful state. By the end of the Thirty Years' War he understood that his power depended upon having a standing army, and at the height of the war against the Dutch his army totaled forty-five thousand. Brandenburg was among the first states in Europe to provide standard uniforms, and a military school was established, as well as the general war commissary and a war office. By the year of the elector's death, the military bureaucracy dominated the government.

Another consequence of his military ambitions was the alliance between the elector and the nobility of Bran-denburg and Prussia, that is, between the elector and the Junkers (landowners, who controlled territories in the east). In exchange for supporting Frederick William's policies, the Junkers' own taxes remained relatively light and they were given greater control over their peasants, largely free of royal interference. Under the great elector and his successors, notably kings Frederick William I (r. 1713-1740) and Frederick the Great (r. 1740-1786), the Junker class became, in essence, servants of the state, particularly in the military and civil bureaucracies.

In pursuing his military goals and strengthening the government, the elector worsened the plight of the middle classes and urban inhabitants. Königsberg, in East Prussia, declined in wealth and population because of the high economic tolls and duties that were placed on the city's commerce, while non-Prussian cities such as Riga and Danzig (Gdansk) prospered. The peasants, both free and enserfed, suffered the most, and many fled the electorate to escape their plight.

Aware of the negative domestic consequences of his military aims, Frederick William followed the prevailing economic doctrine of mercantilism, or cameralism as it was known in Germany, which advocated state leadership in guiding the economy. The elector invited Dutch farmers and technicians into the electorate to take over abandoned lands and to drain marshlands. A model experimental farm, influenced by the elector's wife, Louise Henrietta, was established at Oranienburg, near Berlin. The elector also encouraged immigration from Piedmont, and especially France, where Louis XIV's pro-Catholic religious policies led twenty thousand Protestant Huguenots, many of them professionals and skilled artisans, to settle in Brandenburg, along with fifty Jewish families who were given special trading privileges.

To encourage domestic production, foreign imports of wool, glass, iron, and other items were prohibited. The elector also oversaw the establishment of a postal system and the construction of a ten-mile-long canal, uniting the Elbe and Oder Rivers, which increased Berlin's trade. Towns and cities in the west were more prosperous than those in the east, but only Berlin benefited from the great elector's reign, with the population growing from five thousand in 1648 to twenty thousand by his death. Generally, Frederick William was more successful upon building up the infrastructure of his lands than in promoting prosperous industries, but unlike his eighteenth century successors, he had little interest in developing an educational system. The great elector followed a policy of religious toleration, but as much by necessity as by principle. He favored Calvinist advisers, but to gain toleration for his Calvinism, he had to accept toleration for the majority Lutheran population.

Frederick William, preferring hunting rather than the arts, left court culture to Louise Henrietta, although Frederick William had neither the inclination nor, more important, the finances to emulate Louis XIV's Versailles Palace. Notable for apparently having no mistresses, Frederick William married Dorothea of Hanover a year after the death of Louise Henrietta in 1667. The elector was perhaps happier with Dorothea, who was more willing to join him in hunting and drinking than was Louise Henrietta. However, there was considerable friction between Dorothea, focused upon her children, and the elector's son and heir, Frederick, born to his first wife.

SIGNIFICANCE

The forty-eight-year reign of the great elector laid the foundation for modern Prussia, but he was more of a consolidator than an innovator. His economic endeavors failed to transform Brandenburg-Prussia. He was successful in achieving greater recognition for his Hohen-

zollern Dynasty, and his son and successor, Elector Frederick III, became king in 1701.

Although committed to the Protestant Calvinist faith, Frederick William formed alliances with Catholic rulers when it was to his advantage. Like other rulers of the seventeenth century, he often practiced political absolutism, but on practical grounds more so than on philosophical or theological grounds. By 1688, his various territories had come under more centralized rule, his standing army was the second largest in Germany, and Brandenburg-Prussia had become the leading north German state. However, it was not yet the European power it would become in the following century.

—Eugene Larson

FURTHER READING

Carsten, F. L. *The Origins of Prussia*. Oxford, England: Clarendon Press, 1954. Carsten's book is a first-rate scholarly study, more than one-third of which is devoted to Frederick William and his accomplishments.

McKay, Derek. *The Great Elector: Frederick William of Brandenburg-Prussia*. New York: Longman, 2001. The first English biography in more than fifty years, McKay's study describes Frederick William as a product of his time—an unusually tough and opportunistic ruler able to overcome the hostility of local nobles and surrounding nations.

Schevill, Ferdinand. *The Great Elector*. Chicago: University of Chicago Press, 1947. Schevill's work is the classic but dated biography of the great elector.

Shennan, Margaret. *The Rise of Brandenburg Prussia*. New York: Routledge, 1995. An excellent study of the great elector, placing his accomplishments in the context of the emergence of Prussia as a major power.

SEE ALSO: May 30, 1635: Peace of Prague; July 10, 1655-June 21, 1661: First Northern War; 1667: Pufendorf Advocates a Unified Germany; Apr. 6, 1672-Aug. 10, 1678: French-Dutch War; Aug. 10, 1678-Sept. 26, 1679: Treaties of Nijmegen; 1685: Louis XIV Revokes the Edict of Nantes.

RELATED ARTICLES in *Great Lives from History: The Seventeenth Century, 1601-1700:* Charles X Gustav; Christina; Ferdinand II; Frederick Henry; Frederick V; Frederick William, the Great Elector; Gustavus II Adolphus; Leopold I; Louis XIV; Axel Oxenstierna; Samuel von Pufendorf; Cardinal de Richelieu; Justine Siegemundin; Albrecht Wenzel von Wallenstein; William III.

1640's

May, 1640-January 23, 1641
REVOLT OF THE CATALANS

The revolt of the Catalans revealed political dissension within Spain, resulting in the secession of Catalonia until 1652. The rebellion confirmed the decline of Spain.

LOCALE: Madrid and Catalonia, Spain
CATEGORIES: Government and politics; wars, uprisings, and civil unrest

KEY FIGURES

Pau Claris (1586-1641), canon of the cathedral chapter of Urgell and leader of the Catalan revolutionaries
Count-Duke of Olivares (Gaspar de Guzmán y Pimental; 1587-1645), chief minister and court favorite of King Philip IV
Luis de Haro (1598-1661), duke of Carpio, nephew of Olivares, and chief minister of Philip IV, 1643-1661
Philip IV (1605-1665), king of Spain, r. 1621-1665
Count of Santa Coloma (d. 1640), viceroy of Catalonia

SUMMARY OF EVENT

Since the reign of Philip III (1598-1621), the defense of Spanish interests in Europe and overseas was more than Castile could bear alone. Long years of fighting Habsburg wars in central Europe had depleted the Spanish treasury, despite gold and silver shipments from America. These shipments were beginning to fall off as English raiders made incursions into Spanish America. Spain had not had a balanced budget for almost a century. Yet the Spanish government had not been able to make the Aragonese principalities (including Catalonia) share part of the expenses. It was not Castilian prejudice but fiscal and military emergencies that caused the central government in Castile to tap the resources of non-Castilian provinces.

Although aware of these problems, the new king, Philip IV, continued his father's policy of turning over affairs of government to a court favorite (*privado*) and occupying himself with the social duties of the monarchy. The new favorite and chief minister was the count-duke of Olivares. Unlike his predecessors, Olivares was conscientious and worked hard. He heeded the suggestions of *arbitristas* (reform writers) such as Fernández Navarrete that there should be a just and proportionate adjustment of taxation in the provinces and that the center ought not to bear all responsibilities of revenue. A champion not of Castile but of Spain, Olivares sought to create a unified integrated monarchy, and hence at-

tempted two reforms: First, he wanted equitably distributed taxation throughout the country to produce revenue; second, he wanted to abolish all regional privileges to achieve administrative reform. These reforms, if implemented, would rejuvenate Spain economically as well as militarily.

Olivares's plans attacked the privileges and sentiments of the principality of Catalonia in the kingdom of Aragon. Once the thriving center of maritime trade in the peninsula, Catalonia and its capital city, Barcelona, had been declining since the middle of the fifteenth century. The Catalans had exacted a series of concessions from the Crown dating back to the fourteenth century, the most important of which was the privilege of taxing themselves and voting subsidies to the Crown only if they wanted to do so. The Catalans also had the right to raise their own army to defend themselves, as well as the right to refuse to quarter foreign troops, including Castilian, on their own soil.

Throughout the 1630's, Olivares tried to persuade the Catalans to surrender their concessions, offering them positions within Castilian officialdom to make up for their lost privileges. The Catalan Cortes (parliament) voted small subsidies to the Crown but denied Olivares the major gains he sought. The financial problem became even more acute after Spain's international involvement following the outbreak of war with France in 1635. Taxes in Castile were raised arbitrarily, new loans made, the currency devalued, and offices sold. By 1637, Spain's annual expenditure doubled its income. The war itself went badly in both the Holy Roman Empire and the Netherlands. In 1638, the French invaded the Spanish Basque country and besieged Fuenterrabia. The relief force that drove them out included contingents from all major Spanish provinces except Catalonia.

Determined to get the Catalans to contribute to the war effort, Olivares decided to route the campaign of 1639 directly through Catalonia. Though the Catalans participated in sizable numbers, they suffered heavy casualties in their bid to relieve the border fortress of Salcés from French occupation. Thoroughly exhausted and weakened, the Catalans were in no mood to fight. It was necessary for Olivares to send Castilian troops to hold the frontier against the French. These forces were billeted among the Catalans, and further subsidies were demanded. The greatest discontent was among the peasantry; their crops had failed, they had lost men in battles, and then they were forced to billet "foreign" troops. By May of 1640, the north Catalan countryside was in revolt as peasants attacked Spanish troops throughout the district.

By June, the harvester rebels had moved into Barcelona, where they mobilized the *segadors* (farm laborers) into a revolutionary mob and murdered royal officials, including the viceroy, the count of Santa Coloma, who had been acting under orders from Madrid. Pau Claris, canon of Urgell, member of the Diputació (standing committee of the Catalan Cortes), and a leader of resistance to Madrid, took over control of the city. Olivares dispatched troops from the frontier to Barcelona to end the revolt, meanwhile offering the Catalans certain concessions. Claris, caught between the mob and the Castilian army, took the only course available. On January 23, 1641, he declared the independence of Catalonia from Spain and placed it under allegiance to King Louis XIII of France, now hailed as the count of Barcelona.

While the Catalan revolt was going on, the Portuguese took advantage of the confusion and declared their independence from Spain by proclaiming the duke of Braganza as King John IV of Portugal in Lisbon in December, 1640. A similar movement for independence appeared in Andalusia. Olivares's usefulness had come to an end. In 1643, the king dismissed him and appointed his nephew Luis de Haro as the Crown chief minister. Much less ambitious and more careful than Olivares, Haro simply waited.

SIGNIFICANCE

By the late 1640's, the Catalans had tired of French rule. They discovered that chief ministers Cardinal de Richelieu and his successor Cardinal Jules Mazarin were more exacting than Olivares. Furthermore, the Catalan nobility had discovered overtones of social rebellion in the uprising and they began to fear for their property. Haro offered to restore Catalan privileges.

In 1652, when Mazarin was occupied with the Wars of the Fronde (1648-1653), Philip sent an army under his illegitimate son John Joseph of Austria to Barcelona. The city surrendered and was restored to Spain on October 13, 1652, accepting the sovereignty of Philip IV, with John as his viceroy, in return for a general amnesty and the king's promise to preserve the constitutions. The rebellion and separation of Catalonia, along with the loss of Portugal, remained as a striking confirmation of the decline of Spain.

—*José M. Sánchez and Narasingha P. Sil*

FURTHER READING

Carr, Raymond, ed. *Spain: A History*. New York: Oxford University Press, 2000. A collection of essays on Spanish history. Chapter 6 examines "Vicissitudes of a World Power, 1500-1700."

Elliott, John H. "The Decline of Spain." In *Crisis in Europe, 1560-1660*, edited by Trevor Aston. Garden City, N.Y.: Doubleday, 1967. Elliott analyzes the Catalan revolt as the outcome of the economic crisis of 1590-1620 and "the psychological crisis which impelled it (Catalonia) into its final bid for world supremacy."

_____. *The Revolts of the Catalans: A Study in the Decline of Spain, 1598-1640*. Cambridge, England: Cambridge University Press, 1963. This classic study remains the most authoritative work on the subject. Chapter 16 deals specifically with the revolt, and the six-hundred-page book also analyzes the decline of Spain in the seventeenth century. Elliott is especially useful for a critical assessment of the policies of the count-duke of Olivares.

_____. "The Spanish Peninsula, 1598-1648." In *The New Cambridge History of Europe: Decline of Spain and the Thirty Years' War, 1609-1648/1659*, edited by J. P. Cooper. Cambridge, England: Cambridge University Press, 1970. Through a critical study of the ministerial regimes of the duke of Lerma and of the count-duke of Olivares, Elliott examines the domestic developments and international policies of Spain leading to its involvement in the Thirty Years' War. He also discusses the revolt of Catalonia and the independence of Portugal.

Kamen, Henry. *Spain, 1469-1714: A Society in Conflict*. 2d ed. Harlow, England: Longman, 1991. A good general history of the Golden Age of Spain and its subsequent decline, though rather brief on the revolt.

Lynch, John. *The Hispanic World in Crisis and Change, 1598-1700*. Oxford, England: Blackwell, 1992. This is a vastly improved and updated version of Lynch's much acclaimed *Spain Under the Habsburgs*. Chapter 5 contains a succinct scholarly analysis of the revolt and its consequences.

Payne, Stanley G. *A History of Spain and Portugal*. 2 vols. Madison: University of Wisconsin Press, 1973. Volume 1 provides a reliable general history of the Iberian Peninsula from the time of ancient Hispanica to the seventeenth century. Chapter 15, titled "The Seventeenth-Century Decline," is particularly helpful.

Stradling, R. A. *Spain's Struggle for Europe, 1598-1668*. London: Hambledon Press, 1994. Stradling focuses

1640's

on Spanish politics and international relations, emphasizing the leadership abilities of Philip IV and Olivares. Also stresses the survival of the Spanish monarchy, refuting other historians who maintain the seventeenth century was a time of Spanish decline.

SEE ALSO: Mar. 31, 1621-Sept. 17, 1665: Reign of Philip IV; Nov. 7, 1659: Treaty of the Pyrenees;

Feb. 13, 1668: Spain Recognizes Portugal's Independence; Feb., 1669-Jan., 1677: John of Austria's Revolts. **RELATED ARTICLES** in *Great Lives from History: The Seventeenth Century, 1601-1700:* Catherine of Braganza; Charles II (of Spain); John of Austria; John IV; Jules Mazarin; Count-Duke of Olivares; Philip III; Philip IV; Cardinal de Richelieu.

June-August, 1640
BANDEIRANTES EXPEL THE JESUITS

Portuguese frontiersmen settled southern and western Brazil looking for precious metals. The heavy concentration of Brazilian Indian populations in these regions meant there was plentiful slave labor for these frontiersmen, but it also attracted Jesuit missionaries who sought to protect the Indians they wished to convert. The resulting conflict between the Jesuits and the settlers climaxed when the priests were violently expelled from the area.

LOCALE: Brazil
CATEGORIES: Wars, uprisings, and civil unrest; social issues and reform; religion and theology; economics

KEY FIGURES
José de Anchieta (1534-1597), Jesuit pioneer of southern Brazil who relocated Indians to reservations
António Vieira (1608-1697), leading Brazilian Jesuit orator, writer, and government adviser
António Raposo Tavares (c. 1598-1658), São Paulo official who led expeditions into the Brazilian interior

SUMMARY OF EVENT
Although the Portuguese discovered Brazil in 1500, only after three decades did they begin organizing settlements along its coast, ranging from the equator to the tropic of Capricorn. The southernmost of these settlements was São Vicente. Behind it rose mountains that undulated into a vast, hilly plateau stretching into the interior. Portugal's settlement policy failed, however, to achieve a significant Portuguese presence along the coast, which was increasingly coveted by other European powers. Therefore, in 1543, the Portuguese crown established a formal government for Brazil with a capital at Salvador. It also sent missionaries to evangelize the natives and incorporate them into the Portuguese domain.

The Portuguese missionaries belonged to a new order of Roman Catholic clergy, the Society of Jesus, or Jesuits. They were committed to countering the advances of the Protestant Reformation. The Jesuits had appeared at the same time that the Catholic countries of Portugal and Spain were discovering and settling new territories in Asia, Africa, and the Americas and believed they could compensate for the losses of Catholicism in Europe by advancing their religion in the rest of the world. The first Jesuits in Brazil encountered Indian populations along the Atlantic coast, down the Amazon River Valley, and over the southern plateau that drained into the vast Paraná and Paraguay River system. The latter region, well watered and subtropical, had a particularly dense native population, mostly Guaraní- and Tupi-speaking Indians.

Two of the leading Jesuits first to evangelize in Brazil were Fathers Manuel de Nóbrega and José de Anchieta. They converted masses of Indians and organized them into a type of reservation known as an *aldeia*, or small village. Father Anchieta led the conversion of Indians in southern Brazil, founding the city of São Paulo in 1554. Located at the base of the plateau above São Vicente, the settlement became the center from which evangelizing missions set out, establishing other *aldeias*. Meanwhile, the Jesuits were also evangelizing in adjacent areas of Spanish America, organizing them into large-scale reservations known as *reducciones*. The region now occupied by southern Brazil, eastern Paraguay, and northern Argentina became a vast settlement of Indian missions under Portuguese and Spanish Jesuit control.

São Paulo also attracted Portuguese settlers seeking their fortunes in the region. Since few Portuguese women accompanied these adventurers, the men mated with local Indian women, rapidly creating a large mixed-race population known as *mamelucos*. The *mamelucos* became the dominant racial group of early southern Brazil. They were as skilled in using European technology, such as guns, as they were in using native implements or weapons, such as the bow and arrow, and were as likely to speak Portuguese as an Indian language.

Convinced that Portuguese America must have the same wealth of gold, silver, and precious gems that was being found in Spanish America, the *mamelucos* organized themselves in bands to explore the interior. On horseback, by foot, and in riverboats, they explored and settled vast reaches of inner Brazil. Organized like medieval troops around a *bandeira*, or flag, these groups came themselves to be called *bandeiras*, and their ventures into the interior were known as *entradas* (entries). Eventually, the frontiersmen who joined these groups came to be known as *bandeirantes* and, since they originated from São Paulo, they were also identified as *paulistas*. A famed *bandeirante* noted for his pursuit of precious gems was Fernão Dias, the so-called Emerald Hunter.

A crucial problem of colonial Brazil was an insufficient labor supply for its plantations. The most profitable crop grown in the colony was sugar. The preferred source of labor for sugar plantations was slaves from Africa. Indians as slaves were considered less satisfactory than Africans. However, shortages of African slaves grew in early seventeenth century Brazil because of Dutch occupation (1630-1654) of the northeast of the country. At the same time, southern Portuguese Brazil experienced a growth of sugar and wheat cultivation, which in turn increased the demand for slave labor. As a result of the simultaneous growth in demand and lack of supply of African slaves, the Portuguese turned to the native population for forced labor. Hunting Indians in order to enslave them became a growing economic objective of the *bandeiras*, and the Indians held in Jesuit missions became coveted and easy targets.

A standard *bandeira* consisted of several hundred men, including a few dozen Europeans, many more *mamelucos*, and often a majority of Indians, who were accustomed to a warrior life and enslaving each other. These bands traveled using the many rivers that coursed from São Paulo, especially westward and southward. Along the banks of these rivers, the *paulistas* would raid Portuguese Jesuit *aldeias* and Spanish Jesuit *reducciones*. The greatest concentration of Indians was in Paraguay, which during the colonial period included much of what is today the central area of the Southern Cone countries of South America. The Jesuits estimated that several

hundred thousand Indians were taken from the reservations in raids over a period of decades. In 1629, one of the most formidable of the *bandeiras* raided an area known as Guaira, east of the central Paraná River. Headed by a *paulista* official, António Raposo Tavares, it consisted of more than five dozen whites, almost a thousand *mamelucos*, and two thousand Indians.

The Jesuits vehemently opposed these raids. A leading voice of this opposition was a rising young Brazilian Jesuit orator, Father António Vieira. Having significant influence in the courts of Europe, the Jesuits obtained numerous royal and papal condemnations of the enslavement of Indians. Since an Indian labor force was vital to frontier economic activity, *paulista* hostility to the Jesuits was equally vehement. This hostility culminated in June, 1640, when a new papal bull was announced condemning the enslavement of Indians.

In response to the bull, the municipal councils of São Paulo and São Vicente, supported by the populace and other clergy, drove the Jesuits from the cities. By August, all Jesuits were evacuated from the region. The expulsions stayed in effect until 1642 in Santos and 1653 in São Paulo. Crucial to reversing the expulsions was the reduced pressure during the 1640's for Indian enslavement. During this period, Portugal regained control of its slave-trading posts in Africa, and this source of slaves, to which the Jesuits were much less opposed, restored a steady labor supply to Brazil.

SIGNIFICANCE

The expulsion of the Jesuits by the *paulistas* was brief but highlighted a dramatic socioeconomic development in colonial Brazil. Slave labor had grown to be of such vital importance to the colony that its economic necessity took priority over any moral or cultural considerations. Over the course of the seventeenth and eighteenth centuries, Brazil would become the largest importer of African slaves of any country in the Americas or in history.

The drive of the *bandeirantes* for mineral wealth and territorial dominance became a vital force in determining the borders of Brazil, eventually making it the largest country in South America. Tavares led an expedition of thousands of miles from 1648 to 1652 that crossed westward to Paraguay, arched along the eastern edge of the Andes, and then coursed down the Amazon to the mouth of the river.

The most consequential *entrada* occurred in 1695, when a son-in-law of Fernão Dias discovered gold in central Brazil. This incident led, during the next century, to the largest discoveries of gold in the world. The dis-

1640's

covery of gold and diamonds caused a massive influx of prospectors, increasing the population of Brazil tenfold during the eighteenth century. Brazil became a greater economic power than Portugal, its mother country. The nation's wealth of precious minerals prompted the greatest migration in history of slave labor from Africa and became the source of capital to help fund the Industrial Revolution in Britain.

—*Edward A. Riedinger*

FURTHER READING

Cohen, Thomas M. *The Fire of Tongues: António Vieira and the Missionary Church in Brazil and Portugal.* Stanford, Calif.: Stanford University Press, 1998. Examines sermons, letters, and oratory of the greatest Brazilian Jesuit opponent of slavery.

Goodman, Edward J. *The Explorers of South America.* Norman: University of Oklahoma Press, 1992. Places the early colonial frontier explorations of the *bandeirantes* within the context of other frontiersmen in South America and later types of scientific exploration on the continent.

Hemming, John. *Red Gold: The Conquest of the Brazilian Indians.* Cambridge, Mass.: Harvard University Press, 1978. Classic work in English on Portuguese colonial contact with and subordination of native populations of Brazil.

Moog, Clodomir Vianna. *Bandeirantes and Pioneers.* New York: G. Braziller, 1964. Classic work in English on the frontiersmen of the Brazilian interior, comparing and contrasting them to pioneers of the American West.

Morse, Richard M., ed. *The Bandeirantes: The Historical Role of the Brazilian Pathfinders.* New York: Knopf, 1965. Collection of articles indicating the scope of *paulista* frontiersmen in the geographic, historic, and cultural development of Brazil.

SEE ALSO: 17th cent.: Europe Endorses Slavery; Dec., 1601: Dutch Defeat the Portuguese in Bantam Harbor; 1608: Jesuits Found Paraguay; 1619-c. 1700: The Middle Passage to American Slavery; Oct., 1625-1637: Dutch and Portuguese Struggle for the Guinea Coast; 1630's-1694: Slaves Resist Europeans at Palmares; 1630-1660's: Dutch Wars in Brazil; Aug. 26, 1641-Sept., 1648: Conquest of Luanda; 1644-1671: Ndongo Wars; 1654: Portugal Retakes Control of Brazil; Feb. 13, 1668: Spain Recognizes Portugal's Independence; Beginning 1680's: Guerra dos Bárbaros; Early 1690's: Brazilian Gold Rush.

RELATED ARTICLES in *Great Lives from History: The Seventeenth Century, 1601-1700:* Frederick Henry; Piet Hein; John IV; António Vieira.

November 3, 1640-May 15, 1641
BEGINNING OF ENGLAND'S LONG PARLIAMENT

The opening months of the Long Parliament offered Charles I and his opponents a final opportunity for a peaceful resolution of their differences through compromise. Unfortunately, they failed, and England was soon plunged into civil war.

LOCALE: London, England
CATEGORIES: Government and politics; laws, acts, and legal history

KEY FIGURES
Charles I (1600-1649), king of England, r. 1625-1649
John Pym (1584-1643), leader of the Long Parliament
First Earl of Strafford (Thomas Wentworth; 1593-1641), chief military adviser of King Charles before the outbreak of the English Civil Wars
John Hampden (1595-1643), Pym's "lieutenant" and his staunchest supporter in Parliament

Sir Henry Vane the Younger (1613-1662), member of Parliament, supporter of Pym, and negotiator of the Solemn League and Covenant
William Laud (1573-1645), archbishop of Canterbury, 1633-1645

SUMMARY OF EVENT
In 1637, at the urging of William Laud, the high church archbishop of Canterbury, Charles I attempted to impose a new Anglican prayer book, modeled after the Book of Common Prayer, on the Kirk (church) of Scotland. The Kirk was Presbyterian and Calvinist in character and was opposed to the overt ceremonialism of the new book. The Scots were a factious nation, but the issue of the so-called Scottish Prayer Book united them. The Presbyterian clergy and Scottish nobility led their countrymen in endorsing a covenant that rejected the reforms imposed upon them by the king and Laud. Their defiance

led to the First Bishops' War against King Charles in 1639.

A staunch believer in absolutism and divine right monarchy, Charles I had, from the day he took office, found the advice of Parliament irritating and its interference with what he considered his prerogatives intolerable. Thus, in 1629, he had dissolved Parliament, and he had resolved to govern his realm without calling another one. This decision required the strictest economy, however, because only Parliament was capable of instituting new taxes.

England's role in European affairs was minimal. Except in Ireland, there was no standing army, and the navy received only the barest minimum of support. When the Scots prepared to invade England, the king had the county militia units as his only ready military force, and they refused to fight outside the borders of their respective counties. Charles I was forced to open negotiations with his rebellious Scottish subjects, concluding the Pacification of Berwick in June of 1639. Neither side was willing to fulfill the terms of the treaty, however, creating the possibility of another war early in 1640. Charles could not afford to raise an army to fight such a war without more taxes. Reluctantly, he called Parliament for the first time in eleven years, in a session since known as the Short Parliament. The Short Parliament met from April 13 until May 5, but the House of Commons repeatedly answered the king's demands for money with conditions of its own. Charles dissolved Parliament and had a number of his opponents arrested.

Thomas Wentworth, earl of Strafford and lord lieutenant of Ireland, urged Charles I to use the Irish army he had created against the Scots. The king sought financial aid from Spain, France, and the pope, but with no success. Meanwhile, the Scots seized the English city of Newcastle. With the Scots demanding £850 a day for the maintenance of their forces and public sentiment for the Scottish cause growing daily, Charles I had no choice but to call the fifth Parliament of his reign. The Long Parliament opened its first session on November 3, 1640. It would not be dissolved until 1660.

At the urging of the king, and with his solemn promise of protection, Strafford hurried to London to arrest the leaders of the House of Commons. John Pym, the leader of the parliamentary opposition to royal power, had no doubts of Strafford's intentions, and he countered the king's strategy by beginning impeachment proceedings against the earl. Charged with high treason, Strafford was arrested and held in the Tower of London. Another supposed traitor, Archbishop Laud, soon joined him

Thomas Wentworth, earl of Strafford, Charles I's chief military adviser, attempted to arrest the leaders of the Long Parliament. Instead, the earl was imprisoned and ultimately executed as a result of a parliamentary Bill of Attainder. (R. S. Peale and J. A. Hill)

there. Strafford was charged with advising the king to use the Irish army to subdue England. The earl countered that he meant Scotland, not England. The testimony of two witnesses was necessary to gain a conviction for treason, but there was only one witness to the alleged statement concerning the Irish army, Sir Henry Vane the Elder, a bitter enemy of Strafford.

Vane's notes on the conversation had been destroyed on the order of the king, but there were copies made by Vane's son, Sir Henry Vane the Younger, and they were permitted to stand as the second witness. Treason could be committed only against the king, however, and Strafford maintained that he was acting on the orders of Charles I. The trial promised to be a lengthy one until, over the protests of Pym and John Hampden, a Bill of Attainder was introduced against Strafford. It required no witnesses and no proof, merely a majority vote to convict. Thus began an often-acrimonious debate that dragged on for months.

On February 8, 1641, the House of Commons began to debate the Root and Branch Petition, which bore fif-

1640's

teen thousand signatures. It called for the complete abolition of episcopacy. When a Root and Branch Bill was introduced in the Commons, one of its sponsors was Oliver Cromwell, who would play a pivotal role in the English Civil Wars and the brief replacement of the monarchy by a republic during the Interregnum from 1649 to 1660. Opposition to the bill was so strong in both houses that it was temporarily dropped. The Root and Branch Bill caused some members to reconsider their opposition to the king, and slowly a Royalist faction began to form in both houses.

In the midst of the Strafford debate, the House of Commons passed the Triennial Act on February 16, 1641. Designed to protect its members from royal reprisals, it provided for parliamentary elections without royal assent. It had already been resolved that Parliament could not be dissolved without its consent. Charles I capitulated on both counts and offered no resistance when the prerogative courts, which had been one of the main supports of his regime, were abolished. The other expedients that had provided him with revenue during the eleven years he had governed England without a Parliament—including levying ship money, or money to support the navy, from landlocked counties—were declared illegal. Those who been punished for violating these laws were released from prison or recompensed by Parliament. Meanwhile, the king and his closest advisers desperately sought help from abroad, but with little success. Charles even married his eldest daughter, Mary, to William of Orange, the future stadtholder of the Netherlands and future king of England as William III (r. 1689-1702), in the hope of gaining support from that quarter.

Strafford defended himself with great courage, but he was ultimately condemned to death. Charles I could have pardoned him, but the rumor that he intended to do so provoked riots in London. Fearing for the safety of his family, the king capitulated to the pressure of Pym. Strafford was executed on May 12, 1641, the victim of a judicial murder. Charles I never forgave himself for what he came to see as the rank betrayal of a loyal servant. The public rejoicing in response to the earl's death and the Parliamentary tactics employed to accomplish it seemed to stiffen the king's resolve to resist any further encroachments on what he considered his prerogatives. Charles I began to intrigue in earnest with anyone and everyone who might rid him of Pym and his gang of murderers. The time for moderation and compromise had ended. Fifteen months later, England was torn apart by civil war.

SIGNIFICANCE

The Long Parliament was one of the most important episodes in the evolution of the English concept of representative government. In the seventeenth century, while continental legislative bodies were vanishing, Parliament and especially the House of Commons stood firm against the pretensions of royal absolutism personified by Charles I. Although during the Civil Wars and the Commonwealth the legislature would come under the control of zealots and extremists, their excesses could not erase the achievements of Pym and his colleagues during the first year of the Long Parliament. By May, 1641, Parliament was firmly established as the equal partner of the monarch in governing the realm.

—*Clifton W. Potter, Jr.*

FURTHER READING

Aylmer, G. E. *Rebellion or Revolution? England, 1640-1660.* New York: Oxford University Press, 1986. A study of the transformation of England between the Long Parliament and the Restoration, this work is well written and contains extensive notes and a very useful bibliography.

Brunton, Douglas, and Donald H. Pennington. *Members of the Long Parliament.* Reprint. North Haven, Conn.: Archon Books, 1968. Although in print for more than fifty years, this work remains the standard work on the subject.

Jansson, Maija, ed. *Proceedings in the Opening Session of the Long Parliament: House of Commons.* 3 vols. Rochester, N.Y.: University of Rochester Press, 2000. The definitive work on the initial session of the Long Parliament. It is the standard by which all future books on this critical moment in England's history must be judged.

MacLachlan, Alastair. *The Rise and Fall of Revolutionary England: An Essay on the Fabrication of Seventeenth-Century History.* New York: St. Martin's Press, 1996. Essentially a study of the controversy that has raged over the historiography of the period in the late twentieth and early twenty-first century.

Woolrych, Austin. *Britain in Revolution, 1625-1660.* New York: Oxford University Press, 2002. This is an excellent synthesis of the histories of the various components that composed Great Britain in the seventeenth century.

SEE ALSO: Dec. 18, 1621: The Great Protestation; May 6-June 7, 1628: Petition of Right; Mar., 1629-

1640: "Personal Rule" of Charles I; Mar.-June, 1639: First Bishops' War; 1642-1651: English Civil Wars; Aug. 17-Sept. 25, 1643: Solemn League and Covenant; Dec. 6, 1648-May 19, 1649: Establishment of the English Commonwealth; Dec. 16, 1653-Sept. 3, 1658: Cromwell Rules England as Lord Protector; May, 1659-May, 1660: Restoration of Charles II;

1688-1702: Reign of William and Mary; Nov., 1688-Feb., 1689: The Glorious Revolution.

RELATED ARTICLES in *Great Lives from History: The Seventeenth Century, 1601-1700:* Charles I; Oliver Cromwell; William Laud; Mary II; John Pym; First Earl of Strafford; Sir Henry Vane the Younger; William III.

January 14, 1641
CAPTURE OF MALACCA

The capture of the Portuguese-controlled Malayan port of Malacca by the Dutch allowed the small but powerful European nation to dominate European trade with Southeast Asia and ended Portugal's monopoly on trade in the Indian Ocean.

LOCALE: Malacca, Malay Peninsula (now Melaka, Malaysia)

CATEGORIES: Expansion and land acquisition; trade and commerce; transportation; wars, uprisings, and civil unrest; colonization

KEY FIGURES

Minne Williemson Kaartokoe (fl. early seventeenth century), Dutch captain

Manuel de Sousa Coutinho (d. 1641), Portuguese governor of Malacca

Adrian Antonissoon (fl. early seventeenth century), Dutch sergeant major

Abdul Jalil Shah III (1590-1677), sultan of Johore, r. 1623-1677

SUMMARY OF EVENT

Located on the southwest coast of what is today mainland Malaysia, the port of Malacca (or Melaka) was founded early in the fourteenth century, according to legend by a prince of a once-powerful empire on the large island of Sumatra. The port's deep waters and its strategic location on what would become known as the Strait of Malacca, separating the Malay Peninsula from Sumatra, ensured that it would share in the rich commerce passing among India, China, and the East Indies. Its position near the mouth of the Malacca River also ensured it a share of the trade in tin being mined inland.

Malacca became the largest city in Southeast Asia by the time Portuguese explorer Vasco da Gama entered the Indian Ocean in 1497. The militarily superior Portuguese were determined to control the rich spice trade of the Indian Ocean, and one of da Gama's successors,

Afonso de Albuquerque, laid siege to the city in 1511. The Portuguese quickly overwhelmed the Malay forces, beginning a heavy-handed and largely disruptive occupation that would last for 130 years. By the early seventeenth century, however, the aggressive Dutch East India Company (Verenigde Oost-Indische Compagnie) was contesting Portuguese control of the region and its trade and, in some cases, enlisting the aid of Portugal's Malay enemies.

Dutch designs on Malacca date from 1606. In May of that year, Admiral Cornelis Matelieff de Jonge concluded a treaty with the nearby Malay kingdom of Johore (Johor), whose ruling family had once controlled Malacca. Under the pact, the sultan agreed to allow the Dutch to remain in Malacca if they drove out the hated Portuguese. That summer, the admiral laid siege to the city, but the arrival of a fleet under the command of the viceroy of the Portuguese colony of Goa in India frustrated his plans.

The Dutch made further vain attempts on Malacca in 1608, in 1615, and throughout the 1620's. A blockade in 1633 also proved unsuccessful, but by the mid-1630's, the Dutch had assumed virtual control of the strait itself. In 1636, they managed to sink several Portuguese ships in Malacca's harbor, and in June of 1640, under the direction of Sergeant Major Adrian Antonissoon, they began a long and eventually successful siege of the Portuguese-controlled port. Although they had failed to obtain help from one enemy of the Portuguese, the sultan of Aceh in Sumatra, the Dutch were assisted by another: the sultan of Johore, Abdul Jalil Shah III.

Malacca, whose population then numbered about 20,000, was defended by 250 to 350 Portuguese soldiers and 2,000 to 3,000 Asian troops under the command of its governor, Manuel de Sousa Coutinho. The city's main fortress, known as A Famosa (the famous), had been built more than a century before atop St. Paul's Hill and was guarded by four bastion towers, a series of walls almost 8 feet (2.4 meters) thick, and a keep tower, or dungeon, 118 feet (36 meters) high. Its walls enclosed a governor's palace, a school, a bishop's palace, five churches, the houses of several religious orders, a prison, two hospitals, and a number of administrative buildings. One side of the fortress lay along the Malacca River, allowing for easy provisioning during siege, and two wells assured a supply of water. Toward the end of the sixteenth century Portuguese armaments included seventy cannon and fifty smaller guns.

At the onset of the siege, Dutch sergeant major Antonissoon had twelve large ships, six smaller sloops, and some fifteen hundred men under his command. In July of 1640, the sultan of Johore supplied significant reinforcements: a fleet of forty ships and another fifteen hundred men. Antonissoon landed his men north of Malacca near the settlement of Tranquerah and drove the settlement's Portuguese defenders into the walls of A Famosa. The Dutch were then able to set up sixteen cannon and bombard the city. At the same time the Johorese maintained a blockade of the harbor and destroyed the crops growing in the surrounding fields, denying food to the city's defenders.

Under such siege conditions, starvation spread throughout Malacca, reducing its surviving inhabitants to eating cats, rats, and, in some cases, the bodies of their fallen comrades. Sickness broke out among both the Portuguese and the Dutch, with the Dutch losing Antonissoon and two successors. Finally, on January 14, 1641, under the direction of Admiral Minne Williemson Kaartokoe, the Dutch crossed the shallow Leleh River south of the city and succeeded in storming the bastion of São Domingo. The other bastions followed in quick succession, and Governor Sousa, himself gravely ill, surrendered. He died two days later and was buried with military honors by the Dutch victors.

Under the Portuguese, Malacca had been attacked twenty-four times, but this was the only occasion in which its massive walls had been breached. Most Portuguese buildings had been completely destroyed, and the fortress was in ruins. The siege had resulted directly or indirectly in the death of some seven thousand soldiers, sailors, and civilians, including fifteen hundred Dutch troops.

SIGNIFICANCE

The Dutch conquest of Malacca was a pivotal event in the history of Southeast Asia. It spelled the end of Portuguese domination of trade in the Indian Ocean and signaled Dutch ascendancy throughout the region. Al-

though for a time Portuguese traders redirected their efforts toward other ports, they had already lost momentum to their European rival.

More important, however, the Dutch conquest of Malacca resulted in further weakening of the city itself and in thwarting wider Malay aspirations. The sultan of Johore had, perhaps naïvely, expected the Dutch to turn over Malacca to his control, but found that the port had simply traded one master for another. Most Portuguese inhabitants of Malacca departed for Portuguese settlements in India and Ceylon (now called Sri Lanka), and many Indian Hindus, who had collaborated with the Portuguese and so were distrusted by the Dutch, left as well. Soon after the Portuguese capitulation, a Dutch inspector recorded Malacca's population at a mere 2,150, scarcely more than one-tenth of its size under the Portuguese. In a 1678 report to his superiors, the city's Dutch governor cited a population of only 5,000.

Although Malacca eventually rebounded, the Dutch East India Company showed little interest in developing the Malay port, concentrating its resources instead on its new headquarters at Batavia (now called Jakarta) on the island of Java in Indonesia. Ultimately, the Dutch would prove as harmful as the Portuguese to Malacca and the Malay world.

—Grove Koger

FURTHER READING

Hoyt, Sarnia Hayes. *Old Malacca*. New York: Oxford University Press, 1993. A brief history, with successive chapters dealing specifically with the Portuguese and Dutch periods. Includes color and black-and-white illustrations, maps, and a bibliography.

Lewis, Dianne. *Jan Compagnie in the Straits of Malacca, 1641-1795*. Athens: Ohio University Center for International Studies, 1995. Lewis emphasizes the aftermath of Dutch conquest and occupation. Includes notes, appendices, a glossary, and a substantial bibliography.

Longmire, R. A. "Malacca and the Throat of Venice." *Asian Affairs* 15 (1984): 179-185. A substantial review article discussing Sandhu and Wheatley's 1983 book on Malacca.

Prakash, Om. "The Portuguese and the Dutch in Asian Maritime Trade: A Comparative Analysis." In *Merchants, Companies, and Trade: Europe and Asia in the Early Modern Era*, edited by Sushil Chaudhury and Michel Morineau. New York: Cambridge University Press, 1999. An overview contrasting the Asian mercantile practices of the two nations.

Sandhu, Kernial Singh, and Paul Wheatley, eds. *Melaka: The Transformation of a Malay Capital, c. 1400-1980*. New York: Oxford University Press, 1983. The standard work on the city, although the Portuguese period is slighted. Includes black-and-white and color illustrations and an extensive bibliography.

SEE ALSO: 17th cent.: Age of Mercantilism in Southeast Asia; 17th cent.: The Pepper Trade; Dec., 1601: Dutch Defeat the Portuguese in Bantam Harbor; Mar. 20, 1602: Dutch East India Company Is Founded;

1606-1674: Europeans Settle in India; Apr. 29, 1606: First European Contact with Australia; 1609: Bank of Amsterdam Invents Checks; Oct., 1625-1637: Dutch and Portuguese Struggle for the Guinea Coast; 1639-1640: British East India Company Establishes Fort Saint George; Apr., 1652: Dutch Begin to Colonize Southern Africa.

RELATED ARTICLES in *Great Lives from History: The Seventeenth Century, 1601-1700:* Piet Hein; John IV; Michiel Adriaanszoon de Ruyter; Abel Janszoon Tasman; Maarten Tromp; Zheng Chenggong.

August 26, 1641-September, 1648
CONQUEST OF LUANDA

Luanda, a major outpost for slave-trading in Angola, southwest Africa, was founded by the Portuguese to supply labor primarily for their sugar plantations in Brazil. The Dutch occupied northeast Brazil from 1630 to 1654, and from 1641 to 1648 they held the Angolan slave trade.

LOCALE: Luanda Island and Ndongo kingdom (now west-central Angola)

CATEGORIES: Wars, uprisings, and civil unrest; colonization; trade and commerce; social issues and reform

KEY FIGURES

John Maurice of Nassau (1604-1679), principal governor of New Holland, organized Dutch conquest of Luanda

Salvador Correia de Sá e Benevides (1594-1688), Brazilian-born governor for Portugal in Brazil, who led reconquest of Luanda

João de Almeida (1571-1653), principal adviser to Sá e Benevides

SUMMARY OF EVENT

In the fifteenth century the Portuguese steadily explored the west coast of Africa, seeking a monopoly route to the riches of Asia. However, they found much wealth along the African coast itself, including gold, ivory, and slaves. Along the Guinea coast in the north, south to the Congo River, they established fortifications and trading posts. Luanda Island was a key location to them, and so they occupied it in 1575.

Luanda is situated off the coast of northwest Angola, south of the Congo River. Near the mouth of the Cuanza River, the Portuguese formed Luanda as a commercial

and transportation nexus for the slave trade from the interior of Angola. The Portuguese earlier had established a prospering slave trade through the Congo River. Into this region they introduced food crops from Brazil, including cassava, which would become the starch staple of the southern African continent. Local kings and chieftains amassed wealth by supplying the slave trade, allowing them to purchase European luxury goods and contract European artisans and craftsmen. Portuguese Baroque buildings emerged over the landscape of the Guinea coast and in the Congo and Cuanza valleys.

As Brazilian sugar plantations became ever more important economically, the demand mounted for slaves to supply labor, especially from Angola. Although Portugal had led the exploration of Africa and the Americas, it was ill-equipped to hold its position. Other countries increasingly coveted their possessions. The Dutch were key competitors of the Portuguese. Portugal, a principal but weak ally of Spain, the most bitter Dutch enemy, became easy prey for the growing maritime power of the Netherlands. Wherever the Portuguese maintained colonies—in Brazil, Africa, or Asia—the Dutch succeeded during the early part of the seventeenth century in capturing and occupying parts of them. Most spectacularly, the Dutch succeeded in occupying the northeast of Brazil from 1630 to 1654, establishing their capital at Recife, Pernambuco, and naming the region New Holland.

The Dutch wanted Brazil's sugar plantations, but for the plantations to function, they needed the slave labor the Portuguese obtained from Africa. To this end, therefore, the Dutch descended along the coast of West Africa. In the first decades of the seventeenth century, they wrested dominance of the African gold, slave, and ivory

1640's

393

trade from the Portuguese along the Guinea, or upper, coast. In both Brazil and Africa, Dutch operations functioned as part of a monopoly trading corporation, the Dutch West India Company. It was the military and naval forces of this entity that had conquered and occupied Dutch Brazil and that sought slave labor for the sugar plantations on the other side of the Atlantic Ocean.

In May of 1641, Count John Maurice of Nassau, principal governor of New Holland, mounted a Dutch expedition that successfully captured and occupied Luanda. The force of three thousand men in twenty-one ships was led by Cornelis Jol (d. 1641), the peg-legged Dutch commander also known as Houtebeen (wooden leg). The island of Luanda fronted a bay on the mainland, where the city of São Paulo was located. A short peninsula jutted from the eastern edge of the bay, where the Portuguese had built two fortifications. The Dutch landed on August 25 between the two forts to prevent Portuguese firepower from reaching them. Panicked, the Portuguese abandoned the forts and the city overnight, so the next morning the Dutch were able to enter São Paulo unopposed. The Portuguese fled up the Cuanza River, holding up primarily in two fortifications.

For the next seven years the Portuguese held out, though they were constantly besieged by an alliance of the Dutch with African troops of the Kongo and Matamba kingdoms. The Matamba were commanded by their notorious leader, Queen Njinga (r. 1624-1663). The crucial supply of slaves for Portuguese Brazil was soon cut off. Portugal made futile attempts to rescue its besieged colonists. However, a decisive reversal of the Luanda defeat occurred only with the determination of Portuguese Brazilian landowners to regain their African labor supply.

The king of Portugal, John IV, and the Portuguese governor-general of Brazil persuaded the governor of Rio de Janeiro, Salvador Correia de Sá e Benevides, to lead a joint Brazilian-Portuguese expedition in 1648 to retake Luanda. As throughout his life, he was advised in his strategies and planning for the Angola expedition by Father João de Almeida. Financed and supported more by Brazilian funds and troops than by those of Portugal, Sá e Benevides left Rio de Janeiro in May, 1648, with one thousand men on more than a dozen ships.

In August, Sá e Benevides stationed his squadron opposite the Dutch-occupied fortifications of São Paulo. Before dawn of August 18, the Portuguese attacked these strongholds but were brutally driven back. It seemed as if they were defeated, but it was the Dutch who raised the white flag of surrender. Some of their largest cannon exploded during the defense. Aware of their vulnerability, they also thought the Portuguese had more troops because Sá e Benevides had placed stuffed dummies (for soldiers) on his ship.

The Portuguese were quick to round up not only the Dutch opponents in the city but also those arriving from the interior to support them. By the beginning of September, the Portuguese had exiled from Angola almost all the Dutch occupiers and relieved, at the last hour, the besieged Portuguese in the interior. They then began to subdue the indigenous allies of the Dutch, banishing Queen Njinga to the eastern interior. As governor-general of Angola, Sá e Benevides soon resumed the slave trade to Brazil, where the Dutch were to be definitively removed six years later, in 1654.

SIGNIFICANCE

With their defeat at Luanda, the Dutch not only failed to acquire a stable labor supply for their sugar plantations in Dutch Brazil but shortly thereafter also lost their Brazilian possessions. They were, however, able to hold their victories against the Portuguese in Southeast Asia, developing the colony of Indonesia.

The victory of the Portuguese at Luanda demonstrated the power of indigenous Brazilian forces to act outside their country in their own interests and on behalf of Portugal. This action is often considered the initial phase in forming a Brazilian national character. It also represents the role Pernambuco would develop in the forefront of provincial leadership in Brazil in the following centuries.

Securing Angola meant that for the next two centuries Portugal would become the supplier of more than one million slaves for Brazil. They were the crucial force in exploiting the wealth of the gold rush in Brazil during the eighteenth century. The victory at Luanda meant that Brazil would become demographically and culturally the most African-influenced country in Latin America. Since these slaves came from Bantu-speaking nations, the victory further meant that Bantu linguistic, religious, and sociocultural characteristics would become a paramount feature of Afro-Brazilian culture. Like few military victories in history, Luanda assured a consequent massive, forced, transoceanic migration from one continent that would definitively determine the character and future of another.

—*Edward A. Riedinger*

FURTHER READING

Bender, Gerald J. *Angola Under the Portuguese: The Myth and the Reality.* Trenton, N.J.: African World

Press, 2004. Bender investigates the myths and realities of racism in Portuguese policies.

Boxer, Charles R. *The Dutch Seaborne Empire, 1600-1800*. New York: Knopf, 1965. A classic account of the rise of the Dutch maritime empire in competition with Portugal.

_____. *Salvador de Sá and the Struggle for Brazil and Angola, 1602-1686*. London: Athlone Press, 1952. A definitive biography in English of the Brazilian-born Portuguese colonial administrator who conquered Luanda from the Dutch.

Curto, José C. *Enslaving Spirits: The Portuguese-Brazilian Alcohol Trade at Luanda and Its Hinterland, c. 1550-1830*. Leiden, the Netherlands: Brill, 2004. Chapter 3 details trading operations in Luanda and the interior of Angola from 1550 to 1649.

Egerton, F. Clement C. "The Beginnings." In *Angola in Perspective: Endeavor and Achievement in Portuguese West Africa*. London: Routledge & Kegan Paul, 1973. This chapter traces the origins of Angola from the first settlement by Portugal on Luanda to its settlement of the interior, occupying Mbundu territory.

Price, J. L. *The Dutch Republic in the Seventeenth Century*. New York: St. Martin's Press, 2002. A concise overview of the internal economic, political, and socio-cultural issues propelling the international expansion of the Netherlands in the seventeenth century.

Russell-Wood, A. J. R. *A World on the Move: The Portuguese in Africa, Asia, and America, 1415-1808*. New York: St. Martin's Press, 1992. This work examines Portuguese king John's efforts to recover and develop the Portuguese Empire.

Schwarz-Bart, Simone. "Ana de Sousa Nzinga: The Queen Who Resisted the Portuguese Conquest." In *Ancient African Queens*. Vol. 1 in *In Praise of Black Women*. Madison: University of Wisconsin Press, 2001. This article reviews the life of Njinga as an early Angolan hero of anticolonialist resistance.

SEE ALSO: c. 1625: Formation of the Kuba Kingdom; Oct., 1625-1637: Dutch and Portuguese Struggle for the Guinea Coast; 1630-1660's: Dutch Wars in Brazil; 1644-1671: Ndongo Wars; Mid-17th cent.: Emergence of the Guinea Coast States; Apr., 1652: Dutch Begin to Colonize Southern Africa; Late 17th cent.: Rise of Buganda.

RELATED ARTICLES in *Great Lives from History: The Seventeenth Century, 1601-1700:* Piet Hein; John IV; Njinga.

October 23, 1641-1642
ULSTER INSURRECTION

Native Irish Gaelic Catholics in the northern province of Ulster rebelled against the English crown and against the Scottish, Welsh, and English Protestant settlers who had taken their lands. Thousands of settlers were massacred by the rebels, and many Catholics died as well in subsequent retaliatory massacres that began an entrenched pattern of religious and nationalist violence in northern Ireland.

LOCALE: Ulster, Ireland (now in Ireland and Northern Ireland)

CATEGORIES: Wars, uprisings, and civil unrest; religion and theology; government and politics

KEY FIGURES

Rory O'More (c. 1592-in or after 1666), leader of the Ulster rebellion

Charles I (1600-1649), king of England, Scotland, and Ireland, r. 1625-1649

Sir Phelim Roe O'Neill (1603-1653), Ulster rebel who was regarded as "chief of his name"

Conor Maguire (d. 1644), Dublin-based conspirator in the 1641 insurrection

James Butler (1610-1688), twelfth earl and first marquis of Ormond and a Royalist, anti-Catholic leader

Owen Roe O'Neill (c. 1583-1649), cousin of Sir Phelim Roe O'Neill who served in the Spanish army

Richard Preston (fl. 1642), earl of Desmond, leader of the Old English, and leader of the Catholic confederacy

SUMMARY OF EVENT

Before the Protestant Reformation, the population of Ireland was made up primarily of two distinct groups, Gaelic Irish and Old English. The tensions between these two groups predate the arrival of Protestantism in the

British Isles, but with the advent of the English Reformation in the 1530's, Catholic Irish nobles intensified their efforts to destroy English power in Ireland. These redoubled efforts included seeking aid from Catholic monarchs on the Continent. To the English crown, Ireland had suddenly transformed itself from a backwater to a back door, a threat to the security of the kingdom. Over the next seventy-five years, in a series of wars against various Irish chieftains, the Protestant English monarchs overwhelmed the Catholic Gaelic Irish. The native Irish nobility was displaced, and its lands were confiscated. The last bastion of native Irish resistance, Ulster, submitted to England in 1602. Ulster was left bereft of Irish leadership when the earls of Tyrone and of Tyrconnel, as well as more than one hundred other chiefs, fled to the Continent in 1607.

Feuds, local wars, intrusions by various Scottish clans, and forays by an occasional English monarch had long kept Ulster in a perpetual state of political upheaval. In a region heavily wooded and cut by bogs, rivers, and lakes, the majority of the Irish inhabitants survived through subsistence farming. Population centers were few and far apart, and familial bonds divided the region even further, as clan boundaries were established by Ulster's geographic features. In the early decades of the seventeenth century, James I of England and Scotland sought a solution to the instability of the region. He encouraged a "non-Celtic" settlement (mostly of Lowland Scots), via the Ulster Plantation, which, he trusted, would assist in transforming the Irish Irish into British Irish.

Although land grants, long-term leases, and other incentives encouraged some emigration of Lowland Scots to northern Ireland, the hoped-for large-scale influx of Scots simply did not occur. Modern estimates vary widely, ranging from ten thousand to about forty thousand Scots being established in Ulster by 1639. In addition, there were perhaps another forty thousand immigrants from Wales and northern England. It is impossible, however, to verify any number absolutely.

The presence of these settlers was widely resented by the original inhabitants, for, while the total size of the land grants (80,555 acres, or 32,600 hectares) was only 1.67 percent of the land area of Ulster, the grants were often drawn from the very best lands, which had been confiscated by the Crown from the Irish nobility. Additionally, between 1607 and 1641, large tracts of land were mortgaged, leaving many Catholic landowners near destitution. Crown policy also encouraged Protestantism and tended to disenfranchise Catholics, thereby coupling economic loss with religious and political disqualification. This resulted in a hatred that was never far below the surface.

In 1641, while Charles I was occupied with Scottish Covenanters and a recalcitrant English parliament, opponents of the new order in Ireland saw an opportunity to regain their rights. Sir Rory O'More, chief instigator of the conspiracy, met with

ULSTER INSURRECTION

= The Pale (Royalist Anglo-Irish landowners) in 1641

= Areas controlled by the Scots and Parliamentarians in 1642

Conor Maguire in Dublin in February. O'More's family was originally from the Irish midlands, and he still had widespread support in that area. He suggested that it was time to reverse the pro-English, anti-Irish trends of the preceding three decades. The conspirators hoped that Catholic help from the Continent would quickly manifest itself once a rebellion was under way, but it was clear that the initial action would have to come from the Irish themselves. The plot was developed over the next few months, additional conspirators were recruited, and October 23 was set as the date for the rising in Ulster. A simultaneous attack on Dublin Castle was also planned, for its capture would strengthen the position of the rebels.

The insurrection began on the appointed day, but it quickly went awry. In Dublin, the plot had been betrayed; the leaders, Hugh Og MacMahon and Conor Maguire, were captured, and Dublin Castle remained in royal hands. In Ulster, Sir Phelim Roe O'Neill issued a proclamation stating that the rebellion wanted only the restoration of traditional rights and that no subjects of the king were to be harmed. The situation was already out of hand, however. Although there probably was no planned massacre, insurgents methodically murdered Protestant settlers wherever possible. While there were certainly religious issues involved, this massacre was as much an effort by original Irish owners to take back their land as anything else. An estimated four thousand Protestants were murdered, and another eight thousand died from exposure after being expelled from their homesteads. Moreover, as they recovered from their initial shock, Protestants carried out retaliatory attacks on Catholics. It is impossible to say who was ultimately the more brutal in their atrocities.

When the English Civil Wars erupted in 1642, the insurrection in Ulster was reduced to a mere sideshow, albeit an important one. Both Parliament and the king viewed Ireland as an important source of soldiers and war materiel, and both were determined to control it. Because the Scots were allied with Parliament, a Scottish army was sent to protect the Protestants of Ulster. A Catholic confederacy was established at Kilkenny in May of 1642, "to defend religion and the king." Owen Roe O'Neill returned from abroad to lead the king's army in Ulster, and Richard Preston, earl of Desmond, led the Old English in the south. Support by James Butler, twelfth earl of Ormond, was also vital to Charles, for he kept most of Ireland until 1647. (Butler was rewarded for his service by being raised to marquis of Ormond in 1642, duke in the Irish peerage in 1661, and duke in the English peerage in 1682.) By 1647, however, royal military disasters in England had cost Charles his crown; they would ultimately cost him his head. In 1650, Parliamentary forces under Oliver Cromwell invaded Ireland, and, during the following two years, the Irish rebellion was finally crushed.

SIGNIFICANCE

Although Irish massacres of Scottish settlers during the English Civil Wars resulted in a siege mentality, the real foundations of the cultural differences that exist in Ulster to this day lie in the events of the rest of the seventeenth century. After the crushing of the Irish rebellion, the Cromwellian settlement confiscated and redistributed more than one-half of the land in Ireland. Following the Glorious Revolution (1688) and the Battle of the Boyne (1690), further confiscations almost completely dispossessed Gaelic and Catholic Irish leaders, and the Gaelic population at large lost most of their hope for land ownership. Tens of thousands of Scots migrated to Ireland after 1690, entrenching themselves as a distinct and separate minority in Ulster. When the group memories of earlier experiences were grafted onto this population, there ultimately resulted an Ulster Protestant nationalism, which continued to compete with Irish Catholic nationalism through the early twenty-first century.

—*William S. Brockington, Jr.*

FURTHER READING

Barnard, Toby. *Irish Protestant Ascents and Descents, 1641-1770*. Portland, Oreg.: Four Courts Press, 2004. Chapter 4 examines "The Uses of the 23rd of October 1641 and Irish Protestant Celebrations."

_____. *The Kingdom of Ireland, 1641-1760*. New York: Palgrave Macmillan, 2004. Describes Catholic attempts to gain control of Ireland in the 1640's and in subsequent years.

Beckett, J. C. *The Making of Modern Ireland, 1603-1923*. London: Faber & Faber, 1966. Provides an overview of the issues that have divided Ireland.

Canny, Nicholas. *Kingdom and Colony: Ireland in the Atlantic World, 1560-1800*. Baltimore: Johns Hopkins University Press, 1988. Canny's work discusses Ireland's role in the international conflicts of the early modern era.

Corish, P. J. "The Rising of 1641 and the Confederacy, 1641-1645." In *Early Modern Ireland, 1534-1691*. Vol. 3 in *A New History of Ireland*, edited by T. W. Moody, F. X. Martin, and F. J. Byrne. Oxford, England: Clarendon Press, 1976-2003. Corish's chapter

1640's

gives a concise summary of the events and personages involved in the insurrection.

Lecky, William Edward Hartpole. *A History of Ireland in the Eighteenth Century.* 5 vols. London: Longmans, Green, 1892. Reprint. New York: AMS Press, 1969. Volume 1 provides detailed and dispassionate analysis of the massacre of 1641.

O'Dowd, Mary. "Land and Lordship in Sixteenth- and Early Seventeenth-Century Ireland." In *Economy and Society in Scotland and Ireland, 1500-1939,* edited by Rosalind Mitchison and Peter Roebuck. Edinburgh: John Donald, 1988. Analyzes the issue of land ownership as a factor in Irish-Scottish antipathy.

Ohlmeyer, Jane H., ed. *Ireland from Independence to Occupation, 1641-1660.* New York: Cambridge University Press, 1995. Collection of essays describing how Ireland was transformed by the events of the 1640's and 1650's. Includes an essay by historian Nicholas Canny, "What Really Happened in Ireland in 1641?"

Robinson, P. S. *The Plantation of Ulster: British Settlement in an Irish Landscape, 1600-1670.* New York: St. Martin's Press, 1984. Provides significant information regarding the English, Irish, and Scottish competition for land in Ulster.

Stevenson, David. *Scottish Covenanters and Irish Confederates.* Belfast, Northern Ireland: Ulster Historical Foundation, 1981. Stevenson analyzes the insurrection in Ulster as part of the English Civil Wars.

SEE ALSO: Mar. 24, 1603: James I Becomes King of England; Mar.-June, 1639: First Bishops' War; 1642-1651: English Civil Wars; Aug. 17-Sept. 25, 1643: Solemn League and Covenant; Dec. 6, 1648-May 19, 1649: Establishment of the English Commonwealth; Dec. 16, 1653-Sept. 3, 1658: Cromwell Rules England as Lord Protector; Mar. 12-14, 1655: Penruddock's Uprising; May, 1659-May, 1660: Restoration of Charles II; May 19, 1662: England's Act of Uniformity; 1673-1678: Test Acts; Aug. 13, 1678-July 1, 1681: The Popish Plot; Apr. 4, 1687, and Apr. 27, 1688: Declaration of Liberty of Conscience; Nov., 1688-Feb., 1689: The Glorious Revolution; May 24, 1689: Toleration Act.

RELATED ARTICLES in *Great Lives from History: The Seventeenth Century, 1601-1700:* Charles I; Charles II (of England); Oliver Cromwell; James I; James II; Mary II; Rory O'More; William III.

November, 1641
MASSACHUSETTS RECOGNIZES SLAVERY

The Massachusetts Bay Colony adopted a formal code of laws known as the Body of Liberties. A provision in the code designed to set limits upon slavery in the colony indirectly granted legitimacy to the practice, thereby inaugurating the institution of slavery in the British colonies.

LOCALE: Massachusetts Bay Colony

CATEGORIES: Laws, acts, and legal history; social issues and reform; government and politics; trade and commerce

KEY FIGURES

John Cotton (1584-1652), Puritan clergyman and church leader

Nathaniel Ward (1578-1652), Puritan clergyman and lawmaker

John Winthrop (1588-1649), governor of Massachusetts, 1629-1633, 1637-1640, 1642-1644, 1646-1649

SUMMARY OF EVENT

From its outset, the Massachusetts Bay Colony endorsed the idea of unfree labor. The original colonists brought with them 180 indentured servants. Subsequent food shortages led to the surviving servants being set free in 1630. Unfree labor, however, continued on a private basis, and some white criminals were made slaves to court-appointed masters. Captives from the Pequot War of 1636-1637 were enslaved. Some of these captives were subsequently transported to a Puritan enclave off the coast of Nicaragua, and black slaves were introduced from that enclave to the Massachusetts Bay Colony. The colony, however, remained without a formal endorsement of slavery until the promulgation of a legal code called the Body of Liberties in 1641.

The Body of Liberties was controversial in many respects. It evolved out of the gradually weakening authority of Governor John Winthrop and his first Board of Assistants and the emergence of the General Court as a representative body of freemen. The document was crafted and adopted by Elizabethan men who had grown up in the age of Shakespeare and the King James Bible. They were not democrats, but they had a strong sense of destiny and a healthy fear of absolute authority. In a larger sense, the document came to reflect the classic and ancient struggle between church and state.

In 1635, the General Court had appointed a committee to draw up a body of laws codifying the rights and duties of the colonists. This committee stalled over the church-state conflict, however, and another committee was impaneled in 1636. John Cotton sat on the new committee. Cotton was a devout churchman who envisioned a government based on the theocracy of Israel and drafted a document that derived much of its authority from Scripture. Cotton did, however, believe in limitations on authority. He also resisted adopting biblical statutes wholesale. Winthrop, who was lukewarm to the entire idea, called Cotton's code "Moses his Judicialls."

Cotton's counterpart in drawing up the code was Nathaniel Ward. Ward was a Puritan with a sense of humor and a literary bent. He later penned a humorous pamphlet of observations titled *The Simple Cobler of Aggawam in America* (1647). Like most Puritans, he was a friend to strict discipline, but he also was a foe to arbitrary authority. He could agree with Winthrop and Cotton that all law was the law of God, but with a view toward local conditions and universal morality. He insisted that the code of laws for Massachusetts be based on English common law rather than on the Bible. He became the chief architect and intellectual godfather of the "Massachusetts Magna Charta," the Body of Liberties. His contribution would be a government of laws and not men. The Pequot War slowed deliberations, but by 1638, the committee had a fresh start, and by 1639, it had ordered a document that combined Cotton's and Ward's work. The final document, however, owed more to Ward than to Cotton and was adopted in November, 1641.

In many ways, the Body of Liberties was an enlightened document, and it was certainly remarkable by seventeenth century standards. A compilation of one hundred laws, the Body of Liberties, though not democratic, allowed for wide judicial discretion and for each case to be judged on its merits. It also effectively barred members of the legal profession from defending anyone for pay, and it protected married women from assault. The code addressed the liberties of servants in relatively humanitarian terms for the time: The number of lashes given to servants was limited to forty, and the capital laws were more lenient than those of England.

The distinguished historian Samuel Eliot Morison wrote that the Body of Liberties was "an enlightened body of laws and of principles that would have done credit to any commonwealth in the seventeenth century. . . ." The one problem, however, was slavery. This bold document addressed the slavery issue thus:

> There shall never be any bond slaverie, villainage or captivitie amongst us unles it be lawfull captive, taken in just warres, and such strangers as willingly selle themselves or are sold to us. And these shall have all the liberties and Christian usages which the law of God established in Israell concerning such persons doeth morally require. This exempts none from servitude who shall be judged thereto by authoritie.

Although not a ringing endorsement of slavery, the Body of Liberties nevertheless formally recognized it. Thus it opened the way for the official sanction of slavery. Later and stricter codes would formalize the institution in New England on a colony-by-colony basis.

The recognition of slavery in the Body of Liberties was at base a business decision. An early realization that the price of slaves was greater than their worth as laborers led businessmen in New England to market some of their slave cargoes to the plantation colonies farther south. Indeed, in the triangular trade of West Africa, the West Indies, and North America, the vast majority of slaves taken by New England traders ended up in the West Indies. Shrewd New England traders shipped rum, fish, and dairy products out; they imported slaves, molasses, and sugar. Those few slaves who were not dropped off in the West Indies or on Southern plantations were heavily taxed. In 1705, Massachusetts imposed a duty of £4 for each slave imported into the colony.

By 1680, Governor Simon Bradstreet estimated the number of "blacks or slaves" in the Massachusetts colony at one hundred to two hundred. Some special laws were passed restricting the movement of African Americans in white society, but the Puritans encouraged Christian conversion and honored black marriages. Northern slavery was somewhat milder than the Southern variety. Slaves needed to read and write to do their jobs. Although there were occasional isolated rebellions, the slaves benefited from the New England love for learning and the strong Puritan emphasis on marriage and family.

SIGNIFICANCE

Slavery gradually faded away in Massachusetts, perhaps because of its vague legal status. In the aftermath of the American Revolution, a national clamor for a Bill of

1640's

Rights led individual colonies to adopt their own. While none expressly forbade slavery, the institution seemed at odds with the rhetoric of fundamental human rights prevalent in the nascent United States. By 1776, the white population of Massachusetts was 343,845 and the black population was 5,249. In the census of 1790, Massachusetts was the only state in which no slaves were listed.

As John Winthrop stated,

> wee shall be as a Citty upon a Hill, the Eies of all people are uppon us; soe that if wee shall deale falsely with our god in this worke wee have undertaken and soe cause him to withdrawe his present help from us, wee shall be made a story and a by-word through the world. . . .

Despite the legalization of slavery in the Body of Liberties, slavery was never popular in Massachusetts except as incidental to trade; the slave trade was an accepted practice by seventeenth century European standards. The Puritans themselves were products of a rigorous, harsh, isolated experience. They were humanists and intellectuals with contradictions. They prized sincerity and truthfulness yet practiced repression and inhibition to steel themselves against life's ills. They had a strong element of individualism in their creed, believing that each person must face his Maker alone. Puritan humanism thus never squared with the institution of slavery.

—*Brian G. Tobin*

FURTHER READING

Franklin, John Hope, and Alfred A. Moss, Jr. *From Slavery to Freedom: A History of African Americans.* 8th ed. New York: A. A. Knopf, 2000. Classic text on the evolution of American slavery.

Miller, Perry. *Errand into the Wilderness.* Cambridge, Mass.: Belknap Press of Harvard University Press, 1984. Delves into the theological underpinnings of Puritanism.

_____, ed. *The American Puritans: Their Prose and Poetry.* New York: Columbia University Press, 1982. Includes selected writings from John Cotton, Nathaniel Ward, and John Winthrop.

Morison, Samuel Eliot. *Builders of the Bay Colony.* Boston: Northeastern University Press, 1981. Contains individual chapters on the Elizabethan architects of Massachusetts, including John Cotton, Nathaniel Ward, and John Winthrop.

Phillips, Ulrich B. *American Negro Slavery.* Baton Rouge: Louisiana State University Press, 1966. Rich in original source material about the development of slavery.

Towner, Lawrence William. *A Good Master Well Served: Masters and Servants in Colonial Massachusetts, 1620-1750.* New York: Garland, 1998. Examines the master-servant relationship in colonial Massachusetts, focusing on the living conditions and experiences of African American and white bonded servants.

Wood, Betty. *The Origins of American Slavery: The English Colonies.* New York: Hill and Wang, 1997. Explains the religious and economic rationale for the use of slave labor in English colonies. Chapter 5 focuses on slavery among the Puritans and Quakers.

SEE ALSO: 17th cent.: Europe Endorses Slavery; c. 1601-1613: Shakespeare Produces His Later Plays; 1611: Publication of the King James Bible; Beginning c. 1619: Indentured Servitude Becomes Institutionalized in America; 1619-c. 1700: The Middle Passage to American Slavery; Aug. 20, 1619: Africans Arrive in Virginia; Dec. 26, 1620: Pilgrims Arrive in North America; May, 1630-1643: Great Puritan Migration; July 20, 1636-July 28, 1637: Pequot War; Sept. 8, 1643: Confederation of the United Colonies of New England; Mar., 1661-1705: Virginia Slave Codes; June, 1686-Apr., 1689: Dominion of New England Forms.

RELATED ARTICLES in *Great Lives from History: The Seventeenth Century, 1601-1700:* John Cotton; John Winthrop.

1642 and 1644
TASMAN PROVES AUSTRALIA IS A SEPARATE CONTINENT

On his two exploratory voyages, Dutch navigator Abel Janszoon Tasman unwittingly completed the circumnavigation of Australia. He was too far off the coast, however, to confirm and then chart what was the elusive sixth continent. Because of his southerly and easterly route, he was able to find Tasmania, the South Island of New Zealand, the Tonga Islands, and the Fiji Islands.

LOCALE: New Holland (now Australia); Van Diemen's Land (now Tasmania); New Zealand; the Tonga Islands; the Fiji Islands; Batavia, Java (now Jakarta, Indonesia)

CATEGORY: Exploration and discovery

KEY FIGURES

Abel Janszoon Tasman (c. 1603-1659), Dutch navigator and explorer

Anthony van Diemen (1593-1645), governor-general of the Dutch East India Company during the time of Tasman's voyages

Frans Jacobszoon Visscher (d. 1645), Tasman's chief pilot

Jan Pieterszoon Coen (1587-1629), governor-general of the Dutch East Indies who is credited with establishing the Dutch presence in the region

SUMMARY OF EVENT

From the time they first arrived in the Pacific at the end of the sixteenth century, the Dutch had one goal in mind: profit. Whenever a ship captain reported that some coastal area did not look inviting, no one was sent out to investigate the land even more. As a result, many years passed before anyone realized that some of their sightings, which they assumed were the coastlines of various islands, were actually part of the vast continent that for centuries had been referred to as Terra Australis Incognito (now called Australia).

Those who might have ventured farther inland merely to satisfy their curiosity were discouraged by the fact that their actions were strictly regulated by the commercial enterprise called the Dutch East India Company, which was established in 1602. The company had a virtual monopoly in the area, and it dictated the movements of explorers. After arriving in Batavia (now Jakarta, Indonesia) in 1616, announcing that they had been the first to round Cape Horn at the southern tip of Africa, Dutch navigators Willem Schouten and Jacob Le Maire learned of the hostility of company officials toward anyone who ventured into the Pacific without obtaining explicit permission from company officials: The two were not believed, their ship was confiscated, and they were sent back to Holland.

Even though officials based in Indonesia at later times were no less jealous of the company's prerogatives, they understood the need to explore areas not appearing to have immediate commercial value. Jan Pieterszoon Coen, who was governor-general of the company from 1618 to 1623, not only built forts throughout Indonesia so that Dutch interests would be safeguarded but also drew up a plan to explore and chart the coastline of the area that had been called the Southland (later New Holland), which either adjoined New Guinea or lay to the south of it. However, Coen's plan was not implemented,

Dutch explorer Abel Janszoon Tasman and his crew navigated the waters off the western and southern coasts of Australia and landed at islands such as Tasmania, proving that Australia is a large land mass, previously unknown to Europeans. (Hulton|Archive by Getty Images)

401

TASMAN'S EXPLORATIONS, 1642-1644

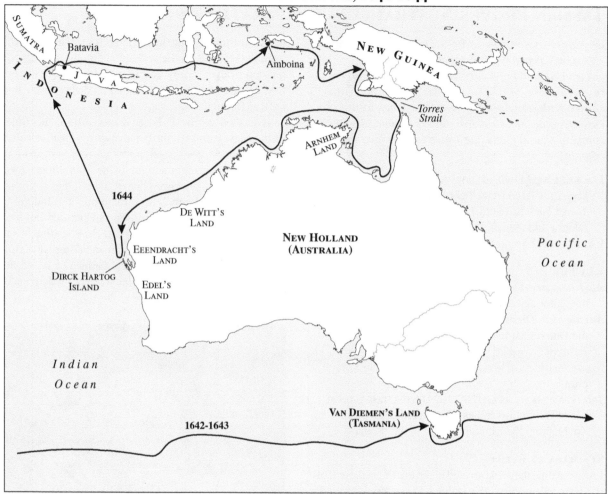

and though in the years that followed, vessels would occasionally land on one or another part of what is now Australia, it was not until after Anthony van Diemen became governor-general in 1636 that the company again became committed to a course of systematic exploration.

Van Diemen chose two men to carry out his plans: Abel Janszoon Tasman would lead the expedition, and Frans Jacobszoon Visscher would serve as chief pilot. Both were well qualified. Tasman was an experienced ship captain with an interest in exploration, and Visscher was a pilot, known for his surveying skills and for his meticulous charts and maps. In fact, the instructions van Diemen eventually formulated were based on a memoir regarding the Southland's discovery that Visscher had finished in 1642; van Diemen, though, reduced the scope

of the project. Tasman was to explore the known coastal areas of the Southland to discover and chart the location of the unknown Terra Australis, ascertain its commercial potential, and find a new route from Java to Chile (across the Pacific Ocean in South America) that would enable Dutch sea raiders to surprise and loot treasure-laden Spanish ships.

As Visscher had suggested, van Diemen instructed the expedition to start at Mauritius in the Indian Ocean off the coast of Africa, head south to about the 52d latitude, sail east to the longitude of New Guinea, and return north toward New Guinea and then east to Java along the known northern coast of Australia. Van Diemen and Tasman, at this time, had no idea that had Tasman sailed north at the longitude of New Guinea, he and his crew would have sighted the southern tip of the Australian continent. Also, Tasman had been given the option of turning north sooner and sailing along what they believed was the unexplored *eastern* coast of the landmass to find out whether or not that area was joined to New Guinea. In fact, had he taken this option, once again, he would have sighted the southern coast of the continent.

Tasman was put in charge of two ships, the *Heemskerck* and the *Zeehaen*, carrying a total of 110 men. The ships and their crew set out for Mauritius on August 14, 1642, and sailed eastward on October 8. Because of bad weather, Visscher persuaded Tasman to alter his course and sail along a latitude that was more southerly. Had he taken the second option and turned north and then east, Tasman would have become the discoverer of the south and east coasts of Australia. Instead, on November 14, the explorers were far south of the continent, and so they sighted the island now called Tasmania (the explorers had named it Van Diemen's Land in honor of the governor-general). Unfortunately, however, they decided not to investigate further; if they had sailed to the north of Van Diemen's Land, they would have found the southeastern coast of the continent they sought.

Still sailing east, they discovered New Zealand's South Island, but the hostility of the island's indigenous Maori made a landing there impossible. From South Island, the expedition turned northeast and sighted the Tonga Islands, where they spent two weeks with the islands' indigenous peoples. After sighting the Fiji Islands, they found their way back to New Guinea and finally to Batavia, arriving on June 14, 1643.

Before long, van Diemen began to plan a new expedition, even though he first was disappointed because Tasman did not explore the areas he had found. Van Diemen ordered Tasman to find out whether or not New Guinea and the Southland were connected and to look for a strait leading from the Gulf of Carpenteria, off the northern coast of the Southland, that might lead south to Van Diemen's Land. The 1644 voyage was much shorter than the voyage of 1642. After more than six months at sea, Tasman returned to Batavia and reported that he had been unsuccessful. He had not been able to make his way through the Torres Strait, which he thought was a bay, and therefore could neither confirm nor deny if New Guinea and the Southland were connected by land. Moreover, Tasman had found no outlet in the Gulf of Carpenteria.

The Amsterdam managers of the Dutch East India Company were not happy, and they soon made it clear that they did not intend to fund voyages that returned empty-handed, that is, without knowledge of new trade possibilities. To make matters worse, the death of van Diemen in 1645 silenced the only voice that could have persuaded the managers otherwise. Several years later, Tasman left the company but remained in Batavia, where he became a wealthy merchant.

SIGNIFICANCE

Although Tasman was wrong in believing that New Guinea and Van Diemen's Land were part of the Southland and that it extended to New Zealand, he knew more about the approximate location of Australia than any of his predecessors. A map of the area that he drew after his second voyage evidently became the basis of charts and globes produced by Dutch cartographers later in the seventeenth century, which were amended as new discoveries were made. However, it was not until the middle of the nineteenth century that the extent of Tasman's achievements became clear. Scholars unearthed the manuscript of Tasman's journal, which contains a large number of drawings and charts, and they also recovered the journal of one of his sailors. The publication of these documents led to the discovery of other early maps and charts, which were then used to study and confirm Tasman's cartography.

—*Rosemary M. Canfield Reisman*

FURTHER READING

Allen, Oliver E. *The Pacific Navigators*. Alexandria, Va.: Time-Life Books, 1980. One of the most accessible accounts of Tasman's voyages. Lavishly illustrated.

Clark, C. M. H. *A History of Australia*. 3 vols. London: Cambridge University Press, 1963-1978. This definitive work has a detailed account of the events that led up to the 1642 voyage, including the reasons Tasman's instructions were so self-contradictory.

Day, Alan Edwin. *Historical Dictionary of the Discovery and Exploration of Australia*. Lanham, Md.: Scarecrow Press, 2003. An excellent, detailed source, with cross-references and an extensive bibliography.

Estensen, Miriam. *Discovery: The Quest for the Great South Land*. New York: St. Martin's Press, 1999. Beginning with the speculations of the ancient Greeks, this work details the search for the sixth continent. Includes maps and illustrations.

Fischer, Steven Roger. *A History of the Pacific Islands*. New York: Palgrave, 2002. Fischer emphasizes the degree to which the Dutch East India Company guarded its monopoly of commercial ventures and exploration.

1640's

Robert, Willem C. H. *The Dutch Explorations, 1605-1756, of the North and Northwest Coast of Australia.* Amsterdam: Philo Press, 1973. Extracts from journals, logbooks, and other documents relating to the voyages of Dutch explorers of Australia. Includes original Dutch texts, edited and with English translations; a critical introduction; and notes. Also includes appendices, a bibliography, and indexes.

Sharp, Andrew. *The Voyages of Abel Janszoon Tasman.* Oxford, England: Clarendon Press, 1968. Contains Tasman's journals and charts, along with commentaries by the author. The final chapter explains how scholars came to understand the scope of Tasman's achievements.

Tasman, Abel Janszoon. *Abel Janszoon Tasman's Journal of His Discovery of Van Diemen's Land and New Zealand in 1642, with Documents Relating to His Exploration of Australia in 1644. . . .* Translated by J. de Hoop Scheffer and C. Stoffel. Amsterdam: F. Muller, 1898. A facsimile of Tasman's journal with English translation. Includes the articles "Life and Labours of Abel Janszoon Tasman" by J. E. Heeres and "Observations Made with the Compass on Tasman's Voyage" by W. van Bemmelen. Maps, illustrations.

SEE ALSO: 17th cent.: The Pepper Trade; Dec., 1601: Dutch Defeat the Portuguese in Bantam Harbor; Mar. 20, 1602: Dutch East India Company Is Founded; Beginning Spring, 1605: Dutch Dominate Southeast Asian Trade; Apr. 29, 1606: First European Contact with Australia; 1609: Bank of Amsterdam Invents Checks; Oct., 1625-1637: Dutch and Portuguese Struggle for the Guinea Coast; Jan. 14, 1641: Capture of Malacca; Aug. 26, 1641-Sept., 1648: Conquest of Luanda; Apr., 1652: Dutch Begin to Colonize Southern Africa; c. 1690: Extinction of the Dodo Bird.

RELATED ARTICLE in *Great Lives from History: The Seventeenth Century, 1601-1700:* Abel Janszoon Tasman.

1642-1651
ENGLISH CIVIL WARS

The escalating political struggle between Royalists, who supported absolute power for the English monarch, and Parliamentarians, who sought constitutional limits upon royal power, finally erupted into overt civil war. King Charles I was ultimately defeated, executed, and replaced by a commonwealth government. Although the Commonwealth was short-lived, the eventually restored monarchy was indebted to the will of Parliament, and the civil wars permanently ended British monarchs' absolutist ambitions.

LOCALE: England
CATEGORIES: Wars, uprisings, and civil unrest; government and politics

KEY FIGURES
Oliver Cromwell (1599-1658), a leader of Parliamentary forces and lord protector of England, 1653-1658
Charles I (1600-1649), king of England, r. 1625-1649
Third Earl of Essex (Robert Devereux; 1591-1646), lord general of the Parliamentary army, 1642-1645
Third Baron Fairfax (Thomas Fairfax; 1612-1671), commander in chief of Cromwell's New Model Army, 1645-1650

Prince Rupert (1619-1682), nephew of King Charles and Royalist military leader
Alexander Leslie (c. 1580-1661), commander of the Scottish Covenanters' army and first earl of Leven
Charles II (1630-1685), disenfranchised heir to the English throne and later king of England, r. 1660-1685

SUMMARY OF EVENT
The English Civil Wars, also called the English Revolution, grew out of a conflict between the Stuart monarchy and the English parliament that began almost as soon as James I was crowned in 1603. The Stuarts believed in the divine right of kings, which meant that they saw themselves as God's representatives on Earth and believed their will should therefore be absolute. England, however, had a common-law constitution that had placed limits upon the monarch's powers from the time of the Magna Carta (1215), and Parliament had a vested interest in preserving those limits and enhancing its own powers at the expense of the king. Most important in the first decades of the seventeenth century, the king was absolutely forbidden from levying new taxes upon any of his subjects. Only Parliament had the power to create new taxes, although the Stuarts could and did find creative

ways to generate revenue by expanding enforcement of existing taxes, forcing wealthy subjects to give them loans, and imprisoning those who refused their requests for money.

As soon as Charles I came to the throne in 1625, it became apparent not only that he believed he should have absolute authority but also that he lacked the tact to hide that belief from Parliament. The relationship between the legislature and the king, who had the power to call and dissolve Parliament as he saw fit, was thus adversarial from the beginning. The conflict between them intensified in 1628, when Charles I was forced to sign the Petition of Right, agreeing to limits on his powers in return for tax money, but then ignored the limits established in the document. The following year, Charles dissolved Parliament and inaugurated the period of Personal Rule (1629-1640), in which he sought to reign without a Parliament.

The period of Personal Rule came to an end when Charles's religious policies in Scotland led to the Bishops' Wars being fought there in 1639 and 1640. Lacking the funds to raise an effective English army to fight the Scots, Charles had no choice but to call a Parliament in 1640. The first,

Ultimately defeated by Parliament, King Charles I was found guilty of treason. He was beheaded on January 30, 1649. (R. S. Peale and J. A. Hill)

the so-called Short Parliament, was dissolved after less than a month, but Charles called what came to be known as the Long Parliament in November, 1640. The reinstated Parliaments refused to obey the king's will: He wanted them simply to pass the taxation bills he needed as quickly as possible. Instead, Parliament ignored the issue of taxes and instead began to air grievances against the king and once again to debate appropriate limits on his powers.

In 1642, the conflict erupted into open war. The English Civil Wars are divided into two phases, sometimes referred to as separate wars. The first phase, often referred to as the First Civil War or sometimes simply as the English Civil War, lasted from 1642 to 1646. The Second Civil War began in 1647, and the Civil Wars came to an end in 1651. The Second Civil War is some-

times said to have lasted from 1647 to 1651, but some historians say that it ended in 1649 and a Third Civil War occurred from 1650 to 1651. Despite having built up over a period of four decades, it came as a shock to the English people that, only forty years after the death of their beloved Queen Elizabeth I, there was now war against their monarch. People struggled to choose a side or to avoid involving themselves in the conflict.

The war had political, economic, and religious causes. There was relative social diversity within each side. Those who supported Charles I were collectively called the Royalists or Cavaliers. The foundation of the Cavaliers was the nobility, the great majority of which had views and interests similar to those of the king. Religiously, the Anglicans, or members of the Church of England, backed the Royalists, since the king was the Supreme Head of that church. The minority Roman Catholics also sided largely with the king, whose expansion of the ceremonial liturgy within the Anglican Church appealed to them. The geographic center of Royalist power was in the north and west of England.

The forces of Parliament were unified largely through their religious affiliations, specifically the Puritans of England and the Presbyterians of Scotland. Parliamentarians are thus sometimes called Roundheads because of the distinctive Puritan haircut. The landed gentry, merchants, and artisans of southeastern England, including London, supported Parliament. A major factor in the war was the fact that Parliament also controlled the nation's naval forces. Each side's army in 1642 numbered about thirteen thousand men.

The precipitating event that finally led to the outbreak of war was the order by Charles I, on January 4, 1642, to arrest five members of Parliament. The baseless or politically motivated arrest of his subjects was one of the central acts forbidden to the king in the Petition of Right, and it infuriated the members of the House of Commons. The men escaped arrest, Charles left London, and both sides began gathering men and weapons. In August, Charles raised his standard in Nottingham as a challenge to Parliament, which responded by naming the third earl of Essex its lord general.

On October 12, 1642, Charles marched his army, led by his nephew, Prince Rupert, back toward London. Almost simultaneously, Essex led the Parliamentary forces west. The two armies met in the Battle of Edgehill, the first battle of the war, on October 23. Charles deployed his infantry on the slopes of the hill with his cavalry on the outside. Essex lined his forces up the same way. Prince Rupert attacked first: He initiated a cavalry attack on both flanks of the opposing army that routed the opposition but ended with his horsemen looting a nearby town rather than supporting the infantry in the rest of the battle. The Parliamentary forces made mistakes as well, and the battle ended in a draw. When the Royalist forces resumed their march the next day, they were not pursued. The route of Charles to London seemed open.

By November 12, the king had advanced to Turnham Green, west of London, where opposition to him was increasing rapidly. He now faced an army of twenty-four thousand, twice the size of his own forces. Charles did not engage the Parliamentary force but instead retired to Oxford for the winter.

The next year, 1643, was one of indecisive combat. Three Royalist victories—one in June at Adwalton Moor in the north and two in July at Lansdown Hill and Roundway Down in the east—gave the king the momentum. The tide began to turn in September, however. The First Battle of Newbury (September 20) was indecisive, but the Royalists were defeated at Winceby, in the northeast, in October. Winceby marked the rise as well of Colonel Oliver Cromwell, a previously insignificant member of Parliament who would become the dominant leader of the Parliamentary forces and of the new government. Cromwell's army of Puritans soon became known as the Ironsides. The third baron Fairfax also emerged from Winceby as a major leader for Parliament. In December, Parliament won another victory at Alton in the south.

A new phase of the war began early in 1644, when Alexander Leslie led his Scottish Presbyterian army, which had defeated Charles in the Bishops' Wars, into England to aid the primarily Puritan Parliamentary armies. He was joined by Fairfax and the now Lieutenant-General Cromwell to win the most decisive battle of the war so far at Marston Moor on July 2, 1644. This victory led to the surrender of the northern Royalist

MAJOR BATTLES OF THE ENGLISH CIVIL WARS

Date	Battle	Victor/Outcome
1642-1646	**First Civil War**	
Oct. 23, 1642	Edgehill	Draw
Nov. 12, 1642	Turnham Green	Parliament by default
June 30, 1643	Adwalton Moor	Royalists
July 5, 1643	Lansdown Hill	Royalists
July 13, 1643	Roundway Down	Royalists
Sept. 20, 1643	First Battle of Newbury	Inconclusive
Oct. 11, 1643	Winceby	Parliament
Dec. 12, 1643	Alton	Parliament
July 2, 1644	Marston Moor	Parliament
Aug. 31-Sept. 2, 1644	Lostwithiel	Royalists
Oct. 27, 1644	Second Battle of Newbury	Inconclusive
June 14, 1645	Naseby	Parliament
July 10, 1645	Langport	Parliament
1647-1651	**Second Civil War**	
Sept. 3, 1650	Dunbar	Parliament
Sept. 3, 1651	Worcester	Parliament

ENGLISH CIVIL WARS

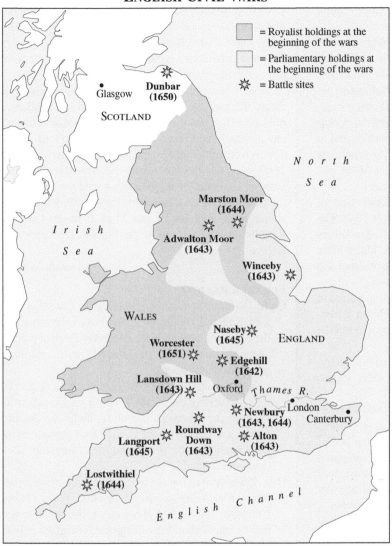

= Royalist holdings at the beginning of the wars

= Parliamentary holdings at the beginning of the wars

✹ = Battle sites

to leave the military. The earl of Essex and others therefore resigned their military positions but remained active politically. Only Cromwell, because of his proven military ability, was exempt from the ordinance. The New Model Army was established in April, 1645, with Fairfax replacing Essex as commander in chief. Cromwell now had his professional army with about twenty-two thousand men.

The next decisive battle of the First Civil War was the Battle of Naseby, northwest of London, on June 14, 1645. Prince Rupert had sacked the nearby city of Leister on May 31 and was rejoined by Charles I. They then marched to relieve a siege of Oxford by Fairfax. They succeeded on June 7, but Fairfax moved up to Naseby, where he was able to choose the next battleground. His infantry was commanded by Sir Henry Ireton, his left flank cavalry by Phillip Skippon, and his right flank cavalry by Cromwell.

Rupert commanded the right flank cavalry for the Royalists and initiated the battle by charging through Ireton's left flank cavalry. However, Cromwell's right flank held its ground and forced the Royalist left flank to retreat. The professionalism of the New Model Army was proven when part of Cromwell's horsemen separated and attacked the Royalist infantry in the center. The Royalist infantry began to retreat along with its left flank cavalry. Charles I was in command of the Royalist reserves, but he fled the area rather than face almost certain death if he had tried to support the retreating Royalist forces. The majority of the Royalist infantry was either killed or captured by the advancing New Model Army. Fairfax recaptured Leister a few days later.

On July 10, Fairfax defeated the Royalists again at Langport, in the southwest. The army of Lord George Goring, the Royalist commander, mostly deserted following this defeat. The Battles of Naseby and Langport sealed the fate of Charles I. His armies almost nonexis-

stronghold at York on July 16. However, Charles led his Royalist troops to a victory of their own at Lostwithiel in the west in September, and the Second Battle of Newbury in October was indecisive.

By the end of 1644, Cromwell, now dominant in the Parliamentary forces, realized they needed a more professional army. At his urging, Parliament passed the Self-Denying Ordinance, which stipulated that no member of Parliament could simultaneously hold a military commission. Members of the House of Commons could choose to resign their positions in Parliament to remain in the army, but members of the House of Lords, whose seats in Parliament were not elective, had no choice but

tent, he fled north in 1646 and surrendered to the Scots. The town of Oxford surrendered in June, 1646, ending the first and major phase of the Civil Wars.

The second phase of the English Civil Wars, also referred to as the Second Civil War, began in 1647, after Charles had been ransomed from the Scots by Parliament and imprisoned at Holmby House while Parliament debated his future. A series of Royalist rebellions, including a new Scottish invasion, allowed the king the opportunity for conspiracy, which some in Parliament and in the army classified as treason by the king. The rebellions were all quickly crushed by the New Model Army, and the king's future was left extremely uncertain.

Disagreement in Parliament on the future role of Charles I led to Pride's Purge of Parliament in 1648. The army, led by Thomas Pride, arrested forty-five members who wanted to retain Charles as monarch. Many more were banned from taking their seats. Those arrested and banned were mostly Scottish Presbyterians. Seventy-five members of the original Long Parliament elected in 1640, mostly Puritans, now formed the Rump Parliament. The army ordered the Rump Parliament to put the king on trial for treason.

The trial of King Charles I was conducted in January, 1649. He was found guilty of treason against the English people and beheaded on January 30.

The second phase of the Civil War was not yet over, however. Royalist uprisings in Ireland had to be crushed by Cromwell in August, 1649. In Scotland, the son of Charles I was crowned as King Charles II. He prepared to lead an army of Scots into England to claim the rest of his throne. Cromwell was sent into Scotland and destroyed a large Scottish army at Dunbar on September 3, 1650. Charles II was still able to march deep into England, but he was defeated by Cromwell at Worcester exactly a year after Dunbar, on September 3, 1651. Charles II escaped and made his way to France, where he stayed until 1660.

SIGNIFICANCE

The execution of King Charles I began a period of English history called the Interregnum, which means a temporary break in a monarchial line. Power was now divided between the army and the Rump Parliament. Since Oliver Cromwell was part of both, he became the link between them. Much of the English population was shocked by the execution of Charles I, but they were not yet ready to accept his son Charles II as their next monarch. They were also not ready to abandon the monarchy entirely. The immediate need was to reestablish peace

and security to the realm. For that reason, the next eleven years were years of political experimentation and continued political turmoil. The experimentation began with a government called the Commonwealth in 1649. Cromwell was named lord protector of England, in effect the ruler of the country, in 1653.

After Cromwell's death, an opportunity existed to create the kind of government that many of England's politicians had desired all along, a constitutional monarchy in which the Crown shared power with Parliament. The movement toward establishing this system began in 1660, when Charles II was restored to the throne by Parliament. Constitutional monarchy would not be fully established in England, however, until 1689, with the installation of William III and Mary II in the Glorious Revolution and passage of the English Declaration of Rights.

—Glenn L. Swygart

FURTHER READING

Carlin, Norah. *The Causes of the English Civil War*. Oxford, England: Blackwell, 1999. Detailed coverage of the causes of the war, in the context of English politics and government from 1603 to 1649. Bibliographical references and index.

Davies, Norman. *The Isles: A History*. New York: Oxford University Press, 1999. Has a long chapter devoted to the seventeenth century, including detailed coverage and a map of the Civil Wars. Emphasizes the parts relating to the three kingdoms of England, Scotland, and Ireland.

Hill, Christopher. *Intellectual Origins of the English Revolution Revisited*. Rev. ed. New York: Oxford University Press, 1997. Revision of 1965 work, covering the intellectual life of England during the period, the Puritan Revolution, and other related topics. Bibliographic references.

Kenyon, John, and Jane Ohlmeyer, eds. *The Civil Wars: A Military History of England, Scotland, and Ireland, 1638-1660*. New York: Oxford University Press, 1998. Essays cover the background, the war in each kingdom, naval operations, logistics and supply, and other major topics.

SEE ALSO: Mar. 24, 1603: James I Becomes King of England; Dec. 18, 1621: The Great Protestation; May 6-June 7, 1628: Petition of Right; Mar., 1629-1640: "Personal Rule" of Charles I; Mar.-June, 1639: First Bishops' War; Nov. 3, 1640-May 15, 1641: Beginning of England's Long Parliament; Aug. 17-Sept. 25, 1643: Solemn League and Covenant; July 2, 1644:

Battle of Marston Moor; Spring, 1645-1660: Puritan New Model Army; 1646-1649: Levellers Launch an Egalitarian Movement; Dec. 6, 1648-May 19, 1649: Establishment of the English Commonwealth; Dec. 16, 1653-Sept. 3, 1658: Cromwell Rules England as Lord Protector; May, 1659-May, 1660: Restoration of Charles II; 1679: Habeas Corpus Act; Nov., 1688-

Feb., 1689: The Glorious Revolution; Feb. 13, 1689: Declaration of Rights.

RELATED ARTICLES in *Great Lives from History: The Seventeenth Century, 1601-1700:* Charles I; Charles II (of England); Oliver Cromwell; Third Baron Fairfax; James I; James II; Mary II; Thomas Pride; Prince Rupert; William III.

1642-1666
REIGN OF SHAH ʿABBĀS II

ʿAbbās II, who considered Ṣafavid rulers to be sacred and infallible, took an active role in government matters and intervened in provincial affairs on the side of the peasants. Under ʿAbbās and his successors, however, Jews, Christians, and nonconformist Muslims faced persecution, and the declining Ṣafavid Empire was plagued by mismanagement, corruption, injustice, and social polarization.

LOCALE: Iran
CATEGORIES: Government and politics; wars, uprisings, and civil unrest; diplomacy and international relations; economics

KEY FIGURES
ʿAbbās II (1633-1666), Ṣafavid shah, r. 1642-1666
Süleyman I (d. 1694), Ṣafavid shah, r. 1666-1694

SUMMARY OF EVENT
ʿAbbās II came to power in the shadow of a domineering and dissolute father, Shah Ṣafī I (r. 1629-1642), who was the grandson of ʿAbbās the Great (r. 1588-1620), the renowned Ṣafavid ruler. Ṣafī was an alcoholic, a paranoid, and cruel. He executed the ablest generals, courtiers, and provincial authorities left behind by ʿAbbās the Great as well as several wives, a sister, and even his own mother.

International affairs bored him, so he left such business to his grand vizier, Saru Taqi (1634-1645). In 1639, the vizier negotiated a peace treaty with the Ottoman Empire (the Treaty of Kasr-i Shirin), which established sound defensible boundaries between the Ṣafavid Persians and their hostile neighbor to the west. However, terms of the treaty compelled the Ṣafavids to relinquish Iraq to Ottoman control, placing the Shia Muslims of that territory under the control of a Sunni government. As a result, factions and intrigues soon arose in the Ṣafavid court between "peace" and "war" parties.

When Ṣafī died after a drinking binge, ʿAbbās II took the throne in 1642 at the age of eight or nine. Although

virtually unprepared for leadership, he learned quickly and soon impressed the regency and his tutors with his energy, sharpness, and sense of justice. His first test came in 1645 with the murder of Saru Taqi by a faction of army officers and courtiers angered by the treaty of 1639. Despite his youth, ʿAbbās demanded an exhaustive investigation and insisted on imposing the death penalty for even the highest officers involved. Out of this crisis, the young shah emerged as an unexpectedly energetic ruler who took the reins of power as soon as he attained maturity.

ʿAbbās II soon revived the old custom of holding public hearings on chosen cases involving corruption, venality, or abuse of authority by public officials and officers. Over time, he also heard cases outside government affairs where peasants or the urban poor might seek redress from some powerful landlord, tribal leader, or merchant house. In so doing, ʿAbbās II quickly gained a popular image for his strong sense of justice, for morality in rule, and for protecting the weak from those who might exploit them. Of course, because of this sense, he reasserted also the absolutist ideal that the shah held final—and ultimately total—power over all his subjects and their affairs. ʿAbbās thereby laid the groundwork that made other major changes appear legitimate and beneficial to the public.

Change, ʿAbbās believed, was vital to the power of the dynasty. More than a century before, when the Ṣafavids had come to power in Iran, they had established an absolutist ruling style. Their shahs combined their Islam with the traditions of Persian divine-right rule, the ancient alliance of semipastoral tribes, and the control of the peasantry by rural landlords, and they brought it all together with a support for progress: urban centers of commerce, culture, and bureaucracy.

The Ṣafavids seized power with a vision of spreading *ithna-ashari*, or Twelver, Shiism throughout Islam, and they had imposed this vision upon most Persians through

409

a mix of persuasion, co-optation, and brute force. Their rulers, therefore, presented themselves to the Persian people as agents of God, divinely commissioned by Allah and mystically directed by the twelve imams of the House of Ali to lead the Muslim people to truth and justice. To support this image of charismatic religious rule, the state filled Persia with Shia law courts, mosques, and madrasas (schools), and patronized recruitment of Shia clergy, who were known as *mujtahids*.

However, under Ṣafī, the power of the shahs had corroded. The Ṣafavid army, in the beginning, had drawn its numbers from various Turkic tribes and people of the northeast who became fanatic partisans of the Shia cause. These forces were known as the *qizilbash* (feudal armies). To their ranks, the shahs had added slave-soldiers called *ghulam*, militias drawn from the towns and rural nobles, nomadic levies, and mercenary cannoneers. These additions had been required not only because of technological change but also because many of the *qizilbash* leaders became landlords and intrigued to preserve their privileges instead of serving the state. The civil service, which also had been recruited from the best families of the towns, also had begun to usurp power. Rivalries among officers and between military and civilians led to defeats in war, local revolts, murders, and state paralysis. Finally, the Shia clergy had begun to challenge the status of the shahs as divinely ordained, arguing that their leaders truly represented the reign of the Hidden Imam and the shah was merely a "guided law enforcer." ʿAbbās intended to meet these forces head-on.

ʿAbbās realized that to attain his ambitions, he needed peace with his neighbors. Shortly after the 1639 treaty, his Ottoman rivals fell into a series of wars on other fronts and into internal revolts that prevented them from launching new attacks on Persian territory. Although ʿAbbās might have taken advantage of these upheavals to attack the Turkish empire, instead, he negotiated improved boundaries and promises that the Sunni Muslim Turks would give greater religious freedoms to the Shia of Iraq. In 1648, however, ʿAbbās did lead a series of expeditions against the Mughals of India, driving them out of the city of Qandahār, which the Mughals had taken from ʿAbbās's father. Once Persian frontiers with India stood secure, the shah made peace quickly with the Mughals and turned to his real concerns: building the power of the dynasty.

With his prestige and credentials as a warrior for Islam now unassailable, ʿAbbās began the systematic confiscation of *qizilbash* lands and the private revenues of their officers. The lands so acquired then became *khassa*,

"royal domains," administered directly by the Ṣafavid household. The shah also shrank many of the *qizilbash* units, demilitarizing them or assigning their members to civilian duties. Some units he ordered to patrol frontier zones, beyond the imperial heartlands where these troops had sometimes raised revolts or oppressed the local folk. This process brought more revenue directly into the royal coffers, allowing the shah to lower some taxes. Benefiting from peace at home and abroad, ʿAbbās could afford to shrink the military, even discharging some of the more advanced forces, such as the artillery corps. Thus, in his own reign, the danger posed by army revolts virtually evaporated.

Increased revenue also allowed ʿAbbās to enlarge his patronage in the public arena by building or refurbishing palaces, mosques, marketplaces, schools, hospitals, and infrastructure, such as roads and bridges. Persian crafts in carpets, armor, ceramics, miniature paintings, and lacquerware still commanded high prices. Eṣfahān, the Ṣafavid capital, reaped much of this largesse, including the Chehel Sotun (Forty Pillars) palace and gardens as well as several grand mosques. The Khaju bridge over the Zayandeh River was another architectural achievement. The emphasis on pious buildings, of course, was also intended to underline the religious charisma of the regime, a charisma that was being increasingly challenged by some of Persia's Shia *mujtahids*.

Like Ṣafavids before him, ʿAbbās claimed to rule in the name of the Hidden Imam of Shiism. After all, Iran was Shia now because the Ṣafavids had converted it from Sunni Islam, and that bold stroke certainly bespoke of divine favor and guidance. Indeed, some Ṣafavids had allowed their supporters to address them with titles and poems that suggested these shahs enjoyed such divine favor that they virtually incarnated the imam himself. ʿAbbās, too, allowed these flatteries and, as a demonstration of his own religious standing, he frequently violated Islamic traditions of religious toleration by imposing discriminatory restrictions on Jews, Zoroastrians, and non-Shia Muslims. At one point, he ordered all the Jews and Zoroastrians of Eṣfahān to convert to Shiism, an act flagrantly in disregard of Qurʾānic protections for religious minorities.

However grateful they may have been to the Ṣafavids for imposing their Shia faith on Persia, a growing number of *mujtahids* refused to tolerate such political excesses. First, the absolutist claims of the shahs struck them as virtual blasphemy against the imam. They noted the moral degeneracy of many of the Ṣafavid shahs, insisting that no person, even the shah, dare place himself above

God's law. Second, they cataloged the offenses of the rulers, arguing that even good rulers still did evil things. Third, others began to posit that, since no secular ruler had the knowledge or uprightness to represent the Hidden Imam, then the most logical institution to provide truly inspired leadership had to be that of the shahs. How *mujtahids* would exercise such power was, of course, the question, and many religious leaders felt that the clergy should serve as advisers rather than take any formal leadership role. Nonetheless, some Muslim leaders had begun to challenge the divine-right absolutism of the shahs just as English Puritans, half a continent away, were defying the Stuarts over the religious vocabulary of political power.

Shah ʿAbbās died at the age of thirty-three. Although not in the same league as some of the great debauchers of the Ṣafavid Dynasty, he, too, had begun to succumb to the temptations of indulgence and the arrogance of power. According to one story, the army had deteriorated so badly that, at one state parade held shortly before ʿAbbās's death, the generals circled the same troops past him several times, hoping he would not notice.

Like ʿAbbās, the son who succeeded him also was a teenager, Ṣafī II. Superstitious and decadent, he changed his regal title from Ṣafī II to Süleyman two years into his reign, hoping to reap the possible blessings that could come from changing his name—that of a despised tyrant—to that of a legendary statesman (Süleyman the Magnificent, who had reigned from 1520 to 1566). The strategy failed, however, and the regime slid into a downward spiral from which it never fully recovered, even though the dynasty survived five decades more.

SIGNIFICANCE

The reign of Shah ʿAbbās II saw the final flowering of Ṣafavid power and culture. ʿAbbās proved adept at making war as well as making peace. His reforms and reductions in the military, although self-serving, might have eventually led to a more loyal, professional corps. However, under less-vigilant supervision, the Ṣafavid army shrank to where it could not effectively defend the regime and intrigues between border units. Ṣafavid rivals soon led to repeated invasions and collapse.

The reign of ʿAbbās deserves note as well for key cultural and religious developments that remained vibrant through the following several centuries. The most persistent development is the long-standing tension and debate among Iranians over the proper political roles of religious and secular leaders in modern Iran.

—*Weston F. Cook, Jr.*

FURTHER READING

Arjomand, Said Amir. *The Shadow of God and the Hidden Imam: Political Order and Social Change in Shiite Iran from the Beginning to 1890.* Chicago: University of Chicago Press, 1984. An excellent overview of religious and social issues within and beyond Iran.

Foran, John. "The Long Fall of the Safavid Dynasty: Moving Beyond the Standard Views." *International Journal of Middle Eastern Studies* 24 (1992): 281-304. A good article that does not moralize about the character of individual shahs but instead seeks to find wider answers as to why the dynasty collapsed.

Morgan, David. *Medieval Persia, 1040-1797.* New York: Longman, 1994. An engaging narrative history that focuses on not only personalities but also social, ethnographic, economic, and religious matters.

Savory, Roger. *Iran Under the Safavids.* New York: Cambridge University Press, 1980. The English-language starting point for a general history of the dynasty and its rulers.

Shaw, Stanford J. *History of the Ottoman Empire and Modern Turkey.* Vol. 1. New York: Cambridge University Press, 1976. Provides excellent, detailed analysis of primary sources.

SEE ALSO: 1602-1639: Ottoman-Ṣafavid Wars; Beginning c. 1615: Coffee Culture Flourishes; 1623-1640: Murad IV Rules the Ottoman Empire; 1629: Ṣafavid Dynasty Flourishes Under ʿAbbās the Great; 1632-c. 1650: Shah Jahan Builds the Taj Mahal; 1656-1662: Persecution of Iranian Jews; 1656-1676: Ottoman Empire's Brief Recovery.

RELATED ARTICLES in *Great Lives from History: The Seventeenth Century, 1601-1700:* ʿAbbās the Great; Shah Jahan.

1640's

1642-1684
BEAVER WARS

The Iroquois Five Nations challenged the French-Huron trade monopoly in pelts, leading to large-scale intertribal warfare.

LOCALE: Northeastern woodlands of New France (now in Canada) and New England

CATEGORIES: Wars, uprisings, and civil unrest; trade and commerce; colonization

KEY FIGURES

Tandihetsi (fl. 1640's), Huron chief married to an Algonquian woman

Kiotsaeton (fl. 1640's), Mohawk orator who presented wampum belts at a peace council

Iroquet (fl. 1609-1615), Algonquian chief

Edmond Andros (1637-1714), English governor of New York and partner in the Covenant Chain

Saint Isaac Jogues (1607-1646), Jesuit priest and intermediary between the Hurons and the Iroquois

Paul Le Jeune (1592-1664), Jesuit priest who wrote extensively about the Hurons

Peter Stuyvesant (c. 1610-1672), director-general of New Netherland, 1647-1664

Henry Hudson (1560's?-1611), English explorer who was employed by the Dutch at Albany

Samuel de Champlain (c. 1567/1570-1635), French explorer, fur trader, and founder of Quebec

SUMMARY OF EVENT

During the seventeenth century, the principal mode of subsistence for the Iroquois changed from farming to trapping. After the Iroquois had traded successfully with the Dutch for several decades, a seemingly insatiable demand for furs to make fashionable top hats for European gentlemen had depleted the Iroquois's source of beaver pelts. Meanwhile, the French had become allies with the Algonquians and Hurons to the north, establishing a lucrative monopoly on the fur trade in the upper Great Lakes. Acting as middlemen, the Hurons bought huge quantities of furs from the Ottawa then sold them to the French. Seeking an expedient solution to the problem of a diminishing supply of furs, the Iroquois began attacking Huron villages and intercepting and confiscating fur shipments along trade routes, provoking a series of conflicts known as the Beaver Wars.

The name "Iroquois" refers both to the members of the Iroquois Confederacy, or League of Five Nations (Seneca, Cayuga, Onondaga, Oneida, and Mohawk), and

to their common language. Consolidation of the league in 1570 (although it had existed informally for several decades before that) helped end centuries of warring among these neighboring tribes and protected them from attacks by surrounding tribes. Although known throughout the woodlands as fierce warriors, the Iroquois had met European advances into their territory peacefully and created profitable alliances, such as their trade agreement with the Dutch at Albany.

In 1608, French explorer Samuel de Champlain established Quebec at a deserted Iroquois site on the Saint Lawrence River. In that area, the Huron Confederacy of four tribes and their Algonquian allies began a trade agreement with the French that was coveted by the Iroquois. This rivalry increased long-existing hostility between Hurons and Iroquois.

In July, 1609, Champlain, two soldiers, and sixty Algonquians and Hurons followed a war party of two hundred Mohawks along what is now called Lake Champlain. In the traditional manner, both sides agreed to engage in battle in the morning. Iroquois warriors preferred close, hand-to-hand fighting with wooden clubs and leather shields, and they were accustomed to using bows and arrows only for ambushes. As the battle began, both sides advanced, but the French remained hidden among the Hurons. Advancing closely, the French fired their guns, killing two Mohawk chiefs instantly and mortally wounding the third. Many Mohawks died and a dozen captives were taken, one of whom was tortured during the victory celebration. This dramatic battle was the Iroquois's first encounter with Europeans and their dreadful weapons. Their humiliation left the Iroquois with a fierce hatred of the French. A few weeks later, Henry Hudson arrived at Albany to initiate the Dutch fur trade, which eventually brought guns to the Iroquois.

In the next three decades, the Hurons and Iroquois lost many warriors in battle. Moreover, the Jesuit priests who brought Christianity to Quebec also brought European diseases. By 1640, through warfare and epidemics, only ten thousand Hurons remained, less than half of their previous number. However, they retained their alliance with the French. Iroquois offers of peace with the Hurons were dissuaded by the French. In 1640, five hundred Iroquois approached a French village to negotiate for peace and trade a French captive for guns. When French offers were not acceptable, the council disbanded and the Iroquois began planning for war.

Early Iroquois warfare was guerrilla-style fighting by small bands, so the beginning date of the Beaver Wars is difficult to determine with certainty, but an attack by a Seneca war party on the Huron village of Arendaronon in 1642 is commonly marked as the first event of the war. In that year, Iroquois also raided the Algonquian village of Chief Iroquet on the Ottawa River, capturing and later releasing Saint Isaac Jogues.

In 1645, the French bargained for peace, using Iroquois captives. The Iroquois wanted to share the middleman role with the Hurons and continue trading with the Dutch. At the council, the great Mohawk orator Kiotsaeton appealed to the French, Hurons, and Algonquians, presenting fifteen wampum belts. He translated the symbolic messages coded in the shell beads. After the council, Father Jogues and Father Paul Le Jeune continued to support the peace effort.

Months later, some Mohawks reported to Huron chief Tandihetsi about secrecy and intrigue involving the possible exclusion of the Algonquians. The chief had a wife and many relatives among the Algonquians. Finally, a trade-related treaty was made, honored for a time, then broken when a huge shipment of furs passed down the Ottawa River and the Iroquois were given no share. In retaliation, the popular Father Jogues was killed when he next returned to visit a Mohawk village.

European presence in North America affected Iroquois social and cultural systems that had provided earlier stability. Ecological balance was upset by the high demand for beaver pelts, economic balance was upset by the shift from farming to trapping, and political balance was upset by rivalries among tribes. The Iroquois had become dependent upon the Dutch for food, metal tools, weapons, and ammunition. Since the primary commodity valued by both Indians and colonists was beaver pelts and the agreement had been broken, the Iroquois began attacking Huron villages and intercepting travel along their trade routes, confiscating whole shipments of pelts. In times of warfare, one gun was well worth the price of twenty beaver pelts.

By March of 1649, the Iroquois had declared open warfare, and one thousand Iroquois set out for the Huron homeland. The starving Hurons, fearing annihilation, burned their villages and escaped into the woods, some to a Jesuit encampment, others divided into clan groups. Eventually, several thousand Hurons were adopted into the five Iroquois tribes themselves. By late 1649, the Iroquois had defeated the Tobaccos; from 1650 to 1656, they warred against the Neutrals on the Niagara peninsula and the Eries on southern Lake Erie, devastating

both and taking over their hunting territories. They successfully maintained trade with the Dutch under Director-General Peter Stuyvesant.

By 1654, the Ottawas had taken over the Hurons' position as middlemen for French pelt traders. When the Iroquois attempted to displace them, the Ottawas moved westward to the Straits of Mackinac. For the next thirty years, they supplied two-thirds of the furs sent to France. By 1670, the Iroquois controlled the woodland territory surrounding the eastern Great Lakes, while the French claimed Lakes Huron and Superior.

In 1680, several hundred Iroquois invaded the territory of the Illini and Miami tribes. In 1684, an unsuccessful attempt to take Fort Saint Louis from the Illinis marked the end of the nearly century-long Iroquois campaign to overturn the French-Huron trade monopoly.

SIGNIFICANCE

During the Beaver Wars, the Iroquois had established a political agreement with the English through Governor Edmond Andros. This Covenant Chain was forged for two purposes: safe access to Albany for Iroquois traders and easy entry into the Indians' affairs for the English. By 1685, the League of Five Nations had been consolidated to deal with external affairs.

Native American leagues, alliances, treaties, covenants, and confederacies all worked against the Europeans' ability to establish a niche in the New World. The powers of France and England had been balanced almost equally for many years, but the long-held Iroquois hostility unleashed in the Beaver Wars turned the scale against the French, and their magnificent schemes of colonization in the northern part of America were lost. Had it not been for the determination of the Iroquois, the official language throughout North America might have become French.

—*Gale M. Thompson*

FURTHER READING

Brandão, José António. *Your Fyre Shall Burn No More: Iroquois Policy Towards New France and Its Native Allies to 1701.* Lincoln: University of Nebraska Press, 1997. In this book about the Beaver Wars, Brandão refutes the conventional wisdom that the Iroquois fought to secure their position in the fur trade. He maintains they fought the war to replenish their population, safeguard their hunting territories, protect their homes, and regain their honor.

Cleland, Charles E. *Rites of Conquest: The History and Culture of Michigan's Native Americans.* Ann Arbor: University of Michigan Press, 1992. A multiethnic, regional approach to the history of the Ojibwa, Ot-

1640's

tawa, and Potawatomi, describing their lives from the period before their contact with Europeans until the late twentieth century.

Grinde, Donald A., Jr. *The Iroquois and the Founding of the American Nation.* San Francisco, Calif.: Indian Historian Press, 1977. Provides cultural and historical background, and discusses Iroquois relationships with colonists before and after the American Revolution. Constitution of the Five Nations and Albany Plan of Union are included as appendices.

Harvey, Karen D., and Lisa D. Harjo. *Indian Country: A History of Native People in America.* Golden, Colo.: North American Press, 1994. Written and illustrated by American Indians. Presents ten culture areas, historical perspectives, contemporary issues, major ceremonies, and time lines from 50,000 B.C.E. to the twentieth century.

Magill, Frank N., and Harvey Markowitz, eds. *Ready Reference: American Indians.* Pasadena, Calif.: Salem Press, 1995. Comprehensive survey of Indians of the Americas, prehistory to late twentieth century. Discusses archaeology, architecture, arts, crafts, culture, history, language, religion, and social organization of tribes in ten culture areas. Contains features on well-known persons, events, acts, and treaties.

Richter, Daniel K. *The Ordeal of the Longhouse: The Peoples of the Iroquois League in the Era of European Colonization.* Chapel Hill: University of North Carolina Press, 1922. Describes the political, social, and economic life of the Iroquois League during the colonial era, including their experiences in the Beaver Wars.

Steele, Ian K. *Warpaths: Invasions of North America.* New York: Oxford University Press, 1994. Discusses American Indian-European warfare in eastern North America, from the defeat of Juan Ponce de León (1513) to negotiated peace with the British (1765). Combines social and military history for a balanced perspective.

SEE ALSO: Mar. 15, 1603-Dec. 25, 1635: Champlain's Voyages; Spring, 1604: First European Settlement in North America; Beginning June, 1610: Hudson Explores Hudson Bay; 1611-1630's: Jesuits Begin Missionary Activities in New France; 1617-c. 1700: Smallpox Epidemics Kill Native Americans; Apr. 27, 1627: Company of New France Is Chartered; 1642-1700: Westward Migration of Native Americans; May, 1642: Founding of Montreal; Sept. 13, 1660-July 27, 1663: British Navigation Acts; Mar. 22, 1664-July 21, 1667: British Conquest of New Netherland; May 2, 1670: Hudson's Bay Company Is Chartered; Apr. 6, 1672-Aug. 10, 1678: French-Dutch War; Beginning 1673: French Explore the Mississippi Valley; May 1, 1699: French Found the Louisiana Colony.

RELATED ARTICLES in *Great Lives from History: The Seventeenth Century, 1601-1700:* Samuel de Champlain; Henry Hudson; Saint Isaac Jogues; Peter Stuyvesant.

1642-1700
WESTWARD MIGRATION OF NATIVE AMERICANS

Expansion into North America by the French, English, and Dutch empires led to wars and rivalry for dominance that embroiled Native Americans in an intense competition for trade and land. Diseases, wars, and uprisings brought destruction to many tribes and forced others to move ever westward. Tribal migrations into the trans-Mississippi West led eventually to the formation of the Great Plains Indian culture.

LOCALE: North America
CATEGORIES: Expansion and land acquisition; social issues and reform; wars, uprisings, and civil unrest

KEY FIGURES
Metacom (King Philip; c. 1639-1676), Wampanoag grand sachem, r. 1662-1676

Sieur de La Salle (René-Robert Cavelier; 1643-1687), French explorer of the Mississippi River
Jacques Marquette (1637-1675), Jesuit missionary and explorer in New France
Willem Kieft (1597-1647), director-general of New Netherland, 1638-1647
Peter Stuyvesant (c. 1610-1672), director-general of New Netherland, 1647-1664

SUMMARY OF EVENT
By the early 1640's, competition among European empires for commerce and colonies in North America was intense. England was expanding its permanent settlements in Virginia, Massachusetts, Connecticut, and Rhode Island. Primarily interested in agriculture and col-

onization, England joined the fur trade rivalry. France claimed the Saint Lawrence River Valley, founded Quebec in Canada, and formed trade alliances with the Indians. By the mid-1600's, converting the Indians to Christianity and exploring the continental waterways had become major goals for the French. Holland claimed the Hudson River Valley as New Netherland and founded New Amsterdam on Manhattan Island. The Dutch engaged in the fur trade, agriculture, shipbuilding, fishing, and whaling. The stage was set for imperial conflicts among the Dutch, French, and English over American trade and territory. These conflicts inevitably involved the American Indians who hunted, farmed, and traded throughout the contested lands.

By 1642, the Beaver Wars (1642-1684) were underway among the French, the Dutch, the English, and their Indian allies. Intense hunting depleted the fur-bearing animals of the Northeast, and to satisfy European demand for furs, Indian hunters and traders were forced to travel ever westward, raiding and trading for furs along the Indian trails that crisscrossed the continent. The first of the Beaver Wars was a conflict between the Hurons, allied with the French, and the Iroquois Confederacy, allied with the Dutch. The Iroquois, supplied with firearms by the Dutch, attacked the Huron hunters and raided their villages, killing or capturing thousands of Hurons. The surviving Hurons fled westward to the Mississippi River but were forced back east by the Sioux who inhabited the wild rice marshlands of the Mississippi headwaters. Finally, joined by the Ottawas, the Hurons settled in fortified villages at the head of Black River and on the southwest shore of Lake Superior.

The Native Americans of the eastern woodlands suffered as a result of European colonists' growing need for land. In February, 1643, Willem Kieft, the director-general of New Netherland, decided to exterminate the lower Delaware River tribes to make room for more Dutch settlers. Hundreds of the lower river Indians were massacred. Survivors were adopted by the Iroquois or shipped to the Caribbean as slaves. When other Indians took revenge on the settlers, retaliation came from both the Dutch and English militaries. In 1643-1644, Dutch and English troops killed more than five hundred Indians in their winter camp in Connecticut.

Peter Stuyvesant, named director-general of New Netherland in 1647, continued the policy of exterminating Indians. In 1655, the tribes retaliated against Dutch settlers when a farmer killed an Indian woman for picking peaches from his orchard. In the ensuing Peach Wars, the Dutch and their Iroquois allies relentlessly attacked the rebel tribes. In 1660, Stuyvesant called upon the Mohawks to destroy the warring tribes, and by 1664, the Mohawks succeeded in forcing them to peace talks. The defeated tribes were required to cede all their remaining lands to the Dutch and stop attacking the settlers. Driven from their lands, the Indian survivors moved west.

The same year, 1664, English troops marched into New Amsterdam, took possession of the Dutch West India Company, and declared that all Dutch holdings in North America were now part of the English Empire. New Netherland was renamed New York, and New Amsterdam became New York City. England continued the established Dutch trade alliance with the Iroquois and thereby gained control of the fur trade. This brought England and its new Iroquois allies into conflict with France and its allies among the Canadian Indians and the tribes of the trans-Appalachian West.

After the Hurons' defeat, France had turned to the Ottawas, Wyandots, and other Native tribes in the Great Lakes region to supply trade furs. The dominant Iroquois began to harass the western tribes along the Illinois and Wisconsin Rivers. Concentrated attacks in 1656-1657 laid waste the villages of the Illinis, who fled west of the Mississippi. The Miami, Kickapoo, Oto, and Wisconsin Indians, fearing the Iroquois, fled down the Mississippi and went west into eastern Iowa.

In 1663, King Louis XIV of France began to build more forts, increase the military, and encourage colonization into Canada. Jesuit missionaries joined the explorers who moved into the Great Lakes region and the Ohio River Valley. Father Jacques Marquette made several expeditions, identifying Indian tribes and making converts to Christianity. On June 17, 1673, he followed the Wisconsin River to its juncture with the Mississippi River and located the Mississippi headwaters in Minnesota. In 1677, the sieur de La Salle secured a commission to explore beyond the Great Lakes. He established Fort Frontenac at the mouth of the Niagara River and explored the Ohio River. His discovery that the Ohio River emptied into the Mississippi River earned him a commission to explore the Mississippi Valley. In 1681-1682, La Salle followed the Mississippi River from its headwaters to the Gulf of Mexico. Claiming the entire territory for France, he named it Louisiana in honor of King Louis XIV and established a chain of military posts to guard France's claim to the mightiest waterway in North America.

Continued territorial expansion by England caused a rebellion known as Metacom's War (King Philip's War; 1675-1676). Led by Metacom (King Philip), the

Wampanoag, Abenaki, and Narrragansett Indians attacked Plymouth Colony. When the warriors reached western New England, they came under attack by England's Iroquois allies. Three thousand Indians and one thousand colonists died before the uprising ended. The English executed Metacom and sold his wife, children, and followers into slavery.

In the 1680's, England's attempt to extend its fur trade to the west provoked retaliation by the French. In June, 1687, French and Indian allies defeated the Seneca, the westernmost nation of the Iroquois Confederacy. By constantly attacking their towns, the French severely reduced the Iroquois population. In 1689-1697, King William's War (also known as Wars of the League of Augsburg) began the French and English struggle for control of North America. French and Indian troops raided English settlements in New York and New England. When English-Iroquois armies marched into the Saint Lawrence Valley in 1693, French and Indian troops attacked their winter camp, destroying shelters and looting supplies. Even more destructive raids against the Iroquois in 1696 destroyed crops and further reduced their population. By 1697, even the Mohawks were defeated. Defying England's protest, the Iroquois Confederacy committed to neutrality and swore friendship with France. The seventeenth century came to a close in a period of temporary and uneasy peace.

By 1700, European diseases, destructive wars, and forced loss of lands had pushed thirty different tribes across the Mississippi into the Great Plains. Nomadic Plains Indians included some Sioux tribes (including the Blackfoot), as well as the Crow, Cheyenne, and Arapaho. Other tribes of Sioux, Algonquians, and Iroquois entered the Northern and Central Plains and began trading with the nomadic tribes, the southwestern Pueblos and Apaches, and the Caddoans on the Southern Plains. The availability of horses, reintroduced into North America by the Spaniards, greatly benefited the Plains Indians. The Pueblo, or Popé's, Revolt of 1680 had scattered the horse herds of the Spaniards who were killed or driven from New Mexico. The Indians used these horses for hunting and transportation and bred them for trade. The horse became a shared symbol of wealth among the Plains Indians.

The tribes retained their own languages but developed a common hand sign language that allowed them to trade, hold joint ceremonies, and build alliances. The synthesis of religion, commerce, and politics produced a common culture that became known as the Plains Indian culture.

SIGNIFICANCE

By 1700, a successful Plains Indians culture came into being, blending the preexisting Plains Indians and the migrating tribes displaced into the region by European imperial expansion. The Indian tribes developed networks of trade from Canada south to Mexico and lived in relative peace for several decades, but their experiences with European empires presaged future migrations. Ultimately, the massive changes would be forced upon Native Americans in the eighteenth and nineteenth centuries by imperial conflicts and the creation and expansion of a new nation, the United States of America.

—*Marguerite R. Plummer*

FURTHER READING

Bancroft-Hunt, Norman. *The Indians of the Great Plains*. Photographs by Werner Forman. Reprint. New York: P. Bedrick Books, 1989. Describes the new culture of the Great Plains Indians after the migrations of the 1600's.

Gibson, Arrell Morgan. *The American Indian: Prehistory to the Present*. Lexington, Ky.: D. C. Heath, 1980. History of incursions of Dutch, Spanish, French, English, and Russian empires into North America and their consequences to Native American societies.

Hyde, George E. *Indians of the Woodlands: From Prehistoric Times to 1725*. Norman: University of Oklahoma Press, 1962. Focuses on Indian tribes between the Ohio and the Great Lakes, from the Hudson to the Mississippi River.

Kehoe, Alice B. *North American Indians: A Comprehensive Account*. Englewood Cliffs, N.J.: Prentice-Hall, 1981. Overview of Indian cultural groups after European contact.

Milner, Clyde A., Carol A. O'Conner, and Martha A. Sandweiss, eds. *The Oxford History of the American West*. New York: Oxford University Press, 1994. Describes European-Indian relationships and changes in native societies between the 1600's and 1800's.

Turner, Geoffrey. *Indians of North America*. New York: Sterling, 1992. Identifies Indian language groups, societies, and economies by locale.

SEE ALSO: 17th cent.: Rise of the Gunpowder Empires; 1611-1630's: Jesuits Begin Missionary Activities in New France; 1617-c. 1700: Smallpox Epidemics Kill Native Americans; Mar. 22, 1622-Oct., 1646: Powhatan Wars; July, 1625-Aug., 1664: Founding of New Amsterdam; May 6, 1626: Algonquians "Sell" Manhattan Island; Apr. 27, 1627: Company of New

France Is Chartered; May, 1630-1643: Great Puritan Migration; Feb. 22-27, 1632: Zuñi Rebellion; July 20, 1636-July 28, 1637: Pequot War; 1642-1684: Beaver Wars; Mar. 22, 1664-July 21, 1667: British Conquest of New Netherland; Beginning 1673: French Explore the Mississippi Valley; June 20, 1675: Metacom's

War Begins; Dec., 1678-Mar. 19, 1687: La Salle's Expeditions; Aug. 10, 1680: Pueblo Revolt; May 1, 1699: French Found the Louisiana Colony.

RELATED ARTICLES in *Great Lives from History: The Seventeenth Century, 1601-1700:* Sieur de La Salle; Louis XIV; Metacom; Peter Stuyvesant.

May, 1642
FOUNDING OF MONTREAL

The sieur de Maisonneuve and forty-one of his followers established the first European settlement at the foot of Mount Royal and called it Ville-Marie de Montreal.

LOCALE: Montreal, New France (now in Canada)
CATEGORIES: Colonization; expansion and land acquisition; government and politics

KEY FIGURES
Sieur de Maisonneuve (Paul de Chomedey; 1612-1676), Montreal's founder and first governor, 1642-1665
Samuel de Champlain (c. 1567/1570-1635), French explorer who sailed up the Saint Lawrence River to Hochelaga in 1603
Jeanne Mance (1606-1673), nurse who established the first hospital in Ville-Marie de Montreal
Marguerite Bourgeoys (1620-1700), established the first school in Montreal in 1653 and founded Sisters of the Congregation of Notre Dame

SUMMARY OF EVENT
In May, 1642, Paul de Chomedey, sieur de Maisonneuve, led a band of forty-one followers, most of them religious mystics devoted to working among the native people, up the Saint Lawrence River from Quebec City, 160 miles (260 kilometers) to the south. They disembarked on a spot between the Saint Lawrence River and the palisades of the mountain behind it, where they built a community. Thus, Chomedey is generally credited with founding what grew into the city of Montreal, although some historians contend that he cofounded the community with Jeanne Mance, the first lay nurse in North America.

The original purpose of those who established this settlement was to create a missionary center in the wilderness to convert Canadian Indians to Christianity. Their method was to encourage the Indians to live among

the French and gradually to adopt their ways. The Indians had little interest in doing this, however, and by the 1650's, the missionary emphasis of the settlement was replaced by commercial interests based on a thriving fur trade.

Montreal was named by Jacques Cartier, who, in 1535, had sailed up the Saint Lawrence River to the Indian settlement of Hochelaga, where he was greeted by over a thousand "First People," as the Canadians call the early Indians. Cartier scaled the mountain against which Hochelaga was built. From its peaks, he saw the Saint Lawrence River extending west to the vanishing line. He named this mountain Monte-Real, or the Royal Mountain. Cartier left Hochelaga the same day he arrived, realizing that the Saint Lawrence River's raging rapids west of the settlement would prevent him from proceeding further.

There is no record of Europeans visiting Hochelaga again until 1603, when Samuel de Champlain explored the area. By this time, the original Indian settlement was gone. However, another settlement, which Champlain named Place Royal, had replaced it. Vestiges of the first settlement remained.

Hochelaga and subsequent settlements on the same site were ideally situated for habitation, being strategically placed on a river that gave them access to the south but whose fierce rapids protected them to the north. The mountain, with its high palisades, offered additional natural protection from aggressive intruders.

When Champlain ventured into the area, the riverbanks between the former Hochelaga and Quebec City were occupied by three groups of First People: the Hurons, the Algonquians, and the Iroquois. The Huron and Algonquian Indians were frequently attacked by the aggressive Iroquois, who, by the middle of the seventeenth century, had brought the Hurons almost to the point of extinction. At Champlain's instigation, a treaty was drawn up between the Hurons and the Algonquians, who

1640's

joined forces to protect themselves from the Iroquois. Savage fighting continued in the area, however, throughout the rest of the seventeenth century, ending only in 1701, when a stronger treaty was forged and agreed to by all three tribes.

After Maisonneuve and his followers arrived on the site, which they named Ville-Marie de Montreal, they spent the summer building houses in which to live, as well as a chapel, a substantial barricade to protect them from attack, and a few outbuildings. Creating a community and erecting the necessary buildings before winter set in were remarkable but necessary accomplishments.

The French king, Louis XIV, gave the community its first charter in 1644. Chomedey became the first governor. A genuinely devout man, he viewed as his foremost goal the conversion to the Catholic faith of the First People. In the same year that the community was granted its charter, Jeanne Mance opened the first hospital there and became the first lay nurse in North America. Mance, one of those among the original colonists, belonged to a wealthy family in Langres, France, and wanted to dedicate herself to a life of service to humankind. Her cousin, Nicholas Dolebeau, a priest in Paris, first planted in her mind the idea of going to New France, as Canada was then called, to work among the indigenous peoples. Mance had gained considerable medical experience when she worked as a nurse during the Thirty Years' War that raged from 1618 to 1648.

Before she left for the New World, Mance had a number of meetings with Angelique de Bullion, whose husband, before his death, had been Louis XIII's superintendent of finance. She urged Mance to establish a hospital like the Hôtel-Dieu de Quebec in the undeveloped area that became Montreal. Angelique de Bullion offered financial support and continuing encouragement to this effort. With her help and under Mance's direction, the Hôtel-Dieu de Montreal was opened in 1645. The hospital, an unpretentious wooden structure 60 feet (18 meters) long and 24 feet (7 meters) wide, had accommodations for six male and two female patients. This arrangement reflected the fact that the early settlement had a preponderance of male inhabitants.

By 1653, the community had 719 male residents but a mere 65 single women, a condition that King Louis XIV sought to remedy by offering a generous dowry to orphan girls who immigrated to Montreal for the purpose of marrying. Mance, although she eventually returned to France, remained devoted to Ville-Marie de Montreal for the rest of her life, returning several times when the community's continued existence was threatened.

Education was not the highest immediate priority as Ville-Marie de Montreal was struggling to establish itself. In its early days, survival was a primary concern. This changed, however, in 1653, with the arrival from France of Marguerite Bourgeoys, who established the first school for girls in the community, housing it in an abandoned stable. She also founded the teaching order of the Sisters of the Congregation of Notre Dame. With impetus from Bourgeoys, a group of priests established the order of Les Messieurs de Saint-Sulpice, which took charge of the education of boys in the community.

Ville-Marie de Montreal became a thriving community, largely through the fur trade in which it engaged with the First People. There was a great demand for furs in France, as well as in the rest of Europe, so the fur merchants of the community became quite affluent. Those with commercial interests did all that they could to keep the three major tribes of First People from fighting among themselves, because it was these Indians who were their suppliers, and wars would interfere with the free exchange of furs. The fur traders therefore worked strenuously to draft and enforce treaties among the tribes.

By 1672, Montreal had grown to a community of fifteen hundred people, but it took it more than another one hundred years to achieve city status. Meanwhile, the religious motives that accounted for the founding of the community were supplanted by an ever-increasing commercial emphasis.

SIGNIFICANCE

Montreal has grown from its humble beginnings into one of the leading cities in Canada. Throughout its history, it has taken full advantage of its propitious location on a major river with mountains near its banks to offer protection from intruders, a very important factor in the community's early days. Montreal's origins as a center of New France is also significant, as many of the city's inhabitants value their French heritage at least as much as their Canadian identity.

The transformation of the early community from one bent on converting the First People to Christianity to one sustained by commerce is not surprising. The missionaries, as well-meaning and dedicated as they obviously were, sought to win over the First People by making them more like themselves. Such efforts required those being saved to forsake much of their heritage, which they valued and were unwilling to relinquish. A more successful approach to converting natives to Catholicism was that practiced by the Jesuits. They learned the native languages of the people among whom they worked, and they adapted themselves to the lives and cultures of those they hoped to save.

—*R. Baird Shuman*

FURTHER READING

Brebner, J. Bartlet. *Canada: A Modern History*. Ann Arbor: University of Michigan Press, 1957. Provides excellent information about Montreal's early days.

Brown, Craig, ed. *The Illustrated History of Canada*. Toronto: Lester & Orpen Dennys, 1987. This comprehensive history of Canada, beautifully and profusely illustrated, deals only briefly with the founding of Montreal.

Riendeau, Roger. *A Brief History of Canada*. New York: Facts On File, 2000. Useful text on Canadian history with passing reference to the founding of Montreal.

Rogers, Stillman D. *Montreal*. Danbury, Conn.: Children's Press, 2000. Directed at an adolescent audience, this attractive, well-illustrated book provides a

good starting point for those seeking information about Montreal and its history.

SEE ALSO: Mar. 15, 1603-Dec. 25, 1635: Champlain's Voyages; Spring, 1604: First European Settlement in North America; 1610-1643: Reign of Louis XIII; Beginning June, 1610: Hudson Explores Hudson Bay; 1611-1630's: Jesuits Begin Missionary Activities in New France; 1618-1648: Thirty Years' War; Apr. 27, 1627: Company of New France Is Chartered; 1642-1684: Beaver Wars; Aug., 1658-Aug. 24, 1660: Explorations of Radisson and Chouart des Groseilliers; May 2, 1670: Hudson's Bay Company Is Chartered; Beginning 1673: French Explore the Mississippi Valley; Dec., 1678-Mar. 19, 1687: La Salle's Expeditions; May 1, 1699: French Found the Louisiana Colony.

RELATED ARTICLES in *Great Lives from History: The Seventeenth Century, 1601-1700:* Saint Marguerite Bourgeoys; Samuel de Champlain; Saint Isaac Jogues; Louis XIII; Louis XIV; Jacques Marquette.

September 2, 1642
CLOSING OF THE THEATERS

The closing of England's commercial theaters by Parliament in 1642 marked the end of Caroline drama and effected a twenty-year hiatus for virtually all licensed theatrical performance in England. Although the parliamentary act was an immediate response to specific political events surrounding the outbreak of the English Civil Wars, it followed closely upon several decades of intense Puritan hostility toward the theater.

LOCALE: England
CATEGORIES: Theater; laws, acts, and legal history; government and politics

KEY FIGURES

Charles I (1600-1649), king of England, r. 1625-1649
William Prynne (1600-1669), Puritan zealot who wrote a vehement attack against the stage
William Laud (1573-1645), archbishop of Canterbury, 1633-1645
Stephen Gosson (1554-1624), English satirist who had published attacks on the theater

SUMMARY OF EVENT

On September 2, 1642, the English parliament issued a proclamation banning the performance of stage plays,

citing as its primary reason the imminent threat of civil war. Although the actual reasons for the closing of the theaters in England have been the subject of much scholarly debate, the actions taken by Parliament in 1642 followed upon several decades of increasing opposition to the commercial theater in London, much of which had been fueled by Puritan polemicists. By the time the theaters were officially reopened in 1660, after the English Civil Wars had ended and as the Restoration of the monarchy was under way, the political landscape in England had changed dramatically. As a result, the dramas that appeared at the start of the Restoration were markedly different from their forebears, both in style and in their relation to politics.

Beginning with the publication of Stephen Gosson's *The Schoole of Abuse* (1579), Puritan reformers in England regularly attacked the theater as an immoral institution that needed to be abolished. This antitheatrical movement produced a steady stream of treatises and pamphlets throughout the next several decades, including a second treatise by Gosson, *Playes Confuted in Five Actions* (1582), as well as Phillip Stubbes's *The Anatomie of Abuses* (1583) and John Rainolds's *The Overthrow of Stage-Plays* (1599). The most notorious example of this polemical genre was William Prynne's *Histrio-Mastix:*

The Players Scourge or Actors Tragedie (1633), a veritable compendium of previous antitheatrical works that ran more than eight hundred pages. The hysteria of Prynne's writing was arguably matched by the punishment he received for it: He was charged with invective against the queen (who had herself acted in some theatrical productions at court) and subsequently had his ears chopped off.

Like most cultural biases, the Puritan antipathy toward the theater in seventeenth century England cannot be attributed to a single concern. Most of the antitheatrical treatises cited classical sources (such as Plato and Saint Augustine) in order to justify their attacks on the stage, but it is more likely that the theater became a nexus for contemporary social, cultural, and political anxieties. Women were not permitted to perform in the commercial theaters, so many antitheatricalists cited the stage's habit of cross-dressing as yet another example of its moral depravity. In truth, opponents of the theater frequently lumped it in with a laundry list of other purported vices, such as mixed dancing, gambling, polyphonic music, classical poetry, makeup, and extravagant clothing, so the reason for the prejudice is likely to be overdetermined.

During the early decades of the seventeenth century, the theater came to be increasingly associated with Royalist politics, and this fact inevitably further polarized Reformist attitudes. William Laud, the royal chaplain and later the archbishop of Canterbury, had become an intensely polarizing figure during the reigns of James I and Charles I, and he was effectively seen as the epitome of Catholic-leaning Royalist politics by most Puritan reformers. Laud's advocacy of extravagant ceremony in church ritual (a practice particularly despised by Reformists) and his tacit approval of courtly theatrical productions, such as the court masque, made it easy for Puritans to associate the theater with a "Laudian" brand of politics that seemed to be dominating royal policy. The idea that the theater was a Royalist institution was further bolstered by the fact that many of the leading dramatists in the 1630's and 1640's, such as William Davenant, themselves had strong ties to the court.

By 1642, tensions between the king and Parliament had escalated. When fighting finally broke out, Parliament issued an order closing the theaters as an emergency response to the growing sense of crisis. The theater was recognized as providing an opportunity for large gatherings of people to foment political causes, and this was precisely what the government wished to control.

The closing of the theaters was likely not intended as a permanent state, at least initially, and over the next several years the ban on commercial acting had to be periodically reinstated.

The ban on theaters did not mean the cessation of dramatic writing, or even of dramatic performance, during the years between 1642 and 1660. The government conducted periodic raids on playhouses throughout the 1640's, and actors were periodically charged with violating the 1642 law. Moreover, after the theaters were closed, dramatic writing became subsumed in the proliferation of pamphlets, which arguably became the principal medium for disseminating political news and debate in England during this period. These pamphlets, which regularly voiced disparate views on contemporary political events, were often composed as dialogues—in a sense, as plays intended to be read rather than performed.

Rather than closing off drama as a venue for political expression, the 1642 edict had the effect of solidifying the theater's reputation as a politically charged medium. Dramatic writing during this period, whether published or performed, was received as political or social commentary, and many of the plays produced immediately after the Restoration in 1660 (particularly those written by John Dryden, Thomas Killigrew, and Roger Boyle, first earl of Orrery) were more explicitly Royalist than anything that had been staged before 1642. This self-conscious politicization of the theaters may also account for the subsequent development of Restoration drama, represented by writers such as Aphra Behn and William Congreve, which has often been described by critics as excessively light and lascivious in comparison to the more weighty drama of the English Renaissance. Restoration dramatists, who placed a high value on brilliant wit and incisive social commentary, had undoubtedly been affected by the often violent intersection of theatrical and political expression during the Civil War.

SIGNIFICANCE

Recent scholarship has shown that the closing of the theaters in 1642 cannot be interpreted simply as the culmination of decades of Puritan attacks on the London stage. More likely, Parliament's decision to close the theaters was as much an effort at social control as it was a response to the theater's perceived immorality. For one thing, the closing of the theaters was most immediately intended to curb opportunities for political assembly in the first waves of civil war, and it was almost surely intended to be only a temporary ban. However, the coincidence of Puritan antitheatricalism and increasing Reformist dissatisfaction with the monarchy had invested the theater with political significance over the first few decades of the seventeenth century, and the 1642 proclamation further encouraged the idea that theatrical performance was an inherently political event.

The relationship between theater and politics was thus significantly transformed by the English Civil Wars, and plays were subsequently seen as viable outlets for overt political and social commentary. After the theaters were officially reinstated in 1660, plays produced during the Restoration period tended to be more focused on domestic affairs, rather than on mythological or historical themes, as they had been during the age of Christopher Marlowe and William Shakespeare.

—Joseph M. Ortiz

FURTHER READING

Barish, Jonas. *The Antitheatrical Prejudice*. Berkeley: University of California Press, 1981. The preeminent study of the historical bias toward the theater, beginning with a careful study of classical Platonic antitheatricalism and ending with a consideration of twentieth century works. The chapters on Renaissance England are extremely useful for their ample references to a large number of primary sources.

Butler, Martin. *Theatre and Crisis, 1632-1642*. New York: Cambridge University Press, 1984. A concise, lucid study of English drama immediately preceding the closing of the theaters, which problematizes the common assumption that the drama of the 1630's and 1640's was Royalist.

Smith, Nigel. *Literature and Revolution in England, 1640-1660*. New Haven, Conn.: Yale University Press, 1994. An impressively comprehensive and well-argued study of the various literary forms that produced political expression during the English Civil Wars. Includes a chapter on the status of drama during the Interregnum. Illustrations.

Wikander, Matthew H. *Fangs of Malice: Hypocrisy, Sincerity, and Acting*. Iowa City: University of Iowa Press, 2002. A study of the rise of Puritan antitheatricalism and responses to it during the early modern period, although it erroneously asserts that the theater of Shakespeare simply dissolved in 1642.

Wiseman, Susan. *Drama and Politics in the English Civil War*. New York: Cambridge University Press, 1998. An extremely cogent and well-written account of the status of drama during the English Civil Wars; persuasively undercuts the long-standing idea that the Civil War represented a "gap" in English drama. Illustrations, bibliography.

SEE ALSO: Early 17th cent.: Revenge Tragedies Become Popular in England; c. 1601-1613: Shakespeare Produces His Later Plays; June 29, 1613: Burning of the Globe Theatre; Feb. 24, 1631: Women First Appear on the English Stage; 1642-1651: English Civil Wars; Dec. 6, 1648-May 19, 1649: Establishment of the English Commonwealth; Dec. 16, 1653-Sept. 3, 1658: Cromwell Rules England as Lord Protector; May, 1659-May, 1660: Restoration of Charles II.

RELATED ARTICLES in *Great Lives from History: The Seventeenth Century, 1601-1700:* Aphra Behn; Charles I; Charles II (of England); John Dryden; Henrietta Maria; James I; William Laud.

1640's

1643

TORRICELLI MEASURES ATMOSPHERIC PRESSURE

Torricelli was the first to define clearly the fundamental concept of "atmospheric pressure," confirming that air has weight. He invented the mercury barometer to measure this atmospheric pressure and to demonstrate that nature does not abhor a vacuum. His work supported Galileo's idea that Earth could move through space without losing its atmosphere, and he also noted the day-to-day variation in the height of mercury in a column, thus initiating the scientific study of meteorology.

LOCALE: Florence, Tuscany (now in Italy)
CATEGORIES: Science and technology; inventions; physics; cultural and intellectual history

KEY FIGURES

Evangelista Torricelli (1608-1647), Italian mathematician and physicist who invented the mercury barometer

Galileo (1564-1642), Italian physicist and astronomer who discovered the laws of falling bodies and projectiles

Benedetto Castelli (1577/1578-1643), student of Galileo and teacher of Torricelli

Ferdinand II de' Medici (1610-1670), grand duke of Tuscany, r. 1621-1670

Blaise Pascal (1623-1662), French philosopher, mathematician, and physicist who supported and developed Torricelli's air pressure concepts

Otto von Guericke (1602-1686), German engineer who invented the air pump

Robert Boyle (1627-1691), Irish physicist who experimented with reduced pressures

Robert Hooke (1635-1703), English experimenter and associate of Boyle

Edmé Mariotte (1620-1684), French Catholic priest and scientist who coined the word "barometer"

SUMMARY OF EVENT

Evangelista Torricelli studied the work of Galileo in Rome as a student of Benedetto Castelli, Galileo's favorite student who recommended him to Galileo. Torricelli invented the mercury barometer two years after serving as Galileo's secretary and assistant for the last three months of his long life. After Galileo died, Grand Duke Ferdinand II de' Medici of Tuscany appointed Torricelli to succeed Galileo as court mathematician at the Florentine Academy.

The invention of the mercury barometer followed a question raised by Galileo, who was curious why the grand duke's pump makers could raise water by suction to a height of only about 34 feet. Ironically, Galileo had appealed to the scholastic idea that "nature abhors a vacuum" to suggest that the "horror" extends to only about 34 feet. It occurred to Torricelli that Galileo's concept of gravity—applied to air—was the true explanation, suggesting that the weight of the air raises the water being pumped. He proposed that humans live at the bottom of a "sea of air," which extends up some 50 miles. To test this idea, he sealed one end of a two-cubit (each cubit equals about 20 inches) glass tube (called the Torricelli tube) and filled it with mercury. When he inverted the tube with the open end in a bowl of mercury, the column did not empty completely, but instead fell to a height of about 30 inches. Torricelli maintained that this 30-inch column of mercury, weighing about the same as 34 feet of water in a column of the same diameter, is held up by the weight of the air.

Torricelli expected this result because he knew that mercury is 13.6 times as heavy as water and, thus, 34 feet of water divided by 13.6 matches the 30 inches of mercury needed to counterbalance the weight of the air. Since a 30-inch column of mercury with one square inch of cross-sectional area weighs about 15 pounds, the air pressure is about 15 pounds per square inch, or 2,100 pounds per square foot at sea level. Torricelli also observed that the height of the mercury column varied from day to day because of changes in atmospheric pressure. These ideas later became important in the development of meteorology and of the steam engine.

Torricelli also maintained that the space above the mercury column is a vacuum, contrary to the scholastic opinion of the day, which held to Aristotle's argument that a void is logically impossible. The "Torricellian vacuum" was the first sustained vacuum. Demonstrating the two concepts, that a vacuum can exist and that the sea of air is held to Earth by gravity, was critical to support the new idea that Earth moves through the vacuum of space.

The first description of the mercury barometer was in a letter that Torricelli wrote on June 11, 1644, to his friend Michelangelo Ricci in Rome, a fellow student of Castelli. (Torricelli's letters on atmospheric pressure are translated into English in a volume of his *Collected Works*, 1919.) Later in 1644, he published in Florence his *Opera geometrica* (geometric works), which included original geometric theorems on the cycloid, his studies on projectile motion, and his work on fluids that led to his equation, known as Torricelli's law, to determine the speed of fluid flow from an opening in a vessel.

Unfortunately, Torricelli died of typhoid fever on October 25, 1647, at the young age of thirty-nine. He is honored in low-pressure research by the unit for pressure called the torr, equivalent to the pressure of one millimeter of mercury. Standard atmospheric pressure is defined as 760 torrs (76 cm of mercury).

Torricelli's ideas on atmospheric pressure and the vacuum were quickly confirmed and extended by other experimenters. In France, Blaise Pascal recognized that if air has weight, it should diminish with altitude. In 1646, he engaged his brother-in-law to climb the Puy-de-Dôme with a mercury barometer, finding that the mercury level dropped from its sea-level value of 76 centimeters to about 70 centimeters at a height of about one mile. In addition to inventing this altimeter concept, he suggested using the barometer to predict weather after noting that stormy conditions were usually preceded by falling air pressure.

In a famous experiment, Pascal refuted the idea that the mercury column is held up by vapor at the top of the column, thereby preventing a vacuum. He repeated Torricelli's experiment with red wine in a 14-meter tube. If the gap at the top of the column indeed were made of vapor instead of being a vacuum, then the volatile wine should fall lower than water; but if it were a vacuum, the lower-density wine should fall less than water to balance the weight of the air, as was observed. Pascal is honored by the International System of Units and the meter-kilogram-second (MKS) system for pressure called the Pascal.

The ideas of "air pressure" and "the vacuum" led to the invention of the air pump in 1650 by the German engineer Otto von Guericke, the burgomaster of Magdeburg. He showed that a close-fitting piston in an evacuated cylinder could not be removed by the effort of twenty men. In 1654, he gave a public demonstration of the power of a vacuum by evacuating two large metal hemispheres fitted together along a greased flange. Air pressure held these "Magdeburg hemispheres" together so tightly that even a team of sixteen horses could not pull them apart.

At Oxford University in England, Robert Boyle engaged Robert Hooke in 1657 to build an improved version of the air pump, and together they began to experiment with reduced air pressures. They showed that a ringing bell produced no sound in a vacuum and that a feather and lead ball fall at the same rate in an evacuated jar. In his first scientific work, *New Experiments Physico-Mechanicall, Touching the Spring of the Air and Its Effects* (pb. 1660), Boyle described his experiments in both physics and the physiology of respiration. By gradually exhausting the air in a jar containing a mouse and a candle, he observed the resulting expiration of the candle at about the same time as the mouse.

In 1662, Boyle found the pressure-volume law now known by his name: He showed that the volume of a gas is inversely proportional to the applied pressure. The same law was discovered independently several years later by the French physi-

Italian physicist and mathematician Evangelista Torricelli, demonstrating his barometer, which measures atmospheric pressure. (The Granger Collection)

1640's

cist Edmé Mariotte, who coined the word "barometer" in his *Discours de la nature de l'air* (pb. 1676; discourse on the nature of air).

SIGNIFICANCE
The invention of the mercury barometer by Evangelista Torricelli introduced the concept of "air pressure" and demonstrated the existence of a vacuum. His ideas solved one of the problems raised by the Copernican theory and Galileo's emphasis on a moving Earth: If Earth is in motion, it must carry its "sea of air" with it. Gravity acting on the air and producing air pressure holds the air in its place around the earth, and the surrounding space must be a vacuum if the atmosphere is not to be stripped away.

The barometer and the concept of "air pressure" led to many other important discoveries and inventions. It opened up the scientific field of meteorology in the development of the weather barometer, and it led to the work of Blaise Pascal and the concept of the "altimeter" to measure altitude above sea level. It also led to the invention of the air pump and to partial-vacuum experiments in both physics and physiology. The air pump in turn led to the invention of the steam engine, in which a vacuum can be produced by condensing steam in a cylinder and the resulting air pressure used to drive a piston, as first suggested by Robert Hooke.

—Joseph L. Spradley

FURTHER READING
Crump, Thomas. *A Brief History of Science as Seen Through the Development of Scientific Instruments.* New York: Carroll & Graf, 2001. This book includes a brief discussion of Torricelli's invention of the barometer.

Magie, William Francis. *A Source Book in Physics.* New York: McGraw-Hill, 1935. This book contains Torricelli's "Letter to Michelangelo Ricci Concerning the Barometer," taken from Torricelli's *Collected Works*, vol. 3 (wr. 1644, pb. 1919).

Margolis, Howard. *It Started with Copernicus.* New York: McGraw-Hill, 2002. About five pages in this book discuss the work of Torricelli.

Rossi, Paoli. *The Birth of Modern Science.* Translated by Cynthia De Nardi Ipsen. Oxford, England: Blackwell, 2001. This translation of *La nascita della scienza moderna in Europa* (2000) includes a brief discussion of Torricelli's work on the barometer in chapter 15, "Instruments and Theories," along with the confirming work of Pascal, von Guericke, and Boyle.

SEE ALSO: 1601-1672: Rise of Scientific Societies; 1660-1692: Boyle's Law and the Birth of Modern Chemistry; 1686: Halley Develops the First Weather Map; Summer, 1687: Newton Formulates the Theory of Universal Gravitation; July 25, 1698: Savery Patents the First Successful Steam Engine.

RELATED ARTICLES in *Great Lives from History: The Seventeenth Century, 1601-1700:* Robert Boyle; Galileo; Otto von Guericke; Edmond Halley; Robert Hooke; Sir Isaac Newton; Blaise Pascal; Evangelista Torricelli.

July, 1643-October 24, 1648
PEACE OF WESTPHALIA

The Peace of Westphalia brought an end to the Thirty Years' War and guaranteed the rights of Catholics and Protestants within the constitution of the Holy Roman Empire.

LOCALE: Osnabrück and Münster, Westphalia (now in Germany)
CATEGORIES: Diplomacy and international relations; wars, uprisings, and civil unrest

KEY FIGURES
Ferdinand III (1608-1657), Holy Roman Emperor, r. 1637-1657
Duc de Longueville (d. 1663), French ambassador to the peace conference

Axel Oxenstierna (1583-1654), Swedish ambassador to the peace conference and chancellor of Sweden, 1612-1654
Cardinal de Richelieu (Armand-Jean du Plessis; 1585-1642), chief minister of France, 1624-1642
Lennart Torstenson (1603-1651), Swedish commanding general whose military victories brought the imperial forces to the peace table
Count Maximilian von Trauttmansdorff (1584-1650), Ferdinand III's ambassador during the negotiations and the leading figure at the conference

SUMMARY OF EVENT
The Peace of Westphalia, which terminated the Thirty

Years' War, was drawn up at the first modern peace congress of European powers. Two major agreements, one drafted at Osnabrück between the Holy Roman Empire and Sweden, and the other at Münster between the empire and France, were both concluded, after protracted negotiations, on October 24, 1648. The very length and scope of the Westphalian peace conference reflected the complex nature of the many problems emanating from the long war, which had begun in 1618 with the Defenestration of Prague.

Within a few years, this initially isolated incident in Prague expanded into a general European war. Indeed, the four phases that can be distinguished in the conflict emphasize its international scope: the Bohemian-Palatinate period, 1618-1625; the Danish period, 1625-1629; the Swedish period, 1630-1635; and the Swedish-French period, 1635-1648. The major battleground was the Holy Roman Empire. During the first two periods of the war, the Catholic forces under Emperor Ferdinand II completely overwhelmed the Protestant opposition. The revolt in Bohemia was suppressed and the Rhenish Palatinate was conquered, as was Denmark, which had entered the conflict on behalf of the Protestant cause. The year 1629 found the Catholic cause everywhere triumphant; only the Netherlands, engaged since 1621 in a continuation of the Wars of Independence with Habsburg Spain, managed to hold its own.

Although religious issues played an important role throughout the conflict, they became increasingly subordinated to political interests during the last two periods of the war, when the Swedes and the French cooperated in an attempt to break the power of the Austrian and Spanish Habsburgs. The entry of Sweden into the war in 1630, led by King Gustavus II Adolphus and subsidized by Cardinal de Richelieu, chief minister of France, brought initial success over the imperial forces. Gustavus II Adolphus had entered the war reluctantly, hesitant to become involved in the sectarian cauldron of German politics. Nevertheless, he did so because he believed the success of imperial forces in the early stages of the war threatened the balance of the constitution of the Holy Roman Empire and the protection it offered to both Catholics and Protestants.

Once the Swedes had been deprived of the brilliant generalship of Gustavus II Adolphus through his death in battle in 1632, however, the imperial armies experienced a partial recovery, and a stalemate ensued. This situation was not substantially altered by the direct participation of France in the war after 1635 against the empire and Spain or the continued strength of the Swedish armies, led af-

ter the king's death by the generals Johan Banér and Lennart Torstenson. Hence, on December 25, 1641, the new emperor, Ferdinand III, agreed to begin peace negotiations the following year with Sweden and France in the Westphalian cities of Osnabrück and Münster, respectively.

Because fighting continued, diplomatic and military events delayed the formal opening of the peace conference at Osnabrück until July, 1643, and that at Münster until April, 1644. For all practical purposes, however, the congress, plagued by incredible problems of protocol and lack of a definite agenda, did not settle down to serious work until the end of 1645, when Count Maximilian von Trauttmansdorff arrived. Trauttmansdorff, chief ambassador of the emperor, was the leading personality of the peace conference. From the outset he demonstrated singular ability to establish good relations with his Swedish and French counterparts, Axel Oxenstierna and the duc de Longueville. Once such an atmosphere had been created, the major powers, together with Spain and the Netherlands, found it somewhat easier to resolve the many complicated issues that divided them. Even so, it took the imperial negotiators almost three years to hammer out peace treaties with the Swedes, who were joined at Osnabrück by Protestant representatives from the empire, and the French.

Because of their close interrelationship, the major provisions of the Treaties of Münster and Osnabrück, both signed on October 24, 1648, as well as a separate agreement signed earlier between Spain and the Netherlands, may be considered as parts of a single settlement, known as the Peace of Westphalia. The stipulations of the settlement can be divided into matters touching the religious affairs of the Holy Roman Empire and those relating to the political affairs of the several European powers concerned. The religious side of the Peace of Westphalia was designed to reconcile Protestant and Catholic elements in the empire; Calvinism received equal, legal status with Catholicism and Lutheranism.

This purely religious equality had its political counterpart in that the Catholic and Protestant states of the empire were now considered to have equal status in imperial affairs. The victory of equality, however, was limited as to the free exercise of religion by individuals. The princes in several states still had the unqualified right to determine the religion of their territories, a principle rigorously enforced in Austria long after 1648. This principle, known as *cuius regio, eius religio* and roughly translated as "The religion of the ruler determines the religion of the ruled," did not solve the problem of individual civil

EUROPE AFTER THE PEACE OF WESTPHALIA, 1648

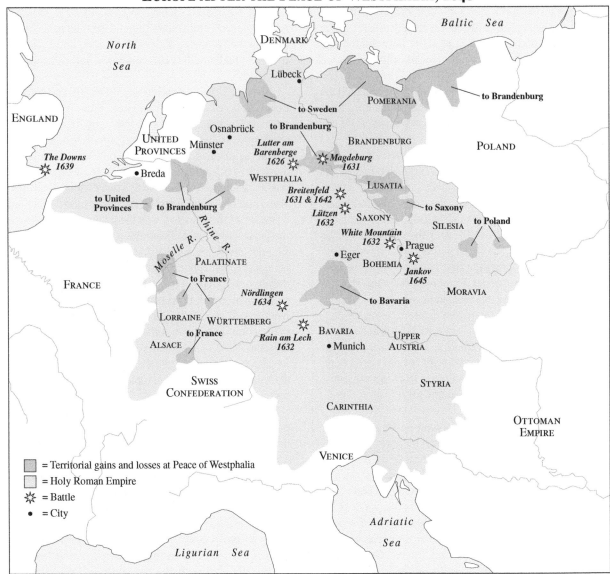

rights, but it made sure that there would always be places where persecuted Catholics or Protestants could find toleration. Finally, ecclesiastical territories were to remain in the possession of the upholders of whichever religion held them on January 1, 1624.

As to the major political provisions of the treaties, Sweden obtained a foothold on the southern Baltic coast through the acquisition of lands in the Holy Roman Empire: Western Pomerania and the secularized bishoprics of Bremen and Verden. Sweden thus reached its apogee as a world power. This development was of more than lo-

cal significance, for the existence of the Protestant world power of Sweden guaranteed the long-term survival of Protestantism. Protestantism was no longer in danger of being a mere hundred-year heresy; it was a permanent part of the European cultural landscape. Although Sweden declined as a power for internal reasons shortly thereafter, its place as a Protestant world power was taken by Great Britain in the 1700's. France, likewise, secured holdings within the empire: Metz, Toul, and Verdun, all of which had actually been under French control since 1522, and Alsace. Brandenburg-Prussia received Eastern Pomerania and several secularized bishoprics. Other stipulations of the settlement recognized the complete independence of the Spanish Netherlands and of Switzerland of the empire, and the virtual independence and sovereignty of each of the German states of the Holy Roman Empire.

SIGNIFICANCE

The Peace of Westphalia of 1648 was a landmark in European history. On the religious side, the Reformation and the Counter-Reformation had ended. Religion no longer played a critical role in the issues that divided European states. Politically, Sweden emerged as a great power in northern Europe for at least the following sixty years. Likewise, the position of Brandenburg-Prussia was greatly strengthened. The Holy Roman Empire, however, became more loosely organized than before. Modern historians tend to criticize the near-anarchy of hundreds of basically self-ruling principalities that were unleashed within the empire; eighteenth century thinkers such as Voltaire and Edward Gibbon, though, praised the pluralism of the revised imperial constitution.

Spain's decline, obvious by 1648, was all the more evident when peace was finally made with France in 1659. France under Louis XIV emerged in the second half of the seventeenth century as the leading Continental power, eager to challenge anew its old adversaries, the Spanish and the Austrian Habsburgs.

As historian C. V. Wedgwood has commented, "the Peace of Westphalia was like most peace treaties, a rearrangement of the European map ready for the next war."

—Edward P. Keleher and Nicholas Birns

FURTHER READING

Asch, Ronald G. *The Thirty Years' War: The Holy Roman Empire and Europe, 1618-1648*. New York: St. Martin's Press, 1997. The work focuses on the Holy Roman Empire's role in the war, including the empire's disagreements with Bohemia that precipitated the conflict.

Croxton, Derek. *Peacemaking in Early Modern Europe: Cardinal Mazarin and the Congress of Westphalia, 1643-1648*. Selinsgrove, Pa.: Susquehanna University Press, 1999. Croxton provides a detailed explanation of the five-year negotiations that eventually ended the Thirty Years' War. The book focuses on Mazarin's role, refuting conventional wisdom that the French minister sought to prolong the conflict.

Guthrie, William P. *Battles of the Thirty Years' War: From White Mountain to Nordlingen, 1618-1635*. Westport, Conn.: Greenwood Press, 2002. The best and most comprehensive account of the military actions during the Bohemian, Danish, and Swedish phases of the Thirty Years' War. Guthrie's excellent appendices provide valuable information on many aspects of the battles.

_____. *The Later Thirty Years' War: From the Battle of Wittstock to the Treaty of Westphalia*. Westport, Conn.: Greenwood Press, 2003. Guthrie's account of the French phase of the Thirty Years' War is the best and the most detailed account in English. Provides excellent, detailed appendices.

Lee, Stephen J. *The Thirty Years' War*. London: Routledge & Kegan Paul, 1991. Lee offers an excellent introduction to the causes and major issues of the war. He examines the motives of the participants, their gains and losses, and the religious, military, social, and economic aspects of the war.

Parker, Geoffrey. *Europe in Crisis, 1598-1648*. Ithaca, N.Y.: Cornell University Press, 1980. This work is useful for understanding the diplomatic strategies of France, Sweden, and the Holy Roman Empire.

_____, ed. *The Thirty Years' War*. 2d ed. New York: Routledge, 1997. A collection of essays examining the military and diplomatic aspects of the war from the perspectives of all participants. Incorporates research that updates the original 1984 edition. Good general introduction.

Wedgwood, C. V. *The Thirty Years' War*. New York: Methuen, 1981. A good narrative history of the conflict. First published in 1938, this revision is somewhat out-of-date when compared to the essay collection edited by Geoffrey Parker.

SEE ALSO: July 5, 1601-Apr., 1604: Siege of Oostende; 1618-1648: Thirty Years' War; May 23, 1618: Defenestration of Prague; Nov. 8, 1620: Battle of White Mountain; Mar. 6, 1629: Edict of Restitution; 1630-1648: Destruction of Bavaria; May 30, 1635: Peace of Prague; Nov. 7, 1659: Treaty of the Pyrenees; 1667: Pufendorf Advocates a Unified Germany.

RELATED ARTICLES in *Great Lives from History: The Seventeenth Century, 1601-1700:* Alexander VII; Christina; The Great Condé; Gustavus II Adolphus; Louis XIV; Jules Mazarin; Axel Oxenstierna; Samuel von Pufendorf; Cardinal de Richelieu; Lennart Torstenson.

August 17-September 25, 1643
SOLEMN LEAGUE AND COVENANT

The Kirk of Scotland and the English parliament approved an agreement under which Reformed Protestantism and Presbyterianism were to be preserved in Scotland. In return, the Scots agreed to join the English Civil War on the side of Parliament to defeat the Episcopalian king.

LOCALE: British Isles
CATEGORIES: Religion and theology; government and politics

KEY FIGURES

Alexander Henderson (1583?-1646), principal author of the Solemn League and Covenant
Charles I (1600-1649), king of England, r. 1625-1649
James I (1566-1625), king of England, r. 1603-1625, and king of Scotland as James VI, r. 1567-1625
James II (1633-1701), king of England, r. 1685-1688
William III (1650-1702), king of England, r. 1689-1702

SUMMARY OF EVENT

By 1560, Protestantism had become the official religion of Scotland, where the first General Assembly of the new national church (the Kirk of Scotland) adopted a Presbyterian form of polity and the Calvinistic system of doctrine. Resistance from the Catholic Mary, Queen of Scots (r. 1542-1567), led Protestant nobles to force her abdication in favor of her infant son, whom the lords made King James VI of Scotland. In 1603, James became king of England as well under the title James I, and he soon displayed a preference for the episcopal polity that administered the Church of England. Episcopacy, or rule within the Church by bishops, threatened the more democratic Presbyterian settlement that had established the Kirk of Scotland.

In addition to potential Scottish unrest, moreover, James encountered opposition from English Puritans who, like their Scottish counterparts, rejected the rule of bishops. In both of his kingdoms, James desired to reduce the church to a department of the state, and he suppressed Presbyterian leaders who resisted his scheme. James saw the hierarchy of the episcopacy, in which the archbishop commanded the bishops and the bishops commanded the rest, as analogous to the absolutist power he believed was the divine right of monarchs. He resolved to require the Scots to adopt the Anglican Book of Common Prayer and to accept authoritative bishops.

He manipulated both the Parliament and the Kirk of Scotland to comply with his requirements. As a result, pronounced tensions developed between the Presbyterians and the Crown.

Upon the death of James I in 1625, Charles I became king and proved even more authoritarian than his father had been. To his hatred of Presbyterianism, Charles added an unqualified rejection of Calvinist theology. His demand that the Scots adopt the Book of Common Prayer provoked riots in which zealous nobles were involved. Scots organized to resist their king, and to do so they pledged themselves to God and to one another by covenant at Greyfriars' Church, Edinburgh, on March 1, 1638.

The meeting at Greyfriars' produced a reaffirmation of the National Covenant that James had accepted in 1580. Across Scotland, Presbyterians vowed to restore the character and polity of their church according to Scripture and following the example of Reformed churches elsewhere. "For Christ's Crown and Covenant" became their slogan. The war against bishops that followed this meeting in 1639 became known as the First Bishops' War.

In 1640, Charles was forced to call a Parliament for the first time in eleven years in order to levy taxes to support a war to suppress the Scots. Parliament, which alone had the power to levy new taxes, refused the king's request, and in 1642, England itself erupted in civil war between king and Parliament. In this English Civil War, the beleaguered Parliament sought Scottish aid, which was forthcoming only after the English joined the Solemn League and Covenant. In this agreement, both kingdoms promised to preserve the Reformed faith in Scotland and to seek further Reformation in England and Ireland. Elimination of popery and prelacy, plus affirmation of Christ's kingship over all, was the declared goal of their agreement. Alexander Henderson, moderator of the General Assembly in Scotland, had composed the Covenant in 1638. The Kirk of Scotland approved it on August 17, 1643, and the English parliament followed suit on September 25 of that year. To the Scots, the Solemn League and Covenant was a religious pact, not just a military alliance.

Large numbers of people from all classes in Scotland signed the Covenant, a document with an introduction, six articles, and a conclusion. The Covenant reflected the Scots' desire to retain the monarchy while requiring the king to submit to the rule of Christ. It lamented the poor state of religion in Ireland and the internal strife wracking England, and it warned of dangers to the Kirk of Scotland. The avowed intention of the signatories was to maintain and propagate the Reformed faith in theology, polity, discipline, and worship, which would require removal of Catholicism and any other objectionable teachings. Subscribers promised to prosecute enemies of the Reformed religion and any who opposed the Solemn League and Covenant. The document closed with a confession of sins and a declaration of desire for the glory of God and the peace of the three kingdoms under the authority of Christ.

The Covenant was a Scottish creation, and in Scotland it had its most dramatic and lasting effects. There, subscription to the Covenant was mandatory. People who refused to sign could not attend universities, and the law required all government and military officials to subscribe. Clergymen who refused lost their positions. Many who did sign were insincere.

The English Civil Wars, in which the Scots participated, brought the execution of Charles I in 1649, an event that estranged Scottish Presbyterians from their Puritan comrades. The Scots had no desire to eliminate the monarchy. For eleven years, the English throne was vacant, while Oliver Cromwell governed a Commonwealth as lord protector. The disenfranchised Prince Charles was declared King Charles II in Scotland in 1651, however. Charles signed the Solemn League and Covenant to gain Scottish support for his cause, but he had no intention of implementing it. When he became king of England in 1660, he at first ignored the Covenant. Within two years, the Scottish Parliament abrogated the Covenant and required public officials to renounce it. There were burnings of the document in England and Scotland.

Although the Puritans cared sincerely for the religious principles enunciated in the Covenant, the rule of the Commonwealth alienated most of the populace, so there was little interest in England in maintaining its provisions. In Scotland, a minority of devout Presbyterians, who came to be known as Covenanters, contended that maintaining the Solemn League and Covenant was a

---

THE SOLEMN LEAGUE AND COVENANT

The Solemn League and Covenant is part treaty, part doctrinal statement, melding religion and politics. The heart of the document is the section reproduced below, in which all Covenanters swear to preserve the Reformed Scottish Church.

That we shall sincerely, really and constantly, through the grace of God, endeavour in our several places and callings, the preservation of the reformed religion in the Church of Scotland, in doctrine, worship, discipline and government, against our common enemies; the reformation of religion in the kingdoms of England and Ireland, in doctrine, worship, discipline and government, according to the Word of God, and the example of the best reformed Churches; and we shall endeavour to bring the Churches of God in the three kingdoms to the nearest conjunction and uniformity in religion, confession of faith, form of Church government, directory for worship and catechising, that we, and our posterity after us, may, as brethren, live in faith and love, and the Lord may delight to dwell in the midst of us.

Source: From http://www.constitution.org/eng/conpur058.htm. Accessed April 26, 2005.

---

moral duty for all Christians. During the reigns of Charles II and James II, those dissidents suffered cruel persecution, and about four hundred pastors were ejected from their pulpits when they refused to disavow the Covenant.

The last two Stuart monarchs tried once again to destroy Presbyterianism in favor of episcopacy, and resistance to the rule of bishops was largely ineffective. When such resistance did occur, severe reprisals followed in what the Covenanters called the Killing Time. James II, however, undermined his own position by extending favors to Catholics, actions that aroused broad Protestant opposition in Scotland and England. In 1688-1689, James was peacefully deposed, and William III and Mary II ascended the throne in the Glorious Revolution. These joint monarchs initiated toleration for all Protestants and some favor toward Presbyterians. In 1690, the Scottish parliament ratified the Westminster Confession of Faith and Presbyterian Polity for the Kirk of Scotland, although the church remained, to a degree, subject to the state.

SIGNIFICANCE

The Revolution Settlement of 1689 allowed broad freedom of religion in England, Scotland, and Ireland. Thus, followers of the Reformed faith were free to worship as they desired, but their religion was not ratified or preferred over other brands of Protestantism. Strict Covenanters objected to the freedoms granted to competing religions and insisted government had no right to regulate such matters. The General Assembly of the National Church ignored their protests, as most Scotsmen rejoiced over the new toleration. A separate Reformed Presbyterian Church maintained that the Covenant was morally binding upon the nation, of which Christ was the ultimate monarch.

The Kirk of Scotland after 1689 allowed ministers to serve even when they made only a perfunctory subscription to the confession of faith, and the Moderate party gained enough strength within the Kirk to dilute its traditional theology. An opposing Evangelical party tried unsuccessfully to preserve that doctrine, at least in some measure. The Moderates espoused an ethical conception of religion and acceptance of critical approaches to Scripture. The Evangelicals stressed the need for repentance and personal piety.

With the support of the Moderates, Parliament restored lay patronage, a practice that permitted wealthy landowners to choose some pastors. This conflicted with Presbyterian polity, which leaves election of ministers solely to the congregations. Secessions from the Kirk of Scotland occurred because the General Assembly failed to oppose patronage vigorously. Covenanters never relinquished their demand that church and state, though distinct, must submit to the Lordship of Christ. The expectation that the state should support and protect the church while refraining from interference in ecclesiastical affairs proved to be a delusion. Only the autonomous denominations remained free from state control.

—James Edward McGoldrick

FURTHER READING

Cameron, Nigel M. de S., ed. *Dictionary of Scottish Church History and Theology*. Downers Grove, Ill.: InterVarsity Press, 1993. This triumph of historical and religious scholarship is rich in entries pertaining to the Solemn League and Covenant.

The Covenant: With a Narrative of the Proceedings and Solemn Manner of Taking It by the Honourable House of Commons and Reverent Assembly of Divines. London: Thomas Underhill, 1643. The text of the Covenant combined with a description of the debate within the English House of Commons and of its passage on September 25, 1643. Also includes the text of speeches given by Alexander Henderson and Philip Nye.

Moore, Edwin Nisbet. *Our Covenant Heritage*. Ross-shire, Scotland: Christian Focus, 2000. An exciting account of the Covenanters' struggle for freedom and the cruel persecutions they endured. The author is a talented amateur historian with family roots in the crises of the seventeenth century.

Stevenson, David. *The Covenanters*. Edinburgh: Saltire Society, 1988. A lucid and brief introduction by a dispassionate author; an excellent place to begin a study of this subject.

Vos, Johannes. *The Scottish Covenanters*. 1940. Reprint. Edinburgh: Blue Banner, 1998. A frankly partisan history written in nontechnical style; extols sacrifices of the dissidents in resisting state tyranny over the church.

SEE ALSO: Mar. 24, 1603: James I Becomes King of England; 1611: Publication of the King James Bible; Mar., 1629-1640: "Personal Rule" of Charles I; Mar.-June, 1639: First Bishops' War; Nov. 3, 1640-May 15, 1641: Beginning of England's Long Parliament; Oct. 23, 1641-1642: Ulster Insurrection; 1642-1651: English Civil Wars; July 2, 1644: Battle of Marston Moor; Dec. 6, 1648-May 19, 1649: Establishment of the English Commonwealth; Dec. 16, 1653-Sept. 3, 1658: Cromwell Rules England as Lord Protector; May, 1659-May, 1660: Restoration of Charles II; 1688-1702: Reign of William and Mary; Nov., 1688-Feb., 1689: The Glorious Revolution; May 24, 1689: Toleration Act.

RELATED ARTICLES in *Great Lives from History: The Seventeenth Century, 1601-1700:* Charles I; Charles II (of England); Oliver Cromwell; James I; James II; Mary II; William III.

September 8, 1643
CONFEDERATION OF THE UNITED COLONIES OF NEW ENGLAND

Plymouth, Connecticut, and New Haven joined with the larger Massachusetts Bay Colony to form a military alliance. Although not always free from disputes, the early cooperation among the colonies embodied in their treaty set a precedent for their 1686 union.

LOCALE: Massachusetts Bay, Plymouth, Connecticut, and New Haven colonies

CATEGORIES: Government and politics; diplomacy and international relations

KEY FIGURES

William Collier (c. 1612-1670), Plymouth commissioner of the United Colonies of New England

Thomas Dudley (1576-1653), deputy governor of Massachusetts Bay Colony and commissioner of the United Colonies of New England

Theophilus Eaton (1590-1658), governor of the New Haven Colony and commissioner of the United Colonies of New England

George Fenwick (c. 1603-1657), Connecticut commissioner of the United Colonies of New England

John Haynes (1594-1654), governor of Connecticut and commissioner of the United Colonies of New England

Thomas Hooker (1586-1647), Connecticut theologian and framer of the Connecticut constitution

Edward Hopkins (c. 1602-1657), governor of Connecticut and commissioner of the United Colonies of New England

Edward Winslow (1595-1655), Plymouth commissioner of the United Colonies of New England

SUMMARY OF EVENT

In 1607, a shipload of English settlers arrived in the New World and established Jamestown, in what is now Virginia. The next English colonial settlement was founded in 1620 at Plymouth, in New England, by the Pilgrims, religious separatists who had been persecuted in Britain. They had intended to settle in Virginia as well, but when their ship, the *Mayflower*, was blown off course and arrived farther north than expected, the Pilgrims decided to create a new community there.

As New England settlement expanded north, south, and west during the 1630's, territorial conflicts became inevitable. Not only did the Puritan colonies attempt to encroach upon one another's territory, but they also came into hostile contact with American Indians, the Dutch, and the French. Although the English nearly destroyed the native population of New England in the brief Pequot War of 1636-1637, the lack of coordinated effort in that war convinced the British that some form of intercolonial cooperation was necessary to determine military policies, ensure participation, arbitrate territorial disputes, and regulate trade. Religious and political turmoil in England in the 1630's and 1640's prevented the mother country from supervising colonial affairs directly, and the colonies preferred it that way. In the absence of formal control from above, however, the Puritan colonies recognized a need to defend their expanding boundaries against foreign aggression.

The joint action between New England's colonies in the Pequot War apparently had fostered a feeling of unity among the Puritan colonies. Furthermore, the leaders of the smaller, weaker colonies of Plymouth, Connecticut, and New Haven realized that if they could enter into an agreement with the Massachusetts Bay Colony as political equals, they would be free from that powerful colony's attempts to encroach upon their territory. The Massachusetts Bay Colony, in turn, would profit from such a union by gaining legal approval from the other member colonies for its efforts to annex territory in Maine.

In the late summer of 1637, a synod of New England church leaders meeting in Cambridge seriously broached the subject of union for the first time, but disagreements marred that and several other attempts to achieve union during the next few years. Fear of an American Indian uprising in 1642, however, spurred Plymouth to send representatives to negotiate with the Massachusetts Bay Colony about their mutual defense. About the same time, Connecticut also sent a proposal for mutual defense efforts to Massachusetts. The Massachusetts General Court, therefore, ordered the magistrates to meet with the deputies of Connecticut, Plymouth, and New Haven on the matters of unification and defense.

Meeting in Boston on May 29, 1643, the American colonies of Massachusetts Bay, Connecticut, New Haven, and Plymouth formed a military alliance. The members of the alliance agreed to coordinate their military operations while retaining independence in internal affairs. The representatives "readily yielded each to the other, in such things as tended to the common good," and drew up articles of confederation. When the last of the four General Courts ratified them on September 8, 1643, these articles of confederation became binding. The newly established United Colonies of New England encompassed all the settlements along the coast and rivers from Long Island to New Hampshire. Rhode Island, which the Puritans disdainfully considered anarchical, and Maine were not included.

As stated in the preamble to the articles of confederation, the purposes of the confederation were to preserve the purity of the Puritans' religion and their ability to worship free of interference, to promote cooperation, and to provide for defense. The articles themselves specified the duties and powers of the confederation's commissioners, the structure of the confederation, and the rules of procedure. Because there was no judicial authority over all the members, each colony could interpret the articles of confederation to its own liking—a situation that was to cause problems later.

The governing body of the confederation was to consist of two annually chosen commissioners from each colony. The only qualifications demanded were that they be church members and that they bring full power from their general courts. The commissioners—William Collier, Thomas Dudley, Theophilus Eaton, George Fenwick, John Haynes, Thomas Hooker, Edward Hopkins, and Edward Winslow—were to convene each September and meet in each colony successively. Anyone who had advice to offer was welcome to speak before them. Three magistrates from any colony could call a special meeting if necessary. Approval of a matter required the votes of six commissioners, although war could be declared by only four during a state of emergency. Thus, the Massachusetts Bay Colony could not veto the wishes of the other three colonies if they were united.

The United Colonies of New England did not consider themselves a nation, but rather individual governments allied by a treaty. Each commissioner actually served as one of his colony's ambassadors to the others. In matters of military preparation, declaration of war, and arbitration, however, the four colonies did surrender to the commissioners their individual powers to act. Although the confederation's commissioners, in theory, possessed vague executive and judicial powers, in actuality they had only advisory powers in most areas.

The articles of confederation specified that each colony's military obligation should be in proportion to its means and population. Each colony was expected to send aid if one of the other three colonies should be invaded and was to participate in all just wars. The commissioners were empowered to decide if the confederation should wage an offensive war, and no colony could do so without their approval.

Apart from military affairs, actual power rested with the general courts of the member colonies. The commissioners could not pass legislation binding on the general courts, nor were they directly responsible to the people. They could neither levy taxes nor requisition supplies. Because the commissioners had no powers of enforcement, a colony that disagreed with a particular decision could nullify it simply by refusing to comply. To avoid conflict, the remaining colonies usually compromised.

Although lacking in power, the Board of Commissioners did perform numerous important services for the four participating colonies. It established various civil agreements of interest to all four colonies and arbitrated intercolonial disputes. Policies concerning American Indians and regulations governing runaway slaves and the extradition of criminals were also within its domain. In the judicial realm, the commissioners established uniform standards for probating wills and served as an admiralty court. Other duties included fund-raising for Harvard College, settling tariff disputes, and promoting religious orthodoxy.

SIGNIFICANCE

The major specific achievement of the military alliance of the confederation was the successful cooperation of its members in Metacom's War (King Philip's War) of 1675-1676, in which the colonies crushed an uprising of Wampanoag Indians. On a less tangible but more significant level, the confederation of the United Colonies of New England was essential to the colonies' survival in the colonies' early years and, despite its flaws, offered a means of coordinating intercolonial resources and resolving disputes.

The confederation was hampered in the successful achievement of some of its aims, however, when bitter rivalries developed among the member colonies. Massachusetts Bay Colony, for example, attempted to win a predominant position within the confederation on the grounds that it had the largest population; failing in this attempt, it refused, in 1653, to participate in a projected war against the Dutch colonies in America. In 1684, shortly after the charter of the Massachusetts Bay Colony was revoked by the English government, the confederation was dissolved.

Unquestionably, serious flaws were inherent in the confederation of the United Colonies of New England. The illusion of power survived only for the first decade of its existence. It was, however, the longest-lived interstate confederation in American history. The leadership that the confederation provided was essential to the existence of the colonies in their early years. It concentrated the colonies' resources in military emergencies and protected the three weaker colonies from encroachment by the Massachusetts Bay Colony. Most important of all, it preserved the peace in New England.

—*Warren M. Billings and Susan M. Taylor*

FURTHER READING

Andrews, Charles M. *The Settlements*. Vols. 1 and 2 in *The Colonial Period of American History*. New Haven, Conn.: Yale University Press, 1964. The chapters on the New England colonies contain frequent references to the affairs and problems of the Confederation of the United Colonies of New England.

Francis, Mark. *Governors and Settlers: Images of Authority in the British Colonies*. London: Macmillan, 1992. Discusses administration and cooperation in the early New England colonies and provides historical background.

Fraser, Gary. *Ambivalent Anti-Colonialism: The United States and the Genesis of West Indian Independence*. Westport, Conn.: Greenwood Press, 1994. Provides a detailed discussion of the early history of the colonies and British relations with the United States.

Greene, Jack P. *Pursuits of Happiness: Social Development of Early Modern British Colonies and the Formation of American Culture*. Chapel Hill: University of North Carolina Press, 1988. Explains the models of English colonization from 1600 to 1660.

Lister, Frederick K. *The Early Security Confederations: From the Ancient Greeks to the United Colonies of New England*. Westport, Conn.: Greenwood Press, 1999. Describes the development of security confederations from their inception in ancient Greece through creation of the United Colonies of New England.

Osgood, Herbert L. *The American Colonies in the Seventeenth Century*. Gloucester, Mass.: Peter Smith, 1957. Provides an institutional history of England's mainland colonies, focusing on the commercial relationship between Great Britain and America.

Ward, Harry M. *The United Colonies of New England, 1643-1690*. New York: Vantage Press, 1961. Examines the ideas that influenced the Founding Fathers and explains what prompted attempts at unification.

SEE ALSO: May 14, 1607: Jamestown Is Founded; Dec. 26, 1620: Pilgrims Arrive in North America; May, 1630-1643: Great Puritan Migration; Fall, 1632-Jan. 5, 1665: Settlement of Connecticut; June, 1636: Rhode Island Is Founded; Nov., 1641: Massachusetts Recognizes Slavery; 1642-1651: English Civil Wars; May 30-31, 1650: First College in North America; June 20, 1675: Metacom's War Begins; June, 1686-Apr., 1689: Dominion of New England Forms.

RELATED ARTICLES in *Great Lives from History: The Seventeenth Century, 1601-1700:* William Bradford; Thomas Hooker; Anne Hutchinson; Miles Standish; Roger Williams.

1644-1671
NDONGO WARS

Queen Njinga of Ndongo and Matamba led an African resistance to Portuguese expansion into Angola that developed into the Battle of Ngolome and the start of the Ndongo Wars. The battle was lost by Njinga's fighters, however, which led, ultimately, to the region's domination by the Portuguese and their perpetuation of the slave trade.

LOCALE: Ndongo kingdom, near the Kwanza River, Angola

CATEGORIES: Wars, uprisings, and civil unrest; expansion and land acquisition; colonization; government and politics; economics

KEY FIGURES

Njinga (1582-1663), queen of Ndongo and Matamba, r. 1624-1663

Ari (d. 1664), Portuguese-supported ruler of Ndongo, r. 1627-1664

Luís Mendes de Sousa Chicorro (d. 1658), Portuguese governor of Angola, 1655-1658

Salvador Correia de Sá e Benevides (1594-1688), Portuguese commander on the Angolan coast and governor of Angola

SUMMARY OF EVENT

Seeking access to the African interior for slaves, Paulo Dias founded in 1576 the city of Luanda for Portugal, near the mouth of the Kwanza River on the west coast of Africa. This territory, named "Angola," comes from the title "Ngola a kiluanje," which named the ruler of the Ndongo kingdom, a kingdom that extended inland 250 miles. The Ndongo, along with the Matamba and Imbangala, make up the Mbundu people, one of the larger ethnic groups in Angola.

Initially, the Mbundu were optimistic about Portuguese relations, hoping to diminish the influence of the rival Kongo Kingdom to the north. However, attitudes changed as Paulo Dias began a military conquest. Stiff resistance came from the Ndongo ruler Ngola Kiluanji, Njinga's father, who opposed the Portuguese forces from his capital in Kabasa. By 1604, the *conquista* (the area conquered by Portugal) had expanded only about 100 miles inland to Massangano, where the Portuguese established a fortress. Not a single Mbundu chief had been paying tribute to the Portuguese. However, captives from these military campaigns were channeled into the growing slave market.

In 1617, following the death of Kiluanji and four decades of his rule, the Portuguese met a measure of success against Kiluanji's son Mbandi. Kabasa was attacked and burned to the ground. After his mother and wife were killed Mbandi had to seek refuge at an island fortress on the Kwanza River.

A rather influential African ruler, Njinga, found herself center stage. Her name first appeared in Portuguese records (1622) in Luanda as the emissary of Mbandi, who was her half brother. When the Portuguese governor John Correia de Sousa left Njinga standing in his presence, one of the Ndongo soldiers kneeled behind her to form a human chair. With dignity she negotiated a peace treaty, recognized Mbandi as a legitimate and independent king, and returned a key fortress. In turn, the Portuguese gained trade rights. Njinga accepted Christian baptism and took the name Dona Ana de Sousa.

The following year, after Mbandi mysteriously died in 1623, Njinga emerged as ruler of the Ndongo. While a proven diplomat with the Portuguese, she was less successful with the Ndongo. In their matrilineal society, she was not in line to the throne. Many were suspicious of the new Christian missionaries within her kingdom. A greater problem was that a new governor neglected the promises made in Luanda. Njinga retreated inland for refuge on the Kindonga islands. There she began to build up a coalition against the Portuguese. Although she had earlier accepted the reality of the slave trade, she would soon welcome to her cause runaway slaves. In 1627, a new governor, Fernão de Sousa, appointed in her place a chieftain from Pungu as Portugal's puppet king. Though a Ndongo himself, the new king, Ari, saw continued popular support for Njinga.

The Imbangala, who had lived south of the Kwanza River and had been migrating east, were made up of fugitives from the Portuguese, marginalized members of the Ndongo court, and mercenary warrior bands. Eventually, they established a new kingdom—Kasanje—that offered large numbers of bowmen to Njinga. She would adopt some of the combat practices of the Imbangala warriors, which made her fighting force all the more fierce and threatening.

Sometime between 1630 and 1635, Njinga turned her eye on another Mbundu kingdom to the east. Following the death of the Matamba king, she took his daughter captive, which led to Njinga becoming ruler over both

Ndongo and Matamba. She soon began her attacks on Ari near Mbaka fort.

During the 1640's, Njinga found another unexpected ally against Portugal. With Portugal drawn into inter-European wars, the Dutch made inroads upon Portuguese territory, first in Kongo and then Luanda. The Portuguese governor fled inland to Massangano to govern a *conquista* that had been reduced to the size of a tribal chiefdom. Njinga negotiated an alliance with the Dutch to provide prisoners of war from her battles with Ari, which would bolster the Dutch slave trade.

The Battle of Ngolome at Kweta (Kiata) in 1644 marked the start of the Ndongo Wars. Even though the Portuguese sent a significant force, Njinga and her general, Amona, were successful in capturing Kanini, the chief of Mbaka, whom they converted to their side. The Portuguese were on the brink of total defeat, and outside reinforcements sailing from Bahia seemed pointless. The new troops were marched toward Massangano in the spring of 1645, only to be annihilated along the way. Only a second group of reinforcements arriving with a new governor, Francisco Sotomaior, managed to reach Massangano safely.

Sotomaior made every effort to halt Njinga's continued raids on Ndongo territory. At a confrontation near the Dande River in 1646, Njinga seemed to have strategic advantage, as Dutch soldiers supported her troops in battle and provided them with guns. However, her forces where overwhelmed by Ari and the Portuguese, who even managed to enter the queen's compound to take her sister Mukambu prisoner. They also recovered intelligence reports sent to Njinga from the Kongo and from another imprisoned sister, Kifunji. Njinga retreated back to Matamba lands, while the Portuguese moved to break

up the queen's alliances. Among the first was the king of Kasanje, who agreed to support Portugal in return for promised economic benefits.

Njinga planned a raid to rescue her sister Kifunji. The Portuguese pulled back to the fortress Massangano and drowned Kifunji in the Kwanza River. Njinga made a tactical error by not launching an immediate attack. On August 24, 1648, Salvador Correia de Sá e Benevides arrived with Brazilian troops and retook the city of Luanda, expelling the Dutch. The Portuguese began consolidating their own holdings, and they subjugated local Ndongo chiefdoms. The capture of warriors restarted the flow of slaves to Brazil. Portugal also turned its attention north in a long campaign against Kongo, which culminated in the successful Battle of Mbwila in 1665.

In the meantime, governor Luís Mendes de Sousa Chicorro was instructed to not attack Matamba and instead seek diplomatic ties with Njinga to reopen trade routes east. A key element was the release of Njinga's imprisoned sister Mukambu. The peace treaty was finally signed on October 12, 1656, resulting in the establishment of trade and Christian missions in Matamba. Mukambu married Njinga's chief military general, Amona. On December 17, 1663, Queen Njinga died, leaving her sister and husband as rulers. Mukambu died three years later.

Njinga always saw herself as legitimate ruler of Ndongo, yet she failed to remove from power the Portuguese puppet king Ari. Once Portugal reasserted itself, however, a period of neglect began, with many Ndongo reduced to slaves and with the ignoring of long-standing promises. Ari's complaints went unheeded, and he died in 1664.

The new ruler of Matamba and of Ndongo attempted to reassert their independence from the Portuguese. Luís Lopes de Sequeira, fresh from successful campaigns against Kongo, responded by attacking the Ndongo capital fortress at Pungu a Ndongo. With reinforcements from Brazil, the fortress was sacked by the Portuguese on November 29, 1671, and the Ndongo ruler was killed. The Ndongo kingdom had been crushed, and Matamba's demise soon followed.

Significance

The defeat of the Ndongo and Matamba changed the political landscape of central Africa. Portugal built a new fort at Pungu a Ndongo, instituting direct rule over the Mbundu. Previously, Ndongo had been a source for slaves, but after the Ndongo Wars, the region became a corridor to the interior of Africa. New kingdoms in the east, such as Kasanje and Lunda, emerged. By the eigh-

NDONGO RULERS	
Dates	*Ruler*
Unknown	Ngana Ngombe
d. 1557	Ngola Inene Kiluanji
r. 1557-1563	Ngola Ndambi
Unknown	Ngola Kiluanji
Unknown	Njinga Ngola Kilombo
r. 1563-1617	Mbandi Ngola Kiluanji
r. 1617-1623	Ngola Mbandi
r. 1624-1663	Njinga
r. 1627-1664	Ngola Ari (appointed by Portuguese)
r. 1664-1671	Ngola Ari II

1640's

teenth century, the number of slaves who were moved through Ndongo territory grew to more than ten thousand per year.

While the Portuguese emerged victorious over the interests of the Dutch, it was the economic stability of Brazil—and its maintenance—that would determine the Ndongo region's fate. Some have thus described the Angola of this time period as a de facto Brazilian colony. Soon, other European interests joined the West African slave trade, and other routes were established to the interior.

—*Fred Strickert*

FURTHER READING

Bender, Gerald J. *Angola Under the Portuguese: The Myth and the Reality.* Trenton, N.J.: African World Press, 2004. Bender investigates the racism of Portuguese colonial policies.

Birmingham, David. *Trade and Conflict in Angola: The Mbundu and Their Neighbors Under the Influence of the Portuguese, 1483-1790.* Oxford, England: Clarendon Press, 1966. A scholarly analysis based on Portuguese documents, Mbundu historical traditions collected in the 1660's, and oral traditions.

Broadhead, Susan H. *Historical Dictionary of Angola.* Metuchen, N.J.: Scarecrow Press, 1992. A compendium of helpful articles, including descriptions of proper names and a chronology, historic maps, a table comparing colonial and modern names, and a bibliography of primary and secondary sources.

Collelo, Thomas. *Angola: A Country Study.* Washington, D.C.: Government Printing Office, 1991. Collelo examines both modern and contemporary sources on the history of Angola.

McKissack, Pat. *Nzingha: Warrior Queen of Matamba.* New York: Scholastic, 2000. A biographical sketch of Queen Njinga for general readers ages 9 to 13.

Miller, Joseph C. "Njinga of Matamba in a New Perspective." *Journal of African History* 16, no. 2 (1975): 201-216. Original analysis of the objectives, assumptions, tactics, and effectiveness of Njinga in claiming and occupying the rulership of Ndongo and Matamba.

Ogot, B. A., ed. *Africa from the Sixteenth to the Eighteenth Century.* Vol. 5 in *General History of Africa.* Berkeley, Calif.: Heinemann, 1992. A comprehensive history of Africa.

Schwarz-Bart, Simone. "Ana de Sousa Nzinga: The Queen Who Resisted the Portuguese Conquest." In *Ancient African Queens.* Vol. 1 in *In Praise of Black Women.* Madison: University of Wisconsin Press, 2001. Reviews the life of Njinga as an early hero of anticolonialist resistance.

Thorton, John K. "The Art of War in Angola, 1575-1680." *Comparative Studies in Society and History* 30, no. 2 (1988): 360-378. Explores the military strategy of the period that includes the Ndongo Wars.

SEE ALSO: 17th cent.: Emergence of Luba Governance; 1619-c. 1700: The Middle Passage to American Slavery; c. 1625: Formation of the Kuba Kingdom; 1630-1660's: Dutch Wars in Brazil; Aug. 26, 1641-Sept., 1648: Conquest of Luanda; Oct. 29, 1665: Battle of Mbwila; Beginning c. 1682: Decline of the Solomonid Dynasty.

RELATED ARTICLES in *Great Lives from History: The Seventeenth Century, 1601-1700:* John IV; Njinga; Philip IV.

April 25, 1644
END OF THE MING DYNASTY

A series of crises, internal and external, led to the downfall of the nearly three-hundred-year-old Ming Dynasty, leaving China vulnerable to the Manchu invasion that resulted in the creation of the Qing Dynasty and ushered in a new era in Chinese history.

LOCALE: China
CATEGORY: Government and politics

KEY FIGURES
Tianqi (1605-1627), Ming emperor of China, r. 1621-1627
Chongzhen (Ch'ung-chen; 1611-1644), last Ming emperor of China, r. 1628-1644
Li Zicheng (Li Tzu-ch'eng; 1605?-1645), Chinese bandit and rebel leader
Wei Zhongxian (1568-1627), Tianqi's chief eunuch and de facto ruler of China, 1624-1627
Wanli (1563-1620), Ming emperor of China, r. 1573-1620

SUMMARY OF EVENT
The Ming Dynasty (1368-1644), after extended periods of expansion and prosperity, entered its period of final decline in the first half of the seventeenth century, when the dynasty was confronted with a series of significant problems and challenges. These problems included a severe decline in governmental efficiency, a worsening financial situation, frequent popular uprisings, and the rapid deterioration of defenses on the northeastern frontier coupled with steady intrusions by the nomadic Juchen tribes into Chinese territory. Under the weight of these crises, the Ming Dynasty eventually crumbled in 1644. At the same time, the Juchens were becoming a unified, bureaucratic rather than nomadic, society. They eventually changed their name to the Manchus, conquered China, and founded a new dynasty, the Qing.

The Ming government in the early seventeenth century was notoriously inefficient. The emperors were inept, inattentive, and irresponsible, and the central government was dominated by endless and debilitating factional struggles. For different reasons in each case, the seventeenth century Ming emperors failed to engage in state affairs. Instead, they chose to live in seclusion in the deep recesses of the imperial palace, pursuing personal pleasures with their favorite women and hobbies. For nearly three decades beginning in the 1590's, the Wanli emperor suspended almost all public audiences with his bureaucrats, whom he detested and who constantly frustrated his plans and contradicted his decisions. Wanli's inaction contributed significantly to the demoralization of the bureaucrats and the exacerbation of factionalism among them, and it left many official positions long unfilled.

The Tianqi emperor was perhaps the most ineffective emperor of the Ming dynasty and was certainly most instrumental in creating the situation that led to its downfall. Only fifteen years old and poorly educated when he ascended the throne, Tianqi showed no interest in governmental affairs. Instead, he became obsessed with his favorite hobby of carpentry, leaving decisions on important governmental matters to his trusted personal attendants, especially eunuchs. Tianqi's neglect of his imperial duties led to the rise of the most powerful and notorious eunuch of Ming times, Wei Zhongxian. Wei was appointed to head the Chinese secret service (the Eastern Depot) in 1623, and for the next four years he dominated the central governmental bureaucracy so completely that he essentially functioned as the dictator of China, instituting a reign of terror.

Aside from the years of Wei's dictatorship (1624-1627), the late Ming Dynasty was characterized by rampant factionalism, as various groups and individuals within the government, especially career civil officials and court eunuchs, struggled to amass power. Mostly, this factionalism involved the persons who were associated with the Donglin Clique. This clique arose during Wanli's reign and persisted until the end of the Ming Dynasty. It included incumbent and retired scholar-officials and scholars who claimed to follow the Confucian system of ethics.

Members of the Donglin Clique were particularly concerned with conducting moral evaluations of central government officials, with the proclaimed goal of removing officials of deficient moral character from office. The evaluations caused so many accusations and counteraccusations and such frequent changes in bureaucratic personnel that they helped paralyze the central Chinese bureaucracy. In the 1620's, the Donglin partisans came into conflict with the eunuch dictator Wei Zhongxian. The conflict proved disastrous for the Donglin Clique, as hundreds of its members were persecuted, imprisoned, or murdered. The factional struggle not only destabilized the civil administration but also had an adverse impact on the military. For example, in 1625,

Xiong Tingbi, the distinguished supreme commander of the Ming armies in the northeast, was first recalled and then beheaded by anti-Donglin forces for his alleged association with the Donglin Clique.

Parallel to the decline in governmental efficiency was the increasing deterioration of the dynasty's finances. During the early seventeenth century, powerful Chinese landowners found ways to avoid paying taxes, small farmers went bankrupt because of poor harvests, production and trade were generally disrupted by recurring popular unrest, and the flow of bullion from the New World to the Old was reduced. As a result, there was a significant decrease in state revenues. At the same time that the imperial government's income diminished, however, its expenditures continued to rise. The higher expenditures were necessary to meet the increasingly extravagant lifestyle of the imperial household, to sustain the empire's costly northeastern frontier defenses against the Juchens, and to pay for internal military operations to repress the various peasant rebellions.

For the Ming rulers, those peasant rebellions represented the most immediate threat to their power. The most significant rebellion against the Ming was Li Zicheng's revolt, which broke out in the northwestern province of Shaanxi (Shensi) in 1631 following a severe drought and famine. Within a little more than a decade, Li's rebel forces had defeated the government's forces, and Li's influence and control had expanded eastward to the vast areas between the Yellow River and the Yangtze River. Finally, the rebels advanced toward the Ming capital, Beijing, and on April 25, 1644, they entered the capital without encountering any resistance. Knowing his reign was at an end, the last Ming emperor, Chongzhen, had already committed suicide earlier that same day. Li Zicheng and his forces, however, ultimately fared no better. They were driven out of Beijing on June 4, 1644, by another Ming enemy, the Manchus.

The Manchus, who had lived in Manchuria, beyond the northeastern frontier, had become a powerful force under Nurhaci (r. 1586-1629), and they began to chal-

Unwilling to be captured alive by rebel invaders, the last Ming emperor, Chongzhen, ordered the women of his household to commit suicide and killed several himself. He then hanged himself from a tree. (Hulton\Archive by Getty Images)

lenge the Ming Dynasty militarily in 1618. For the next twenty-six years, the Manchus and Ming troops were at constant war with each other, and the Manchus almost always had the upper hand. This war proved devastating to the Ming Dynasty: Large numbers of the dynasty's troops were annihilated, large areas of its territory were lost, and a significant portion of its financial resources was drained. By contrast, the Manchus steadily strengthened themselves in the war, so when the government fell to Li Zicheng, they were in a perfect position to exploit the situation, defeat Li's forces, and establish themselves as China's ruling class.

The many problems that dominated Chinese politics in the first four decades of the seventeenth century were both signs and causes of the decline and fall of the Ming Dynasty. Although the dynasty fell and was replaced by foreign conquerors, however, Chinese culture survived and continued to develop.

SIGNIFICANCE

The decline and end of the Ming Dynasty revealed once again that the hereditary monarchical system based on the principle of primogeniture was an ineffective political system in the long run. This system dictated that the eldest son of an emperor must also be emperor and that all important decision-making powers be concentrated in his hands, no matter whether he had interest in politics or had the ability to run the government.

Such a rigid system certainly could not always produce qualified occupants of the imperial throne and guarantee the making and implementation of sound state policies. As late Ming history proved, the opposite was often the case. Almost all the major problems the dynasty faced during its last years resulted from the ill functioning of this imperial system, a system of which even the emperors themselves were ultimately victims.

The demise of the Ming Dynasty and the foundation of the Manchu Qing Dynasty marked the beginning of another era of foreign rule in China—a bitter humiliation that many Chinese subjects would never forget and that would ultimately inspire modern Chinese nationalism. Sun Yat-sen (Sun Yixian), the leader of the 1911 revolution, for example, put forward the slogan of "expelling the barbarians (the Manchus) and reviving the Chinese rule," and he made nationalism one of his Three Principles of the People.

— *Yunqiu Zhang*

FURTHER READING

Brook, Timothy. *The Confusion of Pleasure: Commerce and Culture in Ming China.* Berkeley: University of California Press, 1998. An account of the impact of commercialization on social and cultural life during the Ming Dynasty.

Cass, Victoria Baldwin. *Dangerous Women: Warriors, Grannies, and Geishas of the Ming.* Lanham, Md.: Rowman & Littlefield, 1999. Contains valuable information about official attitudes toward women and women's situation in Ming times.

Mote, Frederick W., and Denis Twitchett, eds. *The Ming Dynasty, 1368-1644, Part 1.* Vol. 7 in *The Cambridge History of China.* New York: Cambridge University Press, 1988. An account of the political history of the Ming Dynasty, including chapters on Wanli's reign.

Mungello, David E. *Great Encounter of China and the West, 1500-1800.* New York: Rowman & Littlefield, 1999. Contains information about the Jesuits' experiences in late Ming China.

Parsons, James Bunyan. *The Peasant Rebellions of the Late Ming Dynasty.* Tuscon: University of Arizona Press, 1970. Examines the rise and fall of the peasant rebellions under Li Zicheng and Zhang Xianzhong.

Tong, James W. *Disorder Under Heaven: Collective Violence in the Ming Dynasty.* Stanford, Calif.: Stanford University Press, 1991. A study of various kinds of collective violence, ranging from banditry to popular rebellions.

Twitchett, Denis, and Frederick W. Mote, eds. *The Ming Dynasty, 1368-1644, Part 2.* Vol. 8 in *The Cambridge History of China.* New York: Cambridge University Press, 1998. Concerned with the Ming Dynasty's governmental structure, fiscal and legal systems, socioeconomic situations, and intellectual trends.

SEE ALSO: 1616-1643: Rise of the Manchus; 1631-1645: Li Zicheng's Revolt; June 6, 1644: Manchus Take Beijing; 1645-1683: Zheng Pirates Raid the Chinese Coast; Feb. 17, 1661-Dec. 20, 1722: Height of Qing Dynasty; 1670: Promulgation of the Sacred Edict; Dec., 1673-1681: Rebellion of the Three Feudatories.

RELATED ARTICLES in *Great Lives from History: The Seventeenth Century, 1601-1700:* Abahai; Chongzhen; Dorgon; Shunzhi; Tianqi; Zheng Chenggong.

1640's

June 6, 1644
MANCHUS TAKE BEIJING

The Manchus seized control of Beijing mere weeks after the last Ming emperor had killed himself and the city had fallen to Chinese rebel leader Li Zicheng. They established themselves as the new rulers of China, founding the Qing Dynasty.

LOCALE: Beijing, China
CATEGORIES: Government and politics; wars, uprisings, and civil unrest; expansion and land acquisition

KEY FIGURES
Dorgon (1612-1650), Manchu prince and imperial regent
Wu Sangui (Wu San-kuei; 1612-1678), Ming general who helped the Manchus take Beijing
Li Zicheng (Li Tzu-ch'eng; 1605?-1645), Chinese rebel leader who was driven from Beijing by Manchu forces
Chongzhen (Ch'ung-chen; 1611-1644), last Ming emperor of China, r. 1628-1644
Shunzhi (Shun-chih; 1638-1661), first Qing emperor of China, r. 1644-1661
Zheng Chenggong (Cheng Ch'eng-kung, or Koxinga; 1624-1662), Chinese pirate leader who fought for the Ming against the Manchus
Abahai (Qing Taizong; 1592-1643), Manchu leader, r. 1626-1643, and emperor of China, r. 1636-1643
Nurhaci (Qing Taizu; 1559-1626), Juchen warlord who took the first steps to establish the Manchu nation

SUMMARY OF EVENT
By the early seventeenth century, the Ming Dynasty was in a state of decline. The empire's military was unable to check the aggressive movements of the northern nomadic tribes. Its governmental bureaucracy was corrupt and dangerously inefficient. In addition, the peasant community was being ravaged by a combination of high taxes and famine. These events destabilized the Ming government and gave rise to widespread peasant uprisings.

At the same time, China's northern provinces were dealing with incursions by an aggressive group of nomadic warriors who were part of the Manchurian Juchen tribe. These warriors were quickly becoming an important force on the frontier. Their location in Manchuria allowed them to interact with the Ming Dynasty. Over time, the Manchurian tribes developed a less nomadic

society that was influenced culturally, economically, and technologically by Chinese civilization. The Manchus were also important military allies of the Ming in their fight against other nomadic tribes in northeast Asia.

The individual who began the process of forming the Manchu nation was Nurhaci. He used his successful military alliance with the Chinese to solidify his position among his own people. Capitalizing on his vast knowledge of the Ming bureaucracy, Nurhaci created a military and administrative structure modeled on the Chinese paradigm. This structure was known as the Eight Banner System; it was the basic organizational model for the military and also provided for census counts and taxation.

When Nurhaci died, his son Abahai succeeded him and drew on his father's success to begin the process of bringing East Asia under Manchurian control. He first defeated Chinese forces in 1631, and this victory allowed him to establish a dynasty with its capital in Mukden, in 1635. The following year, Abahai changed the name of his dynasty to Qing, changed the name of his people from Juchen to Manchu, and declared himself the emperor of China. The Ming Chongzhen emperor still ruled in Beijing, but Abahai's assumed title was more than false bravado. His Qing Dynasty already rivaled the declining Mings in power.

When Abahai died in 1643, his six-year-old son, Fulin, replaced him. Abahai's brother, Prince Dorgon, was appointed regent to advise the young boy in matters of state. It was under the leadership of Dorgon that the Manchus would capture Beijing and become the rulers of China.

By the time of Dorgon's appointment, China and the Ming Dynasty were being devastated by peasant rebellions. A rebel leader named Li Zicheng led the most important of these uprisings. Li's forces prevailed on April 25, 1644, when the Chongzhen emperor killed himself; Li occupied the capital at Beijing on the same day. His men soon began looting and mistreating Beijing's inhabitants. Thus, Li's army confirmed their reputation as brutal conquerors. Over a period of a decade of rebellion against the Ming, Li's war crimes had alienated most of the peasantry; therefore, by the time of the battle for Beijing, the population held as much antipathy for the rebels as they had for the Ming Dynasty.

Many Ming generals who had become disenchanted with the corruption and incompetence of the dynasty's leadership willingly joined forces with the Manchu military; one such important commander was Wu Sangui. Wu Sangui's significance was based on two factors: He was a superb tactician, and he occupied the strategic Shanhai Pass. This gave him control of an important avenue to the capital. Wu was thus in the enviable position of being able to negotiate with both Li Zicheng and Dorgon. Li had offered Wu an impressive package if he would ally himself with the rebel cause. While Wu was impressed with the offer, he also knew that he would have to maintain a subordinate status in his relationship with Li. Therefore, he opened up communication with Dorgon, the leader of the Manchu military.

Wu also knew that many of the Ming generals who had sided with Dorgon and the Manchu forces had received both monetary compensation and vast tracts of land in which they could develop great estates. The potential power attached to the ownership of land convinced Wu that the Manchus had made the better offer. He also realized that the Chinese people hated Li for causing the death of the Chongzhen emperor. No matter what the outcome of the current military situation, Wu knew the Chinese people would never forgive Li; therefore, the Ming general decided to join the Manchu cause. When Li Zicheng was informed that Wu had allowed Dorgon's forces to move safely through the Shanhai Pass, he decided he had to attack this new threat before it reached Beijing. The forces of Li, Wu, and Dorgon collided in the Battle of Shanhaiguan (Shan-hai-kuan). Each army was potentially formidable and used a combination of infantry, cavalry, and artillery when engaging the enemy.

Of the three military forces, Li Zicheng's army had the most serious discipline and morale problems. His force was mostly made up of peasants who had been confined to Beijing for months. During these months, discipline had broken down, and it was then that the occupying force had ravaged the inhabitants of the capital. Wu Sangui, by contrast, had a strong, well-disciplined, professional army that was more than ready to engage the enemy.

Wu and Dorgon agreed that Wu's forces would lead the attack against the rebel army. Dorgon was still unsure about the extent of Wu's power and wanted to make sure his own forces would be strong enough to defeat Li, if the rebel leader were able to overcome Wu's army. The armies of Wu and Li engaged each other and fought in bloody combat for a number of hours, until it became evident that Wu was securing the upper hand. Dorgon then unleashed his Manchu army, and the impact of these fresh fighters broke Li's lines. The peasant general began

to withdraw. Wu quickly capitalized on Li's weakness, pursued the retreating army, and dismantled the rest of Li's force. Li escaped with a small contingent, but he never again had an impact on Chinese history. Dorgon led his forces into Beijing, where on June 6, 1644, he was greeted by thousands of grateful Chinese, who were glad to be free of rebel occupation. Dorgon responded by declaring the beginning of the Qing Dynasty's rule of China. F87ulin was crowned emperor and given the reign name of Shunzhi, inaugurating the dynasty.

The Manchus then began the systematic elimination of the remaining forces that were loyal to the Ming Dynasty. Manchu military leaders were able to defeat the majority of the rebel groups quite easily. The Qing Dynasty's forces did encounter substantial resistance from some of the Ming generals who had been their former allies, however. These extremely competent military men had used the land they had received from the Qing to enhance their wealth and military power. Many of the generals, including Wu Sangui, believed they could create independent feudal fiefdoms that would be beyond the control of the Manchu government. The Qing Dynasty responded to these challenges by launching a series of military campaigns that in time successfully neutralized the warlords and brought all of China under their control.

The Manchus also faced a serious naval threat from groups of pirates who operated along China's eastern seacoast. In the late 1650's, the charismatic Chinese leader Zheng Chenggong (Koxinga) led a force of almost 200,000 men in an attack against the city of Nanjing (Nan-ching). The armies of the Qing Dynasty successfully repelled the onslaught, and Zheng had to withdraw his forces. He then marched back to his power base along the coast and began to plan an attack against the strategic island of Taiwan. In 1661, he executed a successful military operation, defeating the Dutch who were occupying the island and bringing Taiwan under his control. The Qing Dynasty eventually defeated Zheng, however, and this important island became part of the Qing Empire.

SIGNIFICANCE

The Qing Dynasty brought China under its control and was thus able finally to end the chaos that had gripped the country for decades. The foreign Manchus maintained many basic aspects of Chinese civilization under their reign by adapting many Chinese cultural and bureaucratic practices for their own use. However, the Manchus also implemented a number of negative regulations and forced some of their own cultural traditions upon their Chinese subjects. All Chinese men were required to

1640's

shave the front of their heads and wear their hair in a ponytail as a sign of submission to Qing authority. The Manchu government also forbade intermarriage between the two peoples. Over time, these practices caused disunity, and they eventually created the opportunity for China to become dominated by European powers. In time, this led to the Revolution of 1911, which brought the Qing Dynasty to an end.

The Qing Dynasty brought the island of Taiwan under Chinese domination as well. This initially expanded Chinese power and control over the strategic Taiwanese Strait and subsequently increased the nation's economic and military strength. The impact of this conquest still plays an import role in Chinese geostrategic thought.

—*Richard D. Fitzgerald*

FURTHER READING
Crossley, Pamela Kyle. *The Manchus.* Oxford, England: Blackwell, 1997. Excellent introduction to the Manchu culture. Index.

_____. *Orphan Warriors: Three Manchu Generations and the End of the Qing World.* Princeton, N.J.: Princeton University Press, 1990. Explores the important events of the later Qing Dynasty. Index.
_____. *A Translucent Mirror: History and Identity in Qing Imperial Ideology.* Berkeley: University of California Press, 1999. Describes the evolution of Qing political philosophy. Index.

SEE ALSO: 1616-1643: Rise of the Manchus; 1631-1645: Li Zicheng's Revolt; Apr. 25, 1644: End of the Ming Dynasty; 1645-1683: Zheng Pirates Raid the Chinese Coast; Feb. 17, 1661-Dec. 20, 1722: Height of Qing Dynasty; Dec., 1673-1681: Rebellion of the Three Feudatories; Aug. 29, 1689: Treaty of Nerchinsk Draws Russian-Chinese Border; 1699: British Establish Trading Post in Canton.
RELATED ARTICLES in *Great Lives from History: The Seventeenth Century, 1601-1700:* Abahai; Chongzhen; Dorgon; Shunzhi; Zheng Chenggong.

July 2, 1644
BATTLE OF MARSTON MOOR

The Battle of Marston Moor, during the English Civil War, marked a decisive defeat of Royalist forces by Cromwell's Parliamentary forces, acting in conjunction with the Scottish army. The battle led to the loss of the Royalist stronghold of York and Cromwell's eventual victory.

LOCALE: Marston Moor, near York, England
CATEGORIES: Wars, uprisings, and civil unrest; government and politics

KEY FIGURES
Alexander Leslie (c. 1580-1661), commander of the Parliamentary forces at Marston Moor and first earl of Leven
Prince Rupert (1619-1682), nephew of Charles I and commander of the Royalist forces
Oliver Cromwell (1599-1658), general of Parliamentary cavalry and infantry and lord protector of England, 1653-1658
George Goring (1585-1663), commander of the left wing of the Royalist forces
Edward Montagu (1602-1671), second earl of Manchester and commander in chief of the Eastern Association

Third Baron Fairfax (Thomas Fairfax; 1612-1671), commander of the right wing of the Parliamentary forces
William Cavendish (1592-1676), marquis of Newcastle and Royalist commander of the city of York
Charles I (1600-1649), king of England, r. 1625-1649
Lord Eythin (James King; 1589-1652), military adviser to Cavendish

SUMMARY OF EVENT
When English king Charles I decided to resort to armed conflict after his frustrating struggle with Parliament in 1642, he called upon all loyal Englishmen to assist him in asserting his rights and regaining control of the government. The king believed that the members of Parliament had pushed him too far when they proposed that he should govern England in conjunction with them. Charles believed it was his divine right to be the sole ruler of England, and he was both personally unwilling and philosophically opposed to sharing royal power with Parliament. All over England, then, the people were forced to choose between a Parliament demanding its rights and a king who believed that he was chosen by God to rule by divine right.

For two years, the opposing sides prepared. Parliament's forces were larger and better trained. The first battle, an indecisive skirmish at Edgehill in October of 1642, had made each side wary of committing its forces until such time as the prospect of victory seemed to make it worth the risk. During those first two years, most of the country took the side of Parliament. Charles's main support was in the area around Oxford and in the north around the city of York.

The balance of power was drastically altered against the king in September of 1643, when Parliament decided to accept the offer of the Scots to enter the Civil War on their side if members of Parliament and all other important people in England would agree to swear to the Solemn League and Covenant, an agreement by which both the Kirk (church) of Scotland and the Church of England would be reformed along Presbyterian lines. When the Scottish army crossed the border into England in January of 1644, Charles realized that his northern stronghold at York was in imminent danger.

At that time, the city of York was the responsibility of William Cavendish, marquis of Newcastle, who had retreated there after maneuvering with the Scots near Durham. Three units of the Parliamentary army—one under Edward Montagu, second earl of Manchester (later first earl of Sandwich); another under the Scottish commander, Alexander Leslie, earl of Leven; and the third under the third baron Fairfax—surrounded the city of York. Charles, whose headquarters were near Oxford, decided that it was absolutely necessary that York be saved. He detached forces from his own army and sent them under the command of his nephew, Prince Rupert, to the relief of the city. Rupert proceeded to the north, and the officers who were besieging York decided that they should raise the siege and proceed to intercept the forces that were coming to the rescue of Cavendish. It was the deployment of the forces involved that set the stage for the Battle of Marston Moor.

Rupert, however, had not advanced directly upon York. Instead, he had taken a more difficult and roundabout route, marching his army to seize a bridge of boats guarded by Parliamentarian dragoons and so relieving the siege of York without battle. Cavendish, although thankful for the lifting of the siege, urged Rupert to await reinforcements, since the Parliamentarian forces so outnumbered the Royalists. Rupert insisted, however, that King Charles had ordered him not only to break the siege but also to fight a battle. Faced with this order, Cavendish relented, and the Royalist forces prepared to advance early in the morning of July 2, 1644.

The Parliamentarians had their headquarters in the village of Long Marston, about six miles west of the city of York. The generals were not certain of the size of the Royalist army but were convinced that they would have to fight under any circumstances. They were pleasantly surprised when they discovered that the forces of Prince Rupert, encamped on Marston Moor, to the north of Long Marston beside a lane leading to Tockwith, numbered approximately seventeen thousand. The Parliamentarians, commanded by Leslie, could count on twenty-seven thousand.

The disposition of the various units pitted Oliver Cromwell against Prince Rupert, Fairfax opposite Royalist general George Goring, and Manchester and Leslie opposite Lord Eythin. Rupert's forces, which held the northern end of the field, were arranged in a shallow semicircle with cavalry on the flanks and infantry in the center. Rupert, with an elite force of cavalry, was in the rear center. Rupert, who awaited Lord Eythin's arrival with reinforcements throughout most of the day, had stationed his army behind a ditch and a hedge as a defensive measure.

The Parliamentarian troops were arranged in a conventional pattern almost identical to Rupert's, with cavalry on the flanks and a larger force of infantry in the center. On the left, the troops of Cromwell were stationed along a ridge that allowed them to charge downhill, across Marston Field and into the Royalist ranks. In addition, Cromwell had secured his flank by seizing a hill and a rabbit warren to his left, which meant his troops could not be taken in the flank or rear by surprise.

During the afternoon of July 2, there was some probing by artillery as commanders tried to estimate enemy position and strength, but this activity ended about 5:00 P.M. Prince Rupert then decided that the enemy would not attack that evening, and he retired to his coach for the night. He was sadly mistaken, however, for Leslie ordered his army to attack shortly after 7:00 P.M., and Cromwell sent his troops against Prince Rupert.

Despite the element of surprise, the battle did not go easily for Cromwell, and Rupert's men put up a gallant defense. The reserve behind Cromwell, which was under the command of David Leslie, turned the tide against the Royalist right wing. On the left wing, matters developed better for the Royalists. General Goring was able to scatter Fairfax's forces to gain the initiative, at least for a time. Fairfax did manage, however, to join with the cavalry of Cromwell, which was sweeping to its right. With the tide of battle running in favor of its cavalry and with the help of its own infantry, the Parliamentary army defeated the Royalists. The Royalist soldiers of William Cavendish put up a stout defense before they went down to defeat.

SIGNIFICANCE

The Battle of Marston Moor proved to be a disaster for the cause of Charles I. As a result of the battle, he lost York and most of the north. Thereafter, he could not draw on the resources of the north, and he found the Parliamentary noose drawn tighter around Oxford. Although the Battle of Marston Moor was not as important as the Battle of Naseby, which was fought a year later, it can be said that Marston Moor made Naseby possible. With the Royalist force's defeat at Marston Moor, the Royalist cause was doomed, and the balance was tipped inexorably in favor of the Parliamentarians.

—Harold L. Stansell and Michael Witkoski

FURTHER READING

Ashley, Maurice. *The English Civil War*. New York: St. Martin's Press, 1990. An accessible and well-illustrated general history of the events by a distinguished historian of the period, with a revealing section on the engagement.

Barratt, John. *Cavaliers: The Royalist Army at War, 1642-1646*. Stroud, Gloucestershire, England: Sutton, 2000. Comprehensive study of the Royalist armies, examining their organization, recruitment, training, arms, and equipment. Compares Royalist forces, recounts some engagements, and discusses some notable Royalist officers.

Hibbert, Christopher. *Cavaliers and Roundheads*. New York: Charles Scribner's Sons, 1993. A popular history of the period, well researched and well written. Provides the setting and consequences of the battle.

Kenyon, John. *The Civil Wars of England*. London: Weidenfeld & Nicolson, 1988. A careful study of the various phases of the struggle among the various parties in the increasingly complex internal struggle of the times. Good for placing Marston Moor in its context.

Kitson, Frank. *Prince Rupert: Portrait of a Soldier*. London: Constable, 1994. A sympathetic biography of Rupert that attempts to assess as fairly as possible his considerable talents and contributions to the Royalist cause. Contains a good section on the Battle of Marston Moor.

Wanklyn, Malcolm, and Frank Jones. *A Military History of the English Civil War, 1642-1646: Strategy and Tactics*. New York: Longman/Pearson Education, 2004. Describes the military tactics and strategies of the various parties in the war.

Young, Peter. *Marston Moor*. London: Roundwood Press, 1970. Young, a brigadier in the British army and a keen student of military history, provides a clear and understandable account of the engagement.

SEE ALSO: Mar.-June, 1639: First Bishops' War; Nov. 3, 1640-May 15, 1641: Beginning of England's Long Parliament; 1642-1651: English Civil Wars; Aug. 17-Sept. 25, 1643: Solemn League and Covenant; Dec. 6, 1648-May 19, 1649: Establishment of the English Commonwealth; Dec. 16, 1653-Sept. 3, 1658: Cromwell Rules England as Lord Protector; May, 1659-May, 1660: Restoration of Charles II.

RELATED ARTICLES in *Great Lives from History: The Seventeenth Century, 1601-1700:* Charles I; Oliver Cromwell; Third Baron Fairfax; Prince Rupert.

1645-1683
ZHENG PIRATES RAID THE CHINESE COAST

During the upheavals occasioned by the fall of the Ming Dynasty and the subsequent consolidation of the Qing Dynasty, pirate leader Zheng Chenggong waged war against the Qing in pursuit of profits, power, and the possible restoration of the Ming.

LOCALE: Chinese and Taiwanese coasts
CATEGORIES: Wars, uprisings, and civil unrest; government and politics

KEY FIGURES
Zheng Chenggong (Cheng Ch'eng-kung, or Koxinga; 1624-1662), Chinese pirate leader and trader
Kangxi (K'ang-hsi; 1654-1722), Qing emperor of China, r. 1661-1722
Shi Lang (1621-1696), Chinese admiral
Zheng Zhilong (1604-1661), Chinese pirate, trader, and father of Zheng Chenggong
Zheng Keshuang (c. 1670-1707), grandson of Zheng Chenggong

SUMMARY OF EVENT
The rulers of China traditionally saw their world as "all under heaven," and the emperors justified their reigns as having the "mandate of heaven." The mandate could be lost through natural disaster, foreign invasion, incompetent rulers, or peasant uprisings, and a new dynasty would come to the fore, claiming the mandate of heaven. In 1644, the Ming ("bright") Dynasty lost the mandate and was replaced by the non-Chinese Manchus from the north, who established the Qing ("pure") Dynasty, which continued to rule China until 1911.

However, "all under heaven" before the seventeenth century did not encompass the island of Taiwan, located 120 miles (193 kilometers) off the southeast coast of the Chinese mainland. The rulers of China had traditionally turned their backs on the sea. There were exceptions, notably in the early fifteenth century, when Chinese fleets sailed all the way to Africa, but generally China was a land rather than a sea power. Largely inhabited by its aboriginal peoples, Taiwan had been ignored by the Chinese emperors.

Before the seventeenth century, there had been some contacts between Taiwan and the mainland. Chinese merchants from Fujian (Fukien) and Guangdong (Kwangtung) provinces imported deer horns (believed to be an aphrodisiac) and hides from the island. In addition, pirates from China and Japan had made Taiwan a base of their operations. Western nations also had contact with the island. The Portuguese had named the island Ilha Formosa, or Beautiful Isle, but made Macao, near Guangzhou (Canton), their main settlement for Chinese trade. Spain, which had incorporated the Philippines into its far-flung empire, established an outpost in north Taiwan at Chi-lung. The Dutch, who had driven the Portuguese out of the Indonesian Spice Islands, founded a fortified settlement in southwestern Taiwan called Zeelandia in order better to trade with the Chinese mainland, and by the 1640's, the Dutch had driven the Spanish from the island.

As a consequence of the Ming collapse and the Qing takeover in 1644, southern China was anything but peaceful. As late as the 1660's, there were several Ming claimants to the imperial throne who refused to concede that the foreign Qing held the mandate of heaven. The Ming prince of Fu established his court at Nanjing (Nanching) but was captured and soon died. He was followed by two brothers who were Ming descendants as well. One brother's court was centered at Fuzhou (Foochow) across from Taiwan, and the other's was farther south at Guangzhou, but the former was executed by the Qing in 1646 and the latter in 1647. Another claimant was based at Xiamen (Amoy), between Fuzhou and Guangzhou, but he abandoned his claim in 1653. Ming hopes continued in China's southwest until the capture and execution of the prince of Gui in 1662.

Among the other individuals caught up in the Ming resistance to the advancing Qing was the head of the Zheng family, Zheng Zhilong, who combined trade and piracy between Japan, Taiwan, and Fujian province on China's mainland. Initially on the side of the Ming claimants, he joined the Qing in 1646. Changing sides was not uncommon during that turbulent era. However, Zheng's son, Zheng Chenggong, did not follow his father's lead: He remained loyal to the Ming and supported several Ming claimants militarily. Zheng Chenggong was given the Ming imperial surname, pronounced "kok-sehng-yah" in the local dialect, and became known in the West as Koxinga. Nothing if not multicultural, Koxinga had a Japanese mother, and his Chinese father had trading interests extending from Nagasaki in Japan to Taiwan to the Chinese mainland, including the Portuguese enclave of Macao. Black slaves from Macao guarded the Zheng compound at Xiamen, which included a chapel with both Buddhist and Christian features.

While supporting the rebel Ming against the Qing, Zheng Chenggong also enriched himself economically, trading in silks and sugar for his required military supplies. In 1658, he invaded central China with a force of 130,000 troops and one thousand ships, and the following year he attempted to seize the city of Nanjing on the Yangtze River. Repulsed by the Qing forces, he abandoned his base on the island of Quemoy (Jinmen), in Xiamen harbor, and turned to Taiwan, attacking the Dutch fort at Zeelandia. The citadel survived a nine-month siege, and the surviving Dutch surrendered only when allowed to retreat to the port of Batavia in the Dutch East Indies. In spite of the vast booty he captured, however, Zheng's victory came at a cost. His father and brothers, held hostage in Beijing, were executed in 1661 because of his anti-Qing campaigns. According to some accounts, Zheng became mentally unstable, violently lashing out even against his own children. He died in 1662, perhaps a suicide, at the age of thirty-eight.

Zheng's legacy continued after his death. His sons and grandson built on his accomplishments and established a commercial network on Taiwan, trading in salt, sugar, and the building of ships. In 1660, before Zheng Chenggong's death, Qing officials in the southern coastal provinces moved much of the population 20 miles (32 kilometers) into the interior to deprive the Zhengs and other pirate-traders of their economic base. This draconian policy caused considerable hardship and many deaths, and as a result some mainland Chinese fled to Taiwan, which soon had a Chinese population of more than 100,000. In 1664 and 1665, attempts to launch two invasions of Taiwan to wipe out the Zhengs and their supporters failed.

The Qing Kangxi emperor ascended the throne in 1661, at the age of seven, but by the 1670's he had personally begun to take control of the government. During that decade, his focus was less on the Zhengs and Taiwan and more on the rebellion of three Chinese generals who had ruled for the Qing in the south. This Rebellion of the Three Feudatories ended in 1681, allowing the emperor to turn to the problem of Taiwan. His solution was to appoint a former associate of Zheng Chenggong to mount a naval invasion of the island. Shi Lang, described by Kangxi as arrogant and uneducated but with outstanding military abilities, had his own personal reasons for rooting out the Zhengs: Zheng Chenggong had murdered Shi Lang's father and other relatives when Shi Lang switched sides and joined the Qing in the 1650's. With a fleet of three hundred ships, Shi Lang inflicted a devastating defeat upon the Zheng base in the Pescadores in

July, 1683. Three months later, the last resistance on Taiwan came to an end with the surrender of Zheng Keshuang, Zheng Chenggong's grandson, effectively ending the Zhengs' piratical rebellion against the Qing.

SIGNIFICANCE

With the end of the Zheng threat, the Qing government rescinded its coastal evacuation policy and allowed the local populace to return to China's southern provinces. Kangxi treated the surviving Zheng with clemency, allowing them to take up residence in Beijing. Most of the Zheng forces were shifted to northern China to assist in protecting the borders against possible Russian incursions. The fate of Taiwan itself was subject to considerable debate, with some arguing that the island should be abandoned, while others, including Shi Lang, demanded that Taiwan be incorporated into China. Kangxi accepted the latter argument, and Taiwan was formally annexed to China in 1684, becoming a prefecture of Fujian province.

Under Kangxi's imperial order, eight thousand Chinese troops were to be permanently stationed on the island. However, the tribal lands of the aboriginal population were to be preserved, and immigration from the mainland to Taiwan was to be restricted. The island was thus left in a sort of no-man's-land economically and socially, remaining an underpopulated frontier region. The Qing Dynasty, like most Chinese dynasties through the nation's long history, had a preference for agriculture and a disdain for merchants and traders because they created nothing concrete, unlike the peasant farmers who produced food.

After the Sino-Japanese War of 1894, Japan occupied Taiwan until the Japanese defeat at the end of World War II in 1945. As a result of the Communist victory under Mao Zedong (Mao Tse-tung) in the Chinese Civil War, the defeated Nationalists of Jiang Jie-shí (Chiang Kai-shek) retreated to Taiwan, where they established a rival government to the People's Republic.

—*Eugene Larson*

FURTHER READING

Croizier, Ralph C. *Koxinga and Chinese Nationalism.* Cambridge, Mass.: Harvard University Press, 1997. A discussion of Zheng Chenggong as hero and the myths associated with him and his era.

Mote, F. W. *Imperial China, 900-1800.* Cambridge, Mass.: Harvard University Press, 1999. An excellent survey that includes an extensive discussion of Zheng Chenggong.

Spence, Jonathan D. *Emperor of China.* New York: Random House, 1974. A brilliant reconstruction of the ideas, policies, and personality of the Kangxi emperor.

_____. *The Search for Modern China*. New York: Norton, 1990. The best one-volume study of China from the end of the Ming Dynasty to the present.

SEE ALSO: 1616-1643: Rise of the Manchus; 1631-1645: Li Zicheng's Revolt; Apr. 25, 1644: End of the

Ming Dynasty; June 6, 1644: Manchus Take Beijing; Feb. 17, 1661-Dec. 20, 1722: Height of Qing Dynasty; Dec., 1673-1681: Rebellion of the Three Feudatories; Aug. 29, 1689: Treaty of Nerchinsk Draws Russian-Chinese Border.

RELATED ARTICLES in *Great Lives from History: The Seventeenth Century, 1601-1700:* Kangxi; Zheng Chenggong.

Spring, 1645-1660
PURITAN NEW MODEL ARMY

During the English Civil Wars, Parliament created a professional army, the New Model Army. Under the command first of Fairfax and later of Oliver Cromwell, this army defeated the forces of King Charles I and won the Civil War. The New Model Army was England's first standing army and established many of the traditions of the British army, such as uniforms, impressment, discipline, and professionalism.

LOCALE: England
CATEGORIES: Wars, uprisings, and civil unrest; government and politics

KEY FIGURES
Oliver Cromwell (1599-1658), Parliamentary military leader and lord protector of England, 1653-1658
Third Earl of Essex (Robert Devereux; 1591-1646), lord general of the Parliamentary army, 1642-1645
Third Baron Fairfax (Thomas Fairfax; 1612-1671), commander in chief of the New Model Army, 1645-1650
Charles I (1600-1649), king of England, r. 1625-1649

SUMMARY OF EVENT
Historians identify two phases in the English Civil Wars. During the first, the Parliamentary and Royalist armies were fairly well matched, and no single battle secured victory. In response to the inadequate performance of both troops and generals, Parliament passed laws in the spring of 1645 that created the New Model Army. With improved professional leadership, discipline, training, and coherent logistical support, this army was able to defeat the king. The decision of Charles I to renew hostilities in 1647 led to the wars' second phase and his defeat, trial, and execution in 1649. After the execution, the New Model Army saw action in Jamaica, Scotland, and Ireland. After Lord Protector Oliver Cromwell died and his

son, Richard Cromwell, proved incapable of ruling in his place, the Stuart monarchy was returned to power. Following this Stuart Restoration in 1660, the New Model Army was disbanded.

The New Model Army is generally associated with Oliver Cromwell, who became its most famous—and successful—general. Likewise, the Parliamentary forces that became the New Model Army are often portrayed as entirely Puritan, although that characterization is not entirely accurate. Although Puritan voices were influential in Parliament, the Civil Wars stemmed from a wide variety of religious, economic, and political issues. When the Civil Wars began in 1642, many Parliamentary leaders sought not a revolution to replace the monarchy or to institute religious reform, but instead a way to force the king to follow the wishes of the nation as expressed by Parliament.

At first, some Parliamentarian leaders, most notably the third earl of Essex, also held field commands and seemed either unwilling to seek or incapable of seeking a conclusive battle. By 1645, leaders in the House of Commons had begun to demand more aggressive military leadership in the field and better performance from the troops. To accomplish these goals, Parliament needed to remove the existing commanders and eliminate their semi-independent forces. The result was the passage in February, 1645, of the New Model Ordinance and in April, 1645, of the Self-Denying Ordinance: The first created the New Model Army, and the second forbade members of Parliament from holding field commands.

These ordinances were intended to rectify the inherent weaknesses of the Parliamentary armies. Since no standing army existed when the war began, Parliament's forces were an amalgam of local militias and household troops—often grandiosely characterized as regiments—that had been raised by local magnates. The local mili-

1640's

tias, often called "trained bands," saw their role as defensive and therefore often refused to participate in operations outside the boundaries of their counties or municipalities. The personal forces of aristocratic lords, like the third earl of Essex, also exhibited systemic weaknesses. Some in Parliament feared a *coup d'état* from troops who might owe their primary loyalty to the lord who raised and equipped them. Since some of the existing commanders were members of Parliament, it was feared that increasing their regional forces would give such leaders tyrannical powers or, at the very least, too much influence in Parliament. Finally, these armies were plagued by the logistic difficulty of providing equipment, supplies, and wages. Periodic interruption of supplies fostered poor morale and desertion.

The new ordinances were crafted to neutralize these existing forces and assert Parliament's supremacy. The Self-Denying Ordinance prevented existing members of Parliament such as Essex from holding commands in the army. Only Oliver Cromwell, already popular in Parliament based on the reputation he had won through military successes in the field, was given an exemption from this new law. Even then, Cromwell was at first given only a subordinate command, not overall command of the New Model Army. The third baron Fairfax, a young and vigorous officer whose behavior was seen to be reliably neutral and less self-promoting than Cromwell's, was chosen to be the commander in chief of the New Model Army. In addition, logistical support was guaranteed by raising taxes to pay for equipment as well as the salaries for all troops. This ensured that the soldiers' loyalty would be to their paymaster, the nation, rather than to the king or any powerful lord.

The New Model Ordinance called for an army of twenty-two thousand men. The soldiers would be organized into consistently sized regiments on the basis of twelve regiments of infantry, eleven regiments of cavalry, one regiment of dragoons, and two companies of "firelock" armed cavalry (cavalry armed with early flintlocks) that were tasked with protecting the artillery train. For consistency, regimental sizes were to be standardized and all were issued uniforms of "Venetian red" fabric with colored facings to identify the separate regiments.

Many of the personnel were recruited from the existing Parliamentary armies, but Parliament appointed officers in order to eliminate pre-existing loyalties. Since the ordinance was passed after two years of campaigning, too few new recruits came forward. To reach the required troop levels, Parliament passed ordinances allowing the army to impress (conscript) men into service. Addi-

tionally, many prisoners taken in battle were encouraged to switch sides and enlist in the New Model Army. Thus, throughout its existence, the New Model Army contained a significant number of men with little religious conviction or dedication to Parliament.

The New Model Army was created during a time of technological and tactical ferment, which was a significant reason for the high cost of raising and maintaining an army. During the Civil Wars, commanders sought to determine which tactical system was best—the Dutch system used by Maurice of Nassau or the Swedish system of Gustavus II Adolphus. The New Model Army's cavalry under Cromwell's tutelage generally adopted the tactics of Gustavus. During this period, the armor of horsemen and pike men was lightened, mounted musketeers were introduced as dragoons, improved handguns and artillery became more common, and the ratio of pikes to muskets declined. The New Model Army embraced these changes and was generally victorious.

To keep the pressed men in service and improve their performance, strict discipline was imposed. Exercises with arms honed skills, and sanitary discipline enhanced their health. As the war continued, many officers and men became more passionate about religious discipline. Regulations forbidding swearing, for example, were enforced rigorously. This was in line with the increasingly intolerant nature of behavior in Parliament. Recent studies have shown that the growing religious dedication improved morale and cohesion. In addition, men were able to rise in the ranks through merit and skill. This improved social mobility was limited, however, for the regimental commanders and their superiors continued to be aristocrats, like Fairfax, or came from the gentry. Those soldiers who did rise in the ranks became noncommissioned or junior officers.

Parliament's increasing radicalization and the execution of Charles I proved too much for Fairfax, who resigned following the trial. After Fairfax's retirement, Cromwell became the commander in chief of the New Model Army, as well as the leader in Parliament. Under Cromwell's command, the New Model Army achieved its greatest victories. Throughout its last years, the New Model Army remained potent and successful wherever it fought.

SIGNIFICANCE

The New Model Army was England's first standing army. As such, it established many of the traditions associated with the British army. Significant traditions include a uniform that spawned the nickname "redcoats," conscription of citizens into the army, permanent wages based on taxation, standardization of regiments, strict discipline, and professionalism based in part on merit. Most important, because the army was created, paid, and led by the command of Parliament, it established the twin conventions of loyalty to the nation rather than to a lord or king and of civilian control of the military.

—*Kevin B. Reid*

FURTHER READING

Asquith, Stuart. *New Model Army, 1645-60.* London: Osprey, 1999. This volume in the Osprey Men-At-Arms series provides a short, yet detailed, look at the New Model Army's equipment, organization, and tactics.

Firth, C. H. *Cromwell's Army: A History of the English Soldier During the Civil Wars, the Commonwealth, and the Protectorate.* 1912. Reprint. Novato, Calif.: Presidio Press, 1992. Filled with details about the organization of the army and the daily life of its men. It is the standard upon which later works are based.

Gentles, Ian. *The New Model Army in England, Ireland, and Scotland, 1645-1653.* Oxford, England: Blackwell, 1992. This is an excellent study of the politics that formed the New Model Army and a detailed look into the realities of its inner workings.

_____. "The New Model Officer Corps in 1647: A Collective Portrait." *Social History* 22, no. 2 (May, 1997). This article provides invaluable insight into the origins and expectations of the middle-level and junior officers who ran the army.

Roberts, Keith. *Soldiers of the English Civil War I: Infantry.* London: Osprey, 1996. This work provides a good description of the evolution of arms, tactics, and organizations that occurred during the wars.

Tincey, John. *Ironsides: English Cavalry, 1588-1688.* London: Osprey, 2002. This title provides an excellent look at the decisive arm of the New Model Army. This is especially useful for its insight into the tactics that were used both before and during the civil war.

SEE ALSO: 1642-1651: English Civil Wars; Aug. 17-Sept. 25, 1643: Solemn League and Covenant; July 2, 1644: Battle of Marston Moor; 1646-1649: Levellers Launch an Egalitarian Movement; Dec. 6, 1648-May 19, 1649: Establishment of the English Commonwealth; Oct., 1651-May, 1652: Navigation Act Leads to Anglo-Dutch Wars; Dec. 16, 1653-Sept. 3, 1658: Cromwell Rules England as Lord Protector; Mar. 12-14, 1655: Penruddock's Uprising; May, 1659-May, 1660: Restoration of Charles II.

RELATED ARTICLES in *Great Lives from History: The Seventeenth Century, 1601-1700:* Charles I; Charles II (of England); Oliver Cromwell; Third Baron Fairfax; Gustavus II Adolphus; Maurice of Nassau.

August 22, 1645-September, 1669
TURKS CONQUER CRETE

The declining Ottoman Empire still coveted the last and largest of Venice's Mediterranean possessions, so it invaded Crete and provoked a quarter century war, even amid its own internal crises.

LOCALE: Eastern Mediterranean Sea

CATEGORIES: Wars, uprisings, and civil unrest; expansion and land acquisition

KEY FIGURES

İbrahim (1615-1648), Ottoman sultan, r. 1640-1648

Mehmed IV Avci (1642-1693), Ottoman sultan, r. 1648-1687

Köprülü Mehmed Paşa (d. 1661), Ottoman grand vizier, 1656-1661

Köprülü Fazıl Ahmed Paşa (1635-1676), Ottoman grand vizier, 1661-1676

Francesco Morosini (1618-1694), Venetian captain general, 1660-1669, and Venetian doge, 1688-1694

SUMMARY OF EVENT

Venice had acquired the island of Crete as the largest of its maritime spoils of the Fourth Crusade (1202-1204). Subduing the Greek population and establishing an orderly regime had been a painful process, fraught with recurrent setbacks and local rebellions. Culturally, the regime had positive aspects, and for some four centuries Crete was the ultimate anchor of Venice's naval and mercantile position in the eastern Mediterranean.

By the seventeenth century, administrative incompetence had mounted, while the home government was hard-pressed and declining in resources and prestige. Economic decay, rampant poverty, and mounting dissidence made Crete an ever more vulnerable target for the

1640's

Ottoman Empire, which had long resented this Venetian obstacle to its full command of the sea lanes.

The Ottoman Empire was in disarray by the seventeenth century. Gone was the heyday under Süleyman the Magnificent (r. 1520-1566). In 1571, the Turks had conquered Cyprus from Venice and weathered the naval defeat at the Battle of Lepanto. However, the throne was occupied by dynastic successors of weak character and erratic behavior, while the exercise of power was increasingly assumed by the powerful chief minister, the grand vizier. A bloody struggle for the throne ended with the accession of the teenaged Murad IV (r. 1623-1640) who, by ruthless assertion of will, brought a brief restoration of energy and expansionist success. His premature death, however, undid much of his work and disarray resumed. He was succeeded by his brother İbrahim, who was emotionally unstable and eventually quite insane.

In March, 1644, some corsairs of the Hospitaler Order of Malta seized a Turkish vessel carrying distinguished pilgrims to Mecca. Venice was implicated in the episode. İbrahim was enraged and his fury was channeled toward the capture of Crete. A pretense of Malta as the target masked preparations, but Venice suspected the worst and sent a flotilla to strengthen Crete's defenses, though one that had been critically delayed. After heading toward Malta in late April, 1645, the Turkish expeditionary fleet, as a feint, changed course and landed on June 25 at Canea on Crete's northwestern shore. The town held out briefly, surrendering on August 22. The relief fleet arrived too late, and subsequent Venetian efforts to recover Canea failed.

As desperation and confusion marked Venetian countermeasures, the Turks moved out to seize or beleaguer a number of important points. By summer of 1647, they began a siege of Candia (now Iráklion), the island's capital. Heavily fortified, and with a small but stubborn population, the city could be regularly provisioned, since Venetian patrol of the sea lanes kept it accessible. The result was a siege that was to last twenty-two years, one of the longest of any city in history.

With a stalemate at Candia, the Turkish attempt to conquest the remaining island was undermined by government confusion in Constantinople. Venice's economy still was resilient and had considerable resources, but the Venetian Republic was not equal to the burden of defense, so it desperately appealed for outside help. Since the fifteenth century, Venice had taken up the role of Christian champion in the eastern Mediterranean through recurrent naval wars with the Ottoman Empire.

From that ideological position, Venice asked the great powers of Christian Europe for support. Preoccupied with their own affairs and never interested in disinterested causes, the European rulers were indifferent. Nevertheless, individual countries did provide small spurts of aid. The old spirit of crusading was moribund by the mid-sixteenth century, though armchair theorists still discussed it. The opportunity once again to fight infidels on behalf of the Christian faith inspired many young adventurers, noble and otherwise, to go to Crete and perform often heroic service there. The defense of Candia was, in a way, the last crusade.

Though Venice could not recover the lost parts of Crete or break the Siege of Candia, it was still capable of counteractions. In the spring of 1648, a Venetian fleet smashed its way into the Dardanelles (narrow strait between Turkey's Gallipoli Peninsula in Europe and Turkey in Asia) and established a maritime blockade of Constantinople that lasted one year. This outrage was the last straw for the Turkish leadership, exasperated by the irresponsible behavior of İbrahim. A palace coup brought about his deposition and execution, replacing him with his son, Mehmed IV Avci, a child of six. Actual power was left to shifting court and military factions, producing some eight years of confusion and drift.

A new Venetian exertion brought matters to a head. In June, 1656, the republic's fleet met and smashed the Turkish fleet at the mouth of the Dardanelles; only the death in action of the Venetian admiral prevented movement all the way to Constantinople, the center of the Ottoman Empire. Both in symbolic and practical terms, this setback was far graver than the defeat at Lepanto eighty-five years earlier. Once again, the Venetians imposed a blockade on the straits and the Aegean coasts. There was panic in Constantinople, where communications were cut off and food prices skyrocketed.

In this crisis the court agreed to place an able leader in full power as grand vizier. This was the aged but energetic Köprülü Mehmed Paşa. Of Albanian background, a product of one of the final rounds of the *devshirme* system (the "recruitment" of children from subject nations as slave-soldiers), he founded a family dynasty of viziers that would mask the weakness of sultans with a revitalized ministerial rule in place of dynastic autocracy.

Mehmed Paşa marshaled forces to break the Venetian blockade. While Ottoman naval strength would never fully recover, serious renewal of the Candian war was now possible. Through the next five years, Mehmed Paşa instituted a relentless program of reform. When he died in 1661, he could pass on to his son and successor as grand vizier, Fazıl Ahmed Paşa, a secure momentum. Operations in the Balkans, capped by a pivotal defeat by Habsburg forces in 1664, distracted Ahmed's regime, but by 1666, he was ready to end the Cretan stalemate. He took personal command of a new force directed at Candia, to press its siege with renewed vigor.

Candia now had an able new commander, Francesco Morosini, son of a former duke of Crete and kin to several Morosini leaders who had given their lives for Crete. He was aided at times by flamboyant volunteer forces from France who, however, were unruly and soon departed. Faced with Ahmed's relentless pressures, his resources gravely depleted, Morosini recognized the hopelessness of his situation by September of 1669. Though lacking home authorization, he negotiated directly with the vizier, who proved pragmatically generous. Venice was allowed to retain Souda on Crete and a few small offshore islands, but Candia and the rest of the island was surrendered to the Turks formally; Morosini and his diminished troops were allowed to depart in peace, and Venice's trading rights with the Ottoman Empire were renewed.

SIGNIFICANCE

Köprülü Fazıl Ahmed Paşa continued to rule energetically, even achieving expansionist successes in the Ukraine. When he died, still young, in 1676, the dynastic vizierate passed to his brother-in-law, Merzifonlu Kara Mustafa Paşa. Kara Mustafa's recklessness led to the ill-fated Turkish Siege of Vienna in 1683, and his failure further proved Ottoman slippage in the Balkans. The Köprülü leadership was renewed by Ahmed's younger brother Mustafa, but only briefly (1689-1691), and Ottoman reverses and misrule only multiplied.

Shorn of Crete, with Corfu in the Ionian Sea as its only important maritime holding, Venice sought a scapegoat. Morosini's enemies arraigned him on a range of mostly trumped charges. He refuted them triumphantly and, in 1684, was confirmed as captain general in a new campaign against the Turks in Greece. In the middle of this last great display of Venetian strength, he was elected doge of Venice, dying while still in field command (1694).

Betrayed by its allies, Venice saw its Greek conquests evaporate and lost even its last token holdings around Crete (1715). The Venetian Republic entered its final century definitively reduced to minor-power status in the European order.

—John W. Barker

FURTHER READING

Georgopoulou, Maria. *Venice's Mediterranean Colonies: Architecture and Urbanism.* New York: Cambridge University Press, 2001. A fascinating study of Venetian colonial practices, with special focus on Crete.

Kinross, J. P. D. *The Ottoman Centuries: The Rise and Fall of the Turkish Empire.* New York: Morrow Quill, 1977. A basic historical narrative, with the Cretan war traced in context.

McKee, Sally. *Uncommon Dominion: Venetian Crete and the Myth of Ethnic Purity.* Philadelphia: University of Pennsylvania Press, 2000. A provocative study of the island's colonial demography.

Murphey, Rhoads. *Ottoman Warfare, 1500-1700.* New Brunswick, N.J.: Rutgers University Press, 1999. A useful work that examines seventeenth century Ottoman military campaigning.

Norwich, John Julius. *A History of Venice.* New York: Knopf, 1982. A popular, solid narrative account, with particularly full treatment of the Cretan War and on Morosini's Greek campaign.

Richardson, Aubrey. *The Doges of Venice.* London: Methuen, 1914. Old and dated, but a colorful narrative of the Candian war and Morosini's career.

Shaw, Stanford J. *History of the Ottoman Empire and Modern Turkey.* Vol. 1 in *Empire of the Gazis: The Rise and Decline of the Ottoman Empire, 1280-1808.* New York: Cambridge University Press, 1996. A standard scholarly history, with integrated treatment of the Candian war and Ottoman governmental developments.

Smith, Michael Llewellyn. *The Great Island: A Study of Crete.* New York: Longman, 1965. A broad general history of Crete. Illustrated.

Turnbull, Stephen. *The Ottoman Empire, 1326-1699.* New York: Routledge, 2003. A very brief history of Ottoman rule, imperial expansion, and military tactics that focuses especially on Ottoman battles against European powers and on control of the Balkans. Handsomely illustrated.

Wheatcroft, Andrew. *Infidels: A History of the Conflict Between Christendom and Islam.* New York: Random House, 2004. Examines the continuing religious conflicts between the Christian West and the Islamic Middle East.

Wiel, Alethea. *Venice.* New York: T. Fisher Unwin & Putnam's Sons, 1894. Reprint. *A History of Venice: From Its Founding to the Unification of Italy.* New York: Barnes & Noble Books, 1995. A quite old-fashioned popular history, but with extensive treatment of the Candian and Peloponnesian wars.

1640's

SEE ALSO: 1603-1617: Reign of Sultan Ahmed I; 1623-1640: Murad IV Rules the Ottoman Empire; 1638: Waning of the *Devshirme* System; 1656-1676: Ottoman Empire's Brief Recovery; Summer, 1672-Fall, 1676: Ottoman-Polish Wars; July 14-Sept. 12, 1683: Defeat of the Ottomans at Vienna; 1684-1699: Holy League Ends Ottoman Rule of the Danubian Basin; Beginning 1687: Decline of the Ottoman Empire; 1697-1702: Köprülü Reforms of Hüseyin Paşa; Jan. 26, 1699: Treaty of Karlowitz.

RELATED ARTICLES in *Great Lives from History: The Seventeenth Century, 1601-1700:* John III Sobieski; Merzifonlu Kara Mustafa Paşa; Leopold I; Murad IV.

1646-1649
LEVELLERS LAUNCH AN EGALITARIAN MOVEMENT

An egalitarian reform movement, closely associated with Cromwell's New Model Army, was launched in England. The so-called Levellers sought to establish universal male suffrage and government accountability and they provided the foundation for republican political thought.

LOCALE: England
CATEGORIES: Social issues and reform; government and politics; wars, uprisings, and civil unrest

KEY FIGURES
John Lilburne (c. 1615-1657), popular Leveller pamphleteer
John Wildman (1621/1623-1693), Leveller pamphleteer and participant in the Putney Debates
Oliver Cromwell (1599-1658), Parliamentary military leader and lord protector of England, 1653-1658
Richard Overton (d. 1663), Leveller pamphleteer
William Walwyn (1600-1680), Leveller pamphleteer and party organizer
Henry Ireton (1611-1651), officer in the New Model Army
Charles I (1600-1649), king of England, r. 1625-1649

SUMMARY OF EVENT
The English Civil Wars of the 1640's provided a historical precedent for open political debate and dialogue, mass petitions, and popular demonstrations upon Parliament, from which the group now known as the Levellers were able to generate momentum and support for their movement and crystallize a radical political and social agenda. This agenda included the institution of democracy, popular sovereignty, active citizen participation in government, communal action in the public interest, and an individualistic political philosophy emphasizing natural rights and individual and civil liberties. The label "Levellers" was originally coined and used with a pejo-

rative connotation by their opponents to deny the legitimacy of the reform movement and to imply that its members desired to level or equalize property holdings among the population.

Leveller political writing was stimulated by the multiple and complex political, religious, social, and economic conflicts of the period. From 1646 to 1649, severe adverse transformations in manufacturing and landholding upon the English lower middle class led to mass discontent in both urban and rural areas throughout the country. In particular, the Civil Wars were promoting poor trade conditions, sharply accelerated inflated prices, very high unemployment, poor wages, and diminished purchasing power. These factors unfortunately coincided with a prolonged period of bad harvests in the latter part of the 1640's. The Levellers' proposed remedies to such problems provided them immediate, although short-lived, influence and visibility.

Throughout the early 1640's, the Levellers had allied themselves with the radical republican forces in Parliament and various members of the gentry elite in their opposition to monarchical absolutism and to the political theory of the divine right of kings. By the end of the first phase of the Civil Wars in 1646 and in the context of Parliament's various successes, the Levellers echoed the army's skepticism of the Presbyterian-dominated Parliament's negotiation with Royalist forces and King Charles I. By mid-1647, major Leveller leaders had forged an alliance with the rank and file of the army and assisted them to gain greater leverage in the negotiated settlement with the Royalist forces. This was due primarily to a belief, shared by both the Levellers and the Parliamentary army, that the Presbyterian majority in Parliament had treated the army poorly and had failed to promote the general welfare effectively.

In their pamphlets, the Levellers often relied upon a nostalgic glorification of a golden age prior to the Norman invasion of 1066. The Norman Conquest was depicted as the critical watershed event in English constitutional history, since it represented the imposition of the arbitrary power of the "Norman Yoke" on the people and an immediate loss of fundamental rights and liberties. The Levellers argued that Norman rule also led to a perversion of the revered ancient Anglo-Saxon constitution, the subsequent servitude of the English population, and the loss of traditional English representative government. The Levellers insisted that only comprehensive constitutional, political, social, and economic reforms could recover the lost rights and liberties of the English people.

The main intellectual leaders of the Leveller movement included John Lilburne, Richard Overton, William Walwyn, and John Wildman. Most of these Leveller leaders were well educated and had demonstrated the excellent political skills necessary to drive a truly populist democratic movement. As political activists, they had extensive experience and expertise in mass mobilization, political persuasion, agitation, and the writing of political pamphlets. The Levellers' philosophical program was often derived from the personal political experiences of many of their leaders.

John Lilburne's critical commentary on the abuses of a tyrannical government reflected his own protracted periods of arbitrary arrest and imprisonment. The Puritan Lilburne, referred to as Free-born John, was imprisoned, whipped, and pilloried in 1638 for publishing several Puritan works that attacked the Church of England. He was a prolific author, having written many political tracts and petitions promoting individual rights, religious freedom of conscience and toleration, freedom of speech, and limited governmental and church authority. He opposed any form of oligarchical or hierarchical power, such as trading monopolies or church tithes. Lilburne served as a lieutenant-colonel fighting against the Royalist army of King Charles I during the First English Civil War. He had the reputation of being the most popular and charismatic of the Leveller leaders. This was demonstrated by his intensely loyal followers, who supported him throughout his trial for high treason, and by the jury of Londoners who acquitted him in August, 1649.

The Levellers were for the most part drawn from segments of the "middling" class and consisted of small traders, artisans, merchants, apprentices, craftsmen, and husbandmen. They were primarily from London and considered themselves spokespersons and representatives of the politically unrepresented and disenfranchised men of the English population. Certain revolutionary

segments of the New Model Army and various independent congregations were enthusiastic activists in support of the Leveller platform, primarily because of its radical objectives of religious toleration and freedom of religious thought.

The Levellers were highly skilled at writing and circulating effective political pamphlets and petitions and submitting petitions to Parliament to mobilize the masses and increase public support for their movement. Their persuasive rhetoric was articulated in classic political pamphlets and tracts, such as Lilburne's *The Case of the Army Truly Stated* (1647) and *Foundations of Freedom* (1647). Some of the more significant and influential of the Leveller petitions included the Large Petition (March, 1647), the Earnest Petition (January, 1648), the Humble Petition (September, 1648), and the very popular Remonstrance of Many Thousands of the Free People of England (September, 1649). The latter petition, justifying armed resistance to oppressive authority, garnered 98,064 signatures.

As prolific authors of radical political literature (for example, Overton wrote forty essays, and Lilburne authored eighty pamphlets), the Levellers sacrificed intellectual sophistication and logical coherence for the pragmatic party objective of persuasive political rhetoric. The newspaper *The Moderate*, edited by Gilbert Mabbott and printed from July, 1648, to September, 1649, was a major source of Leveller doctrine. Instead of relying upon a political discourse based upon tradition, precedent, or biblical references, Leveller writings provided a then-innovative appeal to rational argumentation.

The Levellers' progressive social, economic, and legal program insisted upon removing trading monopolies, opening up greater tracts of public land and reducing land enclosure, and creating more equitable property ownership laws. They called for comprehensive legal reforms, including equal legal rights for all citizens, and the elimination of church taxes. The Levellers quickly rejected Parliament's attempt in 1646 to impose a Presbyterian theocracy or national church. The most influential Leveller leaders (Lilburne, Walwyn, and Overton) were strongly committed to the positions of religious toleration, freedom of spiritual conscience, and congregational autonomy. These Leveller Calvinist Puritan positions were very popular among numerous independent congregations throughout England.

In the early months of 1647, the New Model Army was influenced by a very strong Leveller faction. In April, 1647, agitators who were proponents of Leveller political theory were popularly elected by the rank and

1640's

file of the army. The grandees (or generals) of the army were compelled to allow for an army council that included these radical soldiers, in addition to the officers who were generally supportive of Oliver Cromwell. From early October to November 8, 1647, a series of intense meetings and debates of the council of the New Model Army were held in the Putney Church.

In addition to Cromwell and Henry Ireton (Cromwell's son-in-law), several officers and so-called Agitators participated in the Putney Debates, which focused on an evaluation and potential adoption of the Levellers' proposed constitution, the Agreement of the People. This radical document was written as a social contract to reestablish a legitimate state, since Parliament's victory over King Charles I in the Civil War had led to the disintegration of the traditional English political system of monarchical absolutism. The various versions of the Agreement of the People were actually popular political petitions, supported by mass signatures and purposely designed as reform constitutions for a new, democratic commonwealth. The central principles of the Agreement of the People were to defend popular sovereignty and to reject arbitrary, despotic power of either the monarchy or the Parliament. At Putney, the Levellers proposed that a republican government replace the traditional rule of an absolute monarchy, hereditary House of Lords, and the more recently oppressive House of Commons.

Both the Putney Debates and the Whitehall Debates (December, 1648) demonstrated the serious disagreements between the Levellers and the grandees concerning political and economic issues. Cromwell and Ireton, for example, rejected the Leveller demands for a republican constitution and universal male suffrage. It was the Leveller Agitators' expansion of the franchise position in particular that promoted the deadlock and breakdown of negotiations at Putney. The proposal to give all men the vote was interpreted by Ireton as a means for promoting mob rule, anarchy, and the abolition or "levelling" of property.

The Agitators returned from Putney to their regiments on November 8, 1647, and a growing army mistrust of the House of Commons and Cromwell led to mutiny among the soldiers on November 15, 1647. The generals quickly crushed the army uprising and restored order among the ranks. Subsequently, the brief success of the Leveller agenda was based upon mobilizing the New Model Army against its officers. Leveller leaders, such as Lilburne, became more aggressive in asserting a more radical program at the initiation of Cromwell's Commonwealth in 1649. They demanded the immediate abo-

lition of the House of Lords, the dissolution of the Rump Parliament, annually elected Parliaments, the dissolution of the council of state, and decentralization of public authority. Again, these radical proposals were rejected by the army officers, and several army mutinies resulted.

Cromwell quickly prompted the arrest and imprisonment of Lilburne, Overton, and Walwyn in the Tower of London in March, 1649. A mutiny among the Leveller troops who refused to follow a command to leave London occurred on April 25, 1649. This rebellion was suppressed by Cromwell, however, and several of the soldiers were court-martialed. Subsequent rebellions among the troops spread throughout England but without much success; many of these army mutinies were stimulated by the soldiers' fear of not receiving payment previously owed to them. In May, 1649, between one thousand and two thousand soldiers mutinied at Banbury and two regiments mutinied at Salisbury. One thousand mutineers from Salisbury moved along the Thames Valley toward London, but they were defeated by Cromwell at Burford, and the Leveller movement was crushed.

SIGNIFICANCE

The Leveller movement was one of the first widespread egalitarian movements in European history. Ideas that have since become commonplace, such as government by the people and for the people, were at the time so unprecedented and radical as to border on insanity in the minds of the English rulers. The immediate consequences of the movement were negative: It resulted in the forcible removal or silencing of advocates of popular democracy in England and consolidated Cromwell's power over the New Model Army and by extension the nation. Cromwell would become lord protector in 1653. The long-term consequences of the movement were a different matter. The Levellers demonstrated that there was a genuine populist spirit present in the hearts of many English subjects, providing both a rational and an empirical basis for future democratic reforms. Their ideas and their fate served as both an example and a cautionary tale to democratic and socialist movements for centuries afterward.

—Mitchel Gerber

FURTHER READING

Brailsford, H. N. *The Levellers and the English Revolution*. Nottingham, Nottinghamshire, England: Spokesman, 1983. This classic study by an outstanding historian provides compelling argumentation that the Levellers provided the intellectual initiative for the English Revolution.

Frank, Joseph. *The Levellers*. Cambridge, Mass.: Harvard University Press, 1955. A landmark work focusing on the writings of Lilburne, Overton, and Walwyn, and the organizational strategies of the Leveller party.

Manning, Brian. *The English People and the English Revolution*. London: Bookmarks, 1991. Manning's controversial study contends that the English Revolution should be interpreted as a class struggle, and that the "middling sort" played a central role in the Leveller movement.

Mendle, Michael, ed. *The Putney Debates of 1647: The Army, the Levellers, and the English State*. Cambridge, England: Cambridge University Press, 2001. Collection of revised papers originally presented at a conference about the Putney Debates held in 1997.

Petegorsky, David W. *Left-Wing Democracy in the English Civil War*. New York: Haskell House, 1972. A sophisticated study of the ideological origins of radical political thought during the Civil Wars.

Sanderson, John. *"But the People's Creatures": The Philosophical Basis of the English Civil War*. New York: Manchester University Press, 1989. Sanderson offers new insights into the radical nature of the Levellers'

political philosophy and the arguments of the movement's critics.

Sharp, Andrew, ed. *The English Levellers*. Cambridge, England: Cambridge University Press, 1998. Collection of writings by Lilburne, Overton, Walwyn, and others expressing the Levellers' political philosophy. Includes an introduction providing an overview of the Leveller movement from 1645 through 1649.

SEE ALSO: Dec. 18, 1621: The Great Protestation; Mar., 1629-1640: "Personal Rule" of Charles I; Mar.-June, 1639: First Bishops' War; Nov. 3, 1640-May 15, 1641: Beginning of England's Long Parliament; 1642-1651: English Civil Wars; Aug. 17-Sept. 25, 1643: Solemn League and Covenant; Spring, 1645-1660: Puritan New Model Army; Dec. 6, 1648-May 19, 1649: Establishment of the English Commonwealth; Dec. 16, 1653-Sept. 3, 1658: Cromwell Rules England as Lord Protector; May, 1659-May, 1660: Restoration of Charles II; Feb. 13, 1689: Declaration of Rights.

RELATED ARTICLES in *Great Lives from History: The Seventeenth Century, 1601-1700:* Charles I; Charles II (of England); Oliver Cromwell; John Lilburne.

1648
CULT OF THE VIRGIN OF GUADALUPE

Miguel Sánchez published his Imagen de la Virgen Maria, *a celebration of the image of the Virgin of Guadalupe, which spawned the most important Catholic cult in the Americas. This book was the first written account of the apparition and became the focus of native devotion dating to 1531. The cult itself became an important component of criollo culture.*

LOCALE: Mexico City, Mexico (formerly New Spain)
CATEGORIES: Religion and theology; cultural and intellectual history

KEY FIGURES

Miguel Sánchez (1594-1674), creole priest and author of *Imagen de la Virgen Maria*
Juan Diego (1474-1548), purported witness to the miracle of the Virgin of Guadalupe
Juan de Zumárraga (1468-1548), first bishop of Mexico, 1527-1547, and archbishop of Mexico, 1547-1548

SUMMARY OF EVENT

In 1648, the creole priest Miguel Sánchez wrote *Imagen de la Virgen Maria* (image of the Virgin Mary), the first published account of the Mexican Virgin of Guadalupe and her miraculous appearance to the native convert Juan Diego. According to Sánchez, this event occurred in December of 1531, only ten years after the fall of the Aztec capital Tenochtitlán to the Spanish conquistador Hernán Cortés. Writing more than one hundred years later, Sánchez recounted the story of the recently Christianized Juan Diego, who was passing by the hill of Tepeyac when the Virgin Mary appeared to him as a native Mexican woman.

Speaking Náhuatl, the Aztec language, she told Juan Diego to descend the hill to see the bishop of Mexico, Juan de Zumárraga, and instruct him to build a church in her honor on the site. Juan Diego dutifully did as he was told, but Zumárraga refused the request. Upon Juan Diego's return to Tepeyac, the Virgin reappeared, repeating her demand. Juan Diego returned to the bishop, who, this time, requested a sign from the Virgin Mary. Returning to Tepeyac a third time, the Virgin assured Juan Diego that she would provide the requested sign but first instructed him to return to his village. There, he discovered his uncle, Juan Bernardino, sick and near death.

Rushing to the church at Tlatelolco to find a confessor, Juan Diego hurried past Tepeyac. The Virgin stopped him, telling Juan Diego that his uncle was cured, and instructed him to ascend the hill to gather roses, miraculously blooming in December, to show to the bishop. Carrying the roses in his native cloak, or *tilma*, Juan Diego returned to Zumárraga. When he opened his cloak to reveal the blooms, an image of the Virgin of Guadalupe was miraculously revealed, imprinted on the fabric. Awestruck by the miracle, the bishop fell to his knees, promising to build the church. This is the image venerated in Mexico City's Basílica de la Virgen de Guadalupe.

The *tilma* is widely regarded as miraculous in origin by Catholics, particularly in Mexico. It represents a dark-skinned Virgin, head bowed and hands clasped in prayer, wearing a crown and starry blue cloak. A mandorla of light surrounds her figure. She stands on a crescent moon, ancient fertility symbol and traditional attribute of the Immaculate Conception, held aloft by a single angel. The depiction appears on a support of maguey cloth, a type of rough native fabric.

Although today the Virgin of Guadalupe is associated with the struggle of native and *mestizo* peoples for justice, recent historians have convincingly demonstrated the creole origins of the cult. In fact, the 1648 publication of Miguel Sánchez's Guadalupan text was instrumental in fomenting creole nationalism. This creole movement, originating in the seventeenth century, eventually led to the Mexican fight for independence from Spain, attained in 1821. Sánchez's text emphasizes the divine favor the Virgin bestowed upon the creoles, people of Spanish origin born in the Americas, recounting miracles worked on their behalf. Indeed, according to Sánchez and others, the Virgin's appearance in Mexico in 1531 was proof of the special status of Mexico, or New Spain, as it was then known.

The book, which contains little about indigenous devotion to the Virgin of Guadalupe, inspired the publication of similar texts, most importantly a simplified revision issued in 1660 by the Jesuit Mateo de la Cruz that circulated widely. Books by Luis Becerra Tanco (1666 and 1685) and one by Francisco de Florencia (1688) followed. Other events testify to the creole orientation of the cult in the seventeenth century, most notably the rebuilding of the church on the original site under Archbishop Juan Pérez de la Serna, an occasion commemorated in a 1615 print by Samuel Stradanus.

Only six short months after the appearance of Sánchez's historic text, another version of the Guadalupan story in the native language of Náhuatl was published, entitled *Huey tlamahuiçoltica* (1649; by a great miracle). This text, composed of writings from the late sixteenth and seventeenth centuries by various authors, was compiled by the creole priest Luis Laso de la Vega. He intended his version, which focuses on indigenous devotion to the Virgin, for native readers. It had no influence on Mexico's creole population and only became widely known in the twentieth century.

The evolution of the Virgin of Guadalupe's cult highlights one of the major problems facing historians who work on Latin America, that is, disentangling the European and indigenous origins of cultural phenomena. Although scholars are increasingly coming to the conclusion that devotion to the Virgin of Guadalupe was initially propagated by those of Spanish descent, many others still insist on its native genealogy. They believe that the devotion was passed down orally among native worshipers, thus explaining the lack of written documentation.

A third group of scholars has proposed that the figure of the Virgin of Guadalupe was foisted upon native converts by missionaries eager to replace the Aztec mother goddess with a similar Catholic figure. This argument is strengthened by the claims of the Franciscan friar Bernardino de Sahagún, who, writing around 1576, claimed that Indians' devotion to the Virgin of Guadalupe was a clever pretense masking worship of the Aztec goddess he identified as Tonantzin, or Our Mother. While many historians have accepted Sahagún's claim, some specialists in Precolumbian culture have questioned the existence of such a goddess, the name of which does not correspond to any documentable native deity.

The *tilma* painting, regarded by many believers as a divinely crafted image, similarly presents scholars with interpretive challenges. Close analysis of the textile, including radiography, has revealed numerous changes and additions to the original, particularly in the areas of the mandorla, moon, angel, and the Virgin's hands. Furthermore, its combination of indigenous drawing technique and Christian iconography closely resembles other Indo-Christian Mexican artworks of the sixteenth century. Based on stylistic analysis, the art historian Jeanette Favrot Peterson has posited a date in the 1550's for the image. Others have suggested a possible author, the celebrated sixteenth century Indian painter Marcos Aquino. Finally, the Mexican image closely resembles a Spanish sculpture found on a choir stall in the monastery of the Virgin of Guadalupe in Extremadura, Spain, after which the former was probably named.

SIGNIFICANCE

The cult of the Virgin of Guadalupe is the most important Catholic cult in the Americas and one of the most widespread throughout the world today. In addition, the Virgin is a major icon of Mexican national identity. Although the origins of her cult remain shrouded in mystery, her image has taken on powerful political meanings over time. Most notably, she is viewed as a symbol representing the rights and humanity of native and *mestizo* peoples. Some view her as the perfect hybrid symbol, representing the confluence of European and Precolumbian cultures. Others insist she is a thinly disguised Aztec mother goddess.

The cult attained its greatest success in the eighteenth century. After being credited with stopping a deadly epidemic of disease in Mexico City in 1737, the Virgin of Guadalupe was named patron of Mexico City and was elevated principal patron of both Mexico and Guatemala in 1746. At the same time, the Virgin of Guadalupe became the object of increasing indigenous devotion, as indicated by surviving Náhuatl sermons and religious dramas. Despite claims of the indigenous origins of the cult, there is little tangible evidence of the cult's popularity among native worshipers until the eighteenth century.

As the meanings attached to her figure shifted, representations of the Mexican Virgin expressed different points of view. Beginning in the eighteenth century, the story of her apparition to Juan Diego was understood as proof of Mary's love for native peoples. In the nineteenth century, pro-independence forces, led by Miguel Hidalgo, deployed her image as a symbol of national pride. During the Mexican Revolution (1910-1920), she came to represent social justice for the disenfranchised. In the 1960's and 1970's in the United States, Mexican American farmworkers carried her image in demonstrations as an emblem of peace and justice. Today, representations of the Virgin of Guadalupe can be found throughout Mexico, Latin America, and the American Southwest, a sign of Catholic faith and Latino identity.

Beginning in the 1970's, however, feminist artists, particularly in the United States, began to question the pious, humble image of the Virgin as a model for women to follow, producing iconoclastic representations of her in high heels, as the Aztec goddess Coatlicue, and even in a bikini (Alma López, 1999). In the 1970's, the Mexican American artist Yolanda M. López created portraits of her grandmother, her mother, and herself in the guise of *La Guadalupana*, activating what many Chicanas see as a passive, traditional image.

Despite historians' challenges to the cult's facticity, devotion to the Virgin of Guadalupe continues to thrive today. A new basilica in the Villa de Guadalupe, built by Pedro Ramírez Vázquez in the 1970's, holds ten thousand worshipers. Pilgrims continue to flock to the site, and Mexicans and other Latinos regard the dark-skinned Virgin as their special protector. As a measure of the cult's continued vitality, in 2002, Pope John Paul II canonized Juan Diego. It matters little to the Catholic faithful that some historians believe he never existed.

—*Charlene Villaseñor Black*

FURTHER READING

Burkhart, Louise. "The Cult of the Virgin of Guadalupe in Mexico." In *South and Meso-American Native Spirituality: From the Cult of the Feathered Serpent to the Theology of Liberation*, edited by Gary H. Gossen and Miguel León-Portilla. Vol. 4 in *World Spirituality: An Encyclopedic History of the Religious Quest*. New York: Crossroad, 1993. Important analysis of the Precolumbian context of the cult of the Virgin of Guadalupe with critique of her supposed conflation with the goddess called Tonantzin.

Lafaye, Jacques. *Quetzalcóatl and Guadalupe: The Formation of Mexican National Consciousness, 1531-1813*. Translated by Benjamin Keen. Chicago: University of Chicago Press, 1976. A classic study of two important nationalist symbols. The author locates the flowering of the Virgin of Guadalupe's cult in the first third of the seventeenth century.

Peterson, Jeanette Favrot. "The Virgin of Guadalupe: Symbol of Conquest or Liberation?" *Art Journal* (1992): 39-47. The definitive art historical study of the subject.

Poole, C. M. Stafford. *Our Lady of Guadalupe: The Origins and Sources of a Mexican Nationalist Symbol, 1531-1797*. Tucson: University of Arizona Press, 1996. The only thorough study of the primary sources documenting the history of the cult, with methodical analysis of their credibility. The author is a major promoter of the idea of the cult as creole in origin.

Taylor, William B. "The Virgin of Guadalupe: An Inquiry into the Social History of Marian Devotion." *American Ethnologist* 14 (1987): 9-33. An important article that focuses on the creole development of the cult.

SEE ALSO: 1604-1680: Rise of Criollo Identity in Mexico.

RELATED ARTICLE in *Great Lives from History: The Seventeenth Century, 1601-1700:* Sor Juana Inés de la Cruz.

1640's

June, 1648
WARS OF THE FRONDE BEGIN

The Wars of the Fronde in France pitted the privileged leaders of the bourgeoisie against the abuses of absolute monarchy, marking the emergence of the bourgeoisie as a serious contender in French politics.

LOCALE: France
CATEGORIES: Wars, uprisings, and civil unrest; government and politics; social issues and reform

KEY FIGURES
Anne of Austria (1601-1666), queen of France, r. 1615-1643, queen regent, r. 1643-1651, and mother of Louis XIV
The Great Condé (Louis II de Bourbon; 1621-1686), cousin of Louis XIV, noted military leader, and participant in the Fronde
Particelli d'Émery (1596-1650), French minister of finance, 1643-1648
Louis XIV (1638-1715), king of France, r. 1643-1715
Jules Mazarin (1602-1661), chief minister of France, 1643-1661
Omer Talon (1595-1652), member of the Parlement of Paris

SUMMARY OF EVENT
As the kingdom of France entered the year 1648, it was beset by a multitude of serious problems. King Louis XIII, who had ruled the country since 1610, had died in 1643, leaving his five-year-old son, Louis XIV, as the new monarch. Until he became old enough to rule in his own right, the government of the kingdom was controlled by a regent, Anne of Austria (Louis XIV's mother), and her first minister and chief adviser, Cardinal Jules Mazarin.

Mazarin, an Italian who had been a protégé of Cardinal de Richelieu (former first minister of Louis XIII who had died in 1642), was resented by many members of the French nobility and by the French people at large. Part of the reason for this resentment was classic xenophobia; many French people simply did not like being ruled by a "foreigner," especially one who appeared to become extraordinarily wealthy as a result of his position. The rumor that Mazarin was Anne's lover, and even perhaps secretly married to the queen, also fueled the popular image that the cardinal was an opportunistic place-seeker who was using his position to further his own ambitions and fortune at the expense of the well-being of France.

This foundation of personal resentment against Mazarin was reinforced by extreme dissatisfaction with many of his policies. The regent and her first minister had inherited a war against the Habsburg Dynasty of Austria and Spain from the previous reign. This conflict, known as the Thirty Years' War, had been a tremendous drain on French resources for years and had prompted a series of dramatic tax increases and administrative innovations that had pushed most of the country's taxpayers to the brink of endurance and had placed the finances of the kingdom in serious jeopardy. Mazarin's decision to continue the war effort meant that there was little chance for improvement in the kingdom's appalling financial condition or for any decrease in taxes. It also did not appear likely that any of Richelieu's administrative reforms, which generally aimed to increase the power of the king's agents at the expense of such semiautonomous institutions as *parlements* (local assemblies of notables, which had the power to register, and thereby implicitly approve or disapprove, royal edicts), would be reversed. Mazarin actually intensified these problems by allowing his minister of finance, Particelli d'Émery, to engage routinely in a number of unscrupulous tactics (such as withholding the salaries of venal state officials) to raise the necessary revenue to keep the country running.

These various grievances culminated in 1648, which ironically marked the successful conclusion of the Thirty Years' War. In January of that year, Louis XIV visited the Parlement of Paris and received a very cool reception. Omer Talon, one of the chief members of this body, gave a speech in which he outlined the financial troubles of the kingdom, the misery of the peasantry, and the heavy burden of taxation. He did congratulate Louis for presiding over the French victory in the Thirty Years' War but argued that victory in and of itself would not be enough to satisfy the problems facing his people. He instead urged the young king to recognize that France was a kingdom where "men are born free" and to "think of these things and of the misery of the people."

As would become evident in the months to come, this speech represented the first gauntlet to be thrown by *parlement* at the policies of the regency. Hoping to take advantage of the king's youth and the unpopularity of Mazarin and his policies, this body wanted to use its right to register royal edicts to gain control of taxation policy and to weaken the power of the royal council and its agents in the field, the intendants. Talon may have expressed their opposition by stressing the misery of the common people, but the main issue was a struggle for control of the future of the kingdom.

As the opposition of the *parlement* grew during the spring and early summer of 1648, Mazarin hesitated to take any firm steps to confront it, fearing that he simply was not strong enough to deal with it effectively. In June, 1648, Louis II of Bourbon, prince of Condé (the Great Condé), won an important victory over the Spanish at the Battle of Lens and provided Mazarin with the confidence he needed to stand up to his critics. He ordered the arrest of three of the most outspoken leaders of the opposition in *parlement* in the hope that this act would intimidate the others into acquiescence.

The public response to this arbitrary act led to the outbreak of the Fronde. The common people of Paris, many of whom actually believed that *parlement* had their best interests at heart, rioted and seized virtual control of the capital. At the same time, the remaining leaders of *parlement* presented a list of grievances to the regency and demanded their immediate resolution. Mazarin quickly and accurately recognized the seriousness of the situation and, despite the pleas of the queen regent to fight back, he released the three imprisoned *parlement* members and agreed to accept a "charter" that *parlement* had drawn up that greatly limited royal power in the areas of taxation, justice, and administration. In January of 1649, Mazarin made another tactical retreat and convinced the young Louis XIV and his mother to flee the capital and temporarily take up residence outside Paris in St. Germain.

Although Condé wanted to then launch a direct frontal assault on the capital and force it back into submission, Mazarin preferred to have his commander establish a siege and thereby gradually bring the city back under royal control with a minimum of bloodshed. This siege did gradually cut off the flow of food into Paris, and as the population's suffering increased, so did the intensity of popular hostility toward Mazarin. "Mazarinades," vicious printed personal attacks on the cardinal, poured from the city's popular presses, as did a torrent of obscene songs about his relationship with the queen regent.

King Louis XIV and Queen-Mother Anne of Austria fled Paris and the Wars of the Fronde around 1650 to the safety of Saint-Germain Palace. (R. S. Peale and J. A. Hill)

1640's

Yet Mazarin knew he held the advantage now that Condé's troops encircled the city, and he began to negotiate with his enemies within Paris. Both sides ultimately had to retreat from their original positions.

SIGNIFICANCE

In the Treaty of Reuil, signed in 1649, Mazarin was unable to obtain the complete humiliation of *parlement* that he originally wanted, but *parlement*, for its part, did not receive its demand for the cardinal's dismissal. Many of the promises of reform that Mazarin had granted immediately before his flight from the city were retained in this agreement. Yet their fulfillment depended on the good will of the Crown and it was clear that this would not be forthcoming once Mazarin had regained his strength. Cardinal Mazarin, Anne, and the king returned to Paris shortly thereafter. Royal power had been seriously tested by this first phase of the Fronde, but it had survived to face new tests that lay on the horizon.

—*Christopher E. Guthrie*

FURTHER READING

Beik, William. *Absolutism and Society in Seventeenth-Century France: State Power and Provincial Aristocracy in Languedoc*. Princeton, N.J.: Princeton University Press, 1985. An excellent case study of the impact of the Fronde on the policies and administration of Louis XIV.

Berce, Yves Marie. *The Birth of Absolutism: A History of France, 1598-1661*. Translated by Richard Rex. New York: St. Martin's Press, 1996. An analysis of the Fronde is included in this history of France from the Edict of Nantes through Mazarin's death.

Briggs, Robin. *Early Modern France, 1560-1715*. New York: Oxford University Press, 1977. One of the best textbooks in English on the early modern period in French history. The work includes a thorough summary on the Fronde and preceding events.

Moote, A. L. *The Revolt of the Judges*. Princeton, N.J.: Princeton University Press, 1971. Although subsequent scholarship has revealed several important errors of interpretation in this study, it remains one of the most complete accounts of this complex event.

Ranum, Orest. *The Fronde: A French Revolution*. Baltimore: Johns Hopkins University Press, 1993. In this analysis of the Fronde, Ranum argues that the conflict represented a precursor to the Great Revolution of 1789.

Treasure, Geoffrey. *Mazarin: The Crisis of Absolutism in France*. New York: Routledge, 1995. Among other topics, this biography discusses how Mazarin worked to retain an absolute French monarchy during the upheavals of the Fronde.

Wolf, John B. *Louis XIV*. New York: W. W. Norton, 1974. The early chapters of this classic biography of Louis XIV include a thorough account of the Fronde, emphasizing this event's impact on Louis's future attitude.

SEE ALSO: Nov. 7, 1659: Treaty of the Pyrenees; 1661: Absolute Monarchy Emerges in France; 1689-1694: Famine and Inflation in France.

RELATED ARTICLES in *Great Lives from History: The Seventeenth Century, 1601-1700:* Anne of Austria; The Great Condé; Louis XIII; Louis XIV; Jules Mazarin; Cardinal de Richelieu; Viscount de Turenne.

December 6, 1648-May 19, 1649
ESTABLISHMENT OF THE ENGLISH COMMONWEALTH

The establishment of the Commonwealth in England ushered in the first modern republic to be founded upon the trial and execution of a king, anticipating the French Revolution of 1789.

LOCALE: England

CATEGORIES: Government and politics; social issues and reform

KEY FIGURES

Oliver Cromwell (1599-1658), Parlimentary military commander, political leader, and lord protector of England, 1653-1658

Thomas Pride (c. 1605-1658), Parliamentary military commander

Henry Ireton (1611-1651), officer in the New Model Army and Cromwell's lieutenant

Charles I (1600-1649), king of England, r. 1625-1649

SUMMARY OF EVENT

Historian have located the crest of the English Civil Wars at various dates—in 1645, after Parliament's army decisively defeated the Royalists; in the Second Civil War of 1647-1649, when the Royalists backed by the Scots attempted to rescue the imprisoned king and were crushed by Parliament's army; at the initial founding of the Commonwealth in 1649 or at its dissolution by Oliver Cromwell four years later; and even in 1658, when Cromwell's death unleashed a new surge of republican radicalism that led to ultimate reaction and the 1660 restoration of the Stuart monarchy. Most historians, however, place the Civil Wars as a shorter period within the English Interregnum. That term refers to the years between 1642, when Charles I fled from his throne in London, and 1660, when his son returned. Even during those years, Cromwell's reign as lord protector resembled a monarchy. If a republic is defined as government by the people without a king, then England's only genuine republic was the Commonwealth of 1649-1653.

The Commonwealth was established with a dramatic event, the trial and execution of King Charles I in January, 1649. As the poet Andrew Marvell later wrote, "This was that memorable hour/ Which first assur'd the forced Pow'r." He meant the power of the people, who, guided by Cromwell and the other regicides, dared for the first time in history to call their king to account for the bloodshed of the Civil Wars. The new democracy had to be a "forced" power because it made a revolutionary break with England's constitutional monarchy. Kings had been dethroned and killed before but had always been replaced by a new king. In 1649, the people—represented by what was left of Parliament and acting through the army—did away with the institution of kingship itself. Americans can easily understand this because their republic, too, had its birth in the repudiation of monarchy. Marvell's poem reminds people, however, that the act of regicide is not just symbolic. Regicide is politically necessary to "assure" the transfer of power from king to people.

Most of the members of the Long Parliament—so called because it was elected in 1641 and legally continued to sit until there was a king to dissolve it officially in 1660—shrank from this transfer of power. When Parliament had originally rebelled against the king and launched the Civil Wars, the reformers did not dream of abolishing monarchical government. Rather, Parliament merely wanted a greater share in the traditional monarchy, specifically, the power to control the army, to choose the king's ministers, or cabinet, and to override his veto. Above all, Parliament wanted to be recognized as the supreme court of the land, the final interpreter of England's laws and constitution. It was really the king's rival claim to appoint judges and interpret laws that put him at odds with Parliament and that led to civil war.

Once they had defeated the Royalist army and captured the king, Parliament was divided sharply for two years (1647-1648) over what to do next. The majority of its members were relatively conservative and willing to accept a Presbyterian church in place of the episcopalian system of bishops who, under the king, had ruled the Church of England ever since Henry VIII. The Parliamentary Presbyterians, in other words, expected the king to continue as the head of church and state but with curtailed powers to appoint the chief officers—the bishops and the ministers—in both institutions.

Vehemently opposed to these Presbyterians were the Parliamentary Independents, who considered the Presbyterian clergy worse even than bishops and who believed that the king and his ministers could not be relied on to govern justly. The cause of the Independents was strengthened by the imprisoned king's treacherous dealings with the Scots, which brought on the Second Civil War and the bloody summer of 1648. When Parliament returned to Westminster that autumn, it immediately fell

1640's

The Great Seal of England adopted by the Commonwealth government. (R. S. Peale and J. A. Hill)

The remaining third of Parliament continued to sit in what was later known as the Rump Parliament. This Parliament included Cromwell among its leaders, and with the army at its back, it quickly proceeded to appoint judges to try the king. Charles I's trial and sentencing took place the week of January 20-27, and he was beheaded on January 30, 1649.

The Commonwealth of England was proclaimed during the next couple of weeks by a series of pronouncements in the House of Commons. Two days after Charles's execution, the Commons resolved to ban from government anyone who had been in favor of negotiating with the late king. On February 6, the Commons voted to abolish the House of Lords. On February 13, the executive functions of the dissolved monarchy were vested for a year in a Council of State with forty councillors, thirty-one of them members of Parliament. Not until May 19, however, was an act passed declaring England to be "a Commonwealth or Free State."

into a heated debate over whether it should continue to negotiate with the king. The Presbyterians insisted that whatever his faults, the king's office, like that of Parliament itself, was constitutionally established. Independents retorted by calling the king "Charles Stuart, that man of blood"—their point being that the king was answerable for his crimes just like any other citizen.

After listening to Parliament debate for two months, members of the army decided to act on their own. Apparently, their decision was made not by Cromwell, who was out of the country, but by his son-in-law, Henry Ireton. On December 6, Colonel Thomas Pride engaged in an action later known as Pride's Purge. Pride and his troops took up a station at the door of the House of Commons and read a list of Presbyterians to be excluded from Parliament. Those who had voted to continue negotiations with the king—perhaps two-thirds of the Parliament's elected members—were effectively retired from public life for the next twelve years. Some of the more vociferous members were even imprisoned.

During the next two years, the army, headed by Cromwell but taking their orders from Parliament and its Council, went on to establish the new government's authority by a string of victories, first in Ireland and Scotland (1649-1650), and finally by defeating the king's son at Worcester in 1651.

SIGNIFICANCE

Despite its political and military success, the new government rested on too narrow a basis for it to endure for long. The Commonwealth was a bold innovation that the English proved unwilling to support. Although it claimed to represent the people, the Rump was a mere oligarchy and was promptly rejected by the Levellers, who wanted a genuine government by the people. At the other extreme, England's powerful landed interests, who had been represented by the Presbyterian members now excluded from Parliament, soon grew weary of a military government, and Cromwell no doubt hoped to appeal to them when he turned out the Rump in April, 1653, and set himself up as lord protector at the end of the same year. His Protectorate, therefore, was a counterrevolutionary government: It stopped radical reform in its tracks. Not until 1688 and the Glorious Revolution did a king come to the throne of England prepared to acknowledge many of the democratic principles first asserted by the Commonwealth. In the wake of the accession of William III and Mary II, the Declaration of Rights and the Toleration Act instituted several of these principles.

—*David B. Haley*

FURTHER READING

Coward, Barry. *The Stuart Age: A History of England, 1603-1714*. New York: Longman, 1980. The best single-volume survey of the four generations of the Stuart dynasty.

Hill, Christopher. *God's Englishman: Oliver Cromwell and the English Revolution*. London: Penguin, 1970. Biography written by a prolific scholar of seventeenth century British history.

Hirst, Derek. *Authority and Conflict: England, 1603-1658*. Cambridge, Mass.: Harvard University Press, 1986. The best survey of the Civil Wars and Commonwealth.

Kennedy, D. E. *The English Revolution, 1642-1649*. New York: St. Martin's Press, 2000. The final chapter focuses on the revolutionary events that occurred from January through March, 1649.

Underdown, David. *Pride's Purge: Politics in the Puritan Revolution*. Oxford, England: Clarendon Press,

1971. Underdown presents a brilliant reconstruction of the events of 1648-1649.

Wedgwood, C. V. *The Trial of Charles I*. London: Collins, 1964. Vivid narrative account of January, 1649, with the king's trial and beheading.

Woolrych, Austin. *Britain in Revolution, 1625-1660*. New York: Oxford University Press, 2003. Part 4 focuses on the British Commonwealth from 1649 through 1653.

Worden, Blair. *The Rump Parliament, 1648-1653*. Cambridge, England: Cambridge University Press, 1974. The best study of Parliament during the Commonwealth period, providing an original explanation of why Cromwell suddenly ended it in April, 1653.

SEE ALSO: Nov. 3, 1640-May 15, 1641: Beginning of England's Long Parliament; 1642-1651: English Civil Wars; Aug. 17-Sept. 25, 1643: Solemn League and Covenant; July 2, 1644: Battle of Marston Moor; Dec. 16, 1653-Sept. 3, 1658: Cromwell Rules England as Lord Protector; May, 1659-May, 1660: Restoration of Charles II; 1688-1702: Reign of William and Mary; Nov., 1688-Feb., 1689: The Glorious Revolution; Feb. 13, 1689: Declaration of Rights; May 24, 1689: Toleration Act.

RELATED ARTICLES in *Great Lives from History: The Seventeenth Century, 1601-1700:* Charles I; Charles II (of England); Oliver Cromwell; Andrew Marvell; Mary II; Thomas Pride; William III.

January 29, 1649
CODIFICATION OF RUSSIAN SERFDOM

The codification of serfdom in Russia completed a process begun by the Muscovite state in the first half of the fifteenth century and marked the legalization of an institution that would remain a fundamental feature of Russia's society and economy until the second half of the nineteenth century.

LOCALE: Muscovy (now Russia)
CATEGORIES: Laws, acts, and legal history; government and politics; social issues and reform; economics; agriculture

KEY FIGURES

Ivan the Terrible (1530-1584), czar of Muscovy, r. 1547-1584
Fyodor I (1557-1598), czar of Muscovy, r. 1584-1598

Vasily Shuysky (1552-1612), czar of Muscovy, r. 1606-1610
Michael Romanov (1596-1645), czar of Muscovy, r. 1613-1645
Alexis (1629-1676), grand prince of Muscovy, r. 1645-1676

SUMMARY OF EVENT

On January 29, 1649, Muscovy's *zemskii sobor* (assembly of the land), a consultative assembly consisting of representatives from the Muscovite elites, ratified the Ulozhenie, Russia's fundamental law code that lasted until the 1830's. Drawn up by a five-man commission, headed by Prince Nikita Odoevsky, and consisting of twenty-five chapters, the Ulozhenie, chapter 11 specifically, effectively turned peasants residing on both seigniorial and nonseigniorial lands into serfs by abolishing a previously established statute of limitations on landlords. The statute had restricted the amount of time a landlord had to recover fugitive peasants, gave the state responsibility for recovering fugitive peasants, and threatened dire consequences for anyone found harboring fugitive peasants. The term "serf" means a peasant possessed by a noble, who is tied to land for sustenance and subject to the landlord's will.

The codification of serfdom found in the 1649 Ulozhenie represented the culmination of a relatively lengthy process by which the Muscovite state limited the movements of peasants in Russia. This process commenced during the Moscow Civil War of 1433 to 1450, when Michael Andreyevich, the appanage prince of Beloozero and Vereia and a loyal ally of Muscovite grand prince Vasily II, decreed that peasants residing on lands of Kirillov and Ferapontov monasteries could leave only during the week before and the week after Saint George's Day (November 26), which marked the traditional end of Russia's agricultural season.

RUSSIA'S CODE OF 1649

The Ulozhenie, Russia's law code, was created in 1649 and became the most comprehensive in Russian history, lasting nearly two centuries. The excerpt here is from "Legal Procedure Concerning the Peasants," a section consisting of thirty-four articles that outlines the rights and obligations of landowners and the legal and property status of peasants, or serfs.

1. All peasants who have fled from lands belonging to the Tsar and are now living on lands belonging to church officials, *votchinniki* [hereditary landowners], and *pomeshchiki* [landholders in service to the czar] are to be returned to the Tsar's lands according to the land cadastres [a real-estate tax register] of 1626 regardless of the *urochnye leta* [a time limit on searching for and returning fugitive peasants]. . . .

10. A person who harbors another's peasants must pay the tsar's taxes and ten rubles per year for each peasant to make up for the plaintiff's lost income from the work of the peasant and must surrender the fugitive peasants to the plaintiff. . . .

22. Peasant children who deny their parents must be tortured. . . .

27. A peasant who is the subject of a suit and states that he does not belong to the defendant will be given to the plaintiff with all his own moveable property. He who is guilty of taking false oath must be severely punished, beaten with a whip around the market place for three days, and jailed for a year. . . .

Source: "The Law Code of 1649," excerpted in *Readings in Russian Civilization*, edited by Thomas Riha (Chicago: University of Chicago Press, 1964), pp. 175-178.

Probably issued at the request of Grand Prince Vasily, who wanted to maintain the support of key Orthodox monasteries against rival claimants to the throne, Prince Michael's decrees established a precedent that soon became applicable first to all monastery peasants and ultimately to all peasants living in the territories of the Muscovite state. This precedent became law in Ivan the Great's Code (*sudebnik*) of 1497, which reiterated, this time explicitly, restrictions on peasant movement. The *sudebnik* of 1497 further established that peasants could depart only after having given prior notice, having cleared up any existing debts, and having paid an exit fee determined by the length of time the peasant in question had been resident on the land.

Although Czar Ivan the Terrible's Code of 1550 also reiterated the provisions of 1497 (and of the mid-fifteenth century decree of Michael Andreyevich), the Muscovite state placed no new limitations on peasant mobility during the first three-quarters of the sixteenth century. Moreover, there is evidence that many peasants ignored the existing provisions, moving at their own discretion without paying off existing debts or the compulsory exit fee, or both. Still, as long as peasant movement had no adverse impact on the interests of the Muscovite state, Muscovy's rulers showed no genuine concern to restrict where or when peasants could be mobile. However, once peasant movement, both legal and illegal, began to affect the state in an adverse fashion, which it did in the late 1570's and early 1580's, Moscow's czars were quick to respond.

In 1581, Ivan the Terrible, whose disastrous domestic and foreign policies produced major chaos and dislocation within the Muscovite state, declared the first so-called Forbidden Year, prohibiting peasant movement for one year, even during the Saint George's Day period. Many historians believe this was Ivan's response to the flight of a significant amount of peasants from the estates of the middle service-class cavalrymen. The cavalrymen, by the end of the sixteenth century, became the backbone of Muscovy's army. They could not fulfill their military obligations to the state without peasant labor on their land. Also losing peasant labor were the estates of the wealthy and powerful magnates (boyars) as well as the church. Although the Forbidden Year of 1581 was intended to be a temporary expedient, the Muscovite state renewed it annually until 1592, when the government of Czar Fyodor I issued an even stricter decree that prohibited all peasant movement until further notice.

Five years later, in 1597, Fyodor's government established a statute of limitations that gave landlords the right to seek out and reclaim peasants who had run away within five years of the decree's issuance. The legislation establishing the statute of limitations declared that fugitive peasants, their families, and their personal (movable) property be returned to their former residences. Yet, the law simultaneously stated, explicitly, that peasants who had fled more than five years before the decree was issued could not be made to return to their former residences if no formal complaint had been made to the appropriate authorities. Also, the seigniors who had received these peasants could not be prosecuted.

Russia's catastrophic Time of Troubles (1584-1613), which featured ongoing dynastic crises, social unrest, rebellion, and foreign invasion, promoted a renewed increase in significant peasant flight from landed estates in general and the estates of the middle service-class cavalry in particular. Once again, Muscovy's rulers responded to the plight of its military servitors (servants). In 1607, Czar Vasily Shuysky issued a decree extending the statute of limitations to fifteen years and imposing fines on any landlord, including the church, who gave refuge to fugitive peasants. Henceforth, any landlord found guilty of harboring a fugitive peasant had to pay the czar ten rubles for each fugitive discovered on his land. In addition, the landlord had to pay the peasant's rightful seignior three rubles for each year the fugitive in question had been given refuge. The evidence suggests that Shuysky's decree did little to halt the flight of peasants, who simply ignored all restrictions on their freedom of movement and relocated, taking maximum advantage of the chaos that reigned in Muscovy. Moreover, by 1613—the end of the Time of Troubles and the election of Michael Romanov as Russia's new czar—the statute of limitations had reverted to the five-year period first established in the legislation of 1597.

The Muscovite state's provisions on peasant movement remained unchanged until the late 1630's, when a new increase in peasant flight and the concomitant concern for the middle service-class cavalry led to renewed governmental measures to restrict peasant mobility. Serving as a catalyst was the cost of Muscovy's Smolensk War (1632-1634) against Poland, which required a tax increase that fell disproportionately on the peasants. Faced with a heavier tax burden, many peasants fled, a development adversely affecting the cavalry, whose representatives, yet again, petitioned the government for assistance. In response, Czar Michael raised the statute of limitations to nine years in 1637 and to fifteen years in 1642. Ultimately, in 1645, the czar even promised to repeal the statute completely as soon as the new census, scheduled for 1646-1647, was completed. Though Michael died shortly thereafter and thus could not fulfill his promise, his successor, Czar Alexis, appointed in 1648 the commission that produced the codification of serfdom found in the 1649 Ulozhenie.

SIGNIFICANCE

The Ulozhenie of 1649 effectively legalized serfdom. It prohibited peasants and their descendants from legally leaving the lands of the landlord with whom they were registered. A famous, brutal uprising of peasants, led by Don Cossack leader Stenka Razin, occurred between 1667 and 1671 and has become legendary. Serfdom as it was codified by Czar Alexis would remain a fundamental feature of Russia's society and economy until it was abolished by Czar Alexander II (r. 1855-1881) on February 19, 1861.

—Bruce J. DeHart

FURTHER READING

Blum, Jerome. *Lord and Peasant in Russia: From the Ninth to the Nineteenth Century*. Princeton, N.J.: Princeton University Press, 1961. A classic analysis of the complex relationship between peasant, noble, and state in Russia from the origins of the Russian state to the emancipation of the serfs. Especially good on serfdom's origins and development.

Hellie, Richard. *Enserfment and Military Change in Muscovy*. Chicago: University of Chicago Press, 1971. The definitive history of the enserfment of the peasant in Muscovy, emphasizing the role of the state and its concern for the well-being of the middle service-class cavalry.

_____, ed. and trans. *The Muscovite Law Code (Ulozhenie) of 1649*. Irvine, Calif.: Charles Schlacks, 1988. A wonderful English translation of the Code of 1649, which codified Russian serfdom.

1640's

SEE ALSO: 17th cent.: Rise of Proto-Industrial Economies; Feb. 7, 1613: Election of Michael Romanov as Czar; 1632-1667: Polish-Russian Wars for the Ukraine; 1652-1667: Patriarch Nikon's Reforms; Apr., 1667-June, 1671: Razin Leads Peasant Uprising

in Russia; 1672-c. 1691: Self-Immolation of the Old Believers.

RELATED ARTICLES in *Great Lives from History: The Seventeenth Century, 1601-1700:* Alexis; Nikon; Stenka Razin; Michael Romanov; Vasily Shuysky.

April 21, 1649
MARYLAND ACT OF TOLERATION

The Act of Toleration formally codified the relative religious freedom that Maryland had enjoyed since its founding. While requiring all members of the colony to espouse Trinitarian Christianity, the act recognized the equal validity of Protestantism and Catholicism and forbade anyone from mistreating a colonist based on their affiliation with either of those forms of Christianity.

LOCALE: Saint Marys (now Saint Marys City), Maryland

CATEGORIES: Laws, acts, and legal history; religion and theology; social issues and reform; colonization

KEY FIGURES

George Calvert (1579/1580-1632), first Lord Baltimore, who secured the Maryland charter from Charles I

Cecilius Calvert (1605-1675), second Lord Baltimore, son of George Calvert, and the first proprietor of Maryland

Leonard Calvert (1606-1647), son of George Calvert and first governor of Maryland

SUMMARY OF EVENT

In his instructions to his brother Leonard Calvert and to the commissioners leading the first settlers to Maryland in 1633, the colony's first proprietor, Cecilius Calvert, second Lord Baltimore, cautioned that "they be very carefull to preserve unity and peace amongst all the passengers on Shipp-board, and that they suffer no scandall nor offence to be given to any of the Protestants. . . ." George Calvert, the first Lord Baltimore and father of Cecilius and Leonard, had died the previous year, before his goal of founding a colony free from religious animosity could be realized. While the sincerity of Lord Baltimore's position is unquestionable, it was nonetheless also quite necessary to the recruitment of Protestant settlers for the venture. Maryland was envisioned as a colony of religious freedom for all, but especially for Catho-

lics. It would have been impossible, however, to find enough British Catholics willing to emigrate to support an entire colony, so advantages had to be offered men of humbler rank, usually loyal practicing members of the Church of England, to persuade them to participate in an undertaking led by Catholic gentlemen.

Some Catholics took advantage of the freedom of religion to proselytize among colonists, as well as among the native populations of the colony. To seek to convert colonists was illegal, however, and it was punished, because religious toleration was practiced from the first. Maryland was indeed unique. Nowhere else had anyone experimented with the concept that Protestants and Catholics could live together amicably and enjoy political and religious equality. Anyone who dared attempt to force his beliefs upon another could expect to meet the fate of one William Lewis, a Catholic who was fined heavily in 1638 for proselytizing among the Protestants.

Cecilius Calvert, loyal to his father's purpose, encouraged missionary work by all Christians among the Maryland Indians, and Catholics and Protestants used the same chapel for their services of worship. Cecilius Calvert had determined that there should be no established church in Maryland; likewise, he believed that the government should not interfere in spiritual matters. Because of this policy, Maryland was able to attract non-Catholics from England and even Puritans and Anglicans from New England.

In ensuring the first of these tenets, the first proprietor became involved in a long dispute with the Jesuit missionaries in the colony. Claiming that they were exempt from civil authority, the Jesuits wanted to obtain land directly from the Indians rather than through the proprietary, as the charter specified. They also demanded special privileges, such as exemption from paying quitrents and preferred treatment for their retainers and servants. Lord Baltimore finally prevailed when the Jesuits' father provincial ordered them to renounce their claims.

The decade between 1640 and 1650 was an inauspicious time to try to stabilize a colony founded on the principle of religious toleration. Leonard Calvert barely managed to recover the province after he was forced to flee to Virginia in 1644 by William Claiborne, a troublemaker of long standing. Claiborne captured Kent Island, and Richard Ingle took the village of Saint Marys and plundered the colony. The combination of American discord and England's Civil War was almost fatal for Lord Baltimore's proprietorship. Only through his shrewdness was he able to ward off revocation of his charter by the triumphant Puritans, and as it was, Catholics and loyalists were threatened with imprisonment and confiscation of their property.

Amid this turmoil, Lord Baltimore drafted the famous document "An Act Concerning Religion," which has come to be known as the Toleration Act. The General Assembly passed the measure on April 21, 1649. Since toleration had been practiced from the colony's founding, the act represented no change in Lord Baltimore's policy. It apparently was passed in order to refute the charge by those who had tried to annul the charter that the colony was a hotbed of popery.

The act had two parts, each with its own preamble, but the second part, positive in its sentiment, was apparently framed by Cecilius Calvert. This section proclaimed that no person "professing to believe in Jesus Christ shall from henceforth be any waies troubled, molested or discountenanced, for or in respect of his or her Religion, nor in the free Exercise thereof within this Province." It further provided for the punishment of anyone failing to respect these rights. The first clause of the act was added later by the General Assembly, then controlled by a Protestant-Puritan majority, to accord with an act passed by Britain's Long Parliament in 1648 to punish heresies and blasphemies. As punishment for blasphemy, or for denying the Holy Trinity or that Jesus Christ was the Son of God, it prescribed the penalty of death and confiscation of property. Paradoxically, the next section again emphasized toleration, prohibiting disparagement "in a reproachful manner" of any religious group and stipulating penalties for offenders. Finally, the act forbade swearing, drunkenness, recreation, and labor on the Sabbath.

SIGNIFICANCE

The Toleration Act did not guarantee complete religious liberty, freedom of thought, or separation of church and state. The first part, added by the General Assembly, actually represented a regression, since it formally limited toleration to Trinitarian Christians. What the act did accomplish was the official, formal expression of the toleration of Catholics and Protestants for each other's beliefs that had been practiced since 1634. It was the first such document in the New World, where several other groups of European settlers had come seeking religious freedom but always in relatively homogeneous religious communities.

Following an investigation into the colony by Parliamentary commissioners, a Puritan-dominated assembly was called on October 30, 1654. The assembly repudiated Lord Baltimore's authority, repealed the Toleration Act, and replaced it with an act denying Catholics protection. When the Calverts regained control in 1657, however, Lord Baltimore promised to stand firm for "An Act Concerning Religion."

—*Warren M. Billings and Daniel A. Brown*

FURTHER READING

Andrews, Charles M. *The Settlements*. Vol. 2 in *The Colonial Period of American History*. New Haven, Conn.: Yale University Press, 1964. Writing from the English point of view, the author places the Calverts into their British context, demonstrating the practical nature of the proprietors in promoting religious toleration.

Andrews, Matthew P. *The Founding of Maryland*. Baltimore: Williams and Wilkins, 1933. The Catholic founders of the colony, from the start, promoted religious toleration and punished only those who bothered their colonial neighbors by proselytizing.

Craven, Wesley F. *The Southern Colonies in the Seventeenth Century, 1607-1689*. Baton Rouge: Louisiana State University Press, 1949. Chapters 6 and 7 provide an introduction to Maryland's beginnings, especially in religious matters.

Hall, Clayton C., ed. *Narratives of Early Maryland, 1633-1684*. New York: Barnes and Noble Books, 1946. This collection of original documents includes Lord Baltimore's instructions to the colonists, the text of the Act of Toleration, and various firsthand accounts of the early years of the Maryland colony.

Hanley, Thomas. *Their Rights and Liberties: The Beginnings of Religious and Political Freedom in Maryland*. Westminster, Md.: Newman Press, 1959. Argues that the principles of religious freedom were in evidence long before the Act of Toleration, and those principles were much more extensive than the Puritan Assembly eventually permitted.

Hennessey, James. "Catholics in an American Environment: The Early Years." *Theological Studies* 50

1640's

(1989): 657-675. Lord Baltimore considered conscience, not political expedience or civil authority, as paramount when it came to colonists. However, he did not extend his concept of conscience to the natives of the colony, whom he considered idolaters.

Krugler, John D. *English and Catholic: The Lord Baltimores in the Seventeenth Century.* Baltimore: Johns Hopkins University Press, 2004. Describes how the Calverts' resolved the conflict between their loyalty to England and their Catholic faith, including their experiments with religious freedom in Maryland. Focuses on George Calvert's career, nationalism, desire for fame and fortune, and deepening sense of Catholicism.

Lasson, Kenneth. "Free Exercise in the Free State: Maryland's Role in Religious Liberty and the First Amendment." *Journal of Church and State* 31 (1989): 419-449. The author argues that Maryland colonial experience helped shape the eventual policy of the new nation.

Steiner, Bernard C. *Beginnings of Maryland.* Baltimore: Johns Hopkins University Press, 1903. Relations between Protestants and Catholics are covered well in this general history.

Terrar, Edward. "Was There a Separation Between Church and State in Mid-Seventeenth Century England and Colonial Maryland?" *Journal of Church and State* 35 (1993): 61-82. Terrar maintains there was not only religious toleration in the colony, but there was also an inchoate separation of church and state, largely through the leadership of the Calverts.

SEE ALSO: Dec. 26, 1620: Pilgrims Arrive in North America; May, 1630-1643: Great Puritan Migration; Fall, 1632-Jan. 5, 1665: Settlement of Connecticut; June, 1636: Rhode Island Is Founded; 1642-1651: English Civil Wars; 1662: Half-Way Covenant; May 19, 1662: England's Act of Uniformity; Mar. 4, 1681: "Holy Experiment" Establishes Pennsylvania; Apr. 4, 1687, and Apr. 27, 1688: Declaration of Liberty of Conscience; May 24, 1689: Toleration Act.

RELATED ARTICLES in *Great Lives from History: The Seventeenth Century, 1601-1700:* George Calvert; Charles I; Anne Hutchinson; Roger Williams.

Mid-17th century
DUTCH SCHOOL OF PAINTING FLOURISHES

In the northern provinces of the Netherlands, Dutch Baroque artists, appealing to a prosperous merchant class, achieved a heightened sense of realism in portraiture and in landscape and genre painting. The representation of native Dutch themes, domestic interiors, and objects became distinctive features of the Dutch school of art.

LOCALE: United Provinces (now the Netherlands)
CATEGORIES: Art; cultural and intellectual history

KEY FIGURES

Frans Hals (c. 1583-1666), Flemish-Dutch portraitist and genre painter
Rembrandt (1606-1669), Dutch painter, draftsman, and etcher
Jan Vermeer (1632-1675), Dutch master of genre painting
Meindert Hobbema (1638-1709), Dutch master of wooded landscapes
Jan Josephszoon van Goyen (1596-1656), Dutch landscape painter and draftsman
Jacob van Ruisdael (1628/1629-1682), Dutch landscape artist, draftsman, and etcher
Jan Steen (c. 1626-1679), Dutch genre painter
Pieter de Hooch (1629-c. 1684), Dutch genre painter

SUMMARY OF EVENT

The Dutch Wars of Independence from Spain, also known as the Eighty Years' War (1568-1648), witnessed a scission of the former Spanish Netherlands into two separate regions. To the south and east, the Flemish and Walloon provinces of what is now Belgium remained under Spanish rule, and an independent United Provinces (now called Holland, or the Netherlands), emerged in the north, proclaiming Calvinism its official religion.

In the early seventeenth century, the Dutch (northern) Netherlands, free from Spanish dominion but plagued by numerous wars, assumed a leading role among European nations in art, scholarship, science, and trade. The thriving Dutch East India Company, founded in 1602, followed by the creation of the Amsterdam exchange bank in 1609 and the Dutch West India Company in 1621, brought tremendous wealth into the country. The expansion of local industry, notably in shipyards, sugar refineries, fishing, and textiles, contributed to the growth of a prosperous merchant class.

Along with the nation's increased wealth and independence came an atmosphere of tolerance and innovation. Lacking support from the Roman Catholic Church and the Habsburg nobility, Dutch artists were compelled to seek new clients and adapt their craft if they were to survive in the evolving marketplace. The nascent Calvinist church, fraught with controversy and iconoclastic zeal, did not offer a suitable alternative. Appealing instead to the republican tastes of wealthy merchants, patricians, aristocrats, guilds, and local government, innovative artists abandoned the flamboyant Baroque style favored by Church and aristocracy in other parts of Europe and offered instead a greater sense of realism in portraiture and in landscape and genre painting.

In the absence of munificent patrons, artists produced noncommissioned art for sale on an open market. This represented a noteworthy evolution in the way art was produced. Paintings tended to be smaller in size, not only to limit the artist's production expenditures but also to accommodate the average Dutch burgher's budget and the space available for artistic display in homes. According to Philips Angel's *Lof der schilder-konst* (in praise of painting), a speech before the Leiden painters' guild in 1641 and published the following year, a painter's primary task was to delight the beholder's eye. Although academic theory from Carel van Mander's *Het schilderboeck* (1604; *The Lives of the Illustrious Netherlandish and German Painters*, 6 vols., 1994-1999) to Samuel van Hoogstraten's *Inleyding tot de hooge schoole der schilderkonst* (1678; introduction to the academy of painting) continued to play an important role in artists' choice of subjects, composition, and techniques, Angel's golden rule proved especially well suited to the practical constraints of a buyer's market. Hence, the producers of noncommissioned art, particularly genre and landscape paintings, strived to delight the eye while appealing to

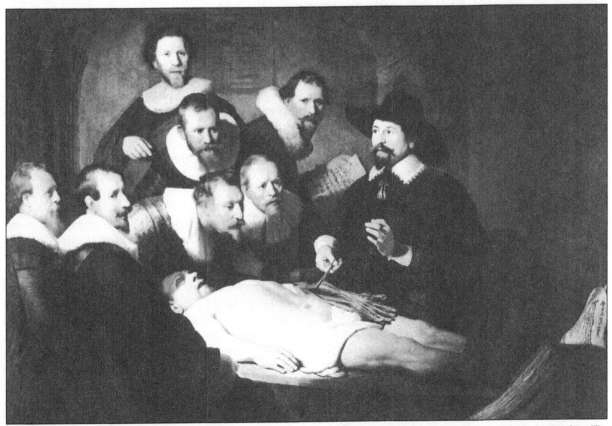

The Anatomy of Dr. Tulp *(1632) established Rembrandt as a master painter in the competitive world of portraiture in Amsterdam. The work was his first major group portrait, depicting an anatomist and his students.* (Harry N. Abrams)

1650's

469

Jan Vermeer's well-known, oft-reproduced painting, The Artist and His Studio *(1665-1670), is a premier example of Dutch genre painting, with its attention to detail, intense natural light, and its reverence for the common.* (Harry N. Abrams)

ate texture and space and to focus attention. In addition to group portraits such as *The Anatomy Lesson of Dr. Tulp* (1632) and *The Night Watch* (1642), Rembrandt also produced individual portraits, self-portraits, etchings, drawings, dramatic historical pieces based on biblical and classical themes, and landscapes.

Specialization in one style of painting was also common among Dutch artists. A host of painters sometimes referred to as the Little Masters specialized in specific types of small-format still life, landscape, or genre painting. Jan Josephszoon van Goyen, Jacob van Ruisdael, and Hobbema garnered international acclaim in landscape artistry, where dunes, windmills, livestock, verdant meadows, river scenes with sails and masts, isolated country roads, and panoramic horizons abound. Adriaen van Ostade (1610-1685), dean of the Haarlem painters' guild of Saint Luke in 1662, painted scenes of peasant life filled with local color. An early master of still life, Ambrosius Bosschaert, the Elder (1573-1621), introduced a vogue of flower painting that remained a favorite Dutch theme until the time of Vincent van Gogh (1853-1890) and beyond. The Dutch expression *stilleven*, from which the English term "still life" derives, came into use as a genre definition around 1653. Successive generations of artists, from Pieter Claesz van Haarlem (1597/1598-1661) to Willem Kalff (1619-1693) and Jan Weenix (1640?-1719), attained distinction as still life painters.

"Genre painting," a term introduced by eighteenth and nineteenth century art historians, refers to scenes of everyday life, depictions of anonymous people engaged in ordinary activities in their natural surroundings. Closely related to portraiture, Dutch genre painting reflects the unique qualities of middle-class and peasant culture in the United Netherlands in the manner of realism, or a credible illusion thereof. Jan Steen and Pieter de Hooch stand out as two of the period's most accomplished painters of Dutch life. Domestic interiors and tavern scenes, featuring regional dress, architectural ele-

the lifestyle, preoccupations, and moral values of the Dutch middle class.

The Golden Age of Dutch painting spans roughly three generations of artists, including Frans Hals, Rembrandt, Jan Vermeer, and Meindert Hobbema. Among early seventeenth century Dutch painters, Hals stands out both in portraiture and genre painting for his ability to seize the vitality and spontaneity of his subjects. His *Banquet of the Officers of the St. George Civic Guard Company* (1616) and *Regents of the St. Elizabeth Hospital at Haarlem* (c. 1641) are examples of the commemorative group portrait common in Dutch painting of the period. Typically, individuals represented in group portraits would each pay a portion of the artist's fee. Rembrandt, some twenty years younger than Hals, also was a master of portraiture and excelled in the use of light and shadow to crements, musical instruments, families at mealtime, mothers and daughters, and music and merriment, were common motifs in their paintings.

Vermeer, a master in the genre, included maps, globes, and Asian tapestries as part of his interior decor, reminding viewers of the preeminent status of the Netherlands as a seafaring and trading nation. Vermeer's *The Astronomer* (1668) and *The Allegory of Painting* (1666-1667) are two well-known examples of his work in genre painting. Gerrit Dou (1613-1675), a leading member of the Leiden group of fine painters (*fijnschilders*), produced genre paintings of remarkable detail. By the last quarter of the seventeenth century, genre painting became the most expensive category of painting on the Dutch market.

SIGNIFICANCE

As art historians readily confirm, the catalog of Dutch artists active during the seventeenth century is quite extensive. Only about one percent of the 17 million paintings thought to have been produced in the northern provinces of the Netherlands between 1600 and 1700 are believed to still exist, yet they are among the most valued pieces in museums throughout the Western world, attracting throngs of admirers each year.

The Little Masters were, above all, intent on creating objects of beauty pleasing to the eye. Also, in the absence of hidden narratives, their paintings typically reveal more than the artists consciously intended. As documents of social history, they are reminders of a period when the middle-class became major consumers of art, a defining moment in European history, when market trends and popular demand dictated an artist's choice of genre, subject, style, and methods of production.

One of the most endearing features of Dutch landscape and genre paintings lies in their representations of regional themes and motifs that seem to capture the very essence of seventeenth century Dutch society. Partly an illusion, perhaps, but one of enduring artistic charm.

—*Jan Pendergrass*

FURTHER READING

Brown, Christopher. *Dutch Landscape, the Early Years: Haarlem and Amsterdam, 1590-1650*. London: Westerman Press, 1986. Multiple prefaces to this catalog of 118 prints provide detailed discussion of Dutch landscape painting.

Ebert-Schifferer, Sybille. *Still Life: A History*. Translated by Russell Stockman. New York: Abrams, 1999. A comprehensive study of still life painting and its history, from antiquity to seventeenth century Dutch painting and beyond.

Franits, Wayne. *Looking at Seventeenth-Century Dutch Art: Realism Reconsidered*. New York: Cambridge University Press, 1997. A collection of articles by fourteen specialists covering major research trends.

Grijzehout, Frans, and Henk van Veen. *The Golden Age of Dutch Painting in Historical Perspective*. Translated by Andrew McCormick. New York: Cambridge University Press, 1999. Thirteen chapters by art historians investigate the reception of Dutch Baroque art from its origins to modern trends in research.

Muizelaar, Klaske, and Derek Phillips. *Picturing Men and Women in the Dutch Golden Age: Paintings and People in Historical Perspective*. New Haven, Conn.: Yale University Press, 2003. Examines some of the ideological underpinnings of Dutch Golden Age painting.

North, Michael. *Art and Commerce in the Dutch Golden Age*. Translated by Catherine Hill. New Haven, Conn.: Yale University Press, 1997. Statistics on the historical, sociological, and economic context of Golden Age artists and art patrons.

Riegl, Alois. *The Group Portraiture of Holland*. Translations by Evelyn M. Kain and David Britt. Los Angeles: Getty Research Institute for the History of Art and the Humanities, 1999. A classic collection of writings by the German art historian Alois Riegl (1858-1909), covering three stages of Dutch portraiture, including two in the seventeenth century. Includes an introduction by Wolfgang Kemp.

Slive, Seymour. *Dutch Painting, 1600-1800*. New Haven, Conn.: Yale University Press, 1995. A survey of Dutch painting, with sections devoted to Hals, Rembrandt, Vermeer, and de Hooch, and to portraiture and still life, landscape, marine, and architectural painting.

SEE ALSO: c. 1601-1620: Emergence of Baroque Art; c. 1601-1682: Spanish Golden Age.
RELATED ARTICLES in *Great Lives from History: The Seventeenth Century, 1601-1700:* Giovanna Garzoni; Frans Hals; Rembrandt; Jan Vermeer.

1650's

Mid-17th century
EMERGENCE OF THE GUINEA COAST STATES

The emergence and consolidation of states and kingdoms along the Gulf of Guinea in West Africa owed as much to the external stimulus provided by trade with Europeans as to the internal dynamics of the region's African states and societies.

LOCALE: Coastal Ghana, Benin, and Nigeria (West Africa)

CATEGORIES: Government and politics; trade and commerce

KEY FIGURES

Ansa Sasraku (d. 1689), chief of the Abrade of Nyanaoase, r. 1660-1689

Boadu Akafo Brempon (fl. c. 1657-1668), ruler of Denkyira, r. c. 1657-1668

Ajagbo (d. late 1690's), king of Oyo, r. c. 1650-late 1690's

SUMMARY OF EVENT

The West African coastline between the Gold Coast and the Bight of Benin was home to speakers of languages in the Kwa subgroup of the Niger-Congo group of languages, including Fante, Ewe, Yoruba, Edo, and Ijo (Izon). By the beginning of the seventeenth century, a number of states of varying sizes had emerged in this coastal zone on the strength of local or internal dynamics and subsequently developed in response to European trade. A major event during this period was the consolidation of these states into substantial polities.

The first years of the seventeenth century saw as many as thirty states along the Gold Coast and its hinterland. These states had been established at least one hundred years earlier and had traded with the Mande and Hausa to the north and with the Europeans at the coast. The growth of trade in both directions imposed demands of effective political authority on these states, and the ongoing internal processes of change were affected by external developments, such as the intrigues of the European traders, who had established trading posts on the coast. Consequently, states located along the coast were drawn into conflicts among the rival European nations. Hence, it was along the Gold Coast that two powerful states, Denkyira and Akwamu, emerged and expanded at the expense of their African neighbors.

Akwamu had been founded about 1500 by migrants from the northern Akan region, who had settled in the forest just off the coast where the Portuguese had estab-

lished a settlement at Elmina. The migrants, known as the Abrade, became clients of the indigenous Accra, whose ruler permitted them to settle on the northern frontier at Nyanaoase. The Abrade, with their ruler Ansa Sasraku, then participated actively in the gold trade with the hinterland, resulting in the emergence of a major market at Abonse near Nyanaoase. By the mid-seventeenth century, the Abrade had created the Akwamu kingdom of Nyanaoase, which was to become more influential than its Accra patron. From its nucleus at Nyanaoase, the rising Akwamu kingdom soon incorporated the Guan, Ewe, Ga, and Adangme as well as the southern Akan Akyem and Kwahu. Akwamu had hitherto expanded largely by colonization.

Akwamu's preeminence along the Gold Coast was accomplished by the capture in 1677 of the capital, Greater Accra, and the takeover of their patron state of Accra. The displaced rulers of Accra eventually resettled in Little Popo, which Akwamu also attacked in 1702. Thus, beginning in 1677, Akwamu expanded by a series of conquests as far east as Little Popo and Whydah in the Aja country. In the 1680's, Akwamu launched major campaigns against the Adangme and Agona. By 1688, European accounts noted that the Akwamu king was being addressed as king of Accra and that he was rich in gold and slaves. Like Akwamu, Denkyira expanded its territory from the mid-seventeenth century with the aid of firearms procured from the Dutch stationed at the coast. Akwamu's greatest expansion occurred during the reign of Boadu Akafo Brempon. By the end of the century, Akwamu had established its control over Wassaw and Aowin to the west and Twifo and Assin to the south. This feat ensured its control over the centers of gold production and trade.

To the east of the Gold Coast in what is now the republics of Togo and Benin, the coastal states did not achieve as much economic and political success. Inhabited by Aja-speaking peoples, including the Ewe and Fon, the zone exhibited a contrast between the western section, inhabited by the Ewe, which did not produce any significant kingdom, and the eastern section, occupied by the Fon, in which were established three major states—Allada (Ardra), Ouidah (Hueda or Whydah), and Abomey. Abomey later developed into the powerful empire of Dahomey in the eighteenth century. The eastern Aja, unlike the Ewe, were influenced by their Yoruba neighbors, whose leading state of Oyo, under ruler Ajagbo, attacked Allada and Dahomey between 1680 and 1682. With the subjugation of Allada in 1698, Oyo extended its reach to the Aja coast, especially during the eighteenth century. In addition, the involvement of the eastern Aja in the transatlantic slave trade was accompanied by the establishment of European trading posts along their coast, unlike that of the Ewe.

In the first decade of the seventeenth century, the Dutch established a trading post at Assim, capital of Allada. French Capuchin missionaries settled there, too, in 1640, and French traders visited the state and inaugurated an exchange of delegations between the Allada court and France. When the French could not secure a treaty from Allada, they turned to Whydah, where they were able to establish a trading post, sparking a trade rivalry between Allada and Whydah. Between 1670 and 1700, the French were joined by other European nations that established trading posts, marking a significant time for the economic and political systems of the Aja coastal states. The rivalry among the states was exploited by European traders, who instigated wars and political instability to weaken the rivals. Indeed, European traders interfered in the succession to the throne, installing puppets who were willing to do their bidding.

In 1698, the leading Aja state of Allada had been conquered by Oyo, facilitating the rise of its rival Whydah, which became the leading slave port in West Africa by 1701.

To the east of the Aja country, Lagos and Warri were the only significant coastal settlements by the beginning of the seventeenth century. They already were involved in the transatlantic slave trade and both were subject to the Benin kingdom in the hinterland of what is now south-central Nigeria. Lagos and Badagry were later to develop into major outlets for the slave trade in the next century. Hence, their relative unimportance during the seventeenth century spared them the kind of European interference experienced by the Aja states. Neither kingdom embarked on territorial expansion, possibly because of their lack of military capacity and subjection to the Benin kingdom.

SIGNIFICANCE

Intense rivalry, conflict, political consolidation, and external interference characterized relations among the states of this region in the seventeenth century. However, Denkyira and Akwamu consolidated their conquests with differing outcomes. Denkyira utilized political and administrative reforms to incorporate its conquests but failed because of its oppressive rule, precipitating the formation of a hostile coalition that led to its defeat and collapse by the 1730's.

The Guinea coastal states experienced major political and economic changes during the seventeenth century, largely because of their participation in the growing transatlantic slave trade, their use of firearms, internal reforms, their invasion by inland states such as Oyo, and the intervention of European traders in local politics. Akwamu, Denkyira, and Whydah exploited these opportunities to their political and economic advantage. Allada declined largely because it was reduced to vassalage by Oyo, whose intervention in Aja politics and trade had been facilitated by internal crisis in that region.

The developments of the seventeenth century shed light on the process of state formation, intergroup

---

GOLD TRADE ALONG THE GUINEA COAST

William Bosman, an official with the Dutch West India Company, lived on the Guinea Coast for fourteen years and documented gold mining by the indigenous peoples of the region, for whom the gold trade was lucrative.

The gold thus digged or found, is of two sorts; one is called Dust-Gold or Gold-Dust, which is almost as fine as Flower, and is the best, bearing also the greatest Price in *Europe*: The other sort is in pieces of different sizes; some being hardly the weight of a Farthing [early English monetary unit], others weighing as heavy as twenty or thirty Guineas [an English gold coin]; though of the last sort now many occur. The *Negroes* indeed tell us, that in the Country Pieces as heavy as one or two hundred Guineas, are found. These Lumps or Pieces are called Mountain-Gold; which being melted, touch better that Dust-Gold; but the multitude of small Stones which always adhere to 'em, occasion a great loss in the melting; for which reason Gold-Dust is most esteemed. Thus much of the good and pure Gold; and now to touch upon the false. The first sort is that mixed with Silver or Copper, and cast into *Fetiches* [ingots], . . . These *Fetiches* are cut into small bits by the *Negroes*. . . . The *Negroe* Women know the exact value of these bits so well at sight, that they never are mistaken; and accordingly they tell them to each other without weighing, as we do coined Money.

Source: Bosman, *New and Accurate Description of the Coast of Guinea* (1705), excerpted in *The Horizon History of Africa*, edited by Alvin M. Josephy, Jr. (New York: American Heritage, 1971), pp. 206-207.

1650's

relations, and the conduct of international trade along the Guinea coast of West Africa. The developments also help to explain the rise of Asante in the Gold Coast hinterland and of Dahomey in the Aja hinterland, and they contextualize the events that culminated in the European conquest and colonization of West Africa during the nineteenth and twentieth centuries.

—*Ayodeji Olukoju*

FURTHER READING

Ajayi, J. F. A., and Michael Crowder, eds. *History of West Africa*. 3d ed. Vol. 1. London: Longman, 1985. An authoritative text containing several relevant chapters.

Akinjogbin, I. A. *Dahomey and Its Neighbours, 1708-1818*. Cambridge, England: Cambridge University Press, 1967. Contains background information on seventeenth century developments in the Aja country.

Daaku, K. Y. *Trade and Politics on the Gold Coast, 1600-1720: A Study of the African Reaction to European Trade*. Oxford, England: Clarendon Press, 1970. A major text on commercial and political developments along the Gold Coast.

Kea, Ray. "Firearms and Warfare on the Gold and Slave Coasts from the Sixteenth to the Nineteenth Centuries." *Journal of African History* 12 (1971): 185-213. Kea considers a critical element in state formation and intergroup relations in the region.

Law, Robin. "Trade and Politics Behind the Slave Coast: The Lagoon Traffic and the Rise of Lagos, 1500-1800." *Journal of African History* 24 (1983): 321-348. Law focuses on trade, intergroup relations, and state formation in the Lagos area.

Ogot, B. A., ed. *Africa from the Sixteenth to the Eighteenth Century*. Vol. 5 in *UNESCO General History of Africa*. Berkeley: University of California Press, 1992. An authoritative collection of essays by leading experts on the Africa of the sixteenth to eighteenth centuries.

SEE ALSO: 17th cent.: Europe Endorses Slavery; 17th cent.: Songhai Empire Dissolves; Beginning c. 1601: Expansion of the Oyo Kingdom; 1612: Rise of the Arma in Timbuktu; 1617-1693: European Powers Vie for Control of Gorée; 1619-c. 1700: The Middle Passage to American Slavery; Oct., 1625-1637: Dutch and Portuguese Struggle for the Guinea Coast; 1630-1660's: Dutch Wars in Brazil; Aug. 26, 1641-Sept., 1648: Conquest of Luanda; 1644-1671: Ndongo Wars; Apr., 1652: Dutch Begin to Colonize Southern Africa; 1660-1677: A Jihad Is Called in Senegambia; 1670-1699: Rise of the Asante Empire; Late 17th cent.: Decline of Benin.

RELATED ARTICLE in *Great Lives from History: The Seventeenth Century, 1601-1700:* Njinga.

1650-1698
WARS FOR THE RED SEA TRADE

With the decline of Portuguese influence along the East African coast, the sultanate of Oman asserted political and economic dominance over the region through a fierce struggle with Portugal. The growth of Omani maritime power together with new European imports of coffee led to a rapid development in Red Sea trade.

LOCALE: East coast of Africa, Oman, and Yemen
CATEGORIES: Wars, uprisings, and civil unrest; expansion and land acquisition; trade and commerce

KEY FIGURES

Sulṭān bin Saif (d. 1679), imam of Oman, r. 1648-1679
Balʿarab bin Sulṭān (d. 1692), imam of Oman,
  r. 1679-1692
Saif bin Sulṭān (d. 1711), imam of Oman, r. 1692-1711

SUMMARY OF EVENT

The Portuguese captured the Indian Ocean spice trade in the sixteenth century by seizing control of the high seas as well as a number of strategic ports, including Mozambique, Mombasa, and Kilwa on the East African coast; Socotra, near the entrance to the Red Sea; Hormuz in the Persian Gulf; and Cochin on the west coast of India. By the seventeenth century, however, the Portuguese had lost control of the Indian Ocean to their Dutch and English rivals.

At the end of the sixteenth century, England became one of the strongest naval powers in Europe. Coveting the wealth and resources of the East, which were already being exploited by other European powers, England entered into direct competition with the Portuguese. In 1600, the English East India Company was established by royal decree. The East India Company began its activities in the Arabian Gulf region by selling English wool to Iran in exchange for silk. In January, 1622, Anglo-Persian forces attacked Hormuz, inflicted considerable damage on the Portuguese, and succeeded in expelling them from their outpost. Three years later, in 1625, a joint Anglo-Dutch fleet defeated the Portuguese fleet near Hormuz. Alongside the English, the Dutch played a key role in the seventeenth century Portuguese decline. This process began with the establishment of the Dutch East India Company in 1602.

As the Portuguese lost influence in the Middle East, they lost control first of the Arabian Gulf waters and then of the Indian Ocean. Oman, located on the western end of the Arabian Peninsula, was able to throw off the colonial yoke as a result of this waning of Portugal's sea power. The Omani Arabs expelled the Portuguese from their country and established the Al-Ya'ruba Dynasty there in 1624.

The dynasty increased its power in the western basin of the Indian Ocean until it was ready to compete directly with Portugal for control of the Red Sea trade routes and strategic posts along the way. In 1650, Oman seized Muscat from Portuguese hands. The Omanis continued to struggle against the Portuguese and struck their centers in India and in Eastern Africa. They managed to sever all communication between the last Portuguese outpost in the Persian Gulf, the trading post in Kanj, and India and East Africa. This led the Portuguese to abandon the post and put an end to Portugal's presence in the region.

Meanwhile, the Omani navy was growing in sophistication and power. It came to rely entirely on modern ships and to employ highly developed cannons with the same capacity as European cannons. The Omanis used huge ships on the European model. These advances in naval technology enabled the Omanis, after expelling the Portuguese from the Persian Gulf, to go even further on the offensive, attempting to take control of East Africa away from Portugal as well.

Whereas the Portuguese had built their eastern African empire relatively quickly during the sixteenth century, basing it simply on controlling the gold trade of the Zimbabwean Plateau, the Omanis had been traveling to East Africa and gaining influence of various sorts since the dawn of history, by way of the monsoon trade winds of the Indian Ocean. They had settled throughout the region from R'as Jurdafun in the north to the Gulf of Delgado in the south, the region now known as the Swahili Coast. With the passing of time, Omanis mixed with Africans, intermarried, and established important cen-

ters of trade. Those Omani Africans were part of the Portuguese eastern African empire.

Following the Omani success in expelling the Portuguese from the Persian Gulf, the people of Mombasa turned to the Omanis, their fellow countrymen and coreligionists, for help against the Portuguese. The Omanis, for their part, encouraged Swahili resistance to the Portuguese, since they feared that Portugal might be tempted to launch a counter-attack against the Persian Gulf from East Africa if they maintained their strength there. Thus, Oman successfully attacked Zanzibar and Pate in 1655, taking a large number of Portuguese captives and seizing a number of warships and trading vessels. As a result, Zanzibar came under the total control of Oman, and its ruler agreed to pay a yearly poll tax in return for protection against the Portuguese.

In 1660, the Omani fleet was in the midst of a siege of Bombay when it received orders to abandon the siege and sail for Mombasa. The Omanis besieged Mombasa for nearly five years (1660-1665). The Portuguese ultimately broke the siege, but it acted as an effective draw on their resources while it lasted. Sulṭān bin Saif, ruler and imam of Oman, made his way to the islands of Pemba and Zanzibar and succeeded in freeing them from all Portuguese control. In 1679, the Portuguese were temporarily forced to withdraw from Pate as well.

Following the death of Sulṭān bin Saif in 1679, his son, Balʿarab bin Sulṭān, ascended the throne. The new ruler made an oath to free Mombasa or die. In 1680, Balʿarab prepared a fleet of twenty-eight boats and laid siege to Mombasa once more, but Mombasa was one of the strongest Portuguese centers in East Africa. Its strong fortifications proved too much for the siege to break. Balʿarab next decided to lay siege to Mozambique's fortress, but the Portuguese defenses there were able to withstand his siege as well. The Omanis began to dig a tunnel beneath the fortress, intending to penetrate inside. The defenders responded by placing charges, which exploded with such tremendous force that they distressed the Omanis, who refused to continue their siege.

The strife between Balʿarab bin Sulṭān and his brother Saif bin Sulṭān over the throne of Oman enabled the Portuguese to regain control over some of the cities on the Swahili Coast, including Malindi, Faza, Pate, and Lamu. In 1686, Pate revolted against Portuguese rule, and its sultan was taken to Goa and beheaded on Christmas Day. However, when Saif became the ruler of Oman, the Omanis won massive victories, the most important of

1650's

which was the capitulation of Mombasa on December 14, 1698, after the fall of Fort Jesus.

The fort fell following a long siege that had commenced in March, 1696. A fleet of seven sails from Oman had arrived in Kilindini harbor and laid siege to Fort Jesus after Pemba called in Omani aid against the Portuguese in 1694. The Omani fleet seized the small fort at the entrance to the channel in Mombasa. The siege lasted thirty-three months and although the fort was never subjected to any serious attack until the final assault was launched, the hardships undergone by the Portuguese garrison through lack of supplies and the ravages of sickness were severe in the extreme. At length, disease exacted so great a toll that the last fierce resistance of the defenders was overcome.

SIGNIFICANCE

The 1698 fall of Mombasa marked the beginning of the expulsion of the Portuguese from the Swahili Coast, and in 1699, the Omanis decisively conquered Pemba, Kilwa, Pate, and Zanzibar. Thus, the Omanis completely expelled the Portuguese from all their strongholds north of Mozambique, and this region became one of Oman's dependencies until the very end of the nineteenth century, when Britain and Germany conquered it. Following the expulsion of the Portuguese from the Swahili Coast, Mombasa became an important state under the Omani-derived Mazrui Dynasty, while the southern coast, controlled by the Busaidi Dynasty, enjoyed a period of prosperity as well.

The growth of Omani maritime power in the western Indian Ocean, as well as new European imports of coffee from Mocha, located in the Red Sea coast nation of Yemen, resulted in rapid development in Red Sea trade throughout the eighteenth century. After the maritime struggles of the second half of the seventeenth century, the Red Sea remained out of bounds to European commercial companies. Yet, the situation changed in the beginning of the eighteenth century, following the rise in popularity of coffee drinking in Europe, which provided the coffee growers of Yemen with additional demand

and motivated them to establish and maintain friendly contact with Europe.

—*Moshe Terdiman*

FURTHER READING

Brouwer, C. G. *Dutch-Yemeni Encounters: Activities of the United East India Company (VOC) in South Arabian Waters Since 1614*. Amsterdam: D'Fluyte Rarob, 1999. A description of Dutch commercial activity in southern Arabia and in the Red Sea coast of Yemen.

Casey-Vine, Paula, ed. *Oman in History*. London: Ministry of Information, Sultanate of Oman and Immel, 1995. A detailed discussion of the struggle between the Omanis and the Portuguese for the control of eastern Africa.

Chaudhuri, K. N. *Trade and Civilisation in the Indian Ocean: An Economic History From the Rise of Islam to 1750*. New York: Cambridge University Press, 1985. A description of the development in the Red Sea trade in the end of the seventeenth century and throughout the eighteenth century.

Freeman-Grenville, G. S. P. "Some Aspects of Portuguese-Swahili Relations, 1498-1698." In *The Swahili Coast, Second to Nineteenth Centuries: Islam, Christianity, and Commerce in Eastern Africa*. London: Variorum Reprints, 1988. A detailed description of the Siege of Fort Jesus in 1696-1698.

Ingham, Kenneth. *A History of East Africa*. London: Longmans, Green, 1966. A short description of the struggle between the Omanis and the Portuguese for control of the Swahili Coast.

Toussaint, Auguste. *History of The Indian Ocean*. Translated by June Guicharnaud. London: Routledge and Kegan Paul, 1966. A short description of the struggle between the Dutch, English and Portuguese for the Indian Ocean trade and the Omani expansion.

SEE ALSO: Early 17th cent.: Rise of Rwanda; 1602-1639: Ottoman-Ṣafavid Wars; Nov. 11, 1606: Treaty of Zsitvatorok.

March 31, 1650
EARTHQUAKE DESTROYS CUZCO

A violent earthquake shook the Peruvian city of Cuzco and the area surrounding it, leveling most of its colonial buildings and resulting in considerable loss of life.

LOCALE: Cuzco (Cusco), viceroyalty of Peru (now in Peru)

CATEGORIES: Natural disasters; environment; architecture

KEY FIGURES

Manuel de Mollinedo y Angulo (d. 1699), bishop who supervised the rebuilding of Cuzco

Marcos Zapata (1675-1765), painter who provided important canvases during the reconstruction of Cuzco

Garcilaso de la Vega (1539-1616), colonial historian of Peru

Gil González Dávila (1578-1658), chronicler of South American history, particularly Peru

SUMMARY OF EVENT

On March 31, 1650, quite unaccountably, the sound of church bells clanging unharmoniously filled the air of Cuzco, Peru. They were neither announcing a holy day nor summoning worshipers to Sunday mass: March 31 in 1650 fell on a Thursday. Rather, the bells were ringing because the earth below the churches in whose belfries they hung was undulating wildly, as an earthquake struck the area, one that by modern standards would have measured at least 7.5 on the Richter scale.

The Spanish historian of South America, Garcilaso de la Vega, has written a great deal about early Peru. The Inca Empire was conquered by Francisco Pizarro, after which Spanish settlement developed quickly. Cuzco, the capital city of the Inca Empire, which stretched from Argentina to the southern border of what is now Colombia, was a thriving city when Pizarro and a band of his Spanish followers arrived there one and one-half centuries before the earthquake.

At that time, Cuzco's indigenous population was estimated to exceed 200,000. By 1650, the year of the great earthquake, with a growing population of Spanish settlers and increasing numbers of Incas, probably at least 250,000 people lived in the city and its environs.

Cuzco, high in the Andes Mountains of Peru, is the oldest continuously inhabited city in the Americas and has the greatest altitude of any major city on the Ameri-

can continents, with an elevation of slightly over 11,000 feet (3,353 meters). The mountains near it reach skyward to almost 18,000 feet (5,486 meters), with El Huascaran, its tallest peak, spiraling to 22,205 feet (6,768 meters). The regular volcanic activity in these mountains is directly related to the frequent earthquakes in the area. The activity of the Nazca Plate, which runs along the Pacific Ocean west of the Peruvian coastline, constantly pushes the land upward, spawning recurrent earthquakes. Since 1568, more than seventy major earthquakes have been recorded in Peru, including the devastating 1650 quake. Peru, therefore, has an average of a major earthquake every six years. Besides its major tremors, Peru records more than two hundred smaller earthquakes every year.

The Incas, well aware of the dangers that earthquakes posed, had developed long before the seventeenth century a type of construction that made their cities almost impervious to earthquakes. When Cuzco was virtually leveled in 1650, nearby Machu Picchu, although it experienced tremors about equal in force to those that destroyed Cuzco, remained essentially intact. The Spanish settlers in Cuzco in the sixteenth and seventeenth centuries constructed their buildings very much in the way they were used to constructing buildings in their native Spain, building them along verticallines that left them vulnerable to earthquake damage. The Inca structures had unique trapezoidal lines that made them almost impregnable.

The Spanish often anchored their new structures to the Inca foundations that remained after they dismantled Inca buildings to make room for more European structures. When the earthquake of 1650 struck, nearly all the European-style colonial buildings crumbled, but their Inca foundations and the few Inca buildings that had not been dismantled survived the earthquake nearly intact. These Inca structures, like all the Inca buildings in the area, were built with huge stones that often weighed between 2-3 tons (1,814-2,722 kilograms). These colossal stones were fitted together so intricately and precisely that a blade of the thinnest knife could not be inserted between them. The Incas used no mortar in their construction, yet their buildings possessed a structural integrity that has never been equaled.

Gil González Dávila, a noted Spanish chronicler of Peru and an eyewitness to the earthquake of 1650, wrote, "Cuzco, how can he who saw you yesterday, and who sees you today, not be moved to tears?" The destruction of the quake was immediate and extensive. Moreover, although the major tremor probably lasted for less than one minute, the area was wracked by continuing aftershocks that terrified an already demoralized populace.

At the height of the seismic activity, a statue of Christ was brought from the cathedral onto the adjoining square, whereupon the tremors ceased. People attributed the respite to a miracle related to this figure, which they venerated and named El Señor de los Temblores, or the Lord of the Earthquakes. The statue is still paraded around Cuzco's Plaza de Armas every Easter Monday on a silver litter supported by forty-five litter bearers, in commemoration of the great earthquake of 1650. Many paintings of this statue have been made and are found in churches throughout the area, placed there to protect the churches from future earthquake damage.

Cuzco's cathedral, although badly shaken, sustained less damage from the earthquake than that suffered by the colonial residences and the churches of San Agustín, Belén, Santo Domingo, La Compañía de Jesus, and La Merced, all of which were badly damaged and, in some cases, were reduced to little more than heaps of rubble. The construction of the Cuzco cathedral, begun in 1556, was nearly complete in 1650. Because it was damaged minimally by the earthquake, the cathedral was finally completed in 1654, just short of one century after construction was started. This Renaissance style structure was built in the shape of a Latin cross.

The construction by the Jesuits of the church of La Compañía de Jesus, which has a most intricate interior, was begun in 1576 and was nearing completion in 1650 when the earthquake struck, causing its completion to be delayed until 1668. It remains one of Cuzco's best examples of the Andean Baroque style of architecture that dominated the area after the almost total reconstruction of the city that was occasioned by the earthquake and that went on unrelentingly until about 1700.

SIGNIFICANCE

The earthquake and the subsequent reconstruction brought about notable changes in the way future colonial buildings in the Andes were constructed. The former vertical style of the Spanish settlers was drastically modified and became more in keeping with the trapezoidal style of the Incas. As a result, when an earthquake of approximately the same intensity as the quake of 1650 struck Cuzco on May 21, 1950, structural damage to the city's buildings was considerably less than the overall destruction that had marked the earlier disaster.

Because most of the valuable wall murals, or frescos, in the churches of Cuzco were lost to the quake, the re-

built churches used fewer wall murals for decoration, replacing them with huge canvases of religious scenes. These could be stored easily and safely as circumstances demanded, and they would suffer little damage in earthquakes. One such canvas in Cuzco's cathedral depicts the earthquake and its aftermath.

Bishop Manuel de Mollinedo y Angulo was a patron of the arts who brought much of his valuable art collection to Cuzco from Spain and played a considerable role in the reconstruction of the city, as did such Jesuit architects as Juan Bautista Egidiario and Diego Martinez de Oviedo, major figures in the reconstruction of La Compañía de Jesus. The bishop helped to establish the Escuela Cuzqueña de Pintura, a noteworthy art school, in which students were trained to produce the kinds of religious art that the reconstructed churches required. Among those who studied there were Basilio Santa Cruz Pumacallao, Marcos Zapata, and Basilio Pacheco, all of whom produced religious paintings that can be seen in Cuzco today.

—R. Baird Shuman

FURTHER READING

Dobyns, Henry E., and Paul L. Doughty. *Peru: A Cultural History*. New York: Oxford University Press, 1976. A clear, concise account of early Peru under the Spanish with several references to the earthquake that leveled Cuzco in 1650.

Falconer, Kieran. *Peru*. New York: Marshall Cavendish, 1995. This beautifully illustrated book, aimed at juvenile readers, has sporadic references to the earthquake that struck Cuzco in 1650.

Fisher, John R., ed. *Peru*. Santa Barbara, Calif.: ABC-CLIO, 1990. Several of the contributions to this useful collection address the role earthquakes have played in Peruvian history.

Hudson, Rex A. *Peru: A Country Study*. Washington, D.C.: Government Printing Office, 1993. A comprehensive overview of Peru with occasional references to the earthquake of 1650.

Meyerson, Julia. *Tambo: Life in an Andean Village*. Austin: University of Texas Press, 1990. An easily accessible account of life in the high country of Peru. Excellent for background reading.

SEE ALSO: Nov. 28, 1607: Martin Begins Draining Lake Texcoco; 1608: Jesuits Found Paraguay; 1615: Guamán Poma Pleas for Inca Reforms.

RELATED ARTICLE in *Great Lives from History: The Seventeenth Century, 1601-1700:* Saint Rose of Lima.

May 30-31, 1650
FIRST COLLEGE IN NORTH AMERICA

Harvard College was the first institution of higher education in North America and, together with the first North American printing press, marked Massachusetts as the intellectual center of the New World.

LOCALE: Massachusetts Bay Colony
CATEGORIES: Education; organizations and institutions

KEY FIGURES
Henry Dunster (1609-1659), first president of Harvard College
Thomas Dudley (1576-1653), governor of Massachusetts Bay Colony, 1634, 1640, 1645, 1650, and member of Harvard's Board of Overseers
Nathaniel Eaton (c. 1610-1674), first professor to be appointed by the Board of Overseers
John Harvard (1607-1638), first benefactor of Harvard College
Anne Hutchinson (1591-1643), central figure in the Antinomian crisis that delayed the founding of Harvard

SUMMARY OF EVENT
In *New England's First Fruits*, the famous tract extolling the virtues of New England to possible supporters in the old country, the Puritans proclaimed that one of their first concerns had been "to advance *Learning* and perpetuate it to Posterity; dreading to leave an illiterate Ministry to the Churches, when our present Ministers shall be in the Dust." Because the Puritan church's tenets emphasized interpretation and discussion of the Scriptures rather than mere ritual or emotion, it required a learned clergy. Therefore, on October 28, 1636, the Massachusetts General Court passed a legislative act to found "a schoale or colledge" and voted four hundred pounds sterling for its support. The Antinomian crisis revolving around Anne Hutchinson delayed action on the matter until November 15, 1637, when, after debating whether the college should be built in Salem, the Massachusetts General Court passed an order that the college be built at Newetowne. A few days later, the building of the college was committed to the first Board of Overseers, which consisted of six magistrates and six church elders. The location for the school was chosen partly because of its resemblance to Oxford and Cambridge in England; hence, Newetowne was renamed Cambridge on May 2, 1638.

By June, 1638, Nathaniel Eaton, the professor engaged by the overseers, had moved into the house acquired for him in the midst of a cow pasture, and the Massachusetts General Court had granted three lots to him for the college. Within a few months, the first classes were being taught, the building was being constructed, and a library was being assembled.

The college already was operating when, on September 14, 1638, a young clergyman named John Harvard died and left his library and half of his estate, amounting to about eight hundred pounds sterling, to the new institution. Although Harvard was not responsible for the founding of the college, nor did his legacy make its establishment possible, his gift was a remarkable one for the times, and the Massachusetts General Court voted on March 13, 1639, to name the college after him.

Unfortunately, Professor Eaton's most praiseworthy accomplishment was the planting and fencing of the yard to keep the cows out and the students in. His tyrannical tenure was marred by beatings and dismal living conditions for the students who boarded at his home. Mistress Eaton's "loathsome catering," featuring such items as "goat's dung in their hasty pudding," provided an inauspicious beginning for that much-maligned institution, the college dining hall. When Eaton's cruelty finally came to the attention of the Massachusetts General Court, he was fined and dismissed, and the college closed its doors at the beginning of its second year. Lacking an instructor, the school remained closed for nearly a full year, although construction work continued.

On August 27, 1640, Henry Dunster, a graduate of Magdalene College, Cambridge, was invited to become the school's first president. He accepted and began teaching classes that fall, infusing life into the college and providing a firm foundation for its growth. The class of 1642 returned, a new freshman class entered, and a three-year course in the arts was established. A thorough knowledge of Greek and Latin was required for admission. Dunster personally instructed the three classes in the arts, philosophies, and Asian languages, and he also moderated the students' disputes. Although the Puritans believed that knowledge without Christ was vain, Harvard College was less ecclesiastical than the universities at Oxford and Cambridge, for it strove to provide a course in philosophy and the liberal arts that would be

1650's

A view of Harvard College in 1725. The single building of 1642 has grown into a "quad." (Library of Congress)

suitable either for a general education or as a basis for entering one of the professions.

The establishment and support of a college was an ambitious undertaking for such a new, economically insecure community. Only the strong religious faith of the Puritans in the purpose of their endeavor carried it through. Contrary to the claims of various educational historians, the Puritans took a greater interest in intellectual pursuits than other Englishmen of their day. Their concentrated system of settlement in towns rendered the accomplishment of popular education easier than in Virginia, where the population was dispersed. Even before the law required it, a number of Puritan towns established schools: Boston had hired a schoolmaster in 1635, as had Charlestown in 1636. The first New England school legislation, the Massachusetts Act of 1642, required the heads of families to teach their children and

servants "to read and understand the principles of religion and the capital laws of the country" and to see that they were employed in useful occupations. Thus, the Puritans understood education as serving social and economic needs: It provided training for citizenship and service in the community.

The laissez-faire system apparently proved to be unsatisfactory: In 1647, the Massachusetts General Court passed a law requiring every town of fifty families to appoint a schoolmaster "to teach all such children as shall resort to him to write and read." His wages were to be paid by the parents or the town, as the town should choose. Towns of one hundred families were to establish grammar schools to instruct youth "so far as they may be fitted for the Universitie." The cost of supporting the schools was a hardship on some of the smaller communities, and the uneducated complained of the ruling class trying to force its high standards upon the poor. Thus, interest in public education did not work its way up from the bottom but down from the top.

Determined to establish in America the collegiate system as it was practiced in England, under which the students lived, studied, ate, and disputed together with their tutors, Dunster and the overseers were anxious to complete the first building despite an economic depression. Donations made possible the occupation of the "Old College" in September, 1642, in time for the commencement of the first nine graduates. Within this building, the students attended classes, studied, ate, and slept.

During its early years, Harvard College had serious financial problems. Lacking any sort of endowment or income-producing lands, it struggled along on tuition fees, as well as the ferry rents and town levies that it was granted. A fund-raising mission to England met with moderate success, and in 1644, representatives at the meeting of the United Colonies of New England agreed that all the Puritan colonies should share in supporting the college. Each family was obligated to give a peck of wheat or one shilling annually. Governor Thomas Dudley signed Harvard College's first official charter on May 30-31, 1650.

SIGNIFICANCE

The establishment of Harvard College among what were in many ways still the fledgling colonies of New England was an event of great cultural import. Alongside the importation of the first American printing press to Cambridge in 1638, it instantly established Massachusetts as the intellectual capital of the New World. More important, it established that there was an intellectual capital among the English colonists, that they were not content with a mere agrarian existence. It is also quite notable that Harvard, while designed to produce religious, Puritan citizens, was not dominated wholly by religion. While this may seem unremarkable by modern standards, among the Puritan theocracy of Massachusetts, the establishment of an institution as given to general learning as to the inculcation of Puritan tenets indicated just how firmly the colonists believed in the importance of education for education's sake.

—*Warren M. Billings and Geralyn Strecker*

FURTHER READING

Bailyn, Bernard, et al., eds. *Glimpses of the Harvard Past.* Cambridge, Mass.: Harvard University Press, 1986. Contains essays on each major phase of the school's development. Bailyn's essay, "Foundations," deals with Harvard's early years.

Lipset, Seymour Martin, and David Riesman. *Education and Politics at Harvard.* New York: McGraw-Hill, 1975. Critical discussion of political controversies at Harvard. The chapter on "The Colonial Period" deals with discipline and academic freedom, among other issues.

Maddocks, Melvin. "Harvard Was Once, Unimaginably, Small and Humble." *Smithsonian* 17, no. 6 (June, 1986): 140-160. Describes the hardships faced by Harvard students from the school's beginnings through the nineteenth century.

Morison, Samuel Eliot. *The Founding of Harvard College.* 1935. Reprint. Cambridge, Mass.: Harvard University Press, 1995. This first volume of Harvard's official tercentennial history sets the school's founding and early development up to 1650 in context with the rise of liberal arts and European universities during the Renaissance.

_____. *Harvard College in the Seventeenth Century.* 2 vols. Cambridge, Mass.: Harvard University Press, 1936. These books continue Morison's tercentennial history of the college, from the granting of its first charter in 1650 through 1708.

_____. "The Puritan Age, 1636-1707." In *Three Centuries of Harvard: 1636-1936.* Cambridge, Mass.: Harvard University Press, 1936. A condensed history of Harvard's founding.

Quincy, Josiah. *The History of Harvard University.* 2 vols. Cambridge, Mass.: John Owen, 1840. Reprint. New York: Arno Press, 1977. The official history of the college, written in celebration of its bicentennial.

SEE ALSO: Dec. 26, 1620: Pilgrims Arrive in North America; May, 1630-1643: Great Puritan Migration; 1638: First Printing Press in North America; Sept. 8, 1643: Confederation of the United Colonies of New England.

RELATED ARTICLES in *Great Lives from History: The Seventeenth Century, 1601-1700:* Anne Hutchinson; Sir Henry Vane the Younger; John Winthrop.

1650's

1651
HOBBES PUBLISHES *LEVIATHAN*

Hobbes published Leviathan, *marking a pivotal moment not only in the ongoing debates about the most reasonable form of government and the proper relationship between church and state but also in the evolution of European philosophy.*

LOCALE: London, England
CATEGORIES: Philosophy; literature

KEY FIGURES

Thomas Hobbes (1588-1679), English social and political philosopher
Oliver Cromwell (1599-1658), general of Parliamentary forces in the English Civil Wars and lord protector of England, 1653-1658
Charles I (1600-1649), king of England, r. 1625-1649
Charles II (1630-1685), king of England, r. 1660-1685

SUMMARY OF EVENT

The seventeenth century was a turbulent period in the evolution of scientific, political, and philosophical thought and of governmental models and political alliances in Europe. The legacy of the Reformation and the Renaissance was quite evident in the almost universal questioning of traditional authorities and truths. Continental Europe was disrupted and Germany decimated by the Thirty Years' War (1618-1648), a struggle between the Protestant princes of Germany, Denmark, England, Sweden, and France and the Catholic princes of the Habsburgs and the Holy Roman Empire. The role of the church in the political arena and the institution of monarchy were the focus of considerable debate and controversy.

In the universities, the long-established authority of Aristotle was under attack, and modern science was taking shape as thinkers such as Galileo struggled to free themselves from the repressive grip of Scholasticism. In England, the debate about political authority was particularly animated and acrimonious. The fundamental questions concerned the nature and limits of power. On the one hand, there were the Royalists, who asserted the divine right of a king to rule with, if not absolute, at least essentially unencumbered power. On the other hand were the Parliamentarians, who advocated limitation of the rights of a king by law and argued for a system under which power would be shared between the king and Parliament.

Thomas Hobbes was educated at Oxford University. Upon his graduation in 1607, he was recommended to William Cavendish, who later became the first earl of Devonshire, as a tutor for his son. Thus began Hobbes's lifelong association with the Cavendish family, a connection that provided Hobbes not only with access to influential people and to a fine library but also with the opportunity to travel in Europe as a guide and tutor. On his travels, Hobbes became acquainted with René Descartes and Galileo and, by his own account, fell in love with geometry and the axiomatic (deductive) method.

Hobbes seems to have developed his political views early in his life. In 1628, the year Parliament drew up the Petition of Right—a document that ranks with the Magna Carta and the Bill of Rights in placing constitutional limits on absolute monarchy—Hobbes published a translation of Thucydides with the expressed intention of showing the evils of democracy. King Charles I was forced to agree to the Petition of Right, because he was in dire need of funds to support English involvement in the religious wars on the Continent. Nevertheless, Charles continued to struggle with Parliament over his right to rule as he pleased and his control of religious policy. In 1629, the king dissolved Parliament and governed for eleven years without calling another session.

During these years, known as the period of Personal Rule, the people became increasingly restive, and the religious climate became steadily more bitter as William Laud, who became archbishop of Canterbury in 1633, persecuted English Puritans. Hobbes supported the king throughout the Personal Rule, because he firmly believed that only a strong monarchy could save England from the chaos of civil war.

Upon his return from a tour of Europe in 1637, as the tutor to the third earl of Devonshire, Hobbes found his country drifting inexorably toward civil war. In April of 1640, King Charles called Parliament into session to ask for money to fight the rebellious Scots, but Parliament was in no mood to grant funds. Instead, it wanted to debate the grievances of the past eleven years. Charles dissolved the so-called Short Parliament after only three weeks but was forced to recall Parliament in the fall "to buy the Scots out of England." On November 3, 1640, the famous Long Parliament assembled, and rebellion was in the air. Hobbes chose this year to publish *The Elements of*

Law Natural and Politic (1640), in which he demonstrated the need for absolute sovereignty. When Parliament arrested the earl of Strafford and Archbishop Laud and charged Strafford with high treason, Hobbes fled to France.

In Paris, Hobbes associated with other Royalists and with the intellectual circle of the friar Marin Mersenne, which included Descartes. For a brief period, Hobbes served as a tutor of mathematics to Prince Charles (the future King Charles II). These years of exile were Hobbes's most productive as a political philosopher. During the eleven years he spent in Paris, civil war did break out in England. The bitter and divisive struggle began in August of 1642 and went on intermittently until Charles I was executed on January 30, 1649, and Prince Charles's supporters in Ireland and Scotland were crushed by Oliver Cromwell in 1650 and 1651. Even after the victory of the Parliamentary forces, the political situation in England was chaotic and unstable. There was continuous debate and experimentation in the struggle to find an appropriate form of government. The situation did not become stable until Cromwell was made lord protector in 1653.

Because of the deteriorating situation in England, Hobbes abandoned his scientific studies and his work on optics and devoted himself instead to an empirical analysis of human nature and society. His masterwork was *Leviathan* (1651), which became highly controversial as soon as it was published. Hobbes offended the Royalists by failing to acknowledge the divine right of kings and offended the Parliamentarians by dismissing both democracy and a constitutional monarchy as impractical and unrealistic. Moreover, he offended both Catholics and Protestants by asserting that religious choice should be the prerogative of the ruler. His French patron, Mersenne, had died in 1648, and Hobbes became increasingly isolated and ill at ease in France for alleged atheism and for holding views antithetical to Catholicism. Shortly after the publication of *Leviathan*, Hobbes made his peace with Parliament and returned to England, where he lived until his death. He remained active in intellectual circles throughout his long life.

In the first part of *Leviathan*, Hobbes deals with people as individuals and with such general philosophical issues as he deems necessary. Hobbes is scientific in his approach to the individual and society. He postulates a state of nature in which all people are equal and are primarily motivated by a desire to preserve their liberty and to dominate others and by a fear of death. In this state of nature, there is no property, no justice or injustice, no good or evil; there is only a war of all against all. Human life in such a state, Hobbes asserts, would be "nasty, brutish, and short."

In the second part of *Leviathan*, Hobbes explains how humanity can escape these evils. Prompted by their fear of death and chaos, people come together and give up their "right" of unlimited self-assertion in choosing a sovereign or sovereign body that shall exercise authority over them, thus putting an end to universal war. Hobbes deduced that the chosen sovereign must have absolute power; otherwise, people would always be in danger of falling back into the anarchy of the state of nature.

In Hobbes's vision, once people have chosen their sovereign, their political power is at an end. Citizens lose all rights, except those that the government may find it expedient to grant and the right of self-defense in extreme circumstances. The powers of the sovereign

Thomas Hobbes. (Library of Congress)

1650's

HOBBES ON COMMONWEALTH

One of the pivotal sections of Hobbes's Leviathan *is his discussion of the nature of the political unit he calls a commonwealth. In the following excerpt, Hobbes defines a commonwealth and explains both why commonwealths are necessary and where their rulers' powers derive from.*

The only way to erect such a Common Power, as may be able to defend them from the invasion of Forraigners, and the injuries of one another, and thereby to secure them in such sort, as that by their owne industrie, and by the fruites of the Earth, they may nourish themselves and live contentedly; is, to conferre all their power and strength upon one Man, or upon one Assembly of men, that may reduce all their Wills, by plurality of voices, unto one Will: which is as much as to say, to appoint one man, or Assembly of men, to beare their Person; and every one to owne, and acknowledge himselfe to be Author of whatsoever he that so beareth their Person, shall Act, or cause to be Acted, in those things which concerne the Common Peace and Safetie; and therein to submit their Wills, every one to his Will, and their Judgements, to his Judgment. This is more than Consent, or Concord; it is a reall Unitie of them all, in one and the same Person, made by Covenant of every man with every man, in such manner, as if every man should say to every man, *I Authorise and give up my Right of Governing my selfe, to this Man, or to this Assembly of men, on this condition, that thou give up thy Right to him, and Authorise all his Actions in like manner.* This done, the Multitude so united in one Person, is called a COMMON-WEALTH, in latine CIVITAS.

Source: From *Leviathan*, by Thomas Hobbes. Edited by C. B. Macpherson (Baltimore: Penguin Books, 1968), p. 227.

evitably differ in their visions of good and evil, for he was convinced that each individual called "good" that which pleased him or her at the moment. Life itself was the only objective good Hobbes recognized. Since human beings were antisocial by nature and since their individual interests must differ, Hobbes concluded that there was no stable alternative to anarchy except yielding all power to a single authority.

SIGNIFICANCE

Scholars have made a case that *Leviathan* is the most influential work in political science to have been written between the Middle Ages and the Enlightenment. Its only rival is Niccolò Machiavelli's *Il principe* (wr. 1513, pb. 1532; *The Prince*, 1640), which is narrower in scope. *Leviathan* is important not only because of its incisive vision of humankind and society but also because of its philosophical methods and assumptions.

The work secured Hobbes's position as one of the foremost thinkers of his time. Since then, he has proved to be an extremely influential philosopher who made three significant contributions to Western thought. Hobbes's conviction that the axiomatic method applies to all thought helped make mathematics and mathematicians foremost in European philosophy. He popularized the idea that the world was fundamentally mathematical by expressing that idea in nonmathematical language and by using the axiomatic method in his philosophical constructions. Hobbes also emphatically and convincingly established a case for a materialist view of the universe. Perhaps most important, he saw the world as an endless chain of cause and effect and established the doctrine of causality. Hobbes translated the methods of the new science of the seventeenth century into a general explanation of humanity and the universe.

—Hal Holladay

are unlimited. He defines law, property, and justice and has the unquestionable right to censor or punish as he sees fit. Hobbes prefers monarchy, but his abstract arguments are equally applicable to all forms of government in which there is one supreme authority not limited by the legal rights of other bodies. According to Hobbes, the English Civil Wars occurred because power was divided among the king, the Lords, and the Commons.

In the third part of *Leviathan*, Hobbes explains that there is no universal church. In each country, the king or chosen power must be the head of the church. Hobbes regarded religion as a system of law, not a system of truth. The fourth part of the work is concerned with criticism of the Roman Catholic Church and of "vain philosophy," by which Hobbes generally refers to the philosophy of Aristotle.

Hobbes did not believe humans to be either innately moral or innately rational creatures. Instead, he believed that rationality was learned, and he was convinced that humanity's basic qualities were pride, avarice, ambition, and fear of death. Hobbes believed that individuals would in-

FURTHER READING

Kraynak, Robert P. *History and Modernity in the Thought of Thomas Hobbes*. Ithaca, N.Y.: Cornell

University Press, 1990. Insightful and original examination of Hobbes's philosophy, which Kraynak maintains, initiated the Enlightenment.

Rogow, Arnold A. *Thomas Hobbes*. New York: W. W. Norton, 1986. A stimulating biographical account of Hobbes. Rogow's analysis of Hobbes's intellectual influences is particularly useful.

Shelton, George. *Morality and Sovereignty in the Philosophy of Hobbes*. New York: St. Martin's Press, 1992. A thoughtful interpretation of Hobbes's doctrine of the laws of nature and a defense of a Hobbesian approach to moral theory.

Sorell, Tom, ed. *The Cambridge Companion to Hobbes*. New York: Cambridge University Press, 1996. A useful guide to Hobbes's life, work, and scholarship.

Sorell, Tom, and Luc Foisneau, eds. *Leviathan After 350 Years*. New York: Oxford University Press, 2004. Collection of essays analyzing *Leviathan*'s place among Hobbes's other works of political philosophy, the connection between Hobbes's politics and psychology, and Hobbes's views on the Bible and the church.

Thornton, Helen. *State of Nature or Eden? Thomas Hobbes and His Contemporaries on the Natural Condition of Human Beings*. Rochester, N.Y.: University of Rochester Press, 2004. Examines the reaction of Hobbes's contemporaries to *Leviathan*, including the book's ideas about religion, natural law, and the fall of man.

SEE ALSO: 1618-1648: Thirty Years' War; Dec. 18, 1621: The Great Protestation; Mar., 1629-1640: "Personal Rule" of Charles I; Nov. 3, 1640-May 15, 1641: Beginning of England's Long Parliament; 1642-1651: English Civil Wars; Dec. 6, 1648-May 19, 1649: Establishment of the English Commonwealth; Dec. 16, 1653-Sept. 3, 1658: Cromwell Rules England as Lord Protector; May, 1659-May, 1660: Restoration of Charles II.

RELATED ARTICLES in *Great Lives from History: The Seventeenth Century, 1601-1700:* Charles I; Charles II (of England); Oliver Cromwell; René Descartes; Galileo; Thomas Hobbes; William Laud; Marin Mersenne.

1651-1652
EDO REBELLIONS

Masterless samurai, or rōnin, *whom the Tokugawa shogunate had deprived of their lords and livelihood, attempted to overthrow or at least disrupt the shogun's government, but they were quickly subdued, marking the end of major resistance to Tokugawa rule for more than two hundred years.*

LOCALE: Edo (now Tokyo), Japan
CATEGORIES: Wars, uprisings, and civil unrest

KEY FIGURES

Yui Shōsetsu (1605-1651), teacher of military science and leader of the first Edo rebellion

Marubashi Chūya (d. 1651), martial arts teacher and fellow leader of the first Edo rebellion

Tokugawa Ietsuna (1641-1680), Japanese shogun, r. 1651-1680

Matsudaira Nobutsuna (1596-1662), senior councillor, or *rōjū*, of the shogun, 1633-1662, who crushed both rebellions

SUMMARY OF EVENT

When the third Tokugawa shogun, Tokugawa Iemitsu, died in 1651, to be succeeded by his ten-year-old son Tokugawa Ietsuna, a determined group of masterless samurai, called *rōnin*, attempted to change the government through violence. The roots of their rebellion stemmed from the Tokugawa shogunate's aggressive reorganization of power in feudal Japan since 1603. The rebellious *rōnin* felt that these policies had left them at a severe disadvantage. They planned to use violence to change their position.

By the middle of the seventeenth century, samurai were the exclusive warriors of Japan. Since 1588, they had been the only ones allowed to bear arms. For their livelihood, samurai depended on a master or lord, called a daimyo. A daimyo had to be granted rule over a territory, called a han, worth at least 10,000 koku. Feudal Japan measured arable land by the average yield of rice. One koku yielded about 5 bushels (175 liters) of rice, and 10 koku corresponded to 2.5 acres (1 hectare) of land. Out of the revenue from his domain, a daimyo would engage the services of samurai. In return for their sustenance, the samurai swore absolute loyalty to their daimyo. Should the daimyo lose his land and thus his lordship, his samurai became *rōnin*, without obvious means of support. Japan's feudal system forbade samurai to work or switch social class to become an artisan or merchant. Thus, almost the only legitimate hope for a *rōnin* lay in finding another daimyo.

When Tokugawa Ieyasu had assumed the title of shogun from the emperor in 1603, founding the Tokugawa shogunate, he had quickly used his position to consolidate his powers, and his next two successors followed suit. According to the Japanese feudal system, the shogun ruled the nation in the name of the emperor, but under the Tokugawa, the emperor was a mere figurehead. The shogunate had all the real power, including the crucial right to allocate land to the daimyos of Japan. Thus, each of the roughly 270 daimyos governed his domain, conditional upon the shogun's approval.

To reward their own loyal followers and to punish their opponents, the first three Tokugawa shoguns made intensive use of this right to determine holder and size of daimyo domains. From 1600 to 1650, they created 172 new daimyos, enlarged the hans of 206 others, and transferred 281 daimyos from one domain to another. However, 213 daimyos lost their hans or saw them significantly reduced. It was from the ranks of their former samurai, now *rōnin*, that the rebels recruited their followers.

One of these *rōnin* was Marubashi Chūya. To survive, he had founded a martial arts school in Edo, the capital of the shogunate. Since samurai were expected to be moral leaders, teaching was one of the few occupations not considered work in the strict sense and therefore allowed to samurai. Since he was famous for his skill with the lance, Marubashi's school quickly attracted both *rōnin* and samurai, eager to improve their fighting skills. Soon, talks of a plot to change the behavior of the shogunate toward the *rōnin* arose.

When Marubashi joined forces with Yui Shōsetsu, the plans of the rebels became more concrete. Yui had studied military arts and founded his own school in Edo, where he taught military science. His fame attracted even daimyos and lower-ranking senior Tokugawa vassals, yet he also attracted many *rōnin*, who became his ardent followers. In turn, Yui looked for ways to help these desperate men who began to crowd the shogunal capital in search of opportunities to support themselves. One solution Yui proposed to them was to become samurai for daimyo Tokugawa Yorinobu of Kii Province (modern Wakayama Province), in the heart of feudal Japan. The *rōnin* clung to this hope, but it failed to materialize.

The death of Tokugawa Iemitsu in the summer of 1651 inspired Yui and Marubashi to form a concrete plan for a rebellion. Their goals differed, however. Both leaders agreed to create a massive disruption of public life to focus attention on the sorrows of the *rōnin*. Whether both Yui and Marubashi agreed on overthrowing the Tokugawa shogunate has remained in dispute. However, the massive scale of their plans shows that they planned a major rebellion. In Japan, their endeavor is referred to as the Keian incident, since it took place in the last Keian year of the traditional calendar.

For drastic effect, the two leaders planned to blow up the arsenal of the shogun's forces. This became a possibility after the traitorous deputy commander of the facility, Kawara Jūrōbei, secretly allied himself with the rebels. The conspirators also planned to burn the city of Edo, assassinate senior ministers, and take over Edo Castle, where the ten-year-old boy shogun Ietsuna resided with his advisers.

While rebel operations in Edo were left to Marubashi, Yui left for the town of Sumpu (modern Shizuoka City) to the west, between Edo and Kyōto. He took with him ten devoted *rōnin*. Simultaneous with Marubashi's attack on Edo, Yui planned to set fire to Sumpu. He envisioned using the chaos caused by the conflagration to seize the sacred shogun shrine at Kunōzan, outside the city gates.

Most likely as a result of Marubashi talking about the plans of the rebels in increasingly boastful terms, government informers learned of the planned rebellion. They brought the information to senior councillor Matsudaira Nobutsuna. Matsudaira had been a loyal adviser to the late shogun. He carried the nickname Chie Izu (Clever Izu), a play on his noble title of Izu no Kami. Clever Izu acted immediately and decisively, bringing the Keian incident to a quick end. He arrested Marubashi and thirty-three of his fellow plotters, including some of their male family members, interrogated them, and had them executed on September 24, 1651.

Learning of the arrest and execution of the Edo rebels, Yui Shōsetsu committed suicide in Sumpu. To add controversy to the issue of the true goals of the rebels, Yui left behind a suicide note. In it, he stated that the goal of his rebellion had not been the overthrow of the Tokugawa shogunate. Instead, his intention had merely been to call attention to the dire position of the *rōnin*. Whether this was true has been the subject of sustained scholarly debate.

Indicative of the persistent dissatisfaction of the *rōnin*, Marubashi had to suppress a second rebellion, called the Jōō incident, in 1652. Again, it was bands of dissatisfied *rōnin*, as well as outlaw soldiers called *hatamoto yakko* (renegade Tokugawa bannermen) and *machi yakko* who caused the unrest. Marubashi put the rebels to death, and revolts against Tokugawa rule ceased to recur.

SIGNIFICANCE

The failure of the rebels to disturb Tokugawa rule during the prematurely discovered Keian incident and the Jōō incident led to a full consolidation of the shogunate. There would be no more major armed challenges to the Tokugawa shoguns for more than two hundred years, and Japan enjoyed in a very long period of domestic peace.

The claim of Yui Shōsetsu's suicide note that the rebellion was merely intended to launch serious consideration of the dire situation of the *rōnin* seemed to have some effect on shogunate policy. While the first three Tokugawa shoguns had taken away from disfavored daimyos an average of 3.6 million koku, or land of 900,000 acres (360,000 hectares), in each of their reigns, that figure dropped for the fourth shogun. Under Tokugawa Ietsuna, from 1651 to 1680, only 728,000 koku, equivalent to 182,000 acres (74,000 hectares), were taken from some daimyos and reassigned to others. The figures crept up again under the next shogun, reaching 1.7 million koku, or 425,000 acres (172 hectares). Thus, while the Edo rebellions failed to disrupt Tokugawa authority, they were indirectly successful in causing a moderation and stabilization of government policy. As fewer daimyos were dispossessed, fewer *rōnin* roamed the capital as a potential source of unrest.

The leaders of the Keian incident, Yui Shōsetsu and Marubashi Chūya, soon became popular heroes. As early as the late seventeenth century, historical fiction about them began to be written, and they were not cast as villains. This trend continued in the 1700's. Many Kabuki plays were written about them as well during the reign of later Tokugawa shoguns. It appears that the Tokugawa rulers were more tolerant of rebels on the stage and in fiction than in real life.

—R. C. Lutz

FURTHER READING

De Benneville, James. *The Haunted House: More Samurai Tales of the Tokugawa.* 2d ed. London: Kegan Paul, 2001. Historical fiction based on contemporary Japanese chronicles of the era that also features some of the samurai rebels as characters. Illustrated.

Ikegami, Eiko. *The Taming of the Samurai.* Cambridge, Mass.: Harvard University Press, 1995. Academic study of the development of samurai culture. Chapter 4 deals with samurai in the Tokugawa shogunate and sheds light on the forces leading to the rebellions. Illustrated, notes, index.

Jansen, Marius. *The Making of Modern Japan.* Cambridge, Mass.: Belknap Press of Harvard University Press, 2000. Begins with a comprehensive look at the Tokugawa shogunate that outlines how the Tokugawa state was set up and successfully enforced its powers against its enemies. Illustrated, notes, index, bibliography.

McClain, James. *Japan: A Modern History.* New York: Norton, 2001. First three chapters deal with the Tokugawa period, provide an excellent overview of the politics of the shogunate that led to the rebellions, and explain why the shogunate remained successful. Illustrated, maps, index.

Turnbull, Stephen. *Samurai: The World of the Warrior.* Oxford, England: Osprey, 2003. Richly illustrated book that brings to life people like the *rōnin* rebels.

SEE ALSO: 1603: Tokugawa Shogunate Begins; Beginning 1607: Neo-Confucianism Becomes Japan's Official Philosophy; 1614-1615: Siege of Ōsaka Castle; 1615: Promulgation of the *Buke shohatto* and *Kinchū narabini kuge shohatto*; 1624-1640's: Japan's Seclusion Policy; Oct., 1637-Apr. 15, 1638: Shimabara Revolt; 1651-1680: Ietsuna Shogunate; 1680-1709: Reign of Tsunayoshi as Shogun.

RELATED ARTICLES in *Great Lives from History: The Seventeenth Century, 1601-1700:* Tokugawa Ieyasu; Tokugawa Tsunayoshi; Yui Shōsetsu.

1651-1680
IETSUNA SHOGUNATE

After a dangerous beginning, when his councillors foiled two rebellions, the fourth Tokugawa shogun, Ietsuna, presided over a consolidation of Tokugawa rule of Japan. Ietsuna and his councillors continued politics and laws initiated by his three predecessors, with occasional changes toward a less aggressive position.

LOCALE: Japan
CATEGORIES: Government and politics; wars, uprisings, and civil unrest

KEY FIGURES

Tokugawa Ietsuna (1641-1680), shogun of Japan, r. 1651-1680
Hoshina Masayuki (1611-1672), guardian, or *hosa*, of the infant shogun Ietsuna, 1651-1661
Sakai Tadakiyo (1624-1681), great elder, or *tairō*, and senior councillor, or *rōjū*, to Ietsuna, 1651-1681
Matsudaira Nobutsuna (1596-1662), *rōjū* to Ietsuna, 1633-1662
Yui Shōsetsu (1605-1651), leader of the first Edo rebellion, the Keian incident
Marubashi Chūya (d. 1651), fellow leader of first Edo rebellion

SUMMARY OF EVENT

When Shogun Tokugawa Iemitsu died in 1651, his eldest son, the ten-year-old Tokugawa Ietsuna, was appointed the next shogun for Japan. The official confirmation of this appointment by the emperor was a mere ceremonial formality. Because of Ietsuna's young age, his uncle, Hoshina Masayuki, became his guardian, or *hosa*, as his father had planned.

Upon Ietsuna's succession, the Tokugawa shogunate faced a rebellion, the Keian incident (so-called because it happened in the last year of Keian according to the traditional Japanese calendar). Two teachers of military science and martial arts, Yui Shōsetsu and Marubashi Chūya, led the revolt. Both men proclaimed that they acted out of sympathy for the plight of the *rōnin*, those samurai who had been deprived of their masters and thus their livelihood by the policies of the first three Tokugawa shoguns.

Since 1600, the Tokugawa had made ample use of their power to assign and reassign the land of Japan to the daimyos, or lords, who in turn employed samurai. To make room for daimyos loyal to the shogunate, by 1651 the Tokugawa had either removed 213 of the existing hostile daimyos or had significantly reduced their land. When a daimyo's land holdings fell below the minimum of 2,500 acres (1,000 hectares) of arable land, he was required to dismiss his samurai. These dismissed warriors became *rōnin*, forbidden from performing labor and yet without military positions to support them either.

In 1651, Yui and Marubashi plotted to blow up the shogun's arsenal and set fire to the shogun's capital city of Edo (modern Tokyo), as well as the city of Sumpu (modern Shizuoka). In the chaos of this urban conflagration, the rebels planned to assassinate senior Tokugawa officials, seize Edo Castle, where Ietsuna resided with his councillors, and take over the shogun's shrine at Kunōzan, outside of Sumpu.

Most likely, it was Marubashi's boasting that led to premature discovery of the plot. At Edo, senior councillor, or *rōjū*, Matsudaira Nobutsuna, who was called Clever Izu, immediately arrested, interrogated, and had executed Marubashi and thirty-three fellow plotters and male members of their families. They died on September 24, 1651. Yui Shōsetsu, who had moved with ten *rōnin* to Sumpu, committed suicide. In a note he claimed that he had not intended to overthrow the shogun. Instead, the foiled revolt was meant merely to call public attention to the plight of the *rōnin*. In 1652, Matsudaira had to suppress a second rebellion, called the Jōō incident. After this, Tokugawa rule was no longer violently opposed by the *rōnin*. Their numbers also dwindled, as far fewer daimyos lost their land under Ietsuna's reign.

During the guardianship of Hoshina Masayuki, the Tokugawa shogunate continued the policies set by Ietsuna's predecessors. The emperor remained virtually confined at his castle at Kyōto, ruling in name only, while the shogunate held all real power. The Tokugawa upheld the policy of national seclusion, or *sakoku*, strictly in place since 1639. This policy forbade most foreigners from entering Japan and prohibited almost all Japanese from leaving the country. Foreign trade was limited to a single artificial island at the port of Nagasaki, on the western end of Japan, on the island of Kyūshū. There, far away from Edo, the Chinese and the Dutch were allowed to trade with the country. Christianity remained forbidden in Japan under penalty of death.

The lives of the samurai and their daimyos continued to be regulated in Ietsuna's reign. Their conduct and position in society was subject to a series of important laws that were continuously enforced. The *Buke shohatto* (laws for military houses, passed 1615) and *Shoshi hatto* (regulations for the vassals, passed 1633 and 1635) held samurai and their lords to the highest ethical standards and strict moral conduct.

To control the daimyo effectively and prevent them from rebelling, Ietsuna's father had formally issued the law of *sankin kōtai* (alternate attendance). Under this law, vigorously enforced in Ietsuna's reign, the daimyos had to spend every other year outside their own domains and live in Edo, where their families had to reside, effectively becoming hostages of the shogun. Moderating previous Tokugawa law, Ietsuna allowed daimyos to adopt an heir shortly before their death. This increased stability for the daimyo's family, because failure to produce an heir meant reassignment of his domain to another family when he died.

In 1657, a major fire devastated Edo. The increased aristocratic population used the sad opportunity to rebuild their palaces and residences in an even more ornate style, typical for the new Edo period. In addition to these architectural innovations, the large number of educated, sophisticated, powerful, and rich people in the shogun's capital also led to a flourishing of literature, philosophy, arts, and religious study.

Of fragile health, the adult Ietsuna continued to rely on his trusted *rōjū* to guide the affairs of Japan. One of them, Sakai Tadakiyo, was appointed *tairō*, or great elder, a position that previous shoguns had not always filled. Because of his great power, Sakai Tadakiyo was known as "Geba Shogun" (dismount shogun). His nickname came from the position of his residence right at the gate to Edo Castle, where a sign admonished all who entered to dismount. Most of Ietsuna's advisers had strong family ties to the Tokugawa clan.

Another sign of humanization under Ietsuna was the abolition of *junshi* in 1663. This was the practice of ritual suicide by the followers of a nobleman upon his death. Since the tenth century, samurai had committed hara-kiri (disembowelment) if their daimyos were killed in battle. By the early seventeenth century, the custom had spread to instances where the lord died of natural causes. The Tokugawa shoguns found this practice distasteful, especially when it became expected rather than offered voluntarily. Upon the advice of his former guardian Hoshina Masayuki, Ietsuna forbade *junshi*. To enforce the rule, the successors of daimyos were made responsible for ensuring that no samurai followed *junshi*. When this occurred in Utsunomiya domain in 1668, the land of the new daimyo was cut by 5,000 acres (2,000 hectares) as punishment, twice the minimum size of a daimyo's domain.

In 1669, an Ainu rebellion occurred on the northernmost island of Hokkaidō because of the sufferings of Japan's ancient native ethnic minority. The shogunate showed little sympathy for the Ainu, however, who had been pushed to the remote North.

The year 1670 saw the publication of a major historical work, *Honchō tsūgan* (historical survey of Japan), which sought to use history to legitimize Tokugawa rule. It was the work of the combative Neo-Confucian scholar Hayashi Razan and, after his death, his son Hayashi Gahō. The elder Hayashi had fiercely fought for the acceptance of the Zhu Xi branch of Neo-Confucianism, and attacked both Christianity and Buddhism. His incorporation of Japanese Shintoism made his philosophy very popular during Ietsuna's reign.

Tokugawa Ietsuna died childless in 1680. His *tairō*, Sakai Tadakiyo, had tried to persuade Ietsuna to adopt an imperial prince, but the shogun had refused. Instead, Ietsuna's younger brother, Tokugawa Tsunayoshi, succeeded him, and Sakai resigned. He died in 1681.

SIGNIFICANCE

After a challenging start, the reign of Tokugawa Ietsuna became one of consolidation and some moderation of Tokugawa rule. During the first years, Ietsuna's guardian and senior councillors governed in his name, and they continued to follow the policies and laws of the preceding three shoguns, which formed the basis of much public life in Japan.

Perhaps in response to the Keian incident of 1651, Ietsuna's reign saw a drastic reduction in the practice of reassigning daimyos. It is also possible that the councillors felt that the practice had achieved its desired effect, and loyal men and their families were already ruling the Japanese domains, making continued reassignment unnecessary and undesirable. The Ainu rebellion of 1669 did not shatter the general sense of domestic peace during Ietsuna's reign.

Ietsuna's continuous reliance on his senior councillors created a climate of government by consensus. Ietsuna did not leave a powerful personal imprint on his reign. Nevertheless, moderation prevailed, and political consensus gave his reign great stability. Ietsuna's final insistence upon keeping the office of the shogun in the Tokugawa family bestowed a flamboyant next ruler on Japan, and continued Tokugawa rule would not end until 1868. His support for Neo-Confucianism—collective subordination to ideals of peace, harmony, and a warrior spirit taught if not tested in battle—quietly reinforced Tokugawa power. Due to the active and far-ranging

1650's

work of his predecessors, Ietsuna did not need to rule aggressively, and he steered a tranquil course.

—*R. C. Lutz*

FURTHER READING

Gerhart, Karen. *The Eyes of Power: Art and Early Tokugawa Authority.* Honolulu: University of Hawaii Press, 1999. Focus on the art commissioned for two castles and the Tokugawa mausoleum by Ietsuna's father; useful discussion of how the early Tokugawa used art to strengthen their power. Notes, bibliography, index.

Jansen, Marius. *The Making of Modern Japan.* Cambridge, Mass.: Harvard University Press, 2000. Begins with comprehensive look at the Tokugawa shogunate that includes an analysis of the Tokugawa state, foreign relations, social groups, education, thought and religion, and a section on rulers and ruled in the first ten chapters. Illustrated, notes, index, bibliography.

McClain, James. *Japan: A Modern History.* New York: Norton, 2001. First three chapters deal with the Toku-

gawa period and provide an excellent overview of politics, lifestyle, culture and samurai ethics of the time. Illustrated, maps, index.

Nishiyama, Matsunosuke. *Edo Culture.* Honolulu: University of Hawaii Press, 1997. Focus on daily city life in the Tokugawa era, emphasis on the common city dweller. Illustrations, index.

SEE ALSO: 1603: Tokugawa Shogunate Begins; Beginning 1607: Neo-Confucianism Becomes Japan's Official Philosophy; 1614-1615: Siege of Ōsaka Castle; Jan. 27, 1614: Japanese Ban Christian Missionaries; 1615: Promulgation of the *Buke shohatto* and *Kinchū narabini kuge shohatto*; 1651-1652: Edo Rebellions; 1657: Work Begins on Japan's National History; Jan. 18-20, 1657: Meireki Fire Ravages Edo; 1680-1709: Reign of Tsunayoshi as Shogun.

RELATED ARTICLES in *Great Lives from History: The Seventeenth Century, 1601-1700:* Tokugawa Ieyasu; Tokugawa Tsunayoshi; Yui Shōsetsu.

October, 1651-May, 1652
NAVIGATION ACT LEADS TO ANGLO-DUTCH WARS

The Navigation Act, Britain's attempt to regulate foreign trade by a national statute, led to three naval wars between former Protestant allies England and the Netherlands. The conflict marked the first modern war waged from nonreligious motives on a global scale. Moreover, it was the first global war between two representative governments or republics.

LOCALE: England and the Netherlands
CATEGORIES: Laws, acts, and legal history; wars, uprisings, and civil unrest

KEY FIGURES

Robert Blake (1599-1657), British admiral under the Commonwealth

Oliver Cromwell (1599-1658), general of Parliamentary forces in the English Civil War and lord protector of England, Scotland, and Ireland, 1653-1658

Maarten Tromp (1598-1653), Dutch admiral

SUMMARY OF EVENT

The Navigation Act passed in 1651 stated that all imports to England had to be in English ships or else in ships of

the producer country (Royalist colonies such as Virginia routinely used Dutch shipping), and it forbade fishing in English waters by foreigners (the Dutch had fished in the English Channel since at least 1295).

This act by England's newly established republic hit its mark: It crippled Dutch trade and shipping, and within two months Holland sent a delegation to Parliament to ask that the Navigation Act be repealed. The Dutch, however, offered no concessions in return. Parliament ignored their request, and England's navy continued to seize Dutch merchant vessels on the grounds that their cargo was contraband. In May of 1652, Maarten Tromp, a Dutch admiral sailing to protect a merchant fleet, clashed near Dover with English warships under Admiral Robert Blake. The encounter was the beginning of the Anglo-Dutch War.

Both sides had been spoiling for this war as a test of strength. The closeness between the two Protestant nations arose from the circumstance that Holland had come into existence by rebelling from Spain not long after Queen Elizabeth I had come to the British throne in 1588 after the death of her half sister Mary I, who had been the wife of King Philip II of Spain. English volunteers, with Elizabeth's blessing, served Holland in its struggle against Spain. In trade, the Dutch originally relied on Portugal, which had discovered the route to India through the efforts of explorer Vasco da Gama. When Spain annexed Portugal, the Dutch had to make their own way to the Far East.

In 1602, they founded the celebrated Dutch East India Company, which before long was disputing with Portugal the command of the Indian Ocean. A second company that launched in 1621, the Dutch West India Company, gained control over the Atlantic from the Cape of Good Hope in South Africa to the Straits of Magellan in South America. These powerful trading companies were authorized by Amsterdam to establish colonies in both Indies, to coin money, and to make war or peace. Besides settling New Amsterdam (later ceded to the English and renamed New York), the Dutch kept up their conquests in Brazil until 1661.

By the time of the English Civil Wars (1642-1648), Amsterdam was the financial center of Europe, where businessmen established their credit and raised loans, and Holland became a vast entry point to which goods were brought for exporting overseas. Holland had more ships than all the navies of Europe combined. With no rivals to their commercial shipping, the Dutch naturally upheld the doctrine of *mare liberum* (an open sea). English merchants looked on enviously as Holland imported Gloucestershire woolens and then reexported them as Dutch products. When the Civil Wars ended, the English Parliament, purged of Royalist sympathizers, beheaded King Charles I and established the Commonwealth. They expected support from Holland, a sister republic. Having only recently been delivered from the Thirty Years' War, Holland kept a wary distance from the new English republic. The Dutch waited to see whether Charles II, proclaimed king in Scotland, would succeed in getting back his father's throne. Only when Oliver Cromwell defeated Charles at Worcester in September, 1651, was Holland forced to take the Commonwealth seriously.

In its Navigation Act the next month, Parliament answered Holland's doctrine of the *mare liberum* with an English doctrine of *mare clausum* (a closed or private sea). The idea that anyone should have exclusive right to part of the ocean—in this case, the English Channel and the seas around England's colonies—sounds odd to modern observers, because the complex notion of free trade across international waters has become so commonplace. In the seventeenth century, however, international law was unheard of and foreign relations were based on what might be called the law of the jungle. A nation expected its king to protect it and to increase its trade by cowing its rivals. For nearly half a century after the 1620's, Europe was in a recession. Not yet having developed technologies to increase their industry, European countries found their best profits in carrying and shipping, and with each decade, the Dutch were claiming a larger share.

English merchants had first clashed with the Dutch in the East Indies in 1623, when the Dutch overran and massacred some English traders at Amboina. When the Navigation Act was passed and the Dutch sent ambassadors to remonstrate, England responded by raking up old grievances against Holland. Besides Amboina, various Dutch acts of piracy were scored against them. For years, England had issued letters of reprisal authorizing its captains to seize Dutch merchant vessels; then as now, a country always pretended it took up war solely to defend its interests (particularly its merchants and trade). Just like a monarch, the new English republic sought to establish its sovereignty by protecting its merchants against an enemy. This kind of patronage is feudal rather than patriotic. (One should note that the urge to further the good of the whole nation played no part in the Dutch wars themselves, as it would do when England fought with France in the next century.) The Navigation Act required, for example, that the Dutch strike their sail in salute to an English ship, which in turn had the right to search any Dutch vessel. That the Commonwealth's navy could enforce such a humiliating provision shows how far the Commonwealth and Protectorate governments increased England's might and prestige.

SIGNIFICANCE

Coming at the end of the wars of religion that had been concluded by the Peace of Westphalia (1648), the Anglo-Dutch War was the first modern war waged from nonreligious motives on a global scale. Moreover, it was the first global war between two representative governments or republics. Historians who believe that the war resulted from commercial rivalry alone ignore the significant motive behind the Navigation Act, which was intended to shape a national policy. Up to that time, the English trading companies were supported by money from investors and by royal grants of monopolies in a commodity, such as tin, or in a geographical area, such as the Baltic. Yet in 1651, with the monarchy abolished, English merchants looked to Parliament instead of the king, and Parliament obliged them by even challenging allies such as Holland and Sweden. In other words, the

Navigation Act signaled that the Commonwealth had thrown off the old ties to religion and to the feudal hierarchy that used to bind the crowned heads of states, and had replaced them by something like a sense of the national interest.

This new sense of a national interest was born of the republic. When Cromwell put an end to the Commonwealth with his Protectorate (1654-1658), he strove to identify the national interest with the Reformation dream of a Protestant crusade against the pope, beginning with war on Spain. He died without having succeeded in rallying the country to his cause, however, and with the restoration of monarchy in 1660, feudal motives of self-interest were reasserted by the restored nobility and gentry who demanded the old privileges. The second and third Anglo-Dutch Wars were not in England's interest but were started by factions of courtiers and by King Charles II. Yet the memory of a united republic was not forgotten. Restoration Parliaments renewed the Navigation Act, and eventually the rival parties—country and court, Whigs and Tories—would rediscover the national interest in the Revolution of 1688.

—David B. Haley

FURTHER READING

Gardiner, Samuel Rawson, ed. *Letters and Papers Relating to the First Dutch War, 1652-1654.* 6 vols. London: Navy Records Society, 1899. Edited by one of the greatest nineteenth century historians of England, this work attempts to exculpate England for its role in the First Anglo-Dutch War.

Groenveld, Simon. "The English Civil War as a Cause of the First Anglo-Dutch War, 1640-1642." *Historical Journal* 30 (1987): 541-566. Groenveld's account tells the story of the First Anglo-Dutch War from the Dutch perspective.

Hainsworth, Roger, and Christine Churches. *The Anglo-Dutch Naval Wars, 1652-1674.* Stroud, England: Sutton, 1998. Establishes the background and causes of the wars, describes major battles, and discusses the role of Robert Blake, the Tromps, and other naval leaders.

Jones, James Rees. *Britain and the World, 1649-1815.* Sussex, England: Harvester Press, 1980. Jones presents a useful analysis of international politics of the period on pages 60-70 of this work.

Pincus, Steven C. A. *Protestantism and Patriotism: Ideologies and the Making of English Foreign Policy, 1650-1668.* New York: Cambridge University Press, 1996. Outlines the causes and consequences of the first two Anglo-Dutch Wars, focusing on the religious and political ideologies that led to the conflict.

Schama, Simon. *The Embarrassment of Riches: An Interpretation of Dutch Culture in the Golden Age.* New York: Alfred A. Knopf, 1987. In this already classic work of popular history, Schama provides an informative survey of Holland's glorious century of expansion.

SEE ALSO: Mar. 20, 1602: Dutch East India Company Is Founded; Beginning Spring, 1605: Dutch Dominate Southeast Asian Trade; 1618-1648: Thirty Years' War; Dec. 18, 1621: The Great Protestation; July, 1625-Aug., 1664: Founding of New Amsterdam; Oct., 1625-1637: Dutch and Portuguese Struggle for the Guinea Coast; May 6, 1626: Algonquians "Sell" Manhattan Island; 1642-1651: English Civil Wars; Sept. 8, 1643: Confederation of the United Colonies of New England; Dec. 6, 1648-May 19, 1649: Establishment of the English Commonwealth; May, 1659-May, 1660: Restoration of Charles II; Sept. 13, 1660-July 27, 1663: British Navigation Acts; Mar. 22, 1664-July 21, 1667: British Conquest of New Netherland; Mar. 4, 1665-July 31, 1667: Second Anglo-Dutch War.

RELATED ARTICLES in *Great Lives from History: The Seventeenth Century, 1601-1700:* Robert Blake; Charles II (of England); Oliver Cromwell; George Monck; Prince Rupert; Michiel Adriaanszoon de Ruyter; Maarten and Cornelis Tromp.